AFAQ

"An Anarchist FAQ", Version 12.0

Copyright © 2012
The Anarchist FAQ Editorial Collective:
Iain McKay, Gary Elkin, Dave Neal, Ed Boraas

Catalogue records for this book are available from the British Library and from the Library of Congress.

ISBN	9781849351225
Library of Congress Control Number	2007939197

First published 2012 by:

AK Press	AK Press
PO Box 12766	674-A 23rd Street
Edinburgh	Oakland
Scotland	CA 94612-1163
EH8 9YE	USA
www.akuk.com	www.akpress.org
ak@akedin.demon.co.uk	akpress@akpress.org

Design, layout and typesetting by:

Euan Sutherland
www.agitcollage.org

An Anarchist FAQ

AFAQ volume two
Iain McKay

AK
PRESS
EDINBURGH • OAKLAND • BALTIMORE

Contents

Introduction to Volume 2 567

Section G : Is individualist anarchism capitalistic? 574

An explanation of individualist anti-capitalism, the individualist critique of social anarchism, the social anarchist response and why 'anarcho'-capitalism is not a variant of individualist anarchism. A look at the ideas of two quite different individualists, Tucker and Stirner.

G.1 Are individualist anarchists anti-capitalist? 577
G.2 Why do individualist anarchists reject social anarchism?.............................596
G.3 Is "anarcho"-capitalism a new form of individualist anarchism? 605
G.4 Why do social anarchists reject individualist anarchism?.............................623
G.5 Benjamin Tucker: Capitalist or Anarchist?...639
G.6 What are the ideas of Max Stirner?..643

Section H: Why do anarchists oppose state socialism? 652

The anarchist critique of statist variants of socialism, with the Russian Revolution as a case study.

H.1 Have anarchists always opposed state socialism? 654
H.2 What parts of anarchism do Marxists particularly misrepresent?.....................680
H.3 What are the myths of state socialism?..714
H.4 Didn't Engels refute anarchism in "On Authority"? 771
H.5 What is vanguardism and why do anarchists reject it?................................783
H.6 Why did the Russian Revolution fail?...807

Section I : What would an anarchist society look like? 834

No blueprints but an explanation of possible anarchist social and economic structures, with lessons learned from the Spanish Revolution.

I.1 Isn't libertarian socialism an oxymoron? 837
I.2 Is this a blueprint for an anarchist society? 863
I.3 What could the economic structure of anarchy look like?..............................872
I.4 How could an anarchist economy function?...897
I.5 What could the social structure of anarchy look like? 936
I.6 What about the "Tragedy of the Commons"?...965
I.7 Won't Libertarian Socialism destroy individuality?...................................972
I.8 Does revolutionary Spain show that libertarian socialism can work in practice?......974

Section J : What do anarchists do? 1008

From child rearing to social revolution via direct action, social struggles and building organisations.

J.1 Are anarchists involved in social struggles? 1009

J.2 What is direct action?.. 1017

J.3 What kinds of organisation do anarchists build? 1034

J.4 What trends in society aid anarchist activity?.. 1058

J.5 What alternative social organisations do anarchists create? 1065

J.6 What methods of child rearing do anarchists advocate? 1098

J.7 What do anarchists mean by social revolution? 1108

Bibliography 1126

Anarchist Anthologies.. 1126

Anarchist and Libertarian Works 1126

Works about Anarchism 1130

Non-Anarchist Works... 1131

Introduction to Volume 2

"Conquer or die – such is the dilemma that faces the … peasants and workers at this historic moment … But we will not conquer in order to repeat the errors of the past years, the error of putting our fate into the hands of new masters; we will conquer in order to take our destinies into our own hands, to conduct our lives according to our own will and our own conception of the truth."

Nestor Makhno[1]

Welcome to volume 2 of **An Anarchist FAQ** (**AFAQ**)!

If the core of volume 1 was based on outlining anarchist ideas and history as well as presenting the anarchist critique of authority, capitalism and statism, then this volume is focused around two threads. The first is the critique of Marxism, historically anarchism's main alternative within the socialist movement. The second is what anarchists aim for and how we get there.

Needless to say, the second theme is by far the more important as anarchism is more than just analysing what is wrong with the world, it also aims to change it.

First, though, we start with an account of individualist anarchism (section G). It is fair to say that individualist anarchism has generally been on the margin of accounts of anarchism. This, undoubtedly, reflects the fact it has been predominantly a North American movement and was always a small minority within the global anarchist movement. Even in the USA, it was eclipsed by social anarchism.

As such, it has been somewhat overlooked in accounts of anarchism and **AFAQ** seeks to correct that. Unfortunately, it has also to address claims that "anarcho"-capitalism is a form of individualist anarchism and so it spends some time refuting such assertions. We do so with a heavy heart, as this will tend to exaggerate the importance of that ideology and its influence but it needs to be done simply in order to counteract those ideologues and academics who seek to confuse the two either out of ignorance (for the latter) or self-interest (for the former). In addition, section G is shaped by the history of **AFAQ**, when it started as an anti-"anarcho"-capitalist FAQ rather than a pro-anarchist one. If it had been started as the pro-anarchist FAQ it has now become, that section would have been substantially different (most obviously, the material on "anarcho"-capitalism being placed in an appendix where it belongs).

This means that in some regards, section G can be considered as a continuation of section F (which is on why "anarcho"-capitalism is not a form of anarchism). Individualist anarchism **is** the form of anarchism closest to liberalism and, as a consequence, to "anarcho"-capitalism. However, similarities do not equate to the former being a (flawed, from an "anarcho"-capitalist perspective) forerunner of the latter. If this were the case then some would assert that social anarchism is a form of Marxism. There are overlaps, of course, but then again there are overlaps between individualist anarchism, Marxism and social anarchism. Yet, for all its differences with social anarchism, individualist anarchism shared a critique of capitalism and the state which has significant commonality.

Individualist anarchism is a unique political theory and it does it a disservice to reduce it to simply a flawed precursor of an ideology whose origins and aims are radically at odds with it. It is no coincidence that individualist anarchism found its home in the broader labour and socialist movements while propertarianism views these with disdain. Nor is it a coincidence that the main influences on individualist anarchism were labour, monetary and land reform movements plus the economics of Proudhon and other socialists while, for "anarcho"-capitalism, it is "Austrian" economics which developed, in part, precisely to combat such popular movements. This leads to fundamentally different analyses, strategies and aims that show beyond doubt that the two cannot be confused. The individualist anarchists cannot be considered as forerunners of propertarianism in any more than the most superficial terms. So it is a shame this needs to be discussed at all, but it has.

Ironically, a sadly unpublished article from the 1950s by the founder of that ideology, Murray Rothbard, has come to light which came to the same conclusion (inaccurately entitled, given the history of anarchist use of libertarian, **Are Libertarians 'Anarchists'?**). Ignoring the errors, distortions and inventions about anarchism Rothbard inflicts on the reader, this essay came to the following (correct!) conclusion: *"We must therefore conclude that we are **not** anarchists, and that those who call us anarchists are not on firm etymological ground, and are being completely unhistorical."* This was applicable to both the *"dominant anarchist doctrine … of 'anarchist communism'"* (*"which has also been called 'collectivist anarchism,' 'anarcho-syndicalism,' and 'libertarian communism'*) as well as individualist anarchists, considered by Rothbard *"the best of them"*, as **both** had *"socialistic elements in their doctrines."* He suggested that there were thinkers *"in that Golden Age of liberalism"* who had ideas *"similar"* to his ideology but these *"never referred to themselves as anarchists"* while *"all the anarchist groups … possessed socialistic **economic** doctrines in common."* If only he had kept to that analysis and called his ideology something more accurate then this FAQ would have been much shorter!

Also significant is Rothbard's use of the term "libertarian communism" which indicates he was well aware of the traditional use of libertarian as an alternative to anarchist. Interestingly, while reminiscing about the origins of the so-called "libertarian" right in America Rothbard publicly acknowledged their stealing of the word libertarian from genuine anarchists:

> *"One gratifying aspect of our rise to some prominence is that, for the first time in my memory, we, 'our side,' had captured a crucial word from the enemy … 'Libertarians' … had long been simply a polite word for left-wing [sic!] anarchists, that is for anti-private property anarchists, either of the communist or syndicalist variety. But now we had taken it over …"[2]*

Today, of course, propertarians shrilly denounce anarchists using the term libertarian in its original and correct meaning as attempting to appropriate *their* name and associate it with socialism! Oh, the irony...

Unlike the propertarians who are so busy degrading the good name "libertarian" and the memories of individualist anarchism, adherents of both schools of anarchism considered themselves socialists. Of course there *are* real differences between individualist and social anarchism, and we explore these. We show that attempts by some members of each school to excommunicate the others are, ultimately, pointless (in general, the individualists seemed keener to do that than the social anarchists but both sides had their intolerant ones). There is significant overlap between both sections of the movement and so it is perfectly possible for each to coexist happily in a free society as well as, on certain issues and tactics, to work fruitfully together in resisting capitalism and the state.[3]

We then turn to discuss Marxism and its flaws (section H). To be honest, it is staggering that this section even needs to be written given that the anarchist critique of Marxism has been validated time and time again. It is like writing a book on evolution and spending a significant time refuting the claims of Lamarckian theory. Sadly, though, many radicals seem unable to grasp the facts of history, namely that the predictions made by anarchists as regards Marxism have come to pass. Bakunin was right: social democracy did become reformist and the dictatorship of the proletariat became the dictatorship *over* the proletariat.

This critique is not to suggest that anarchists should reject everything Marx argued.[4] In terms of his critique of capitalism, there is much that libertarians can agree with (undoubtedly because much of it was built on Proudhon's analysis!). In part, it is this analysis which ensures that Marxism remains alive as a distinct ideology in the radical movement rather than Marx's positive contributions being integrated along with others (such as Proudhon and Bakunin) into libertarian socialism. It is a powerful and, in large parts, a correct analysis of that system but in terms of constructive ideas on what socialism would be and how to achieve it, Marxism comes up as deeply flawed. So, as with anarchist thinkers, we should recognise the important and valid parts of Marx's contribution to the socialist movement while rejecting its negative aspects – particularly as many so-called "Marxist" positions were first expounded by anarchists!

In part, because as well as his critique of capitalism the other main reason for Marxism's continued existence is, undoubtedly, its apparent success. Needless to say, most Marxists are keen to forget that the first apparently successful Marxist movement was social democracy. Engels lavish praise for it is rarely mentioned these days, given social democracy's quick descent into reformism and, worse, explicit counter-revolution during the German revolution. Rather, it is the apparent success of Leninism[5] during the Russian Revolution that accounts for why so many radicals are attracted to it. As such, what Alexander Berkman termed **The Bolshevik Myth** is alive and well – and needs to be combated.

Suffice to say, the promises of Lenin's **State and Revolution** did not last the night and within six months there was a *de facto* party dictatorship presiding over a state capitalist economy (by early 1919, the need for party dictatorship in a revolution was considered a truism by all the leaders of the party). If that counts as a success, what would failure be? Luckily, unlike Berkman's generation, the numbers blinded by wishful thinking about "socialism" in Russia are fewer although we do have those who, while denouncing Stalin, seem incapable of seeing the obvious links with Lenin's regime and its ideological conceptions (most notably, but not limited to, its vanguardism). As we show in section H.6, the standard modern-day Leninist excuses for Bolshevik tyranny have nothing to recommend them – both in terms of theory and empirical evidence. So as well as presenting a theoretical critique of Marxism, we seek to root it in the experiences of Marxism in practice. This involves, in the main, focusing on the Social-Democratic movement, Bolshevism and the Russian Revolution.

We also spend some time refuting numerous Marxist distortions of anarchist ideas. I've lost count of the times I have seen blatantly false claims about anarchism raised by Marxists. I'm not that surprised, as few Marxists actually bother to read the likes of Proudhon, Bakunin and Kropotkin. Instead, they simply repeat what other Marxists have claimed about anarchism (starting, of course, with Marx and Engels). This explains why section H.2 has so many quotes in it, simply to drive home what would be obvious to anyone familiar with anarchist theory and practice. A few quotes could be dismissed as selective, a multitude cannot. I'm sorry that has to be done, but the regularity of abysmally bad Marxist diatribes against anarchism means that it had to be done in such detail. Sadly, I'm sure that refuting these habitual false assertions in **AFAQ** it will not stop Marxists repeating them.

Marxist myths on anarchism also feed into section G, given that many Marxists have been at pains to portray anarchism as being simply "anti-state" (in this, they share common-ground with the propertarians). Yet even a cursory glance of anarchist theory and history shows that it has *never* limited itself to just a critique of the state. As long as anarchism has been a named socio-economic theory we have directed our fire at both state **and** property. *Property is Theft!*, my new anthology of Proudhon's writings, shows how interlinked the anarchist opposition to the state and capitalism has been from the start. Thus we find Proudhon arguing that *"the capitalist principle"* and the *"governmental principle are one and the same principle"* and so *"the abolition of the exploitation of man by man and the abolition of government of man by man are one and the same formula."* Moreover, it is *"to protect this exploitation of man by man that the State exists"* Unsurprisingly, then, anarchists are *"simultaneously striving for the abolition of capital and of the State"* and *"if you do away with the former, you still have to do away with the latter, and vice versa.*"[6]

So the notion of an anarchism which is simply anti-state is completely alien to our tradition. However, falsely limiting anarchism to purely opposition to the state does allow Marxists to portray their tradition as the only form of socialism and so exclude anarchism, by definition, from anti-capitalism.

After Marxism, we move onto more constructive and fruitful subjects, namely anarchist ideas of what a free society could be like (section I) and what we do in the here and now to bring it closer and to make our lives better (section J).

Section I is important, simply because it presents a rough outline of what anarchists have suggested would characterise a free society. So we discuss workers self-management, community self-government, economic and social federalism, anti-social behaviour in a free society, and a host of other issues. While many people, particularly Marxists, question the wisdom of discussing the future society (Marx's comment on "writing the cookbooks of the future" springs to mind[7]), anarchists have been more willing to sketch out a rough vision of what a free society could be like. This may come as a surprise for some (infatuated with Bakunin's pre-anarchist comment that *"the urge to destroy is a creative urge"*) but in reality anarchism has always been a constructive socio-economic theory and anarchist thinkers have always been more than willing to sketch what a free society *could* be.

And that is the key, this is what anarchy *could* be like. As we are at pains to stress, we are not presenting a blueprint: it is a series of suggestions based on our critique of capitalism, anarchist principles and the experiences of the struggle against oppression as well as social revolutions that have taken place. This is important, as anarchists have never abstractly postulated ideal social organisations to the oppression of hierarchy but, rather, developed our ideas of what a free society could look like by critically analysing the current exploitative and oppressive one as well as the self-activity and self-organisation of those resisting it. Anarchy will be created from below, by the people themselves, for, as Kropotkin put it, the *"work of demolition can only be accomplished by the direct participation of the whole of the people. And they will only act in the name of their immediate and popular needs. The land to the peasant; the factory, the workshop, the railway and the rest to the worker."*[8]

This anti-utopian perspective has been a significant aspect of anarchism since Proudhon who (especially his **System of Economic Contradictions**) attacked utopian socialists like Fourier and Saint-Simon for presenting fantastical visions (and appealing for rich benefactors!) rather than studying tendencies within capitalism which could transcend it (particularly working class self-activity). Thus social transformation *"must not emanate from the powers that be; it ought to be SPONTANEOUS."* It must come *"from below"* as only this ensured change *"by the concerted action of the citizens, by the experience of the workers, by the progress and diffusion of enlightenment, revolution by the means of liberty."*[9] Echoing Proudhon, Kropotkin argued that *"the method followed by the anarchist thinker"* is *"entirely different from that followed by the utopists ... He studies human society as it is now and was in the past ... tries to discover its tendencies, past and present, its growing needs, intellectual and economic, and in his ideal he merely points out in which direction evolution goes."*[10] A key aspect of this is looking at the self-organisation and struggles of working class people, these being the means by which anarchists link the current to the future.

So we discuss in **AFAQ** the perennial issues of both transition and how the new world gestates within the old. As section I.2.3 shows in detail, anarchists have always stressed that the new world is created in our struggles against the old. The fight for freedom transforms those who take part as well as creating the organisations (such as community assemblies, workers' councils, factory committees and their federations) which will be the framework of a free society. So the IWW slogan of *"building a new world in the shell of the old"* has been a key aspect of anarchism for some time, with Proudhon proclaiming during the 1848 Revolution that *"a new society be founded in the heart of the old society"* based on *"a body representative of the proletariat be[ing] formed ... in opposition to the bourgeoisie's representation."*[11]

Which brings us nicely to the last section, on what do anarchists do? In section J we summarise how anarchists see social change happening. There are substantial discussions on alternative forms of social organisation we advocate and how they are the embryonic forms of a free society we create while resisting the current oppressive one. Thus, for example, we discuss how the federations of workplace assemblies we urge to fight the bosses become the means by which co-operative production is organised in a free society while the neighbourhood assemblies created as a counter-power to the state become the means by which free individuals manage their communities. As will soon become clear, Marxist myths not withstanding, anarchists stress the importance of working class struggle in changing the world. Kropotkin summarised the libertarian perspective well in 1907:

> *"Workmen's organisations are the real force capable of accomplishing the social revolution – after the awakening of the proletariat has been accomplished, first by individual action, then by collective action, by strikes and revolts extending more and more; and where workmen's organisations have not allowed themselves to be dominated by the gentlemen who advocate 'the conquest of political power', but have continued to walk hand in hand with anarchists – as they have done in Spain – they have obtained, on the one hand, immediate results (an eight-hour day in certain trades in Catalonia), and on the other have made good propaganda for the social revolution – the one to come, not from the efforts of those highly-placed gentlemen, but from below, from workmen's organisations."*[12]

We also outline why anarchists support direct action and reject voting ("political action") as the means of social change, as well as the role of libertarians in social struggle and revolution and how we organise to influence both. As well as summarising our ideas on the important issues of how we organise and how we change the world, we take the time to refute some of the more common false claims against abstentionism and whether we are "a-political" or not. Suffice to say, the anarchist critique of electioneering has been validated (as can be seen by the numbers of ex-radical politicians and ex-socialist parties in the world). Our arguments on the transforming power of direct action, solidarity and working class self-organisation from below have, likewise, been vindicated time and time again.

Few, if any, anarchists place all their hopes in spontaneity (if that were all that was required we would be in an anarchist society by now!). So we organise *as anarchists* and participate in the class struggle to push it in libertarian directions. Kropotkin words are extremely relevant here:

> *"The syndicate[union] is absolutely necessary. It is the only form of working-men's group that permits of maintaining the direct struggle against capital, without falling into parliamentarianism. But evidently it does not take that trend mechanically, since we have in Germany, France and England syndicates rallying to parliamentarianism … The **other** element is necessary, the element of which Malatesta speaks and which Bakunin has always practised."*[13]

So section J also addresses the issue of how anarchists organise, the kinds of associations we create and how we seek to influence social movements and the class struggle. Suffice to say, while we reject Leninism and its vanguardism we do not reject organising anarchist groups and federations to explain our ideas in order to see them gain predominance in popular organisations and social conflicts.

It must also be noted that the sections within this volume have been slightly edited to ensure that it approximates volume 1 in size. This has involved trimming around a tenth of the material. I have tried to cut non-essential paragraphs and sub-sections to ensure that the core of the arguments remain intact. This means that, for example, section H.2 (which debunks various Marxist myths about anarchism) ends on section H.2.11 in print but goes to section H.2.14 on-line. This was done with a heavy heart.

Since volume 1 has been published, significant changes have occurred in the world. Neo-liberalism has taken a battering as the inevitable consequences of its policies resolved themselves in economic crisis. While reality has struck a blow to that ideology, it is fair to say that it will survive – after all, the ideology is so unrealistic already why should mere reality impact on its beauty for the true believer? Not to mention, of course, the significant class interests expressed in it. One thing is true, unless working class people organise and resist then governments, political discourse, economies and economic ideology will simply continue on as before – and those who will pay the costs of the crisis will not be the ruling class that created it.

On a more positive note, section B.1 of **AFAQ** indicated how hierarchies of wealth and power adversely affect those subject to them. **The Spirit Level: Why More Equal Societies Almost Always Do Better** by Richard Wilkinson and Kate Pickett presents more evidence on this subject, noting that on almost every index of quality of life or wellness there is a strong correlation between a country's level of economic inequality and its social outcomes. Significantly, it is not just the poor that are adversely affected by inequality, but society as a whole. So more equal societies have less crime and smaller prison populations as well as consistently delivering other advantages such as better physical and mental health, lower rates of teenage pregnancy and obesity, and higher rates of literacy and social trust. All of which confirm the anarchist analysis of the harmful effects of inequality in wealth and power.

AFAQ has moved its main site location (although the various aliases we have remain the same).[14] As a result, it also has a blog in which we post supplemental material on anarchism and news about the FAQ itself (such as updates).[15] Notable postings include the 2008 article marking the 150th anniversary of the use of the term "libertarian" by anarchists (*150 years of libertarian*), a supplement to our appendix on anarchist symbols contained in volume 1 (*The Red Flag of Anarchy*) and an unfinished appendix to section C explaining classical economics from a socialist perspective.

Finally, on a personal note, I dedicate this volume, like the first, to my family. I hope that this work will help, however slightly, to make the world a better place for them and that my children will grow up in a freer, more sustainable, world. Whether they do or not really is up to us, the current generation. Are we up for the challenge? Are we ready to fight for freedom and equality? The answer to that lies in your hands.

Either you can read **AFAQ** and leave it at that or you can join in the struggle for freedom and equality. The anarchist movement is not perfect, nor does it have all the answers. However, it remains for all that our best chance of making the world a fit place for unique individuals to live and flourish in. The question is whether we will remain happy to keep surviving within capitalism or whether we will seek to transform ourselves and our world for the better. We may fail. We may not stop the slide towards increased authoritarianism and atomisation. One thing is sure, if we do not resist then that slide will accelerate.

And if we do resist? Well, we may well change the world...

Iain McKay

www.anarchistfaq.org.uk

Endnotes

1   quoted by Peter Arshinov, **The History of the Makhnovist Movement**, p. 58

2   **The Betrayal of the American Right**, Ludwig von Mises Institute, p. 83

3   I would also like to take the opportunity to thank individualist anarchist Shawn Wilbur for his valued input into section G and the suggestions he made after reading the first drafts sent to him. Without this help, and the numerous works of nineteenth century anarchism he has placed on-line, this section would not be as comprehensive as it has become.

4   Nor, for that matter, that there are no libertarian Marxists. There are, as we indicated in section A.4.4 of volume 1 of **AFAQ**. Why they continue to call themselves Marxists while rejecting Marx's ideas on numerous key issues (and implicitly agreeing with Bakunin in the process) is a mystery.

5   We are aware that many Marxists reject the suggestion that Leninism is actually Marxist – a position we show has some validity. We argue that it was not only anarchism which Lenin distorted in **State and Revolution** but also important aspects of the ideas of Marx and Engels on such key issues as the state (see section H.3.10, for example).

6   **Property is Theft!**, p. 496, p. 535, p. 503 and p. 506

7   If Marx had been a bit more forthcoming then the likes of Stalin would have found it harder to label their nightmare regimes "socialist."

8   quoted by G. Woodcock and I. Avakumovic, **The Anarchist Prince**, p. 369.

9   Proudhon, **Op. Cit.**, p. 325 and p. 398

10   **Anarchism**, p. 47

11   **Op. Cit.**, p. 321. Proudhon had made a similar call in 1846, arguing that *"an agricultural and industrial combination must be found by means of which power, today the ruler of society, shall become its slave"* as the state is *"inevitably enchained to capital and directed against the proletariat."* (pp. 225-6)

12   quoted by Woodcock and Avakumovic, **Op. Cit.**, pp. 294-5. As noted in the introduction to volume 1, the words used by previous generations of anarchists are dated and would appear sexist if uttered today. Suffice to say, Kropotkin was in favour of working women unionising. As discussed in section A.3.5, with the notable exception of Proudhon, anarchists are for equality between the sexes – even if they unthinkingly used the sexist terminology of their time (Emma Goldman, for example, used "man" to describe all humanity).

13   quoted by Woodcock and Avakumovic, **Op. Cit.**, p. 295

14   Namely: www.anarchistfaq.org, www.anarchismfaq.org, www.anarchyfaq.org and www.anarchistfaq.org.uk.

15   It can be found at: http://anarchism.pageabode.com/blogs/afaq

Section G
Is individualist anarchism capitalistic?

Section G - Is individualist anarchism capitalistic?...................... 574

G.1 Are individualist anarchists anti-capitalist? 577
G.1.1 What about their support of the free market? 581
G.1.2 What about their support of "private property"? 585
G.1.3 What about their support for wage labour? 588
G.1.4 Why is the social context important in evaluating Individualist Anarchism? 593

G.2 Why do individualist anarchists reject social anarchism? 596
G.2.1 Is communist-anarchism compulsory? 596
G.2.2 Is communist-anarchism violent? 599
G.2.3 Does communist-anarchism aim to destroy individuality? 602
G.2.4 What other reasons do individualists give for rejecting communist-anarchism? 604

G.3 Is "anarcho"-capitalism a new form of individualist anarchism? 605
G.3.1 Is "anarcho"-capitalism American anarchism? 608
G.3.2 What are the differences between "anarcho"-capitalism and individualist anarchism? 611
G.3.3 What about "anarcho"-capitalists' support of "defence associations"? 614
G.3.4 Why is individualist anarchist support for equality important? 617
G.3.5 Would individualist anarchists have accepted "Austrian" economics? 618
G.3.6 Would mutual banking simply cause inflation? 619

G.4 Why do social anarchists reject individualist anarchism? 623
G.4.1 Is wage labour consistent with anarchist principles? 632
G.4.2 Why do social anarchists think individualism is inconsistent anarchism? 635

G.5 Benjamin Tucker: Capitalist or Anarchist? 639

G.6 What are the ideas of Max Stirner? 643

Section G
Is individualist anarchism capitalistic?

The short answer is, no, it is not. While a diverse tendency, the individualist anarchists were opposed to the exploitation of labour, all forms of non-labour income (such as profits, interest and rent) as well as capitalist property rights (particularly in land). While aiming for a free market system, they considered laissez-faire capitalism to be based on various kinds of state enforced class monopoly which ensured that labour was subjected to rule, domination and exploitation by capital. As such it is deeply **anti**-capitalist and many individualist anarchists, including its leading figure Benjamin Tucker, explicitly called themselves socialists (indeed, Tucker often referred to his theory as ***"Anarchistic-Socialism"***).

So, in this section of our anarchist FAQ we indicate why the individualist anarchists cannot be classified as "ancestors" of the bogus libertarians of the "anarcho"-capitalist school. Rather, they must be classified as libertarian **socialists** due to their opposition to exploitation, critique of capitalist property rights and concern for equality, albeit being on the liberal wing of anarchist thought. Moreover, while all wanted to have an economy in which all incomes were based on labour, many also opposed wage labour, i.e. the situation where one person sells their labour to another rather than the product of that labour (a position which, we argue, their ideas logically imply). So while **some** of their ideas do overlap with those of the "anarcho"-capitalist school they are not capitalistic, no more than the overlap between their ideas and anarcho-communism makes them communistic.

In this context, the creation of "anarcho"-capitalism may be regarded as yet another tactic by capitalists to reinforce the public's perception that there are no viable alternatives to capitalism, i.e. by claiming that "even anarchism implies capitalism." In order to justify this claim, they have searched the history of anarchism in an effort to find some thread in the movement that can be used for this purpose. They think that with the individualist anarchists they have found such a thread. However, such an appropriation requires the systematic ignoring or dismissal of key aspects of individualist-anarchism (which, of course, the right-"libertarian" does). Somewhat ironically, this attempt by right-"libertarians" to exclude individualist anarchism from socialism parallels an earlier attempt by state socialists to do the same. Tucker furiously refuted such attempts in an article entitled *"Socialism and the Lexicographers"*, arguing that *"the Anarchistic Socialists are not to be stripped of one half of their title by the mere dictum of the last lexicographer."* [**Instead of a Book**, p. 365]

Nevertheless, in the individualists we find anarchism coming closest to "classical" liberalism and being influenced by the ideas of Herbert Spencer, a forefather of "libertarian" capitalism (of the minimal state variety). As Kropotkin summarised, their ideas were *"a combination of those of Proudhon with those of Herbert Spencer."* [**Anarchism**, p. 296] What the "anarcho"-capitalist is trying is to ignore Proudhon's influence (i.e. the socialist aspect of their

theories) which just leaves Spencer, who was a right-wing liberal. To reduce individualist anarchism so is to destroy what makes it a unique political theory and movement. While both Kropotkin and Tucker praised Spencer as a synthetic philosopher and social scientist, they were both painfully aware of the limitations in his socio-political ideas. Tucker considered his attacks on all forms of socialism (including Proudhon) as authoritarian as being, at best, misinformed or, at worse, dishonest. He also recognised the apologetic and limited nature of his attacks on state intervention, noting that *"amid his multitudinous illustrations ... of the evils of legislation, he in every instance cites some law passed ostensibly at least to protect labour, alleviating suffering, or promote the people's welfare. But never once does he call attention to the far more deadly and deep-seated evils growing out of the innumerable laws creating privilege and sustaining monopoly."* Unsurprisingly, he considered Spencer as a *"champion of the capitalistic class."* [quoted by James J. Martin, **Men Against the State**, p. 240] As we will discuss in section G.3, it is likely that he would have drawn the same conclusion about "anarcho"-capitalism.

This does not mean that the majority thread within the anarchist movement is uncritical of individualist anarchism. Far from it! Social anarchists have argued that this influence of non-anarchist ideas means that while its *"criticism of the State is very searching, and [its] defence of the rights of the individual very powerful,"* like Spencer it *"opens ... the way for reconstituting under the heading of 'defence' all the functions of the State."* [Kropotkin, **Op. Cit.**, p. 297] This flows, social anarchists argue, from the impact of liberal principles and led some individualist anarchists like Benjamin Tucker to support contract theory in the name of freedom, without being aware of the authoritarian social relationships that could be implied by it, as can be seen under capitalism (other individualist anarchists were more aware of this contradiction as we will see). Therefore, social anarchists tend to think of individualist anarchism as an inconsistent form of anarchism, one which could become consistent by simply logically applying its own principles (see section G.4). On their part, many individualist anarchists simply denied that social anarchists were anarchists, a position other anarchists refute (see section G.2). As such, this section can also be considered, in part, as a continuation of the discussion begun in section A.3.

Few thinkers are completely consistent. Given Tucker's adamant anti-statism and anti-capitalism, it is likely that had he realised the authoritarian social relationships which contract theory tends to produce (and justify) when involving employing labour, he would have modified his views in such a way as to eliminate the contradiction (particularly as contracts involving wage labour directly contradict his support for "occupancy and use"). It is understandable why he failed to do so, however, given the social context in which he lived and agitated. In Tucker's America, self-employment was still a possibility on a wide scale (in fact, for much of the nineteenth century it was the dominant form of economic activity). His reforms were aimed at making it easier for workers to gain access to both land and machinery, so allowing wage workers to become independent farmers or artisans. Unsurprisingly, therefore, he viewed individualist anarchism as a society of workers, not one of capitalists and workers. Moreover, as we will argue in section G.4.1, his love for freedom and opposition to usury logically implies artisan and co-operative labour — people selling the products of their labour, as opposed to the labour itself — which itself implies self-management in production (and society in general), not authoritarianism within the workplace (this was the conclusion of Proudhon as well as Kropotkin). Nevertheless, it is this inconsistency — the non-anarchist aspect of individualist anarchism — which right "libertarians" like Murray Rothbard select and concentrate on, ignoring the anti-capitalist context in which this aspect of individualist thought exists. As David Wieck pointed out:

> "Out of the history of anarchist thought and action Rothbard has pulled forth a single thread, the thread of individualism, and defines that individualism in a way alien even to the spirit of a Max Stirner or a Benjamin Tucker, whose heritage I presume he would claim — to say nothing of how alien is his way to the spirit of Godwin, Proudhon, Bakunin, Kropotkin, Malatesta, and the historically anonymous persons who through their thoughts and action have tried to give anarchism a living meaning. Out of this thread Rothbard manufactures one more bourgeois ideology." [**Anarchist Justice**, pp. 227-228]

It is with this in mind that we discuss the ideas of people like Tucker. As this section of the FAQ will indicate, even at its most liberal, individualist, extreme anarchism was fundamentally **anti-**capitalist. Any concepts which "anarcho"-capitalism imports from the individualist tradition ignore both the theoretical underpinnings of their ideas as well as the social context of self-employment and artisan production within which those concepts arose, thus turning them into something radically different from what was intended by their originators. As we discuss in section G.1.4 the social context in which individualist anarchism developed is essential to understanding both its politics and its limitations ("*Anarchism in America is not a **foreign importation** but a product of the social conditions of this country and its historical traditions,*" although it is "*true that American anarchism was also influenced later by European ideas.*" [Rudolf Rocker, **Pioneers of American Freedom**, p. 163]).

Saying that, it would be a mistake to suggest (as some writers have) that individualist anarchism can be viewed purely in American terms. While understanding the nature of American society and economy at the time is essential to understanding individualist anarchism, it would be false to imply that only individualist anarchism was the product of American conditions and subscribed to by Americans while social anarchism was imported from Europe by immigrants. After all, Albert and Lucy Parsons were both native-born Americans who became communist-anarchists while Emma Goldman and Alexander Berkman only become anarchists once they had arrived in America. Native-born Voltairine de Cleyre moved from individualist to communist anarchism. Josiah Warren may have been born in Boston, but he developed his anarchism after his experiences in an experimental community set up by Welsh socialist Robert Owen (who, in turn, was inspired by William Godwin's ideas). While Warren and Proudhon may have developed their ideas independently, American libertarians became aware of Proudhon and other European socialists as radical journals had correspondents in France during the 1848 revolution and partial translations of radical writings from Europe appeared as quickly as they could be transmitted and translated. Individualist anarchists like William Greene and Tucker were heavily influenced by the ideas of Proudhon and so imported aspects of European anarchism into American individualist anarchism while the likes of the French individualist E. Armand brought aspects of American anarchism into the European movement. Similarly, both Spooner and Greene had been members of the First International while individualist anarchists Joseph Labadie and Dyer Lum were organisers of the **Knights of Labor** union along with Albert and Lucy Parsons. Lum later joined the anarcho-communist inspired **International Working People's Association** (IWPA) and edited its English language paper (the **Alarm**) when Parsons was imprisoned awaiting execution. All forms of anarchism were, in other words, a combination of European and American influences, both in terms of ideas and in terms of social experiences and struggles, even organisations.

While red-baiting and cries of "Un-American" may incline some to stress the "native-born" aspect of individualist anarchism (particularly those seeking to appropriate that tendency for their own ends), both wings of the US movement had native-born and foreign members, aspects and influences (and, as Rocker noted, the "*so-called white civilisation of [the American] continent is the work of European immigrants.*" [**Op. Cit.**, p. 163]). While both sides tended to denounce and attack the other (particularly after the Haymarket events), they had more in common than the likes of Benjamin Tucker and Johann Most would have been prepared to admit and each tendency, in its own way, reflected aspects of American society and the drastic transformation it was going through at the time. Moreover, it was changes in American society which lead to the steady rise of social anarchism and its eclipse of individualist anarchism from the 1880s onwards. While there has been a tendency to stress an individualist tendency in accounts of American anarchism due to its unique characteristics, only those "*without a background in anarchist history*" would think "*that the individualist anarchists were the larger segment of the anarchist movement in the U.S. at the time. Nothing could be farther from the truth. The collectivist branch of anarchism was much stronger among radicals and workers during the late nineteenth century and early twentieth century than the individualist brand. Before the Civil War, the opposite would be true.*" [Greg Hall, **Social Anarchism**, no. 30, pp. 90-91]

By the 1880s, social anarchism had probably exceeded the size of the "home-grown" individualists in the United States. The IWPA had some five thousand members at its peak with perhaps three times as many supporters. [Paul Avrich, **The Haymarket Tragedy**, p. 83] Its journals had an aggregate circulation of over 30,000. [George Woodcock, **Anarchism**, p. 395] In contrast, the leading individualist newspaper **Liberty** "*probably never had more than 600 to 1000 subscribers, but it was undoubtedly read by more than that.*" [Charles H. Hamilton, "*Introduction*", pp. 1-19, **Benjamin R. Tucker and the Champions of Liberty**, Coughlin, Hamilton and Sullivan (eds.), p. 10] The repression after Haymarket took its toll and the progress of social anarchism was hindered for a decade. However, "*[b]y the turn of the century, the anarchist movement in America had become predominantly communist in orientation.*" [Paul Avrich, **Anarchist Voices**, p. 5] As an added irony for those who stress the individualist nature of anarchism in America while dismissing social anarchism as a foreign import, the first American newspaper to use the name **"An-archist"** was published in Boston in 1881 by anarchists within the social revolutionary branch of the movement. [Paul Avrich, **The Haymarket Tragedy**, p. 57] Equally ironic, given the appropriation of the term by the American right, the first anarchist journal to use the term "libertarian" (**La Libertaire, Journal du Mouvement Social**) was published in New York between 1858 and 1861 by French communist-anarchist Joseph Déjacque. [Max Nettlau, **A Short History of Anarchism**, pp. 75-6]

All this is not to suggest that individualist anarchism does not have American roots nor that many of its ideas and visions were not significantly shaped by American social conditions and developments. Far from it! It is simply to stress that it did not develop in complete isolation of European anarchism during the latter half of the nineteenth century and that the social anarchism which overtook by the end of that century was also a product of American conditions (in this case, the transformation of a pre-capitalist society into a capitalist one). In other words, the rise of communist anarchism and the decline of individualist anarchism by the end of the nineteenth century reflected American society just as much as the development of the latter in the first place. Thus the rise of capitalism in America meant the rise of an anarchism more suitable to the social conditions and social relationships produced by that change. Unsurprisingly, therefore, individualist anarchism remains the minority trend in American anarchism to this day with such comrades as Joe Peacott (see his pamphlet **Individualism Reconsidered**), Kevin Carson (see his book **Studies in Mutualist Political Economy**) and Shawn Wilbur (who has painstakingly placed many rare early individualist and mutualist anarchist works onto the internet) keeping its ideas alive.

So like social anarchism, individualist anarchism developed as a response to the rise of capitalism and the transformation of American society this produced. As one academic put it, the *"early anarchists, though staunchly individualistic, did not entertain a penchant for … capitalism. Rather, they saw themselves as socialists opposed to the state socialism of Karl Marx. The individualist anarchists saw no contradiction between their individualist stance and their rejection of capitalism."* She stresses that they were *"fervent anti-capitalists"* and thought that *"workers created value through their labour, a value appropriated by owners of businesses … The individualist anarchists blamed capitalism for creating inhumane working conditions and for increasing inequalities of wealth. Their self-avowed 'socialism' was rooted in their firm belief in equality, material as well as legal."* This, however, did not stop her asserting that *"contemporary anarcho-capitalists are descendants of nineteenth-century individualist anarchists such as Josiah Warren, Lysander Spooner, and Benjamin Tucker."* [Susan Love Brown, pp. 99-128, *"The Free Market as Salvation from Government"*, **Meanings of the Market**, James G. Carrier (ed.), p. 104, p. 107, p. 104 and p. 103] Trust an academic to ignore the question of how related **are** two theories which differ on such a key issue as whether to be anti-capitalist or not!

Needless to say, some "anarcho"-capitalists are well aware of the fact that individualist anarchists were extremely hostile to capitalism while supporting the "free market." Unsurprisingly, they tend to downplay this opposition, often arguing that the anarchists who point out the anti-capitalist positions of the likes of Tucker and Spooner are quoting them out of context. The truth is different. In fact, it is the "anarcho"-capitalist who takes the ideas of the individualist anarchists from both the historical and theoretical context. This can be seen from the "anarcho"-capitalist dismissal of the individualist anarchists' "bad" economics as well as the nature of the free society wanted by them.

It is possible, no doubt, to trawl through the many issues of, say, **Liberty** or the works of individualist anarchism to find a few comments which may be used to bolster a claim that anarchism need not imply socialism. However, a few scattered comments here and there are hardly a firm basis to ignore the vast bulk of anarchist theory and its history as a movement. This is particularly the case when applying this criteria consistently would mean that communist anarchism, for example, would be excommunicated from anarchism simply because of the opinions of **some** individualist anarchists. Equally, it may be possible to cobble together all the non-anarchist positions of individualist anarchists and so construct an ideology which justified wage labour, the land monopoly, usury, intellectual property rights, and so on but such an ideology would be nothing more than a mockery of individualist anarchism, distinctly at odds with its spirits and aims. It would only convince those ignorant of the anarchist tradition.

It is not a fitting tribute to the individualist anarchists that their ideas are today being associated with the capitalism that they so clearly despised and wished to abolish. As one modern day Individualist Anarchist argues:

> *"It is time that anarchists recognise the valuable contributions of … individualist anarchist theory and take advantage of its ideas. It would be both futile and criminal to leave it to the capitalist libertarians, whose claims on Tucker and the others can be made only by ignoring the violent opposition they had to capitalist exploitation and monopolistic 'free enterprise' supported by the state."* [J.W. Baker, *"Native American Anarchism,"* pp. 43-62, **The Raven**, vol. 10, no. 1, pp. 61-2]

We hope that this section of the FAQ will go some way to explaining the ideas and contributions of individualist anarchism to a new generation of rebels. Given the diversity of individualist anarchism, it is hard to generalise about it (some are closer to classical liberalism than others, for example, while a few embraced revolutionary means of change such as Dyer Lum). However, we will do our best to draw out the common themes of the movement, indicating where certain people differed from others. Similarly, there are distinct differences between European and American forms of mutualism, regardless of how often Tucker invoked Proudhon's name to justify his own interpretations of anarchism and we will indicate these (these differences, we think, justify calling the American branch individualist anarchism rather than mutualism). We will also seek to show why social anarchism rejects individualist anarchism (and vice versa) as well as giving a critical evaluation of both positions. Given the diverse nature of individualist anarchism, we are sure that we will not cover all the positions and individuals associated with it but we hope to present enough to indicate why the likes of Tucker,

Labadie, Yarros and Spooner deserve better than to be reduced to footnotes in books defending an even more extreme version of the capitalism they spent their lives fighting.

G.1

Are individualist anarchists anti-capitalist?

To answer this question, it is necessary to first define what we mean by capitalism and socialism. While there is a tendency for supporters of capitalism (and a few socialists!) to equate it with the market and private property, this is not the case. It is possible to have both and not have capitalism (as we discuss in section G.1.1 and section G.1.2, respectively). Similarly, the notion that "socialism" means, by definition, state ownership and/or control, or that being employed by the state rather than by private capital is "socialism" is distinctly wrong. While some socialists have, undoubtedly, defined socialism in precisely such terms, socialism as a historic movement is much wider than that. As Proudhon put it, *"[m]odern Socialism was not founded as a sect or church; it has seen a number of different schools."* [**Selected Writings of Pierre-Joseph Proudhon**, p. 177]

As Proudhon, Bakunin, Kropotkin and Tucker all stressed, anarchism is one of those schools. For Kropotkin, anarchism was *"the no-government system of socialism."* [**Anarchism**, p. 46] Likewise, for Tucker, there were *"two schools of socialistic thought"*, one of which represented authority and the other liberty, namely *"State Socialism and Anarchism."* [**The Individualist Anarchists**, pp. 78-9] It was *"not Socialist Anarchism against Individualist Anarchism, but of Communist Socialism against Individualist Socialism."* [Tucker, **Liberty**, no. 129, p. 2] As one expert on Individualist Anarchism noted, Tucker *"looked upon anarchism as a branch of the general socialist movement."* [James J. Martin, **Men Against the State**, pp. 226-7] Thus we find Individualist anarchist Victor Yarros, like Tucker, talking about *"the position and teachings of the Anarchistic Socialists"* when referring to his ideas. [**Liberty**, no. 98, p. 5]

Part of the problem is that in the 20th century, the statist school of socialism prevailed both within the labour movement (at least in English speaking countries or until fascism destroyed it in mainland Europe and elsewhere) and within the revolutionary movement (first as social democracy, then as Communism after the Russian Revolution). This lead to anarchists not using the term "socialist" to describe their ideas as they did not want to be confused with either reformed capitalism (social democracy) or state capitalism (Leninism and Stalinism). As anarchism was understood as being inherently anti-capitalist, this did not become an issue until certain right-wing liberals started calling themselves "anarcho"-capitalists (somewhat ironically, these liberals joined with the state socialists in trying to limit anarchism to anti-statism and denying their socialist credentials). Another part of the problem is that many, particularly those in America, derive their notion of what socialism is from right-wing sources who are more than happy to agree with the Stalinists that socialism **is** state ownership. This is the case

with right-"libertarians", who rarely study the history or ideas of socialism and instead take their lead from such fanatical anti-socialists as Ludwig von Mises and Murray Rothbard. Thus they equate socialism with social democracy or Leninism/Stalinism, i.e. with state ownership of the means of life, the turning of part or the whole working population into employees of the government or state regulation and the welfare state. In this they are often joined by social democrats and Marxists who seek to excommunicate all other kinds of socialism from the anti-capitalist movement.

All of which leads to some strange contradictions. If "socialism" **is** equated to state ownership then, clearly, the individualist anarchists are not socialists but, then, neither are the social anarchists! Thus if we assume that the prevailing socialism of the 20th century defines what socialism is, then quite a few self-proclaimed socialists are not, in fact, socialists. This suggests that socialism cannot be limited to state socialism. Perhaps it would be easier to define "socialism" as restrictions on private property? If so, then, clearly, social anarchists are socialists but then, as we will prove, so are the individualist anarchists!

Of course, not all the individualist anarchists used the term "socialist" or "socialism" to describe their ideas although many did. Some called their ideas Mutualism and explicitly opposed socialism (William Greene being the most obvious example). However, at root the ideas were part of the wider socialist movement and, in fact, they followed Proudhon in this as he both proclaimed himself a socialist while also attacking it. The apparent contradiction is easily explained by noting there are two schools of socialism, state and libertarian. Thus it is possible to be both a (libertarian) socialist and condemn (state) socialism in the harshest terms.

So what, then, is socialism? Tucker stated that *"the bottom claim of Socialism"* was *"that labour should be put in possession of its own,"* that *"the natural wage of labour is its product"* and *"interest, rent, and profit … constitute the trinity of usury."* [**The Individualist Anarchists**, p. 78 and p. 80] This definition also found favour with Kropotkin who stated that socialism *"in its wide, generic, and true sense"* was an *"effort to **abolish** the exploitation of labour by capital."* [**Anarchism**, p. 169] For Kropotkin, anarchism was *"brought forth by the same critical and revolutionary protest which gave rise to Socialism in general"*, socialism aiming for *"the negation of Capitalism and of society based on the subjection of labour to capital."* Anarchism, unlike other socialists, extended this to oppose *"what constitutes the real strength of Capitalism: the State and its principle supports."* [**Environment and Evolution**, p. 19] Tucker, similarly, argued that Individualist anarchism was a form of socialism and would result in the *"emancipation of the workingman from his present slavery to capital."* [**Instead of a Book**, p. 323]

The various schools of socialism present different solutions to this exploitation and subjection. From the nationalisation of capitalist property by the state socialists, to the socialisation of property by the libertarian communists, to the co-operatives of mutualism, to the free market of the individualist anarchists, all are seeking, in one way or the other, to ensure the end of the domination and exploitation of labour by capital. The disagreements between them all rest in whether their solutions achieve this aim and whether they will make life worth living and enjoyable (which also explains why individualist and social anarchists disagree so much!). For anarchists, state socialism is little more than state **capitalism**, with a state monopoly replacing capitalist monopolies and workers being exploited by one boss (the state) rather than many. So all anarchists would agree with Yarrows when he argued that *"[w]hile* **State** *Socialism removes the disease by killing the patient,* **no**-*State Socialism offers him the means of recovering strength, health, and vigour."* [**Liberty**, no. 98, p. 5]

So, why are the individualist anarchists anti-capitalists? There are two main reasons.

Firstly, the Individualist Anarchists opposed profits, interest and rent as forms of exploitation (they termed these non-labour incomes **"usury"**, but as Tucker stressed usury was *"but another name for the exploitation of labour."* [**Liberty**, no. 122, p. 4]). To use the words of Ezra Heywood, the Individualist Anarchists thought *"Interest is theft, Rent Robbery, and Profit Only Another Name for Plunder."* [quoted by Martin Blatt, *"Ezra Heywood & Benjamin Tucker,"*, pp. 28-43, **Benjamin R. Tucker and the Champions of Liberty**, Coughlin, Hamilton and Sullivan (eds.), p. 29] Non-labour incomes are merely *"different methods of levying tribute for the use of capital."* Their vision of the good society was one in which *"the usurer, the receiver of interest, rent and profit"* would not exist and Labour would *"secure its natural wage, its entire product."* [Tucker, **The Individualist Anarchists**, p. 80, p. 82 and p. 85] This would also apply to dividends, *"since no idle shareholders could continue in receipt of dividends were it not for the support of monopoly, it follows that these dividends are no part of the proper reward of ability."* [Tucker, **Liberty**, no. 282, p. 2]

In addition, as a means of social change, the individualists suggested that activists start *"inducing the people to steadily refuse the payment of rents and taxes."* [**Instead of a Book** pp. 299-300] These are hardly statements with which capitalists would agree. Tucker, as noted, also opposed interest, considering it usury (exploitation and a *"crime"*) pure and simple and one of the means by which workers were denied the full fruits of their labour. Indeed, he looked forward to the day when *"any person who charges more than cost for any product"* will *"be regarded very much as we now regard a pickpocket."* This *"attitude of hostility to usury, in any form"* hardly fits into the capitalist mentality or belief system. [**Op. Cit.**, p. 155] Similarly, Ezra Heywood considered profit-taking *"an injustice which ranked second only to legalising titles to absolute ownership of land or raw-materials."* [James J. Martin, **Op. Cit.**, p. 111] Opposition to profits, rent or interest is hardly capitalistic — indeed, the reverse.

Thus the Individualist Anarchists, like the social anarchists, opposed the exploitation of labour and desired to see the end of capitalism by ensuring that labour would own what it produced. They desired a society in which there would no longer be capitalists and workers, only workers. The worker would receive the full product of his/her labour, so ending the exploitation of labour by capital. In Tucker's words, a free society would see *"each man reaping the fruits of his labour and no man able to live in idleness on an income from capital"* and so society would *"become a great hive of Anarchistic workers, prosperous and free individuals"* combining *"to carry on their production and distribution on the cost principle."* [**The Individualist Anarchists**, p. 276]

Secondly, the Individualist Anarchists favoured a new system of land ownership based on **"occupancy and use."** So, as well as this opposition to capitalist usury, the individualist anarchists also expressed opposition to capitalist ideas on property (particularly property in land). J.K. Ingalls, for example, considered that *"the private domination of the land"* originated in *"usurpation only, whether of the camp, the court or the market. Whenever such a domination excludes or deprives a single human being of his equal opportunity, it is a violation, not only of the public right, and of the social duty, but of the very principle of law and morals upon which property itself is based."* [quoted by Martin, **Op. Cit.**, p. 148f] As Martin comments, for Ingalls, *"[t]o reduce land to the status of a commodity was an act of usurpation, enabling a group to 'profit by its relation to production' without the expenditure of labour time."* [**Op. Cit.**, p. 148] These ideas are identical to Proudhon's and Ingalls continues in this Proudhonian *"occupancy and use"* vein when he argues that possession *"remains* **possession**, *and can never become* **property**, *in the sense of absolute dominion, except by positive statue [i.e. state action]. Labour can only claim* **occupancy**, *and can lay no claim to more than the usufruct."* Current property ownership in land were created by *"forceful and fraudulent taking"* of land, which *"could give no justification to the system."* [quoted by Martin, **Op. Cit.**, p. 149]

The capitalist system of land ownership was usually termed the **"land monopoly"**, which consisted of *"the enforcement by government of land titles which do not rest upon personal occupancy and cultivation."* Under anarchism, individuals would *"no longer be protected by their fellows in anything but personal occupancy and cultivation of land"* and so *"ground rent would disappear."* [Tucker, **The Individualist Anarchists**, p. 85] This applied to what was on the land as well, such as housing:

> *"If a man exerts himself by erecting a building on land which afterward, by the operation of the principle of occupancy and use, rightfully becomes another's, he must, upon demand of the subsequent occupant, remove from this land the results of his self-exertion, or, failing so to do, sacrifice his property therein."* [**Liberty**, no. 331, p. 4]

This would apply to both the land and what was on it. This meant that *"tenants would not be forced to pay ... rent"* nor would landlords *"be allowed to seize their property."* This, as Tucker noted, was a complete rejection of the capitalist system of property rights and saw anarchism being dependent on *"the Anarchistic view that occupancy and use should condition and limit landholding becom[ing] the prevailing view."* [**The Individualist Anarchists**, p. 162 and p. 159] As Joseph Labadie put it, socialism includes any theory *"which has for its object the* **changing of the present status of property** *and the relations one person or class holds to another. In other words, any movement which has for its aim the changing of social relations, of companionships, of associations, of powers of one class over another class, is Socialism."* [our emphasis, **Liberty**, no. 158, p. 8] As such, both social and individualist anarchists are socialists as both aimed at changing the present status of property.

It should also be noted here that the individualist anarchist ideal that competition in banking would drive interest to approximately zero is their equivalent to the social anarchist principle of free access to the means of life. As the only cost involved would be an administration charge which covers the labour involved in running the mutual bank, all workers would have access to "capital" for (in effect) free. Combine this with "occupancy and use" in terms of land use and it can be seen that both individualist and social anarchists shared a common aim to make the means of life available to all without having to pay a tribute to an owner or be dependent on a ruling capitalist or landlord class.

For these reasons, the Individualist Anarchists are clearly anti-capitalist. While an Individualist Anarchy would be a market system, it would not be a capitalist one. As Tucker argued, the anarchists realised "the fact that one class of men are dependent for their living upon the sale of their labour, while another class of men are relieved of the necessity of labour by being legally privileged to sell something that is not labour... . And to such a state of things I am as much opposed as any one. But the minute you remove privilege... every man will be a labourer exchanging with fellow-labourers ... What Anarchistic-Socialism aims to abolish is usury ... it wants to deprive capital of its reward." As noted above, the term "usury," for Tucker, was simply a synonym for "the exploitation of labour." [**Instead of a Book**, p. 404 and p. 396]

The similarities with social anarchism are obvious. Like them, the individualist anarchists opposed capitalism because they saw that profit, rent and interest were all forms of exploitation. As communist-anarchist Alexander Berkman noted, "[i]f the worker would get his due — that is, the things he produces or their equivalent — where would the profits of the capitalist come from? If labour owned the wealth it produced, there would be no capitalism." Like social anarchists they opposed usury, to have to pay purely for access/use for a resource. It ensured that a "slice of their daily labour is taken from [the workers] for the privilege of **using** these factories" [**What is Anarchism?**, p. 44 and p. 8] For Marx, abolishing interest and interest-bearing capital "means the abolition of capital and of capitalist production itself." [**Theories of Surplus Value**, vol. 3, p. 472] A position, incidentally, also held by Proudhon who maintained that "reduction of interest rates to vanishing point is itself a revolutionary act, because it is destructive of capitalism." [quoted by Edward Hyams, **Pierre-Joseph Proudhon: His Revolutionary Life, Mind and Works**, p. 188] Like many socialists, Individualist Anarchists used the term "interest" to cover all forms of surplus value: "the use of money" plus "house-rent, dividends, or share of profits" and having to "pay a tax to somebody who owns the land." "In doing away with interest, the cause of inequality in material circumstances will be done away with." [John Beverley Robinson, **The Individualist Anarchists**, pp. 144-5]

Given that Individualist Anarchism aimed to abolish interest along with rent and profit it would suggest that it is a socialist theory. Unsurprisingly, then, Tucker agreed with Marx's analysis on capitalism, namely that it lead to industry concentrating into the hands of a few and that it robbed workers of the fruits of the toil (for Francis Tandy it was a case of "the Marxian theory of surplus value, upon which all Socialistic philosophy — whether State or Anarchistic — is necessarily based" [**Op. Cit.**, no. 312, p. 3]). Tucker quoted a leading Marxist's analysis of capitalism and noted that "Liberty endorses the whole of it, excepting a few phrases concerning the nationalisation of industry and the assumption of political power by working people." However, he was at pains to argue that this analysis was first expounded by Proudhon, "that the tendency and consequences of capitalistic production ... were demonstrated to the world time and time again during the twenty years preceding the publication of 'Das Kapital'" by the French anarchist. This included "the historical persistence of class struggles in successive manifestations" as well as "the theory that labour is the source and measure of value." "Call Marx, then, the father of State socialism, if you will," argued Tucker, "but we dispute his paternity of the general principles of economy on which all schools of socialism agree." [**Liberty**, no. 35, p. 2]

This opposition to profits, rent and interest as forms of exploitation and property as a form of theft clearly makes individualist anarchism anti-capitalist and a form of (libertarian) socialism. In addition, it also indicates well the common ground between the two threads of anarchism, in particular their common position to capitalism. The social anarchist Rudolf Rocker indicates well this common position when he argues:

"it is difficult to reconcile personal freedom with the existing economic system. Without doubt the present inequality of economic interests and the resulting class conflicts in society are a continual danger to the freedom of the individual ... [T]he undisturbed natural development of human personality is impossible in a system which has its root in the shameless exploitation of the great mass of the members of society. One cannot be free either politically or personally so long as one is in economic servitude of another and cannot escape from this condition. This was recognised by men like Godwin, Warren, Proudhon, Bakunin, [and women like Goldman and de Cleyre, we must add!] and many others who subsequently reached the conviction that the domination of man over man will not disappear until there is an end of the exploitation of man by man." [**Nationalism and Culture**, p. 167]

There are other, related, reasons why the individualist anarchists must be considered left-wing libertarians rather than propertarians. Given their opposition to non-labour income, they saw their proposals as having egalitarian implications. As regards equality, we discover that they saw their ideas as promoting it. Thus we find Tucker arguing that that the "happiness possible in any society that does not improve upon the present in the matter of distribution of wealth, can hardly be described as beatific." He was clearly opposed to "the inequitable distribution of wealth" under capitalism and equally clearly saw his proposals as a means of reducing it substantially. The abolition of those class monopolies which create interest, rent and profit would reduce income and wealth inequalities substantially. However, there was "one exception, and that a comparatively trivial one", namely economic rent (the natural differences between different bits of land and individual labour). This "will probably remain with us always. Complete liberty will very much lessen it; of that I have no doubt ... At the worst, it will be a small matter, no more worth consideration in comparison with the liberty than the slight disparity that will always exist in consequence *of inequalities of skill."* [**Why I am an Anarchist**, pp. 135-6] Another individualist anarchist, John Beverley Robinson, agreed:

> *"When privilege is abolished, and the worker retains all that he produces, then will come the powerful trend toward equality of material reward for labour that will produce substantial financial and social equality, instead of the mere political equality that now exists."* [**Patterns of Anarchy**, pp. 278-9]

As did Lysander Spooner, who pointed out that the *"wheel of fortune, in the present state of things, is of such enormous diameter"* and *"those on its top are on so showy a height"* while *"those underneath it are in such a pit of debt, oppression, and despair."* He argued that under his system *"fortunes could hardly be represented by a wheel; for it would present no such height, no such depth, no such irregularity of motion as now. It should rather be represented by an extended surface, varied somewhat by inequalities, but still exhibiting a general level, affording a safe position for all, and creating no necessity, for either force or fraud, on the part of anyone to secure his standing."* Thus Individualist anarchism would create a condition *"neither of poverty, nor riches; but of moderate competency — such as will neither enervate him by luxury, nor disable him by destitution; but which will at once give him and opportunity to labour, (both mentally and physically) and stimulate him by offering him all the fruits of his labours."* [quoted by Stephan L. Newman, **Liberalism at Wit's End**, p. 72 and p. 73]

As one commentator on individualist anarchism, Wm. Gary Kline, correctly summarised:

> *"Their proposals were designed to establish true equality of opportunity ... and they expected this to result in a society without great wealth or poverty. In the absence of monopolistic factors which would distort competition, they expected a society of largely self-employed workmen with no significant disparity of wealth between any of them since all would be required to live at their own expense and not at the expense of exploited fellow human beings."* [**The Individualist Anarchists: A Critique of Liberalism**, pp. 103-4]

Hence, like social anarchists, the Individualist Anarchists saw their ideas as a means towards equality. By eliminating exploitation, inequality would soon decrease as wealth would no longer accumulate in the hands of the few (the owners). Rather, it would flow back into the hands of those who produced it (i.e. the workers). Until this occurred, society would see *"[o]n one side a dependent class of wage-workers and on the other a privileged class of wealth-monopolisers, each become more and more distinct from the other as capitalism advances."* This has *"resulted in a grouping and consolidation of wealth which grows apace by attracting all property, no matter by whom produced, into the hands of the privileged, and hence property becomes a social power, an economic force destructive of rights, a fertile source of injustice, a means of enslaving the dispossessed."* [William Ballie, **The Individualist Anarchists**, p. 121]

Moreover, like the social anarchists, the Individualist Anarchists were aware that the state was not some neutral machine or one that exploited all classes purely for its own ends. They were aware that it was a vehicle of **class rule,** namely the rule of the capitalist class over the working class. Spooner thought that that *"holders of this monopoly [of the money supply] now rule and rob this nation; and the government, in all its branches, is simply their tool"* and that *"the employers of wage labour ... are also the monopolists of money."* [Spooner, **A Letter to Grover Cleveland**, p. 42 and p. 48] Tucker recognised that *"capital had so manipulated legislation"* that they gained an advantage on the capitalist market which allowed them to exploit labour. [**The Individualist Anarchists**, pp. 82-3] He was quite clear that the state was a **capitalist** state, with *"Capitalists hav[ing] placed and kept on the statute books all sorts of prohibitions and taxes"* to ensure a "free market" skewed in favour of themselves. [**Instead of a Book**, p. 454] A.H. Simpson argued that the Individualist Anarchist *"knows very well that the present State ... is simply the tool of the property-owning class."* [**The Individualist Anarchists**, p. 92] Thus both wings of the anarchist movement were united in their opposition to capitalist exploitation and their common recognition that the state was a tool of the capitalist class, used to allow them to exploit the working class.

Tucker, like other individualist anarchists, also supported labour unions, and although he opposed violence during strikes he recognised that it was caused by frustration due to an unjust system. Indeed, like social anarchists, he considered *"the labourer in these days [as] a soldier... His employer is ... a member of an opposing army. The whole industrial and commercial world is in a state of internecine war, in which the proletaires are massed on one side and the proprietors on the other."* The cause of strikes rested in the fact that *"before ... strikers violated the equal liberty of others, their own right to equality of liberty had been wantonly and continuously violated"* by the capitalists using the state, for the *"capitalists ... in denying [a free market] to [the workers] are guilty of criminal invasion."* [**Instead of a Book**, p. 460 and p. 454] *"With our present economic system,"* Tucker stressed, *"almost every strike is just. For what is justice in production and distribution? That labour, which creates all, shall have **all**."* [**Liberty**, no. 19, p. 1]

Another important aspects of unions and strikes were that they represented both a growing class consciousness and the ability to change society. *"It is the power of the great unions to paralyse industry and **ignore** the government that has alarmed the political burglars,"* argued Victor Yarrows. This explained why unions and strikes were crushed by force as *"the State can have no rival, say the plutocrats, and the trades unions, with the sympathetic strike and boycott as weapons, are becoming too formidable."* Even defeated strikes were useful as they ensured that *"the strikers and their sympathisers will have acquired some additional knowledge of the essential nature of the beast, government, which plainly has no other purpose at present than to protect monopoly and put down all opposition to it." "There is such a thing as the solidarity of labour,"* Yarrows went on, *"and it is a healthy and encouraging sign that workmen recognise the need of mutual support and co-operation in their conflict with monopoly and its official and unofficial servants. Labour has to fight government as well as capital, 'law and order' as well as plutocracy. It cannot make the slightest movement against monopoly without colliding with some sort of 'authority', Federal,*

State, or municipal." The problem was that the unions *"have no clear general aims and deal with results rather than causes."* [**Liberty**, no. 291, p. 3]

This analysis echoed Tucker's, who applauded the fact that *"[a]nother era of strikes apparently is upon us. In all trades and in all sections of the country labour is busy with its demands and its protests. Liberty rejoices in them. They give evidence of life and spirit and hope and growing intelligence. They show that the people are beginning to know their rights, and, knowing, dare to maintain them. Strikes, whenever and wherever inaugurated, deserve encouragement from all true friends of labour."* [**Op. Cit.**, no. 19, p. 1] Even failed strikes were useful, for they exposed *"the tremendous and dangerous power now wielded by capital."* [**Op. Cit.**, no. 39, p. 1] The *"capitalists and their tools, the legislatures, already begin to scent the impending dangers of trades-union socialism and initiatory steps are on foot in the legislatures of several states to construe labour combinations as conspiracies against commerce and industry, and suppress them by law."* [**Op. Cit.**, no. 22, p. 3]

Some individualist anarchists, like Dyer Lum and Joseph Labadie, were union organisers while Ezra Heywood *"scoffed at supporters of the status quo, who saw no evidence of the tyranny on the part of capital, and who brought up the matter of free contract with reference to labourers. This argument was no longer valid. Capital controlled land, machinery, steam power, waterfalls, ships, railways, and above all, money and public opinion, and was in a position to wait out recalcitrancy at its leisure."* [Martin, **Op. Cit.**, p. 107] For Lum, *"behind the capitalist ... privilege stands as support"* and so social circumstances matter. *"Does liberty exist,"* he argued, *"where rent, interest, and profit hold the employee in economic subjection to the legalised possessor of the means of life? To plead for individual liberty under the present social conditions, to refuse to abate one jot of control that legalised capital has over individual labour, and to assert that the demand for restrictive or class legislation comes only from the voluntary associations of workmen [i.e., trade unions] is not alone the height of impudence, but a barefaced jugglery of words."* [**Liberty**, no. 101, p. 5]

Likewise, Tucker advocated and supported many other forms of non-violent direct action as well as workplace strikes, such as boycotts and rent strikes, seeing them as important means of radicalising the working class and creating an anarchist society. However, like social anarchists the Individualist Anarchists did not consider labour struggle as an end in itself — they considered reforms (and discussion of a *"fair wage"* and *"harmony between capital and labour"*) as essentially *"conservative"* and would be satisfied with no less than *"the abolition of the monopoly privileges of capital and interest-taking, and the return to labour of the full value of its production."* [Victor Yarros, quoted by Martin, **Op. Cit.**, p. 206f]

Therefore, it is clear that both social and Individualist Anarchists share much in common, including an opposition to capitalism. The former may have been in favour of free exchange but between equally situated individuals. Only given a context of equality can free exchange be considered to benefit both parties equally and not generate growing inequalities which benefit the stronger of the parties involved which, in turn, skews the bargaining position of those involved in favour of the stronger (also see section F.3).

It is unsurprising, therefore, that the individualist anarchists considered themselves as socialists. Like Proudhon, they desired a (libertarian) socialist system based on the market but without exploitation and which rested on possession rather than capitalist private property. With Proudhon, only the ignorant or mischievous would suggest that such a system was capitalistic. The Individualist Anarchists, as can be seen, fit very easily into Kropotkin's comments that *"the anarchists, in common with all socialists ... maintain that the now prevailing system of private ownership in land, and our capitalist production for the sake of profits, represent a monopoly which runs against both the principles of justice and the dictates of utility."* [**Anarchism**, p. 285] While they rejected the communist-anarchist solution to the social question, they knew that such a question existed and was rooted in the exploitation of labour and the prevailing system of property rights.

So why is Individualist Anarchism and Proudhon's mutualism socialist? Simply because they opposed the exploitation of labour by capital and proposed a means of ending it. The big debate between social and individualist anarchists revolves around whether the other school can **really** achieve this common goal and whether its proposed solution would, in fact, secure meaningful individual liberty for all.

G.1.1 What about their support of the free market?

Many, particularly on the "libertarian"-right, would dismiss claims that the Individualist Anarchists were socialists. By their support of the "free market" the Individualist Anarchists, they would claim, show themselves as really supporters of capitalism. Most, if not all, anarchists would reject this claim. Why is this the case?

This because such claims show an amazing ignorance of socialist ideas and history. The socialist movement has had a many schools, many of which, but not all, opposed the market and private property. Given that the right "libertarians" who make such claims are usually not well informed of the ideas they oppose (i.e. of socialism, particularly **libertarian** socialism) it is unsurprising they claim that the Individualist Anarchists are not socialists (of course the fact that many Individualist Anarchists argued they **were** socialists is ignored). Coming from a different tradition, it is unsurprising they are not aware of the fact that socialism is not monolithic. Hence we discover right-"libertarian" guru von Mises claiming that the *"essence of socialism is the entire elimination of the market."* [**Human Action**, p. 702] This would have come as something of a surprise to, say, Proudhon, who argued that *"[t]o suppress competition is to suppress liberty itself."* [**General Idea of the Revolution**, p. 50] Similarly, it would have surprised Tucker, who called himself a socialist while supporting a freer market than von Mises ever dreamt of. As Tucker put it:

> *"**Liberty** has always insisted that Individualism and Socialism are not antithetical terms; that, on the contrary, the most perfect Socialism is possible only on condition of the most perfect Individualism; and that Socialism includes, not only Collectivism and Communism, but also*

that school of Individualist Anarchism which conceives liberty as a means of destroying usury and the exploitation of labour." [**Liberty**, no. 129, p. 2]

Hence we find Tucker calling his ideas both *"Anarchistic Socialism"* and *"Individualist Socialism"* while other individualist anarchists have used the terms *"free market anti-capitalism"* and *"free market socialism"* to describe the ideas.

The central fallacy of the argument that support for markets equals support for capitalism is that many self-proclaimed socialists are not opposed to the market. Indeed, some of the earliest socialists were market socialists (people like Thomas Hodgskin and William Thompson, although the former ended up rejecting socialism and the latter became a communal-socialist). Proudhon, as noted, was a well known supporter of market exchange. German sociologist Franz Oppenheimer expounded a similar vision to Proudhon and called himself a *"liberal socialist"* as he favoured a free market but recognised that capitalism was a system of exploitation. [*"Introduction"*, **The State**, p. vii] Today, market socialists like David Schweickart (see his **Against Capitalism** and **After Capitalism**) and David Miller (see his **Market, State, and community: theoretical foundations of market socialism**) are expounding a similar vision to Proudhon's, namely of a market economy based on co-operatives (albeit one which retains a state). Unfortunately, they rarely, if ever, acknowledge their debt to Proudhon (needless to say, their Leninist opponents do as, from their perspective, it damns the market socialists as not being real socialists).

It could, possibly, be argued that these self-proclaimed socialists did not, in fact, understand what socialism "really meant." For this to be the case, **other**, more obviously socialist, writers and thinkers would dismiss them as not being socialists. This, however, is not the case. Thus we find Karl Marx, for example, writing of *"the socialism of Proudhon."* [**Capital**, vol. 1, p. 161f] Engels talked about Proudhon being *"the Socialist of the small peasant and master-craftsman"* and of *"the Proudhon school of Socialism."* [Marx and Engels, **Selected Works**, p. 254 and p. 255] Bakunin talked about Proudhon's *"socialism, based on individual and collective liberty and upon the spontaneous action of free associations."* He considered his own ideas as *"Proudhonism widely developed and pushed right to these, its final consequences"* [**Michael Bakunin: Selected Writings**, p. 100 and p. 198] For Kropotkin, while Godwin was the *"first theoriser of Socialism without government — that is to say, of Anarchism"* Proudhon was the second as he, *"without knowing Godwin's work, laid anew the foundations of Anarchism."* He lamented that *"many modern Socialists"* supported *"centralisation and the cult of authority"* and so *"have not yet reached the level of their two predecessors, Godwin and Proudhon."* [**Evolution and Environment**, pp. 26-7] These renowned socialists did not consider Proudhon's position to be in any way anti-socialist (although, of course, being critical of whether it would work and its desirability if it did). Tucker, it should be noted, called Proudhon *"the father of the Anarchistic school of Socialism."* [**Instead of a Book**, p. 381] Little wonder, then, that the likes of Tucker considered themselves socialists and stated numerous times that they were.

Looking at Tucker and the Individualist anarchists we discover that other socialists considered them socialists. Rudolf Rocker stated that

*"it is not difficult to discover certain fundamental principles which are common to all of them and which divide them from all other varieties of socialism. They all agree on the point that man be given the full reward of his labour and recognise in this right the economic basis of all personal liberty. They all regard the free competition of individual and social forces as something inherent in human nature … They answered the socialists of other schools who saw in **free competition** one of the destructive elements of capitalist society that the evil lies in the fact we have too little rather than too much competition, since the power of monopoly has made competition impossible."* [**Pioneers of American Freedom**, p. 160] Malatesta, likewise, saw many schools of socialism, including *"anarchist or authoritarian, mutualist or individualist."* [**Errico Malatesta: His Life and Ideas**, p. 95]

Adolph Fischer, one of the Haymarket Martyrs and contemporary of Tucker, argued that *"every anarchist is a socialist, but every socialist is not necessarily an anarchist. The anarchists are divided into two factions: the communistic anarchists and the Proudhon or middle-class anarchists."* The former *"advocate the communistic or co-operative method of production"* while the latter *"do not advocate the co-operative system of production, and the common ownership of the means of production, the products and the land."* [**The Autobiographies of the Haymarket Martyrs**, p. 81] However, while not being communists (i.e. aiming to eliminate the market), he obviously recognised the Individualists Anarchists as fellow socialists (we should point out that Proudhon **did** support co-operatives, but they did not carry this to communism as do most social anarchists — as is clear, Fischer means communism by the term *"co-operative system of production"* rather than co-operatives as they exist today and Proudhon supported — see section G.4.2).

Thus claims that the Individualist Anarchists were not "really" socialists because they supported a market system cannot be supported. The simple fact is that those who make this claim are, at best, ignorant of the socialist movement, its ideas and its history or, at worse, desire, like many Marxists, to write out of history competing socialist theories. For example, Leninist David McNally talks of the *"anarcho-socialist Pierre-Joseph Proudhon"* and how Marx combated *"Proudhonian socialism"* before concluding that it was *"non-socialism"* because it has *"wage-labour and exploitation."* [**Against the Market**, p. 139 and p. 169] Of course, that this is not true (even in a Marxist sense) did not stop him asserting it. As one reviewer correctly points out, *"McNally is right that even in market socialism, market forces rule workers' lives"* and this is *"a serious objection. But it is not tantamount to capitalism or to wage labour"* and it *"does not have exploitation in Marx's sense (i.e., wrongful expropriation of surplus by non-producers)"* [Justin Schwartz, **The American Political Science Review**, Vol. 88, No. 4, p. 982] For Marx, as we noted in section C.2, commodity production only becomes capitalism when there is the exploitation of wage labour. This is the case with Proudhon as well, who differentiated between possession and private property and argued that co-operatives should replace capitalist firms. While their specific solutions may have differed (with Proudhon aiming for a market economy consisting of artisans, peasants and co-operatives while Marx aimed for communism, i.e. the abolition of money via state ownership of capital) their analysis of capitalism and private property were identical — which Tucker consistently noted (as regards the theory of surplus value, for example, he argued that *"Proudhon propounded and proved [it] long before Marx advanced it."* [**Liberty**, no. 92, p. 1])

As Tucker argued, *"the fact that State Socialism ... has overshadowed other forms of Socialism gives it no right to a monopoly of the Socialistic idea."* [**Instead of a Book**, pp. 363-4] It is no surprise that the authoritarian left and "libertarian" right have united to define socialism in such a way as to eliminate anarchism from its ranks — they both have an interest in removing a theory which exposes the inadequacies of their dogmas, which explains how we can have both liberty **and** equality and have a decent, free and just society.

There is another fallacy at the heart of the claim that markets and socialism do not go together, namely that all markets are capitalist markets. So another part of the problem is that the same word often means different things to different people. Both Kropotkin and Lenin said they were "communists" and aimed for "communism." However, it does not mean that the society Kropotkin aimed for was the same as that desired by Lenin. Kropotkin's communism was decentralised, created and run from the bottom-up while Lenin's was fundamentally centralised and top-down. Similarly, both Tucker and the Social-Democrat (and leading Marxist) Karl Kautsky called themselves a "socialist" yet their ideas on what a socialist society would be like were extremely different. As J.W. Baker notes, *"Tucker considered himself a socialist ... as the result of his struggle against 'usury and capitalism,' but anything that smelled of 'state socialism' was thoroughly rejected."* ["*Native American Anarchism,"* pp. 43-62, **The Raven**, vol. 10, no. 1, p. 60] This, of course, does not stop many "anarcho"-capitalists talking about "socialist" goals as if all socialists were Stalinists (or, at best, social democrats). In fact, "socialist anarchism" has included (and continues to include) advocates of truly free markets as well as advocates of a non-market socialism which has absolutely nothing in common with the state capitalist tyranny of Stalinism. Similarly, "anarcho"-capitalists accept a completely ahistorical definition of "capitalism," so ignoring the massive state violence and support by which that system was created and is maintained.

The same with terms like "property" and the "free market," by which the "anarcho"-capitalist assumes the individualist anarchist means the same thing as they do. We can take land as an example. The individualist anarchists argued for an **"occupancy and use"** system of "property" (see next section for details). Thus in their "free market," land would not be a commodity as it is under capitalism and so under individualist anarchism absentee landlords would be considered as aggressors (for under capitalism they use state coercion to back up their collection of rent against the actual occupiers of property). Tucker argued that local defence associations should treat the occupier and user as the rightful owner, and defend them against the aggression of an absentee landlord who attempted to collect rent. An "anarcho"-capitalist would consider this as aggression **against** the landlord and a violation of "free market" principles. Such a system of "occupancy and use" would involve massive violations of what is considered normal in a capitalist "free market." Equally, a market system which was based on capitalist property rights in land would **not** be considered as genuinely free by the likes of Tucker.

This can be seen from Tucker's debates with supporters of laissez-faire capitalism such as Auberon Herbert (who, as discussed in section F.7.2, was an English minimal statist and sometimes called a forerunner of "anarcho"-capitalism). Tucker quoted an English critic of Herbert, who noted that *"When we come to the question of the ethical basis of property, Mr. Herbert refers us to 'the open market'. But this is an evasion. The question is not whether we should be able to sell or acquire 'in the open market' anything which we rightfully possess, but how we come into rightful possession."* [**Liberty**, no. 172, p. 7] Tucker rejected the idea *"that a man should be allowed a title to as much of the earth as he, in the course of his life, with the aid of all the workmen that he can employ, may succeed in covering with buildings. It is occupancy **and** use that Anarchism regards as the basis of land ownership, ... A man cannot be allowed, merely by putting labour, to the limit of his capacity and beyond the limit of his person use, into material of which there is a limited supply and the use of which is essential to the existence of other men, to withhold that material from other men's use; and any contract based upon or involving such withholding is as lacking in sanctity or legitimacy as a contract to deliver stolen goods."* [**Op. Cit.**, no. 331, p. 4]

In other words, an individualist anarchist would consider an "anarcho"-capitalist "free market" as nothing of the kind and vice versa. For the former, the individualist anarchist position on "property" would be considered as forms of regulation and restrictions on private property and so the "free market." The individualist anarchist would consider the "anarcho"-capitalist "free market" as another system of legally maintained privilege, with the free market distorted in favour of the wealthy. That capitalist property rights were being maintained by private police would not stop that regime being unfree. This can be seen when "anarcho"-capitalist Wendy McElroy states that *"radical individualism hindered itself ... Perhaps most destructively, individualism clung to the labour theory of value and refused to incorporate the economic theories arising within other branches of individualist thought, theories such as marginal utility. Unable to embrace statism, the stagnant movement failed to adequately comprehend the logical alternative to the state — a free market."* ["*Benjamin Tucker, **Liberty**, and Individualist Anarchism*", pp. 421-434, **The Independent Review**, vol. II, No. 3, p. 433] Therefore, rather than being a source of commonality, individualist anarchism and "anarcho"-capitalism actually differ quite considerably on what counts as a genuinely free market.

So it should be remembered that "anarcho"-capitalists at best agree with Tucker, Spooner, et al on fairly vague notions like the "free market." They do not bother to find out what the individualist anarchists meant by that term. Indeed, the "anarcho"-capitalist embrace of different economic theories means that they actually reject the reasoning that leads up to these nominal "agreements." It is the "anarcho"-capitalists who, by rejecting the underlying economics of the mutualists, are forced to take any "agreements" out of context. It also means that when faced with obviously anti-capitalist arguments and conclusions of the individualist anarchists, the "anarcho"-capitalist cannot explain them and are reduced to arguing that the anti-capitalist concepts and opinions expressed by the likes of Tucker are somehow "out of context." In contrast, the anarchist can explain these so-called "out of context" concepts by placing them into the context of the ideas of the individualist anarchists and the society which shaped them.

The "anarcho"-capitalist usually admits that they totally disagree with many of the essential premises and conclusions of the individualist anarchist analyses (see next section). The most basic difference is that the individualist anarchists rooted their ideas in the labour theory of value while the "anarcho"-capitalists favour mainstream marginalist theory. It does not take much thought to realise that advocates of socialist theories and those of capitalist ones will naturally develop differing notions of what is and what should be happening within a given economic system. One difference that **has** in fact arisen is that the notion of what constitutes a "free market" has differed according to the theory of value applied. Many things can be attributed to the workings of a "free" market under a capitalist analysis that would be considered symptoms of economic unfreedom under most socialist driven analyses.

This can be seen if you look closely at the case of Tucker's comments that anarchism was simply *"consistent Manchesterianism."* If this is done then a simple example of this potential confusion can be found. Tucker argued that anarchists *"accused"* the Manchester men *"of being inconsistent,"* that while being in favour of laissez faire for *"the labourer in order to reduce his wages"* they did not believe *"in liberty to compete with the capitalist in order to reduce his usury."* [**The Individualist Anarchists**, p. 83] To be consistent in this case is to be something other — and more demanding in terms of what is accepted as "freedom" — than the average Manchesterian (i.e. a supporter of "free market" capitalism). By *"consistent Manchesterism"*, Tucker meant a laissez-faire system in which class monopolies did not exist, where capitalist private property in land and intellectual property did not exist. In other words, a free market purged of its capitalist aspects. Partisans of the capitalist theory see things differently, of course, feeling justified in calling many things "free" that anarchists would not accept, and seeing "constraint" in what the anarchists simply thought of as "consistency." This explains both his criticism of capitalism **and** state socialism:

> *"The complaint of the Archist Socialists that the Anarchists are bourgeois is true to this extent and no further — that, great as is their detestation for a bourgeois society, they prefer its partial liberty to the complete slavery of State Socialism."* [**Why I am an Anarchist**, p. 136]

It should be clear that a "free market" will look somewhat different depending on your economic presuppositions. Ironically, this is something "anarcho"-capitalists implicitly acknowledge when they admit they do not agree with the likes of Spooner and Tucker on many of their key premises and conclusions (but that does not stop them claiming — despite all that — that their ideas are a modern version of individualist anarchism!). Moreover, the "anarcho"-capitalist simply dismisses all the reasoning that got Tucker there — that is like trying to justify a law citing Leviticus but then saying "but of course all that God stuff is just absurd." You cannot have it both ways. And, of course, the "anarcho"-capitalist support for non-labour based economics allow them to side-step (and so ignore) much of what anarchists — communists, collectivists, individualists, mutualists and syndicalists alike — consider authoritarian and coercive about "actually existing" capitalism. But the difference in economic analysis is critical. No matter what they are called, it is pretty clear that individualist anarchist standards for the freedom of markets are far more demanding than those associated with even the freest capitalist market system.

This is best seen from the development of individualist anarchism in the 20th century. As historian Charles A. Madison noted, it *"began to dwindle rapidly after 1900. Some of its former adherents joined the more aggressive communistic faction … many others began to favour the rising socialist movement as the only effective weapon against billion-dollar corporations."* [*"Benjamin R. Tucker: Individualist and Anarchist,"* pp. 444-67, **The New England Quarterly**, Vol. 16, No. 3, pp. p. 464] Other historians have noted the same. *"By 1908,"* argued Eunice Minette Schuster *"the industrial system had fastened its claws into American soil"* and while the *"Individualist Anarchists had attempted to destroy monopoly, privilege, and inequality, originating in the lack of opportunity"* the *"superior force of the system which they opposed … overwhelmed"* them. Tucker left America in 1908 and those who remained *"embraced either Anarchist-Communism as the result of governmental violence against the labourers and their cause, or abandoned the cause entirely."* [**Native American Anarchism**, p. 158, pp. 159-60 and p. 156] While individualist anarchism did not entirely disappear with the ending of **Liberty**, social anarchism became the dominant trend in America as it had elsewhere in the world.

As we note in section G.4, the apparent impossibility of mutual banking to eliminate corporations by economic competition was one of the reasons Voltairine de Cleyre pointed to for rejecting individualist anarchism in favour of communist-anarchism. This problem was recognised by Tucker himself thirty years after **Liberty** had been founded. In the postscript to a 1911 edition of his famous essay *"State Socialism and Anarchism"*, he argued that when he wrote it 25 years earlier *"the denial of competition had not effected the enormous concentration of wealth that now so gravely threatens social order"* and so while a policy of mutual banking might have stopped and reversed the process of accumulation in the past, the way now was *"not so clear."* This was because the tremendous capitalisation of industry now made the money monopoly a convenience, but no longer a necessity. Admitted Tucker, the *"trust is now a monster which … even the freest competition, could it be instituted, would be unable to destroy"* as *"concentrated capital"* could set aside a sacrifice fund to bankrupt smaller competitors and continue the process of expansion of reserves. Thus the growth of economic power, producing as it does natural barriers to entry from the process of capitalist production and accumulation, had resulted in a situation where individualist anarchist solutions could no longer reform capitalism away. The centralisation of capital had *"passed for the moment beyond their reach."* The problem of the trusts, he argued, *"must be grappled with for a time solely by forces political or revolutionary,"* i.e., through confiscation either through the machinery of government *"or in denial of it."* Until this *"great levelling"* occurred, all individualist anarchists could do was to spread their ideas as those trying to *"hasten it by joining in the propaganda of State Socialism or revolution make a sad mistake indeed."* [quoted by James J. Martin, **Op. Cit.**, pp. 273-4]

In other words, the economic power of *"concentrated capital"* and *"enormous concentration of wealth"* placed an insurmountable obstacle to the realisation of anarchy. Which means that the abolition of usury and relative equality were considered **ends** rather than side effects for Tucker and if free competition could not achieve these then such a society would **not** be anarchist. If economic inequality was large enough, it meant anarchism was impossible as the rule of capital could be maintained by economic power alone without the need for extensive state intervention (this was, of course, the position of revolutionary anarchists like Bakunin, Most and Kropotkin in the 1870s and onwards whom Tucker dismissed as not being anarchists).

Victor Yarros is another example, an individualist anarchist and associate of Tucker, who by the 1920s had abandoned anarchism for social democracy, in part because he had become convinced that economic privilege could not be fought by economic means. As he put it, the most *"potent"* of the *"factors and forces [which] tended to undermine and discredit that movement"* was *"the amazing growth of trusts and syndicates, of holding companies and huge corporations, of chain banks and chain stores."* This *"gradually and insidiously shook the faith of many in the efficacy of mutual banks, co-operative associations of producers and consumers, and the competition of little fellows. Proudhon's plan for a bank of the people to make industrial loans without interest to workers' co-operatives, or other members, seemed remote and inapplicable to an age of mass production, mechanisation, continental and international markets."* [*"Philosophical Anarchism: Its Rise, Decline, and Eclipse"*, pp. 470-483, **The American Journal of Sociology**, vol. 41, no. 4, p. 481]

If the individualist anarchists shared the "anarcho"-capitalist position or even shared a common definition of "free markets" then the *"power of the trusts"* would simply not be an issue. This is because "anarcho"-capitalism does not acknowledge the existence of such power, as, by definition, it does not exist in capitalism (although as noted in section F.1 Rothbard himself proved critics of this assertion right). Tucker's comments, therefore, indicate well how far individualist anarchism actually is from "anarcho"-capitalism. The "anarcho"-capitalist desires free markets no matter their result or the concentration of wealth existing at their introduction. As can be seen, Tucker saw the existence of concentrations of wealth as a problem and a hindrance towards anarchy. Thus Tucker was well aware of the dangers to individual liberty of inequalities of wealth and the economic power they produce. Equally, if Tucker supported the "free market" above all else then he would not have argued this point. Clearly, then, Tucker's support for the "free market" cannot be abstracted from his fundamental principles nor can it be equated with a "free market" based on capitalist property rights and massive inequalities in wealth (and so economic power). Thus individualist anarchist support for the free market does not mean support for a **capitalist** "free market."

In summary, the "free market" as sought by (say) Tucker would not be classed as a "free market" by right-wing "libertarians." So the term "free market" (and, of course, "socialism") can mean different things to different people. As such, it would be correct to state that **all** anarchists oppose the "free market" by definition as all anarchists oppose the **capitalist** "free market." And, just as correctly, "anarcho"-capitalists would oppose the individualist anarchist "free market," arguing that it would be no such thing as it would be restrictive of property rights (**capitalist** property rights of course). For example, the question of resource use in an individualist society is totally different than in a capitalist "free market" as landlordism would not exist. This is a restriction on capitalist property rights and a violation of a capitalist "free market." So an individualist "free market" would not be considered so by right-wing "libertarians" due to the substantial differences in the rights on which it would be based (with no right to capitalist private property being the most important).

All this means that to go on and on about individualist anarchism and its support for a free market simply misses the point. No one denies that individualist anarchists were (and are) in favour of a "free market" but this did not mean they were not socialists nor that they wanted the same kind of "free market" desired by "anarcho"-capitalism or that has existed under capitalism. Of course, whether their economic system would actually result in the abolition of exploitation and oppression is another matter and it is on this issue which social anarchists disagree with individualist anarchism **not** whether they are socialists or not.

G.1.2 What about their support of "private property"?

The notion that because the Individualist Anarchists supported "private property" they supported capitalism is distinctly wrong. This is for two reasons. Firstly, private property is not the distinctive aspect of capitalism — exploitation of wage labour is. Secondly and more importantly, what the Individualist Anarchists meant by "private property" (or "property") was distinctly different than what is meant by theorists on the "libertarian"-right or what is commonly accepted as "private property" under capitalism. Thus support of private property does not indicate a support for capitalism.

On the first issue, it is important to note that there are many different kinds of private property. If quoting Karl Marx is not **too** out of place:

> *"Political economy confuses, on principle, two very different kinds of private property, one of which rests on the labour of the producer himself, and the other on the exploitation of the labour of others. It forgets that the latter is not only the direct antithesis of the former, but grows on the former's tomb and nowhere else.*
>
> *"In Western Europe, the homeland of political economy, the process of primitive accumulation is more or less accomplished …*
>
> *"It is otherwise in the colonies. There the capitalist regime constantly comes up against the obstacle presented by the producer, who, as owner of his own conditions of labour, employs that labour to enrich himself instead of the capitalist. The contradiction of these two diametrically opposed economic systems has its practical manifestation here in the struggle between them."* [**Capital**, vol. 1, p. 931]

So, under capitalism, *"property turns out to be the right, on the part of the capitalist, to appropriate the unpaid labour of others, or its product, and the impossibility, on the part of the worker, of appropriating his own product."* In other words, property is not viewed as being identical with capitalism. *"The historical conditions of [Capital's] existence are by no means given with the mere circulation of money and commodities. It arises only when the owner of the means of production and subsistence finds the free worker available on the market, as the seller of his own labour-power."* Thus wage-labour, for Marx, is the necessary pre-condition for capitalism, **not** "private property" as such as *"the means of production and subsistence, while they remain the property of the immediate producer, are not capital. They only become capital under circumstances in which they serve at the same time as means of exploitation of, and domination over, the worker."* [**Op. Cit.**, p. 730, p. 264 and p. 933]

For Engels, *"[b]efore capitalistic production"* industry was *"based upon the private property of the labourers in their means of production"*, i.e., *"the agriculture of the small peasant"* and *"the handicrafts organised in guilds."* Capitalism, he argued, was based on capitalists owning *"**social** means of production only workable by a collectivity of men"* and so they *"appropriated ... the product of the **labour of others**."* Both, it should be noted, had also made this same distinction in the **Communist Manifesto**, stating that *"the distinguishing feature of Communism is not the abolition of property generally, but the abolition of bourgeois property."* Artisan and peasant property is *"a form that preceded the bourgeois form"* which there *"is no need to abolish"* as *"the development of industry has to a great extent already destroyed it."* This means that communism *"deprives no man of the power to appropriate the products of society; all that it does is to deprive him of the power to subjugate the labour of others by means of such appropriation."* [Marx and Engels, **Selected Works**, p. 412, p. 413, p. 414, p. 47 and p. 49]

We quote Marx and Engels simply because as authorities on socialism go, they are ones that right-"libertarians" (or Marxists, for that matter) cannot ignore or dismiss. Needless to say, they are presenting an identical analysis to that of Proudhon in **What is Property?** and, significantly, Godwin in his **Political Justice** (although, of course, the conclusions drawn from this common critique of capitalism were radically different in the case of Proudhon). This is, it must be stressed, simply Proudhon's distinction between property and possession (see section B.3.1). The former is theft and despotism, the latter is liberty. In other words, for genuine anarchists, "property" is a **social relation** and that a key element of anarchist thinking (both social and individualist) was the need to redefine that relation in accord with standards of liberty and justice.

So what right-"libertarians" do when they point out that the individualist anarchists supported property is to misunderstand the socialist critique of capitalism. They, to paraphrase Marx, confuse two very different kinds of "property," one of which rests on the labour of the producers themselves and the other on the exploitation of the labour of others. They do not analyse the social relationships between people which the property in question generates and, instead, concentrate on **things** (i.e. property). Thus, rather than

being interested in people and the relationships they create between themselves, the right-"libertarian" focuses on property (and, more often than not, just the word rather than what the word describes). This is a strange position for someone seeking liberty to take, as liberty is a product of social interaction (i.e. the relations we have and create with others) and not a product of things (property is not freedom as freedom is a relationship between people, not things). They confuse property with possession (and vice versa).

So artisan and co-operative property is not capitalist. It does not generate relationships of exploitation and domination as the worker owns and controls their own means of production. It is, in effect, a form of socialism (a *"petit bourgeois"* form of socialism, to use the typical insulting Marxist phrase). Thus support for "private property" need not mean support for capitalism (as shown, for example, by the Individualist Anarchists). To claim otherwise is to ignore the essential insight of socialism and totally distort the socialist case against capitalism.

To summarise, from an anarchist (and Marxist) perspective capitalism is **not** defined by "property" as such. Rather, it is defined by private property, property which is turned into a means of exploiting the labour of those who use it. For most anarchists, this is done by means of wage labour and abolished by means of workers' associations and self-management (see next section for a discussion of individualist anarchism and wage labour). To use Proudhon's terminology, there is a fundamental difference between property and possession.

Secondly, and more importantly, what the Individualist Anarchists meant by "private property" (or "property") was distinctly different than what is meant by supporters of capitalism. Basically, the "libertarian" right exploit, for their own ends, the confusion generated by the use of the word "property" by the likes of Tucker to describe a situation of "possession." Proudhon recognised this danger. He argued that *"it is proper to call different things by different names, if we keep the name 'property' for the former [individual possession], we must call the latter [the domain of property] robbery, rapine, brigandage. If, on the contrary, we reserve the name 'property' for the latter, we must designate the former by the term **possession** or some other equivalent; otherwise we should be troubled with an unpleasant synonym."* [**What is Property?**, p. 373] Unfortunately Tucker, who translated this work, did not heed Proudhon's words of wisdom and called possession in an anarchist society by the word "property" (but then, so did Proudhon in the latter part of his life!) Looking at Tucker's arguments, it is clear that the last thing Tucker supported was capitalist property rights. For example, he argued that *"property, in the sense of individual possession, is liberty"* and contrasted this with capitalist property. [**Instead of a Book**, p. 394] That his ideas on "property" were somewhat different than that associated with right-"libertarian" thinkers is most clearly seen with regards to land. Here we discover him advocating *"occupancy and use"* and rejecting the "right" of land owners to bar the landless from any land they owned but did not **personally** use. Rent was *"due to that denial of liberty which takes the shape of land monopoly, vesting titles to land in individuals and associations which do not use it, and thereby compelling the non-owning users to pay tribute to the non-using owners as a condition of admission to the competitive market."* Anarchist opposition of rent did *"not* mean simply the freeing of unoccupied land. It means the freeing of all land not occupied **by the owner**. In other words, it means land ownership limited by occupancy and use." [Tucker, **The Individualist Anarchists**, p. 130 and p. 155]

A similar position was held by John Beverley Robinson. He argued that there "are two kinds of land ownership, proprietorship or property, by which the owner is absolute lord of the land, to use it or to hold it out of use, as it may please him; and possession, by which he is secure in the tenure of land which he uses and occupies, but has no claim upon it at all if he ceases to use it." Moreover, "[a]ll that is necessary to do away with Rent is to away with absolute property in land." [**Patterns of Anarchy**, p. 272] Joseph Labadie, likewise, stated that "the two great sub-divisions of Socialists" (anarchists and State Socialists) both "agree that the resources of nature — land, mines, and so forth — should not be held as private property and subject to being held by the individual for speculative purposes, that use of these things shall be the only valid title, and that each person has an equal right to the use of all these things. They all agree that the present social system is one composed of a class of slaves and a class of masters, and that justice is impossible under such conditions." [**What is Socialism?**]

Thus the Individualist Anarchists definition of "property" differed considerably from that of the capitalist definition. As they themselves acknowledge. Robinson argued that "the only real remedy is a change of heart, through which land using will be recognised as proper and legitimate, but land holding will be regarded as robbery and piracy." [**Op. Cit.**, p. 273] Tucker, likewise, indicated that his ideas on "property" were not the same as existing ones when he argued that "the present system of land tenure should be changed to one of occupancy and use" and that "no advocate of occupancy-and-use tenure of land believes that it can be put in force, until as a theory it has been as generally ... seen and accepted as the prevailing theory of ordinary private property." [**Occupancy and Use verses the Single Tax**] Thus, for Tucker, anarchism is dependent on "the Anarchistic view that occupancy and use should condition and limit landholding becom[ing] the prevailing view." [**The Individualist Anarchists**, p. 159]

Based on this theory of "property" Tucker opposed landlords and rent, arguing that anarchy "means the freeing of all land not occupied **by the owner**" that is, "land ownership limited by occupancy and use." He extended this principle to housing, arguing that "Anarchic associations" would "not collect your rent, and might not even evict your tenant" and "tenants would not be forced to pay you rent, nor would you be allowed to seize their property. The Anarchic Associations would look upon your tenants very much as they would look upon your guests." [**Op. Cit.**, p. 155 and p. 162] In fact, individualist anarchism would "accord the actual occupant and user of land the right to that which is upon the land, who left it there when abandoning the land." [Tucker, **Liberty**, no. 350, p. 4]

In the case of land and housing, almost all Individualist Anarchists argued that the person who lives or works on it (even under lease) would be regarded "as the occupant and user of the land on which the house stands, and as the owner of the house itself," that is they become "the owner of both land and house as soon as he becomes the occupant." [Tucker, **Occupancy and Use Versus the Single Tax**] For Tucker, occupancy and use was "the Anarchistic solution

of the land question" as it allowed free access to land to all, to be "enjoyed by the occupant without payment of tribute to a non-occupant." This applied to what was on the land as well, for if A builds a house, and rents it to B, who lives or works in it under the lease then Tucker would "regard B as the occupant and user of the land on which the house stands, and as **the owner of the house itself**." [**Liberty**, no. 308, p. 4]

Needless to say, the individualist anarchists were just as opposed to that mainstay of modern capitalism, the corporation. For Greene corporations "disarrange our social organisation, and make the just distribution of the products of labour impossible." [quoted by Wm. Gary Kline, **The Individualist Anarchists: A Critique of Liberalism**, p. 94] While opposing state attempts to limit trusts (it did not get to the root of the problem which lay in class privilege), Tucker took it for granted that "corporate privileges are in themselves a wrong." [**The Individualist Anarchists**, p. 129] Given that "occupancy and use" applies to what is on the land, it logically follows that for those workplaces with absentee owners (i.e., owners who hire managers to run them) then these are abandoned by their owners. By the "occupancy and use" criteria, the land and what is on it reverts to those actually using them (i.e., the workers in question). Corporations and shareowners, in other words, are extremely unlikely to exist in individualist anarchism.

Hence to claim that the Individualist Anarchists supported capitalist property rights is false. As can be seen, they advocated a system which differed significantly to the current system, indeed they urged the restriction of property rights to a form of possession. Unfortunately, by generally using the term "property" to describe this new system of possession they generated exactly the confusion that Proudhon foretold. Sadly, right-"libertarians" use this confusion to promote the idea that the likes of Tucker supported capitalist property rights and so capitalism. As Tucker argued, "[d]efining it with Proudhon as the sum total of legal privileges bestowed upon the holder of wealth, [individualist anarchism] agrees with Proudhon that property is robbery. But using the word in the commoner acceptation, as denoting the labour's individual possession of his product or of his proportional share of the joint product of himself and others, [it] holds that property is liberty." [**Liberty**, no. 122, p. 4]

If, as it is sometimes suggested, the difference between right "libertarians" and left libertarians is that the former despise the state because it hinders the freedom of property while the latter condemn it because it is a bastion of property, it is worthwhile to note two important facts. Firstly, that individualist anarchism condemns the state because it protects the land monopoly, i.e., capitalist property rights in land and what is on it, rather than a system of "occupancy and use." Secondly, that all schools of anarchist oppose capitalism because it is based on the exploitation of labour, an exploitation which the state protects. Hence de Cleyre: "I wish a sharp distinction made between the legal institution of property, and property in the sense that what a man definitely produces by his own labour is his own." The inequality and oppressions of capitalism are "the inevitable result of the whole politico-economic lie that man can be free and the institution of property continue to exist." [**Exquisite Rebel**, p. 297] Given this, given these bastions of property against which the both the individualist and social anarchists turn their fire, it is obvious that both schools are left libertarians.

For these reasons it is clear that just because the Individualist Anarchists supported (a form of) "property" does not mean they are capitalists. After all, as we note in the section G.2 communist-anarchists recognise the necessity of allowing individuals to own and work their own land and tools if they so desire yet no one claims that they support "private property." Equally, that many of the Individualist Anarchists used the term "property" to describe a system of possession (or "occupancy-and-use") should not blind us to the non-capitalist nature of that "property." Once we move beyond looking at the words they used to what they meant by those words we clearly see that their ideas are distinctly different from those of supporters of capitalism. In fact, they share a basic commonality with social anarchism ("*Property will lose a certain attribute which sanctifies it now. The absolute ownership of it — 'the right to use or abuse' will be abolished — and possession, use, will be the only title.*" [Albert R. Parsons, **Anarchism: Its Philosophy and Scientific Basis**, p. 173]). This should be unsurprising given the influence of Proudhon on both wings of the movement.

As Malatesta noted, recognising the "*the right of workers to the products of their own labour,*" demanding "*the abolition of interest*" and "*the division of land and the instruments of labour among those who wish to use them*" would be "*a socialist school different from [communist-anarchism], but it is still socialism.*" It would be a "*mutualist*" socialism. [**At the Café**, p. 54 and p. 56] In other words, property need not be incompatible with socialism. It all depends on the type of property being advocated.

G.1.3 What about their support for wage labour?

As we have argued in section A.2.8 and elsewhere, a consistent anarchist must oppose wage labour as this is a form of hierarchical authority. While social anarchism has drawn this logical conclusion from anarchist principles, individualist anarchism has not. While many of its supporters have expressed opposition to wage labour along with other forms hierarchical organisation, some (like Tucker) did not. The question is whether supporting wage labour disqualifies them from the socialist movement or not.

Within individualist anarchism, there are two different positions on this matter. Some of them clearly opposed wage labour as inherently exploitative and saw their socio-economic ideas as a means of ending it. Others argued that it was not wage labour **as such** which was the problem and, as a consequence, they did not expect it to disappear under anarchy. So opposition to exploitation of labour was a universal thread in Individualist Anarchist thought, as it was in the social anarchist movement. However, opposition to wage slavery was a common, but not universal, thread within the individualist anarchist tradition. As we discuss in section G.4, this is one of the key reasons why social anarchists reject individualist anarchism, arguing that this makes it both inconsistent in terms of general anarchist principles as well in the principles of individualist anarchism.

Voltairine de Cleyre in her overview of anarchism put the difference in terms of individualist anarchism and mutualist anarchism. As she put it, the "*extreme individualists*" held that the "*essential institutions of Commercialism are in themselves good, and are rendered vicious merely by the interference by the State.*" This meant "*the system of employer and employed, buying and selling, banking, and all the other essential institutions of Commercialism*" would exist under their form of anarchism. Two key differences were that property in land would be modified so that it could be "*held by individuals or companies for such time and in such allotments as they use only*" and that "*wages would rise to the full measure of the individual production, and forever remain there*" as "*bosses would be hunting for men rather than men bosses.*" In other words, land would no longer be owned as under capitalism and workers would no longer be exploited as profit, interest and rent could not exist and the worker would get the full product of his or her labour in wages. In contrast, mutualist anarchism "*is a modification of the program of Individualism, laying more emphasis upon organisation, co-operation and free federation of the workers. To these the trade union is the nucleus of the free co-operative group, which will obviate the necessity of an employer … The mutualist position on the land question is identical with that of the Individualists.*" The "*material factor which accounts for such differences as there are between Individualists and Mutualists*" was due to the former being intellectual workers and so "*never know[ing] directly the oppressions of the large factory, nor mingled with workers' associations. The Mutualists had; consequently their leaning towards a greater Communism.*" ["*Anarchism*", **Exquisite Rebel**, pp. 77-8]

Next, we must clarify what is meant by **"wage labour"** and the related term **"wages system."** They are not identical. Marx, for example, corrected the Gotha Programme's "*abolition of the wage system*" by saying "*it should read: system of wage labour*" (although that did not stop him demanding "*the ultimate abolition of the wages system*" elsewhere). [Marx and Engels, **Selected Works**, p. 324 and p. 226] The difference lies in whether there is communism (distribution according to need) or socialism (distribution according to work done), as in Marx's (in)famous difference between a lower and higher phase of communism. It is the difference between a distribution of goods based on deeds and one based on needs and Kropotkin's famous polemic "*The collectivist Wages System*" rests on it. He argued that the wages system was based on "*renumeration to each according to the time spent in producing, while taking into account the productivity of his labour*". In other words: "*To each according to his deeds.*" [**The Conquest of Bread**, p. 162 and p. 167] Such a wages system could exist in different forms. Most obviously, and the focus of Kropotkin's critique, it could be a regime where the state owned the means of production and paid its subjects according to their labour (i.e., state socialism). It could also refer to a system of artisans, peasants and co-operatives which sold the product of their labour on a market or exchanged their goods with others based on labour-time notes (i.e., associational socialism).

This should not be confused with wage labour, in which a worker sells their labour to a boss. This results in a hierarchical social relationship being created in which the worker is the servant of the employer. The employer, as they own the labour of the worker, also keeps the product of said labour and as we argued in section C.2, this places the boss is in a position to get the worker to produce more than they get back in wages. In other words, wage labour is based on oppression and can result in exploitation as the bosses control both the production process (i.e., the labour of the workers) and the goods it produces. It is this which explains socialist opposition to wage labour — it is the means by which labour is exploited under capitalism (anarchist opposition to wage labour includes this but also extends it to include its denial of freedom to those subject to workplace hierarchy).

So for the purposes of this discussion **"wage labour"** refers to hierarchical social relationships **within** production while **"wages system"** refers to how goods are distributed once they are produced. Thus you can have a wages system without wage labour but not wage labour without a wages system. Communist-anarchists aim for the abolition of both wage labour and the wages system while mutualist-anarchists only aim to get rid of the first one. The problem is that the terms are sometimes mixed up, with "wages" and "wages system" being confused with "wage labour." This is the case with the nineteenth century American labour movement which tended to use the term "wages system" to refer to wage labour and the expression *"abolition of the wages system"* to refer to the aim of replacing capitalism with a market system based on producer co-operatives.

So after this unfortunately essential diversion, we can now discuss the position of individualist anarchism on wage labour. Unfortunately, there is no consistent position on this issue within the tradition. Some follow social anarchism in arguing that a free society would see its end, others see no contradiction between their ideas and wage labour. We will discuss each in turn.

Joshua King Ingalls, for example, praised attempts to set up communities based on libertarian principles as *"a demonstration … that none need longer submit to the tyranny and exactions of the swindler and speculator in the products of others toil. The example would be speedily followed by others who would break away from the slavery of wages, and assert their independence of capital."* [*"Method of Transition for the Consideration of the True Friends of Human Rights and Human Progress,"* **Spirit of the Age**, Vol. I, No. 25, pp. 385-387] The *"present relation of 'Capital and Labor' is … really a mixed relation between contract and status; held by fiction of law as one of 'freedom of contract,' while it retains potentially all the essential features of serfdom. Industrially and economically, the relation is substantially the same as that which existed between the chattel and his owner, and the serf and his lord."* Ingalls pointed to *"the terrible fear of being 'out of a job,' which freedom of contract means to a wage-worker."* [*"Industrial Wars and Governmental Interference,"* **The Twentieth Century**, September 6, 1894, pp. 11-12] *"To reward capital,"* he argued, *"is a direct inversion of natural right, as the right of man must be acknowledged paramount to that of property … Any system, securing a premium to capital, however small, must result in the want, degradation and servitude of one class, and in bestowing unearned wealth and power upon another."* [*"Man and Property, their Rights and Relations,"* **Spirit of the Age**, vol. I, no. 8, pp. 114-116] Like Proudhon, he recognised that joint productive activity resulted in an output greater than that possible by the same number of people working in isolation, an

output monopolised by those who owned the workplace or land in question:

> *"That the operation of any wealth increasing enterprise is co-operative needs only stating … and its logic in division of the product of the conjoint labour, can only be frustrated by the fiction that the worker has contracted away his share of the increase by accepting wages. But, being dispossessed of his common right to land, and to opportunity to use the common materials and forces, he can make no equitable contract and cannot be lawfully thus concluded … The only pretence which prevents this distribution, is the plea that the worker in accepting wages, has tacitly contracted away his share of the increase, has made a sale of his interest. Even this subterfuge fails logically however, whenever the operators reduce the rate of compensation without the full concurrence of the co-operative workers, and their just claim to joint ownership obtains again. It is altogether too late, to urge that this is a mere matter of exchange; so much money, so much labour-; and that the operator may lay off and take on whom he pleases. It never was, as economists teach, a matter of exchange, but one of co-operative endeavour."* [*"Industrial Wars and Governmental Interference,"* **The Twentieth Century**, September 6, 1894, pp. 11-12]

Unsurprisingly given this analysis he saw the need to replace wage labour (which he called *"false and immoral"*) with a better system: *"the adoption of honesty in our useful industries, and a reciprocal system of exchange, would unfold a grand and universal cooperative movement, seems so clear to me."* [*"The Wage Question"*, **The American Socialist**, Vol. 2, No. 38, p. 298] This would result in a boost to economic activity:

> *"No one, say they, will do anything but for profits. But the man who works for wages has no profits; and is not only destitute of this stimulus, but his labour product is minus the profits of the capitalist, landlord, and forestaller. A rational economy would seem to require, that if any one received extra inducement to act, it should be that one who did the most labourious and repulsive work. It is thus seen, that while exorbitant profits afford an unnatural stimulus, in mere wages we have an inadequate motive to action."* [*"Labor, Wages, And Capital. Division Of Profits Scientifically Considered"*, **Brittan's Quarterly Journal**, No. I, pp. 66-79]

The land monopoly was *"the foundation of class dominion and of poverty and industrial subjection."* [quoted by Bowman N. Hall, *"Joshua K. Ingalls, American Individualist: Land Reformer, Opponent of Henry George and Advocate of Land Leasing, Now an Established Mode"*, pp. 383-96, **American Journal of Economics and Sociology**, Vol. 39, No. 4, p. 387] Without access to land, people would have no option to sell their liberty to others and, as such, the abolition of slavery and wage labour were related:

> *"The right to life involves the right to land to live and labour upon. Commercial ownership of land which enables one to exclude another from it, and thus enforces*

involuntary idleness, is as destructive of human freedom as ownership of the person, enforcing involuntary service ... Liberation of the slaves would bring their labour in more direct competition with our over-crowded and poorly paid wage-workers. I did not offer this as a reason against the abolition of chattel slavery, but as a reason why the friends of emancipation from chattel slavery should unite with the friends for the emancipation of the wage worker, by restoring him the right to land, for the production of the means of life ... The real issue was between the rights of labour and the rights of ownership." [quoted by Bowman N. Hall, **Op. Cit.**, p. 385]

This analysis was a common theme in pre-civil war libertarian circles. As historian James J. Martin noted, *"[t]o men like Warren and Evens chattel slavery was merely one side of a brutal situation, and although sympathetic with its opponents, refused to take part in the struggle [against slavery] unless it was extended to a wholesale attack on what they termed 'wage slavery' in the states where Negro slavery no longer existed."* [**Men Against the State**, p. 81] Such a view, we may add, was commonplace in radical working class journals and movements of the time. Thus we find George Henry Evans (who heavily influenced Individualist Anarchists like Warren and Ingalls with the ideas of land reform based on *"occupancy and use"*) writing:

"I was formally, like yourself, sir, a very warm advocate of the abolition of (black) slavery. This was before I saw that there was white slavery. Since I saw this, I have materially changed my views as to the means of abolishing Negro slavery. I now see clearly, I think, that to give the landless black the privilege of changing masters now possessed by the landless white, would hardly be a benefit to him in exchange for his surety of support in sickness and old age, although he is in a favourable climate." [quoted by Martin, **Op. Cit.**, p. 81f]

Ingalls, likewise, *"considered the only 'intelligent' strike [by workers as] one which would be directed against wage work altogether."* For Lysander Spooner, liberty meant that the worker was entitled to *"all the fruits of his own labour"* and argued that this *"might be feasible"* only when *"every man [was] his own employer or work[s] for himself in a direct way, since working for another resulted in a portion being diverted to the employer."* [Martin, **Op. Cit.**, p. 153 and p. 172] To quote Spooner:

*"When a man knows that he is to have **all** the fruits of his labour, he labours with more zeal, skill, and physical energy, than when he knows — as in the case of one labouring for wages — that a portion of the fruits of his labour are going to another... In order that each man may have the fruits of his own labour, it is important, as a general rule, that each man should be his own employer, or work directly for himself, and not for another for wages; because, in the latter case, a part of the fruits of his labour go to his employer, instead of coming to himself ... That each man may be his own employer, it is necessary that he have materials, or capital, upon which*

to bestow his labour." [**Poverty: Its Illegal Causes and Legal Cure**, p. 8]

Wage labour had a negative impact on those subject to it in terms of their personal development. *"The mental independence of each individual would be greatly promoted by his pecuniary independence,"* Spooner argued. *"Freedom of thought, and the free utterance of thought, are, to a great degree, suppressed ... by their dependence upon the will and favour of others, for that employment by which they must obtain their daily bread. They dare not investigate, or if they investigate, dare not freely avow and advocate those moral, social, religious, political, and economical truths, which alone can rescue them from their degradation, lest they should thereby sacrifice their bread by stirring the jealousy of those out whom they are dependent, and who derive their power, wealth, and consequence from the ignorance and servitude of the poor."* [**Op. Cit.**, p. 54] As we argued in section B.1, all forms of hierarchy (including wage labour) distorts the personality and harms the individual psychologically.

Spooner argued that it was state restrictions on credit and money (the *"money monopoly"* based on banks requiring gold/silver to operate) as the reason why people sell themselves to others on the labour market. As he put it, *"a monopoly of money ... . put[s] it wholly out of the power of the great body of wealth-producers to hire the capital needed for their industries; and thus compel them ... — by the alternative of starvation — to sell their labour to the monopolists of money ... [who] plunder all the producing classes in the prices of their labour."* Spooner was well aware that it was capitalists who ran the state (*"the employers of wage labour ... are also the monopolists of money"*). In his ideal society, the *"amount of money capable of being furnished ... is so great that every man, woman, and child... could get it, and go into business for himself, or herself — either singly, or in partnerships — and be under no necessity to act as a servant, or sell his or her labour to others. All the great establishments, of every kind, now in the hands of a few proprietors, but employing a great number of wage labourers, would be broken up; for few, or no persons, who could hire capital, and do business for themselves, would consent to labour for wages for another."* [**A Letter to Grover Cleveland**, p. 20, p. 48 and p. 41]

As Eunice Minette Schuster noted, Spooner's *"was a revolt against the industrial system"*, a **return to pre-industrial** *society."* He *"would destroy the factory system, wage labour ... by making every individual a small capitalist, an independent producer"* and *"turn the clock of time backwards, not forward."* This position seems to have been a common one, for *"the early American Individualists aimed to return ... to an economic system where everyone would be a small, independent proprietor."* [**Native American Anarchism**, p. 148, pp. 151-2 and p. 157] As another commentator on individualist anarchism also noted, *"the dominant vision of the future was obviously that of a relatively modest scale of production ... underpinned by individual, self-employed workers"* and so the individualist anarchists *"expected a society of largely self-employed workmen with no significant disparity of wealth between any of them."* [Wm. Gary Kline **The Individualist Anarchists**, p. 95 and p. 104]

This is not to say that all the individualist anarchists ignored the rise of large scale industrial production. Far from it. Tucker, Greene and Lum all recognised that anarchism had to adjust to the industrial system and proposed different solutions for it. Greene and Lum followed Proudhon and advocated co-operative production while Tucker argued that mutual banks could result in a non-exploitative form of wage labour developing.

William Greene pronounced that *"[t]here is no device of the political economists so infernal as the one which ranks labour as a commodity, varying in value according to supply and demand … To speak of labour as merchandise is treason; for such speech denies the true dignity of man … Where labour is merchandise in fact … there man is merchandise also, whether in England or South Carolina."* This meant that, *"[c]onsidered from this point of view, the price of commodities is regulated not by the labour expended in their production, but by the distress and want of the labouring class. The greater the distress of the labourer, the more willing will he be to work for low wages, that is, the higher will be the price he is willing to give for the necessaries of life. When the wife and children of the labourer ask for bread, and he has none to give them, then, according to the political economists, is the community prosperous and happy; for then the rate of wages is low, and commodities command a high price in labour."* [**Mutual Banking**, pp. 49-50 and p. 49]

Greene's alternative was co-operation in production, consumption and exchange. *"The triple formula of practical mutualism"*, he argued, was *"the associated workshop"* for production, the *"protective union store"* for consumption and the *"the Mutual Bank"* for exchange. All three were required, for *"the Associated Workshop cannot exist for a single day without the Mutual Bank and the Protective Union Store."* Without mutual banking, the productive co-operatives would not survive as it would not gain access to credit or at a high rate (*"How do you advance the cause of labour by putting your associated neck under the heel of capital? Your talk about 'the emancipation of labour' is wind and vapour; labour cannot be emancipated by any such process."*) Thus the *"Associated Workshop ought to be an organisation of personal credit. For what is its aim and purpose? Is it not the emancipation of the labourer from all dependence upon capital and capitalists?"* [**Op. Cit.**, p. 37, p. 34, p. 35 and p. 34] The example of the Mondragon co-operative complex in the Basque country confirms the soundness of Greene's analysis.

Here we see a similar opposition to the commodification of labour (and so labourers) within capitalism that also marks social anarchist thought. As Rocker notes, Greene *"emphasised more strongly the **principle of association** than did Josiah Warren and more so than Spooner had done."* He had a *"strong sympathy for the **principle of association**. In fact, the theory of Mutualism is nothing less than co-operative labour based on the cost principle."* He also *"rejected … the designation of labour as a **commodity**"* and *"constantly endeavoured to introduce his ideas into the youthful labour movement … so as to prevent the social problem being regarded by labour as only a question of wages."* [**Pioneers of American Freedom**,, p. 108, p. 109, pp. 111-2 and p. 112] This support for producers' associations alongside mutual banks is identical to Proudhon's ideas — which is unsurprising as Greene was a declared follower of the French anarchist. Martin also indicates Greene's

support for co-operation and associative labour and its relation to the wider labour movement:

> *"Coming at a time when the labour and consumer groups were experimenting with 'associated workshops' and 'protective union stores,' Greene suggested that the mutual bank be incorporated into the movement, forming what he called 'complementary units of production, consumption, and exchange … the triple formula of practical mutualism.'"* [**Op. Cit.**, pp. 134-5]

Dyer Lum was another individualist anarchist who opposed wage labour and supported co-operative production. Like Greene, Lum took an active part in the labour movement and was a union organiser. As he put it, the Knights of Labor aimed to work for the *"abolishment of the wage-system"* as well as the right of life requiring the right to the means of living. Dyer, while rejecting their infatuation with political action, had *"the fullest sympathy"* for their aims and supported their economic measures. [**Liberty**, no. 82, p. 7] Unsurprisingly, as one historian notes, *"Lum began to develop an ideology that centred on the labour reformers' demand: 'The Wage System must go!'"* He joined *"the ideological path of labour reformers who turned to a radicalised laissez-faire explanation of wage slavery."* [Frank H. Brooks, *"Ideology, Strategy, and Organization: Dyer Lum and the American Anarchist Movement"*, pp. 57-83, **Labor History**, vol. 34, No. 1, p. 63 and p. 67] Like the communist-anarchists of the IWPA, for Lum trade unions were both the means of fighting capitalism and the way to abolish wage labour:

> *"Anarchists in Chicago tended to be much more sympathetic to class organisation, specifically unions, because they had many contacts to local unions and the Knights of Labor. The issue was not resolved at the founding conference of the IWPA, but the Chicago anarchists did manage to get a resolution passed stating that 'we view in trades unions based upon progressive principles — the abolition of the wages-system — the corner-stone of a better society structure than the present one.'*
>
> *"Lum agreed wholeheartedly with this resolution, particularly the phrase 'abolition of the wages-system.' This phrase not only confirmed the ideological link between anarchism and labour reform, but also paralleled similar language in the declaration of principles of the Knights of Labor. By 1886, Lum had joined the Knights and he urged other anarchists, particularly individualists, to support their struggles. Lum continued to be involved with organised labour for the next seven years, seeing unions as a practical necessity in the struggle against class politics and state repression."* [Brooks, **Op. Cit.**, pp. 70-1]

However, *"[d]espite the similarity between the evolution of Lum's strategy and that of the revolutionary anti-statist socialists in the IWPA, his analysis of 'wage slavery' was considerably more individualistic."* [Brooks, **Op. Cit.**, p. 66] Lum saw it as resulting primarily from state interference in the economy which reduced the options available to working class people. With a genuine free market based on free land and free credit workers would work for themselves, either as independent producers or in co-operatives ("*where capital seeks labour … where authority dissolves under the genial glow of liberty, and necessity for wage-labour disappears.*" [Dyer D. Lum, contained in Albert Parsons, **Anarchism**, p. 153]). Thus a key element of "*Lum's anarchism was his mutualist economics, an analysis of 'wage slavery' and a set of reforms that would 'abolish the wage system.'*" [Brooks, **Op. Cit.**, p. 71] Voltairine de Cleyre, in her individualist anarchist days, concurred with her mentor Lum, arguing for a "*complete international federation of labour, whose constituent groups shall take possession of land, mines, factories, all the instruments of production, issue their own certificates of exchange, and, in short, conduct their own industry without regulative interference from law-makers or employers.*" [**The Voltairine de Cleyre Reader**, p. 6]

European individualist anarchists, it should be noted had a similar perspective. As mentioned in section A.3.1, Frenchman E. Armand argued that "*ownership of the means of production and free disposal of his produce*" was "*the quintessential guarantee of the autonomy of the individual*" but only as long as "*the proprietor does not transfer it to someone else or reply upon the services of someone else in operating it.*" ["*Mini-Manual of the Anarchist Individualist*", pp. 145-9, **Anarchism**, Robert Graham (ed.), p. 147] Another French individualist anarchist, Ernest Lesigne, argued that in a free society, "*there should be no more proletaires*" as "*everybody*" would be "*proprietor.*" This would result in "*The land to the cultivator. The mine to the miner. The tool to the labourer. The product to the producer.*" [quoted approvingly by Tucker, **Instead of a Book**, p. 17 and p. 18] Lesigne considered "*co-operative production*" as "*a solution to the great problem of social economy, — the delivery of products to the consumer at cost*" and as a means of producers to "*receive the value of your product, of your effort, without having to deal with a mass of hucksters and exploiters.*" [**The Individualist Anarchists**, p. 123]

In other words, many individualist anarchists envisioned a society without wage labour and, instead, based upon peasant, artisan and associated/co-operative labour (as in Proudhon's vision). In other words, a **non**-capitalist society or, more positively, a (libertarian) socialist one as the workers' own and control the means of production they use. Like social anarchists, they opposed capitalist exploitation, wage slavery and property rights. However, not all individualist anarchists held this position, a notable exception being Benjamin Tucker and many of his fellow contributors to **Liberty**. Tucker asserted against the common labour movement and social anarchist equation of capitalism with wage slavery that "*[w]ages is not slavery. Wages is a form of voluntary exchange, and voluntary exchange is a form of Liberty.*" [**Liberty**, no. 3, p. 1]

The question now is, does this support of wage labour equate to support for capitalism? The answer to that depends on whether you see such a system as resulting in the exploitation of labour. If socialism is, to requote Kropotkin, "*understood in its wide, generic, and true sense*" as "*an effort to **abolish** the exploitation of labour by capital*" then even those Individualist Anarchists who support wage labour must be considered as socialists due to their opposition to usury. It is for this reason we discover Rudolf Rocker arguing that

Stephan P. Andrews was "*one of the most versatile and significant exponents of libertarian socialism*" in the USA in spite of his belief that "*the specific cause of the economic evil [of capitalism] is founded not on the existence of the wage system*" but, rather, on the exploitation of labour, "*on the unjust compensation of the worker*" and the usury that "*deprives him of a part of his labour.*" [**Op. Cit.**, p. 85 and pp. 77-8] His opposition to exploitation meant he was a socialist, an opposition which individualist anarchism was rooted in from its earliest days and the ideas of Josiah Warren:

> "*The aim was to circumvent the exploitation inherent in capitalism, which Warren characterised as a sort of 'civilised cannibalism,' by exchanging goods on co-operative rather than supply and demand principles.*" [J.W. Baker, "*Native American Anarchism,*" pp. 43-62, **The Raven**, vol. 10, no. 1, p. 51]

So it should not be implied that the term socialist is restricted simply to those who oppose wage labour. It should be noted that for many socialists, wage labour is perfectly acceptable — as long as the state is the boss. As Tucker noted, State Socialism's "*principle plank*" is "*the confiscation of **all** capital by the State*", so stopping "*the liberty of those non-aggressive individuals who are thus prevented from carrying on business for themselves or assuming relations between themselves as employer and employee if they prefer, and who are obliged to become employees of the State against their will.*" [**Instead of a Book**, p. 378] Of course, such a position is not a very good form of socialism which is why anarchists have tended to call such schemes state-capitalism (an analysis which was confirmed once the Soviet Union was created, incidentally). If state bureaucrats own and control the means of production, it would not come as too great a surprise if they, like private bosses, did so to maximise their incomes and minimise that of their employees.

Which explains why the vast majority of anarchists do not agree with Tucker's position. Individualist anarchists like Tucker considered it as a truism that in their society the exploitation of labour could not exist. Thus even if some workers did sell their liberty, they would still receive the full product of their labour. As Tucker put it, "*when interest, rent and profit disappear under the influence of free money, free land, and free trade, it will make no difference whether men work for themselves, or are employed, or employ others. In any case they can get nothing but that wage for their labour which free competition determines.*" [**Op. Cit.**, p. 274] Whether this could actually happen when workers sell their liberty to an employer is, of course, where other anarchists disagree. The owner of a workplace does not own simply his (labour) share of the total product produced within it. He (and it usually is a he) owns everything produced while workers get their wages. The employer, therefore, has an interest in getting workers to produce as much as they can during the period they are employed. As the future price of the commodity is unknown, it is extremely unlikely that workers will be able to accurately predict it and so it is unlikely that their wages will always equal the cost price of the product. As such, the situation that an individual worker would get his "natural" wage would be unlikely and so they would be exploited by their employer. At best, it could be argued that in the long run wages will rise to that level but, as Keynes noted, in the long run we are all dead and Tucker did not say that the free market would end exploitation eventually. So individual ownership of large-scale workplaces would not, therefore, end exploitation.

In other words, if (as Tucker argued) individualist anarchism desires "[n]ot to abolish wages, but to make **every** man dependent upon wages and to secure every man his **whole** wages" then this, logically, can only occur under workers control. We discuss this in more detail in section G.4.1, where we also indicate how social anarchists consider Tucker's position to be in a basic contradiction to anarchist principles. Not only that, as well as being unlikely to ensure that labour received its full product, it also contradicts his own principle of **"occupancy and use"**. As such, while his support for non-exploitative wage labour does not exclude him from the socialist (and so anarchist) movement, it does suggest an inconsistent anarchism, one which can (fortunately) be easily made consistent by bringing it fully in line with its own stated ideals and principles.

Finally, we must note that there is a certain irony in this, given how keenly Tucker presented himself as a follower of Proudhon. This was because Proudhon agreed with Tucker's anarchist opponents, arguing continually that wage labour needed to be replaced by co-operative production to end exploitation and oppression in production. We discuss this aspect of Proudhon's ideas in section G.4.2.

So, to conclude, it can be seen that individualist anarchists hold two positions on wage labour. Some are closer to Proudhon and the mainstream anarchist tradition than others while a few veer extremely close to liberalism. While all are agreed that their system would end the exploitation of labour, some of them saw the possibility of a non-exploitative wage labour while others aimed for artisan and/or co-operative production to replace it. Suffice to say, while few social anarchists consider non-exploitative wage labour as being very likely it is the opposition to non-labour income which makes individualist anarchism socialist (albeit, an inconsistent and flawed version of libertarian socialism).

G.1.4 Why is the social context important in evaluating Individualist Anarchism?

When reading the work of anarchists like Tucker and Warren, we must remember the social context of their ideas, namely the transformation of America from a pre-capitalist to a capitalist society. The individualist anarchists, like other socialists and reformers, viewed with horror the rise of capitalism and its imposition on an unsuspecting American population, supported and encouraged by state action (in the form of protection of private property in land, restricting money issuing to state approved banks using specie, government orders supporting capitalist industry, tariffs, suppression of unions and strikes, and so on). In other words, the individualist anarchists were a response to the social conditions and changes being inflicted on their country by a process of "primitive accumulation" (see section F.8).

The non-capitalist nature of the early USA can be seen from the early dominance of self-employment (artisan and peasant production). At the beginning of the 19th century, around 80% of the working (non-slave) male population were self-employed. The great majority of Americans during this time were farmers working their own land, primarily for their own needs. Most of the rest were self-employed artisans, merchants, traders, and professionals. Other classes — employees (wage workers) and employers (capitalists) in the North, slaves and planters in the South — were relatively small. The great majority of Americans were independent and free from anybody's command — they owned and controlled their means of production. Thus early America was, essentially, a pre-capitalist society. However, by 1880, the year before Tucker started **Liberty**, the number of self-employed had fallen to approximately 33% of the working population. Now it is less than 10%. [Samuel Bowles and Herbert Gintis, **Schooling in Capitalist America**, p. 59] As the US Census described in 1900, until about 1850 "the bulk of general manufacturing done in the United States was carried on in the shop and the household, by the labour of the family or individual proprietors, with apprentice assistants, as contrasted with the present system of factory labour, compensated by wages, and assisted by power." [quoted by Jeremy Brecher and Tim Costello, **Common Sense for Hard Times**, p. 35] Thus the post-civil war period saw "the factory system become general. This led to a large increase in the class of unskilled and semi-skilled labour with inferior bargaining power. Population shifted from the country to the city … It was this milieu that the anarchism of Warren-Proudhon wandered." [Eunice Minette Schuster, **Native American Anarchism**, pp. 136-7]

It is **only** in this context that we can understand individualist anarchism, namely as a revolt against the destruction of working-class independence and the growth of capitalism, accompanied by the growth of two opposing classes, capitalists and proletarians. This transformation of society by the rise of capitalism explains the development of **both** schools of anarchism, social and individualist. "American anarchism," Frank H. Brooks argues, "like its European counterpart, is best seen as a nineteenth century development, an ideology that, like socialism generally, responded to the growth of industrial capitalism, republican government, and nationalism. Although this is clearest in the more collectivistic anarchist theories and movements of the late nineteenth century (Bakunin, Kropotkin, Malatesta, communist anarchism, anarcho-syndicalism), it also helps to explain anarchists of early- to mid-century such as Proudhon, Stirner and, in America, Warren. For all of these theorists, a primary concern was the 'labour problem' — the increasing dependence and immiseration of manual workers in industrialising economies." ["Introduction", **The Individualist Anarchists**, p. 4]

The Individualist Anarchists cannot be viewed in isolation. They were part of a wider movement seeking to stop the capitalist transformation of America. As Bowles and Ginitis note, this "process has been far from placid. Rather, it has involved extended struggles with sections of U.S. labour trying to counter and temper the effects of their reduction to the status of wage labour." The rise of capitalism "marked the transition to control of work by nonworkers" and "with the rise of entrepreneurial capital, groups of formerly independent workers were increasingly drawn into the wage-labour system. Working people's organisations advocated alternatives to this system; land reform, thought to allow all to become an independent producer, was a common demand. Worker co-operatives were a widespread and influential part of the labour movement as early as the 1840s ... but failed because sufficient capital could not be raised." [**Op. Cit.**, p. 59 and p. 62] It is no coincidence that the issues raised by the Individualist Anarchists (land reform via "*occupancy-and-use*", increasing the supply of money via mutual banks and so on) reflect these alternatives raised by working class people and their organisations. Little wonder Tucker argued that:

> "*Make capital free by organising credit on a mutual plan, and then these vacant lands will come into use ... operatives will be able to buy axes and rakes and hoes, and then they will be independent of their employers, and then the labour problem will solved.*" [**Instead of a Book**, p. 321]

Thus the Individualist Anarchists reflect the aspirations of working class people facing the transformation of an society from a pre-capitalist state into a capitalist one. Changing social conditions explain why Individualist Anarchism must be considered socialistic. As Murray Bookchin noted:

> "*Th[e] growing shift from artisanal to an industrial economy gave rise to a gradual but major shift in socialism itself. For the artisan, socialism meant producers' co-operatives composed of men who worked together in small shared collectivist associations, although for master craftsmen it meant mutual aid societies that acknowledged their autonomy as private producers. For the industrial proletarian, by contrast, socialism came to mean the formation of a mass organisation that gave factory workers the collective power to expropriate a plant that no single worker could properly own. These distinctions led to two different interpretations of the 'social question' ... The more progressive craftsmen of the nineteenth century had tried to form networks of co-operatives, based on individually or collectively owned shops, and a market knitted together by a moral agreement to sell commodities according to a 'just price' or the amount of labour that was necessary to produce them. Presumably such small-scale ownership and shared moral precepts would abolish exploitation and greedy profit-taking. The class-conscious proletarian ... thought in terms of the complete socialisation of the means of production, including land, and even of abolishing the market **as such**, distributing goods according to needs rather than labour ... They advocated **public** ownership of the means of production, whether by the state or by the working class organised in trade unions.*" [**The Third Revolution**, vol. 2, p. 262]

So, in this evolution of socialism we can place the various brands of anarchism. Individualist anarchism is clearly a form of artisanal socialism (which reflects its American roots) while communist anarchism and anarcho-syndicalism are forms of industrial (or proletarian) socialism (which reflects its roots in Europe). Proudhon's mutualism bridges these extremes, advocating as it does artisan

socialism for small-scale industry and agriculture and co-operative associations for large-scale industry (which reflects the state of the French economy in the 1840s to 1860s). With the changing social conditions in the US, the anarchist movement changed too, as it had in Europe. Hence the rise of communist-anarchism in addition to the more native individualist tradition and the change in Individualist Anarchism itself:

> "*Green emphasised more strongly the **principle of association** than did Josiah Warren and more so than Spooner had done. Here too Proudhon's influence asserts itself... In principle there is essentially no difference between Warren and Proudhon. The difference between them arises from a dissimilarity of their respective environments. Proudhon lived in a country where the sub-division of labour made co-operation in social production essential, while Warren had to deal with predominantly small individual producers. For this reason Proudhon emphasised the **principle of association** far more than Warren and his followers did, although Warren was by no means opposed to this view.*" [Rudolf Rocker, **Pioneers of American Freedom**, p. 108]

As noted in section A.3, Voltairine de Cleyre subscribed to a similar analysis, as does another anarchist, Peter Sabatini, more recently:

> "*The chronology of anarchism within the United States corresponds to what transpired in Europe and other locations. An organised anarchist movement imbued with a revolutionary collectivist, then communist, orientation came to fruition in the late 1870s. At that time, Chicago was a primary centre of anarchist activity within the USA, due in part to its large immigrant population...*

> "*The Proudhonist anarchy that Tucker represented was largely superseded in Europe by revolutionary collectivism and anarcho-communism. The same changeover occurred in the US, although mainly among subgroups of working class immigrants who were settling in urban areas. For these recent immigrants caught up in tenuous circumstances within the vortex of emerging corporate capitalism, a revolutionary anarchy had greater relevancy than go slow mutualism.*" [**Libertarianism: Bogus Anarchy**]

Looking at the society in which their ideas developed (rather than ahistorically projecting modern ideas backward) we can see the socialist core of Individualist Anarchism. It was, in other words, an un-Marxian form of socialism (as was mutualism and communist-anarchism). Thus, to look at the Individualist Anarchists from the perspective of "modern socialism" (say, communist-anarchism or Marxism) means to miss the point. The social conditions which produced Individualist Anarchism were substantially different from those existing today (and those which produced communist-anarchism and Marxism) and so what was a possible solution to the "*social problem*" **then** may not be one suitable **now** (and, indeed, point to a different kind of socialism than that which developed later). Moreover, Europe in the 1870s was distinctly different than America (although, of course, the USA **was** catching up). For example, there was still vast tracks of unclaimed land (once the Native Americans had been removed, of course) available to workers. In the towns and cities, artisan production *"remained important … into the 1880s"* [David Montgomery, **The Fall of the House of Labour**, p. 52] Until the 1880s, the possibility of self-employment was a real one for many workers, a possibility being hindered by state action (for example, by forcing people to buy land via Homestead Acts, restricting banking to those with specie, suppressing unions and strikes and so on — see section F.8.5). Little wonder that Individualist Anarchism was considered a real solution to the problems generated by the creation of capitalism in the USA and that, by the 1880s, Communist Anarchist became the dominant form of anarchism. By that time the transformation of America was nearing completion and self-employment was no longer a real solution for the majority of workers.

This social context is essential for understanding the thought of people like Greene, Spooner and Tucker. For example, as Stephen L. Newman points out, Spooner *"argues that every man ought to be his own employer, and he envisions a world of yeoman farmers and independent entrepreneurs."* [**Liberalism at Wit's End**, p. 72] This sort of society was in the process of being destroyed when Spooner was writing. Needless to say, the Individualist Anarchists did not think this transformation was unstoppable and proposed, like other sections of US labour, various solutions to problems society faced. Given the commonplace awareness in the population of artisan production and its advantages in terms of liberty, it is hardly surprising that the individualist anarchists supported "free market" solutions to social problems. For, given the era, this solution implied workers' control and the selling of the product of labour, not the labourer him/herself. Unsurprisingly, therefore, the *"greatest part [of **Liberty**'s readers] proves to be of the professional/intellectual class: the remainder includes independent manufacturers and merchants, artisans and skilled workers … The anarchists' hard-core supporters were the socio-economic equivalents of Jefferson's yeoman-farmers and craftsworkers: a freeholder-artisan-independent merchant class allied with freethinking professionals and intellectuals. These groups — in Europe as well as in America — had socio-economic independence, and through their desire to maintain and improve their relatively free positions, had also the incentive to oppose the growing encroachments of the capitalist State."* [Morgan Edwards, *"Neither Bombs Nor Ballots: **Liberty** & the Strategy of Anarchism"*, pp. 65-91, **Benjamin R. Tucker and the Champions of Liberty**, Coughlin, Hamilton and Sullivan (eds.), p. 85]

Individualist anarchism is obviously an aspect of a struggle between the system of peasant and artisan production of early America and the state encouraged system of capitalism. Indeed, their analysis of the change in American society from one of mainly independent producers into one based mainly upon wage labour has many parallels with Karl Marx's analysis of *"primitive accumulation"* in the Americas and elsewhere presented in chapter 33 of **Capital** (*"The Modern Theory of Colonization"*). It is this process which Individualist Anarchism protested against, the use of the state to favour the rising capitalist class. So the social context the individualist anarchists lived in must be remembered. America at the times was a predominantly rural society and industry was not

as developed as it is now. Wage labour would have been minimised. As Wm. Gary Kline argues:

> *"Committed as they were to equality in the pursuit of property, the objective for the anarchist became the construction of a society providing equal access to those things necessary for creating wealth. The goal of the anarchists who extolled mutualism and the abolition of all monopolies was, then, a society where everyone willing to work would have the tools and raw materials necessary for production in a non-exploitative system … the dominant vision of the future society … [was] underpinned by individual, self-employed workers."* [**The Individualist Anarchists: A Critique of Liberalism**, p. 95]

This social context helps explain why some of the individualist anarchists were indifferent to the issue of wage labour, unlike most anarchists. A limited amount of wage labour within a predominantly self-employed economy does not make a given society capitalist any more than a small amount of governmental communities within an predominantly anarchist world would make it statist. As Marx put it, in such socities *"the separation of the worker from the conditions of labour and from the soil … does not yet exist, or only sporadically, or on too limited a scale … Where, amongst such curious characters, is the 'field of abstinence' for the capitalists? … Today's wage-labourer is tomorrow's independent peasant or artisan, working for himself. He vanishes from the labour-market — but not into the workhouse."* There is a *"constant transformation of wage-labourers into independent producers, who work for themselves instead of for capital"* and so *"the degree of exploitation of the wage-labourer remain[s] indecently low."* In addition, the *"wage-labourer also loses, along with the relation of dependence, the feeling of dependence on the abstemious capitalist."* [**Op. Cit.**, pp. 935-6] Within such a social context, the anti-libertarian aspects of wage labour are minimised and so could be overlooked by otherwise sharp critics of authoritarianism as Tucker and Andrews.

Therefore Rocker was correct when he argued that Individualist Anarchism was *"above all … rooted in the peculiar social conditions of America which differed fundamentally from those of Europe."* [**Op. Cit.**, p. 155] As these conditions changed, the viability of Individualist Anarchism's solution to the social problem decreased (as acknowledged by Tucker in 1911, for example — see section G.1.1). Individualist Anarchism, argued Morgan Edwards, *"appears to have dwindled into political insignificance largely because of the erosion of its political-economic base, rather than from a simple failure of strategy. With the impetus of the Civil War, capitalism and the State had too great a head start on the centralisation of economic and political life for the anarchists to catch up. This centralisation reduced the independence of the intellectual/professional and merchant artisan group that were the mainstay of the **Liberty** circle."* [**Op. Cit.**, pp. 85-6] While many of the individualist anarchists adjusted their own ideas to changing social circumstances, as can be seen by Greene's support for co-operatives (*"the principle of association"*) as the only means of ending exploitation of labour by capital, the main forum of the movement (**Liberty**) did not consistently subscribe to this position nor did their support for union struggles play a major role in their strategy. Faced with another form of anarchism which supported both, unsurprisingly communist-anarchism replaced it as the dominant form of anarchism by the start of the 20th century in America.

If these social conditions are not taken into account then the ideas of the likes of Tucker and Spooner will be distorted beyond recognition. Similarly, by ignoring the changing nature of socialism in the face of a changing society and economy, the obvious socialistic aspects of their ideas will be lost. Ultimately, to analyse the Individualist Anarchists in an a-historic manner means to distort their ideas and ideals. Moreover, to apply those ideas in a non-artisan economy without the intention of radically transforming the socio-economic nature of that society towards one based on artisan production one would mean to create a society distinctly different than one they envisioned (see section G.3 for further discussion).

G.2

Why do individualist anarchists reject social anarchism?

As noted in section G.1, the individualist anarchists considered themselves as anti-capitalists and many called themselves mutualists and socialists. It may be objected that they opposed the more obviously socialist types of anarchism like communist-anarchism and, as a consequence, should be considered as supporters of capitalism. This is not the case as can be seen from **why** they rejected communist-anarchism. The key thing to remember is that capitalism does not equal the market. So while the individualist anarchists advocated a market economy, it *"is evident from their writings that they rejected both capitalism and communism — as did Proudhon."* [Brian Morris, *"Global Anti-Capitalism"*, pp. 170-6, **Anarchist Studies**, vol. 14, no. 2, p. 175]

It should noted that while Tucker came to excommunicate non-individualist forms of anarchism from the movement, his initial comments on the likes of Bakunin and Kropotkin were very favourable. He reprinted articles by Kropotkin from his paper **La Revolte**, for example, and discussed *"the Anarchistic philosophy, as developed by the great Proudhon and actively propagated by the heroic Bakunin and his successors on both sides of the Atlantic."* [**Liberty**, no. 26, p. 3] After the rise of the IWPA in the early 1880s and the Haymarket police riot of 1886, Tucker changed his position. Now it was a case that the *"Anarchistic social ideal"* was *"utterly inconsistent with that of those Communists who falsely call themselves Anarchists while at the same time advocating a **regime** of Archism fully as despotic as that of the State Socialists themselves."* For Tucker, real anarchists did not advocate, like communist anarchists, *"forcible expropriation"* nor *"force as a revolutionary agent and authority as a safeguard of the new social order."* [**The Individualist Anarchists**, pp. 88-9] As will become clear, Tucker's summation of communist-anarchism leaves a lot to be desired. However, even after the break between individualist and communist anarchism in America, Tucker saw that both had things in common as both were socialists:

"To be sure, there is a certain and very sincere comradeship that must exist between all honest antagonists of the exploitation of labour, but the word comrade cannot gloss over the vital difference between so-called Communist-Anarchism and Anarchism proper." [**Liberty**, no. 172, p. 1]

Social anarchists would agree with Tucker in part, namely the need not to gloss over vital differences between anarchist schools but most reject Tucker's attempts to exclude other tendencies from *"Anarchism proper."*

It is these disagreements to which we now turn. It should be stressed, though, that the individualist anarchists, while tending to excommunicate social anarchism, also had many inclusive moments and so it makes these objections often seem petty and silly. Yes, there was certainly pettiness involved and it worked both ways and there was a certain amount of tit-for-tat, just as there is now (although to a much lesser degree these days). Anarchist-communist opposition to what some of them sadly called *"bourgeois anarchism"* was a fact, as was individualist anarchist opposition to communist-anarchism. Yet this should not blind us to what both schools had in common. However, if it were not for some opponents of anarchism (particularly those seeking to confuse libertarian ideas with propertarian ones) dragging these (mostly resolved) disagreements back into the light of day this section would be a lot shorter. As it is, covering these disagreements and showing how they could be resolved is a useful task — if only to show how individualist and communist anarchism are not as alien as some make out.

There were four main objections made to communist-anarchism by the individualists. Firstly, that communist-anarchism was compulsory and any compulsory system could not be anarchist. Secondly, that a revolution would be imposing anarchism and so contradicted its principles. Thirdly, that distribution by need was based on altruism and, consequently, unlikely to succeed. Fourthly, that the communist-anarchists are determining how a free society would be organised which is authoritarian. Needless to say, communist-anarchists rejected these claims as being false and while we have already sketched these arguments, objections and replies in section A.3.1 it is worthwhile to repeat (and expand on) them here as these disagreements are sometimes highlighted by those who fail to stress what both schools have in common and, consequently, distort the debates and issues involved.

We will discuss these objections in the following sections.

G.2.1 Is communist-anarchism compulsory?

Some individualist anarchists argued that communist-anarchists wanted to force everyone to be communists and, as such, this proved they were not anarchists. This objection is, ironically, both the most serious **and** the easiest to refute. As Tucker noted, *"to eliminate the compulsory element from Communism is to remove, in the view of every man who values liberty above aught else, the* *chief* objection to it." [**Liberty**, no. 122, p. 5] For Henry Appleton, there was "*a class of ranting enthusiasts who falsely call themselves Anarchists*" who advocated both violence and "*levelling*". "*All Communism,*" he asserted, "*under whatever guise, is the natural enemy of Anarchism and a Communist sailing under the flag of Anarchism is as false a figure as could be invented.*" Yet, ironically, A. H. Simpson disproved that particular claim for while attacking communism he ended by stating his "*argument applies only to aggressive Communists*" and that "*[v]oluntary Communism can exist and, if successful, flourish under Anarchy.*" So, apparently, **some** kinds of communism are compatible with anarchism after all! Victor Yarrows, likewise, pointed to "*two different schools*" of communists, those who support "*voluntary Communism, which they intend to reach by the Anarchistic method*" and those who "*plot the forcible suppression of the entire system*" of private property. Only the former was "*voluntary or Anarchistic Communism.*" [**The Individualist Anarchists**, pp. 89-90, p. 94, p. 95 and p. 96] This, it should be noted, is more than enough to disprove any claims that genuine anarchists cannot be communists.

So, the question is whether communist-anarchists are in favour of forcing people to be communists. If their communism is based on voluntary association then, according to the Individualist Anarchists themselves, it is a form of anarchism. Unsurprisingly, we discover that communist-anarchists have long argued that their communism was voluntary in nature and that working people who did not desire to be communists would be free not to be.

This position can be found in Kropotkin, from his earliest writings to his last. Thus we discover him arguing that an anarchist revolution "*would take care not to touch the holding of the peasant who cultivates it himself ... without wage labour. But we would expropriate all land that was not cultivated by the hands of those who at present possess the land.*" This was compatible with communism because libertarian communists aimed at "*the complete expropriation of all those who have the means of exploiting human beings; the return to the community of the nation of everything that in the hands of anyone can be used to exploit others.*" Following Proudhon's analysis, private property was different from individual possession and as long as "*social wealth remains in the hands of the few who possess it today*" there would be exploitation. Instead, the aim was to see such social wealth currently monopolised by the capitalist class "*being placed, on the day of the revolution, at the free disposition of all the workers.*" This would "*create the situation where each person may live by working freely, without being forced to sell his work and his liberty to others.*" [**Words of a Rebel**, p. 214, pp. 207-8, p. 207 and p. 208] If someone desired to work outside of the commune, then that was perfectly compatible with this aim.

This position was followed in later works. The "*scope of Expropriation,*" Kropotkin argued was clear and would only "*apply to everything that enables any man — be he financier, mill-owner, or landlord — to appropriate the product of others' toil.*" Thus only those forms of property based on wage labour would be expropriated. In terms of housing, the same general rule applies ("*the expropriation of dwellings contains the whole social revolution*"). Kropotkin explicitly discusses the man who "*by dint of privation has contrived to buy a house just large enough to hold his family. And we are going*

to deprive him of his hard-earned happiness, to turn him into the street! Certainly not ... Let him work in his little garden, too." Anarchist-communism "*will make the lodger understand that he need not pay his former landlord any more rent. Stay where you are, but rent free.*" [**The Conquest of Bread**, p. 61, p. 95, pp. 95-6 and p. 96]

Which, incidentally, was **exactly** the same position as Tucker (see section G.1.2) and so Kropotkin's analysis of the land monopoly was identical:

> "*when we see a peasant who is in possession of just the amount of land he can cultivate, we do not think it reasonable to turn him off his little farm. He exploits nobody, and nobody would have the right to interfere with his work. But if he possesses under the capitalist law more than he can cultivate himself, we consider that we must not give him the right of keeping that soil for himself, leaving it uncultivated when it might be cultivated by others, or of making others cultivate it for his benefit.*"
> [**Act for Yourselves**, p. 104]

For Kropotkin, communism "*must be the work of all, a natural growth, a product of the constructive genius of the great mass. Communism cannot be imposed from above; it could not live even for a few months if the constant and daily co-operation of all did not uphold it. It must be free.*" [**Anarchism**, p. 140]

Malatesta agreed. Anarchism, he stressed, "*cannot be imposed, both on moral grounds in regard to freedom, as well as because it is impossible to apply 'willy nilly' a regime of justice for all. It cannot be imposed on a minority by a majority. Neither can it be imposed by a majority on one or more minorities.*" Thus "*anarchists who call themselves communists*" do so "*not because they wish to impose their particular way of seeing things on others*" but because "*they are convinced, until proved wrong, that the more human beings are joined in brotherhood, and the more closely they co-operate in their efforts for the benefit of all concerned, the greater is the well-being and freedom which each can enjoy.*" Imposed communism,*" he stressed, "*would be the most detestable tyranny that the human mind could conceive. And free and voluntary communism is ironical if one has not the right and the possibility to live in a different regime, collectivist, mutualist, individualist — as one wishes, always on condition that there is no oppression or exploitation of others.*" He agreed with Tucker that "*State communism, which is authoritarian and imposed, is the most hateful tyranny that has ever afflicted, tormented and handicapped mankind.*" [**Errico Malatesta: His Life and Ideas**, p. 21, p. 34, p. 103 and p. 34]

Therefore, arguing that the land and machinery should be common property does **not** preclude individuals possessing it independently of communes as both are rooted in individual possession (or "occupancy and use") rather than private property. The key anarchist difference between property and possession explains any perceived contradiction in the communist position. Thus we find Kropotkin arguing that a communist-anarchist society is one "*without having the soil, the machinery, the capital in short, in the hands of private owners. We all believe that free organisations of workers would be able to carry on production on the farm and on the factory, as well, and probably much better, than it is conducted* now under the individual ownership of the capitalist." The commune "*shall take into possession of all the soil, the dwelling-houses, the manufactures, the mines and the means of communication.*" [**Act for Yourselves**, p. 103 and p. 104]

This in no way contradicts his argument that the individuals will not be forced to join a commune. This is because the aim of anarchist-communism is, to quote another of Kropotkin's works, to place "*the product reaped or manufactured at the disposal of all, leaving to each the liberty to consume them as he pleases in his own home.*" [**The Place of Anarchism in the Evolution of Socialist Thought**, p. 7] Thus individual ownership meant individual ownership of resources used by others rather than individual possession of resources which individuals used. This can be seen from his comment that "*some poor fellow*" who "*has contrived to buy a house just large enough to hold his family*" would not be expropriated by the commune ("*by all means let him stay there*") while also asserting "*[w]ho, then, can appropriate for himself the tiniest plot of ground in such a city, without committing a flagrant injustice?*" [**Conquest of Bread**, pp. 95-6 and p. 90]

Kropotkin's opposition to private appropriation of land can only be understood in context, namely from his discussion on the "*abolition of rent*" and the need for "*free dwellings*", i.e. the end of landlordism. Kropotkin accepted that land could and would be occupied for personal use — after all, people need a place to live! In this he followed Proudhon, who also argued that "*Land cannot be appropriated*" (Chapter 3, part 1 of **What is Property?**). For the French anarchist, the land "*is limited in amount*" and so "*it ought not to be appropriated*" ("*let any living man dare change his right of territorial possession into the right of property, and I will declare war upon him, and wage it to the death!*"). This meant that "*the land is indispensable to our existence, — consequently a common thing, consequently insusceptible of appropriation.*" Overall, "*labour has no inherent power to appropriate natural wealth.*" [**Property is Theft!**, p. 105 and p. 109] As we discuss in section G.4.2, Proudhon extended this to workplaces as well.

Proudhon, it is well known, supported the use of land (and other resources) for personal use. How, then, can he argue that the "*land cannot be appropriated*"? Is Proudhon subject to the same contradiction as Kropotkin? Of course not, once we take into account the fundamental difference between private property and possession, appropriation and use which underlies both individualist **and** communist anarchism. As Malatesta argued:

> "*Communism is a free agreement: who doesn't accept it or maintain it remains outside of it ... Everyone has **the right to land, to the instruments of production** and all the advantages that human beings can enjoy in the state of civilisation that humanity has reached. If someone does not want to accept a communist life and the obligations that it supposes, it is their business. They and those of a like mind will come to an agreement ... [They] will have **the same rights as the communists** over the natural wealth and accumulated products of previous generations ... I have always spoken of free agreement, of free communism. How can there be liberty without a possible alternative?*" [our emphasis, **At the café**, pp. 69-70]

Compare this to individualist anarchist Stephen Byington's comment that "*[t]hose who wish to unite in the communistic enjoyment of their labour will be free to do so; those who wish to hold the products of their labour as private property will be equally free to do so.*" [quoted by Wm. Gary Kline, **The Individualist Anarchists: A Critique of Liberalism**, p. 93] The similarities are as obvious as between Proudhon's and Kropotkin's arguments.

The same, it must be stressed, can be said of the "*Chicago Anarchists*" whom Tucker labelled as authoritarians. Thus we find Albert Parsons, for example, denouncing that kind of private property which allows exploitation to happen. The key problem was that "*the necessary means for the existence of all has been appropriated and monopolised by a few. The land, the implements of production and communication, the resources of life, are now held as private property, and its owners exact tribute from the propertyless*" ("*Wealth is power*"). The aim of communist-anarchism was to ensure the "*[f]ree access to the means of production [which] is the natural right of every man able and willing to work.*" This implied that "*[a]ll organisation will be voluntary with the sacred right forever reserved for each individual 'to think and to rebel.'*" This meant that as far as the "*final outcome*" of social change was involved "*many disciples of anarchism believe [it] will be communism — the common possession of the resources of life and the productions of united labour. No anarchist is compromised by this statement, who does not reason out the future outlook in this way.*" [**Anarchism: Its Philosophy and Scientific Basis**, p. 97, p. 99, p. 96 ,p. 174 and pp. 174-5] This did not exclude mutualism or individualist anarchism:

> "*Many expedients will be tried by which a just return may be awarded the worker for his exertions. The time check or labour certificate, which will be honoured at the store-houses hour for hour, will no doubt have its day. But the elaborate and complicated system of book-keeping this would necessitate, the impossibility of balancing one man's hour against another's with accuracy, and the difficulty in determining how much more one man owed natural resources, condition, and the studies and achievements of past generations, than did another, would, we believe, prevent this system from obtaining a thorough and permanent establishment. The mutual banking system ... may be in operation in the future free society. Another system, more simple ... appears the most acceptable and likely to prevail. Members of the groups ... if honest producers ... will be honoured in any other group they may visit, and given whatever is necessary for their welfare and comfort.*" [**Op. Cit.**, p. 175]

As we discuss in section G.4, this was the same conclusion that Voltairine de Cleyre reached three decades later. This was rooted in a similar analysis of property as Proudhon and Tucker, namely "*possession*" or "*occupancy and use*": "*The workshops will drop into the hands of the workers, the mines will fall to the miners, and the land and all other things will be controlled by those who posses and use them. There will be, there can then be no title to anything aside from its possession and use.*" The likes of Parsons supported communism not because of an opposition between "communism" and "occupancy and use" but rather, like Kropotkin, because of *"the utter impossibility of awarding to each an exact return for the amount of labour performed will render absolute communism a necessity sooner or later."* [**Op. Cit.**, p. 105 and p. 176] So while capitalism *"expropriates the masses for the benefit of the privileged class ... socialism teaches how all may possess property ... [and] establish a universal system of co-operation, and to render accessible to each and every member of the human family the achievements and benefits of civilisation which, under capitalism, are being monopolised by a privileged class."* [August Spies, contained in Parsons, **Op. Cit.**, pp. 63-4]

All of which indicates that Tucker did not really understand communist-anarchism when he argued that communism is *"the force which compels the labourer to pool his product with the products of all and forbids him to sell his labour or his products."* [**Instead of a Book**, p. 400] Rather, communist-anarchists argue that communism must be free and voluntary. In other words, a communist-anarchist society would not "forbid" anything as those who are part of it must be in favour of communism for it to work. The option of remaining outside the communist-anarchist society is there, as (to requote Kropotkin) expropriation would *"apply to everything that enables any man [or woman] ... to appropriate the product of others' toil."* [**The Conquest of Bread**, p. 61] Thus communist-anarchism would "forbid" exactly what Individualist Anarchism would "forbid" — property, not possession (i.e. any form of "ownership" not based on "occupancy and use").

Tucker, at times, admits that this is the case. For example, he once noted that *"Kropotkin says, it is true, that he would allow the individual access to the land; but he proposes to strip him of capital entirely, and as he declares a few pages further on that without capital agriculture is impossible, it follows that such access is an empty privilege not at all equivalent to the liberty of individual production."* [quoted by George Woodcock and Ivan Avakumovic, **The Anarchist Prince**, p. 279] However, as two biographers of Kropotkin note, Tucker *"partly misinterprets his opponent, as when he suggests that the latter's idea of communist anarchism would **prevent** the individual from working on his own if he wished (a fact which Kropotkin always explicitly denied, since the basis of his theory was the voluntary principle)."* [Woodcock and Avakumovic, **Op. Cit.**, p. 280] To quote Kropotkin himself:

> *"when we see a Sheffield cutler, or a Leeds clothier working with their own tools or handloom, we see no use in taking the tools or the handloom to give to another worker. The clothier or cutler exploit nobody. But when we see a factory whose owners claim to keep to themselves the instruments of labour used by 1,400 girls, and consequently exact from the labour of these girls ... profit ... we consider that the people ... are fully entitled to take possession of that factory and to let the girls produce ... for themselves and the rest of the community ... and take what they need of house room, food and clothing in return."* [**Act for Yourselves**, p. 105]

So Kropotkin argued that a communist-anarchist revolution would **not** expropriate the tools of self-employed workers who exploited no-one. Malatesta also argued that in an anarchist society *"the peasant [is free] to cultivate his piece of land, alone if he wishes; free is the shoe maker to remain at his last or the blacksmith in his small forge."* Thus these two very famous communist-anarchists also supported "property" but they are recognised as obviously socialists. This apparent contradiction is resolved when it is understood that for communist-anarchists (like all anarchists) the abolition of property does not mean the end of possession and so *"would not harm the independent worker whose real title is possession and the work done"* unlike capitalist property. [Malatesta, **Op. Cit.**, p. 103] Compare this with Yarros' comment that *"[s]mall owners would not suffer from the application of the 'personal use' principle, while large owners, who have come into possession of the landed property, or the capital with which they purchased the landed property, by means that equal liberty could not sanction, would have no principle to base any protest on."* [**Liberty**, no. 197, p. 2] In other words, **all** anarchists (as we argue in section B.3) oppose private property but support possession (we return to this issue in section I.6.2 as it is an all too common fallacy).

G.2.2 Is communist-anarchism violent?

Having shown that communist-anarchism is a valid form of anarchism even in terms of individualist anarchism in the last section, it is now necessary to discuss the issue of methods, i.e., the question of revolution and violence. This is related to the first objection, with Tucker arguing that *"their Communism is another State, while my voluntary cooperation is not a State at all. It is a very easy matter to tell who is an Anarchist and who is not. Do you believe in any form of imposition upon the human will by force?"* [**Liberty**, no. 94, p. 4] However, Tucker was well aware that the state imposed its will on others by force and so the question was whether revolution was the right means of ending its oppression.

To a large degree, discussion on the question of revolution was clouded by the fact it took place during the height of the *"propaganda by the deed"* period in anarchist history (see section A.2.18). As George Woodcock noted, a *"cult of violence ... marked and marred"* the IWPA and alienated the individualist anarchists. [**Anarchism**, p. 393] Johann Most was the focus for much of this rhetoric (see Paul Avrich's **The Haymarket Tragedy**, particularly the chapter entitled *"Cult of Dynamite"*). However, the reason why talk of dynamite found an audience had nothing to do with anarchism but rather because of the violence regularly directed against striking workers and unions. As we discuss more fully in section G.3.1, strikes were habitually repressed by violence (by the state or by the employer's private police). The massive 1877 strike wave, for example, saw the **Chicago Times** urge the use of hand grenades against strikers while employers organised *"private guards and bands of uniformed vigilantes"* which *"roamed the streets, attacking and dispersing groups of workers.* Business leaders concluded that *"the chief lesson of the strike as the need for a stronger apparatus of repression"* and presented the city of Chicago with two Gatling guns to aid that task. *"The erection of government armouries in the centres of American cities dates from this period."* This repression and the vitriolic ruling class rhetoric used *"set a pattern for the future and fuelled the hatreds and passions without which the Haymarket tragedy would not have occurred."* [Paul Avrich, **The Haymarket Tragedy**, p. 33 and p. 35]

Given the general infatuation with dynamite and violence which this state and employer violence provoked, the possibility for misunderstanding was more than likely (as well as giving the enemies of anarchism ample evidence to demonise it while allowing the violence of the system they support to be downplayed). Rather than seeing communist-anarchists as thinking a revolution was the product of mass struggle, it was easy to assume that by revolution they meant acts of violence or terrorism conducted by a few anarchists on behalf of everyone else (this false perspective is one which Marxists to this day tend to repeat when dismissing anarchism). In such a situation, it is easy to see why so many individualist anarchists thought that a small group of anarchists sought to impose communism by means of violence. However, this was not the case. According to Albert Parsons, the communist-anarchists argued that the working class *"will be driven to use [force] in self-defence, in self-preservation against those who are degrading, enslaving and destroying them."* [**The Autobiographies of the Haymarket Martyrs**, p. 46] As August Spies put it, *"[t]o charge us with an attempt to overthrow the present system on or about May 4th, and then establish anarchy, is too absurd a statement, I think, even for a political office-holder to make ... Only mad men could have planned such a brilliant scheme."* Rather, *"we have predicted from the lessons history teaches, that the ruling classes of to-day would no more listen to the voice of reason than their predecessors; that they would attempt by brute force to stay the wheel of progress."* [contained in Parsons, **Anarchism: Its Philosophy and Scientific Basis**, p. 55] Subsequent events have proven that Spies and Parsons had a point!

Thus arguments about violence should not result in the assumption that the individualist anarchists were pacifists as the subject usually is not violence as such but rather assassinations and attempts of minorities to use violence to create "anarchy" by destroying the state on behalf of the general population. *"To brand the policy of terrorism and assassination as immoral is ridiculously weak,"* argued Tucker. *"**Liberty** does not assume to set any limit on the right of an invaded individual to choose his own methods of defence. The invader, whether an individual or a government forfeits all claim to consideration from the invaded. This truth is independent of the character of the invasion."* This meant that the *"right to resist oppression by violence is beyond doubt. But its exercise would be unwise unless the suppression of free thought, free speech, and a free press were enforced so stringently that all other means of throwing it off had become hopeless."* Ultimately, though, the *"days of armed revolution have gone by. It is too easily put down."* [**Instead of a Book**, p. 430, p. 439 and p. 440]

Except for a small group of hard-core insurrectionists, few social anarchists think that violence should be the first recourse in social struggle. The ultra-revolutionary rhetoric associated with the 1883-6 period is not feature of the anarchist movement in general and so lessons have been learned. As far as strategy goes, the tactics advocated by social anarchists involve the same ones that individualist anarchists support, namely refusal of obedience to all forms of authority. This would include workplace, rent and tax strikes, occupations, protests and such like. Violence has always been seen as the last option, to be used only in self-defence (or, sometimes, in revenge for greater acts of violence by oppressors). The problem is that any effective protest will result in the protesters coming into conflict with either the state or property owners. For example, a rent strike will see the agents of the property owner trying to evict tenants, as would a workers strike which occupied the workplace. Similarly, in the Seattle protests in 1999 the police used force against the non-violent protesters blocking the roads long before the Black Bloc started breaking windows (which is, in itself, non-violent as it was directed against corporate property, not people — unlike the police action). Unless the rebels simply did what they were told, then any non-violent protest could become violent — but only because private property ultimately rests on state violence, a fact which becomes obvious when people refuse to acknowledge it and its privileges (*"There is only one law for the poor, to wit: Obey the rich."* [Parsons, **Op. Cit.**, p. 97]). Thus Adolph Fischer, one of the Haymarket Martyrs:

> *"Would a peaceful solution of the social question be possible, the anarchists would be the first ones to rejoice over it.*
>
> *"But is it not a fact that on occasion of almost every strike the minions of the institutions of private property — militia, police, deputy sheriffs; yes, even federal troops — are being called to the scenes of conflict between capital and labour, in order to protect the interests of capital? ... What peaceful means should the toilers employ? There is, for example, the strike? If the ruling classes want to enforce the 'law' they can have every striker arrested and punished for 'intimidation' and conspiracy. A strike can only be successful if the striking workingmen prevent their places being occupied by others. But this prevention is a crime in the eyes of the law. Boycott? In several states the 'courts of justice' have decided that the boycott is a violation of the law, and in consequence thereof, a number of boycotts have had the pleasure of examining the inner construction of penitentiaries 'for 'conspiracy' against the interests of capital."* [**The Autobiographies of the Haymarket Martyrs**, pp. 85-6]

Some individualist anarchists did agree with this position. Dyer Lum, for example, *"supported revolutionary violence on practical and historical grounds. Practically speaking, Lum did not believe that 'wage slavery' could be ended by non-violence because capitalists would surely use force to resist."* [Frank H. Brooks, *"Ideology, Strategy, and Organization: Dyer Lum and the American Anarchist Movement"*, pp. 57-83, **Labor History**, vol. 34, No. 1, p. 71] Spooner's rhetoric could be as violent sounding as Johann Most at his worse and he called upon the subjects of the British Empire to rise in revolt (see his pamphlet **Revolution**). Equally, many social anarchists are pacifists or believe that anarchism can come about by means of reform and not revolution. Thus the reform/revolution divide does not quite equal the individualist/social anarchist divide, although it is fair to say that most individualist anarchists were and are reformists.

So, it must be stressed that most individualist anarchists did not oppose revolution **as such**. Rather they considered it as both unlikely to succeed and unnecessary. They rejected revolutionary expropriation *"not because we deem such expropriation unjust, invasive, criminal, but solely because we are we are convinced that there is a better, safer, and wiser way for labour to pursue with a view to emancipation."* With mutual banks, they argued, it became possible *"for labour to gradually lift itself into the position to command its full share of wealth, and absorb in the shape of wages all that is now alienated from it in the forms of profit, interest proper, and monopoly rent."* [Yarrows, **Liberty**, no. 171, p. 5] As such, their aims were the same as communist-anarchism (namely to end exploitation of labour and the abolition of the state) but their means were different. Both, however, were well aware that capitalism could not be ended by political action (i.e., voting). *"That the privileged class"*, argued William Bailie *"will submit to expropriation, even if demanded at the ballot-box, is a delusion possible only to him who knows not the actual situation confronting the people of this country."* [*"The Rule of the Monopolists"*, **Liberty**, no. 368, p. 4]

However, there was one area of life that was excluded from their opposition to expropriation: the land. As Yarros put it, *"the Anarchists' position on the land question, which involves the dispossession of present landlords and the entire abolition of the existing system of land tenure ... They wish to expropriate the landlords, and allow the landless to settle on land which does not now belong to them."* This *"[o]ne exception ... we are compelled to make"* involved *"believ[ing] that the landless **will**, individually and for the purpose of occupying ownership, take possession of the land not personally occupied and used by landlord, and **will** protect each other in the possession of such lands against any power hostile to them."* [**Op. Cit.**, no. 171, p. 4 and p. 5]

Yet as subsequent history has shown, landlords are just as likely to organise and support violent counter-revolutionary movements in the face of land reform as are industrial capitalists. Both sections of the capitalist class supported fascists like Mussolini, Franco and Pinochet in the face of even moderate attempts at expropriation by either reformist governments or the peasants themselves. So as the history of land reform shows, landlords are more than willing to turn to death squads and fascism to resist it. To suggest that squatting land would provoke less capitalist violence than, say, expropriating workplaces simply cannot be supported in the light of 20th century history. The choice, then, is simply to allow the landlords and capitalists to keep their property and try to buy it back from them or use political or revolutionary means to expropriate them. Communist-anarchists thought that the mutual banks would not work and so supported expropriation by means of a mass revolt, a social revolution.

As such, communist-anarchists are not revolutionaries by choice but rather because they do not think capitalism can be reformed away nor that the ruling class will freely see their power, property and privileges taken from them. They reject the mutualist and individualist anarchist suggestion that mutual banks could provide enough credit to compete capitalism away and, even if it could, the state would simply outlaw it. This perspective does **not** imply, as many enemies of anarchism suggest, that social anarchists always seek to use violence but rather that we are aware that the state and capitalists will use violence against any effective protest. So, the methods social anarchists urge — strikes, occupations, protests, and so forth — are all inherently non-violent but resistance by the state and capitalist class to these acts of rebellion often results in violence (which is dutifully reported as violence by the rebels, not the powerful, in the media). That the capitalist class will use violence and force to maintain its position *"is demonstrated in every strike which threatens their power; by every lock-out, by every discharge; by every black-list."* [Parsons, **Anarchism: Its Philosophy and Scientific Basis**, p. 105] Ultimately, the workings of capitalism itself provokes resistance to it. Even if no anarchist participated in, or helped organise, strikes and protests they would occur anyway and the state would inevitably intervene to defend "law and order" and "private property" — as the history of every class system proves. So communist-anarchism does not produce the class war, the class war produces communist-anarchism.

In addition, Tucker thought that a violent revolution would not succeed for without an awareness of anarchist ideals in the general public, the old system would soon return. *"If government should be abruptly and entirely abolished tomorrow,"* he argued, *"there would probably ensue a series of physical conflicts about land and many other things, ending in reaction and a revival of the old tyranny."* [**Instead of a Book**, p. 329] Almost all revolutionary anarchists would agree with his analysis (see section A.2.16). Such anarchists have always seen revolution as the end of a long process of self-liberation and self-education through struggle. All anarchists reject the idea that all that was required was to eliminate the government, by whatever means, and the world would be made right. Rather, we have seen anarchism as a social movement which, like anarchy itself, requires the participation of the vast majority to be viable. Hence anarchist support for unions and strikes, for example, as a means of creating more awareness of anarchism and its solutions to the social question (see section J.1). This means that communist-anarchists do not see revolution as imposing anarchism, but rather as an act of self-liberation by a people sick of being ruled by others and acting to free themselves of tyranny.

So, in summary, in terms of tactics there is significant overlap between the strategies advocated by both social and individualist anarchists. The key difference is that the former do not think that the latter's mutual banks make expropriation unnecessary while the individualist anarchists think that expropriation of capital would provoke the state into attacking and it would be unlikely that the rebels would win. Both, however, can agree that violence should only be used in self-defence and that for most of the time it is not required as other forms of resistance are far more effective.

G.2.3 Does communist-anarchism aim to destroy individuality?

Then there is the desirability of communism as such. A. H. Simpson argued that *"Anarchism is egoism; Communism is altruism"* and altruism in any form will involve *"the duty of the individual to sacrifice himself to God, the State, the community, the 'cause' of anything, superstition that always makes for tyranny. This idea, whether under Theocracy or Communism, will result in the same thing — always authority."* He did, though, argue that in a free society people who *"desire to have their individuality submerged in the crowd"* would be free to set up their own communes. [**The Individualist Anarchists**, p. 92 and p. 94] This flows from Joshua Warren's experiences on Robert Owen's co-operative community **New Harmony** and the conclusions he drew from its collapse. Warren essentially began the individualist anarchist tradition by concluding that any sort of collective emphasis was bound to fail because it prevented people from sufficiently addressing individual concerns, since supposed collective concerns would inevitably take their place. The failure of these communities was rooted in a failure to understand the need for individual self-government. Thus, for Warren, it *"seemed that the differences of opinion, tastes, and purposes **increased** just in proportion to the demand for conformity"* and so it *"appeared that it was nature's own inherent law of diversity that had conquered us ... Our 'united interests' were directly at war with the individualities of persons and circumstances."* [quoted by George Woodcock, **Anarchism**, p. 390] Thus, property within the limits of occupancy and use, and within an economy dominated by the cost principle or some close equivalent, had to be a necessary protection for the individual from both the potential tyranny of the group (communism) and from inequalities in wealth (capitalism).

In return, communist-anarchists would agree. *"Phalansteries,* argued Kropotkin, *"are repugnant to millions of human beings."* While most people feel *"the necessity of meeting his [or her] fellows for the pursuit of common work ... it is not so for the hours of leisure"* and such communities *"do not take this into account."* Thus a commune system does not imply communal living (although such arrangements *"can please some"*). Rather it was a case of *"isolated apartments ... Isolation, alternating with time spent in society, is the normal desire of human nature."* [**The Conquest of Bread**, pp. 123-4] Kropotkin in his discussion on why intentional communities like that of Owen's failed repeated many of Warren's points and stressed that they were based on the authoritarian spirit and violated the need for individual liberty, isolation and diversity (see his **Small Communal Experiments and Why They Fail**). The aim of communist-anarchism is to create a communist society based on individual liberty and freely joined functional groups. It does not aim to burden individuals with communal issues beyond those required by said groupings. Thus self-managed communities involve managing only those affairs which truly rest in joint needs, with the interests of individuals and other groups only being discussed if they are harming others and other means of resolving disputes have failed. Whether this can actually happen, of course, will be discovered in a free society. If it did not, the communist-

anarchists would be the first to seek alternative economic and social arrangements which guaranteed liberty.

It should also go without saying that no communist-anarchist sought a system by which individuals would have their personality destroyed. As Kropotkin stressed:

> *"Anarchist Communism maintains that most valuable of all conquests — individual liberty — and moreover extends it and gives it a solid basis — economic liberty — without which political liberty is delusive; it does not ask the individual who has rejected god, god the king, and god the parliament, to give himself unto himself a god more terrible than any of the preceding — god the Community, or to abdicate upon its alter his independence, his will, his tastes, and to renew the vow of asceticism which he formally made before the crucified god. It says to him, on the contrary, 'No society is free so long as the individual is not so! Do not seek to modify society by imposing upon it an authority which shall make everything right; if you do you will fail ... abolish the conditions which allow some to monopolise the fruit of labour of others.'"* [**The Place of Anarchism in Socialistic Evolution**, pp. 14-5]

Of course, denying that communist-anarchists seek such a regime is not the same as saying that such a regime would not be created by accident. Unsurprisingly, communist-anarchists have spent some time arguing that their system would not be subject to such a degeneration as its members would be aware of the danger and act to stop it (see, for example, section I.5.6). The key to understanding communist-anarchism is to recognise that it is based on free access. It does not deny an individual (or even a group of individuals) the ability to work their own land or workplace, it simply denies them the ability to exclude others from it unless they agree to be their servant first. The sharing of the products of labour is considered as the means to reduce even more any authority in society as people can swap workplaces and communities with ease, without worrying about whether they can put food on their table or not.

Of course, there is slight irony to Simpson's diatribe against communism in that it implicitly assumes that private property is not a god and that individuals should respect it regardless of how it impacts on them and their liberty. Would it not be altruism of the worse kind if working class people did not simply take the land and capital they need to survive rather than sell their labour and liberty to its owners? So why exclude private property (even in a modified form) from individualist anarchist scorn? As we argue in section G.6 this was Max Stirner's position and, fundamentally, the communist-anarchist one too. Communist-anarchists oppose private property as it generates relationships of authority and these harm those subject to them and, as a consequence, they argue that it is in the **self**-interest of the individuals so oppressed to expropriate private property and share the whole world.

The issue of sharing and what it implied also caused some individualist anarchists to oppose it. Henry Appleton argued that *"all communism rests upon an artificial attempt to level things, as against a social development resting upon untrammelled individual sovereignty."* The *"true Anarchist ... is opposed to all manner of artificial levelling machines. How pitiful the ignorance which* accuses him of wanting to level everything, when the very integral thought of Anarchism is opposed to levelling!" [**The Individualist Anarchists**, p. 89] However, as we have indicated in section A.2.5, all genuine anarchists, **including communist-anarchists**, are opposed to making or treating people as if they were identical. In fact, the goal of communist-anarchism has always been to ensure and protect the natural diversity of individuals by creating social conditions in which individuality can flourish. The fundamental principle of communism is the maxim **"from each according to their abilities, to each according to their needs."** There is nothing there about *"levelling"* or (which amounts to the same thing), *"equality of outcome."* To make an obvious point: *"If one person need medical treatment and another is more fortunate, they are not to be granted an equal amount of medical care, and the same is true of other human needs.* Hence Chomsky talks of the *"authentic left"* who recognise that individuals *"will differ in their aspirations, their abilities, and their personal goals"* and seek a society which allows that diversity to fully flourish. [**The Chomsky Reader**, p. 191 and p. 192] In the words of Rudolf Rocker:

> *"a far greater degree of economic equality … would … be no guarantee against political and social oppression. Economic equality alone is not social liberation. It is just this which Marxism and all the other schools of authoritarian Socialism have never understood. Even in prison, in the cloister, or in the barracks one finds a fairly high degree of economic equality, as all the inmates are provided with the same dwelling, the same food, the same uniform, and the same tasks … [this was] the vilest despotism … the human being was merely the automation of a higher will, on whose decisions he had not the slightest influence. It was not without reason that Proudhon saw in a 'Socialism' without freedom the worst form of slavery. The urge for social justice can only develop properly and be effective, when it grows out of man's sense of personal freedom and is based on that. In other words **Socialism will be free, or it will not be at all**. In its recognition of this lies the genuine and profound justification for the existence of Anarchism."* [**Anarcho-Syndicalism**, p. 14]

Therefore, anarchists *"demand the abolition of all economic monopolies and the common ownership of the soil and all other means of production, the use of which must be available to all without distinction; for personal and social freedom is conceivable only on the basis of equal economic advantages for everybody.* [**Op. Cit.**, p. 11] As Kropotkin stressed, anarchists recognise that there are two types of communism, libertarian and authoritarian and *"our communism, is not that of the authoritarian school: it is anarchist communism, communism without government, free communism. It is a synthesis of the two chief aims pursued by humanity since the dawn of its history — economic freedom and political freedom."* It is based on *"everybody, contributing for the common well-being to the full extent of his [or her] capacities … enjoy[ing] also from the common stock of society to the fullest possible extent of his [or her] needs."* Thus it is rooted in individual tastes and diversity, on *"putting the wants of the individual **above** the valuation of the services he [or she] has rendered, or might render, to society."* Thus

communism was *"the best basis for individual development and freedom"* and so *"the full expansion of man's faculties, the superior development of what is original in him, the greatest fruitfulness of intelligences, feeling and will."* It would ensure the *"most powerful development of individuality, of individual originality."* The *"most powerful development of individuality, of individual originality … can only be produced when the first needs of food and shelter are satisfied"* and this was why *"communism and anarchism"* are *"a necessary complement to one another."* [**Anarchism**, p. 61, p. 59, p. 60 and p. 141]

So, communist-anarchists would actually agree with individualist anarchists like Simpson and oppose any notion of *"levelling"* (artificial or otherwise). The aim of libertarian communism is to increase diversity and individuality, **not** to end it by imposing an abstract equality of outcome or of consumption that would utterly ignore individual tastes or preferences. Given that communist-anarchists like Kropotkin and Malatesta continually stressed this aspect of their ideas, Simpson was simply confusing libertarian and authoritarian forms of communism for polemical effect rather than presenting a true account of the issues at hand.

A firmer critique of communist-anarchism can be found when Tucker argued that *"Kropotkinian anarchism means the liberty to eat, but not to cook; to drink, but not to brew; to wear, but not to spin; to dwell, but not to build; to give, but not to sell or buy; to think, but not to print; to speak, but not to hire a hall; to dance, but not to pay the fiddler."* [quoted by George Woodcock and Ivan Avakumovic, **Op. Cit.**, p. 279] Yet even this contains a distortion, as it is clear that communist-anarchism is based on the assumption that members of a communist society **would** have to contribute (if physically able, of course) to the common resources in order to gain access to them. The notion that Kropotkin thought that a communist society would only take into account *"to each according to their needs"* while ignoring *"from each according to their abilities"* seems hard to square with his published arguments. While it is true that individual contributions would not be exactly determined, it is false to suggest that communist-anarchism ignores the obvious truism that in order to consume you first need to produce. Simply put, if someone seeks to live off the work of others in a free society those within it would be asked to leave and provide for themselves. By their actions, they have shown that they do not want to live in a communist commune and those who do wish to live as communists would feel no particular need to provide for those who do not (see section I.4.14).

This can be seen when Tucker quoted **Freedom** saying that *"in the transitional revolutionary period communities and individuals may be obliged in self-defence to make it their rule that 'He who will not work neither shall he eat.' It is not always possible for us to act up to our principles and … expediency may force us to confine our Communism to those who are willing to be our brothers and equals."* Somewhat incredibly, Tucker stated *"I am not quite clear as to the meaning of this, and would ask to be enlightened on the question whether those objectionable individuals are to be let alone to live in their own way, or whether the State Socialistic plan would be pursued in dealing with them."* [**Liberty**, no. 149, p. 1] Clearly, his anti-communism got in the way of any attempt to build bridges or acknowledge that communist-anarchists had no desire (as noted above) to force people to be communists nor to have the "communism" of those unwilling (rather than unable) to contribute imposed on them!

G.2.4 What other reasons do individualists give for rejecting communist-anarchism?

The other differences are not as major. Some individualist anarchists took umbrage because the communist-anarchists predicted that an anarchist society would take a communal form, so prescribing the future development of a free society in potentially authoritarian ways. As James Martin summarised, it was Tucker's *"belief that 'in all subsequent social co-operation no manner of organisation or combination whatsoever shall be binding upon any individual without his consent,' and to decide in advance upon a communal structure violated this maxim from the start."* [**Men Against the State**, p. 222] Others took umbrage because the communist-anarchists refused to spell out in sufficient detail exactly how their vision would work.

Communist-anarchists reply in four main ways. Firstly, the individualist anarchists themselves predicted roughly how they thought a free society would look and function, namely one based on individual ownership of production based around mutual banks. Secondly, communist-anarchists presented any vision as one which was consistent with libertarian principles, i.e., their suggestions for a free society was based on thinking about the implication of anarchist principles in real life. There seemed little point in advocating anarchism if any future society would be marked by authority. To not discuss how a free society could work would result in authoritarian solutions being imposed (see section I.2.1). Thirdly, they were at pains to link the institutions of a free society to those already being generated within capitalism but in opposition to its hierarchical nature (see section I.2.3). Fourthly, presenting more than a sketch would be authoritarian as it is up to a free people to create their own society and solve their problems themselves (see section I.2).

Clearly, A. H. Simpson was wrong when he asserted that communist-anarchists argued thusly: *"Abolish private property by instituting compulsory Communism, and the State will go."* No communist-anarchist has ever argued for compulsory communism. Somewhat ironically, Simpson went on to argue that the *"difference between Communism and Anarchy is plainly observable in their methods. Abolish the State … that bulwark of the robber system … says the Anarchist. Abolish private property, the source of all evil and injustice, parent of the State, says the Communist."* [**The Individualist Anarchists**, p. 92] Yet communist-anarchists do **not** subscribe to the position of abolishing private property first, **then** the state. As we note when refuting the opposite assertion by Marxists in section H.2.4, anarchists like Kropotkin and Malatesta followed Bakunin in arguing that **both** needed to be abolished at the same time. Kropotkin, for example, did not divide economic and political issues, for him it was a case of *"the political and economic principles of Anarchism."* [**Anarchism**, p. 159]

This unity of economic and political aspects of anarchism exists within Individualist Anarchism too, but it is hidden by the unfortunate tendency of its supporters of discussing certain forms of private property as state enforced monopolies. So to a large degree many of the disagreements between the two schools of anarchism were rooted in semantics. Thus we find William Bailie arguing that the anarchist-communist *"assumption that rent and interest are due to private property is not proven"* as *"both rent and interest are the result of monopoly, of restricted individual liberty."* [**Liberty**, no. 261, p. 1] In other words, rent is caused because the state enforces property rights which the individualist anarchists disagree with. Thus when individualist anarchists argue they seek to get rid of the state, they **also** mean the end of capitalist property rights (particularly in land). That this can lead to confusion is obvious as, in the usual sense of the word, rent **is** caused by private property. The communist-anarchists, in contrast, generally used the term "private property" and "property" in the same way that Proudhon used it in 1840, namely property which allows its owner to exploit the labour of another. As such, they had no problem with those who laboured by themselves on their own property.

The lack of a market in communist-anarchism led some individualist anarchists like William Bailie to argue that it *"ignores the necessity for any machinery to adjust economic activities to their ends."* Either its supporters *"exalt a chaotic and unbalanced condition"* or they will produce an *"insufferable hierarchy."* [**The Individualist Anarchists**, p. 116] Thus, to use modern terms, either communist-anarchists embrace central planning or their system simply cannot produce goods to meet demand with over-production of unwanted goods and under-production of desired ones. Needless to say, communist-anarchists argue that it is possible to bring the demand and production of goods into line without requiring centralised planning (which would be inefficient and a dire threat to individual freedom — Kropotkin's arguments against state capitalism were proved right in Soviet Russia). It would require a system of horizontal links between self-managed workplaces and the transmission of appropriate information to make informed decisions (see section I for a discussion of some possibilities).

In summary, then, while individualist anarchism opposed communist-anarchism much of this opposition was rooted in misunderstandings and, at times, outright distortion. Once these are corrected, it becomes clear that both schools of anarchism share significant ideas in common. This is unsurprising, given the impact of Proudhon on both of them as well as their common concerns on the social question and participation in the labour and other popular movements. As both are (libertarian) socialists inspired by many of the same intellectual and social influences, this should come as no surprise. That a few individualist and communist anarchists tried to deny those common influences should not blind us to them or the fact that both schools of anarchism are compatible.

Ultimately, though, anarchism should be wide enough and generous enough to include both communist and individualist anarchism. Attempts to excommunicate one or the other seem petty given how much each has in common and, moreover, given that both are compatible with each other as both are rooted in similar perspectives on possession, capitalist property rights and voluntary association. Once the differences in terminology are understood, the differences are not impossible to reconcile.

G.3
Is "anarcho"-capitalism a new form of individualist anarchism?

No. As Carole Pateman once pointed out, *"[t]here has always been a strong radical individualist tradition in the USA. Its adherents have been divided between those who drew anarchist, egalitarian conclusions, and those who reduced political life to the capitalist economy writ large, to a series of exchanges between unequally situated individuals."* [**The Problem of Political Obligation**, p. 205] What right-"libertarians" and "anarcho"-capitalists do is to confuse these two traditions, ignoring fundamental aspects of individualist anarchism in order to do so. Thus anarchist Peter Sabatini:

> *"in those rare moments when [Murray] Rothbard (or any other [right-wing] Libertarian) does draw upon individualist anarchism, he is always highly selective about what he pulls out. Most of the doctrine's core principles, being decidedly anti-Libertarianism, are conveniently ignored, and so what remains is shrill anti-statism conjoined to a vacuous freedom in hackneyed defence of capitalism. In sum, the 'anarchy' of Libertarianism reduces to a liberal fraud."* [**Libertarianism: Bogus Anarchy**]

As class struggle anarchist Benjamin Franks notes, individualist anarchism *"has similarities with, but is not identical to, anarcho-capitalism."* [**Rebel Alliances**, p. 44] For Colin Ward, while the *"mainstream"* of anarchist propaganda *"has been **anarchist-communism**"* there are *"several traditions of **individualist anarchism**"*, including that associated with Max Stirner and *"a remarkable series of 19th-century American figures"* who *"differed from free-market liberals in their absolute mistrust of American capitalism, and in their emphasis on mutualism."* Ward was careful to note that by the *"late 20th century the word 'libertarian' ... was appropriated by a new group of American thinkers"* and so *"it is necessary to examine the modern individualist 'libertarian' response from the standpoint of the anarchist tradition."* It was found to be wanting, for while Rothbard was *"the most aware of the actual anarchist tradition among the anarcho-capitalist apologists"* he may have been *"aware of a tradition, but he is singularly unaware of the old proverb that freedom for the pike means death for the minnow."* The individualist anarchists were *"busy social inventors exploring the potential of autonomy."* The *"American 'libertarians' of the 20th century are academics rather than social activists, and their inventiveness seems to be limited to providing an ideology for untrammelled market capitalism."* [**Anarchism: A Short Introduction**, pp. 2-3, p. 62, p. 67, and p. 69]

In this section we will sketch these differences between the genuine libertarian ideas of Individualist Anarchism and the bogus "anarchism" of right-"libertarian" ideology. This discussion builds upon our general critique of "anarcho"-capitalism we presented in section F. However, here we will concentrate on presenting individualist anarchist analysis of "anarcho"-capitalist positions rather than, as before, mostly social anarchist ones (although, of course, there are significant overlaps and similarities). In this way, we can show the fundamental differences between the two theories for while there are often great differences between specific individualist anarchist thinkers all share a vision of a free society distinctly at odds with the capitalism of their time as well as the "pure" system of economic textbooks and right-"libertarian" dreams (which, ironically, so often reflects the 19th century capitalism the individualist anarchists were fighting).

First it should be noted that some "anarcho"-capitalists shy away from the term, preferring such expressions as "market anarchist" or "individualist anarchist." This suggests that there is some link between their ideology and that of Tucker and his comrades. However, the founder of "anarcho"-capitalism, Murray Rothbard, refused that label for, while *"strongly tempted,"* he could not do so because *"Spooner and Tucker have in a sense pre-empted that name for their doctrine and that from that doctrine I have certain differences."* Somewhat incredibly Rothbard argued that on the whole politically *"these differences are minor,"* economically *"the differences are substantial, and this means that my view of the consequences of putting our more of less common system into practice is very far from theirs."* [*"The Spooner-Tucker Doctrine: An Economist's View"*, pp. 5-15, **Journal of Libertarian Studies**, vol. 20, no. 1, p. 7]

What an understatement! Individualist anarchists advocated an economic system in which there would have been very little inequality of wealth and so of power (and the accumulation of capital would have been minimal without profit, interest and rent). Removing this social and economic basis would result in **substantially** different political regimes. In other words, politics is not isolated from economics. As anarchist David Wieck put it, Rothbard *"writes of society as though some part of it (government) can be extracted and replaced by another arrangement while other things go on as before, and he constructs a system of police and judicial power without any consideration of the influence of historical and economic context."* [**Anarchist Justice**, p. 227]

Unsurprisingly, the political differences he highlights **are** significant, namely *"the role of law and the jury system"* and *"the land question."* The former difference relates to the fact that the individualist anarchists *"allow[ed] each individual free-market court, and more specifically, each free-market jury, totally free rein over judicial decision."* This horrified Rothbard. The reason is obvious, as it allows real people to judge the law as well as the facts, modifying the former as society changes and evolves. For Rothbard, the idea that ordinary people should have a say in the law is dismissed. Rather, *"it would not be a very difficult task for Libertarian lawyers and jurists to arrive at a rational and objective code of libertarian legal principles and procedures."* [**Op. Cit.**, pp. 7-8] Of course, the fact that *"lawyers"* and *"jurists"* may have a radically different idea of what is just than those subject to their laws is not raised by Rothbard, never mind answered. While Rothbard notes that juries may defend the people against the state, the notion that they may defend the people against the authority and power of the rich is not even raised. That is why the rich have tended to oppose juries as well as popular assemblies. Unsurprisingly, as we indicated in section F.6.1, Rothbard wanted laws to be made by judges, lawyers, jurists and other "libertarian" experts rather than jury judged and driven. In other words, to exclude the general population from any say in the law and how it changes. This hardly a *"minor"* difference! It is like a supporter of the state saying that it is a *"minor"* difference if you favour a dictatorship rather than a democratically elected government. As Tucker argued, *"it is precisely in the tempering of the rigidity of enforcement that one of the chief excellences of Anarchism consists ... under Anarchism all rules and laws will be little more than suggestions for the guidance of juries, and that all disputes ... will be submitted to juries which will judge not only the facts but the law, the justice of the law, its applicability to the given circumstances, and the penalty or damage to be inflicted because of its infraction ... under Anarchism the law ... will be regarded as **just** in proportion to its flexibility, instead of now in proportion to its rigidity."* [**The Individualist Anarchists**, pp. 160-1] In others, the law will evolve to take into account changing social circumstances and, as a consequence, public opinion on specific events and rights. Tucker's position is fundamentally **democratic** and evolutionary while Rothbard's is autocratic and fossilised.

This is particularly the case if you are proposing an economic system that is based on inequalities of wealth, power and influence and the means of accumulating more. As we note in section G.3.3, one of the few individualist anarchists that remained pointed this out and opposed Rothbard's arguments. As such, while Rothbard may have subscribed to a system of competing defence companies like Tucker, he expected them to operate in a substantially different legal system, enforcing different (capitalist) property rights and within a radically different socio-economic system. These differences are hardly *"minor"*. As such, to claim that "anarcho"-capitalism is simply individualist anarchism with "Austrian" economics shows an utter lack of understanding of what individualist anarchism stood for and aimed for.

On the land question, Rothbard opposed the individualist position of *"occupancy and use"* as it *"would automatically abolish all rent payments for land."* Which was precisely **why** the individualist anarchists advocated it! In a predominantly rural economy, as was the case during most of the 19th century in America, this would result in a significant levelling of income and social power as well as bolstering the bargaining position of non-land workers by reducing the numbers forced onto the labour market (which, as we note in section F.8.5, was the rationale for the state enforcing the land monopoly in the first place). He bemoans that landlords cannot charge rent on their *"justly-acquired private property"* without noticing that is begging the question as anarchists deny that this is *"justly-acquired"* land in the first place. Unsurprisingly, Rothbard considered *"the proper theory of justice in landed property can be found in John Locke"*, ignoring the awkward fact that the first self-proclaimed anarchist book was written **precisely** to refute that kind of theory and expose its anti-libertarian implications. His argument simply shows how far from anarchism his ideology is. For Rothbard, it goes without saying that the landlord's *"freedom of contract"* tops the worker's freedom to control their own work and live and, of course, their right to life. [**Op. Cit.**, p. 8 and p. 9]

For anarchists, *"the land is indispensable to our existence, consequently a common thing, consequently insusceptible of appropriation."* [Proudhon, **What is Property?**, p. 107] Tucker

looked forward to a time when capitalist property rights in land were ended and *"the Anarchistic view that occupancy and use should condition and limit landholding becomes the prevailing view."* This *"does not simply mean the freeing of unoccupied land. It means the freeing of all land not occupied **by the owner**"* and *"tenants would not be forced to pay you rent, nor would you be allowed to seize their property. The Anarchic associations would look upon your tenants very much as they would look upon your guests."* [**The Individualist Anarchists**, p. 159, p. 155 and p. 162] The ramifications of this position on land use are significant. At its most basic, what counts as force and coercion, and so state intervention, are fundamentally different due to the differing conceptions of property held by Tucker and Rothbard. If we apply, for example, the individualist anarchist position on land to the workplace, we would treat the workers in a factory as the rightful owners, on the basis of occupation and use; at the same time, we could treat the share owners and capitalists as aggressors for attempting to force their representatives as managers on those actually occupying and using the premises. The same applies to the landlord against the tenant farmer. Equally, the outcome of such differing property systems will be radically different — in terms of inequalities of wealth and so power (with having others working for them, it is unlikely that would-be capitalists or landlords would get rich). Rather than a *"minor"* difference, the question of land use fundamentally changes the nature of the society built upon it and whether it counts as genuinely libertarian or not.

Tucker was well aware of the implications of such differences. Supporting a scheme like Rothbard's meant *"departing from Anarchistic ground,"* it was *"Archism"* and, as he stressed in reply to one supporter of such property rights, it opened the door to other authoritarian positions: *"Archism in one point is taking him to Archism in another. Soon, if he is logical, he will be an Archist in all respects."* It was a *"fundamentally foolish"* position, because it *"starts with a basic proposition that must be looked upon by all consistent Anarchists as obvious nonsense."* *"What follows from this?"* asked Tucker. *"Evidently that a man may go to a piece of vacant land and fence it off; that he may then go to a second piece and fence that off; then to a third, and fence that off; then to a fourth, a fifth, a hundredth, a thousandth, fencing them all off; that, unable to fence off himself as many as he wishes, he may hire other men to do the fencing for him; and that then he may stand back and bar all other men from using these lands, or admit them as tenants at such rental as he may choose to extract."* It was *"a theory of landed property which all Anarchists agree in viewing as a denial of equal liberty."* It is *"utterly inconsistent with the Anarchistic doctrine of occupancy and use as the limit of property in land."* [**Liberty**, No. 180, p. 4 and p. 6] This was because of the dangers to liberty capitalist property rights in land implied:

> *"I put the right of occupancy and use above the right of contract ... principally by my interest in the right of contract. Without such a preference the theory of occupancy and use is utterly untenable; without it ... it would be possible for an individual to acquire, and hold simultaneously, virtual titles to innumerable parcels of land, by the merest show of labour performed thereon*

... [This would lead to] the virtual ownership of the entire world by a small fraction of its inhabitants ... [which would see] the right of contract, if not destroyed absolutely, would surely be impaired in an intolerable degree." [**Op. Cit.**, no. 350, p. 4]

Clearly a position which Rothbard had no sympathy for, unlike landlords. Strange, though, that Rothbard did not consider the obvious liberty destroying effects of the monopolisation of land and natural resources as *"rational grounds"* for opposing landlords but, then, as we noted in section F.1 when it came to private property Rothbard simply could not see its state-like qualities — even when he pointed them out himself! For Rothbard, the individualist anarchist position involved a *"hobbling of land sites or of optimum use of land ownership and cultivation and such arbitrary misallocation of land injures all of society."* [Rothbard, **Op. Cit.**, p. 9] Obviously, those subject to the arbitrary authority of landlords and pay them rent are not part of *"society"* and it is a strange coincidence that the interests of landlords just happen to coincide so completely with that of *"all of society"* (including their tenants?). And it would be churlish to remind Rothbard's readers that, as a methodological individualist, he was meant to think that there is no such thing as *"society"* — just individuals. And in terms of these individuals, he clearly favoured the landlords over their tenants and justifies this by appealing, like any crude collectivist, to an abstraction (*"society"*) to which the tenants must sacrifice themselves and their liberty. Tucker would not have been impressed.

For Rothbard, the nineteenth century saw *"the establishment in North America of a truly libertarian land system."* [**The Ethics of Liberty**, p. 73] In contrast, the Individualist Anarchists attacked that land system as the *"land monopoly"* and looked forward to a time when *"the libertarian principle to the tenure of land"* was actually applied [Tucker, **Liberty**, no. 350, p. 5] So given the central place that "occupancy and use" lies in individualist anarchism, it was extremely patronising for Rothbard to assert that *"it seems ... a complete violation of the Spooner-Tucker 'law of equal liberty' to prevent the legitimate owner from selling his land to someone else."* [*"The Spooner-Tucker Doctrine: An Economist's View"*, **Op. Cit.**, p. 9] Particularly as Tucker had explicitly addressed this issue and indicated the logical and common sense basis for this so-called "violation" of their principles. Thus "occupancy and use" was *"the libertarian principle to the tenure of land"* because it stopped a class of all powerful landlords developing, ensuring a real equality of opportunity and liberty rather than the formal "liberty" associated with capitalism which, in practice, means selling your liberty to the rich.

Somewhat ironically, Rothbard bemoaned that it *"seems to be a highly unfortunate trait of libertarian and quasi-libertarian groups to spend the bulk of their time and energy emphasising their most fallacious or unlibertarian points."* [**Op. Cit.**, p. 14] He pointed to the followers of Henry George and their opposition to the current land holding system and the monetary views of the individualist anarchists as examples (see section G.3.6 for a critique of Rothbard's position on mutual banking). Of course, both groups would reply that Rothbard's positions were, in fact, both fallacious and unlibertarian in nature. As, indeed, did Tucker decades before

Rothbard proclaimed his private statism a form of "anarchism." Yarros' critique of those who praised capitalism but ignored the state imposed restrictions that limited choice within it seems as applicable to Rothbard as it did Herbert Spencer:

"A system is voluntary when it is voluntary all round ... not when certain transactions, regarded from certain points of view, appear voluntary. Are the circumstances which compel the labourer to accept unfair terms law-created, artificial, and subversive of equal liberty? That is the question, and an affirmative answer to it is tantamount to an admission that the present system is not voluntary in the true sense." [**Liberty**, no. 184, p. 2]

So while "anarcho"-capitalists like Walter Block speculate on how starving families renting their children to wealthy paedophiles is acceptable *"on libertarian grounds"* it is doubtful that any individualist anarchist would be so blasé about such an evil. [*"Libertarianism vs. Objectivism: A Response to Peter Schwartz,"* pp. 39-62, **Reason Papers**, Vol. 26, Summer 2003, p. 20] Tucker, for example, was well aware that liberty without equality was little more than a bad joke. *"If,"* he argued, *"after the achievement of all industrial freedoms, economic rent should prove to be the cause of such inequalities in comfort that an effective majority found themselves at the point of starvation, they would undoubtedly cry, 'Liberty be damned!' and proceed to even up; and I think that at that stage of the game they would be great fools if they didn't. From this it will be seen that I am no[t] ... a stickler for absolute equal liberty under all circumstances."* Needless to say, he considered this outcome as unlikely and was keen to *"[t]ry freedom first."* [**Liberty**, no. 267, p. 2 and p. 3]

The real question is why Rothbard considered this a **political** difference rather than an economic one. Unfortunately, he did not explain. Perhaps because of the underlying **socialist** perspective behind the anarchist position? Or perhaps the fact that feudalism and monarchism was based on the owner of the land being its ruler suggests a political aspect to propertarian ideology best left unexplored? Given that the idea of grounding rulership on land ownership receded during the Middle Ages, it may be unwise to note that under "anarcho"-capitalism the landlord and capitalist would, likewise, be sovereign over the land **and** those who used it? As we noted in section F.1, this is the conclusion that Rothbard does draw. As such, there **is** a political aspect to this difference, namely the difference between a libertarian social system and one rooted in authority.

Ultimately, *"the expropriation of the mass of the people from the soil forms the basis of the capitalist mode of production."* [Marx, **Capital**, vol. 1, p. 934] For there are *"two ways of oppressing men: either directly by brute force, by physical violence; or indirectly by denying them the means of life and this reducing them to a state of surrender."* In the second case, government is *"an organised instrument to ensure that dominion and privilege will be in the hands of those who ... have cornered all the means of life, first and foremost the land, which they make use of to keep the people in bondage and to make them work for their benefit."* [Malatesta, **Anarchy**, p. 21] Privatising the coercive functions of said government hardly makes much difference.

As such, Rothbard was right to distance himself from the term individualist anarchism. It is a shame he did not do the same with libertarian as well!

G.3.1 Is "anarcho"-capitalism American anarchism?

Unlike Rothbard, some "anarcho"-capitalists are more than happy to proclaim themselves "individualist anarchists" and so suggest that their notions are identical, or nearly so, with the likes of Tucker, Ingalls and Labadie. As part of this, they tend to stress that individualist anarchism is uniquely American, an indigenous form of anarchism unlike social anarchism. To do so, however, means ignoring not only the many European influences on individualist anarchism itself (most notably, Proudhon) but also downplaying the realities of American capitalism which quickly made social anarchism the dominant form of Anarchism in America. Ironically, such a position is deeply contradictory as "anarcho"-capitalism itself is most heavily influenced by a European ideology, namely "Austrian" economics, which has lead its proponents to reject key aspects of the indigenous American anarchist tradition.

For example, "anarcho"-capitalist Wendy McElroy does this in a short essay provoked by the Seattle protests in 1999. After property destruction in Seattle placed American anarchists back in the media, she stated that social anarchism *"is not American anarchism. Individualist anarchism, the indigenous form of the political philosophy, stands in rigorous opposition to attacking the person or property of individuals."* While Canadian, her rampant American nationalism is at odds with the internationalism of the individualist anarchists and like an ideological protectionist she argued that *"Left [sic!] anarchism (socialist and communist) are foreign imports that flooded the country like cheap goods during the 19th century."* [**Anarchism: Two Kinds**] Apparently Albert and Lucy Parsons were un-Americans, as was Voltairine de Cleyre who turned from individualist to communist anarchism. And best not mention the social conditions in America which quickly made communist-anarchism predominant in the movement or that individualist anarchists like Tucker proudly proclaimed their ideas socialist!

She argued that *"[m]any of these anarchists (especially those escaping Russia) introduced lamentable traits into American radicalism"* such as *"propaganda by deed"* as well as a class analysis which *"divided society into economic classes that were at war with each other."* Taking the issue of *"propaganda by the deed"* first, it should be noted that use of violence against person or property was hardly alien to American traditions. The Boston Tea Party was just as *"lamentable"* an attack on *"property of individuals"* as the window breaking at Seattle while the revolution and revolutionary war were hardly fought using pacifist methods or respecting the *"person or property of individuals"* who supported imperialist Britain. Similarly, the struggle against slavery was not conducted purely by means Quakers would have supported (John Brown springs to mind), nor was (to use just one example) Shay's rebellion. So *"attacking the person or property of individuals"* was hardly alien to

American radicalism and so was definitely **not** imported by *"foreign"* anarchists.

Of course, anarchism in America became associated with terrorism (or *"propaganda by the deed"*) due to the Haymarket events of 1886 and Berkman's assassination attempt against Frick during the Homestead strike. Significantly, McElroy makes no mention of the substantial state and employer violence which provoked many anarchists to advocate violence in self-defence. For example, the great strike of 1877 saw the police open fire on strikers on July 25th, killing five and injuring many more. *"For several days, meetings of workmen were broken up by the police, who again and again interfered with the rights of free speech and assembly."* The **Chicago Times** called for the use of hand grenades against strikers and state troops were called in, killing a dozen strikers. *"In two days of fighting, between 25 and 50 civilians had been killed, some 200 seriously injured, and between 300 and 400 arrested. Not a single policeman or soldier had lost his life."* This context explains why many workers, including those in reformist trade unions as well as anarchist groups like the IWPA, turned to armed self-defence (*"violence"*). The Haymarket meeting itself was organised in response to the police firing on strikers and killing at least two. The Haymarket bomb was thrown after the police tried to break-up a peaceful meeting by force: *"It is clear then that … it was the police and not the anarchists who were the perpetrators of the violence at the Haymarket."* All but one of the deaths and most of the injuries were caused by the police firing indiscriminately in the panic after the explosion. [Paul Avrich, **The Haymarket Tragedy**, pp. 32-4, p. 189, p. 210, and pp. 208-9] As for Berkman's assassination attempt, this was provoked by the employer's Pinkerton police opening fire on strikers, killing and wounding many. [Emma Goldman, **Living My Life**, vol. 1, p. 86]

In other words, it was **not** foreign anarchists or alien ideas which associated anarchism with violence but, rather, the reality of American capitalism. As historian Eugenia C. Delamotte puts it, *"the view that anarchism stood for violence … spread rapidly in the mainstream press from the 1870s"* because of *"the use of violence against strikers and demonstrators in the labour agitation that marked these decades — struggles for the eight-hour day, better wages, and the right to unionise, for example. Police, militia, and private security guards harassed, intimidated, bludgeoned, and shot workers routinely in conflicts that were just as routinely portrayed in the media as worker violence rather than state violence; labour activists were also subject to brutal attacks, threats of lynching, and many other forms of physical assault and intimidation … the question of how to respond to such violence became a critical issue in the 1870s, with the upswelling of labour agitation and attempts to suppress it violently."* [**Gates of Freedom**, pp. 51-2]

Joseph Labadie, it should be noted, thought the *"Beastly police"* got what they deserved at Haymarket as they had attempted to break up a peaceful public meeting and such people should *"go at the peril of their lives. If it is necessary to use dynamite to protect the rights of free meeting, free press and free speech, then the sooner we learn its manufacture and use … the better it will be for the toilers of the world."* The radical paper he was involved in, the **Labor Leaf**, had previously argued that *"should trouble come, the capitalists will use the regular army and militia to shoot down those who are* not satisfied. It won't be so if the people are equally ready." Even reformist unions were arming themselves to protect themselves, with many workers applauding their attempts to organise union militias. As one worker put it: "With union men well armed and accustomed to military tactics, we could keep Pinkerton's men at a distance ... Employers would think twice, too, before they attempted to use troops against us ... Every union ought to have its company of sharpshooters." [quoted by Richard Jules Oestreicher, **Solidarity and Fragmentation**, p. 200 and p. 135]

While the violent rhetoric of the Chicago anarchists was used at their trial and is remembered (in part because enemies of anarchism take great glee in repeating it), the state and employer violence which provoked it has been forgotten or ignored. Unless this is mentioned, a seriously distorted picture of both communist-anarchism **and** capitalism are created. It is significant, of course, that while the **words** of the Martyrs are taken as evidence of anarchism's violent nature, the actual violence (up to and including murder) against strikers by state and private police apparently tells us nothing about the nature of the state or capitalist system (Ward Churchill presents an excellent summary of such activities in his article "From the Pinkertons to the PATRIOT Act: The Trajectory of Political Policing in the United States, 1870 to the Present" [**CR: The New Centennial Review**, Vol. 4, No. 1, pp. 1-72]).

So, as can be seen, McElroy distorts the context of anarchist violence by utterly ignoring the far worse capitalist violence which provoked it. Like more obvious statists, she demonises the resistance to the oppressed while ignoring that of the oppressor. Equally, it should also be noted Tucker rejected violent methods to end class oppression not out of principle, but rather strategy as there "was no doubt in his mind as to the righteousness of resistance to oppression by recourse to violence, but his concern now was with its expedience ... he was absolutely convinced that the desired social revolution would be possible only through the utility of peaceful propaganda and passive resistance." [James J. Martin, **Men Against the State**, p. 225] For Tucker "as long as freedom of speech and of the press is not struck down, there should be no resort to physical force in the struggle against oppression." [quoted by Morgan Edwards, "Neither Bombs Nor Ballots: Liberty & the Strategy of Anarchism", pp. 65-91, **Benjamin R. Tucker and the Champions of Liberty**, Coughlin, Hamilton and Sullivan (eds.), p. 67] Nor should we forget that Spooner's rhetoric could be as blood-thirsty as Johann Most's at times and that American individualist anarchist Dyer Lum was an advocate of insurrection.

As far as class analysis goes, which allegedly "divided society into economic classes that were at war with each other", it can be seen that the "left" anarchists were simply acknowledging the reality of the situation — as did, it must be stressed, the individualist anarchists. As we noted in section G.1, the individualist anarchists were well aware that there was a class war going on, one in which the capitalist class used the state to ensure its position (the individualist anarchist "knows very well that the present State is an historical development, that it is simply the tool of the property-owning class; he knows that primitive accumulation began through robbery bold and daring, and that the freebooters then organised the State in its present form for their own self-preservation." [A.H. Simpson, **The Individualist Anarchists**, p. 92]). Thus workers had a right

to a genuinely free market for "[i]f the man with labour to sell has not this free market, then his liberty is violated and his property virtually taken from him. Now, such a market has constantly been denied ... to labourers of the entire civilised world. And the men who have denied it are ... Capitalists ... [who] have placed and kept on the statute-books all sorts of prohibitions and taxes designed to limit and effective in limiting the number of bidders for the labour of those who have labour to sell." [**Instead of a Book**, p. 454] For Joshua King Ingalls, "[i]n any question as between the worker and the holder of privilege, [the state] is certain to throw itself into the scale with the latter, for it is itself the source of privilege, the creator of class rule." [quoted by Bowman N. Hall, "Joshua K. Ingalls, American Individualist: Land Reformer, Opponent of Henry George and Advocate of Land Leasing, Now an Established Mode," pp. 383-96, **American Journal of Economics and Sociology**, Vol. 39, No. 4, p. 292] Ultimately, the state was "a police force to regulate the people in the interests of the plutocracy." [Ingalls, quoted by Martin, **Op. Cit.**, p. 152]

Discussing Henry Frick, manager of the Homestead steelworkers who was shot by Berkman for using violence against striking workers, Tucker noted that Frick did not "aspire, as I do, to live in a society of mutually helpful equals" but rather it was "his determination to live in luxury produced by the toil and suffering of men whose necks are under his heel. He has deliberately chosen to live on terms of hostility with the greater part of the human race." While opposing Berkman's act, Tucker believed that he was "a man with whom I have much in common, — much more at any rate than with such a man as Frick." Berkman "would like to live on terms of equality with his fellows, doing his share of work for not more than his share of pay." [**The Individualist Anarchists**, pp. 307-8] Clearly, Tucker was well aware of the class struggle and why, while not supporting such actions, violence occurred when fighting it.

As Victor Yarros summarised, for the individualist anarchists the "State is the servant of the robbers, and it exists chiefly to prevent the expropriation of the robbers and the restoration of a free and fair field for legitimate competition and wholesome, effective voluntary cooperation." ["Philosophical Anarchism: Its Rise, Decline, and Eclipse", pp. 470-483, **The American Journal of Sociology**, vol. 41, no. 4, p. 475] For "anarcho"-capitalists, the state exploits all classes subject to it (perhaps the rich most, by means of taxation to fund welfare programmes and legal support for union rights and strikes).

So when McElroy states that, "Individualist anarchism rejects the State because it is the institutionalisation of force against peaceful individuals", she is only partly correct. While it may be true for "anarcho"-capitalism, it fails to note that for the individualist anarchists the modern state was the institutionalisation of force by the capitalist class to deny the working class a free market. The individualist anarchists, in other words, like social anarchists also rejected the state because it imposed certain class monopolies and class legislation which ensured the exploitation of labour by capital — a significant omission on McElroy's part. "Can it be soberly pretended for a moment that the State ... is purely a defensive institution?" asked Tucker. "Surely not ... you will find that a good nine-tenths of existing legislation serves ... either to prescribe the individual's personal habits, or, worse still, to create and sustain *commercial, industrial, financial, and proprietary monopolies which deprive labour of a large part of the reward that it would receive in a perfectly free market."* [Tucker, **Instead of a Book**, pp. 25-6] In fact:

> *"As long as a portion of the products of labour are appropriated for the payment of fat salaries to useless officials and big dividends to idle stockholders, labour is entitled to consider itself defrauded, and all just men will sympathise with its protest."* [Tucker, **Liberty**, no. 19, p. 1]

It goes without saying that almost all "anarcho"-capitalists follow Rothbard in being totally opposed to labour unions, strikes and other forms of working class protest. As such, the individualist anarchists, just as much as the "left" anarchists McElroy is so keen to disassociate them from, argued that *"[t]hose who made a profit from buying or selling were class criminals and their customers or employees were class victims. It did not matter if the exchanges were voluntary ones. Thus, left anarchists hated the free market as deeply as they hated the State."* [McElroy, **Op. Cit.**] Yet, as any individualist anarchist of the time would have told her, the "free market" did not exist because the capitalist class used the state to oppress the working class and reduce the options available to choose from so allowing the exploitation of labour to occur. Class analysis, in other words, was not limited to *"foreign"* anarchism, nor was the notion that making a profit was a form of exploitation (usury). As Tucker continually stressed: *"Liberty will abolish interest; it will abolish profit; it will abolish monopolistic rent; it will abolish taxation; it will abolish the exploitation of labour."* [**The Individualist Anarchists**, p. 157]

It should also be noted that the "left" anarchist opposition to the individualist anarchist "free market" is due to an analysis which argues that it will not, in fact, result in the anarchist aim of ending exploitation nor will it maximise individual freedom (see section G.4). We do not "hate" the free market, rather we love individual liberty and seek the best kind of society to ensure free people. By concentrating on markets being free, "anarcho"-capitalism ensures that it is wilfully blind to the freedom-destroying similarities between capitalist property and the state (as we discussed in section F.1). An analysis which many individualist anarchists recognised, with the likes of Dyer Lum seeing that replacing the authority of the state with that of the boss was no great improvement in terms of freedom and so advocating co-operative workplaces to abolish wage slavery. Equally, in terms of land ownership the individualist anarchists opposed any voluntary exchanges which violated *"occupancy and use"* and so they, so, *"hated the free market as deeply as they hated the State."* Or, more correctly, they recognised that voluntary exchanges can result in concentrations of wealth and so power which made a mockery of individual freedom. In other words, that while the market may be free the individuals within it would not be.

McElroy partly admits this, saying that *"the two schools of anarchism had enough in common to shake hands when they first met. To some degree, they spoke a mutual language. For example, they both reviled the State and denounced capitalism. But, by the latter, individualist anarchists meant 'state-capitalism' the alliance of government and business."* Yet this *"alliance of government and business"* has been the only kind of capitalism that has ever existed. They were well aware that such an alliance made the capitalist system what it was, i.e., a system based on the exploitation of labour. William Bailie, in an article entitled *"The Rule of the Monopolists"* simply repeated the standard socialist analysis of the state when he talked about the *"gigantic monopolies, which control not only our industry, but all the machinery of the State, — legislative, judicial, executive, — together with school, college, press, and pulpit."* Thus the *"preponderance in the number of injunctions against striking, boycotting, and agitating, compared with the number against locking-out, blacklisting, and the employment of armed mercenaries."* The courts could not ensure justice because of the *"subserviency of the judiciary to the capitalist class … and the nature of the reward in store for the accommodating judge."* Government *"is the instrument by means of which the monopolist maintains his supremacy"* as the law-makers *"enact what he desires; the judiciary interprets his will; the executive is his submissive agent; the military arm exists in reality to defend **his** country, protect **his** property, and suppress **his** enemies, the workers on strike."* Ultimately, *"when the producer no longer obeys the State, his economic master will have lost his power."* [**Liberty**, no. 368, p. 4 and p. 5] Little wonder, then, that the individualist anarchists thought that the end of the state and the class monopolies it enforces would produce a radically different society rather than one essentially similar to the current one but without taxes. Their support for the "free market" implied the end of capitalism and its replacement with a new social system, one which would end the exploitation of labour.

She herself admits, in a roundabout way, that "anarcho"-capitalism is significantly different from individualist anarchism. *"The schism between the two forms of anarchism has deepened with time,"* she asserts. This was *"[l]argely due to the path breaking work of Murray Rothbard"* and so, unlike genuine individualist anarchism, the new *"individualist anarchism"* (i.e., "anarcho"-capitalism) *"is no longer inherently suspicious of profit-making practices, such as charging interest. Indeed, it embraces the free market as the voluntary vehicle of economic exchange"* (does this mean that the old version of it did not, in fact, embrace *"the free market"* after all?) This is because it *"draws increasingly upon the work of Austrian economists such as Mises and Hayek"* and so *"it draws increasingly farther away from left anarchism"* and, she fails to note, the likes of Warren and Tucker. As such, it would be churlish to note that "Austrian" economics was even more of a *"foreign import"* much at odds with American anarchist traditions as communist anarchism, but we will! After all, Rothbard's support of usury (interest, rent and profit) would be unlikely to find much support from someone who looked forward to the development of *"an attitude of hostility to usury, in any form, which will ultimately cause any person who charges more than cost for any product to be regarded very much as we now regard a pickpocket."* [Tucker, **The Individualist Anarchists**, p. 155] Nor, as noted above, would Rothbard's support for an *"Archist"* (capitalist) land ownership system have won him anything but dismissal nor would his judge, jurist and lawyer driven political system have been seen as anything other than rule by the few rather than rule by none.

Ultimately, it is a case of influences and the kind of socio-political analysis and aims they inspire. Unsurprisingly, the main influences in individualist anarchism came from social movements and protests. Thus poverty-stricken farmers and labour unions seeking monetary and land reform to ease their position and subservience to capital all plainly played their part in shaping the theory, as did the Single-Tax ideas of Henry George and the radical critiques of capitalism provided by Proudhon and Marx. In contrast, "anarcho"-capitalism's major (indeed, predominant) influence is "Austrian" economists, an ideology developed (in part) to provide intellectual support against such movements and their proposals for reform. As we will discuss in the next section, this explains the quite fundamental differences between the two systems for all the attempts of "anarcho"-capitalists to appropriate the legacy of the likes of Tucker.

G.3.2 What are the differences between "anarcho"-capitalism and individualist anarchism?

The key differences between individualist anarchism and "anarcho"-capitalism derive from the fact the former were socialists while the latter embrace capitalism with unqualified enthusiasm. Unsurprisingly, this leans to radically different analyses, conclusions and strategies. It also expresses itself in the vision of the free society expected from their respective systems. Such differences, we stress, all ultimately flow from fact that the individualist anarchists were/are socialists while the likes of Rothbard are wholeheartedly supporters of capitalism.

As scholar Frank H. Brooks notes, "*the individualist anarchists hoped to achieve socialism by removing the obstacles to individual liberty in the economic realm.*" This involved making equality of opportunity a reality rather than mere rhetoric by ending capitalist property rights in land and ensuring access to credit to set-up in business for themselves. So while supporting a market economy "*they were also advocates of socialism and critics of industrial capitalism, positions that make them less useful as ideological tools of a resurgent capitalism.*" [**The Individualist Anarchists**, p. 111] Perhaps unsurprisingly, most right-"libertarians" get round this problem by hiding or downplaying this awkward fact. Yet it remains essential for understanding both individualist anarchism and why "anarcho"-capitalism is not a form of anarchism.

Unlike both individualist and social anarchists, "anarcho"-capitalists support capitalism (a "pure" free market type, which has never existed although it has been approximated occasionally as in 19th century America). This means that they totally reject the ideas of anarchists with regards to property and economic analysis. For example, like all supporters of capitalists they consider rent, profit and interest as valid incomes. In contrast, all Anarchists consider these as exploitation and agree with Tucker; "**Whoever** contributes to production is alone entitled. **What** has no rights that **who** is bound to respect. **What** is a thing. **Who** is a person. Things have no claims; they exist only to be claimed. The possession of a right cannot be predicted of dead material, but only a living person." [quoted by Wm. Gary Kline, **The Individualist Anarchists**, p. 73]

This, we must note, is the fundamental critique of the capitalist theory that capital is productive. In and of themselves, fixed costs do not create value. Rather, value is created depends on how investments are developed and used once in place and because of this the Individualist Anarchists, like other anarchists, considered non-labour derived income as usury, unlike "anarcho"-capitalists. Similarly, anarchists reject the notion of capitalist property rights in favour of possession (including the full fruits of one's labour). For example, anarchists reject private ownership of land in favour of a "occupancy and use" regime. In this we follow Proudhon's **What is Property?** and argue that "*property is theft*" as well as "*despotism*". Rothbard, as noted in the section F.1, rejected this perspective.

As these ideas are an **essential** part of anarchist politics, they cannot be removed without seriously damaging the rest of the theory. This can be seen from Tucker's comments that "*Liberty insists... [on] the abolition of the State and the abolition of usury; on no more government of man by man, and no more exploitation of man by man.*" [quoted by Eunice Schuster, **Native American Anarchism**, p. 140] Tucker indicates here that anarchism has specific economic **and** political ideas, that it opposes capitalism along with the state. Therefore anarchism was never purely a "political" concept, but always combined an opposition to oppression with an opposition to exploitation. The social anarchists made exactly the same point. Which means that when Tucker argued that "*Liberty insists on Socialism... — true Socialism, Anarchistic Socialism: the prevalence on earth of Liberty, Equality, and Solidarity*" he knew exactly what he was saying and meant it wholeheartedly. [**Instead of a Book**, p. 363] So because "anarcho"-capitalists embrace capitalism and reject socialism, they cannot be considered anarchists or part of the anarchist tradition.

There are, of course, overlaps between individualist anarchism and "anarcho"-capitalism, just as there are overlaps between it and Marxism (and social anarchism, of course). However, just as a similar analysis of capitalism does not make individualist anarchists Marxists, so apparent similarities between individualist anarchism and "anarcho"-capitalism does not make the former a forerunner of the latter. For example, both schools support the idea of "free markets." Yet the question of markets is fundamentally second to the issue of property rights, for what is exchanged on the market is dependent on what is considered legitimate property. In this, as Rothbard noted, individualist anarchists and "anarcho"-capitalists differ and different property rights produce different market structures and dynamics. This means that capitalism is not the only economy with markets and so support for markets cannot be equated with support for capitalism. Equally, opposition to markets is **not** the defining characteristic of socialism. As such, it **is** possible to be a market socialist (and many socialists are) as "markets" and "property" do not equate to capitalism as we proved in sections G.1.1 and G.1.2 respectively.

One apparent area of overlap between individualist anarchism and "anarcho"-capitalism is the issue of wage labour. As we noted in section G.1.3, unlike social anarchists, some individualist anarchists were not consistently against it. However, this similarity is more apparent than real as the individualist anarchists were opposed to exploitation and argued (unlike "anarcho"-capitalism) that in their system workers bargaining powers would be raised to such a level that their wages would equal the full product of their labour and so it would not be an exploitative arrangement. Needless to say, social anarchists think this is unlikely to be the case and, as we discuss in section G.4.1, individualist anarchist support for wage labour is in contradiction to many of the stated basic principles of the individualist anarchists themselves. In particular, wage labour violates "occupancy and use" as well as having more than a passing similarity to the state.

However, these problems can be solved by consistently applying the principles of individualist anarchism, unlike "anarcho"-capitalism, and that is why it is a real (if inconsistent) school of anarchism. Moreover, the social context these ideas were developed in and would have been applied ensure that these contradictions would have been minimised. If they had been applied, a genuine anarchist society of self-employed workers would, in all likelihood, have been created (at least at first, whether the market would increase inequalities is a moot point between anarchists). Thus we find Tucker criticising Henry George by noting that he was *"enough of an economist to be very well aware that, whether it has land or not, labour which can get no capital — that is, which is oppressed by capital — cannot, without accepting the alternative of starvation, refuse to reproduce capital for the capitalists."* Abolition of the money monopoly will increase wages, so allowing workers to *"steadily lay up money, with which he can buy tools to compete with his employer or to till his bit of land with comfort and advantage. In short, he will be an independent man, receiving what he produces or an equivalent thereof. How to make this the lot of all men is the labour question. Free land will not solve it. Free money, supplemented by free land, will."* [**Liberty**, no. 99, p. 4 and p. 5] Sadly, Rothbard failed to reach George's level of understanding (at least as regards his beloved capitalism).

Which brings us another source of disagreement, namely on the effects of state intervention and what to do about it. As noted, during the rise of capitalism the bourgeoisie were not shy in urging state intervention against the masses. Unsurprisingly, working class people generally took an anti-state position during this period. The individualist anarchists were part of that tradition, opposing what Marx termed *"primitive accumulation"* in favour of the pre-capitalist forms of property and society it was destroying.

However, when capitalism found its feet and could do without such obvious intervention, the possibility of an "anti-state" capitalism could arise. Such a possibility became a definite once the state started to intervene in ways which, while benefiting the system as a whole, came into conflict with the property and power of individual members of the capitalist and landlord class. Thus social legislation which attempted to restrict the negative effects of unbridled exploitation and oppression on workers and the environment were having on the economy were the source of much outrage in certain bourgeois circles:

> *"Quite independently of these tendencies [of individualist anarchism] … the anti-socialist bourgeoisie (which is also anti-statist, being hostile to any social intervention on the part of the State to protect the victims of exploitation — in the matter of working hours, hygienic working conditions and so on), and the greed of unlimited exploitation, had stirred up in England a certain agitation in favour*

> *of pseudo-individualism, an unrestrained exploitation. To this end, they enlisted the services of a mercenary pseudo-literature … which played with doctrinaire and fanatical ideas in order to project a species of 'individualism' that was absolutely sterile, and a species of 'non-interventionism' that would let a man die of hunger rather than offend his dignity."* [Max Nettlau, **A Short History of Anarchism**, p. 39]

This perspective can be seen when Tucker denounced Herbert Spencer as a champion of the capitalistic class for his vocal attacks on social legislation which claimed to benefit working class people but staying strangely silent on the laws passed to benefit (usually indirectly) capital and the rich. "Anarcho"-capitalism is part of that tradition, the tradition associated with a capitalism which no longer needs obvious state intervention as enough wealth has been accumulated to keep workers under control by means of market power.

In other words, there are substantial differences between the victims of a thief trying to stop being robbed and be left alone to enjoy their property and the successful thief doing the same! Individualist Anarchist's were aware of this. For example, Victor Yarros stressed this key difference between individualist anarchism and the proto-"libertarian" capitalists of "voluntaryism":

> *"[Auberon Herbert] believes in allowing people to retain all their possessions, no matter how unjustly and basely acquired, while getting them, so to speak, to swear off stealing and usurping and to promise to behave well in the future. We, on the other hand, while insisting on the principle of private property, in wealth honestly obtained under the reign of liberty, do not think it either unjust or unwise to dispossess the landlords who have monopolised natural wealth by force and fraud. We hold that the poor and disinherited toilers would be justified in expropriating, not alone the landlords, who notoriously have no equitable titles to their lands, but **all** the financial lords and rulers, all the millionaires and very wealthy individuals… . Almost all possessors of great wealth enjoy neither what they nor their ancestors rightfully acquired (and if Mr. Herbert wishes to challenge the correctness of this statement, we are ready to go with him into a full discussion of the subject)…*

> *"If he holds that the landlords are justly entitled to their lands, let him make a defence of the landlords or an attack on our unjust proposal."* [quoted by Carl Watner, *"The English Individualists As They Appear In Liberty,"* pp. 191-211, **Benjamin R. Tucker and the Champions of Liberty**, Coughlin, Hamilton and Sullivan (eds.), pp. 199-200]

It could be argued, in reply, that some "anarcho"-capitalists do argue that stolen property should be returned to its rightful owners and, as a result, do sometimes argue for land reform (namely, the seizing of land by peasants from their feudal landlords). However, this position is, at best, a pale shadow of the individualist anarchist position or, at worse, simply rhetoric. As leading "anarcho"-capitalist

Walter Block pointed out:

"While this aspect of libertarian theory sounds very radical, in practice it is less so. This is because the claimant always needs proof. Possession is nine tenths of the law, and to overcome the presumption that property is now in the hands of its rightful owners required that an evidentiary burden by overcome. The further back in history was the initial act of aggression (not only because written evidence is less likely to be available), the less likely it is that there can be proof of it." [**Op. Cit.,** pp. 54-5]

Somewhat ironically, Block appears to support land reform in Third World countries in spite of the fact that the native peoples have no evidence to show that they are the rightful owners of the land they work. Nor does he bother himself to wonder about the wider social impact of such theft, namely in the capital that was funded using it. If the land was stolen, then so were its products and so was any capital bought with the profits made from such goods. But, as he says, this aspect of right-"libertarian" ideology *"sounds very radical"* but *"in practice it is less so."* Apparently, theft **is** property! Not to mention that nine tenths of property is currently possessed (that is, used) not by its "rightful owners" but rather those who by economic necessity have to work for them. This is a situation the law was designed to protect, including (apparently) a so-called "libertarian" one.

This wider impact is key. As we indicated in section F.8, state coercion (particularly in the form of the land monopoly) was essential in the development of capitalism. By restricting access to land, working class people had little option but to seek work from landlords and capitalists. Thus the stolen land ensured that workers were exploited by the landlord and the capitalist and so the exploitation of the land monopoly was spread throughout the economy, with the resulting exploited labour being used to ensure that capital accumulated. For Rothbard, unlike the individualist anarchists, the land monopoly had limited impact and can be considered separately from the rise of capitalism:

"the emergence of wage-labour was an enormous boon for many thousands of poor workers and saved them from starvation. If there is no wage labour, as there was not in most production before the Industrial Revolution, then each worker must have enough money to purchase his own capital and tools. One of the great things about the emergence of the factory system and wage labour is that poor workers did not have to purchase their own capital equipment; this could be left to the capitalists." [**Konkin on Libertarian Strategy**]

Except, of course, **before** the industrial revolution almost all workers did, in fact, have their own capital and tools. The rise of capitalism was based on the exclusion of working people from the land by means of the land monopoly. Farmers were barred, by the state, from utilising the land of the aristocracy while their access to the commons was stripped from them by the imposition of capitalist property rights by the state. Thus Rothbard is right, in a sense. The emergence of wage-labour was based on the fact that workers had

to purchase access to the land from those who monopolised it by means of state action — which was precisely what the individualist anarchists opposed. Wage labour, after all, first developed **on the land** not with the rise of the factory system. Even Rothbard, we hope, would not have been so crass as to say that landlordism was an enormous boon for those poor workers as it saved them from starvation for, after all, one of the great things about landlordism is that poor workers did not have to purchase their own land; that could be left to the landlords.

The landless workers, therefore, had little option but to seek work from those who monopolised the land. Over time, increasing numbers found work in industry where employers happily took advantage of the effects of the land monopoly to extract as much work for as little pay as possible. The profits of both landlord and capitalist exploitation were then used to accumulate capital, reducing the bargaining power of the landless workers even more as it became increasingly difficult to set-up in business due to natural barriers to competition. It should also be stressed that once forced onto the labour market, the proletariat found itself subjected to numerous state laws which prevented their free association (for example, the banning of unions and strikes as conspiracies) as well as their ability to purchase their own capital and tools. Needless to say, the individualist anarchists recognised this and considered the ability of workers to be able to purchase their own capital and tools as an essential reform and, consequently, fought against the money monopoly. They reasoned, quite rightly, that this was a system of class privilege designed to keep workers in a position of dependency on the landlords and capitalists, which (in turn) allowed exploitation to occur. This was also the position of many workers, who rather than consider capitalism a boon, organised to defend their freedom and to resist exploitation — and the state complied with the wishes of the capitalists and broke that resistance.

Significantly, Tucker and other individualist anarchists saw state intervention as a result of capital manipulating legislation to gain an advantage on the so-called free market which allowed them to exploit labour and, as such, it benefited the **whole** capitalist class (*"If, then, the capitalist, by abolishing the free market, compels other men to procure their tools and advantages of him on less favourable terms than they could get before, while it may be better for them to come to his terms than to go without the capital, does he not deduct from their earnings?"* [Tucker, **Liberty**, no. 109, p. 4]). Rothbard, at best, acknowledges that **some** sections of big business benefit from the current system and so fails to have a comprehensive understanding of the dynamics of capitalism as a **system** (rather as an ideology). This lack of understanding of capitalism as a historic and dynamic system rooted in class rule and economic power is important in evaluating "anarcho"-capitalist claims to anarchism.

Then there is the issue of strategy, with Rothbard insisting on *"political action,"* namely voting for the Libertarian Party. *"I see no other conceivable strategy for the achievement of liberty than political action,"* he stated. Like Marxists, voting was seen as the means of achieving the abolition of the state, as *"a militant and abolitionist"* Libertarian Party *"in control of Congress could wipe out all the [non-'libertarian'] laws overnight ... No other strategy for liberty can work."* [**Op. Cit.**] The individualist anarchists, like other anarchists, rejected such arguments as incompatible with genuine libertarian principles. As Tucker put it, voting could not be libertarian as it would make the voter *"an accomplice in aggression."* [**The Individualist Anarchists**, p. 305]

Rothbard's position indicates an interesting paradox. Rothbard wholeheartedly supported *"political action"* as the only means of achieving the end of the state. Marxists (when not excommunicating anarchism from the socialist movement) often argue that they agree with the anarchists on the ends (abolition of the state) but only differ on the means (i.e., political action over direct action). Obviously, no one calls Marx an anarchist and this is precisely because he aimed to use political action to achieve the abolition of the state. Yet, for some reason, Rothbard's **identical** position on tactics makes some call him an anarchist. So, given Rothbard's argument that the state must be seized first by a political party by means of *"political action"* in order to achieve his end, the question must be raised why he is considered an anarchist at all. Marx and Engels, like Lenin, all made identical arguments against anarchism, namely that political action was essential so that the Socialist Party could seize state power and implement the necessary changes to ensure that the state withered away. No one has ever considered them anarchists in spite of the common aim of ending the state yet many consider Rothbard to be an anarchist despite advocating the same methods as the Marxists. As we noted in section F.8, a better term for "anarcho"-capitalism could be "Marxist-capitalism" and Rothbard's argument for "political action" confirms that suggestion.

So the claims that "anarcho"-capitalism is a new form of individualist anarchism can only be done on the basis of completely ignoring the actual history of capitalism as well as ignoring the history, social context, arguments, aims and spirit of individualist anarchism. This is only convincing if the actual ideas and aims of individualist anarchism are unknown or ignored and focus is placed on certain words used (like "markets" and "property") rather than the specific meanings provided to them by its supporters. Sadly, this extremely superficial analysis is all too common — particularly in academic circles and, of course, in right-"libertarian" ones.

G.3.3 What about "anarcho"-capitalists' support of "defence associations"?

It would be fair to say that "anarcho"-capitalist interest in individualist anarchism rests on their argument that, to quote Tucker, *"defense is a service, like any other service"*, and that such a service could and should be provided by private agencies paid for like any other commodity on the market. [**Liberty**, no. 104, p. 4] Therefore:

> *"Anarchism means no government, but it does not mean no laws and no coercion. This may seem paradoxical, but the paradox vanishes when the Anarchist definition of government is kept in view. Anarchists oppose government, not because they disbelieve in punishment of crime and resistance to aggression, but because they disbelieve in compulsory protection. Protection*

> *and taxation without consent is itself invasion; hence Anarchism favours a system of voluntary taxation and protection."* [**Op. Cit.**, no. 212, p. 2]

While most of the rest of the theory is ignored or dismissed as being the product of "bad" economics, this position is considered the key link between the two schools of thought. However, it is not enough to say that both the individualist anarchists and "anarcho"-capitalists support a market in protection, you need to look at what forms of property are being defended and the kind of society within which it is done. Change the social context, change the kinds of property which are being defended and you change the nature of the society in question. In other words, defending capitalist property rights within an unequal society is radically different in terms of individual liberty than defending socialistic property rights within an equal society — just as a market economy based on artisan, peasant and co-operative production is fundamentally different to one based on huge corporations and the bulk of the population being wage slaves. Only the most superficial analysis would suggest that they are the same and label both as being "capitalist" in nature.

It should, therefore, not be forgotten that the individualist anarchists advocated a system rooted in individual possession of land and tools plus the free exchange of the products of labour between self-employed people or wage workers who receive the full equivalent of their product. This means that they supported the idea of a market in "defence associations" to ensure that the fruits of an individual's labour would not be stolen by others. Again, the social context of individualist anarchism — namely, an egalitarian economy without exploitation of labour (see section G.3.4) — is crucial for understanding these proposals. However, as in their treatment of Tucker's support for contract theory, "anarcho"-capitalists remove the individualist anarchists' ideas about free-market defence associations and courts from the social context in which they were proposed, using those ideas in an attempt to turn the individualists into defenders of capitalism.

As indicated in section G.1.4, the social context in question was one in which an economy of artisans and peasant farmers was being replaced by a state-backed capitalism. This context is crucial for understanding the idea of the "defence associations" that Tucker suggested. For what he proposed was clearly **not** the defence of capitalist property relations. This can be seen, for example, in his comments on land use. Thus:

> *"The land for the people' … means the protection by … voluntary associations for the maintenance of justice … of all people who desire to cultivate land in possession of whatever land they personally cultivate … and the positive refusal of the protecting power to lend its aid to the collection of any rent, whatsoever."* [**Instead of a Book**, p. 299]

There is no mention here of protecting **capitalist** farming, i.e. employing wage labour; rather, there is explicit mention that only land being used for **personal** cultivation — thus **without** employing wage labour — would be defended. In other words, the defence association would defend *"occupancy and use"* (which is a clear break with capitalist property rights) and not the domination of the landlord over society or those who use the land the landlord claims to own. This means that certain contracts were not considered valid within individualist anarchism even if they were voluntarily agreed to by the parties involved and so would not be enforceable by the "defence associations." As Tucker put it:

> "A man cannot be allowed, merely by putting labour, to the limit of his capacity and beyond the limit of his personal use, into material of which there is a limited supply and the use of which is essential to the existence of other men, to withhold that material from other men's use; and any contract based upon or involving such withholding is lacking in sanctity or legitimacy as a contract to deliver stolen goods." [**Liberty**, No. 321, p. 4]

Refusal to pay rent on land is a key aspect of Tucker's thought, and it is significant that he explicitly rejects the idea that a defence association can be used to collect it. In addition, as a means towards anarchy, Tucker suggests *"inducing the people to steadily refuse the payment of rent and taxes."* [**Instead of a Book**, p. 299] It is hard to imagine that a landowner influenced by Murray Rothbard or David Friedman would support such an arrangement or a "defence association" that supported it. As such, the individualist anarchist system would impose restrictions on the market from an "anarcho"-capitalist perspective. Equally, from an individualist anarchist perspective, "anarcho"-capitalism would be enforcing a key class monopoly by force and so would simply be another kind of state. As Tucker put it in reply to the proto-right-"libertarian" Auberon Herbert:

> "It is true that Anarchists … do, in a sense, propose to get rid of ground-rent by force. That is to say, if landlords should try to evict occupants, the Anarchists advise the occupants to combine to maintain their ground by force … But it is also true that the Individualists … propose to get rid of theft by force … The Anarchists justify the use of machinery (local juries, etc.) to adjust the property question involved in rent just as the Individualists justify similar machinery to adjust the property question involved in theft." [**Op. Cit.**, no. 172, p. 7]

It comes as no surprise to discover that Tucker translated Proudhon's **What is Property?** and subscribed to its conclusion that *"property is theft"*!

This opposition to the *"land monopoly"* was, like all the various economic proposals made by the individualist anarchists, designed to eliminate the vast differences in wealth accruing from the *"usury"* of industrial capitalists, bankers, and landlords. Such a system, the individualist anarchists argued, would be unlikely to reproduce the massive inequalities of wealth associated with capitalism and have a dynamic utterly different to that system. They did not consider the state as some alien body grafted onto capitalism which could be removed and replaced with "defence associations" leaving the rest of society more or less the same. Rather, they saw the state as being an essential aspect of capitalism, defending key class monopolies and restricting freedom for the working class. By abolishing the state, they automatically abolished these class monopolies and so capitalism. In other words, they had political **and** economic goals

and ignoring the second cannot help but produce **different** results. As Voltairine de Cleyre put it in her individualist days, Anarchism *"means not only the denial of authority, not only a new economy, but a revision of the principles of morality. It means the development of the individual as well as the assertion of the individual."* [**The Voltairine de Cleyre Reader**, p. 9]

Right-"libertarians" reject all of this, the social context of Tucker's ideas on "defence associations." They do not aim for a *"new economy"*, but simply the existing one without a public state. They have no critique of capitalist property rights nor any understanding of how such rights can produce economic power and limit individual freedom. In fact, they attack what they consider the "bad economics" of the individualists without realising it is **precisely** these "bad" (i.e. anti-capitalist) economics which will minimise, if not totally eliminate, any potential threat to freedom associated with "defence associations." Without the accumulations of wealth inevitable when workers' do not receive the full product of their labour, it is unlikely that a "defence association" would act like the private police forces American capitalists utilised to break unions and strikes both in Tucker's time and now. Unless this social context exists, any defence associations will soon become mini-states, serving to enrich the elite few by protecting the usury they gain from, and their power and control (i.e. government) over, those who toil. In other words, the "defence associations" of Tucker and Spooner would not be private states, enforcing the power of capitalists and landlords upon wage workers. Instead, they would be like insurance companies, protecting possessions against theft (as opposed to protecting capitalist theft from the dispossessed as would be the case in "anarcho"-capitalism — an important difference lost on the private staters). Where social anarchists disagree with individualist anarchists is on whether a market system will actually produce such equality, particularly one without workers' self-management replacing the authority inherent in the capitalist-labourer social relationship. As we discuss in section G.4, without the equality and the egalitarian relationships of co-operative and artisan production there would be a tendency for capitalism and private statism to erode anarchy.

In addition, the emphasis given by Tucker and Lysander Spooner to the place of juries in a free society is equally important for understanding how their ideas about defence associations fit into a non-capitalist scheme. For by emphasising the importance of trial by jury, they knock an important leg from under the private statism associated with "anarcho"-capitalism. Unlike a wealthy judge, a jury made up mainly of fellow workers would be more inclined to give verdicts in favour of workers struggling against bosses or of peasants being forced off their land by immoral, but legal, means. As Lysander Spooner argued in 1852: *"If a jury have not the right to judge between the government and those who disobey its laws, and resist its oppressions, the government is absolute, and the people, legally speaking, are slaves. Like many other slaves they may have sufficient courage and strength to keep their masters somewhat in check; but they are nevertheless known to the law only as slaves."* [**Trial by Jury**] It is hardly surprising that Rothbard rejects this in favour of a legal system determined and interpreted by lawyers, judges and jurists. Indeed, as we noted in section F.6.1, Rothbard explicitly rejected the idea that juries should be able to judge the law as well as the facts of a case under his system. Spooner would have had no problem recognising that replacing government imposed laws with those made by judges, jurists and lawyers would hardly change the situation much. Nor would he have been too surprised at the results of a free market in laws in a society with substantial inequalities in income and wealth.

Individualist Anarchist Laurance Labadie, the son of Tucker associate Joseph Labadie, argued in response to Rothbard as follows:

> *"Mere common sense would suggest that any court would be influenced by experience; and any free-market court or judge would in the very nature of things have some precedents guiding them in their instructions to a jury. But since no case is exactly the same, a jury would have considerable say about the heinousness of the offence in each case, realising that circumstances alter cases, and prescribing penalty accordingly. This appeared to Spooner and Tucker to be a more flexible and equitable administration of justice possible or feasible, human beings being what they are ...*

> *"But when Mr. Rothbard quibbles about the jurisprudential ideas of Spooner and Tucker, and at the same time upholds **presumably in his courts** the very economic evils which are at bottom the very reason for human contention and conflict, he would seem to be a man who chokes at a gnat while swallowing a camel."* [quoted by Mildred J. Loomis and Mark A. Sullivan, *"Laurance Labadie: Keeper Of The Flame"*, pp. 116-30, **Benjamin R. Tucker and the Champions of Liberty**, Coughlin, Hamilton and Sullivan (eds.), p. 124]

As we argued in detail in section F.6, a market for "defence associations" within an unequal system based on extensive wage labour would simply be a system of private states, enforcing the authority of the property owner over those who use but do not own their property. Such an outcome can only be avoided within an egalitarian society where wage-labour is minimised, if not abolished totally, in favour of self-employment (whether individually or co-operatively). In other words, the kind of social context which the individualist anarchists explicitly or implicitly assumed and aimed for. By focusing selectively on a few individualist proposals taken out of their social context, Rothbard and other "anarcho"-capitalists have turned the libertarianism of the individualist anarchists into yet another ideological weapon in the hands of (private) statism and capitalism.

When faced with the actual visions of a good society proposed by such people as Tucker and Spooner, "anarcho"-capitalists tend to dismiss them as irrelevant. They argue that it does not matter what Tucker or Spooner thought would emerge from the application of their system, it is the fact they advocated the "free market", "private property" and "defence associations" that counts. In response anarchists note three things. Firstly, individualist anarchists generally held radically different concepts of what a "free market" and "private property" would be in their system and so the tasks of any "defence association" would be radically different. As such, anarchists argue that "anarcho"-capitalists simply look at the

words people use rather than what they meant by them and the social context in which they are used. Secondly, it seems a strange form of support to rubbish the desired goals of people you claim to follow. If someone claimed to be a Marxist while, at the same time, arguing that Marx was wrong about socialism people would be justified in questioning their use of that label. Thirdly, and most importantly, no one advocates a means which would not result in their desired ends. If Tucker and Spooner did not think their system would result in their goals they would have either changed their goals or changed their method. As noted in section G.1.1, Tucker explicitly argued that concentrations of wealth under capitalism had reached such levels that his system of free competition would not end it. Clearly, then, outcomes were important to individualist anarchists.

The lack of commonality can also be seen from the right-"libertarian" response to Kevin Carson's excellent **Studies in Mutualist Political Economy**, an impressive modern restatement of the ideas of Tucker and other individualist anarchists. Leading "anarcho"-capitalist Walter Block dismissed *"Marxists like Carson"* and labelled him *"a supposed anarchist"* who on many issues *"is out there, way, way out there in some sort of Marxist never-never land."* [*"Kevin Carson as Dr. Jeryll and Mr. Hyde"*, pp. 35-46, **Journal of Libertarian Studies**, vol. 20, no. 1, p. 40, p. 43 and p. 45] Another right-"libertarian", George Reisman, concurred stating that for the most part *"Carson is a Marxist"*, while arguing that *"the 'individualist' anarchist shows himself to be quite the collectivist, attributing to the average person qualities of independent thought and judgement that are found only in exceptional individuals."* Carson's *"views on the nature of ownership give full support to the conception of anarchy ... as being nothing but chaos."* Overall, *"Carson is essentially a Marxist and his book filled with ignorant Marxist diatribes against capitalism."* [*"Freedom is Slavery: Laissez-Faire capitalism is government intervention"*, pp. 47-86, **Op. Cit.**, p. 47, p. 55, p. 61 and p. 84] Needless to say, all the issues which Block and Geisman take umbridge at can be found in the works of individualist anarchists like Tucker (Carson's excellent dissection of these remarkably ignorant diatribes is well worth reading [*"Carson's Rejoinders"*, pp. 97-136, **Op. Cit.**]).

So the notion that a joint support for a market in "defence services" can allow the social and theoretical differences between "anarcho"-capitalism and individualist anarchism to be ignored is just nonsense. This can best be seen from the fate of any individualist anarchist defence association within "anarcho"-capitalism. As it would not subscribe to Rothbard's preferred system of property rights it would be in violation of the *"general libertarian law code"* drawn up and implemented by right-"libertarian" jurists, judges and lawyers. This would, by definition, make such an association *"outlaw"* when it defended tenants against attempts to extract rents from them or to evict them from the land or buildings they used but did not own. As it is a judge-run system, no jury would be able to judge the law as well as the crime, so isolating the capitalist and landlord class from popular opposition. Thus the ironic situation arises that the **"Benjamin Tucker defence association"** would be declared an outlaw organisation under "anarcho"-capitalism and driven out of business (i.e., destroyed) as it broke the land monopoly which the law monopoly enforces. Even more ironically, such an organisation would survive in an communist anarchist society (assuming it could find enough demand to make it worthwhile).

If the world had had the misfortune of having "anarcho"-capitalism imposed on it in the nineteenth century, individualist anarchists like Warren, Tucker, Labadie, Ingalls and Lum would have joined Proudhon, Bakunin, Kropotkin, Parsons and Goldman in prison for practising *"occupancy and use"* in direct violation of the *"general libertarian law code."* That it was private police, private courts and private prisons which were enforcing such a regime would not have been considered that much of an improvement.

Unsurprisingly, Victor Yarros explicitly distanced himself from those who *"want liberty to still further crush and oppress the people; liberty to enjoy their plunder without fear of the State's interfering with them ... liberty to summarily deal with impudent tenants who refuse to pay tribute for the privilege of living and working on the soil."* [**Liberty**, no. 102, p. 4] He would have had little problem recognising "anarcho"-capitalism as being a supporter of *"that particular kind of freedom which the **bourgeoisie** favours, and which is championed by the **bourgeoisie's** loyal servants, [but] will never prove fascinating to the disinherited and oppressed."* [**Op. Cit.**, no. 93, p. 4]

G.3.4 Why is individualist anarchist support for equality important?

Another another key difference between genuine individualist anarchism and "anarcho"-capitalism is the former's support for equality and the latter's a lack of concern for it.

In stark contrast to anarchists of all schools, inequality is not seen to be a problem with "anarcho"-capitalists (see section F.3). However, it is a truism that not all "traders" are equally subject to the market (i.e., have the same market power). In many cases, a few have sufficient control of resources to influence or determine price and in such cases, all others must submit to those terms or not buy the commodity. When the commodity is labour power, even this option is lacking — workers have to accept a job in order to live. As we argued in section C.9, workers are usually at a disadvantage on the labour market when compared to capitalists, and this forces them to sell their liberty in return for making profits for others. These profits increase inequality in society as the property owners receive the surplus value their workers produce. This increases inequality further, consolidating market power and so weakens the bargaining position of workers further, ensuring that even the freest competition possible could not eliminate class power and society (something Tucker eventually recognised as occurring with the development of trusts within capitalism — see section G.1.1).

By removing the underlying commitment to abolish non-labour income, any "anarchist" capitalist society would have vast differences in wealth and so power. Instead of government imposed monopolies in land, money and so on, the economic power flowing from private property and capital would ensure that the majority remained in (to use Spooner's words) *"the condition of servants"* (see sections F.2 and F.3.1 for more on this). The Individualist Anarchists were aware of this danger and so supported economic ideas that opposed usury (i.e. rent, profit and interest) and ensured the worker the full value of her labour. While not all of them called these ideas "socialist" it is clear that these ideas **are** socialist in nature and in aim (similarly, not all the Individualist Anarchists called themselves anarchists but their ideas are clearly anarchist in nature and in aim). This combination of the political and economic is essential as they mutually reinforce each other. Without the economic ideas, the political ideas would be meaningless as inequality would make a mockery of them. As Spooner argued, inequality lead to many social evils:

> *"Extremes of difference, in their pecuniary circumstances, divide society into castes; set up barriers to personal acquaintance; prevent or suppress sympathy; give to different individuals a widely different experience, and thus become the fertile source of alienation, contempt, envy, hatred, and wrong. But give to each man all the fruits of his own labour, and a comparative equality with others in his pecuniary condition, and caste is broken down; education is given more equally to all; and the object is promoted of placing each on a social level with all: of introducing each to the acquaintance of all; and of giving to each the greatest amount of that experience, which, being common to all, enables him to sympathise with all, and insures to himself the sympathy of all. And thus the social virtues of mankind would be greatly increased."* [**Poverty: Its Illegal Causes and Legal Cure**, pp. 46-7]

Because of the evil effects of inequality on freedom, both social and individualist anarchists desire to create an environment in which circumstances would not drive people to sell their liberty to others at a disadvantage. In other words, they desired an equalisation of market power by opposing interest, rent and profit and capitalist definitions of private property. Kline summarises this by saying *"the American [individualist] anarchists exposed the tension existing in liberal thought between private property and the ideal of equal access. The Individual Anarchists were, at least, aware that existing conditions were far from ideal, that the system itself working against the majority of individuals in their efforts to attain its promises. Lack of capital, the means to creation and accumulation of wealth, usually doomed a labourer to a life of exploitation. This the anarchists knew and they abhorred such a system."* [**The Individualist Anarchists: A critique of liberalism**, p. 102]

This desire for bargaining equality is reflected in their economic ideas and by removing these underlying economic ideas of the individualist anarchists, "anarcho"-capitalism makes a mockery of any ideas they do appropriate. Essentially, the Individualist Anarchists agreed with Rousseau that in order to prevent extreme inequality of fortunes you deprive people of the means to accumulate in the first place and **not** take away wealth from the rich. An important point which "anarcho"-capitalism fails to understand or appreciate.

The Individualist Anarchists assumed that exploitation of labour would be non-existent in their system, so a general equality would prevail and so economic power would not undermine liberty. Remove this underlying assumption, assume that profits could be made and capital accumulated, assume that land can be monopolised by landlords (as the "anarcho"-capitalists do) and a radically different society is produced. One in which economic power means that the vast majority have to sell themselves to get access to the means of life and are exploited by those who own them in the process. A condition of "free markets" may exist, but as Tucker argued in 1911, it would not be anarchism. The **deus ex machina** of invisible hands takes a beating in the age of monopolies.

So we must stress that the social situation is important as it shows how apparently superficially similar arguments can have radically different aims and results depending on who suggests them and in what circumstances. Hence the importance of individualist anarchist support for equality. Without it, genuine freedom would not exist for the many and "anarchy" would simply be private statism enforcing rule by the rich.

G.3.5 Would individualist anarchists have accepted "Austrian" economics?

One of the great myths perpetrated by "anarcho"-capitalists is the notion that "anarcho"-capitalism is simply individualist anarchism plus "Austrian" economics. Nothing could be further from the truth, as is clear once the individualist anarchist positions on capitalist property rights, exploitation and equality are understood. Combine this with their vision of a free society as well as the social and political environment they were part of and the ridiculous nature of such claims become obvious.

At its most basic, Individualist anarchism was rooted in socialist economic analysis as would be expected of a self-proclaimed socialist theory and movement. The "anarcho"-capitalists, in a roundabout way, recognise this with Rothbard dismissing the economic fallacies of individualist anarchism in favour of "Austrian" economics. *"There is,"* he stated, *"in the body of thought known as 'Austrian economics,' a scientific [sic!] explanation of the workings of the free market … which individualist anarchists could easily incorporate into their so political and social **Weltanshauung**. But to do this, they must throw out the worthless excess baggage of money-crankism and reconsider the nature and justification of the economic categories of interest, rent and profit."* Yet Rothbard's assertion is nonsense, given that the individualist anarchists were well aware of various justifications for exploitation expounded by the defenders of capitalism and rejected everyone. He himself noted that the *"individualist anarchists were exposed to critiques of their economic fallacies; but, unfortunately, the lesson, despite the weakness of Tucker's replies, did not take."* [*"The Spooner-Tucker Doctrine: An Economist's View"*, **Op. Cit.**, p. 14] As such, it seems like extremely wishful thinking that the likes of Tucker would have rushed to embrace an economic ideology whose basic aim has always been to refute the claims of socialism and defend capitalism from attacks on it.

Nor can it be suggested that the individualist anarchists were ignorant of the developments within bourgeois economics which the "Austrian" school was part of. Both Tucker and Yarros, for example, attacked marginal productivity theory as advocated by

John B. Clark. [**Liberty**, no. 305] Tucker critiqued another anarchist for once being an *"Anarchistic socialist, standing squarely upon the principles of Liberty and Equity"* but then *"abandon[ing] Equity by repudiating the Socialistic theory of value and adopting one which differs but little, if any, from that held by the ordinary economist."* [**Op. Cit.**, no. 80, p. 4] So the likes of Tucker were well aware of the so-called marginalist revolution and rejected it.

Somewhat ironically, a key founder of "Austrian" economics was quoted favourably in **Liberty** but only with regards to his devastating critique of existing theories of interest and profit. Hugo Bilgram asked a defender of interest whether he had *"ever read Volume 1 of Böhm-Bawerk's 'Capital and Interest'"* for in this volume *"the fructification theory is … completely refuted."* Bilgram, needless to say, did not support Böhm-Bawerk's defence of usury, instead arguing that restrictions in the amount of money forced people to pay for its use and *"[t]his, and nothing else, [causes] the interest accruing to capital, regarding which the modern economists are doing their utmost to find a theory that will not expose the system of industrial piracy of today."* He did not exclude Böhm-Bawerk's theory from his conclusion that *"since every one of these pet theories is based on some fallacy, [economists] cannot agree upon any one."* The abolition of the money monopoly will *"abolish the power of capital to appropriate a net profit."* [**Op. Cit.**, no. 282, p. 11] Tucker himself noted that Böhm-Bawerk *"has refuted all these ancient apologies for interest — productivity of capital, abstinence, etc."* [**Op. Cit.**, no. 287, p. 5] **Liberty** also published a synopsis of Francis Tandy's **Voluntary Socialism**, whose chapter 6 was *"devoted to an analysis of value according to the marginal utility value of Böhm-Bawerk. It also deals with the Marxian theory of surplus value, showing that all our economic ills are due to the existence of that surplus value."* [**Op. Cit.**, no. 334, p. 5] Clearly, then, the individualist anarchists were aware of the "Austrian" tradition and only embraced its critique of previous defences of non-labour incomes.

We have already critiqued the "time preference" justification for interest in section C.2.7 so will not go into it in much detail here. Rothbard argued that it *"should be remembered by radicals that, if they wanted to, all workers could refuse to work for wages and instead form their own producers' co-operatives and wait for years for their pay until the products are sold to the consumers; the fact that they do not do so, shows the enormous advantage of the capital investment, wage-paying system as a means of allowing workers to earn money far in advance of the sale of their products."* And how, Professor Rothbard, are these workers to live during the years they wait until their products are sold? The reason why workers do not work for themselves has nothing to do with "time preference" but their lack of resources, their **class** position. Showing how capitalist ideology clouds the mind, Rothbard asserted that interest (*"in the shape of 'long-run' profit"*) would still exist in a *"world in which everyone invested his own money and nobody loaned or borrowed."* [**Op. Cit.**, p. 12] Presumably, this means that the self-employed worker who invests her own money into her own farm pays herself interest payments just as her labour income is, presumably, the "profits" from which this "interest" payment is deducted along with the "rent" for access to the land she owns!

So it seems extremely unlikely that the individualist anarchists would have considered "Austrian" economics as anything other than an attempt to justify exploitation and capitalism, like the other theories they spent so much time refuting. They would quickly have noted that "time preference", like the "waiting"/"abstinence" justifications for interest, is based on taking the current class system for granted and ignoring the economic pressures which shape individual decisions. In Tucker's words (when he critiqued Henry George's argument that interest is related to time) *"increase which is purely the work of time bears a price only because of monopoly."* The notion that "time" produced profit or interest was one Tucker was well aware of, and refuted on many occasions. He argued that it was class monopoly, restrictions on banking, which caused interest and *"where there is no monopoly there will be little or no interest."* If someone *"is to be rewarded for his mere time, what will reward him save [another]'s labour? There is no escape from this dilemma. The proposition that the man who for time spent in idleness receives the product of time employed in labour is a parasite upon the body industrial is one which ... [its supporters] can never successfully dispute with men who understand the rudiments of political economy."* [**Liberty**, no. 109, p. 4 and p. 5] For Joshua King Ingalls, *"abstinence"* (or the ability to *"wait,"* as it was renamed in the late nineteenth century) was *"a term with which our cowardly moral scientists and political economists attempt to conjure up a spirit that will justify the greed of our land and money systems; by a casuistry similar to that which once would have justified human slavery."* [*"Labor, Wages, And Capital. Division Of Profits Scientifically Considered,"* **Brittan's Quarterly Journal**, I (1873), pp. 66-79]

What of the economic justification for that other great evil for individualist anarchists, rent? Rothbard attacked Adam Smith's comment that landlords were monopolists who demanded rent for nature's produce and liked to reap what they never sowed. As he put it, Smith showed *"no hint of recognition here that the landlord performs the vital function of allocating the land to its most productive use."* [**An Austrian Perspective on the History of Economic Thought**, vol. 1, p. 456] Yet, as Smith was well aware, it is the farmer who has to feed himself and pay rent who decides how best to use the land, not the landlord. All the landlord does is decide whether to throw the farmer off the land when a more profitable business opportunity arrives (as in, say, the Highland clearances) or that it is more "productive" to export food while local people starve (as in, say, the great Irish famine). It was precisely this kind of arbitrary power which the individualist anarchists opposed. As John Beverley Robinson put it, the *"land owner gives nothing whatever, but permission to you to live and work on his land. He does not give his product in exchange for yours. He did not produce the land. He obtained a title at law to it; that is, a privilege to keep everybody off his land until they paid him his price. He is well called the lord of the land — the landlord!"* [**Patterns of Anarchy**, p. 271]

Liberty also favourably quoted a supporter of the silver coinage, General Francis A. Walker, and his arguments in favour of ending the gold standard. It praised his argument as *"far more sound and rational than that of the supercilious, narrow, bigoted monomentallists."* Walker attacked those *"economists of the **a priori** school, who treat all things industrial as if they were in a state of flux, ready to be poured indifferently into any kind of mould or pattern."* These economists *"are always on hand with the answer that industrial society will 'readjust' itself to the new conditions"* and *"it would not matter if wages were at any time unduly depressed by combinations of employers, inasmuch as the excess of profits resulting would infallibly become capital, and as such, constitute an additional demand for labour ... It has been the teaching of the economists of this sort which has so deeply discredited political economy with the labouring men on the one hand, and with practical business men on the other."* The *"greatest part of the evil of a diminishing money supply is wrought through the discouragement of enterprise."* [**Liberty**, no. 287, p. 11] Given that the "Austrian" school takes the **a priori** methodology to ridiculous extremes and is always on hand to defend *"excess of profits"*, *"combinations of employers"* and the gold standard we can surmise Tucker's reaction to Rothbard's pet economic ideology.

Somewhat ironically, given Rothbard's attempts to inflict bourgeois economics along with lots of other capitalist ideology onto individualist anarchism, Kropotkin noted that supporters of *"individualist anarchism ... soon realise that the individualisation they so highly praise is not attainable by individual efforts, and ... [some] abandon the ranks of the anarchists, and are driven into the liberal individualism of the classical economists."* [**Anarchism**, p. 297] "Anarcho"-capitalists confuse the ending place of **ex**-anarchists with their starting point. As can be seen from their attempt to co-opt the likes of Spooner and Tucker, this confusion only appears persuasive by ignoring the bulk of their ideas as well as rewriting the history of anarchism.

So it can, we think, be safe to assume that Tucker and other individualist anarchists would have little problem in refuting Rothbard's economic fallacies as well as his goldbug notions (which seem to be the money monopoly in another form) and support for the land monopoly. Significantly, modern individualist anarchists like Kevin Carson have felt no need to embrace "Austrian" economics and retain their socialist analysis while, at the same time, making telling criticisms of Rothbard's favourite economic ideology and the apologetics for "actually existing" capitalism its supporters too often indulge in (Carson calls this *"vulgar libertarianism"*, wherein right-"libertarians" forget that the current economy is far from their stated ideal when it is a case of defending corporations or the wealthy).

G.3.6 Would mutual banking simply cause inflation?

One of the arguments against Individualist and mutualist anarchism, and mutual banking in general, is that it would just produce accelerating inflation. The argument is that by providing credit without interest, more and more money would be pumped into the economy. This would lead to more and more money chasing a given set of goods, so leading to price rises and inflation.

Rothbard, for example, dismissed individualist anarchist ideas on mutual banking as being *"totally fallacious monetary views."* He based his critique on "Austrian" economics and its notion of *"time preference"* (see section C.2.7 for a critique of this position). Mutual banking would artificially lower the interest rate by generating credit, Rothbard argued, with the new money only benefiting those who initially get it. This process "exploits" those further down the line in the form accelerating inflation. As more and more money was be pumped into the economy, it would lead to more and more money chasing a given set of goods, so leading to price rises and inflation. To prove this, Rothbard repeated Hume's argument that *"if everybody magically woke up one morning with the quantity of money in his possession doubled"* then prices would simply double. [*"The Spooner-Tucker Doctrine: An Economist's View"*, **Journal of Libertarian Studies**, vol. 20, no. 1, p. 14 and p. 10]

However, Rothbard is assuming that the amount of goods and services are fixed. This is just wrong and shows a real lack of understanding of how money works in a real economy. This is shown by the lack of agency in his example, the money just "appears" by magic (perhaps by means of a laissez-fairy?). Milton Friedman made the same mistake, although he used the more up to date example of government helicopters dropping bank notes. As post-Keynesian economist Nicholas Kaldor pointed out with regards to Friedman's position, the *"transmission mechanism from money to income remained a 'black box' — he could not explain it, and he did not attempt to explain it either. When it came to the question of **how** the authorities increase the supply of bank notes in circulation he answered that they are scattered over populated areas by means of a helicopter — though he did not go into the ultimate consequences of such an aerial Santa Claus."* [**The Scourge of Monetarism**, p. 28]

Friedman's and Rothbard's analysis betrays a lack of understanding of economics and money. This is unsurprising as it comes to us via neo-classical economics. In neo-classical economics inflation is always a monetary phenomena — too much money chasing too few goods. Milton Friedman's Monetarism was the logical conclusion of this perspective and although "Austrian" economics is extremely critical of Monetarism it does, however, share many of the same assumptions and fallacies (as Hayek's one-time follower Nicholas Kaldor noted, key parts of Friedman's doctrine are *"closely reminiscent of the Austrian school of the twenties and the early thirties"* although it *"misses some of the subtleties of the Hayekian transmission mechanism and of the money-induced distortions in the 'structure of production.'"* [**The Essential Kaldor**, pp. 476-7]). We can reject this argument on numerous points.

Firstly, the claim that inflation is always and everywhere a monetary phenomena has been empirically refuted — often using Friedman's own data and attempts to apply his dogma in real life. As we noted in section C.8.3, the growth of the money supply and inflation have no fixed relationship, with money supply increasing while inflation falls. As such, *"the claim that inflation is always and everywhere caused by increases in the money supply, and that the rate of inflation bears a stable, predictable relationship to increases in the money supply is ridiculous."* [Paul Ormerod, **The Death of Economics**, p. 96] This means that the assumption that increasing the money supply by generating credit will always simply result in inflation cannot be supported by the empirical evidence we have. As Kaldor stressed, the *"the 'first-round effects' of the helicopter operation could be anything, depending on where the scatter occurred ... there is no reason to suppose that the ultimate effect on the amount of money in circulation or on incomes would bear any close relation to the initial injections."* [**The Scourge of Monetarism**, p. 29]

Secondly, even if we ignore the empirical record (as "Austrian" economics tends to do when faced with inconvenient facts) the "logical" argument used to explain the theory that increases in money will increase prices is flawed. Defenders of this argument usually present mental exercises to prove their case (as in Hume and Friedman). Needless to say, such an argument is spurious in the extreme simply because money does not enter the economy in this fashion. It is generated to meet specific demands for money and is so, generally, used productively. In other words, money creation is a function of the demand for credit, which is a function of the needs of the economy (i.e. it is endogenous) and **not** determined by the central bank injecting it into the system (i.e. it is **not** exogenous). And this indicates why the argument that mutual banking would produce inflation is flawed. It does not take into account the fact that money will be used to generate ***new*** goods and services.

As leading Post-Keynesian economist Paul Davidson argued, the notion that *"inflation is always and everywhere a monetary phenomenon"* (to use Friedman's expression) is *"ultimately based on the old homily that inflation is merely 'too many dollars chasing too few goods.'"* Davidson notes that *"[t]his 'too many dollars cliché is usually illustrated by employing a two-island parable. Imagine a hypothetical island where the only available goods are 10 apples and the money supply consists of, say, 10 $1 bills. If all the dollars are used to purchase the apples, the price per apple will be $1. For comparison, assume that on a second island there are 20 $1 bills and only 10 apples. All other things being equal, the price will be $2 per apple. Ergo, inflation occurs whenever the money supply is excessive relative to the available goods."* The similarities with Rothbard's argument are clear. So are its flaws as *"no explanation is given as to why the money supply was greater on the second island. Nor is it admitted that, if the increase in the money supply is associated with entrepreneurs borrowing 'real bills' from banks to finance an increase in payrolls necessary to harvest, say, 30 additional apples so that the $20 chases 40 apples, then the price will be only $0.50 per apple. If a case of 'real bills' finance occurs, then an increase in the money supply is not associated with higher prices but with greater output."* [**Controversies in Post Keynesian Economics**, p. 100] Davidson is unknowingly echoing Tucker (*"It is the especial claim of free banking that it will increase production ... If free banking were only a picayanish attempt to distribute more equitably the small amount of wealth now produced, I would not waste a moment's energy on it."* [**Liberty**, no. 193, p. 3]).

This, in reply to the claims of neo-classical economics, indicates why mutual banking would not increase inflation. Like the neo-classical position, Rothbard's viewpoint is static in nature and does not understand how a real economy works. Needless to say, he (like Friedman) did not discuss how the new money gets into circulation. Perhaps, like Hume, it was a case of the money fairy placing the money into people's wallets. Maybe it was a case, like Friedman, of government (black?) helicopters dropping it from the skies. Rothbard did not expound on the mechanism by which money would be created or placed into circulation, rather it just appears one day out of the blue and starts chasing a given amount of goods. However, the individualist anarchists and mutualists did not think in such bizarre (typically, economist) ways. Rather than think that mutual banks would hand out cash willy-nilly to passing strangers, they realistically considered the role of the banks to be one of evaluating useful investment opportunities (i.e., ones which would be likely to succeed). As such, the role of credit would be to **increase** the number of goods and services in circulation along with money, so ensuring that inflation is not generated (assuming that it is caused by the money supply, of course). As one Individualist Anarchist put it: *"In the absence of such restrictions [on money and credit], imagine the rapid growth of wealth, and the equity in its distribution, that would result."* [John Beverley Robinson, **The Individualist Anarchists**, p. 144] Thus Tucker:

> *"A is a farmer owning a farm. He mortgages his farm to a bank for $1,000, giving the bank a mortgage note for that sum and receiving in exchange the bank's notes for the same sum, which are secured by the mortgage. With the bank-notes A buys farming tools off B. The next day B uses the notes to buy off C the materials used in the manufacture of tools. The day after, C in turn pays them to D in exchange for something he needs. At the end of a year, after a constant succession of exchanges, the notes are in the hands of Z, a dealer in farm produce. He pays them to A, who gives in return $1,000 worth of farm products which he has raised during the year. Then A carries the notes to the bank, receives in exchange for them his mortgage note, and the bank cancels the mortgage. Now, in this whole circle of transactions, has there been any lending of capital? If so, who was the lender? If not, who is entitled to interest?"* [**Instead of a Book**, p. 198]

Obviously, in a real economy, as Rothbard admits *"inflation of the money supply takes place a step at a time and that the first beneficiaries, the people who get the new money first, gain at the expense of the people unfortunate enough to come last in line."* This process is *"plunder and exploitation"* as the *"prices of things they [those last in line] have to buy shooting up before the new injection [of money] filters down to them."* [**Op. Cit.**, p. 11] Yet this expansion of the initial example, again, assumes that there is no increase in goods and services in the economy, that the *"first beneficiaries"* do nothing with the money bar simply buying more of the existing goods and services. It further assumes that this existing supply of goods and services is unchangeable, that firms do not have inventories of goods and sufficient slack to meet unexpected increases in demand. In reality, of course, a mutual bank would be funding productive investments and any firm will respond to increasing demand by increasing production as their inventories start to decline. In effect, Rothbard's analysis is just as static and unrealistic as the notion of money suddenly appearing overnight in people's wallets. Perhaps unsurprisingly Rothbard compared the credit generation of banks to the act of counterfeiters so showing his utter lack of awareness of how banks work in a credit-money (i.e., real) economy.

The "Austrian" theory of the business cycle is rooted in the notion that banks artificially lower the rate of interest by providing more credit than their savings and specie reverses warrant. Even in terms of pure logic, such an analysis is flawed as it cannot reasonably be asserted that all "malinvestment" is caused by credit expansion as capitalists and investors make unwise decisions all the time, irrespective of the supply of credit. Thus it is simply false to assert, as Rothbard did, that the *"process of inflation, as carried out in the real [sic!] world"* is based on *"new money"* entering the market by means of *"the loan market"* but *"this fall is strictly temporary, and the market soon restores the rate to its proper level."* A crash, according to Rothbard, is the process of restoring the rate of interest to its *"proper"* level yet a crash can occur even if the interest rate is at that rate, assuming that the banks can discover this equilibrium rate and have an incentive to do so (as we discussed in section C.8 both are unlikely). Ultimately, credit expansion fails under capitalism because it runs into the contradictions within the capitalist economy, the need for capitalists, financiers and landlords to make profits via exploiting labour. As interest rates increase, capitalists have to service their rising debts putting pressure on their profit margins and so raising the number of bankruptcies. In an economy without non-labour income, the individualist anarchists argued, this process is undercut if not eliminated.

So expanding this from the world of fictional government helicopters and money fairies, we can see why Rothbard is wrong. Mutual banks operate on the basis of providing loans to people to set up or expand business, either as individuals or as co-operatives. When they provide a loan, in other words, they **increase** the amount of goods and services in the economy. Similarly, they do not simply increase the money supply to reduce interest rates. Rather, they reduce interest rates to increase the demand for money in order to increase the productive activity in an economy. By producing new goods and services, inflation is kept at bay. Would increased demand for goods by the new firms create inflation? Only if every firm was operating at maximum output, which would be a highly unlikely occurrence in reality (unlike in economic textbooks).

So what, then does case inflation? Inflation, rather than being the result of monetary factors, is, in fact, a result of profit levels and the dynamic of the class struggle. In this most anarchists agree with post-Keynesian economics which views inflation as *"a symptom of an on-going struggle over income distribution by the exertion of market power."* [Paul Davidson, **Op. Cit.**, p. 102] As workers' market power increases via fuller employment, their organisation, militancy and solidarity increases so eroding profits as workers keep more of the value they produce. Capitalists try and maintain their profits by rising prices, thus generating inflation (i.e. general price rises). Rather than accept the judgement of market forces in the form of lower profits, capitalists use their control over industry and market power of their firms to maintain their profit levels at the expense of the consumer (i.e., the workers and their families).

In this sense, mutual banks **could** contribute to inflation — by reducing unemployment by providing the credit needed for workers to start their own businesses and co-operatives, workers' power would increase and so reduce the power of managers to extract more work for a given wage and give workers a better economic environment to ask for better wages and conditions. This was, it should be stressed, a key reason why the individualist anarchists supported mutual banking:

> *"people who are now deterred from going into business by the ruinously high rates which they must pay for capital*

with which to start and carry on business will find their difficulties removed … This facility of acquiring capital will give an unheard of impetus to business, and consequently create an unprecedented demand for labour — a demand which will always be in excess of the supply, directly to the contrary of the present condition of the labour market … Labour will then be in a position to dictate its wages." [Tucker, **The Individualist Anarchists**, pp. 84-5]

And, it must also be stressed, this was a key reason why the capitalist class turned against Keynesian full employment policies in the 1970s (see section C.8.3). Lower interest rates and demand management by the state lead precisely to the outcome predicted by the likes of Tucker, namely an increase in working class power in the labour market as a result of a lowering of unemployment to unprecedented levels. This, however, led to rising prices as capitalists tried to maintain their profits by passing on wage increases rather than take the cut in profits indicated by economic forces. This could also occur if mutual banking took off and, in this sense, mutual banking could produce inflation. However, such an argument against the scheme requires the neo-classical and "Austrian" economist to acknowledge that capitalism cannot produce full employment and that the labour market must always be skewed in favour of the capitalist to keep it working, to maintain the inequality of bargaining power between worker and capitalist. In other words, that capitalism needs unemployment to exist and so cannot produce an efficient and humane allocation of resources.

By supplying working people with money which is used to create productive co-operatives and demand for their products, mutual banks increase the amount of goods and services in circulation as they increase the money supply. Combined with the elimination of profit, rent and interest, inflationary pressures are effectively undercut (it makes much more sense to talk of a interest/rent/profits-prices spiral rather than a wages-prices spiral when discussing inflation). Only in the context of the ridiculous examples presented by neo-classical and "Austrian" economics does increasing the money supply result in rising inflation. Indeed, the "sound economic" view, in which if the various money-substitutes are in a fixed and constant proportion to "real money" (i.e. gold or silver) then inflation would not exist, ignores the history of money and the nature of the banking system. It overlooks the fact that the emergence of bank notes, fractional reserve banking and credit was a spontaneous process, not planned or imposed by the state, but rather came from the profit needs of capitalist banks which, in turn, reflected the real needs of the economy (*"The truth is that, as the exchanges of the world increased, and the time came when there was not enough gold and silver to effect these exchanges, so … people had to resort to paper promises."* [John Beverley Robinson, **Op. Cit.**, p. 139]). What **was** imposed by the state, however, was the imposition of legal tender, the use of specie and a money monopoly (*"attempt after attempt has been made to introduce credit money outside of government and national bank channels, and the promptness of the suppression has always been proportional to the success of the attempt."* [Tucker, **Liberty**, no. 193, p. 3]).

Given that the money supply is endogenous in nature, any attempt to control the money supply will fail. Rather than control the money supply, which would be impossible, the state would have to use interest rates. To reduce the demand for money, interest rates would be raised higher and higher, causing a deep recession as business cannot maintain their debt payments and go bankrupt. This would cause unemployment to rise, weakening workers' bargaining power and skewing the economy back towards the bosses and profits — so making working people pay for capitalism's crisis. Which, essentially, is what the Thatcher and Reagan governments did in the early 1980s. Finding it impossible to control the money supply, they raised interest rates to dampen down the demand for credit, which provoked a deep recession. Faced with massive unemployment, workers' market power decreased and their bosses increased, causing a shift in power and income towards capital.

So, obviously, in a capitalist economy the increasing of credit is a source of instability. While not causing the business cycle, it does increase its magnitude. As the boom gathers strength, banks want to make money and increase credit by lowering interest rates below what they should be to match savings. Capitalists rush to invest, so soaking up some of the unemployment which always marks capitalism. The lack of unemployment as a disciplinary tool is why the boom turns to bust, not the increased investment. Given that in a mutualist system, profits, interest and rent do not exist then erosion of profits which marks the top of a boom would not be applicable. If prices drop, then labour income drops. Thus a mutualist society need not fear inflation. As Kaldor argued with regard to the current system, *"under a 'credit-money' system … unwanted or excess amounts of money **could never come into existence**; it is the increase in the value of transactions … which calls forth an increase in the 'money supply' (whether in the form of bank balances or notes in circulation) as a result of the net increase in the value of working capital at the various stages of production and distribution."* [**Op. Cit.**, p. 46] The gold standard cannot do what a well-run credit-currency can do, namely tailor the money supply to the economy's demand for money. The problem in the nineteenth century was that a capitalist credit-money economy was built upon a commodity-money base, with predictably bad results. Would this be any different under Rothbard's system? Probably not. For Rothbard, each bank would have 100% reserve of gold with a law passed that defined fractional reserve banking as fraud. How would this affect mutual banks? Rothbard argued that attempts to create mutual banks or other non-gold based banking systems would be allowed under his system. Yet, how does this fit into his repeated call for a 100% gold standard for banks? Why would a mutual bank be excluded from a law on banking? Is there a difference between a mutual bank issuing credit on the basis of a secured loan rather than gold and a normal bank doing so? Needless to say, Rothbard never did address the fact that the customers of the banks **know** that they practised fractional reserve banking and still did business with them. Nor did he wonder why no enterprising banker exploited a market niche by advertising a 100% reserve policy. He simply assumed that the general public subscribed to his gold-bug prejudices and so would not frequent mutual banks. As for other banks, the full might of the law would be used to stop them practising the same policies and freedoms he allowed for mutual ones. So rather than give people the freedom to choose whether to save with a fractional reserve bank or not, Rothbard simply outlawed that option. Would a regime inspired by Rothbard's goldbug dogmas really allow mutual banks to operate when it refuses other banks the freedom to issue credit and money on the same basis? It seems illogical for that to be the case and so would such a regime not, in fact, simply be a new form of the money monopoly Tucker and his colleagues spent so much time combating? One thing is sure, though, even a 100% gold standard will not stop credit expansion as firms and banks would find ways around the law and it is doubtful that private defence firms would be in a position to enforce it.

Once we understand the absurd examples used to refute mutual banking plus the real reasons for inflation (i.e., *"a symptom of a struggle over the distribution of income."* [Davidson, **Op. Cit.**, p. 89]) and how credit-money actually works, it becomes clear that the case against mutual banking is far from clear. Somewhat ironically, the post-Keynesian school of economics provides a firm understanding of how a real credit system works compared to Rothbard's logical deductions from imaginary events based on propositions which are, at root, identical with Walrasian general equilibrium theory (an analysis "Austrians" tend to dismiss). It may be ironic, but not unsurprising as Keynes praised Proudhon's follower Silvio Gesell in **The General Theory** (also see Dudley Dillard's essay *"Keynes and Proudhon"* [**The Journal of Economic History**, vol. 2, No. 1, pp. 63-76]). Libertarian Marxist Paul Mattick noted Keynes debt to Proudhon, and although Keynes did not subscribe to Proudhon's desire to use free credit to fund *"independent producers and workers' syndicates"* as a means create an economic system *"without exploitation"* he did share the Frenchman's *"attack upon the payment of interest"* and wish to see the end of the rentier. [**Marx and Keynes**, p. 5 and p. 6]

Undoubtedly, given the "Austrian" hatred of Keynes and his economics (inspired, in part, by the defeat inflicted on Hayek's business cycle theory in the 1930s by the Keynesians) this will simply confirm their opinion that the Individualist Anarchists did not have a sound economic analysis! As Rothbard noted, the individualist anarchist position was *"simply pushing to its logical conclusion a fallacy adopted widely by preclassical and by current Keynesian writers."* [**Op. Cit.**, p. 10] However, Keynes was trying to analyse the economy as it is rather than deducing logically desired conclusions from the appropriate assumptions needed to confirm the prejudices of the assumer (like Rothbard). In this, he did share the same method if not exactly the same conclusions as the Individualist Anarchists and Mutualists.

Needless to say, social anarchists do not agree that mutual banking can reform capitalism away. As we discuss in section G.4, this is due to many factors, including the natural barriers to competition capital accumulation creates. However, this critique is based on the real economy and does not reflect Rothbard's abstract theorising based on pre-scientific methodology. While other anarchists may reject certain aspects of Tucker's ideas on money, we are well aware, as one commentator noted, that his *"position regarding the State and money monopoly derived from his Socialist convictions"* where socialism *"referred to an intent to fundamentally reorganise the societal systems so as to return the full product of labour to the labourers."* [Don Werkheiser, *"Benjamin R. Tucker: Champion of Free Money"*, pp. 212-221, **Benjamin R. Tucker and the Champions of Liberty**, Coughlin, Hamilton and Sullivan (eds.), p. 212]

G.4
Why do social anarchists reject individualist anarchism?

As James J. Martin notes, *"paralleling"* European social anarchism *"chronologically was a kindred but nearly unconnected phenomenon in America, seeking the same ends through individualistic rather than collectivistic dynamics."* [**Men Against the State**, p. ix] When the two movements meet in America in the 1880s, the similarities and differences of both came into sharp relief. While both social and individualist anarchists reject capitalism as well as the state and seek an end to the exploitation of labour by capital (i.e. to usury in all its forms), both schools of anarchism rejected each others solutions to the social problem. The vision of the social anarchists was more communally based, urging social ownership of the means of life. In contrast, reflecting the pre-dominantly pre-capitalist nature of post-revolution US society, the Individualist Anarchists urged possession of the means of life and mutual banking to end profit, interest and rent and ensure every worker access to the capital they needed to work for themselves (if they so desired). While social anarchists placed co-operatives (i.e., workers' self-management) at the centre of their vision of a free society, many individualist anarchists did not as they thought that mutual banking would end exploitation by ensuring that workers received the full product of their labour.

Thus their vision of a free society and the means to achieve it were somewhat different (although, we stress, **not** mutually exclusive as communist anarchists supported artisan possession of the means of production for those who rejected communism and the Individualist Anarchists supported voluntary communism). Tucker argued that a communist could not be an anarchist and the communist-anarchists argued that Individualist Anarchism could not end the exploitation of capital by labour. Here we indicate why social anarchists reject individualist anarchism (see section G.2 for a summary of why Individualist Anarchists reject social anarchism).

Malatesta summarises the essential points of difference as well as the source of much of the misunderstandings:

> *"The individualists assume, or speak as if they assumed, that the (anarchist) communists wish to impose communism, which of course would put them right outside the ranks of anarchism.*
>
> *"The communists assume, or speak as if they assumed, that the (anarchist) individualists reject every idea of association, want the struggle between men, the domination of the strongest — and this would put them not only outside the anarchist movement but outside humanity.*
>
> *"In reality those who are communists are such because they see in communism freely accepted the realisation of brotherhood, and the best guarantee for individual freedom. And individualists, those who are really*

anarchists, are anti-communist because they fear that communism would subject individuals nominally to the tyranny of the collectivity and in fact to that of the party or caste which, with the excuse of administering things, would succeed in taking possession of the power to dispose of material things and thus of the people who need them. Therefore they want each individual, or each group, to be in a position to enjoy freely the product of their labour in conditions of equality with other individuals and groups, with whom they would maintain relations of justice and equity.

"In which case it is clear that there is no basic difference between us. But, according to the communists, justice and equity are, under natural conditions impossible of attainment in an individualistic society, and thus freedom too would not be attained.

"If climatic conditions throughout the world were the same, if the land were everywhere equally fertile, if raw materials were evenly distributed and within reach of all who needed them, if social development were the same everywhere in the world ... then one could conceive of everyone ... finding the land, tools and raw materials needed to work and produce independently, without exploiting or being exploited. But natural and historical conditions being what they are, how is it possible to establish equality and justice between he who by chance finds himself with a piece of arid land which demands much labour for small returns with him who has a piece of fertile and well sited land?" Of between the inhabitant of a village lost in the mountains or in the middle of a marshy area, with the inhabitants of a city which hundreds of generations of man have enriched with all the skill of human genius and labour? [**Errico Malatesta: His Life and Ideas**, pp. 31-2]

The social anarchist opposition to individualist anarchism, therefore, resolves around the issues of inequality, the limitations and negative impact of markets and whether wage-labour is consistent with anarchist principles (both in general and in terms of individualist anarchism itself). We discuss the issue of wage labour and anarchist principles in the next section and argue in section G.4.2 that Tucker's support for wage-labour, like any authoritarian social relationship, ensures that this is an inconsistent form of anarchism. Here we concentrate on issues of inequality and markets.

First, we must stress that individualist anarchism plays an important role in reminding all socialists that capitalism does **not** equal the market. Markets have existed before capitalism and may, if we believe market socialists like David Schweickart and free market socialists like Benjamin Tucker and Kevin Carson, even survive it. While some socialists (particularly Leninists echoing, ironically, supporters of capitalism) equate capitalism with the market, this is not the case. Capitalism is a specific form of market economy based on certain kinds of property rights which result in generalised wage labour and non-labour incomes (exploitation). This means that the libertarian communist critique of capitalism is to a large

degree independent of its critique of markets and their negative impact. Equally, the libertarian communist critique of markets, while applicable to capitalism, applies to other kinds of economy. It is fair to say, though, that capitalism tends to intensify and worsen the negative effects of markets.

Second, we must also note that social anarchists are a diverse grouping and include the mutualism of Proudhon, Bakunin's collectivism and Kropotkin's communism. All share a common hostility to wage labour and recognise, to varying degrees, that markets tend to have negative aspects which can undermine the libertarian nature of a society. While Proudhon was the social anarchist most in favour of competition, he was well aware of the need for self-managed workplaces to federate together to protect themselves from its negative aspects — aspects he discussed at length. His *"agro-industrial federation"* was seen as a means of socialising the market, of ensuring that competition would not reach such levels as to undermine the freedom and equality of those within it. Individualist anarchists, in contrast, tended not to discuss the negative effects of markets in any great depth (if at all), presumably because they thought that most of the negative effects would disappear along with capitalism and the state. Other anarchists are not so optimistic.

So, two key issues between social and individualist anarchism are the related subjects of property and competition. As Voltairine de Cleyre put it when she was an individualist anarchist:

> *"She and I hold many differing views on both Economy and Morals ... Miss Goldmann [sic] is a communist; I am an individualist. She wishes to destroy the right of property, I wish to assert it. I make my war upon privilege and authority, whereby the right of property, the true right in that which is proper to the individual, is annihilated. She believes that co-operation would entirely supplant competition; I hold that competition in one form or another will always exist, and that it is highly desirable it should."* [**The Voltairine de Cleyre Reader**, p. 9]

The question of "property" is subject to much confusion and distortion. It should be stressed that both social and individualist anarchists argue that the only true property is that produced by labour (mental and physical) and capitalism results in some of that being diverted to property owners in the form of interest, rent and profits. Where they disagree is whether it is possible and desirable to calculate an individual's contribution to social production, particularly within a situation of joint labour. For Tucker, it was a case of creating *"the economic law by which every man may get the equivalent of his product."* [quoted by George Woodcock and Ivan Avakumovic, **The Anarchist Prince**, p. 279] Social anarchists, particularly communist ones, question whether it is possible in reality to discover such a thing in any society based on joint labour (*"which it would be difficult to imagine could exist in any society where there is the least complexity of production."* [George Woodcock and Ivan Avakumovic, **Op. Cit.**, p. 280]).

This was the crux of Kropotkin's critique of the various schemes of "labour money" and "labour vouchers" raised by other schools of socialism (like mutualism, collectivism and various state socialist systems). They may abolish wage labour (or, at worse, create state capitalism) but they did not abolish the wages system, i.e., payment according to work done. This meant that a system of individualist distribution was forced upon a fundamentally co-operative system of production and so was illogical and unjust (see Kropotkin's *"The Collectivist Wage System"* in **The Conquest of Bread**). Thus Daniel Guérin:

> *"This method of remuneration, derived from modified individualism, is in contradiction to collective ownership of the means of production, and cannot bring about a profound revolutionary change in man. It is incompatible with anarchism; a new form of ownership requires a new form of remuneration. Service to the community cannot be measured in units of money. Needs will have to be given precedence over services, and all the products of the labour of all must belong to all, each to take his share of them freely. **To each according to his need** should be the motto of libertarian communism."* [**Anarchism**, p. 50]

Simply put, wages rarely reflect the actual contribution of a specific person to social well-being and production nor do they reflect their actual needs. To try and get actual labour income to reflect the actual contribution to society would be, communist-anarchists argued, immensely difficult. How much of a product's price was the result of better land or more machinery, luck, the willingness to externalise costs, and so on? Voltairine de Cleyre summarised this problem and the obvious solution:

> *"I concluded that as to the question of exchange and money, it was so exceedingly bewildering, so impossible of settlement among the professors themselves, as to the nature of value, and the representation of value, and the unit of value, and the numberless multiplications and divisions of the subject, that the best thing ordinary workingmen or women could do was to organise their industry so as to get rid of money altogether. I figured it this way: I'm not any more a fool than the rest of ordinary humanity; I've figured and figured away on this thing for years, and directly I thought myself middling straight, there came another money reformer and showed me the hole in that scheme, till, at last, it appears that between 'bills of credit,' and 'labour notes' and 'time checks,' and 'mutual bank issues,' and 'the invariable unit of value,' none of them have any sense. How many thousands of years is it going to get this sort of thing into people's heads by mere preaching of theories. Let it be this way: Let there be an end of the special monopoly on securities for money issues. Let every community go ahead and try some member's money scheme if it wants; - let every individual try it if he pleases. But better for the working people let them all go. Let them produce together, co-operatively rather than as employer and employed; let them fraternise group by group, let each use what he needs of his own product, and deposit the rest in the storage-houses, and let those others who need goods have them as occasion arises."* [**Exquisite Rebel**, p. 62]

And, obviously, it must be stressed that "property" in the sense of personal possessions would still exist in communist-anarchism. As the co-founder of **Freedom** put it:

> *"Does Anarchism, then, it may be asked, acknowledge no **Meum** or **Tuum**, no personal property? In a society in which every man is free to take what he requires, it is hardly conceivable that personal necessaries and conveniences will not be appropriated, and difficult to imagine why they should not … When property is protected by no legal enactments, backed by armed force, and is unable to buy personal service, its resuscitation on such a scale as to be dangerous to society is little to be dreaded. The amount appropriated by each individual, and the manner of his appropriation, must be left to his own conscience, and the pressure exercised upon him by the moral sense and distinct interests of his neighbours."* [Charlotte Wilson, **Anarchist Essays**, p. 24]

To use an appropriate example, public libraries are open to all local residents and they are free to borrow books from the stock available. When the book is borrowed, others cannot come along and take the books from a person's home. Similarly, an individual in a communist society can take what they like from the common stocks and use it as they see fit. They do not need permission from others to do so, just as people freely go to public parks without requiring a vote by the local community on whether to allow access or not. Communism, in other words, does not imply community control of personal consumption nor the denial of individuals to appropriate and use the common stock of available goods. Socialised consumption does **not** mean "society" telling people what to consume but rather ensuring that all individuals have free access to the goods produced by all. As such, the issue is not about "property" in the sense of personal property but rather "property" in the sense of access to the means of life by those who use them. Will owner occupiers be able to exclude others from, say, their land and workplaces unless they agree to be their servants?

Which brings us to a key issue between certain forms of individualist anarchism and social anarchism, namely the issue of wage labour. As capitalism has progressed, the size of workplaces and firms have increased. This has lead to a situation where ownership and use has divorced, with property being used by a group of individuals distinct from the few who are legally proclaimed to be its owners. The key problem arises in the case of workplaces and how do non-possessors gain access to them. Under social anarchism, any new members of the collective automatically become part of it, with the same rights and ability to participate in decision making as the existing ones. In other words, socialised production does **not** mean that "society" will allocate individuals work tasks but rather it ensures that all individuals have free access to the means of life. Under individualist anarchism, however, the situation is not as clear with some (like Tucker) supporting wage labour. This suggests that the holders of workplaces can exclude others from the means of life they possess and only allow them access under conditions which create hierarchical social relationships between them. Thus we could have a situation in which the owners who actually manage their own workplaces are, in effect, working capitalists who hire others to do specific tasks in return for a wage.

The problem is highlighted in Tucker's description of what would replace the current system of statism (and note he calls it *"scientific socialism"* thus squarely placing his ideas in the anti-capitalist camp):

> *"we have something very tangible to offer , . . We offer non-compulsive organisation. We offer associative combination. We offer every possible method of voluntary social union by which men and women may act together for the furtherance of well-being. In short, we offer voluntary scientific socialism in place of the present compulsory, unscientific organisation which characterises the State and all of its ramifications."* [quoted by Martin, **Op. Cit.**, p. 218]

Yet it is more than possible for voluntary social unions to be authoritarian and exploitative (we see this every day under capitalism). In other words, not every form of non-compulsive organisation is consistent with libertarian principles. Given Tucker's egoism, it is not hard to conclude that those in stronger positions on the market will seek to maximise their advantages and exploit those who are subject to their will. As he put it, *"[s]o far as inherent right is concerned, might is the only measure. Any man ... and any set of men ... have the right, if they have the power, to kill or coerce other men and to make the entire world subservient to their ends. Society's right to enslave the individual and the individual's right to enslave society are only unequal because their powers are unequal."* In the market, all contracts are based on ownership of resources which exist before any specific contract is made. If one side of the contract has more economic power than the other (say, because of their ownership of capital) then it staggers belief that egoists will not seek to maximise said advantage and so the market will tend to increase inequalities over time rather than reduce them. If, as Tucker argued, *"Anarchic associations would recognise the right of individual occupants to combine their holdings and work them under any system they might agree upon, the arrangement being always terminable at will, with reversion to original rights"* then we have the unfortunate situation where inequalities will undermine anarchism and defence associations arising which will defend them against attempts by those subject to them to use direct action to rectify the situation. [**The Individualist Anarchists**, p. 25 and p. 162]

Kropotkin saw the danger, arguing that such an idea *"runs against the feelings of equality of most of us"* and *"brings the would-be 'Individualists' dangerously near to those who imagine themselves to represent a 'superior breed' — those to whom we owe the State ... and all other forms of oppression."* [**Evolution and Environment**, p. 84] As we discuss in the next section, it is clear that wage labour (like any hierarchical organisation) is not consistent with general anarchist principles and, furthermore, in direct contradiction to individualist anarchist principles of "occupancy and use." Only if "occupancy and use" is consistently applied and so wage labour replaced by workers associations can the inequalities associated with market exchanges not become so great as to destroy the equal freedom of all required for anarchism to work.

Individualist anarchists reply to this criticism by arguing that this is derived from a narrow reading of Stirner's ideas and that they are in favour of universal egoism. This universal egoism and the increase in competition made possible by mutual banking will ensure that workers will have the upper-hand in the market, with the possibility of setting up in business themselves always available. In this way the ability of bosses to become autocrats is limited, as is their power to exploit their workers as a result. Social anarchists argue, in response, that the individualists tend to underestimate the problems associated with natural barriers to entry in an industry. This could help generate generalised wage labour (and so a new class of exploiters) as workers face the unpleasant choice of working for a successful firm, being unemployed or working for low wages in an industry with lower barriers to entry. This process can be seen under capitalism when co-operatives hire wage workers and not include them as members of the association (i.e. they exercise their ownership rights to exclude others). As Proudhon argued:

> *"I have shown the entrepreneur, at the birth of industry, negotiating on equal terms with his comrades, who have since become his workers. It is plain, in fact, that this original equality was bound to disappear through the advantageous position of the master and the dependence of the wage-workers. In vain does the law assure the right of each to enterprise ... When an establishment has had leisure to develop itself, enlarge its foundations, ballast itself with capital, and assure itself a body of patrons, what can a workman do against a power so superior?"* [**Property is Theft!**, p. 192]

Voltairine de Cleyre also came to this conclusion. Discussing the limitations of the Single Tax land reform, she noted that *"the stubborn fact always came up that no man would employ another to work for him unless he could get more for his product than he had to pay for it, and that being the case, the inevitable course of exchange and re-exchange would be that the man having received less than the full amount, could buy back less than the full amount, so that eventually the unsold products must again accumulate in the capitalist's hands; and again the period of non-employment arrives."* This obviously applied to individualist anarchism. In response to objections like this, individualists tend to argue that competition for labour would force wages to equal output. Yet this ignores natural barriers to competition: *"it is well enough to talk of his buying hand tools, or small machinery which can be moved about; but what about the gigantic machinery necessary to the operation of a mine, or a mill? It requires many to work it. If one owns it, will he not make the others pay tribute for using it?"* [**Op. Cit.**, p. 60 and p. 61]

As such, a free market based on wage labour would be extremely unlikely to produce a non-exploitative society and, consequently, it would not be socialist and so not anarchist. Moreover, the successful business person would seek to secure his or her property and power and so employ police to do so. *"I confess that I am not in love with all these little states,"* proclaimed de Cleyre, *"and it is ... the thought of the anarchist policeman that has driven me out of the individualist's camp, wherein I for some time resided."* [quoted by Eugenia C. Delamotte, **Gates of Freedom**, p. 25] This outcome can only be avoided by consistently applying "occupancy and use" in such as way as to eliminate wage labour totally. Only this can achieve a society based on freedom **of** association as well as freedom **within** association.

As we noted in section G.2, one of the worries of individualist anarchists is that social anarchism would subject individuals to group pressures and concerns, violating individual autonomy in the name of collective interests. Thus, it is argued, the individual will become a slave of the group in practice if not in theory under social anarchism. However, an inherent part of our humanity is that we associate with others, that we form groups and communities. To suggest that there are no group issues within anarchism seems at odds with reality. Taken literally, of course, this implies that such a version of "anarchy" there would be no forms of association at all. No groups, no families, no clubs: nothing bar the isolated individual. It implies no economic activity beyond the level of peasant farming and one-person artisan workplaces. Why? Simply because any form of organisation implies "group issues." Two people deciding to live together or one hundred people working together becomes a group, twenty people forming a football club becomes a group. And these people have joint interests and so group issues. In other words, to deny group issues is implying a social situation that has never existed nor ever will. Thus Kropotkin:

> "to reason in this way is to pay … too large a tribute to metaphysical dialectics, and to ignore the facts of life. It is impossible to conceive a society in which the affairs of any one of its members would not concern many other members, if not all; still less a society in which a continual contact between its members would not have established an interest of every one towards all others, which would render it **impossible** to act without thinking of the effects which our actions may have on others." [**Evolution and Environment**, p. 85]

Once the reality of "group issues" is acknowledged, as most individualist anarchists do, then the issue of collective decision making automatically arises. There are two ways of having a group. You can be an association of equals, governing yourselves collectively as regards collective issues. Or you can have capitalists and wage slaves, bosses and servants, government and governed. Only the first, for obvious reasons, is compatible with anarchist principles. Freedom, in other words, is a product of how we interact with each other, not of isolation. Simply put, anarchism is based on self-management of group issues, not in their denial. Free association is, in this perspective, a necessary but not sufficient to guarantee freedom. Therefore, social anarchists reject the individualists' conception of anarchy, simply because it can, unfortunately, allow hierarchy (i.e. government) back into a free society in the name of "liberty" and "free contracts." Freedom is fundamentally a social product, created in and by community. It is a fragile flower and does not fare well when bought and sold on the market.

Moreover, without communal institutions, social anarchists argue, it would be impossible to specify or supply group or public goods. In addition, occupancy and use would, on the face of it, preclude such amenities which are utilised by members of a community such as parks, roads or bridges — anything which is used but not occupied continually. In terms of roads and bridges, who actually occupies and uses them? The drivers? Those who maintain them? The occupiers of the houses which the road passes? Those who funded its construction? If the last, then why does this not apply to housing and other buildings left on land? And how are the owners to collect a return on their investment unless by employing police to bar access to non-payers? And would such absentee owners not also seek to extend their appropriations to other forms of property? Would it not be far easier to simply communalise such forms of commonly used "property" rather than seek to burden individuals and society with the costs of policing and restricting access to them?

After all, social anarchists note, for Proudhon there was a series of industries and services that he had no qualms about calling "*public works*" and which he considered best handled by communes and their federations. Thus "*the initiative of communes and departments as to works that operate within their jurisdiction*" with "*the initiative of the workers companies as to carrying the works out.*" This was due to both their nature and libertarian values and so the "*direct, sovereign initiative of localities, in arranging for public works that belong to them, is a consequence of the democratic principle and the free contract: their subordination to the State is … a return to feudalism.*" Workers' self-management of such public works was, again, a matter of libertarian principles for "*it becomes necessary for the workers to form themselves into democratic societies, with equal conditions for all members, on pain of a relapse into feudalism.*" [**Op. Cit.**, pp. 595-6]

In the case of a park, either it is open to all or it is fenced off and police used to bar access. Taking "occupancy and use" as our starting point then it becomes clear that, over time, either the community organises itself communally or a park becomes private property. If a group of people frequent a common area then they will have to discuss how to maintain it — for example, arrange for labour to be done on it, whether to have a play-ground for children or to have a duck pond, whether to increase the numbers and types of trees, and so forth. That implies the development of communal structures. In the case of new people using the amenity, either they are excluded from it (and have to pay for access) or they automatically join the users group and so the park is, in effect, common property and socialised. In such circumstances, it would be far easier simply to ignore the issue of individual contributions and base access on need (i.e., communistic principles). However, as already indicated in section G.2.1, social anarchists reject attempts to coerce other workers into joining a co-operative or commune. Freedom cannot be given, it must be taken and social anarchism, like all forms of anarchy, cannot be imposed. How those who reject social anarchism will gain access to common property will depend, undoubtedly, on specific circumstances and who exactly is involved and how they wish to utilise it. As such, it will be difficult to generalise as each commune will determine what is best and reach the appropriate contracts with any individualist anarchists in their midst or vicinity.

Most social anarchists also are critical of the means which individualist anarchists support to achieve anarchy, namely to abolish capitalism by the creation of mutual banks which would compete exploitation and oppression away. While mutual banks could aid the position of working class people under capitalism (which is why Bakunin and other social anarchists recommended them), they cannot

Is individualist anarchism capitalistic?

undermine or eliminate it. This is because capitalism, due to its need to accumulate, creates **natural** barriers to entry into a market (see section C.4). Thus the physical size of the large corporation would make it immune to the influence of mutual banking and so usury could not be abolished. Even if we look at the claimed indirect impact of mutual banking, namely an increase in the demand of labour and so wages, the problem arises that if this happens then capitalism would soon go into a slump (with obvious negative effects on small firms and co-operatives). In such circumstances, the number of labourers seeking work would rise and so wages would fall and profits rise. Then it is a case of whether the workers would simply tolerate the slump and let capitalism continue or whether they would seize their workplaces and practice the kind of expropriation individualist anarchists tended to oppose.

This problem was recognised by many individualist anarchists themselves and it played a significant role in its decline as a movement. By 1911 Tucker had come to the same conclusions as communist-anarchists on whether capitalism could be reformed away. As we noted in section G.1.1, he *"had come to believe that free banking and similar measures, even if inaugurated, were no longer adequate to break the monopoly of capitalism or weaken the authority of the state."* [Paul Avrich, **Anarchist Voices**, p. 6] While admitting that political or revolutionary action was required to destroy the concentrations of capital which made anarchy impossible even with free competition, he rejected the suggestion that individualist anarchists should join in such activity. Voltairine de Cleyre came to similar conclusions earlier and started working with Emma Goldman before becoming a communist-anarchist sometime in 1908. Perhaps unsurprisingly, one historian argues that as the *"native American variety of anarchism dissolved in the face of increasing State repression and industrialisation, rationalisation, and concentration of capital, American anarchists were forced either to acquiesce or to seek a more militant strain of anarchism: this latter presented itself in the form of Communist Anarchism ... Faith in peaceful evolution toward an anarchist society seemed archaic and gradually faded."* [Kline, **The Individualist Anarchists**, p. 83]

So while state action may increase the degree of monopoly in an industry, the natural tendency for any market is to place barriers (natural ones) to new entries in terms of set-up costs and so on. This applies just as much to co-operatives as it does to companies based on wage-labour. It means that if the relation between capital and labour was abolished **within** the workplace (by their transformation into co-operatives) but they remained the property of their workers, it would only be a matter of time before the separation of the producers from their means of production reproduced itself. This is because, within any market system, some firms fail and others succeed. Those which fail will create a pool of unemployed workers who will need a job. The successful co-operatives, safe behind their natural barriers to entry, would be in a stronger position than the unemployed workers and so may hire them as wage labourers — in effect, the co-operative workers would become "collective capitalists" hiring other workers. This would end workers' self-management (as not all workers are involved in the decision making process) as well as workers' ownership, i.e. "occupancy and use," (as not all workers' would own the means of production they used). The individual workers involved may "consent" to becoming wage

slaves, but that is because it is the best option available rather than what they really want. Which, of course, is the same as under capitalism.

This was why Proudhon argued that *"every individual employed in the association"* must have *"an undivided share in the property of the company"* in order to ensure workers' self-management. [**Op. Cit.**, p. 585] Only this could ensure *"occupancy and use"* and so self-management in a free society (i.e. keep that society free). Thus in anarchism, as de Cleyre summarised, it is *"a settled thing that to be free one must have liberty of access to the sources and means of production"* Without socialisation of the means of life, liberty of access could be denied. Little wonder she argued that she had become *"convinced that a number of the fundamental propositions of individualistic economy would result in the destruction of equal liberty."* The only logical anarchist position is *"that some settlement of the whole labour question was needed which would not split up the people again into land possessors and employed wage-earners."* Hence her movement from individualism towards, first, mutualism and then communism — it was the only logical position to take in a rapidly industrialising America which had made certain concepts of individualism obsolete. It was her love of freedom which made her sensitive to the possibility of any degeneration back into capitalism: *"the instinct of liberty naturally revolted not only at economic servitude, but at the outcome of it, class-lines."* [**Op. Cit.**, p. 58, p. 105, p. 61 and p. 55] As we argue in section G.4.2 such a possibility can be avoided only by a consistent application of "occupancy and use" which, in practice, would be nearly identical to the communalisation or socialisation of the means of life.

This issue is related to the question of inequality within a market economy and whether free exchanges tend to reduce or increase any initial inequalities. While Individualist Anarchists argue for the *"cost principle"* (i.e. cost being the limit of price) the cost of creating the same commodity in different areas or by different people is not equal. Thus the market price of a good **cannot** really equal the multitude of costs within it (and so price can only equal a workers' labour in those few cases where that labour was applied in average circumstances). This issue was recognised by Tucker, who argued that *"economic rent ... is one of nature's inequalities. It will probably remain with us always. Complete liberty will very much lessen it; of that I have no doubt."* [**Why I am an Anarchist**, pp. 135-6] However, argue social anarchists, the logic of market exchange produces a situation where the stronger party to a contract seeks to maximise their advantage. Given this, free exchange will tend to **increase** differences in wealth and income over time, not eliminate them. As Daniel Guérin summarised:

> *"Competition and the so-called market economy inevitably produce inequality and exploitation, and would do so even if one started from complete equality. They could not be combined with workers' self-management unless it were on a temporary basis, as a necessary evil, until (1) a psychology of 'honest exchange' had developed among the workers; (2) most important, society as a whole had passed from conditions of shortage to the stage of abundance, when competition would lose its purpose ... The libertarian communist would condemn Proudhon's*

version of a collective economy as being based on a principle of conflict; competitors would be in a position of equality at the start, only to be hurled into a struggle which would inevitably produce victors and vanquished, and where goods would end up by being exchanged according to the principles of supply and demand." [**Op. Cit.**, pp. 53-4]

Thus, even a non-capitalist market could evolve towards inequality and away from fair exchange. It was for this reason that Proudhon argued that a portion of income from agricultural produce be paid into a central fund which would be used to make equalisation payments to compensate farmers with less favourably situated or less fertile land. As he put it, economic rent *"in agriculture has no other cause than the inequality in the quality of land ... if anyone has a claim on account of this inequality ... [it is] the other land workers who hold inferior land. That is why in our scheme for liquidation [of capitalism] we stipulated that every variety of cultivation should pay a proportional contribution, destined to accomplish a balancing of returns among farm workers and an assurance of products."* [**Op. Cit.**, p. 582] His advocacy of federations of workers' associations was, likewise, seen as a means of abolishing inequalities.

Unlike Proudhon, however, individualist anarchists did not propose any scheme to equalise income. Perhaps Tucker was correct and the differences would be slight, but in a market situation exchanges tend to magnify differences, **not** reduce them as the actions of self-interested individuals in unequal positions will tend to exacerbate differences. Over time these slight differences would become larger and larger, subjecting the weaker party to relatively increasingly worse contracts. Without equality, individualist anarchism would quickly become hierarchical and non-anarchist. As the communist-anarchist paper **Freedom** argued in the 1880s:

"*Are not the scandalous inequalities in the distribution of wealth today merely the culminate effect of the principle that every man is justified in securing to himself everything that his chances and capacities enable him to lay hands on?*

"*If the social revolution which we are living means anything, it means the destruction of this detestable economic principle, which delivers over the more social members of the community to the domination of the most unsocial and self-interested.*" [**Freedom**, vol. 2, no. 19]

Freedom, it should be noted, is slightly misrepresenting the position of individualist anarchists. They did **not** argue that every person could appropriate all the property he or she could. Most obviously, in terms of land they were consistently opposed to a person owning more of it than they actually used. They also tended to apply this to what was on the land as well, arguing that any buildings on it were abandoned when the owner no longer used them. Given this, individualist anarchists have stressed that such a system would be unlikely to produce the inequalities associated with capitalism (as Kropotkin noted, equality was essential and was implicitly acknowledged by individualists themselves who argued that their system *"would offer no danger, because the rights of each individual would have been limited by the equal rights of all*

others."* [**Evolution and Environment**, p. 85]). Thus contemporary individualist anarchist Joe Peacott:

"*Although individualists envision a society based on private property, we oppose the economic relationships of capitalism, whose supporters misuse words like private enterprise and free markets to justify a system of monopoly ownership in land and the means of production which allows some to skim off part or even most of the wealth produced by the labour of others. Such a system exists only because it is protected by the armed power of government, which secures title to unjustly acquired and held land, monopolises the supply of credit and money, and criminalises attempts by workers to take full ownership of the means of production they use to create wealth. This state intervention in economic transactions makes it impossible for most workers to become truly independent of the predation of capitalists, banks, and landlords. Individualists argue that without the state to enforce the rules of the capitalist economy, workers would not allow themselves to be exploited by these thieves and capitalism would not be able to exist ...*

"*One of the criticisms of individualist economic proposals raised by other anarchists is that a system based on private ownership would result in some level of difference among people in regard to the quality or quantity of possessions they have. In a society where people are able to realise the full value of their labour, one who works harder or better than another will possess or have the ability to acquire more things than someone who works less or is less skilled at a particular occupation ...*

"*The differences in wealth that arise in an individualist community would likely be relatively small. Without the ability to profit from the labour of others, generate interest from providing credit, or extort rent from letting out land or property, individuals would not be capable of generating the huge quantities of assets that people can in a capitalist system. Furthermore, the anarchist with more things does not have them at the expense of another, since they are the result of the owner's own effort. If someone with less wealth wishes to have more, they can work more, harder, or better. There is no injustice in one person working 12 hours a day and six days a week in order to buy a boat, while another chooses to work three eight hour days a week and is content with a less extravagant lifestyle. If one can generate income only by hard work, there is an upper limit to the number and kind of things one can buy and own.*" [**Individualism and Inequality**]

However, argue social anarchists, market forces may make such an ideal impossible to achieve or maintain. Most would agree with Peter Marshall's point that *"[u]ndoubtedly real difficulties exist with the economic position of the individualists. If occupiers became owners overnight as Benjamin Tucker recommended, it would mean in practice that those with good land or houses would merely become better off than those with bad. Tucker's advocacy of 'competition everywhere and always' among occupying owners, subject to the only moral law of minding your own business might will encourage individual greed rather than fair play for all."* [**Demanding the Impossible**, p. 653]

Few social anarchists are convinced that all the problems associated with markets and competition are purely the result of state intervention. They argue that it is impossible to have most of the underlying pre-conditions of a competitive economy without the logical consequences of them. It is fair to say that individualist anarchists tend to ignore or downplay the negative effects of markets while stressing their positive ones.

While we discuss the limitations of markets in section I.1.3, suffice to say here that competition results in economic forces developing which those within the market have to adjust to. In other words, the market may be free but those within it are not. To survive on the market, firms would seek to reduce costs and so implement a host of dehumanising working practices in order to compete successfully on the market, things which they would resist if bosses did it. Work hours could get longer and longer, for example, in order to secure and maintain market position. This, in turn, affects our quality of life and our relationship with our partners, children, parents, friends, neighbours and so on. That the profits do not go to the executives and owners of businesses may be a benefit, it matters little if people are working longer and harder in order to invest in machinery to ensure market survival. Hence **survival,** not **living,** would be the norm within such a society, just as it is, unfortunately, in capitalism.

Ultimately, Individualist Anarchists lose sight of the fact that success and competition are not the same thing. One can set and reach goals without competing. That we may loose more by competing than by co-operating is an insight which social anarchists base their ideas on. In the end, a person can become a success in terms of business but lose sight of their humanity and individuality in the process. In contrast, social anarchists stress community and co-operation in order to develop us as fully rounded individuals. As Kropotkin put it, *"the **individualisation** they so highly praise is not attainable by individual efforts."* [**Anarchism**, p. 297]

As we noted in section D.1, the capitalist state intervenes into the economy and society to counteract the negative impact of market forces on social life and the environment as well as, of course, protecting and enhancing the position of itself and the capitalist class. As individualist anarchism is based on markets (to some degree), it seems likely that market forces would have similar negative impacts (albeit to a lesser degree due to the reduced levels of inequality implied by the elimination of non-labour incomes). Without communal institutions, social anarchists argue, individualist anarchism has no means of counteracting the impact of such forces except, perhaps, by means of continual court cases and juries. Thus social issues would not be discussed by all affected but rather by small sub-groups retroactively addressing individual cases.

Moreover, while state action may have given the modern capitalist an initial advantage on the market, it does not follow that a truly free market will not create similar advantages naturally over time. And if it did, then surely a similar system would develop? As such,

it does not follow that a non-capitalist market system would remain such. In other words, it is true that extensive state intervention was required to **create** capitalism but after a time economic forces can usually be relied upon to allow wage workers to be exploited. The key factor is that while markets have existed long before capitalism, that system has placed them at the centre of economic activity. In the past, artisans and farmers produced for local consumers, with the former taking their surplus to markets. In contrast, capitalism has produced a system where producers are primarily geared to exchanging **all** goods they create on an extensive market rather simply a surplus locally. This implies that the dynamics of a predominantly market system may be different from those in the past in which the market played a much smaller role and where self-sufficiency was always a possibility. It is difficult to see how, for example, car workers or IT programmers could produce for their own consumption using their own tools.

So in a market economy with a well-developed division of labour it is possible for a separation of workers from their means of production to occur. This is particularly the case when the predominant economic activity is not farming. Thus the net effect of market transactions could be to re-introduce class society simply by their negative long-term consequences. That such a system developed without state aid would make it no less unfree and unjust. It is of little use to point out that such a situation is **not** what the Individualist Anarchists desired for it is a question of whether their ideas would actually result in what they wanted. Social anarchists have fears that they will not. Significantly, as we noted in section G.3, Tucker was sensible enough to argue that those subject to such developments should rebel against them.

In response, individualist anarchists could argue that the alternative to markets would be authoritarian (i.e., some form of central planning) and/or inefficient as without markets to reward effort most people would not bother to work well and provide for the consumer. So while markets do have problems with them, the alternatives are worse. Moreover, when social anarchists note that there is a remarkable correlation between competitiveness in a society and the presence of clearly defined "have" and "have-not" groups individualist anarchists would answer that the causation flows not from competitiveness to inequality but from inequality to competitiveness. In a more equal society people would be less inclined to compete as ruthlessly as under capitalism and so the market would not generate as many problems as it does today. Moreover, eliminating the artificial barriers erected by the state would allow a universal competition to develop rather than the one sided form associated with capitalism. With a balance of market power, competition would no longer take the form it currently does.

Yet, as noted above, this position ignores natural barriers to competition The accumulation needs of a competitive market economy do not disappear just because capitalism has been replaced by co-operatives and mutual credit banks. In any market economy, firms will try to improve their market position by investing in new machinery, reducing prices by improving productivity and so on. This creates barriers to new competitors who have to expend more money in order to match the advantages of existing firms. Such amounts of money may not be forthcoming from even the biggest mutual bank and so certain firms would enjoy a privileged position on the market. Given that Tucker defined a monopolist as *"any person, corporation, or institution whose right to engage in any given pursuit of life is secured, either wholly or partially, by any agency whatsoever — whether the nature of things or the force of events or the decree of arbitrary power — against the influence of competition"* we may suggest that due to **natural** barriers, an individualist anarchist society would not be free of monopolists and so of usury. [quoted by James J. Martin, **Men Against the State**, p. 210]

For this reason, even in a mutualist market certain companies would receive a bigger slice of profits than (and at the expense of) others. This means that exploitation would still exist as larger companies could charge more than cost for their products. It could be argued that the ethos of an anarchist society would prevent such developments happening but, as Kropotkin noted, this has problems, firstly because of *"the difficulty of estimating the **market value**"* of a product based on *"average time"* or cost necessary to produce it and, secondly, if that could be done then to get people *"to agree upon such an estimation of their work would already require a deep penetration of the Communist principles into their ideas."* [**Environment and Evolution**, p. 84] In addition, the free market in banking would also result in **its** market being dominated by a few big banks, with similar results. As such, it is all fine and well to argue that with rising interest rates more competitors would be drawn into the market and so the increased competition would automatically reduce them but that is only possible if there are no serious natural barriers to entry.

This obviously impacts on how we get from capitalism to anarchism. Natural barriers to competition limit the ability to compete exploitation away. So as to its means of activism, individualist anarchism exaggerates the potential of mutual banks to fund co-operatives. While the creation of community-owned and -managed mutual credit banks would help in the struggle for a free society, such banks are not enough in themselves. Unless created as part of the social struggle against capitalism and the state, and unless combined with community and strike assemblies, mutual banks would quickly die, because the necessary social support required to nurture them would not exist. Mutual banks must be part of a network of other new socio-economic and political structures and cannot be sustained in isolation from them. This is simply to repeat our earlier point that, for most social anarchists, capitalism cannot be reformed away. As such, social anarchists would tend to agree with the summary provided by this historian:

> *"If [individualist anarchists] rejected private ownership of property, they destroyed their individualism and 'levelled' mankind. If they accepted it, they had the problem of offering a solution whereby the inequalities [of wealth] would not amount to a tyranny over the individual. They meet the same dilemma in 'method.' If they were consistent libertarian individualists they could not force from 'those who had' what they had acquired justly or unjustly, but if they did not force it from them, they perpetuated inequalities. They met a stone wall."* [Eunice Minette Schuster, **Native American Anarchism**, p. 158]

So while Tucker believed in direct action, he opposed the "forceful" expropriation of social capital by the working class, instead favouring the creation of a mutualist banking system to replace capitalism with a non-exploitative system. Tucker was therefore fundamentally a **reformist,** thinking that anarchy would evolve from capitalism as mutual banks spread across society, increasing the bargaining power of labour. And reforming capitalism over time, by implication, always means tolerating boss's control during that time. So, at its worst, this is a reformist position which becomes little more than an excuse for tolerating landlord and capitalist domination.

Also we may note, in the slow transition towards anarchism, we would see the rise of pro-capitalist "defence associations" which **would** collect rent from land, break strikes, attempt to crush unions and so on. Tucker seemed to have assumed that the anarchist vision of *"occupancy-and-use"* would become universal. Unfortunately, landlords and capitalists would resist it and so, ultimately, an Individualist Anarchist society would have to either force the minority to accept the majority wishes on land use (hence his comments on there being *"no legal power to collect rent"*) or the majority are dictated to by the minority who are in favour of collecting rent and hire "defence associations" to enforce those wishes. With the head start big business and the wealthy have in terms of resources, conflicts between pro- and anti-capitalist "defence associations" would usually work against the anti-capitalist ones (as trade unions often find out). In other words, reforming capitalism would not be as non-violent or as simple as Tucker maintained. The vested powers which the state defends will find other means to protect themselves when required (for example, when capitalists and landlords backed fascism and fascist squads in Italy after workers "occupied and used" their workplaces and land-workers and peasants "occupied and used" the land in 1920). We are sure that economists will then rush to argue that the resulting law system that defended the collection of rent and capitalist property against "occupancy and use" was the most "economically efficient" result for "society."

In addition, even if individualist mutualism **did** result in an increase in wages by developing artisan and co-operative ventures that decreased the supply of labour in relation to its demand, this would not eliminate the subjective and objective pressures on profits that produce the business cycle within capitalism (see section C.7). In fact, it would increase the subjective pressures considerably as was the case under the social Keynesianism of the post-war period. Unsurprisingly, business interests sought the necessary "reforms" and ruthlessly fought the subsequent strikes and protests to achieve a labour market more to their liking (see section C.8.2 for more on this). This means that an increase in the bargaining power of labour would soon see capital moving to non-anarchist areas and so deepening any recession caused by a lowering of profits and other non-labour income. This could mean that during an economic slump, when workers' savings and bargaining position were weak, the gains associated with mutualism could be lost as co-operative firms go bust and mutual banks find it hard to survive in a hostile environment.

Mutual banks would not, therefore, undermine modern capitalism, as recognised by social anarchists from Bakunin onward. They placed their hopes in a social revolution organised by workplace and community organisations, arguing that the ruling class would be as unlikely to tolerate being competed away as they would be voted away. The collapse of social Keynesianism into neo-liberalism shows that even a moderately reformed capitalism which increased working class power will not be tolerated for too long. In other words, there was a need for social revolution which mutual banks do not, and could not, eliminate.

However, while social anarchists disagree with the proposals of individualist anarchists, we do still consider them to be a form of anarchism — one with many flaws and one perhaps more suited to an earlier age when capitalism was less developed and its impact upon society far less than it is now (see section G.1.4). Individualist and social anarchism could co-exist happily in a free society and neither believes in forcing the other to subscribe to their system. As Paul Nursey-Bray notes *"linking all of these approaches … is not just the belief in individual liberty and its corollary, the opposition to central or state authority, but also a belief in community, and an equality of community members."* The *"discussion over forms of property … should not be allowed to obscure the commonality of the idea of the free community of self-regulating individuals."* And so *"there are meeting points in the crucial ideas of individual autonomy and community that suggest, at least, a basis for the discussion of equality and property relations."* [**Anarchist Thinkers and Thought**, p. xvi]

G.4.1 Is wage labour consistent with anarchist principles?

No, it is not. This can be seen from social anarchism, where opposition to wage labour as hierarchical and exploitative is taken as an obvious and logical aspect of anarchist principles. However, ironically, this conclusion must also be drawn from the principles expounded by individualist anarchism. However, as noted in section G.1.3, while many individualist anarchists opposed wage labour and sought its end not all did. Benjamin Tucker was one of the latter. To requote him:

> *"Wages is not slavery. Wages is a form of voluntary exchange, and voluntary exchange is a form of Liberty."* [**Liberty**, no. 3, p. 1]

The question of wage labour was one of the key differences between Tucker and communist-anarchist Johann Most. For Most, it signified that Tucker supported the exploitation of labour. For Tucker, Most's opposition to it signified that he was not a real anarchist, seeking to end freedom by imposing communism onto all. In response to Most highlighting the fact that Tucker supported wage labour, Tucker argued as followed:

> *"If the men who oppose wages — that is, the purchase and sale of labour — were capable of analysing their thought and feelings, they would see that what really excites their anger is not the fact that labour is bought and sold, but the fact that one class of men are dependent for their living upon the sale of their labour, while another class of men are relieved of the necessity of labour by being legally privileged to sell something that is not labour, and that,*

> *but for the privilege, would be enjoyed by all gratuitously. And to such a state of things I am as much opposed as any one. But the minute you remove privilege, the class that now enjoy it will be forced to sell their labour, and then, when there will be nothing but labour with which to buy labour, the distinction between wage-payers and wage-receivers will be wiped out, and every man will be a labourer exchanging with fellow-labourers. Not to abolish wages, but to make every man dependent upon wages and secure to every man his whole wages is the aim of Anarchistic Socialism. What Anarchistic Socialism aims to abolish is usury. It does not want to deprive labour of its reward; it wants to deprive capital of its reward. It does not hold that labour should not be sold; it holds that capital should not be hired at usury."* [**Liberty**, no. 123, p. 4]

Social anarchists, in reply, would argue that Tucker is missing the point. The reason why almost all anarchists are against wage labour is because it generates social relationships based on authority and, as such, it sets the necessary conditions for the exploitation of labour to occur. If we take the creation of employer-employee relationships within an anarchy, we see the danger of private statism arising (as in "anarcho"-capitalism) and so the end of anarchy. Such a development can be seen when Tucker argued that if, in an anarchy, *"any labourers shall interfere with the rights of their employers, or shall use force upon inoffensive 'scabs,' or shall attack their employers' watchmen … I pledge myself that, as an Anarchist and in consequence of my Anarchistic faith, I will be among the first to volunteer as a member of a force to repress these disturbers of order, and, if necessary, sweep them from the earth."* [**Op. Cit.**, p. 455] Tucker's comments were provoked by the Homestead strike of 1892, where the striking steelworkers fought with, and defeated, their employer's Pinkerton thugs sent to break the strike (Tucker, it should be stressed supported the strikers but not their methods and considered the capitalist class as responsible for the strike by denying workers a free market).

In such a situation, these defence associations would be indeed "private states" and here Tucker's ideas unfortunately do parallel those of the "anarcho"-capitalists (although, as Tucker thought that the employees would not be exploited by the employer, this does not suggest that Tucker can be considered a forefather of "anarcho"-capitalism). As Kropotkin warned, *"[f]or their self-defence, both the citizen and group have a right to any violence [within individualist anarchy] … Violence is also justified for enforcing the duty of keeping an agreement. Tucker … opens … the way for reconstructing under the heading of the 'defence' all the functions of the State."* [**Anarchism**, p. 297]

Such an outcome is easy to avoid, however, by simply consistently applying individualist anarchist principles and analysis to wage labour. To see why, it is necessary simply to compare private property with Tucker's definition of the state.

How did Tucker define the state? All states have two common elements, *"aggression"* and *"the assumption of sole authority over a given area and all within it, exercised generally for the double purpose of more complete oppression of its subjects and extension* of its boundaries." This monopoly of authority is important, as "I am not aware that any State has ever tolerated a rival State within its borders." So the state, Tucker stated, is "the embodiment of the principle of invasion in an individual, or a band of individuals, assuming to act as representatives or masters of the entire people within a given area." The "essence of government is control, or the attempt to control. He who attempts to control another is a governor, an aggressor, an invader … he who resists another's attempt to control is not an aggressor, an invader, a governor, but simply a defender, a protector." In short, "the Anarchistic definition of government: the subjection of the non-invasive individual to an external will." [**The Individualist Anarchists**, p. 24]

The similarities with capitalist property (i.e., one based on wage labour) is obvious. The employer assumes and exercises "sole authority over a given area and all within it," they are the boss after all and so capitalists are the "masters of the entire people within a given area." That authority is used to control the employees in order to maximise the difference between what they produce and what they get paid (i.e., to ensure exploitation). As August Spies, one of the Haymarket Martyrs, noted:

> "I was amazed and was shocked when I became acquainted with the condition of the wage-workers in the New World.
>
> "The factory: the ignominious regulations, the surveillance, the spy system, the servility and lack of manhood among the workers and the arrogant arbitrary behaviour of the boss and his associates — all this made an impression upon me that I have never been able to divest myself of. At first I could not understand why the workers, among them many old men with bent backs, silently and without a sign of protest bore every insult the caprice of the foreman or boss would heap upon them. I was not then aware of the fact that the opportunity to work was a privilege, a favour, and that it was in the power of those who were in the possession of the factories and instruments of labour to deny or grant this privilege. I did not then understand how difficult it was to find a purchaser for ones labour, I did not know then that there were thousands and thousands of idle human bodies in the market, ready to hire out upon most any conditions, actually begging for employment. I became conscious of this, very soon, however, and I knew then why these people were so servile, they suffered the humiliating dictates and capricious whims of their employers." [**The Autobiographies of the Haymarket Martyrs**, pp. 66-7]

That this is a kind of state-like authority becomes clear when we consider company towns. As Ward Churchill notes, the "extent of company power over workers included outright ownership of the towns in which they lived, a matter enabling employers to garner additional profits by imposing exorbitant rates of rent, prices for subsistence commodities, tools, and such health care as was available. Conditions in these 'company towns' were such that, by 1915, the Commission on Industrial Relations was led to observe that they displayed 'every aspect of feudalism except the recognition of special duties on the part of the employer.' The job of the Pinkertons — first for the railroads, then more generally — was to prevent workers from organising in a manner that might enable them to improve their own circumstances, thus reducing corporate profits." ["From the Pinkertons to the PATRIOT Act: The Trajectory of Political Policing in the United States, 1870 to the Present", pp. 1-72, **CR: The New Centennial Review**, vol. 4, No. 1, pp. 11-2] In the words of one historian of the Pinkerton Agency "[b]y the mid-1850s a few businessmen saw the need for greater control over their employees; their solution was to sponsor a private detective system. In February 1855, Allan Pinkerton, after consulting with six midwestern railroads, created such an agency in Chicago." [Frank Morn, quoted by Churchill, **Op. Cit.**, p. 4] As we have noted in section F.7.1, such regimes remained into the 1930s, with corporations having their own well armed private police to enforce the propertarian hierarchy (see also section F.6.2).

So, in terms of monopoly of authority over a given area the capitalist company and the state share a common feature. The reason why wage labour violates Individualist Anarchist principles is clear. If the workers who use a workplace do not own it, then someone else will (i.e. the owner, the boss). This in turn means that the owner can tell those who use the resource what to do, how to do it and when. That is, they are the sole authority over the workplace and those who use it. However, according to Tucker, the state can be defined (in part) as "the assumption of sole authority over a given area and all within it." Tucker considered this element as "common to all States" and so opposition to the state logically implies support for workers' self-management for only in this case can people govern themselves during the working day (see section B.4 for more discussion). Even with Tucker's other aspect, "aggression", there are issues. Competition is inherently aggressive, with companies seeking to expand their market share, go into new markets, drive their competitors out of business, and so forth. Within the firm itself, bosses always seek to make workers do more work for less, threatening them with the sack if they object.

Tucker's comments on strikers brings to light an interesting contradiction in his ideas. After all, he favoured a system of "property" generally defined by use and occupancy, that is whoever uses and possesses is to be consider the owner. As we indicated in section G.1.2, this applied to both the land and what was on it. In particular, Tucker pointed to the example of housing and argued that rent would not be collected from tenants nor would they be evicted for not paying it. Why should this position change when it is a workplace rather than a house? Both are products of labour, so that cannot be the criteria. Nor can it be because one is used for work as Tucker explicitly includes the possibility that a house could be used as a workplace.

Thus we have a massive contradiction between Tucker's "occupancy and use" perspective on land use and his support for wage labour. One letter to **Liberty** (by "Egoist") pointed out this contradiction: "if production is carried on in groups, as it now is, who is the legal occupier of the land? The employer, the manager, or the ensemble of those engaged in the co-operative work? The latter appearing the only rational answer." [**Op. Cit.**, no. 143, p. 4] Sadly, Tucker's reply did not address this particular question and so we are left with an unresolved contradiction.

Thus we have numerous contradictions in Tucker's position. On the one hand, occupancy and use precludes landlords renting land and housing but includes capitalists hiring workers to "occupancy and use" their land and workplaces; the state is attacked for being a monopoly of power over a given area while the boss can have the same authority; opposing voluntary wage labour shows that you are an authoritarian, but opposing voluntary landlordism is libertarian. Yet, there is no logical reason for workplaces to be excluded from "occupancy and use." As Tucker put it:

> "Occupancy and use is the only title to land in which we will protect you; if you attempt to use land which another is occupying and using, we will protect him against you; if another attempts to use land to which you lay claim, but which you are not occupying and using, we will not interfere with him; but of such land as you occupy and use you are the sole master, and we will not ourselves take from you, or allow anyone else to take from you, whatever you may get out of such land." [**Liberty**, no. 252, p. 3]

Needless to say, capitalists are not occupying and using the workplaces nor are any of the other shareholders. As we discuss in the next section, this is precisely why most anarchists have opposed wage labour as being incompatible with general anarchist principles. In other words, a consistent anarchism precludes all forms of authoritarian social relationships.

There is another reason why wage labour is at odds with anarchist principles. This is to do with our opposition to exploitation and usury. Simply put, there are the problems in determining what are the "whole wages" of the employer and the employee. The employer, of course, does not simply get his "share" of the collectively produced output, they get the whole amount. This would mean that the employer's "wages" are simply the difference between the cost of inputs and the price the goods were sold on the market. This would imply that the market wage of the labour has to be considered as equalling the workers' "whole wage" and any profits equalling the bosses "whole wage" (some early defences of profit did argue precisely this, although the rise of shareholding made such arguments obviously false). The problem arises in that the employer's income is not determined independently of their ownership of capital and their monopoly of power in the workplace. This means that the boss can appropriate for themselves all the advantages of co-operation and self-activity within the workplace simply because they owned it. Thus, "profits" do not reflect the labour ("wages") of the employer.

It was this aspect of ownership which made Proudhon such a firm supporter of workers associations. As he put it, a "*hundred men, uniting or combining their forces, produce, in certain cases, not a hundred times, but two hundred, three hundred, a thousand times as much. This is what I have called **collective force**. I even drew from this an argument ... against certain forms of appropriation: that it is not sufficient to pay merely the wages of a given number of workers, in order to acquire their product legitimately; that they must be paid twice, thrice or ten times their wages, or an equivalent service rendered to each one of them.*" This analysis of

exploitation occurring **within** production meant that the workplace must be self-managed for as "*all labour must leave a surplus, all wages [must] be equal to product*" and "*[b]y virtue of the principle of collective force, workers are the equals and associates of their leaders.*" Thus, "*all workers must associate, inasmuch as collective force and division of labour exist everywhere, to however slight a degree*" because of "*the immorality, tyranny and theft suffered.*" Industrial democracy, in which "*all positions are elective, and the by-laws subject to the approval of the members,*" would ensure that "*the collective force, which is a product of the community, ceases to be a source of profit to a small number of managers*" and becomes "*the property of all the workers.*" [**Property is Theft!**, p. 554, p. 77, p. 584 and p. 586]

Proudhon had first expounded this analysis in **What is Property?** in 1840 and, as K. Steven Vincent notes, this was "*[o]one of the reasons Proudhon gave for rejecting 'property' [and] was to become an important motif of subsequent socialist thought.*" Thus "*collective endeavours produced an additional value*" which was "*unjustly appropriated by the **proprietaire.***" [**Pierre-Joseph Proudhon the Rise of French Republican Socialism** p. 64 and p. 65] Marx, it should be noted, concurred. Without mentioning Proudhon, he stressed how a capitalist buys the labour-power of 100 men and "*can set the 100 men to work. He pays them the value of 100 independent labour-powers, but does not pay them for the combined labour power of the 100.*" [**Capital**, Vol. 1, p. 451] Only co-operative workplaces can ensure that the benefits of co-operative labour are not monopolised by the few who happen to own, and so control, the means of production.

If this is not done, then it becomes a case of simply renaming "profits" to "wages" and saying that they are the result of the employers work rather than their ownership of capital. However, this is not the case as some part of the "wages" of the employer is derived purely from their owning capital (and is usury, charging to allow use) while, for the workers, it is unlikely to equal their product in the short run.

The logic is simple — which boss would employ a worker unless they expected to get more out of their labour than they pay in wages? And why does the capitalist get this reward? They own "capital" and, consequently, their "labour" partly involves excluding others from using it and ordering about those whom they do allow in — in exchange for keeping the product of their labour. Thus exploitation takes place within production and so a contract for wages made beforehand simply cannot be expected to anticipate the use-value extracted by the boss from the workers subjected to his authority. Thus wage labour and exploitation would go hand-in-hand — and so Most's horror at Tucker's support for it.

As best, it could be argued that such "wages" would be minimal as workers would be able to swap jobs to get higher wages and, possibly, set up co-operatives in competition. However, this amounts to saying that, in the long run, labour gets its full product and to say that is to admit in the short term that labour **is** exploited. Yet nowhere did Tucker argue that labour would get its full product **eventually** in a free society, rather he stressed that liberty would result in the end of exploitation. Nor should we be blind to the fact that a market economy is a dynamic one, making the long run unlikely to ever appear ("*in the long run we are all dead*" as

Keynes memorably put it). Combine this with the natural barriers to competition we indicated in section G.4 and we are left with problems of usury/exploitation in an individualist anarchist system.

The obvious solution to these problems is to be found in Proudhon, namely the use of co-operatives for any workplace which cannot be operated by an individual. This was the also the position of the Haymarket anarchists, with August Spies (for example) arguing that *"large factories and mines, and the machinery of exchange and transportation ... have become too vast for private control. Individuals can no longer monopolise them."* [contained in Albert Parsons, **Anarchism: Its Philosophy and Scientific Basis**, pp. 60-1] Proudhon denounced property as *"despotism"*, for Albert Parsons the *"wage system of labour is a despotism."* [**Op. Cit.**, p. 21]

> As Frank H. Brooks notes, *"producer and consumer co-operatives were a staple of American labour reform (and of Proudhonian anarchism)."* This was because they *"promised the full reward of labour to the producer, and commodities at cost to the consumer."* [**The Individualist Anarchists**, p. 110] This was the position of Voltairine de Cleyre (during her individualist phase) as well as her mentor Dyer Lum.

So, somewhat ironically given his love of Proudhon, it was, in fact, Most who was closer to the French anarchist's position on this issue than Tucker. Kropotkin echoed Proudhon's analysis when he noted that *"the only guarantee not to be robbed of the fruits of your labour is to possess the instruments of labour."* [**The Conquest of Bread**, p. 145] In other words, for a self-proclaimed follower of Proudhon, Tucker ignored the French anarchist's libertarian arguments against wage labour. The key difference between the communist-anarchists and Proudhon was on the desirability of making the product of labour communal or not (although both recognised the right of people to share as they desired). However, it must be stressed that Proudhon's analysis was not an alien one to the individualist anarchist tradition. Joshua King Ingalls, for example, presented a similar analysis to Proudhon on the issue of joint production as well as its solution in the form of co-operatives (see section G.1.3 for details) and Dyer Lum was a firm advocate of the abolition of wage labour. So integrating the insights of social anarchism on this issue with individualist anarchism would not be difficult and would build upon existing tendencies within it.

In summary, social anarchists argue that individualist anarchism does not solve the social question. If it did, then they would be individualists. They argue that in spite of Tucker's claims, workers would still be exploited in any form of individualist anarchism which retained significant amounts of wage labour as well as being a predominantly hierarchical, rather than libertarian, society. As we argue in the next section, this is why most anarchists consider individualist anarchism as being an inconsistent form of anarchism.

G.4.2 Why do social anarchists think individualism is inconsistent anarchism?

From our discussion of wage labour in the last section, some may consider that Tucker's support for wage labour would place him outside the ranks of anarchism. After all, this is one of the key reasons why most anarchists reject "anarcho"-capitalism as a form of anarchism. Surely, it could be argued, if Murray Rothbard is not an anarchist, then why is Tucker?

That is not the case and the reason is obvious — Tucker's support for wage labour is inconsistent with his ideas on "occupancy and use" while Rothbard's are in line with his capitalist property rights. Given the key place self-management holds in almost all anarchist thought, unsurprisingly we find Chomsky summarising the anarchist position as follows:

> *"A consistent anarchist must oppose private ownership of the means of production and the wage slavery which is a component of this system, as incompatible with the principle that labour must be freely undertaken and under the control of the producer ... A consistent anarchist must oppose not only alienated labour but also the stupefying specialisation of labour that takes place when the means for developing production [as Marx put it] 'mutilate the worker into a fragment of a human being...' "* [**Chomsky on Anarchism**, p. 123]

Thus the *"consistent anarchist, then, will be a socialist, but a socialist of a particular sort."* [**Op. Cit.**, p. 125] Which suggests that Tucker's position is one of inconsistent anarchism. While a socialist, he did not take his libertarian positions to their logical conclusions — the abolition of wage labour. There is, of course, a certain irony in this. In response to Johann Most calling his ideas *"Manchesterism"*, Tucker wrote *"what better can a man who professes Anarchism want than that? For the principle of Manchesterism is liberty, and consistent Manchesterism is consistent adherence to liberty. The only inconsistency of the Manchester men lies in their infidelity to liberty in some of its phases. And this infidelity to liberty in some of its phases is precisely the fatal inconsistency of the 'Freiheit' school ... Yes, genuine Anarchism is consistent Manchesterism, and Communistic or pseudo-Anarchism is inconsistent Manchesterism."* [**Liberty**, no. 123, p. 4]

In other words, if individualist anarchism is, as Tucker claimed, *"consistent Manchesterism"* then, argue social anarchists, individualist anarchism is "inconsistent" anarchism. This means that some of Tucker's arguments contradict some of his own fundamental principles, most obviously his indifference to wage labour. This, as argued, violates "occupancy and use", his opposition to exploitation and his anarchism as it is a form of hierarchy.

To see what we mean we must point out that certain individualist anarchists are not the only "inconsistent" ones that have existed. The most obvious example is Proudhon, whose sexism is well known, utterly disgraceful and is in direct contradiction to his other ideas and principles. While Proudhon attacked hierarchy in politics and economics, he fully supported patriarchy in the home. This support for a form of archy does not refute claims that Proudhon was an anarchist, it just means that certain of his ideas were inconsistent with his key principles. As one French anarcha-feminist critic of Proudhon put it in 1869: *"These so-called lovers of liberty, if they are unable to take part in the direction of the state, at least they will be able to have a little monarchy for their personal use, each in his own home ... Order in the family without hierarchy seems impossible to them — well then, what about in the state?"* [André Léo, quoted by Carolyn J. Eichner, *"Vive La Commune!' Feminism, Socialism, and Revolutionary Revival in the Aftermath of the 1871 Paris Commune,"*, pp. 68-98, **Journal of Women's History**, Vol. 15, No.2, p. 75] Rejecting monarchy and hierarchy on the state level and within the workplace while supporting it — in the form of rule by the father — on the family level was simply illogical and inconsistent. Subsequent anarchists (from Bakunin onwards) solved this obvious contradiction by consistently applying anarchist principles and opposing sexism and patriarchy. In other words, by critiquing Proudhon's sexism by means of the very principles he himself used to critique the state and capitalism.

Much the same applies to individualist anarchists. The key issue is that, given their own principles, individualist anarchism can easily become **consistent** anarchism. That is why it is a school of anarchism, unlike "anarcho"-capitalism. All that is required is to consistently apply "occupancy and use" to workplaces (as Proudhon advocated). By consistently applying this principle they can finally end exploitation along with hierarchy, so bringing all their ideas into line.

Tucker's position is also in direct opposition to Proudhon's arguments, which is somewhat ironic since Tucker stressed being inspired by and following the French anarchist and his ideas (Tucker referred to Proudhon as being both *"the father of the Anarchistic school of socialism"* as well as *"being the Anarchist par excellence"* [Tucker, **Instead of a Book**, p. 391]). Tucker is distinctly at odds with Proudhon who consistently opposed wage-labour and so, presumably, was also an advocate of *"pseudo-Anarchism"* alongside Kropotkin and Most.

For Proudhon, the worker has *"sold and surrendered his liberty"* to the proprietor, with the proprietor being *"a man, who, having absolute control of an instrument of production, claims the right to enjoy the product of the instrument without using it himself."* This leads to exploitation and if *"the labourer is proprietor of the value which he creates, it follows"* that *"all production being necessarily collective, the labourer is entitled to a share of the products and profits commensurate with his labour"* and that, *"all accumulated capital being social property, no one can be its exclusive proprietor."* With *"machinery and the workshop, divine right — that is, the principle of authority — makes its entrance into political economy. Capital ... Property ... are, in economic language, the various names of ... Power, Authority."* Thus, under capitalism, the workplace has a *"hierarchical organisation."* There are three alternatives, capitalism (*"that is, monopoly and what follows"*), state socialism (*"exploitation by the State"*) *"or else ... a solution based on equality, — in other words, the organisation of labour, which involves the negation of political economy and the end of property."* In short, *"all property becomes ... collective and undivided."* [**Property is Theft!**, p. 21,

p. 139, p. 114, pp. 117-8, p. 193, p. 202 and p. 137] Indeed, in 1849 he angrily rejected the assertion that he wanted *"individual ownership and non-organisation of the instruments of labour"*:

> *"I have never penned nor uttered any such thing: and have argued the opposite a hundred times over ... I deny all kinds of proprietary domain. I deny it, precisely because I believe in an order wherein the instruments of labour will cease to be appropriated and instead become shared."* [**Op. Cit.**, p. 499]

So *"under universal association, ownership of the land and of the instruments of labour is **social** ownership."* This was because wage-workers were *"subordinated, exploited,"* their *"permanent condition is one of obedience"* and so, therefore, a *"slave."* Capitalist companies *"plunder the bodies and souls of wage workers"* and they are *"an outrage upon human dignity and personality."* However, in a co-operative the situation changes and the worker is an *"associate"* and *"forms a part of the producing organisation"* and *"forms a part of the sovereign power, of which he was before but the subject."* Without association, people *"would remain related as subordinates and superiors, and there would ensue two industrial castes of masters and wage-workers, which is repugnant to a free and democratic society."* [**Op. Cit.**, p. 377, p. 583, p. 584 and p. 583]

This analysis lead Proudhon to call for co-operatives to end wage labour and it appears repeatedly in his work. Thus we find him arguing in 1851 that socialism is *"the elimination of misery, the abolition of capitalism and of wage-labour, the transformation of property, ... the effective and direct sovereignty of the workers, ... the substitution of the contractual regime for the legal regime."* [quoted by John Ehrenberg, **Proudhon and his Age**, p. 111] Fourteen years later, he argued the same, with the aim of his mutualist ideas being *"the complete emancipation of the workers ... the abolition of the wage worker."* [quoted by K. Steven Vincent, **Pierre-Joseph Proudhon and the Rise of French Republican Socialism** p. 222] Thus a key idea of Proudhon's politics is the abolition of wage labour: *"Industrial Democracy must follow Industrial Feudalism."* [**Property is Theft!**, p. 610]

(As an aside, it is deeply significant how different Proudhon's analysis of hierarchy and wage-labour is to Murray Rothbard's. For Rothbard, both *"hierarchy"* and *"wage-work"* were part of *"a whole slew of institutions necessary to the triumph of liberty"* (others included *"granting of funds by libertarian millionaires, and a libertarian political party"*). He strenuously objected to those *"indicting"* such institutions *"as non-libertarian or non-market"*. [**Konkin on Libertarian Strategy**] For Proudhon — as well as Bakunin, Kropotkin, and others — both wage-labour and hierarchy were anti-libertarian by their very nature. How could hier-archy be *"necessary"* for the triumph of an-archy? Logically, it makes no sense. An-**archy**, by definition, means no-archy rather than wholehearted support for a specific form of **archy**, namely hier-**archy**! At best, Rothbard was a "voluntary archist" not an anarchist.)

As Charles A. Dana put it (in a work published by Tucker and described by him as *"a really intelligent, forceful, and sympathetic exposition of mutual banking"*), *"[b]y introducing mutualism into exchanges and credit we introduce it everywhere, and labour will assume a new aspect and become truly democratic."* Labour *"must be reformed by means of association as well as banking" for "if labour be not organised, the labourers will be made to toil for others to receive the fruit thereof as heretofore." These co-operatives "to a great extent abolish the exploitation of the employed worker by the employing capitalist, and make the worker his own employer; but, in order to completely gain that end, the associations must be associated, united in one body for mutual aid." This is "the Syndicate of Production." [**Proudhon and His "Bank of the People"**, p. 45, p. 50 and p. 54] Tucker, however, asserted that Proudhon included the syndicate of production "to humour those of his associates who placed stress on these features. He did not consider them of any value." [**Op. Cit.**, pp. 51-2] However, he was simply incorrect. Industrial democracy was a key aspect of Proudhon's ideas, as was the creation of an "agro-industrial federation" based on these self-managed associations. This can be seen from Tucker's own comparison of Marx and Proudhon made on the formers death:

> "For Karl Marx, the 'egalitaire', we feel the profoundest respect; as for Karl Marx, the 'authoritaire', we must consider him an enemy… . Proudhon was years before Marx [in discussing the struggle of the classes and the privileges and monopolies of capital]… . The vital difference between Proudhon and Marx [was] to be found in their respective remedies which they proposed. Marx would nationalise the productive and distributive forces; Proudhon would individualise and associate them. Marx would make the labourers political masters; Proudhon would abolish political mastership entirely … Marx believed in compulsory majority rule; Proudhon believed in the voluntary principle. In short, Marx was an 'authoritaire'; Proudhon was a champion of Liberty." [**Liberty**, no. 35, p. 2]

Ironically, therefore, by Tucker placing so much stress in opposing capitalist **exploitation,** instead of capitalist **oppression,** he was actually closer to the "authoritaire" Marx than Proudhon and, like Marx, opened the door to various kinds of domination and restrictions on individual self-government within anarchism. Again we see a support for contract theory creating authoritarian, not libertarian, relationships between people. Simply put, the social relationships produced by wage labour share far too much in common with those created by the state **not** to be of concern to any genuine libertarian. Arguing that it is based on consent is as unconvincing as those who defend the state in similar terms.

Tucker himself pointed out that "the essence of government is control… He who attempts to control another is a governor, an aggressor, an invader." [**Instead of a Book**, p. 23] So when Tucker suggests that (non-exploitative, and so non-capitalist) wage labour could exist in individualist anarchy there is a distinct contradiction. Unlike wage labour under capitalism, workers would employ other workers and all would (in theory) receive the full product of their labour. Be that as it may, such relationships are not libertarian and so contradict Tucker's own theories on individual liberty (as Proudhon and Mill recognised with their own, similar, positions). Wage labour is based on the control of the worker by the employer; hence Tucker's contract theory can lead to a form of "voluntary" and "private" government within the workplace. This means that,

while outside of a contract an individual is free, within it he or she is governed. This violates Tucker's concept of "equality of liberty," since the boss has obviously more liberty than the worker during working hours.

Therefore, logically, individualist anarchism must follow Proudhon and support co-operatives and self-employment in order to ensure the maximum individual self-government and labour's "natural wage." So Tucker's comments about strikers and wage labour show a basic inconsistency in his basic ideas. This conclusion is not surprising. As Malatesta argued:

> "The individualists give the greatest importance to an abstract concept of freedom and fail to take into account, or dwell on the fact, that real, concrete freedom is the outcome of solidarity and voluntary co-operation … They certainly believe that to work in isolation is fruitless and that an individual, to ensure a living as a human being and to materially and morally enjoy all the benefits of civilisation, must either exploit — directly or indirectly — the labour of others … or associate with his [or her] fellows and share their pains and the joys of life. And since, being anarchists, they cannot allow the exploitation of one by another, they must necessarily agree that to be free and live as human beings they have to accept some degree and form of voluntary communism." [**The Anarchist Revolution**, p. 16]

Occupancy and use, therefore, implies the collective ownership of resources used by groups which, in turn, implies associative labour and self-management. In other words, "some degree and form of voluntary communism." Ultimately, as John P. Clark summarised, opposition to authority which is limited to just the state hardly makes much sense from a libertarian perspective:

> "Neither … is there any reason to consider such a position a very consistent or convincing form of anarchism … A view of anarchism which seeks to eliminate coercion and the state, but which overlooks other ways in which people dominate other people, is very incomplete and quite contradictory type of anarchism. The most thorough-going and perceptive anarchist theories have shown that all types of domination are interrelated, all are destructive, and all must be eliminated … Anarchism may begin as a revolt against political authority, but if followed to its logical conclusion it becomes an all-encompassing critique of the will to dominate and all its manifestations." [**Max Stirner's Egoism**, pp. 92-3]

Certain individualist anarchists were keenly aware of the fact that even free association need not be based on freedom for both parties. Take, for example, marriage. Marriage, correctly argued John Beverley Robinson, is based on "the promise to obey" and this results in "a very real subordination." As part of "the general progress toward freedom in all things," marriage will "become the union of those who are both equal and both free." [**Liberty**, no. 287, p. 2] Why should property associated subordination be any better than patriarchal subordination? Does the fact that one only lasts 8 or 12 hours rather than 24 hours a day really make one consistent with libertarian principles and the other not?

Thus Tucker's comments on wage labour indicates a distinct contradiction in his ideas. It violates his support for *"occupancy and use"* as well as his opposition to the state and usury. It could, of course, be argued that the contradiction is resolved because the worker consents to the authority of the boss by taking the job. However, it can be replied that, by this logic, the citizen consents to the authority of the state as a democratic state allows people to leave its borders and join another one — that the citizen does not leave indicates they consent to the state (this flows from Locke). When it came to the state, anarchists are well aware of the limited nature of this argument (as one individualist anarchist put it: *"As well say that the government of New York or even of the United States is voluntary, and, if you don't like New York Sunday laws, etc., you can secede and go to — South Carolina."* [A. H. Simpson, **The Individualist Anarchists**, p. 287]). In other words, consent of and by itself does not justify hierarchy for if it did, the current state system would be anarchistic. This indicates the weakness of contract theory as a means of guaranteeing liberty and its potential to generate, and justify, authoritarian social relationships rather than libertarian and liberty enhancing ones.

This explains anarchist opposition to wage labour, it undermines liberty and, as a result, allows exploitation to happen. Albert Parsons put it well. Under capitalism labour *"is a commodity and wages is the price paid for it. The owner of this commodity — of labour — sells it, that is himself, to the owner of capital in order to live ... The reward of the wage labourer's activity is not the product of his labour — far from it."* This implies exploitation and so class struggle as there is a *"irreconcilable conflict between wage labourers and capitalists, between those who buy labour or sell its products, and the wage worker who sells labour (himself) in order to live."* This is because the boss will seek to use their authority over the worker to make them produce more for the agreed wage. Given this, during a social revolution the workers *"first act will, of necessity, be the application of communistic principles. They will expropriate all wealth; they will take possession of all foundries, workshops, factories, mines, etc., for in no other way could they be able to continue to produce what they require on a basis of equality, and be, at the same time, independent of any authority."* [**Anarchism: Its Philosophy and Scientific Basis**, p. 99, p. 104 and p. 166] Hence Kropotkin's comment that *"anarchism ... refuses all hierarchical organisation and preaches free agreement."* [**Anarchism**, p. 137] To do otherwise is to contradict the basic ideas of anarchism.

Peter Kropotkin recognised the statist implications of some aspects of anarchist individualism which Tucker's strike example highlights. Tucker's anarchism, due to its uncritical support for contract theory, could result in a few people dominating economic life, because *"no force"* would result in the perpetuation of authority structures, with freedom simply becoming the *"right to full development"* of *"privileged minorities."* But, Kropotkin argued, *"as such monopolies cannot be maintained otherwise than under the protection of a monopolist legislation and an organised coercion by the State, the claims of these individualists necessarily end up in a return to the State idea and to that same coercion which they so fiercely attack themselves. Their position is thus the same as that of Spencer and of the so-called 'Manchester school' of economists, who also begin by a severe criticism of the State and end up in its full recognition in order to maintain the property monopolies, of which the State is the necessary stronghold."* [**Op. Cit.**, p. 162]

Such would be the possible (perhaps probable) result of the individualists' contract theory of freedom without a social background of communal self-management and ownership. As can be seen from capitalism, a society based on the abstract individualism associated with contract theory would, in practice, produce social relationships based on power and authority (and so force — which would be needed to back up that authority), **not** liberty. As we argued in section A.2.14, voluntarism is **not** enough in itself to preserve freedom. This result, as noted in section A.3, could **only** be avoided by workers' control, which is in fact the logical implication of Tucker's and other individualists' proposals. This is hardly a surprising implication, since as we've seen, artisan production was commonplace in 19th-century America and its benefits were extolled by many individualists. Without workers' control, individualist anarchism would soon become a form of capitalism and so statism — a highly unlikely intention of individualists like Tucker, who hated both.

Therefore, given the assumptions of individualist anarchism in both their economic and political aspects, it is forced along the path of co-operative, not wage, labour. In other words, individualist anarchism is a form of socialism as workers receive the full product of their labour (i.e. there is no non-labour income) and this, in turn, logically implies a society in which self-managed firms compete against each other on the free market, with workers selling the product of their labour and not the labour itself. As this unites workers with the means of production they use, it is **not** capitalism and instead a form of socialism based upon worker ownership and control of the places they work.

For individualist anarchists not to support co-operatives results in a contradiction, namely that the individualist anarchism which aims to secure the worker's *"natural wage"* cannot in fact do so, while dividing society into a class of order givers and order takers which violates individual self-government. It is this contradiction within Tucker's thought which the self-styled "anarcho"-capitalists take advantage of in order to maintain that individualist anarchism in fact implies capitalism (and so private-statism), not workers' control. In order to reach this implausible conclusion, a few individualist anarchist ideas are ripped from their social context and applied in a way that makes a mockery of them.

Given this analysis, it becomes clear why few social anarchists exclude individualist anarchism from the anarchist tradition while almost all do so for "anarcho"-capitalism. The reason is simple and lies in the analysis that any individualist anarchism which supports wage labour is **inconsistent** anarchism. It **can** easily be made **consistent** anarchism by applying its own principles consistently. In contrast, "anarcho"-capitalism rejects so many of the basic, underlying, principles of anarchism and has consistently followed the logical conclusions of such a rejection into private statism and support for hierarchical authority associated with private property that it cannot be made consistent with the ideals of anarchism. In contrast, given its **own** principles, individualist anarchism can easily become **consistent** anarchism. That is why it is a school of anarchism, unlike "anarcho"-capitalism. All that is required is to consistently apply "occupancy and use" to workplaces (as Proudhon advocated as did many individualist anarchists). By consistently applying this principle it finally ends exploitation along with hierarchy, so bringing all its ideals into line.

As Malatesta argued, "*anarchy, as understood by the anarchists and as only they can interpret it, is based on socialism. Indeed were it not for those schools of socialism which artificially divide the natural unity of the social question, and consider some aspects out of context … we could say straight out that anarchy is synonymous with socialism, for both stand for the abolition of the domination and exploitation of man by man, whether exercised at bayonet point or by a monopoly of the means of life.*" Without socialism, liberty is purely "*liberty … for the strong and the property owners to oppress and exploit the weak, those who have nothing … [so] lead[ing] to exploitation and domination, in other words, to authority … for freedom is not possible without equality, and real anarchy cannot exist without solidarity, without socialism.*" [**Anarchy**, p. 48 and p. 47]

G.5
Benjamin Tucker: Capitalist or Anarchist?

Benjamin Tucker, like all genuine anarchists, was against both the state and capitalism, against both oppression and exploitation. While not against the market and property he was firmly against capitalism as it was, in his eyes, a state-supported monopoly of social capital (tools, machinery, etc.) which allows owners to exploit their employees, i.e., to avoid paying workers the full value of their labour. He thought that the "*labouring classes are deprived of their earnings by usury in its three forms, interest, rent and profit.*" [quoted by James J. Martin, **Men Against the State**, p. 210f] Therefore "*Liberty will abolish interest; it will abolish profit; it will abolish monopolistic rent; it will abolish taxation; it will abolish the exploitation of labour; it will abolish all means whereby any labourer can be deprived of any of his product.*" [**The Individualist Anarchists**, p. 157]

This stance puts him squarely in the libertarian socialist tradition and, unsurprisingly, Tucker referred to himself many times as a socialist and considered his philosophy to be "*Anarchistic socialism.*" For Tucker, capitalist society was exploitative and stopped the full development of all and so had to be replaced:

> "*[This] society is fundamentally anti-social. The whole so-called social fabric rests on privilege and power, and is disordered and strained in every direction by the inequalities that necessarily result therefrom. The welfare of each, instead of contributing to that of all, as it naturally should and would, almost invariably detracts from that of all. Wealth is made by legal privilege a hook with which to filch from labour's pockets. Every man who gets rich thereby makes his neighbours poor. The better off one is, the worse the rest are … Labour's Deficit is precisely equal to the Capitalist's Efficit.*

> "*Now, Socialism wants to change all this. Socialism says … that no man shall be able to add to his riches except by labour; that is adding to his riches by his labour alone no man makes another man poorer; that on the contrary every man thus adding to his riches makes every other man richer; … that every increase in capital in the hands of the labourer tends, in the absence of legal monopoly, to put more products, better products, cheaper products, and a greater variety of products within the reach of every man who works; and that this fact means the physical, mental, and moral perfecting of mankind, and the realisation of human fraternity.*" [**Instead of a Book**, pp. 361-2]

It is true that he also sometimes railed against "socialism," but in those cases it is clear that he was referring to **state** socialism. Like many anarchists (including Proudhon, Bakunin and Kropotkin), he argued that there are two kinds of socialism based upon two different principles:

> "*The two principles referred to are Authority and Liberty, and the names of the two schools of Socialistic thought which fully and unreservedly represent one or the other of them are, respectively, State Socialism and Anarchism. Whoso knows what these two schools want and how they propose to get it understands the Socialistic movement. For, just as it has been said that there is no half-way house between Rome and Reason, so it may be said that there is no half-way house between State Socialism and Anarchism.*" [**The Anarchist Reader**, p. 150]

Like other socialists, Tucker argued that profits "*to a few mean robbery of others, — monopoly. Andrews and Warren, realising this, make individual sovereignty **and** the cost principle the essential conditions of a true civilisation.*" [**Liberty**, no. 94, p. 1] Like Proudhon, he argued that "*property, in the sense of individual possession, is liberty.*" [**Op. Cit.**, no. 122, p. 4] However, unlike state socialists and communist-anarchists, Tucker saw a key role for a market system under socialism. In this he followed Proudhon who also argued that competition was required to ensure that prices reflected the labour costs involved in producing it and so interest, rent and profit were opposed because they did not reflect actual costs but simply usury paid to the wealthy for being allowed to use part of their wealth, a part the rich could comfortably lend out to others as they were not using it. Once capitalism was abolished, the market would be able to reach its full promise and become a means of enriching all rather than the few:

> "*Liberty's aim — universal happiness — is that of all Socialists, in contrast with that of the Manchester men — luxury fed by misery. But its principle — individual sovereignty — is that of the Manchester men, in contrast with that of the Socialists — individual subordination. But individual sovereignty, **when logically carried out**, leads, not to luxury fed by misery, but to comfort for all industrious persons and death for all idle ones.*" [**Liberty**, no. 89, p. 1]

As other anarchists have also argued, likewise for Tucker — the state is the *"protector"* of the exploiter. *"Usury is the serpent gnawing at labour's vitals, and only liberty can detach and kill it. Give labourers their liberty and they will keep their wealth."* [**The Individualist Anarchists**, p. 89] From this it is clear that he considered laissez-faire capitalism to be opposed to genuine individual sovereignty. This was because it was based on the state interfering in the market by enforcing certain restrictions on competition in favour of the capitalist class and certain types of private property. Thus his opposition to the state reflected his opposition to capitalist property rights and the abolition of the state automatically meant their abolition as well.

Tucker spent considerable time making it clear that he was against capitalist private property rights, most notably in land and what was on it. He supported Proudhon's argument that *"property is theft,"* even translating many of Proudhon's works including the classic *"What is Property?"* where that phrase originated. Tucker advocated **possession** (or *"occupancy and use,"* to use his preferred expression for the concept) but not private property, believing that empty land, houses, and so on should be squatted by those who could use them, as labour (i.e. use) would be the only title to "property" (Tucker opposed all non-labour income as usury). For Tucker, the true *"Anarchistic doctrine"* was *"occupancy and use as the basis and limit of land ownership."* Supporting the current property rights regime meant *"departing from Anarchistic ground."* It was *"Archism"* and *"all Anarchists agree in viewing [it] as a denial of equal liberty"* and *"utterly inconsistent with the Anarchistic doctrine of occupancy and use as the limit of property in land."* [**Liberty**, no. 180, p. 4 and p. 6] He looked forward to the day when *"the Anarchistic view that occupancy and use should condition and limit landholding becomes the prevailing view."* [**Op. Cit.**, no. 162, p. 5]

This was because Tucker did not believe in a *"natural right"* to property nor did he approve of unlimited holdings of scarce goods and *"in the case of land, or of any other material the supply of which is so limited that all cannot hold it in unlimited quantities, Anarchism undertakes to protect no titles except such as are based on actual occupancy and use."* [**Instead of a Book**, p. 61] He clearly recognised that allowing "absolute" rights to private property in land would result in the liberty of non-owners being diminished and so *"I put the right of occupancy and use above the right of contract ... principally by my interest in the right of contract. Without such a preference the theory of occupancy and use is utterly untenable; without it ... it would be possible for an individual to acquire, and hold simultaneously, virtual titles to innumerable parcels of land, by the merest show of labour performed thereon. This would lead to "the virtual ownership of the entire world by a small fraction of its inhabitants"* which would result in *"the right of contract, if not destroyed absolutely, would surely be impaired in an intolerable degree."* [**Liberty**, no. 350, p. 4] Thus *"[i]t is true ... that Anarchism does not recognise the principle of human rights. But it recognises human equality as a necessity of stable society."* [**Instead of a Book**, p. 64]

So Tucker considered private property in land use (which he called the *"land monopoly"*) as one of the four great evils of capitalism. According to Tucker, *"the land monopoly ... consists in the enforcement by government of land titles which do not rest upon personal occupancy and cultivation ... the individual should no longer be protected by their fellows in anything but personal occupation and cultivation of land."* *"Rent"*, he argued, *"is due to the denial of liberty which takes the shape of the land monopoly, vesting titles to land in individuals and associations which do not use it, and thereby compelling the non-owning users to pay tribute to the non-using owners as a condition of admission to the competitive market."* the land *"should be free to all, and no one would control more than he [or she] used."* [**The Individualist Anarchists**, p. 85, p. 130 and p. 114] Ending this monopoly would, he thought, reduce the evils of capitalism and increase liberty (particularly in predominantly agricultural societies such as the America of his era). For those who own no property have no room for the soles of their feet unless they have the permission of those who do own property, hardly a situation that would increase, never mind protect, freedom for all. Significantly, Tucker extended this principle to what was on the land, and so Tucker would *"accord the actual occupant and user of land the right to that which is upon the land, who left it there when abandoning the land."* [**Liberty**, no. 350, p. 4] The freedom to squat empty land and buildings would, in the absence of a state to protect titles, further contribute to the elimination of rent:

> *"Ground rent exists only because the State stands by to collect it and to protect land titles rooted in force or fraud. Otherwise land would be free to all, and no one could control more than he used."* [quoted by James J. Martin, **Op. Cit.**, p. 210]

This would lead to *"the abolition of landlordism and the annihilation of rent."* [**Instead of a Book**, p. 300] Significantly, Tucker considered the **Irish Land League** (an organisation which used non-payment of rent to secure reforms against the British state) as *"the nearest approach, on a large scale, to perfect Anarchistic organisation that the world has yet seen. An immense number of local groups ... each group autonomous, each free ... each obeying its own judgement ... all co-ordinated and federated."* [**The Individualist Anarchists**, p. 263]

The other capitalist monopolies were based on credit, tariffs and patents and all were reflected in (and supported by) the law. As far as tariffs went, this was seen as a statist means of *"fostering production at high prices"* which the workers paid for. Its abolition *"would result in a great reduction in the prices of all articles taxed.* [**Op. Cit.**, p. 85 and p. 86] With capitalists in the protected industries being unable to reap high profits, they would be unable to accumulate capital to the same degree and so the market would also become more equal. As for patents, Tucker considered that there was *"no more justification for the claim of the discoverer of an idea to exclusive use of it than there would have been for a claim on the part of the man who first 'struck oil' to ownership of the entire oil region or petroleum product ... The central injustice of copyright and patent law is that it compels the race to pay an individual through a long term of years a monopoly price for knowledge that he has discovered today, although some other man or men might, and in many cases very probably would, have discovered it tomorrow."* [**Liberty**, no. 173, p. 4] The state, therefore, protects the inventors (or, these days, the company the inventors work for) *"against competition for a period long enough to enable them to extort from the people a reward enormously in excess of the labour* measure of their services — in other words, in giving certain people a right of property for a term of years in laws and facts of Nature, and the power to extract tribute from others for the use of this natural wealth, which should be open to all." [**The Individualist Anarchists**, p. 86]

However, the key monopoly was the credit monopoly. Tucker believed that bankers monopoly of the power to create credit and currency was the linchpin of capitalism. Although he thought that all forms of monopoly are detrimental to society, he maintained that the banking monopoly is the worst, since it is the root from which both the industrial-capitalist and landlordist monopolies grow and without which they would wither and die. For, if credit were not monopolised, its price (i.e. interest rates) would be much lower, which in turn would drastically lower the price of capital goods and buildings — expensive items that generally cannot be purchased without access to credit. This would mean that the people currently *"deterred from going into business by the ruinously high rates they must pay for capital with which to start and carry on business will find their difficulties removed"* (they would simply *"pay for the labour of running the banks"*). This *"facility of acquiring capital will give an unheard of impetus to business, and consequently create an unprecedented demand for labour — a demand which will always be in excess of the supply, directly to the contrary of the present condition of the labour market ... Labour will then be in a position to dictate its wages."* [**Op. Cit.**, p. 84 and p. 85]

Following Proudhon, Tucker argued that if any group of people could legally form a "mutual bank" and issue credit based on any form of collateral they saw fit to accept, the price of credit would fall to the labour cost of the paperwork involved in running the bank. He claimed that banking statistics show this cost to be less than one percent of principal, and hence, that a one-time service fee which covers this cost and no more is the only **non-usurious** charge a bank can make for extending credit. This charge should not be called "interest" since, as it represented the labour-cost in providing, it is non-exploitative. This would ensure that workers could gain free access to the means of production (and so, in effect, be the individualist equivalent of the communist-anarchist argument for socialisation).

Tucker believed that under mutual banking, capitalists' ability to extract surplus value from workers in return for the use of tools, machinery, etc. would be eliminated because workers would be able to obtain zero-interest credit and use it to buy their own instruments of production instead of "renting" them, as it were, from capitalists. *"Make capital free by organising credit on a mutual plan,"* stressed Tucker, *"and then these vacant lands will come into use ... operatives will be able to buy axes and rakes and hoes, and then they will be independent of their employers, and then the labour problem will solved."* [**Instead of a Book**, p. 321] Easy access to mutual credit would result in a huge increase in the purchase of capital goods, creating a high demand for labour, which in turn would greatly increase workers' bargaining power and thus raise their wages toward equivalence with the value their labour produces.

For Tucker, reforms had to be applied at the heart of the system and so he rejected the notion of setting up intentional communities based on anarchist principles in the countryside or in other countries. *"Government makes itself felt alike in city and in country,"* he

argued, *"capital has its usurious grip on the farm as surely as on the workshop, and the oppression and exactions of neither government nor capital can be avoided by migration. The State is the enemy, and the best means of fighting it can be found in communities already existing."* He stressed that *"I care nothing for any reform that cannot be effected right here in Boston among the every day people whom I meet in the streets."* [quoted by Martin, **Op. Cit.**, p. 249 and p. 248]

It should be noted that while his social and political vision remained mostly the same over his lifetime, Tucker's rationale for his system changed significantly. Originally, like the rest of the American individualist anarchist tradition he subscribed to a system of natural rights. Thus he advocated "occupancy and use" based on a person's right to have access to the means of life as well as its positive effects on individual liberty. However, under the influence of Max Stirner's book **The Ego and Its Own**, Tucker along with many of his comrades, became egoists (see next section for a discussion of Stirner). This resulted in Tucker arguing that while previously *"it was my habit to talk glibly of the right of man to land"* this was *"a bad habit, and I long ago sloughed it off."* Now a person's *"only right over the land is his might over it."* [**Instead of a Book**, p. 350] Contracts were seen as the means of securing the peaceful preservation of the ego's personality as it would be against a person's self-interest to aggress against others (backed-up, of course, by means of freely joined defence associations). It should be noted that the issue of egoism split the individualist anarchist movement and lead to its further decline.

He looked to alternative institutions such as co-operative banks and trade unions, combined with civil disobedience in the form of strikes, general strikes, tax and rent strikes and boycotts to bring anarchism closer. He was firm supporter of the labour movement and *"strikes, whenever and wherever inaugurated, deserve encouragement from all the friends of labour ... They show that people are beginning to know their rights, and knowing, dare to maintain them."* Echoing Bakunin's thoughts on the subject, Tucker maintained that strikes should be supported and encouraged because *"as an awakening agent, as an agitating force, the beneficent influence of a strike is immeasurable ... with our present economic system almost every strike is just. For what is justice in production and distribution? That labour, which creates all, shall have **all**."* [**Liberty**, no. 19, p. 7] While critical of certain aspects of trade unionism, Tucker was keen to stress that *"it is not to be denied for a moment that workingmen are obliged to unite and act together in order, not to successfully contend with, but to defend themselves at least to some extent from, the all-powerful possessors of natural wealth and capital."* [**Op. Cit.**, no. 158, p. 1]

Like the anarcho-syndicalists and many other social anarchists, Tucker considered Labour unions as a positive development, being a *"crude step in the direction of supplanting the State"* and involved a *"movement for self-government on the part of the people, the logical outcome of which is ultimate revolt against those usurping political conspiracies which manifest themselves in courts and legislatures. Just as the [Irish] Land League has become a formidable rival of the British State, so the amalgamated trades unions may yet become a power sufficiently strong to defy the legislatures and overthrow them."* Thus unions were *"a potent sign of emancipation."* Indeed, he called the rise of the unions *"trades-union socialism,"* saw in it a means of *"supplanting"* the state by *"an intelligent and self-governing socialism"* and indicated that *"imperfect as they are, they are the beginnings of a revolt against the authority of the political State. They promise the coming substitution of industrial socialism for usurping legislative mobism."* [**The Individualist Anarchists**, pp. 283-284] Hence we see the co-operative nature of the voluntary organisations supported by Tucker and a vision of socialism being based on self-governing associations of working people.

In this way working people would reform capitalism away by non-violent social protest combined with an increase in workers' bargaining power by alternative voluntary institutions and free credit. Exploitation would be eliminated and workers would gain economic liberty. His ideal society would be classless, with *"each man reaping the fruit of his labour and no man able to live in idleness on an income from capital"* and society *"would become a great hive of Anarchistic workers, prosperous and free individuals."* While, like all anarchists, he rejected *"absolute equality"* he did envision an egalitarian society whose small differences in wealth were rooted in labour, not property, and so liberty, while abolishing exploitation, would *"not abolish the limited inequality between one labourer's product and another's ... Liberty will ultimately make all men rich; it will not make all men equally rich."* [**The Individualist Anarchists**, p. 276, p. 156 and p. 157] He firmly believed that the *"most perfect Socialism is possible only on the condition of the most perfect individualism."* [quoted by Peter Marshall, **Demanding the Impossible**, p. 390]

As we noted in section G.1.3, there is one apparent area of disagreement between Tucker and most other socialists, namely the issue of wage labour. For almost all anarchists the employer/employee social relationship does not fit in well with Tucker's statement that *"if the individual has the right to govern himself, all external government is tyranny."* [**The Individualist Anarchists**, p. 86] However, even here the differences are not impossible to overcome. It is important to note that because of Tucker's proposal to increase the bargaining power of workers through access to mutual credit, his individualist anarchism is not only compatible with workers' control but would in fact **promote** it (as well as logically requiring it — see section G.4.1).

For if access to mutual credit were to increase the bargaining power of workers to the extent that Tucker claimed it would, they would then be able to: (1) demand and get workplace democracy; and (2) pool their credit to buy and own companies collectively. This would eliminate the top-down structure of the firm and the ability of owners to pay themselves unfairly large salaries as well as reducing capitalist profits to zero by ensuring that workers received the full value of their labour. Tucker himself pointed this out when he argued that Proudhon (like himself) *"would individualise and associate"* workplaces by mutualism, which would *"place the means of production within the reach of all."* [quoted by Martin, **Op. Cit.**, p. 228] Proudhon used the word *"associate"* to denote co-operative (i.e. directly democratic) workplaces (and given Proudhon's comments — quoted in section G.4.2 — on capitalist firms we can dismiss any attempt to suggest that the term *"individualise"* indicates support for capitalist rather than artisan/peasant production, which is the classic example of individualised

production). For as Proudhon recognised, only a system without wage slavery (and so exploitation) would ensure the goal of all anarchists: *"the greatest amount of liberty compatible with equality of liberty."* [Tucker, **Instead of a Book**, p. 131]

Thus the logical consequence of Tucker's proposals would be a system equivalent in most important respects to the kind of system advocated by other left libertarians. In terms of aspirations, Tucker's ideas reflected those of social anarchists — a form of socialism rooted in individual liberty. His fire was directed against the same targets, exploitation and oppression and so state and capital. He aimed for a society without inequalities of wealth where it would be impossible to exploit another's labour and where free access to the means of life were secured by mutual banking and "occupancy and use" applied to land and what was on it. He considered laissez-faire capitalism to be a system of state-supported privilege rather than as an ideal to be aimed for. He argued extensively that getting rid of the state would mean getting rid of capitalist property rights and so, like other anarchists, he did not artificially divide economic and political issues. In other words, like social anarchists, he was against the state because it protected specific kinds of private property, kinds which allowed its owners to extract tribute from labour.

In summary, then, Tucker *"remained a left rather than a right-wing libertarian."* [Marshall, **Op. Cit.**, p. 391] When he called himself a socialist he knew well what it meant and systematically fought those (usually, as today, Marxists and capitalists) who sought to equate it with state ownership. John Quail, in his history of British Anarchism, puts his finger on the contextual implications and limitations of Tucker's ideas when he wrote:

> *"Tucker was a Proudhonist and thus fundamentally committed to a society based on small proprietorship. In the American context, however, where the small landowner was often locked in battle with large capitalist interests, this did not represent the reactionary position it often did later where it could easily degenerate into an 'Anarchism for small business-men.' Tucker had a keen sense of the right of the oppressed to struggle against oppression."* [**The Slow Burning Fuse**, p. 19]

As we stressed in section G.1.4, many of Tucker's arguments can only be fully understood in the context of the society in which he developed them, namely the transformation of America from a pre-capitalist into a capitalist one by means of state intervention (the process of *"primitive accumulation"* to use Marx's phrase — see section F.8.5). At that time, it was possible to argue that access to credit would allow workers to set-up business and undermine big business. However, eventually Tucker had come to argue that this possibility had effectively ended and even the freest market would not be able to break-up the economic power of corporations and trusts (see section G.1.1).

In this, ironically, Tucker came to the same conclusion as his old enemy Johann Most had done three decades previously. In the 1880s, Tucker had argued that wage labour would be non-exploitative under individualist anarchy. This was part of the reason why Most had excommunicated Tucker from anarchism, for he thought that Tucker's system could not, by definition, end exploitation due to its tolerance of wage labour, an argument Tucker disputed but did not disprove (see section G.4.1 for more discussion on this issue). In 1888 Tucker had speculated that *"the question whether large concentrations of capital for production on the large scale confronts us with the disagreeable alternative of either abolishing private property or continuing to hold labour under the capitalistic yoke."* [**Liberty**, no. 122, p. 4] By 1911, he had come to the conclusion that the latter had come to pass and considered revolutionary or political action as the only means of breaking up such concentrations of wealth (although he was against individualist anarchists participating in either strategy). [Martin, **Op. Cit.**, pp. 273-4] In other words, Tucker recognised that economic power existed and, as a consequence, free markets were not enough to secure free people in conditions of economic inequality.

There are, of course, many differences between the anarchism of, say, Bakunin and Kropotkin and that of Tucker. Tucker's system, for example, does retain some features usually associated with capitalism, such as competition between firms in a free market. However, the fundamental socialist objection to capitalism is not that it involves markets or "private property" but that it results in exploitation. Most socialists oppose private property and markets because they result in exploitation and have other negative consequences rather than an opposition to them as such. Tucker's system was intended to eliminate exploitation and involves a radical change in property rights, which is why he called himself a socialist and why most other anarchists concurred. This is why we find Kropotkin discussing Tucker in his general accounts of anarchism, accounts which note that the anarchists *"constitute the left wing"* of the socialists and which make no comment that Tucker's ideas were any different in this respect. [**Anarchism**, p. 285] A position, needless to say, Tucker also held as he considered his ideas as part of the wider socialist movement.

So while it is true that Tucker placed "property" and markets at the heart of his vision of anarchy, this does not make him a supporter of capitalism (see sections G.1.1 and G.1.2). Unlike supporters of capitalism, the individualist anarchists identified "property" with simple "possession," or *"occupancy and use"* and considered profit, rent and interest as exploitation. Indeed, Tucker explicitly stated that *"all property rests on a labour title, and no other property do I favour."* [**Instead of a Book**, p. 400] Because of their critique of capitalist property rights and their explicit opposition to usury (profits, rent and interest) individualist anarchists like Tucker could and did consider themselves as part of the wider socialist movement, the libertarian wing as opposed to the statist/Marxist wing.

To some extent, Stirner's work **The Ego and Its Own** is like a Rorschach test. Depending on the reader's psychology, he or she can interpret it in drastically different ways. Hence, a few have tried to use Stirner's ideas to defend capitalism while others have used them to argue for anarcho-syndicalism. For example, many in the anarchist movement in Glasgow, Scotland, took Stirner's *"Union of Egoists"* literally as the basis for their anarcho-syndicalist organising in the 1940s and beyond. Similarly, we discover the noted anarchist historian Max Nettlau stating that *"[o]n reading Stirner, I maintain that he cannot be interpreted except in a socialist sense."* [**A Short History of Anarchism**, p. 55] In this section of the FAQ, we will indicate why, in our view, the latter, syndicalistic, interpretation of egoism is far more appropriate than the capitalistic one.

It should be noted, before continuing, that Stirner's work has had a bigger impact on individualist anarchism than social anarchism. Benjamin Tucker and many of his comrades embraced egoism when they became aware of **The Ego and Its Own** (a development which provoked a split in individualist circles which, undoubtedly, contributed to its decline). However, his influence was not limited to individualist anarchism. As John P. Clark notes, Stirner *"has also been seen as a significant figure by figures who are more in the mainstream of the anarchist tradition. Emma Goldman, for example, combines an acceptance of many of the principles of anarcho-syndicalism and anarcho-communism with a strong emphasis on individuality and personal uniqueness. The inspiration for this latter part of her outlook comes from thinkers like ... Stirner. Herbert Read has commented on the value of Stirner's defence of individuality."* [**Max Stirner's Egoism**, p. 90] Daniel Guérin's classic introduction to anarchism gives significant space to the German egoist, arguing he *"rehabilitated the individual at a time when the philosophical field was dominated by Hegelian anti-individualism and most reformers in the social field had been led by the misdeeds of bourgeois egotism to stress its opposite"* and pointed to *"the boldness and scope of his thought."* [**Anarchism**, p. 27] From meeting anarchists in Glasgow during the Second World War, long-time anarchist activist and artist Donald Rooum likewise combined Stirner and anarcho-communism. In America, the short-lived Situationist influenced group *"For Ourselves"* produced the inspired **The Right to Be Greedy: Theses on the Practical Necessity of Demanding Everything**, a fusion of Marx and Stirner which proclaimed a *"communist egoism"* based on the awareness that greed *"in its fullest sense is the **only possible** basis of communist society."*

It is not hard to see why so many people are influenced by Stirner's work. It is a classic, full of ideas and a sense of fun that is lacking in many political writers. For many, it is only known through the criticism Marx and Engels subjected it too in their book **The German Ideology**. As with their later attacks on Proudhon and Bakunin, the two Germans did not accurately reflect the ideas they were attacking and, in the case of Stirner, they made it their task to make them appear ridiculous and preposterous. That they took so much time and energy to do so suggests that Stirner's work is far more important and difficult to refute than their notoriously misleading diatribe suggests. That in itself should prompt interest in his work.

As will become clear from our discussion, social anarchists have much to gain from understanding Stirner's ideas and applying what is useful in them. While some may object to our attempt to place egoism and communism together, pointing out that Stirner rejected "communism". Quite! Stirner did not subscribe to libertarian communism, because it did not exist when he was writing and so he was directing his critique against the various forms of **state** communism which did. Moreover, this does not mean that anarcho-communists and others may not find his work of use to them. And Stirner would have approved, for nothing could be more foreign to his ideas than to limit what an individual considers to be in their best interest. Unlike the narrow and self-defeating "egoism" of, say, Ayn Rand, Stirner did not prescribe what was and was not in a person's self-interest. He did not say you should act in certain ways because he preferred it, he did not redefine selfishness to allow most of bourgeois morality to remain intact. Rather he urged the individual to think for themselves and seek their own path. Not for Stirner the grim "egoism" of "selfishly" living a life determined by some guru and which only that authority figure would approve of. True egoism is not parroting what Stirner wrote and agreeing with everything he expounded. Nothing could be more foreign to Stirner's work than to invent "Stirnerism." As Donald Rooum put it:

> "I am happy to be called a Stirnerite anarchist, provided 'Stirnerite' means one who agrees with Stirner's general drift, not one who agrees with Stirner's every word. Please judge my arguments on their merits, not on the merits of Stirner's arguments, and not by the test of whether I conform to Stirner." ["Anarchism and Selfishness", pp. 251-9, **The Raven**, no. 3, p. 259fn]

With that in mind, we will summarise Stirner's main arguments and indicate why social anarchists have been, and should be, interested in his ideas. Saying that, John P. Clark presents a sympathetic and useful social anarchist critique of his work in **Max Stirner's Egoism**. Unless otherwise indicated all quotes are from Stirner's **The Ego and Its Own**.

So what is Stirner all about? Simply put, he is an Egoist, which means that he considers self-interest to be the root cause of an individual's every action, even when he or she is apparently doing "altruistic" actions. Thus: *"I am everything to myself and I do everything **on my account**."* Even love is an example of selfishness, *"because love makes me happy, I love because loving is natural to me, because it pleases me."* He urges others to follow him and *"take courage now to really make **yourselves** the central point and the main thing altogether."* As for other people, he sees them purely as a means for self-enjoyment, a self-enjoyment which is mutual: *"For me you are nothing but my food, even as I am fed upon and turned to use by you. We have only one relation to each other, that of **usableness**, of utility, of use."* [p. 162, p. 291 and pp. 296-7]

For Stirner, all individuals are unique (*"My flesh is not their flesh, my mind is not their mind,"*) and should reject any attempts to restrict or deny their uniqueness: *"To be looked upon as a mere **part**, part of society, the individual cannot bear — because he is **more**; his uniqueness puts from it this limited conception."* Individuals, in order to maximise their uniqueness, must become aware of the **real** reasons for their actions. In other words they must become conscious, not unconscious, egoists. An unconscious, or involuntary, egoist is one *"who is always looking after his own and yet does not count himself as the highest being, who serves only himself and at the same time always thinks he is serving a higher being, who knows nothing higher than himself and yet is infatuated about something higher."* [p. 138, p. 265 and p. 36] In contrast, egoists are aware that they act purely out of self-interest, and if they support a "higher being," it is not because it is a noble thought but because it will benefit them.

Stirner himself, however, has no truck with "higher beings." Indeed, with the aim of concerning himself purely with his own interests, he attacks all "higher beings," regarding them as a variety of what he calls *"spooks,"* or ideas to which individuals sacrifice themselves and by which they are dominated. First amongst these is the abstraction *"Man"*, into which all unique individuals are submerged and lost. As he put it, *"liberalism is a religion because it separates my essence from me and sets it above me, because it exalts 'Man' to the same extent as any other religion does to God … it sets me beneath Man."* Indeed, he *"who is infatuated with **Man** leaves persons out of account so far as that infatuation extends, and floats in an ideal, sacred interest. **Man**, you see, is not a person, but an ideal, a spook."* [p. 176 and p.79] Among the many *"spooks"* Stirner attacks are such notable aspects of capitalist life as private property, the division of labour, the state, religion, and (at times) society itself. We will discuss Stirner's critique of capitalism before moving onto his vision of an egoist society and how it relates to social anarchism.

For the egoist, private property is a spook which *"lives by the grace of **law**"* and it *"becomes 'mine' only by effect of the law".* In other words, private property exists purely *"through the **protection of the State**, through the State's grace."* Recognising its need for state protection, Stirner is also aware that *"[i]t need not make any difference to the 'good citizens' who protects them and their principles, whether an absolute King or a constitutional one, a republic, if only they are protected. And what is their principle, whose protector they always 'love'? Not that of labour"*, rather it is *"**interest-bearing possession** … **labouring capital**, therefore … labour certainly, yet little or none at all of one's own, but labour of capital and of the — subject labourers."* [p. 251, p. 114, p. 113 and p. 114]

As can be seen from capitalist support for fascism, Stirner was correct — as long as a regime supports capitalist interests, the 'good citizens' (including many on the so-called "libertarian" right) will support it. Stirner sees that not only does private property require state protection, it also leads to exploitation and oppression. As noted in section D.10, like subsequent anarchists like Kropotkin, Stirner attacked the division of labour resulting from private property for its deadening effects on the ego and individuality of the worker:

*"When everyone is to cultivate himself into man, condemning a man to **machine-like labour** amounts to the same thing as slavery ... Every labour is to have the intent that the man be satisfied. Therefore he must become a **master** in it too, be able to perform it as a totality. He who in a pin-factory only puts on heads, only draws the wire, works, as it were mechanically, like a machine; he remains half-trained, does not become a master: his labour cannot **satisfy** him, it can only **fatigue** him. His labour is nothing by itself, has no object **in itself,** is nothing complete in itself; he labours only into another's hands, and is **used** (exploited) by this other."* [p. 121]

Stirner had nothing but contempt for those who defended property in terms of "natural rights" and opposed theft and taxation with a passion because it violates said rights. *"Rightful, or legitimate property of another,"* he stated, *"will be only that which **you** are content to recognise as such. If your content ceases, then this property has lost legitimacy for you, and you will laugh at absolute right to it."* After all, *"what well-founded objection could be made against theft"* [p. 278 and p. 251] He was well aware that inequality was only possible as long as the masses were convinced of the sacredness of property. In this way, the majority ends up without property:

*"Property in the civic sense means **sacred** property, such that I must **respect** your property ... Be it ever so little, if one only has somewhat of his own - to wit, a **respected** property: The more such owners ... the more 'free people and good patriots' has the State."*

*"Political liberalism, like everything religious, counts on **respect**, humaneness, the virtues of love ... For in practice people respect nothing, and everyday the small possessions are bought up again by greater proprietors, and the 'free people' change into day labourers."* [p. 248]

Thus free competition *"is not 'free,' because I lack the **things** for competition."* Due to this basic inequality of wealth (of "things"), *"[u]nder the **regime** of the commonality the labourers always fall into the hands of the possessors ... of the capitalists, therefore. The labourer cannot **realise** on his labour to the extent of the value that it has for the customer."* [p. 262 and p. 115] In other words, the working class is exploited by the capitalists and landlords.

Moreover, it is the exploitation of labour which is the basis of the state, for the state *"rests on the **slavery of labour**. If **labour becomes free**, the State is lost."* Without surplus value to feed off, a state could not exist. For Stirner, the state is the greatest threat to his individuality: *"**I am free in no State**."* This is because the state claims to be sovereign over a given area, while, for Stirner, only the ego can be sovereign over itself and that which it uses (its *"property"*): *"I am my **own** only when I am master of myself."* Thus the state *"is not thinkable without lordship and servitude (subjection); for the State must will to be the lord of all that it embraces."* Stirner also warned against the illusion in thinking that political liberty means that the state need not be a cause of concern

for *"[p]olitical liberty means that the **polis**, the State, is free; ... not, therefore, that I am free of the State... It does not mean **my** liberty, but the liberty of a power that rules and subjugates me; it means that one of my **despots** ... is free."* [p. 116, p. 226, p. 169, p. 195 and p. 107]

Therefore Stirner urges insurrection against all forms of authority and **dis**-respect for property. For *"[i]f man reaches the point of losing respect for property, everyone will have property, as all slaves become free men as soon as they no longer respect the master as master."* And in order for labour to become free, all must have *"property."* *"The poor become free and proprietors only when they **rise.**"* Thus, *"[i]f we want no longer to leave the land to the landed proprietors, but to appropriate it to ourselves, we unite ourselves to this end, form a union, a **société**, that makes **itself** proprietor ... we can drive them out of many another property yet, in order to make it **our** property, the property of the — **conquerors**."* Thus property *"deserves the attacks of the Communists and Proudhon: it is untenable, because the civic proprietor is in truth nothing but a propertyless man, one who is everywhere **shut out**. Instead of owning the world, as he might, he does not own even the paltry point on which he turns around."* [p. 258, p. 260, p. 249 and pp. 248-9]

Stirner recognises the importance of self-liberation and the way that authority often exists purely through its acceptance by the governed. As he argues, *"no thing is sacred of itself, but my **declaring it sacred,** by my declaration, my judgement, my bending the knee; in short, by my conscience."* It is from this worship of what society deems *"sacred"* that individuals must liberate themselves in order to discover their true selves. And, significantly, part of this process of liberation involves the destruction of **hierarchy.** For Stirner, *"Hierarchy is domination of thoughts, domination of mind!,"* and this means that we are *"kept down by those who are supported by thoughts."* [p. 72 and p. 74] That is, by our own willingness to not question authority and the sources of that authority, such as private property and the state:

*"Proudhon calls property 'robbery' (**le vol**) But alien property — and he is talking of this alone — is not less existent by renunciation, cession, and humility; it is a **present**. Who so sentimentally call for compassion as a poor victim of robbery, when one is just a foolish, cowardly giver of presents? Why here again put the fault on others as if they were robbing us, while we ourselves do bear the fault in leaving the others unrobbed? The poor are to blame for there being rich men."* [p. 315]

For those, like modern-day "libertarian" capitalists, who regard "profit" as the key to "selfishness," Stirner has nothing but contempt. Because "greed" is just one part of the ego, and to spend one's life pursuing only that part is to deny all other parts. Stirner called such pursuit *"self-sacrificing,"* or a *"one-sided, unopened, narrow egoism,"* which leads to the ego being possessed by one aspect of itself. For *"he who ventures everything else for **one thing,** one object, one will, one passion ... is ruled by a passion to which he brings the rest as sacrifices."* [p. 76]

For the true egoist, capitalists are *"self-sacrificing"* in this sense, because they are driven only by profit. In the end, their behaviour is just another form of self-denial, as the worship of money leads them to slight other aspects of themselves such as empathy and critical thought (the bank balance becomes the rule book). A society based on such "egoism" ends up undermining the egos which inhabit it, deadening one's own and other people's individuality and so reducing the vast potential "utility" of others to oneself. In addition, the drive for profit is not even based on self-interest, it is forced upon the individual by the workings of the market (an alien authority) and results in labour "claim[ing] all our time and toil," leaving no time for the individual "to take comfort in himself as the unique." [pp. 268-9]

Stirner also turns his analysis to "socialism" and "communism," and his critique is as powerful as the one he directs against capitalism. This attack, for some, gives his work an appearance of being pro-capitalist, while, as indicated above, it is not. Stirner did attack socialism, but he (rightly) attacked **state** socialism, not libertarian socialism, which did not really exist at that time (the only well known anarchist work at the time was Proudhon's **What is Property?**, published in 1840 and this work obviously could not fully reflect the developments within anarchism that were to come). He also indicated why moralistic (or altruistic) socialism is doomed to failure, and laid the foundations of the theory that socialism will work only on the basis of egoism (communist-egoism, as it is sometimes called). Stirner correctly pointed out that much of what is called socialism was nothing but warmed up liberalism, and as such ignores the individual: "Whom does the liberal look upon as his equal? Man! …, In other words, he sees in you, not **you**, but the **species**." A socialism that ignores the individual consigns itself to being state capitalism, nothing more. "Socialists" of this school forget that "society" is made up of individuals and that it is individuals who work, think, love, play and enjoy themselves. Thus: "That society is no ego at all, which could give, bestow, or grant, but an instrument or means, from which we may derive benefit … of this the socialists do not think, because they — as liberals — are imprisoned in the religious principle and zealously aspire after — a sacred society, such as the State was hitherto." [p. 123]

Of course, for the egoist libertarian communism can be just as much an option as any other socio-political regime. As Stirner stressed, egoism "is not hostile to the tenderest of cordiality … nor of socialism: in short, it is not inimical to any interest: it excludes no interest. It simply runs counter to un-interest and to the uninteresting: it is not against love but against sacred love … not against socialists, but against the sacred socialists." [**No Gods, No Masters**, vol. 1, p. 23] After all, if it aids the individual then Stirner had no more problems with libertarian communism that, say, rulers or exploitation. Yet this position does not imply that egoism tolerates the latter. Stirner's argument is, of course, that those who are subject to either have an interest in ending both and should unite with those in the same position to end it rather than appealing to the good will of those in power. As such, it goes without saying that those who find in egoism fascistic tendencies are fundamentally wrong. Fascism, like any class system, aims for the elite to rule and provides various spooks for the masses to ensure this (the nation, tradition, property, and so on). Stirner, on the other hand, urges an universal egoism rather than one limited to just a few. In other words, he would wish those subjected to fascistic domination to reject such spooks and to unite

and rise against those oppressing them:

> "Well, who says that every one can do everything? What are you there for, pray, you who do not need to put up with everything? Defend yourself, and no one will do anything to you! He who would break your will has to do with you, and is your **enemy**. Deal with him as such. If there stand behind you for your protection some millions more, then you are an imposing power and will have an easy victory." [p. 197]

That Stirner's desire for individual autonomy becomes transferred into support for rulership for the few and subjection for the many by many of his critics simply reflects the fact we are conditioned by class society to accept such rule as normal — and hope that our masters will be kind and subscribe to the same spooks they inflict on their subjects. It is true, of course, that a narrow "egoism" would accept and seek such relationships of domination but such a perspective is not Stirner's. This can be seen from how Stirner's egoist vision could fit with social anarchist ideas.

The key to understanding the connection lies in Stirner's idea of the "union of egoists," his proposed alternative mode of organising society. Stirner believed that as more and more people become egoists, conflict in society will decrease as each individual recognises the uniqueness of others, thus ensuring a suitable environment within which they can co-operate (or find "truces" in the "war of all against all"). These "truces" Stirner termed **"Unions of Egoists."** They are the means by which egoists could, firstly, "annihilate" the state, and secondly, destroy its creature, private property, since they would "multiply the individual's means and secure his assailed property." [p. 258]

The unions Stirner desires would be based on free agreement, being spontaneous and voluntary associations drawn together out of the mutual interests of those involved, who would "care best for their welfare if they **unite** with others." [p. 309] The unions, unlike the state, exist to ensure what Stirner calls "intercourse," or "union" between individuals. To better understand the nature of these associations, which will replace the state, Stirner lists the relationships between friends, lovers, and children at play as examples. [**No Gods, No Masters**, vol. 1, p. 25] These illustrate the kinds of relationships that maximise an individual's self-enjoyment, pleasure, freedom, and individuality, as well as ensuring that those involved sacrifice nothing while belonging to them. Such associations are based on mutuality and a free and spontaneous co-operation between equals. As Stirner puts it, "intercourse is mutuality, it is the action, the **commercium**, of individuals." [p. 218] Its aim is "pleasure" and "self-enjoyment." Thus Stirner sought a broad egoism, one which appreciated others and their uniqueness, and so criticised the narrow egoism of people who forgot the wealth others are:

> "But that would be a man who does not know and cannot appreciate any of the delights emanating from an interest taken in others, from the consideration shown to others. That would be a man bereft of innumerable pleasures, a wretched character … would he not be a wretched egoist, rather than a genuine Egoist? … The person who loves a

human being is, by virtue of that love, a wealthier man that someone else who loves no one." [**No Gods, No Masters**, vol. 1, p. 23]

In order to ensure that those involved do not sacrifice any of their uniqueness and freedom, the contracting parties have to have roughly the same bargaining power and the association created must be based on self-management (i.e. equality of power). Only under self-management can all participate in the affairs of the union and express their individuality. Otherwise, we have to assume that some of the egoists involved will stop being egoists and will allow themselves to be dominated by another, which is unlikely. As Stirner himself argued:

"But is an association, wherein most members allow themselves to be lulled as regards their most natural and most obvious interests, actually an Egoist's association? Can they really be 'Egoists' who have banded together when one is a slave or a serf of the other?...

"Societies wherein the needs of some are satisfied at the expense of the rest, where, say, some may satisfy their need for rest thanks to the fact that the rest must work to the point of exhaustion, and can lead a life of ease because others live in misery and perish of hunger, or indeed who live a life of dissipation because others are foolish enough to live in indigence, etc., such societies ... [are] more of a religious society, a communion held as sacrosanct by right, by law and by all the pomp and circumstance of the courts." [**Op. Cit.**, p. 24]

Therefore, egoism's revolt against all hierarchies that restrict the ego logically leads to the end of authoritarian social relationships, particularly those associated with private property and the state. Given that capitalism is marked by extensive differences in bargaining power outside its "associations" (i.e. firms) and power within these "associations" (i.e. the worker/boss hierarchy), from an egoist point of view it is in the self-interest of those subjected to such relationships to get rid of them and replace them with unions based on mutuality, free association, and self-management. Ultimately, Stirner stresses that it is in the workers' **self-interest** to free themselves from both state and capitalist oppression. Sounding like an anarcho-syndicalist, Stirner recognised the potential for strike action as a means of self-liberation:

"The labourers have the most enormous power in their hands, and, if they once become thoroughly conscious of it and used it, nothing could withstand them; they would only have to stop labour, regard the product of labour as theirs, and enjoy it. This is the sense of the labour disturbances which show themselves here and there." [p. 116]

Given the holistic and egalitarian nature of the union of egoists, it can be seen that it shares little with the so-called free agreements of capitalism (in particular wage labour). The hierarchical structure of capitalist firms hardly produces associations in which the individual's experiences can be compared to those involved in friendship or play, nor do they involve equality. An essential aspect

of the *"union of egoists"* for Stirner was such groups should be "owned" by their members, not the members by the group. That points to a **libertarian** form of organisation within these "unions" (i.e. one based on equality and participation), **not** a hierarchical one. If you have no say in how a group functions (as in wage slavery, where workers have the "option" of "love it or leave it") then you can hardly be said to own it, can you? Indeed, Stirner argues, for *"[o]nly in the union can you assert yourself as unique, because the union does not possess you, but you possess it or make it of use to you."* [p. 312]

Thus, Stirner's *"union of egoists"* cannot be compared to the employer-employee contract as the employees cannot be said to "own" the organisation resulting from the contract (nor do they own themselves during work time, having sold their labour/liberty to the boss in return for wages — see section B.4). Only within a participatory association can you *"assert"* yourself freely and subject your maxims, and association, to your *"ongoing criticism"* — in capitalist contracts you can do both only with your bosses' permission.

And by the same token, capitalist contracts do not involve "leaving each other alone" (a la "anarcho"-capitalism). No boss will "leave alone" the workers in his factory, nor will a landowner "leave alone" a squatter on land he owns but does not use. Stirner rejects the narrow concept of "property" as private property and recognises the **social** nature of "property," whose use often affects far more people than those who claim to "own" it: *"I do not step shyly back from your property, but look upon it always as **my** property, in which I 'respect' nothing. Pray do the like with what you call my property!"* [p. 248] This view logically leads to the idea of both workers' self-management and grassroots community control (as will be discussed more fully in section I) as those affected by an activity will take a direct interest in it and not let "respect" for "private" property allow them to be oppressed by others.

Moreover, egoism (self-interest) must lead to self-management and mutual aid (solidarity), for by coming to agreements based on mutual respect and social equality, we ensure non-hierarchical relationships. If I dominate someone, then in all likelihood I will be dominated in turn. By removing hierarchy and domination, the ego is free to experience and utilise the full potential of others. As Kropotkin argued in **Mutual Aid**, individual freedom and social co-operation are not only compatible but, when united, create the most productive conditions for all individuals within society.

Stirner reminds the social anarchist that communism and collectivism are not sought for their own sake but to ensure individual freedom and enjoyment. As he argued: *"But should competition some day disappear, because concerted effort will have been acknowledged as more beneficial than isolation, then will not every single individual inside the associations be equally egoistic and out for his own interests?"* [**Op. Cit.**, p. 22] This is because competition has its drawbacks, for *"[r]estless acquisition does not let us take breath, take a calm **enjoyment**. We do not get the comfort of our possessions... Hence it is at any rate helpful that we come to an agreement about **human** labours that they may not, as under competition, claim all our time and toil."* [p. 268] In other words, in the market only the market is free not those subject to its pressures and necessities — an important truism which defenders of capitalism always ignore.

Forgetting about the individual was, for Stirner, the key problem with the forms of communism he was familiar with and so this *"organisation of labour touches only such labours as others can do for us … the rest remain egoistic, because no one can in your stead elaborate your musical compositions, carry out your projects of painting, etc.; nobody can replace Raphael's labours. The latter are labours of a unique person, which only he is competent to achieve."* He went on to ask *"for whom is time to be gained [by association]? For what does man require more time than is necessary to refresh his wearied powers of labour? Here Communism is silent."* Unlike egoism, which answers: *"To take comfort in himself as unique, after he has done his part as man!"* In other words, competition *"has a continued existence"* because *"all do not attend to **their affair** and come to an **understanding** with each other about it."* [p. 269 and p. 275] As can be seen from Chapter 8 of Kropotkin's **Conquest of Bread** (*"The Need for Luxury"*), communist-anarchism builds upon this insight, arguing that communism is required to ensure that all individuals have the time and energy to pursue their own unique interests and dreams (see section I.4).

Stirner notes that socialising property need not result in genuine freedom if it is not rooted in individual use and control. He states *"the lord is proprietor. Choose then whether you want to be lord, or whether society shall be!"* He notes that many communists of his time attacked alienated property but did not stress that the aim was to ensure access for all individuals. *"Instead of transforming the alien into own,"* Stirner noted, *"they play impartial and ask only that all property be left to a third party, such as human society. They revindicate the alien not in their own name, but in a third party's"* Ultimately, of course, under libertarian communism it is not "society" which uses the means of life but individuals and associations of individuals. As Stirner stressed: *"Neither God nor Man ('human society') is proprietor, but the individual."* [p. 313, p. 315 and p. 251] This is why social anarchists have always stressed self-management — only that can bring collectivised property into the hands of those who utilise it. Stirner places the focus on decision making back where it belongs — in the individuals who make up a given community rather than abstractions like "society."

Therefore Stirner's union of egoists has strong connections with social anarchism's desire for a society based on freely federated individuals, co-operating as equals. His central idea of "property" — that which is used by the ego — is an important concept for social anarchism because it stresses that hierarchy develops when we let ideas and organisations own us rather than vice versa. A participatory anarchist community will be made up of individuals who must ensure that it remains their "property" and be under their control; hence the importance of decentralised, confederal organisations which ensure that control. A free society must be organised in such a way to ensure the free and full development of individuality and maximise the pleasure to be gained from individual interaction and activity. Lastly, Stirner indicates that mutual aid and equality are based not upon an abstract morality but upon self-interest, both for defence against hierarchy and for the pleasure of co-operative intercourse between unique individuals.

Stirner demonstrates brilliantly how abstractions and fixed ideas (*"spooks"*) influence the very way we think, see ourselves, and act. He shows how hierarchy has its roots within our own minds, in how we view the world. He offers a powerful defence of individuality in an authoritarian and alienated world, and places subjectivity at the centre of any revolutionary project, where it belongs. Finally, he reminds us that a free society must exist in the interests of all, and must be based upon the self-fulfilment, liberation and enjoyment of the individual.

Section H

Why do anarchists oppose state socialism?

Section H - Why do anarchists oppose state socialism?.............. 652

H.1 Have anarchists always opposed state socialism? 654

H.1.1 What was Bakunin's critique of Marxism? 656
H.1.2 What are the key differences between Anarchists and Marxists? 663
H.1.3 Why do anarchists wish to abolish the state "overnight"? 666
H.1.4 Do anarchists have "absolutely no idea" of what to put in place of the state? 668
H.1.5 Why do anarchists reject "utilising the present state"? 670
H.1.6 Why do anarchists try to "build the new world in the shell of the old"? 673
H.1.7 Haven't you read Lenin's "State and Revolution"? 676

H.2 What parts of anarchism do Marxists particularly misrepresent? 680

H.2.1 Do anarchists reject defending a revolution? 683
H.2.2 Do anarchists reject "class conflict" and "collective struggle"? 687
H.2.3 Does anarchism yearn "for what has gone before"? 690
H.2.4 Do anarchists think "the state is the main enemy"? 692
H.2.5 Do anarchists think "full blown" socialism will be created overnight? 695
H.2.6 How do Marxists misrepresent Anarchist ideas on mutual aid? 697
H.2.7 Who do anarchists see as their "agents of social change"? 699
H.2.8 What is the relationship of anarchism to syndicalism? 702
H.2.9 Do anarchists have "liberal" politics? 705
H.2.10 Are anarchists against leadership? 706
H.2.11 Are anarchists "anti-democratic"? 708

H.3 What are the myths of state socialism? 714

H.3.1 Do Anarchists and Marxists want the same thing? 716
H.3.2 Is Marxism "socialism from below"? 720
H.3.3 Is Leninism "socialism from below"? 724
H.3.4 Don't anarchists just quote Marxists selectively? 726
H.3.5 Has Marxist appropriation of anarchist ideas changed it? 728
H.3.6 Is Marxism the only revolutionary politics which have worked? 732
H.3.7 What is wrong with the Marxist theory of the state? 733
H.3.8 What is wrong with the Leninist theory of the state? 738
H.3.9 Is the state simply an agent of economic power? 743
H.3.10 Has Marxism always supported the idea of workers' councils? 748
H.3.11 Does Marxism aim to give power to workers organisations? 755
H.3.12 Is big business the precondition for socialism? 758
H.3.13 Why is state socialism just state capitalism? 763
H.3.14 Don't Marxists believe in workers' control? 767

H.4 Didn't Engels refute anarchism in "On Authority"? 771

H.4.1 Does organisation imply the end of liberty? 774
H.4.2 Does free love show the weakness of Engels' argument? 775
H.4.3 How do anarchists propose to run a factory? 776
H.4.4 How does the class struggle refute Engels' arguments? 777
H.4.5 Is the way industry operates "independent of all social organisation"? 778
H.4.6 Why does Engels' "On Authority" harm Marxism? 780
H.4.7 Is revolution "the most authoritarian thing there is"? 781

H.5 What is vanguardism and why do anarchists reject it? 783

H.5.1 Why are vanguard parties anti-socialist? 784
H.5.2 Have vanguardist assumptions been validated? 786
H.5.3 Why does vanguardism imply party power? 787
H.5.4 Did Lenin abandon vanguardism? 789
H.5.5 What is "democratic centralism"? 792
H.5.6 Why do anarchists oppose "democratic centralism"? 794
H.5.7 Is the way revolutionaries organise important? 796
H.5.8 Are vanguard parties effective? 796
H.5.9 What are vanguard parties effective at? 798
H.5.10 Why does "democratic centralism" produce "bureaucratic centralism"? 798
H.5.11 Can you provide an example of the negative nature of vanguard parties? 801
H.5.12 Surely the Russian Revolution proves that vanguard parties work? 802

H.6 Why did the Russian Revolution fail? 807

H.6.1 Can objective factors explain the failure of the Russian Revolution? 810
H.6.2 Did Bolshevik ideology influence the outcome of the Russian Revolution? 815
H.6.3 Were the Russian workers "declassed" and "atomised"? 823

Section H
Why do anarchists oppose state socialism?

The socialist movement has been continually divided, with various different tendencies and movements. The main tendencies of socialism are state socialism (Social Democracy, Leninism, Maoism and so on) and libertarian socialism (anarchism mostly, but also libertarian Marxists and others). The conflict and disagreement between anarchists and Marxists is legendary.

In addition to this divide between libertarian and authoritarian forms of socialism, there is another divide between reformist and revolutionary wings of these two tendencies. *"The term 'anarchist,'"* Murray Bookchin wrote, *"is a generic word like the term 'socialist,' and there are probably as many different kinds of anarchists are there are socialists. In both cases, the spectrum ranges from individuals whose views derive from an extension of liberalism (the 'individualist anarchists', the social-democrats) to revolutionary communists (the anarcho-communists, the revolutionary Marxists, Leninists and Trotskyites)."* [**Post-Scarcity Anarchism**, p. 138f]

In this section of the FAQ we concentrate on the conflict between the revolutionary wings of both movements. Here we discuss why communist-anarchists, anarcho-syndicalists and other revolutionary anarchists reject Marxist theories, particularly the ideas of Leninists and Trotskyites. We will concentrate almost entirely on the works of Marx, Engels, Lenin and Trotsky as well as the Russian Revolution. This is because many Marxists reject the Chinese, Cuban and other revolutions as being infected from the start by Stalinism. In contrast, there is a general agreement in Marxist circles that the Russian Revolution was a true socialist revolution and the ideas of Lenin (and usually Trotsky) follow in Marx's footsteps. What we say against Marx and Lenin is also applicable to their more controversial followers and, therefore, we ignore them. We also dismiss out of hand any suggestion that the Stalinist regime was remotely socialist. Unfortunately many serious revolutionaries consider Lenin's regime to be an example of a valid socialist revolution so we have to discuss why it was not.

As noted, two main wings of the revolutionary socialist movement, anarchism and Marxism, have always been in conflict. While, with the apparent success of the Russian revolution, the anarchist movement was overshadowed by Leninism in many countries, this situation has been changing. In recent years anarchism has seen a revival as more and more people recognise the fundamentally anti-socialist nature of the Russian "experiment" and the politics that inspired it. With this re-evaluation of socialism and the Soviet Union, more and more people are rejecting Marxism and embracing libertarian socialism. As can be seen from the press coverage from such events as the anti-Poll Tax riots in the UK at the start of the 1990s, the London J18 and N30 demonstrations in 1999 as well as those in Prague, Quebec, Genoa and Gothenburg anarchism has become synonymous with anti-capitalism.

Needless to say, when anarchists re-appear in the media and news bulletins the self-proclaimed "vanguard(s) of the proletariat" become worried and hurriedly write patronising articles on "anarchism" (without bothering to really understand it or its arguments against Marxism). These articles are usually a mishmash of lies, irrelevant personal attacks, distortions of the anarchist position and the ridiculous assumption that anarchists are anarchists because no one has bothered to inform of us of what "Marxism" is "really" about. We do not aim to repeat such "scientific" analysis in our FAQ so we shall concentrate on politics and history. By so doing we will indicate that anarchists are anarchists because we understand Marxism and reject it as being unable to lead to a socialist society.

It is unfortunately common for many Marxists, particularly Leninist influenced ones, to concentrate on personalities and not politics when discussing anarchist ideas. In other words, they attack **anarchists** rather than present a critique of **anarchism**. This can be seen, for example, when many Leninists attempt to "refute" the whole of anarchism, its theory and history, by pointing out the personal failings of specific anarchists. They say that Proudhon was anti-Jewish and sexist, that Bakunin was racist, that Kropotkin supported the Allies in the First World War and so anarchism is flawed. Yet this is irrelevant to a critique of anarchism as it does not address anarchist ideas but rather points to when anarchists fail to live up to them. Anarchist ideas are ignored by this approach, which is understandable as any critique which tried to do this would not only fail but also expose the authoritarianism of mainstream Marxism in the process.

Even taken at face value, you would have to be stupid to assume that Proudhon's misogyny or Bakunin's racism had equal weighting with Lenin's and the Bolsheviks' behaviour (for example, the creation of a party dictatorship, the repression of strikes, free speech, independent working class organisation, the creation of a secret police force, the attack on Kronstadt, the betrayal of the Makhnovists, the violent repression of the Russian anarchist movement, etc.) in the league table of despicable activity. It seems strange that personal bigotry is of equal, or even more, importance in evaluating a political theory than its practice during a revolution.

Moreover, such a technique is ultimately dishonest. Looking at Proudhon, for example, his anti-Semitic outbursts remained unpublished in his note books until well after his ideas and, as Robert Graham points out, *"a reading of **General Idea of the Revolution** will show, anti-Semitism forms no part of Proudhon's revolutionary programme."* [*"Introduction"*, **General Idea of the Revolution**, p. xxxvi] Similarly, Bakunin's racism is an unfortunate aspect of his life, an aspect which is ultimately irrelevant to the core principles and ideas he argued for. As for Proudhon's sexism it should be noted that Bakunin and subsequent anarchists totally rejected it and argued for complete equality between the sexes. Likewise, anarchists from Kropotkin onwards have opposed racism in all its forms (and the large Jewish anarchist movement saw that Bakunin's anti-Semitic comments were not a defining aspect to his ideas). Why mention these aspects of their ideas at all?

Nor were Marx and Engels free from racist, sexist or homophobic comments yet no anarchist would dream these were worthy of mention when critiquing their ideology (for those interested in such matters, Peter Fryer's essay **"Engels: A Man of his Time"** should be consulted). This is because the anarchist critique of Marxism is robust and confirmed by substantial empirical evidence (namely, the failures of social democracy and the Russian Revolution).

If we look at Kropotkin's support for the Allies in the First World War we discover a strange hypocrisy on the part of Marxists as well as an attempt to distort history. Why hypocrisy? Simply because Marx and Engels supported Prussia during the Franco-Prussian war while, in contrast, Bakunin argued for a popular uprising and social revolution to stop the war. As Marx wrote to Engels on July 20th, 1870:

> "The French need to be overcome. If the Prussians are victorious, the centralisation of the power of the State will be useful for the centralisation of the German working class. Moreover, German ascendancy will transfer the centre of gravity of the European worker's movement from France to Germany ... On a world scale, the ascendancy of the German proletariat over the French proletariat will at the same time constitute the ascendancy of **our** theory over Proudhon's." [quoted by Arthur Lehning, **Michael Bakunin: Selected Writings**, p. 284]

Marx, in part, supported the deaths of working class people in war in order to see **his** ideas become more important than Proudhon's! The hypocrisy of the Marxists is clear - if anarchism is to be condemned for Kropotkin's actions, then Marxism must be equally condemned for Marx's.

This analysis also rewrites history as the bulk of the Marxist movement supported their respective states during the conflict. A handful of the parties of the Second International opposed the war (and those were the smallest ones as well). The father of Russian Marxism, George Plekhanov, supported the Allies while the German Social Democratic Party (the jewel in the crown of the Second International) supported its nation-state in the war. There was just one man in the German Reichstag in August 1914 who did not vote for war credits (and he did not even vote against them, he abstained). While a small minority of the German Social-Democrats did not support the war, initially many of this anti-war minority went along with the majority of the party in the name of "discipline" and "democratic" principles.

In contrast, only a **very** small minority of anarchists supported any side during the conflict. The bulk of the anarchist movement (including such leading lights as Malatesta, Rocker, Goldman and Berkman) opposed the war, arguing that anarchists must "*capitalise upon every stirring of rebellion, every discontent in order to foment insurrection, to organise the revolution to which we look for the ending of all of society's iniquities."* [**No Gods, No Masters**, vol. 2., p. 36] As Malatesta noted at the time, the pro-war anarchists were *"not numerous, it is true, but [did have] amongst them comrades whom we love and respect most."* He stressed that the *"almost all"* of the anarchists *"have remained faithful to their convictions"* namely *"to awaken a consciousness of the antagonism of interests between dominators and dominated, between exploiters and workers, and to develop the class struggle inside each country, and solidarity among all workers across the frontiers, as against any prejudice and any passion of either race or nationality."* [**Errico Malatesta: His Life and Ideas**, p. 243, p. 248 and p. 244] By pointing to Kropotkin, Marxists hide the facts that he was very much in a

minority within the anarchist movement and that it was the official Marxist movement which betrayed the cause of internationalism, not anarchism. Indeed, the betrayal of the Second International was the natural result of the *"ascendancy"* of Marxism over anarchism that Marx had hoped. The rise of Marxism in the form of social-democracy, ended as Bakunin predicted, with the corruption of socialism in the quagmire of electioneering and statism. As Rudolf Rocker correctly argued, *"the Great War of 1914 was the exposure of the bankruptcy of political socialism."* [**Marx and Anarchism**]

Here we will analyse Marxism in terms of its theories and how they worked in practice. Thus we will conduct a scientific analysis of Marxism, looking at its claims and comparing them to what they achieved in practice. Few, if any, Marxists present such an analysis of their own politics, which makes Marxism more a belief system than analysis. For example, many Marxists point to the success of the Russian Revolution and argue that while anarchists attack Trotsky and Lenin for being statists and authoritarians, that statism and authoritarianism saved the revolution. In reply, anarchists point out that the revolution did, in fact, **fail.** The aim of that revolution was to create a free, democratic, classless society of equals. It created a one party dictatorship based around a class system of bureaucrats exploiting and oppressing working class people and a society lacking equality and freedom. As the stated aims of the Marxist revolution failed to materialise, anarchists would argue that it failed even though a "Communist" Party remained in power for over 70 years. And as for statism and authoritarianism "saving" the revolution, they saved it for Stalin, not socialism. That is nothing to be proud of.

From an anarchist perspective, this makes perfect sense as *"[n]o revolution can ever succeed as a factor of liberation unless the MEANS used to further it be identical in spirit and tendency with the PURPOSE to be achieved."* [Emma Goldman, **My Disillusionment in Russia**, p. 261] In other words, statist and authoritarian means will result in statist and authoritarian ends. Calling a new state a "workers state" will not change its nature as a form of minority (and so class) rule. It has nothing to do with the intentions of those who gain power, it has to do with the nature of the state and the social relationships it generates. The state structure is an instrument of minority rule, it **cannot** be used by the majority because it is based on hierarchy, centralisation and the empowerment of the minority at the top at the expense of everyone else. States have certain properties **just because they are states.** They have their own dynamics which place them outside popular control and are not simply a tool in the hands of the economically dominant class. Making the minority Socialists within a "workers' state" just changes the minority in charge, the minority exploiting and oppressing the majority. As Emma Goldman put it:

> "It would be an error to assume that the failure of the Revolution was due entirely to the character of the Bolsheviki. Fundamentally, it was the result of the principles and methods of Bolshevism. It was the authoritarian spirit and principles of the State which stifled the libertarian and liberating aspirations [unleashed by the revolution] ... Only this understanding of the underlying forces that crushed the Revolution can present the true lesson of that world-stirring event." [**Op. Cit.**, p. 250]

Similarly, in spite of over 100 years of socialists and radicals using elections to put forward their ideas and the resulting corruption of every party which has done so, most Marxists still call for socialists to take part in elections. For a theory which calls itself scientific this ignoring of empirical evidence, the facts of history, is truly amazing. Marxism ranks with economics as the "science" which most consistently ignores history and evidence.

As this section of the FAQ will make clear, this name calling and concentration on the personal failings of individual anarchists by Marxists is not an accident. If we take the ability of a theory to predict future events as an indication of its power then it soon becomes clear that anarchism is a far more useful tool in working class struggle and self-liberation than Marxism. After all, anarchists predicted with amazing accuracy the future development of Marxism. Bakunin argued that electioneering would corrupt the socialist movement, making it reformist and just another bourgeois party (see section J.2). This is what in fact happened to the Social-Democratic movement across the world by the turn of the twentieth century (the rhetoric remained radical for a few more years, of course).

If we look at the "workers' states" created by Marxists, we discover, yet again, anarchist predictions proved right. Bakunin argued that "[b]y popular government they [the Marxists] mean government of the people by a small number of representatives elected by the people... [That is,] government of the vast majority of the people by a privileged minority. But this minority, the Marxists say, will consist of workers. Yes, perhaps, of **former** workers, who, as soon as they become rulers or representatives of the people will cease to be workers and will begin to look upon the whole workers' world from the heights of the state. They will no longer represent the people but themselves and their own pretensions to govern the people." [**Statism and Anarchy**, p. 178] The history of every Marxist revolution proves his critique was correct.

Due to these "workers' states" socialism has become associated with repressive regimes, with totalitarian state capitalist systems the total opposite of what socialism is actually about. Nor does it help when self-proclaimed socialists (such as Trotskyites) obscenely describe regimes that exploit, imprison and murder wage labourers in Cuba, North Korea, and China as 'workers' states'. While some neo-Trotskyists (like the British SWP) refuse to defend, in any way, Stalinist states (as they argue - correctly, even if their analysis is flawed - that they are state capitalist) most Trotskyists do not. Little wonder many anarchists do not use the terms "socialist" or "communist" and just call themselves "anarchists." This is because such terms are associated with regimes and parties which have nothing in common with our ideas, or, indeed, the ideals of socialism as such.

This does not mean that anarchists reject everything Marx wrote. Far from it. Much of his analysis of capitalism is acceptable to anarchists, for example both Bakunin and Tucker considered Marx's economic analysis as important. Indeed, there are some schools of Marxism which are very libertarian and are close cousins to anarchism (for example, council communism and Autonomist Marxism are close to revolutionary anarchism). Unfortunately, these forms of Libertarian Marxism are a minority current within that movement. So, Marxism is not all bad - unfortunately the vast bulk of it is and those elements which are not are found in anarchism anyway. For most, Marxism is the school of Marx, Engels, Lenin and Trotsky, not Marx, Pannekoek, Gorter, Ruhle and Mattick.

The minority libertarian trend of Marxism is based, like anarchism, on a rejection of party rule, electioneering and creating a "workers' state." Its supporters also, like anarchists, advocate direct action, self-managed class struggle, working class autonomy and a self-managed socialist society. These Marxists oppose the dictatorship of the party over the proletariat and, in effect, agree with Bakunin on many key issues (such as anti-parliamentarianism, direct action, workers' councils, etc.).

These libertarian forms of Marxism should be encouraged and not tarred with the same brush as Leninism and social democracy (indeed Lenin commented upon *"the anarchist deviation of the German Communist Workers' Party"* and the *"semi-anarchist elements"* of the very groups we are referring to here under the term libertarian Marxism. [**Collected Works**, vol. 32, p. 252 and p. 514]). Over time, hopefully, such comrades will see that the libertarian element of their thought outweighs the Marxist legacy. So our comments in this section of the FAQ are mostly directed to the majority form of Marxism, not to its libertarian wing.

One last point. We must note that in the past many leading Marxists have slandered anarchists. Engels, for example, wrote that the anarchist movement survived because *"the governments in Europe and America are much too interested in its continued existence, and spend too much money on supporting it."* [**Collected Works**, vol. 27, p. 414] So there is often no love lost between the two schools of socialism. Indeed, Marxists have argued that anarchism and socialism were miles apart and some even asserted that anarchism was not even a form of socialism. Lenin (at times) and leading American Marxist Daniel De Leon took this line, along with many others. This is true, in a sense, as anarchists are not **state** socialists - we reject such "socialism" as deeply authoritarian. However, all anarchists **are** members of the socialist movement and we reject attempts by Marxists to monopolise the term. Be that as it may, sometimes in this section we may find it useful to use the term socialist/communist to describe "state socialist" and anarchist to describe "libertarian socialist/communist." This in no way implies that anarchists are not socialists. It is purely a tool to make our arguments easier to read.

H.1
Have anarchists always opposed state socialism?

Yes. Anarchists have always argued that real socialism cannot be created using a state. The basic core of the argument is simple. Socialism implies equality, yet the state signifies inequality - inequality in terms of power. As we argued in section B.2, anarchists consider one of the defining aspects of the state is its hierarchical nature. In other words, the delegation of **power** into the hands of a few. As such, it violates a core idea of socialism, namely social equality. Those who make up the governing bodies in a state have more power than those who have elected them (see section I.1).

It is with this perspective that anarchists have combated the idea of state socialism and Marxism (although we should stress that libertarian forms of Marxism, such as council communism, have strong similarities to anarchism). In the case of the Russian Revolution, the anarchists were amongst the first on the left to be suppressed by the Bolsheviks. Indeed, the history of Marxism is, in part, a history of its struggles against anarchists just as the history of anarchism is also, in part, a history of its struggle against the various forms of Marxism and its offshoots.

While both Stirner and Proudhon wrote many pages against the evils and contradictions of state socialism, anarchists have only really been fighting the Marxist form of state socialism since Bakunin. This is because, until the First International, Marx and Engels were relatively unknown socialist thinkers. Proudhon was aware of Marx (they had meant in France in the 1840s and had corresponded) but Marxism was unknown in France during his life time and so Proudhon did not directly argue against Marxism (he did, however, critique Louis Blanc and other French state socialists).

Before discussing Bakunin's opposition and critique of Marxism in the next section, we should consider the thoughts of Proudhon on state socialism. It is worth noting that when Proudhon was writing communist ideas were all authoritarian in nature. Libertarian communism only developed after Bakunin's death in 1876. This means that when Proudhon was critiquing "communism" he was attacking a specific form of communism, the form which subordinated the individual to the community. Anarchist communists like Kropotkin and Malatesta also opposed such kinds of "communism." As Kropotkin put it, *"before and in 1848"* communism *"was put forward in such a shape as to fully account for Proudhon's distrust as to its effect upon liberty. The old idea of Communism was the idea of monastic communities … The last vestiges of liberty and of individual energy would be destroyed, if humanity ever had to go through such a communism."* [**Act for Yourselves**, p. 98] Of course, it may be likely that Proudhon would have rejected libertarian communism as well, but bear in mind that not all forms of "communism" are identical.

He particularly attacked the ideas of Louis Blanc. Blanc, whose most famous book was **Organisation du Travail** (**Organisation of Work**, first published in 1840) argued that social ills resulted from competition and they could be solved by means of eliminating it via government initiated and financed reforms. More specifically, Blanc argued that it was *"necessary to use the whole power of the state"* to ensure the creation and success of workers' associations (or *"social workshops"*). Since that *"which the proletarians lack to free themselves are the tools of labour,"* the government *"must furnish them"* with these. *"The state,"* in short, *"should place itself resolutely at the head of industry."* [quoted by K. Steven Vincent, **Pierre-Joseph Proudhon and the Rise of French Republican Socialism**, p. 139] Capitalists would be encouraged to invest money in these workshops, for which they would be guaranteed interest payments but the workers would keep the remaining profits generated by the workshops. Such state-initiated workshops would soon prove to be more efficient than privately owned industry and, by charging lower prices, force privately owned industry either out of business or to change into social workshops, so eliminating competition.

Proudhon objected to this scheme on many levels. He argued that Blanc's scheme appealed *"to the state for its silent partnership; that is, he gets down on his knees before the capitalists and recognises the sovereignty of monopoly."* Given that Proudhon saw the state as an instrument of the capitalist class, asking that state to abolish capitalism was illogical and impossible. Moreover, by getting the funds for the "social workshop" from capitalists, Blanc's scheme was hardly undermining their power. *"Capital and power,"* Proudhon argued, *"secondary organs of society, are always the gods whom socialism adores; if capital and power did not exist, it would invent them."* [**Property is Theft!**, p. 215 and p. 217] He stressed the authoritarian nature of Blanc's scheme:

"M. Blanc is never tired of appealing to authority, and socialism loudly declares itself anarchistic; M. Blanc places power above society, and socialism tends to subordinate it to society; M. Blanc makes social life descend from above, and socialism maintains that it springs up and grows from below; M. Blanc runs after politics, and socialism is in quest of science. No more hypocrisy, let me say to M. Blanc: you desire neither Catholicism nor monarchy nor nobility, but you must have a God, a religion, a dictatorship, a censorship, a hierarchy, distinctions, and ranks. For my part, I deny your God, your authority, your sovereignty, your judicial State, and all your representative mystifications." [**Op. Cit.**, p. 205]

Equally, Proudhon opposed the "top-down" nature of Blanc's ideas. As it was run by the state, the system of workshops would hardly be libertarian as *"hierarchy would result from the elective principle … as in constitutional politics … Who will make the law? The government."* Such a regime, Proudhon argued, would be unlikely to function well and the net result would be *"all reforms ending, now in hierarchical corporation, now in State monopoly, or the tyranny of community."* [**Op. Cit.**, p. 21 and p. 207] This was because of the perspective of state socialists:

"As you cannot conceive of society without hierarchy, you have made yourselves the apostles of authority; worshippers of power, you think only of strengthening it and muzzling liberty; your favourite maxim is that the welfare of the people must be achieved in spite of the people; instead of proceeding to social reform by the extermination of power and politics, you insist on a reconstruction of power and politics." [**Op. Cit.**, pp. 225-6]

Instead of reform from above, Proudhon stressed the need for working class people to organise themselves for their own liberation. As he put it, the *"problem before the labouring classes … [is] not in capturing, but in subduing both power and monopoly, - that is, in generating from the bowels of the people, from the depths of labour, a greater authority, a more potent fact, which shall envelop capital and the state and subjugate them."* For, *"to combat and reduce power, to put it in its proper place in society, it is of no use to change the holders of power or introduce some variation into its workings: an agricultural and industrial combination must be found by means of which power, today the ruler of society, shall become its slave."* This was because the state *"finds itself inevitably enchained to capital and directed against the proletariat."* Unsurprisingly, Proudhon stressed in 1848 that *"the proletariat must emancipate itself without the help of the government."* [**Op. Cit.,** pp. 225-6 and p. 306] In addition, by guaranteeing interest payments, Blanc's scheme insured the continued exploitation of labour by capital and, of course, while opposing capitalist competition, Proudhon did not consider it wise to abolish all forms of the market.

So while none of Proudhon's arguments were directly aimed at Marxism, his critiques are applicable to much of mainstream Marxism as this inherited many of the ideas of the state socialism they attacked. Much of their analysis was incorporated in the collectivist and communist ideas of the anarchists that followed them. This can be seen from the fact that Proudhon's ideas on the management of production by workers' associations, opposition to nationalisation as state-capitalism and the need for action from below by working people themselves, all found their place in communist-anarchism and anarcho-syndicalism and in their critique of mainstream Marxism (such as social democracy) and Leninism. Echoes of these critiques can be found Bakunin's comments of 1868:

> *"I hate Communism because it is the negation of liberty and because for me humanity is unthinkable without liberty. I am not a Communist, because Communism concentrates and swallows up in itself for the benefit of the State all the forces of society, because it inevitably leads to the concentration of property in the hands of the State ... I want to see society and collective or social property organised from below upwards, by way of free associations, not from above downwards, by means of any kind of authority whatsoever ... That is the sense in which I am a Collectivist and not a Communist."* [quoted by K.J. Kenafick, **Michael Bakunin and Karl Marx**, pp. 67-8]

It is with Bakunin that Marxism and Anarchism came into direct conflict as it was Bakunin who lead the struggle against Marx in the **International Workingmen's Association** between 1868 and 1872. It was in these exchanges that the two schools of socialism (the libertarian and the authoritarian) clarified themselves. With Bakunin, the anarchist critique of Marxism (and state socialism in general) starts to reach its mature form. We discuss Bakunin's critique in the next section.

H.1.1 What was Bakunin's critique of Marxism?

Bakunin and Marx famously clashed in the first **International Working Men's Association** between 1868 and 1872. This conflict helped clarify the anarchist opposition to the ideas of Marxism and can be considered as the first major theoretical analysis and critique of Marxism by anarchists. Later critiques followed, of course, particularly after the degeneration of Social Democracy into reformism and the failure of the Russian Revolution (both of

which allowed the theoretical critiques to be enriched by empirical evidence) but the Bakunin/Marx conflict laid the ground for what came after. As such, an overview of Bakunin's critique is essential as anarchists continued to develop and expand upon it (particularly after the experiences of actual Marxist movements and revolutions confirmed it).

First, however, we must stress that Marx and Bakunin had many similar ideas. They both stressed the need for working people to organise themselves to overthrow capitalism by a social revolution. They argued for collective ownership of the means of production. They both constantly stressed that the emancipation of the workers must be the task of the workers themselves. They differed, of course, in exactly how these common points should be implemented in practice. Both, moreover, had a tendency to misrepresent the opinions of the other on certain issues (particularly as their struggle reached its climax). Anarchists, unsurprisingly, argue Bakunin has been proved right by history, so confirming the key aspects of his critique of Marx.

So what was Bakunin's critique of Marxism? There are six main areas. Firstly, there is the question of current activity (i.e. whether the workers' movement should participate in "politics" and the nature of revolutionary working class organisation). Secondly, there is the issue of the form of the revolution (i.e. whether it should be a political **then** an economic one, or whether it should be both at the same time). Thirdly, there is the prediction that state socialism will be exploitative, replacing the capitalist class with the state bureaucracy. Fourthly, there is the issue of the "dictatorship of the proletariat." Fifthly, there is the question of whether political power **can** be seized by the working class as a whole or whether it can only be exercised by a small minority. Sixthly, there was the issue of whether the revolution be centralised or decentralised in nature. We shall discuss each in turn.

On the issue of current struggle, the differences between Marx and Bakunin are clear. For Marx, the proletariat had to take part in bourgeois elections as an organised political party. As the resolution of the (gerrymandered) Hague Congress of First International put it: *"In its struggle against the collective power of the propertied classes the proletariat cannot act as a class except by constituting itself a political party, distinct from and opposed to, all old parties formed by the propertied classes ... The conquest of political power has therefore become the great duty of the working class."* [**Collected Works**, vol. 23, p. 243]

This political party must stand for elections and win votes. As Marx argued in the preamble of the French Workers' Party, the workers must turn the franchise *"from a means of deception ... into an instrument of emancipation."* This can be considered as part of the process outlined in the **Communist Manifesto**, where it was argued that the *"immediate aim of the Communists is the same as that of all the other proletarian parties,"* namely the *"conquest of political power by the proletariat,"* the *"first step in the revolution by the working class"* being *"to raise the proletariat to the position of ruling class, to win the battle of democracy."* Engels later stressed (in 1895) that the **"Communist Manifesto** *had already proclaimed the winning of universal suffrage, of democracy, as one of the first and most important tasks of the militant proletariat"* and that German Social Democracy had showed workers of all countries *"how* to make use of universal suffrage." [**Marx and Engels Reader**, p. 566, p. 484, p. 490 and p. 565]

With this analysis in mind, Marxist influenced political parties have consistently argued for and taken part in election campaigns, seeking office as a means of spreading socialist ideas and as a means of pursuing the socialist revolution. The Social Democratic parties which were the first Marxist parties (and which developed under the watchful eyes of Marx and Engels) saw revolution in terms of winning a majority within Parliamentary elections and using this political power to abolish capitalism (once this was done, the state would "wither away" as classes would no longer exist). In effect, as we discuss in section H.3.10, these parties aimed to reproduce Marx's account of the forming of the Paris Commune on the level of the national Parliament.

Bakunin, in contrast, argued that while the communists "imagine they can attain their goal by the development and organisation of the political power of the working classes ... aided by bourgeois radicalism" anarchists "believe they can succeed only through the development and organisation of the non-political or anti-political power of the working classes." The Communists "believe it necessary to organise the workers' forces in order to seize the political power of the State," while anarchists "organise for the purpose of destroying it." Bakunin saw this in terms of creating new organs of working class power in opposition to the state, organised "from the bottom up, by the free association or federation of workers, starting with the associations, then going on to the communes, the region, the nations, and, finally, culminating in a great international and universal federation." In other words, a system of workers' councils. As such, he constantly argued for workers, peasants and artisans to organise into unions and join the **International Workingmen's Association**, so becoming "a real force ... which knows what to do and is therefore capable of guiding the revolution in the direction marked out by the aspirations of the people: a serious international organisation of workers' associations of all lands capable of replacing this departing world of **states**." [**Bakunin on Anarchism**, pp. 262-3, p. 270 and p. 174] To Marx's argument that workers should organise politically (i.e., send their representations to Parliament) Bakunin realised that when "common workers" are sent "to Legislative Assemblies" the result is that the "worker-deputies, transplanted into a bourgeois environment, into an atmosphere of purely bourgeois ideas, will in fact cease to be workers and, becoming Statesmen, they will become bourgeois ... For men do not make their situations; on the contrary, men are made by them." [**The Basic Bakunin**, p. 108]

As far as history goes, the experience of Social Democracy confirmed Bakunin's analysis. A few years after Engels death in 1895, German Social Democracy was racked by the "revisionism" debate. This debate did not spring from the minds of a few leaders, isolated from the movement, but rather expressed developments **within** the movement itself. In effect, the revisionists wanted to adjust the party rhetoric to what the party was actually doing and so the battle against the revisionists basically represented a battle between what the party **said** it was doing and its actual practice. As one of the most distinguished historians of this period put it, the "distinction between the contenders remained largely a subjective one, a difference of ideas in the evaluation of reality rather than a difference in the realm of action." [C. Schorske, **German Social Democracy**, p. 38] By the start of the First World War, the Social Democrats had become so corrupted by their activities in bourgeois institutions they supported its state (and ruling class) and voted for war credits rather than denounce the war as Imperialist slaughter for profits. Clearly, Bakunin was proved right. (see also section J.2.6 for more discussion on the effect of electioneering on radical parties).

However, we must stress that because Bakunin rejected participating in bourgeois politics, it did not mean that he rejected "politics" or "political struggle" in general (see section J.2.10). Bakunin clearly advocated what would later be termed a syndicalist strategy (see section H.2.8). This union movement would be complemented by a specific anarchist organisation which would work within it to influence it towards anarchist aims by the "natural influence" of its members (see section J.3.7).

Comparing Bakunin and Marx, it is clear whom history has validated. Even that anti-anarchist Stalinist hack Eric Hobsbawn could not avoid admitting "the remarkable achievement of Spanish anarchism which was to create a working-class movement that remained genuinely revolutionary. Social democratic and ... even communist trade unions have rarely been able to escape either schizophrenia [i.e., revolutionary rhetoric hiding reformist practice] or betrayal of their socialist convictions." [**Revolutionaries**, p. 104] This is probably the only accurate comment made in his various diatribes on anarchism but, of course, he did not allow the implications of his statement to bother his faith in Leninist ideology. So given the long history of reformism and betrayal of socialist principles by radicals utilising elections and political parties, it comes as no surprise that anarchists consider both Bakunin's critique and alternative to be confirmed by experience (section J.2 discusses direct action and electioneering).

Which brings us to the second issue, namely the nature of the revolution itself. For Bakunin, a revolution meant a **social** revolution from below. This involved both the abolition of the state **and** the expropriation of capital. In his words, "the revolution must set out from the first radically and totally to destroy the State." The "natural and necessary consequences" of which will be the "confiscation of all productive capital and means of production on behalf of workers' associations, who are to put them to collective use ... the federative Alliance of all working men's associations ... will constitute the Commune." There "can no longer be any successful political ... revolution unless the political revolution is transformed into social revolution." [**Michael Bakunin: Selected Writings**, p. 170 and p. 171]

So economic and political transformation "must be accomplished together and simultaneously." [**The Basic Bakunin**, p. 106] Given that Bakunin thought the state was the protector of capitalism, no economic change could be achieved until such time as it was abolished. This also meant that Bakunin considered a political revolution before an economic one to mean the continued slavery of the workers. As he argued, "[t]o win political freedom first can signify no other thing but to win this freedom only, leaving for the first days at least economic and social relations in the same old state, - that is, leaving the proprietors and capitalists with their insolent wealth, and the workers with their poverty." With capitalists' economic power intact, could the workers' **political** power remain strong? As such, *"every political revolution taking place prior to and consequently without a social revolution must necessarily be a bourgeois revolution, and a bourgeois revolution can only be instrumental in bringing about bourgeois Socialism - that is, it is bound to end in a new, more hypocritical and more skilful, but no less oppressive, exploitation of the proletariat by the bourgeois."* [**The Political Philosophy of Bakunin**, p. 294 and p. 289]

Did Marx and Engels hold this position? Apparently so. Discussing the Paris Commune, Marx noted that it was *"the political form at last discovered under which to work out the economic emancipation of labour,"* and as the *"political rule of the producer cannot coexist with the perpetuation of his social slavery"* the Commune was to *"serve as a lever for uprooting the economic foundations upon which rests the existence of classes."* Engels argued that the *"proletariat seizes the public power, and by means of this transforms the ... means of production ... into public property."* In the **Communist Manifesto** they argued that *"the first step in the revolution by the working class"* is *"rais[ing] the proletariat to the position of ruling class, to win the battle of democracy."* The proletariat *"will use its political supremacy to wrest, by degrees, all capital from the bourgeois, to centralise all instruments of production in the hands of the State, i.e. of the proletariat organised as the ruling class."* [**Op. Cit.**, p. 635, p. 717 and p. 490]

This is made even clearer in Engels' *"Principles of Communism"* (often considered as a draft of the **Manifesto**). That document stressed that it was not possible for *"private property to be abolished at one stroke"*, arguing that *"the proletarian revolution will transform existing society gradually."* The revolution *"will establish a **democratic constitution**, and through this, the direct or indirect dominance of the proletariat. Direct in England, where the proletarians are already a majority of the people."* *"Democracy"*, Engels went on, *"would be quite useless to the proletariat if it were not immediately used as a means of carrying through further measures directly attacking private ownership."* [**Collected Works**, vol. 6, p. 350] Decades later, when Marx discussed what the "dictatorship of the proletariat" meant, he argued (in reply to Bakunin's question of *"over whom will the proletariat rule?"*) that it simply meant *"that so long as other classes continue to exist, the capitalist class in particular, the proletariat fights it (for with the coming of the proletariat to power, its enemies will not yet have disappeared), it must use measures of **force**, hence governmental measures; if it itself still remains a class and the economic conditions on which the class struggle and the existence of classes have not yet disappeared, they must be forcibly removed or transformed, and the process of their transformation must be forcibly accelerated."* [**The Marx-Engels Reader**, pp. 542-3] Note, "capitalists," not "former capitalists," so implying that the members of the proletariat are, in fact, still proletarians after the "socialist" revolution and so still subject to wage slavery under economic masters. Which makes perfect sense, as otherwise the term *"dictatorship of the proletariat"* would be meaningless.

Then there is the issue of when the working class could seize political power. As Engels put it, the conflict *"between bourgeoisie and proletariat can only be fought out in a republic"* as this is *"the form in which the struggle must be fought out."* Workers would have to create a republic in countries without one (such as Germany at the time). [Marx and Engels, **The Socialist Revolution**, p. 264] Decades previously, Engels had argued that the *"first, fundamental condition for the introduction of community of property is the political liberation of the proletariat through a democratic constitution."* [**Collected Works**, vol. 6, p. 102] Thus the bourgeois revolution would come first, then the proletarian one. The **Communist Manifesto** had raised the possibility of a bourgeois revolution in Germany being *"but a prelude to an immediately following proletarian revolution."* [**Selected Writings**, p. 63] Within two years, Marx and Engels argued that this was wrong, that a socialist revolution was not possible in Continental Europe for some time. Even in the 1880s, Engels was still arguing that a proletarian revolution was not immediately possible in Germany and the first results of any revolution would be a bourgeois republic within which the task of social democracy was to build its forces and influence.

Clearly, then, Marx and Engels considered the creation of a republic in a well developed capitalist economy as the basis for seizing of state power as the key event and, later, the expropriation of the expropriators would occur. Thus the economic power of the capitalists would remain, with the proletariat utilising political power to combat and reduce it. Anarchists argue that if the proletariat does not hold economic power, its political power would at best be insecure and would in fact degenerate. Would the capitalists just sit and wait while their economic power was gradually eliminated by political action? And what of the proletariat during this period? Will they patiently obey their bosses, continue to be oppressed and exploited by them until such time as the end of their "social slavery" has been worked out (and by whom)? Would they be happy to fight for a bourgeois republic first, then wait for an unspecified period of time before the party leadership proclaimed that the time was ripe to introduce socialism?

As the experience of the Russian Revolution showed, the position of Marx and Engels proved to be untenable. Bakunin's perspective was repeated by a Russian worker in 1906 when he expressed his impatience with Menshevik strategy:

> *"[The Mensheviks tell] us that the workers' congress is the best means of assuring the independence of the proletariat in the bourgeois revolution; otherwise, we workers will play the role of cannon fodder in it. So I ask: what is the insurance for? Will we really make the bourgeois revolution? Is it possible that we will spill blood twice - once for the victory of the bourgeois revolution, and the time for the victory of our proletarian revolution? No, comrades, it is not to be found in the party programme [that this must be so]; but if we workers are to spill blood, then only once, for freedom and socialism."* [quoted by Abraham Ascher, **The Mensheviks in the Russian Revolution**, p. 43]

In 1917, this lesson was well learned and the Russian workers initially followed Bakunin's path (mostly spontaneously and without significant influence by libertarians). The Mensheviks repeated their mistakes of 1905 as they *"proved unable to harness this revolutionary potential to any practical purpose. They were blinded by their rigid marxist formula of 'bourgeois revolution first, socialist revolution later' and tried to restrain the masses. They preached self-abnegation to them, told them to stand aside until such times as the bourgeoisie had built a solid capitalist system. This made no sense to workers and peasants - why should they renounce the power that was in their hands already?"* Leading Menshevik Fedor Dan *"admitted in 1946 that the Menshevik concept of the bourgeois revolution rested on 'illusions'"* [Vera Broido, **Lenin and the Mensheviks**, p 14 and p. 15] Once Lenin returned to Russia, the Bolsheviks broke with this previously shared perspective and started to support and encourage the radicalisation of the workers and so managed to gain popular support. However, they did so partially and incompletely and, as a consequence, finally held back and so fatally undermined the revolution.

After the February revolution paralysed the state, the workers organised factory committees and raised the idea and practice of workers self-management of production. The Russian anarchists supported this movement whole-heartedly, arguing that it should be pushed as far as it would go. In contrast, Lenin argued for *"workers' control over the capitalists."* [**The Lenin Anthology**, p. 402] This was, unsurprisingly, the policy applied immediately after the Bolshevik seizure of power. However, as one Leninist writer admits, *"[t]wo overwhelmingly powerful forces obliged the Bolsheviks to abandon this 'reformist' course."* One was the start of the civil war, the other *"was the fact that the capitalists used their remaining power to make the system unworkable. At the end of 1917 the All Russian Congress of employers declared that those 'factories in which the control is exercised by means of active interference in the administration will be closed.' The workers' natural response to the wave of lockouts which followed was to demand that their [sic!] state nationalise the factories."* [John Rees, *"In Defence of October"*, pp. 3-82, **International Socialism**, no. 52, p. 42] By July 1918, only one-fifth of nationalised firms had been done so by the state, the rest by local committees from below (which, incidentally, shows the unresponsiveness of centralised power). Clearly, the idea that a social revolution can come after a political was shown to be a failure - the capitalist class used its powers to disrupt the economic life of Russia.

Faced with the predictable opposition by capitalists to their system of "control" the Bolsheviks nationalised the means of production. Sadly, **within** the nationalised workplace the situation of the worker remained essentially unchanged. Lenin had been arguing for one-man management (appointed from above and armed with "dictatorial" powers) since late April 1918 (see section H.3.14). This aimed at replacing the capitalists with state appointed managers, **not** workers self-management. In fact, as we discuss in section H.6.2 the party leaders repeatedly overruled the factory committees' suggestions to build socialism based on their management of the economy in favour of centralised state control. Bakunin's fear of what would happen if a political revolution preceded a social one came true. The working class continued to be exploited and oppressed as before, first by the bourgeoisie and then by the new bourgeoisie of state appointed managers armed with all the powers of the old ones (plus a few more). Russia confirmed Bakunin's analysis that a revolution must immediately combine political and economic goals in order for it to be successful.

The experience of Bolshevik Russia also confirms Bakunin's prediction that state socialism would simply be state capitalism. As Bakunin stressed, the state *"is the government from above downwards of an immense number of men [and women], very different from the point of view of the degree of their culture, the nature of the countries or localities that they inhabit, the occupations they follow, the interests and aspirations directing them - the State is the government of all these by one or another minority."* The state *"has always been the patrimony of some privileged class"* and *"when all other classes have exhausted themselves"* it *"becomes the patrimony of the bureaucratic class."* The Marxist state *"will not content itself with administering and governing the masses politically"* it will *"also administer the masses economically, concentrating in the hands of the State the production and distribution of wealth."* This will result in *"a new class, a new hierarchy of real and counterfeit scientists and scholars, and the world will be divided into a minority ruling in the name of knowledge, and an immense ignorant majority. And then, woe unto the mass of ignorant ones!"* Thus exploitation by a new bureaucratic class would be the only result when the state becomes *"the sole proprietor"* and *"the only banker, capitalist, organiser, and director of all national labour, and the distributor of all its products."* [**Bakunin on Anarchism**, pp. 317-8, p. 318 and p. 217] Subsequent anarchists have tended to call such a regime **state capitalism** (see section H.3.13).

The Bolshevik leadership's rejection of the factory committees and their vision of socialism also confirmed Bakunin's fear that Marxism urges the people *"not only not abolish the State, but, on the contrary, they must strengthen it and enlarge it, and turn it over to ... the leaders of the Communist party ... who will then liberate them in their own way."* The economic regime imposed by the Bolsheviks, likewise, confirmed Bakunin's critique as the state *"control[led] all the commerce, industry, agriculture, and even science. The mass of the people will be divided into two armies, the agricultural and the industrial under the direct command of the state engineers, who will constitute the new privileged political-scientific class."* Unsurprisingly, this new state-run economy was a disaster which, again, confirmed his warning that unless this minority *"were endowed with omniscience, omnipresence, and the omnipotence which the theologians attribute to God, [it] could not possibly know and foresee the needs of its people, or satisfy with an even justice those needs which are most legitimate and pressing."* [**Op. Cit.**, p. 332, pp. 332-3 and p. 318]

Which brings us to the "dictatorship of the proletariat." While many Marxists basically use this term to describe the defence of the revolution and so argue that anarchists do not see the need for that, this is incorrect. Anarchists from Bakunin onwards have argued that a revolution would have to defend itself from counter revolution and yet we reject the concept totally (see section H.2.1 for a refutation of claims that anarchists think a revolution does not need defending). To understand why Bakunin rejected the concept, we must provide some historical context.

Anarchists in the nineteenth century rejected the idea of the "dictatorship of the proletariat" in part because the proletariat was a **minority** of working class people at the time. To argue for a dictatorship of the proletariat meant to argue for the dictatorship of a **minority** class, a class which excluded the majority of toiling people. When Marx and Engels wrote the **Communist Manifesto**, for example, over 80% of the population of France and Germany were peasants or artisans - what they termed the "petit-bourgeois". This meant that their claim that the *"proletarian movement is the self-conscious, independent movement of the immense majority, in the interests of the immense majority"* was simply not true. Rather, for Marx's life-time (and for many decades afterwards) the proletarian movement was like *"[a]ll previous movements,"* namely *"movements of minorities, or in the interests of minorities."* Not that Marx and Engels were unaware of this for they also noted that *"[i]n countries like France"* the peasants *"constitute far more than half of the population."* In 1875 Marx commented that *"the majority of the 'toiling people' in Germany consists of peasants, and not of proletarians."* He stressed elsewhere around the same time that *"the peasant ... forms a more of less considerable majority ... in the countries of the West European continent."* [**The Marx-Engels Reader**, p. 482, p. 493, p. 536 and p. 543]

Clearly, then, Marx and Engels vision of proletarian revolution was one which involved a minority dictating to the majority and so Bakunin rejected it. His opposition rested on the fact that a "dictatorship of the proletariat," at the time, actually meant a dictatorship by a **minority** of working people and so a "revolution" which excluded the majority of working people (i.e. artisans and peasants). As he argued in 1873:

> *"If the proletariat is to be the ruling class ... then whom will it rule? There must be yet another proletariat which will be subject to this new rule, this new state. It may be the peasant rabble ... which, finding itself on a lower cultural level, will probably be governed by the urban and factory proletariat."* [**Statism and Anarchy**, pp. 177-8]

For Bakunin, to advocate the "dictatorship of the proletariat" in an environment where the vast majority of working people were peasants would be a disaster. It is only when we understand this social context that we can understand Bakunin's opposition to Marx's "dictatorship of the proletariat" - it would be a dictatorship of a minority class over the rest of the working population (he took it as a truism that the capitalist and landlord classes should be expropriated and stopped from destroying the revolution!). Bakunin continually stressed the need for a movement and revolution of **all** working class people (see section H.2.7) and that the peasants *"will join cause with the city workers as soon as they become convinced that the latter do not pretend to impose their will or some political or social order invented by the cities for the greater happiness of the villages; they will join cause as soon as they are assured that the industrial workers will not take their lands away."* For an *"uprising by the proletariat alone would not be enough; with that we would have only a political revolution which would necessarily produce a natural and legitimate reaction on the part of the peasants, and that reaction, or merely the indifference of the peasants, would strangle the revolution of the cities."* [**The Political Philosophy of Bakunin**, p. 401 and p. 378]

This explains why the anarchists at the St. Imier Congress argued that *"every political state can be nothing but organised domination for the benefit of one class, to the detriment of the masses, and that should the proletariat itself seize power, it would in turn become a new dominating and exploiting class."* As the proletariat was a minority class at the time, their concerns can be understood. For anarchists then and now, a social revolution has to be truly popular and involve the majority of the population in order to succeed. Unsurprisingly, the congress stressed the role of the proletariat in the struggle for socialism, arguing that *"the proletariat of all lands ... must create the solidarity of revolutionary action ... independently of and in opposition to all forms of bourgeois politics."* Moreover, the aim of the workers' movement was *"free organisations and federations ... created by the spontaneous action of the proletariat itself, [that is, by] the trade bodies and the autonomous communes."* [quoted in **Bakunin on Anarchism**, p. 438, p. 439 and p. 438]

Hence Bakunin's comment that *"the designation of the proletariat, the world of the workers, as **class** rather than as **mass**"* was *"deeply antipathetic to us revolutionary anarchists who unconditionally advocate full popular emancipation."* To do so, he argued, meant *"[n]othing more or less than a new aristocracy, that of the urban and industrial workers, to the exclusion of the millions who make up the rural proletariat and who ... will in effect become subjects of this great so-called popular State."* [**Michael Bakunin: Selected Writings**, pp. 253-4]

Again, the experiences of the Russian Revolution confirm Bakunin's worries. The Bolsheviks implemented the dictatorship of the city over the countryside, with disastrous results (see section H.6.2 for more details).

One last point on this subject. While anarchists reject the "dictatorship of the proletariat" we clearly do not reject the key role the proletariat must play in any social revolution (see section H.2.2 on why the Marxist assertion anarchists reject class struggle is false). We only reject the idea that the proletariat must dictate over other working people like peasants and artisans. We do not reject the need for working class people to defend a revolution, nor the need for them to expropriate the capitalist class nor for them to manage their own activities and so society.

Then there is the issue of whether, even if the proletariat **does** seize political power, whether the whole class can actually exercise it. Bakunin raised the obvious questions:

> *"For, even from the standpoint of that urban proletariat who are supposed to reap the sole reward of the seizure of political power, surely it is obvious that this power will never be anything but a sham? It is bound to be impossible for a few thousand, let alone tens or hundreds of thousands of men to wield that power effectively. It will have to be exercised by proxy, which means entrusting it to a group of men elected to represent and govern them, which in turn will unfailingly return them to all the deceit and subservience of representative or bourgeois rule. After a brief flash of liberty or orgiastic revolution, the citizens of the new State will wake up slaves, puppets and victims of a new group of ambitious men."* [**Op. Cit.**, pp. 254-5]

He repeated this argument: *"What does it mean, 'the proletariat raised to a governing class?' Will the entire proletariat head the government? The Germans number about 40 million. Will all 40 millions be members of the government? The entire nation will rule, but no one will be ruled. Then there will be no government, no* state; but if there is a state, there will also be those who are ruled, there will be slaves." Bakunin argued that Marxism resolves this dilemma *"in a simple fashion. By popular government they mean government of the people by a small number of representatives elected by the people. So-called popular representatives and rulers of the state elected by the entire nation on the basis of universal suffrage - the last word of the Marxists, as well as the democratic school - is a lie behind which the despotism of a ruling minority is concealed, a lie all the more dangerous in that it represents itself as the expression of a sham popular will."* [**Statism and Anarchy**, p. 178]

So where does Marx stand on this question. Clearly, the self-proclaimed followers of Marx support the idea of "socialist" governments (indeed, many, including Lenin and Trotsky, went so far as to argue that party dictatorship was essential for the success of a revolution - see next section). Marx, however, is less clear. He argued, in reply to Bakunin's question if all Germans would be members of the government, that *"[c]ertainly, because the thing starts with the self-government of the township."* However, he also commented that *"[c]an it really be that in a trade union, for example, the entire union forms its executive committee,"* suggesting that there **will** be a division of labour between those who govern and those who obey in the Marxist system of socialism. [**The Marx-Engels Reader**, p. 545 and p. 544] Elsewhere he talks about *"a socialist government"* coming *"to the helm in a country".* [**Collected Works**, vol. 46, p. 66] As we discuss in section H.3.10, both Marx and Engels saw universal suffrage in a republic as expressing the political power of the working class.

So Bakunin's critique holds, as Marx clearly saw the "dictatorship of the proletariat" involving a socialist government having power. For Bakunin, like all anarchists, if a political party is the government, then clearly its leaders are in power, not the mass of working people they claim to represent. Anarchists have, from the beginning, argued that Marx made a grave mistake confusing working class power with the state. This is because the state is the means by which the management of people's affairs is taken from them and placed into the hands of a few. It signifies **delegated** power. As such, the so-called "workers' state" or "dictatorship of the proletariat" is a contradiction in terms. Instead of signifying the power of the working class to manage society it, in fact, signifies the opposite, namely the handing over of that power to a few party leaders at the top of a centralised structure. This is because *"all State rule, all governments being by their very nature placed outside the people, must necessarily seek to subject it to customs and purposes entirely foreign to it. We therefore declare ourselves to be foes … of all State organisations as such, and believe that the people can be happy and free, when, organised from below upwards by means of its own autonomous and completely free associations, without the supervision of any guardians, it will create its own life."* [Bakunin, **Marxism, Freedom and the State**, p. 63] Hence Bakunin's constant arguments for a decentralised, federal system of workers councils organised from the bottom-up. Again, the transformation of the Bolshevik government into a dictatorship **over** the proletariat during the early stages of the Russian Revolution supports Bakunin's critique of Marxism.

Related to this issue is Bakunin's argument that Marxism created a privileged position for socialist intellectuals in both the current social movement and in the social revolution. This was because Marx stressed that his theory was a "scientific socialism" and, Bakunin argued, that implied *"because thought, theory and science, at least in our times, are in the possession of very few, these few ought to be the leaders of social life"* and they, not the masses, should organise the revolution *"by the dictatorial powers of this learned minority, which presumes to express the will of the people."* This would be *"nothing but a despotic control of the populace by a new and not at all numerous aristocracy of real and pseudoscientists"* and so there would *"be a new [ruling] class, a new hierarchy of real and counterfeit scientists and scholars, and the world will be divided into a minority ruling in the name of knowledge, and an immense ignorant majority. And then, woe unto the mass of ignorant ones!"* Thus *"every state, even the pseudo-People's State concocted by Mr. Marx, is in essence only a machine ruling the masses from above, through a privileged minority of conceited intellectuals who imagine that they know what the people need and want better than do the people themselves."* The Russian anarchist predicted that *"the organisation and the rule of the new society by socialist savants"* would be *"the worse of all despotic governments!"* [**Bakunin on Anarchism**, pp. 328-9, p. 331, p. 319, p. 338 and p. 295] History proved Bakunin right, with the Bolshevik regime being precisely that. As we discuss in section H.5, Lenin's vanguardism did produce such a result, with the argument that the party leadership knew the objective needs of working class people better than they themselves did being used to justify party dictatorship and the strict centralisation of social life in the hands of its leadership.

Which brings us to the last issue, namely whether the revolution will be decentralised or centralised. For Marx, the issue is somewhat confused by his support for the Paris Commune and its federalist programme (written, we must note, by a follower of Proudhon). However, in 1850, Marx stood for extreme centralisation of power, arguing that the workers *"must not only strive for a single and indivisible German republic, but also within this republic for the most determined centralisation of power in the hands of the state authority."* He argued that in a nation like Germany *"where there are so many relics of the Middle Ages to be abolished"* it *"must under no circumstances be permitted that every village, every town and every province should put a new obstacle in the path of revolutionary activity, which can proceed with full force from the centre."* He stressed that *"[a]s in France in 1793 so today in Germany it is the task of the really revolutionary party to carry through the strictest centralisation."* [**The Marx-Engels Reader**, pp. 509-10] Lenin followed this aspect of Marx's ideas, arguing that *"Marx was a centralist"* and applying this perspective both in the party and once in power [**The Essential Works of Lenin**, p. 310] Obviously, this issue dove-tails into the question of whether the whole class exercises power under the "dictatorship of the proletariat." In a centralised system, obviously, power **has to be** exercised by a few (as Marx's argument in 1850 showed). Centralism, by its very nature excludes the possibility of extensive participation in the decision making process. Moreover, the decisions reached by such a body could not reflect the real needs of society. In the words of Bakunin:

"What man, what group of individuals, no matter how great their genius, would dare to think themselves able to embrace and understand the plethora of interests, attitudes and activities so various in every country, every province, locality and profession." [**Michael Bakunin: Selected Writings**, p. 240]

He stressed that *"the revolution should be and should everywhere remain independent of the central point, which must be its expression and product - not its source, guide and cause ... the awakening of all local passions and the awakening of spontaneous life at all points, must be well developed in order for the revolution to remain alive, real and powerful."* Anarchists reject centralisation because it destroys the mass participation a revolution requires in order to succeed. Therefore we do *"not accept, even in the process of revolutionary transition, either constituent assemblies, provisional governments or so-called revolutionary dictatorships; because we are convinced that revolution is only sincere, honest and real in the hands of the masses, and that when it is concentrated in those of a few ruling individuals it inevitably and immediately becomes reaction."* Rather, the revolution *"everywhere must be created by the people, and supreme control must always belong to the people organised into a free federation of agricultural and industrial associations ... organised from the bottom upwards by means of revolutionary delegation."* [**Op. Cit.**, pp. 179-80, p. 237 and p. 172]

This, we must stress, does not imply isolation. Bakunin always emphasised the importance of federal organisation to co-ordinate struggle and defence of the revolution. As he put it, all revolutionary communes would need to federate in order *"to organise the necessary common services and arrangements for production and exchange, to establish the charter of equality, the basis of all liberty - a charter utterly negative in character, defining what has to be abolished for ever rather than the positive forms of local life which can be created only by the living practice of each locality - and to organise common defence against the enemies of the Revolution."* [**Op. Cit.**, p. 179]

Ironically, it is a note by Engels to the 1885 edition of Marx's 1850 article which shows the fallacy of the standard Marxist position on centralisation and the validity of Bakunin's position. As Engels put it, *"this passage is based on a misunderstanding"* and it was now *"a well known fact that throughout the whole [Great French] revolution ... the whole administration of the departments, arrondissements and communes consisted of authorities elected by the respective constituents themselves, and that these authorities acted with complete freedom within general state laws [and] that precisely this provincial and local self-government ... became the most powerful lever of the revolution."* [**The Marx-Engels Reader**, p. 510f] Marx's original comments imply the imposition of freedom by the centre on a population not desiring it (and how could the centre be representative of the majority in such a case?). Moreover, how could a revolution be truly social if it was not occurring in the grassroots across a country? Unsurprisingly, local autonomy has played a key role in every real revolution.

As such, Bakunin has been proved right. Centralism has always killed a revolution and, as he always argued, real socialism can only be worked from below, by the people of every village, town, and city. The problems facing the world or a revolution cannot be solved by a few people at the top issuing decrees. They can only be solved by the active participation of the mass of working class people, the kind of participation centralism and government by their nature exclude.

Given Marx's support for the federal ideas of the Paris Commune, it can be argued that Marxism is not committed to a policy of strict centralisation (although Lenin, of course, argued that Marx **was** a firm supporter of centralisation). What is true is, to quote Daniel Guérin, that Marx's comments on the Commune differ *"noticeably from Marx's writings of before and after 1871"* while Bakunin's were *"in fact quite consistent with the lines he adopted in his earlier writings."* [**No Gods, No Masters**, vol. 1, p. 167] Indeed, as Bakunin himself noted, while the Marxists *"saw all their ideas upset by the uprising"* of the Commune, they *"found themselves compelled to take their hats off to it. They went even further, and proclaimed that its programme and purpose were their own, in face of the simplest logic and their own true sentiments."* This modification of ideas by Marx in the light of the Commune was not limited just to federalism, he also praised its system of mandating recallable delegates. This was a position which Bakunin had been arguing for a number of years previously but which Marx had never advocated. In 1868, for example, Bakunin was talking about a *"Revolutionary Communal Council"* composed of *"delegates ... vested with plenary but accountable and removable mandates."* [**Michael Bakunin: Selected Writings**, p. 261 and pp. 170-1] As such, the Paris Commune was a striking confirmation of Bakunin's ideas on many levels, **not** Marx's (who adjusted his ideas to bring them in line with Bakunin's!).

Since Bakunin, anarchists have deepened this critique of Marxism and, with the experience of both Social-Democracy and Bolshevism, argue that he predicted key failures in Marx's ideas. Given that his followers, particularly Lenin and Trotsky, have emphasised (although, in many ways, changed them) the centralisation and "socialist government" aspects of Marx's thoughts, anarchists argue that Bakunin's critique is as relevant as ever. Real socialism can only come from below.

For more on Bakunin's critique of Marxism, Mark Leier's excellent biography of the Russian Anarchist (**Bakunin: The Creative Passion**) is worth consulting, as is Brian Morris's **Bakunin: The Philosophy of Freedom**. John Clark has two useful essays on this subject in his **The Anarchist Moment** while Richard B. Saltman's **The Social and Political Thought of Michael Bakunin** contains an excellent chapter on Bakunin and Marx. A good academic account can be found in Alvin W. Gouldner's *"Marx's Last Battle: Bakunin and the First International"* (**Theory and Society**, Vol. 11, No. 6) which is a revised and shortened version of a chapter of his **Against Fragmentation: the Origins of Marxism and the Sociology of Intellectuals**. Obviously, though, Bakunin's original writings should be the first starting point.

H.1.2 What are the key differences between Anarchists and Marxists?

There are, of course, important similarities between anarchism and Marxism. Both are socialist, oppose capitalism and the current state, support and encourage working class organisation and see class struggle as the means of creating a social revolution which will transform society into a new one. However, the differences between these socialist theories are equally important. In the words of Errico Malatesta:

> "The important, fundamental dissension [between anarchists and Marxists] is [that] … [Marxist] socialists are authoritarians, anarchists are libertarians.

> "Socialists want power … and once in power wish to impose their programme on the people… Anarchists instead maintain, that government cannot be other than harmful, and by its very nature it defends either an existing privileged class or creates a new one; and instead of inspiring to take the place of the existing government anarchists seek to destroy every organism which empowers some to impose their own ideas and interests on others, for they want to free the way for development towards better forms of human fellowship which will emerge from experience, by everyone being free and, having, of course, the economic means to make freedom possible as well as a reality." [**Errico Malatesta: His Life and Ideas**, p. 142]

The other differences derive from this fundamental one. So while there are numerous ways in which anarchists and Marxists differ, their root lies in the question of power. Marxists seek power (in the name of the working class and usually hidden under rhetoric arguing that party and class power are the same). Anarchists seek to destroy hierarchical power in all its forms and ensure that everyone is free to manage their own affairs (both individually and collectively). From this comes the differences on the nature of a revolution, the way the working class movement should organise and the tactics it should apply and so on. A short list of these differences would include the question of the "dictatorship of the proletariat", the standing of revolutionaries in elections, centralisation versus federalism, the role and organisation of revolutionaries, whether socialism can only come *"from below"* or whether it is possible for it come *"from below"* and *"from above"* and a host of others (i.e. some of the differences we indicated in the last section during our discussion of Bakunin's critique of Marxism). Indeed, there are so many it is difficult to address them all here. As such, we can only concentrate on a few in this and the following sections.

One of the key issues is on the issue of confusing party power with popular power. The logic of the anarchist case is simple. In any system of hierarchical and centralised power (for example, in a state or governmental structure) then those at the top are in charge (i.e. are in positions of power). It is **not** "the people," nor "the proletariat," nor "the masses," it is those who make up the government who have and exercise real power. As Malatesta argued, government means *"the delegation of power, that is the abdication of initiative and sovereignty of all into the hands of a few"* and *"if … , as do the authoritarians, one means government action when one talks of social action, then this is still the resultant of individual forces, but only of those individuals who form the government."* [**Anarchy**, p. 40 and p. 36] Therefore, anarchists argue, the replacement of party power for working class power is inevitable because of the nature of the state. In the words of Murray Bookchin:

> "Anarchist critics of Marx pointed out with considerable effect that any system of representation would become a statist interest in its own right, one that at best would work against the interests of the working classes (including the peasantry), and that at worst would be a dictatorial power as vicious as the worst bourgeois state machines. Indeed, with political power reinforced by economic power in the form of a nationalised economy, a 'workers' republic' might well prove to be a despotism (to use one of Bakunin's more favourite terms) of unparalleled oppression …

> "Republican institutions, however much they are intended to express the interests of the workers, necessarily place policy-making in the hands of deputies and categorically do not constitute a 'proletariat organised as a ruling class.' If public policy, as distinguished from administrative activities, is not made by the people mobilised into assemblies and confederally co-ordinated by agents on a local, regional, and national basis, then a democracy in the precise sense of the term does not exist. The powers that people enjoy under such circumstances can be usurped without difficulty … [I]f the people are to acquire real power over their lives and society, they must establish - and in the past they have, for brief periods of time established - well-ordered institutions in which they themselves directly formulate the policies of their communities and, in the case of their regions, elect confederal functionaries, revocable and strictly controllable, who will execute them. Only in this sense can a class, especially one committed to the abolition of classes, be mobilised as a class to manage society." ["The Communist Manifesto: Insights and Problems", pp. 14-17, **Black Flag**, no. 226, pp. 16-7]

This is why anarchists stress direct democracy (self-management) in free federations of free associations. It is the only way to ensure that power remains in the hands of the people and is not turned into an alien power above them. Thus Marxist support for statist forms of organisation will inevitably undermine the liberatory nature of the revolution.

Thus the **real** meaning of a workers state is simply that the **party** has the real power, not the workers. That is the nature of a state. Marxist rhetoric tends to hide this reality. As an example, we can point to Lenin's comments in October, 1921. In an essay marking the fourth anniversary of the Bolshevik Revolution, Lenin stated that the Soviet system *"provides the maximum of democracy* for the workers and peasants; at the same time, it marks a break with **bourgeois** democracy and the rise of a new, epoch-making type of democracy, namely, proletarian democracy, or the dictatorship of the proletariat." [**Collected Works**, vol. 33, p. 55] Yet Lenin's comments came just a few months after factions within the Communist Party had been banned and after the Kronstadt rebellion and a wave of strikes calling for free soviet elections had been repressed. It was written years after Lenin had asserted that "[w]hen we are reproached with having established a dictatorship of one party ... we say, 'Yes, it is a dictatorship of one party! This is what we stand for and we shall not shift from that position ...'" [**Op. Cit.**, vol. 29, p. 535] And, of course, they had not shifted from that position! Clearly, the term "proletarian democracy" had a drastically different meaning to Lenin than to most people!

The identification of party power and working class power reaches its height (or, more correctly, depth) in the works of Lenin and Trotsky. Lenin, for example, argued that "the Communists' correct understanding of his tasks" lies in "correctly gauging the conditions and the moment when the vanguard of the proletariat can successfully assume power, when it will be able - during and after the seizure of power - to win adequate support from sufficiently broad strata of the working class and of the non-proletarian working masses, and when it is able thereafter to maintain, consolidate, and extend its rule by educating, training and attracting ever broader masses of the working people." Note, the vanguard (the party) seizes power, **not** the masses. Indeed, he stressed that the "mere presentation of the question - 'dictatorship of the party **or** dictatorship of the class: dictatorship (party) of the leaders **or** dictatorship (party) of the masses?' - testifies to most incredible and hopelessly muddled thinking" and "[t]o go so far ... as to contrast, **in general**, the dictatorship of the masses with a dictatorship of the leaders is ridiculously absurd, and stupid." [**The Lenin Anthology**, p. 575, p. 567 and p. 568]

Lenin stressed this idea numerous times. For example, he argued that "the dictatorship of the proletariat cannot be exercised through an organisation embracing the whole of the class, because in all capitalist countries (and not only over here, in one of the most backward) the proletariat is still so divided, so degraded, and so corrupted in parts ... that an organisation taking in the whole proletariat cannot directly exercise proletarian dictatorship. It can be exercised only by a vanguard ... Such is the basic mechanism of the dictatorship of the proletariat, and the essentials of transition from capitalism to communism ... for the dictatorship of the proletariat cannot be exercised by a mass proletarian organisation." [**Collected Works**, vol. 32, p. 21] This position had become Communist orthodoxy both in Russia and internationally since early 1919. The American socialist John Reed, author of **Ten Days that Shook the World**, was a defender of "the value of centralisation" and "the dictatorship of a revolutionary minority" (noting that "the Communist Party is supreme in Russia"). [**Shaking the World**, p. 238] Similarly with the likes of Amedeo Bordiga, the first leader of the Communist Party in Italy.

Victor Serge, the ex-anarchist and enthusiastic convert to Bolshevism, argued this mainstream Bolshevik position until the mid-1930s. In 1919, it was a case that "dictatorship" was not some kind of "proletarian" dictatorship by the masses. He, like the leading

Bolsheviks, explicitly argued against this. Yes, he wrote, "if we are looking at what should, that is at what **ought to**, be the case" but this "seems doubtful" in reality. "For it appears that by force of circumstances one group is obliged to impose itself on the others and to go ahead of them, breaking them if necessary, in order then to exercise exclusive dictatorship." The militants "leading the masses ... cannot rely on the consciousness, the goodwill or the determination of those they have to deal with; for the masses who will follow them or surround them will be warped by the old regime, relatively uncultivated, often unaware, torn by feelings and instincts inherited from the past." So "revolutionaries will have to take on the dictatorship without delay." The experience of Russia "reveals an energetic and innovative minority which is compelled to make up for the deficiencies in the education of the backward masses by the use of compulsion." And so the party "is in a sense the nervous system of the class. Simultaneously the consciousness and the active, physical organisation of the dispersed forces of the proletariat, which are often ignorant of themselves and often remain latent or express themselves contradictorily." And what of the masses? What was their role? Serge was equally blunt. While the party is "supported by the entire working population," strangely enough, "it maintains its unique situation in dictatorial fashion" while the workers are "[b]ehind" the communists, "sympathising instinctively with the party and carrying out the menial tasks required by the revolution." [**Revolution in Danger**, p. 106, p. 92, p. 115, p. 67, p. 66 and p. 6]

Such are the joys of socialist liberation. The party thinks for the workers while they carry out the "menial tasks" of the revolution. Like doing the work and following the orders - as in any class system.

Trotsky agreed with this lesson and in 1926 opined that the "dictatorship of the party does not contradict the dictatorship of the class either theoretically or practically; but is the expression of it, if the regime of workers' democracy is constantly developed more and more." [**The Challenge of the Left Opposition (1926-27)**, p. 76] The obvious contradictions and absurdities of this assertion are all too plain. Needless to say, when defending the concept of "the dictatorship of the party" he linked it to Lenin (and so to Leninist orthodoxy):

> "Of course, the foundation of our regime is the dictatorship of a class. But this in turn assumes ... it is a class that has come to self-consciousness through its vanguard, which is to say, through the party. Without this, the dictatorship could not exist ... Dictatorship is the most highly concentrated function of a class, and therefore the basic instrument of a dictatorship is a party. In the most fundamental aspects a class realises its dictatorship through a party. That is why Lenin spoke not only of the dictatorship of the class but also the dictatorship of the party and, **in a certain sense**, made them identical." [**Op. Cit.**, pp. 75-6]

He repeated this position on party dictatorship into the late 1930s, long after it had resulted in the horrors of Stalinism:

"The revolutionary dictatorship of a proletarian party is for me not a thing that one can freely accept or reject: It is an objective necessity imposed upon us by the social realities - the class struggle, the heterogeneity of the revolutionary class, the necessity for a selected vanguard in order to assure the victory. The dictatorship of a party belongs to the barbarian prehistory as does the state itself, but we can not jump over this chapter, which can open (not at one stroke) genuine human history... The revolutionary party (vanguard) which renounces its own dictatorship surrenders the masses to the counter-revolution ... Abstractly speaking, it would be very well if the party dictatorship could be replaced by the 'dictatorship' of the whole toiling people without any party, but this presupposes such a high level of political development among the masses that it can never be achieved under capitalist conditions. The reason for the revolution comes from the circumstance that capitalism does not permit the material and the moral development of the masses." [**Writings of Leon Trotsky 1936-37**, pp. 513-4]

Significantly, this was the year after his apparent (and much belated) embrace of soviet democracy in **The Revolution Betrayed**. Moreover, as we discuss in section H.3.8, he was just repeating the same arguments he had made while in power during the Russian Revolution. Nor was he the only one. Zinoviev, another leading Bolshevik, argued in 1920 along the same lines:

"soviet rule in Russia could not have been maintained for three years - not even three weeks - without the iron dictatorship of the Communist Party. Any class conscious worker must understand that the dictatorship of the working class can be achieved only by the dictatorship of its vanguard, i.e., by the Communist Party ... All questions of economic reconstruction, military organisation, education, food supply - all these questions, on which the fate of the proletarian revolution depends absolutely, are decided in Russia before all other matters and mostly in the framework of the party organisations ... Control by the party over soviet organs, over the trade unions, is the single durable guarantee that any measures taken will serve not special interests, but the interests of the entire proletariat." [quoted by Oskar Anweiler, **The Soviets**, pp. 239-40]

Three years later, at the Communist Party's congress, he made light of *"comrades who think that the dictatorship of the party is a thing to be realised in practice but not spoken about."* He went on to argue that what was needed was *"a **single** powerful central committee which is leader of everything ... in this is expressed the dictatorship of the party."* The Congress itself resolved that *"the dictatorship of the working class cannot be assured otherwise than in the form of a dictatorship of its leading vanguard, i.e., the Communist Party."* [quoted by E.H. Carr, **The Bolshevik Revolution 1917-1923**, vol. 1, p. 236, pp. 236-7 and p. 237]

How these positions can be reconciled with workers' democracy,

power or freedom is not explained. As such, the idea that Leninism (usually considered as mainstream Marxism) is inherently democratic or a supporter of power to the people is clearly flawed. Equally flawed are the attempts by Leninists to distance themselves from, and rationalise, these positions in terms of the "objective circumstances" (such as civil war) facing the Russian Revolution. As we discuss in section H.6, Bolshevik authoritarianism started **before** these problems began and continued long after they ended (in part because the policies pursued by the Bolshevik leadership had roots in their ideology and, as a result, that ideology itself played a key role in the failure of the revolution).

Ultimately, though, the leading lights of Bolshevism concluded from their experiences that the dictatorship of the proletariat could only be achieved by the dictatorship of the party and they generalised this position for **all** revolutions. Even in the prison camps in the late 1920s and early 1930s, *"almost all the Trotskyists continued to consider that 'freedom of party' would be 'the end of the revolution.' 'Freedom to choose one's party - that is Menshevism,' was the Trotskyists' final verdict."* [Ante Ciliga, **The Russian Enigma**, p. 280] While few Leninists today would subscribe to this position, the fact is when faced with the test of revolution the founders of their ideology not only practised the dictatorship of the party, they raised it to an ideological truism. Sadly, most modern day Trotskyists ignore this awkward fact in favour of inaccurate claims that Trotsky's **Left Opposition** *"framed a policy along [the] lines"* of *"returning to genuine workers' democracy"*. [Chris Harman, **Bureaucracy and Revolution in Eastern Europe**, p. 19] In reality, as "Left Oppositionist" Victor Serge pointed out, *"the greatest reach of boldness of the Left Opposition in the Bolshevik Party was to demand the restoration of inner-Party democracy, and it never dared dispute the theory of single-party government - by this time, it was too late."* [**The Serge-Trotsky Papers**, p. 181]

Significantly, this position on party rule has its roots in the uneven political development within the working class (i.e. that the working class contains numerous political perspectives within it). As the party (according to Leninist theory) contains the most advanced ideas and (again according to Leninist theory) the working class cannot reach beyond a trade union consciousness by its own efforts, the party must take power to ensure that the masses do not make "mistakes" or "waver" (show "vacillation") during a revolution. From such a perspective to the position of party dictatorship is not far (and a journey that all the leading Bolsheviks, including Lenin and Trotsky did in fact take).

These arguments by leading Bolsheviks confirm Bakunin's fear that the Marxists aimed for *"a tyranny of the minority over a majority in the name of the people - in the name of the stupidity of the many and the superior wisdom of the few."* [**Marxism, Freedom and the State**, p. 63]

In contrast, anarchists argue that precisely because of political differences we need the fullest possible democracy and freedom to discuss issues and reach agreements. Only by discussion and self-activity can the political perspectives of those in struggle develop and change. In other words, the fact Bolshevism uses to justify its support for party power is the strongest argument against it. For anarchists, the idea of a revolutionary government is a contradiction. As Malatesta put it, *"if you consider these worthy* electors as unable to look after their own interests themselves, how is it that they will know how to choose for themselves the shepherds who must guide them? And how will they be able to solve this problem of social alchemy, of producing a genius from the votes of a mass of fools?" [**Anarchy**, pp. 53-4] As such, anarchists think that power should be in the hands of the masses themselves. Only freedom or the struggle for freedom can be the school of freedom. That means that, to quote Bakunin, "since it is the people which must make the revolution everywhere … the ultimate direction of it must at all times be vested in the people organised into a free federation of agricultural and industrial organisations … organised from the bottom up through revolutionary delegation." [**No God, No Masters**, vol. 1, pp. 155-6]

Clearly, then, the question of state/party power is one dividing anarchists and most Marxists. Again, though, we must stress that libertarian Marxists agree with anarchists on this subject and reject the whole idea that rule/dictatorship of a party equals the dictatorship of the working class. As such, the Marxist tradition as a whole does not confuse this issue, although the majority of it does. So not all Marxists are Leninists. A few (council communists, Situationists, and so on) are far closer to anarchism. They also reject the idea of party power/dictatorship and the use of elections and instead argue for direct action, the abolition of wage slavery by workers' self-management of production and so on. They represent the best in Marx's work and should not be lumped with the followers of Bolshevism. Sadly, they are in the minority.

Finally, we should indicate other important areas of difference as summarised by Lenin in his work **The State and Revolution**:

> "The difference between the Marxists and the anarchists is this: 1) the former, while aiming at the complete abolition of the state, recognise that this aim can only be achieved after classes have been abolished by the socialist revolution, as the result of the establishment of socialism which leads to the withering away of the state. The latter want to abolish the state completely overnight, failing to understand the conditions under which the state can be abolished 2) the former recognise that after the proletariat has conquered political power it must utterly destroy the old state machine and substitute for it a new one consisting of the organisation of armed workers, after the type of the Commune. The latter, while advocating the destruction of the state machine, have absolutely no idea of **what** the proletariat will put in its place and **how** it will use its revolutionary power; the anarchists even deny that the revolutionary proletariat should utilise its state power, its revolutionary dictatorship; 3) the former demand that the proletariat be prepared for revolution by utilising the present state; the latter reject this."
> [**Essential Works of Lenin**, p. 358]

We will discuss each of these points in the next three sections. Point one will be discussed in section H.1.3, the second in section H.1.4 and the third and final one in section H.1.5.

H.1.3 Why do anarchists wish to abolish the state "overnight"?

As indicated at the end of the last section, Lenin argued that while Marxists aimed "at the complete abolition of the state" they "recognise that this aim can only be achieved after classes have been abolished by the socialist revolution" while anarchists "want to abolish the state completely overnight." This issue is usually summarised by Marxists arguing that a new state is required to replace the destroyed bourgeois one. This new state is called by Marxists **"the dictatorship of the proletariat"** or a workers' state. Anarchists reject this transitional state while Marxists embrace it. Indeed, according to Lenin "a Marxist is one who **extends** the acceptance of the class struggle to the acceptance of the **dictatorship of the proletariat**." [**Essential Works of Lenin**, p. 358 and p. 294]

So what does the "dictatorship of the proletariat" actually mean? Generally, Marxists seem to imply that this term simply means the defence of the revolution and so the anarchist rejection of the dictatorship of the proletariat means, for Marxists, the denial of the need to defend a revolution. This particular straw man was used by Lenin in **The State and Revolution** when he quoted Marx's article "Indifference to Politics" to suggest that anarchists advocated workers "laying down their arms" after a successful revolution. Such a "laying down [of] their arms" would mean "abolishing the state" while keeping their arms "in order to crush the resistance of the bourgeoisie" would mean "giv[ing] the state a revolutionary and transitory form," so setting up "their revolutionary dictatorship in place of the dictatorship of the bourgeoisie." [Marx, quoted by Lenin, **Op. Cit.**, p. 315]

That such an argument can be made, never mind repeated, suggests a lack of honesty. It assumes that the Marxist and Anarchist definitions of "the state" are identical. They are not. For anarchists the state, government, means "the delegation of power, that is the abdication of initiative and sovereignty of all into the hands of a few." [Malatesta, **Anarchy**, p. 41] For Marxists, the state is "an organ of class **rule**, an organ for the **oppression** of one class by another." [Lenin, **Op. Cit.**, p. 274] That these definitions are in conflict is clear and unless this difference is made explicit, anarchist opposition to the "dictatorship of the proletariat" cannot be clearly understood.

Anarchists, of course, agree that the current state is the means by which the bourgeois class enforces its rule over society. In Bakunin's words, "the political state has no other mission but to protect the exploitation of the people by the economically privileged classes." [**The Political Philosophy of Bakunin**, p. 221] "Throughout history, just as in our time, government is either the brutal, violent, arbitrary rule of the few over the many or it is an organised instrument to ensure that domination and privilege will be in the hands of those who … have cornered all the means of life." Under capitalism, as Malatesta succulently put, the state is "the bourgeoisie's servant and **gendarme**." [**Op. Cit.**, p. 21 and p. 23] The reason why the state is marked by centralised power is due to its role as the protector of (minority) class rule. As such, a state cannot be anything but a defender of minority power as its centralised and hierarchical structure is designed for that purpose. If the working class really were running society, as Marxists claim they would be in the "dictatorship of the proletariat," then it would not be a state. As Bakunin put it: *"Where all rule, there are no more ruled, and there is no State."* [**Op. Cit.**, p. 223]

The idea that anarchists, by rejecting the "dictatorship of the proletariat," also reject defending a revolution is false. We do not equate the "dictatorship of the proletariat" with the need to defend a revolution or expropriating the capitalist class, ending capitalism and building socialism. Anarchists from Bakunin onwards have taken both of these necessities for granted. As we discuss this particular Marxist straw man in section H.2.1, we will leave our comments on anarchist awareness of the need to defend a revolution at this.

Anarchists, then, do not reject defending a revolution and our opposition to the so-called "revolutionary" or "socialist" state is not based on this, regardless of what Marx and Lenin asserted. Rather, we argue that the state can and must be abolished "overnight" during a social revolution because any state, including the so-called "dictatorship of the proletariat", is marked by hierarchical power and can only empower the few at the expense of the many. The state will not "wither away" as Marxists claim simply because it excludes, by its very nature, the active participation of the bulk of the population and ensures a new class division in society: those in power (the party) and those subject to it (the working class). Georges Fontenis sums up anarchist concerns on this issue:

> *"The formula 'dictatorship of the proletariat' has been used to mean many different things. If for no other reason it should be condemned as a cause of confusion. With Marx it can just as easily mean the centralised dictatorship of the party which claims to represent the proletariat as it can the federalist conception of the Commune.*
>
> *"Can it mean the exercise of political power by the victorious working class? No, because the exercise of political power in the recognised sense of the term can only take place through the agency of an exclusive group practising a monopoly of power, separating itself from the class and oppressing it. And this is how the attempt to use a State apparatus can reduce the dictatorship of the proletariat to the dictatorship of the party over the masses.*
>
> *"But if by dictatorship of the proletariat is understood collective and direct exercise of 'political power', this would mean the disappearance of 'political power' since its distinctive characteristics are supremacy, exclusivity and monopoly. It is no longer a question of exercising or seizing political power, it is about doing away with it all together!*
>
> *"If by dictatorship is meant the domination of the majority by a minority, then it is not a question of giving power to the proletariat but to a party, a distinct political group. If by dictatorship is meant the domination of a minority by the majority (domination by the victorious proletariat of*

the remnants of a bourgeoisie that has been defeated as a class) then the setting up of dictatorship means nothing but the need for the majority to efficiently arrange for its defence its own social Organisation.

[...]

"The terms 'domination', 'dictatorship' and 'state' are as little appropriate as the expression 'taking power' for the revolutionary act of the seizure of the factories by the workers.

We reject then as inaccurate and causes of confusion the expressions 'dictatorship of the proletariat', 'taking political power', 'workers state', 'socialist state' and 'proletarian state'." [**Manifesto of Libertarian Communism**, pp. 22-3]

So anarchists argue that the state has to be abolished "overnight" simply because a state is marked by hierarchical power and the exclusion of the bulk of the population from the decision making process. It cannot be used to implement socialism simply because it is not designed that way. To extend and defend a revolution a state is not required. Indeed, it is a hindrance:

> *"The mistake of authoritarian communists in this connection is the belief that fighting and organising are impossible without submission to a government; and thus they regard anarchists ... as the foes of all organisation and all co-ordinated struggle. We, on the other hand, maintain that not only are revolutionary struggle and revolutionary organisation possible outside and in spite of government interference but that, indeed, that is the only effective way to struggle and organise, for it has the active participation of all members of the collective unit, instead of their passively entrusting themselves to the authority of the supreme leaders.*
>
> *"Any governing body is an impediment to the real organisation of the broad masses, the majority. Where a government exists, then the only really organised people are the minority who make up the government; and ... if the masses do organise, they do so against it, outside it, or at the very least, independently of it. In ossifying into a government, the revolution as such would fall apart, on account of its awarding that government the monopoly of organisation and of the means of struggle."* [Luigi Fabbri, *"Anarchy and 'Scientific' Communism"*, pp. 13-49, **The Poverty of Statism**, Albert Meltzer (ed.), p. 27]

This is because of the hierarchical nature of the state, its delegation of power into the hands of the few and so a so-called "revolutionary" government can have no other result than a substitution of the few (the government) for the many (the masses). This, in turn, undermines the mass participation and action from below that a revolution needs to succeed and flourish. *"Instead of acting for themselves,"* Kropotkin argued, *"instead of marching forward, instead of advancing in the direction of the new order of things,* the people, confiding in their governors, entrusted to them the charge of taking the initiative." However, social change is the product of "the people in action" and "the brain of a few individuals [are] absolutely incapable of finding solutions" to the problems it will face "which can only spring from the life of the people." For anarchists, a revolution "is not a simple change of governors. It is the taking possession by the people of all social wealth" and this cannot be achieved "be decrees emanating from a government." This "economic change" will be "so immense and so profound" that it is "impossible for one or any individual to elaborate the different social forms which must spring up in the society of the future. This elaboration of new social forms can only be made by the collective work of the masses" and "[a]ny authority external to it will only be an obstacle, a "drag on the action of the people." A revolutionary state, therefore, "becomes the greatest obstacle to the revolution" and to "dislodge it" requires the people "to take up arms, to make another revolution." [**Anarchism**, p. 240, p. 241, pp. 247-8, p. 248, p. 249, p. 241 and p. 242] Which, we should stress, was exactly what happened in Russia, where anarchists and others (such as the Kronstadt rebels) called for a "Third Revolution" against the Bolshevik state and the party dictatorship and state capitalism it had created.

For anarchists, the abolition of the state does not mean rejecting the need to extend or defend a revolution (quite the reverse!). It means rejecting a system of organisation designed by and for minorities to ensure their rule. To create a state (even a "workers' state") means to delegate power away from the working class and eliminate their power in favour of party power ("the principle error of the [Paris] Commune, an unavoidable error, since it derived from the very principle on which power was constituted, was precisely that of being a government, and of substituting itself for the people by force of circumstances." [Elisée Reclus, quoted John P. Clark and Camille Martin, **Anarchy, Geography, Modernity**, p. 72]).

In place of a state anarchists' argue for a free federation of workers' organisations as the means of conducting a revolution (and the framework for its defence). Most Marxists seem to confuse centralism and federalism, with Lenin stating that "if the proletariat and the poor peasants take state power into their own hands, organise themselves quite freely in communes, and unite the action of all the communes in striking at capital ... won't that be centralism? Won't that be the most consistent democratic centralism and, moreover, proletarian centralism?" No, it would be federalism, the most consistent federalism as advocated by Proudhon and Bakunin and, under the influence of the former, suggested by the Paris Commune. Lenin argued that some "simply cannot conceive of the possibility of voluntary centralism, of the voluntary fusion of the proletarian communes, for the sole purpose of destroying bourgeois rule and the bourgeois state machine." [**The Lenin Anthology**, p. 348] Yet "voluntary centralism" is, at best, just another why of describing federalism - assuming that "voluntary" really means that, of course. At worst, and in practice, such centralism simply places all the decision making at the centre, at the top, and all that is left is for the communes to obey the decisions of a few party leaders.

As we discuss in the next section, anarchists see this federation of workers' associations and communes (the framework of a free society) as being based on the organisations working class people create in their struggle against capitalism. These self-managed organisations, by refusing to become part of a centralised state, will ensure the success of a revolution.

H.1.4 Do anarchists have "absolutely no idea" of what to put in place of the state?

Lenin's second claim was that anarchists, "while advocating the destruction of the state machine, have absolutely no idea of **what** the proletariat will put in its place" and compared this to the Marxists who argued for a new state machine "consisting of armed workers, after the type of the [Paris] Commune." [**Essential Works of Lenin**, p. 358]

For anarchists, Lenin's assertion simply shows his unfamiliarity with anarchist literature and need not be taken seriously - anyone familiar with anarchist theory would simply laugh at such comments. Sadly, most Marxists are **not** familiar with that theory, so we need to explain two things. Firstly, anarchists have very clear ideas on what to "replace" the state with (namely a federation of communes based on working class associations). Secondly, that this idea is based on the idea of armed workers, inspired by the Paris Commune (although predicted by Bakunin).

Moreover, for anarchists Lenin's comment seems somewhat incredulous. As George Barrett put it, in reply to the question "if you abolish government, what will you put it its place," this "seems to an Anarchist very much as if a patient asked the doctor, 'If you take away my illness, what will you give me in its place?' The Anarchist's argument is that government fulfils no useful purpose ... It is the headquarters of the profit-makers, the rent-takers, and of all those who take from but who do not give to society. When this class is abolished by the people so organising themselves to run the factories and use the land for the benefit of their free communities, i.e. for their own benefit, then the Government must also be swept away, since its purpose will be gone. The only thing then that will be put in the place of government will be the free organisation of the workers. When Tyranny is abolished, Liberty remains, just as when disease is eradicated health remains." [**Objections to Anarchism**, p. 356]

Barrett's answer contains the standard anarchist position on what will be the organisational basis of a revolutionary society, namely that the "only thing then that will be put in the place of government will be the free organisation of the workers." This is a concise summary of anarchist theory and cannot be bettered. This vision, as we discuss in section I.2.3 in some detail, can be found in the work of Bakunin, Kropotkin, Malatesta and a host of other anarchist thinkers. Since anarchists from Bakunin onwards have stressed that a federation of workers' associations would constitute the framework of a free society, to assert otherwise (as Lenin did) is little more than a joke or a slander. To quote Bakunin:

> "The future social organisation must be made solely from the bottom up, by the free association or federation of

workers, firstly in their unions, then in the communes, regions, nations and finally in a great federation, international and universal." [**Michael Bakunin: Selected Writings**, p. 206]

Similar ideas can easily be found in the works of other anarchists. While the actual names and specific details of these federations of workers' associations may change (for example, the factory committees and soviets in the Russian Revolution, the collectives in Spain, the section assemblies in the French Revolution are a few of them) the basic ideas are the same. Bakunin also pointed to the means of defence, a workers' militia (the people armed, as per the Paris Commune - section H.2.1).

A major difference between anarchism and Marxism which Lenin points to is, clearly, false. Anarchists are well aware of what should "*replace*" the bourgeois state and have always been so. The **real** difference is simply that anarchists say what they mean while Lenin's "new" state did not, in fact, mean working class power but rather party power.

As for Lenin's comment that we have "*absolutely no ideas*" of how the working class "*will use its revolutionary power*" suggests more ignorance, as we have urged working people to expropriate the expropriators, reorganise production under workers' self-management and start to construct society from the bottom upwards (a quick glance at Kropotkin's **Conquest of Bread**, for example, would soon convince any reader of the inaccuracy of Lenin's comment). This summary by the anarchist Jura Federation (written in 1880) gives a flavour of anarchist ideas on this subject:

"*The bourgeoisie's power over the popular masses springs from economic privileges, political domination and the enshrining of such privileges in the laws. So we must strike at the wellsprings of bourgeois power, as well as its various manifestations.*

"*The following measures strike us as essential to the welfare of the revolution, every bit as much as armed struggle against its enemies:*

"*The insurgents must confiscate social capital, landed estates, mines, housing, religious and public buildings, instruments of labour, raw materials, gems and precious stones and manufactured products:*

"*All political, administrative and judicial authorities are to be deposed … What should the organisational measures of the revolution be?*

"*Immediate and spontaneous establishment of trade bodies: provisional assumption by those of … social capital …: local federation of a trades bodies and labour organisation:*

"*Establishment of neighbourhood groups and federations of same …*

"*Organisation of the insurgent forces … the federation of all the revolutionary forces of the insurgent Communes …*

Federation of Communes and organisation of the masses, with an eye to the revolution's enduring until such time as all reactionary activity has been completely eradicated … Once trade bodies have been have been established, the next step is to organise local life. The organ of this life is to be the federation of trades bodies and it is this local federation which is to constitute the future Commune." [**No Gods, No Masters**, vol. 1, pp. 246-7]

Clearly, anarchists do have some ideas on what the working class will "*replace*" the state with and how it will use its "*revolutionary power*"!

Similarly, Lenin's statement that "*the anarchists even deny that the revolutionary proletariat should utilise its state power, its revolutionary dictatorship*" again distorts the anarchist position. As we argued in the last section, our objection to the "state power" of the proletariat is precisely **because** it cannot, by its very nature as a state, actually allow the working class to manage society directly (and, of course, it automatically excludes other sections of the working masses, such as the peasantry and artisans). We argued that, in practice, it would simply mean the dictatorship of a few party leaders. This position, we must stress, was one Lenin himself was arguing in the year after completing **State and Revolution** and so the leading Bolsheviks confirmed the anarchist argument that the "dictatorship of the proletariat" would, in fact, become a dictatorship **over** the proletariat by the party.

Italian anarchist Camillo Berneri summed up the differences well:

"*The Marxists … foresee the natural disappearance of the State as a consequence of the destruction of classes by the means of 'the dictatorship of the proletariat,' that is to say State Socialism, whereas the Anarchists desire the destruction of the classes by means of a social revolution which eliminates, with the classes, the State. The Marxists, moreover, do not propose the armed conquest of the Commune by the whole proletariat, but they propose the conquest of the State by the party which imagines that it represents the proletariat. The Anarchists allow the use of direct power by the proletariat, but they understand by the organ of this power to be formed by the entire corpus of systems of communist administration-corporate organisations [i.e. industrial unions], communal institutions, both regional and national-freely constituted outside and in opposition to all political monopoly by parties and endeavouring to a minimum administrational centralisation.*" ["*Dictatorship of the Proletariat and State Socialism*", pp. 51-2, **Cienfuegos Press Anarchist Review**, no. 4, p. 52]

Clearly, Lenin's assertions are little more than straw men. Anarchists are not only well aware of the need for a federation of working class associations (workers' councils or soviets) to replace the state, they were advocating it long before Lenin took up this perspective in 1917 (as we discuss in section H.3.10). The key difference being, of course, anarchists meant it while Lenin saw it as a means of securing Bolshevik party power.

Lastly, it should also be noted that Marxists, having taken so long to draw the same conclusions as anarchists like Proudhon and Bakunin, have tended to make a fetish of workers councils. As an example, we find Chris Harman of the British SWP complaining that the Argentinean masses organised themselves in the wrong way as part of their revolt against neo-liberalism which started in December 2001. He states that the *"neighbourhood committees and popular assemblies"* created by the revolt *"express the need of those who have overthrown presidents to organise themselves"* and notes *"they have certain similarities with the characteristic forms of mass self organisation that arose in the great working class struggles of the 20th century - the workers' councils or soviets."* But, he stressed, *"they also have very important differences from these."* Yet Harman's complaints show his own confusions, seriously arguing that *"the popular assemblies are not yet bodies of delegates. The people at them represent themselves, but do not have an organic connection with some group of people who they represent - and who can recall them if they do not carry out their will."* [*"Argentina: rebellion at the sharp end of the world crisis"*, pp. 3-48, **International Socialism**, vol. 94, p. 25] That, of course, is the whole point - they are popular **assemblies**! A popular assembly does not "represent" anyone because its members govern themselves, i.e. are directly democratic. They are the elemental bodies which recall any delegates who do not implement their mandate! But given that Leninism aims at party power, this concern for representation is perfectly understandable, if lamentable.

So rather than celebrate this rise in mass self-management and self-organisation, Harman complains that these *"popular assemblies are not anchored in the workplaces where millions of Argentineans are still drawn together on a daily basis to toil."* Need it be said that such an SWP approved organisation will automatically exclude the unemployed, housewives, the elderly, children and other working class people who were taking part in the struggle? In addition, any capitalist crisis is marked by rising unemployment, firms closing and so on. While workplaces must and have been seized by their workers, it is a law of revolutions that the economic disruption they cause results in increased unemployment (in this Kropotkin's arguments in **The Conquest of Bread** have been confirmed time and time again). Significantly, Harman admits that they include *"organisations of unemployed workers"* as well as *"that in some of the assemblies an important leading role is played by unemployed activists shaped by their role in past industrial struggles."* He does not, however, note that creating workers' councils would end their active participation in the revolt. [**Op. Cit.**, p. 25]

That the Argentine working class formed organs of power which were not totally dependent on the workplace was, therefore, a good sign. Factory assemblies and federations must be formed but as a complement to, rather than as a replacement of, the community assemblies. Harman states that the assemblies were *"closer to the sections - the nightly district mass meetings - of the French Revolution than to the workers' councils of 1905 and 1917 in Russia"* and complains that a *"21st century uprising was taking the form of the archetypal 18th century revolution!"* [**Op. Cit.**. p. 25 and p. 22] Did the Argentineans not realise that a 21st century uprising should mimic *"the great working class struggles of the 20th century"*, particularly that which took place in a mostly pre-capitalist Tsarist regime which was barely out of the 18th century itself? Did they

not realise that the leaders of the vanguard party know better than themselves how they should organise and conduct their struggles? That the people of the 21st century knew best how to organise their own revolts is lost on Harman, who prefers to squeeze the realities of modern struggles into the forms which Marxists took so long to recognise in the first place. Given that anarchists have been discussing the possibilities of community assemblies for some time, perhaps we can expect Leninists to recognise their importance in a few decades? After all, the Bolsheviks in Russia were slow to realise the significance of the soviets in 1905 so Harman's position is hardly surprising.

So, it is easy to see what anarchists think of Lenin's assertion that *"Anarchism had failed to give anything even approaching a true solution of the concrete political problems, **viz.**, must the old state machine be **smashed**? and **what** should supersede it?"* [**Op. Cit.**, p. 350] We simply point out that Lenin was utterly distorting the anarchist position on social revolution. Revolutionary anarchists had, since the 1860s, argued that workers' councils (soviets) could be both a weapon of class struggle against capitalism and the state as well as the framework of the future (libertarian) socialist society. Lenin only came to superficially similar conclusions in 1917. Which means that when he talked of workers' councils, Lenin was only repeating Bakunin - the difference being we anarchists mean it!

H.1.5 Why do anarchists reject "utilising the present state"?

This is another key issue, the question of Marxists demanding (in the words of Lenin) *"that the proletariat be prepared for revolution by utilising the present state"* while anarchists *"reject this."* [**Essential Works of Lenin**, p. 358] By this, Lenin meant the taking part of socialists in bourgeois elections, standing candidates for office and having socialist representatives in Parliament and other local and national state bodies. In other words, what Marx termed *"political action"* and the Bolsheviks *"revolutionary Parliamentarianism."*

For anarchists, the use of elections does not "prepare" the working class for revolution (i.e. managing their own affairs and society). Rather, it prepares them to follow leaders and let others act for them. In the words of Rudolf Rocker:

> *"Participation in the politics of the bourgeois States has not brought the labour movement a hair's-breadth nearer to Socialism, but thanks to this method, Socialism has almost been completely crushed and condemned to insignificance ... Participation in parliamentary politics has affected the Socialist Labour movement like an insidious poison. It destroyed the belief in the necessity of constructive Socialist activity, and, worse of all, the impulse to self-help, by inoculating people with the ruinous delusion that salvation always comes from above."* [**Anarcho-Syndicalism**, p. 54]

While electoral ("political") activity ensures that the masses become accustomed to following leaders and letting them act on their behalf, anarchists' support direct action as *"the best available means for preparing the masses to manage their own personal and collective interests; and besides, anarchists feel that even now the working people are fully capable of handling their own political and administrative interests."* Political action, in contrast, needs centralised *"authoritarian organisations"* and results in *"ceding power by all to someone, the delegate, the representative".* "For direct pressure put against the ruling classes by the masses, the Socialist Party has substituted representation" and *"instead of fostering the class struggle ... it has adopted class collaboration in the legislative arena, without which all reforms would remain a vain hope."* [Luigi Galleani, **The End of Anarchism?**, pp. 13-4, p. 14 and p. 12]

Anarchists, therefore, argue that we need to reclaim the power which has been concentrated into the hands of the state. That is why we stress direct action. Direct action means action by the people themselves, that is action directly taken by those directly affected. Through direct action, we dominate our own struggles, it is we who conduct it, organise it, manage it. We do not hand over to others our own acts and task of self-liberation. That way, we become accustomed to managing our own affairs, creating alternative, libertarian, forms of social organisation which can become a force to resist the state, win reforms and, ultimately, become the framework of a free society. In other words, direct action creates organs of self-activity (such as community assemblies, factory committees, workers' councils, and so on) which, to use Bakunin's words, are *"creating not only the ideas but also the facts of the future itself."*

The idea that socialists standing for elections somehow prepares working class people for revolution is simply wrong. Utilising the state, standing in elections, only prepares people for following leaders - it does not encourage the self-activity, self-organisation, direct action and mass struggle required for a social revolution. Moreover, as Bakunin predicted, participation in elections has a corrupting effect on those who do so. The history of radicals using elections has been a long one of betrayal and the transformation of revolutionary parties into reformist ones (see section J.2.6 for more discussion). Using the existing state ensures that the division at the heart of existing society (namely a few who govern and the many who obey) is reproduced in the movements trying to abolish it. It boils down to handing effective leadership to special people, to "leaders," just when the situation requires working people to solve their own problems and take matters into their own hands:

> *"The Social Question will be put ... long before the Socialists have conquered a few seats in Parliament, and thus the solution of the question will be actually in the hands of the workmen [and women] themselves ...*
>
> *"Under the influence of government worship, they may try to nominate a new government ... and they may entrust it with the solution of all difficulties. It is so simple, so easy, to throw a vote into the ballot-box, and to return home! So gratifying to know that there is somebody who will arrange your own affairs for the best, while you are quietly smoking your pipe and waiting for orders which you have only to execute, not to reason about."* [Kropotkin, **Act for Yourselves**, p. 34]

Only the struggle for freedom (or freedom itself) can be the school for freedom, and by placing power into the hands of leaders, utilising the existing state ensures that socialism is postponed rather than prepared for. As such, strikes and other forms of direct action *"are of enormous value; they create, organise, and form a workers' army, an army which is bound to break down the power of the bourgeoisie and the State, and lay the ground for a new world."* [Bakunin, **The Political Philosophy of Bakunin**, pp. 384-5] In contrast, utilising the present state only trains people in following leaders and so socialism *"lost its creative initiative and became an ordinary reform movement ... content with success at the polls, and no longer attributed any importance to social upbuilding."* [Rocker, **Op. Cit.**, p. 55]

Which highlights another key problem with the notion of utilising the present state as Marxist support for electioneering is somewhat at odds with their claims of being in favour of collective, mass action. There is nothing more isolated, atomised and individualistic than voting. It is the act of one person in a box by themselves. It is the total opposite of collective struggle. The individual is alone before, during and after the act of voting. Indeed, unlike direct action, which, by its very nature, throws up new forms of organisation in order to manage and co-ordinate the struggle, voting creates no alternative social structures. Nor can it as it is not based on nor does it create collective action or organisation. It simply empowers an individual (the elected representative) to act on behalf of a collection of other individuals (the voters). This will hinder collective organisation and action as the voters expect their representative to act and fight for them - if they did not, they would not vote for them in the first place!

Given that Marxists usually slander anarchists as "individualists" the irony is delicious!

If we look at the anti-Poll-Tax campaign in the UK in the late 1980s and early 1990s, we can see what would happen to a mass movement which utilised electioneering. Various left-wing parties spent a lot of time and effort lobbying Labour Councillors not to implement the tax (with no success). Let us assume they had succeeded and the Labour Councillors had refused to implement the tax (or "socialist" candidates had been elected to stop it). What would have happened? Simply that there would not have been a mass movement or mass organisation based on non-payment, nor self-organised direct action to resist warrant sales, nor community activism of any form. Rather, the campaign would have consisted of supporting the councillors in their actions, mass rallies in which the leaders would have informed us of their activities on our behalf and, perhaps, rallies and marches to protest any action the government had inflicted on them. The leaders may have called for some form of mass action but this action would not have come from below and so not be a product of working class self-organisation, self-activity and self-reliance. Rather, it would have been purely re-active and a case of follow the leader, without the empowering and liberating aspects of taking action by yourself, as a conscious and organised group. It would have replaced the struggle of millions with the actions of a handful of leaders.

Of course, even discussing this possibility indicates how remote it is from reality. The Labour Councillors were not going to act - they were far too "practical" for that. Years of working within the system, of using elections, had taken their toll decades ago. Anarchists, of course, saw the usefulness of picketing the council meetings, of protesting against the Councillors and showing them a small example of the power that existed to resist them if they implemented the tax. As such, the picket would have been an expression of direct action, as it was based on showing the power of our direct action and class organisations. Lobbying, however, was building illusions in "leaders" acting for us and based on pleading rather than defiance. But, then again, Militant desired to replace the current leaders with themselves and so had an interest in promoting such tactics and focusing the struggle on leaders and whether they would act for people or not.

Unfortunately, the Socialists never really questioned **why** they had to lobby the councillors in the first place - if utilising the existing state **was** a valid radical or revolutionary tactic, why has it always resulted in a de-radicalising of those who use it? This would be the inevitable result of any movement which "complements" direct action with electioneering. The focus of the movement will change from the base to the top, from self-organisation and direct action from below to passively supporting the leaders. This may not happen instantly, but over time, just as the party degenerates by working within the system, the mass movement will be turned into an electoral machine for the party - even arguing against direct action in case it harms the election chances of the leaders. Just as the trade union leaders have done again and again in Britain and elsewhere.

So anarchists point to the actual record of Marxists "utilising the present state". Murray Bookchin's comments about the German Social Democrats are appropriate here:

> "the party's preoccupation with parliamentarism was taking it ever away from anything Marx had envisioned. Instead of working to overthrow the bourgeois state, the SPD, with its intense focus on elections, had virtually become an engine for getting votes and increasing its Reichstag representation within the bourgeois state … The more artful the SPD became in these realms, the more its membership and electorate increased and, with the growth of new pragmatic and opportunistic adherents, the more it came to resemble a bureaucratic machine for acquiring power under capitalism rather than a revolutionary organisation to eliminate it." [**The Third Revolution**, vol. 2, p. 300]

The reality of working within the state soon transformed the party and its leadership, as Bakunin predicted. If we look at Leninism, we discover a similar failure to consider the evidence:

> "From the early 1920s on, the Leninist attachment to pre-WWI social democratic tactics such as electoral politics and political activity within pro-capitalist labour unions dominated the perspectives of the so-called Communists. But if these tactics were correct ones, why didn't they lead to a less dismal set of results? We must be materialists, not idealists. What was the actual outcome of the Leninist strategies? Did Leninist strategies result in successful proletarian revolutions, giving rise to societies worthy of

> the human beings that live in them? The revolutionary movement in the inter-war period was defeated." [Max Anger, "The Spartacist School of Falsification", pp. 50-2, **Anarchy: A Journal of Desire Armed**, no. 43, pp. 51-2]

As Scottish Anarchist Ethel McDonald argued in 1937, the tactics urged by Lenin were a disaster in practice:

> "At the Second Congress of the Third International, Moscow, a comrade who is with us now in Spain, answering Zinoviev, urged faith in the syndicalist movement in Germany and the end of parliamentary communism. He was ridiculed. Parliamentarianism, communist parliamentarianism, but still parliamentarianism would save Germany. And it did … Saved it from Socialism. Saved it for Fascism. Parliamentary social democracy and parliamentary communism have destroyed the socialist hope of Europe, has made a carnage of human liberty. In Britain, parliamentarianism saved the workers from Socialism … Have you not had enough of this huge deception? Are you still prepared to continue in the same old way, along the same old lines, talking and talking and doing nothing?" ["The Volunteer Ban", pp. 72-5, **Workers City**, Farquhar McLay (ed.), p. 74]

When the Nazis took power in 1933 in Germany the 12 million Socialist and Communist voters and 6 million organised workers took no action. In Spain, it was the anarcho-syndicalist CNT which lead the battle against fascism on the streets and helped create one of the most important social revolutions the world has seen. The contrast could not be more clear. And many Marxists urge us to follow Lenin's advice today!

All in all, the history of socialists actually using elections has been a dismal failure and was obviously a failure long before 1917. Subsequent experience has only confirmed that conclusion. Rather than prepare the masses for revolution, it has done the opposite. As we argue in section J.2, this is to be expected. That Lenin could still argue along these lines even after the rise of reformism ("revisionism") in the 1890s and the betrayal of social democracy in 1914 indicates a lack of desire to learn the lessons of history.

The negative effects of "utilising" the present state are, sometimes, acknowledged by Marxists although this rarely interferes with their support for standing in elections. Thus we find that advocate of "revolutionary" parliamentarianism, Trotsky, noting that [i]f parliamentarianism served the proletariat to a certain extent as a training school for revolution, then it also served the bourgeoisie to a far greater extent as the school of counter-revolutionary strategy. Suffice it to say that by means of parliamentarianism the bourgeoisie was able so to educate the Social Democracy that it is today [1924] the main prop of private property." [**Lessons of October**, pp. 170-1] Of course, the followers of Lenin and Trotsky are made of sterner stuff than those of Marx and Engels and so utilising the same tactics will have a different outcome. As one-time syndicalist William Gallacher put it in reply to Lenin's question "[i]f the workers sent you to represent them in Parliament, would you become corrupt?": "No, I'm sure that under no circumstances could the bourgeoisie corrupt me." [quoted by Mark Shipway, **Anti-Parliamentary Communism**, p. 21] Mere will-power, apparently, is sufficient to counteract the pressures and influences of parliamentarianism which Marx and Engels, unlike Bakunin, failed to predict but whose legacy still haunts the minds of those who claim to be *"scientific socialists"* and so, presumably, base their politics on facts and experience rather than wishful thinking.

This is why anarchists reject the notion of radicals utilising the existing state and instead urge direct action and solidarity outside of bourgeois institutions. Only this kind of struggle creates the spirit of revolt and new popular forms of organisation which can fight and replace the hierarchical structures of capitalist society. Hence anarchists stress the need of working class people to *"rely on themselves to get rid of the oppression of Capital, without expecting that the same thing can be done for them by anybody else. The emancipation of the workmen [and women] must be the act of the workmen [and women] themselves."* [Kropotkin, **Op. Cit.**, p. 32] Only this kind of movement and struggle can maximise the revolutionary potential of struggles for reforms within capitalism. As history shows, the alternative has repeatedly failed.

It should be noted, however, that not all Marxists have refused to recognise the lessons of history. Libertarian Marxists, such as council communists, also reject *"utilising the present state"* to train the proletariat for revolution (i.e. for socialists to stand for elections). Lenin attacked these Marxists who had drawn similar conclusions as the anarchists (**after** the failure of social-democracy) in his 1920 diatribe **Left-wing Communism: An Infantile Disorder**. In that pamphlet he used the experiences of the Bolsheviks in semi-Feudal Tsarist Russia to combat the conclusions drawn by socialists in the advanced capitalist countries with sizeable social democratic parties. Lenin's arguments for revolutionary Parliamentarianism did not convince the anti-Parliamentarians who argued that its *"significance lies not in its content, but in the person of the author, for the arguments are scarcely original and have for the most part already been used by others ... their fallacy resides mainly in the equation of the conditions, parties, organisations and parliamentary practice of Western Europe with their Russian counterparts."* [Anton Pannekoek, **Pannekoek and Gorter's Marxism**, p. 143] While anarchists would disagree with the underlying assumption that Marx was right in considering parliamentarianism as essential and it only became problematic later, we would agree whole-heartedly with the critique presented (unsurprisingly, as we made it first).

Pannekoek's article along with Herman Gorter's **Open Letter to Comrade Lenin** are essential reading for those who are taken in with Lenin's arguments, along with the chapter on *"Socialism"* in Alexander Berkman's **What is Anarchism?**. Interestingly, the Comintern asked Berkman to translate Lenin's **Left-Wing Communism** and he agreed until he read its contents. He then said he would continue if he could write a rebuttal, a request which was rejected. For anarchists, placing the word "revolutionary" in front of "parliamentarianism" does not provide a shield against the negative influences and pressures which naturally arise by utilising that tactic. Given the sorry history of radicals doing so, this is unsurprising. What is surprising is how so many Marxists are willing to ignore that history in favour of Lenin's pamphlet.

H.1.6 Why do anarchists try to "build the new world in the shell of the old"?

Another key difference between anarchists and Marxists is on how the movement against capitalism should organise in the here and now. Anarchists argue that it should prefigure the society we desire - namely it should be self-managed, decentralised, built and organised from the bottom-up in a federal structure. This perspective can be seen from the justly famous *"Circular of the Sixteen"* issued at the Sonvillier congress by the libertarian wing of the First International:

"The future society must be nothing else than the universalisation of the organisation that the International has formed for itself. We must therefore take care to make this organisation as close as possible to our ideal. How could one want an equalitarian and free society to issue from an authoritarian organisation? It is impossible. The International, the embryo of the future human society is held to be henceforward, the faithful image of our principles of liberty and of federation, and is considered to reject any principle tending to authority and dictatorship." [quoted by K.J. Kenafick, **Michael Bakunin and Karl Marx**, pp. 262-3]

Anarchists apply this insight to all organisations they take part in, stressing that the only way we can create a self-managed society is by self-managing our own struggles and organisations today. It is an essential part of our politics that we encourage people to *"learn how to participate in the life of the organisation and to do without leaders and permanent officials"* and *"practice direct action, decentralisation, autonomy and free initiative."* This flows logically from our politics, as it is *"obvious that anarchists should seek to apply to their personal and political lives this same principle upon which, they believe, the whole of human society should be based."* [Malatesta, **The Anarchist Revolution**, p. 94] In this way we turn our class organisations (indeed, the class struggle itself) into practical and effective *"schools of anarchism"* in which we learn to manage our own affairs without hierarchy and bosses and so popular organisations become the cells of the new society:

"Libertarian forms of organisation have the enormous responsibility of trying to resemble the society they are seeking to develop. They can tolerate no disjunction between ends and means. Direct action, so integral to the management of a future society, has its parallel in the use of direct action to change society. Communal forms, so integral to the structure of a future society, have their parallel in the use of communal forms - collectives, affinity groups, and the like - to change society. The ecological ethics, confederal relationships, and decentralised structures we would expect to find in a future society, are fostered by the values and networks we try to use in achieving an ecological society." [Murray Bookchin, **The Ecology of Freedom**, pp. 446-7]

Marxists reject this argument. Instead they stress the importance of centralisation and consider the anarchist argument as utopian. For effective struggle, strict centralisation is required as the capitalist class and state is also centralised. In other words, to fight for socialism there is a need to organise in a way which the capitalists have utilised - to fight fire with fire. Unfortunately they forget to extinguish a fire you have to use water. Adding more flame will only increase the combustion, **not** put it out!

Of course, Marx and Engels misrepresented the anarchist position. They asserted that the anarchist position implied that the Paris Communards *"would not have failed if they had understood that the Commune was 'the embryo of the future human society' and had cast away all discipline and all arms, that is, the things which must disappear when there are no more wars!"* [**Collected Works**, vol. 23, p. 115] Needless to say this is simply a slander on the anarchist position particularly as anarchists are well aware of the need to defend a revolution (see section H.2.1) and the need for **self**-discipline (see section H.4). Anarchists, as the Circular makes clear, recognise that we cannot totally reflect the future and so the current movement can only be *"as near as possible to our ideal."* Thus we have to do things, such as fighting the bosses, rising in insurrection, smashing the state or defending a revolution, which we would not have to do in a socialist society. However, we can do these things in a manner which is consistent with our values and our aims. For example, a strike can be run in two ways. Either it can be managed via assemblies of strikers and co-ordinated by councils of elected, mandated and recallable delegates or it can be run from the top-down by a few trade union leaders. The former, of course, is the anarchist way and it reflects *"the future human society"* (and, ironically, is paid lip-service to by Marxists).

Such common sense, unfortunately, was lacking in Marx and Engels, who instead decided to utter nonsense for a cheap polemical point. Neither answered the basic point - how do people become able to manage society if they do not directly manage their own organisations and struggles today? How can a self-managed society come about unless people practice it in the here and now? Can people create a socialist society if they do not implement its basic ideas in their current struggles and organisations? Equally, it would be churlish to note that the Commune's system of federalism by mandated delegates had been advocated by Bakunin for a number of years before 1871 and, unsurprisingly, he took the revolt as a striking, if incomplete, confirmation of anarchism (see section A.5.1).

The Paris Commune, it must be stressed, brought the contradictions of the Marxist attacks on anarchism to the surface. It is deeply sad to read, say, Engels attacking anarchists for holding certain positions yet praising the 1871 revolution when it implemented exactly the same ideas. For example, in his deeply inaccurate diatribe *"The Bakuninists at Work"*, Engels was keen to distort the federalist ideas of anarchism, dismissing *"the so-called principles of anarchy, free federation of independent groups."* [**Collected Works**, vol. 23, p. 297] Compare this to his praise for the Paris Commune which, he gushed, refuted the Blanquist notion of a revolution sprung by a vanguard which would create *"the strictest, dictatorial centralisation of all power in the hands of the new revolutionary government."* Instead the Commune *"appealed to [the provinces] to form a*

free federation of all French Communes … a national organisation which for the first time was really created by the nation itself. It was precisely the oppressing power of the former centralised government … which was to fall everywhere, just as it had fallen in Paris." [**Selected Writings**, pp. 256-7]

Likewise, Engels praised the fact that, to combat the independence of the state from society, the Commune introduced wages for officials the same as that *"received by other workers"* and the use of *"the binding mandate to delegates to representative bodies."* [**Op. Cit.**, p. 258] Compare this to Engels attack on anarchist support for binding mandates (which, like our support for free federation, pre-dated the Commune). Then it was a case of this being part of Bakunin's plans to control the international *"for a secret society … there is nothing more convenient than the imperative mandate"* as all its members vote one way, while the others will *"contradict one another."* Without these binding mandates, *"the common sense of the independent delegates will swiftly unite them in a common party against the party of the secret society."* Obviously the notion that delegates from a group should reflect the wishes of that group was lost on Engels. He even questioned the utility of this system for *"if all electors gave their delegates imperative mandates concerning all points in the agenda, meetings and debates of the delegates would be superfluous."* [**Collected Works**, vol. 22, p. 281 and p. 277] It should be noted that Trotsky shared Engels dislike of "representatives" being forced to actually represent the views of their constituents within the party. [**In Defense of Marxism**, pp. 80-1]

Clearly a *"free federation"* of Communes and binding mandates are bad when anarchists advocate them but excellent when workers in revolt implement them! Why this was the case Engels failed to explain. However, it does suggest that the anarchist idea that we must reflect the future in how we organise today is no hindrance to revolutionary change and, in fact, reflects what is required to turn a revolt into a genuine social revolution.

Engels asserted that the anarchist position meant that *"the proletariat is told to organise not in accordance with the requirements of the struggle … but according to the vague notions of a future society entertained by some dreamers."* [**Op. Cit.**, vol. 23, p. 66] In this he was wrong, as he failed to understand that the anarchist position was produced by the class struggle itself. He failed to understand how that struggle reflects our aspirations for a better world, how we see what is wrong with modern society and seek to organise to end such abuses rather than perpetuate them in new forms. Thus the trade unions which Bakunin argued would be the basis of a free society are organised from the bottom-up and based upon the direct participation of the workers. This form of organisation was not forced upon the workers by some intellectuals thinking they were a good idea. Rather they were created to fight the bosses and reflected the fact that workers were sick of being treated as servants and did not wish to see that repeated in their own organisations.

As Bakunin argued, when a union delegates authority to its officials it may be *"very good for the committees, but [it is] not at all favourable for the social, intellectual, and moral progress of the collective power of the International."* The committees *"substituted their own will and their own ideas for that of the membership"* while the membership expressed *"indifference to general problems"* and left *"all problems to the decisions of committees."* This could only be solved by *"call[ing] general membership meetings,"* that is *"popular assemblies."* Bakunin goes on to argue that the *"organisation of the International, having as its objective not the creation of new despotism but the uprooting of all domination, will take on an essentially different character than the organisation of the State."* This must be the *"organisation of the trade sections and their representation by the Chambers of Labour"* and these *"bear in themselves the living seeds of the new society which is to replace the old world. They are creating not only the ideas, but also the facts of the future itself."* [**Bakunin on Anarchism**, pp. 246-7 and p. 255]

Ou Shengbai, a Chinese anarchist, argued that libertarians *"deeply feel that the causes of popular misery are these: (1) Because of the present political system power is concentrated in a few hands with the result that the majority of the people do not have the opportunity for free participation. (2) Because of the capitalist system all means of production are concentrated in the hands of the capitalists with the results that the benefits that ought to accrue to labourers are usurped by capitalists.* [quoted by Arif Dirlik, **Anarchism in the Chinese Revolution**, p. 235] Does it make much sense to organise in ways which reflect these problems? Surely the reason why people become socialists is because they seek to change society, to give the mass of the population an opportunity for free participation and to manage their own affairs. Why destroy those hopes and dreams by organising in a way which reflects the society we oppose rather than the one we desire?

Ultimately, Engels dismissed the practical experiences of working class people, dismissed our ability to create a better world and our ability to dream. In fact, he seems to think there is some division of labour between *"the proletariat"* who do the struggling and *"some dreamers"* who provide the ideas. The notion that working class people can both struggle **and** dream was lost on him, as was the notion that our dreams shape our struggles and our struggles shape our dreams. People resist oppression and exploitation because we want to determine what goes on in our lives and to manage our own affairs. In that process, we create new forms of organisation which allows that to happen, ones that reflect our dreams of a better world. This is not in opposition to the needs of the struggle, as Engels asserted, but is rather an expression of it. To dismiss this process, to advocate organisational methods which are the very antithesis of what working class people have shown, repeatedly, that they want, is the height of arrogance and, ultimately, little more than a dismissal of the hopes, dreams and creative self-activity of working class people. As libertarian socialist Cornelius Castoriadis put it:

> *"the organisation's inspiration can come only from the socialist structures created by the working class in the course of its own history. It must let itself be guided by the principles on which the soviet and the factory council were founded … the principles of workers' management must govern the operation and structure of the organisation. Apart from them, there are only capitalist principles, which, as we have seen, can only result in the establishment of capitalist relationships."* [**Political and Social Writings**, vol. 2, pp. 217-8]

Ironically enough, given their own and their followers claims of Marxism's proletarian core, it was Marx and Engels who were at odds with the early labour movement, **not** Bakunin and the anarchists. Historian Gwyn A. Williams notes in the early British labour movement there were *"to be no leaders"* and the organisations were *"consciously modelled on the civil society they wished to create."* [**Artisans and Sans-Culottes**, p. 72] Lenin, unsurprisingly, dismissed the fact that the British workers *"thought it was an indispensable sign of democracy for all the members to do all the work of managing the unions"* as *"primitive democracy"* and *"absurd."* He also complained about *"how widespread is the 'primitive' conception of democracy among the masses of the students and workers"* in Russia. [**Essential Works of Lenin**, pp. 162-3] Clearly, the anarchist perspective reflects the ideas of the workers' movement before it degenerates into reformism and bureaucracy while Marxism reflects it during this process of degeneration. Needless to say, the revolutionary nature of the early union movement clearly shows who was correct!

Anarchists, in other words, simply generalised the experiences of the workers in struggle and Bakunin and his followers were expressing a common position held by many in the International. Even Marx paid lip-service to this when he stated *"in contrast to old society … a new society is springing up"* and the *"Pioneer of that new society is the International Working Men's Association."* [**Selected Works**, p. 263] Clearly, considering the International as the embryo of the future society is worthy only of scorn as the correct position is to consider it merely as a pioneer!

As such, libertarians *"lay no claims to originality in proposing this [kind of prefigurative organisation]. In every revolution, during most strikes and daily at the level of workshop organisation, the working class resorts to this type of direct democracy."* [Maurice Brinton, **For Workers' Power**, p. 48] Given how Marxists pay lip-service to such forms of working class self-organisation, it seems amusing to hear them argue that this is correct for everyone else but not themselves and their own organisations! Apparently, the same workers who are expected to have the determination and consciousness necessary to overthrow capitalism and create a new world in the future are unable to organise themselves in a socialist manner today. Instead, we have to tolerate so-called "revolutionary" organisations which are just as hierarchical, top-down and centralised as the system which provoked our anger at its injustice in the first and which we are trying to end!

Related to this is the fact that Marxists (particularly Leninists) favour centralisation while anarchists favour decentralisation within a federal organisation. Anarchists do not think that decentralisation implies isolation or narrow localism. We have always stressed the importance of federalism to co-ordinate decisions. Power would be decentralised, but federalism ensures collective decisions and action. Under centralised systems, anarchists argue, power is placed into the hands of a few leaders. Rather than the real interests and needs of the people being co-ordinated, centralism simply means the imposition of the will of a handful of leaders, who claim to "represent" the masses. Co-ordination from below, in other words, is replaced by coercion from above in the centralised system and the needs and interests of all are replaced by those of a few leaders at the centre.

Such a centralised, inevitably top-down, system can only be counter-productive, both practically and in terms of generating socialist consciousness:

> "Bolsheviks argue that to fight the highly centralised forces of modern capitalism requires an equally centralised type of party. This ignores the fact that capitalist centralisation is based on coercion and force and the exclusion of the overwhelming majority of the population from participating in any of its decisions ...
>
> "The very structure of these organisations ensures that their personnel do not think for themselves, but unquestioningly carry out the instructions of their superiors ...
>
> "Advocates of 'democratic centralism' insist that it is the only type of organisations which can function effectively under conditions of illegality. This is nonsense. The 'democratic centralist' organisation is particularly vulnerable to police persecution. When all power is concentrated in the hands of the leaders, their arrest immediately paralyses the whole organisation. Members trained to accept unquestioningly the instruction of an all-wise Central Committee will find it very difficult to think and act for themselves. The experiences of the German Communist Party [under the Nazis] confirm this. With their usual inconsistency, the Trotskyists even explain the demise of their Western European sections during World War II by telling people how their leaders were murdered by the Gestapo!" [Maurice Brinton, **Op. Cit.**, p. 43]

As we discuss in depth in section H.5 the Leninist vanguard party does, ironically, create in embryo a new world simply because once in power it refashions society in **its** image. However, no anarchist would consider such a centralised, hierarchical top-down class system rooted in bureaucratic power as being remotely desirable or remotely socialist.

Therefore anarchists "recognised neither the state nor pyramidal organisation" Kropotkin argued, while Marxists "recognised the state and pyramidal methods of organisation" which "stifled the revolutionary spirit of the rank-and-file workers." [**Conquest of Bread and Other Writings**, p. 212] The Marxist perspective inevitably places power into the hands of a few leaders, who then decree which movements to support and encourage based on what is best for the long term benefit of the party itself rather than the working class. Thus we find Engels arguing while Marxists were "obliged to support every **real** popular movement" they also had to ensure "that the scarcely formed nucleus of our proletarian Party is not sacrificed in vain and that the proletariat is not decimated in futile local revolts," for example "a blood-letting like that of 1871 in Paris." [Marx and Engels, **The Socialist Revolution**, p. 294 and p. 320] This produces a conservative approach to social struggle, with mass actions and revolutionary situations ignored or warned against because of the potential harm it could inflict on the party. Unsurprisingly, every popular revolution has occurred against the advice of the so-called "revolutionary" Marxist leadership including

the Paris Commune and the 1917 February revolution in Russia (even the October seize of power was done in the face of resistance from the Bolshevik party machine).

It is for these reasons that anarchists "[a]s much as is humanly possible ... try to reflect the liberated society they seek to achieve" and "not slavishly duplicate the prevailing system of hierarchy, class and authority." Rather than being the abstract dreams of isolated thinkers, these "conclusions ... emerge from an exacting study of past revolutions, of the impact centralised parties have had on the revolutionary process" and history has more than confirmed the anarchist warning that the "revolutionary party, by duplicating these centralistic, hierarchical features would reproduce hierarchy and centralism in the post revolutionary society." [Murray Bookchin, **Post-Scarcity Anarchism**, p. 138, p. 139 and p. 137] Moreover, we base our arguments on how social movements should organise on the experiences of past struggles, of the forms of organisation spontaneously produced by those struggles and which, therefore, reflect the needs of those struggles and the desire for a better way of life which produced them. Ultimately, no one knows when a revolution turns the hopes and aspirations of today into tomorrow's reality and it would be wise to have some experience of managing our own affairs before hand.

By failing to understand the importance of applying a vision of a free society to the current class struggle, Marxists help ensure that society never is created. By copying bourgeois methods within their "revolutionary" organisations (parties and unions) they ensure bourgeois ends (inequality and oppression).

H.1.7 Haven't you read Lenin's "State and Revolution"?

This question is often asked of people who critique Marxism, particularly its Leninist form. Lenin's **State and Revolution** is often considered his most democratic work and Leninists are quick to point to it as proof that Lenin and those who follow his ideas are not authoritarian. As such, it is an important question. So how do anarchists reply when people point them to Lenin's work as evidence of the democratic (even libertarian) nature of Marxism? Anarchists reply in two ways.

Firstly, we argue many of the essential features of Lenin's ideas are to be found in anarchist theory and, in fact, had been aspects of anarchism for decades **before** Lenin put pen to paper. Bakunin, for example, talked about mandated delegates from workplaces federating into workers' councils as the framework of a (libertarian) socialist society in the 1860s as well as popular militias to defend a revolution. Moreover, he was well aware that revolution was a **process** rather than an event and so would take time to develop and flourish. Hence Murray Bookchin:

> "Bakunin, Kropotkin, and Malatesta were not so naive as to believe that anarchism could be established over night. In imputing this notion to Bakunin, Marx and Engels wilfully distorted the Russian anarchist's views. Nor did the anarchists ... believe that abolition of the state involved

'laying down of arms' immediately after the revolution, to use Marx's obscurantist choice of terms, thoughtlessly repeated by Lenin in **State and Revolution**. *Indeed, much that passes for 'Marxism' in* **State and Revolution** *is pure anarchism - for example, the substitution of revolutionary militias for professional armed bodies and the substitution of organs of self-management for parliamentary bodies. What is authentically Marxist in Lenin's pamphlet is the demand for 'strict centralism,' the acceptance of a 'new' bureaucracy, and the identification of soviets with a state."* [**Post-Scarcity Anarchism**, p. 137]

That this is the case is hidden in Lenin's work as he deliberately distorts anarchist ideas in it (see sections H.1.3 and H.1.4 for example). Therefore, when Marxists ask whether anarchists have read Lenin's **State and Revolution** we reply by arguing that most of Lenin's ideas were first expressed by anarchists and his work just strikes anarchists as little more than a re-hash of many of our own ideas but placed in a statist context which totally and utterly undermines them in favour of party rule.

Secondly, anarchists argue that regardless of what Lenin argued for in **State and Revolution**, he did not apply those ideas in practice (indeed, he did the exact opposite). Therefore, the question of whether we have read Lenin's work simply drives home the ideological nature and theoretical bankruptcy of Leninism. This is because the person is asking you to evaluate their politics based on what they say rather than on what they do, like any politician.

To use an analogy, what would you say to a politician who has cut welfare spending by 50% and increased spending on the military and who argues that this act is irrelevant and that you should look at their manifesto which states that they were going to do the opposite? You would dismiss this argument as laughable and them as liars as you would evaluate them by their actions, not by what they say. Leninists, by urging you to read Lenin's **State and Revolution** are asking you to evaluate them by what their manifesto says and ignore what they did. Anarchists, on the other hand, ask you to evaluate the Leninist manifesto by comparing it to what they actually did in power. Such an evaluation is the only means by which we can judge the validity of Leninist claims and politics.

As we discuss the role of Leninist ideology in the fate of the Russian Revolution in section H.6 we will provide a summary of Lenin's claims in his famous work **State and Revolution** and what he did in practice here. Suffice to say the difference between reality and rhetoric was extremely large and, therefore, it is a damning indictment of Bolshevism. Post-October, the Bolsheviks not only failed to introduce the ideas of Lenin's book, they in fact introduced the exact opposite.

Simply put, if the **State and Revolution** is the manifesto of Bolshevism, then not a single promise in that work was kept by the Bolsheviks when they got into power. As such, Lenin's work cannot be used to evaluate Bolshevik ideology as Bolshevism paid no attention to it once it had taken state power. While Lenin and his followers chant rhapsodies about the Soviet State (this 'highest and most perfect system of democracy") they quickly turned its

democratic ideas into a fairy-tale, and an ugly fairy-tale at that, by simply ignoring it in favour of party power (and party dictatorship). To state the obvious, to quote theory and not relate it to the practice of those who claim to follow it is a joke. If you look at the actions of the Bolsheviks after the October Russian Revolution you cannot help draw the conclusion that Lenin's **State and Revolution** has nothing to do with Bolshevik policy and presents a false image of what Leninists desire. As such, we must present a comparison between rhetoric and realty.

In order to show that this is the case, we need to summarise the main ideas contained in Lenin's work. Moreover, we need to indicate what the Bolsheviks did, in fact, do. Finally, we need to see if the various rationales justifying these actions hold water.

So what did Lenin argue for in **State and Revolution**? Writing in the mid-1930s, anarchist Camillo Berneri summarised the main ideas of that work as follows:

"The Leninist programme of 1917 included these points: the discontinuance of the police and standing army, abolition of the professional bureaucracy, elections for all public positions and offices, revocability of all officials, equality of bureaucratic wages with workers' wages, the maximum of democracy, peaceful competition among the parties within the soviets, abolition of the death penalty." ["*The Abolition and Extinction of the State,*" pp. 50-1, **Cienfuegos Press Anarchist Review**, no. 4, p. 50]

As he noted, *"[n]ot a single one of the points of this programme has been achieved."* This was, of course, under Stalinism and most Leninists will concur with Berneri. However what Leninists tend not to mention is that by the end of the 7 month period of Bolshevik rule before the start of the civil war (i.e., from November 1917 to May 1918) none of these points existed. So, as an example of what Bolshevism "really" stands for it seems strange to harp on about a work which was never really implemented when the author was in a position to do so (i.e. before the onslaught of a civil war Lenin thought was inevitable anyway!). Similarly, if **State and Revolution** indicates the features a "workers' state" must have then, by May 1918, Russia did not have such a state and so, logically, it can be considered as such only if we assume that the good intentions of its rulers somehow overcome its political and economic structure (which, sadly, **is** the basic Trotskyist defence of Leninism against Stalinism!).

To see that Berneri's summary is correct, we need to quote Lenin directly. Obviously the work is a wide ranging defence of Lenin's interpretation of Marxist theory on the state. As it is an attempt to overturn decades of Marxist orthodoxy, much of the work is quotes from Marx and Engels and Lenin's attempts to enlist them for his case (we discuss this issue in section H.3.10). Equally, we need to ignore the numerous straw men arguments about anarchism Lenin inflicts on his reader. Here we simply list the key points as regards Lenin's arguments about his "workers' state" and how the workers would maintain control of it:

1) Using the Paris Commune as a prototype, Lenin argued for the abolition of *"parliamentarianism"* by turning *"representative institutions from mere 'talking shops'*

into working bodies." This would be done by removing *"the division of labour between the legislative and the executive."* [**Essential Works of Lenin**, p. 304 and p. 306]

2) *"All officials, without exception, to be elected and subject to recall **at any time**"* and so *"directly responsible to their constituents."* [**Op. Cit.**, p. 302 and p. 306]

3) The *"immediate introduction of control and superintendence by **all**, so that **all** shall become 'bureaucrats' for a time and so that, therefore, **no one** can become a 'bureaucrat'."* Proletarian democracy would *"take immediate steps to cut bureaucracy down to the roots ... to the complete abolition of bureaucracy"* as the *"**essence** of bureaucracy"* is officials becoming transformed"* into privileged persons divorced from the masses and **superior to** the masses."* [**Op. Cit.**, p. 355 and p. 360]

4) There should be no *"special bodies of armed men"* standing apart from the people *"since the majority of the people itself suppresses its oppressors, a 'special force' is no longer necessary."* Using the example of the Paris Commune, Lenin suggested this meant *"abolition of the standing army"* by the *"armed masses."* [**Op. Cit.**, p. 275, p. 301 and p. 339]

5) The new (workers) state would be *"the organisation of violence for the suppression of ... the exploiting class, i.e. the bourgeoisie. The toilers need a state only to overcome the resistance of the exploiters"* who are *"an insignificant minority,"* that is *"the landlords and the capitalists."* This would see *"an immense expansion of democracy ... for the poor, democracy for the people"* while, simultaneously, imposing *"a series of restrictions on the freedom of the oppressors, the exploiters, the capitalists ... their resistance must be broken by force: it is clear that where there is suppression there is also violence, there is no freedom, no democracy."* [**Op. Cit.**, p. 287 and pp. 337-8]

This would be implemented after the current, bourgeois, state had been smashed. This would be the *"dictatorship of the proletariat"* and be *"the introduction of complete democracy for the people."* [**Op. Cit.**, p. 355] However, the key practical ideas on what the new "semi-state" would be are contained in these five points. He generalised these points, considering them valid for all countries. The first point was the combining of legislative and executive functions in "working bodies". The first body to be created by the Bolshevik revolution was the "Council of People's Commissars" (CPC) This was a government separate from and above the Central Executive Committee (CEC) of the soviets congress which, in turn, was separate from and above the national soviet congress. It was an executive body elected by the soviet congress, but the soviets themselves were not turned into "working bodies." The promises of Lenin's **State and Revolution** did not last the night.

The Bolsheviks, it must be stressed, clearly recognised that the Soviets had alienated their power to this body with the party's Central Committee arguing in November 1917 that *"it is impossible to refuse a purely Bolshevik government without treason to the slogan of the power of the Soviets, since a majority at the Second All-Russian Congress of Soviets ... handed power over to this government."* [contained in Robert V. Daniels (ed.), **A Documentary History of Communism**, vol. 1, pp. 128-9] However, it could be argued that Lenin's promises were kept as the new government simply gave itself legislative powers four days later. Sadly, this is not the case. In the Paris Commune the delegates of the people took executive power into their own hands. Lenin reversed this and his executive took legislative power from the hands of the people's delegates. As we discuss in section H.6.1, this concentration of power into executive committees occurred at all levels of the soviet hierarchy. What of the next principle, namely the election and recall of all officials? This lasted slightly longer, namely around 5 months. By March of 1918, the Bolsheviks started a systematic campaign against the elective principle in the workplace, in the military and even in the soviets. In the workplace, Lenin was arguing for appointed one-man managers *"vested with dictatorial powers"* by April 1918 (see section H.3.14). In the military, Trotsky simply decreed the end of elected officers in favour of appointed officers. As far as the soviets go, the Bolsheviks were refusing to hold elections because they *"feared that the opposition parties would show gains."* When elections were held, *"Bolshevik armed force usually overthrew the results"* in provincial towns. Moreover, the Bolsheviks *"pack[ed] local soviets"* with representatives of organisations they controlled *"once they could not longer count on an electoral majority."* [Samuel Farber, **Before Stalinism**, p. 22, p. 24 and p. 33] This kind of packing was even practised at the national level when the Bolsheviks gerrymandered a Bolshevik majority at the Fifth Congress of Soviets. So much for competition among the parties within the soviets! And as far as the right of recall went, the Bolsheviks only supported this when the workers were recalling the opponents of the Bolsheviks, not when the workers were recalling them.

Then there was the elimination of bureaucracy. The new state soon had a new bureaucratic and centralised system quickly emerge around it. Rather than immediately cutting the size and power of the bureaucracy, it *"grew by leaps and bounds. Control over the new bureaucracy constantly diminished, partly because no genuine opposition existed. The alienation between 'people' and 'officials,' which the soviet system was supposed to remove, was back again. Beginning in 1918, complaints about 'bureaucratic excesses,' lack of contact with voters, and new proletarian bureaucrats grew louder and louder."* [Oskar Anweiler, **The Soviets**, p. 242] So the rise of a state bureaucracy started immediately with the seizure of power by the Bolsheviks, particularly as the state's functions grew to include economic decisions as well as political ones. Instead of the state starting to *"wither away"* it grew:

> *"The old state's political apparatus was 'smashed,' but in its place a new bureaucratic and centralised system emerged with extraordinary rapidity. After the transfer of government to Moscow in March 1918 it continued to expand ... As the functions of the state expanded so did*

the bureaucracy, and by August 1918 nearly a third of Moscow's working population were employed in offices. The great increase in the number of employees … took place in early to mid-1918 and, thereafter, despite many campaigns to reduce their number, they remained a steady proportion of the falling population" [Richard Sakwa, *"The Commune State in Moscow in 1918,"* pp. 429-449, **Slavic Review**, vol. 46, no. 3/4, pp. 437-8]

This, anarchists would stress, is an inherent feature of centralised systems. As such, this rise of bureaucracy confirmed anarchist predictions that centralisation will recreate bureaucracy. After all, some means were required to gather, collate and provide information by which the central bodies made their decisions. Overtime, this permanent collection of bodies would become the real power in the state, with the party members nominally in charge really under the control of an unelected and uncontrolled officialdom. Thus a necessary side-effect of Bolshevik centralism was bureaucracy and it soon became the real power in the state (and, ultimately, in the 1920s became the social base for the rise of Stalin). This is to be expected as any state *"is already a privileged class and cut off from the people"* and would *"seek to extend its powers, to be beyond public control, to impose its own policies and to give priority to special interests."* Moreover, *"what an all-powerful, oppressive, all-absorbing oligarchy must be one which has at its services, that is at its disposal, all social wealth, all public services."* [Malatesta, **Anarchy**, p. 36 and p. 37]

Then there is the fourth point, namely the elimination of the standing army, the suppression of *"special bodies of armed men"* by the *"armed masses."* This promise did not last two months. On the 20th of December, 1917, the Council of People's Commissars decreed the formation of a political (secret) police force, the *"Extraordinary Commission to Fight Counter-Revolution."* This was more commonly known by the Russian initials of the first two terms of its official name: The Cheka.

While it was initially a small organisation, as 1918 progressed it grew in size and activity. The Cheka soon became a key instrument of Bolshevik rule and it was most definitely a *"special body of armed men"* and not the same as the *"armed workers."* In other words, Lenin's claims in **State and Revolution** did not last two months and in under six months the Bolshevik state had a mighty group of *"armed men"* to impose its will. This is not all. The Bolsheviks also conducted a sweeping transformation of the military within the first six months of taking power. During 1917, the soldiers and sailors (encouraged by the Bolsheviks and other revolutionaries) had formed their own committees and elected officers. In March 1918, Trotsky simply abolished all this by decree and replaced it with appointed officers (usually ex-Tsarist ones). In this way, the Red Army was turned from a workers' militia (i.e. an armed people) into a *"special body"* separate from the general population.

Both the army and the Cheka were special, professional, armed forces standing apart from the people and unaccountable to them. Indeed, they were used to repress strikes and working class unrest which refutes the idea that Lenin's "workers' state" would simply be an instrument of violence directed at the exploiters. As the Bolsheviks lost popular support, they turned the violence of the

"worker's state" against the workers (and, of course, the peasants). When the Bolsheviks lost soviet elections, force was used to disband them. Faced with strikes and working class protest during this period, the Bolsheviks responded with state violence (see section H.6.3). So, as regards the claim that the new ("workers") state would repress only the exploiters, the truth was that it was used to repress whoever opposed Bolshevik power, including workers and peasants. If, as Lenin stressed, *"where there is suppression there is also violence, there is no freedom, no democracy"* then there cannot be working class freedom or democracy if the "workers' state" is suppressing that class.

As can be seen, after the first six months of Bolshevik rule not a single measure advocated by Lenin in **State and Revolution** existed in "revolutionary" Russia. Some of the promises were broken quite quickly (overnight, in one case). Most took longer. Yet Leninists may object by noting that many Bolshevik degrees did, in fact, reflect **State and Revolution**. For example, the democratisation of the armed forces was decreed in late December 1917. However, this was simply acknowledging the existing revolutionary gains of the military personnel. Similarly, the Bolsheviks passed a decree on workers' control which, again, simply acknowledged the actual gains by the grassroots (and, in fact, limited them for further development).

Yet this cannot be taken as evidence of the democratic nature of Bolshevism as most governments faced with a revolutionary movement will acknowledge and "legalise" the facts on the ground (until such time as they can neutralise or destroy them). For example, the Provisional Government created after the February Revolution also legalised the revolutionary gains of the workers (for example, legalising the soviets, factory committees, unions, strikes and so forth). The real question is whether Bolshevism continued to encourage these revolutionary gains once it had consolidated its power. It did not. Indeed, it can be argued that the Bolsheviks simply managed to do what the Provisional Government it replaced had failed to do, namely destroy the various organs of popular self-management created by the revolutionary masses. So the significant fact is not that the Bolsheviks recognised the gains of the masses but that their toleration of the application of what their followers say were their real principles did not last long and, significantly, the leading Bolsheviks did not consider the abolition of such principles as harming the "communist" nature of the regime.

"All Power to the Soviets" became, very quickly, "All Power to the Bolsheviks." Unsurprisingly, as this was Lenin's aim all along and so we find him in 1917 continually repeating this basic idea (see section H.3.3). Given this, the almost utter non-mention of the party and its role in **State and Revolution** is deeply significant. Given the emphasis that Lenin had always placed on the party, it's absence is worrying. When the party is mentioned in that work, it is done so in an ambiguous manner. For example, Lenin noted that *"[b]y educating the workers' party, Marxism educates the vanguard of the proletariat which is capable of assuming power and of **leading the whole people** to socialism, of directing and organising the new order."* It is not clear whether it is the vanguard or the proletariat as a whole which assumes power. Later, he stated that *"the dictatorship of the proletariat"* was *"the organisation of the vanguard of the oppressed as the ruling class for the purpose*

of crushing the oppressors." [**Essential Works of Lenin**, p. 288 and p. 337] Based on subsequent Bolshevik practice after the party seized power, it seems clear that it is the vanguard which assumes power rather than the whole class.

As such, given this clear and unambiguous position throughout 1917 by Lenin, it seems incredulous, to say the least, for Leninist Tony Cliff to assert that "*[t]o start with Lenin spoke of the **proletariat, the class** - not the Bolshevik Party - assuming state power.*" [**Lenin**, vol. 3, p. 161] Surely the title of one of Lenin's most famous pre-October essays, usually translated as "*Can the Bolsheviks Retain State Power?*", should have given the game away? As would, surely, quoting numerous calls by Lenin for the Bolsheviks to seize power? Apparently not.

Where does that leave Lenin's **State and Revolution**? Well, modern-day Leninists still urge us to read it, considering it his greatest work and the best introduction to what Leninism really stands for. For example, we find Leninist Tony Cliff calling that book "*Lenin's real testament*" while, at the same time, acknowledging that its "*message … which was the guide for the first victorious proletarian revolution, was violated again and again during the civil war.*" Not a very good "*guide*" or that convincing a "*message*" if it was not applicable in the very circumstances it was designed to be applied in (a bit like saying you have an excellent umbrella but it only works when it is not raining). Moreover, Cliff is factually incorrect. As we discuss in section H.6, the Bolsheviks "*violated*" that "*guide*" before the civil war started (i.e. when "*the victories of the Czechoslovak troops over the Red Army in June 1918, that threatened the greatest danger to the Soviet republic,*" to quote Cliff). [**Op. Cit.**, p. 161 and p. 18] Similarly, much of the economic policies implemented by the Bolsheviks had their roots in that book and the other writings by Lenin from 1917.

The conclusions of dissident Marxist Samuel Farber seem appropriate here. As he puts it, "*the very fact that a Sovnarkom had been created as a separate body from the CEC [Central Executive Committee] of the soviets clearly indicates that, Lenin's **State and Revolution** notwithstanding, the separation of at least the top bodies of the executive and the legislative wings of the government remained in effect in the new Soviet system.*" This suggests "*that **State and Revolution** did not play a decisive role as a source of policy guidelines for 'Leninism in power.'*" After all, "*immediately after the Revolution the Bolsheviks established an executive power … as a clearly separate body from the leading body of the legislature … Therefore, some sections of the contemporary Left appear to have greatly overestimated the importance that **State and Revolution** had for Lenin's government. I would suggest that this document … can be better understood as a distant, although doubtless sincere [!], socio-political vision … as opposed to its having been a programmatic political statement, let alone a guide to action, for the period immediately after the successful seizure of power.*" [**Op. Cit.**, pp. 20-1 and p. 38]

That is **one** way of looking at it. Another would be to draw the conclusion that a "*distant … socio-political vision*" drawn up to sound like a "*guide to action*" which was then immediately ignored is, at worse, little more than a deception, or, at best, a theoretical justification for seizing power in the face of orthodox Marxist dogma. Whatever the rationale for Lenin writing his book, one thing is true -

it was never implemented. Strange, then, that Leninists today urge us to read it to see what "Lenin really wanted." Particularly given that so few of its promises were actually implemented (those that were just recognised the facts on the ground) and **all** of them were no longer applied in less than six months after the seize of power.

It will be objected in defence of Leninism that it is unfair to hold Lenin responsible for the failure to apply his ideas in practice. The terrible Civil War, in which Soviet Russia was attacked by numerous armies, and the resulting economic chaos meant that the objective circumstances made it impossible to implement his democratic ideas. This argument contains flaws. Firstly, as we indicated above, the undemocratic policies of the Bolsheviks started **before** the start of the Civil War (so suggesting that the hardships of the Civil War were not to blame). Secondly, Lenin himself mocked those who argued that revolution was out of the question because of difficult circumstances and so to blame these for the failure of the Bolsheviks to apply the ideas in **State and Revolution** means to argue that those ideas are inappropriate for a revolution (which, we must stress, is what the leading Bolsheviks actually **did** end up arguing by their support for party dictatorship). You cannot have it both ways.

Lenin at no time indicated in **State and Revolution** that it was impossible or inapplicable to apply those ideas during a revolution in Russia (quite the reverse!). Given that Marxists, including Lenin, argue that a "dictatorship of the proletariat" is required to defend the revolution against capitalist resistance it seems incredulous to argue that Lenin's major theoretical work on that regime was impossible to apply in precisely the circumstances it was designed for.

The Russian Revolution shows that a workers state, as anarchists have long argued, means minority power, not working class self-management of society. As such, Lenin's work indicates the contradictory nature of Marxism - while claiming to support democratic/libertarian ideals they promote structures (such as centralised states) which undermine those values in favour of party rule. The lesson is clear, only libertarian means can ensure libertarian ends and they have to be applied consistently within libertarian structures to work. To apply them to statist ones will simply fail.

H.2

What parts of anarchism do Marxists particularly misrepresent?

Many people involved in politics will soon discover that Marxist groups (particularly Leninist ones) organise "debates" about anarchism. These meetings are usually entitled "*Marxism and Anarchism*" and are usually organised after anarchists have been active in the area or have made the headlines somewhere.

These meetings, contrary to common sense, are usually not a debate as (almost always) no anarchists are invited to argue the anarchist viewpoint and, therefore, they present a one-sided account of *"Marxism and Anarchism"* in a manner which benefits the organisers. Usually, the format is a speaker distorting anarchist ideas and history for a long period of time (both absolutely in terms of the length of the meeting and relatively in terms of the boredom inflicted on the unfortunate attendees). It will soon become obvious to those attending that any such meeting is little more than an unprincipled attack on anarchism with little or no relationship to what anarchism is actually about. Those anarchists who attend such meetings usually spend most of their allotted (usually short) speaking time refuting the nonsense that is undoubtedly presented. Rather than a **real** discussion between the differences between anarchism and "Marxism" (i.e. Leninism), the meeting simply becomes one where anarchists correct the distortions and misrepresentations of the speaker in order to create the basis of a real debate. If the reader does not believe this summary we would encourage them to attend such a meeting and see for themselves.

In addition, many of the founding fathers of Marxism (and Leninism) also decided to attack anarchism in similar ways, so this activity does have a long tradition in Marxist circles (particularly in Leninist and Trotskyist ones). Sadly, Max Nettlau's comments on Marx and Engels are applicable to many of their followers today. He argued that they *"acted with that shocking lack of honesty which was characteristic of **all** their polemics. They worked with inadequate documentation, which, according to their custom, they supplemented with arbitrary declarations and conclusions - accepted as truth by their followers although they were exposed as deplorable misrepresentations, errors and unscrupulous perversions of the truth."* [**A Short History of Anarchism**, p. 132] As the reader will discover, this summary has not lost its relevance today. If you read Marxist "critiques" of anarchism you will soon discover the same repetition of "accepted" truths, the same inadequate documentation, the same arbitrary declarations and conclusions as well as an apparent total lack of familiarity with the source material they claim to be analysing.

This section of the FAQ lists and refutes many of the most common distortions Marxists make with regards to anarchism. As will become clear, many of the most common Marxist attacks on anarchism have little or no basis in fact but have simply been repeated so often by Marxists that they have entered the ideology (the idea that anarchists think the capitalist class will just disappear being, probably, the most famous one).

Moreover, Marxists make many major and minor distortions of anarchist theory in passing. For example, Eric Hobsbawm wrote of the *"extremism of the anarchist rejection of state and organisation"* while being well aware, as a leading Marxist historian, of numerous anarchist organisations. [**Revolutionaries**, p. 113] This kind of nonsense has a long history, with Engels asserting in his infamous diatribe *The Bakuninists at work* that Bakunin *"[a]s early as September 1870 (in his **Lettres a un francais** [Letters to a Frenchman]) ... had declared that the only way to drive the Prussians out of France by a revolutionary struggle was to do away with all forms of centralised leadership and leave each town, each village, each parish to wage war on its own."* For Engels anarchist federalism *"consisted precisely in the fact that each town acted on its own, declaring that the important thing was not co-operation with other towns but separation from them, this precluding any possibility of a combined attack."* This meant *"the fragmentation and*

isolation of the revolutionary forces which enabled the government troops to smash one revolt after the other." According to Engels, the anarchists *"proclaimed [this] a principle of supreme revolutionary wisdom."* [**Collected Works**, vol. 23, p. 592]

In fact, the truth is totally different. Bakunin did, of course, reject *"centralised leadership"* as it would be *"necessarily very circumscribed, very short-sighted, and its limited perception cannot, therefore, penetrate the depth and encompass the whole complex range of popular life."* However, it is a falsehood to state that he denied the need for co-ordination of struggles and federal organisations from the bottom up. As he put it, the revolution must *"foster the self-organisation of the masses into autonomous bodies, federated from the bottom upwards."* With regards to the peasants, he thought they will *"come to an understanding, and form some kind of organisation ... to further their mutual interests ... the necessity to defend their homes, their families, and their own lives against unforeseen attack ... will undoubtedly soon compel them to contract new and mutually suitable arrangements."* The peasants would be *"freely organised from the bottom up."* Rather than deny the need for co-ordination, Bakunin stressed it: *"the peasants, like the industrial city workers, should unite by federating the fighting battalions, district by district, assuring a common co-ordinated defence against internal and external enemies."* [*"Letters to a Frenchman on the present crisis"*, **Bakunin on Anarchism**, p. 196, p. 206, p. 207 and p. 190]

In this Bakunin was repeating his earlier arguments concerning social revolution - arguments that Engels was well aware of and so he deliberately misrepresented Bakunin's ideas. Moreover, far from exposing the flaws of federalism, Engels recounts a revolt in which federalism was **not** actually implemented. It should also be mentioned that Engels opposed the Spanish workers rising in revolt in the first place. *"A few years of peaceful bourgeois republic,"* he argued, *"would prepare the ground in Spain for a proletarian revolution"* and *"instead of staging isolated, easily crushed rebellions,"* he hoped that the *"Spanish workers will make use of the republic"* with a *"view to an approaching revolution."* He ended by asking them not to give the bourgeois government *"an excuse to suppress the revolutionary movement."* [**Op. Cit.**, pp. 420-1] In his post-revolt diatribe, Engels repeated this analysis and suggested that the "Bakuninists" should have simply stood for election:

> *"At quiet times, when the proletariat knows beforehand that at best it can get only a few representatives to parliament and have no chance whatever of winning a parliamentary majority, the workers may sometimes be made to believe that it is a great revolutionary action to sit out the elections at home, and in general, not to attack the State in which they live and which oppresses them, but to attack the State as such which exists nowhere and which accordingly cannot defend itself."* [**Op. Cit.**, p. 583]

For some reason, few Leninists quote these recommendations to the Spanish workers nor do they dwell on the reformist and bureaucratic nature of the Socialist party inspired by this advice. As we discuss in section H.3.10, the notion that voting in elections was to *"attack the State"* fits in well with the concept that universal suffrage equalled the *"political power"* of the proletariat and the democratic republic was the *"specific form"* of its dictatorship. Again, for some strange reason, few Leninists mention that either.

We could go on, but space precludes discussing every example. Suffice to say, it is not wise to take any Marxist assertion of anarchist thought or history at face value. A common technique is to quote anarchist writers out of context or before they become anarchists. For example, Marxist Paul Thomas argues that Bakunin favoured *"blind destructiveness"* and yet quotes more from Bakunin's pre-anarchist works (as well as Russian nihilists) than Bakunin's anarchist works to prove his claim. Similarly, Thomas claims that Bakunin *"defended the **federes** of the Paris Commune of 1871 on the grounds that they were strong enough to dispense with theory altogether,"* yet his supporting quote clearly does not, in fact, say this. [**Karl Marx and the Anarchists**, pp. 288-90 and p. 285] What Bakunin was, in fact, arguing was simply that theory must progress from experience and that any attempt to impose a theory on society would be doomed to create a *"Procrustean bed"* as no government could *"embrace the infinite multiplicity and diversity of the real aspirations, wishes and needs whose sum total constitutes the collective will of a people."* He explicitly contrasted the Marxist system of *"want[ing] to impose science upon the people"* with the anarchist desire *"to diffuse science and knowledge among the people, so that the various groups of human society, when convinced by propaganda, may organise and spontaneously combine into federations, in accordance with their natural tendencies and their real interests, but never according to a plan traced in advance and **imposed upon the ignorant masses** by a few 'superior' minds."* [**The Political Theory of Bakunin**, p. 300] A clear misreading of Bakunin's argument but one which fits nicely into Marxist preconceptions of Bakunin and anarchism in general.

Ultimately, though, these kinds of articles by Marxists simply show the ideological nature of their own politics and say far more about Marxism than anarchism. After all, if their politics were strong they would not need to distort anarchist ideas! In addition, these essays are usually marked by a lot of (usually inaccurate) attacks on the ideas (or personal failings) of individual anarchists (usually Proudhon and Bakunin and sometimes Kropotkin). No modern anarchist theorist is usually mentioned, never mind discussed. Obviously, for most Marxists, anarchists must repeat parrot-like the ideas of these "great men." However, while Marxists may do this, anarchists have always rejected this approach. We deliberately call ourselves **anarchists** rather than Proudhonists, Bakuninists, Kropotkinists, or after any other person. As Malatesta argued in 1876 (the year of Bakunin's death) *"[w]e follow ideas and not men, and rebel against this habit of embodying a principle in a man."* [**Errico Malatesta: His Life and Ideas**, p. 198]

Therefore, anarchists, unlike many (most?) Marxists do not believe that some prophet wrote down the scriptures in past centuries and if only we could reach a correct understanding of these writings today we would see the way forward. Chomsky put it extremely well:

> *"The whole concept of Marxist or Freudian or anything like that is very odd. These concepts belong to the history of organised religion. Any living person, no matter how gifted, will make some contributions intermingled with error and partial understanding. We try to understand and improve on their contributions and eliminate the errors. But how can you identify yourself as a Marxist, or a Freudian, or an X-ist, whoever X may be? That would be to treat the person as a God to be revered, not a human being whose contributions are to be assimilated and transcended. It's a crazy idea, a kind of idolatry."* [**The Chomsky Reader**, pp. 29-30]

This means that anarchists recognise that any person, no matter how great or influential, is only human. They make mistakes, they fail to live up to all the ideals they express, they are shaped by the society they live in, and so on. Anarchists recognise this fact and extract the positive aspects of past anarchist thinkers, reject the rest and develop what we consider the living core of their ideas, learn from history and constantly try to bring anarchist ideas up-to-date (after all, a lot has changed since the days of Proudhon, Bakunin and Kropotkin and this has to be taken into account). As Max Nettlau put it with regards to Proudhon, *"we have to extract from his work useful teachings that would be of great service to our modern libertarians, who nevertheless have to find their own way from theory to practice and to the critique of our present-day conditions, as Proudhon did in his time. This does not call for a slavish imitation; it implies using his work to inspire us and enable us to profit by his experience."* [**A Short History of Anarchism**, pp. 46-7] Similarly for other anarchists - we see them as a source of inspiration upon which to build rather than a template which to copy. This means to attack anarchism by, say, attacking Bakunin's or Proudhon's personal failings is to totally miss the point. While anarchists may be inspired by the ideas of, say, Bakunin or Proudhon it does not mean we blindly follow all of their ideas. Far from it! We critically analyse their ideas and keep what is living and reject what is useless or dead. Sadly, such common sense is lacking in many who critique anarchism.

However, the typical Marxist approach does have its benefits from a political perspective. It is very difficult for Marxists and Leninists to make an objective criticism of Anarchism for, as Albert Meltzer pointed out, *"by its nature it undermines all the suppositions basic to Marxism. Marxism was held out to be the basic working class philosophy (a belief which has utterly ruined the working class movement everywhere). It holds that the industrial proletariat cannot owe its emancipation to anyone but themselves alone. It is hard to go back on that and say that the working class is not yet ready to dispense with authority placed over it ... Marxism normally tries to refrain from criticising anarchism as such - unless driven to doing so, when it exposes its own authoritarianism ... and concentrates its attacks not on Anarchism, but on Anarchists."* [**Anarchism: Arguments for and Against**, p. 62] Needless to say, this technique is the one usually applied by Marxists (although, we must stress that usually their account of the ideas of Proudhon, Bakunin, and Kropotkin are so distorted that they fail even to do this!).

So anarchist theory has developed since Proudhon, Bakunin and Kropotkin. At each period in history anarchism advanced in its understanding of the world, the anarchism of Bakunin was a development of that of Proudhon, these ideas were again developed by the anarcho-communists of the 1880s and by the syndicalists of the 1890's, by the Italian Malatesta, the Russian Kropotkin, the Mexican Flores Magon and many other individuals and movements. Today we stand on their shoulders, not at their feet.

As such, to concentrate on the ideas of a few *"leaders"* misses the point totally. While anarchism contains many of the core insights of, say, Bakunin, it has also developed them and added to them. It has, concretely, taken into account, say, the lessons of the Russian and Spanish revolutions and so on. As such, even assuming that Marxist accounts of certain aspects of the ideas of Proudhon, Bakunin and Kropotkin were correct, they would have to be shown to be relevant to modern anarchism to be of any but historical interest. Sadly, Marxists generally fail to do this and, instead, we are subject to a (usually inaccurate) history lesson.

In order to understand, learn from and transcend previous theorists we must honestly present their ideas. Unfortunately many Marxists do not do this and so this section of the FAQ involves correcting the many mistakes, distortions, errors and lies that Marxists have subjected anarchism to. Hopefully, with this done, a real dialogue can develop between Marxists and anarchists. Indeed, this has happened between libertarian Marxists (such as council communists and Situationists) and anarchists and both tendencies have benefited from it. Perhaps this dialogue between libertarian Marxists and anarchists is to be expected, as the mainstream Marxists have often misrepresented the ideas of libertarian Marxists as well - when not dismissing them as anarchists!

H.2.1 Do anarchists reject defending a revolution?

According to many Marxists anarchists either reject the idea of defending a revolution or think that it is not necessary. The Trotskyists of **Workers' Power** present a typical Marxist account of what **they** consider as anarchist ideas on this subject:

> *"the anarchist conclusion is not to build any sort of state in the first place - not even a democratic workers' state. But how could we stop the capitalists trying to get their property back, something they will definitely try and do?*
>
> *"Should the people organise to stop the capitalists raising private armies and resisting the will of the majority? If the answer is yes, then that organisation - whatever you prefer to call it - is a state: an apparatus designed to enable one class to rule over another.*
>
> *"The anarchists are rejecting something which is necessary if we are to beat the capitalists and have a chance of developing a classless society."* ["What's wrong with anarchism?", pp. 12-13, **World Revolution: Prague S26 2000**, p. 13]

It would be simple to quote Malatesta from 1891 on this issue and leave it at that. As he put it some seem to suppose *"that anarchists,*

*in the name of their principles, would wish to see that strange freedom respected which violates and destroys the freedom and life of others. They seem almost to believe that after having brought down government and private property we would allow both to be quietly built up again, because of respect for the **freedom** of those who might feel the need to be rulers and property owners. A truly curious way of interpreting our ideas."* [**Anarchy**, pp. 42-3] Pretty much common sense, so you would think! Sadly, this appears to not be the case. As such, we have to explain anarchist ideas on the defence of a revolution and why this necessity need not imply a state and, if it did, then it signifies the end of the revolution.

The argument by **Workers' Power** is very common within the Leninist left and contains three fallacies, which we expose in turn. Firstly, we have to show that anarchists have always seen the necessity of defending a revolution. This shows that the anarchist opposition to the *"democratic workers' state"* (or *"dictatorship of the proletariat"*) has nothing to do with beating the ruling class and stopping them regaining their positions of power. Secondly, we have to discuss the anarchist and Marxist definitions of what constitutes a *"state"* and show what they have in common and how they differ. Thirdly, we must summarise why anarchists oppose the idea of a *"workers' state"* in order for the **real** reasons why anarchists oppose it to be understood. Each issue will be discussed in turn.

For revolutionary anarchists, it is a truism that a revolution will need to defend itself against counter-revolutionary threats. Bakunin, for example, while strenuously objecting to the idea of a *"dictatorship of the proletariat"* also thought a revolution would need to defend itself:

> *"Immediately after established governments have been overthrown, communes will have to reorganise themselves along revolutionary lines ... In order to defend the revolution, their volunteers will at the same time form a communal militia. But no commune can defend itself in isolation. So it will be necessary to radiate revolution outward, to raise all of its neighbouring communes in revolt ... and to federate with them for common defence."* [**No Gods, No Masters**, vol. 1, p. 142]

And:

> *"the Alliance of all labour associations ... will constitute the Commune ... there will be a standing federation of the barricades and a Revolutionary Communal Council ... [made up of] delegates ... invested with binding mandates and accountable and revocable at all times ... all provinces, communes and associations ... [will] delegate deputies to an agreed place of assembly (all ... invested with binding mandated and accountable and subject to recall), in order to found the federation of insurgent associations, communes and provinces ... and to organise a revolutionary force with the capacity of defeating the reaction ... it is through the very act of extrapolation and organisation of the Revolution with an eye to the mutual defences of insurgent areas that the universality of the Revolution ... will emerge triumphant."* [**Op. Cit.**, pp. 155-6]

Malatesta agreed, explicitly pointing to "corps of volunteers (anarchist formations)" as a means of defending a revolution from "attempts to reduce a free people to a state of slavery again." To defend a revolution required "the necessary geographical and mechanical knowledge, and above all large masses of the population willing to go and fight. A government can neither increase the abilities of the former nor the will and courage of the latter." [**Anarchy**, p. 42] Decades later, his position had not changed and he was still arguing for the "creation of voluntary militia, without powers to interfere as militia in the life of the community, but only to deal with any armed attacks by the forces of reaction to re-establish themselves, or to resist outside intervention" for only "the people in arms, in possession of the land, the factories and all the natural wealth" could "defend ... the revolution." [**Errico Malatesta: His Life and Ideas**, p. 166 and p. 170]

Alexander Berkman concurred. In his classic introduction to anarchism, he devoted a whole chapter to the issue which he helpfully entitled "Defense of the Revolution". He noted that it was "your duty, as an Anarchist, to protect your liberty, to resist coercion and compulsion ... the social revolution ... will defend itself against invasion from any quarter ... The armed workers and peasants are the only effective defence of the revolution. By means of their unions and syndicates they must always be on guard against counter-revolutionary attack." [**What is Anarchism?**, pp. 231-2] Emma Goldman clearly and unambiguously stated that she had "always insisted that an armed attack on the Revolution must be met with armed force" and that "an armed counter-revolutionary and fascist attack can be met in no way except by an armed defence." [**Vision on Fire**, p. 222 and p. 217] Kropotkin, likewise, took it as a given that "a society in which the workers would have a dominant voice" would require a revolution to create and "each time that such a period of accelerated evolution and reconstruction on a grand scale begins, civil war is liable to break out on a small or large scale." The question was "how to attain the greatest results with the most limited amount of civil war, the smallest number of victims, and a minimum of mutual embitterment." To achieve this there was "only one means; namely, that the oppressed part of society should obtain the clearest possible conception of what they intend to achieve, and how, and that they should be imbued with the enthusiasm which is necessary for that achievement." Thus, "there are periods in human development when a conflict is unavoidable, and civil war breaks out quite independently of the will of particular individuals." [**Memoirs of a Revolutionist**, pp. 270-1]

So Durruti, while fighting at the front during the Spanish revolution, was not saying anything new or against anarchist theory when he stated that "the bourgeois won't let us create a libertarian communist society simply because we want to. They'll fight back and defend their privileges. The only way we can establish libertarian communism is by destroying the bourgeoisie" [quoted by Abel Paz, **Durruti in the Spanish Revolution**, p. 484] Clearly, anarchism has always recognised the necessity of defending a revolution and proposed ideas to ensure it (ideas applied with great success by, for example, the Makhnovists in the Ukrainian Revolution and the CNT militias during the Spanish). As such, any assertion that anarchism rejects the necessity of defending a revolution is simply false. Sadly, it is one Marxists make repeatedly (undoubtedly inspired by Engels

similar distortions - see section H.4.7).

Which, of course, brings us to the second assertion, namely that any attempt to defend a revolution means that a state has been created (regardless of what it may be called). For anarchists, such an argument simply shows that Marxists do not really understand what a state is. While the Trotskyist definition of a "state" may be (to quote **Workers' Power**) "an apparatus designed to enable one class to rule another," the anarchist definition is somewhat different. Anarchists, of course, do not deny that the modern state is (to use Malatesta's excellent expression) "the bourgeoisie's servant and **gendarme**." [**Anarchy**, p. 23] However, as we discuss in section H.3.7, the Marxist analysis is superficial and fundamentally metaphysical rather than scientific. Anarchists take an evolutionary perspective on the state and, as a result, argue that every state that has ever existed has defended the power of a minority class and, unsurprisingly, has developed certain features to facilitate this. The key one is centralisation of power. This ensures that the working people are excluded from the decision making process and power remains a tool of the ruling class. As such, the centralisation of power (while it may take many forms) is the key means by which a class system is maintained and, therefore, a key aspect of a state. As Kropotkin put it, the State idea "includes the existence of a power situated above society" as well as "a **territorial concentration** as well as the concentration of many functions of the life of societies in the hands of a few." It "implies some new relationships between members of society ... in order to subject some classes to the domination of others" and this becomes obvious "when one studies the origins of the State." [**The State: Its Historic Role**, p. 10] This was the case with representative democracy:

> "To attack the central power, to strip it of its prerogatives, to decentralise, to dissolve authority, would have been to abandon to the people the control of its affairs, to run the risk of a truly popular revolution. That is why the bourgeoisie sought to reinforce the central government even more." [Kropotkin, **Words of a Rebel**, p. 143]

This meant, Kropotkin continued, that the "representative system was organised by the bourgeoisie to ensure their domination, and it will disappear with them. For the new economic phase that is about to begin we must seek a new form of political organisation, based on a principle quite different from that of representation. The logic of events imposes it." [**Op. Cit.**, p. 125] This suggests that the Marxist notion that we can use a state (i.e., any centralised and hierarchical social structure) to organise and defend a social revolution is based on flawed reasoning in which it "seems to be taken for granted that Capitalism and the workers' movement both have the same end in view. If this were so, they might perhaps use the same means; but as the capitalist is out to perfect his system of exploitation and government, whilst the worker is out for emancipation and liberty, naturally the same means cannot be employed for both purposes." [George Barrett, **Objections to Anarchism**, p. 343]

To reproduce in the new society social structures which share the same characteristics (such as centralisation and delegation of power) which mark the institutions of class society would be a false step, one which can only recreate a new form of class system in which a new ruling elite govern and exploit the many. So while we agree with Marxists that the main function of the state is to defend class society, we also stress the structure of the state has evolved to execute that role. In the words of Rudolf Rocker:

> "social institutions … do not arise arbitrarily, but are called into being by special needs to serve definite purposes … The newly arisen possessing classes had need of a political instrument of power to maintain their economic and social privileges over the masses of their own people … Thus arose the appropriate social conditions for the evolution of the modern state, as the organ of political power of privileged castes and classes for the forcible subjugation and oppression of the non-possessing classes … Its external forms have altered in the course of its historical development, but its functions have always been the same … And just as the functions of the bodily organs of … animals cannot be arbitrarily altered, so that, for example, one cannot at will hear with his eyes and see with his ears, so also one cannot at pleasure transform an organ of social oppression into an instrument for the liberation of the oppressed. The state can only be what it is: the defender of mass-exploitation and social privileges, and creator of privileged classes."
> [**Anarcho-Syndicalism**, pp. 14-5]

As such, a new form of society, one based on the participation of all in the affairs of society (and a classless society can be nothing else) means the end of the state. This is because it has been designed to **exclude** the participation a classless society needs in order to exist. In anarchist eyes, it is an abuse of the language to call the self-managed organisations by which the former working class manage (and defend) a free society a state.

However, as **Workers Power** indicate, it could be objected that the anarchist vision of a federation of communal and workplace assemblies and volunteer militias to defend it is simply a new form of state. In other words, that the anarchists advocate what most people (including most Marxists) would call a state as this federal system is based on social organisation, collective decision making and (ultimately) the armed people. This was the position of Marx and Engels, who asserted against Bakunin that *"to call this machine a 'revolutionary Commune organised from the bottom to top' makes little difference. The name changes nothing of the substance"* for to be able to do anything at all the communal councils *"must be vested with some power and supported by a public force."* [**Collected Works**, vol. 23, p. 469]

Anarchists reject this argument. To quote Daniel Guérin, initially anarchists used terms like the state or revolutionary state as a synonym for *"social collective"* but *"soon saw, however, that it was rather dangerous for them to use the same word as the authoritarians while giving it a quite different meaning. They felt that a new concept called for a new word and that the use of the old term could be dangerously ambiguous; so they ceased to give the name 'State' to the social collective of the future."* [**Anarchism**, pp. 60-1] This is more than mere labels or semantics as it gets to the heart of the difference between libertarian and authoritarian conceptions of society and social change. Anarchists argue that the state is structured to ensure minority rule and,

consequently, a "workers' state" would be a new form of minority rule over the workers. For this reason we argue that working class self-management from the bottom-up cannot be confused with a "state." The Russian Revolution showed the validity of this, with the Bolsheviks calling their dictatorship a "workers' state" in spite of the workers having no power in it.

Anarchists have long pointed out that government is not the same as collective decision making and to call the bottom-up communal system anarchists aim for a "state" when its role is to promote and ensure mass participation in social life is nonsense. That Marxists are vaguely aware of this obvious fact explains why they often talk of a "semi-state", a "new kind of state", a state "unique in history," or use some other expression to describe their post-revolutionary system. This would be a state (to use Engels words) which is *"no longer a state in the proper sense of the word."* [quoted by Lenin, **Op. Cit.**, p. 319] If that **is** the case, then why call it state?

Somewhat ironically, Engels provided more than enough support for the anarchist position. It is perfectly possible to have social organisation and it **not** be a state. When discussing the Native American Iroquois Confederacy, Engels noted that *"organ of the Confederacy was a Federal Council"* which was *"elected … and could always be removed"* by popular assemblies. There was *"no chief executive"* but *"two supreme war chiefs"* and *"[w]hen war broke out it was carried on mainly by volunteers."* Yet this was *"the organisation of a society which as yet knows no **state**."* [**Selected Works**, p. 517, p. 518 and p. 516] In the anarchist commune there is a federal council elected and mandated by popular assemblies. These, in turn, are federated in a similar bottom-up manner. The means of production have been expropriated and held by society as a whole and so classes have been abolished. Volunteer militias have been organised for self-defence against counter-revolutionary attempts to subject the free people to authority. Why is this **not** a society which *"knows no **state**"*? Is it because the anarchist commune is fighting against the capitalist class? If so, does this mean that the Iroquois Confederacy became a state when it waged war against those seeking to impose bourgeois rule on it? That is doubtful and so Marx's assertion is simply wrong and reflects both the confusion at the heart of the Marxist theory of the state and the illogical depths Marxists sink to when attacking anarchism.

This not a matter of mere "labels" as Marxists assert, but rather gets to the key issue of who has the real power in a revolution - the people armed or a new minority (the "revolutionary" government). In other words, most Marxists cannot tell the difference between libertarian organisation (power to the base and decision making from the bottom-up) and the state (centralised power in a few hands and top-down decision making). Which helps explain why the Bolshevik revolution was such a failure. The confusion of working class power with party power is one of the root problems with Marxism. So why do most Marxists tend to call their post-revolutionary organisation a state? Simply because, at some level, they recognise that, in reality, the working class does not wield power in the so-called "workers' state": the party does. This was the case in Russia. The working class never wielded power under the Bolsheviks and here is the most obvious contradiction in the Marxist theory of the state - a contradiction which, as we discuss in section H.3.8 the Leninists solved by arguing that the party had to assert its power **over** the working class for its own good.

Moreover, as we discuss in section H.3.9, it is both simplistic and wrong to argue that the state is simply the tool of economic classes. The state is a source of social inequality in and of itself and, consequently, can oppress and exploit the working class just as much as, and independently of, any economically dominant class:

> "*All political power inevitably creates a privileged situation* for the men who exercise it. Thus it violates, from the beginning, the equalitarian principle and strikes at the heart of the Social Revolution ... [It] inevitably becomes a source of other privileges, even if it does not depend on the bourgeoisie. Having taken over the Revolution, having mastered it, and bridled it, *power is compelled to create a bureaucratic apparatus*, indispensable to all authority which wants to maintain itself, to command, to order - in a word, 'to govern'. Rapidly, it attracts around itself all sorts of elements eager to dominate and exploit.
>
> "*Thus it forms a new privileged caste*, at first politically and later economically ... It sows everywhere the seed of inequality and soon infects the whole social organism." [Voline, **The Unknown Revolution**, p. 249]

So if it **were** simply a question of consolidating a revolution and its self-defence then there would be no argument:

> "*But perhaps the truth is simply this: ... [some] take the expression 'dictatorship of the proletariat' to mean simply the revolutionary action of the workers in taking possession of the land and the instruments of labour, and trying to build a society and organise a way of life in which there will be no place for a class that exploits and oppresses the producers.*
>
> "*Thus constructed, the 'dictatorship of the proletariat' would be the effective power of all workers trying to bring down capitalist society and would thus turn into Anarchy as soon as resistance from reactionaries would have ceased and no one can any longer seek to compel the masses by violence to obey and work for him. In which case, the discrepancy between us would be nothing more than a question of semantics. Dictatorship of the proletariat would signify the dictatorship of everyone, which is to say, it would be a dictatorship no longer, just as government by everybody is no longer a government in the authoritarian, historical and practical sense of the word.*
>
> "*But the real supporters of 'dictatorship of the proletariat' do not take that line, as they are making quite plain in Russia. Of course, the proletariat has a hand in this, just as the people has a part to play in democratic regimes, that is to say, to conceal the reality of things. In reality, what we have is the dictatorship of one party, or rather, of one party's leaders: a genuine dictatorship, with its decrees, its penal sanctions, its henchmen and above all its armed*

> *forces, which are at present [1919] also deployed in the defence of the revolution against its external enemies, but which will tomorrow be used to impose the dictator's will upon the workers, to apply a break on revolution, to consolidate the new interests in the process of emerging and protect a new privileged class against the masses.*" [Malatesta, **No Gods, No Masters**, vol. 2, pp. 38-9]

The question is, therefore, one of **who** "*seizes power*" - will it be the mass of the population or will it be a party claiming to represent it. The difference is vital and it confuses the issue to use the same word "state" to describe two such fundamentally different structures as a "bottom-up" self-managed communal federation and a "top-down" hierarchical centralised organisation (such as has been every state that has existed). This explains why anarchists reject the idea of a "*democratic workers' state*" as the means by which a revolution defends itself. Rather than signify working class power or management of society, it signifies the opposite - the seizure of power of a minority (in this case, the leaders of the vanguard party).

This is why anarchists reject the idea of a "*democratic workers' state.*" Simply put, as far as it is a state, it cannot be democratic and in as far as it is democratic, it cannot be a state. The Leninist idea of a "*workers' state*" means, in fact, the seizure of power by the party. This, we must stress, naturally follows from the reality of the state. It is designed for minority rule and excludes, by its very nature, mass participation and this aspect of the state was one which the leading lights of Bolshevism agreed with. Little wonder, then, that in practice the Bolshevik regime suppressed of any form of democracy which hindered the power of the party. Maurice Brinton summed up the issue well when he argued that "*'workers' power' cannot be identified or equated with the power of the Party - as it repeatedly was by the Bolsheviks ... What 'taking power' really implies is that the vast majority of the working class at last realises its ability to manage both production and society - and organises to this end.*" [**The Bolsheviks and Workers' Control**, p. xiv]

In summary, therefore, anarchists reject the idea that the defence of a revolution can be conducted by a state. As Bakunin once put it, there is the "*Republic-State*" and there is "*the system of the Republic-Commune, the Republic-Federation, i.e. the system of* **Anarchism.** *This is the politics of the Social Revolution, which aims at the abolition of the* **State** *and establishment of the economic, entirely free organisation of the people - organisation from bottom to top by means of federation.*" [**The Political Philosophy of Bakunin**, p. 314] Indeed, creating a new state will simply destroy the most important gain of any revolution - working class autonomy - and its replacement by another form of minority rule (by the party). Anarchists have always argued that the defence of a revolution must not be confused with the state and so argue for the abolition of the state **and** the defence of a revolution. Only when working class people actually run society themselves will a revolution be successful. For anarchists, this means that "*effective emancipation can be achieved only by the* **direct, widespread, and independent action** *...* **of the workers themselves,** *grouped ... in their own class organisations ... on the basis of concrete action and self-government,* **helped but not governed,** *by revolutionaries working in the very midst of, and not above the mass and the professional, technical, defence and other branches."* [Voline, **Op. Cit.**, p. 197]

This means that anarchists argue that the state cannot be transformed or adjusted, but has to be smashed by a social revolution and replaced with organisations and structures created by working class people during their own struggles (see section H.1.4 for details). Anarchist opposition to the so-called workers' state has absolutely **nothing** to do with the issue of defending a revolution, regardless of what Marxists assert.

H.2.2 Do anarchists reject "class conflict" and "collective struggle"?

Of course not. Anarchists have always taken a keen interest in the class struggle, in the organisation, solidarity and actions of working class people. Anarchist Nicholas Walter summarised the obvious and is worth quoting at length:

"Virtually all forms of revolutionary socialism during the nineteenth century, whether authoritarian or libertarian, were based on the concept of class struggle ... The term anarchist was first adopted by Pierre-Joseph Proudhon in 1840, and although he disliked the class struggle, he recognised it existed, and took sides in it when he had to ... during the French Revolution of 1848, he insisted that he was on the side of the proletariat against the bourgeoisie ... his last book was a positive study of the need for specifically proletarian politics ...

"The actual anarchist movement was founded later, by the anti-authoritarian sections of the First International ... They accepted [its] founding Address ..., drafted by Karl Marx, which assumed the primacy of the class struggle and insisted that 'the emancipation of the working classes must be conquered by the working classes themselves'; they accepted the Programme of the International Alliance of Social Democracy (1869), drafted by Michael Bakunin, which assumed the primacy of the class struggle ... and they accepted the declaration of the St. Imier Congress which assumed the primacy of the class struggle and insisted that 'rejecting all compromise to arrive at the accomplishment of the social revolution, the proletarians of all countries must establish, outside all bourgeois politics, the solidarity of revolutionary action' ... This was certainly the first anarchist movement, and this movement was certainly based on a libertarian version of the concept of the class struggle.

"Most of the leaders of this movement - first Michael Bakunin, James Guillaume, Errico Malatesta, Carlo Caliero, later Peter Kropotkin, Louise Michel, Emile Pouget, Jean Grave, and so on - took for granted that there was a struggle between the proletariat and the bourgeoisie and that the social revolution would be conducted by the

former against the latter. They derived such ideas ... from the traditional theory of revolutionary socialism and the traditional practice of working-class action ...

"The great revolutions of the early twentieth century - in Mexico, Russia, Spain - all derived from the class struggle and all involved anarchist intervention on the side of the working class. The great martyrs of the anarchist movement - from Haymarket in 1887 through Francisco Ferrer in 1909 to Sacco and Vanzetti in 1927 - were killed in the class struggle. The great partisans of anarchist warfare - from Emiliano Zapata through Nestor Makhno to Buenaventura Durruti - were all fighting in the class struggle.

"So ... class struggle in anarchism ... [and] its importance in the anarchist movement is incontrovertible." [**The Anarchist Past and other essays**, pp. 60-2]

Anyone even remotely aware of anarchism and its history could not fail to notice that class struggle plays a key role in anarchist theory, particularly (but not exclusively) in its revolutionary form. To assert otherwise is simply to lie about anarchism. Sadly, Marxists have been known to make such an assertion.

For example, Pat Stack of the British SWP argued that anarchists *"dismiss ... the importance of the collective nature of change"* and so *"downplays the centrality of the working class"* in the revolutionary process. This, he argues, means that for anarchism the working class *"is not the key to change."* He stresses that for Proudhon, Bakunin and Kropotkin *"revolutions were not about ... collective struggle or advance"* and that anarchism *"despises the collectivity."* Therefore, *"[i]t follows that if class conflict is not the motor of change, the working class is not the agent and collective struggle not the means."* [*"Anarchy in the UK?"*, **Socialist Review**, no. 246] Needless to say, he makes the usual exception for anarcho-syndicalists, thereby showing his total ignorance of anarchism **and** syndicalism (see section H.2.8).

Assertions like these are simply incredible. It is hard to believe that anyone who is a leading member of a Leninist party could write such nonsense which suggests that Stack is aware of the truth and simply decides to ignore it. All in all, it is **very** easy to refute these assertions. All we have to do is, unlike Stack, to quote from the works of Bakunin, Kropotkin and other anarchists. Even the briefest familiarity with the writings of revolutionary anarchism would soon convince the reader that Stack really does not know what he is talking about.

Take, for example, Bakunin. Rather than reject class conflict, collective struggle or the key role of the working class, Bakunin based his political ideas on all three. As he put it, there was, *"between the proletariat and the bourgeoisie, an irreconcilable antagonism which results inevitably from their respective stations in life."* He stressed that *"war between the proletariat and the bourgeoisie is unavoidable"* and would only end with the *"abolition of the bourgeoisie as a distinct class."* In order for the worker to *"become strong"* he *"must unite"* with other workers in *"the union of all local and national workers' associations into a world-wide association, **the great International Working-Men's Association.**"* It was only *"through* practice and collective experience" and "the progressive expansion and development of the economic struggle [that] will bring [the worker] more to recognise his [or her] true enemies: the privileged classes, including the clergy, the bourgeoisie, and the nobility; and the State, which exists only to safeguard all the privileges of those classes." There was "but a single path, that of **emancipation through practical action**" which "has only one meaning. It means workers' solidarity in their struggle against the bosses. It means **trades-unions, organisation, and the federation of resistance funds.**" Then, "when the revolution - brought about by the force of circumstances - breaks out, the International will be a real force and know what it has to do", namely to "take the revolution into its own hands" and become "an earnest international organisation of workers' associations from all countries" which will be "capable of replacing this departing political world of States and bourgeoisie." [**The Basic Bakunin**, pp. 97-8, p. 103 and p. 110]

Hardly the words of a man who rejected class conflict, the working class and the collective nature of change! Nor is this an isolated argument from Bakunin, it recurs continuously throughout Bakunin's works. For Bakunin, the "initiative in the new movement will belong to the people ... in Western Europe, to the city and factory workers - in Russia, Poland, and most of the Slavic countries, to the peasants." However, "in order that the peasants rise up, it is absolutely necessary that the initiative in this revolutionary movement be taken up by the city workers ... who combine in themselves the instincts, ideas, and conscious will of the Social Revolution." [**The Political Philosophy of Bakunin**, p. 375] Similarly, he argued that "equality" was the "aim" of the International Workers' Association and "the organisation of the working class its strength, the unification of the proletariat the world over ... its weapon, its only policy." He stressed that "to create a people's force capable of crushing the military and civil force of the State, it is necessary to organise the proletariat." [quoted by K.J. Kenafick, **Michael Bakunin and Karl Marx**, p. 95 and p. 254]

Strikes played a very important role in Bakunin's ideas (as they do in all revolutionary anarchist thought). He saw the strike as "the beginnings of the social war of the proletariat against the bourgeoisie ... Strikes are a valuable instrument from two points of view. Firstly, they electrify the masses ... awaken in them the feeling of the deep antagonism which exists between their interests and those of the bourgeoisie ... secondly they help immensely to provoke and establish between the workers of all trades, localities and countries the consciousness and very fact of solidarity: a twofold action, both negative and positive, which tends to constitute directly the new world of the proletariat, opposing it almost in an absolute way to the bourgeois world." [quoted by Caroline Cahm, **Kropotkin and the Rise of Revolutionary Anarchism 1872-1886**, pp. 216-217] For Bakunin, strikes train workers for social revolution as they "create, organise, and form a workers' army, an army which is bound to break down the power of the bourgeoisie and the State, and lay the ground for a new world." [**The Political Philosophy of Bakunin**, pp. 384-5]

As we argue in section I.2.3, the very process of collective class struggle would, for Bakunin and other anarchists, create the basis of a free society. Thus, in Bakunin's eyes, the "future social organisation must be made solely from the bottom upwards, by the free association or federation of workers, firstly in their unions, then in the communes, regions, nations and finally in a great federation, international and universal." [**Michael Bakunin: Selected Writings**, p. 206] In other words, the basic structure created by the revolution would be based on the working classes own combat organisations, as created in their struggles against oppression and exploitation. The link between present and future would be labour unions (workers' associations), which played the key role of both the means to abolish capitalism and the state and as the framework of a socialist society.

For Bakunin, the "very essence of socialism" lies in "the irrepressible conflict between the workers and the exploiters of labour." A "living, powerful, socialist movement" can "be made a reality only by the awakened revolutionary consciousness, the collective will, and the organisation of the working masses themselves." [**Bakunin on Anarchism**, p. 191 and p. 212] Therefore, it was essential to "[o]rganise always more and more the practical militant international solidarity of the toilers of all trades and of all countries, and remember ... you will find an immense, an irresistible force in this universal collectivity." Hence Bakunin's support for self-discipline within self-managed organisations, which came directly from the his awareness of the **collective** nature of social change: "Today, in revolutionary action as in labour itself, collectivism must replace individualism. Understand clearly that in organising yourselves you will be stronger than all the political leaders in the world." [quoted by Kenafick, **Op. Cit.**, p. 291 and p. 244]

All of which is quite impressive for someone who was a founding father of a theory which, according to Stack, downplayed the "centrality of the working class," argued that the working class was "not the key to change," dismissed "the importance of the collective nature of change" as well as "collective struggle or advance" and "despises the collectivity"! Clearly, to argue that Bakunin held any of these views simply shows that the person making such statements does not have a clue what they are talking about.

The same, needless to say, applies to all revolutionary anarchists. Kropotkin built upon Bakunin's arguments and, like him, based his politics on collective working class struggle and organisation. He consistently stressed that "the Anarchists have always advised taking an active part in those workers' organisations which carry on the **direct** struggle of Labour against Capital and its protector - the State." Such struggle, "better than any other indirect means, permits the worker to obtain some temporary improvements in the present conditions of work, while it opens his eyes to the evil done by Capitalism and the State that supports it, and wakes up his thoughts concerning the possibility of organising consumption, production, and exchange without the intervention of the capitalist and the State." [**Evolution and Environment**, pp. 82-3] In his article on "Anarchism" for the **Encyclopaedia Britannica**, Kropotkin stressed that anarchists "have endeavoured to promote their ideas directly amongst the labour organisations and to induce those unions to a direct struggle against capital, without placing their faith in parliamentary legislation." [**Anarchism**, p. 287]

Far from denying the importance of collective class struggle, he actually stressed it again and again. As he once wrote, "to make the revolution, the mass of workers will have to organise themselves. Resistance and the strike are excellent means of organisation for doing this." He argued that it was "a question of organising societies of resistance for all trades in each town, of creating resistance funds against the exploiters, of giving more solidarity to the workers' organisations of each town and of putting them in contact with those of other towns, of federating them ... Workers' solidarity must no longer be an empty word but practised each day between all trades and all nations." [quoted by Cahm, **Op. Cit.**, pp. 255-6]

As can be seen, Kropotkin was well aware of the importance of popular, mass, struggles. As he put it, anarchists "know very well that any popular movement is a step towards the social revolution. It awakens the spirit of revolt, it makes men [and women] accustomed to seeing the established order (or rather the established disorder) as eminently unstable." [**Words of a Rebel**, p. 203] As regards the social revolution, he argues that "a decisive blow will have to be administered to private property: from the beginning, the workers will have to proceed to take over all social wealth so as to put it into common ownership. This revolution can only be carried out by the workers themselves." In order to do this, the masses have to build their own organisation as the "great mass of workers will not only have to constitute itself outside the bourgeoisie ... it will have to take action of its own during the period which will precede the revolution ... and this sort of action can only be carried out when a strong **workers' organisation** exists." This meant, of course, it was "the mass of workers we have to seek to organise. We ... have to submerge ourselves in the organisation of the people ... When the mass of workers is organised and we are with it to strengthen its revolutionary idea, to make the spirit of revolt against capital germinate there ... then it will be the social revolution." [quoted by Caroline Cahm, **Op. Cit.**, pp. 153-4]

He saw the class struggle in terms of "a multitude of acts of revolt in all countries, under all possible conditions: first, individual revolt against capital and State; then collective revolt - strikes and working-class insurrections - both preparing, in men's minds as in actions, a revolt of the masses, a revolution." Clearly, the mass, collective nature of social change was not lost on Kropotkin who pointed to a "multitude of risings of working masses and peasants" as a positive sign. Strikes, he argued, "were once 'a war of folded arms'" but now were "easily turning to revolt, and sometimes taking the proportions of vast insurrections." [**Anarchism**, p. 144]

Kropotkin could not have been clearer. Somewhat ironically, given Stack's assertions, Kropotkin explicitly opposed the Marxism of his time (Social Democracy) precisely **because** it had "moved away from a pure labour movement, in the sense of a direct struggle against capitalists by means of strikes, unions, and so forth." The Marxists, he stated, opposed strikes and unions because they "diverted forces from electoral agitation" while anarchists "reject[ed] a narrowly political struggle [and] inevitably became a more revolutionary party, both in theory and in practice." [**The Conquest of Bread and Other Writings**, pp. 207-8, p. 208 and p. 209]

And Pat Stack argues that Kropotkin did not see "class conflict as the dynamic for social change," nor "class conflict" as "the motor of change" and the working class "not the agent and collective struggle not the means"! Truly incredible and a total and utter distortion of Kropotkin's ideas on the subject.

As for other anarchists, we discover the same concern over class

conflict, collective struggle and organisation and the awareness of a mass social revolution by the working class. Emma Goldman, for example, argued that anarchism "stands for direct action" and that "[t]rade unionism, the economic arena of the modern gladiator, owes its existence to direct action ... In France, in Spain, in Italy, in Russia, nay even in England (witness the growing rebellion of English labour unions), direct, revolutionary economic action has become so strong a force in the battle for industrial liberty as to make the world realise the tremendous importance of labour's power. The General Strike [is] the supreme expression of the economic consciousness of the workers ... Today every great strike, in order to win, must realise the importance of the solidaric general protest." [**Anarchism and Other Essays**, pp. 65-6] She placed collective class struggle at the centre of her ideas and, crucially, she saw it as the way to create an anarchist society:

> "It is this war of classes that we must concentrate upon, and in that connection the war against false values, against evil institutions, against all social atrocities. Those who appreciate the urgent need of co-operating in great struggles ... must organise the preparedness of the masses for the overthrow of both capitalism and the state. Industrial and economic preparedness is what the workers need. That alone leads to revolution at the bottom ... That alone will give the people the means to take their children out of the slums, out of the sweat shops and the cotton mills ... That alone leads to economic and social freedom, and does away with all wars, all crimes, and all injustice." [**Red Emma Speaks**, pp. 355-6]

For Malatesta, "the most powerful force for social transformation is the working class movement ... Through the organisations established for the defence of their interests, workers acquire an awareness of the oppression under which they live and of the antagonisms which divide them from their employers, and so begin to aspire to a better life, get used to collective struggle and to solidarity." This meant that anarchists "must recognise the usefulness and importance of the workers' movement, must favour its development, and make it one of the levers of their action, doing all they can so that it ... will culminate in a social revolution." Anarchists must "deepen the chasm between capitalists and wage-slaves, between rulers and ruled; preach expropriation of private property and the destruction of State." The new society would be organised "by means of free association and federations of producers and consumers." [**Errico Malatesta: His Life and Ideas**, p. 113, pp. 250-1 and p. 184] Alexander Berkman, unsurprisingly, argued the same thing. As he put it, only "the workers" as "the worst victims of present institutions," could abolish capitalism an the state as "it is to their own interest to abolish them ... labour's emancipation means at the same time the redemption of the whole of society." He stressed that "**only the right organisation of the workers** can accomplish what we are striving for ... Organisation from the bottom up, beginning with the shop and factory, on the foundation of the joint interests of the workers everywhere ... alone can solve the labour question and serve the true emancipation of man[kind]." [**What is Anarchism?**, p. 187 and p. 207]

As can be seen, the claim that Kropotkin or Bakunin, or anarchists in general, ignored the class struggle and collective working class struggle and organisation is either a lie or indicates ignorance. Clearly, anarchists have placed working class struggle, organisation and collective direct action and solidarity at the core of their politics (and as the means of creating a libertarian socialist society) from the start. Moreover, this perspective is reflected in the anarchist flag itself as we discuss in our appendix on the symbols of anarchism. According to Louise Michel the *"black flag is the flag of strikes."* [**The Red Virgin: Memoirs of Louise Michel**, p. 168] If anarchism does, as some Marxists assert, reject class conflict and collective struggle then using a flag associated with an action which expresses both seems somewhat paradoxical. However, for those with even a basic understanding of anarchism and its history there is no paradox as anarchism is obviously based on class conflict and collective struggle.

H.2.3 Does anarchism yearn "for what has gone before"?

Leninist Pat Stack states that one of the *"key points of divergence"* between anarchism and Marxism is that the former, *"far from understanding the advances that capitalism represented, tended to take a wistful look back. Anarchism shares with Marxism an abhorrence of the horrors of capitalism, but yearns for what has gone before."* [*"Anarchy in the UK?"*, **Socialist Review**, no. 246] Like his other *"key point"* (namely the rejection of class struggle - see last section), Stack is simply wrong. Even the quickest look at the works of Proudhon, Bakunin and Kropotkin would convince the reader that this is simply distortion. Rather than look backwards for our ideas of social life, anarchists have always been careful to base our ideas on the current state of society and what anarchist thinkers considered positive current trends within it.

The dual element of progress is important to remember. Capitalism is a class society, marked by exploitation, oppression and various social hierarchies. In such a society progress can hardly be neutral. It will reflect vested interests, the needs of those in power, the rationales of the economic system (e.g. the drive for profits) and those who benefit from it, the differences in power between states and companies and so on. Equally, it will be shaped by the class struggle, the resistance of the working classes to exploitation and oppression, the objective needs of production, etc. As such, trends in society will reflect the various class conflicts, social hierarchies, power relationships and so on which exist within it.

This is particularly true of the economy. The development of the industrial structure of a capitalist economy will be based on the fundamental need to maximise the profits and power of the capitalists. As such, it will develop (either by market forces or by state intervention) in order to ensure this. This means that various tendencies apparent in capitalist society exist specifically to aid the development of capital. It does not follow that because a society which places profits above people has found a specific way of organising production "efficient" that a socialist society will do so. As such, anarchist opposition to specific tendencies within capitalism (such as the increased concentration and centralisation

of companies) does not mean a *"yearning"* for the past. Rather, it shows an awareness that capitalist methods are precisely that and that they need not be suited for a society which replaces the profit system with human and ecological need as the criteria for decision making.

For anarchists, this means questioning the assumptions of capitalist progress and so the first task of a revolution after the expropriation of the capitalists and the destruction of the state will be to transform the industrial structure and how it operates, not keep it as it is. Anarchists have long argued that capitalist methods cannot be used for socialist ends. In our battle to democratise and socialise the workplace, in our awareness of the importance of collective initiatives by the direct producers in transforming their work situation, we show that factories are not merely sites of production, but also of reproduction - the reproduction of a certain structure of social relations based on the division between those who give orders and those who take them. Moreover, the structure of industry has developed to maximise profits. Why assume that this structure will be equally as efficient in producing useful products by meaningful work which does not harm the environment, society or those who do the actual tasks? A further aspect of this is that many of the struggles today, from the Zapatistas in Chiapas to those against Genetically Modified (GM) food and nuclear power are precisely based on the understanding that capitalist "progress" can not be uncritically accepted. To resist the expulsion of people from the land in the name of progress or the introduction of terminator seeds is not to look back to *"what had gone"*, although this is also precisely what the proponents of capitalist globalisation often accuse us of. Rather, it is to put *"**people before profit.**"*

That so many Marxists fail to understand this suggests that their ideology subscribes to notions of "progress" which simply build upon capitalist ones. As such, only a sophist would confuse a critical evaluation of trends within capitalism with a yearning for the past. It means to buy into the whole capitalist notion of "progress" which has always been part of justifying the inhumanities of the status quo. Simply put, just because a process is rewarded by the profit driven market it does not mean that it makes sense from a human or ecological perspective. For example, as we argue in section J.5.11, the capitalist market hinders the spread of co-operatives and workers' self-management in spite of their well documented higher efficiency and productivity. From the perspective of the needs of the capitalists, this makes perfect sense. In terms of the workers and efficient allocation and use of resources, it does not. Would Marxists argue that because co-operatives and workers' self-management of production are marginal aspects of the capitalist economy it means that they will play no part in a sane society or that if a socialist expresses interest in them it means that are *"yearning"* for a past mode of production? We hope not.

This common Marxist failure to understand anarchist investigations of the future is, ironically enough, joined with a total failure to understand the social conditions in which anarchists have put forward their ideas. For all his claims that anarchists ignore *"material conditions,"* it is Pat Stack (and others like him) who does so in his claims against Proudhon. Stack calls the Frenchman *"the founder of modern anarchism"* and states that Marx dubbed Proudhon *"the socialist of the small peasant or master craftsman."* Typically,

Stack gets even this wrong as it was Engels who used those words, although Marx would probably have not disagreed if he had been alive when they were penned. [**The Marx-Engels Reader**, p. 626] From this, Stack implies that Proudhon was *"yearning for the past"* when he advanced his mutualist ideas.

Nothing, however, could be further from the truth. This is because the society in which the French anarchist lived was predominately artisan and peasant in nature. This was admitted by Marx and Engels in the **Communist Manifesto** (*"[i]n countries like France"* the peasants *"constitute far more than half of the population."* [**Op. Cit.**, p. 493]). As such, for Proudhon to incorporate the aspirations of the majority of the population is not to *"yearn for what has gone before"* but rather an extremely sensible position to take. This suggests that for Engels to state that the French anarchist was *"the socialist of the small peasant or master craftsman"* was unsurprising, a simple statement of fact, as the French working classes were, at the time, predominately small peasants or master craftsmen (or artisans). It, in other words, reflected the society Proudhon lived in and, as such, did not reflect desires for the past but rather a wish to end exploitation and oppression **now** rather than some unspecified time in the future.

Moreover, Proudhon's ideas cannot be limited to just that as Marxists try to do. As K. Steven Vincent points out Proudhon's *"social theories may not be reduced to a socialism for only the peasant class, nor was it a socialism only for the petite bourgeois; it was a socialism of and for French workers. And in the mid-nineteenth century ... most French workers were still artisans."* Indeed, *"[w]hile Marx was correct in predicting the eventual predominance of the industrial proletariat vis-à-vis skilled workers, such predominance was neither obvious nor a foregone conclusion in France during the nineteenth century. The absolute number of small industries even increased during most of the century."* [**Pierre-Joseph Proudhon and the Rise of French Republican Socialism**, p. 5 and p. 282] Proudhon himself noted in 1851 that of a population of 36 million, 24 million were peasants and 6 million were artisans. Of the remaining 6 million, these included wage-workers for whom *"workers' associations"* would be essential as *"a protest against wage-labour,"* the *"negation of the capitalist regime"* and for *"the management of large instruments of labour."* [**Property is Theft!**, p. 558]

To summarise, if the society in which you live is predominately made-up of peasants and artisans then it is hardly an insult to be called *"the socialist of the small peasant or master craftsman."* Equally, it can hardly represent a desire for *"what has gone before"* to tailor your ideas to the actual conditions in the country in which you live! And Stack accuses **anarchists** of ignoring *"material conditions"*!

Neither can it be said that Proudhon ignored the development of industrialisation in France during his lifetime. Quite the reverse, in fact, as indicated above. Proudhon did **not** ignore the rise of large-scale industry and argued that such industry should be managed by the workers' themselves via workers associations. As he put it, *"certain industries"* required *"the combined employment of a large number of workers"* and so the producer is *"a collectivity."* In such industries *"we have no choice"* and so *"it is necessary to form an ASSOCIATION among the workers"* because *"without that they would remain related as subordinates and superiors, and there*

would ensue two industrial castes of masters and wage-workers, which is repugnant to a free and democratic society." [**Op. Cit.**, p. 583] Even Engels had to grudgingly admit that Proudhon supported *"the association of workers"* for *"large-industry and large establishments, such as railways."* [**Op. Cit.**, p. 626]

All in all, Stack is simply showing his ignorance of both Proudhon's ideas **and** the society (the *"material conditions"*) in which they were shaped and were aimed for. As can be seen, Proudhon incorporated the development of large-scale industry within his mutualist ideas and so the need to abolish wage labour by workers' associations and workers' control of production. After distorting Proudhon's ideas on industry, Stack does the same with Bakunin:

> *"Similarly, the Russian anarchist leader Bakunin argued that it was the progress of capitalism that represented the fundamental problem. For him industrialisation was an evil. He believed it had created a decadent western Europe, and therefore had held up the more primitive, less industrialised Slav regions as the hope for change."*

Now, it would be extremely interesting to find out where, exactly, Stack discovered that Bakunin made these claims. After all, they are at such odds with Bakunin's anarchist ideas that it is tempting to conclude that Stack is simply making it up.

It is, of course, simple to refute Stack's claims. We need only do that which he does not, namely quote Bakunin. For someone who thought *"industrialisation was an evil,"* a key aspect of Bakunin's ideas on social revolution was the seizing of industry and its placing under social ownership. As he put it, *"capital and all tools of labour belong to the city workers - to the workers associations. The whole organisation of the future should be nothing but a free federation of workers - agricultural workers as well as factory workers and associations of craftsmen."* [**The Political Philosophy of Bakunin**, p. 410] Bakunin argued that *"to destroy ... all the instruments of labour ... would be to condemn all humanity - which is infinitely too numerous today to exist ... on the simple gifts of nature ... - to ... death by starvation. Thus capital cannot and must not be destroyed. It must be preserved."* Only when workers *"obtain not individual but **collective** property in capital"* and when capital is no longer *"concentrated in the hands of a separate, exploiting class"* will they be able *"to smash the tyranny of capital."* [**The Basic Bakunin**, pp. 90-1] He stressed that only *"associated labour, this is labour organised upon the principles of reciprocity and co-operation, is adequate to the task of maintaining the existence of a large and somewhat civilised society."* Moreover, the *"whole secret of the boundless productivity of human labour consists first of all in applying ... scientifically developed reason ... and then in the division of that labour."* [**The Political Philosophy of Bakunin**, pp. 341-2] Hardly the thoughts of someone opposed to industrialisation! Unsurprisingly, then, Eugene Pyziu noted that *"[i]n an article printed in 1868 [Bakunin] rejected outright the doctrine of the rottenness of the West and of the messianic destiny of Russia."* [**The Doctrine of Anarchism of Michael A. Bakunin**, p. 61] Rather than oppose industrialisation and urge the destruction of industry, Bakunin considered one of the first acts of the revolution would be workers' associations taking over the means of production and turning them into collective property managed by the workers themselves. Hence Daniel Guérin's comment:

> *"Proudhon and Bakunin were 'collectivists,' which is to say they declared themselves without equivocation in favour of the common exploitation, not by the State but by associated workers of the large-scale means of production and of the public services. Proudhon has been quite wrongly presented as an exclusive enthusiast of private property."* [*"From Proudhon to Bakunin"*, pp. 23-33, **The Radical Papers**, Dimitrios I. Roussopoulos (ed.), p. 32]

Clearly, Stack does not have the faintest idea of what he is talking about! Nor is Kropotkin any safer than Proudhon or Bakunin from Stack's distortions:

> *"Peter Kropotkin, another famous anarchist leader to emerge in Russia, also looked backwards for change. He believed the ideal society would be based on small autonomous communities, devoted to small scale production. He had witnessed such communities among Siberian peasants and watchmakers in the Swiss mountains."*

Stack must be hoping that the reader has, like himself, not read Kropotkin's classic work **Fields, Factories and Workshops** for if they have then they would be aware of the distortion Stack subjects Kropotkin's ideas to. Kropotkin while stressing the importance of decentralising industry within a free society did not look backward for his inspiration. Rather, he looked to trends within existing society, trends he thought pointed in an anti-capitalist direction. This can be seen from the fact he based his ideas on detailed analysis of current developments in the economy and came to the conclusion that industry would spread across the globe (which has happened) and that small industries will continue to exist side by side with large ones (which also has been confirmed). From these facts he argued that a socialist society would aim to decentralise production, combining agriculture with industry and both using modern technology to the fullest. This was possible only after a social revolution which expropriated industry and the land and placed social wealth into the hands of the producers. Until then, the positive trends he saw in modern society would remain circumscribed by the workings of the capitalist market and the state.

As we discuss the fallacy that Kropotkin (or anarchists in general) have argued for *"small autonomous communities, devoted to small scale production"* in section I.3.8, we will not do so here. Suffice to say, he did not, as is often asserted, argue for *"small-scale production"* (he still saw the need for factories, for example) but rather for production geared to **appropriate** levels, based on the objective needs of production (without the distorting effects generated by the needs of capitalist profits and power) and, of necessity, the needs of those who work in and live alongside industry (and today we would add, the needs of the environment). In other words, the transformation of capitalism into a society human beings could live full and meaningful lives in. Part of this would involve creating an industry based on human needs. *"Have the factory and the workshop at the gates of your fields and gardens and work in them,"* he argued. *"Not those large establishments, of course, in*

which huge masses of metals have to be dealt with and which are better placed at certain spots indicated by Nature, but the countless variety of workshops and factories which are required to satisfy the infinite diversity of tastes among civilised men [and women]." The new factories and workplaces would be *"airy and hygienic, and consequently economical, … in which human life is of more account than machinery and the making of extra profits."* [**Fields, Factories and Workshops Tomorrow**, p. 197] Under capitalism, he argued, the whole discourse of economics (like industrial development itself) was based on the logic and rationale of the profit motive:

> *"Under the name of profits, rent and interest upon capital, surplus value, and the like, economists have eagerly discussed the benefits which the owners of land or capital, or some privileged nations, can derive, either from the under-paid work of the wage-labourer, or from the inferior position of one class of the community towards another class, or from the inferior economical development of one nation towards another nation…*
>
> *"In the meantime the great question - 'What have we to produce, and how?' necessarily remained in the background … The main subject of social economy - that is, the **economy of energy required for the satisfaction of human needs** - is consequently the last subject which one expects to find treated in a concrete form in economical treatises."* [**Op. Cit.**, p. 17]

Kropotkin's ideas were, therefore, an attempt to discuss how a post-capitalist society could develop, based on an extensive investigation of current trends within capitalism, and reflecting the needs which capitalism ignores. To fetishise big industry, as Leninists tend to do, means locking socialism itself into the logic of capitalism and, by implication, sees a socialist society which will basically be the same as capitalism, using the technology, industrial structure and industry developed under class society without change (see section H.3.12). Rather than condemn Kropotkin, Stack's comments (and those like them) simply show the poverty of the Leninist critique of capitalism and its vision of the socialist future.

All in all, anyone who claims that anarchism is *"backward looking"* or *"yearns for the past"* simply has no idea what they are talking about.

H.2.4 Do anarchists think "the state is the main enemy"?

Pat Stack argues that *"the idea that dominates anarchist thought"* is *"that the state is the main enemy, rather than identifying the state as one aspect of a class society that has to be destroyed."* [*"Anarchy in the UK?"*, **Socialist Review**, no. 246] Marxist Paul Thomas states that *"Anarchists insist that the basis source of social injustice is the state."* [**Karl Marx and the Anarchists**, p. 2]

On the face of it, such assertions make little sense. After all, was not the first work by the first self-declared anarchist called **What is Property?** and contained the revolutionary maxim **"property** *is theft"*? Surely this fact alone would be enough to put to rest the notion that anarchists view the state as the main problem in the world? Obviously not. Flying in the face of this well known fact as well as anarchist theory, Marxists have constantly repeated the falsehood that anarchists consider the state as the main enemy. Indeed, Stack and Thomas are simply repeating an earlier assertion by Engels:

> *"Bakunin has a peculiar theory of his own, a medley of Proudhonism and communism. The chief point concerning the former is that he does not regard capital, i.e. the class antagonism between capitalists and wage workers which has arisen through social development, but the* **state** *as the main enemy to be abolished … our view [is] that state power is nothing more than the organisation which the ruling classes - landowners and capitalists - have provided for themselves in order to protect their social privileges, Bakunin maintains that it is the* **state** *which has created capital, that the capitalist has his capital* **only by the grace of the state.** *As, therefore, the state is the chief evil, it is above all the state which must be done away with and then capitalism will go to blazes of itself. We, on the contrary, say: Do away with capital, the concentration of all means of production in the hands of a few, and the state will fall of itself. The difference is an essential one … the abolition of capital* **is** *precisely the social revolution."* [Marx, Engels and Lenin, **Anarchism and Anarcho-Syndicalism**, p. 71]

As will come as no surprise, Engels did not bother to indicate where he discovered Bakunin's ideas on these matters. Similarly, his followers raise this kind of assertion as a truism, apparently without the need for evidence to support the claim. This is hardly surprising as anarchists, including Bakunin, have expressed an idea distinctly at odds with Engels' claims, namely that the social revolution would be marked by the abolition of capitalism and the state at the same time. That this is the case can be seen from John Stuart Mill who, unlike Engels, saw that Bakunin's ideas meant *"not only the annihilation of all government, but getting all property of all kinds out of the hands of the possessors to be used for the general benefit."* [*"Chapters on Socialism,"* **Principles of Political Economy**, p. 376] If the great liberal thinker could discern this aspect of anarchism, why not Engels?

After all, this vision of a **social** revolution (i.e. one that combined political, social **and** economic goals) occurred continuously throughout Bakunin's writings when he was an anarchist. Indeed, to claim that he, or anarchists in general, just opposed the state suggests a total unfamiliarity with anarchist theory. For Bakunin, like all anarchists, the abolition of the state occurs at the same time as the abolition of capital. This joint abolition **is** precisely the social revolution. As one academic put it:

> *"In Bakunin's view, the struggle against the main concentration of power in society, the state, was* **no less necessary** *than the struggle against capital. Engels, however, puts the matter somewhat differently, arguing that for Bakunin the state was the main enemy, as if*

Bakunin had not held that capital, too, was an enemy and that its expropriation was a necessary even if not sufficient condition for the social revolution … [Engels'] formulation … distorts Bakunin's argument, which also held capital to be an evil necessary to abolish" [Alvin W. Gouldner, *"Marx's Last Battle: Bakunin and the First International"*, pp. 853-884, **Theory and Society**, Vol. 11, No. 6, pp. 863-4]

In 1865, for example, we discover Bakunin arguing that anarchists *"seek the destruction of all States"* in his *"Program of the Brotherhood."* Yet he also argued that a member of this association *"must be socialist"* and see that *"labour"* was the *"sole producer of social assets"* and so *"anyone enjoying these without working is an exploiter of another man's labour, a thief."* They must also *"understand that there is no liberty in the absence of equality"* and so the *"attainment of the widest liberty"* is possible only *"amid the most perfect (de jure and de facto) political, economic and social equality."* The *"sole and supreme objective"* of the revolution *"will be the effective political, economic and social emancipation of the people."* This was because political liberty *"is not feasible without political equality. And the latter is impossible without economic and social equality."* This means that the *"land belongs to everyone. But usufruct of it will belong only to those who till it with their own hands."* As regards industry, *"through the unaided efforts and economic powers of the workers' associations, capital and the instruments of labour will pass into the possession of those who will apply them … through their own labours."* He opposed sexism, for women are *"equal in all political and social rights."* Ultimately, *"[n]o revolution could succeed … unless it was simultaneously a political and a social revolution. Any exclusively political revolution … will, insofar as it consequently does not have the immediate, effective, political and economic emancipation of the people as its primary objective, prove to be … illusory, phoney."* [**No Gods, No Masters**, vol. 1, pp. 134-41]

In 1868, Bakunin was arguing the same ideas. The *"Association of the International Brethren seeks simultaneously universal, social, philosophical, economic and political revolution, so that the present order of things, rooted in property, exploitation, domination and the authority principle"* will be destroyed. The *"revolution as we understand it will … set about the … complete destruction of the State … The natural and necessary upshot of that destruction"* will include the *"[d]issolution of the army, magistracy, bureaucracy, police and clergy"* and *"[a]ll productive capital and instruments of labour … be[ing] confiscated for the benefit of toilers associations, which will have to put them to use in collective production"* as well as the *"[s]eizure of all Church and State properties."* The *"federated Alliance of all labour associations … will constitute the Commune."* The people *"must make the revolution everywhere, and … ultimate direction of it must at all times be vested in the people organised into a free federation of agricultural and industrial associations … organised from the bottom up."* [**Op. Cit.**, pp. 152-6]

Are these the words of a person who considered the state as the *"chief evil"* or *"that the state is the main enemy"*? Of course not, rather Bakunin clearly identified the state as one aspect of a class society that has to be destroyed. As he put it, the *"State, which* has never had any task other than to regularise, sanction and ... protect the rule of the privileged classes and exploitation of the people's labour for the rich, must be abolished. Consequently, this requires that society be organised from the bottom up through the free formation and free federation of worker associations, industrial, agricultural, scientific and artisan alike, ... founded upon collective ownership of the land, capital, raw materials and the instruments of labour, which is to say, all large-scale property ... leaving to private and hereditary possession only those items that are actually for personal use." [**Op. Cit.**, p. 182] Clearly, as Wayne Thorpe notes, for Bakunin "[o]nly the simultaneous destruction of the state and of the capitalist system, accompanied by the organisation from below of a federalist system of administration based upon labour's economic associations ... could achieve true liberty." [**"The Workers Themselves"**, p. 6]

Rather than seeing the state as the main evil to be abolished, Bakunin always stressed that a revolution must be economic **and** political in nature, that it must ensure political, economic and social liberty and equality. As such, he argued for **both** the destruction of the state and the expropriation of capital (both acts conducted, incidentally, by a federation of workers' associations or workers' councils). While the apparatus of the state was being destroyed ("Dissolution of the army, magistracy, bureaucracy, police and clergy"), capitalism was also being uprooted and destroyed ("All productive capital and instruments of labour ... confiscated for the benefit of toilers associations"). To assert, as Engels did, that Bakunin ignored the necessity of abolishing capitalism and the other evils of the current system while focusing exclusively on the state, is simply distorting his ideas. As Mark Leier summarises in his excellent biography of Bakunin, Engels "was just flat-out wrong ... What Bakunin did argue was that the social revolution had to be launched against the state and capitalism simultaneously, for the two reinforced each other." [**Bakunin: The Creative Passion**, p. 274]

Kropotkin, unsurprisingly, argued along identical lines as Bakunin. He stressed that "the revolution will burn on until it has accomplished its mission: the abolition of property-owning and of the State." This revolution, he re-iterated, would be a "mass rising up against property and the State." Indeed, Kropotkin always stressed that "there is one point to which all socialists adhere: the expropriation of capital must result from the coming revolution." This meant that "the area of struggle against capital, and against the sustainer of capital - government" could be one in which "various groups can act in agreement" and so "any struggle that prepares for that expropriation should be sustained in unanimity by all the socialist groups, to whatever shading they belong." [**Words of a Rebel**, p. 75 and p. 204] Little wonder Kropotkin wrote his famous article "Expropriation" on this subject! As he put it:

> "Expropriation - that is the guiding word of the coming revolution, without which it will fail in its historic mission: the complete expropriation of all those who have the means of exploiting human beings; the return to the community of the nation of everything that in the hands of anyone can be used to exploit others." [**Op. Cit.**, pp. 207-8]

This was because he was well aware of the oppressive nature of

capitalism: "For the worker who **must sell** his labour, it is impossible to remain **free**, and it is precisely because it is impossible that we are anarchists and communists." [**Selected Writings on Anarchism and Revolution**, p. 305] For Kropotkin, "the task we impose ourselves" is to acquire "sufficient influence to induce the workmen to avail themselves of the first opportunity of taking possession of land and the mines, of railways and factories," to bring working class people "to the conviction that they must rely on themselves to get rid of the oppression of Capital." [**Act for Yourselves**, p. 32] Strange words if Marxist assertions were true. As can be seen, Kropotkin is simply following Bakunin's ideas on the matter. He, like Bakunin, was well aware of the evils of capitalism and that the state protects these evils.

For Kropotkin, the "State is there to protect exploitation, speculation and private property; it is itself the by-product of the rapine of the people. The proletarian must rely on his own hands; he can expect nothing of the State. It is nothing more than an organisation devised to hinder emancipation at all costs." [**Words of a Rebel**, p. 27] Rather than see the state as the main evil, he clearly saw it as the protector of capitalism - in other words, as one aspect of a class system which needed to be replaced by a better society:

> "The very words Anarchist-Communism show in what direction society, in our opinion, is already going, and on what lines it can get rid of the oppressive powers of Capital and Government ... The first conviction to acquire is that nothing short of expropriation on a vast scale, carried out by the workmen themselves, can be the first step towards a reorganisation of our production on Socialist principles." [Kropotkin, **Act for Yourselves**, pp. 32-3]

Similarly with other anarchists. Emma Goldman summarised the libertarian position when she argued that anarchism "really stands for" the "liberation of the human body from the domination of property; liberation from the shackles and restraint of government." Goldman was well aware that wealth "means power; the power to subdue, to crush, to exploit, the power to enslave, to outrage, to degrade." She considered property "not only a hindrance to human well-being, but an obstacle, a deadly barrier, to all progress." A key problem of modern society was that "man must sell his labour" and so "his inclination and judgement are subordinated to the will of a master." Anarchism, she stressed, was the "the only philosophy that can and will do away with this humiliating and degrading situation ... There can be no freedom in the large sense of the word ... so long as mercenary and commercial considerations play an important part in the determination of personal conduct." The state, ironically for Stack's claim, was "necessary **only** to maintain or protect property and monopoly." [**Red Emma Speaks**, p. 73, p. 66, p. 50 and p. 51]

Errico Malatesta, likewise, stressed that, for "all anarchists," it was definitely a case that the "abolition of political power is not possible without the simultaneous destruction of economic privilege." The "Anarchist Programme" he drafted listed "Abolition of private property" before "Abolition of government" and argued that "the present state of society" was one in "which some have inherited the land and all social wealth, while the mass of the people, disinherited in all respects, is exploited and oppressed by a small possessing class." It ends by arguing that anarchism wants "the complete destruction of the domination and exploitation of man by man" and for "expropriation of landowners and capitalists for the benefit of all; and the abolition of government." [**Errico Malatesta: His Life and Ideas**, p. 158, p. 184, p. 183, p. 197 and p. 198] Nearly three decades previously, we find Malatesta arguing the same idea. As he put it in 1891, anarchists "struggle for anarchy, and for socialism, because we believe that anarchy and socialism must be realised immediately, that is to say that in the revolutionary act we must drive government away, abolish property … human progress is measured by the extent government power and private property are reduced." [**Anarchy**, p. 54]

Little wonder Bertrand Russell stated that anarchism "is associated with belief in the communal ownership of land and capital" because, like Marxism, it has the "perception that private capital is a source of tyranny by certain individuals over others." [**Roads to Freedom**, p. 40] Russell was, of course, simply pointing out the obvious. As Brian Morris correctly summarises:

> "Another criticism of anarchism is that it has a narrow view of politics: that it sees the state as the fount of all evil, ignoring other aspects of social and economic life. This is a misrepresentation of anarchism. It partly derives from the way anarchism has been defined, and partly because Marxist historians have tried to exclude anarchism from the broader socialist movement. But when one examines the writings of classical anarchists… as well as the character of anarchist movements… it is clearly evident that it has never had this limited vision. It has always challenged all forms of authority and exploitation, and has been equally critical of capitalism and religion as it has been of the state." ["Anthropology and Anarchism," pp. 35-41, **Anarchy: A Journal of Desire Armed**, no. 45, p, p. 40]

All in all, Marxist claims that anarchists view the state as the "chief evil" or see the destruction of the state as the "main idea" of anarchism are simply talking nonsense. In fact, rather than anarchists having a narrow view of social liberation, it is, in fact, Marxists who do so. By concentrating almost exclusively on the (economic) class source of exploitation, they blind themselves to other forms of exploitation and domination that can exist independently of (economic) class relationships. This can be seen from the amazing difficulty that many of them got themselves into when trying to analyse the Stalinist regime in Russia. Anarchists are well aware that the state is just one aspect of the current class system but unlike Marxists we recognise that "class rule must be placed in the much **larger** context of hierarchy and domination as a whole." [Murray Bookchin, **The Ecology of Freedom**, p. 28] This has been the anarchist position from the nineteenth century onwards and one which is hard not to recognise if you are at all familiar with the anarchist movement and its theory. As one historian notes, we have never been purely anti-state, but also anti-capitalist and opposed to all forms of oppression:

> "Anarchism rejected capitalism … not only because it viewed it as inimical to social equality, but also because

it saw it as a form of domination detrimental to individual freedom. Its basic tenet regarded hierarchical authority - be it the state, the church, the economic elite, or patriarchy - as unnecessary and deleterious to the maximisation of human potential." [Jose Moya, **Italians in Buenos Aires's Anarchist Movement**, p. 197]

So we oppose the state because it is just one aspect of a class ridden and hierarchical system. We just recognise that all the evils of that system must be destroyed at the same time to ensure a **social** revolution rather than just a change in who the boss is.

H.2.5 Do anarchists think "full blown" socialism will be created overnight?

Another area in which Marxists misrepresent anarchism is in the assertion that anarchists believe a completely socialist society (an ideal or "utopian" society, in other words) can be created "overnight." As Marxist Bertell Ollman puts it, "[u]nlike anarcho-communists, none of us [Marxists] believe that communism will emerge full blown from a socialist revolution. Some kind of transition and period of indeterminate length for it to occur are required." [**Market Socialism: The Debate among Socialists**, Bertell Ollman (ed.), p. 177] This assertion, while it is common, fails to understand the anarchist vision of revolution. We consider it a **process** and not an event: "By revolution we do not mean just the insurrectionary act." [Malatesta, **Errico Malatesta: His Life and Ideas**, p. 156]

Once this is understood, the idea that anarchists think a "full blown" anarchist society will be created "overnight" is a fallacy. As Murray Bookchin pointed out, "Bakunin, Kropotkin, Malatesta were not so naive as to believe that anarchism could be established overnight. In imputing this notion to Bakunin, Marx and Engels wilfully distorted the Russian anarchist's views." [**Post-Scarcity Anarchism**, p. 137] Indeed, Kropotkin stressed that anarchists "do not believe that in any country the Revolution will be accomplished at a stroke, in the twinkling of a eye, as some socialists dream." Moreover, "[n]o fallacy more harmful has ever been spread than the fallacy of a 'One-day Revolution.'" [**The Conquest of Bread**, p. 81] Bakunin argued that a "more or less prolonged transitional period" would "naturally follow in the wake of the great social crisis" implied by social revolution. [**The Political Philosophy of Bakunin**, p. 412] The question, therefore, is not whether there will be a "transitional" society after a revolution but what **kind** of transition it will be.

So anarchists are aware that a "full blown" communist society will not come about immediately. Rather, the creation of such a society will be a **process** which the revolution will start off. As Alexander Berkman put it in his classic introduction to communist-anarchist ideas "you must not confuse the social revolution with anarchy. Revolution, in some of its stages, is a violent upheaval; anarchy is a social condition of freedom and peace. The revolution is the **means** of bringing anarchy about but it is not anarchy itself. It is to pave the road for anarchy, to establish conditions which will make a life of liberty possible." However, the "end shapes the means" and so "to achieve its purpose the revolution must be imbued with and directed by the anarchist spirit and ideas ... the social revolution must be anarchist in method as in aim." [**What is Anarchism?**, p. 231]

Berkman also acknowledged that "full blown" communism was not likely after a successful revolution. "Of course," he argued, "when the social revolution has become thoroughly organised and production is functioning normally there will be enough for everybody. But in the first stages of the revolution, during the process of re-construction, we must take care to supply the people as best we can, and equally, which means rationing." Clearly, in such circumstances "full blown" communism would be impossible and, unsurprisingly, Berkman argued that would not exist. However, the principles that inspire communism and anarchism could be applied immediately. This meant that both the state and capitalism would be abolished. While arguing that "[t]here is no other way of securing economic equality, which alone is liberty" than communist anarchism, he also stated that it is "likely ... that a country in social revolution may try various economic experiments ... different countries and regions will probably try out various methods, and by practical experience learn the best way. The revolution is at the same time the opportunity and justification for it." Rather than "dictate to the future, to prescribe its mode of conduct", Berkman argued that his "purpose is to suggest, in broad outline the principles which must animate the revolution, the general lines of action it should follow if it is to accomplish its aim - the reconstruction of society on a foundation of freedom and equality." [**Op. Cit.**, p. 215 and p. 230]

Malatesta argued along similar lines. While urging the "complete destruction of the domination and exploitation of man by man" by the "expropriation of landlords and capitalists for the benefit of all" and "the abolition of government," he recognised that in "the post-revolutionary period, in the period of reorganisation and transition, there might be 'offices for the concentration and distribution of the capital of collective enterprises', that there might or might not be titles recording the work done and the quantity of goods to which one is entitled." However, he stressed that this "is something we shall have to wait and see about, or rather, it is a problem which will have many and varied solutions according to the system of production and distribution which will prevail in the different localities and among the many ... groupings that will exist." He argued that while, eventually, all groups of workers (particularly the peasants) will "understand the advantages of communism or at least of the direct exchange of goods for goods," this may not happen "in a day." If some kind of money was used, then people should "ensure that [it] truly represents the useful work performed by its possessors" rather than being that "powerful means of exploitation and oppression" is currently is. [**Errico Malatesta: His Life and Ideas**, pp. 198-9 and pp. 100-1] Emma Goldman, also, saw "a society based on voluntary co-operation of productive groups, communities and societies loosely federated together, eventually developing into a free communism, actuated by a solidarity of interests." [**Red Emma Speaks**, p. 50]

So rather than seeing a "full blown" communist society appearing instantly from a revolution, anarcho-communists see a period of transition in which the degree of communism in a given community or area is dependent on the objective conditions facing it. This period of transition would see different forms of social experimentation but the desire is to see libertarian communist principles as the basis of as much of this experimentation as possible. To claim that anarcho-communists ignore reality and see communism as being created overnight is simply a distortion of their ideas. Rather, they are aware that the development towards communism is dependent on local conditions, conditions which can only be overcome in time and by the liberated community re-organising production and extending it as required. Thus we find Malatesta arguing in 1884 that communism could be brought about immediately only in a very limited number of areas and, "for the rest," collectivism would have to be accepted "for a transitional period." This was because, "[f]or communism to be possible, a high stage of moral development is required of the members of society, a sense of solidarity both elevated and profound, which the upsurge of the revolution may not suffice to induce. This doubt is the more justified in that material conditions favourable to this development will not exist at the beginning." [quoted by Daniel Guérin, **Anarchism**, p. 51]

Clearly, our argument contradicts the widely held view that anarchists believed a utopian world would be created instantly after a revolution. Of course, by asserting that anarchists think "full blown communism" will occur without some form of transitional period, Marxists paint a picture of anarchism as simply utopian, a theory which ignores objective reality in favour of wishful thinking. However, as seen above, such is not the case. Anarchists are aware that "full blown communism" is dependent on objective conditions and, therefore, cannot be implemented until those conditions are met. Until such time as the objective conditions are reached, various means of distributing goods, organising and managing production, and so on will be tried. Such schemes will be based as far as possible on communistic principles.

Such a period of transition would be based on libertarian and communist principles. The organisation of society would be anarchist - the state would be abolished and replaced by a free federation of workers and community associations. The economic structure would be socialist - production would be based on self-managed workplaces and the principles of distribution would be as communistic as possible under the given objective conditions.

It also seems strange for Marxists to claim that anarchists thought a "full blown" communist society was possible "overnight" given that anarchists had always noted the difficulties facing a social revolution. Kropotkin, for example, continually stressed that a revolution would face extensive economic disruption. In his words:

"A political revolution can be accomplished without shaking the foundations of industry, but a revolution where the people lay hands upon property will inevitably paralyse exchange and production ... This point cannot be too much insisted upon; the reorganisation of industry on a new basis ... cannot be accomplished in a few days; nor, on the other hand, will people submit to be half starved for years in order to oblige the theorists who uphold the wage system. To tide over the period of stress they will demand what they have always demanded in such cases - communisation of supplies - the giving of rations." [**The Conquest of Bread**, pp. 72-3]

The basic principles of this "transition" period would, therefore, be based on the *"socialising of production, consumption and exchange."* The state would be abolished and *"federated Communes"* would be created. The end of capitalism would be achieved by the *"expropriation"* of *"everything that enables any man - be he financier, mill-owner, or landlord — to appropriate the product of others' toil."* Distribution of goods would be based on *"no stint or limit to what the community possesses in abundance, but equal sharing and dividing of those commodities which are scarce or apt to run short."* [**Op. Cit.**, p. 136, p. 61 and p. 76] Clearly, while not *"full blown"* communism by any means, such a regime does lay the ground for its eventual arrival. As Max Nettlau summarised: *"Nothing but a superficial interpretation of some of Kropotkin's observations could lead one to conclude that anarchist communism could spring into life through an act of sweeping improvisation, with the waving of a magic wand."* [**A Short History of Anarchism**, p. 80]

This was what happened in the Spanish Revolution, for example. Different collectives operated in different ways. Some tried to introduce free communism, some a combination of rationing and communism, others introduced equal pay, others equalised pay as much as possible and so on. Over time, as economic conditions changed and difficulties developed the collectives changed their mode of distribution to take them into account. These collectives indicate well the practical aspects of anarchism and its desire to accommodate and not ignore reality.

Lastly, and as an aside, it is this anarchist awareness of the disruptive effects of a revolution on a country's economy which, in part, makes anarchists extremely sceptical of pro-Bolshevik rationales that blame the difficult economic conditions facing the Russian Revolution for Bolshevik authoritarianism (see section H.6.1 for a fuller discussion of this). If, as Kropotkin argued, a social revolution inevitably results in massive economic disruption then, clearly, Bolshevism should be avoided if it cannot handle such inevitable events. In such circumstances, centralisation would only aid the disruption, not reduce it. This awareness of the problems facing a social revolution also led anarchists to stress the importance of local action and mass participation. As Kropotkin put it, the *"immense constructive work demanded by a social revolution cannot be accomplished by a central government ... It has need of knowledge, of brains and of the voluntary collaboration of a host of local and specialised forces which alone can attack the diversity of economic problems in their local aspects."* [**Anarchism**, pp. 255-6] Without this local action, co-ordinated joint activity would remain a dead letter.

In summary, anarchists acknowledge that **politically** there is no transitional period (i.e. the state must be abolished and replaced by a free federation of self-managed working class organisations). Economically anarchists recognise that different areas will develop in different ways and so there will be various economical transitional forms. Rather than seeing *"full blown communism"* being the instant result of a socialist revolution, anarchist-communists actually argue the opposite - *"full blown communism"* will develop only after a successful revolution and the inevitable period of social reconstruction which comes after it. A *"full blown"* communist economy will develop as society becomes ready for it. What we **do** argue is that any transitional economic form must be based on the principles of the type of society it desires. In other words, any transitional period must be as communistic as possible if communism is your final aim and, equally, it must be libertarian if your final goal is freedom.

Also see section I.2.2 for further discussion on this issue.

H.2.6 How do Marxists misrepresent Anarchist idea on mutual aid?

Anarchist ideas on mutual aid are often misrepresented by Marxists. Looking at Pat Stack's *"Anarchy in the UK?"* article, for example, we find a particularly terrible misrepresentation of Kropotkin's ideas. Indeed, it is so incorrect that it is either a product of ignorance or a desire to deceive (and as we shall indicate, it is probably the latter). Here is Stack's account of Kropotkin's ideas:

> *"And the anarchist Peter Kropotkin, far from seeing class conflict as the dynamic for social change as Marx did, saw co-operation being at the root of the social process. He believed the co-operation of what he termed 'mutual aid' was the natural order, which was disrupted by centralised states. Indeed in everything from public walkways and libraries through to the Red Cross, Kropotkin felt he was witnessing confirmation that society was moving towards his mutual aid, prevented only from completing the journey by the state. It follows that if class conflict is not the motor of change, the working class is not the agent and collective struggle not the means."* [*"Anarchy in the UK?"*, **Socialist Review**, no. 246]

There are three issues with Stack's summary. Firstly, Kropotkin did not, in fact, reject class conflict as the *"dynamic of social change"* nor reject the working class as its *"agent."* Secondly, all of Stack's examples of *"Mutual Aid"* do not, in fact, appear in Kropotkin's classic book **Mutual Aid**. They do appear in other works by Kropotkin but **not** as examples of *"mutual aid."* Thirdly, in **Mutual Aid** Kropotkin discusses such aspects of working class *"collective struggle"* as strikes and unions. All in all, it is Stack's total and utter lack of understanding of Kropotkin's ideas which immediately stands out from his comments.

As we have discussed how collective, working class direct action, organisation and solidarity in the class struggle were at the core of Kropotkin's politics in section H.2.2, we will not do so here. Rather, we will discuss how Stack lies about Kropotkin's ideas on mutual aid. As just noted, the examples Stack lists are not to be found in Kropotkin's classic work **Mutual Aid**. Now, **if** Kropotkin **had** considered them as examples of *"mutual aid"* then he would have listed them in that work. This does not mean, however, that Kropotkin did not mention these examples. He does, but in other works (notably his essay **Anarchist-Communism: Its Basis and Principles**) and he does **not** use them as examples of mutual aid. [**Anarchism**, pp. 59-60]

The examples Stack selects have nothing to do with mutual aid in Kropotkin's eyes. Rather, they are examples of communistic tendencies within capitalism, empirical evidence that can be used to not only show that communism can work but also that it is not a utopian social solution but an expression of tendencies within society. Simply put, he is using examples from existing society to show that communism is not impossible.

Similarly with Stack's other examples, which are **not** used as expressions of *"mutual aid"* but rather as evidence that social life can be organised without government. [**Op. Cit.**, pp. 65-7] Just as with communism, he gave concrete examples of libertarian tendencies within society to prove the possibility of an anarchist society. And just like his examples of communistic activities within capitalism, his examples of co-operation without the state are not listed as examples of *"mutual aid."*

All this would suggest that Stack has either not read Kropotkin's works or that he has and consciously decided to misrepresent his ideas. In fact, its a combination of the two. Stack (as proven by his talk at **Marxism 2001**) gathered his examples of *"mutual aid"* from Paul Avrich's essay *"Kropotkin's Ethical Anarchism"* contained in his **Anarchist Portraits**. As such, he has not read the source material. Moreover, he simply distorted what Avrich wrote. In other words, not only has he not read Kropotkin's works, he consciously decided to misrepresent the secondary source he used. This indicates the quality of almost all Marxist critiques of anarchism.

For example, Avrich correctly noted that Kropotkin did not *"deny that the 'struggle for existence' played an important role in the evolution of species. In **Mutual Aid** he declares unequivocally that 'life is struggle; and in that struggle the fittest survive.'"* Kropotkin simply argued that co-operation played a key role in determining who was, in fact, the fittest. Similarly, Avrich listed many of the same examples Stack presents but not in his discussion of Kropotkin's ideas on mutual aid. Rather, he correctly did so in his discussion of how Kropotkin saw examples of anarchist communism *"manifesting itself 'in the thousands of developments of modern life.'"* This did not mean that Kropotkin did not see the need for a social revolution, quite the reverse. As Avrich noted, Kropotkin *"did not shrink from the necessity of revolution"* as he *"did not expect the propertied classes to give up their privileges and possessions without a fight."* This *"was to be a **social** revolution, carried out by the masses themselves"* achieved by means of *"expropriation"* of social wealth. [**Anarchist Portraits**, p. 58, p. 62 and p. 66]

So much for Stack's claims. As can be seen, they are not only a total misrepresentation of Kropotkin's work, they are also a distortion of his source!

A few more points need to be raised on this subject.

Firstly, Kropotkin never claimed that mutual aid *"was the natural order."* Rather, he stressed that Mutual Aid was (to use the subtitle of his book on the subject) *"a factor of evolution."* As he put it, mutual aid *"represents one of the factors of evolution"*, another being *"the self-assertion of the individual, not only to attain personal or caste superiority, economical, political, and spiritual, but also in its much more important although less evident function of breaking through the bonds, always prone to become crystallised, which the tribe, the village community, the city, and the State impose upon the individual."* Thus Kropotkin recognised that there is class struggle within society as well as *"the self-assertion of the individual taken as a progressive element"* (i.e., struggle against forms of social

association which now hinder individual freedom and development). Kropotkin did not deny the role of struggle, in fact the opposite as he stressed that the book's examples concentrated on mutual aid simply because mutual struggle (between individuals of the same species) had *"already been analysed, described, and glorified from time immemorial"* and, as such, he felt no need to illustrate it. He did note that it *"was necessary to show, first of all, the immense part which this factor plays in the evolution of both the animal world and human societies. Only after this has been fully recognised will it be possible to proceed to a comparison between the two factors."* [**Mutual Aid**, p. 231 and pp. 231-2] So at no stage did Kropotkin deny either factor (unlike the bourgeois apologists he was refuting).

Secondly, Stack's argument that Kropotkin argued that co-operation was the natural order is in contradiction with his other claims that anarchism *"despises the collectivity"* and *"dismiss[es] the importance of the collective nature of change"* (see section H.2.2). How can you have co-operation without forming a collective? And, equally, surely support for co-operation clearly implies the recognition of the *"collective nature of change"*? Moreover, had Stack bothered to **read** Kropotkin's classic he would have been aware that both unions and strikes are listed as expressions of *"mutual aid"* (a fact, of course, which would undermine Stack's silly assertion that anarchists reject collective working class struggle and organisation). Thus we find Kropotkin stating that *"Unionism"* expressed the *"worker's need of mutual support"* as well as discussing how the state *"legislated against the workers' unions"* and that these were *"the conditions under which the mutual-aid tendency had to make its way." "To practise mutual support under such circumstances was anything but an easy task."* This repression failed, as *"the workers' unions were continually reconstituted"* and spread, forming *"vigourous federal organisations ... to support the branches during strikes and prosecutions."* In spite of the difficulties in organising unions and fighting strikes, he noted that *"every year there are thousands of strikes ... the most severe and protracted contests being, as a rule, the so-called 'sympathy strikes,' which are entered upon to support locked-out comrades or to maintain the rights of the unions."* Anyone (like Kropotkin) who had *"lived among strikers speak with admiration of the mutual aid and support which are constantly practised by them."* [**Op. Cit.**, pp. 210-3]

Kropotkin, as noted, recognised the importance of struggle or competition as a means of survival but also argued that co-operation within a species was the best means for it to survive in a hostile environment. This applied to life under capitalism. In the hostile environment of class society, then the only way in which working class people could survive would be to practice mutual aid (in other words, solidarity). Little wonder, then, that Kropotkin listed strikes and unions as expressions of mutual aid in capitalist society. Moreover, if we take Stack's arguments at face value, then he clearly is arguing that solidarity is not an important factor in the class struggle and that mutual aid and co-operation cannot change the world! Hardly what you would expect a socialist to argue. In other words, his inaccurate diatribe against Kropotkin backfires on his own ideas.

Thirdly, **Mutual Aid** is primarily a work of popular science and not a work on revolutionary anarchist theory like, say, **The Conquest** of Bread or Words of a Rebel. As such, it does not present a full example of Kropotkin's revolutionary ideas and how mutual aid fits into them. However, it does present some insights on the question of social progress which indicate that he did not think that *"co-operation"* was *"at the root of the social process,"* as Stack claims. For example, Kropotkin noted that *"[w]hen Mutual Aid institutions … began … to lose their primitive character, to be invaded by parasitic growths, and thus to become hindrances to process, the revolt of individuals against these institutions took always two different aspects. Part of those who rose up strove to purify the old institutions, or to work out a higher form of commonwealth."* But at the same time, others *"endeavoured to break down the protective institutions of mutual support, with no other intention but to increase their own wealth and their own powers."* In this conflict *"lies the real tragedy of history."* He also noted that the mutual aid tendency *"continued to live in the villages and among the poorer classes in the towns."* Indeed, *"in so far as"* as new *"economical and social institutions"* were *"a creation of the masses"* they *"have all originated from the same source"* of mutual aid. [**Op. Cit.**, pp. 18-9 and p. 180] Clearly, Kropotkin saw history marked by both co-operation and conflict as you would expect in a society divided by class and hierarchy.

Significantly, Kropotkin considered **Mutual Aid** as an attempt to write history from below, from the perspective of the oppressed. As he put it, history, *"such as it has hitherto been written, is almost entirely a description of the ways and means by which theocracy, military power, autocracy, and, later on, the richer classes' rule have been promoted, established, and maintained."* The *"mutual aid factor has been hitherto totally lost sight of; it was simply denied, or even scoffed at."* [**Op. Cit.**, p. 231] He was well aware that mutual aid (or solidarity) could not be applied between classes in a class society. Indeed, as noted, his chapters on mutual aid under capitalism contain the strike and union. As he put it in an earlier work:

> *"What solidarity can exist between the capitalist and the worker he exploits? Between the head of an army and the soldier? Between the governing and the governed?"* [**Words of a Rebel**, p. 30]

In summary, Stack's assertions about Kropotkin's theory of *"Mutual Aid"* are simply false. He distorts the source material and shows a total ignorance of Kropotkin's work (which he obviously has not bothered to read before criticising it). A truthful account of *"Mutual Aid"* would involve recognising that Kropotkin showed it being expressed in both strikes and labour unions and that he saw solidarity between working people as the means of not only surviving within the hostile environment of capitalism but also as the basis of a mass revolution which would end it.

H.2.7 Who do anarchists see as their "agents of social change"?

It is often charged, usually without any evidence, that anarchists do not see the working class as the *"agent"* of the social revolution. Pat Stack, for example, states *"the failure of anarchism [is] to understand the centrality of the working class itself."* He argues that for Marx, *"the working class would change the world and in the process change itself. It would become the agent for social advance and human liberty."* For Bakunin, however, *"skilled artisans and organised factory workers, far from being the source of the destruction of capitalism, were 'tainted by pretensions and aspirations'. Instead Bakunin looked to those cast aside by capitalism, those most damaged, brutalised and marginalised. The lumpen proletariat, the outlaws, the 'uncivilised, disinherited, illiterate', as he put it, would be his agents for change."* [*"Anarchy in the UK?"*, **Socialist Review**, no. 246] He fails to provide any references for his accusations. This is unsurprising, as to do so would mean that the reader could check for themselves the validity of Stack's claims.

Take, for example, the quote *"uncivilised, disinherited, illiterate"* Stack uses as evidence. This expression is from an essay written by Bakunin in 1872 and which expressed what he considered the differences between his ideas and those of Marx. The quote can be found on page 294 of **Bakunin on Anarchism**. On the previous page, we discover Bakunin arguing that *"for the International to be a real power, it must be able to organise within its ranks the immense majority of the proletariat of Europe, of America, of all lands."* [p. 293] Clearly Stack is quoting out of context, distorting Bakunin's position to present a radically false image of anarchism. Moreover, as we will indicate, Stack's also quotes them outside the historical context as well.

Let us begin with Bakunin's views on *"skilled artisans and organised factory workers."* In **Statism and Anarchy**, for example, we discover Bakunin arguing that the *"proletariat … must enter the International [Workers' Association] en masse, form factory, artisan, and agrarian sections, and unite them into local federations"* for *"the sake of its own liberation."* [p. 51] This perspective is the predominant one in Bakunin's ideas with the Russian continually arguing that anarchists saw *"the new social order"* being *"attained … through the social (and therefore anti-political) organisation and power of the working masses of the cities and villages."* He argued that *"only the trade union sections can give their members … practical education and consequently only they can draw into the organisation of the International the masses of the proletariat, those masses without whose practical co-operation … the Social Revolution will never be able to triumph."* The International, in Bakunin's words, *"organises the working masses … from the bottom up"* and that this was *"the proper aim of the organisation of trade union sections."* He stressed that revolutionaries must *"[o]rganise the city proletariat in the name of revolutionary Socialism … [and] unite it into one preparatory organisation together with the peasantry."* [**The Political Philosophy of Bakunin**, p. 300, p. 310, p. 319 and p. 378]

This support for organised workers and artisans can also be seen from the rest of the essay Stack distorts, in which Bakunin discusses the *"flower of the proletariat"* as well as the policy that the **International Workingmen's Association** should follow (i.e. the organised revolutionary workers). He argued that its *"sections and federations [must be] free to develop its own policies ... [to] attain real unity, basically economic, which will necessarily lead to real political unity ... The foundation for the unity of the International ... has already been laid by the common sufferings, interests, needs, and real aspirations of the workers of the whole world."* He stressed that *"the International has been ... the work of the proletariat itself ... It was their keen and profound instinct as workers ... which impelled them to find the principle and true purpose of the International. They took the common needs already in existence as the foundation and saw the **international organisation of economic conflict against capitalism** as the true objective of this association. In giving it exclusively this base and aim, the workers at once established the entire power of the International. They opened wide the gates to all the millions of the oppressed and exploited."* The International, as well as *"organising local, national and international strikes"* and *"establishing national and international trade unions,"* would discuss *"political and philosophical questions."* The workers *"join the International for one very practical purpose: solidarity in the struggle for full economic rights against the oppressive exploitation by the bourgeoisie."* [**Bakunin on Anarchism**, pp. 297-8, pp. 298-9 and pp. 301-2]

All this, needless to say, makes a total mockery of Stack's claim that Bakunin did not see *"skilled artisans and organised factory workers"* as *"the source of the destruction of capitalism"* and *"agents for change."* Indeed, it is hard to find a greater distortion of Bakunin's ideas. Rather than dismiss *"skilled artisans"* and *"organised factory workers"* Bakunin desired to organise them along with agricultural workers into unions and get these unions to affiliate to the **International Workers' Association**. He argued again and again that the working class, organised in unions, were the means of making a revolution (i.e. *"the source of the destruction of capitalism,"* to use Stack's words).

Only in **this** context can we understand Bakunin's comments which Stack (selectively) quotes. Any apparent contradiction generated by Stack's quoting out of context is quickly solved by looking at Bakunin's work. This reference to the *"uncivilised, disinherited, illiterate"* comes from a polemic against Marx. From the context, it can quickly be seen that by these terms Bakunin meant the bulk of the working class. In his words:

> *"To me the flower of the proletariat is not, as it is to the Marxists, the upper layer, the aristocracy of labour, those who are the most cultured, who earn more and live more comfortably than all the other workers. Precisely this semi-bourgeois layer of workers would, if the Marxists had their way, constitute their **fourth governing class.** This could indeed happen if the great mass of the proletariat does not guard against it. By virtue of its relative well-being and semi-bourgeois position, this upper layer of workers is unfortunately only too deeply saturated with all the political and social prejudices and all the narrow*

aspirations and pretensions of the bourgeoisie. Of all the proletariat, this upper layer is the least socialist, the most individualist.

> *"By the **flower of the proletariat**, I mean above all that great mass, those millions of the uncultivated, the disinherited, the miserable, the illiterates ... I mean precisely that eternal 'meat' (on which governments thrive), that great **rabble of the people** (underdogs, 'dregs of society') ordinarily designated by Marx and Engels by the phrase ... Lumpenproletariat"* [**Bakunin on Anarchism**, p. 294]

Thus Bakunin contrasted a *"semi-bourgeois"* layer to the *"great mass of the proletariat."* In a later work, Bakunin makes the same point, namely that there was *"a special category of relatively affluent workers, earning higher wages, boasting of their literary capacities and ... impregnated by a variety of bourgeois prejudices ... in Italy ... they are insignificant in number and influence ... In Italy it is the extremely poor proletariat that predominates. Marx speaks disdainfully, but quite unjustly, of this **Lumpenproletariat.** For in them, and only in them, and not in the bourgeois strata of workers, are there crystallised the entire intelligence and power of the coming Social Revolution."* [**Op. Cit.**, p. 334] Again it is clear that Bakunin is referring to a small minority within the working class and **not** dismissing the working class as a whole. He explicitly pointed to the *"**bourgeois-influenced** minority of the urban proletariat"* and contrasted this minority to *"the mass of the proletariat, both rural and urban."* [**Michael Bakunin: Selected Writings**, p. 254]

Clearly, Stack is distorting Bakunin's ideas on this subject when he claims that Bakunin thought **all** workers were *"tainted by pretensions and aspirations."* In fact, like Marx, Engels and Lenin, Bakunin differentiated between different types of workers. This did not mean he rejected organised workers or skilled artisans nor the organisation of working people into revolutionary unions, quite the reverse. As can be seen, Bakunin argued there was a group of workers who accepted bourgeois society and did relatively well under it. It was **these** workers who were *"frequently no less egoistic than bourgeois exploiters, no less pernicious to the International than bourgeois socialists, and no less vain and ridiculous than bourgeois nobles."* [**The Basic Bakunin**, p. 108] It is comments like this that Marxists quote out of context and use for their claims that Bakunin did not see the working class as the agent of social change. However, rather than refer to the whole working class, Stack quotes Bakunin's thoughts in relation to a minority strata within it. Clearly, from the context, Bakunin **did not** mean **all** working class people. Also, let us not forget the historical context. After all, when Bakunin was writing the vast majority of the working population across the world was, in fact, illiterate and disinherited. To get some sort of idea of the numbers of working people who would have been classed as *"the uncultivated, the disinherited, the miserable, the illiterates"* we have to provide some numbers. In Spain, for example, *"in 1870, something like 60 per cent of the population was illiterate."* [Gerald Brenan, **The Spanish Labyrinth**, p. 50] In Russia, in 1897 (i.e. 21 years after Bakunin's death), *"only 21% of the total population of European Russia was literate. This was mainly because of the* *appallingly low rate of literacy in the countryside - 17% compared to 45% in the towns."* [S.A. Smith, **Red Petrograd**, p. 34] Stack, in effect, is excluding the majority of the working masses from the working class movement **and** the revolution in the 1860-70s by his comments. Little wonder Bakunin said what he said. By ignoring the historical context (as he ignores the context of Bakunin's comments), Stack misleads the reader and presents a distinctly distorted picture of Bakunin's thought.

In other words, Bakunin's comments on the *"flower of the proletariat"* apply to the majority of the working class during his lifetime and for a number of decades afterwards and **not** to an underclass, not to what Marx termed the "lumpenproletariat". As proven above, Bakunin's *"lumpenproletariat"* is not what Marxists mean by the term. If Bakunin had meant the same as Marx by the "lumpenproletariat" then this would not make sense as the "lumpenproletariat" for Marx were not wage workers. This can best be seen when Bakunin argues that the International must organise this *"flower of the proletariat"* and conduct economic collective struggle against the capitalist class. In his other works (and in the specific essay these quotes are derived from) Bakunin stressed the need to organise all workers and peasants into unions to fight the state and bosses and his arguments that workers associations should not only be the means to fight capitalism but also the framework of an anarchist society. Clearly, Sam Dolgoff's summary of Bakunin's ideas on this subject is the correct one:

> *"Bakunin's **Lumpenproletariat** ... was broader than Marx's, since it included all the submerged classes: unskilled, unemployed, and poor workers, poor peasant proprietors, landless agricultural labourers, oppressed racial minorities, alienated and idealistic youth, declasse intellectuals, and 'bandits' (by whom Bakunin meant insurrectionary 'Robin Hoods' like Pugachev, Stenka Razin, and the Italian Carbonari)."* ["Introduction", **Bakunin on Anarchism**, pp. 13-4]

Moreover, the issue is clouded by translation issues as well. As Mark Leier notes Bakunin *"rarely used the word 'lumpenproletariat.' While he does use the French word **canaille**, this is better translated as 'mob' or 'rabble' ... When Bakunin does talk about the **canaille** or rabble, he usually refers not to the lumpenproletariat as such but to the poorer sections of the working class ... While we might translate 'destitute proletariat' as 'lumpenproletariat,' Bakunin himself ... is referring to a portion of the proletariat and the peasantry, not the lumpenproletariat."* [**Bakunin: The Creative Passion**, p. 221]

Nor is Stack the only Marxist to make such arguments as regards Bakunin. Paul Thomas quotes Bakunin arguing that the working class *"remains socialist without knowing it"* because of *"the very force of its position"* and *"all the conditions of its material existence"* and then, incredulously, adds that *"[i]t is for this reason that Bakunin turned away from the proletariat and its scientific socialism"* towards the peasantry. [**Karl Marx and the Anarchists**, p. 291] A more distorted account of Bakunin's ideas would be hard to find (and there is a lot of competition for that particular honour). The quotes Thomas provides are from Bakunin's *"The Policy of the International"* in which he discussed his ideas on how the International Working-Men's Association should operate (namely *"the collective struggle*

of the workers against the bosses"). At the time (and for some time after) Bakunin called himself a revolutionary socialist and argued that by class struggle, the worker would soon *"recognise himself [or herself] to be a revolutionary socialist, and he [or she] will act like one."* [**The Basic Bakunin**, p. 103] As such, the argument that the social position workers are placed in makes them *"socialist without knowing"* does not, in fact, imply that Bakunin thought they would become Marxists (*"scientific socialism"*) and, therefore, he turned against them. Rather, it meant that, for Bakunin, anarchist ideas were a product of working class life and it was a case of turning instinctive feelings into conscious thought by collective struggle. As noted above, Bakunin did not *"turn away"* from these ideas nor the proletariat. Indeed, Bakunin held to the importance of organising the proletariat (along with artisans and peasants) to the end of his life. Quite simply, Thomas is distorting Bakunin's ideas.

Lastly, we have to point out a certain irony (and hypocrisy) in Marxist attacks on Bakunin on this subject. This is because Marx, Engels and Lenin held similar views on the corrupted *"upper strata"* of the working class as Bakunin did. Indeed, Marxists have a specific term to describe this semi-bourgeois strata of workers, namely the *"labour aristocracy."* Marx, for example, talked about the trade unions in Britain being *"an aristocratic minority"* and the *"great mass of workers ... has long been outside"* them (indeed, *"the most wretched mass has never belonged."*) [**Collected Works**, vol. 22, p. 614] Engels also talked about *"a small, privileged, 'protected' minority"* within the working class, which he also called *"the working-class aristocracy."* [**Op. Cit.**, vol. 27, p. 320 and p. 321] Lenin approvingly quotes Engels arguing that the *"English proletariat is actually becoming more and more bourgeois, so that this most bourgeois of all nations is apparently aiming at the possession of ... a bourgeois proletariat **alongside** the bourgeoisie."* [quoted by Lenin, **Collected Works**, vol. 22, p. 283] Like Lenin, Engels explained this by the dominant position of Britain within the world market. Indeed, Lenin argued that *"a section of the British proletariat becomes bourgeois."* For Lenin, imperialist *"superprofits"* make it *"**possible to bribe** the labour leaders and the upper stratum of the labour aristocracy."* This *"stratum of workers-turned-bourgeois, or the labour aristocracy, who are quite philistine in their mode of life, in the size of their earnings and in their entire outlook ... are the real **agents of the bourgeoisie in the working-class** movement, the labour lieutenants of the capitalist class."* [**Op. Cit.**, p. 284 and p. 194]

As can be seen, this is similar to Bakunin's ideas and, ironically enough, nearly identical to Stack's distortion of those ideas (particularly in the case of Marx). However, only someone with a desire to lie would suggest that any of them dismissed the working class as their *"agent of change"* based on this (selective) quoting. Unfortunately, that is what Stack does with Bakunin. Ultimately, Stack's comments seem hypocritical in the extreme attacking Bakunin while remaining quiet on the near identical comments of his heroes.

It should be noted that this analysis is confirmed by non-anarchists who have actually studied Bakunin. Wayne Thorpe, an academic who specialises in syndicalism, presents an identical summary of Bakunin's ideas on this matter. [**"The Workers Themselves"**, p. 280] Marxist selective quoting not withstanding, for Bakunin (as another academic noted) *"it seemed self-evident that the revolution, even in Eastern Europe, required the unity of peasantry and city workers because of the latter's more advanced consciousness."* The notion that Bakunin stressed the role of the lumpenproletariat is a *"popular stereotype"* but is one *"more distorted by its decisive omissions than in what it says."* *"Marx"*, he correctly summarised, *"accented the revolutionary role of the urban proletariat and tended to deprecate the peasantry, while Bakunin, although **accepting** the vanguard role of the proletariat in the revolution, felt that the peasantry, too, approached correctly, also had great potential for revolution."* [Alvin W. Gouldner, *"Marx's Last Battle: Bakunin and the First International"*, pp. 853-884, **Theory and Society**, Vol. 11, No. 6, p. 871, p. 869 and p. 869] This flowed from Bakunin's materialist politics:

> *"Not restricting the revolution to those societies in which an advanced industrialism had produced a massive urban proletariat, Bakunin observed sensibly that the class composition of the revolution was bound to differ in industrially advanced Western Europe and in Eastern Europe where the economy was still largely agricultural … This is a far cry, then, from the Marxist stereotype of Bakunin-the-anarchist who relied exclusively on the backward peasantry and ignored the proletariat."* [**Op. Cit.**, p. 870]

All in all, once a historic and textual context is placed on Bakunin's words, it is clear which social class was considered as the social revolution's *"agents of change"*: the working class (i.e. wage workers, artisans, peasants and so on). In this, other revolutionary anarchists follow him. Looking at Kropotkin we find a similar perspective to Bakunin's. In his first political work, Kropotkin explicitly raised the question of *"where our activity be directed"* and answered it *"categorically"* - *"unquestionably among the peasantry and urban workers."* In fact, he *"consider[ed] this answer the fundamental position in our practical program."* This was because *"the insurrection must proceed among the peasantry and urban workers themselves"* if it were to succeed. As such, revolutionaries *"must not stand outside the people but among them, must serve not as a champion of some alien opinions worked out in isolation, but only as a more distinct, more complete expression of the demands of the people themselves."* [**Selected Writings on Anarchism and Revolution**, pp. 85-6]

That was in 1873. Nearly 30 years later, Kropotkin expressed identical opinions stating that he *"did not need to overrate the qualities of the workers in order to espouse the cause of the social, predominantly workers' revolution."* The need was to *"forge solidarity"* between workers and it was *"precisely to awaken this solidarity - without which progress would be difficult - that we must work to insure that the syndicates and the trade unions not be pushed aside by the bourgeois."* The social position of the working class people ensured their key role in the revolution: *"Being exploited today at the bottom of the social ladder, it is to his advantage to demand equality. He has never ceased demanding it, he has fought for it and will fight for it again, whereas the bourgeois … thinks it is to his advantage to maintain inequality."* Unsurprisingly, Kropotkin stressed that *"I have always preached active participation in the*

*workers' movement, in the **revolutionary workers' movement"*** [**Op. Cit.**, p. 299, pp. 299-300, p. 300 and p. 304]

Much the same can be said for the likes of Goldman, Berkman, Malatesta and so on - as even a basic familiarity with their writings and activism would confirm.

To conclude, for anarchists, the social revolution will be made by the working class (*"Anarchists, like Socialists, usually believe in the doctrine of class war."* [Bertrand Russell, **Roads to Freedom**, p. 38]). However, as British anarchist Benjamin Franks summarises, *"[b]ecause anarchists hold to a broader view of the working class, which includes the lumpenproletariat, they have been accused of promoting this section above others. This standard marxist interpretation of anarchism is inaccurate; anarchists simply include the lumpenproletariat as part of the working class, rather than exclude or exalt it."* [**Rebel Alliances**, p. 168] Ultimately, for anyone to claim that Bakunin, or any social anarchist, rejects the working class as an agent of social change simply shows their ignorance of the politics they are trying to attack.

H.2.8 What is the relationship of anarchism to syndicalism?

One of the most common Marxist techniques when they discuss anarchism is to contrast the likes of Bakunin and Kropotkin to the revolutionary syndicalists. The argument runs along the lines that "classical" anarchism is individualistic and rejects working class organisation and power while syndicalism is a step forward from it (i.e. a step closer to Marxism). Sadly, such arguments simply show the ignorance of the author rather than any form of factual basis. When the ideas of revolutionary anarchists like Bakunin and Kropotkin are compared to revolutionary syndicalism, the similarities are soon discovered.

This kind of argument can be found in Pat Stack's essay *"Anarchy in the UK?"* After totally distorting the ideas of anarchists like Bakunin and Kropotkin, Stack argues that anarcho-syndicalists *"tended to look to the spontaneity and anti-statism of anarchism, the economic and materialist analysis of Marxism, and the organisational tools of trade unionism. Practically every serious anarchist organisation came from or leant on this tradition … The huge advantage they had over other anarchists was their understanding of the power of the working class, the centrality of the point of production (the workplace) and the need for collective action."* [**Socialist Review**, no. 246]

Given that Stack's claims that anarchists reject the *"need for collective action,"* do not understand *"the power of the working class"* and the *"centrality"* of the workplace are simply inventions, it would suggest that Stack's *"huge advantage"* does not, in fact, exist and is pure nonsense. Bakunin, Kropotkin and all revolutionary anarchists, as proven in section H.2.2, already understood all this and based their politics on the need for collective working class struggle at the point of production. As such, by contrasting anarcho-syndicalism with anarchism (as expressed by the likes of Bakunin and Kropotkin) Stack simply shows his utter and total ignorance of his subject matter.

Moreover, if he bothered to read the works of the likes of Bakunin and Kropotkin he would discover that many of their ideas were identical to those of revolutionary syndicalism. For example, Bakunin argued that the *"organisation of the trade sections, their federation in the International, and their representation by Chambers of Labour, ... [allow] the workers ... [to] combin[e] theory and practice ... [and] bear in themselves the living germs of **the social order**, which is to replace the bourgeois world. They are creating not only the ideas but also the facts of the future itself."* [quoted by Rudolf Rocker, **Anarcho-Syndicalism**, p. 50] Like the syndicalists, he argued *"the natural organisation of the masses ... is organisation based on the various ways that their various types of work define their day-to-day life; it is organisation by trade association"* and once *"every occupation ... is represented within the International [Working-Men's Association], its organisation, the organisation of the masses of the people will be complete."* Moreover, Bakunin stressed that the working class had *"but a single path, that of **emancipation through practical action**"* which meant *"workers' solidarity in their struggle against the bosses"* by *"**trades-unions, organisation, and the federation of resistance funds**"* [**The Basic Bakunin**, p. 139 and p. 103]

Like the syndicalists, Bakunin stressed working class self-activity and control over the class struggle:

> *"Toilers count no longer on anyone but yourselves. Do not demoralise and paralyse your growing strength by being duped into alliances with bourgeois Radicalism ... Abstain from all participation in bourgeois Radicalism and organise outside of it the forces of the proletariat. The bases of this organisation are already completely given: they are the workshops and the federation of workshops, the creation of fighting funds, instruments of struggle against the bourgeoisie, and their federation, not only national, but international.*

> *"And when the hour of revolution sounds, you will proclaim the liquidation of the State and of bourgeois society, anarchy, that is to say the true, frank people's revolution ... and the new organisation from below upwards and from the circumference to the centre."* [quoted by K.J. Kenafick, **Michael Bakunin and Karl Marx**, pp. 120-1]

Like the later syndicalists, Bakunin was in favour of a general strike as a means of bringing about a social revolution. As *"strikes spread from one place to another, they come close to turning into a general strike. And with the ideas of emancipation that now hold sway over the proletariat, a general strike can result only in a great cataclysm which forces society to shed its old skin."* He raised the possibility that this could *"arrive before the proletariat is sufficiently organised"* and dismissed it because the strikes expressed the self-organisation of the workers for the *"necessities of the struggle impel the workers to support one another"* and the *"more active the struggle becomes ... the stronger and more extensive this federation of proletarians must become."* Thus strikes *"indicate a certain collective strength already"* and *"each strike becomes the point of departure for the formation of new groups."* He rejected the idea that a revolution could be *"arbitrarily"* made by *"the most powerful associations."*

Rather they were produced by *"the force of circumstances."* As with the syndicalists, Bakunin argued that not all workers needed to be in unions before a general strike or revolution could take place. A minority (perhaps *"one worker in ten"*) needed to be organised and they would influence the rest so ensuring *"at critical moments"* the majority would *"follow the International's lead."* [**The Basic Bakunin**, pp. 149-50, p. 109 and p. 139]

As with the syndicalists, the new society would be organised *"by free federation, from below upwards, of workers' associations, industrial as well as agricultural ... in districts and municipalities at first; federation of these into regions, of the regions into nations, and the nations into a fraternal Internationalism."* Moreover, *"capital, factories, all the means of production and raw material"* would be owned by *"the workers' organisations"* while the land would be given *"to those who work it with their own hands."* [quoted by Kenafick, **Op. Cit.**, p. 241 and p. 240] Compare this to the syndicalist CGT's 1906 **Charter of Amiens** which declared *"the trade union today is an organisation of resistance"* but *"in the future [it will] be the organisation of production and distribution, the basis of social reorganisation."* [quoted by Wayne Thorpe, **"The Workers Themselves"**, p. 201]

The similarities with revolutionary syndicalism could not be clearer. Little wonder that all serious historians see the obvious similarities between anarcho-syndicalism and Bakunin's anarchism. For example, George R. Esenwein's (in his study of early Spanish anarchism) comments that syndicalism *"had deep roots in the Spanish libertarian tradition. It can be traced to Bakunin's revolutionary collectivism."* He also notes that the class struggle was *"central to Bakunin's theory."* [**Anarchist Ideology and the Working Class Movement in Spain, 1868-1898**, p. 209 and p. 20] Caroline Cahm, likewise, points to *"the basic syndicalist ideas of Bakunin"* and that he *"argued that trade union organisation and activity in the International [Working Men's Association] were important in the building of working-class power in the struggle against capital ... He also declared that trade union based organisation of the International would not only guide the revolution but also provide the basis for the organisation of the society of the future."* Indeed, he *"believed that trade unions had an essential part to play in the developing of revolutionary capacities of the workers as well as building up the organisation of the masses for revolution."* [**Kropotkin and the Rise of Revolutionary Anarchism**, p. 219, p. 215 and p. 216] Paul Avrich, in his essay *"The Legacy of Bakunin,"* agreed. *"Bakunin,"* he stated, *"perhaps even more than Proudhon, was a prophet of revolutionary syndicalism, who believed that a free federation of trade unions would be the 'living germs of a new social order which is to replace the bourgeois world.'"* [**Anarchist Portraits**, pp. 14-15] Bertrand Russell noted that *"[h]ardly any of these ideas [associated with syndicalism] are new: almost all are derived from the Bakunist [sic!] section of the old International"* and that this was *"often recognised by Syndicalists themselves."* [**Roads to Freedom**, p. 52] The syndicalists, notes Wayne Thorpe, *"identified the First International with its federalist wing ... [r]epresented ... initially by the Proudhonists and later and more influentially by the Bakuninists."* [**Op. Cit.**, p. 2]

Needless to say, anarchists agree with this perspective. Arthur Lehning, for example, summarises the anarchist perspective when he commented that *"Bakunin's collectivist anarchism ... ultimately formed the ideological and theoretical basis of anarcho-syndicalism."* ["Introduction", **Michael Bakunin: Selected Writings**, p. 29] Anarchist academic David Berry also notes that *"anarchist syndicalists were keen to establish a lineage with Bakunin ... the anarchist syndicalism of the turn of the century was a revival of a tactic"* associated with *"the Bakuninist International."* [**A History of the French Anarchist Movement, 1917-1945**, p. 17] Another, Mark Leier, points out that *"the Wobblies drew heavily on anarchist ideas pioneered by Bakunin."* [**Bakunin: The Creative Passion**, p. 298] Kropotkin argued that syndicalism *"is nothing other than the rebirth of the International - federalist, worker, Latin."* [quoted by Martin A. Miller, **Kropotkin**, p. 176] Malatesta stated in 1907 that he had *"never ceased to urge the comrades into that direction which the syndicalists, forgetting the past, call **new**, even though it was already glimpsed and followed, in the International, by the first of the anarchists."* [**The Anarchist Reader**, p. 221] Little wonder that Rudolf Rocker stated in his classic introduction to the subject that anarcho-syndicalism was *"a direct continuation of those social aspirations which took shape in the bosom of the First International and which were best understood and most strongly held by the libertarian wing of the great workers' alliance."* [**Anarcho-Syndicalism**, p. 54] Murray Bookchin just stated the obvious:

> *"Long before syndicalism became a popular term in the French labour movement of the late [eighteen]nineties, it already existed in the Spanish labour movement of the early seventies. The anarchist-influenced Spanish Federation of the old IWMA was ... distinctly syndicalist."* ["Looking Back at Spain," pp. 53-96, Dimitrios I. Roussopoulos (ed.), **The Radical Papers**, p. 67]

Perhaps, in the face of such evidence (and the writings of Bakunin himself), Marxists could claim that the sources we quote are either anarchists or "sympathetic" to anarchism. To counter this is very easy, we need only quote Marx and Engels. Marx attacked Bakunin for thinking that the *"working class ... must only organise themselves by trades-unions"* and *"not occupy itself with **politics.**"* Engels argued along the same lines, having a go at the anarchists because in the *"Bakuninist programme a general strike is the lever employed by which the social revolution is started"* and that they admitted *"this required a well-formed organisation of the working class"* (i.e. a trade union federation). Indeed, he summarised Bakunin's strategy as being to *"organise, and when **all** the workers, hence the majority, are won over, dispose all the authorities, abolish the state and replace it with the organisation of the International."* [Marx, Engels and Lenin, **Anarchism and Anarcho-Syndicalism**, p. 48, p. 132, p. 133 and p. 72] Ignoring the misrepresentations of Marx and Engels about the ideas of their enemies, we can state that they got the basic point of Bakunin's ideas - the centrality of trade union organisation and struggle as well as the use of strikes and the general strike. Therefore, you do not have to read Bakunin to find out the similarities between his ideas and syndicalism, you can read Marx and Engels. Clearly, most Marxist critiques of anarchism have not even done that!

Later anarchists, needless to say, supported the syndicalist movement and, moreover, drew attention to its anarchist roots.

Emma Goldman noted that in the First International *"Bakunin and the Latin workers"* forged ahead *"along industrial and Syndicalist lines"* and stated that syndicalism *"is, in essence, the economic expression of Anarchism"* and that *"accounts for the presence of so many Anarchists in the Syndicalist movement. Like Anarchism, Syndicalism prepares the workers along direct economic lines, as conscious factors in the great struggles of to-day, as well as conscious factors in the task of reconstructing society."* After seeing syndicalist ideas in action in France in 1900, she *"immediately began to propagate Syndicalist ideas."* The *"most powerful weapon"* for liberation was *"the conscious, intelligent, organised, economic protest of the masses through direct action and the general strike."* [**Red Emma Speaks**, p. 89, p. 91, p. 90 and p. 60]

Kropotkin argued anarchist communism *"wins more and more ground among those working-men who try to get a clear conception as to the forthcoming revolutionary action. The syndicalist and trade union movements, which permit the workingmen to realise their solidarity and to feel the community of their interests better than any election, prepare the way for these conceptions."* [**Anarchism**, p. 174] His support for anarchist participation in the labour movement was strong, considering it a key method of preparing for a revolution and spreading anarchist ideas amongst the working classes: *"The **syndicat** is absolutely necessary. It is the sole force of the workers which continues the direct struggle against capital without turning to parliamentarism."* [quoted by Miller, **Op. Cit.**, p. 177]

"Revolutionary Anarchist Communist propaganda within the Labour Unions," Kropotkin stressed, *"had always been a favourite mode of action in the Federalist or 'Bakuninist' section of the International Working Men's Association. In Spain and in Italy it had been especially successful. Now it was resorted to, with evident success, in France and **Freedom** [the British Anarchist paper he helped create in 1886] eagerly advocated this sort of propaganda."* [**Act For Yourselves**, pp. 119-20] Caroline Cahm notes in her excellent account of Kropotkin's ideas between 1872 and 1886, he *"was anxious to revive the International as an organisation for aggressive strike action to counteract the influence of parliamentary socialists on the labour movement."* This resulted in Kropotkin advocating a *"remarkable fusion of anarchist communist ideas with both the bakuninist [sic!] internationalist views adopted by the Spanish Federation and the syndicalist ideas developed in the Jura Federation in the 1870s."* This included seeing the importance of revolutionary labour unions, the value of strikes as a mode of direct action and syndicalist action developing solidarity. *"For Kropotkin,"* she summarises, *"revolutionary syndicalism represented a revival of the great movement of the Anti-authoritarian International ... It seems likely that he saw in it the [strikers International] which he had advocated earlier."* [**Op. Cit.**, p. 257 and p. 268]

Clearly, any one claiming that there is a fundamental difference between anarchism and syndicalism is talking nonsense. Syndicalist ideas were being argued by the likes of Bakunin and Kropotkin before syndicalism emerged in the French CGT in the 1890s as a clearly labelled revolutionary theory. Rather than being in conflict, the ideas of syndicalism find their roots in the ideas of Bakunin and "classical" anarchism. This would be quickly seen if the actual writings of Bakunin and Kropotkin were consulted. There **are,** of course, differences between anarchism and syndicalism, but they are **not** those usually listed by Marxists (section J.3.9 discusses these differences and, as will quickly be discovered, they are **not** based on a rejection of working class organisation, direct action, solidarity and collective struggle!).

Ultimately, claims like Pat Stack's simply show how unfamiliar the author is with the ideas they are pathetically attempting to critique. Anarchists from Bakunin onwards shared most of the same ideas as syndicalism (which is unsurprising as most of the ideas of anarcho-syndicalism have direct roots in the ideas of Bakunin). In other words, for Stack, the *"huge advantage"* anarcho-syndicalists have *"over other anarchists"* is that they, in fact, share the same *"understanding of the power of the working class, the centrality of the point of production (the workplace) and the need for collective action"*! This, in itself, shows the bankruptcy of Stack's claims and those like it.

H.2.9 Do anarchists have "liberal" politics?

Another assertion by Marxists is that anarchists have *"liberal"* politics or ideas. For example, one Marxist argues that the *"programme with which Bakunin armed his super-revolutionary vanguard called for the 'political, economic and social equalisation of classes and individuals of both sexes, beginning with the abolition of the right of inheritance.' This is **liberal** politics, implying nothing about the abolition of capitalism."* [Derek Howl, *"The Legacy of Hal Draper,"* pp. 137-49, **International Socialism**, no. 52, p. 148]

That Howl is totally distorting Bakunin's ideas can quickly be seen by looking at the whole of the programme. The passage quoted is from item 2 of the *"Programme of the Alliance."* Strangely Howl fails to quote the end of that item, namely when it states this *"equalisation"* was *"in pursuance of the decision reached by the last working men's Congress in Brussels, the land, the instruments of work and all other capital may become the collective property of the whole of society and be utilised only by the workers, in other words by the agricultural and industrial associations."* If this was not enough to indicate the abolition of capitalism, item 4 states that the Alliance *"repudiates all political action whose target is anything except the triumph of the workers' cause over Capital."* [**Michael Bakunin: Selected Writings**, p. 174]

Howl's dishonesty is clear. Bakunin **explicitly** argued for the abolition of capitalism in the same item Howl (selectively) quotes from. If the socialisation of land and capital under the control of workers' associations is not the abolition of capitalism, we wonder what is!

Equally as dishonest as this quoting out of context is Howl's non-mention of the history of the expression *"political, economic and social equalisation of classes and individuals of both sexes."* After Bakunin sent the Alliance programme to the General Council of the **International Workingmen's Association**, he received a letter dated March 9, 1869 from Marx which stated that the term *"the equalisation of classes"* *"literally interpreted"* would mean *"harmony of capital and labour"* as *"persistently preached by the bourgeois socialists."* Marx argued that it was *"not the logically*

impossible *'equalisation of classes',* but the historically necessary, superseding *'abolition of classes'"* which was the *"true secret of the proletarian movement"* and which *"forms the great aim of the International Working Men's Association."* Significantly, the letter adds the following: *"Considering, however, the context in which that phrase 'equalisation of classes' occurs, it seems to be a mere slip of the pen, and the General Council feels confident that you will be anxious to remove from your program an expression which offers such a dangerous misunderstanding."* [**Collected Works**, vol. 21, p. 46]

Given the context, Marx was right. The phrase *"equalisation of classes"* placed in the context of the political, economic and social equalisation of individuals obviously implies the abolition of classes. The logic is simple. If both worker and capitalist shared the same economic and social position then wage labour would not exist (in fact, it would be impossible as it is based on social and economic **inequality**) and so class society would not exist. Similarly, if the tenant and the landlord were socially equal then the landlord would have no power over the tenant, which would be impossible. Bakunin agreed with Marx on the ambiguity of the term and the Alliance changed its Programme to call for *"the final and total abolition of classes and the political, economic and social equalisation of individuals of either sex."* [Bakunin, **Op. Cit.** p. 174] This change ensured the admittance of the Alliance sections into the International Workingmen's Association (although this did not stop Marx, like his followers, bringing up this *"mere slip of the pen"* years later). However, Howl repeating the changed phrase *"equalisation of classes"* out of context helps discredit anarchism and so it is done.

Simply put, anarchists are **not** liberals. We are well aware of the fact that without equality, liberty is impossible except for the rich. As Nicolas Walter put it: *"Like liberals, anarchists want freedom; like socialists, anarchists want equality. But we are not satisfied by liberalism alone or by socialism alone. Freedom without equality means that the poor and weak are less free than the rich and strong, and equality without freedom means that we are all slaves together. Freedom and equality are not contradictory, but complementary; in place of the old polarisation of freedom versus equality - according to which we are told that more freedom equals less equality, and more equality equals less freedom - anarchists point out that in practice you cannot have one without the other. Freedom is not genuine if some people are too poor or too weak to enjoy it, and equality is not genuine is some people are ruled by others."* [**About Anarchism**, p. 29] Clearly, anarchists do **not** have liberal politics. Quite the reverse, as we subject these to extensive critique from a working class perspective.

To the claim that anarchism *"combines a socialist critique of capitalism with a liberal critique of socialism,"* anarchists reply that it is mistaken. [Paul Thomas, **Karl Marx and the Anarchists**, p. 7] Rather, anarchism is simply a socialist critique of both capitalism and the state. Freedom under capitalism is fatally undermined by inequality - it simply becomes the freedom to pick a master. This violates liberty and equality, as does the state. *"Any State at all,"* argued Bakunin, *"no matter what kind, is a domination and exploitation. It is a negation of Socialism, which wants an equitable human society delivered from all tutelage, from all authority and* political domination as well as economic exploitation." [quoted by Kenafick, **Op. Cit.**, pp. 95-6] As such, state structures violate not only liberty but also equality. There is no real equality in power between, say, the head of the government and one of the millions who may, or may not, have voted for them. As the Russian Revolution proved, there can be no meaningful equality between a striking worker and the "socialist" political police sent to impose the will of the state, i.e., the "socialist" ruling elite.

This means that if anarchists are concerned about freedom (both individual **and** collective) it is not because we are influenced by liberalism. Quite the reverse, as liberalism happily tolerates hierarchy and the restrictions of liberty implied by private property, wage labour and the state. As Bakunin argued, capitalism turns *"the worker into a subordinate, a passive and obedient servant."* [**The Political Philosophy of Bakunin**, p. 188] So anarchism rejects liberalism (although, as Bakunin put it, *"[i]f socialism disputes radicalism, this is hardly to reverse it but rather to advance it."* [**The Basic Bakunin**, p. 87]). Therefore, anarchism rejects liberalism, not because it supports the idea of freedom, but precisely because it does not go far enough and fails to understand that without equality, freedom is little more than freedom for the master. In fact, as we argue in section H.4, it is Marxism itself which has a distinctly liberal perspective of freedom, seeing it restricted by association rather than association being an expression of it.

Lastly, a few words on the mentality that could suggest that anarchist concern for liberty means that it is a form of liberalism. Rather than suggest the bankruptcy of anarchism it, in fact, suggests the bankruptcy of the politics of the person making the accusation. After all, the clear implication is that a concern with individual, collective and social freedom is alien to socialist ideas. It also strikes at the heart of socialism - its concern for equality - as it clearly implies that some have more power (namely the right to suppress the liberty of others) than the rest. As such, it suggests a superficial understanding of **real** socialism (see also our discussion of Marxist claims about anarchist "elitism" in section H.2.11).

To argue that a concern for freedom means *"liberalism"* (or, equally, *"individualism"*) indicates that the person is not a socialist. After all, a concern that every individual controls their daily lives (i.e. to be free) means a wholehearted support for collective self-management of group affairs. It means a vision of a revolution (and post-revolutionary society) based on direct working class participation and management of society from below upwards. To dismiss this vision by dismissing the principles which inspire it as *"liberalism"* means to support rule from above by the "enlightened" elite (i.e. the party) and the hierarchical state structures. It means arguing for **party** power, not **class** power, as liberty is seen as a **danger** to the revolution and so the people must be protected against the "petty-bourgeois"/"reactionary" narrowness of the people (to requote Bakunin, *"every state, even the pseudo-People's State concocted by Mr. Marx, is in essence only a machine ruling the masses from above, through a privileged minority of conceited intellectuals who imagine that they know what the people need and want better than do the people themselves."* [**Bakunin on Anarchism**, p. 338]). Rather than seeing free debate of ideas and mass participation as a source of strength, it sees it as a source of "bad influences" which the masses must be protected from.

Moreover, it suggests a total lack of understanding of the difficulties that a social revolution will face. Unless it is based on the active participation of the majority of a population, any revolution will fail. The construction of socialism, of a new society, will face thousands of unexpected problems and seek to meet the needs of millions of individuals, thousands of communities and hundreds of cultures. Without the individuals and groups within that society being in a position to freely contribute to that constructive task, it will simply wither under the bureaucratic and authoritarian rule of a few party leaders. As such, individual liberties are an essential aspect of **genuine** social reconstruction - without freedom of association, assembly, organisation, speech and so on, the active participation of the masses will be replaced by an isolated and atomised collective of individuals subjected to autocratic rule from above.

As ex-anarchist turned Bolshevik Victor Serge concluded in the late 1930s (when it was far too late) the *"fear of liberty, which is the fear of the masses, marks almost the entire course of the Russian Revolution. If it is possible to discover a major lesson, capable of revitalising Marxism ... one might formulate it in these terms: Socialism is essentially democratic — the word, 'democratic', being used here in its libertarian sense."* [**The Serge-Trotsky Papers**, p. 181]

Ultimately, as Rudolf Rocker suggested, the *"urge for social justice can only develop properly and be effective, when it grows out of man's sense of personal freedom and it based on that. In other words **Socialism will be free, or it will not be at all.** In its recognition of this lies the genuine and profound justification for the existence of Anarchism."* [**Anarcho-Syndicalism**, p. 14]

H.2.10 Are anarchists against leadership?

It is a common assertion by Marxists that anarchists reject the idea of *"leadership"* and so think in terms of a totally spontaneous revolution. This is also generally understood to imply that anarchists do not see the need for revolutionaries to organise together to influence the class struggle in the here and now. Hence the British SWP's Duncan Hallas:

> *"That an organisation of socialist militants is necessary is common ground on the left, a few anarchist purists apart. But what kind of organisation? One view, widespread amongst newly radicalised students and young workers, is that of the libertarians ... [They have] hostility to centralised, co-ordinated activity and profound suspicion of anything smacking of 'leadership.' On this view nothing more than a loose federation of working groups is necessary or desirable. The underlying assumptions are that centralised organisations inevitably undergo bureaucratic degeneration and that the spontaneous activities of working people are the sole and sufficient basis for the achievement of socialism ... some libertarians draw the conclusion that a revolutionary socialist party is a contradiction in terms. This, of course, is the traditional*

anarcho-syndicalist position." [**Towards a revolutionary socialist party**, p. 39]

Ignoring the usual patronising references to the age and experience of non-Leninists, this argument can be faulted on many levels. Firstly, while libertarians do reject centralised structures, it does **not** mean we reject co-ordinated activity. This may be a common Marxist argument, but it is a straw man one. Secondly, anarchists do **not** reject the idea of *"leadership."* We simply reject the idea of hierarchical leadership. Thirdly, while all anarchists do think that a *"revolutionary socialist party"* is a contradiction in terms, it does not mean that we reject the need for revolutionary organisations (i.e. organisations of anarchists). While opposing centralised and hierarchical political parties, anarchists have long saw the need for anarchist groups and federations to discuss and spread our ideas and influence. We will discuss each issue in turn.

The first argument is the least important. For Marxists, co-ordination equals centralism and to reject centralisation means to reject co-ordination of joint activity. For anarchists, co-ordination does not equal centralism or centralisation. This is why anarchism stresses federation and federalism as the means of co-ordinating joint activity. Under a centralised system, the affairs of all are given over to a handful of people at the centre. Their decisions are then binding on the mass of the members of the organisation whose position is simply that of executing the orders of those whom the majority elect. This means that power rests at the top and decisions flow from the top downwards. As such, the "revolutionary" party simply mimics the very society it claims to oppose (see section H.5.6) as well as being extremely ineffective (see section H.5.8)

In a federal structure, in contrast, decisions flow from the bottom up by means of councils of elected, mandated and recallable **delegates**. In fact, we discover anarchists like Bakunin and Proudhon arguing for elected, mandated and recallable delegates rather than for representatives in their ideas of how a free society worked years before the Paris Commune applied them in practice. The federal structure exists to ensure that any co-ordinated activity accurately reflects the decisions of the membership. As such, anarchists *"do not deny the need for co-ordination between groups, for discipline, for meticulous planning, and for unity in action. But they believe that co-ordination, discipline, planning, and unity in action must be achieved **voluntarily,** by means of a self-discipline nourished by conviction and understanding, not by coercion and a mindless, unquestioning obedience to orders from above."* This means we *"vigorously oppose the establishment of an organisational structure that becomes an end in itself, of committees that linger on after their practical tasks have been completed, of a 'leadership' that reduces the 'revolutionary' to a mindless robot."* [Murray Bookchin, **Post-Scarcity Anarchism**, p. 139] In other words, co-ordination comes *from below* rather than being imposed from above by a few leaders. To use an analogy, federalist co-ordination is the co-ordination created in a strike by workers resisting their bosses. It is created by debate amongst equals and flows from below upwards. Centralised co-ordination is the co-ordination imposed from the top-down by the boss.

Secondly, anarchists are not against all forms of *"leadership."* We are against hierarchical and institutionalised forms of leadership. In other words, of giving **power** to leaders. This is the key difference, as Albert Meltzer explained. *"In any grouping some people,"* he argued, *"do naturally 'give a lead.' But this should not mean they are a class apart. What they always reject is institutionalised leadership. That means their supporters become blind followers and the leadership not one of example or originality but of unthinking acceptance."* Any revolutionary in a factory where the majority have no revolutionary experience, will at times, "give a lead." However, *"no real Anarchist … would agree to be part of an **institutionalised leadership**. Neither would an Anarchist wait for a lead, but give one."* [**Anarchism: Arguments for and against**, p. 58 and p. 59]

This means, as we argue in section J.3.6, that anarchists seek to influence the class struggle as **equals.** Rather than aim for positions of power, anarchists want to influence people by the power of their ideas as expressed in the debates that occur in the organisations created in the social struggle itself. This is because anarchists recognise that there is an unevenness in the level of ideas within the working class. This fact is obvious. Some workers accept the logic of the current system, others are critical of certain aspects, others (usually a minority) are consciously seeking a better society (and are anarchists, ecologists, Marxists, etc.) and so on. Only constant discussion, the clash of ideas, combined with collective struggle can develop political awareness and narrow the unevenness of ideas within the oppressed: *"Only freedom or the struggle for freedom can be the school for freedom."* [Malatesta, **Errico Malatesta: His Life and Ideas**, p. 59]

From this perspective, it follows that any attempt to create an institutionalised leadership structure means the end of the revolutionary process. Such "leadership" automatically means a hierarchical structure, one in which the leaders have power and make the decisions for the rest. This just reproduces the old class division of labour between those who think and those who act (i.e. between order givers and order takers). Rather than the revolutionary masses taking power in such a system, it is the "leaders" (i.e. a specific party hierarchy) who do so and the masses role becomes, yet again, simply that of selecting which boss tells them what to do.

So the anarchist federation does not reject the need of "leadership" in the sense of giving a lead, of arguing its ideas and trying to win people to them. It does reject the idea that "leadership" should become separated from the mass of the people. Simply put, no party, no group of leaders have all the answers and so the active participation of all is required for a successful revolution. It is not a question of organisation versus non-organisation, or "leadership" versus non-"leadership" but rather what **kind** of organisation and the **kind** of leadership.

Clearly, then, anarchists do not reject or dismiss the importance of politically aware minorities organising and spreading their ideas within social struggles. As Caroline Cahm summarised in her excellent study of Kropotkin's thought, *"Kropotkin stressed the role of heroic minorities in the preparation for revolution."* [**Kropotkin and the Rise of Revolutionary Anarchism, 1872-86**, p. 276] Yet, as John Crump correctly argued, the *"key words here are **in the preparation for revolution**. By their courage and daring in opposing capitalism and the state, anarchist minorities could teach* by example and thereby draw increasing numbers into the struggle. But Kropotkin was not advocating substitutionism; the idea that a minority might carry out the revolution in place of the people was as alien to him as the notion that a minority would exercise rule after the revolution. In fact, Kropotkin recognised that the former would be a prescription for the latter." [**Hatta Shuzo and Pure Anarchism in Interwar Japan**, p. 9] In Kropotkin's own words:

> "The idea of anarchist communism, today represented by feeble minorities, but increasingly finding popular expression, will make its way among the mass of the people. Spreading everywhere, the anarchist groups … will take strength from the support they find among the people, and will raise the red flag of the revolution … On that day, what is now the minority will become the People, the great mass, and that mass rising against property and the State, will march forward towards anarchist communism." [**Words of a Rebel**, p. 75]

This influence would be gained simply by the correctness of our ideas and the validity of our suggestions. This means that anarchists seek influence "through advice and example, leaving the people … to adopt our methods and solutions if these are, or seem to be, better than those suggested and carried out by others." As such, any anarchist organisation would "strive to acquire overwhelming influence in order to draw the [revolutionary] movement towards the realisation of our ideas. But such influence must be won by doing more and better than others, and will be useful if won in that way." This means rejecting "taking over command, that is by becoming a government and imposing one's own ideas and interests through police methods." [Malatesta, **The Anarchist Revolution**, pp. 108-9]

Moreover, unlike leading Marxists like Lenin and Karl Kautsky, anarchists think that socialist ideas are developed **within** the class struggle rather than outside it by the radical intelligentsia (see section H.5). Kropotkin argued that "modern socialism has emerged out of the depths of the people's consciousness. If a few thinkers emerging from the bourgeoisie have given it the approval of science and the support of philosophy, the basis of the idea which they have given their own expression has nonetheless been the product of the collective spirit of the working people. The rational socialism of the International is still today our greatest strength, and it was elaborated in working class organisation, under the first influence of the masses. The few writers who offered their help in the work of elaborating socialist ideas have merely been giving form to the aspirations that first saw their light among the workers." [**Op. Cit.**, p. 59] In other words, anarchists are a part of the working class (either by birth or by rejecting their previous class background and becoming part of it), the part which has generalised its own experiences, ideas and needs into a theory called "anarchism" and seeks to convince the rest of the validity of its ideas and tactics. This would be a dialogue, based on both learning **and** teaching.

As such, this means that the relationship between the specifically anarchist groups and oppressed peoples in struggle is a two way one. As well as trying to influence the social struggle, anarchists also try and learn from the class struggle and try to generalise from the experiences of their own struggles and the struggles of other working class people. Rather than seeing the anarchist group as some sort of teacher, anarchists see it as simply part of the social struggle and its ideas can and must develop from active participation within that struggle. As anarchists agree with Bakunin and reject the idea that their organisations should take power on behalf of the masses, it is clear that such groups are not imposing alien ideas upon people but rather try to clarify the ideas generated by working class people in struggle. It is an objective fact that there is a great difference in the political awareness within the masses of oppressed people. This uneven development means that they do not accept, all at once or in their totality, revolutionary ideas. There are layers. Groups of people, by ones and twos and then in larger numbers, become interested, read literature, talk with others, and create new ideas. The first groups that explicitly call their ideas "anarchism" have the right and duty to try to persuade others to join them. This is not opposed to the self-organisation of the working class, rather it is how working class people self-organise.

Lastly, most anarchists recognise the need to create specifically anarchist organisations to spread anarchist ideas and influence the class struggle. Suffice to say, the idea that anarchists reject this need to organise politically in order to achieve a revolution is not to be found in the theory and practice of all the major anarchist thinkers nor in the history and current practice of the anarchist movement itself. As Leninists themselves, at times, admit. Ultimately, if spontaneity was enough to create (and ensure the success of) a social revolution then we would be living in a libertarian socialist society. The fact that we are not suggests that spontaneity, however important, is not enough in itself. This simple fact of history is understood by anarchists and we organise ourselves appropriately.

See section J.3 for more details on what organisations anarchists create and their role in anarchist revolutionary theory. For a discussion of the role of anarchists in a revolution, see section J.7.5.

H.2.11 Are anarchists "anti-democratic"?

One of the common arguments against anarchism is that it is "anti-democratic" (or "elitist"). For example, a member of the British **Socialist Workers Party** denounces anarchism for being "necessarily deeply anti-democratic" due to its "thesis of the absolute sovereignty of the individual ego as against the imposition of **any** 'authority' over it," which, it is claimed, is the "distinctly anarchist concept." This position is an "idealist conception" in which "**any** authority is seen as despotic; 'freedom' and 'authority' (and therefore 'freedom' and 'democracy') are opposites. This presumption of opposition to 'authority' was fostered by liberalism." This is contrasted with the Marxist "materialist understanding of society" in which it "was clear that 'authority' is necessary in **any** society where labour is collaborative." [Derek Howl, "The Legacy of Hal Draper," pp. 137-49, **International Socialism**, no. 52, p. 145] Hal Draper is quoted arguing that:

By the 'principle of authority' the consistent anarchist means principled opposition to any exercise of authority, including opposition to authority derived from the most complete democracy and exercised in completely democratic fashion ... Of all ideologies, anarchism is the one most fundamentally anti-democratic in principle, since it is not only unalterably hostile to democracy in general but particularly to any socialist democracy of the most ideal kind that could be imagined."

Such an argument is just ridiculous. Indeed, it is flawed on so many levels its hard to know where to start. The obvious place is the claim that anarchism is the most *"fundamentally anti-democratic in principle."* Now, given that there are fascists, monarchists, supporters (like Trotsky) of *"party dictatorship"* and a host of others who advocate minority rule (even by one person) over everyone else, can it be argued with a straight face that anarchism is the most *"anti-democratic"* because it argues for the liberty of all? Is the idea and practice of absolute monarchy and fascism **really** more democratic than anarchism? Clearly not, although this does indicate the quality of this kind of argument. Equally, the notion that liberalism rests on a *"presumption of opposition to 'authority'"* cannot be supported by even a casual understanding of the subject. That ideology has always sought ways to justify the authority structures of the liberal state not to mention the hierarchies produced by capitalist private property. So the notion that liberalism is against "authority" is hard to square with both its theory and reality.

Another obvious point is that anarchists do not see **any** authority as *"despotic."* As we discuss in section H.4, this common Marxist assertion is simply not true. Anarchists have always been very clear on the fact they reject specific kinds of authority and not *"authority"* as such. In fact, by the term *"principal of authority,"* Bakunin meant **hierarchical** authority, and not all forms of *"authority"*. This explains why Kropotkin argued that *"the origin of the anarchist conception of society"* lies in *"the criticism"* of the *"hierarchical organisations and the authoritarian conceptions of society"* and stressed that anarchism *"refuses all hierarchical organisation."* [**Anarchism**, p. 158 and p. 137]

This means, just to state the obvious, that making and sticking by collective decisions are **not** acts of authority. Rather they are simply expressions of individual autonomy. Clearly in most activities there is a need to co-operate with other people. Indeed, **living** involves the *"absolute sovereignty of the individual ego"* (as if anarchists like Bakunin used such terms!) being *"restricted"* by exercising that *"sovereignty."* Take, for example, playing football. This involves finding others who seek to play the game, organising into teams, agreeing on rules and so on. All terrible violations of the *"absolute sovereignty of the individual ego,"* yet it was precisely the *"sovereignty"* of the *"individual"* which produced the desire to play the game in the first place. What sort of *"sovereignty"* is it that negates itself when it is exercised? Clearly, then, the Marxist "summary" of anarchist ideas on this matter, like of many others, is poverty stricken.

And, unsurprisingly enough, we find anarchist thinkers like Bakunin and Kropotkin attacking this idea of *"the absolute sovereignty of the individual ego"* in the most severe terms. Indeed, they thought it

was a bourgeois theory which simply existed to justify the continued domination and exploitation of working class people by the ruling class. Kropotkin quite clearly recognised its anti-individual and unfree nature by labelling it *"the authoritarian individualism which stifles us"* and stressing its *"narrow-minded, and therefore foolish"* nature. [**Conquest of Bread**, p. 130] Similarly, it would do the Marxist argument little good if they quoted Bakunin arguing that the *"freedom of individuals is by no means an individual matter. It is a collective matter, a collective product. No individual can be free outside of human society or without its co-operation"* or that he considered *"individualism"* as a *"bourgeois principle."* [**The Basic Bakunin**, p. 46 and p. 57] He had nothing but contempt for, as he put it, *"that individualistic, egotistical, malicious and illusory freedom"* which was *"extolled"* by all the *"schools of bourgeois liberalism."* [**Michael Bakunin: Selected Writings**, p. 196]

Perhaps, of course, these two famous anarchists were not, in fact, *"consistent"* anarchists, but that claim is doubtful.

The notion that anarchism is inherently an extreme form of "individualism" seems to be the great assumption of Marxism. Hence the continual repetition of this "fact" and the continual attempt to link revolutionary anarchism with Stirner's ideas (the only anarchist to stress the importance of the *"ego"*). Thus we find Engels talking about *"Stirner, the great prophet of contemporary anarchism - Bakunin has taken a great deal from him ... Bakunin blended [Stirner] with Proudhon and labelled the blend 'anarchism'"* For Marx, *"Bakunin has merely translated Proudhon's and Stirner's anarchy into the crude language of the Tartars."* [Marx, Engels and Lenin, **Anarchism and Anarcho-Syndicalism**, p. 175 and p. 153] In reality, of course, Stirner was essentially unknown to the anarchist movement until his book was rediscovered in the late nineteenth century and even then his impact was limited. In terms of Bakunin, while his debt to Proudhon is well known and obvious, the link with Stirner seems to have existed only in the heads of Marx and Engels. As Mark Leier notes, *"there is no evidence of this ... Bakunin mentions Stirner precisely once in his collected works, and then only in passing ... as far as can be determined, Bakunin had no interest, even a negative one, in Stirner's ideas."* [**Bakunin: The Creative Passion**, p. 97] Nor was Proudhon influenced by Stirner (it is doubtful he even knew of him) while Stirner criticised the French anarchist. Does that mean Stirner is the only "consistent" anarchist? Moreover, even in terms of Stirner, Marxist diatribes about the *"absolute sovereignty of the individual ego"* fail to note that the egoist himself advocated organisation (*"the union of egos"*) and was well aware that it required agreements between individuals which, in the abstract, reduced "liberty" (the union *"offer[s] a greater measure of liberty"* while containing a lesser amount of *"unfreedom"* [**The Ego and Its Own**, p. 308]).

Anarchism does, of course, derive from the Greek for *"without authority"* or *"without rulers"* and this, unsurprisingly, informs anarchist theory and visions of a better world. This means that anarchism is against the *"domination of man by man"* (and woman by woman, woman by man, and so on). However, *"[a]s knowledge has penetrated the governed masses ... the people have revolted against the form of authority then felt most intolerable. This spirit of revolt in the individual and the masses, is the natural and necessary fruit of the spirit of domination; the vindication of human dignity, and the saviour of social life."* Thus *"freedom is the necessary preliminary to any true and equal human association."* [Charlotte Wilson, **Anarchist Essays**, p. 54 and p. 40] In other words, anarchism comes from the struggle of the oppressed against their rulers and is an expression of individual and social freedom. Anarchism was born from the class struggle.

Taking individual liberty as a good thing, the next question is how do free individuals co-operate together in such a way as to ensure their continued liberty (*"The belief in freedom assumes that human beings can co-operate."* [Emma Goldman, **Red Emma Speaks**, p. 442]). This suggests that any association must be one of equality between the associating individuals. This can only be done when everyone involved takes a meaningful role in the decision making process and because of this anarchists stress the need for **self-government** (usually called **self-management**) of both individuals and groups. Self-management within free associations and decision making from the bottom-up is the only way domination can be eliminated. This is because, by making our own decisions ourselves, we automatically end the division of society into governors and governed (i.e. end hierarchy). As Anarchism clearly means support for freedom and equality, it automatically implies opposition to all forms of hierarchical organisation and authoritarian social relationships. This means that anarchist support for individual liberty does not end, as many Marxists assert, in the denial of organisation or collective decision making but rather in support for **self-managed** groups. Only this form of organisation can end the division of society into rulers and ruled, oppressor and oppressed, exploiter and exploited and create an environment in which individuals can associate without denying their freedom and equality.

Therefore, the **positive** side of anarchism (which naturally flows from its opposition to authority) results in a political theory which argues that people must control their own struggles, organisations and affairs directly. This means we support mass assemblies and their federation via councils of mandated delegates subject to recall if they break their mandates (i.e. they act as they see fit, i.e. as politicians or bureaucrats, and not as the people who elected them desire). This way people directly govern themselves and control their own lives, allowing those affected by a decision to have a say in it and so they manage their own affairs directly and without hierarchy. Rather than imply an "individualism" which denies the importance of association and the freedom it can generate, anarchism implies an opposition to hierarchy in all its forms and support for the free association of equals. In other words, anarchism can generally be taken to mean support for self-government or self-management, both by individuals and by groups.

In summary, anarchist support for individual liberty incurs a similar support for self-managed groups. In such groups, individuals co-operate as equals to maximise their liberty. This means, for anarchists, Marxists are just confusing co-operation with coercion, agreement with authority, association with subordination. Thus the Marxist *"materialist"* concept of authority distorts the anarchist position and, secondly, is supra-historical in the extreme. Different forms of decision making are lumped together, independent of the various forms it may assume. To equate hierarchical and self-managed decision making, antagonistic and harmonious forms of organisation, alienated authority or authority retained in the hands of those directly affected by it, can only be a source of confusion. Rather than being a *"materialistic"* approach, the Marxist one is pure philosophical idealism - the postulating of a-historic concepts independently of the individuals and societies that generate specific social relationships and ways of working together.

Similarly, it would be churlish to note that Marxists themselves have habitually rejected democratic authority when it suited them. Even that *"higher type of democracy"* of the soviets was ignored by the Bolshevik party once it was in power. As we discuss in section H.6.1, faced with the election of non-Bolshevik majorities to the soviets, Bolshevik armed force was used to overthrow the results. In addition, they also gerrymandered soviets once they could no longer count on an electoral majority. In the workplace, the Bolsheviks replaced workers' economic democracy with *"one-man management"* appointed from above, by the state, armed with *"dictatorial power"* (see section H.3.14). As discussed in section H.3.8, the Bolsheviks generalised their experiences exercising power into explicit support for party dictatorship. Throughout the 1920s and 30s, Trotsky repeated this conclusion and repeatedly advocated party dictatorship, urging the party to use its power to crush opposition in the working class to its rule. For the Bolshevik tradition, the power of the party to ignore the wishes of the class it claims to represent is a fundamental ideological position.

So remember, when Lenin or Trotsky argue for *"party dictatorship"*, the over-riding of the democratic decisions of the masses by the party, the elimination of workers factory committees in favour of appointed managers armed with *"dictatorial"* power or when the Bolsheviks disbanded soviets with non-Bolshevik majorities, it is **anarchism** which is fundamentally *"anti-democratic"*! All in all, that anyone can claim that anarchism is more *"anti-democratic"* than Leninism is a joke.

However, all these anti-democratic acts do fit in nicely with Howl's *"materialist"* Marxist concept that *"'authority' is necessary in **any** society where labour is collaborative."* Since *"authority"* is essential and all forms of collective decision making are necessarily *"authoritarian"* and involve *"subordination,"* then it clearly does not really matter how collectives are organised and how decisions are reached. Hence the lack of concern for the liberty of the working people subjected to the (peculiarly bourgeois-like) forms of authority preferred by Lenin and Trotsky. It was precisely for this reason, to differentiate between egalitarian (and so libertarian) forms of organisation and decision making and authoritarian ones, that anarchists called themselves *"anti-authoritarians."*

Even if we ignore all the anti-democratic acts of Bolshevism (or justify them in terms of the problems facing the Russian Revolution, as most Leninists do), the anti-democratic nature of Leninist ideas still comes to the fore. The Leninist support for centralised state power brings their attack on anarchism as being *"anti-democratic"* into clear perspective and, ultimately, results in the affairs of millions being decided upon by a handful of people in the Central Committee of the vanguard party. As an example, we will discuss Trotsky's arguments against the Makhnovist movement in the Ukraine.

For Trotsky, the Makhnovists were against *"Soviet power."* This, he argued, was simply *"the authority of all the local soviets in the Ukraine"* as they all *"recognise the central power which they themselves have elected."* Consequently, the Makhnovists rejected not only central authority but also the local soviets as well. Trotsky also suggested that there were no *"appointed"* persons in Russia as *"there is no authority in Russia but that which is elected by the whole working class and working peasantry. It follows [!] that commanders appointed by the central Soviet Government are installed in their positions by the will of the working millions."* He stressed that one can speak of *"appointed"* persons *"only under the bourgeois order, when Tsarist officials or bourgeois ministers appointed at their own discretion commanders who kept the soldier masses subject to the bourgeois classes."* When the Makhnovists tried to call the fourth regional conference of peasants, workers and partisans to discuss the progress of the Civil War in early 1919, Trotsky, unsurprisingly enough, *"categorically banned"* it. With typical elitism, he noted that the Makhnovist movement had *"its roots in the ignorant masses"*! [**How the Revolution Armed**, vol. II, p. 277, p. 280, p. 295 and p. 302]

In other words, because the Bolshevik government had been given power by a national Soviet Congress in the past (and only remained there by gerrymandering and disbanding soviets), he (as its representative) had the right to ban a conference which would have expressed the wishes of millions of workers, peasants and partisans fighting for the revolution! The fallacious nature of his arguments is easily seen. Rather than executing the will of millions of toilers, Trotsky was simply executing his own will. He did not consult those millions nor the local soviets which had, in Bolshevik ideology, surrendered their power to the handful of people in the central committee of the Bolshevik Party. By banning the conference he was very effectively undermining the practical, functional democracy of millions and replacing it with a purely formal "democracy" based on empowering a few leaders at the centre. Yes, indeed, truly democracy in action when one person can deny a revolutionary people its right to decide its own fate!

Unsurprisingly, the anarchist Nestor Makhno replied by arguing that he considered it *"an inviolable right of the workers and peasants, a right won by the revolution, to call congresses on their own account, to discuss their affairs. That is why the prohibition by the central authorities on the calling of such congresses ... represent a direct and insolent violation of the rights of the workers."* [quoted by Peter Arshinov, **The History of the Makhnovist Movement**, p. 129] We will leave it to the readers to decide which of the two, Trotsky or Makhno, showed the fundamentally *"anti-democratic"* perspective. Moreover, there are a few theoretical issues that need to be raised on this matter. Notice, for example, that no attempt is made to answer the simple question of why having 51% of a group automatically makes you right! It is taken for granted that the minority should subject themselves to the will of the majority before that will is even decided upon. Does that mean, for example, that Marxists refuse minorities the right of civil disobedience if the majority acts in a way which harms their liberties and equality? If, for example, the majority in a community decides to implement race laws, does that mean that Marxists would **oppose** the discriminated minority taking direct action to undermine and abolish them? Or, to take an example closer to Marxism, in 1914 the leaders of the Social Democratic Party in the German Parliament voted for war credits. The anti-war minority of that group went along with the majority in the name of "democracy," "unity" and "discipline". Would Howl

and Draper argue that they were right to do so? If they were not right to betray the ideas of Marxism and international working class solidarity, then why not? They did, after all, subject themselves to the *"most perfect socialist democracy"* and so, presumably, made the correct decision.

Simply put, the arguments that anarchists are *"anti-democratic"* are question-begging in the extreme, when not simply hypocritical.

As a general rule-of-thumb, anarchists have little problem with the minority accepting the decisions of the majority after a process of free debate and discussion. As we argue in section A.2.11, such collective decision making is compatible with anarchist principles - indeed, is based on them. By governing ourselves directly, we exclude others governing us. However, we do not make a fetish of this, recognising that, in certain circumstances, the minority must and should ignore majority decisions. For example, if the majority of an organisation decide on a policy which the minority thinks is disastrous then why should they follow the majority? Equally, if the majority make a decision which harms the liberty and equality of a non-oppressive and non-exploitative minority, then that minority has the right to reject the "authority" of the majority. Hence Carole Pateman:

> *"The essence of liberal social contract theory is that individuals ought to promise to, or enter an agreement to, obey representatives, to whom they have alienated their right to make political decisions ... Promising ... is an expression of individual freedom and equality, yet commits individuals for the future. Promising also implies that individuals are capable of independent judgement and rational deliberation, and of evaluating and changing their own actions and relationships; promises may sometimes justifiably be broken. However, to promise to obey is to deny or limit, to a greater or lesser degree, individuals' freedom and equality and their ability to exercise these capacities. To promise to obey is to state that, in certain areas, the person making the promise is no longer free to exercise her capacities and decide upon her own actions, and is no longer equal, but subordinate."* [**The Problem of Political Obligation**, p. 19]

Thus, for anarchists, a democracy which does not involve individual rights to dissent, to disagree and to practice civil disobedience would violate freedom and equality, the very values Marxists usually claim to be at the heart of their politics. The claim that anarchism is *"anti-democratic"* basically hides the argument that the minority must become the slave of the majority - with no right of dissent when the majority is wrong (in practice, of course, it is usually meant the orders and laws of the minority who are elected to power). In effect, it wishes the minority to be subordinate, not equal, to the majority. Anarchists, in contrast, because we support self-management also recognise the importance of dissent and individuality - in essence, because we are in favour of self-management ("democracy" does not do the concept justice) we also favour the individual freedom that is its rationale. We support the liberty of individuals because we believe in self-management ("democracy") so passionately.

So Howl and Draper fail to understand the rationale for democratic decision making - it is not based on the idea that the majority is always right but that individual freedom requires democracy to express and defend itself. By placing the collective above the individual, they undermine democratic values and replace them with little more than tyranny by the majority (or, more likely, a tiny minority who claim to represent the majority).

Moreover, progress is determined by those who dissent and rebel against the status quo and the decisions of the majority. That is why anarchists support the right of dissent in self-managed groups - in fact, dissent, refusal, revolt by individuals and minorities is a key aspect of self-management. Given that Leninists do not support self-management (rather they, at best, support the Lockean notion of electing a government as being "democracy") it is hardly surprising they, like Locke, view dissent as a danger and something to denounce. Anarchists, on the other hand, recognising that self-management's (i.e. direct democracy's) rationale and base is in individual freedom, recognise and support the rights of individuals to rebel against what they consider as unjust impositions. As history shows, the anarchist position is the correct one - without rebellion, numerous minorities would never have improved their position and society would stagnate. Indeed, Howl's and Draper's comments are just a reflection of the standard capitalist diatribe against strikers and protestors - they do not need to protest, for they live in a "democracy."

This Marxist notion that anarchists are "anti-democratic" gets them into massive contradictions. Lance Selfa's highly inaccurate and misleading article "Emma Goldman: A life of controversy" is an example of this [**International Socialist Review**, no. 34, March-April 2004] Ignoring the far more substantial evidence for Leninist elitism, Selfa asserted that "Goldman never turned away from the idea that heroic individuals, not masses, make history" and quotes from her 1910 essay "Minorities Versus Majorities" to prove this. Significantly, he does not actually refute the arguments Goldman expounded. He does, needless to say, misrepresent them.

The aim of Goldman's essay was to state the obvious - that the mass is not the source for new ideas. Rather, new, progressive, ideas are the product of minorities, which then spread to the majority by the actions of those minorities. Even social movements and revolutions start when a minority takes action. Trade unionism, for example, was (and still is) a minority movement in most countries. Support for racial and sexual equality was long despised (or, at best, ignored) by the majority and it took a resolute minority to advance that cause and spread the idea in the majority. The Russian Revolution did not start with the majority. It started when a minority of women workers (ignoring the advice of the local Bolsheviks) took to the streets and from these hundreds grew into a movement of hundreds of thousands.

The facts are clearly on the side of Goldman, not Selfa. Given that Goldman was expounding such an obvious law of social evolution, it seems incredulous that Selfa has a problem with it. This is particularly the case as Marxism (particularly its Leninist version) implicitly recognises this. As Marx argued, the ruling ideas of any epoch are those of the ruling class. Likewise for Goldman: "Human thought has always been falsified by tradition and custom, and perverted false education in the interests of those who held power ... by the State and the ruling class." Hence the "continuous struggle" against "the State and even against 'society,' that is,

against the majority subdued and hypnotised by the State and State worship." If this were not the case, as Goldman noted, no state could save itself or private property from the masses. Hence the need for people to break from their conditioning, to act for themselves. As she argued, such direct action is "the salvation of man" as it "necessitates integrity, self-reliance, and courage." [**Red Emma Speaks**, p. 111 and p. 76]

Thus Goldman, like other anarchists, was not dismissing the masses, just stressing the obvious: namely that socialism is a process of self-liberation and the task of the conscious minority is to encourage this process by encouraging the direct action of the masses. Hence Goldman's support for syndicalism and direct action, a support Selfa (significantly) fails to inform his readers of.

So was Goldman's rejection of "majorities" the elitism Selfa claims it was? No, far from it. This is clear from looking at that work in context. For example, in a debate between her and a socialist she used the Lawrence strike "as an example of direct action." [**Living My Life**, vol. 1., p. 491] The workers in one of the mills started the strike by walking out. The next day five thousand at another mill struck and marched to another mill and soon doubled their number. The strikers soon had to supply food and fuel for 50,000. [Howard Zinn, **A People's History of the United States**, pp. 327-8] Rather than the strike being the act of the majority, it was the direct action of a minority which started it and it then spread to the majority (a strike, incidentally, Goldman supported and fund raised for). It should also be noted that the Lawrence strike reflected her ideas of how a general strike could be started by "one industry or by a small, conscious minority among the workers" which "is soon taken up by many other industries, spreading like wildfire." [**Red Emma Speaks**, p. 95]

Do Marxists really argue that this was "elitist"? If so, then every spontaneous revolt is "elitist". Every attempt by oppressed minorities to resist their oppression is "elitist." Indeed, every attempt to change society is "elitist" as if it involves a minority not limiting themselves to simply advancing new ideas but, instead, taking direct action to raise awareness or to resist hierarchy in the here and now. Revolutions occur when the ideas of the majority catch up with the minority who inspire others with their ideas and activity. So in his keenness to label the anarchist movement "elitist", Selfa has also, logically, so-labelled the labour, feminist, peace and civil rights movements (among many others).

Equally embarrassing for Selfa, Trotsky (a person whom he contrasts favourably with Goldman despite the fact he was a practitioner and advocate of party dictatorship) agreed with the anarchists on the importance of minorities. As he put it during the debate on Kronstadt in the late 1930s, a "revolution is 'made' directly by a **minority**. The success of a revolution is possible, however, only where this minority finds more or less support, or at least friendly neutrality, on the part of the majority. The shift in different stages of the revolution ... is directly determined by changing political relations between the minority and the majority, between the vanguard and the class." [Lenin and Trotsky, **Kronstadt**, p. 85] Not that this makes Trotsky an elitist for Selfa, of course. The key difference is that Goldman did not argue that this minority should seize power and rule the masses, regardless of the wishes of that majority, as Trotsky did (see section H.1.2). As Goldman noted, the

"Socialist demagogues know that [her argument is true] as well as I, but they maintain the myth of the virtues of the majority, because their very scheme means the perpetuation of power" and *"authority, coercion and dependence rest on the mass, but never freedom."* [**Op. Cit.**, p. 85]

So, yes, anarchists do support individual freedom to resist even democratically made decisions simply because democracy **has to be** based on individual liberty. Without the right of dissent, democracy becomes a joke and little more than a numerical justification for tyranny. This does not mean we are *"anti-democratic,"* indeed the reverse as we hold true to the fundamental rationale for democratic decision-making - it allows individuals to combine as equals and not as subordinates and masters. Moreover, diversity is essential for any viable eco-system and it is essential in any viable society (and, of course, any society worth living in). This means that a healthy society is one which encourages diversity, individuality, dissent and, equally, self-managed associations to ensure the freedom of all. As Malatesta argued:

"There are matters over which it is worth accepting the will of the majority because the damage caused by a split would be greater than that caused by error; there are circumstances in which discipline becomes a duty because to fail in it would be to fail in the solidarity between the oppressed and would mean betrayal in face of the enemy. But when one is convinced that the organisation is pursuing a course which threatens the future and makes it difficult to remedy the harm done, then it is a duty to rebel and to resist even at the risk of provoking a split ... What is essential is that individuals should develop a sense of organisation and solidarity, and the conviction that fraternal co-operation is necessary to fight oppression and to achieve a society in which everyone will be able to enjoy his [or her] own life." [**Errico Malatesta: His Life and Ideas**, pp. 132-3]

This means that anarchists are not against majority decision making as such. We simply recognise it has limitations. In practice, the need for majority and minority to come to an agreement is one most anarchists would recognise:

"But such an adaptation [of the minority to the decisions of the majority] on the one hand by one group must be reciprocal, voluntary and must stem from an awareness of need and of goodwill to prevent the running of social affairs from being paralysed by obstinacy. It cannot be imposed as a principle and statutory norm...

"So ... anarchists deny the right of the majority to govern in human society in general ... how is it possible ... to declare that anarchists should submit to the decisions of the majority before they have even heard what those might be?" [Malatesta, **The Anarchist Revolution**, pp. 100-1]

Therefore, while accepting majority decision making as a key aspect of a revolutionary movement and a free society, anarchists do not make a fetish of it. We recognise that we must use our own judgement in evaluating each decision reached simply because the majority is not always right. We must balance the need for solidarity in the common struggle and needs of common life with critical analysis and judgement. As Malatesta argued:

"In any case it is not a question of being right or wrong; it is a question of freedom, freedom for all, freedom for each individual so long as he [or she] does not violate the equal freedom of others. No one can judge with certainty who is right and who is wrong, who is closer to the truth and which is the best road for the greatest good for each and everyone. Experience through freedom is the only means to arrive at the truth and the best solutions; and there is no freedom if there is not the freedom to be wrong.

"In our opinion, therefore, it is necessary that majority and minority should succeed in living together peacefully and profitably by mutual agreement and compromise, by the intelligent recognition of the practical necessities of communal life and of the usefulness of concessions which circumstances make necessary." [**Errico Malatesta: His Life and Ideas**, p. 72]

Needless to say, our arguments apply with even more force to the decisions of the **representatives** of the majority, who are in practice a very small minority. Leninists usually try and confuse these two distinct forms of decision making. When Leninists discuss majority decision making they almost always mean the decisions of those elected by the majority - the central committee or the government - rather than the majority of the masses or an organisation. Ultimately, the Leninist support for democracy (as the Russian Revolution showed) is conditional on whether the majority supports them or not. Anarchists are not as hypocritical or as elitist as this, arguing that everyone should have the same rights the Leninists usurp for their leaders.

This counterpoising of socialism to "individualism" is significant. The aim of socialism is, after all, to increase individual liberty (to quote the **Communist Manifesto**, to create *"an association, in which the free development of each is the condition for the free development of all."* [**The Marx-Engels Reader**, p. 491]). As such, authentic socialism **is** "individualist" in its aspirations and denounces capitalism for being a partial and flawed individualism which benefits the few at the expense of the many (in terms of their development and individuality). This can be seen when Goldman, for example, argued that anarchism *"alone stresses the importance of the individual, his [or her] possibilities and needs in a free society."* It *"insists that the centre of gravity in society is the individual - that he must think for himself, act freely, and live fully. The aim of Anarchism is that every individual in the world shall be able to do so."* Needless to say, she differentiated her position from bourgeois ideology: *"Of course, this has nothing in common with a much boasted 'rugged individualism.' Such predatory individualism is really flabby, not rugged ... Their 'rugged individualism' is simply one of the many pretences the ruling class makes to unbridled business and political extortion."* [**Op. Cit.**, p. 442 and p. 443] This support for individuality did not preclude solidarity, organising unions, practising direct action, supporting syndicalism, desiring communism and so on, but rather **required** it (as Goldman's own life showed). It flows automatically from a love of freedom for all. Given this, the typical Leninist attacks against anarchism for being "individualism" simply exposes the state capitalist nature of Bolshevism:

> "capitalism promotes egotism, not individuality or 'individualism.' ... the ego it created ... [is] shrivelled ... The term 'bourgeois individualism,' an epithet widely used by the left today against libertarian elements, reflects the extent to which bourgeois ideology permeates the socialist project; indeed, the extent to which the 'socialist' project (as distinguished from the libertarian communist project) is a mode of state capitalism." [Murray Bookchin, **Post-Scarcity Anarchism**, p. 194fn]

Therefore the Marxist attack on anarchism as *"anti-democratic"* is not only false, it is ironic and hypocritical. Firstly, anarchists do **not** argue for *"the absolute sovereignty of the individual ego."* Rather, we argue for individual freedom. This, in turn, implies a commitment to self-managed forms of social organisation. This means that anarchists do not confuse agreement with (hierarchical) authority. Secondly, Marxists do not explain why the majority is always right or why their opinions are automatically the truth. Thirdly, the logical conclusions of their arguments would result in the absolute enserfment of the individual to the representatives of the majority. Fourthly, rather than being supporters of democracy, Marxists like Lenin and Trotsky explicitly argued for minority rule and the ignoring of majority decisions when they clashed with the decisions of the ruling party. Fifthly, their support for "democratic" centralised power means, in practice, the elimination of democracy in the grassroots. As can be seen from Trotsky's arguments against the Makhnovists, the democratic organisation and decisions of millions can be banned by a single individual.

All in all, Marxists claims that anarchists are *"anti-democratic"* just backfire on Marxism.

H.3
What are the myths of state socialism?

Ask most people what socialism means and they will point to the Soviet Union, China, Cuba and a host of other authoritarian, centralised, exploitative and oppressive party dictatorships. These regimes have in common two things. Firstly, the claim that their rulers are Marxists or socialists. Secondly, that they have successfully alienated millions of working class people from the very idea of socialism. Indeed, the supporters of capitalism simply had to describe the "socialist paradises" as they really are in order to put people off socialism. The Stalinist regimes and their various apologists (and even "opponents", like the Trotskyists, who defend them as *"degenerated workers' states"*) let the bourgeoisie have an easy time in dismissing all working-class demands and struggles as so many attempts to set up similar party dictatorships.

The association of "socialism" or "communism" with these dictatorships has often made anarchists wary of calling themselves socialists or communists in case our ideas are associated with them. As Errico Malatesta argued in 1924:

> "I foresee the possibility that the communist anarchists will gradually abandon the term 'communist': it is growing in ambivalence and falling into disrepute as a result of Russian 'communist' despotism. If the term is eventually abandoned this will be a repetition of what happened with the word 'socialist.' We who, in Italy at least, were the first champions of socialism and maintained and still maintain that we are the true socialists in the broad and human sense of the word, ended by abandoning the term to avoid confusion with the many and various authoritarian and bourgeois deviations of socialism. Thus too we may have to abandon the term 'communist' for fear that our ideal of free human solidarity will be confused with the avaricious despotism which has for some time triumphed in Russia and which one party, inspired by the Russian example, seeks to impose world-wide." [**The Anarchist Revolution**, p. 20]

That, to a large degree happened with anarchists simply calling themselves by that name (without adjectives) or libertarians to avoid confusion. This, sadly, resulted in two problems. Firstly, it gave Marxists even more potential to portray anarchism as being primarily against the state and not being as equally opposed to capitalism, hierarchy and inequality (as we argue in section H.2.4, anarchists have opposed the state as just one aspect of class and hierarchical society). Secondly, extreme right-wingers tried to appropriate the names "libertarian" and "anarchist" to describe their vision of extreme capitalism as "anarchism," they claimed, was simply "anti-government" (see section F for discussion on why "anarcho"-capitalism is not anarchist). To counter these distortions of anarchist ideas, many anarchists have re-appropriated the use of the words "socialist" and "communist," although always in combination with the words "anarchist" and "libertarian."

Such combination of words is essential as the problem Malatesta predicted still remains. If one thing can be claimed for the 20th century, it is that it has seen the word *"socialism"* become narrowed and restricted into what anarchists call *"state socialism"* - socialism created and run from above, by the state (i.e. by the state bureaucracy and better described as state capitalism). This restriction of "socialism" has been supported by both Stalinist and Capitalist ruling elites, for their own reasons (the former to secure their own power and gain support by associating themselves with socialist ideals, the latter by discrediting those ideas by associating them with the horror of Stalinism). The Stalinist *leadership thus portrays itself as socialist to protect its right to wield the club, and Western ideologists adopt the same pretence in order to forestall the threat of a more free and just society."* The latter use it as *"a powerful ideological weapon to enforce conformity and obedience,"* tc *"ensure that the necessity to rent oneself to the owners and managers of these [capitalist] institutions will be regarded as virtually a natural law, the only alternative to the 'socialist' dungeon."* In reality, *"if there is a relation"* between Bolshevism and socialism, *"it is the relation of contradiction."* [*"The Soviet Union versus Socialism"*, pp. 47-52, **The Radical Papers**, Dimitrios I. Roussopoulos (ed.), pp. 47-8]

This means that anarchists and other libertarian socialists have a major task on their hands - to reclaim the promise of socialism from the distortions inflicted upon it by both its enemies (Stalinists and capitalists) and its erstwhile and self-proclaimed supporters (Social Democracy and its offspring Bolshevism). A key aspect of this process is a critique of both the practice and ideology of Marxism and its various offshoots. Only by doing this can anarchists prove, to quote Rocker, that ***"Socialism will be free, or it will not be at all."*** [**Anarcho-Syndicalism**, p. 14]

Such a critique raises the problem of which forms of "Marxism" to discuss. There is an extremely diverse range of Marxist viewpoints and groups in existence. Indeed, the different groups spend a lot of time indicating why all the others are not "real" Marxists (or Marxist-Leninists, or Trotskyists, and so on) and are just "sects" without "real" Marxist theory or ideas. This "diversity" is, of course, a major problem (and somewhat ironic, given that some Marxists like to insult anarchists by stating there are as many forms of anarchism as anarchists!). Equally, many Marxists go further than dismissing specific groups. Some even totally reject other branches of their movement as being non-Marxist (for example, some Marxists dismiss Leninism as having little, or nothing, to do with what they consider the *"real"* Marxist tradition to be). This means that discussing Marxism can be difficult as Marxists can argue that our FAQ does not address the arguments of this or that Marxist thinker, group or tendency.

With this in mind, this section of the FAQ will concentrate on the works of Marx and Engels (and so the movement they generated, namely Social Democracy) as well as the Bolshevik tradition started by Lenin and continued (by and large) by Trotsky. These are the core thinkers (and the recognised authorities) of most Marxists and so latter derivations of these tendencies can be ignored (for example Maoism, Castroism and so on). It should also be noted that even this grouping will produce dissent as some Marxists argue that the Bolshevik tradition is not part of Marxism. This perspective can be seen in the *"impossiblist"* tradition of Marxism (e.g. the **Socialist Party of Great Britain** and its sister parties) as well as in the left/council communist tradition (e.g. in the work of such Marxists as Anton Pannekoek and Paul Mattick). The arguments for their positions are strong and well worth reading (indeed, any honest analysis of Marxism and Leninism cannot help but show important differences between the two). However, as the vast majority of Marxists today are also Leninists, we have to reflect this in our FAQ (and, in general, we do so by referring to "mainstream Marxists" as opposed to the small minority of libertarian Marxists).

Another problem arises when we consider the differences not only between Marxist tendencies, but also within a specific tendency before and after its representatives seize power. For example, as Chomsky pointed out, *"there are … very different strains of Leninism … there's the Lenin of 1917, the Lenin of the 'April Theses' and **State and Revolution**. That's one Lenin. And then there's the Lenin who took power and acted in ways that are unrecognisable … compared with, say, the doctrines of 'State and Revolution.' … this [is] not very hard to explain. There's a big difference between the libertarian doctrines of a person who is trying to associate himself with a mass popular movement to acquire power and the authoritarian power of somebody who's taken power and is trying to consolidate it… that is true of Marx also. There are competing strains in Marx."* As such, this section of our FAQ will try and draw out the contradictions within Marxism and indicate what aspects of the doctrine aided the development of the "second" Lenin for the seeds from which authoritarianism grew post-October 1917 existed from the start. Anarchists agree with Chomsky, namely that he considered it *"characteristic and unfortunate that the lesson that was drawn from Marx and Lenin for the later period was the authoritarian lesson. That is, it's the authoritarian power of the vanguard party and destruction of all popular forums in the interests of the masses. That's the Lenin who became known to later generations. Again, not very surprisingly, because that's what Leninism really was in practice."* [**Language and Politics**, p. 152] Which, of course, means evaluating both the theory **and** practice of Marxism. For anarchists, it seems strange that for a body of work whose followers stress is revolutionary and liberating, its results have been so bad. If Marxism is so obviously revolutionary and democratic, then why have so few of the people who read it drawn those conclusions? How could it be transmuted so easily into Stalinism? Why are there so few **libertarian** Marxists, if it were Lenin (or, following Lenin, Social Democracy) which "misinterpreted" Marx and Engels? So when Marxists argue that the problem is in the interpretation of the message not in the message itself, anarchists reply that the reason these numerous, allegedly false, interpretations exist at all simply suggests that there are limitations within Marxism **as such** rather than the readings it has been subjected to. When something repeatedly fails and produces such terrible results in the process then there has to be a fundamental flaw somewhere. Thus Cornelius Castoriadis:

> *"Marx was, in fact, the first to stress that the significance of a theory cannot be grasped independently of the historical and social practice it inspires and initiates, to which it gives rise, in which it prolongs itself and under cover of which a given practice seeks to justify itself.*

> *"Who, today, would dare proclaim that the only significance of Christianity for history is to be found in reading unaltered versions of the Gospels or that the historical practice of various Churches over a period of some 2,000 years can teach us nothing fundamental about the significance of this religious movement? A 'faithfulness to Marx' which would see the historical fate of Marxism as something unimportant would be just as laughable. It would in fact be quite ridiculous. Whereas for the Christian the revelations of the Gospels have a transcendental kernel and an intemporal validity, no theory could ever have such qualities in the eyes of a Marxist. To seek to discover the meaning of Marxism only in what Marx wrote (while keeping quiet about what the doctrine has become in history) is to pretend - in flagrant contradiction with the central ideas of that doctrine - that real history doesn't count and that the truth of a theory is*

always and exclusively to be found 'further on.' It finally comes to replacing revolution by revelation and the understanding of events by the exegesis of texts." ["*The Fate of Marxism,*" pp. 75-84 **The Anarchist Papers**, Dimitrios Roussopoulos (ed.), p. 77]

This does not mean forsaking the work of Marx and Engels. It means rejecting once and for all the idea that two people, writing over a period of decades over a hundred years ago have all the answers. As should be obvious! Ultimately, anarchists think we have to **build** upon the legacy of the past, not squeeze current events into it. We should stand on the shoulders of giants, not at their feet.

Thus this section of our FAQ will attempt to explain the various myths of Marxism and provide an anarchist critique of it and its offshoots. Of course, the ultimate myth of Marxism is what Alexander Berkman called "*The Bolshevik Myth,*" namely the idea that the Russian Revolution was a success. However, given the scope of this revolution, we will not discuss it fully here except when it provides useful empirical evidence for our critique (see section H.6 for more on the Russian Revolution). Our discussion here will concentrate for the most part on Marxist theory, showing its inadequacies, its problems, where it appropriated anarchist ideas and how anarchism and Marxism differ. This is a big task and this section of the FAQ can only be a small contribution to it.

As noted above, there are minority trends in Marxism which are libertarian in nature (i.e. close to anarchism). As such, it would be simplistic to say that anarchists are "anti-Marxist" and we generally do differentiate between the (minority) libertarian element and the authoritarian mainstream of Marxism (i.e. Social-Democracy and Leninism in its many forms). Without doubt, Marx contributed immensely to the enrichment of socialist ideas and analysis (as acknowledged by Bakunin, for example). His influence, as to be expected, was both positive and negative. For this reason he must be read and discussed critically. This FAQ is a contribution to this task of transcending the work of Marx. As with anarchist thinkers, we must take what is useful from Marx and reject the rubbish. But never forget that anarchists are anarchists precisely because we think that anarchist thinkers have got more right than wrong and we reject the idea of tying our politics to the name of a long dead thinker.

H.3.1 Do Anarchists and Marxists want the same thing?

Ultimately, the greatest myth of Marxism is the idea that anarchists and most Marxists want the same thing. Indeed, it could be argued that it is anarchist criticism of Marxism which has made them stress the similarity of long term goals with anarchism. "*Our polemics against [the Marxists],*" Bakunin argued, "*have forced them to recognise that freedom, or anarchy - that is, the voluntary organisation of the workers from below upward - is the ultimate goal of social development.*" He stressed that the means to this apparently similar end were different. The Marxists "*say that [a] state yoke, [a] dictatorship, is a necessary transitional device for*

achieving the total liberation of the people: anarchy, or freedom, is the goal, and the state, or dictatorship, is the means ... We reply that no dictatorship can have any other objective than to perpetuate itself, and that it can engender and nurture only slavery in the people who endure it. Liberty can be created only by liberty, by an insurrection of all the people and the voluntary organisation of the workers from below upwards." [**Statism and Anarchy**, p. 179]

As such, it is commonly taken for granted that the ends of both Marxists and Anarchists are the same, we just disagree over the means. However, within this general agreement over the ultimate end (a classless and stateless society), the details of such a society are somewhat different. This, perhaps, is to be expected given the differences in means. As is obvious from Bakunin's argument, anarchists stress the unity of means and goals, that the means which are used affect the goal reached. This unity between means and ends is expressed well by Martin Buber: "*One cannot in the nature of things expect a little tree that has been turned into a club to put forth leaves.*" [**Paths in Utopia**, p. 127] In summary, we cannot expect to reach our end destination if we take a path going in the opposite direction. As such, the agreement on ends may not be as close as often imagined.

So when it is stated that anarchists and state socialists want the same thing, the following should be borne in mind. Firstly, there are key differences on the question of current tactics. Secondly, there is the question of the immediate aims of a revolution. Thirdly, there is the long term goals of such a revolution. These three aspects form a coherent whole, with each one logically following on from the last. As we will show, the anarchist and Marxist vision of each aspect are distinctly different, so suggesting that the short, medium **and** long term goals of each theory are, in fact, different. We will discuss each aspect in turn.

First, there is the question of the nature of the revolutionary movement. Here anarchists and most Marxists have distinctly opposing ideas. The former argue that both the revolutionary organisation (i.e. an anarchist federation) and the wider labour movement should be organised in line with the vision of society which inspires us. This means that it should be a federation of self-managed groups based on the direct participation of its membership in the decision making process. Power, therefore, is decentralised and there is no division between those who make the decisions and those who execute them. We reject the idea of others acting on our behalf or on behalf of the people and so urge the use of direct action and solidarity, based upon working class self-organisation, self-management and autonomy. Thus, anarchists apply their ideas in the struggle against the current system, arguing what is "efficient" from a hierarchical or class position is deeply inefficient from a revolutionary perspective.

Marxists disagree. Most Marxists are also Leninists. They argue that we must form a "*vanguard*" party based on the principles of "*democratic centralism*" complete with institutionalised and hierarchical leadership. They argue that how we organise today is independent of the kind of society we seek and that the party should aim to become the recognised leadership of the working class. Every thing they do is subordinated to this end, meaning that no struggle is seen as an end in itself but rather as a means to gaining membership and influence for the party until such time as it gathers enough support to seize power. As this is a key point of contention between anarchists and Leninists, we discuss this in some detail in section H.5 and its related sections and so not do so here.

Obviously, in the short term anarchists and Leninists cannot be said to want the same thing. While we seek a revolutionary movement based on libertarian (i.e. revolutionary) principles, the Leninists seek a party based on distinctly bourgeois principles of centralisation, delegation of power and representative over direct democracy. Both, of course, argue that only their system of organisation is effective and efficient (see section H.5.8 on a discussion why anarchists argue that the Leninist model is not effective from a revolutionary perspective). The anarchist perspective is to see the revolutionary organisation as part of the working class, encouraging and helping those in struggle to clarify the ideas they draw from their own experiences and its role is to provide a lead rather than a new set of leaders to be followed (see section J.3.6 for more on this). The Leninist perspective is to see the revolutionary party as the leadership of the working class, introducing socialist consciousness into a class which cannot generate itself (see section H.5.1).

Given the Leninist preference for centralisation and a leadership role by hierarchical organisation, it will come as no surprise that their ideas on the nature of post-revolutionary society are distinctly different from anarchists. While there is a tendency for Leninists to deny that anarchists have a clear idea of what will immediately be created by a revolution (see section H.1.4), we do have concrete ideas on the kind of society a revolution will immediately create. This vision is in almost every way different from that proposed by most Marxists.

Then there is the question of the state. Anarchists, unsurprisingly enough, seek to destroy it. Simply put, while anarchists want a stateless and classless society and advocate the means appropriate to those ends, most Marxists argue that in order to reach a stateless society we need a new "workers'" state, a state, moreover, in which their party will be in charge. Trotsky, writing in 1906, made this clear: "Every political party deserving of the name aims at seizing governmental power and thus putting the state at the service of the class whose interests it represents." [quoted by Israel Getzler, **Marxist Revolutionaries and the Dilemma of Power**, p. 105] This fits in with Marx's and Engels's repeated equation of universal suffrage with the political power or political supremacy of the working class. In other words, "*political power*" simply means the ability to nominate a government (see section H.3.10).

While Marxists like to portray this new government as "*the dictatorship of the proletariat,*" anarchists argue that, in fact, it will be the dictatorship **over** the proletariat. This is because if the working class **is** the ruling class (as Marxists claim) then, anarchists argue, how can they delegate their power to a government and remain so? Either the working class directly manages its own affairs (and so society) or the government does. Any state is simply rule by a few and so is incompatible with socialism (we discuss this issue in section H.3.7). The obvious implication of this is that Marxism seeks party rule, not working class direct management of society (as we discuss in section H.3.8, the Leninist tradition is extremely clear on this matter).

Then there is the question of the building blocks of socialism. Yet again, there is a clear difference between anarchism and Marxism. Anarchists have always argued that the basis of socialism is working class organisations, created in the struggle against capitalism and the state. This applies to both the social and economic structure of a post-revolutionary society. For most forms of Marxism, a radically different picture has been the dominant one. As we discuss in section H.3.10, Marxists only reached a similar vision for the political structure of socialism in 1917 when Lenin supported the soviets as the framework of his workers' state. However, as we prove in section H.3.11, he did so for instrumental purposes only, namely as the best means of assuring Bolshevik power. If the soviets clashed with the party, it was the latter which took precedence. Unsurprisingly, the Bolshevik mainstream moved from "*All Power to the Soviets*" to "*dictatorship of the party*" rather quickly. Thus, unlike anarchism, most forms of Marxism aim for party power, a "revolutionary" government above the organs of working class self-management.

Economically, there are also clear differences. Anarchists have consistently argued that the workers "*ought to be the real managers of industries.*" [Peter Kropotkin, **Fields, Factories and Workshops Tomorrow**, p. 157] To achieve this, we have pointed to various organisations over time, such as factory committees and labour unions. As we discuss in more detail in section H.3.12, Lenin, in contrast, saw socialism as being constructed on the basis of structures and techniques (including management ones) developed under capitalism. Rather than see socialism as being built around new, working class organisations, Lenin saw it being constructed on the basis of developments in capitalist organisation. "*The Leninist road to socialism,*" notes one expert on Lenin, "*emphatically ran through the terrain of monopoly capitalism. It would, according to Lenin, abolish neither its advanced technological base nor its institutionalised means for allocating resources or structuring industry... The institutionalised framework of advanced capitalism could, to put it shortly, be utilised for realisation of specifically socialist goals. They were to become, indeed, the principal (almost exclusive) instruments of socialist transformation.*" [Neil Harding, **Leninism**, p.145]

The role of workers' in this vision was basically unchanged. Rather than demand, like anarchists, workers' self-management of production in 1917, Lenin raised the demand for "*country-wide, all-embracing workers' control over the capitalists*" (and this is the "*important thing*", **not** "*confiscation of the capitalists' property*") [**The Lenin Anthology**, p. 402] Once the Bolsheviks were in power, the workers' own organs (the factory committees) were integrated into a system of state control, losing whatever power they once held at the point of production. Lenin then modified this vision by replacing capitalists with (state appointed) "*one-man management*" over the workers (see section H.3.14). In other words, a form of **state** capitalism in which workers would still be wage slaves under bosses appointed by the state. Unsurprisingly, the "*control*" workers exercised over their bosses (i.e. those with **real** power in production) proved to be as elusive in production as it was in the state. In this, Lenin undoubtedly followed the lead of the **Communist Manifesto** which stressed state ownership of the means of production without a word about workers' self-management of production. As we discuss in section H.3.13, state "socialism" cannot help being "*state *capitalism"* by its very nature.

Needless to say, as far as means go, few anarchists and syndicalists are complete pacifists. As syndicalist Emile Pouget argued, *"[h]istory teaches that the privileged have never surrendered their privileges without having been compelled so to do and forced into it by their rebellious victims. It is unlikely that the bourgeoisie is blessed with an exceptional greatness of soul and will abdicate voluntarily"* and so *"[r]ecourse to force ... will be required."* [**The Party Of Labour**] This does not mean that libertarians glorify violence or argue that all forms of violence are acceptable (quite the reverse!), it simply means that for self-defence against violent opponents violence is, unfortunately, sometimes required.

The way an anarchist revolution would defend itself also shows a key difference between anarchism and Marxism. As we discussed in section H.2.1, anarchists (regardless of Marxist claims) have always argued that a revolution needs to defend itself. This would be organised in a federal, bottom-up way as the social structure of a free society. It would be based on voluntary working class militias. This model of working class self-defence was applied successfully in both the Spanish and Ukrainian revolutions (by the CNT-FAI and the Makhnovists, respectively). In contrast, the Bolshevik method of defending a revolution was the top-down, hierarchical and centralised "Red Army". As the example of the Makhnovists showed, the "Red Army" was not the only way the Russian Revolution could have been defended although it was the only way Bolshevik power could be.

So while Anarchists have consistently argued that socialism must be based on working class self-management of production and society based on working class organisations, the Leninist tradition has not supported this vision (although it has appropriated some of its imagery to gain popular support). Clearly, in terms of the immediate aftermath of a revolution, anarchists and Leninists do not seek the same thing. The former want a free society organised and run from below-upwards by the working class based on workers self-management of production while the latter seek party power in a new state structure which would preside over an essentially state capitalist economy.

Lastly, there is the question of the long term goal. Even in this vision of a classless and stateless society there is very little in common between anarchist communism and Marxist communism, beyond the similar terminology used to describe it. This is blurred by the differences in terminology used by both theories. Marx and Engels had raised in the 1840s the (long term) goal of *"an association, in which the free development of each is the condition for the free development of all"* replacing *"the old bourgeois society, with its classes and class antagonisms,"* in the **Communist Manifesto**. Before this *"vast association of the whole nation"* was possible, the proletariat would be *"raise[d] ... to the position of ruling class"* and *"all capital"* would be *"centralise[d] ... in the hands of the State, i.e. of the proletariat organised as the ruling class."* As economic classes would no longer exist, *"the public power would lose its political character"* as political power *"is merely the organised power of one class for oppressing another."* [**Selected Works**, p. 53]

It was this, the means to the end, which was the focus of much debate (see section H.1.1 for details). However, it cannot be assumed that the ends desired by Marxists and anarchists are identical. The argument that the *"public power"* could stop being *"political"* (i.e. a state) is a tautology, and a particularly unconvincing one at that. After all, if *"political power"* is defined as being an instrument of class rule it automatically follows that a classless society would have a non-political *"public power"* and so be without a state! This does not imply that a *"public power"* would no longer exist as a structure within (or, more correctly, over) society, it just implies that its role would no longer be *"political"* (i.e. an instrument of class rule). Given that, according to the Manifesto, the state would centralise the means of production, credit and transportation and then organise it *"in accordance with a common plan"* using *"industrial armies, especially for agriculture"* this would suggest that the state structure would remain even after its *"political"* aspects had, to use Engels words, *"die[d] out."* [Marx and Engels, **Op. Cit.**, pp. 52-3 and p. 424]

From this perspective, the difference between anarchist communism and Marxist-communism is clear. *"While both,"* notes John Clark, *"foresee the disappearance of the state, the achievement of social management of the economy, the end of class rule, and the attainment of human equality, to mention a few common goals, significant differences in ends still remain. Marxist thought has inherited a vision which looks to high development of technology with a corresponding degree of centralisation of social institutions which will continue even after the coming of the social revolution... . The anarchist vision sees the human scale as essential, both in the techniques which are used for production, and for the institutions which arise from the new modes of association ... In addition, the anarchist ideal has a strong hedonistic element which has seen Germanic socialism as ascetic and Puritanical."* [**The Anarchist Moment**, p. 68] Thus Marx presents *"a formulation that calls not for the ultimate abolition of the State but suggests that it will continue to exist (however differently it is reconstituted by the proletariat) as a 'nonpolitical' (i.e., administrative) source of authority."* [Murray Bookchin, **The Ecology of Freedom**, p. 196fn]

Moreover, it is unlikely that such a centralised system could become stateless and classless in actuality. As Bakunin argued, in the Marxist state *"there will be no privileged class. Everybody will be equal, not only from the judicial and political but also from the economic standpoint. This is the promise at any rate ... So there will be no more class, but a government, and, please note, an extremely complicated government which, not content with governing and administering the masses politically ... will also administer them economically, by taking over the production and **fair** sharing of wealth, agriculture, the establishment and development of factories, the organisation and control of trade, and lastly the injection of capital into production by a single banker, the State."* Such a system would be, in reality, *"the reign of the **scientific mind**, the most aristocratic, despotic, arrogant and contemptuous of all regimes"* based on *"a new class, a new hierarchy of real or bogus learning, and the world will be divided into a dominant, science-based minority and a vast, ignorant majority."* [**Michael Bakunin: Selected Writings**, p. 266]

George Barrett's words also seem appropriate:

> *"The modern Socialist ... have steadily worked for centralisation, and complete and perfect organisation*

and control by those in authority above the people. The anarchist, on the other hand, believes in the abolition of that central power, and expects the free society to grow into existence from below, starting with those organisations and free agreements among the people themselves. It is difficult to see how, by making a central power control everything, we can be making a step towards the abolition of that power." [**Objections to Anarchism**, p. 348]

Indeed, by giving the state increased economic activities it ensures that this so-called "transitional" state grows with the implementation of the Marxist programme. Moreover, given the economic tasks the state now does it hardly makes much sense to assert it will "wither away" - unless you think that the centralised economic planning which this regime does also "withers away." Marx argued that once the *"abolition of classes"* has *"been attained"* then *"the power of the State ... disappears, and the functions of government are transformed into simple administrative functions."* [Marx, Engels and Lenin, **Anarchism and Anarcho-Syndicalism**, p. 76] In other words, the state apparatus does not "wither away" rather its function as an instrument of class rule does. This is an automatic result of classes themselves withering away as private property is nationalised. Yet as class is defined as being rooted in ownership of the means of production, this becomes a meaningless tautology. Obviously, as the state centralises the means of production into its own hands then (the existing) economic classes cease to exist and, as a result, the state "disappears." Yet the power and size of the State is, in fact, increased by this process and so the elimination of economic classes actually increases the power and size of the state machine.

As Brain Morris notes, *"Bakunin's fears that under Marx's kind of socialism the workers would continue to labour under a regimented, mechanised, hierarchical system of production, without direct control over their labour, has been more than confirmed by the realities of the Bolshevik system. Thus, Bakunin's critique of Marxism has taken on an increasing relevance in the age of bureaucratic State capitalism."* [**Bakunin: The Philosophy of Freedom**, p. 132] Thus the *"central confusions of Marxist political theorists"* are found in the discussion on the state in **The Communist Manifesto**. If class is *"an exclusively economic category, and if the old conditions of production are changed so that there is no longer any private ownership of the means of production, then classes no longer exist by definition when they are defined in terms of ... the private ownership of the means of production ... If Marx also defines 'political power' as 'the organised power of one [economic] class for oppressing another', then the ... argument is no more than a tautology, and is trivially true."* Unfortunately, as history has confirmed, *"we cannot conclude ... if it is a mere tautology, that with a condition of no private ownership of the means of production there could be no ... dominant and subordinate strata."* [Alan Carter, **Marx: A Radical Critique**, p. 221 and pp. 221-2]

Unsurprisingly, therefore, anarchists are not convinced that a highly centralised structure (as a state is) managing the economic life of society can be part of a truly classless society. While economic class as defined in terms of ownership of the means of production may

not exist, social classes (defined in terms of inequality of power, authority and control) will continue simply because the state is designed to create and protect minority rule (see section H.3.7). As Bolshevik and Stalinist Russia showed, nationalising the means of production does not end class society. As Malatesta argued:

"When F. Engels, perhaps to counter anarchist criticisms, said that once classes disappear the State as such has no **raison d'être** and transforms itself from a government of men into an administration of things, he was merely playing with words. Whoever has power over things has power over men; whoever governs production also governs the producers; who determines consumption is master over the consumer.

"This is the question; either things are administered on the basis of free agreement of the interested parties, and this is anarchy; or they are administered according to laws made by administrators and this is government, it is the State, and inevitably it turns out to be tyrannical.

"It is not a question of the good intentions or the good will of this or that man, but of the inevitability of the situation, and of the tendencies which man generally develops in given circumstances." [**Errico Malatesta: His Life and Ideas**, p. 145]

The anarchist vision of the future society, therefore, does not exactly match the state communist vision, as much as the latter would like to suggest it does. The difference between the two is authority, which cannot be anything but the largest difference possible. Anarchist economic and organisational theories are built around an anti-authoritarian core and this informs both our means and aims. For anarchists, the Leninist vision of socialism is unattractive. Lenin continually stressed that his conception of socialism and *"state capitalism"* were basically identical. Even in **State and Revolution**, allegedly Lenin's most libertarian work, we discover this particularly unvisionary and uninspiring vision of "socialism":

"**All** citizens are transformed into the salaried employees of the state ... **All** citizens become employees and workers of a **single** national state 'syndicate' ... The whole of society will have become a single office and a single factory with equality of work and equality of pay." [**Essential Works of Lenin**, p. 348]

To which, anarchists point to Engels and his comments on the tyrannical and authoritarian character of the modern factory (as we discuss in section H.4.4). Clearly, Lenin's idea of turning the world into one big factory takes on an extremely frightening nature given Engels' lovely vision of the lack of freedom in the workplace.

For these reasons anarchists reject the simplistic Marxist analysis of inequality being rooted simply in economic class. Such an analysis, as the comments of Lenin and Engels prove, shows that social inequality can be smuggled in by the backdoor of a proposed classless and stateless society. Thus Bookchin:

"Basic to anti-authoritarian Socialism - specifically, to Anarchist Communism - is the notion that hierarchy and *domination cannot be subsumed by class rule and economic exploitation, indeed, that they are more fundamental to an understanding of the modern revolutionary project ... Power of human over human long antedates **the very formation of classes and economic modes of social oppression...** . This much is clear: it will no longer do to insist that a classless society, freed from material exploitation, will necessarily be a liberated society. There is nothing in the social future to suggest that bureaucracy is incompatible with a classless society, the domination of women, the young, ethnic groups or even professional strata.*" [**Toward an Ecological Society**, pp. 208-9]

Ultimately, anarchists see that *"there is a realm of domination that is broader than the realm of material exploitation. The tragedy of the socialist movement is that, steeped in the past, it uses the methods of domination to try to 'liberate' us from material exploitation."* Needless to say, this is doomed to failure. Socialism *"will simply mire us in a world we are trying to overcome. A non-hierarchical society, self-managed and free of domination in all its forms, stands on the agenda today, not a hierarchical system draped in a red flag."* [Bookchin, **Op. Cit.**, p. 272 and pp. 273-4]

In summary, it cannot be said that anarchists and most Marxists want the same thing. While they often use the same terms, these terms often hide radically different concepts. Just because, say, anarchists and mainstream Marxists talk about *"social revolution,"* *"socialism,"* *"all power to the soviets"* and so on, it does not mean that we mean the same thing by them. For example, the phrase *"all power to the soviets"* for anarchists means exactly that (i.e. that the revolution must be directly managed by working class organs). Leninists mean *"all power to a central government elected by a national soviet congress."* Similarly with other similar phrases (which shows the importance of looking at the details of any political theory and its history).

We have shown that discussion over ends is as important as discussion over means as they are related. As Kropotkin once pointed out, those who downplay the importance of discussing the *"order of things which ... should emerge from the coming revolution"* in favour of concentrating on *"practical things"* are being less than honest as *"far from making light of such theories, they propagate them, and all that they do now is a logical extension of their ideas. In the end those words 'Let us not discuss theoretical questions' really mean: 'Do not subject our theory to discussion, but help us to put it into execution.'"* [**Words of a Rebel**, p. 200]

Hence the need to critically evaluate both ends and means. This shows the weakness of the common argument that anarchists and Leftists share some common visions and so we should work with them to achieve those common things. Who knows what happens after that? As can be seen, this is not the case. Many aspects of anarchism and Marxism are in opposition and cannot be considered similar (for example, what a Leninist considers as socialism is extremely different to what an anarchist thinks it is). If you consider "socialism" as being a "workers' state" presided over by a "revolutionary" government, then how can this be reconciled with the anarchist vision of a federation of self-managed communes and workers' associations? As the Russian Revolution shows, only

by the armed might of the *"revolutionary"* government crushing the anarchist vision.

The only thing we truly share with these groups is a mutual opposition to existing capitalism. Having a common enemy does not make someone friends. Hence anarchists, while willing to work on certain mutual struggles, are well aware there are substantial differences in both terms of means and goals. The lessons of revolution in the 20th Century is that once in power, Leninists will repress anarchists, their current allies against the capitalist system. This is does not occur by accident, it flows from the differences in vision between the two movements, both in terms of means and goals.

H.3.2 Is Marxism "socialism from below"?

Some Marxists, such as the **International Socialist Tendency**, like to portray their tradition as being *"socialism from below."* Under *"socialism from below,"* they place the ideas of Marx, Engels, Lenin and Trotsky, arguing that they and they alone have continued this, the true, ideal of socialism (Hal Draper's essay *"The Two Souls of Socialism"* seems to have been the first to argue along these lines). They contrast this idea of socialism *"from below"* with *"socialism from above,"* in which they place reformist socialism (social democracy, Labourism, etc.), elitist socialism (Lassalle and others who wanted educated and liberal members of the middle classes to liberate the working class) and Stalinism (bureaucratic dictatorship over the working class). Anarchism, it is argued, should be placed in the latter camp, with Proudhon and Bakunin showing that anarchist libertarianism is a *"myth"*.

For those who uphold this idea, *"Socialism from below"* is simply the self-emancipation of the working class by its own efforts. To anarchist ears, the claim that Marxism (and in particular Leninism) is socialism *"from below"* sounds paradoxical, indeed laughable. This is because anarchists from Proudhon onwards have used the imagery of socialism being created and run from below upwards. They have been doing so for far longer than Marxists have. As such, *"socialism from below"* simply sums up the **anarchist** ideal!

Thus we find Proudhon in 1846 arguing that socialism *"springs up and grows from below"* and a few years later how *"**from below** signifies the people ... the initiative of the masses."* Every *"serious and lasting Revolution"* was *"made **from below**, by the people."* A *"Revolution **from above**"* was *"pure governmentalism,"* *"the negation of collective activity, of popular spontaneity"* and is *"the oppression of the wills of those below."* The means of this revolution *"from below"* would be federations of working class associations for both credit (mutual banks) and production (workers' associations or co-operatives) as well as federations of communes (democratically organised communities). He *"had always thought that the proletariat must emancipate itself without the help of the government"* and so the *"revolutionary power ... is in you. The people alone, acting upon themselves without intermediary, can achieve the economic Revolution ... The people alone can save civilisation and advance humanity!"* Thus capitalism would be reformed away by the actions of the workers themselves. The *"problem of association,"* he argued, "consists in organising ... the producers, and by this subjecting capital and subordinating power. Such is the war of liberty against authority, a war of the producer against the non-producer; a war of equality against privilege ... An agricultural and industrial combination must be found by means of which power, today the ruler of society, shall become its slave." Ultimately, "any revolution, to be effective, must be spontaneous and emanate, not from the heads of authorities, but from the bowels of the people ... the only connection between government and labour is that labour, in organising itself, has the abrogation of governments as its mission." [**Property is Theft!**, p. 205, p. 398, pp. 26-7, p. 306, p. 336, p. 225 and p. 26]

Similarly, Bakunin saw an anarchist revolution as coming "from below." As he put it, "liberty can be created only by liberty, by an insurrection of all the people and the voluntary organisation of the workers from below upward." [**Statism and Anarchy**, p. 179] Elsewhere he wrote that "popular revolution" would "create its own organisation from the bottom upwards and from the circumference inwards, in accordance with the principle of liberty, and not from the top downwards and from the centre outwards, as in the way of authority." [**Michael Bakunin: Selected Writings**, p. 170] His vision of revolution and revolutionary self-organisation and construction from below was a core aspect of his anarchist ideas and he argued repeatedly for "the free organisation of the people's lives in accordance with their needs - not from the top down, as we have it in the State, but from the bottom up, an organisation formed by the people themselves ... a free union of associations of agricultural and factory workers, of communes, regions, and nations." He stressed that "the politics of the Social Revolution" was "the abolition of the State" and "the economic, altogether free organisation of the people, an organisation from below upward, by means of federation." [**The Political Philosophy of Bakunin**, pp. 297-8]

While Proudhon wanted to revolutionise society, he rejected revolutionary means to do so (i.e. collective struggle, strikes, insurrection, etc.). Bakunin, however, was a revolutionary in this, the popular, sense of the word. Yet he shared with Proudhon the idea of socialism being created by the working class itself. As he put it, in "a social revolution, which in everything is diametrically opposed to a political revolution, the actions of individuals hardly count at all, whereas the spontaneous action of the masses is everything. All that individuals can do is clarify, propagate and work out the ideas corresponding to the popular instinct, and, what is more, to contribute their incessant efforts to revolutionary organisation of the natural power of the masses - but nothing else beyond that; the rest can and should be done by the people themselves ... revolution can be waged and brought to its full development only through the spontaneous and continued mass action of groups and associations of the people." [**Op. Cit.**, pp. 298-9]

Therefore, the idea of "socialism from below" is a distinctly anarchist notion, one found in the works of Proudhon and Bakunin and repeated by anarchists ever since. As such, to hear Marxists appropriate this obviously anarchist terminology and imagery appears to many anarchists as opportunistic and an attempt to cover the authoritarian reality of mainstream Marxism with anarchist rhetoric. Moreover, the attempt to suggest that anarchism is part of the elitist "socialism from above" school rests on little more than selective quoting of Proudhon and Bakunin (including from Bakunin's pre-anarchist days) to present a picture of their ideas distinctly at odds with reality. However, there are "libertarian" strains of Marxism which are close to anarchism. Does this mean that there are no elements of a "socialism from below" to be found in Marx and Engels?

If we look at Marx, we get contradictory impressions. On the one hand, he argued that freedom "consists in converting the state from an organ superimposed upon society into one completely subordinate to it." Combine this with his comments on the Paris Commune (see his "The Civil War in France"), we can say that there are clearly elements of "socialism from below" in Marx's work. On the other hand, he often stresses the need for strict centralisation of power. In 1850, for example, he argued that the workers must "not only strive for a single and indivisible German republic, but also within this republic for the most determined centralisation of power in the hands of the state authority." This was because "the path of revolutionary activity" can "proceed only from the centre." This meant that the workers must be opposed to the "federative republic" planned by the democrats and "must not allow themselves to be misguided by the democratic talk of freedom for the communities, of self-government, etc." This centralisation of power was essential to overcome local autonomy, which would allow "every village, every town and every province" to put "a new obstacle in the path" the revolution due to "local and provincial obstinacy." Decades later, Marx dismissed Bakunin's vision of "the free organisation of the worker masses from bottom to top" as "nonsense." [**Marx-Engels Reader**, p. 537, p. 509 and p. 547]

Thus we have a contradiction. While arguing that the state must become subordinate to society, we have a central power imposing its will on "local and provincial obstinacy." This implies a vision of revolution in which the centre (indeed, "the state authority") forces its will on the population, which (by necessity) means that the centre power is "superimposed upon society" rather than "subordinate" to it. Given his dismissal of the idea of organisation from bottom to top, we cannot argue that by this he meant simply the co-ordination of local initiatives. Rather, we are struck by the "top-down" picture of revolution Marx presents. Indeed, his argument from 1850 suggests that Marx favoured centralism not only in order to prevent the masses from creating obstacles to the revolutionary activity of the "centre," but also to prevent them from interfering with their own liberation.

Looking at Engels, we discover him writing that "[a]s soon as our Party is in possession of political power it has simply to expropriate the big landed proprietors just like the manufacturers in industry ... thus restored to the community [they] are to be turned over by us to the rural workers who are already cultivating them and are to be organised into co-operatives." He even states that this expropriation may "be compensated," depending on "the circumstances which we obtain power, and particularly by the attitude adopted by these gentry." [**Selected Writings**, pp. 638-9] Thus we have the party taking power, then expropriating the means of life **for the workers** and, lastly, "turning over" these to them. While this fits into the general scheme of the **Communist Manifesto**, it cannot be said to be "socialism from below" which can only signify the direct expropriation of the means of production by the workers themselves, organising themselves into free producer associations to do so.

It may be argued that Marx and Engels did not exclude such a solution to the social question. For example, we find Engels stating that *"the question is not whether the proletariat when it comes to power will simply seize by force the tools of production, the raw materials and means of subsistence"* or *"whether it will redeem property therein by instalments spread over a long period."* To attempt to predict this *"for all cases would be utopia-making."* [**Collected Works**, vol. 23, p. 386] However, Engels is assuming that the political revolution (the proletariat *"com[ing] to power"*) comes **before** the social revolution (the seizure of the means of production). In this, we can assume that it is the "revolutionary" government which does the seizing (or redeeming) rather than rebel workers.

This vision of revolution as the party coming to power can be seen from Engels' warning that the *"worse thing that can befall the leader of an extreme party is to be compelled to assume power at a time when the movement is not yet ripe for the domination of the class he represents and for the measures this domination implies."* [**Op. Cit.**, vol. 10, p. 469] Needless to say, such a vision is hard to equate with *"socialism from below"* which implies the active participation of the working class in the direct management of society from the bottom-up. If the leaders *"assume power"* then **they** have the real power, not the class they claim to *"represent."* Equally, it seems strange that socialism can be equated with a vision which equates *"domination"* of a class being achieved by the fact a leader *"represents"* it. Can the working class really be said to be the ruling class if its role in society is to select those who exercise power on its behalf (i.e. to elect representatives)? Bakunin quite rightly answered in the negative. While representative democracy may be acceptable to ensure bourgeois rule, it cannot be assumed that it can be utilised to create a socialist society. It was designed to defend class society and its centralised and top-down nature reflects this role.

Moreover, Marx and Engels had argued in **The Holy Family** that the *"question is not what this or that proletarian, or even the whole of the proletariat at the moment **considers** as its aim. The question is **what the proletariat is**, and what, consequent on that **being**, it will be compelled to do."* [quoted by Murray Bookchin, **The Spanish Anarchists**, p. 280] As Murray Bookchin argued:

> *"These lines and others like them in Marx's writings were to provide the rationale for asserting the authority of Marxist parties and their armed detachments over and even against the proletariat. Claiming a deeper and more informed comprehension of the situation than 'even the whole of the proletariat at the given moment,' Marxist parties went on to dissolve such revolutionary forms of proletarian organisation as factory committees and ultimately to totally regiment the proletariat according to lines established by the party leadership."* [**Op. Cit.**, p. 289]

Thus the ideological underpinning of a *"socialism from above"* is expounded, one which dismisses what the members of the working class actually want or desire at a given point (a position which Trotsky, for one, explicitly argued). A few years later, they argued in **The Communist Manifesto** that *"a portion of the bourgeois goes over to the proletariat, and in particular, a portion of the bourgeois ideologists, who have raised themselves to the level of comprehending theoretically the historical movement as a whole."* They also noted that the Communists are *"the most advanced and resolute section of the working-class parties"* and *"they have over the great mass of the proletariat the advantage of clearly understanding the line of march, the conditions, and the general results of the proletarian movement."* This gives a privileged place to the party (particularly the *"bourgeois ideologists"* who join it), a privileged place which their followers had no problem abusing in favour of party power and hierarchical leadership from above. As we discuss in section H.5, Lenin was just expressing orthodox Social-Democratic (i.e. Marxist) policy when he argued that socialist consciousness was created by bourgeois intellectuals and introduced into the working class from outside. Against this, we have to note that the Manifesto states that the proletarian movement was *"the self-conscious, independent movement of the immense majority, in the interests of the immense majority"* (although, as discussed in section H.1.1, when they wrote this the proletariat was a **minority** in all countries bar Britain). [**Selected Works**, p. 44, p. 46 and p. 45]

Looking at the tactics advocated by Marx and Engels, we see a strong support for *"political action"* in the sense of participating in elections. This support undoubtedly flows from Engels's comments that universal suffrage *"in an England two-thirds of whose inhabitants are industrial proletarians means the exclusive political rule of the working class with all the revolutionary changes in social conditions which are inseparable from it."* [**Collected Works**, vol. 10, p. 298] Marx, likewise, repeatedly argued along identical lines. For example, in 1855, he stated that *"universal suffrage … implies the assumption of political power as means of satisfying [the workers'] social means"* and, in Britain, *"revolution is the direct content of universal suffrage."* [**Op. Cit.**, vol. 11, pp. 335-6] Yet how could an entire class, the proletariat organised as a *"movement"* exercise its power under such a system? While the atomised voting to nominate representatives (who, in reality, held the real power in society) may be more than adequate to ensure bourgeois, i.e. minority, power, could it be used for working class, i.e. majority, power?

This seems highly unlikely because such institutions are designed to place policy-making in the hands of representatives and were created explicitly to **exclude** mass participation in order to ensure bourgeois control (see section B.2.5). They do not (indeed, cannot) constitute a *"proletariat organised as a ruling class."* If public policy, as distinguished from administrative activities, is not made by the people themselves, in federations of self-managed assemblies, then a movement of the vast majority does not, cannot, exist. For people to acquire real power over their lives and society, they must establish institutions organised and run, as Bakunin constantly stressed, from below. This would necessitate that they themselves directly manage their own affairs, communities and workplaces and, for co-ordination, mandate federal assemblies of revocable and strictly controllable delegates, who will execute their decisions. Only in this sense can a majority class, especially one committed to the abolition of all classes, organise as a class to manage society. As such, Marx and Engels tactics are at odds with any idea of *"socialism from below."* While, correctly, supporting strikes and other forms of working class direct action (although, significantly, Engels dismissed the general strike) they placed that support within a general political strategy which emphasised electioneering and representative forms. This, however, is a form of struggle which can only really be carried out by means of leaders. The role of the masses is minor, that of voters. The focus of the struggle is at the top, in parliament, where the duly elected leaders are. As Luigi Galleani argued, this form of action involved the *"ceding of power by all to someone, the delegate, the representative, individual or group."* This meant that rather than the anarchist tactic of *"direct pressure put against the ruling classes by the masses,"* the Socialist Party *"substituted representation and the rigid discipline of the parliamentary socialists,"* which inevitably resulted in it *"adopt[ing] class collaboration in the legislative arena, without which all reforms would remain a vain hope."* It also resulted in the socialists needing *"authoritarian organisations"*, i.e. ones which are centralised and disciplined from above down. [**The End of Anarchism?**, p. 14, p. 12 and p. 14] The end result was the encouragement of a viewpoint that reforms (indeed, the revolution) would be the work of leaders acting on behalf of the masses whose role would be that of voters and followers, not active participants in the struggle (see section J.2 for a discussion on direct action and why anarchists reject electioneering).

By the 1890s, the top-down and essentially reformist nature of these tactics had made their mark in both Engels' politics and the practical activities of the Social-Democratic parties. Engels introduction to Marx's **The Class Struggles in France** indicated how far Marxism had progressed and undoubtedly influenced by the rise of Social-Democracy as an electoral power, it stressed the use of the ballot box as the ideal way, if not the only way, for the party to take power. He noted that *"[w]e, the 'revolutionists', the 'overthrowers'"* were *"thriving far better on legal methods than on illegal methods and overthrow"* and the bourgeoisie *"cry despairingly ... legality is the death of us"* and were *"much more afraid of the legal than of the illegal action of the workers' party, of the results of elections than of those of rebellion."* He argued that it was essential *"not to fitter away this daily increasing shock force [of party voters] in vanguard skirmishes, but to keep it intact until the decisive day."* [**Selected Writings**, p. 656, p. 650 and p. 655]

The net effect of this would simply be keeping the class struggle within the bounds decided upon by the party leaders, so placing the emphasis on the activities and decisions of those at the top rather than the struggle and decisions of the mass of working class people themselves. As we noted in section H.1.1, when the party was racked by the *"revisionism"* controversy after Engels death, it was fundamentally a conflict between those who wanted the party's rhetoric to reflect its reformist tactics and those who sought the illusion of radical words to cover the reformist practice. The decision of the Party leadership to support their state in the First World War simply proved that radical words cannot defeat reformist tactics.

Needless to say, from this contradictory inheritance Marxists had two ways of proceeding. Either they become explicitly anti-state (and so approach anarchism) or become explicitly in favour of party and state power and so, by necessity, *"revolution from above."* The council communists and other libertarian Marxists followed the first path, the Bolsheviks and their followers the second. As we discuss in the next section, Lenin explicitly dismissed the idea that Marxism proceeded *"only from below,"* stating that this was an anarchist principle. Nor was he shy in equating party power with working class power.

All this is to be expected, given the weakness of the Marxist theory of the state. As we discuss in section H.3.7, Marxists have always had an a-historic perspective on the state, considering it as purely an instrument of class rule rather than what it is, an instrument of **minority** class rule. For anarchists, the *"State is the minority government, from the top downward, of a vast quantity of men."* This automatically means that a socialism, like Marx's, which aims for a socialist government and a workers' state automatically becomes, against the wishes of its best activists, *"socialism from above."* As Bakunin argued, Marxists are *"worshippers of State power, and necessarily also prophets of political and social discipline and champions of order established from the top downwards, always in the name of universal suffrage and the sovereignty of the masses, for whom they save the honour and privilege of obeying leaders, elected masters."* [**Michael Bakunin: Selected Writings**, p. 265 and pp. 237-8]

For this reason anarchists from Bakunin onwards have argued for a bottom-up federation of workers' councils as the basis of revolution and the means of managing society after capitalism and the state have been abolished. If these organs of workers' self-management are co-opted into a state structure (as happened in Russia) then their power will be handed over to the real power in any state - the government and its bureaucracy. The state is the delegation of power - as such, it means that the idea of a *"workers' state"* expressing *"workers' power"* is a logical impossibility. If workers are running society then power rests in their hands. If a state exists then power rests in the hands of the handful of people at the top, not in the hands of all. The state was designed for minority rule. No state can be an organ of working class (i.e. majority) self-management due to its basic nature, structure and design.

So, while there are elements of *"socialism from below"* in the works of Marx and Engels they are placed within a distinctly centralised and authoritarian context which undermines them. As John Clark summarises, *"in the context of Marx's consistent advocacy of centralist programmes, and the part these programmes play in his theory of social development, the attempt to construct a **libertarian** Marxism by citing Marx's own proposals for social change would seem to present insuperable difficulties."* [**Op. Cit.**, p. 93]

H.3.3 Is Leninism "socialism from below"?

As discussed in the last section, Marx and Engels left their followers with an ambiguous legacy. On the one hand, there **are** elements of *"socialism from below"* in their politics (most explicitly in Marx's comments on the libertarian influenced Paris Commune). On the other, there are distinctly centralist and statist themes in their work.

From this legacy, Leninism took the statist themes. This explains why anarchists think the idea of Leninism being *"socialism from below"* is incredible. Simply put, the actual comments and actions of Lenin and his followers show that they had no commitment to a *"socialism from below."* As we will indicate, Lenin disassociated himself repeatedly from the idea of politics *"from below,"* considering it (quite rightly) an anarchist idea. In contrast, he stressed the importance of a politics which somehow combined action *"from above"* and *"from below."* For those Leninists who maintain that their tradition is *"socialism from below"* (indeed, the only *"real"* socialism *"from below"*), this is a major problem and, unsurprisingly, they generally fail to mention it.

So what was Lenin's position on *"from below"*? In 1904, during the debate over the party split into Bolsheviks and Mensheviks, Lenin stated that the argument *"[b]ureaucracy **versus** democracy is in fact centralism **versus** autonomism; it is the organisational principle of revolutionary Social-Democracy as opposed to the organisational principle of opportunist Social-Democracy. The latter strives to proceed from the bottom upward, and, therefore, wherever possible ... upholds autonomism and 'democracy,' carried (by the overzealous) to the point of anarchism. The former strives to proceed from the top downward."* [**Collected Works**, vol. 7, pp. 396-7] Thus it is the non-Bolshevik (*"opportunist"*) wing of Marxism which bases itself on the *"organisational principle"* of *"from the bottom upward,"* not the Bolshevik tradition (as we note in section H.5.5, Lenin also rejected the *"primitive democracy"* of mass assemblies as the basis of the labour and revolutionary movements). Moreover, this vision of a party run from the top down was enshrined in the Bolshevik ideal of *"democratic centralism"*. How you can have *"socialism from below"* when your *"organisational principle"* is *"from the top downward"* is not explained by Leninist exponents of *"socialism from below."*

Lenin repeated this argument in his discussion on the right tactics to apply during the near revolution of 1905. He mocked the Mensheviks for only wanting *"pressure from below"* which was *"pressure by the citizens on the revolutionary government."* Instead, he argued for *"pressure ... from above as well as from below,"* where *"pressure from above"* was *"pressure by the revolutionary government on the citizens."* He notes that Engels *"appreciated the importance of action from above"* and that he saw the need for *"the utilisation of the revolutionary governmental power."* Lenin summarised his position (which he considered as being in line with that of orthodox Marxism) by stating: *"Limitation, in principle, of revolutionary action to pressure from below and renunciation of pressure also from above is **anarchism.**"* [**Op. Cit.**, vol. 8, p. 474, p. 478, p. 480

and p. 481] This seems to have been a common Bolshevik position at the time, with Stalin stressing in the same year that *"action only from 'below'"* was *"an anarchist principle, which does, indeed, fundamentally contradict Social-Democratic tactics."* [**Collected Works**, vol. 1, p. 149]

It is in this context of *"above and below"* in which we must place Lenin's comments in 1917 that socialism was *"democracy from below, without a police, without a standing army, voluntary social duty by a **militia** formed from a universally armed people."* [**Op. Cit.**, vol. 24, p. 170] Given that Lenin had rejected the idea of *"only from below"* as an anarchist principle (which it is), we need to bear in mind that this *"democracy from below"* was **always** placed in the context of a Bolshevik government. Lenin always stressed that the *"Bolsheviks must assume power."* The Bolsheviks *"can and **must** take state power into their own hands."* He raised the question of *"will the Bolsheviks dare take over full state power alone?"* and answered it: *"I have already had occasion ... to answer this question in the affirmative."* Moreover, *"a political party ... would have no right to exist, would be unworthy of the name of party ... if it refused to take power when opportunity offers."* [**Op. Cit.**, vol. 26, p. 19 and p. 90] Lenin's *"democracy from below"* always meant representative government, **not** popular power or self-management. The role of the working class was that of voters and so the Bolsheviks' first task was *"to convince the majority of the people that its programme and tactics are correct."* The second task *"that confronted our Party was to capture political power."* The third task was for *"the Bolshevik Party"* to **administer** Russia,*"* to be the *"governing party."* [**Op. Cit.**, vol. 27, pp. 241-2] Thus Bolshevik power was equated with working class power.

Towards the end of 1917, he stressed this vision of a Bolshevik run *"democracy from below"* by arguing that since *"the 1905 revolution Russia has been governed by 130,000 landowners ... Yet we are told that the 240,000 members of the Bolshevik party will not be able to govern Russia, govern her in the interests of the poor."* He even equated rule by the party with rule by the class, noting that *"proletarian revolutionary power"* and *Bolshevik power"* are *"now one the same thing."* He admitted that the proletariat could not actually govern itself for *"[w]e know that an unskilled labourer or a cook cannot immediately get on with the job of state administration ... We demand that **training** in th[is] work ... be conducted by the class-conscious workers and soldiers."* The *"class-conscious workers must lead, but for the work of administration they can enlist the vast mass of the working and oppressed people."* Thus democratic sounding rhetoric, in reality, hid the fact that the party would govern (i.e., have power) and working people would simply administer the means by which its decisions would be implemented. Lenin also indicated that once in power, the Bolsheviks *"shall be fully and unreservedly in favour of a strong state power and of centralism."* [**Op. Cit.**, vol. 26, p. 111, p. 179, p. 113, p. 114 and p. 116]

Clearly, Lenin's position had not changed. The goal of the revolution was simply a Bolshevik government, which, if it were to be effective, had to have the real power in society. Thus, socialism would be implemented from above, by the *"strong"* and centralised government of the *"class-conscious workers"* who would *"lead"* and so the party would *"govern"* Russia, in the *"interests"* of the masses. Rather than govern themselves, they would be subject to *"the power of the Bolsheviks"*. While, eventually, the *"working"* masses would take part in the administration of state decisions, their role would be the same as under capitalism as, we must note, there is a difference between making policy and carrying it out, between the *"work of administration"* and governing, a difference Lenin obscures. In fact, the name of this essay clearly shows who would be in control under Lenin: *"Can the Bolsheviks retain State Power?"*

As one expert noted, the Bolsheviks made *"a distinction between the execution of policy and the making of policy. The 'broad masses' were to be the executors of state decrees, not the formulators of legislation."* However, by *"claiming to draw 'all people' into [the state] administration, the Bolsheviks claimed also that they were providing a greater degree of democracy than the parliamentary state."* [Frederick I. Kaplan, **Bolshevik Ideology and the Ethics of Soviet Labor**, p. 212] The difference is important. Ante Ciliga, a political prisoner under Stalin, once noted how the secret police *"liked to boast of the working class origin of its henchmen."* He quoted a fellow prisoner, and ex-Tsarist convict, who retorted: *"You are wrong if you believe that in the days of the Tsar the gaolers were recruited from among dukes and the executioners from among the princes!"* [**The Russian Enigma**, pp. 255-6]

All of which explains the famous leaflet addressed to the workers of Petrograd immediately after the October Revolution, informing them that *"the revolution has won."* The workers were called upon to *"show ... **the greatest firmness and endurance,** in order to facilitate the execution of all the aims of the new People's Government."* They were asked to *"cease immediately all economic and political strikes, to take up your work, and do it in perfect order ... All to your places"* as the *"best way to support the new Government of Soviets in these days"* was *"by doing your job."* [quoted by John Reed, **Ten Days that Shook the World**, pp. 341-2] Which smacks far more of *"socialism from above"* than *"socialism from below"*!

The implications of Lenin's position became clearer after the Bolsheviks had taken power. Now it was the concrete situation of a "revolutionary" government exercising power *"from above"* onto the very class it claimed to represent. As Lenin explained to his political police, the Cheka, in 1920:

> *"Without revolutionary coercion directed against the avowed enemies of the workers and peasants, it is impossible to break down the resistance of these exploiters. On the other hand, revolutionary coercion is bound to be employed towards the wavering and unstable elements among the masses themselves."* [**Op. Cit.**, vol. 42, p. 170]

It could be argued that this position was forced on Lenin by the problems facing the Bolsheviks in the Civil War, but such an argument is flawed. This is for two main reasons. Firstly, according to Lenin himself civil war was inevitable and so, unsurprisingly, Lenin considered his comments as universally applicable. Secondly, this position fits in well with the idea of pressure *"from above"* exercised by the "revolutionary" government against the masses (and nothing to do with any sort of *"socialism from below"*). Indeed, *"wavering"* and *"unstable"* elements is just another way of saying *"pressure*

from below," the attempts by those subject to the "revolutionary" government to influence its policies. As we noted in section H.1.2, it was in this period (1919 and 1920) that the Bolsheviks openly argued that the *"dictatorship of the proletariat"* was, in fact, the *"dictatorship of the party"* (see section H.3.8 on how the Bolsheviks modified the Marxist theory of the state in line with this). Rather than the result of the problems facing Russia at the time, Lenin's comments simply reflect the unfolding of certain aspects of his ideology when his party held power (as we make clear in section H.6.2 the ideology of the ruling party and the ideas held by the masses are also factors in history).

To show that Lenin's comments were not caused by circumstantial factors, we can turn to his infamous work **Left-Wing Communism**. In this 1920 tract, written for the Second Congress of the Communist International, Lenin lambasted those Marxists who argued for direct working class power against the idea of party rule (i.e. the various council communists around Europe). We have already noted in section H.1.2 that Lenin had argued in that work that it was *"ridiculously absurd, and stupid"* to *"a contrast, **in general**, between the dictatorship of the masses and the dictatorship of the leaders."* [**The Lenin Anthology**, p. 568] Here we provide his description of the *"top-down"* nature of Bolshevik rule:

> *"In Russia today, the connection between leaders, party, class and masses ... are concretely as follows: the dictatorship is exercised by the proletariat organised in the Soviets and is guided by the Communist Party ... The Party, which holds annual congresses ..., is directed by a Central Committee of nineteen elected at the congress, while the current work in Moscow has to be carried on by [two] still smaller bodies ... which are elected at the plenary sessions of the Central Committee, five members of the Central Committee to each bureau. This, it would appear, is a full-fledged 'oligarchy.' No important political or organisational question is decided by any state institution in our republic [sic!] without the guidance of the Party's Central Committee.*

> *"In its work, the Party relies directly on the **trade unions**, which ...have a membership of over four million and are formally **non-Party**. Actually, all the directing bodies of the vast majority of the unions ... are made up of Communists, and carry out all of the directives of the Party. Thus ... we have a formally non-communist ... very powerful proletarian apparatus, by means of which the Party is closely linked up with the **class** and **the masses,** and by means of which, under the leadership of the Party, the **class dictatorship** of the class is exercised."* [**Op. Cit.**, pp. 571-2]

This was *"the general mechanism of the proletarian state power viewed 'from above,' from the standpoint of the practical realisation of the dictatorship"* and so *"all this talk about 'from above' **or** 'from below,' about 'the dictatorship of leaders' **or** 'the dictatorship of the masses,'"* is *"ridiculous and childish nonsense."* [**Op. Cit.**, p. 573] Lenin, of course, did not bother to view *"proletarian"* state power *"from below,"* from the viewpoint of the proletariat. If he had, perhaps he would have recounted the numerous strikes and protests broken by the Cheka under martial law, the gerrymandering and disbanding of soviets, the imposition of *"one-man management"* onto the workers in production, the turning of the unions into agents of the state/party and the elimination of working class freedom by party power? Which suggests that there are fundamental differences, at least for the masses, between *"from above"* and *"from below."*

At the Comintern congress itself, Zinoviev announced that *"the dictatorship of the proletariat is at the same time the dictatorship of the Communist Party."* [**Proceedings and Documents of the Second Congress 1920**, vol. 1, p. 152] Trotsky also universalised Lenin's argument when he pondered the important decisions of the revolution and who would make them in his reply to the delegate from the Spanish anarcho-syndicalist union the CNT:

> *"Who decides this question [and others like it]? We have the Council of People's Commissars but it has to be subject to some supervision. Whose supervision? That of the working class as an amorphous, chaotic mass? No. The Central Committee of the party is convened to discuss ... and to decide ... Who will solve these questions in Spain? The Communist Party of Spain."* [**Op. Cit.**, p. 174]

Clearly, the claim that Leninism (and its various off-shoots like Trotskyism) is *"socialism from below"* is hard to take seriously. As proven above, the Leninist tradition is explicitly against the idea of *"only from below,"* with Lenin explicitly stating that it was an *"anarchist stand"* to be for *"'action only from below', not 'from below and from above'"* which was the position of Marxism. [**Collected Works**, vol. 9, p. 77] Once in power, Lenin and the Bolsheviks implemented this vision of *"from below and from above,"* with the highly unsurprising result that *"from above"* quickly repressed *"from below"* (which was dismissed as *"wavering"* by the masses). This was to be expected, for a government to enforce its laws, it has to have power over its citizens and so socialism *"from above"* is a necessary side-effect of Leninist theory.

Ironically, Lenin's argument in **State and Revolution** comes back to haunt him. In that work he had argued that the *"dictatorship of the proletariat"* meant *"democracy for the people"* which *"imposes a series of restrictions on the freedom of the oppressors, the exploiters, the capitalists."* These must be crushed *"in order to free humanity from wage-slavery; their resistance must be broken by force; it is clear that where there is suppression there is also violence, there is no freedom, no democracy."* [**Essential Works of Lenin**, pp. 337-8] If the working class itself is being subject to *"suppression"* then, clearly, there is *"no freedom, no democracy"* for that class - and the people *"will feel no better if the stick with which they are being beaten is labelled 'the people's stick'."* [Bakunin, **Bakunin on Anarchism**, p. 338]

So when Leninists argue that they stand for the *"principles of socialism from below"* and state that this means the direct and democratic control of society by the working class then, clearly, they are being less than honest. Looking at the tradition they place themselves in, the obvious conclusion which must be reached is that Leninism is **not** based on *"socialism from below"* in the sense of working class self-management of society (i.e. the only condition when the majority can *"rule"* and decisions truly flow from below

upwards). At best, they subscribe to the distinctly bourgeois vision of *"democracy"* as being simply the majority designating (and trying to control) its rulers. At worst, they defend politics which have eliminated even this form of democracy in favour of party dictatorship and *"one-man management"* armed with *"dictatorial"* powers in industry (most members of such parties do not know how the Bolsheviks gerrymandered and disbanded soviets to maintain power, raised the dictatorship of the party to an ideological truism and wholeheartedly advocated *"one-man management"* rather than workers' self-management of production). As we discuss in section H.5, this latter position flows easily from the underlying assumptions of vanguardism which Leninism is based on.

So, Lenin, Trotsky and so on simply cannot be considered as exponents of *"socialism from below."* Any one who makes such a claim is either ignorant of the actual ideas and practice of Bolshevism or they seek to deceive. For anarchists, *"socialism from below"* can only be another name, like libertarian socialism, for anarchism (as Lenin, ironically enough, acknowledged). This does not mean that *"socialism from below,"* like *"libertarian socialism,"* is identical to anarchism, it simply means that libertarian Marxists and other socialists are far closer to anarchism than mainstream Marxism.

H.3.4 Don't anarchists just quote Marxists selectively?

No, far from it. While it is impossible to quote everything a person or an ideology says, it is possible to summarise those aspects of a theory which influenced the way it developed in practice. As such, **any** account is *"selective"* in some sense, the question is whether this results in a critique rooted in the ideology and its practice or whether it presents a picture at odds with both. As Maurice Brinton put it in the introduction to his classic account of workers' control in the Russian Revolution:

> *"Other charges will also be made. The quotations from Lenin and Trotsky will not be denied but it will be stated that they are 'selective' and that 'other things, too' were said. Again, we plead guilty ... It ... seems more relevant to quote those statements of the Bolshevik leaders of 1917 which helped determine Russia's evolution [towards Stalinism] rather those other statements which ... were forever to remain in the realm of rhetoric."* [**The Bolsheviks and Workers' Control**, p. xv]

Hence the need to discuss all aspects of Marxism rather than take what its adherents like to claim for it as granted. In this, we agree with Marx himself who argued that we cannot judge people by what they say about themselves but rather what they do. Unfortunately while many self-proclaimed Marxists (like Trotsky) may quote these comments, fewer apply them to their own ideology or actions (again, like Trotsky).

This can be seen from the almost ritualistic way many Marxists respond to anarchist (or other) criticisms of their ideas. When they complain that anarchists *"selectively"* quote from the leading proponents of Marxism, they are usually at pains to point people to some document which they have selected as being more *"representative"* of their tradition. Leninists usually point to Lenin's **State and Revolution**, for example, for a vision of what Lenin *"really"* wanted. To this anarchists reply by, as we discussed in section H.1.7, pointing out that much of what passes for 'Marxism' in **State and Revolution** is anarchist and, equally important, it was not applied in practice. This explains an apparent contradiction. Leninists point to the Russian Revolution as evidence for the democratic nature of their politics. Anarchists point to it as evidence of Leninism's authoritarian nature. Both can do this because there is a substantial difference between Bolshevism before it took power and afterwards. While the Leninists ask you to judge them by their manifesto, anarchists say judge them by their record!

Simply put, Marxists quote selectively from their own tradition, ignoring those aspects of it which would be unappealing to potential recruits. While the leaders may know their tradition has skeletons in its closet, they try their best to ensure no one else gets to know. Which, of course, explains their hostility to anarchists doing so! That there is a deep divide between aspects of Marxist rhetoric and its practice and that even its rhetoric is not consistent we will now prove. By so doing, we can show that anarchists do not, in fact, quote Marxist's *"selectively."*

As an example, we can point to the leading Bolshevik Grigorii Zinoviev. In 1920, as head of the Communist International he wrote a letter to the **Industrial Workers of the World**, a revolutionary labour union, which stated that the *"Russian Soviet Republic ... is the most highly centralised government that exists. It is also the most democratic government in history. For all the organs of government are in constant touch with the working masses, and constantly sensitive to their will."* [**Proceedings and Documents of the Second Congress 1920**, vol. 2, p. 928] The same year he explained to the Second Congress of the Communist International that *"[t]oday, people like Kautsky come along and say that in Russia you do not have the dictatorship of the working class but the dictatorship of the party. They think this is a reproach against us. Not in the least! We have a dictatorship of the working class and that is precisely why we also have a dictatorship of the Communist Party. The dictatorship of the Communist Party is only a function, an attribute, an expression of the dictatorship of the working class ... the dictatorship of the proletariat is at the same time the dictatorship of the Communist Party."* [**Op. Cit.**, vol. 1, pp. 151-2] It seems redundant to note that the second quote is the accurate one, the one which matches the reality of Bolshevik Russia. Therefore it is hardly *"selective"* to quote the latter and not the former, as it expresses the reality of Bolshevism rather than its rhetoric.

This duality and the divergence between practice and rhetoric comes to the fore when Trotskyists discuss Stalinism and try to counter pose the Leninist tradition to it. For example, we find the British SWP's Chris Harman arguing that the *"whole experience of the workers' movement internationally teaches that only by regular elections, combined with the right of recall by shop-floor meetings can rank-and-file delegates be made really responsible to those who elect them."* [**Bureaucracy and Revolution in Eastern Europe**, pp. 238-9] Significantly, Harman does not mention that both Lenin and Trotsky rejected this experience once in power. As we discuss in section H.3.8, Leninism came not only to practice but to argue

theoretically for state power explicitly to eliminate such control from below. How can the numerous statements of leading Leninists (including Lenin and Trotsky) on the necessity of party dictatorship be reconciled with it?

The ironies do not stop there, of course. Harman correctly notes that under Stalinism, the *"bureaucracy is characterised, like the private capitalist class in the West, by its control over the means of production."* [**Op. Cit.**, p. 147] However, he fails to note that it was **Lenin,** in early 1918, who had raised and then implemented such *"control"* in the form of *"one-man management."* As he put it: *"Obedience, and unquestioning obedience at that, during work to the one-man decisions of Soviet directors, of the directors elected or appointed by Soviet institutions, vested with dictatorial powers."* [**Collected Works**, vol. 27, p. 316] To **fail** to note this link between Lenin and the Stalinist bureaucracy on this issue is quoting *"selectively."*

The contradictions pile up. Harman argues that *"people who seriously believe that workers at the height of revolution need a police guard to stop them handing their factories over to capitalists certainly have no real faith in the possibilities of a socialist future."* [**Op. Cit.**, p. 144] Yet this does not stop him praising the regime of Lenin and Trotsky and contrasting it with Stalinism, in spite of the fact that this was precisely what the Bolsheviks **did** from 1918 onwards! Indeed this tyrannical practice played a role in provoking the strikes in Petrograd which preceded the Kronstadt revolt in 1921, when *"the workers wanted the special squads of armed Bolsheviks, who carried out a purely police function, withdrawn from the factories."* [Paul Avrich, **Kronstadt 1921**, p. 42] It seems equally strange that Harman denounces the Stalinist suppression of the Hungarian revolution for workers' democracy and genuine socialism while he defends the Bolshevik suppression of the Kronstadt revolt for the same goals. Similarly, when Harman argues that if by *"political party"* it is *"meant a party of the usual sort, in which a few leaders give orders and the masses merely obey ... then certainly such organisations added nothing to the Hungarian revolution."* However, as we discuss in section H.5, such a party was **precisely** what Leninism argued for and applied in practice. Simply put, the Bolsheviks were never a party *"that stood for the councils taking power."* [**Op. Cit.**, p. 186 and p. 187] As Lenin repeatedly stressed, its aim was for the Bolshevik party to take power **through** the councils (see section H.3.11). Once in power, the councils were quickly marginalised and became little more than a fig-leaf for party rule.

This confusion between what was promised and what was done is a common feature of Leninism. Felix Morrow, for example, wrote what is usually considered the definitive Trotskyist work on the Spanish Revolution (in spite of it being deeply flawed). Morrow stated that the *"essential points of a revolutionary program [are] all power to the working class, and democratic organs of the workers, peasants and combatants, as the expression of the workers' power."* [**Revolution and Counter-Revolution in Spain**, p. 133] How this can be reconciled with, say, Trotsky's opinion of ten years previously that *"[w]ith us the dictatorship of the party (quite falsely disputed theoretically by Stalin) is the expression of the socialist dictatorship of the proletariat ... The dictatorship of a party is a part of the socialist revolution"*? [**Leon Trotsky on China**, p. 251]

Or with Lenin's and Trotsky's repeated call for the party to seize and exercise power? Or their opinion that an organisation taking in the whole proletariat cannot directly exercise the proletarian dictatorship? How can the working class *have all power"* if power is held not by mass organisations but rather by a vanguard party? Particularly, as we note in section H.1.2 when party dictatorship is placed at the heart of Leninist ideology.

Given all this, who is quoting who *"selectively"*? The Marxists who ignore what the Bolsheviks did when in power and repeatedly point to Lenin's **The State and Revolution** or the anarchists who link what they did with what they said outside of that holy text? Considering this absolutely contradictory inheritance, anarchists feel entitled to ask the question *"Will the real Leninist please stand up?"* What is it to be, popular democracy or party rule? If we look at Bolshevik practice, the answer is the latter anarchists argue. Ironically, the likes of Lenin and Trotsky concurred, incorporating the necessity of party power into their ideology as a key lesson of the Russian revolution. As such, anarchists do not feel they are quoting Leninism *"selectively"* when they argue that it is based on party power, not working class self-management. That Leninists often publicly deny this aspect of their own ideology or, at best, try to rationalise and justify it, suggests that when push comes to shove (as it does in every revolution) they will make the same decisions and act in the same way.

In addition there is the question of what could be called the *"social context."* Marxists often accuse anarchists of failing to place the quotations and actions of, say, the Bolsheviks into the circumstances which generated them. By this they mean that Bolshevik authoritarianism can be explained purely in terms of the massive problems facing them (i.e. the rigours of the Civil War, the economic collapse and chaos in Russia and so on). As we discuss this question in section H.6, we will simply summarise the anarchist reply by noting that this argument has three major problems with it. Firstly, there is the problem that Bolshevik authoritarianism started **before** the start of the Civil War and, moreover, intensified **after** its end. As such, the Civil War cannot be blamed. The second problem is simply that Lenin continually stressed that civil war and economic chaos was inevitable during a revolution. If Leninist politics cannot handle the inevitable then they are to be avoided. Equally, if Leninists blame what they should **know** is inevitable for the degeneration of the Bolshevik revolution it would suggest their understanding of what revolution entails is deeply flawed. The last problem is simply that the Bolsheviks did not care. As Samuel Farber notes, *"there is no evidence indicating that Lenin or any of the mainstream Bolshevik leaders lamented the loss of workers' control or of democracy in the soviets, or at least referred to these losses as a retreat, as Lenin declared with the replacement of War Communism by NEP in 1921. In fact ... the very opposite is the case."* [**Before Stalinism**, p. 44] Hence the continuation (indeed, intensification) of Bolshevik authoritarianism after their victory in the civil war. Given this, it is significant that many of the quotes from Trotsky given above date from the late 1930s. To argue, therefore, that "social context" explains the politics and actions of the Bolsheviks seems incredulous.

Lastly, it seems ironic that Marxists accuse anarchists of quoting *"selectively."* After all, as proven in section H.2, this is **exactly** what Marxists do to anarchism!

H.3.5 Has Marxist appropriation of anarchist ideas changed it?

As is obvious in any account of the history of socialism, Marxists (of various schools) have appropriated key anarchist ideas and (often) present them as if Marxists thought of them first.

For example, as we discuss in section H.3.10, it was anarchists who first raised the idea of smashing the bourgeois state and replacing it with the fighting organisations of the working class (such as unions, workers' councils, etc.). It was only in 1917, decades after anarchists had first raised the idea, that Marxists started to argue these ideas but, of course, with a twist. While anarchists meant that working class organisations would be the basis of a free society, Lenin saw these organs as the best means of achieving Bolshevik party power.

Similarly with the libertarian idea of the *"militant minority."* By this, anarchists and syndicalists meant groups of workers who gave an example by their direct action which their fellow workers could imitate (for example by leading wildcat strikes which would use flying pickets to get other workers to join in). This "militant minority" would be at the forefront of social struggle and would show, by example, practice and discussion, that their ideas and tactics were the correct ones. After the Russian Revolution of 1917, Bolsheviks argued that this idea was similar to their idea of a vanguard party. This ignored two key differences. Firstly that the libertarian *"militant minority"* did not aim to take power on behalf of the working class but rather to encourage it, by example, to manage its own struggles and affairs (and, ultimately, society). Secondly, that *"vanguard parties"* are organised in hierarchical ways alien to the spirit of anarchism. While both the *"militant minority"* and *"vanguard party"* approaches are based on an appreciation of the uneven development of ideas within the working class, vanguardism transforms this into a justification for party rule **over** the working class by a so-called *"advanced"* minority (see section H.5 for a full discussion). Other concepts, such as *"workers' control,"* direct action, and so on have suffered a similar fate.

A classic example of this appropriation of anarchist ideas into Marxism is provided by the general strike. In 1905, Russia had a near revolution in which the general strike played a key role. Unsurprisingly, as anarchists had been arguing for the general strike since the 1870s, we embraced these events as a striking confirmation of our long held ideas on revolutionary change. Marxists had a harder task as such ideas were alien to mainstream Social Democracy. Yet faced with the success and power of the general strike in practice, the more radical Marxists, like Rosa Luxemburg, had to incorporate it into their politics.

Yet they faced a problem. The general strike was indelibly linked with such heresies as anarchism and syndicalism. Had not Engels himself proclaimed the nonsense of the general strike in his diatribe *"The Bakuninists at work"*? Had his words not been repeated ad infinitum against anarchists (and radical socialists) who questioned the wisdom of social democratic tactics, its reformism and bureaucratic inertia? The Marxist radicals knew that Engels would again be invoked by the bureaucrats and reformists in the Social Democratic movement to throw cold water over any attempt to adjust Marxist politics to the economic power of the masses as expressed in mass strikes. The Social Democratic hierarchy would simply dismiss them as "anarchists." This meant that Luxemburg was faced with the problem of proving Engels was right, even when he was wrong.

She did so in an ingenious way. Like Engels himself, she simply distorted what the anarchists thought about the general strike in order to make it acceptable to Social Democracy. Her argument was simple. Yes, Engels had been right to dismiss the "general strike" idea of the anarchists in the 1870s. But today, thirty years later, Social Democrats should support the general strike (or mass strike, as she called it) because the concepts were different. The anarchist "general strike" was utopian. The Marxist "mass strike" was practical.

To discover why, we need to see what Engels had argued in the 1870s. Engels, mocked the anarchists (or "Bakuninists") for thinking that "a general strike is the lever employed by which the social revolution is started." He accusing them of imagining that "[o]ne fine morning, all the workers in all the industries of a country, or even of the whole world, stop work, thus forcing the propertied classes either humbly to submit within four weeks at most, or to attack the workers, who would then have the right to defend themselves and use the opportunity to pull down the entire old society." He stated that at the September 1 1873 Geneva congress of the anarchist Alliance of Social Democracy, it was "universally admitted that to carry out the general strike strategy, there had to be a perfect organisation of the working class and a plentiful funds." He noted that that was "the rub" as no government would stand by and "allow the organisation or funds of the workers to reach such a level." Moreover, the revolution would happen long before "such an ideal organisation" was set up and if they had been "there would be no need to use the roundabout way of a general strike" to achieve it. [**Collected Works**, vol. 23, pp. 584-5]

Rosa Luxemburg repeated Engels arguments in her essay "The Mass Strike, the Political Party and the Trade Unions" in order to show how her support for the general strike was in no way contrary to Marxism. [**Rosa Luxemburg Speaks**, pp. 153-218] Her "mass strike" was different from the anarchist "general strike" as mocked by Engels as it was a dynamic process and could not be seen as one act, one isolated action which overthrows the bourgeoisie. Rather, the mass strike as the product of the everyday class struggle within society, leads to a direct confrontation with the capitalist state and so it was inseparable from the revolution.

The only problem with all this is that the anarchists did not actually argue along the lines Engels and Luxemburg claimed. Most obviously, as we indicated in section H.2.8, Bakunin saw the general strike as a **dynamic** process which would **not** be set for a specific date and did **not** need all workers to be organised before hand. As such, Bakunin's ideas are totally at odds with Engels assertions on what anarchist ideas on the general strike were about (they, in fact, reflect what actually happened in 1905).

But what of the "Bakuninists"? Again, Engels account leaves a lot to be desired. Rather than the September 1873 Geneva congress being, as he claimed, of the (disbanded) Alliance of Social Democracy, it was in fact a meeting of the non-Marxist federations of the First International. Contra Engels, anarchists did not see the general

strike as requiring all workers to be perfectly organised and then passively folding arms "one fine morning." The Belgian libertarians who proposed the idea at the congress saw it as a tactic which could mobilise workers for revolution, "a means of bringing a movement onto the street and leading the workers to the barricades." Moreover, leading anarchist James Guillaume explicitly rejected the idea that it had "to break out everywhere at an appointed day and hour" with a resounding "No!" In fact, he stressed that they did "not even need to bring up this question and suppose things could be like this. Such a supposition could lead to fatal mistakes. The revolution has to be contagious." [quoted by Caroline Cahm, **Kropotkin and the Rise of Revolutionary Anarchism 1872-1886**, p. 223 and p. 224] Another account of this meeting notes that how the general strike was to start was "left unsaid", with Guillaume "recognis[ing] that it is impossible for the anarchists simply to set the hour for the general strike." Another anarchist did "not believe that the strike was a sufficient means to win the social revolution" but could "set the stage for the success of an armed insurrection." Only one delegate, regardless of Engels' claims, thought it "demanded the utmost organisation of the working class" and if that were the case "then the general strike would not be necessary." This was the delegate from the reformist British trade unions and he was "attack[ing]" the general strike as "an absurd and impractical proposition." [Phil H. Goodstein, **The Theory of the General Strike**, pp. 43-5]

Perhaps this is why Engels did not bother to quote a single anarchist when recounting their position on this matter? Needless to say, Leninists continue to parrot Engels assertions to this day. The facts are somewhat different. Clearly, the "anarchist" strategy of overthrowing the bourgeoisie with one big general strike set for a specific date exists only in Marxist heads, nowhere else. Once we remove the distortions promulgated by Engels and repeated by Luxemburg, we see that the 1905 revolution and "historical dialectics" did not, as Luxemburg claim, validate Engels and disprove anarchism. Quite the reverse as the general strikes in Russia followed the anarchist ideas of what a general strike would be like quite closely. Little wonder, then, that Kropotkin argued that the 1905 general strike "demonstrated" that the Latin workers who had been advocating the general strike "as a weapon which would be irresistible in the hands of labour for imposing its will" had been "right." [**Selected Writings on Anarchism and Revolution**, p. 288]

So, contra Luxemburg, "the fatherland of Bakunin" was **not** "the burial-place of [anarchism's] teachings." [**Op. Cit.**, p. 157] As Nicholas Walter argued, while the numbers of actual anarchists was small, "the 1905 Revolution was objectively an anarchist revolution. The military mutinies, peasant uprisings and workers' strikes (culminating in a general strike), led to the establishment of soldiers' and workers' councils ... and peasants' communes, and the beginning of agrarian and industrial expropriation - all along the lines suggested by anarchist writers since Bakunin." [**The Anarchist Past and Other Essays**, p. 122] The real question must be when will Marxists realise that quoting Engels does not make it true?

Moreover, without becoming an insurrection, as anarchists had stressed, the limits of the general strike were exposed in 1905. Unlike some of the syndicalists in the 1890s and 1900s, this limitation was understood by the earliest anarchists. Consequently, they saw the general strike as the start of a revolution and not as the revolution itself. So, for all the Leninist accounts of the 1905 revolution claiming it for their ideology, the facts suggest that it was anarchism, not Marxism, which was vindicated by it. Luxemburg was wrong. The *"land of Bakunin's birth"* provided an unsurpassed example of how to make a revolution precisely because it applied (and confirmed) anarchist ideas on the general strike (and, it should be added, workers' councils). Marxists (who had previously quoted Engels to dismiss such things) found themselves repudiating aspect upon aspect of their dogma to remain relevant. Luxemburg, as Bookchin noted, *"grossly misrepresented the anarchist emphasis on the general strike after the 1905 revolution in Russia in order to make it acceptable to Social Democracy."* (He added that Lenin *"was to engage in the same misrepresentation on the issue of popular control in* **State and Revolution***"*). [**Towards an Ecological Society**, p. 227fn]

As such, while Marxists have appropriated certain anarchist concepts, it does not automatically mean that they mean exactly the same thing by them. Rather, as history shows, radically different concepts can be hidden behind similar sounding rhetoric. As Murray Bookchin argued, many Marxist tendencies *"attach basically alien ideas to the withering conceptual framework of Marxism - not to say anything new but to preserve something old with ideological formaldehyde - to the detriment of any intellectual growth that the distinctions are designed to foster. This is mystification at its worst, for it not only corrupts ideas but the very capacity of the mind to deal with them. If Marx's work can be rescued for our time, it will be by dealing with it as an invaluable part of the development of ideas, not as pastiche that is legitimated as a 'method' or continually 'updated' by concepts that come from an alien zone of ideas."* [**Op. Cit.**, p. 242f]

This is not some academic point. The ramifications of Marxists appropriating such *"alien ideas"* (or, more correctly, the rhetoric associated with those ideas) has had negative impacts on actual revolutionary movements. For example, Lenin's definition of *"workers' control"* was radically different than that current in the factory committee movement during the Russian Revolution (which had more in common with anarchist and syndicalist use of the term). The similarities in rhetoric allowed the factory committee movement to put its weight behind the Bolsheviks. Once in power, Lenin's position was implemented while that of the factory committees was ignored. Ultimately, Lenin's position was a key factor in creating state capitalism rather than socialism in Russia (see section H.3.14 for more details).

This, of course, does not stop modern day Leninists appropriating the term workers' control *"without bating an eyelid. Seeking to capitalise on the confusion now rampant in the movement, these people talk of 'workers' control' as if a) they meant by those words what the politically unsophisticated mean (i.e. that working people should themselves decide about the fundamental matters relating to production) and b) as if they - and the Leninist doctrine to which they claim to adhere - had always supported demands of this kind, or as if Leninism had always seen in workers' control the universally valid foundation of a new social order, rather than just a* **slogan** *to be used for manipulatory purposes in specific and very limited historical contexts."* [Maurice Brinton, **The Bolsheviks**

and Workers' Control, p. iv] This clash between the popular idea of workers' control and the Leninist one was a key reason for the failure of the Russian Revolution precisely because, once in power, the latter was imposed.

Thus the fact that Leninists have appropriated libertarian (and working class) ideas and demands does not, in fact, mean that we aim for the same thing (as we discussed in section H.3.1, this is far from the case). The use of anarchist/popular rhetoric and slogans means little and we need to look at the content of the ideas proposed. Given the legacy of the appropriation of libertarian terminology to popularise authoritarian parties and its subsequent jettison in favour of authoritarian policies once the party is in power, anarchists have strong grounds to take Leninist claims with a large pinch of salt!

Equally with examples of actual revolutions. As Martin Buber noted, while *"Lenin praises Marx for having 'not yet, in 1852, put the concrete question as to what should be set up in place of the State machinery after it had been abolished,'"* Lenin argued that *"it was only the Paris Commune that taught Marx this."* However, as Buber correctly pointed out, the Paris Commune *"was the realisation of the thoughts of people who had put this question very concretely indeed … the historical experience of the Commune became possible only because in the hearts of passionate revolutionaries there lived the picture of a decentralised, very much 'de-Stated' society, which picture they undertook to translate into reality. The spiritual fathers of the Commune had such that ideal aiming at decentralisation which Marx and Engels did not have, and the leaders of the Revolution of 1871 tried, albeit with inadequate powers, to begin the realisation of that idea in the midst of revolution."* [**Paths in Utopia**, pp. 103-4] Thus, while the Paris Commune and other working class revolts are praised, their obvious anarchistic elements (which were usually often predicted by anarchist thinkers) are not mentioned. This results in some strange dichotomies. For example, Bakunin's vision of revolution is based on a federation of workers' councils, predating Marxist support for such bodies by decades, yet Marxists argue that Bakunin's ideas have nothing to teach us. Or, the Paris Commune being praised by Marxists as the first *"dictatorship of the proletariat"* when it implements federalism, delegates being subjected to mandates and recall and raises the vision of a socialism of associations while anarchism is labelled "petit-bourgeois" in spite of the fact that these ideas can be found in works of Proudhon and Bakunin which predate the 1871 revolt!

From this, we can draw two facts. Firstly, anarchism has successfully predicted certain aspects of working class revolution. Anarchist K.J. Kenafick stated the obvious when he argues that any *"comparison will show that the programme set out [by the Paris Commune] is … the system of Federalism, which Bakunin had been advocating for years, and which had first been enunciated by Proudhon. The Proudhonists … exercised considerable influence in the Commune. This 'political form' was therefore not 'at last' discovered; it had been discovered years ago; and now it was proven to be correct by the very fact that in the crisis the Paris workers adopted it almost automatically, under the pressure of circumstance, rather than as the result of theory, as being the form most suitable to express working class aspirations."* [**Michael Bakunin and Karl Marx**, pp. 212-3] Rather than being somehow alien to the working class and its struggle for freedom, anarchism in fact bases itself on the class struggle. This means that it should come as no surprise when the ideas of anarchism are developed and applied by those in struggle, for those ideas are just generalisations derived from past working class struggles! If anarchist ideas are applied spontaneously by those in struggle, it is because those involved are themselves drawing similar conclusions from their own experiences.

The other fact is that while mainstream Marxism often appropriated certain aspects of libertarian theory and practice, it does so selectively and places them into an authoritarian context which undermines their libertarian nature. Hence anarchist support for workers councils becomes transformed by Leninists into a means to ensure party power (i.e. state authority) rather than working class power or self-management (i.e. no authority). Similarly, anarchist support for leading by example becomes transformed into support for party rule (and often dictatorship). Ultimately, the practice of mainstream Marxism shows that libertarian ideas cannot be transplanted selectively into an authoritarian ideology and be expected to blossom.

Significantly, those Marxists who **do** apply anarchist ideas honestly are usually labelled by their orthodox comrades as "anarchists." As an example of Marxists appropriating libertarian ideas honestly, we can point to the council communist and currents within Autonomist Marxism. The council communists broke with the Bolsheviks over the question of whether the party would exercise power or whether the workers' councils would. Needless to say, Lenin labelled them an *"anarchist deviation."* Currents within Autonomist Marxism have built upon the council communist tradition, stressing the importance of focusing analysis on working class struggle as the key dynamic in capitalist society.

In this they go against the mainstream Marxist orthodoxy and embrace a libertarian perspective. As libertarian socialist Cornelius Castoriadis argued, *"the economic theory expounded [by Marx] in **Capital** is based on the postulate that capitalism has managed completely and effectively to transform the worker - who appears there only as labour power - into a commodity; therefore the use value of labour power - the use the capitalist makes of it - is, as for any commodity, completely determined by the use, since its exchange value - wages - is determined solely by the laws of the market ... This postulate is necessary for there to be a 'science of economics' along the physico-mathematical model Marx followed ... But he contradicts the most essential fact of capitalism, namely, that the use value and exchange value of labour power are objectively indeterminate; they are determined rather by the struggle between labour and capital both in production and in society. Here is the ultimate root of the 'objective' contradictions of capitalism ... The paradox is that Marx, the 'inventor' of class struggle, wrote a monumental work on phenomena determined by this struggle in which the struggle itself was entirely absent."* [**Political and Social Writings**, vol. 2, pp. 202-3] Castoriadis explained the limitations of Marx's vision most famously in his *"Modern Capitalism and Revolution."* [**Op. Cit.**, pp. 226-343]

By rejecting this heritage which mainstream Marxism bases itself on and stressing the role of class struggle, Autonomist Marxism breaks decisively with the Marxist mainstream and embraces a position previously associated with anarchists and other libertarian socialists. The key role of class struggle in invalidating all deterministic economic *"laws"* was expressed by French syndicalists at the start of the twentieth century. This insight predated the work of Castoriadis and the development of Autonomist Marxism by over 50 years and is worth quoting at length:

> *"the keystone of socialism ... proclaimed that 'as a general rule, the average wage would be no more than what the worker strictly required for survival'. And it was said: 'That figure is governed by capitalist pressure alone and this can even push it below the minimum necessary for the working man's subsistence ... The only rule with regard to wage levels is the plentiful or scarce supply of man-power ...'*

> *"By way of evidence of the relentless operation of this law of wages, comparisons were made between the worker and a commodity: if there is a glut of potatoes on the market, they are cheap; if they are scarce, the price rises ... It is the same with the working man, it was said: his wages fluctuate in accordance with the plentiful supply or dearth of labour!*

> *"No voice was raised against the relentless arguments of this absurd reasoning: so the law of wages may be taken as right ... for as long as the working man [or woman] is content to be a commodity! For as long as, like a sack of potatoes, she remains passive and inert and endures the fluctuations of the market ... For as long as he bends his back and puts up with all of the bosses' snubs, ... the law of wages obtains.*

> *"But things take a different turn the moment that a glimmer of consciousness stirs this worker-potato into life. When, instead of dooming himself to inertia, spinelessness, resignation and passivity, the worker wakes up to his worth as a human being and the spirit of revolt washes over him: when he bestirs himself, energetic, wilful and active ... [and] once the labour bloc comes to life and bestirs itself ... then, the laughable equilibrium of the law of wages is undone."* [Emile Pouget, **Direct Action**, pp. 9-10]

And Marx, indeed, had compared the worker to a commodity, stating that labour power *"is a commodity, neither more nor less than sugar. The former is measured by the clock, the latter by the scale."* [**Selected Works**, p. 72] However, as Castoridias argued, unlike sugar the extraction of the use value of labour power *"is not a technical operation; it is a process of bitter struggle in which half the time, so to speak, the capitalists turn out to be losers."* [**Op. Cit.**, p. 248] A fact which Pouget stressed in his critique of the mainstream socialist position:

> *"A novel factor has appeared on the labour market: the will of the worker! And this factor, not pertinent when it comes to setting the price of a bushel of potatoes, has a bearing upon the setting of wages; its impact may be large or small, according to the degree of tension of the*

labour force which is a product of the accord of individual wills beating in unison - but, whether it be strong or weak, there is no denying it.

"Thus, worker cohesion conjures up against capitalist might a might capable of standing up to it. The inequality between the two adversaries - which cannot be denied when the exploiter is confronted only by the working man on his own - is redressed in proportion with the degree of cohesion achieved by the labour bloc. From then on, proletarian resistance, be it latent or acute, is an everyday phenomenon: disputes between labour and capital quicken and become more acute. Labour does not always emerge victorious from these partial struggles: however, even when defeated, the struggle workers still reap some benefit: resistance from them has obstructed pressure from the employers and often forced the employer to grant some of the demands put." [**Op. Cit.**, p. 10]

The best currents of Autonomist Marxism share this anarchist stress on the power of working people to transform society and to impact on how capitalism operates. Unsurprisingly, most Autonomist Marxists reject the idea of the vanguard party and instead, like the council communists, stress the need for **autonomist** working class self-organisation and self-activity (hence the name!). They agree with Pouget when he argued that direct action *"spells liberation for the masses of humanity"*, it *"puts paid to the age of miracles - miracles from Heaven, miracles from the State - and, in contraposition to hopes vested in 'providence' (no matter what they may be) it announces that it will act upon the maxim: salvation lies within ourselves!"* [**Op. Cit.**, p. 3] As such, they draw upon anarchistic ideas and rhetoric (for many, undoubtedly unknowingly) and draw anarchistic conclusions. This can be seen from the works of the leading US Autonomist Marxist Harry Cleaver. His excellent essay *"Kropotkin, Self-Valorisation and the Crisis of Marxism"* is by far the best Marxist account of Kropotkin's ideas and shows the similarities between communist-anarchism and Autonomist Marxism. [**Anarchist Studies**, vol.2 , no. 2, pp. 119-36] Both, he points out, share a *"common perception and sympathy for the power of workers to act autonomously"* regardless of the *"substantial differences"* on other issues. [**Reading Capital Politically**, p. 15] As such, the links between the best Marxists and anarchism can be substantial. This means that some Marxists have taken on board many anarchist ideas and have forged a version of Marxism which is basically libertarian in nature. Unfortunately, such forms of Marxism have always been a minority current within it. Most cases have seen the appropriation of anarchist ideas by Marxists simply as part of an attempt to make mainstream, authoritarian Marxism more appealing and such borrowings have been quickly forgotten once power has been seized.

Therefore appropriation of rhetoric and labels should not be confused with similarity of goals and ideas. The list of groupings which have used inappropriate labels to associate their ideas with other, more appealing, ones is lengthy. Content is what counts. If libertarian sounding ideas **are** being raised, the question becomes one of whether they are being used simply to gain influence or

whether they signify a change of heart. As Bookchin argued:

"Ultimately, a line will have to be drawn that, by definition, excludes any project that can tip decentralisation to the side of centralisation, direct democracy to the side of delegated power, libertarian institutions to the side of bureaucracy, and spontaneity to the side of authority. Such a line, like a physical barrier, must irrevocably separate a libertarian zone of theory and practice from the hybridised socialisms that tend to denature it. This zone must build its anti-authoritarian, utopian, and revolutionary commitments into the very recognition it has of itself, in short, into the very way it defines itself... . to admit of domination is to cross the line that separates the libertarian zone from the [state] socialist." [**Op. Cit.**, pp. 223-4]

Unless we know exactly what we aim for, how to get there and who our **real** allies are, we will get a nasty surprise once our self-proclaimed "allies" take power. As such, any attempt to appropriate anarchist rhetoric into an authoritarian ideology will simply fail and become little more than a mask obscuring the real aims of the party in question. As history shows.

H.3.6 Is Marxism the only revolutionary politics which have worked?

Some Marxists will dismiss our arguments, and anarchism, out of hand. This is because anarchism has not lead a "successful" revolution while Marxism has. The fact, they assert, that there has never been a serious anarchist revolutionary movement, let alone a successful anarchist revolution, in the whole of history proves that Marxism works. For some Marxists, practice determines validity. Whether something is true or not is not decided intellectually in wordy publications and debates, but in reality.

For Anarchists, such arguments simply show the ideological nature of most forms of Marxism. The fact is, of course, that there have been many anarchistic revolutions which, while ultimately defeated, show the validity of anarchist theory (the ones in Spain and in the Ukraine being the most significant). Moreover, there have been serious revolutionary anarchist movements across the world, the majority of them crushed by state repression (usually fascist or communist based). However, this is not the most important issue, which is the fate of these "successful" Marxist movements and revolutions. The fact that there has never been a "Marxist" revolution which has not become a party dictatorship proves the need to critique Marxism.

So, given that Marxists argue that Marxism is **the** revolutionary working class political theory, its actual track record has been appalling. After all, while many Marxist parties have taken part in revolutions and even seized power, the net effect of their "success" have been societies bearing little or no relationship to socialism. Rather, the net effect of these revolutions has been to discredit socialism by associating it with one-party states presiding over state capitalist economies.

Equally, the role of Marxism in the labour movement has also been less than successful. Looking at the first Marxist movement, social democracy, it ended by becoming reformist, betraying socialist ideas by (almost always) supporting their own state during the First World War and going so far as crushing the German revolution and betraying the Italian factory occupations in 1920. Indeed, Trotsky stated that the Bolshevik party was *"the only revolutionary"* section of the Second International, which is a damning indictment of Marxism. [**Stalin**, vol. 1, p. 248] Just as damning is the fact that neither Lenin or Trotsky noticed it before 1914! In fact, Lenin praised the *"fundamentals of parliamentary tactics"* of German and International Social Democracy, expressing the opinion that they were *"at the same time implacable on questions of principle and always directed to the accomplishment of the final aim"* in his obituary of August Bebel in 1913! [**Collected Works**, vol. 19, p. 298] For those that way inclined, some amusement can be gathered comparing Engels glowing predictions for these parties and their actual performance (in the case of Spain and Italy, his comments seem particularly ironic).

As regards Bolshevism itself, the one "revolutionary" party in the world, it avoided the fate of its sister parties simply because there was no question of applying social democratic tactics within bourgeois institutions as these did not exist in Tsarist Russia. Moreover, the net result of its seizure of power was, first, a party dictatorship and state capitalism under Lenin, then their intensification under Stalin and the creation of a host of Trotskyist sects who spend a considerable amount of time justifying and rationalising the ideology and actions of the Bolsheviks which helped create the Stalinism. Given the fate of Bolshevism in power, Bookchin simply stated the obvious:

> *"None of the authoritarian technics of change has provided successful 'paradigms', unless we are prepared to ignore the harsh fact that the Russian, Chinese, and Cuban 'revolutions' were massive counterrevolutions that blight our entire century."* [**The Ecology of Freedom**, p. 446]

Clearly, a key myth of Marxism is the idea that it has been a successful movement. In reality, its failures have been consistent and devastating so suggesting it is time to re-evaluate the whole ideology and embrace a revolutionary theory like anarchism. Indeed, it would be no exaggeration to argue that every *"success"* of Marxism has, in fact, proved that the anarchist critique of Marxism was correct. Thus, as Bakunin predicted, the Social-Democratic parties became reformist and the *"dictatorship of the proletariat"* became the *"dictatorship **over** the proletariat."* With "victories" like these, Marxism does not need failures! Thus Murray Bookchin:

> *"A theory which is so readily 'vulgarised,' 'betrayed,' or, more sinisterly, institutionalised into bureaucratic power by nearly all its adherents may well be one that lends itself to such 'vulgarisations,' 'betrayals,' and bureaucratic forms **as a normal condition of its existence**. What may seem to be 'vulgarisations,' 'betrayals,' and bureaucratic manifestations of its tenets in the heated light of doctrinal disputes may prove to be the fulfilment of its tenets in the cold light of historical development."* [**Toward an Ecological Society**, p. 196]

Hence the overwhelming need to critically evaluate Marxist ideas and history (such as the Russian Revolution - see section H.6). Unless we honestly discuss and evaluate all aspects of revolutionary ideas, we will never be able to build a positive and constructive revolutionary movement. By seeking the roots of Marxism's problems, we can enrich anarchism by avoiding possible pitfalls and recognising and building upon its strengths (e.g., where anarchists have identified, however incompletely, problems in Marxism which bear on revolutionary ideas, practice and transformation).

If this is done, anarchists are sure that Marxist claims that Marxism is **the** revolutionary theory will be exposed for the baseless rhetoric they are.

H.3.7 What is wrong with the Marxist theory of the state?

For anarchists, the idea that a state (any state) can be used for socialist ends is simply ridiculous. This is because of the nature of the state as an instrument of minority class rule. As such, it precludes the mass participation required for socialism and would create a new form of class society.

As we discussed in section B.2, the state is defined by certain characteristics (most importantly, the centralisation of power into the hands of a few). Thus, for anarchists, *"the word 'State' … should be reserved for those societies with the hierarchical system and centralisation."* [Peter Kropotkin, **Ethics**, p. 317f] This defining feature of the state has not come about by chance. As Kropotkin argued in his classic history of the state, *"a social institution cannot lend itself to **all** the desired goals, since, as with every organ, [the state] developed according to the function it performed, in a definite direction and not in all possible directions."* This means, by *"seeing the State as it has been in history, and as it is in essence today"* the conclusion anarchists *"arrive at is for the abolition of the State."* Thus the state has *"developed in the history of human societies to prevent the direct association among men [and women] to shackle the development of local and individual initiative, to crush existing liberties, to prevent their new blossoming - all this in order to subject the masses to the will of minorities."* [**The State: Its Historic Role**, p. 56]

So if the state, as Kropotkin stressed, is defined by *"the existence of a power situated above society, but also of a **territorial concentration** as well as the concentration **in the hands of a few of many functions in the life of societies**"* then such a structure has not evolved by chance. Therefore *"the pyramidal organisation which is the essence of the State"* simply *"cannot lend itself to a function opposed to the one for which it was developed in the course of history,"* such as the popular participation from below required by social revolution and socialism. [**Op. Cit.**, p. 10, p. 59 and p. 56] Based on this evolutionary analysis of the state, Kropotkin, like all anarchists, drew the conclusion *"that the State organisation, having been the force to which the minorities resorted for establishing and organising their power over the masses, cannot be the force which will serve to destroy these privileges."* [**Evolution and Environment**, p. 82]

This does **not** mean that anarchists dismiss differences between types of state, think the state has not changed over time or refuse to see that different states exist to defend different ruling minorities. Far from it. Anarchists argue that *"[e]very economic phase has a political phase corresponding to it, and it would be impossible to touch private property unless a new mode of political life be found at the same time."* *"A society founded on serfdom,"* Kropotkin explained, *"is in keeping with absolute monarchy; a society based on the wage system, and the exploitation of the masses by the capitalists finds it political expression in parliamentarianism."* As such, the state form changes and evolves, but its basic function (defender of minority rule) and structure (delegated power into the hands of a few) remains. Which means that *"a free society regaining possession of the common inheritance must seek, in free groups and free federations of groups, a new organisation, in harmony with the new economic phase of history."* [**The Conquest of Bread**, p. 54]

As with any social structure, the state has evolved to ensure that it carries out its function. In other words, the state is centralised because it is an instrument of minority domination and oppression. Insofar as a social system is based on decentralisation of power, popular self-management, mass participation and free federation from below upwards, it is not a state. If a social system is, however, marked by delegated power and centralisation it is a state and cannot be, therefore, a instrument of social liberation. Rather it will become, slowly but surely, *"whatever title it adopts and whatever its origin and organisation may be"* what the state has always been, an instrument for *"oppressing and exploiting the masses, of defending the oppressors and the exploiters."* [Malatesta, **Anarchy**, p. 23] Which, for obvious reasons, is why anarchists argue for the destruction of the state by a free federation of self-managed communes and workers' councils (see section H.1.4 for further discussion).

This explains why anarchists reject the Marxist definition and theory of the state. For Marxists, *"the state is nothing but a machine for the oppression of one class by another."* While it has been true that, historically, it is *"the state of the most powerful, economically dominant class, which, through the medium of the state, becomes also the politically dominant class, and this acquires the means of holding down and exploiting the oppressed class,"* this need not always be the case. The state is *"at best an evil inherited by the proletariat after its victorious struggle for class supremacy,"* although it *"cannot avoid having to lop off at once as much as possible"* of it *"until such time as a generation reared in new, free social conditions is able to throw the entire lumber of the state on the scrap heap."* This new state, often called the *"dictatorship of the proletariat,"* would slowly *"wither away"* (or *"dies out"*) as classes disappear and the state *"at last ... becomes the real representative of the whole of society"* and so *"renders itself unnecessary."* Engels is at pains to differentiate this position from that of the anarchists, who demand *"the abolition of the state out of hand."* [**Selected Works**, p. 258, pp. 577-8, p. 528 and p. 424]

For anarchists, this argument has deep flaws. Simply put, unlike the anarchist one, this is not an empirically based theory of the state. Rather, we find such a theory mixed up with a metaphysical, non-empirical, a-historic definition which is based not on what the state **is** but rather what it **could** be. Thus the argument that the state *"is nothing but a machine for the oppression of one class by another"* is trying to draw out an abstract essence of the state rather than ground what the state is on empirical evidence and analysis. This perspective, anarchists argue, simply confuses two very different things, namely the state and popular social organisation, with potentially disastrous results. By calling the popular self-organisation required by a social revolution the same name as a hierarchical and centralised body constructed for, and evolved to ensure, minority rule, the door is wide open to confuse popular power with party power, to confuse rule by the representatives of the working class with working class self-management of the revolution and society. Indeed, at times, Marx seemed to suggest that **any** form of social organisation is a state. At one point he complained that the French mutualists argued that *"[e]verything [was] to broken down into small '**groupes**' or '**communes**', which in turn form an 'association', but not a state."* [**Collected Works**, vol. 42, p. 287] Unsurprisingly, then, that Kropotkin noted *"the German school which takes pleasure in confusing **State** with **Society**."* This was a *"confusion"* made by those *"who cannot visualise Society without a concentration of the State."* Yet this *"is to overlook the fact that Man lived in Societies for thousands of years before the State had been heard of"* and that *"communal life"* had *"been destroyed by the State."* So *"large numbers of people [have] lived in communes and free federations"* and these were not states as the state *"is only one of the forms assumed by society in the course of history. Why then make no distinction between what is permanent and what is accidental?"* [**The State: Its Historic Role**, pp. 9-10] As we discussed in section H.2.1, anarchist opposition to the idea of a "dictatorship of the proletariat" should not be confused with idea that anarchists do not think that a social revolution needs to be defended. Rather, our opposition to the concept rests on the confusion which inevitably occurs when you mix up scientific analysis with metaphysical concepts. By drawing out an a-historic definition of the state, Engels helped ensure that the *"dictatorship of the proletariat"* became the *"dictatorship over the proletariat"* by implying that centralisation and delegated power into the hands of the few can be considered as an expression of popular power.

To explain why, we need only to study the works of Engels himself. Engels, in his famous account of the **Origin of the Family, Private Property and the State**, defined the state as follows:

> *"The state is ... by no means a power forced on society from without ... Rather, it is a product of society at a certain stage of development; it is an admission ... that it has split into irreconcilable antagonisms ... in order that these antagonisms and classes with conflicting economic interests might not consume themselves and society in fruitless struggle, it became necessary to have power seemingly standing above society that would alleviate the conflict ... this power, arisen out of society but placing itself above it, and alienating itself more and more from it, is the state."* [**Selected Writings**, p. 576]

The state has two distinguishing features, firstly (and least importantly) it *"divides its subjects **according to territory**."* The second *"is the establishment of a **public power** which no longer* directly coincides with the population organising itself as an armed force. This special public power is necessary because a self-acting armed organisation of the population has become impossible since the split into classes … This public power exists in every state; it consists not merely of armed men but also of material adjuncts, prisons and institutions of coercion of all kinds." Thus "an essential feature of the state is a public power distinct from the mass of the people." [**Op. Cit.**, pp. 576-7 and pp. 535-6]

In this, the Marxist position concurs with the anarchist. Engels discussed the development of numerous ancient societies to prove his point. Talking of Greek society, he argued that it was based on a popular assembly which was "sovereign" plus a council. This social system was not a state because "when every adult male member of the tribe was a warrior, there was as yet no public authority separated from the people that could have been set up against it. Primitive democracy was still in full bloom, and this must remain the point of departure in judging power and the status of the council." Discussing the descent of this society into classes, he argued that this required "an institution that would perpetuate, not only the newly-rising class division of society, but the right of the possessing class to exploit the non-possessing class and the rule of the former over the latter." Unsurprisingly, "this institution arrived. The **state** was invented." The original communal organs of society were "superseded by real governmental authorities" and the defence of society ("the actual 'people in arms'") was "taken by an armed 'public power' at the service of these authorities and, therefore, also available against the people." With the rise of the state, the communal council was "transformed into a senate." [**Op. Cit.**, pp. 525-6, p. 528 and p. 525]

Thus the state arises specifically to exclude popular self-government, replacing it with minority rule conducted via a centralised, hierarchical top-down structure ("government … is the natural protector of capitalism and other exploiters of popular labour." [Bakunin, **Michael Bakunin: Selected Writings**, p. 239]).

This account of the rise of the state is at direct odds with Engels argument that the state is simply an instrument of class rule. For the "dictatorship of the proletariat" to be a state, it would have to constitute a power above society, be different from the people armed, and so be "a public power distinct from the mass of the people." However, Marx and Engels are at pains to stress that the "dictatorship of the proletariat" will not be such a regime. However, how can you have something (namely "a public power distinct from the mass of the people") you consider as "an essential feature" of a state missing in an institution you call the same name? It is a bit like calling a mammal a "new kind of reptile" in spite of the former not being cold-blooded, something you consider as "an essential feature" of the latter!

This contradiction helps explains Engels comments that "[w]e would therefore propose to replace **state** everywhere by **Gemeinwesen**, a good old German word which can very well convey the meaning of the French word '**commune**'" He even states that the Paris Commune "was no longer a state in the proper sense of the word." However, this comment does not mean that Engels sought to remove any possible confusion on the matter, for he still talked of "the state" as "only a transitional institution which is used in the struggle, in the revolution, to hold down's one's adversaries by force

… so long as the proletariat still **uses** the state, it does not use it in the interests of freedom but in order to hold down its adversaries, and as soon as it becomes possible to speak of freedom the state as such ceases to exist." [**Op. Cit.**, p. 335] Thus the state would still exist and, furthermore, is **not** identified with the working class as a whole ("a self-acting armed organisation of the population"), rather it is an institution standing apart from the "people armed" which is used, by the proletariat, to crush its enemies.

(As an aside, we must stress that to state that it only becomes possible to "speak of freedom" after the state and classes cease to exist is a serious theoretical error. Firstly, it means to talk about "freedom" in the abstract, ignoring the reality of class and hierarchical society. To state the obvious, in class society working class people have their freedom restricted by the state, wage labour and other forms of social hierarchy. The aim of social revolution is the conquest of liberty by the working class by overthrowing hierarchical rule. Freedom for the working class, by definition, means stopping any attempts to restrict that freedom by its adversaries. To state the obvious, it is not a "restriction" of the freedom of would-be bosses to resist their attempts to impose their rule! As such, Engels failed to consider revolution from a working class perspective - see section H.4.7 for another example of this flaw. Moreover his comments have been used to justify restrictions on working class freedom, power and political rights by Marxist parties once they have seized power. "Whatever power the State gains," correctly argued Bookchin, "it always does so at the expense of popular power. Conversely, whatever power the people gain, they always acquire at the expense of the State. To legitimate State power, in effect, is to delegitimate popular power." [**Remaking Society**, p. 160])

Elsewhere, we have Engels arguing that "the characteristic attribute of the former state" is that while society "had created its own organs to look after its own special interests" in the course of time "these organs, at whose head was the state power, transformed themselves from the servants of society into the masters of society." [**Op. Cit.**, p. 257] Ignoring the obvious contradiction with his earlier claims that the state and communal organs were different, with the former destroying the latter, we are struck yet again by the idea of the state as being defined as an institution above society. Thus, if the post revolutionary society is marked by "the state" being dissolved into society, placed under its control, then it is not a state. To call it a "new and truly democratic" form of "state power" makes as little sense as calling a motorcar a "new" form of bicycle. As such, when Engels argues that the Paris Commune "was no longer a state in the proper sense of the word" or that when the proletariat seizes political power it "abolishes the state as state" we may be entitled to ask what it is, a state or not a state. [**Op. Cit.**, p. 335 and p. 424] It cannot be both, it cannot be a "public power distinct from the mass of the people" **and** "a self-acting armed organisation of the population." If it is the latter, then it does not have what Engels considered as "an essential feature of the state" and cannot be considered one. If it is the former, then any claim that such a regime is the rule of the working class is automatically invalidated. That Engels mocked the anarchists for seeking a revolution "without a provisional government and in the total absence of any state or state-like institution, which are to be destroyed" we can safely say that it is the former. [Marx, Engels and Lenin, **Anarchism and Anarcho-Syndicalism**, p. 156]

Given that *"primitive democracy,"* as Engels noted, defended itself against its adversaries without such an institution shows that to equate the defence of working class freedom with the state is not only unnecessary, it simply leads to confusion. For this reason anarchists do not confuse the necessary task of defending and organising a social revolution with creating a state. Thus, the problem for Marxism is that the empirical definition of the state collides with the metaphysical, the actual state with its Marxist essence. As Italian Anarchist Camillo Berneri argued: *"The Proletariat' which seizes the state, bestowing on it the complete ownership of the means of production and destroying itself as proletariat and the state 'as the state' is a metaphysical fantasy, a political hypostasis of social abstractions."* [*"The Abolition and Extinction of the State,"* pp. 50-1, **Cienfuegos Press Anarchist Review**, no. 4, p. 50]

This is no academic point, as we explain in the next section this confusion has been exploited to justify party power **over** the proletariat. Thus, as Berneri argued, Marxists *"do not propose the armed conquest of the commune by the whole proletariat, but they propose the conquest of the State by the party which imagines it represents the proletariat. The Anarchists allow the use of direct power by the proletariat, but they understand the organ of this power to be formed by the entire corpus of systems of communist administration - corporate organisations [i.e. industrial unions], communal institutions, both regional and national - freely constituted outside and in opposition to all political monopoly by parties and endeavouring to a minimum administrational centralisation."* Thus *"the Anarchists desire the destruction of the classes by means of a social revolution which eliminates, with the classes, the State."* [*"Dictatorship of the Proletariat and State Socialism"*, pp 51-2, **Op. Cit.**, p. 52] Anarchists are opposed to the state because it is not neutral, it cannot be made to serve our interests. The structures of the state are only necessary when a minority seeks to rule over the majority. We argue that the working class can create our own structures, organised and run from below upwards, to ensure the efficient running of everyday life.

By confusing two radically different things, Marxism ensures that popular power is consumed and destroyed by the state, by a new ruling elite. In the words of Murray Bookchin:

> *"Marx, in his analysis of the Paris Commune of 1871, has done radical social theory a considerable disservice. The Commune's combination of delegated policy-making with the execution of policy by its own administrators, a feature of the Commune which Marx celebrated, is a major failing of that body. Rousseau quite rightly emphasised that popular power cannot be delegated without being destroyed. One either has a fully empowered popular assembly or power belongs to the State."* [*"Theses on Libertarian Municipalism"*, pp. 9-22, **The Anarchist Papers**, Dimitrios Roussopoulos (ed.), p. 14]

If power belongs to the state, then the state is a public body distinct from the population and, therefore, not an instrument of working class power. Rather, as an institution designed to ensure minority rule, it would ensure its position within society and become

either the ruling class itself or create a new class which instrument it would be. As we discuss in section H.3.9 the state cannot be considered as a neutral instrument of economic class rule, it has specific interests in itself which can and does mean it can play an oppressive and exploitative role in society independently of an economically dominant class.

Which brings us to the crux of the issue whether this "new" state will, in fact, be unlike any other state that has ever existed. Insofar as this "new" state is based on popular self-management and self-organisation, anarchists argue that such an organisation cannot be called a state as it is **not** based on delegated power. *"As long as,"* as Bookchin stressed, *"the institutions of power consisted of armed workers and peasants as distinguished from a professional bureaucracy, police force, army, and cabal of politicians and judges, they were no[t] a State … These institutions, in fact comprised a revolutionary people in arms … not a professional apparatus that could be regarded as a State in any meaningful sense of the term."* [*"Looking Back at Spain,"* pp. 53-96, **The Radical Papers**, Dimitrios I. Roussopoulos (ed.), p. 86] This was why Bakunin was at pains to emphasis that a *"federal organisation, from below upward, of workers' associations, groups, communes, districts, and ultimately, regions and nations"* could not be considered as the same as *"centralised states"* and were *"contrary to their essence."* [**Statism and Anarchy**, p. 13]

So when Lenin argued in **State and Revolution** that in the *"dictatorship of the proletariat"* the *"organ of suppression is now the majority of the population, and not the minority"* and that *"since the majority of the people itself suppresses its oppressors, a 'special force' for the suppression [of the bourgeoisie] is **no longer necessary**"* he is confusing two fundamentally different things. As Engels made clear, such a social system of *"primitive democracy"* is not a state. However, when Lenin argued that *"the more the functions of state power devolve upon the people generally, the less need is there for the existence of this power,"* he was implicitly arguing that there would be, in fact, a *"public power distinct from mass of the people"* and so a state in the normal sense of the word based on delegated power, *"special forces"* separate from the armed people and so on. [**Essential Works of Lenin**, p. 301]

That such a regime would not *"wither away"* has been proven by history. The state machine does not (indeed, **cannot**) represent the interests of the working classes due to its centralised, hierarchical and elitist nature - all it can do is represent the interests of the party in power, its own bureaucratic needs and privileges and slowly, but surely, remove itself from popular control. This, as anarchists have constantly stressed, is why the state is based on the delegation of power, on hierarchy and centralisation. The state is organised in this way to facilitate minority rule by excluding the mass of people from taking part in the decision making processes within society. If the masses actually did manage society directly, it would be impossible for a minority class to dominate it. Hence the need for a state. Which shows the central fallacy of the Marxist theory of the state, namely it argues that the rule of the proletariat will be conducted by a structure, the state, which is designed to exclude the popular participation such a concept demands!

Considered another way, *"political power"* (the state) is simply the power of minorities to enforce their wills. This means that a social revolution which aims to create socialism cannot use it to further its aims. After all, if the state (i.e. *"political power"*) has been created to further minority class rule (as Marxists and anarchists agree) then, surely, this function has determined how the organ which exercises it has developed. Therefore, we would expect organ and function to be related and impossible to separate. So when Marx argued that the conquest of political power had become the great duty of the working class because landlords and capitalists always make use of their political privileges to defend their economic monopolies and enslave labour, he drew the wrong conclusion.

Building on a historically based (and so evolutionary) understanding of the state, anarchists concluded that it was necessary not to seize political power (which could only be exercised by a minority within any state) but rather to destroy it, to dissipate power into the hands of the working class, the majority. By ending the regime of the powerful by destroying their instrument of rule, the power which was concentrated into their hands automatically falls back into the hands of society. Thus, working class power can only be concrete once *"political power"* is shattered and replaced by the social power of the working class based on its own class organisations (such as factory committees, workers' councils, unions, neighbourhood assemblies and so on). As Murray Bookchin put it:

> *"the slogan 'Power to the people' can only be put into practice when the power exercised by social elites is dissolved into the people. Each individual can then take control of his [or her] daily life. If 'Power to the people' means nothing more than power to the 'leaders' of the people, then the people remain an undifferentiated, manipulated mass, as powerless after the revolution as they were before."* [**Post-Scarcity Anarchism**, p. xif]

This issue is fudged by Marx. When Bakunin, in *"Statism and Anarchy"*, asked the question *"Will the entire proletariat head the government?"*, Marx argued in response:

> *"Does in a trade union, for instance, the whole union constitute the executive committee? Will all division of labour in a factory disappear and also the various functions arising from it? And will everybody be at the top in Bakunin's construction built from the bottom upwards? There will in fact be no below then. Will all members of the commune also administer the common affairs of the region? In that case there will be no difference between commune and region. 'The Germans [says Bakunin] number nearly 40 million. Will, for example, all 40 million be members of the government?' Certainly, for the thing begins with the self-government of the commune."* [Marx, Engels and Lenin, **Anarchism and Anarcho-Syndicalism**, pp. 150-1]

As Alan Carter argues, *"this might have seemed to Marx [over] a century ago to be satisfactory rejoinder, but it can hardly do today. In the infancy of the trade unions, which is all Marx knew, the possibility of the executives of a trade union becoming divorced from the ordinary members may not have seemed to him to be a likely outcome, We, however, have behind us a long history of union leaders 'selling out' and being out of touch with their members. Time*

has ably demonstrated that to reject Bakunin's fears on the basis of the practice of trade union officials constitutes a woeful complacency with regard to power and privilege - a complacency that was born ample fruit in the form of present Marxist parties and 'communist' societies … [His] dispute with Bakunin shows quite clearly that Marx did not stress the continued control of the revolution by the mass of the people as a prerequisite for the transcendence of all significant social antagonisms." [**Marx: A Radical Critique**, pp. 217-8] Non-anarchists have also noticed the poverty of Marx's response. For example, as David W. Lovell puts it, *"[t]aken as a whole, Marx's comments have dodged the issue. Bakunin is clearly grappling with the problems of Marx's transition period, in particular the problem of leadership, while Marx refuses to discuss the political form of what must be (at least in part) class rule by the proletariat."* [**From Marx to Lenin**, p. 64]

As we discussed in section H.3.1, Marx's *"Address to the Communist League,"* with its stress on *"the most determined centralisation of power in the hands of the state authority"* and that *"the path of revolutionary activity … can only proceed with full force from the centre,"* suggests that Bakunin's fears were valid and Marx's answer simply inadequate. [**Marx-Engels Reader**, p. 509] Simply put, if, as Engels argued, *"an essential feature of the state is a public power distinct from the mass of the people,"* then, clearly Marx's argument of 1850 (and others like it) signifies a state in the usual sense of the word, one which has to be *"distinct"* from the mass of the population in order to ensure that the masses are prevented from interfering with their own revolution. This was not, of course, the desire of Marx and Engels but this result flows from their theory of the state and its fundamental flaws. These flaws can be best seen from their repeated assertion that the capitalist democratic state could be captured via universal suffrage and used to introduce socialism (see section H.3.10) but it equally applies to notions of creating new states based on the centralisation of power favoured by ruling elites since class society began.

As Kropotkin stressed, *"one does not make an historical institution follow in the direction to which one points - that is in the opposite direction to the one it has taken over the centuries."* To expect this would be a *"a sad and tragic mistake"* simply because *"the old machine, the old organisation, [was] slowly developed in the course of history to crush freedom, to crush the individual, to establish oppression on a legal basis, to create monopolists, to lead minds astray by accustoming them to servitude"*. [**The State: Its Historic Role**, pp. 57-8] A social revolution needs new, non-statist, forms of social organisation to succeed:

> *"To give full scope to socialism entails rebuilding from top to bottom a society dominated by the narrow individualism of the shopkeeper. It is not as has sometimes been said by those indulging in metaphysical wooliness just a question of giving the worker 'the total product of his labour'; it is a question of completely reshaping all relationships … In every street, in every hamlet, in every group of men gathered around a factory or along a section of the railway line, the creative, constructive and organisational spirit must be awakened in order to rebuild life - in the factory, in the village, in the store, in production and in distribution*

of supplies. All relations between individuals and great centres of population have to be made all over again, from the very day, from the very moment one alters the existing commercial or administrative organisation.

"And they expect this immense task, requiring the free expression of popular genius, to be carried out within the framework of the State and the pyramidal organisation which is the essence of the State! They expect the State … to become the lever for the accomplishment of this immense transformation. They want to direct the renewal of a society by means of decrees and electoral majorities... How ridiculous!" [Kropotkin, **Op. Cit.**, pp. 58-9]

Ultimately, the question, of course, is one of power. Does the *"executive committee"* have the fundamental decision making power in society, or does that power lie in the mass assemblies upon which a federal socialist society is built? If the former, we have rule by a few party leaders and the inevitable bureaucratisation of the society and a state in the accepted sense of the word. If the latter, we have a basic structure of a free and equal society and a new organisation of popular self-management which eliminates the existence of a public power above society. This is not playing with words. It signifies the key issue of social transformation, an issue which Marxism tends to ignore or confuse matters about when discussing. Bookchin clarified what is at stake:

*"To some neo-Marxists who see centralisation and decentralisation merely as difference of degree, the word 'centralisation' may merely be an awkward way of denoting means for **co-ordinating** the decisions made by decentralised bodies. Marx, it is worth noting, greatly confused this distinction when he praised the Paris Commune as a 'working, not a parliamentary body, executive and legislative at the same time.' In point of fact, the consolidation of 'executive and legislative' functions in a single body was regressive. It simply identified the process of policy-making, a function that rightly should belong to the people in assembly, with the technical execution of these policies, a function that should be left to strictly administrative bodies subject to rotation, recall, limitations of tenure … Accordingly, the melding of policy formation with administration placed the institutional emphasis of classical [Marxist] socialism on centralised bodies, indeed, by an ironical twist of historical events, bestowing the privilege of formulating policy on the 'higher bodies' of socialist hierarchies and their execution precisely on the more popular 'revolutionary committees' below."* [**Toward an Ecological Society**, pp. 215-6]

By confusing co-ordination with the state (i.e. with delegation of power), Marxism opens the door wide open to the *"dictatorship of the proletariat"* being a state *"in the proper sense."* In fact, not only does Marxism open that door, it even invites the state *"in the proper sense"* in! This can be seen from Engels comment that just as *"each political party sets out to establish its rule in the state, so the German Social-Democratic Workers' Party is striving to establish **its** rule, the rule of the working class."* [**Collected Works**, vol. 23, p. 372] By confusing rule by the party *"in the state"* with *"rule of the working class,"* Engels is confusing party power and popular power. For the party to *"establish **its** rule,"* the state in the normal sense (i.e. a structure based on the delegation of power) has to be maintained. As such, the *"dictatorship of the proletariat"* signifies the delegation of power by the proletariat into the hands of the party and that implies a *"public power distinct from the mass of the people"* and so minority rule.

In summary, the Marxist theory of the state is simply a-historic and postulates some kind of state "essence" which exists independently of actual states and their role in society. To confuse the organ required by a minority class to execute and maintain its rule and that required by a majority class to manage society is to make a theoretical error of great magnitude. It opens the door to the idea of party power and even party dictatorship. As such, the Marxism of Marx and Engels is confused on the issue of the state. Their comments fluctuate between the anarchist definition of the state (based, as it is, on generalisations from historical examples) and the a-historic definition (based not on historical example but rather derived from a supra-historical analysis). Trying to combine the metaphysical with the scientific, the authoritarian with the libertarian, could only leave their followers with a confused legacy and that is what we find.

Since the death of the founding fathers of Marxism, their followers have diverged into two camps. The majority have embraced the metaphysical and authoritarian concept of the state and proclaimed their support for a *"workers' state."* This is represented by social-democracy and its radical offshoot, Leninism. As we discuss in the next section, this school has used the Marxist conception of the state to allow for rule over the working class by the *"revolutionary"* party. The minority has become increasingly and explicitly anti-state, recognising that the Marxist legacy is contradictory and that for the proletariat to directly manage society then there can be no power above them. To this camp belongs the libertarian Marxists of the council communist, Situationist and other schools of thought which are close to anarchism.

H.3.8 What is wrong with the Leninist theory of the state?

As discussed in the last section, there is a contradiction at the heart of the Marxist theory of the state. On the one hand, it acknowledges that the state, historically, has always been an instrument of minority rule and is structured to ensure this. On the other, it argues that you can have a state (the *"dictatorship of the proletariat"*) which transcends this historical reality to express an abstract essence of the state as an *"instrument of class rule."* This means that Marxism usually confuses two very different concepts, namely the state (a structure based on centralisation and delegated power) and the popular self-management and self-organisation required to create and defend a socialist society.

This confusion between two fundamentally different concepts proved to be disastrous when the Russian Revolution broke out. Confusing party power with working class power, the Bolsheviks aimed to create a "workers' state" in which their party would be in power (see section H.3.3). As the state was an instrument of class rule, it did not matter if the new "workers' state" was centralised, hierarchical and top-down like the old state as the structure of the state was considered irrelevant in evaluating its role in society. Thus, while Lenin seemed to promise a radical democracy in which the working class would directly manage its own affairs in his **State and Revolution**, in practice he implemented a *"dictatorship of the proletariat"* which was, in fact, *"the organisation of the vanguard of the oppressed as the ruling class."* [**Essential Works of Lenin**, p. 337] In other words, the vanguard party in the position of head of the state, governing on behalf of the working class which, in turn, meant that the new "workers' state" was fundamentally a state in the usual sense of the word. This quickly lead to a dictatorship **over**, not of, the proletariat (as Bakunin had predicted). This development did not come as a surprise to anarchists, who had long argued that a state is an instrument of minority rule and cannot change its nature. To use the state to affect socialist change is impossible, simply because it is not designed for such a task. As we argued in section B.2, the state is based on centralisation of power explicitly to ensure minority rule and for this reason has to be abolished during a social revolution.

As Voline summarised, there is *"an explicit, irreconcilable contradiction between the very essence of State Socialist power (if it triumphs) and that of the true Social Revolutionary process."* This was because *"the basis of State Socialism and delegated power is **the explicit non-recognition of [the] principles of the Social Revolution**. The characteristic traits of Socialist ideology and practice ... do not belong to the future, but are wholly a part of the bourgeois past ... Once this model has been applied, the true principles of the Revolution are fatally abandoned. Then follows, inevitably, the rebirth, under another name, of the exploitation of the labouring masses, with all its consequences."* Thus *"the forward march of the revolutionary masses towards real emancipation, towards the creation of new forms of social life, is incompatible with the very principle of State power ... the authoritarian principle and the revolutionary principle are diametrically opposed and mutually exclusive."* [**The Unknown Revolution**, p. 247 and p. 248]

Ironically, the theoretical lessons Leninists gained from the experience of the Russian Revolution confirm the anarchist analysis that the state structure exists to facilitate minority rule and marginalise and disempower the majority to achieve that rule. This can be seen from the significant revision of the Marxist position which occurred once the Bolshevik party become the ruling party. Simply put, after 1917 leading representatives of Leninism stressed that state power was **not** required to repress resistance by the ex-ruling class as such, but, in fact, was also necessitated by the divisions within the working class. In other words, state power was required because the working class was not able to govern itself and so required a grouping (the party) above it to ensure the success of the revolution and overcome any *"wavering"* within the masses

themselves. Needless to say, his latter day followers point to Lenin's apparently democratic, even libertarian, sounding 1917 work, **The State and Revolution** when asked about the Leninist theory of the state. As our discussion in section H.1.7 proved, the ideas expounded in his pamphlet were rarely, if at all, applied in practice by the Bolsheviks. Moreover, it was written before the seizure of power. In order to see the validity of his argument we must compare it to his and his fellow Bolshevik leaders opinions once the revolution had "succeeded." What lessons did they generalise from their experiences and how did these lessons relate to **State and Revolution**?

The change can be seen from Trotsky, who argued quite explicitly that *"the proletariat can take power only through its vanguard"* and that *"the necessity for state power arises from an insufficient cultural level of the masses and their heterogeneity."* Only with *"support of the vanguard by the class"* can there be the *"conquest of power"* and it was in *"this sense the proletarian revolution and dictatorship are the work of the whole class, but only under the leadership of the vanguard."* Thus, rather than the working class as a whole seizing power, it is the *"vanguard"* which takes power - *"a revolutionary party, even after seizing power ... is still by no means the sovereign ruler of society."* Thus state power is required to **govern the masses,** who cannot exercise power themselves. As Trotsky put it: *"Those who propose the abstraction of Soviets to the party dictatorship should understand that only thanks to the Bolshevik leadership were the Soviets able to lift themselves out of the mud of reformism and attain the state form of the proletariat."* [**Writings 1936-37**, p. 490, p. 488 and p. 495]

Logically, though, this places the party in a privileged position. So what happens if the working class no longer supports the vanguard? Who takes priority? Unsurprisingly, in both theory and practice, the party is expected to rule over the masses. This idea that state power was required due to the limitations within the working class is reiterated a few years later in 1939. Moreover, the whole rationale for party dictatorship came from the fundamental rationale for democracy, namely that any government should reflect the changing opinions of the masses:

> *"The very same masses are at different times inspired by different moods and objectives. It is just for this reason that a centralised organisation of the vanguard is indispensable. Only a party, wielding the authority it has won, is capable of overcoming the vacillation of the masses themselves ... if the dictatorship of the proletariat means anything at all, then it means that the vanguard of the proletariat is armed with the resources of the state in order to repel dangers, including those emanating from the backward layers of the proletariat itself."* ["The Moralists and Sycophants against Marxism", pp. 53-66, **Their Morals and Ours**, p. 59]

Needless to say, **by definition** everyone is *"backward"* when compared to the *"vanguard of the proletariat."* Moreover, as it is this *"vanguard"* which is *"armed with the resources of the state"* and **not** the proletariat as a whole we are left with one obvious conclusion, namely party dictatorship rather than working class democracy. How Trotsky's position is compatible with the idea of the working class as the "ruling class" is not explained. However, it fits in well with the anarchist analysis of the state as an instrument designed to ensure minority rule.

Thus the possibility of party dictatorship exists if popular support fades. Which is, significantly, precisely what **had** happened when Lenin and Trotsky were in power. In fact, these arguments built upon other, equally elitist statements which had been expressed by Trotsky when he held the reins of power. In 1920, for example, he argued that while the Bolsheviks have "*more than once been accused of having substituted for the dictatorship of the Soviets the dictatorship of the party,*" in fact "*it can be said with complete justice that the dictatorship of the Soviets became possible only by means of the dictatorship of the party.*" This, just to state the obvious, was his argument seventeen years later. "*In this 'substitution' of the power of the party for the power of the working class,*" Trotsky added, "*there is nothing accidental, and in reality there is no substitution at all. The Communists express the fundamental interests of the working class.*" [**Terrorism and Communism**, p. 109] In early 1921, he argued again for Party dictatorship at the Tenth Party Congress:

> "*The Workers' Opposition has come out with dangerous slogans, making a fetish of democratic principles! They place the workers' right to elect representatives above the Party, as if the party were not entitled to assert its dictatorship even if that dictatorship temporarily clashed with the passing moods of the workers' democracy. It is necessary to create amongst us the awareness of the revolutionary birthright of the party, which is obliged to maintain its dictatorship, regardless of temporary wavering even in the working classes. This awareness is for us the indispensable element. The dictatorship does not base itself at every given moment on the formal principle of a workers' democracy.*" [quoted by Samuel Farber, **Before Stalinism**, p. 209]

The similarities with his arguments of 1939 are obvious. Unsurprisingly, he maintained this position in the intervening years. He stated in 1922 that "*we maintain the dictatorship of our party!*" [**The First Five Years of the Communist International**, vol. 2, p. 255] The next year saw him arguing that "*[i]f there is one question which basically not only does not require revision but does not so much as admit the thought of revision, it is the question of the dictatorship of the Party.*" He stressed that "*[o]ur party is the ruling party*" and that "*[t]o allow any changes whatever in this field*" meant "*bring[ing] into question all the achievements of the revolution and its future.*" He indicated the fate of those who **did** question the party's position: "*Whoever makes an attempt on the party's leading role will, I hope, be unanimously dumped by all of us on the other side of the barricade.*" [**Leon Trotsky Speaks**, p. 158 and p. 160]

By 1927, when Trotsky was in the process of being "*dumped*" on the "*other side of the barricade*" by the ruling bureaucracy, he **still** argued for "*the Leninist principle, inviolable for every Bolshevik, that the dictatorship of the proletariat is and can be realised only through the dictatorship of the party.*" It was stressed that the "*dictatorship of the proletariat [sic!] demands as its very core a*

single proletarian party." [**The Challenge of the Left Opposition (1926-7)**, p. 395 and p. 441] As we noted in section H.1.2, ten years later, he was still explicitly arguing for the "*revolutionary dictatorship of a proletarian party*".

Thus, for Trotsky over a twenty year period, the "*dictatorship of the proletariat*" was fundamentally a "*dictatorship of the party.*" While the working class may be allowed some level of democracy, the rule of the party was repeatedly given precedence. While the party may be placed into power by a mass revolution, once there the party would maintain its position of power and dismiss attempts by the working class to replace it as "*wavering*" or "*vacillation*" due to the "*insufficient cultural level of the masses and their heterogeneity.*" In other words, the party dictatorship was required to protect working class people from themselves, their tendency to change their minds based on changing circumstances, evaluating the results of past decisions, debates between different political ideas and positions, make their own decisions, reject what is in their best interests (as determined by the party), and so on. Thus the underlying rationale for democracy (namely that it reflects the changing will of the voters, their "*passing moods*" so to speak) is used to justify party dictatorship!

The importance of party power **over** the working class was not limited to Trotsky. It was considered of general validity by all leading Bolsheviks and, moreover, quickly became mainstream Bolshevik ideology. In March 1923, for example, the Central Committee of the Communist Party in a statement issued to mark the 25th anniversary of the founding of the Bolshevik Party. This statement summarised the lessons gained from the Russian revolution. It stated that "*the party of the Bolsheviks proved able to stand out fearlessly against the vacillations within its own class, vacillations which, with the slightest weakness in the vanguard, could turn into an unprecedented defeat for the proletariat.*" Vacillations, of course, are expressed by workers' democracy. Little wonder the statement rejects it: "*The dictatorship of the working class finds its expression in the dictatorship of the party.*" ["*To the Workers of the USSR*" in G. Zinoviev, **History of the Bolshevik Party**, p. 213 and p. 214] Trotsky and other leading Bolsheviks were simply following Lenin's lead, who had admitted at the end of 1920 that while "*the dictatorship of the proletariat*" was "*inevitable*" in the "*transition of socialism,*" it is "*not exercised by an organisation which takes in all industrial workers.*" The reason "*is given in the theses of the Second Congress of the Communist International on the role of political parties*" (more on which later). This means that "*the Party, shall we say, absorbs the vanguard of the proletariat, and this vanguard exercises the dictatorship of the proletariat.*" This was required because "*in all capitalist countries … the proletariat is still so divided, so degraded, and so corrupted in parts*" that it "*can be exercised only by a vanguard … the dictatorship of the proletariat cannot be exercised by a mass proletarian organisation.*" [**Collected Works**, vol. 32, p. 20 and p. 21] For Lenin, "*revolutionary coercion is bound to be employed towards the wavering and unstable elements among the masses themselves.*" [**Op. Cit.**, vol. 42, p. 170] Needless to say, Lenin failed to mention this aspect of his system in **The State and Revolution** (a failure usually repeated by his followers). It is, however, a striking confirmation of Bakunin's comments "*the State cannot be sure of its own self-preservation without an armed* force to defend it against its own **internal enemies,** *against the discontent of its own people."* [**Michael Bakunin: Selected Writings**, p. 265]

Looking at the lessons leading leaders of Leninism gained from the experience of the Russian Revolution, we have to admit that the Leninist *"workers' state"* will not be, in fact, a *"new"* kind of state, a *"semi-state,"* or, to quote Lenin, a *"new state"* which *"is no longer a state in the proper sense of the word."* If, as Lenin argued in early 1917, the state *"in the proper sense of the term is domination over the people by contingents of armed men divorced from the people,"* then Bolshevism in power quickly saw the need for a state *"in the proper sense."* [**Op. Cit.**, vol. 24, p. 85] While this state *"in the proper sense"* had existed from the start of Bolshevik rule, it was only from early 1919 onwards (at the latest) that the leaders of Bolshevism had openly brought what they said into line with what they did. Only by being a *"state in the proper sense"* could the Bolshevik party rule and exercise *"the dictatorship of the party"* over the *"wavering"* working class.

This recreation of the state *"in the proper sense"* did not come about by chance or simply because of the *"will to power"* of the leaders of Bolshevism. Rather, there are strong institutional pressures at work within any state structure (even a so-called *"semi-state"*) to turn it back into a *"proper"* state. We discuss this in more detail in section H.3.9. However, we should not ignore that many of the roots of Bolshevik tyranny can be found in the contradictions of the Marxist theory of the state. As noted in the last section, for Engels, the seizure of power by the party meant that the working class was in power. The Leninist tradition builds on this confusion between party and class power. It is clear that the *"dictatorship of the proletariat"* is, in fact, rule by the party. In Lenin's words:

> *"Engels speaks of **a government that is required for the domination of a class** ... Applied to the proletariat, it consequently means a government **that is required for the domination of the proletariat,** i.e. the dictatorship of the proletariat for the effectuation of the socialist revolution."* [**Op. Cit.**, vol. 8, p. 279]

The role of the working class in this state was also indicated, as *"only a revolutionary dictatorship supported by the vast majority of the people can be at all durable."* [**Op. Cit.**, p. 291] In other words the *"revolutionary government"* has the power, not the working class in whose name it governs. In 1921 he made this explicit: *"To govern you need an army of steeled revolutionary Communists. We have it, and it is called the Party."* The *"Party is the leader, the vanguard of the proletariat, which rules directly."* For Lenin, as *"long as we, the Party's Central Committee and the whole Party, continue to run things, that is govern we shall never - we cannot - dispense with ... removals, transfers, appointments, dismissals, etc."* of workers, officials and party members from above. [**Op. Cit.**, vol. 32, p. 62, p. 98 and p. 99] Unsurprisingly, these powers were used by Lenin, and then Stalin, to destroy opposition (although the latter applied coercive measures **within** the party which Lenin only applied to non-party opponents).

So much for *"workers' power,"* *"socialism from below"* and other such rhetoric.

This vision of "socialism" being rooted in party power over the working class was the basis of the Communist International's resolution on the role of the party. This resolution is, therefore, important and worth discussing. It argues that the Communist Party *"is **part** of the working class,"* namely its *"most advanced, most class-conscious, and therefore most revolutionary part."* It is *"distinguished from the working class as a whole in that it grasps the whole historic path of the working class in its entirety and at every bend in that road endeavours to defend not the interests of individual groups or occupations but the interests of the working class as a whole."* [**Proceedings and Documents of the Second Congress 1920**, vol. 1, p. 191] However, in response it can be argued that this simply means the *"interests of the party"* as only it can understand what *"the interests of the working class as a whole"* actually are. Thus we have the possibility of the party substituting its will for that of the working class simply because of what Leninists term the *"uneven development"* of the working class. As Alan Carter argues, these *"conceptions of revolutionary organisation maintain political and ideological domination by retaining supervisory roles and notions of privileged access to knowledge ... the term 'class consciousness' is employed to facilitate such domination over the workers. It is not what the workers think, but what the party leaders think they ought to think that constitutes the revolutionary consciousness imputed to the workers."* The ideological basis for a new class structure is created as the *"Leninist revolutionary praxis ... is carried forward to post-revolutionary institutions,"* [**Marx: A Radical Critique**, p. 175]

The resolution stresses that before the revolution, the party *"will encompass ... only a minority of the workers."* Even after the *"seizure of power,"* it will still *"not be able to unite them all into its ranks organisationally."* Only after the *"final defeat of the bourgeois order"* will *"all or almost all workers begin to join"* it. Thus the party is a **minority** of the working class. It then goes on to state that *"[e]very class struggle is a political struggle. This struggle, which inevitably becomes transformed into civil war, has as its goal the conquest of political power. Political power cannot be seized, organised, and directed other than by some kind of political party."* [**Op. Cit.**, p. 192, p. 193] And as the party is a *"part"* of the working class which cannot *"unite"* all workers *"into its ranks,"* this means that political power can only be *"seized, organised, and directed"* by a **minority.**

Thus we have minority rule, with the party (or more correctly its leaders) exercising political power. The idea that the party *"must **dissolve** into the councils, that the councils can **replace** the Communist Party"* is *"fundamentally wrong and reactionary."* This is because, to *"enable the soviets to fulfil their historic tasks, there must ... be a strong Communist Party, one that does not simply 'adapt' to the soviets but is able to make them renounce 'adaptation' to the bourgeoisie."* [**Op. Cit.**, p. 196] Thus rather than the workers' councils exercising power, their role is simply that of allowing the Communist Party to seize political power.

As we indicated in section H.3.4, the underlying assumption behind this resolution was made clear by Zinoviev during his introductory speech to the congress meeting which finally agreed the resolution: the dictatorship of the party **was** the dictatorship of the proletariat. Little wonder that Bertrand Russell, on his return from Lenin's Russia in 1920, wrote that:

"Friends of Russia here [in Britain] think of the dictatorship of the proletariat as merely a new form of representative government, in which only working men and women have votes, and the constituencies are partly occupational, not geographical. They think that 'proletariat' means 'proletariat,' but 'dictatorship' does not quite mean 'dictatorship.' This is the opposite of the truth. When a Russian Communist speaks of a dictatorship, he means the word literally, but when he speaks of the proletariat, he means the word in a Pickwickian sense. He means the 'class-conscious' part of the proletariat, i.e. the Communist Party. He includes people by no means proletarian (such as Lenin and Tchicherin) who have the right opinions, and he excludes such wage-earners as have not the right opinions, whom he classifies as lackeys of the bourgeoisie." [**The Practice and Theory of Bolshevism**, pp. 26-27]

Significantly, Russell pointed, like Lenin, to the Comintern resolution on the role of the Communist Party. In addition, he noted the reason why this party dictatorship was required: *"No conceivable system of free elections would give majorities to the Communists, either in the town or country."* [**Op. Cit.**, pp. 40-1]

Nor are followers of Bolshevism shy in repeating its elitist conclusions. Founder and leader of the British SWP, Tony Cliff, for example, showed his lack of commitment to working class democracy when he opined that the *"actual level of democracy, as well as centralism, [during a revolution] depends on three basic factors: 1. the strength of the proletariat; 2. the material and cultural legacy left to it by the old regime; and 3. the strength of capitalist resistance. The level of democracy feasible must be in direct proportion to the first two factors, and in inverse proportion to the third. The captain of an ocean liner can allow football to be played on his vessel; on a tiny raft in a stormy sea the level of tolerance is far lower."* [**Lenin**, vol. 3, p. 179] That Cliff compares working class democracy to football says it all. Rather than seeing it as the core gain of a revolution, he relegates it to the level of a **game,** which may or may not be *"tolerated"!* And need we speculate who the paternalistic *"captain"* in charge of the ship of the state would be?

Replacing Cliff's revealing analogies we get the following: *"The party in charge of a workers' state can allow democracy when the capitalist class is not resisting; when it is resisting strongly, the level of tolerance is far lower."* So, democracy will be *"tolerated"* in the extremely unlikely situation that the capitalist class will not resist a revolution! That the party has no right to *"tolerate"* democracy or not is not even entertained by Cliff, its right to negate the basic rights of the working class is taken as a given. Clearly the key factor is that the party is in power. It **may** *"tolerate"* democracy, but ultimately his analogy shows that Bolshevism considers it as an added extra whose (lack of) existence in no way determines the nature of the *"workers' state"* (unless, of course, he is analysing Stalin's regime rather than Lenin's then it becomes of critical importance!). Perhaps, therefore, we may add another *"basic factor"* to Cliff's three; namely *"4. the strength of working class support for the party."* The level of democracy feasible must be in direct proportion to this factor, as the Bolsheviks made clear. As long

as the workers vote for the party, then democracy is wonderful. If they do not, then their *"wavering"* and *"passing moods"* cannot be *"tolerated"* and democracy is replaced by the dictatorship of the party. Which is no democracy at all.

Obviously, then, if, as Engels argued, *"an essential feature of the state is a public power distinct from the mass of the people"* then the regime advocated by Bolshevism is not a *"semi-state"* but, in fact, a normal state. Trotsky and Lenin are equally clear that said state exists to ensure that the *"mass of the people"* do not participate in public power, which is exercised by a minority, the party (or, more correctly, the leaders of the party). One of the key aims of this new state is to repress the *"backward"* or *"wavering"* sections of the working class (although, by definition, all sections of the working class are *"backward"* in relation to the *"vanguard"*). Hence the need for a *"public power distinct from the people"* (as the suppression of the strike wave and Kronstadt in 1921 shows, elite troops are always needed to stop the army siding with their fellow workers). And as proven by Trotsky's comments after he was squeezed out of power, this perspective was **not** considered as a product of *"exceptional circumstances."* Rather it was considered a basic lesson of the revolution, a position which was applicable to all future revolutions. In this, Lenin and other leading Bolsheviks concurred.

The irony (and tragedy) of all this should not be lost. In his 1905 diatribe against anarchism, Stalin had denied that Marxists aimed for party dictatorship. He stressed that there was *"a dictatorship of the minority, the dictatorship of a small group … which is directed against the people … Marxists are the enemies of such a dictatorship, and they fight such a dictatorship far more stubbornly and self-sacrificingly than do our noisy Anarchists."* The practice of Bolshevism and the ideological revisions it generated easily refutes Stalin's claims. The practice of Bolshevism showed that his claim that *"[a]t the head"* of the *"dictatorship of the proletarian majority … stand the masses"* is in sharp contradiction with Bolshevik support for *"revolutionary"* governments. Either you have (to use Stalin's expression) *"the dictatorship of the streets, of the masses, a dictatorship directed against all oppressors"* or you have party power **in the name of the street, of the masses.** [**Collected Works**, vol. 1, p. 371-2] The fundamental flaw in Leninism is that it confuses the two and so lays the ground for the very result anarchists predicted and Stalin denied.

In summary, Bolshevism is based on a substantial revision of the Marxist theory of the state. While Marx and Engels were at pains to stress the accountability of their new state to the population under it, Leninism has made a virtue of the fact that the state has evolved to exclude that mass participation in order to ensure minority rule. Leninism has done so explicitly to allow the party to overcome the *"wavering"* of the working class, the very class it claims is the *"ruling class"* under socialism! In doing this, the Leninist tradition exploited the confused nature of the state theory of traditional Marxism. The Leninist theory of the state is flawed simply because it is based on creating a *"state in the proper sense of the word,"* with a public power distinct from the mass of the people. This was the major lesson gained by the leading Bolsheviks (including Lenin and Trotsky) from the Russian Revolution and has its roots in the common Marxist error of confusing party power with working class power. So when Leninists point to Lenin's **State and Revolution** as the definitive Leninist theory of the state, anarchists simply point to the lessons Lenin himself gained from actually conducting a revolution. Once we do, the slippery slope to the Leninist solution to the contradictions inherit in the Marxist theory of the state can be seen, understood and combated.

H.3.9 Is the state simply an agent of economic power?

As we discussed in section H.3.7, the Marxist theory of the state confuses an empirical analysis of the state with a metaphysical one. While Engels is aware that the state developed to ensure minority class rule and, as befits its task, evolved specific characteristics to execute that role, he also raised the idea that the state (*"as a rule"*) is *"the state of the most powerful, economically dominant class"* and *"through the medium of the state, becomes also the politically dominant class."* Thus the state can be considered, in essence, as *"nothing but a machine for the oppression of one class by another." "At a certain stage of economic development"*, Engels stressed, *"which was necessarily bound up with the split in society into classes, the state became a necessity owing to this split."* [**Selected Works**, pp. 577-8, p. 579 and p. 258] For Lenin, this was *"the basic idea of Marxism on the question of the historical role and meaning of the state,"* namely that *"the state is an organ of class **rule**, the organ for the **oppression** of one class by another."* [**Essential Works of Lenin**, p. 273 and p. 274]

The clear implication is that the state is simply an instrument, without special interests of its own. If this is the case, the use of a state by the proletariat is unproblematic (and so the confusion between working class self-organisation and the state we have discussed in various sections above is irrelevant). This argument can lead to simplistic conclusions, such as once a "revolutionary" government is in power in a "workers state" we need not worry about abuses of power or even civil liberties (this position was commonplace in Bolshevik ranks during the Russian Civil War, for example). It also is at the heart of Trotsky's contortions with regards to Stalinism, refusing to see the state bureaucracy as a new ruling class simply because the state, by definition, could not play such a role.

For anarchists, this position is a fundamental weakness of Marxism, a sign that the mainstream Marxist position significantly misunderstands the nature of the state and the needs of social revolution. However, we must stress that anarchists would agree that the state generally does serve the interests of the economically dominant classes. Bakunin, for example, argued that the State *"is authority, domination, and force, organised by the property-owning and so-called enlightened classes against the masses."* He saw the social revolution as destroying capitalism and the state at the same time, that is *"to overturn the State's domination, and that of the privileged classes whom it solely represents."* [**The Basic Bakunin**, p. 140] However, anarchists do not reduce our analysis and understanding of the state to this simplistic Marxist level. While being well aware that the state is the means of ensuring the domination of an economic elite, as we discussed in section B.2.5,

anarchists recognise that the state machine also has interests of its own. The state, for anarchists, is the delegation of power into the hands of a few. This creates, by its very nature, a privileged position for those at the top of the hierarchy:

> *"A government, that is a group of people entrusted with making the laws and empowered to use the collective force to oblige each individual to obey them, is already a privileged class and cut off from the people. As any constituted body would do, it will instinctively seek to extend its powers, to be beyond public control, to impose its own policies and to give priority to its special interests. Having been put in a privileged position, the government is already at odds with the people whose strength it disposes of."* [Malatesta, **Anarchy**, p. 36]

The Bolshevik regime during the Russia revolution proved the validity of this analysis. The Bolsheviks seized power in the name of the soviets yet soon marginalised, gerrymandered and disbanded them to remain in power while imposing a vision of socialism (more correctly, state capitalism) at odds with popular aspirations.

Why this would be the case is not hard to discover. Given that the state is a highly centralised, top-down structure it is unsurprising that it develops around itself a privileged class, a bureaucracy, around it. The inequality in power implied by the state is a source of privilege and oppression independent of property and economic class. Those in charge of the state's institutions would aim to protect (and expand) their area of operation, ensuring that they select individuals who share their perspectives and to whom they can pass on their positions. By controlling the flow of information, of personnel and resources, the members of the state's higher circles can ensure its, and their own, survival and prosperity. As such, politicians who are elected are at a disadvantage. The state is the permanent collection of institutions that have entrenched power structures and interests. The politicians come and go while the power in the state lies in its institutions due to their permanence. It is to be expected that such institutions would have their own interests and would pursue them whenever they can.

This would not fundamentally change in a new "workers' state" as it is, like all states, based on the delegation and centralisation of power into a few hands. Any "workers' government" would need a new apparatus to enforce its laws and decrees. It would need effective means of gathering and collating information. It would thus create *"an entirely new ladder of administration to extend its rule and make itself obeyed."* While a social revolution needs mass participation, the state limits initiative to the few who are in power and *"it will be impossible for one or even a number of individuals to elaborate the social forms"* required, which *"can only be the collective work of the masses ... Any kind of external authority will merely be an obstacle, a hindrance to the organic work that has to be accomplished; it will be no better than a source of discord and of hatreds."* [Kropotkin, **Words of a Rebel**, p. 169 and pp. 176-7]

Rather than "withering away," any "workers' state" would tend to grow in terms of administration and so the government creates around itself a class of bureaucrats whose position is different from the rest of society. This would apply to production as well. Being unable to manage everything, the state would have to re-introduce hierarchical management in order to ensure its orders are met and that a suitable surplus is extracted from the workers to feed the needs of the state machine. By creating an economically powerful class which it can rely on to discipline the workforce, it would simply recreate capitalism anew in the form of *"state capitalism"* (this is precisely what happened during the Russian Revolution). To enforce its will onto the people it claims to represent, specialised bodies of armed people (police, army) would be required and soon created. All of which is to be expected, as state socialism *"entrusts to a few the management of social life and [so] leads to the exploitation and oppression of the masses by the few."* [Malatesta, **Op. Cit.**, p. 47] Simply put, the vision of the state as merely an instrument of class rule blinds its supporters to the dangers of **political** inequality in terms of power, the dangers inherent in giving a small group of people power over everyone else. The state has certain properties **because it is a state** and one of these is that it creates a bureaucratic class around it due to its centralised, hierarchical nature. Within capitalism, the state bureaucracy is (generally) under the control of the capitalist class. However, to generalise from this specific case is wrong as the state bureaucracy is a class in itself - and so trying to abolish classes without abolishing the state is doomed to failure:

> *"The State has always been the patrimony of some privileged class: the sacerdotal class, the nobility, the bourgeoisie - and finally, when all the other classes have exhausted themselves, the class of the bureaucracy enters upon the stage and then the State falls, or rises, if you please to the position of a machine."* [Bakunin, **The Political Philosophy of Bakunin**, p. 208]

Thus the state cannot simply be considered as an instrument of rule by economic classes. It can be quite an effective parasitical force in its own right, as both anthropological and historical evidence suggest. The former raises the possibility that the state arose before economic classes and that its roots are in inequalities in power (i.e. hierarchy) within society, not inequalities of wealth. The latter points to examples of societies in which the state was not, in fact, an instrument of (economic) class rule but rather pursued an interest of its own.

As regards anthropology, Michael Taylor summarises that the *"evidence does not give [the Marxist] proposition [that the rise of economic classes caused the creation of the state] a great deal of support. Much of the evidence which has been offered in support of it shows only that the primary states, not long after their emergence, were economically stratified. But this is of course consistent also with the simultaneous rise ... of political and economic stratification, or with the **prior** development of the state - i.e. of **political** stratification - and the creation of economic stratification by the ruling class."* [**Community, Anarchy and Liberty**, p. 132] Thus the state is not, initially, a product of economic classes but rather an independent development based on inequalities of social power. Harold Barclay, an anarchist who has studied anthropological evidence on this matter, concurs:

> *"In Marxist theory power derives primarily, if not exclusively, from control of the means of production and distribution of wealth, that is, from economic factors.*

> *Yet, it is evident that power derived from knowledge - and usually 'religious' style knowledge - is often highly significant, at least in the social dynamics of small societies... Economic factors are hardly the only source of power. Indeed, we see this in modern society as well, where the capitalist owner does not wield total power. Rather technicians and other specialists command it as well, not because of their economic wealth, but because of their knowledge."* [quoted by Alan Carter, **Marx: A Radical Critique**, p. 191]

If, as Bookchin summarises, *"hierarchies precede classes"* then trying to use a hierarchical structure like the state to abolish them is simply wishful thinking.

As regards more recent human history, there have been numerous examples of the state existing without being an instrument of (economic) class rule. Rather, the state **was** the ruling class. While the most obvious example is the Stalinist regimes where the state bureaucracy ruled over a state capitalist economy, there have been plenty of others, as Murray Bookchin pointed out:

> *"Each State is not necessarily an institutionalised system of violence in the interests of a specific ruling class, as Marxism would have us believe. There are many examples of States that **were** the 'ruling class' and whose own interests existed quite apart from - even in antagonism to - privileged, presumably 'ruling' classes in a given society. The ancient world bears witness to distinctly capitalistic classes, often highly privileged and exploitative, that were bilked by the State, circumscribed by it, and ultimately devoured by it - which is in part why a capitalist society never emerged out of the ancient world. Nor did the State 'represent' other class interests, such as landed nobles, merchants, craftsmen, and the like. The Ptolemaic State in Hellenistic Egypt was an interest in its own right and 'represented' no other interest than its own. The same is true of the Aztec and the Inca States until they were replaced by Spanish invaders. Under the Emperor Domitian, the Roman State became the principal 'interest' in the empire, superseding the interests of even the landed aristocracy which held such primacy in Mediterranean society...*

> *"Near-Eastern States, like the Egyptian, Babylonian, and Persian, were virtually extended households of individual monarchs ... Pharaohs, kings, and emperors nominally held the land (often co-jointly with the priesthood) in the trust of the deities, who were either embodied in the monarch or were represented by him. The empires of Asian and North African kings were 'households' and the population was seen as 'servants of the palace' ...*

> *"These 'states,' in effect, were not simply engines of exploitation or control in the interests of a privileged 'class.' ... The Egyptian State was very real but it 'represented' nothing other than itself."* [**Remaking Society**, pp. 67-8]

Bakunin pointed to Turkish Serbia, where economically dominant classes *"do not even exist - there is only a bureaucratic class. Thus, the Serbian state will crush the Serbian people for the sole purpose of enabling Serbian bureaucrats to live a fatter life."* [**Statism and Anarchy**, p. 54] Leninist Tony Cliff, in his attempt to prove that Stalinist Russia was state capitalist and its bureaucracy a ruling class, pointed to various societies which *"had deep class differentiation, based not on private property but on state property. Such systems existed in Pharaonic Egypt, Moslem Egypt, Iraq, Persia and India."* He discusses the example of Arab feudalism in more detail, where *"the feudal lord had no permanent domain of his own, but a member of a class which collectively controlled the land and had the right to appropriate rent."* This was *"ownership of the land by the state"* rather than by individuals. [**State Capitalism in Russia**, pp. 316-8] As such, the idea that the state is simply an instrument of class rule seems unsupportable.

Marx's *"implicit theory of the state - a theory which, in reducing political power to the realisation of the interests of the dominant economic classes, precludes any concern with the potentially authoritarian and oppressive outcome of authoritarian and centralised revolutionary methods ... This danger (namely, the dismissal of warranted fears concerning political power) is latent in the central features of Marx's approach to politics."* [Alan Carter, **Op. Cit.**, p. 219] To summarise the obvious conclusion:

> *"By focusing too much attention on the economic structure of society and insufficient attention on the problems of political power, Marx has left a legacy we would have done better not to inherit. The perceived need for authoritarian and centralised revolutionary organisation is sanctioned by Marx's theory because his theoretical subordination of political power to economic classes apparently renders post-revolutionary political power unproblematic."* [**Op. Cit.**, p. 231]

Many factors contributed to Stalinism, including Marxism's defective theory of the state. In stressing that socialism meant nationalising property, it lead to state management which, in turn, expropriated the working class as a vast managerial bureaucracy was required to run it. Moreover, Marxism disguised this new ruling class as it argues that the state 'represents' an economic class and had no interests of itself. Hence Trotsky's utter inability to understand Stalinism and his insane formula that the proletariat remained the ruling class under Stalin (or, for that matter, under himself and Lenin)!

However, there is more to Marxism than its dominant theory of the state. Given the blindness of orthodox Marxism to this issue, it seems ironic that one of the people responsible for it also provides anarchists with evidence to back up our argument that the state is not simply an instrument of class rule but rather has interests of its own. Thus we find Engels arguing that proletariat, *"in order not to lose again its only just conquered supremacy,"* would have *"to safeguard itself against its own deputies and officials, by declaring them all, without exception, subject to recall at any moment."* [**Selected Works**, p. 257] Yet, if the state was simply an instrument of class rule such precautions would not be necessary. Engels comments show an awareness that the state can have interests of its own, that it is not simply a machine of class rule.

Aware of the obvious contradiction, Engels argued that the state *"is, as a rule, the state of the most powerful, economically dominant class which, through the medium of the state, becomes the politically dominant class ... By way of exception, however, periods occur in which the warring classes balance each other, so nearly that the state power, as ostensible mediator, acquires, for the moment, a certain degree of independence of both."* He pointed to the *"absolute monarchy of the seventeenth and eighteenth centuries"*, which held the balance between the nobility and the bourgeoisie against one another as well as *"the Bonapartism of the First, and still more of the Second French Empire."* It should be noted that, elsewhere, Engels was more precise on how long the state was, in fact, controlled by the bourgeoisie, namely two years: *"In France, where the bourgeoisie as such, as a class in its entirety, held power for only two years, 1849 and 1850, under the republic, it was able to continue its social existence only by abdicating its political power to Louis Bonaparte and the army."* [**Op. Cit.**, pp. 577-8 and p. 238] So, in terms of French history, Engels argued that *"by way of exception"* accounted for over 250 years, the 17th and 18th centuries and most of the 19th, bar a two year period! Even if we are generous and argue that the 1830 revolution placed one section of the bourgeoisie (finance capital) into political power, we are still left with over 200 hundred years of state "independence" from classes! Given this, it would be fair to suggest that the "exception" should be when it **is** an instrument of class rule, not when it is not!

So, according to Engels, the executive of the state, like the state itself, can become independent from classes if the opposing classes were balanced. This analysis, it must be pointed out, was an improvement on the earliest assertions of Marx and Engels on the state. In the 1840s, it was a case of the *"independence of the state is only found nowadays in those countries where the estates have not yet completely developed into classes ... where consequently no section of the population can achieve dominance over the others."* [**Collected Works**, vol. 5, p. 90] For Engels, *"[f]rom the moment the state administration and legislature fall under the control of the bourgeoisie, the independence of the bureaucracy ceases to exist."* [**Op. Cit.**, vol. 6, p. 88] It must, therefore, have come as a surprise for Marx and Engels when the state and its bureaucracy appeared to become independent in France under Napoleon III.

Talking of which, it should be noted that, initially for Marx, under Bonapartism *"the state power is not suspended in mid air. Bonaparte represents a class, and the most numerous class of French society at that, the **small-holding [Parzellen] peasants**."* The Bonaparte *"who dispersed the bourgeois parliament is the chosen of the peasantry."* However, this class is *"incapable of enforcing their class interests in their own name ... They cannot represent themselves, they must be represented. Their representative must at the same time appear as their master, as an authority over them, as an unlimited governmental power ... The political influence of the small-holding peasants, therefore, finds its final expression in the executive power subordinating society to itself."* Yet Marx himself admits that this regime experienced *"peasant risings in half of France"*, organised *"raids on the peasants by the army"* and the *"mass incarceration and transportation of peasants."* A strange form of class rule, when the class represented is oppressed by the regime! Rest assured, though, the *"Bonaparte dynasty represents not the revolutionary, but the conservative peasant."* Then Marx, without comment, pronounced Bonaparte to be *"the representative of the **lumpenproletariat** to which he himself, his entourage, his government and his army belong."* [**Selected Works**, p. 170, p. 171 and p. 176]

It would be fair to say that Marx's analysis is somewhat confused and seems an ad hoc explanation to the fact that in a modern society the state appeared to become independent of the economically dominant class. Yet if a regime is systematically oppressing a class then it is fair to conclude that is **not** representing that class in any way. Bonaparte's power did not, in other words, rest on the peasantry. Rather, like fascism, it was a means by which the bourgeoisie could break the power of the working class and secure its own class position against possible social revolution. As Bakunin argued, it was a *"despotic imperial system"* which the bourgeois *"themselves founded out of fear of the Social Revolution."* [**The Basic Bakunin**, p. 63] Thus the abolition of bourgeois rule was more apparent than real:

> *"As soon as the people took equality and liberty seriously, the bourgeoisie ... retreated into reaction ... They began by suppressing universal suffrage ... The fear of Social Revolution ... . hurled this downfallen class ... into the arms of the dictatorship of Napoleon III ... We should not think that the Bourgeois Gentlemen were too inconvenienced ... [Those who] applied themselves earnestly and exclusively to the great concern of the bourgeoisie, the exploitation of the people ... were well protected and powerfully supported ... All went well, according to the desires of the bourgeoisie."* [**Op. Cit.**, pp. 62-3]

Somewhat ironically, then, a key example used by Marxists for the "independence" of the state is no such thing. Bonapartism did not represent a "balance" between the proletariat and bourgeoisie but rather the most naked form of state rule required in the face of working class revolt. It was a counter-revolutionary regime which reflected a defeat for the working class, not a "balance" between it and the capitalist class.

Marx's confusions arose from his belief that, for the bourgeoisie, the parliamentary republic *"was the unavoidable condition of their **common** rule, the sole form of state in which their general class interest subjected to itself at the same time both the claims of their particular factions and all the remaining classes of society."* The abolition of the republic, the replacement of the government, was, for him, the end of the political rule of the bourgeoisie as he argued that *"the industrial bourgeoisie applauds with servile bravos the **coup d'état** of December 2, the annihilation of parliament, the downfall of its own rule, the dictatorship of Bonaparte."* He repeated this identification: *"Passing of the parliamentary regime and of bourgeois rule. Victory of Bonaparte."* [**Selected Works**, pp. 151-2, pp. 164-5 and p. 166] Political rule was equated to which party held power and so, logically, universal suffrage was *"the equivalent of political power for the working class ... where the proletariat forms the large majority of the population."* Its *"inevitable result"* would be *"**the political supremacy of the working class**."* [**Collected Works**, vol. 11, pp. 335-6] This was, of course, simply

wrong (on both counts) as he, himself, seemed to became aware of two decades later.

In 1871 he argued that *"the State power assumed more and more the character of the national power of capital over labour, of a public force organised for social enslavement, of an engine of class despotism."* This meant that *"in view of the threatened upheaval of the proletariat, [the bourgeoisie] now used that State power mercilessly and ostentatiously as the national war-engine of capital against labour"* and so were *"bound not only to invest the executive with continually increased powers of repression, but at the same time to divest their own parliamentary stronghold ... of all its own means of defence against the Executive. The Executive, in the person of Louis Bonaparte, turned them out."* Marx now admitted that this regime only *"professed to rest upon the peasantry"* while, *"[i]n reality, it was the only form of government possible at a time when the bourgeoisie had already lost, and the working class had not yet acquired, the faculty of ruling the nation."* However, *"[u]nder its sway, bourgeois society, freed from political cares, attained a development unexpected even by itself."* [**Selected Works**, p. 285, p. 286, pp. 286-7 and p. 287]

Yet capitalists often do well under regimes which suppress the basic liberties of the working class and so the bourgeoisie remained the ruling class and the state remained its organ. In other words, there is no "balance" between classes under Bonapartism even if the political regime is not subject to electoral control by the bourgeoisie and has more independence to pursue its own agenda.

This is not the only confirmation of the anarchist critique of the Marxist theory of the state which can be found in Marxism itself. Marx, at times, also admitted the possibility of the state **not** being an instrument of (economic) class rule. For example, he mentioned the so-called ***"Asiatic Mode of Production"*** in which *"there are no private landowners"* but rather *"the state ... which confronts"* the peasants *"directly as simultaneously landowner and sovereign, rent and tax coincide ... Here the state is the supreme landlord. Sovereignty here is landed property concentrated on a national scale."* [**Capital**, vol. 3, p. 927] Thus *"the State [is] the real landlord"* in the *"Asiatic system"* [**Collected Works**, vol. 12, p. 215] In other words, the ruling class could be a state bureaucracy and so be independent of economic classes. Unfortunately this analysis remained woefully undeveloped and no conclusions were drawn from these few comments, perhaps unsurprisingly as it undermines the claim that the state is merely the instrument of the economically dominant class. It also, of course, has applicability to state socialism and certain conclusions could be reached that suggested it, as Bakunin warned, would be a new form of class rule.

The state bureaucracy as the ruling class can be seen in Soviet Russia (and the other so-called "socialist" regimes such as China and Cuba). As libertarian socialist Ante Ciliga put it, *"the manner in which Lenin organised industry had handed it over entirely into the hands of the bureaucracy,"* and so the workers *"became once more the wage-earning manpower in other people's factories. Of socialism there remained in Russia no more than the word."* [**The Russian Enigma**, p. 280 and p. 286] Capitalism became state capitalism under Lenin and Trotsky and so the state, as Bakunin predicted and feared, became the new ruling class under Marxism (see section H.3.14 for more discussion of this).

The confusions of the Marxist theory of the state ensured that Trotsky, for example, failed to recognise the obvious, namely that the Stalinist state bureaucracy was a ruling class. Rather, it was the *"new ruling caste"*, or *"the ruling stratum"*. While admitting, at one stage, that the *"transfer of the factories to the State changed the situation of the workers only juridically"* Trotsky then ignored the obvious conclusion that this has left the working class as an exploited class under a (new) form of capitalism to assert that the *"nature"* of Stalinist Russia was *"a proletarian State"* because of its *"nationalisation"* of the means of life (which *"constitute the basis of the Soviet social structure"*). He admitted that the *"Soviet Bureaucracy has expropriated the proletariat politically"* but has done so *"in order by methods of **its own** to defend the social conquests"* of the October Revolution. He did not ponder too deeply the implications of admitting that the *"means of production belong to the State. But the State, so to speak, 'belongs' to the bureaucracy."* [**The Revolution Betrayed**, p. 93, p. 136, p. 228, p. 235 and p. 236] If that is so, only ideology can stop the obvious conclusion being drawn, namely that the state bureaucracy was the ruling class. But that is precisely what happened with Trotsky's confusion expressing itself thusly:

> *"In no other regime has a bureaucracy ever achieved such a degree of independence from the dominating class … it is something more than a bureaucracy. It is in the full sense of the word the sole privileged and commanding stratum in the Soviet society."* [**Op. Cit.**, p. 235]

By this, Trotsky suggested that the working class was the *"dominating class"* under Stalinism! In fact, the bureaucracy *"continues to preserve State property only to the extent it fears the proletariat"* while, at the same time, the bureaucracy has *"become [society's] lord"* and *"the Soviet state has acquired a totalitarian-bureaucratic character"*! This nonsense is understandable, given the unwillingness to draw the obvious conclusion from the fact that the bureaucracy was *"compelled to defend State property as the source of its power and its income. In this aspect of its activity it still remains a weapon of proletarian dictatorship."* [**Op. Cit.**, p. 112, p. 107, p. 238 and p. 236] By commanding nationalised property, the bureaucracy, like private capitalists, could exploit the labour of the working class and did. That the state owned the means of production did not stop this being a form of class system.

It is simply nonsense to claim, as Trotsky did, that the *"anatomy of society is determined by its economic relations. So long as the forms of property that have been created by the October Revolution are not overthrown, the proletariat remains the ruling class."* [**Writings of Leon Trotsky 1933-34**, p. 125] How could the proletariat be the *"ruling class"* if it were under the heel of a totalitarian dictatorship? State ownership of property was precisely the means by which the bureaucracy enforced its control over production and so the source of its economic power and privileges. To state the obvious, if the working class does not control the property it is claimed to own then someone else does. The economic relationship thus generated is a hierarchical one, in which the working class is an oppressed class. Significantly, Trotsky combated those of his followers who drew the same conclusions as had anarchists and libertarian Marxists

while he and Lenin held the reins of power. Perhaps this ideological blindness is understandable, given Trotsky's key role in creating the bureaucracy in the first place. So Trotsky did criticise, if in a confused manner, the Stalinist regime for its *"injustice, oppression, differential consumption, and so on, even if he had supported them when he himself was in the elite."* [Neil C. Fernandez, **Capitalism and Class Struggle in the USSR**, p. 180]). Then there is the awkward conclusion that if the bureaucracy were a ruling class under Stalin then Russia was also state capitalist under Lenin and Trotsky for the economic relations were identical in both (this obvious conclusion haunts those, like the British SWP, who maintain that Stalinism was State Capitalist but not Bolshevism - see section H.3.13). Suffice to say, if the state itself can be the "economically dominant class" then the state cannot be a mere instrument of an economic class.

To summarise, if the state can become *"independent"* of economic classes or even exist without an economically dominant class, then that implies that it is no mere machine, no mere *"instrument"* of class rule. It implies the anarchist argument that the state has interests of its own, generated by its essential features and so, therefore, cannot be used by a majority class as part of its struggle for liberation is correct. Simply put, Anarchists have long *"realised - feared - that any State structure, whether or not socialist or based on universal suffrage, has a certain independence from society, and so may serve the interests of those within State institutions rather than the people as a whole or the proletariat."* [Brian Morris, **Bakunin: The Philosophy of Freedom**, p. 134] Thus *"the state certainly has interests of its own … [,] acts to protect [them] … and protects the interests of the bourgeoisie when these interests happen to coincide with its own, as, indeed, they usually do."* [Carter, **Op. Cit.**, p. 226]

As Mark Leier quips, Marxism *"has usually - save when battling anarchists - argued that the state has some 'relative autonomy' and is not a direct, simple reflex of a given economic system."* [**Bakunin: The Constructive Passion**, p. 275] The reason why the more sophisticated Marxist analysis of the state is forgotten when it comes to attacking anarchism should be obvious - it undermines both the Marxist critique of anarchism and its own theory of the state. Ironically, arguments and warnings about the *"independence"* of the state by Marxists imply that the state has interests of its own and cannot be considered simply as an instrument of class rule. They suggest that the anarchist analysis of the state is correct, namely that any structure based on delegated power, centralisation and hierarchy must, inevitably, have a privileged class in charge of it, a class whose position enables it to not only exploit and oppress the rest of society but also to effectively escape from popular control and accountability. This is no accident. The state is structured to enforce minority rule and exclude the majority.

H.3.10 Has Marxism always supported the idea of workers' councils?

One of the most widespread myths associated with Marxism is the idea that Marxism has consistently aimed to smash the current (bourgeois) state and replace it by a *"workers' state"* based on working class organisations created during a revolution.

This myth is sometimes expressed by those who should know better (i.e. Marxists). According to John Rees (of the British Socialist Workers Party) it has been a *"cornerstone of revolutionary theory"* that *"the soviet is a superior form of democracy because it unifies political and economic power."* This *"cornerstone"* has, apparently, existed *"since Marx's writings on the Paris Commune."* [*"In Defence of October"*, pp. 3-82, **International Socialism**, no. 52, p. 25] In fact, nothing could be further from the truth, as Marx's writings on the Paris Commune prove beyond doubt.

The Paris Commune, as Marx himself noted, was *"formed of the municipal councillors, chosen by universal suffrage in the various wards of the town."* [**Selected Works**, p. 287] As Marx made clear, it was definitely **not** based on delegates from workplaces and so could **not** unify political and economic power. Indeed, to state that the Paris Commune was a soviet is simply a joke, as is the claim that Marxists supported soviets as revolutionary organs to smash and replace the state from 1871. In fact Marxists did not subscribe to this *"cornerstone of revolutionary theory"* until 1917 when Lenin argued that the Soviets would be the best means of ensuring a Bolshevik government. Which explains why Lenin's use of the slogan *"All Power to the Soviets"* and call for the destruction of the bourgeois state came as such a shock to his fellow Marxists. Unsurprisingly, given the long legacy of anarchist calls to smash the state and their vision of a socialist society built from below by workers councils, many Marxists called Lenin an anarchist! Therefore, the idea that Marxists have always supported workers councils' is untrue and any attempt to push this support back to 1871 simply farcical.

Not all Marxists are as ignorant of their political tradition as Rees. As his fellow party member Chris Harman recognised, *"[e]ven the 1905 [Russian] revolution gave only the most embryonic expression of how a workers' state would in fact be organised. The fundamental forms of workers' power - the soviets (workers' councils) - were not recognised."* It was *"[n]ot until the February revolution [of 1917 that] soviets became central in Lenin's writings and thought."* [**Party and Class**, p. 18 and p. 19] Before then, Marxists had held the position, to quote Karl Kautsky from 1909 (who is, in turn, quoting his own words from 1893), that the democratic republic *"was the particular form of government in which alone socialism can be realised."* He added, after the Russian Revolution, that *"not a single Marxist revolutionary repudiated me, neither Rosa Luxemburg nor Klara Zetkin, neither Lenin nor Trotsky."* [**The Road to Power**, p. 34 and p. xlviii]

Lenin himself, even after Social Democracy supported their respective states in the First World War and before his return to Russia, still argued that Kautsky's work contained *"a most complete exposition of the tasks of our times"* and *"it was most advantageous to the German Social-Democrats (in the sense of the promise they held out), and moreover came from the pen of the most eminent writer of the Second International ... Social-Democracy ... wants conquest of political power by the proletariat, the dictatorship of the proletariat."* [**Collected Works**, vol. 21, p. 94] There was no hint that Marxism stood for anything other than seizing power in a republic, as expounded by the likes of Kautsky.

Before continuing it should be stressed that Harman's summary is correct only if we are talking about the Marxist movement. Looking at the wider revolutionary movement, two groups definitely recognised the importance of the soviets as a form of working class power and as the framework of a socialist society. These were the anarchists and the Social-Revolutionary Maximalists, both of whom *"espoused views that corresponded almost word for word with Lenin's April 1917 program of 'All power to the soviets.'"* The *"aims of the revolutionary far left in 1905"* Lenin *"combined in his call for soviet power [in 1917], when he apparently assimilated the anarchist program to secure the support of the masses for the Bolsheviks."* [Oskar Anweiler, **The Soviets**, p. 94 and p. 96]

So before 1917, when Lenin claimed to have discovered what had eluded all the previous followers of Marx and Engels (including himself!), it was only anarchists (or those close to them such as the SR-Maximalists) who argued that the future socialist society would be structurally based around the organs working class people themselves created in the process of the class struggle and revolution. For example, the syndicalists *"regarded the soviets ... as admirable versions of the **bourses du travail**, but with a revolutionary function added to suit Russian conditions. Open to all leftist workers regardless of specific political affiliation, the soviets were to act as nonpartisan labour councils improvised 'from below' ... with the aim of bringing down the old regime."* The anarchists of **Khleb i Volia** *"also likened the 1905 Petersburg Soviet - as a non-party mass organisation - to the central committee of the Paris Commune of 1871."* [Paul Avrich, **The Russian Anarchists**, pp. 80-1] In 1907, it was concluded that the revolution required *"the proclamation in villages and towns of workers' communes with soviets of workers' deputies ... at their head."* [quoted by Alexandre Skirda, **Facing the Enemy**, p. 77] These ideas can be traced back to Bakunin, so, ironically, the idea of the superiority of workers' councils **has** existed from around the time of the Paris Commune, but only in anarchist theory.

So, if Marxists did not support workers' councils until 1917, what **did** Marxists argue should be the framework of a socialist society before this date? To discover this, we must look to Marx and Engels. Once we do, we discover that their works suggest that their vision of socialist transformation was fundamentally based on the bourgeois state, suitably modified and democratised to achieve this task. As such, rather than present the true account of the Marxist theory of the state Lenin interpreted various inexact and ambiguous statements by Marx and Engels (particularly from Marx's defence of the Paris Commune) to justify his own actions in 1917. Whether his 1917 revision of Marxism in favour of workers' councils as the means to socialism is in keeping with the **spirit** of Marx is another matter of course. For the **Socialist Party of Great Britain** and its sister parties, Lenin violated both the letter **and** the spirit of

Marx and they stress his arguments in favour of utilising universal suffrage to introduce socialism (indeed, their analysis of Marx and critique of Lenin is substantially the same as the one presented here). For the council communists, who embraced the idea of workers' councils but broke with the Bolsheviks over the issue of whether the councils or the party had power, Lenin's analysis, while flawed in parts, is in the general spirit of Marx and they stress the need to smash the state and replace it with workers' councils. In this, they express the best in Marx. When faced with the Paris Commune and its libertarian influences he embraced it, distancing himself (for a while at least) from many of his previous ideas.

So what was the original (orthodox) Marxist position? It can be seen from Lenin who, as late December 1916 argued that *"Socialists are in favour of utilising the present state and its institutions in the struggle for the emancipation of the working class, maintaining also that the state should be used for a specific form of transition from capitalism to socialism."* Lenin attacked Bukharin for *"erroneously ascribing this [the anarchist] view to the socialist"* when he had stated socialists wanted to *"abolish"* the state or *"blow it up."* He called this *"transitional form"* the dictatorship of the proletariat, *"which is **also** a state."* [**Collected Works**, vol. 23, p. 165] In other words, the socialist party would aim to seize power within the existing republican state and, after making suitable modifications to it, use it to create socialism.

That this position was the orthodox one is hardly surprising, given the actual comments of both Marx and Engels. For example Engels argued in April 1883 while he and Marx saw *"the gradual dissolution and ultimate disappearance of that political organisation called **the State**"* as *"**one** of the final results of the future revolution,"* they *"at the same time … have always held that … the proletarian class will first have to possess itself of the organised political force of the State and with its aid stamp out the resistance of the Capitalist class and re-organise society."* The idea that the proletariat needs to *"possess"* the existing state is made clear when he notes that the anarchists *"reverse the matter"* by advocating that the revolution *"has to **begin** by abolishing the political organisation of the State."* For Marxists *"the only organisation the victorious working class finds **ready-made** for use, is that of the State. It may require adaptation to the new functions. But to destroy that at such a moment, would be to destroy the only organism by means of which the working class can exert its newly conquered power."* [our emphasis, **Op. Cit.**, vol. 47, p. 10]

Obviously the only institution which the working class *"finds ready-made for use"* is the democratic (i.e., bourgeois) state, although, as Engels stressed, it *"may require adaptation."* In Engels 1891 introduction to Marx's *"The Civil War in France"*, this analysis is repeated when Engels asserted that the state *"is nothing but a machine for the oppression of one class by another"* and that it is *"at best an evil inherited by the proletariat after its victorious struggle for class supremacy, whose worst sides the victorious proletariat, just like the Commune, cannot avoid having to lop off at once as much as possible."* [**Selected Works**, p. 258]

If the proletariat creates a **new** state to replace the bourgeois one, then how can it be *"ready-made for use"* and *"an evil inherited"* by it? If, as Lenin argued, Marx and Engels thought that the working class had to smash the bourgeois state and replace it with a new

one, why would it have *"to lop off at once as much as possible"* from the state it had just *"inherited"*?

Three years later, Engels made his position clear: *"With respect to the proletariat the republic differs from the monarchy only in that it is the **ready-for-use** form for the future rule of the proletariat."* He went on to state that the French socialists *"are at an advantage compared to us in already having it"* and warned against *"baseless"* illusions such as seeking to *"entrust socialist tasks to it while it is dominated by the bourgeoisie."* [Marx and Engels, **The Socialist Revolution**, p. 296] This was, significantly, simply repeating Engels 1891 argument from his critique of the draft of the Erfurt program of the German Social Democrats:

> *"If one thing is certain it is that our Party and the working class can only come to power under the form of a democratic republic. This is even the specific form for the dictatorship of the proletariat, as the Great French Revolution has already shown."* [**Collected Works**, vol. 27, p. 227]

Clearly Engels does not speak of a "commune-republic" or anything close to a soviet republic, as expressed in Bakunin's work or the libertarian wing of the First International with their ideas of a "trade-union republic" or a free federation of workers' associations. Clearly and explicitly he speaks of the democratic republic, the current state (*"an evil inherited by the proletariat"*) which is to be seized and transformed.

Unsurprisingly, when Lenin came to quote this passage in **State and Revolution** he immediately tried to obscure its meaning. *"Engels,"* he wrote, *"repeated here in a particularly striking form the fundamental idea which runs through all of Marx's work, namely, that the democratic republic is the nearest approach to the dictatorship of the proletariat."* [**The Lenin Anthology**, p. 360] However, obviously Engels did nothing of the kind. He did not speak of the political form which *"is the nearest approach"* to the dictatorship, rather he wrote only of *"the specific form"* of the dictatorship, the *"only"* form in which *"our Party"* can come to power. Hal Draper, likewise, denied that Engels meant what he clearly wrote, arguing that he **really** meant the Paris Commune. *"Because of the expression 'great French revolution,'"* Draper asserted, *"the assumption has often been made that Engels meant the French Revolution of 1789; but the idea that he, or anyone else, could view 1789 (or 1793) as a 'dictatorship of the proletariat' is too absurd to entertain."* [**The 'dictatorship of the proletariat' from Marx to Lenin**, p. 37fn]

Yet, contextually, no evidence exists to support such a claim and what does disputes it - Engels discusses French history and makes no mention of the Commune but **does** mention the republic of 1792 to 1799 (significantly, Lenin makes no attempt to suggest that Engels meant the Paris Commune or anything else bar a democratic republic). In fact, Engels goes on to argue that *"[f]rom 1792 to 1799 each French department, each commune, enjoyed complete self-government on the American model, and this is what we too must have. How self-government is to be organised and how we can manage without a bureaucracy has been shown to us by America and the first French Republic."* Significantly, Engels was explicitly discussing the need for a *"republican party programme"*, commenting that it would be impossible for *"our best people to become ministers"* under an Emperor and arguing that, in Germany at the time, they could not call for a republic and had to raise the *"demand for* **the concentration of all political power in the hands of the people's representatives**.*"* Engels stressed that *"the proletariat can only use the form of the one and indivisible republic"* with *"self-government"* meaning *"officials elected by universal suffrage"*. [**Op. Cit.**, pp. 227-9]

Clearly, the *"assumption"* Draper denounced makes more sense than his own or Lenin's. This is particularly the case when it is clear that both Marx and Engels viewed the French Republic under the Jacobins as a situation where the proletariat held political power (although, like Marx with the Paris Commune, they do not use the term "dictatorship of the proletariat" to describe it). Engels wrote of *"the rule of the Mountain party"* as being *"the short time when the proletariat was at the helm of the state in the French Revolution"* and *"from May 31, 1793 to July 26, 1794 ... not a single bourgeois dared show his face in the whole of France."* Marx, similarly, wrote of this period as one in which *"the proletariat overthrows the political rule of the bourgeoisie"* but due to the *"material conditions"* its acts were *"in service"* of the bourgeois revolution. The *"bloody action of the people"* only *"prepared the way for"* the bourgeoisie by destroying feudalism, something which the bourgeoisie was not capable of. [**Op. Cit.**, vol. 6, p. 373, p. 5 and p. 319]

Apparently Engels did **not** consider it *"too absurd to entertain"* that the French Republic of 1793 was *"a 'dictatorship of the proletariat'"* and, ironically, Draper's *"anyone else"* turned out to be Marx! Moreover, this was well known in Marxist circles long before Draper made his assertion. Julius Martov (for example) after quoting Marx on this issue summarised that, for Marx and Engels, the *"Reign of Terror in France was the momentary domination of the democratic petty bourgeoisie and the proletariat over all the possessing classes, including the authentic bourgeoisie."* [**The State and Socialist Revolution**, p. 51]

Similarly, Lenin quoted Engels on the proletariat seizing *"state power"* and nationalising the means of production, an act by which it *"abolishes itself as proletariat"* **and** *"abolishes the state as state."* Significantly, it is **Lenin** who has to write that *"Engels speaks here of the proletarian revolution 'abolishing' the* **bourgeois** *state, while the words about the state withering away refer to the remnants of the* **proletariat** *state* **after** *the socialist revolution."* Yet Engels himself makes no such differentiation and talks purely of *"the state"* and it *"becom[ing] the real representative of the whole of society"* by *"taking possession of the means of production in the name of society."* Perhaps Lenin was right and Engels really meant two different states but, sadly, he failed to make that point explicitly, so allowing Marxism, to use Lenin's words, to be subjected to *"the crudest distortion"* by its followers, *"prune[d]"* and *"reduc[ed] ... to opportunism."* [**Op. Cit.**, pp. 320-2]

Then there are Engels 1887 comments that in the USA the workers *"next step towards their deliverance"* was *"the formation of a political workingmen's party, with a platform of its own, and the conquest of the Capitol and the White House for its goal."* This new party *"like all political parties everywhere ... aspires to the conquest of political power."* Engels then discusses the *"electoral battle"* going on in America. [Marx and Engels, **Collected Works**, vol. 26, p. 435 and

p. 437] Significantly, 40 years previously in 1847, Engels had argued that the revolution *"will establish a* **democratic constitution**, *and through this, the direct ... dominance of the proletariat"* where *"the proletarians are already a majority of the people."* He noted that *"a democratic constitution has been introduced"* in America. [**Op. Cit.**, vol. 6, p. 350 and p. 356] The continuity is significant, particularly as these identical arguments come before and after the Paris Commune of 1871.

This was no isolated statement. Engels had argued along the same lines (and, likewise, echoed early statements) as regards Britain in 1881, *"where the industrial and agricultural working class forms the immense majority of the people, democracy means the dominion of the working class, neither more nor less. Let, then, that working class prepare itself for the task in store for it - the ruling of this great Empire ... And the best way to do this is to use the power already in their hands, the actual majority they possess ... to send to Parliament men of their own order."* In case this was not clear enough, he lamented that *"[e]verywhere the labourer struggles for political power, for direct representation of his class in the legislature - everywhere but in Great Britain."* [**Op. Cit.**, vol. 24, p. 405] For Engels:

> *"In every struggle of class against class, the next end fought for is political power; the ruling class defends its political supremacy, that is to say its safe majority in the Legislature; the inferior class fights for, first a share, then the whole of that power, in order to become enabled to change existing laws in conformity with their own interests and requirements. Thus the working class of Great Britain for years fought ardently and even violently for the People's Charter [which demanded universal suffrage and yearly general elections], which was to give it that political power."* [**Op. Cit.**, p. 386]

The 1st of May, 1893, saw Engels argue that the task of the British working class was not only to pursue economic struggles *"but above all in winning political rights, parliament, through the working class organised into an independent party"* (significantly, the original manuscript stated *"but in winning parliament, the political power"*). He went on to state that the 1892 general election saw the workers give a *"taste of their power, hitherto unexerted."* [**Op. Cit.**, vol. 27, p. 395] This, significantly, is in line with his 1870 comment that in Britain *"the bourgeoisie could only get its real representative ... into government only by extension of the franchise, whose consequences are bound to put an end to all bourgeois rule."* [**Selected Works**, p. 238]

Marx seems to see voting for a government as being the same as political power as the *"fundamental contradiction"* of a democracy under capitalism is that the classes *"whose social slavery the constitution is to perpetuate"* it *"puts in possession of political power through universal suffrage."* [**Collected Works**, vol. 10, p. 79] For Engels in 1847, *"democracy has as its necessary consequence the political rule of the proletariat."* Universal suffrage would *"make political power pass from the middle class to the working class"* and so *"the democratic movement"* is *"striving for the political domination of the proletariat."* [**Op. Cit.**, vol. 7, p. 299, p. 440 and p. 368]

All of which, of course, fits into Marx's account of the Paris Commune where, as noted above, the Commune *"was formed of the municipal councillors"* who had been *"chosen by universal suffrage in the various wards of the town"* in the municipal elections held on March 26th, 1871. Once voted into office, the Commune then smashed the state machine inherited by it, recognising that *"the working class cannot simply lay hold of the ready-made state machinery, and wield it for its own purposes."* The *"first decree of the Commune … was the suppression of the standing army, and the substitution for it of the armed people."* Thus the Commune lops off one of the *"ubiquitous organs"* associated with the *"centralised State power"* once it had inherited the state via elections. [**Selected Works**, p. 287, p. 285, p. 287 and p. 285] Indeed, this is precisely what **was** meant, as confirmed by Engels in a letter written in 1884 clarifying what Marx meant:

> *"It is simply a question of showing that the victorious proletariat must first refashion the old bureaucratic, administrative centralised state power before it can use it for its own purposes: whereas all bourgeois republicans since 1848 inveighed against this machinery so long as they were in the opposition, but once they were in the government they took it over without altering it and used it partly against the reaction but still more against the proletariat."* [**Collected Works**, vol. 47, p. 74]

Interestingly, in the second outline of the **Civil War in France**, Marx used words almost identical to Engels later explanation:

> *"But the proletariat cannot, as the ruling classes and their different rival fractions have done in the successive hours of their triumph, simply lay hold on the existent State body and wield this ready-made agency for their own purpose. The first condition for the holding of political power, is to* **transform its working machinery** *and destroy it as an instrument of class rule."* [our emphasis, **Collected Works**, vol. 22, p. 533]

It is, of course, true that Marx expressed in his defence of the Commune the opinion that new *"Communal Constitution"* was to become a *"reality by the destruction of the State power"* yet he immediately argues that *"the merely repressive organs of the old government power were to be amputated"* and *"its legitimate functions were to be wrestled from"* it and *"restored to the responsible agents of society."* [**Selected Works**, pp. 288-9] This corresponds to Engels arguments about removing aspects from the state inherited by the proletariat and signifies the *"destruction"* of the state machinery (its bureaucratic-military aspects) rather than the republic itself.

In other words, Lenin was right to state that *"Marx's idea is that the working class must* **break up, smash** *the 'ready-made state machinery,' and not confine itself to merely laying hold of it."* This was never denied by thinkers like Karl Kautsky, rather they stressed that for Marx and Engels universal suffrage was the means by which political power would be seized (at least in a republic) while violent revolution would be the means to create a republic and to defend it against attempts to restore the old order. As Engels put it in 1886, Marx had drawn *"the conclusion that, at least in Europe, England*

is the only country where the inevitable social revolution might be effected entirely by peaceful and legal means. He certainly never forgot to add that he hardly expected the English ruling classes to submit, without a 'pro-slavery rebellion,' to this peaceful and legal revolution."* [*"Preface to the English edition"* in Marx, **Capital**, vol. 1, p. 113] Thus Kautsky stressed that the abolition of the standing army was *"absolutely necessary if the state is to be able to carry out significant social reforms"* once the party of the proletariat was in a position to *"control legislation."* This would mean *"the most complete democracy, a militia system"* after, echoing the **Communist Manifesto**, *"the conquest of democracy"* had been achieved. [**The Road to Power**, p. 69, p. 70 and p. 72]

Essentially, then, Lenin was utilising a confusion between smashing the state and smashing the state machine once the workers' party had achieved a majority within a democratic republic. In other words, Lenin was wrong to assert that *"this lesson … had not only been completely ignored, but positively distorted by the prevailing, Kautskyite, 'interpretation' of Marxism."* As we have proved *"the false notion that universal suffrage 'in the* **present-day** *state' is really capable of revealing the will of the majority of the working people and of securing its realisation"* was **not** invented by the *"petty-bourgeois democrats"* nor *"the social-chauvinists and opportunists."* It can be found repeatedly in the works of Engels and Marx themselves and so *"Engels's perfectly clear, concise and concrete statement is distorted at every step"* not only *"at every step in the propaganda and agitation of the 'official' (i.e., opportunist) socialist parties"* but also by Engels himself! [**Op. Cit.** p. 336 and pp. 319-20]

Significantly, we find Marx recounting in 1852 how the *"executive power with its enormous bureaucratic and military organisation, with its wide-ranging and ingenious state machinery … sprang up in the days of the absolute monarchy, with the decay of the feudal system which it had helped to hasten."* After 1848, *"in its struggle against the revolution, the parliamentary republic found itself compelled to strengthen, along with the repressive, the resources and centralisation of governmental power. All revolutions perfected this machine instead of smashing it. The parties that contended in turn for domination regarded the possession of this huge state edifice as the principal spoils of the victor."* However, *"under the absolute monarchy, during the first Revolution, under Napoleon, bureaucracy was only the means of preparing the class rule of the bourgeoisie. Under the Restoration, under Louis Philippe, under the parliamentary republic, it was the instrument of the ruling class, however much it strove for power of its own."* It was *"[o]nly under the second Bonaparte does the state seem to have made itself completely independent."* [**Selected Works**, pp. 169-70]

This analysis is repeated in **The Civil War in France**, except the expression *"the State power"* is used as an equivalent to the *"state machinery."* Again, the state machine/power is portrayed as coming into existence **before** the republic: *"The centralised state power, with its ubiquitous organs of standing army, police, bureaucracy, clergy, and judicature … originates from the days of absolute monarchy."* Again, the *"bourgeois republicans … took the state power"* and used it to repress the working class. Again, Marx called for *"the destruction of the state power"* and noted that the Commune abolished the standing army, the privileged role of the clergy, and so on. The Commune's *"very existence presupposed the non-existence of monarchy, which, in Europe at least, is the normal encumbrance and indispensable cloak of class rule. It supplied the republic with the basis of really democratic institutions."* [**Op. Cit.** p. 285, p. 286, p. 288 and p. 290]

Obviously, then, what the socialist revolution had to smash existed **before** the republican state was created and was an inheritance of pre-bourgeois rule (even if the bourgeoisie utilised it for its own ends). How this machine was to be smashed was left unspecified but given that it was not identical to the *"parliamentary republic"* Marx's arguments cannot be taken as evidence that the democratic state needed to be smashed or destroyed rather than seized by means of universal suffrage (and reformed appropriately, by *"smashing"* the *"state machinery"* as well as including recall of representatives and the combining of administrative and legislative tasks into their hands). Clearly, Lenin's attempt to equate the *"parliamentary republic"* with the *"state machinery"* cannot be supported in Marx's account. At best, it could be argued that it is the spirit of Marx's analysis, perhaps bringing it up to date. However, this was **not** Lenin's position (he maintained that social democracy had hidden Marx's clear call to smash the bourgeois democratic state).

Unsurprisingly, Lenin does not discuss the numerous quotes by Marx and Engels on this matter which clearly contradict his thesis. Nor mention that in 1871, a few months after the Commune, Marx argued that in Britain, *"the way to show [i.e., manifest] political power lies open to the working class. Insurrection would be madness where peaceful agitation would more swiftly and surely do the work."* [**Collected Works**, vol. 22, p. 602] The following year, saw him suggest that America could join it as *"the workers can achieve their aims by peaceful means"* there as well [**Op. Cit.**, vol. 23, p. 255] If Marx **had** concluded that the capitalist state had to be destroyed rather than captured and refashioned then he quickly changed his mind! In fact, during the Commune itself, in April 1871, Marx had written to his friend Ludwig Kugelman *"[i]f you look at the last chapter of my **Eighteenth Brumaire** you will find that I say that the next attempt of the French revolution will be no longer, as before, to transfer the bureaucratic military machine from one hand to another, but to break it, and that is essential for every real people's revolution on the Continent. And this is what our heroic Party [sic!] comrades in Paris are attempting."* [**Op. Cit.**, vol. 44, p. 131] As noted above, Marx explicitly noted that the bureaucratic military machine predated the republic and was, in effect, inherited by it.

Lenin did note that Marx *"restricts his conclusion to the Continent"* on the issue of smashing the state machine, but does not list an obvious factor, that the UK approximated universal suffrage, in why this was the case (thus Lenin did not note that Engels, in 1891, added *"democratic republics like France"* to the list of states where *"the old society may peacefully evolve into the new."* [**Op. Cit.**, vol. 27, p. 226]). In 1917, Lenin argued, *"this restriction"* was *"no longer valid"* as both Britain and America had *"completely sunk into the all-European filthy, bloody morass of bureaucratic-military institutions."* [**Op. Cit.**, pp. 336-7] Subsequently, he repeated this claim in his polemic against Karl Kautsky, stating that notions that reforming the state were now out of date because of *"the existence of **militarism** and a **bureaucracy**"* which *"were **non-existent** in*

Britain and America"* in the 1870s. He pointed to how *"the most democratic and republican bourgeoisie in America … deal with workers on strike"* as further proof of his position. [**Collected Works**, vol. 28, p. 238 and p. 244] However, this does not impact on the question of whether universal suffrage could be utilised in order to be in a position to smash this state machine or not. Equally, Lenin failed to acknowledge the violent repression of strikes in the 1870s and 1880s in America (such as the Great Upheaval of 1877 or the crushing of the 8 hour day movement after the Haymarket police riot of 1886). As Martov argued correctly:

> *"The theoretic possibility [of peaceful reform] has not revealed itself in reality. But the sole fact that he admitted such a possibility shows us clearly Marx's opinion, leaving no room for arbitrary interpretation. What Marx designated as the 'destruction of the State machine' … was the destruction of the **military and bureaucratic apparatus** that the bourgeois democracy had inherited from the monarchy and perfected in the process of consolidating the rule of the bourgeois class. There is nothing in Marx's reasoning that even suggests the destruction of the **State organisation as such** and the replacement of the State during the revolutionary period, that is during the dictatorship of the proletariat, with a social bond formed on a **principle opposed to that of the State.** Marx and Engels foresaw such a substitution only at the end of a process of 'a progressive withering away' of the State and all the functions of social **coercion.** They foresaw this atrophy of the State and the functions of social coercion to be the result of the prolonged existence of the socialist regime."* [**Op. Cit.**, p. 31]

It should also be remembered that Marx's comments on smashing the state machine were made in response to developments in France, a regime that Marx and Engels viewed as **not** being purely bourgeois. Marx notes in his account of the Commune how, in France, *"[p]eculiar historical circumstances"* had *"prevented the classical development … of the bourgeois form of government."* [**Selected Works**, p. 289] For Engels, Proudhon *"confuses the French Bureaucratic government with the normal state of a bourgeoisie that rules both itself and the proletariat."* [**Collected Works**, vol. 11, p. 548] In the 1870s, Marx considered Holland, Britain and the USA to have *"the genuine capitalist state."* [**Op. Cit.**, vol. 24, p. 499] Significantly, it was precisely these states in which Marx had previously stated a peaceful revolution could occur:

> *"We know that the institutions, customs and traditions in the different countries must be taken into account; and we do not deny the existence of countries like America, England, and if I knew your institutions better I might add Holland, where the workers may achieve their aims by peaceful means. That being true, we must admit that in most countries on the continent it is force which must be the lever of our revolution; it is force which will have to be resorted to for a time in order to establish the rule of the workers."* [**Op. Cit.**, vol. 23, p. 255]

Interestingly, in 1886, Engels expanded on Marx's speculation as regards Holland and confirmed it. Holland, he argued, as well as *"a residue of local and provincial self-government"* also had *"an absence of any real bureaucracy in the French or Prussian sense"* because, alone in Western Europe, it did not have an *"absolute monarchy"* between the 16th and 18th century. This meant that *"only a few changes will have to be made to establish that free self-government by the working [people] which will necessarily be our best tool in the organisation of the mode of production."* [**Op. Cit.**, vol. 47, pp. 397-8] Few would argue that smashing the state and its replacement with a new workers' one would really constitute a *"few changes"*! However, Engels position does fit in with the notion that the *"state machine"* to be smashed is a legacy of absolute monarchy rather than the state structure of a bourgeois democratic republic. It also shows the nature of a Marxist revolution in a republic, in a *"genuine capitalist state"* of the type Marx and Engels expected to be the result of the first stage of any revolt.

The source of Lenin's restatement of the Marxist theory of the state which came as such a shock to so many Marxists can be found in the nature of the Paris Commune. After all, the major influence in terms of *"political vision"* of the Commune was anarchism. The *"rough sketch of national organisation which the Commune had no time to develop"* which Marx praises but does not quote was written by a follower of Proudhon. [**Selected Works**, p. 288] It expounded a clearly **federalist** and "bottom-up" organisational structure. It clearly implied *"the destruction of the State power"* rather than seeking to *"inherit"* it. Based on this libertarian revolt, it is unsurprising that Marx's defence of it took on a libertarian twist. As noted by Bakunin, who argued that its *"general effect was so striking that the Marxists themselves, who saw their ideas upset by the uprising, found themselves compelled to take their hats off to it. They went further, and proclaimed that its programme and purpose were their own, in face of the simplest logic … This was a truly farcical change of costume, but they were bound to make it, for fear of being overtaken and left behind in the wave of feeling which the rising produced throughout the world."* [**Michael Bakunin: Selected Writings**, p. 261]

The nature of **The Civil War in France** and the circumstances in which it was written explains why. Marx, while publicly opposing any kind of revolt before hand, did support the Commune once it began. His essay is primarily a propaganda piece in defence of it and is, fundamentally, reporting on what the Commune actually did and advocated. Thus, as well as reporting the Communal Constitution's vision of a federation of communes, we find Marx noting, also without comment, that the Commune decreed *"the surrender to associations of workmen, under reserve of compensation, of all closed workshops and factories."* [**Op. Cit.**, p. 294] While Engels, at times, suggested that this could be a possible policy for a socialist government, it is fair to say that few Marxists consider Marx's reporting of this particular aspect of the Commune as being a key aspect of his ideology. As Marx's account reports on the facts of the Commune it could hardly **not** reflect the libertarian ideas which were so strong in both it and the French sections of the International - ideas he had spent much time and energy opposing. Moreover, given the frenzy of abuse the Communards were subject to by the bourgeoisie, it was unlikely that Marx would have aided the reaction

by being overly critical. Equally, given how positively the Commune had been received in working class and radical circles Marx would have been keen to gain maximum benefit from it for both the International and his own ideology and influence. This would also have ensured that Marx kept his criticisms quiet, particularly as he was writing on behalf of an organisation which was not Marxist and included various different socialist tendencies.

This means that to fully understand Marx and Engels, we need to look at **all** their writings, before and after the Paris Commune. It is, therefore, significant that **immediately** after the Commune Marx stated that workers could achieve socialism by utilising existing democratic states **and** that the labour movement should take part in political action and send workers to Parliament. There is no mention of a federation of communes in these proposals and they reflect ideas both he and Engels had expressed since the 1840s. Ten years after the Commune, Marx stated that it was *"merely an uprising of one city in exceptional circumstances.* [**Collected Works**, vol. 46, p. 66] Similarly, a mere 3 years after the Commune, Engels argued that the key thing in Britain was *"to form anew a strong workers' party with a definite programme, and the best political programme they could wish for was the People's Charter."* [**Op. Cit.**, vol. 23, p. 614] The Commune was not mentioned and, significantly, Marx had previously defined this programme in 1855 as being *"to increase and extend the omnipotence of Parliament by elevating it to people's power. They [the Chartists] are not breaking up parliamentarism but are raising it to a higher power."* [**Op. Cit.**, vol. 14, p. 243]

As such, Marx's defence of the Commune should not mean ignoring the whole body of his and Engels work, nor should Marx's conclusion that the *"state machinery"* must be smashed in a successful revolution be considered to be in contradiction with his comments on utilising the existing democratic republic. It does, however, suggest that Marx's reporting of the Proudhon-influenced ideas of the Communards cannot be taken as a definitive account of his ideas on social transformation.

The fact that Marx did not mention anything about abolishing the existing state and replacing it with a new one in his contribution to the *"Program of the French Workers Party"* in 1880 is significant. It said that the *"collective appropriation"* of the means of production *"can only proceed from a revolutionary action of the class of producers - the proletariat - organised in an independent political party."* This would be *"pursued by all the means the proletariat has at its disposal including universal suffrage which will thus be transformed from the instrument of deception that it has been until now into an instrument of emancipation."* [**Op. Cit.**, vol. 24, p. 340] There is nothing about overthrowing the existing state and replacing it with a new state, rather the obvious conclusion which is to be drawn is that universal suffrage was the tool by which the workers would achieve socialism. It does fit in, however, with Marx's repeated comments that universal suffrage was the equivalent of political power for the working class where the proletariat was the majority of the population. Or, indeed, Engels numerous similar comments. It explains the repeated suggestion by Marx that there were countries like America and Britain *"where the workers can achieve their aims by peaceful means."* There is Engels:

"One can imagine that the old society could peacefully grow into the new in countries where all power is concentrated in the people's representatives, where one can constitutionally do as one pleases as soon as a majority of the people give their support; in democratic republics like France and America, in monarchies such as England, where the dynasty is powerless against the popular will. But in Germany, where the government is virtually all-powerful and the Reichstag and other representative bodies are without real power, to proclaim likewise in Germany … is to accept the fig leaf of absolutism and to bind oneself to it." [**Op. Cit.**, vol. 27, p. 226]

This, significantly, repeats Marx's comments in an unpublished article from 1878 on the Reichstag debates on the anti-socialist laws where, in part, he suggested that *"[i]f in England … or the United States, the working class were to gain a majority in Parliament or Congress, they could by lawful means, rid themselves of such laws and institutions as impeded their development … However, the 'peaceful' movement might be transformed into a 'forcible' one by resistance on the part of those interested in restoring the former state of affairs; if … they are put down by* **force***, it is as rebels against 'lawful' force."* [**Op. Cit.**, vol. 24, p. 248] Sadly, he never finished and published it but it is in line with many of his public pronouncements on this subject.

Marx also excluded countries on the European mainland (with the possible exception of Holland) from his suggestions of peaceful reform. In those countries, presumably, the first stage of the revolution would be, as stressed in the **Communist Manifesto**, creating a fully democratic republic (*"to win the battle for democracy"* - see section H.1.1). As Engels put it, *"the first and direct result of the revolution with regard to the* **form** *can and* **must** *be nothing but the* **bourgeois** *republic. But this will be here only a brief transitional period … The bourgeois republic … will enable us to* **win over the great masses of the workers to revolutionary socialism** *… Only then can we successfully take over."* The *"proletariat can only use the form of the one and indivisible republic"* for it is *"the sole political form in which the struggle between the proletariat and the bourgeoisie can be fought to a finish."* [Marx and Engels, **The Socialist Revolution**, p. 265, p. 283 and p. 294] As he summarised:

> *"Marx and I, for forty years, repeated ad nauseam that for us the democratic republic is the only political form in which the struggle between the working class and the capitalist class can first be universalised and then culminate in the decisive victory of the proletariat."* [**Collected Works**, vol. 27, p. 271]

It is for these reasons that orthodox Marxism up until 1917 held the position that the socialist revolution would be commenced by seizing the existing state (usually by the ballot box, or by insurrection if that was impossible). Martov in his discussion of Lenin's "discovery" of the "real" Marxist theory on the state (in **State and Revolution**) stressed that the idea that the state should be smashed by the workers who would then *"transplant into the structure of society the forms of* **their own** *combat organisations"* was a libertarian idea,

alien to Marx and Engels. While acknowledging that *"in our time, working people take to 'the idea of the soviets' after knowing them as combat organisations formed in the process of the class struggle at a sharp revolutionary stage,"* he distanced Marx and Engels quite successfully from such a position. [**Op. Cit.**, p. 42] As such, he makes a valid contribution to Marxism and presents a necessary counter-argument to Lenin's claims.

This position should not be confused with a totally reformist position, as social-democracy became. Marx and Engels were well aware that a revolution would be needed to create and defend a republic. Engels, for example, noted *"how totally mistaken is the belief that a republic, and not only a republic, but also a communist society, can be established in a cosy, peaceful way."* Thus violent revolution was required to create a republic - Marx and Engels were revolutionaries, after all. Within a republic, both recognised that insurrection would be required to defend democratic government against attempts by the capitalist class to maintain its economic position. Universal suffrage was, to quote Engels, *"a splendid weapon"* which, while *"slower and more boring than the call to revolution"*, was *"ten times more sure and what is even better, it indicates with the most perfect accuracy the day when a call to armed revolution has to be made."* This was because it was *"even ten to one that universal suffrage, intelligently used by the workers, will drive the rulers to overthrow legality, that is, to put us in the most favourable position to make revolution."* *"The big mistake"*, Engels argued, was *"to think that the revolution is something that can be made overnight. As a matter of fact it is a process of development of the masses that takes several years even under conditions accelerating this process."* Thus it was a case of, *"as a revolutionary, any means which leads to the goal is suitable, including the most violent and the most pacific."* [Marx and Engels, **The Socialist Revolution**, p. 283, p. 189, p. 265 and p. 274] However, over time and as social democratic parties and universal suffrage spread, the emphasis did change from insurrection (the **Communist Manifesto**'s *"violent overthrow of the bourgeoisie"*) to Engels last pronouncement that *"the conditions of struggle had essentially changed. Rebellion in the old style, street fighting with barricades … , was to a considerable extent obsolete."* [**Selected Works**, p. 45 and pp. 653-4]

Obviously, neither Marx nor Engels (unlike Bakunin, significantly) saw the rise of reformism which usually made this need for the ruling class to *"overthrow legality"* redundant. Nor, for that matter, did they see the effect of economic power in controlling workers parties once in office. Sure, armed coups have taken place to overthrow even slightly reformist governments but, thanks to the use of "political action", the working class was in no position to *"make revolution"* in response. Not, of course, that these have been required in most republics as utilising Marxist methods have made many radical parties so reformist that the capitalists can easily tolerate their taking office or can utilise economic and bureaucratic pressures to control them.

So far from arguing, as Lenin suggested, for the destruction of the capitalist state, Marx and Engels consistently advocated the use of universal suffrage to gain control over the state, control which then would be used to smash or shatter the *"state machine."* Revolution would be required to create a republic and to defend it against reaction, but the key was the utilisation of political action to take political power within a democratic state. The closest that Marx or Engels came to advocating workers councils was in 1850 when Marx suggested that the German workers "*establish their own revolutionary workers' governments*" alongside of the "*new official governments*". These could be of two forms, either of "*municipal committees and municipal councils*" or "*workers' clubs or workers' committees.*" There is no mention of how these would be organised but their aim would be to supervise and threaten the official governments "*by authorities backed by the whole mass of the workers.*" These clubs would be "*centralised*". In addition, "*workers candidates are [to be] put up alongside of the bourgeois-democratic candidates*" to "*preserve their independence*". (although this "independence" meant taking part in bourgeois institutions so that "*the demands of the workers must everywhere be governed by the concessions and measures of the democrats.*"). [**The Marx-Engels Reader**, p. 507, p. 508 and p. 510] So while these "*workers' committees*" could, in theory, be elected from the workplace Marx made no mention of this possibility (talk of "*municipal councils*" suggests that such a possibility was alien to him). It also should be noted that Marx was echoing Proudhon who, the year before, had argued that the clubs "*had to be organised. The organisation of popular societies was the fulcrum of democracy, the corner-stone of the republican order.*" [**No Gods, No Masters**, vol. 1, p. 48] So, as with the soviets, even the idea of workers' clubs as a means of ensuring mass participation was first raised by anarchists (although, of course, inspired by working class self-organisation during the 1848 French revolution). All this may seem a bit academic to many. Does it matter? After all, most Marxists today subscribe to some variation of Lenin's position and so, in some aspects, what Marx and Engels really thought is irrelevant. Indeed, it is possible that Marx faced with workers' councils, as he was with the Commune, would have embraced them (perhaps not, as he was dismissive of similar ideas expressed in the libertarian wing of the First International). After all, the Mensheviks used Marx's 1850s arguments to support their activities in the soviets in 1905 (while the Bolshevik's expressed hostility to both the policy and the soviets) and, of course, there is nothing in them to exclude such a position. What is important is that the idea that Marxists have always subscribed to the idea that a social revolution would be based on the workers' own combat organisations (be they unions, soviets or whatever) is a relatively new one to the ideology. If, as John Rees asserts, "*the socialist revolution must counterpoise the soviet to parliament … precisely because it needs an organ which combines economic power - the power to strike and take control of the workplaces - with an insurrectionary bid for political power*" and "*breaking the old state*" then the ironic thing is that it was Bakunin, **not** Marx, who advocated such a position. [**Op. Cit.**, p. 25] Given this, the shock which met Lenin's arguments in 1917 can be easily understood.

Rather than being rooted in the Marxist vision of revolution, as it has been in anarchism since at least the 1860s, workers councils have played, rhetoric aside, the role of fig-leaf for party power (libertarian Marxism being a notable exception). They have been embraced by its Leninist wing purely as a means of ensuring party power. Rather than being seen as the most important gain of a revolution as they allow mass participation, workers' councils have been seen, and used, simply as a means by which the party can seize

power. Once this is achieved, the soviets can be marginalised and ignored without affecting the "proletarian" nature of the revolution in the eyes of the party:

> "*while it is true that Lenin recognised the different functions and democratic raison d'être for both the soviets and his party, in the last analysis it was the party that was more important than the soviets. In other words, the party was the final repository of working-class sovereignty. Thus, Lenin did not seem to have been reflected on or have been particularly perturbed by the decline of the soviets after 1918.*" [Samuel Farber, **Before Stalinism**, p. 212]

This perspective can be traced back to the lack of interest Marx and Engels expressed in the forms which a proletarian revolution would take, as exemplified by Engels comments on having to "*lop off*" aspects of the state "*inherited*" by the working class. The idea that the organisations people create in their struggle for freedom may help determine the outcome of the revolution is missing. Rather, the idea that any structure can be appropriated and (after suitable modification) used to rebuild society is clear. This cannot but flow from the flawed Marxist theory of the state we discussed in section H.3.7. If, as Marx and Engels argued, the state is simply an instrument of class rule then it becomes unproblematic to utilise the existing republican state or create a new form of state complete with representative structures. The Marxist perspective, moreover, cannot help take emphasis away from the mass working class organisations required to rebuild society in a socialist manner and place it on the group who will "*inherit*" the state and "*lop off*" its negative aspects, namely the party and the leaders in charge of both it and the new "workers' state."

This focus towards the party became, under Lenin (and the Bolsheviks in general) a purely instrumental perspective on workers' councils and other organisations. They were of use purely in so far as they allowed the Bolshevik party to take power (indeed Lenin constantly identified workers' power and soviet power with Bolshevik power and as Martin Buber noted, for Lenin "***All power to the Soviets!***" meant, at bottom, "***All power to the Party through the Soviets!***"). It can, therefore, be argued that his book **State and Revolution** was a means to use Marx and Engels to support his new found idea of the soviets as being the basis of creating a Bolshevik government rather than a principled defence of workers' councils as the framework of a socialist revolution. We discuss this issue in the next section.

H.3.11 Does Marxism aim to give power to workers organisations?

The short answer depends on which branch of Marxism you mean. If you are talking about libertarian Marxists such as council communists, Situationists and so on, then the answer is a resounding "yes." Like anarchists, these Marxists see a social revolution as being based on working class self-management and, indeed, criticised (and broke with) Bolshevism precisely on this question. Some Marxists, like the **Socialist Party of Great Britain**, stay true to Marx and Engels and argue for using the ballot box (see last section) although this does not exclude utilising such organs once political power is seized by those means. However, if we look at the mainstream Marxist tradition (namely Leninism), the answer has to be an empathic "no."

As we noted in section H.1.4, anarchists have long argued that the organisations created by the working class in struggle would be the initial framework of a free society. These organs, created to resist capitalism and the state, would be the means to overthrow both as well as extending and defending the revolution (such bodies have included the "soviets" and "factory committees" of the Russian Revolution, the collectives in the Spanish revolution, popular assemblies of the 2001 Argentine revolt against neo-liberalism and the French Revolution, revolutionary unions and so on). Thus working class self-management is at the core of the anarchist vision and so we stress the importance (and autonomy) of working class organisations in the revolutionary movement and the revolution itself. Anarchists work within such bodies at the base, in the mass assemblies, and do not seek to replace their power with that of their own organisation (see section J.3.6).

Leninists, in contrast, have a different perspective on such bodies. Rather than placing them at the heart of the revolution, Leninism views them purely in instrumental terms - namely, as a means of achieving party power. Writing in 1907, Lenin argued that "*Social-Democratic Party organisations may, in case of necessity, participate in inter-party Soviets of Workers' Delegates … and in congresses … of these organisations, and may organise such institutions, provided this is done on strict Party lines for the purpose of developing and strengthening the Social-Democratic Labour Party*", that is "*utilise*" such organs "*for the purpose of developing the Social-Democratic movement.*" Significantly, given the fate of the soviets post-1917, Lenin noted that the party "*must bear in mind that if Social-Democratic activities among the proletarian masses are properly, effectively and widely organised, such institutions may actually become superfluous.*" [**Collected Works**, vol. 12, pp. 143-4] Thus the means by which working class can manage their own affairs would become "*superfluous*" once the party was in power. How the working class could be considered the "ruling class" in such a society is hard to understand.

As Oscar Anweiler summarises in his account of the soviets during the two Russian Revolutions:

> "*The drawback of the new 'soviet democracy' hailed by Lenin in 1906 is that he could envisage the soviets only as **controlled** organisations; for him they were instruments by which the party controlled the working masses, rather than true forms of a workers democracy. The basic contradiction of the Bolshevik soviet system - which purports to be a democracy of all working people but in reality recognises only the rule of one party - is already contained in Lenin's interpretation of the soviets during the first Russian revolution.*" [**The Soviets**, p. 85]

Thirteen years later, Lenin repeated this same vision of party power as the goal of revolution in his infamous diatribe against "Left-wing" Communism (i.e. those Marxists close to anarchism) as we noted in section H.3.3. The Bolsheviks had, by this stage, explicitly argued

for party dictatorship and considered it a truism that the whole proletariat could not rule nor could the proletarian dictatorship be exercised by a mass working class organisation. Therefore, rather than seeing revolution being based upon the empowerment of working class organisation and the socialist society being based on this, Leninists see workers organisations in purely instrumental terms as the means of achieving a Leninist government:

> "*With all the idealised glorification of the soviets as a new, higher, and more democratic type of state, Lenin's principal aim was revolutionary-strategic rather than social-structural … The slogan of the soviets was primarily tactical in nature; the soviets were in theory organs of mass democracy, but in practice tools for the Bolshevik Party. In 1917 Lenin outlined his transitional utopia without naming the definitive factor: the party. To understand the soviets' true place in Bolshevism, it is not enough, therefore, to accept the idealised picture in Lenin's state theory. Only an examination of the actual give-and-take between Bolsheviks and soviets during the revolution allows a correct understanding of their relationship.*" [Anweiler, **Op. Cit.**, pp. 160-1]

Simply put, Leninism confuses party power and workers' power. An example of this "confusion" can be found in most Leninist works. For example, John Rees argues that "*the essence of the Bolsheviks' strategy … was to take power from the Provisional government and put it in the hands of popular organs of working class power - a point later made explicit by Trotsky in his **Lessons of October**.*" ["*In Defence of October*", pp. 3-82, **International Socialism**, no. 52, p. 73] However, in reality Lenin had always been clear that the essence of the Bolsheviks' strategy was the taking of power by the Bolshevik party **itself.** He explicitly argued for Bolshevik power during 1917, considering the soviets as the best means of achieving this. He constantly equated Bolshevik rule with working class rule. Once in power, this identification did not change. As such, rather than argue for power to be placed into "*the hands of popular organs of working class power*" Lenin argued this only insofar as he was sure that these organs would then **immediately** pass that power into the hands of a Bolshevik government.

This explains his turn against the soviets after July 1917 when he considered it impossible for the Bolsheviks to gain a majority in them. It can be seen when the Bolshevik party's Central Committee opposed the idea of a coalition government immediately after the overthrow of the Provisional Government in October 1917. As it explained, "*a purely Bolshevik government*" was "*impossible to refuse*" since "*a majority at the Second All-Russian Congress of Soviets … handed power over to this government.*" [quoted by Robert V. Daniels, **A Documentary History of Communism**, pp. 127-8] A mere ten days after the October Revolution the Left Social Revolutionaries charged that the Bolshevik government was ignoring the Central Executive Committee of the Soviets, established by the second Congress of Soviets as the supreme organ in society. Lenin dismissed their charges, stating that "*the new power could not take into account, in its activity, all the rigmarole which would set it on the road of the meticulous observation of all the formalities.*" [quoted by Frederick I. Kaplan, **Bolshevik Ideology**

and the Ethics of Soviet Labour, p. 124] Clearly, the soviets did not have *"All Power,"* they promptly handed it over to a Bolshevik government (and Lenin implies that he was not bound in any way to the supreme organ of the soviets in whose name he ruled). All of which places Rees' assertions into the proper context and shows that the slogan *"All Power to the Soviets"* is used by Leninists in a radically different way than most people would understand by it! It also explains why soviets were disbanded if the opposition won majorities in them in early 1918 (see section H.6.1). The Bolsheviks only supported *"Soviet power"* when the soviets were Bolshevik. As was recognised by leading left-Menshevik Julius Martov, who argued that the Bolsheviks loved Soviets only when they were *"in the hands of the Bolshevik party."* [quoted by Israel Getzler, **Op. Cit.**, p. 174] Which explains Lenin's comment that *"[o]nly the development of this war [Kornilov's counter-revolutionary rebellion in August 1917] can bring **us** to power but we must **speak** of this as little as possible in our agitation (remembering very well that even tomorrow events may put us in power and then we will not let it go)."* [quoted by Neil Harding, **Leninism**, p. 253]

All this can be confirmed, unsurprisingly enough, by looking at the essay Rees references. When studying Trotsky's work we find the same instrumentalist approach to the question of the *"popular organs of working class power."* Yes, there is some discussion on whether soviets or *"some of form of organisation"* like factory committees could become *"organs of state power"* but this is always within the context of party power. This was stated quite clearly by Trotsky in his essay when he argued that the *"essential aspect"* of Bolshevism was the *"training, tempering, and organisation of the proletarian vanguard as enables the latter to seize power, arms in hand."* [**Lessons of October**, p. 167 and p. 127] As such, the vanguard seizes power, **not** *"popular organs of working class power."* Indeed, the idea that the working class can seize power itself is raised and dismissed:

> *"But the events have proved that without a party capable of directing the proletarian revolution, the revolution itself is rendered impossible. The proletariat cannot seize power by a spontaneous uprising … there is nothing else that can serve the proletariat as a substitute for its own party."* [**Op. Cit.**, p. 117]

Hence soviets were not considered as the *"essence"* of Bolshevism, rather the *"fundamental instrument of proletarian revolution is the party."* Popular organs are seen purely in instrumental terms, with such organs of "workers' power" discussed in terms of the strategy and program of the party not in terms of the value that such organs have as forms of working class self-management of society. Why should he, when *"the task of the Communist party is the conquest of power for the purpose of reconstructing society"*? [**Op. Cit.**, p. 118 and p. 174]

This can be clearly seen from Trotsky's discussion of the "October Revolution" of 1917 in **Lessons of October**. Commenting on the Bolshevik Party conference of April 1917, he stated that the *"whole of … [the] Conference was devoted to the following fundamental question: Are we heading toward the conquest of power in the name of the socialist revolution or are we helping (anybody and everybody) to complete the democratic revolution?*

… Lenin's position was this: … the capture of the soviet majority; the overthrow of the Provisional Government; the seizure of power through the soviets." [**Op. Cit.**, p. 134] Note, **through** the soviets not **by** the soviets, thus showing that the Party would hold the real power, not the soviets of workers' delegates. This is confirmed when Trotsky stated that *"to prepare the insurrection and to carry it out under cover of preparing for the Second Soviet Congress and under the slogan of defending it, was of inestimable advantage to us"* and that it was *"one thing to prepare an armed insurrection under the naked slogan of the seizure of power by the party, and quite another thing to prepare and then carry out an insurrection under the slogan of defending the rights of the Congress of Soviets."* The Soviet Congress just provided *"the legal cover"* for the Bolshevik plans. [**Op. Cit.**, p. 134, p. 158 and p. 161]

Thus we have the *"seizure of power through the soviets"* with *"an armed insurrection"* for *"the seizure of power by the party"* being hidden by *"the slogan"* (*"the legal cover"*) of defending the Soviets! Hardly a case of placing power in the hands of working class organisations. Trotsky **did** note that in 1917 the *"soviets had to either disappear entirely or take real power into their hands."* However, he immediately added that *"they could take power … only as the dictatorship of the proletariat directed by a single party."* [**Op. Cit.**, p. 126] Clearly, the *"single party"* has the real power, **not** the soviets and unsurprisingly the rule of *"a single party"* also amounted to the soviets effectively disappearing as they quickly became mere ciphers it. Soon the *"direction"* by *"a single party"* became the dictatorship of that party **over** the soviets, which (it should be noted) Trotsky defended wholeheartedly when he wrote **Lessons of October** (and, indeed, into the 1930s).

This cannot be considered as a one-off. Trotsky repeated this analysis in his **History of the Russian Revolution**, when he stated that the *"question, what mass organisations were to serve the party for leadership in the insurrection, did not permit an **a priori**, much less a categorical, answer."* Thus the *"mass organisations"* serve the party, not vice versa. This instrumentalist perspective can be seen when Trotsky noted that when *"the Bolsheviks got a majority in the Petrograd Soviet, and afterward a number of others,"* the *"phrase 'Power to the Soviets' was not, therefore, again removed from the order of the day, but received a new meaning: All power to the **Bolshevik** soviets."* This meant that the *"party was launched on the road of armed insurrection through the soviets and in the name of the soviets."* As he put it in his discussion of the July days in 1917, the army *"was far from ready to raise an insurrection in order to give power to the Bolshevik Party"* and so *"the state of popular consciousness … made impossible the seizure of power by the Bolsheviks in July."* [vol. 2, p. 303, p. 307, p. 78 and p. 81] So much for *"all power to the Soviets"*! He even quotes Lenin: *"The Bolsheviks have no right to await the Congress of Soviets. They ought to seize the power right **now**."* Ultimately, the *"Central Committee adopted the motion of Lenin as the only thinkable one: to form a government of the Bolsheviks only."* [vol. 3, pp. 131-2 and p. 299]

So where does this leave the assertion that the Bolsheviks aimed to put power into the hands of working class organisations? Clearly, Rees' summary of both Trotsky's essay and the *"essence"* of Bolshevism leave a lot to be desired. As can be seen, the *"essence"* of Trotsky's essay and of Bolshevism is the importance of party power, not workers' power (as recognised by another member of the SWP: *"The masses needed to be profoundly convinced that there was no alternative to Bolshevik power."* [Tony Cliff, **Lenin**, vol. 2, p. 265]).

Thus the key organisation was the party, **not** the mass organisations of the working class. Indeed, Trotsky was quite explicit that such organisations could only become the state form of the proletariat under the party dictatorship. Significantly, Trotsky fails to indicate what would happen when these two powers clash. Certainly Trotsky's role in the Russian revolution tells us that the power of the party was more important to him than democratic control by workers through mass bodies and as we have shown in section H.3.8, Trotsky explicitly argued that a state was required to overcome the *"wavering"* in the working class which could be expressed by democratic decision making.

In contrast, anarchists argue for direct working class self-management of society. When we argue that working class organisations must be the framework of a free society we mean it. We do not equate party power with working class power or think that *"All power to the Soviets"* is possible if they immediately delegate that power to the leaders of the party. This is for obvious reasons:

> *"If the revolutionary means are out of their hands, if they are in the hands of a techno-bureaucratic elite, then such an elite will be in a position to direct to their own benefit not only the course of the revolution, but the future society as well. If the proletariat are to **ensure** that an elite will not control the future society, they must prevent them from controlling the course of the revolution."* [Alan Carter, **Marx: A Radical Critique**, p. 165]

Thus the slogan *"All power to the Soviets"* for anarchists means exactly that - organs for the working class to run society directly, based on mandated, recallable delegates. This slogan fitted perfectly with our ideas, as anarchists had been arguing since the 1860's that such workers' councils were both a weapon of class struggle against capitalism and the framework of the future libertarian society. For the Bolshevik tradition, that slogan simply means that a Bolshevik government will be formed over and above the soviets. The difference is important, *"for the Anarchists declared, if 'power' really should belong to the soviets, it could not belong to the Bolshevik party, and if it should belong to that Party, as the Bolsheviks envisaged, it could not belong to the soviets."* [Voline, **The Unknown Revolution**, p. 213] Reducing the soviets to simply executing the decrees of the central (Bolshevik) government and having their All-Russian Congress be able to recall the government (i.e. those with **real** power) does not equal *"all power,"* quite the reverse - the soviets will simply be a fig-leaf for party power.

In summary, rather than aim to place power into the hands of workers' organisations, most Marxists do not. Their aim is to place power into the hands of the party. Workers' organisations are simply means to this end and, as the Bolshevik regime showed, if they clash with that goal, they will be simply be disbanded. However, we must stress that not all Marxist tendencies subscribe to this. The council communists, for example, broke with the Bolsheviks precisely over this issue, the difference between party and class power.

H.3.12 Is big business the precondition for socialism?

A key idea in most forms of Marxism is that the evolution of capitalism itself will create the preconditions for socialism. This is because capitalism tends to result in big business and, correspondingly, increased numbers of workers subject to the *"socialised"* production process within the workplace. The conflict between the socialised means of production and their private ownership is at the heart of the Marxist case for socialism:

> *"Then came the concentration of the means of production and of the producers in large workshops and manufactories, their transformation into actual socialised means of production and socialised producers. But the socialised producers and means of production and their products were still treated, after this change, just as they had been before … the owner of the instruments of labour … appropriated to himself … exclusively the product of the **labour of others.** Thus, the products now produced socially were not appropriated by those who actually set in motion the means of production and actually produced the commodities, but by the **capitalists** … The mode of production is subjected to this [individual or private] form of appropriation, although it abolishes the conditions upon which the latter rests.*

> *"This contradiction, which gives to the new mode of production its capitalistic character, **contains the germ of the whole of the social antagonisms of today.**"* [Engels, **Marx-Engels Reader**, pp. 703-4]

It is the business cycle of capitalism which show this contradiction between socialised production and capitalist appropriation the best. Indeed, the *"fact that the socialised organisation of production within the factory has developed so far that it has become incompatible with the anarchy of production in society, which exists side by side with and dominates it, is brought home to the capitalists themselves by the violent concentration of capital that occurs during crises."* The pressures of socialised production results in capitalists merging their properties *"in a particular branch of industry in a particular country"* into *"a trust, a union for the purpose of regulating production."* In this way, *"the production of capitalistic society capitulates to the production upon a definite plan of the invading socialistic society."* This *"transformation"* can take the form of *"joint-stock companies and trusts, or into state ownership."* The later does not change the *"capitalist relation"* although it does have *"concealed within it"* the *"technical conditions that form the elements of that solution."* This *"shows itself the way to accomplishing this revolution. **The proletariat seizes political power and turns the means of production into state property.**"* [**Op. Cit.**, p. 709, p. 710, p. 711, p. 712 and p. 713]

Thus the centralisation and concentration of production into bigger and bigger units, into big business, is seen as the evidence of the need for socialism. It provides the objective grounding for socialism, and, in fact, this analysis is what makes Marxism *"scientific socialism."*

This process explains how human society develops through time:

"*In the social production of their life, men enter into definite relations that are indispensable and independent of their will, relations of production which correspond to a definite stage of development of their material productive forces. The sum total of these relations of production constitutes the economic structure of society, the real foundation, on which rises a legal and political superstructure and to which correspond definite forms of social consciousness … At a certain stage of their development, the material productive forces come in conflict with the existing relations of production or - what is but a legal expression for the same thing - with the property relations within which they have been at work hitherto. From forms of development of the productive forces these relations turn into their fetters. Then begins an epoch of social revolution. With the change of the economic foundation the entire immense superstructure is more or less rapidly transformed.*" [Marx, **Op. Cit.**, pp. 4-5]

The obvious conclusion to be drawn from this is that socialism will come about due to tendencies inherent within the development of capitalism. The "*socialisation*" implied by collective labour within a firm grows steadily as capitalist companies grow larger and larger. The objective need for socialism is therefore created and so, for most Marxists, "***big is beautiful.***" Indeed, some Leninists have invented terminology to describe this, which can be traced back to at least as far as Bolshevik (and Left Oppositionist) Evgeny Preobrazhensky (although his perspective, like most Leninist ones, has deep roots in the Social Democratic orthodoxy of the Second International). Preobrazhensky, as well as expounding the need for "*primitive socialist accumulation*" to build up Soviet Russia's industry, also discussed "*the contradiction of the law of planning and the law of value.*" [Hillel Ticktin, "*Leon Trotsky and the Social Forces Leading to Bureaucracy, 1923-29*", pp. 45-64, **The Ideas of Leon Trotsky**, Hillel Ticktin and Michael Cox (eds.), p. 45] Thus Marxists in this tradition (like Hillel Ticktin) argue that the increased size of capital means that more and more of the economy is subject to the despotism of the owners and managers of capital and so the "*anarchy*" of the market is slowly replaced with the conscious planning of resources. Marxists sometimes call this the "*objective socialisation of labour*" (to use Ernest Mandel's term). Thus there is a tendency for Marxists to see the increased size and power of big business as providing objective evidence for socialism, which will bring these socialistic tendencies within capitalism to full light and full development. Needless to say, most will argue that socialism, while developing planning fully, will replace the autocratic and hierarchical planning of big business with democratic, society-wide planning.

This position, for anarchists, has certain problems associated with it. One key drawback, as we discuss in the next section, is it focuses attention away from the internal organisation within the workplace onto ownership and links between economic units. It ends up confusing capitalism with the market relations between firms rather than identifying it with its essence, wage slavery. This meant that many Marxists consider that the basis of a socialist economy was guaranteed once property was nationalised. This perspective tends to dismiss as irrelevant the way production is managed. The anarchist critique that this simply replaced a multitude of bosses with one, the state, was (and is) ignored. Rather than seeing socialism as being dependent on workers' management of production, this position ends up seeing socialism as being dependent on organisational links between workplaces, as exemplified by big business under capitalism. Thus the "*relations of production*" which matter are **not** those associated with wage labour but rather those associated with the market. This can be seen from the famous comment in **The Manifesto of the Communist Party** that the bourgeoisie "*cannot exist without constantly revolutionising the instruments of production, and thereby the relations of production, and with them the whole relations of society.*" [Marx and Engels, **Op. Cit.**, p. 476] But the one relation of production it **cannot** revolutionise is the one generated by the wage labour at the heart of capitalism, the hierarchical relations at the point of production. As such, it is clear that by "*relations of production*" Marx and Engels meant something else than wage slavery, namely, the internal organisation of what they term "*socialised production.*"

Capitalism is, in general, as dynamic as Marx and Engels stressed. It transforms the means of production, the structure of industry and the links between workplaces constantly. Yet it only modifies the form of the organisation of labour, not its content. No matter how it transforms machinery and the internal structure of companies, the workers are still wage slaves. At best, it simply transforms much of the hierarchy which governs the workforce into hired managers. This does not transform the fundamental social relationship of capitalism, however and so the "*relations of production*" which prefigure socialism are, precisely, those associated with the "*socialisation of the labour process*" which occurs **within** capitalism and are no way antagonistic to it.

This mirrors Marx's famous prediction that the capitalist mode of production produces "*the centralisation of capitals*" as one capitalist "*always strikes down many others.*" This leads to "*the further socialisation of labour and the further transformation of the soil and other means of production into socially exploited and therefore communal means of production takes on a new form.*" Thus capitalist progress itself objectively produces the necessity for socialism as it socialises the production process and produces a working class "*constantly increasing in numbers, and trained, united and organised by the very mechanism of the capitalist process of production. The monopolisation of capital becomes a fetter upon the mode of production … The centralisation of the means of production and the socialisation of labour reach a point at which they become incompatible with their capitalist integument. This integument is burst asunder. The knell of capitalist private property sounds. The expropriators are expropriated.*" [**Capital**, vol. 1, pp. 928-9] Note, it is not the workers who organise themselves but rather they are "*organised by the very mechanism of the capitalist process of production.*" Even in his most libertarian work, "*The Civil War in France*", this perspective can be found. He, rightly, praised attempts by the Communards to set up co-operatives (although distinctly failed to mention Proudhon's obvious influence) but then went on to argue that the working class had "*no ready-made utopias to introduce*" and that "*to work out their own emancipation, and along* with it that that higher form to which present society is irresistibly tending by its own economical agencies" they simply had "to set free the elements of the new society with which old collapsing bourgeois society itself is pregnant." [**Marx-Engels Reader**, pp. 635-6]

Then we have Marx, in his polemic against Proudhon, arguing that social relations "are closely bound up with productive forces. In acquiring new productive forces men change their mode of production; and in changing their mode of production, in changing the way of earning their living, they change their social relations. The hand-mill gives you society with the feudal lord; the steam-mill, society with the industrial capitalist." [**Collected Works**, vol. 6, p. 166] On the face of it, this had better **not** be true. After all, the aim of socialism is to expropriate the property of the industrial capitalist. If the social relationships **are** dependent on the productive forces then, clearly, socialism is impossible as it will have to be based, initially, on the legacy of capitalism. Fortunately, the way a workplace is managed is not predetermined by the technological base of society. As is obvious, a steam-mill can be operated by a co-operative, so making the industrial capitalist redundant. That a given technological basis (or productive forces) can produce many different social and political systems can easily be seen from history. Murray Bookchin gives one example:

"Technics ... does not fully or even adequately account for the institutional differences between a fairly democratic federation such as the Iroquois and a highly despotic empire such as the Inca. From a strictly instrumental viewpoint, the two structures were supported by almost identical 'tool kits.' Both engaged in horticultural practices that were organised around primitive implements and wooden hoes. Their weaving and metalworking techniques were very similar ... At the **community** level, Iroquois and Inca populations were immensely similar ...

"Yet at the **political** level of social life, a democratic confederal structure of five woodland tribes obviously differs decisively from a centralised, despotic structure of mountain Indian chiefdoms. The former, a highly libertarian confederation ... The latter, a massively authoritarian state ... Communal management of resources and produce among the Iroquois tribes occurred at the clan level. By contrast, Inca resources were largely state-owned, and much of the empire's produce was simply confiscation ... and their redistribution from central and local storehouses. The Iroquois worked together freely ... the Inca peasantry provided corvee labour to a patently exploitative priesthood and state apparatus under a nearly industrial system of management." [**The Ecology of Freedom**, pp. 331-2]

Marx's claim that a given technological level implies a specific social structure is wrong. However, it does suggest that our comments that, for Marx and Engels, the new "social relationships" which develop under capitalism which imply socialism are relations between workplaces, **not** those between individuals and so classes are correct. The implications of this position became clear during the Russian revolution.

The idea that socialism involved simply taking over the state and nationalising the "objectively socialised" means of production can be seen in both mainstream social-democracy and its Leninist child. Rudolf Hilferding argued that capitalism was evolving into a highly centralised economy, run by big banks and big firms. All what was required to turn this into socialism would be its nationalisation:

"Once finance capital has brought the most important branches of production under its control, it is enough for society, through its conscious executive organ - the state conquered by the working class - to seize finance capital in order to gain immediate control of these branches of production ... taking possession of six large Berlin banks would ... greatly facilitate the initial phases of socialist policy during the transition period, when capitalist accounting might still prove useful." [**Finance Capital**, pp. 367-8]

Lenin basically disagreed with this only in-so-far as the party of the proletariat would take power via revolution rather than by election ("the state conquered by the working class" equals the election of a socialist party). Lenin took it for granted that the difference between Marxists and anarchists is that "the former stand for centralised, large-scale communist production, while the latter stand for disconnected small production." [**Collected Works**, vol. 23, p. 325] The obvious implication of this is that anarchist views "express, not the future of bourgeois society, which is striving with irresistible force towards the socialisation of labour, but the present and even the past of that society, the domination of blind chance over the scattered and isolated small producer." [**Op. Cit.**, vol. 10, p. 73]

Lenin applied this perspective during the Russian Revolution. For example, he argued in 1917 that his immediate aim was for a "state capitalist" economy, this being a necessary stage to socialism. As he put it, "socialism is merely the next step forward from state-capitalist monopoly ... socialism is merely state-capitalist monopoly **which is made to serve the interests of the whole people** and has to that extent **ceased** to be capitalist monopoly." [**Op. Cit.**, vol. 25, p. 358] The Bolshevik road to "socialism" ran through the terrain of state capitalism and, in fact, simply built upon its institutionalised means of allocating recourses and structuring industry. As Lenin put it, "the modern state possesses an apparatus which has extremely close connections with the banks and syndicates [i.e., trusts], an apparatus which performs an enormous amount of accounting and registration work ... This apparatus must not, and should not, be smashed. It must be wrestled from the control of the capitalists," it "must be subordinated to the proletarian Soviets" and "it must be expanded, made more comprehensive, and nation-wide." This meant that the Bolsheviks would "not invent the organisational form of work, but take it ready-made from capitalism" and "borrow the best models furnished by the advanced countries." [**Op. Cit.**, vol. 26, pp. 105-6 and p. 110]

The institutional framework of capitalism would be utilised as the principal (almost exclusive) instruments of "socialist" transformation. **"Without big banks Socialism would be impossible,"** argued Lenin, as they "are the 'state apparatus' which we need to bring about socialism, and which we **take ready-made** from capitalism;

*our task here is merely to **lop off** what capitalistically mutilates this excellent apparatus, to make it **even bigger**, even more democratic, even more comprehensive. A single State Bank, the biggest of the big ... will constitute as much as nine-tenths of the **socialist** apparatus. This will be country-wide book-keeping, country-wide accounting of the production and distribution of goods."* While this is *"not fully a state apparatus under capitalism,"* it *"will be so with us, under socialism."* For Lenin, building socialism was easy. This *"nine-tenths of the socialist apparatus"* would be created *"at one stroke, by a single decree."* [**Op. Cit.**, p. 106] Once in power, the Bolsheviks implemented this vision of socialism being built upon the institutions created by monopoly capitalism. Moreover, Lenin quickly started to advocate and implement the most sophisticated capitalist methods of organising labour, including *"one-man management"* of production, piece-rates and Taylorism (*"scientific management"*). This was not done accidentally or because no alternative existed (as we discuss in section H.6.2, workers were organising federations of factory committees which could have been, as anarchists argued at the time, the basis of a genuine socialist economy).

As Gustav Landuer commented, when mainstream Marxists *"call the capitalist factory system a social production ... we know the real implications of their socialist forms of labour."* [**For Socialism**, p. 70] As can be seen, this glorification of large-scale, state-capitalist structures can be traced back to Marx and Engels, while Lenin's support for capitalist production techniques can be explained by mainstream Marxism's lack of focus on the social relationships at the point of production.

For anarchists, the idea that socialism can be built on the framework provided to us by capitalism is simply ridiculous. Capitalism has developed industry and technology to further the ends of those with power, namely capitalists and managers. Why should they use that power to develop technology and industrial structures which lead to workers' self-management and power rather than technologies and structures which enhance their own position vis-à-vis their workers and society as a whole? As such, technological and industrial development is not "neutral" or just the "application of science." They are shaped by class struggle and class interest and cannot be used for different ends. Simply put, socialism will need to develop **new** forms of economic organisation based on socialist principles. The concept that monopoly capitalism paves the way for socialist society is rooted in the false assumption that the forms of social organisation accompanying capital concentration are identical with the socialisation of production, that the structures associated with collective labour under capitalism are the same as those required under socialism to achieve **genuine** socialisation. This false assumption, as can be seen, goes back to Engels and was shared by both Social Democracy and Leninism despite their other differences.

While anarchists are inspired by a vision of a non-capitalist, decentralised, diverse society based on appropriate technology and appropriate scale, mainstream Marxism is not. Rather, it sees the problem with capitalism is that its institutions are not centralised and big enough. As Alexander Berkman correctly argues:

> *"The role of industrial decentralisation in the revolution is unfortunately too little appreciated... Most people are still*

in the thraldom of the Marxian dogma that centralisation is 'more efficient and economical.' They close their eyes to the fact that the alleged 'economy' is achieved at the cost of the workers' limb and life, that the 'efficiency' degrades him to a mere industrial cog, deadens his soul, kills his body. Furthermore, in a system of centralisation the administration of industry becomes constantly merged in fewer hands, producing a powerful bureaucracy of industrial overlords. It would indeed be the sheerest irony if the revolution were to aim at such a result. It would mean the creation of a new master class." [**What is Anarchism?**, p. 229]

That mainstream Marxism is soaked in capitalist ideology can be seen from Lenin's comments that when *"the separate establishments are amalgamated into a single syndicate, this economy [of production] can attain tremendous proportions, as economic science teaches us."* [**Op. Cit.**, vol. 25, p. 344] Yes, **capitalist** economic science, based on **capitalist** definitions of efficiency and economy and on **capitalist** criteria! That Bolshevism bases itself on centralised, large scale industry because it is more "efficient" and "economic" suggests nothing less than that its "socialism" will be based on the same priorities of capitalism. This can be seen from Lenin's idea that Russia had to learn from the advanced capitalist countries, that there was only one way to develop production and that was by adopting capitalist methods of "rationalisation" and management. Thus, for Lenin in early 1918 *"our task is to study the state capitalism of the Germans, to spare **no effort** in copying it and not to shrink from adopting **dictatorial** methods to hasten the copying of it."* [**Op. Cit.**, vol. 27, p. 340] In the words of Luigi Fabbri:

> *"Marxist communists, especially Russian ones, are beguiled by the distant mirage of big industry in the West or America and mistake for a system of production what is only a typically capitalist means of speculation, a means of exercising oppression all the more securely; and they do not appreciate that that sort of centralisation, far from fulfilling the real needs of production, is, on the contrary, precisely what restricts it, obstructs it and applies a brake to it in the interests of capital.*
>
> *"Whenever [they] talk about 'necessity of production' they make no distinction between those necessities upon which hinge the procurement of a greater quantity and higher quality of products - this being all that matters from the social and communist point of view - and the necessities inherent in the bourgeois regime, the capitalists' necessity to make more profit even should it mean producing less to do so. If capitalism tends to centralise its operations, it does so not for the sake of production, but only for the sake of making and accumulating more money."* ["Anarchy and 'Scientific' Communism", pp. 13-49, **The Poverty of Statism**, Albert Meltzer (ed.), pp. 21-22]

Efficiency, in other words, does not exist independently of a given society or economy. What is considered "efficient" under capitalism may be the worse form of inefficiency in a free society. The idea that socialism may have **different** priorities, need **different** methods of organising production, have **different** visions of how an economy was structured than capitalism, is absent in mainstream Marxism. Lenin thought that the institutions of bourgeois economic power, industrial structure and capitalist technology and techniques could be "captured" and used for other ends. Ultimately, though, capitalist means and organisations can only generate capitalist ends. It is significant that the *"one-man management,"* piece-work, Taylorism, etc. advocated and implemented under Lenin are usually listed by his followers as evils of Stalinism and as proof of its anti-socialist nature.

Equally, it can be argued that part of the reason why large capitalist firms can "plan" production on a large scale is because they reduce the decision making criteria to a few variables, the most significant being profit and loss. That such simplification of input data may result in decisions which harm people and the environment goes without saying. *"The lack of context and particularity,"* James C. Scott correctly notes, *"is not an oversight; it is the necessary first premise of any large-scale planning exercise. To the degree that the subjects can be treated as standardised units, the power of resolution in the planning exercise is enhanced. Questions posed within these strict confines can have definitive, quantitative answers. The same logic applies to the transformation of the natural world. Questions about the volume of commercial wood or the yield of wheat in bushels permit more precise calculations than questions about, say, the quality of the soil, the versatility and taste of the grain, or the well-being of the community. The discipline of economics achieves its formidable resolving power by transforming what might otherwise be considered qualitative matters into quantitative issues with a single metric and, as it were, a bottom line: profit or loss."* [**Seeing like a State**, p. 346] Whether a socialist society could factor in all the important inputs which capitalism ignores within an even more centralised planning structure is an important question. It is extremely doubtful that there could be a positive answer to it. This does not mean, we must stress, that anarchists argue exclusively for "small-scale" production as many Marxists, like Lenin, assert (as we prove in section I.3.8, anarchists have always argued for **appropriate** levels of production and scale). It is simply to raise the possibility of what works under capitalism may be undesirable from a perspective which values people and planet instead of power and profit.

As should be obvious, anarchism is based on critical evaluation of technology and industrial structure, rejecting the whole capitalist notion of "progress" which has always been part of justifying the inhumanities of the status quo. Just because something is rewarded by capitalism it does not mean that it makes sense from a human or ecological perspective. This informs our vision of a free society and the current struggle. We have long argued that capitalist methods cannot be used for socialist ends. In our battle to democratise and socialise the workplace, in our awareness of the importance of collective initiatives by the direct producers in transforming their work situation, we show that factories are not merely sites of production, but also of reproduction - the reproduction of a certain structure of social relations based on the division between those who give orders and those who take them, between those who direct and those who execute.

It goes without saying that anarchists recognise that a social revolution will have to start with the industry and technology which is left to it by capitalism and that this will have to be expropriated by the working class (this expropriation will, of course, involve transforming it and, in all likelihood, rejecting numerous technologies, techniques and practices considered as "efficient" under capitalism). This is **not** the issue. The issue is who expropriates it and what happens to it next. For anarchists, the means of life are expropriated directly by society, for most Marxists they are expropriated by the state. For anarchists, such expropriation is based on workers' self-management and so the fundamental capitalist *"relation of production"* (wage labour) is abolished. For most Marxists, state ownership of production is considered sufficient to ensure the end of capitalism (with, if we are lucky, some form of *"workers' control"* over those state officials who manage production - see section H.3.14).

In contrast to the mainstream Marxist vision of socialism being based around the institutions inherited from capitalism, anarchists have raised the idea that the *"free commune"* would be the *"medium in which the ideas of modern Socialism may come to realisation."* These *"communes would federate"* into wider groupings. Labour unions (or other working class organs created in the class struggle such as factory committees) were *"not only an instrument for the improvement of the conditions of labour, but also … an organisation which might … take into its hands the management of production."* Large labour associations would *"come into existence for the inter-communal service[s]."* Such communes and workers' organisations as the basis of *"Socialist forms of life could find a much easier realisation"* than the *"seizure of all industrial property by the State, and the State organisation of agriculture and industry."* Thus railway networks *"could be much better handled by a Federated Union of railway employees, than by a State organisation."* Combined with co-operation *"both for production and for distribution, both in industry and agriculture,"* workers' self-management of production would create *"samples of the bricks"* of the future society (*"even samples of some of its rooms"*). [Kropotkin, **The Conquest of Bread**, pp. 21-23]

This means that anarchists also root our arguments for socialism in a scientific analysis of tendencies within capitalism. However, in opposition to the analysis of mainstream Marxism which focuses on the objective tendencies within capitalist development, anarchists emphasise the **oppositional** nature of socialism to capitalism. Both the *"law of value"* and the *"law of planning"* are tendencies **within** capitalism, that is aspects of capitalism. Anarchists encourage class struggle, the direct conflict of working class people against the workings of all capitalism's "laws". This struggle produces **mutual aid** and the awareness that we can care best for our own welfare if we **unite** with others - what we can loosely term the *"law of co-operation"* or *"law of mutual aid"*. This law, in contrast to the Marxian *"law of planning"* is based on working class subjectivity and develops within society only in **opposition** to capitalism. As such, it provides the necessary understanding of where socialism will come from, from **below**, in the spontaneous self-activity of the oppressed fighting for their freedom. This means that the basic structures of socialism will be the organs created by working class people in their struggles against exploitation and oppression (see section I.2.3 for more details). Gustav Landauer's basic insight is correct (if his means were not totally so) when he wrote that *"Socialism will not grow out of capitalism but away from it"* [**Op. Cit.**, p. 140] In other words, tendencies **opposed** to capitalism rather than ones which are part and parcel of it.

Anarchism's recognition of the importance of these tendencies towards mutual aid within capitalism is a key to understanding what anarchists do in the here and now, as will be discussed in section J. In addition, it also laid the foundation of understanding the nature of an anarchist society and what creates the framework of such a society in the here and now. Anarchists do not abstractly place a better society (anarchy) against the current, oppressive one. Instead, we analyse what tendencies exist within current society and encourage those which empower and liberate people. Based on these tendencies, anarchists propose a society which develops them to their logical conclusion. Therefore an anarchist society is created not through the developments within capitalism, but in social struggle against it.

H.3.13 Why is state socialism just state capitalism?

For anarchists, the idea that socialism can be achieved via state ownership is simply ridiculous. For reasons which will become abundantly clear, anarchists argue that any such *"socialist"* system would simply be a form of *"state capitalism."* Such a regime would not fundamentally change the position of the working class, whose members would simply be wage slaves to the state bureaucracy rather than to the capitalist class. Marxism would, as Kropotkin predicted, be *"the worship of the State, of authority and of State Socialism, which is in reality nothing but State capitalism."* [quoted by Ruth Kinna, *"Kropotkin's theory of Mutual Aid in Historical Context"*, pp. 259-283, **International Review of Social History**, No. 40, p. 262]

However, before beginning our discussion of why anarchists think this we need to clarify our terminology. This is because the expression *"state capitalism"* has three distinct, if related, meanings in socialist (particularly Marxist) thought. Firstly, "state capitalism" was/is used to describe the current system of big business subject to extensive state control (particularly if, as in war, the capitalist state accrues **extensive** powers over industry). Secondly, it was used by Lenin to describe his immediate aims after the October Revolution, namely a regime in which the capitalists would remain but would be subject to a system of state control inherited by the new "proletarian" state from the old capitalist one. The third use of the term is to signify a regime in which the state **replaces** the capitalist class **totally** via nationalisation of the means of production. In such a regime, the state would own, manage and accumulate capital rather than individual capitalists.

Anarchists are opposed to all three systems described by the term "state capitalism." Here we concentrate on the third definition, arguing that state socialism would be better described as "state capitalism" as state ownership of the means of life does not get to the heart of capitalism, namely wage labour. Rather it simply replaces private bosses with the state and changes the form of

property (from private to state property) rather than getting rid of it.

The idea that socialism simply equals state ownership (nationalisation) is easy to find in the works of Marxism. The **Communist Manifesto**, for example, states that the *"proletariat will use its political supremacy to wrest, by degrees, all capital from the bourgeoisie, to centralise all instruments of production into the hands of the State."* This meant: *"Centralisation of credit in the hands of the State, by means of a national bank with State capital and an exclusive monopoly"*; *"Centralisation of the means of communication and transport in the hands of the State"*; *"Extension of factories and instruments of production owned by the State"*; *"Establishment of industrial armies, especially for agriculture.* [Marx and Engels, **Selected Works**, pp. 52-3] Thus *"feudal estates ... mines, pits, and so forth, would become property of the state"* as well as *"[a]ll means of transport,"* with *"the running of large-scale industry and the railways by the state."* [**Collected Works**, vol. 7, p. 3, p. 4 and p. 299]

Engels repeats this formula thirty-two years later in **Socialism: Utopian and Scientific** by asserting that capitalism itself *"forces on more and more the transformation of the vast means of production, already socialised, into state property.* ***The proletariat seizes political power and turns the means of production into state property.*** *"* Socialism is **not** equated with state ownership of productive forces by a capitalist state, *"but concealed within it are the technical conditions that form the elements of that solution"* to the social problem. It simply *"shows itself the way to accomplishing this revolution.* ***The proletariat seizes political power and turns the means of production into state property.*** *"* Thus state ownership **after** the proletariat seizes power is the basis of socialism, when by this *"first act"* of the revolution the state *"really constitutes itself as the representative of the whole of society."* [**Marx-Engels Reader**, p. 713, p. 712 and p. 713]

What is significant from these programmatic statements on the first steps of socialism is the total non-discussion of what is happening at the point of production, the non-discussion of the social relations in the workplace. Rather we are subjected to discussion of *"the contradiction between socialised production and capitalist appropriation"* and claims that while there is *"socialised organisation of production within the factory,"* this has become *"incompatible with the anarchy of production in society."* The obvious conclusion to be drawn is that "socialism" will inherit, without change, the *"socialised"* workplace of capitalism and that the fundamental change is that of ownership: *"The proletariat seized the public power, and by means of this transforms the socialised means of production ... into public property. By this act, the proletariat frees the means of production from the character of capital they have thus far borne."* [Engels, **Op. Cit.**, p. 709 and p. 717]

That the Marxist movement came to see state ownership rather than workers' management of production as the key issue is hardly surprising. Thus we find leading Social-Democrats arguing that socialism basically meant the state, under Social-Democratic control of course, acquiring the means of production and nationalising them. Rudolf Hilferding presented what was Marxist orthodoxy at the time when he argued that in *"a communist society"* production *"is consciously determined by the social central organ,"* which would decide *"what is to be produced and how much, where and by whom."* While this information is determined by the market forces under capitalism, in socialism it *"is given to the members of the socialist society by their authorities … we must derive the undisturbed progress of the socialist economy from the laws, ordinances and regulations of socialist authorities."* [quoted by Nikolai Bukharin, **Economy Theory of the Leisure Class**, p. 157] The Bolsheviks inherited this concept of "socialism" and implemented it, with terrible results.

This vision of society in which the lives of the population are controlled by *"authorities"* in a *"social central organ"* which tells the workers what to do, while in line with the **Communist Manifesto**, eems less than appealing. It also shows why state socialism is not socialism at all. Thus George Barrett:

> *"If instead of the present capitalist class there were a set of officials appointed by the Government and set in a position to control our factories, it would bring about no revolutionary change. The officials would have to be paid, and we may depend that, in their privileged positions, they would expect good remuneration. The politicians would have to be paid, and we already know their tastes. You would, in fact, have a non-productive class dictating to the producers the conditions upon which they were allowed to use the means of production. As this is exactly what is wrong with the present system of society, we can see that State control would be no remedy, while it would bring with it a host of new troubles … under a governmental system of society, whether it is the capitalism of today or a more a perfected Government control of the Socialist State, the essential relationship between the governed and the governing, the worker and the controller, will be the same; and this relationship so long as it lasts can be maintained only by the bloody brutality of the policeman's bludgeon and the soldier's rifle."* [**The Anarchist Revolution**, pp. 8-9]

The key to seeing why state socialism is simply state capitalism can be found in the lack of change in the social relationships at the point of production. The workers are still wage slaves, employed by the state and subject to its orders. As Lenin stressed in **State and Revolution**: *"All citizens are transformed into hired employees of the state … All citizens become employees and workers of a single country-wide state 'syndicate' … The whole of society will have become a single office and a single factory, with equality of labour and pay."* [**Collected Works**, vol. 25, pp. 473-4] Given that Engels had argued, against anarchism, that a factory required subordination, authority, lack of freedom and *"a veritable despotism independent of all social organisation,"* Lenin's idea of turning the world into one big factory takes on an extremely frightening nature. [**Marx-Engels Reader**, p. 731] A reality which one anarchist described in 1923 as being the case in Lenin's Russia:

> *"The nationalisation of industry, removing the workers from the hands of individual capitalists, delivered them to the yet more rapacious hands of a single, ever-present capitalist boss, the State. The relations between the*

workers and this new boss are the same as earlier relations between labour and capital, with the sole difference that the Communist boss, the State, not only exploits the workers, but also punishes them himself … Wage labour has remained what it was before, except that it has taken on the character of an obligation to the State … It is clear that in all this we are dealing with a simple substitution of State capitalism for private capitalism." [Peter Arshinov, **History of the Makhnovist Movement**, p. 71]

All of which makes Bakunin's comments seem justified (as well as stunningly accurate):

> *"**Labour financed by the State** - such is the fundamental principle of **authoritarian Communism,** of State Socialism. The State, **having become the sole proprietor** … will have become sole capitalist, banker, money-lender, organiser, director of all national work, and the distributor of its profits."* [**The Political Philosophy of Bakunin**, p. 293]

Such a system, based on those countries *"where modern capitalist development has reached its highest point of development"* would see *"the gradual or violent expropriation of the present landlords and capitalists, or of the appropriation of all land and capital by the State. In order to be able to carry out its great economic and social mission, this State will have to be very far-reaching, very powerful and highly centralised. It will administer and supervise agriculture by means of its appointed mangers, who will command armies of rural workers organised and disciplined for that purpose. At the same time, it will set up a single bank on the ruins of all existing banks."* Such a system, Bakunin correctly predicted, would be *"a barracks regime for the proletariat, in which a standardised mass of men and women workers would wake, sleep, work and live by rote; a regime of privilege for the able and the clever."* [**Michael Bakunin: Selected Writings**, p. 258 and p. 259]

Proudhon, likewise was well aware that state ownership did not mean the end of private property, rather it meant a change in who ordered the working class about. *"We do not want,"* he stated, *"to see the State confiscate the mines, canals and railways; that would be to add to monarchy, and more wage slavery. We want the mines, canals, railways handed over to democratically organised workers' associations"* which would be the start of a *"vast federation of companies and societies woven into the common cloth of the democratic social Republic."* He contrasted workers' associations run by and for their members to those *"subsidised, commanded and directed by the State,"* which would crush *"all liberty and all wealth, precisely as the great limited companies are doing."* [**No Gods, No Masters**, vol. 1, p. 62 and p. 105]

Simply put, if workers did not directly manage their own work then it matters little who formally owns the workplaces in which they toil. As Maurice Brinton argued, libertarian socialists *"hold that the 'relations of production' - the relations which individuals or groups enter into with one another in the process of producing wealth - are the essential foundations of any society. A certain pattern of relations of production is the common denominator of all class societies. This pattern is one in which the producer does not dominate the means* of production but on the contrary both is 'separated from them' and from the products of his [or her] own labour. In all class societies the producer is in a position of subordination to those who manage the productive process. Workers' management of production - implying as it does the total domination of the producer over the productive process - is not for us a marginal matter. It is the core of our politics. It is the only means whereby authoritarian (order-giving, order-taking) relations in production can be transcended and a free, communist or anarchist, society introduced." He went on to note that "the means of production may change hands (passing for instance from private hands into those of a bureaucracy, collectively owning them) without this revolutionising the relations of production. Under such circumstances - and whatever the formal status of property - the society is still a class society for production is still managed by an agency other than the producers themselves. Property relations, in other words, do not necessarily reflect the relations of production. They may serve to mask them - and in fact they often have." [**The Bolsheviks and Workers' Control**, pp. vii-vii]

As such, for anarchists (and libertarian Marxists) the idea that state ownership of the means of life (the land, workplaces, factories, etc.) is the basis of socialism is simply wrong. Therefore, "*Anarchism cannot look upon the coming revolution as a mere substitution … of the State as the universal capitalist for the present capitalists.*" [Kropotkin, **Evolution and Environment**, p. 106] Given that the "*State organisation having always been … the instrument for establishing monopolies in favour of the ruling minorities, [it] cannot be made to work for the destruction of these monopolies. The anarchists consider, therefore, that to hand over to the State all the main sources of economic life - the land, the mines, the railways, banking, insurance, and so on - as also the management of all the main branches of industry … would mean to create a new instrument of tyranny. State capitalism would only increase the powers of bureaucracy and capitalism.*" [Kropotkin, **Anarchism**, p. 286] Needless to say, a society which was not democratic in the workplace would not remain democratic politically either. Either democracy would become as formal as it is within any capitalist republic or it would be replaced by dictatorship. So, without a firm base in the direct management of production, any "socialist" society would see working class social power ("*political power*") and liberty wither and die, just like a flower ripped out of the soil.

Unsurprisingly, given all this, we discover throughout history the co-existence of private and state property. Indeed, the nationalisation of key services and industries has been implemented under all kinds of capitalist governments and within all kinds of capitalist states (which proves the non-socialist nature of state ownership). Moreover, anarchists can point to specific events where the capitalist class has used nationalisation to undermine revolutionary gains by the working class. The best example by far is in the Spanish Revolution, when the Catalan government used nationalisation against the wave of spontaneous, anarchist inspired, collectivisation which had placed most of industry into the direct hands of the workers. The government, under the guise of legalising the gains of the workers, placed them under state ownership to stop their development, ensure hierarchical control and so class society. A similar process occurred during the Russian Revolution under the

Bolsheviks. Significantly, "*many managers, at least those who remained, appear to have preferred nationalisation (state control) to workers' control and co-operated with Bolshevik commissars to introduce it. Their motives are not too difficult to understand … The issue of who runs the plants - who makes decisions - is, and probably always will be, the crucial question for managers in any industrial relations system.*" [Jay B. Sorenson, **The Life and Death of Soviet Trade Unionism**, pp. 67-8] As we discuss in the next section, the managers and capitalists were not the only ones who disliked "*workers' control,*" the Bolsheviks did so as well, and they ensured that it was marginalised within a centralised system of state control based on nationalisation.

As such, anarchists think that an utterly false dichotomy has been built up in discussions of socialism, one which has served the interests of both capitalists and state bureaucrats. This dichotomy is simply that the economic choices available to humanity are "private" ownership of productive means (capitalism), or state ownership of productive means (usually defined as "socialism"). In this manner, capitalist nations used the Soviet Union, and continue to use autocracies like North Korea, China, and Cuba as examples of the evils of "public" ownership of productive assets. While the hostility of the capitalist class to such regimes is often used by Leninists as a rationale to defend them (as "*degenerated workers' states*", to use the Trotskyist term) this is a radically false conclusion. As one anarchist argued in 1940 against Trotsky (who first raised this notion):

> "*Expropriation of the capitalist class is naturally terrifying to 'the bourgeoisie of the whole world,' but that does not prove anything about a workers' state … In Stalinist Russia expropriation is carried out … by, and ultimately for the benefit of, the bureaucracy, not by the workers at all. The bourgeoisie are afraid of expropriation, of power passing out of their hands, whoever seizes it from them. They will defend their property against any class or clique. The fact that they are indignant [about Stalinism] proves their fear - it tells us nothing at all about the agents inspiring that fear.*" [J.H., "*The Fourth International*", pp. 37-43, **The Left and World War II**, Vernon Richards (ed.), pp. 41-2]

Anarchists see little distinction between "private" ownership of the means of life and "state" ownership. This is because the state is a highly centralised structure specifically designed to exclude mass participation and so, therefore, necessarily composed of a ruling administrative body. As such, the "public" cannot actually "own" the property the state claims to hold in its name. The ownership and thus control of the productive means is then in the hands of a ruling elite, the state administration (i.e. bureaucracy). The "*means of wealth production*" are "*owned by the state which represents, as always, a privileged class - the bureaucracy.*" The workers "*do not either individually or collectively own anything, and so, as elsewhere, are compelled to sell their labour power to the employer, in this case the state.*" ["*USSR - The Anarchist Position*", pp. 21-24, **Op. Cit.**, p. 23] Thus, the means of production and land of a state "socialist" regime are **not** publicly owned - rather, they are owned by a bureaucratic elite, **in the name of the people**, a subtle but important distinction. As one Chinese anarchist put it:

> *"Marxian socialism advocates the centralisation not only of political power but also of capital. The centralisation of political power is dangerous enough in itself; add to that the placing of all sources of wealth in the hands of the government, and the so-called state socialism becomes merely state capitalism, with the state as the owner of the means of production and the workers as its labourers, who hand over the value produced by their labour. The bureaucrats are the masters, the workers their slaves. Even though they advocate a state of the dictatorship of workers, the rulers are bureaucrats who do not labour, while workers are the sole producers. Therefore, the suffering of workers under state socialism is no different from that under private capitalism."* [Ou Shengbai, quoted by Arif Dirlik, **Anarchism in the Chinese Revolution**, p. 224]

In this fashion, decisions about the allocation and use of the productive assets are not made by the people themselves, but by the administration, by economic planners. Similarly, in "private" capitalist economies, economic decisions are made by a coterie of managers. In both cases the managers make decisions which reflect their own interests and the interests of the owners (be it shareholders or the state bureaucracy) and **not** the workers involved or society as a whole. In both cases, economic decision-making is top-down in nature, made by an elite of administrators - bureaucrats in the state socialist economy, capitalists or managers in the "private" capitalist economy. The much-lauded distinction of capitalism is that unlike the monolithic, centralised state socialist bureaucracy it has a **choice** of bosses (and choosing a master is not freedom). And given the similarities in the relations of production between capitalism and state "socialism," the obvious inequalities in wealth in so-called "socialist" states are easily explained. The relations of production and the relations of distribution are inter-linked and so inequality in terms of power in production means inequality in control of the social product, which will be reflected in inequality in terms of wealth. The mode of distributing the social product is inseparable from the mode of production and its social relationships. Which shows the fundamentally confused nature of Trotsky's attempts to denounce the Stalinist regime's privileges as "bourgeois" while defending its "socialist" economic base (see Cornelius Castoriadis, *"The Relations of Production in Russia"*, pp. 107-158, **Political and Social Writings**, vol. 1).

In other words, private property exists if some individuals (or groups) control/own things which are used by other people. This means, unsurprising, that state ownership is just a form of property rather than the negation of it. If you have a highly centralised structure (as the state is) which plans and decides about all things within production, then this central administration would be the real owner because it has the exclusive right to decide how things are used, **not** those using them. The existence of this central administrative strata excludes the abolition of property, replacing socialism or communism with state owned "property," i.e. **state** capitalism. As such, state ownership does **not** end wage labour and, therefore, social inequalities in terms of wealth and access

to resources. Workers are still order-takers under state ownership (whose bureaucrats control the product of their labour and determine who gets what). The only difference between workers under private property and state property is the person telling them what to do. Simply put, the capitalist or company appointed manager is replaced by a state appointed one.

As anarcho-syndicalist Tom Brown stressed, when *"the many control the means whereby they live, they will do so by abolishing private ownership and establishing common ownership of the means of production, with workers' control of industry."* However, this is *"not to be confused with nationalisation and state control"* as *"ownership is, in theory, said to be vested in the people"* but, in fact *"control is in the hands of a small class of bureaucrats."* Then *"common ownership does not exist, but the labour market and wage labour go on, the worker remaining a wage slave to State capitalism."* Simply put, common ownership *"demands common control. This is possible only in a condition of industrial democracy by workers' control."* [**Syndicalism**, p. 94] In summary:

> *"Nationalisation is not Socialisation, but State Capitalism ... Socialisation ... is not State ownership, but the common, social ownership of the means of production, and social ownership implies control by the producers, not by new bosses. It implies Workers' Control of Industry - and that is Syndicalism."* [**Op. Cit.**, p. 111]

However, many Marxists (in particular Leninists) state they are in favour of both state ownership **and** *"workers' control."* As we discuss in more depth in next section, while they mean the same thing as anarchists do by the first term, they have a radically different meaning for the second (it is for this reason modern-day anarchists generally use the term *"workers' self-management"*). To anarchist ears, the combination of nationalisation (state ownership) and *"workers' control"* (and even more so, self-management) simply expresses political confusion, a mishmash of contradictory ideas which simply hides the reality that state ownership, by its very nature, precludes workers' control. As such, anarchists reject such contradictory rhetoric in favour of *"socialisation"* and *"workers' self-management of production."* History shows that nationalisation will always undermine workers' control at the point of production and such rhetoric always paves the way for state capitalism.

Therefore, anarchists are against both nationalisation **and** privatisation, recognising both as forms of capitalism, of wage slavery. We believe in genuine public ownership of productive assets, rather than corporate/private or state/bureaucratic control. Only in this manner can the public address their own economic needs. Thus, we see a third way that is distinct from the popular "either/or" options forwarded by capitalists and state socialists, a way that is entirely more democratic. This is workers' self-management of production, based on social ownership of the means of life by federations of self-managed syndicates and communes.

Finally, it should be mentioned that some Leninists do have an analysis of Stalinism as "state capitalist," most noticeably the British SWP. According to the creator of this theory, Tony Cliff, Stalinism had to be considered a class system because *"[i]f the state is the repository of the means of production and the workers do not control it, they do not own the means of production, i.e., they are not the ruling class."* Which is fine, as far as it goes (anarchists would stress the social relations **within** production as part of our criteria for what counts as socialism). The problems start to accumulate when Cliff tries to explain why Stalinism was (state) capitalist. For Cliff, internally the USSR could be viewed as one big factory and the division of labour driven by bureaucratic decree. Only when Stalinism was *"viewed within the international economy the basic features of capitalism can be discerned."* Thus it is international competition which makes the USSR subject to "the law of value" and, consequently, capitalist. However, as international trade was tiny under Stalinism *"competition with other countries is mainly military."* It is this indirect competition in military matters which made Stalinist Russia capitalist rather than any internal factor. [**State capitalism in Russia**, pp. 311-2, p. 221 and p. 223]

The weakness of this argument should be obvious. From an anarchist position, it fails to discuss the social relations within production and the obvious fact that workers could, and did, move workplaces (i.e., there was a market for labour). Cliff only mentions the fact that the Stalinist regime's plans were never fulfilled when he shows up the inefficiencies of Stalinist mismanagement. With regards to labour, that appears to be divided according to the plan. Similarly, to explain Stalinism's "capitalist" nature as being a product of military competition with other, more obviously, capitalist states is a joke. It is like arguing that Ford is a capitalist company because BMW is! As one libertarian Marxist put it: *"One can only wonder as to the type of contortions Cliff might have got into if Soviet military competition had been with China alone!"* [Neil C. Fernandez, **Capitalism and Class Struggle in the USSR**, p. 65] Significantly, Cliff raised the possibility of single world-wide Stalinist regime and concluded it would **not** be state capitalist, it would *"be a system of exploitation not subject to the law of value and all its implications."* [**Op. Cit.**, p. 225] As Fernandez correctly summarises:

> *"Cliff's position appears untenable when it is remembered that whatever capitalism may or may not entail, what it **is** is a mode of production, defined by a certain type of social production relations. If the USSR is capitalist simply because it produces weaponry to compete with those countries that themselves would have been capitalist even without such competition, then one might as well say the same about tribes whose production is directed to the provision of tomahawks in the fight against colonialism."* [**Op. Cit.**, p. 65]

Strangely, as a Marxist, Cliff seemed unaware that, for Marx, "competition" did not define capitalism. As far as trade goes, the *"character of the production process from which [goods] derive is immaterial"* and so on the market commodities come *"from all modes of production"* (for example, they could be *"the product of production based on slavery, the product of peasants ..., of a community ... , of state production (such as existed in earlier epochs of Russian history, based on serfdom) or half-savage hunting peoples"*). [**Capital**, vol. 2, pp. 189-90] This means that trade *"exploits a given mode of production but does not create it"* and so relates *"to the mode of production from outside."* [**Capital**, vol. 3, p. 745] Much the same can be said of military competition - it does not define the mode of production.

There are other problems with Cliff's argument, namely that it implies that Lenin's regime was also state capitalist (as anarchists stress, but Leninists deny). If, as Cliff suggests, a "workers' state" is one in which *"the proletariat has direct or indirect control, no matter how restricted, over the state power"* then Lenin's regime was not one within six months. Similarly, workers' self-management was replaced by one-man management under Lenin, meaning that Stalin inherited the (capitalistic) relations of production rather than created them. Moreover, if it were military competition which made Stalinism "state capitalist" then, surely, so was Bolshevik Russia when it was fighting the White and Imperialist armies during the Civil War. Nor does Cliff prove that a proletariat actually existed under Stalinism, raising the clear contradiction that *"[i]f there is only one employer, a 'change of masters' is impossible ... a mere formality"* while also attacking those who argued that Stalinism was *"bureaucratic collectivism"* because Russian workers were **not** proletarians but rather slaves. So this *"mere formality"* is used to explain that the Russian worker is a proletarian, not a slave, and so Russia was state capitalist in nature! [Cliff, **Op. Cit.**, p. 310, p. 219, p. 350 and p. 348]

All in all, attempts to draw a clear line between Leninism and Stalinism as regards its state capitalist nature are doomed to failure. The similarities are far too obvious and simply support the anarchist critique of state socialism as nothing more than state capitalism. Ultimately, *"Trotskyism merely promises socialism by adopting the same methods, and mistakes, which have produced Stalinism."* [J.H., *"The Fourth International"*, pp. 37-43, **The Left and World War II**, Vernon Richards (ed.), p. 43]

H.3.14 Don't Marxists believe in workers' control?

As we discussed in the last section, anarchists consider the usual association of state ownership with socialism to be false. We argue that it is just another form of the wages system, of capitalism, albeit with the state replacing the capitalist and so state ownership, for anarchists, is simply state capitalism. Instead we urge socialisation based on workers' self-management of production. Libertarian Marxists concur.

Some mainstream Marxists, however, say they seek to combine state ownership with *"workers' control."* This can be seen from Trotsky, for example, who argued in 1938 for *"workers' control ... the penetration of the workers' eye into all open and concealed springs of capitalist economy ... workers' control becomes a school for planned economy. On the basis of the experience of control, the proletariat will prepare itself for direct management of nationalised industry when the hour for that eventuality strikes."* This, it is argued, proves that nationalisation (state ownership and control) is not *"state capitalism"* but rather *"control is the first step along the road to the socialist guidance of economy."* [**The Death Agony of Capitalism and the Tasks of the Fourth International**, p. 73 and p. 74] This explains why many modern day Leninists are often heard voicing support for what anarchists consider an obvious oxymoron, namely *"nationalisation under workers' control."*

Anarchists are not convinced. This is because of two reasons. Firstly, because by the term *"workers' control"* anarchists and Leninists mean two radically different things. Secondly, when in **power** Trotsky advocated radically different ideas. Based on these reasons, anarchists view Leninist calls for *"workers' control"* simply as a means of gaining popular support, calls which will be ignored once the real aim, party power, has been achieved: it is an example of Trotsky's comment that *"[s]logans as well as organisational forms should be subordinated to the indices of the movement."* [**Op. Cit.**, p. 72] In other words, rather than express a commitment to the ideas of worker's control of production, mainstream Marxist use of the term *"workers' control"* is simply an opportunistic technique aiming at securing support for the party's seizure of power and once this is achieved it will be cast aside in favour of the first part of the demands, namely state ownership and so control. In making this claim anarchists feel they have more than enough evidence, evidence which many members of Leninist parties simply know nothing about.

We will look first at the question of terminology. Anarchists traditionally used the term *"workers' control"* to mean workers' full and direct control over their workplaces, and their work. However, after the Russian Revolution a certain ambiguity arose in using that term. This is because specific demands which were raised during that revolution were translated into English as *"workers' control"* when, in fact, the Russian meaning of the word (**kontrolia**) was far closer to *"supervision"* or *"steering."* Thus the term *"workers' control"* is used to describe two radically different concepts.

This can be seen from Trotsky when he argued that the workers should *"demand resumption, as public utilities, of work in private businesses closed as a result of the crisis. Workers' control in such case would be replaced by direct workers' management."* [**Op. Cit.**, p. 73] Why workers' employed in open capitalist firms were not considered suitable for *"direct workers' management"* is not explained, but the fact remains Trotsky clearly differentiated between management and control. For him, *"workers' control"* meant *"workers supervision"* over the capitalist who retained power. Thus the *"slogan of workers' control of production"* was not equated to actual workers' control over production. Rather, it was *"a sort of economic dual power"* which meant that *"ownership and right of disposition remain in the hands of the capitalists."* This was because it was *"obvious that the power is not yet in the hands of the proletariat, otherwise we would have not workers' control of production but the control of production by the workers' state as an introduction to a regime of state production on the foundations of nationalisation."* [Trotsky, **The Struggle Against Fascism in Germany**, p. 91 and p. 92]

This vision of *"workers' control"* as simply supervision of the capitalist managers and a prelude to state control and, ultimately, nationalisation can be found in Lenin. Rather than seeing *"workers' control"* as workers managing production directly, he always saw it in terms of workers' *"controlling"* those who did. It simply meant *"the country-wide, all-embracing, omnipresent, most precise and most conscientious **accounting** of the production and distribution of goods."* He clarified what he meant, arguing for *"country-wide, all-embracing workers' control over the capitalists"* who would still manage production. Significantly, he considered that *"as much as*

*nine-tenths of the **socialist** apparatus"* required for this *"country-wide **book-keeping**, country-wide **accounting** of the production and distribution of goods"* would be achieved by nationalising the *"big banks,"* which *"**are** the 'state apparatus' which we **need** to bring about socialism"* (indeed, this was considered *"something in the nature of the **skeleton** of socialist society"*). This structure would be taken intact from capitalism for *"the modern state possesses an apparatus which has extremely close connection with the banks and [business] syndicates … this apparatus must not, and should not, be smashed."* [**Collected Works**, vol. 26, p. 105, p. 107, p. 106 and pp. 105-6] Over time, this system would move towards full socialism.

Thus, what Leninists mean by *"workers' control"* is radically different than what anarchists traditionally meant by that term (indeed, it was radically different from the workers' definition, as can be seen from a resolution of the Bolshevik dominated First Trade Union Congress which complained that *"the workers misunderstand and falsely interpret workers' control."* [quoted by M. Brinton, **The Bolsheviks and Workers' Control**, p. 32]). It is for this reason that from the 1960s English speaking anarchists and other libertarian socialists have been explicit and have used the term *"workers' self-management"* rather than *"workers' control"* to describe their aims. Mainstream Marxists, however have continued to use the latter slogan, undoubtedly, as we note in section H.3.5, to gain members from the confusion in meanings.

Secondly, there is the example of the Russian Revolution itself. As historian S.A. Smith correctly summarises, the Bolshevik party *"had no position on the question of workers' control prior to 1917."* The *"factory committees launched the slogan of workers' control of production quite independently of the Bolshevik party. It was not until May that the party began to take it up."* However, Lenin used *"the term ['workers' control'] in a very different sense from that of the factory committees."* In fact Lenin's proposals were *"thoroughly statist and centralist in character, whereas the practice of the factory committees was essentially local and autonomous."* While those Bolsheviks *"connected with the factory committees assigned responsibility for workers' control of production chiefly to the committees"* this *"never became official Bolshevik party policy."* In fact, *"the Bolsheviks never deviated before or after October from a commitment to a statist, centralised solution to economic disorder. The disagreement between the two wings of the socialist movement [i.e., the Mensheviks and Bolsheviks] was not about state control in the abstract, but what **kind** of state should co-ordinate control of the economy: a bourgeois state or a workers' state?"* They *"did not disagree radically in the specific measures which they advocated for control of the economy."* Lenin *"never developed a conception of workers' self-management. Even after October, workers' control remained for him fundamentally a matter of 'inspection' and 'accounting' … rather than as being necessary to the transformation of the process of production by the direct producers. For Lenin, the transformation of capitalist relations of production was achieved at central-state level, rather than at enterprise level. Progress to socialism was guaranteed by the character of the state and achieved through policies by the central state - not by the degree of power exercised by workers on the shop floor."* [**Red Petrograd**, p. 153, p. 154, p. 159, p. 153, p. 154 and p. 228]

Thus the Bolshevik vision of *"workers' control"* was always placed in a statist context and it would be exercised not by workers' organisations but rather by state capitalist institutions. This has nothing in common with control by the workers themselves and their own class organisations as advocated by anarchists. In May 1917, Lenin was arguing for the *"establishment of state control over all banks, and their amalgamation into a single central bank; also control over the insurance agencies and big capitalist syndicates."* [**Collected Works**, vol. 24, p. 311] He reiterated this framework later that year, arguing that *"the new means of control have been created **not** by us, but by capitalism in its military-imperialist stage"* and so *"the proletariat takes its weapons from capitalism and does not 'invent' or 'create them out of nothing.'"* The aim was *"compulsory amalgamation in associations under state control,"* *"by workers' control of the **workers' state**."* [**Op. Cit.**, vol. 26, p. 108, p. 109 and p. 108] The factory committees were added to this *"state capitalist"* system but they played only a very minor role in it. Indeed, this system of state control was designed to limit the power of the factory committees:

> *"One of the first decrees issued by the Bolshevik Government was the Decree on Workers' Control of 27 November 1917. By this decree workers' control was institutionalised ... Workers' control implied the persistence of private ownership of the means of production, though with a 'diminished' right of disposal. The organs of workers' control, the factory committees, were not supposed to evolve into workers' management organs after the nationalisation of the factories. The hierarchical structure of factory work was not questioned by Lenin ... To the Bolshevik leadership the transfer of power to the working class meant power to its leadership, i.e. to the party. Central control was the main goal of the Bolshevik leadership. The hasty creation of the VSNKh (the Supreme Council of the National Economy) on 1 December 1917, with precise tasks in the economic field, was a significant indication of fact that decentralised management was not among the projects of the party, and that the Bolsheviks intended to counterpoise central direction of the economy to the possible evolution of workers' control toward self-management."* [Silvana Malle, **The Economic Organisation of War Communism, 1918-1921**, p. 47]

Once in power, the Bolsheviks soon turned away from even this limited vision of workers' control and in favour of *"one-man management."* Lenin raised this idea in late April 1918 and it involved granting state appointed *"individual executives dictatorial powers (or 'unlimited' powers)."* Large-scale industry required *"thousands subordinating their will to the will of one,"* and so the revolution *"demands"* that *"the people unquestioningly obey the single will of the leaders of labour."* Lenin's *"superior forms of labour discipline"* were simply hyper-developed capitalist forms. The role of workers in production was the same, but with a novel twist, namely *"unquestioning obedience to the orders of individual representatives of the Soviet government during the work."* This support for wage slavery was combined with support for capitalist management techniques. *"We must raise the question of piece-work and apply and test it in practice,"* argued Lenin, *"we must raise the question of applying much of what is scientific and progressive in the Taylor system; we must make wages correspond to the total amount of goods turned out."* [Lenin, **Op. Cit.**, vol. 27, p. 267, p. 269, p. 271 and p. 258]

This vision had already been applied in practice, with the *"first decree on the management of nationalised enterprises in March 1918"* which had *"established two directors at the head of each enterprise ... Both directors were appointed by the central administrators."* An *"economic and administrative council"* was also created in the workplace, but this *"did not reflect a syndicalist concept of management."* Rather it included representatives of the employees, employers, engineers, trade unions, the local soviets, co-operatives, the local economic councils and peasants. This composition *"weakened the impact of the factory workers on decision-making ... The workers' control organs [the factory committees] remained in a subordinate position with respect to the council."* Once the Civil War broke out in May 1918, this process was accelerated. By 1920, most workplaces were under one-man management and the Communist Party at its Ninth Congress had *"promoted one-man management as the most suitable form of management."* [Malle, **Op. Cit.**, p. 111, p. 112, p. 141 and p. 128] In other words, the manner in which Lenin organised industry had handed it over entirely into the hands of the bureaucracy.

Trotsky did not disagree with all this, quite the reverse - he wholeheartedly defended the imposing of *"one-man management"*. As he put it in 1920, *"our Party Congress ... expressed itself in favour of the principle of one-man management in the administration of industry ... It would be the greatest possible mistake, however, to consider this decision as a blow to the independence of the working class. The independence of the workers is determined and measured not by whether three workers or one are placed at the head of a factory."* As such, it *"would consequently be a most crying error to confuse the question as to the supremacy of the proletariat with the question of boards of workers at the head of factories. The dictatorship of the proletariat is expressed in the abolition of private property in the means of production, in the supremacy over the whole Soviet mechanism of the collective will of the workers, and not at all in the form in which individual economic enterprises are administered."* The term *"collective will of the workers"* is simply a euphemism for the Party which Trotsky had admitted had *"substituted"* its dictatorship for that of the Soviets (indeed, *"there is nothing accidental"* in this *"'substitution' of the power of the party for the power of the working class"* and *"in reality there is no substitution at all."* The *"dictatorship of the Soviets became possible only by means of the dictatorship of the party"*). The unions *"should discipline the workers and teach them to place the interests of production above their own needs and demands."* He even argued that *"the only solution to economic difficulties from the point of view of both principle and of practice is to treat the population of the whole country as the reservoir of the necessary labour power ... and to introduce strict order into the work of its registration, mobilisation and utilisation."* [**Terrorism and Communism**, p. 162, p. 109, p. 143 and p. 135]

Trotsky did not consider this a result of the Civil War. Again, the opposite was the case: *"I consider if the civil war had not plundered our economic organs of all that was strongest, most independent, most endowed with initiative, we should undoubtedly have entered the path of one-man management in the sphere of economic administration much sooner and much less painfully."* [**Op. Cit.**, pp. 162-3] Significantly, discussing developments in Russia since the N.E.P, Trotsky a few years later argued that it was *"necessary for each state-owned factory, with its technical director and with its commercial director, to be subjected not only to control from the top - by the state organs - but also from below, by the market which will remain the regulator of the state economy for a long time to come."* Workers' control, as can be seen, was not even mentioned, nor considered as an essential aspect of control *"from below."* As Trotsky also stated that *"[u]nder socialism economic life will be directed in a centralised manner,"* our discussion of the state capitalist nature of mainstream Marxism we presented in the last section is confirmed. [**The First Five Years of the Communist International**, vol. 2, p. 237 and p. 229]

The contrast between what Trotsky did when he was in power and what he argued for after he had been expelled is obvious. Indeed, the arguments of 1938 and 1920 are in direct contradiction to each other. Needless to say, Leninists and Trotskyists today are fonder of quoting Trotsky and Lenin when they did not have state power rather than when they did. Rather than compare what they said to what they did, they simply repeat ambiguous slogans which meant radically different things to Lenin and Trotsky than to the workers' who thrust them into power. For obvious reasons, we feel. Given the opportunity for latter day Leninists to exercise power, we wonder if a similar process would occur again? Who would be willing to take that chance?

As such, any claim that mainstream Marxism considers *"workers' control"* as an essential feature of its politics is simply nonsense. For a comprehensive discussion of *"workers' control"* during the Russian Revolution Maurice Brinton's account cannot be bettered. As he stressed, *"only the ignorant or those willing to be deceived can still kid themselves into believing that proletarian power **at the point of production** was ever a fundamental tenet or objective of Bolshevism."* [**The Bolsheviks and Workers' Control**, p. 14]

All this is not some academic point. As Brinton noted, faced *"with the bureaucratic monstrosity of Stalinist and post-Stalinist Russia, yet wishing to retain some credibility among their working class supporters, various strands of Bolshevism have sought posthumously to rehabilitate the concept of 'workers' control.'"* The facts show that between 1917 and 1921 *"all attempts by the working class to assert real power over production - or to transcend the narrow role allocated by to it by the Party - were smashed by the Bolsheviks, after first having been denounced as anarchist or anarcho-syndicalist deviations. Today workers' control is presented as a sort of sugar coating to the pill of nationalisation of every Trotskyist or Leninist micro-bureaucrat on the make. Those who strangled the viable infant are now hawking the corpse around."* [**For Workers' Power**, p. 165] Little has changed since Brinton wrote those words in the 1960s, with Leninists today proclaiming with a straight face that they stand for "self-management"!

The roots of this confusion can be found in Marx and Engels. In the struggle between authentic socialism (i.e. workers' self-management) and state capitalism (i.e. state ownership) there **are** elements of the correct solution to be found in their ideas, namely their support for co-operatives. For example, Marx praised the efforts made within the Paris Commune to create co-operatives, so *"transforming the means of production, land and capital ... into mere instruments of free and associated labour."* He argued that *"[i]f co-operative production is not to remain a shame and a snare; if it is to supersede the Capitalist system; if united co-operative societies are to regulate national production upon a common plan, thus taking it under their own control, and putting an end to the constant anarchy and periodical convulsions which are the fatality of Capitalist production - what else ... would it be but Communism, 'possible' Communism?"* [**Selected Works**, pp. 290-1] In the 1880s, Engels suggested as a reform the putting of public works and state-owned land into the hands of workers' co-operatives rather than capitalists. [**Collected Works**, vol. 47, p. 239]

These comments should not be taken as being totally without aspects of nationalisation. Engels argued for *"the transfer - initially on lease - of large estates to autonomous co-operatives under state management and effected in such a way that the State retains ownership of the land."* He stated that neither he nor Marx *"ever doubted that, in the course of transition to a wholly communist economy, widespread use would have to be made of co-operative management as an intermediate stage. Only it will mean so organising things that society, i.e. initially the State, retains ownership of the means of production and thus prevents the particular interests of the co-operatives from taking precedence over those of society as a whole."* [**Op. Cit.**, p. 389] However, Engels comments simply bring home the impossibilities of trying to reconcile state ownership and workers' self-management. While the advocacy of co-operatives is a positive step forward from the statist arguments of the **Communist Manifesto**, Engels squeezes these libertarian forms of organising production into typically statist structures. How *"autonomous co-operatives"* can co-exist with (and under!) *"state management"* and *"ownership"* is not explained, not to mention the fatal confusion of socialisation with nationalisation.

In addition, the differences between the comments of Marx and Engels are obvious. While Marx talks of *"united co-operative societies,"* Engels talks of *"the State."* The former implies a free federation of co-operatives, the latter a centralised structure which the co-operatives are squeezed into and under. The former is socialist, the latter is state capitalist. From Engels argument, it is obvious that the stress is on state ownership and management rather than self-management. This confusion became a source of tragedy during the Russian Revolution when the workers, like their comrades during the Commune, started to form a federation of factory committees while the Bolsheviks squeezed these bodies into a system of state control which was designed to marginalise them. Moreover, the aims of the Paris workers were at odds with the vision of the **Communist Manifesto** and in line with anarchism - most obviously Proudhon's demands for workers associations to replace wage labour and what he called, in 1863, an *"agricultural-industrial federation."* Thus the Commune's idea of co-operative production was a clear expression of what Proudhon called *"industrial democracy"* based on *"democratically organised workers' associations"* forming a *"vast federation of companies and societies woven into the common* cloth of the democratic and social Republic" (for "under universal association, ownership of the land and of the instruments of labour is **social** ownership"). [**Property is Theft!**, p. 711, p. 611, pp. 377-8] Thus, while Engels (in part) echoes Proudhon's ideas, he does not go fully towards a self-managed system of co-operation and co-ordination based on the workers' own organisations. Significantly, Bakunin and later anarchists simply developed these ideas to their logical conclusion.

Marx, to his credit, supported these libertarian visions when applied in practice by the Paris workers during the Commune and promptly revised his ideas. This fact has been obscured somewhat by Engels historical revisionism in this matter. In his 1891 introduction to Marx's "The Civil War in France", Engels painted a picture of Proudhon being opposed to association (except for large-scale industry) and stressed that "to combine all these associations in one great union" was "the direct opposite of the Proudhon doctrine" and so "the Commune was the grave of the Proudhon doctrine." [**Selected Works**, p. 256] However, as noted, this is nonsense. The forming of workers' associations and their federation was a key aspect of Proudhon's ideas and so the Communards were obviously acting in his spirit. Given that the **Communist Manifesto** stressed state ownership and failed to mention co-operatives at all, the claim that the Commune acted in its spirit seems a tad optimistic. He also argued that the "economic measures" of the Commune were driven not by "principles" but by "simple, practical needs." This meant that "the confiscation of shut-down factories and workshops and handing them over to workers' associations" were "not at all in accordance with the spirit of Proudhonism but certainly in accordance with the spirit of German scientific socialism"! This seems unlikely, given Proudhon's well known and long-standing advocacy of co-operatives as well as Marx's comment in 1866 that in France the workers ("particularly those of Paris"!) "are strongly attached, without knowing it [!], to the old rubbish" and that the "Parisian gentlemen had their heads full of the emptiest Proudhonist phrases." [Marx, Engels, Lenin, **Anarchism and Anarcho-Syndicalism**, p. 92, p. 46 and p. 45]

What did this "old rubbish" consist of? Well, in 1869 the delegate of the Parisian Construction Workers' Trade Union argued that "[a]ssociation of the different corporations [labour unions/associations] on the basis of town or country ... leads to the commune of the future ... Government is replaced by the assembled councils of the trade bodies, and by a committee of their respective delegates." In addition, "a local grouping which allows the workers in the same area to liase on a day to day basis" and "a linking up of the various localities, fields, regions, etc." (i.e., international trade or industrial union federations) would ensure that "labour organises for present and future by doing away with wage slavery." This "mode of organisation leads to the labour representation of the future." [**No Gods, No Masters**, vol. 1, p. 184]

To state the obvious, this had clear links with both Proudhon's ideas **and** what the Commune did in practice. Rather than being the "grave" of Proudhon's ideas on workers' associations, the Commune saw their birth, i.e. their application. Rather than the Parisian workers becoming Marxists without knowing it, Marx had become a follower of Proudhon! The idea of socialism being based on a federation of workers' associations was not buried with the

Paris Commune. It was integrated into all forms of social anarchism (including communist-anarchism and anarcho-syndicalism) and recreated every time there is a social revolution.

In ending we must note that anarchists are well aware that individual workplaces could pursue aims at odds with the rest of society (to use Engels expression, their "particular interests"). This is often termed "localism." Anarchists, however, argue that the mainstream Marxist solution is worse than the problem. By placing self-managed workplaces under state control (or ownership) they become subject to even worse "particular interests," namely those of the state bureaucracy who will use their power to further their own interests. In contrast, anarchists advocate federations of self-managed workplaces to solve this problem. This is because the problem of "localism" and any other problems faced by a social revolution will be solved in the interests of the working class only if working class people solve them themselves. For this to happen it requires working class people to manage their own affairs directly and that implies self-managed organising from the bottom up (i.e. anarchism) rather than delegating power to a minority at the top, to a "revolutionary" party or state. This applies economically, socially and politically. As Bakunin argued, the "revolution should not only be made for the people's sake; it should also be made by the people." [**No Gods, No Masters**, vol. 1, p. 141]

H.4

Didn't Engels refute anarchism in "On Authority"?

No, far from it. Engels (in)famous essay "On Authority" is often pointed to by Marxists of various schools as refuting anarchism. Indeed, it is often considered the essential Marxist work for this and is often trotted out (pun intended) when anarchist influence is on the rise. However this is not the case. In fact, his essay is both politically flawed and misrepresentative. As such, anarchists do not think that Engels refuted anarchism in his essay but rather just showed his ignorance of the ideas he was critiquing. This ignorance essentially rests on the fact that the whole concept of authority was defined and understood differently by Bakunin and Engels, meaning that the latter's critique was flawed. While Engels may have thought that they both were speaking of the same thing, in fact they were not.

For Engels, all forms of group activity meant the subjection of the individuals that make it up. As he put it, "whoever mentions combined action speaks of organisation" and so it is not possible "to have organisation without authority," as authority means "the imposition of the will of another upon ours ... authority presupposes subordination." [**Marx-Engels Reader**, p. 731 and p. 730] Given that, Engels considered the ideas of Bakunin to fly in the face of common sense and so show that he, Bakunin, did not know what he was talking about. However, in reality, it was Engels who did this.

The first fallacy in Engels account is that anarchists, as we indicated in section B.1, do not oppose all forms of authority. Bakunin was extremely clear on this issue and differentiated between **types** of authority, of which he opposed only certain kinds. For example, he asked the question *"[d]oes it follow that I reject all authority?"* and answered quite clearly: *"No, far be it from me to entertain such a thought."* He acknowledged the difference between being **an** authority - an expert - and being **in** authority. This meant that *"[i]f I bow before the authority of the specialists and declare myself ready to follow, to a certain extent and so long as it may seem to me to be necessary, their general indications and even their directions, it is because their authority is imposed upon me by no one ... I bow before the authority of specialists because it is imposed upon me by my own reason."* Similarly, he argued that anarchists *"recognise all natural authority, and all influence of fact upon us, but none of right; for all authority and all influence of right, officially imposed upon us, immediately becomes a falsehood and an oppression."* He stressed that the *"only great and omnipotent authority, at once natural and rational, the only one we respect, will be that of the collective and public spirit of a society founded on equality and solidarity and the mutual respect of all its members."* [**The Political Philosophy of Bakunin**, p. 253, p. 241 and p. 255]

Bakunin contrasted this position with the Marxist one, whom he argued were *"champions of the social order built from the top down, always in the name of universal suffrage and the sovereignty of the masses upon whom they bestow the honour of obeying their leaders, their elected masters."* In other words, a system based on delegated **power** and so **hierarchical** authority. This excludes the masses from governing themselves (as in the state) and this, in turn, *"means domination, and any domination presupposes the subjugation of the masses and, consequently, their exploitation for the benefit of some ruling minority."* [**Bakunin on Anarchism**, p. 277]

So while Bakunin and other anarchists, on occasion, **did** argue that anarchists reject *"all authority"* they, as Carole Pateman correctly notes, *"tended to treat 'authority' as a synonym for 'authoritarian,' and so have identified 'authority' with hierarchical power structures, especially those of the state. Nevertheless, their practical proposals and some of their theoretical discussions present a different picture."* [**The Problem of Political Obligation**, p. 141] This can be seen when Bakunin noted that *"the principle of **authority**"* was the *"eminently theological, metaphysical and political idea that the masses, **always** incapable of governing themselves, must submit at all times to the benevolent yoke of a wisdom and a justice, which in one way or another, is imposed from above."* [**Marxism, Freedom and the State**, p. 33] Clearly, by the term *"principle of authority"* Bakunin meant **hierarchy** rather than organisation and the need to make agreements (what is now called self-management).

Bakunin, clearly, did not oppose **all** authority but rather a specific kind of authority, namely **hierarchical** authority. This kind of authority placed power into the hands of a few. For example, wage labour produced this kind of authority, with a *"meeting ... between master and slave ... the worker sells his person and his liberty for a given time."* The state is also hierarchical authority, with *"those who govern"* (i.e. *"those who frame the laws of the country as well as those who exercise the executive power"*) being in an *"exceptional position diametrically opposed to ... popular aspirations"* towards liberty. They end up *"viewing society from the high position in which they find themselves"* and so *"[w]hoever says*

political power says domination" over *"a more or less considerable section of the population."* [**The Political Philosophy of Bakunin**, p. 187 and p. 218]

Thus hierarchical authority is top-down, centralised and imposed. It is **this** kind of authority Bakunin had in mind when he argued that anarchists *"are in fact enemies of all authority"* and it will *"corrupt those who exercise [it] as much as those who are compelled to submit to [it]."* [**Op. Cit.**, p. 249] In other words, "authority" was used as shorthand for "hierarchy" (or "hierarchical authority"), the imposition of decisions rather than agreement to abide by the collective decisions you make with others when you freely associate with them. In place of this kind of authority, Bakunin proposed a *"natural authority"* based on the masses *"governing themselves."* He did not object to the need for individuals associating themselves into groups and managing their own affairs, rather he opposed the idea that co-operation necessitated hierarchy:

> *"Hence there results, for science as well as for industry, the necessity of division and association of labour. I take and I give - such is human life. Each is an authoritative leader and in turn is led by others. Accordingly there is no fixed and constant authority, but continual exchange of mutual, temporary, and, above all, voluntary authority and subordination."* [**Op. Cit.**, pp. 353-4]

This kind of free association would be the expression of liberty rather than (as in hierarchical structures) its denial. Anarchists reject the idea of giving a minority (a government) the power to make our decisions for us. Rather, power should rest in the hands of all, not concentrated in the hands of a few. We are well aware of the need to organise together and, therefore, the need to stick by decisions reached. The importance of solidarity in anarchist theory is an expression of this awareness. However, there are different kinds of organisation. There can be no denying that in a capitalist workplace or army there is "organisation" and "discipline" yet few, if any, sane persons would argue that this distinctly top-down and hierarchical form of working together is something to aspire to, particularly if you seek a free society. This cannot be compared to making and sticking by a collective decision reached by free discussion and debate within a self-governing associations. As Bakunin argued:

> *"Discipline, mutual trust as well as unity are all excellent qualities when properly understood and practised, but disastrous when abused ... [one use of the word] discipline almost always signifies despotism on the one hand and blind automatic submission to authority on the other ...*
>
> *"Hostile as I am to [this,] the authoritarian conception of discipline, I nevertheless recognise that a certain kind of discipline, not automatic but voluntary and intelligently understood is, and will ever be, necessary whenever a greater number of individuals undertake any kind of collective work or action. Under these circumstances, discipline is simply the voluntary and considered co-ordination of all individual efforts for a common purpose. At the moment of revolution, in the midst of the struggle, there is a natural division of functions according to the aptitude of each, assessed and judged by the collective*

whole: Some direct and others carry out orders. But no function remains fixed and it will not remain permanently and irrevocably attached to any one person. Hierarchical order and promotion do not exist, so that the executive of yesterday can become the subordinate of tomorrow. No one rises above the others, and if he does rise, it is only to fall back again a moment later, like the waves of the sea forever returning to the salutary level of equality.

"In such a system, power, properly speaking, no longer exists. Power is diffused to the collectivity and becomes the true expression of the liberty of everyone, the faithful and sincere realisation of the will of all ... this is the only true discipline, the discipline necessary for the organisation of freedom. This is not the kind of discipline preached by the State ... which wants the old, routine-like, automatic blind discipline. Passive discipline is the foundation of every despotism." [**Bakunin on Anarchism**, pp. 414-5]

Clearly Engels misunderstood the anarchist conception of liberty. Rather than seeing it as essentially negative, anarchists argue that liberty is expressed in two different, but integrated, ways. Firstly, there is rebellion, the expression of autonomy in the face of authority. This is the negative aspect of it. Secondly, there is association, the expression of autonomy by working with your equals. This is the positive aspect of it. As such, Engels concentrates on the negative aspect of anarchist ideas, ignoring the positive, and so paints a false picture of anarchism. Freedom, as Bakunin argued, is a product of connection, not of isolation. How a group organises itself determines whether it is authoritarian or libertarian. If the individuals who take part in a group manage the affairs of that group (including what kinds of decisions can be delegated) then that group is based on liberty. If that power is left to a few individuals (whether elected or not) then that group is structured in an authoritarian manner. This can be seen from Bakunin's argument that power must be *"diffused"* into the collective in an anarchist society. Clearly, anarchists do not reject the need for organisation nor the need to make and abide by collective decisions. Rather, the question is how these decisions are to be made - are they to be made from below, by those affected by them, or from above, imposed by a few people in authority.

Only a sophist would confuse hierarchical power with the power of people managing their own affairs. It is an improper use of words to denote equally as "authority" two such opposed concepts as individuals subjected to the autocratic power of a boss and the voluntary co-operation of conscious individuals working together as equals. The lifeless obedience of a governed mass cannot be compared to the organised co-operation of free individuals, yet this is what Engels did. The former is marked by hierarchical power and the turning of the subjected into automatons performing mechanical movements without will and thought. The latter is marked by participation, discussion and agreement. Both are, of course, based on co-operation but to argue that the latter restricts liberty as much as the former simply confuses co-operation with coercion. It also indicates a distinctly liberal conception of liberty, seeing it restricted by association with others rather than seeing association as an expression of liberty. As Malatesta argued:

"The basic error ... is in believing that organisation is not possible without authority.

"Now, it seems to us that organisation, that is to say, association for a specific purpose and with the structure and means required to attain it, is a necessary aspect of social life. A man in isolation cannot even live the life of a beast ... Having therefore to join with other humans ... he must submit to the will of others (be enslaved) or subject others to his will (be in authority) or live with others in fraternal agreement in the interests of the greatest good of all (be an associate). Nobody can escape from this necessity." [**Errico Malatesta: His Life and Ideas**, pp. 84-5]

Therefore, organisation is *"only the practice of co-operation and solidarity"* and is a *"natural and necessary condition of social life."* [Malatesta, **Op. Cit.**, p. 83] Clearly, the question is not whether we organise, but how we do so. This means that, for anarchists, Engels confused vastly different concepts: *"Co-ordination is dutifully confused with command, organisation with hierarchy, agreement with domination - indeed, 'imperious' domination."* [Murray Bookchin, **Towards an Ecological Society**, pp. 126-7]

Socialism will only exist when the discipline currently enforced by the stick in the hand of the boss is replaced by the conscious self-discipline of free individuals. It is not by changing who holds the stick (from a capitalist to a "socialist" boss) that socialism will be created. It is only by the breaking up and uprooting of this slavish spirit of discipline, and its replacement by self-management, that working people will create a new discipline which will be the basis of socialism (the voluntary self-discipline Bakunin talked about). As Kropotkin memorably put it:

"Having been brought up in a serf-owner's family, I entered active life, like all young men of my time, with a great deal of confidence in the necessity of commanding, ordering, scolding, punishing, and the like. But when, at an early stage, I had to manage serious enterprises and to deal with men, and when each mistake would lead at once to heavy consequences, I began to appreciate the difference between acting on the principle of command and discipline and acting on the principle of common understanding. The former works admirably in a military parade, but it is worth nothing where real life is concerned, and the aim can be achieved only through the severe effort of many converging wills." [**Memoirs of a Revolutionist**, p. 202]

Clearly, then, Engels did not refute anarchism by his essay. Rather, he refuted a straw man of his own creation. The question was **never** one of whether certain tasks need co-operation, co-ordination, joint activity and agreement. It was, in fact, a question of **how** that is achieved. As such, Engels diatribe misses the point. Instead of addressing the actual politics of anarchism or their actual use of the word "authority," he rather addressed a series of logical deductions he draws from a false assumption regarding those politics. Engels essay shows, to paraphrase Keynes cutting remarks against von Hayek, the bedlam that can be created when a remorseless logician deduces away from an incorrect starting assumption.

H.4.1 Does organisation imply the end of liberty?

Engels argument in *"On Authority"* can be summed up as any form of collective activity means co-operating with others and that this means the individual subordinates themselves to others, specifically the group. As such, authority cannot be abolished as organisation means that *"the will of a single individual will always have to subordinate itself, which means that questions are settled in an authoritarian way."* [**Op. Cit.**, p. 731]

Engels argument proves too much. As every form of joint activity involves agreement and *"subordination,"* then life itself becomes *"authoritarian."* The only free person, according to Engels' logic, would be the hermit. Anarchists reject such nonsense. As George Barrett argued:

> *"To get the full meaning out of life we must co-operate, and to co-operate we must make agreements with our fellow-men. But to suppose that such agreements mean a limitation of freedom is surely an absurdity; on the contrary, they are the exercise of our freedom.*

> *"If we are going to invent a dogma that to make agreements is to damage freedom, then at once freedom becomes tyrannical, for it forbids men [and women] to take the most ordinary everyday pleasures. For example, I cannot go for a walk with my friend because it is against the principle of Liberty that I should agree to be at a certain place at a certain time to meet him. I cannot in the least extend my own power beyond myself, because to do so I must co-operate with someone else, and co-operation implies an agreement, and that is against Liberty. It will be seen at once that this argument is absurd. I do not limit my liberty, but simply exercise it, when I agree with my friend to go for a walk.*

> *"If, on the other hand, I decide from my superior knowledge that it is good for my friend to take exercise, and therefore I attempt to compel him to go for a walk, then I begin to limit freedom. This is the difference between free agreement and government."* [**Objections to Anarchism**, pp. 348-9]

If we took Engels' argument seriously then we would have to conclude that living makes freedom impossible! After all by doing any joint activity you "subordinate" yourself to others and so, ironically, exercising your liberty by making decisions and associating with others would become a denial of liberty. Clearly Engels argument is lacking something!

Perhaps this paradox can be explained once we recognise that Engels is using a distinctly liberal view of freedom - i.e. freedom from. Anarchists reject this. We see freedom as holistic - freedom from and freedom to. This means that freedom is maintained by the kind of relationships we form with others, **not** by isolation. As Bakunin argued, *"man in isolation can have no awareness of his liberty. Being free for man means being acknowledged, considered and treated as such by another man. Liberty is therefore a feature not of isolation but of interaction, not of exclusion but rather of connection".* [**Michael Bakunin: Selected Writings**, p. 147] Liberty is denied when we form hierarchical relationships with others not necessarily when we associate with others. To combine with other individuals is an expression of individual liberty, **not** its denial! We are aware that freedom is impossible outside of association. Within an association absolute "autonomy" cannot exist, but such a concept of "autonomy" would restrict freedom to such a degree that it would be so self-defeating as to make a mockery of the concept of autonomy and no sane person would seek it. To requote Malatesta, the freedom we want *"is not an absolute metaphysical, abstract freedom"* but *"a real freedom, possible freedom, which is the conscious community of interests, voluntary solidarity."* [**Anarchy**, p. 43]

To state the obvious, anarchists are well aware that *"anyone who associates and co-operates with others for a common purpose must feel the need to co-ordinate his [or her] actions with those of his [or her] fellow members and do nothing that harms the work of others and, thus, the common cause; and respect the agreements that have been made - except when wishing sincerely to leave the association when emerging differences of opinion or changed circumstances or conflict over preferred methods make co-operation impossible or inappropriate."* [Malatesta, **The Anarchist Revolution**, pp. 107-8] For anarchists, collective organisation and co-operation does not mean the end of individuality. Bakunin expressed it well:

> *"You will think, you will exist, you will act collectively, which nevertheless will not prevent in the least the full development of the intellectual and moral faculties of each individual. Each of you will bring to you his own talents, and in all joining together you will multiply your value a hundred fold. Such is the law of collective action ... in giving your hands to each other for this action in common, you will promise to each other a mutual fraternity which will be ... a sort of free contract ... Then proceed collectively to action you will necessarily commence by practising this fraternity between yourselves ... by means of regional and local organisations ... you will find in yourselves strength that you had never imagined, if each of you acted individually, according to his own inclination and not as a consequence of a unanimous resolution, discussed and accepted beforehand."* [quoted by K.J. Kenafick, **Michael Bakunin and Karl Marx**, pp. 244-5]

So, unlike the essentially (classical) liberal position of Engels, anarchists recognise that freedom is a product of how we associate. This need not imply continual agreement nor an unrealistic assumption that conflict and uncooperative behaviour will disappear. For those within an organisation who refuse to co-operate, anarchists argue that this problem is easily solved. Freedom of association implies the freedom **not** to associate and so those who ignore the decisions reached collectively and disrupt the organisation's workings would simply be *"compelled to leave"* the association. In this way, a free association *"could protect itself without the authoritarian organisation we have nowadays."* [Kropotkin, **The Conquest of Bread**, p. 152] Ultimately, Engels is simply confusing obedience with agreement, coercion with co-operation, organisation with authority, objective reality with despotism.

Rather than seeing organisation as restricting freedom, anarchists argue that the **kind** of organisation we create is what matters. We can form relationships with others which are based on equality, not subordination. As an example, we point to the differences between marriage and free love (see next section). Once it is recognised that decisions can be made on the basis of co-operation between equals, Engels essay can be seen for what it is - a deeply flawed piece of cheap and inaccurate diatribe.

H.4.2 Does free love show the weakness of Engels' argument?

Yes! Engels, let us not forget, argued, in effect, that any activities which *"replace isolated action by combined action of individuals"* meant *"the imposition of the will of another upon ours"* and so *"the will of the single individual will have to subordinate itself, which means that questions are settled in an authoritarian manner."* This, for Engels, means that *"authority"* has not *"disappeared"* under anarchism but rather it has only *"changed its form."* [**Op. Cit.**, pp. 730-1]

However, to say that authority just changes its form misses the qualitative differences between authoritarian and libertarian organisation. Precisely the differences which Bakunin and other anarchists tried to stress by calling themselves anti-authoritarians and being against the *"principle of authority."* By arguing that all forms of association are necessarily "authoritarian," Engels is impoverishing the liberatory potential of socialism. He ensures that the key question of liberty within our associations is hidden behind a mass of sophistry.

As an example, look at the difference between marriage and free love. Both forms necessitate two individuals living together, sharing the same home, organising their lives together. The same situation and the same commitments. But do both imply the same social relationships? Are they both *"authoritarian"*?

Traditionally, the marriage vow is based on the wife promising to obey the husband. Her role is simply that of obedience (in theory, at least). As Carole Pateman argues, *"[u]ntil late into the nineteenth century the legal and civil position of a wife resembled that of a slave"* and, in theory, she *"became the property of her husband and stood to him as a slave/servant to a master."* [**The Sexual Contract**, p. 119 and pp. 130-1] As such, an obvious social relationship exists - an authoritarian one in which the man has power over the woman. We have a relationship based on domination and subordination.

In free love, the couple are equals. They decide their own affairs, together. The decisions they reach are agreed between them and no domination takes place (unless you think making an agreement equals domination or subordination). They both agree to the decisions they reach, based on mutual respect and give and take. Subordination to individuals does not meaningfully exist (at best, it could be argued that both parties are "dominated" by their decisions, hardly a meaningful use of the word). Instead of subordination, there is free agreement.

Both types of organisation apply to the same activities - a couple living together. Has "authority" just changed its form as Engels argued? Of course not. There is a substantial difference between the two. The former is authoritarian. One part of the organisation dictates to the other. The latter is libertarian as neither dominates (or they, as a couple, "dominate" each other as individuals - surely an abuse of the language, we hope you agree!). Each part of the organisation agrees to the decision. Do all these differences just mean that we have changed the name of "authority" or has authority been abolished and liberty created? This was the aim of Bakunin's terminology, namely to draw attention to the qualitative change that has occurred in the social relationships generated by the association of individuals when organised in an anarchist way. A few Marxists have also seen this difference. For example, Rosa Luxemburg repeated (probably unknowingly) Bakunin's distinction between forms of discipline and organisation when she argued that:

> *"We misuse words and we practice self-deception when we apply the same term - discipline - to such dissimilar notions as: (1) the absence of thought and will in a body with a thousand automatically moving hands and legs, and (2) the spontaneous co-ordination of the conscious, political acts of a body of men. What is there in common between the regulated docility of an oppressed class and the self-discipline and organisation of a class struggling for its emancipation? ... The working class will acquire the sense of the new discipline, the freely assumed self-discipline of the social democracy, not as a result of the discipline imposed on it by the capitalist state, but by extirpating, to the last root, its old habits of obedience and servility."* [**Rosa Luxemburg Speaks**, pp. 119-20]

Engels is confusing two radically different means of decision making by arguing both involve subordination and authority. The difference is clear: the first involves the domination of an individual over another while the second involves the "subordination" of individuals to the decisions and agreements they make. The first is authority, the second is liberty. As Kropotkin put it:

> *"This applies to all forms of association. Cohabitation of two individuals under the same roof may lead to the enslavement of one by the will of the other, as it may also lead to liberty for both. The same applies to the family or ... to large or small associations, to each social institution ...*
> *"Communism is capable of assuming all forms of freedom or of oppression - which other institutions are unable to do. It may produce a monastery where all implicitly obey the orders of their superior, and it may produce an absolutely free organisation, leaving his full freedom to the individual, existing only as long as the associates wish to remain together, imposing nothing on anybody, being anxious rather to defend, enlarge, extend in all directions the liberty of the individual. Communism may be authoritarian (in which case the community will soon decay) or it may be Anarchist. The State, on the contrary, cannot be this. It is authoritarian or it ceases to be the State."* [**Small Communal Experiments and Why They Fail**, pp. 12-3]

Therefore, the example of free love indicates that, for anarchists, Engels arguments are simply pedantic sophistry. It goes without saying that organisation involves co-operation and that, by necessity, means that individuals come to agreements between themselves to work together. The question is **how** do they do that, not whether they do so or not. As such, Engels' arguments confuse agreement with hierarchy, co-operation with coercion. Simply put, the **way** people conduct joint activity determines whether an organisation is libertarian or authoritarian. That was why anarchists called themselves anti-authoritarians, to draw attention to the different ways of organising collective life.

H.4.3 How do anarchists propose to run a factory?

In his campaign against anti-authoritarian ideas within the First International, Engels asks in a letter written in January 1872 *"how do these people [the anarchists] propose to run a factory, operate a railway or steer a ship without having in the last resort one deciding will, without a single management"*? [**The Marx-Engels Reader**, p. 729]

This could only be asked if Engels was totally ignorant of Bakunin's ideas and his many comments supporting co-operatives as the means by which workers would *"organise and themselves conduct the economy without guardian angels, the state or their former employers."* Bakunin was *"convinced that the co-operative movement will flourish and reach its full potential only in a society where the land, the instruments of production, and hereditary property will be owned and operated by the workers themselves: by their freely organised federations of industrial and agricultural workers."* [**Bakunin on Anarchism**, p. 399 and p. 400] Which meant that Bakunin, like all anarchists, was well aware of how a factory or other workplace would be organised:

> *"Only associated labour, that is, labour organised upon the principles of reciprocity and co-operation, is adequate to the task of maintaining ... civilised society."* [**The Political Philosophy of Bakunin**, p. 341]

By October of that year, Engels had finally *"submitted arguments like these to the most rabid anti-authoritarians"* who replied to run a factory, railway or ship did require organisation *"but here it was not a case of authority which we confer on our delegates, but of a commission entrusted!"* Engels commented that the anarchists *"think that when they have changed the names of things they have changed the things themselves."* He, therefore, thought that authority will *"only have changed its form"* rather than being abolished under anarchism as *"whoever mentions combined action speaks of organisation"* and it is not possible *"to have organisation without authority."* [**Op. Cit.**, p. 732 and p. 731]

However, Engels is simply confusing two different things, authority and agreement. To make an agreement with another person is an exercise of your freedom, not its restriction. As Malatesta argued, *"the advantages which association and the consequent division of labour offer"* meant that humanity *"developed towards solidarity."*

However, under class society *"the advantages of association, the good that Man could drive from the support of his fellows"* was distorted and a few gained *"the advantages of co-operation by subjecting other men to [their] will instead of joining with them."* This oppression *"was still association and co-operation, outside of which there is no possible human life; but it was a way of co-operation, imposed and controlled by a few for their personal interest."* [**Anarchy**, pp. 30-1] Anarchists seek to organise association to eliminate domination. This would be done by workers organising themselves collectively to make their own decisions about their work (workers' self-management, to use modern terminology). This did not necessitate the same authoritarian social relationships as exist under capitalism:

> *"Of course in every large collective undertaking, a division of labour, technical management, administration, etc., is necessary. But authoritarians clumsily play on words to produce a **raison d'être** for government out of the very real need for the organisation of work. Government ... is the concourse of individuals who have had, or have seized, the right and the means to make laws and to oblige people to obey; the administrator, the engineer, etc., instead are people who are appointed or assume the responsibility to carry out a particular job and do so. Government means the delegation of power, that is the abdication of initiative and sovereignty of all into the hands of a few; administration means the delegation of work, that is tasks given and received, free exchange of services based on free agreement... Let one not confuse the function of government with that of administration, for they are essentially different, and if today the two are often confused, it is only because of economic and political privilege."* [**Op. Cit.**, pp. 41-2]

For a given task, co-operation and joint activity may be required by its very nature. Take, for example, a train network. The joint activity of numerous workers are required to ensure that it operates successfully. The driver depends on the work of signal operators, for example, and guards to inform them of necessary information essential for the smooth running of the network. The passengers are dependent on the driver and the other workers to ensure their journey is safe and quick. As such, there is an objective need to co-operate but this need is understood and agreed to by the people involved.

If a specific activity needs the co-operation of a number of people and can only be achieved if these people work together as a team and, therefore, need to make and stick by agreements, then this is undoubtedly a natural fact which the individual can only rebel against by leaving the association. Similarly, if an association considers it wise to elect a delegate whose tasks have been allocated by that group then, again, this is a natural fact which the individuals in question have agreed to and so has not been imposed upon them by any external will - the individual has been convinced of the need to co-operate and does so.

If an activity requires the co-operation of numerous individuals then, clearly, that is a natural fact and there is not much the individuals involved can do about it. Anarchists are not in the habit of denying common sense. The question is simply **how** do these individuals co-ordinate their activities. Is it by means of self-management or by hierarchy (authority)? So anarchists have always been clear on how industry would be run - by the workers' themselves in their own free associations. In this way the domination of the boss would be replaced by agreements between equals.

H.4.4 How does the class struggle refute Engels' arguments?

Engels argued that large-scale industry (or, indeed, any form of organisation) meant that "authority" was required. He stated that factories should have "*Lasciate ogni autonomia, voi che entrate*" ("*Leave, ye that enter in, all autonomy behind*") written above their doors. That is the basis of capitalism, with the wage worker being paid to obey. This obedience, Engels argued, was necessary even under socialism, as applying the "*forces of nature*" meant "*a veritable despotism independent of all social organisation.*" This meant that "*[w]anting to abolish authority in large-scale industry is tantamount to wanting to abolish industry itself.*" [**Op. Cit.**, p. 731]

The best answer to Engels claims can be found in the class struggle. Given that Engels was a capitalist (an actual owner of a factory), he may have not been aware of the effectiveness of "*working to rule*" when practised by workers. This basically involves doing **exactly** what the boss tells you to do, regardless of the consequences as regards efficiency, production and so on. Quite simply, workers refusing to practice autonomy can be an extremely effective and powerful weapon in the class struggle.

This weapon has long been used by workers and advocated by anarchists, syndicalists and wobblies. For example, the IWW booklet **How to fire your boss** argues that "*[w]orkers often violate orders, resort to their own techniques of doing things, and disregard lines of authority simply to meet the goals of the company. There is often a tacit understanding, even by the managers whose job it is to enforce the rules, that these shortcuts must be taken in order to meet production quotas on time.*" It argues, correctly, that "*if each of these rules and regulations were followed to the letter*" then "*[c]onfusion would result - production and morale would plummet. And best of all, the workers can't get in trouble with the tactic because they are, after all, 'just following the rules.'*" The British anarcho-syndicalists of the **Direct Action Movement** agreed and even quoted an industrial expert on the situation:

> "*If managers' orders were completely obeyed, confusion would result and production and morale would be lowered. In order to achieve the goals of the organisation workers must often violate orders, resort to their own techniques of doing things, and disregard lines of authority. Without this kind of systematic sabotage much work could not be done. This unsolicited sabotage in the form of disobedience and subterfuge is especially necessary to enable large bureaucracies to function effectively.*" [J.A.C. Brown, quoted in **Direct Action in Industry**]

Another weapon of workers' resistance is what has been called "*Working without enthusiasm*" and is related to the "work to rule." This tactic aims at "*slowing production*" in order to win gains from management:

> "*Even the simplest repetitive job demands a certain minimum of initiative and in this case it is failing to show any non-obligatory initiative … [This] leads to a fall in production - above all in quality. The worker carries out every operation minimally; the moment there is a hitch of any kind he abandons all responsibility and hands over to the next man above him in the hierarchy; he works mechanically, not checking the finished object, not troubling to regulate his machine. In short he gets away with as much as he can, but never actually does anything positively illegal.*" [Pierre Dubois, **Sabotage in Industry**, p. 51]

The practice of "*working to rule*" and "*working without enthusiasm*" shows how out of touch Engels (like any capitalist) was with the realities of shop floor life. These forms of direct action are extremely effective **because** the workers refuse to act autonomously in industry, to work out the problems they face during the working day themselves, and instead place all the decisions on the authority required, according to Engels, to run the factory. The factory itself quickly grinds to a halt. What keeps it going is not the "*imperious*" will of authority, but rather the autonomous activity of workers thinking and acting for themselves to solve the numerous problems they face during the working day. In contrast, the hierarchical perspective "*ignores essential features of any real, functioning social order. This truth is best illustrated in a work-to-rule strike, which turns on the fact that any production process depends on a host of informal practices and improvisations that could never be codified. By merely following the rules meticulously, the workforce can virtually halt production.*" [James C. Scott, **Seeing like a State**, p. 6] As Cornelius Castoriadis argued:

> "*Resistance to exploitation expresses itself in a drop in* **productivity as well as exertion on the workers' part** *… At the same time it is expressed in the disappearance of the* **minimum** *collective and spontaneous* **management and organisation** *of work that the workers normally and of necessity puts out. No modern factory could function for twenty-four hours without this spontaneous organisation of work that groups of workers, independent of the official business management, carry out by filling in the gaps of official production directives, by preparing for the unforeseen and for regular breakdowns of equipment, by compensating for management's mistakes, etc.*
>
> "*Under 'normal' conditions of exploitation, workers are torn between the need to organise themselves in this way in order to carry out their work - otherwise there are repercussions for them - and their natural desire to do their work, on the one hand, and, on the other, the awareness that by doing so they only are serving the boss's interests. Added to those conflicting concerns are the continual efforts of factory's management*

apparatus to 'direct' all aspects of the workers' activity, which often results only in preventing them from organising themselves." [**Political and Social Writings**, vol. 2, p. 68]

Needless to say, co-operation and co-ordination are required in any collective activity. Anarchists do not deny this fact of nature, but the example Engels considered as irrefutable simply shows the fallacy of his argument. If large-scale industry were run along the lines argued by Engels, it would quickly grind to halt. So trying to eliminate workers' autonomy is difficult as *"[i]ndustrial history shows"* that *"such management attempts to control the freedom of the work force invariably run up against the contradiction that the freedom is necessary for quality production."* [David Noble, **Forces of Production**, p. 277]

Ironically, the example of Russia under Lenin and Trotsky reinforces this fact. *"Administrative centralisation"* was enforced on the railway workers which, in turn, *"led more to ignorance of distance and the inability to respond properly to local circumstances ... 'I have no instructions' became all the more effective as a defensive and self-protective rationalisation as party officials vested with unilateral power insisted all their orders be strictly obeyed. Cheka ruthlessness instilled fear, but repression ... only impaired the exercise of initiative that daily operations required."* [William G. Rosenberg, *"The Social Background to Tsektran"*, pp. 349-373, **Party, State, and Society in the Russian Civil War**, Diane P. Koenker, William G. Rosenberg and Ronald Grigor Suny (eds.), p. 369] Without the autonomy required to manage local problems, the operation of the railways was seriously harmed and, unsurprisingly, a few months after Trotsky subjected railway workers to the *"militarisation of labour"* in September 1920, there was a *"disastrous collapse of the railway network in the winter of 1920-1."* [Jonathan Aves, **Workers against Lenin**, p. 102] There can be no better way to cripple an economy than to impose Lenin's demand that the task of workers was that of *"unquestioningly obeying the will of the Soviet leader, of the dictator, **during** the work."* [**Collected Works**, vol. 27, p. 270]

As the experience of workers' in struggle shows, it is the **abolition** of autonomy which ensures the abolition of large-scale industry, not its exercise. The conscious decision by workers to **not** exercise their autonomy brings industry grinding to a halt and are effective tools in the class struggle. As any worker knows, it is only our ability to make decisions autonomously that keeps industry going.

Rather than abolishing authority making large-scale industry impossible, it is the abolishing of autonomy which quickly achieves this. The issue is how do we organise industry so that this essential autonomy is respected and co-operation between workers achieved based on it. For anarchists, this is done by self-managed workers associations in which hierarchical authority is replaced by collective self-discipline.

H.4.5 Is the way industry operates "independent of all social organisation"?

As noted in the last section, Engels argued that applying the *"forces of nature"* meant *"a veritable despotism independent of all social organisation."* This meant that *"[w]anting to abolish authority in large-scale industry is tantamount to wanting to abolish industry itself."* [**Op. Cit.**, p. 731]

For anarchists, Engels' comments ignore the reality of class society in an important way. Modern (*"large-scale"*) industry has not developed neutrally or naturally, independently of all social organisation as Engels claimed. Rather it has been shaped by the class struggle along with technology (which is often a weapon in that conflict - see section D.10). As Castoriadis argued:

*"Management organises production with a view of achieving 'maximum efficiency.' But the first result of this sort of organisation is to stir up the workers' revolt against production itself ... To combat the resistance of the workers, the management institutes an ever more minute division of labour and tasks ... Machines are invented, or selected, according to one fundamental criterion: Do they assist in the struggle of management against workers, do they reduce yet further the worker's margin of autonomy, do they assist in eventually replacing him [or her] altogether? In this sense, the organisation of production today ... is **class organisation.** Technology is predominantly **class technology.** No ... manager would ever introduce into his plant a machine which would increase the freedom of a particular worker or of a group of workers to run the job themselves, even if such a machine increased production.*

"The workers are by no means helpless in this struggle. They constantly invent methods of self-defence. They break the rules, while 'officially' keeping them. They organise informally, maintain a collective solidarity and discipline." [**The Meaning of Socialism**, pp. 9-10]

So one of the key aspects of the class struggle is the conflict of workers against attempts by management to eliminate their autonomy within the production process. This struggle generates the machines which Engels claims produce a *"veritable despotism independent of all social organisation."* Regardless of what Engels implies, the way industry has developed is not independent of class society and its "despotism" has been engineered that way. For example, it may be a fact of nature that ten people may be required to operate a machine, but that machine is not such a fact, it is a human invention and so can be changed. Nor is it a fact of nature that work organisation should be based on a manager dictating to the workers what to do - rather it could be organised by the workers themselves, using collective self-discipline to co-ordinate their joint effort.

David Noble quotes one shop steward who stated the obvious,

namely that workers are "not automatons. We have eyes to see with, ears to hear with, and mouths to talk." As Noble comments, "[f]or management ... that was precisely the problem. Workers controlled the machines, and through their unions had real authority over the division of labour and job content." [**Forces of Production**, p. 37] This autonomy was what managers constantly struggled against and introduced technology to combat. So Engels' notion that machinery was "despotic" hides the nature of class society and the fact that authority is a social relationship, a relationship between people and not people and things. And, equally, that different kinds of organisation meant different social relationships to do collective tasks. It was precisely to draw attention to this that anarchists called themselves anti-authoritarians.

Clearly, Engels is simply ignoring the actual relations of authority within capitalist industry and, like the capitalism he claims to oppose, is raising the needs of the bosses to the plane of "natural fact." Indeed, is this not the refrain of every boss or supporter of capitalism? Right-wing "libertarian" guru Ludwig von Mises spouted this kind of nonsense when he argued that "[t]he root of the syndicalist idea is to be seen in the belief that entrepreneurs and capitalists are irresponsible autocrats who are free to conduct their affairs arbitrarily... . The fundamental error of this argument is obvious [sic!]. The entrepreneurs and capitalists are not irresponsible autocrats. They are unconditionally subject to the sovereignty of the consumers. The market is a consumers' democracy." [**Human Action**, p. 814] In other words, it is not the bosses fault that they dictate to the worker. No, of course not, it is the despotism of the machine, of nature, of the market, of the customer, anyone and anything **but** the person **with** authority who is actually giving the orders and punishing those who do not obey!

Needless to say, like Engels, von Mises is fundamentally flawed simply because the boss is not just repeating the instructions of the market (assuming that it is a "consumers' democracy," which it is not). Rather, they give their own instructions based on their own sovereignty over the workers. The workers could, of course, manage their own affairs and meet the demands of consumers directly. The "sovereignty" of the market (just like the "despotism" of machines and joint action) is independent of the social relationships which exist within the workplace, but the social relationships themselves are not predetermined by it. Thus the same workshop can be organised in different ways and so the way industry operates **is** dependent on social organisation. The workers can manage their own affairs or be subjected to the rule of a boss. To say that "authority" still exists simply means to confuse agreement with obedience.

The importance of differentiating between types of organisation and ways of making decisions can be seen from the experience of the class struggle. During the Spanish Revolution anarchists organised militias to fight the fascists. One was lead by anarchist militant Durruti. His military adviser, Pérez Farras, a professional soldier, was concerned about the application of libertarian principles to military organisation. Durruti replied:

> "I've said it once and I'll say it again: I've been an anarchist my entire life and the fact that I'm responsible for this human collectivity won't change my convictions. It was as an anarchist that I agreed to carry out the task

that the Central Committee of the Anti-Fascist Militias entrusted me.

> "I don't believe - and everything happening around us confirms this - that you can run a workers' militia according to classic military rules. I believe that discipline, co-ordination, and planning are indispensable, but we shouldn't define them in terms taken from the world that we're destroying. We have to build on new foundations. My comrades and I are convinced that solidarity is the best incentive for arousing an individual's sense of responsibility and a willingness to accept discipline as an act of self-discipline.

> "War has been imposed upon us ... but our goal is revolutionary victory. This means defeating the enemy, but also a radical change in men. For that change to occur, man must learn to live and conduct himself as a free man, an apprenticeship that develops his personality and sense of responsibility, his capacity to be master of his own acts. The worker on the job not only transforms the material on which he works, but also transforms himself through that work. The combatant is nothing more than a worker whose tool is a rifle - and he should strive toward the same objective as a worker. One can't behave like an obedient soldier but rather as a conscious man who understands the importance of what he's doing. I know that it's not easy to achieve this, but I also know that what can't be accomplished with reason will not be obtained by force. If we have to sustain our military apparatus by fear, then we won't have changed anything except the colour of the fear. It's only by freeing itself from fear that society can build itself in freedom." [quoted by Abel Paz, **Durruti: In The Spanish Revolution**, p. 474]

Is it really convincing to argue that the individuals who made up the militia are subject to the same social relationships as those in a capitalist or Leninist army? The same, surely, goes for workers associations and wage labour. Ultimately, the flaw in Engels' argument can be best seen simply because he thinks that the "automatic machinery of a big factory is much more despotic than the small capitalist who employ workers ever have been." [**Op. Cit.**, p. 731] Authority and liberty become detached from human beings, as if authoritarian social relationships can exist independently of individuals! It is a **social** relationship anarchists oppose, not an abstraction.

Engels' argument is applicable to **any** society and to **any** task which requires joint effort. If, for example, a table needs four people to move it then those four people are subject to the "despotism" of gravity! Under such "despotism" can we say its irrelevant whether these four people are slaves to a master who wants the table moved or whether they agree between themselves to move the table and on the best way to do it? In both cases the table movers are subject to the same "despotism" of gravity, yet in the latter example they are **not** subject to the despotism of other human beings as they clearly are in the former. Engels is simply playing with words!

The fallacy of Engels' basic argument can be seen from this simple example. He essentially uses a **liberal** concept of freedom (i.e. freedom exists prior to society and is reduced within it) when attacking anarchism. Rather than see freedom as a product of interaction, as Bakunin did, Engels sees it as a product of isolation. Collective activity is seen as a realm of necessity (to use Marx's phrase) and not one of freedom. Indeed, machines and the forces of nature are considered by Engels' as "despots"! As if despotism were not a specific set of relationships between **humans.** As Bookchin argued:

"To Engels, the factory is a natural fact of technics, not a specifically bourgeois mode of rationalising labour; hence it will exist under communism as well as capitalism. It will persist 'independently of all social organisation.' To co-ordinate a factory's operations requires 'imperious obedience,' in which factory hands lack all 'autonomy.' Class society or classless, the realm of necessity is also a realm of command and obedience, of ruler and ruled. In a fashion totally congruent with all class ideologists from the inception of class society, Engels weds Socialism to command and rule as a natural fact. Domination is reworked from a social attribute into a precondition for self-preservation in a technically advanced society." [**Toward an Ecological Society**, p. 206]

Given this, it can be argued that Engels' *"On Authority"* had a significant impact in the degeneration of the Russian Revolution into state capitalism. By deliberately obscuring the differences between self-managed and authoritarian organisation, he helped provide Bolshevism with ideological justification for eliminating workers self-management in production. After all, if self-management and hierarchical management both involve the same *"principle of authority,"* then it does not really matter how production is organised and whether industry is managed by the workers or by appointed managers (as Engels stressed, authority in industry was independent of the social system and all forms of organisation meant subordination). Murray Bookchin draws the obvious conclusion from Engels' (and Marx's) position: *"Obviously, the factory conceived of as a 'realm of necessity' [as opposed to a 'realm of freedom'] requires no need for self-management."* [**Op. Cit.**, p. 126] Thus it is no great leap from the arguments of Engels in *"On Authority"* to Lenin's arguments justifying the imposition of capitalist organisational forms during the Russian Revolution:

*"Firstly, the question of principle, namely, is the appointment of individuals, dictators with unlimited powers, in general compatible with the fundamental principles of Soviet government? ... concerning the significance of individual dictatorial powers from the point of view of the specific tasks of the present moment, it must be said that large-scale machine industry - which is precisely the material source, the productive source, the foundation of socialism - calls for absolute and strict unity of will, which directs the joint labours of hundreds, thousands and tens of thousands of people ... But how can strict unity of will be ensured? By thousands subordinating their will to the will of one ... **unquestioning subordination** to a single*

*will is absolutely necessary for the success of processes organised on the pattern of large-scale machine industry. On the railways it is twice and three times as necessary ... Today ... revolution demands - precisely in the interests of its development and consolidation, precisely in the interests of socialism - that the people **unquestioningly obey the single will** of the leaders of labour."* [**Collected Works**, vol. 27, pp. 267-9]

Hence the Bolsheviks need not have to consider whether replacing factory committees with appointed managers armed with *"dictatorial powers"* would have any effect on the position of workers in socialism (after all, they were subject to subordination either way). Nor did they have to worry about putting economic power into the hands of a state-appointed bureaucracy as "authority" and subordination were required to run industry no matter what. Engels had used the modern factory system of mass production as a direct analogy to argue against the anarchist call for workers' councils, for autonomy, for participation, for self-management. Authority, hierarchy, and the need for submission and domination is inevitable given the current mode of production, both Engels and Lenin argued. Little wonder, then, the worker became the serf of the state under the Bolsheviks. In his own way, Engels contributed to the degeneration of the Russian Revolution by providing the rationale for the Bolsheviks disregard for workers' self-management of production.

Simply put, Engels was wrong. The need to co-operate and co-ordinate activity may be independent of social development, but the nature of a society does impact on how this co-operation is achieved. If it is achieved by hierarchical means, then it is a class society. If it is achieved by agreements between equals, then it is a socialist one. As such, how industry operates **is** dependent on the society it is part of. An anarchist society would run industry based on the free agreement of workers united in free associations. This would necessitate making and sticking to joint decisions but this co-ordination would be between equals, not master and servant. By not recognising this fact, Engels fatally undermined the cause of socialism.

H.4.6 Why does Engels' "On Authority" harm Marxism?

Ironically, Engels' essay *"On Authority"* also strikes at the heart of Marxism and its critique of anarchism. Forgetting what he had written in 1873, Engels argued in 1894 that for him and Marx the *"ultimate political aim is to overcome the whole state and therefore democracy as well."* [quoted by Lenin, *"State and Revolution"*, **Essential Works of Lenin**, p. 331] Lenin argued that *"the abolition of the state means also the abolition of democracy."* [**Op. Cit.**, p. 332]

The problems arise from the awkward fact that Engels' *"On Authority"* had stated that any form of collective activity meant "authority" and so the subjection of the minority to the majority (*"if possible"*) and *"the imposition of the will of another upon ours."* [**Marx-Engels Reader**, p. 731 and p. 730] Aware of the contradiction, Lenin stresses that *"someone may even begin to fear we are expecting the advent of an order of society in which the subordination of the minority to the majority will not be respected."* That was not the case, however. He simply rejected the idea that democracy was *"the recognition of this principle"* arguing that *"democracy is a* **state** *which recognises the subordination of the minority to the majority, i.e. an organisation for the systematic use of* **violence** *by one class against the other, by one section of the population against another."* He argued that *"the need for violence against people in general, the need for the* **subjection** *of one man to another, will vanish, since people will* **become accustomed** *to observing the elementary conditions of social life* **without force** *and* **without subordination.** *"* [**Op. Cit.**, pp. 332-3]

Talk about playing with words! Earlier in his work Lenin summarised Engels **"On Authority"** by stating that *"is it not clear that ... complex technical units, based on the employment of machinery and the ordered co-operation of many people, could function without a certain amount of subordination, without some authority or power."* [**Op. Cit.**, p. 316] Now, however, he argued that communism would involve no *"subordination"* while, at the same time, be based on the *"the principle of the subordination of the minority to the majority"*! A contradiction? Perhaps not, as he argued that the minority would *"become accustomed"* to the conditions of *"social life"* - in other words the recognition that sticking to your agreements you make with others does not involve "subordination." This, ironically, would confirm anarchist ideas as we argue that making agreements with others, as equals, does not involve domination or subordination but rather is an expression of autonomy, of liberty.

Similarly, we find Engels arguing in **Anti-Duhring** that socialism *"puts an end to the former subjection of men to their own means of production"* and that *"productive labour, instead of being a means of subjugating men, will become a means of their emancipation."* This work was written in 1878, six years after *"On Authority"* where he stressed that *"the automatic machinery of a big factory is much more despotic than the small capitalists who employ workers ever have been"* and *"subdu[ing] the forces of nature ... avenge themselves"* upon *"man"* by *"subjecting him ... to a veritable despotism independent of all social organisation."* [**Op. Cit.**, p. 720, p. 721 and p. 731] Engels is clearly contradicting himself. When attacking the anarchists, he argues that the *"subjection"* of people to the means of production was inevitable and utterly *"independent of all social organisation."* Six years later he proclaims that socialism will abolish this inescapable subjection to the *"veritable despotism"* of modern industry!

As can be seen from both Engels and Lenin, we have a contradiction within Marxism. On the one hand, they argue that authority (*"subjection"*) will always be with us, no matter what, as *"subordination"* and *"authority"* is independent of the specific society we live in. On the other, they argue that Marxist socialism will be without a state, *"without subordination"*, *"without force"* and will end the *"subjection of men to their own means of production."* The two positions cannot be reconciled.

Simply put, if **"On Authority"** is correct then, logically, it means that not only is anarchism impossible but also Marxist socialism. Lenin and Engels are trying to have it both ways. On the one hand, arguing that anarchism is impossible as any collective activity

means subjection and subordination, on the other, that socialism will end that inevitable subjection. And, of course, arguing that democracy will be "overcome" while, at the same time, arguing that it can never be. Ultimately, it shows that Engels essay is little more than a cheap polemic without much merit.

Even worse for Marxism is Engels' comment that authority and autonomy *"are relative things whose spheres vary with the various phases of society"* and that *"the material conditions of production and circulation inevitably develop with large-scale industry and large-scale agriculture, and increasingly tend to enlarge the scope of this authority."* Given that this is *"a veritable despotism"* and Marxism aims at *"one single vast plan"* in modern industry, then the scope for autonomy, for freedom, is continually reduced during the working day. [**Op. Cit.**, p. 732, p. 731 and p. 723] If machinery and industry means despotism, as Engels claimed against Bakunin, then what does that mean for Lenin's aim to ensure *"the transformation of the whole state economic mechanism into a single huge machine ... as to enable hundreds of millions of people to be guided by a single plan?"* [**Collected Works**, vol. 27, pp. 90-1] Surely such an economy would be, to use Engels' words, *"a veritable despotism"*? The only possible solution is reducing the working day to a minimum and so the time spent as a slave to the machine (and plan) is reduced. The idea that work should be transformed into creative, empowering and liberating experience is automatically destroyed by Engels' argument. Like capitalism, Marxist-Socialism is based on "work is hell" and the domination of the producer. Hardly an inspiring vision of the future.

H.4.7 Is revolution "the most authoritarian thing there is"?

As well as the argument that "authority" is essential for every collective activity, Engels raises another argument against anarchism. This second argument is that revolutions are by nature authoritarian. In his words, a *"revolution is certainly the most authoritarian thing there is; it is the act whereby one part of the population imposes its will upon the other part by means of rifles, bayonets and cannon - authoritarian means, if such there be at all; and if the victorious party does not want to have fought in vain, it must maintain this rule by means of the terror its arms inspire in the reactionaries."* [**Marx-Engels Reader**, p. 733]

Yet such an analysis is without class analysis and so will, by necessity, mislead the writer and the reader. Engels argues that revolution is the imposition by *"one part of the population"* on another. Very true - but Engels fails to indicate the nature of class society and, therefore, of a social revolution. In a class society *"one part of the population"* constantly *"imposes its will upon the other part"* - those with power impose their decisions to those beneath them in the social hierarchy. In other words, the ruling class imposes its will on the working class everyday, in work by the hierarchical structure of the workplace and in society by the state. Discussing the "population" as if it were not divided by classes and so subject to specific forms of authoritarian social relationships is liberal nonsense.

Once we recognise that the "population" in question is divided into classes we can easily see the fallacy of Engels argument. In a social revolution, the act of revolution is the overthrow of the power and authority of an oppressing and exploiting class by those subject to that oppression and exploitation. In other words, it is an act of **liberation** in which the hierarchical power of the few over the many is eliminated and replaced by the freedom of the many to control their own lives. It is hardly authoritarian to destroy authority! Thus a social revolution is, fundamentally, an act of liberation for the oppressed who act in their own interests to end the system in which *"one part of the population imposes its will upon the other"* everyday. Malatesta stated the obvious:

> *"To fight our enemies effectively, we do not need to deny the principle of freedom, not even for one moment: it is sufficient for us to want real freedom and to want it for all, for ourselves as well as for others.*

> *"We want to expropriate the property-owning class, and with violence, since it is with violence that they hold on to social wealth and use it to exploit the working class. Not because freedom is a good thing for the future, but because it is a good thing, today as well as tomorrow, and the property owners, by denying us the means of exercising our freedom, in effect, take it away from us.*

> *"We want to overthrow the government, all governments - and overthrow them with violence since it is by the use of violence that they force us into obeying - and once again, not because we sneer at freedom when it does not serve our interests but because governments are the negation of freedom and it is not possible to be free without getting rid of them …*

> *"The freedom to oppress, to exploit … is the denial of freedom: and the fact that our enemies make irrelevant and hypocritical use of the word freedom is not enough to make us deny the principle of freedom which is the outstanding characteristic of our movement and a permanent, constant and necessary factor in the life and progress of humanity."* [**Errico Malatesta: His Life and Ideas**, p. 51]

It seems strange that Engels, in effect, is arguing that the abolition of tyranny is tyranny against the tyrants! As Malatesta so clearly argued, anarchists *"recognise violence only as a means of legitimate self-defence; and if today they are in favour of violence it is because they maintain that slaves are always in a state of legitimate defence."* [**Op. Cit.**, p. 59] As such, Engels fails to understand the revolution from a **working class** perspective (perhaps unsurprisingly, as he was a capitalist). The "authority" of the "armed workers" over the bourgeois is, simply, the defence of the workers' freedom against those who seek to end it by exercising/recreating the very authoritarian social relationships the revolution sought to end in the first place. This explains why, as we discussed in section H.2.1 anarchists have always argued that a revolution would need to defend itself against those seeking to return the masses to their position at the bottom of the social hierarchy.

To equate the defence of freedom with "authority" is, in anarchist eyes, an expression of confused politics. Ultimately, Engels is like the liberal who equates the violence of the oppressed to end oppression with that of the oppressors!

Needless to say, this applies to the class struggle as well. Is, for example, a picket line really authoritarian because it tries to impose its will on the boss, police or scabs? Rather, is it not defending the workers' freedom against the authoritarian power of the boss and their lackeys (the police and scabs)? Is it "authoritarian" to resist authority and create a structure - a strike assembly and picket line - which allows the formally subordinated workers to manage their own affairs directly and without bosses? Is it "authoritarian" to combat the authority of the boss, to proclaim your freedom and exercise it? Of course not.

Structurally, a strikers' assembly and picket line - which are forms of self-managed association - cannot be compared to an "authority" (such as a state). To try and do so fails to recognise the fundamental difference. In the strikers' assembly and picket line the strikers themselves decide policy and do not delegate power away into the hands of an authority (any strike committee executes the strikers decisions or is replaced). In a state, **power** is delegated into the hands of a few who then use that power as they see fit. This by necessity disempowers those at the base, who are turned into mere electors and order takers (i.e. an authoritarian relationship is created). Such a situation can only spell death of a social revolution, which requires the active participation of all if it is to succeed. It also, incidentally, exposes a central fallacy of Marxism, namely that it claims to desire a society based on the participation of everyone yet favours a form of organisation - centralisation - that excludes that participation.

Georges Fontenis summarises anarchist ideas on this subject when he wrote:

> *"And so against the idea of State, where power is exercised by a specialised group isolated from the masses, we put the idea of direct workers power, where accountable and controlled elected delegates (who can be recalled at any time and are remunerated at the same rate as other workers) replace hierarchical, specialised and privileged bureaucracy; where militias, controlled by administrative bodies such as soviets, unions and communes, with no special privileges for military technicians, realising the idea of the armed people, replace an army cut off from the body of Society and subordinated to the arbitrary power of a State or government."* [**Manifesto of Libertarian Communism**, p. 24]

Anarchists, therefore, are no more impressed with this aspect of Engels critique than his "organisation equals authority" argument. In summary, his argument is simply a liberal analysis of revolution, totally without a class basis or analysis and so fails to understand the anarchist case nor answer it. To argue that a revolution is made up of two groups of people, one of which *"imposes its will upon the other"* fails to indicate the social relations that exist between these groups (classes) and the relations of authority between them which the revolution is seeking to overthrow. As such, Engels critique totally misses the point.

Many socialists follow the ideas of Lenin and, in particular, his ideas on vanguard parties. These ideas were expounded by Lenin in his (in)famous work **What is to be Done?** which is considered as one of the important books in the development of Bolshevism.

The core of these ideas is the concept of *"vanguardism,"* or the *"vanguard party."* According to this perspective, socialists need to organise together in a party, based on the principles of *"democratic centralism,"* which aims to gain a decisive influence in the class struggle. The ultimate aim of such a party is revolution and its seizure of power. Its short term aim is to gather into it all *"class conscious"* workers into a *"efficient"* and *"effective"* party, alongside members of other classes who consider themselves as revolutionary Marxists. The party would be strictly centralised, with all members expected to submit to party decisions, speak in one voice and act in one way. Without this *"vanguard,"* injecting its politics into the working class (who, it is asserted, can only reach trade union consciousness by its own efforts), a revolution is impossible.

Lenin laid the foundation of this kind of party in his book **What is to be Done?** and the vision of the *"vanguard"* party was explicitly formalised in the Communist International. As Lenin put it, *"Bolshevism* **has created** *the ideological and tactical foundations of a Third International … Bolshevism* **can serve as a model of tactics for all.***"* [**Collected Works**, vol. 28, pp. 292-3] Using the Russian Communist Party as its model, Bolshevik ideas on party organisation were raised as a model for revolutionaries across the world. Since then, the various followers of Leninism and its offshoots like Trotskyism have organised themselves in this manner (with varying success).

The wisdom of applying an organisational model that had been developed in the semi-feudal conditions of Tsarist Russia to **every** country, regardless of its level of development, has been questioned by anarchists from the start. After all, could it not be wiser to build upon the revolutionary tendencies which had developed in specific countries rather than import a new model which had been created for, and shaped by, radically different social, political and economic conditions? The wisdom of applying the vanguard model is not questioned on these (essentially materialist) points by those who subscribe to it. While revolutionary workers in the advanced capitalist nations subscribed to anarchist and syndicalist ideas, this tradition is rejected in favour of one developed by, in the main, bourgeois intellectuals in a nation which was still primarily feudal and absolutist. The lessons learned from years of struggle in actual capitalist societies were simply rejected in favour of those from a party operating under Tsarism. While most supporters of vanguardism will admit that conditions now are different than in Tsarist Russia, they still subscribe to organisational methods developed in that context and justify it, ironically enough, because of its "success" in the totally different conditions that prevailed in Russia in the early 20th Century! And Leninists claim to be materialists!

Perhaps the reason why Bolshevism rejected the materialist approach was because most of the revolutionary movements in advanced capitalist countries were explicitly anti-parliamentarian, direct actionist, decentralist, federalist and influenced by libertarian ideas? This materialist analysis was a key aspect of the council communist critique of Lenin's **Left-Wing Communism**, for example (see Herman Gorter's **Open Letter to Comrade Lenin** for one excellent reply to Bolshevik arguments, tactics and assumptions). This attempt to squeeze every working class movement into **one** "officially approved" model dates back to Marx and Engels. Faced with any working class movement which did **not** subscribe to their vision of what they should be doing (namely organising in political parties to take part in "political action," i.e. standing in bourgeois elections) they simply labelled it as the product of non-proletarian "sects." They went so far as to gerrymander the 1872 conference of the First International to make acceptance of "political action" mandatory on all sections in an attempt to destroy anarchist influence in it.

So this section of our FAQ will explain why anarchists reject this model. In our view, the whole concept of a *"vanguard party"* is fundamentally anti-socialist. Rather than present an effective and efficient means of achieving revolution, the Leninist model is elitist, hierarchical and highly inefficient in achieving a socialist society. At best, these parties play a harmful role in the class struggle by alienating activists and militants with their organisational principles and manipulative tactics within popular structures and groups. At worse, these parties can seize power and create a new form of class society (a state capitalist one) in which the working class is oppressed by new bosses (namely, the party hierarchy and its appointees).

However, before discussing why anarchists reject "vanguardism" we need to stress a few points. Firstly, anarchists recognise the obvious fact that the working class is divided in terms of political consciousness. Secondly, from this fact most anarchists recognise the need to organise together to spread our ideas as well as taking part in, influencing and learning from the class struggle. As such, anarchists have long been aware of the need for revolutionaries to organise **as revolutionaries.** Thirdly, anarchists are well aware of the importance of revolutionary minorities playing an inspiring and "leading" role in the class struggle. We do not reject the need for revolutionaries to *"give a lead"* in struggles, we reject the idea of institutionalised leadership and the creation of a leader/led hierarchy implicit (and sometimes not so implicit) in vanguardism.

As such, we do not oppose *"vanguardism"* for these reasons. So when Leninists like Tony Cliff argue that it is *"unevenness in the class [which] makes the party necessary,"* anarchists reply that *"unevenness in the class"* makes it essential that revolutionaries organise together to influence the class but that organisation does not and need not take the form of a vanguard party. [Tony Cliff, **Lenin**, vol. 2, p. 149] This is because we reject the concept and practice for three reasons.

Firstly, and most importantly, anarchists reject the underlying assumption of vanguardism. It is based on the argument that *"socialist consciousness"* has to be introduced into the working class from outside. We argue that not only is this position empirically false, it is fundamentally anti-socialist in nature. This is because it logically denies that the emancipation of the working class is the task of the working class itself. Moreover, it serves to justify elite rule. Some Leninists, embarrassed by the obvious anti-socialist nature of this concept, try and argue that Lenin (and so Leninism) does not hold this position. We show that such claims are false.

Secondly, there is the question of organisational structure. Vanguard parties are based on the principle of *"democratic centralism"*. Anarchists argue that such parties, while centralised, are not, in fact, democratic nor can they be. As such, the *"revolutionary"* or *"socialist"* party is no such thing as it reflects the structure of the capitalist system it claims to oppose.

Lastly, anarchists argue that such parties are, despite the claims of their supporters, not actually very efficient or effective in the revolutionary sense of the word. At best, they hinder the class struggle by being slow to respond to rapidly changing situations. At worse, they are "efficient" in shaping both the revolution and the post-revolutionary society in a hierarchical fashion, so re-creating class rule.

So these are key aspects of the anarchist critique of vanguardism, which we discuss in more depth in the following sections. It is a bit artificial to divide these issues into different sections because they are all related. The role of the party implies a specific form of organisation (as Lenin himself stressed), the form of the party influences its effectiveness. It is for ease of presentation we divide up our discussion so.

H.5.1 Why are vanguard parties anti-socialist?

The reason why vanguard parties are anti-socialist is simply because of the role assigned to them by Lenin, which he thought was vital. Simply put, without the party, no revolution would be possible. As Lenin put it in 1900, *"[i]solated from Social-Democracy, the working class movement becomes petty and inevitably becomes bourgeois."* [**Collected Works**, vol. 4, p. 368] In **What is to be Done?**, he expands on this position:

> *"Class political consciousness can be brought to the workers **only from without**, that is, only outside of the economic struggle, outside the sphere of relations between workers and employers. The sphere from which alone it is possible to obtain this knowledge is the sphere of relationships between **all** the various classes and strata and the state and the government - the sphere of the interrelations between **all** the various classes."* [**Essential Works of Lenin**, p. 112]

Thus the role of the party is to inject socialist politics into a class incapable of developing them itself.

Lenin is at pains to stress the Marxist orthodoxy of his claims and quotes the *"profoundly true and important"* comments of Karl Kautsky on the subject. [**Op. Cit.**, p. 81] Kautsky, considered the "pope" of Social-Democracy, stated that it was *"absolutely untrue"* that *"socialist consciousness"* was a *"necessary and direct result of the proletarian class struggle."* Rather, *"socialism and the class

struggle arise side by side and not one out of the other ... Modern socialist consciousness can arise only on the basis of profound scientific knowledge ... The vehicles of science are not the proletariat, but the **bourgeois intelligentsia**: it was in the minds of some members of this stratum that modern socialism originated, and it was they who communicated it to the more intellectually developed proletarians who, in their turn, introduced it into the proletarian class struggle."* Kautsky stressed that *"socialist consciousness is something introduced into the proletarian class struggle from without."* [quoted by Lenin, **Op. Cit.**, pp. 81-2]

So Lenin, it must be stressed, was not inventing anything new here. He was simply repeating the orthodox Marxist position and, as is obvious, wholeheartedly agreed with Kautsky's pronouncements (any attempt to claim that he did not or later rejected them is nonsense, as we prove in section H.5.4). Lenin, with his usual modesty, claimed to speak on behalf of the workers when he wrote that *"intellectuals must talk to us, and tell us more about what we do not know and what we can never learn from our factory and 'economic' experience, that is, you must give us political knowledge."* [**Op. Cit.**, p. 108] Thus we have Lenin painting a picture of a working class incapable of developing *"political knowledge"* or *"socialist consciousness"* by its own efforts and so is reliant on members of the party, themselves either radical elements of the bourgeoisie and petty-bourgeoisie or educated by them, to provide it with such knowledge.

The obvious implication of this argument is that the working class cannot liberate itself by its own efforts. Without the radical bourgeois to provide the working class with "socialist" ideas, a socialist movement, let alone society, is impossible. If the working class cannot develop its own political theory by its own efforts then it cannot conceive of transforming society and, at best, can see only the need to work within capitalism for reforms to improve its position in society. A class whose members cannot develop political knowledge by its own actions cannot emancipate itself. It is, by necessity, dependent on others to shape and form its movements. To quote Trotsky's telling analogy on the respective roles of party and class, leaders and led:

> *"Without a guiding organisation, the energy of the masses would dissipate like steam not enclosed in a piston. But nevertheless, what moves things is not the piston or the box, but the steam."* [**History of the Russian Revolution**, vol. 1, p. 17]

While Trotsky's mechanistic analogy may be considered as somewhat crude, it does expose the underlying assumptions of Bolshevism. After all, did not Lenin argue that the working class could not develop *"socialist consciousness"* by themselves and that it had to be introduced from without? How can you expect steam to create a piston? You cannot. Thus we have a blind, elemental force incapable of conscious thought being guided by a creation of science, the piston (which, of course, is a product of the work of the *"vehicles of science,"* namely the **bourgeois intelligentsia**). In the Leninist perspective, if revolutions are the locomotives of history (to use Marx's words) then the masses are the steam, the party the locomotive and the leaders the train driver. The idea of a future society being constructed democratically from below by the workers themselves rather than through periodically elected leaders seems to have passed Bolshevism past. This is unsurprising, given that the Bolsheviks saw the workers in terms of blindly moving steam in a box, something incapable of being creative unless an outside force gave them direction (instructions).

Libertarian socialist Cornelius Castoriadis provides a good critique of the implications of the Leninist position:

> "No positive content, nothing new capable of providing the foundation for the reconstruction of society could arise out of a mere awareness of poverty. From the experience of life under capitalism the proletariat could derive no new principles either for organising this new society or for orientating it in another direction. Under such conditions, the proletarian revolution becomes ... a simple reflex revolt against hunger. It is impossible to see how socialist society could ever be the result of such a reflex ... Their situation forces them to suffer the consequences of capitalism's contradictions, but in no way does it lead them to discover its causes. An acquaintance with these causes comes not from experiencing the production process but from theoretical knowledge ... This knowledge may be accessible to individual workers, but not to the proletariat **qua** proletariat. Driven by its revolt against poverty, but incapable of self-direction since its experiences does not give it a privileged viewpoint on reality, the proletariat according to this outlook, can only be an infantry in the service of a general staff of specialists. These specialists **know** (from considerations that the proletariat as such does not have access to) what is going wrong with present-day society and how it must be modified. The traditional view of the economy and its revolutionary perspective can only found, and actually throughout history has only founded, a **bureaucratic politics** ... [W]hat we have outlined are the consequences that follow objectively from this theory. And they have been affirmed in an ever clearer fashion within the actual historical movement of Marxism, culminating in Stalinism." [**Social and Political Writings**, vol. 2, pp. 257-8]

Thus we have a privileged position for the party and a perspective which can (and did) justify party dictatorship **over** the proletariat. Given the perspective that the working class cannot formulate its own "ideology" by its own efforts, of its incapacity to move beyond "trade union consciousness" independently of the party, the clear implication is that the party could in no way be bound by the predominant views of the working class. As the party embodies "socialist consciousness" (and this arises outside the working class and its struggles) then opposition of the working class to the party signifies a failure of the class to resist alien influences. As Lenin put it:

> "Since there can be no talk of an independent ideology being developed by the masses of the workers in the process of their movement, **the only choice is**: either bourgeois or socialist ideology. There is no middle course ... Hence, to belittle socialist ideology **in any way, to deviate from it in the slightest degree** means strengthening bourgeois ideology. There is a lot of talk about spontaneity, but the **spontaneous** development of the labour movement leads to its becoming subordinated to bourgeois ideology ... Hence our task, the task of Social-Democracy, is to **combat spontaneity**, to **divert** the labour movement from its spontaneous, trade unionist striving to go under the wing of the bourgeoisie, and to bring it under the wing of revolutionary Social-Democracy." [**Op. Cit.**, pp. 82-3]

The implications of this argument became clear once the Bolsheviks seized power. As a justification for party dictatorship, you would be hard pressed to find any better. If the working class revolts against the ruling party, then we have a "spontaneous" development which, inevitably, is an expression of bourgeois ideology. As the party represents socialist consciousness, any deviation in working class support for it simply meant that the working class was being "subordinated" to the bourgeoisie. This meant, obviously, that to "belittle" the "role" of the party by questioning its rule meant to "strengthen bourgeois ideology" and when workers spontaneously went on strike or protested against the party's rule, the party had to "combat" these strivings in order to maintain working class rule! As the "masses of the workers" cannot develop an "independent ideology," the workers are rejecting socialist ideology in favour of bourgeois ideology. The party, in order to defend the "the revolution" (even the "rule of the workers"!) has to impose its will onto the class, to "combat spontaneity."

As we saw in section H.1.2, none of the leading Bolsheviks were shy about drawing these conclusions once in power and faced with working class revolt against their rule. Indeed, they raised the idea that the "dictatorship of the proletariat" was also, in fact, the "dictatorship of the party" and, as we discussed in section H.3.8 integrated this into their theory of the state. Thus, Leninist ideology implies that "workers' power" exists independently of the workers. This means that the sight of the "dictatorship of the proletariat" (i.e. the Bolshevik government) repressing the proletariat is to be expected.

As well as explaining the subsequent embrace of party dictatorship **over** the working class, vanguardism also explains the notorious inefficiency of Leninist parties faced with revolutionary situations we discuss in section H.5.8. Basing themselves on the perspective that all spontaneous movements are inherently bourgeois they could not help but be opposed to autonomous class struggle and the organisations and tactics it generates. James C. Scott, in his excellent discussion of the roots and flaws in Lenin's ideas on the party, makes the obvious point that since, for Lenin, "authentic, revolutionary class consciousness could never develop autonomously within the working class, it followed that that the actual political outlook of workers was always a threat to the vanguard party." [**Seeing like a State**, p. 155] As Maurice Brinton argued, the "Bolshevik cadres saw their role as the leadership of the revolution. Any movement not initiated by them or independent of their control could only evoke their suspicion." These developments, of course, did not occur by chance or accidentally for "a given ideological premise (the preordained hegemony of the Party) led necessarily to certain conclusions in practice." [**The Bolsheviks and Workers' Control**, p. xi and p. xii]

Bakunin expressed the implications of the vanguardist perspective extremely well. It is worthwhile quoting him at length:

> "Idealists of all sorts, metaphysicians, positivists, those who uphold the priority of science over life, the doctrinaire revolutionists - all of them champion with equal zeal although differing in their argumentation, the idea of the State and State power, seeing in them, quite logically from their point of view, the only salvation of society. **Quite logically,** I say, having taken as their basis the tenet - a fallacious tenet in our opinion - that thought is prior to life, and abstract theory is prior to social practice, and that therefore sociological science must become the starting point for social upheavals and social reconstruction - they necessarily arrived at the conclusion that since thought, theory, and science are, for the present at least, the property of only a very few people, those few should direct social life; and that on the morrow of the Revolution the new social organisation should be set up not by the free integration of workers' associations, villages, communes, and regions from below upward, conforming to the needs and instincts of the people, but solely by the dictatorial power of this learned minority, allegedly expressing the general will of the people." [**The Political Philosophy of Bakunin**, pp. 283-4]

The idea that "socialist consciousness" can exist independently of the working class and its struggle suggests exactly the perspective Bakunin was critiquing. For vanguardism, the abstract theory of socialism exists prior to the class struggle and exists waiting to be brought to the masses by the educated few. The net effect is, as we have argued, to lay the ground for party dictatorship. The concept is fundamentally anti-socialist, a justification for elite rule and the continuation of class society in new, party approved, ways.

H.5.2 Have vanguardist assumptions been validated?

Lenin claimed that workers can only reach a "trade union consciousness" by their own efforts. Anarchists argue that such an assertion is empirically false. The history of the labour movement is marked by revolts and struggles which went far further than just seeking reforms as well as revolutionary theories derived from such experiences.

The category of "economic struggle" corresponds to no known social reality. Every "economic" struggle is "political" in some sense and those involved can, and do, learn political lessons from them. As Kropotkin noted in the 1880s, there "is almost no serious strike which occurs today without the appearance of troops, the exchange of blows and some acts of revolt. Here they fight with the troops; there they march on the factories ... Thanks to government intervention the rebel against the factory becomes the rebel against the State." [quoted by Caroline Cahm, **Kropotkin and the Rise of Revolutionary Anarchism**, p. 256] If history shows anything, it shows that workers are more than capable of going beyond "trade union consciousness." The Paris Commune, the 1848 revolts and, ironically enough, the 1905 and 1917 Russian Revolutions show that the masses are capable of revolutionary struggles in which the self-proclaimed "vanguard" of socialists spend most of their time trying to catch up with them!

The history of Bolshevism also helps discredit Lenin's argument that the workers cannot develop socialist consciousness alone due to the power of bourgeois ideology. Simply put, if the working class is subjected to bourgeois influences, then so are the "professional" revolutionaries within the party. Indeed, the strength of such influences on the "professionals" of revolution **must** be higher as they are not part of proletarian life. If social being influences consciousness then if a revolutionary is no longer part of the working class then they no longer are rooted in the social conditions which generate socialist theory and action. No longer connected with collective labour and working class life, the "professional" revolutionary is more likely to be influenced by the social milieu he or she now is part of (i.e. a bourgeois, or at best petit-bourgeois, environment).

This tendency for the "professional" revolutionary to be subject to bourgeois influences can continually be seen from the history of the Bolshevik party. As Trotsky himself noted:

> "It should not be forgotten that the political machine of the Bolshevik Party was predominantly made up of the intelligentsia, which was petty bourgeois in its origin and conditions of life and Marxist in its ideas and in its relations with the proletariat. Workers who turned professional revolutionists joined this set with great eagerness and lost their identity in it. The peculiar social structure of the Party machine and its authority over the proletariat (neither of which is accidental but dictated by strict historical necessity) were more than once the cause of the Party's vacillation and finally became the source of its degeneration ... In most cases they lacked independent daily contact with the labouring masses as well as a comprehensive understanding of the historical process. They thus left themselves exposed to the influence of alien classes." [**Stalin**, vol. 1, pp. 297-8]

He pointed to the example of the First World War, when, "even the Bolshevik party did not at once find its way in the labyrinth of war. As a general rule, the confusion was most pervasive and lasted longest amongst the Party's higher-ups, who came in direct contact with bourgeois public opinion." Thus the professional revolutionaries "were largely affected by compromisist tendencies, which emanated from bourgeois circles, while the rank and file Bolshevik workingmen displayed far greater stability resisting the patriotic hysteria that had swept the country." [**Op. Cit.**, p. 248 and p. 298] It should be noted that he was repeating earlier comments on the "immense intellectual backsliding of the upper stratum of the Bolsheviks during the war" was caused by "isolation from the masses and isolation from those abroad - that is primarily from Lenin." [**History of the Russian Revolution**, vol. 3, p. 134] As we discuss in section H.5.12, even Trotsky had to admit that during 1917 the working class was far more revolutionary than the party and the party more revolutionary than the *"party machine"* of *"professional revolutionaries."*

Ironically enough, Lenin himself recognised this aspect of intellectuals after he had praised their role in bringing "revolutionary" consciousness to the working class. In his 1904 work **One Step Forward, Two Steps Back**, he argued that it was now the presence of *"large numbers of radical intellectuals in the ranks"* which has ensured that *"the opportunism which their mentality produces had been, and is, bound to exist."* [**Collected Works**, vol. 7, pp. 403-4] According to Lenin's new philosophy, the working class simply needs to have been through the *"schooling of the factory"* in order to give the intelligentsia lessons in political discipline, the very same intelligentsia which up until then had played the leading role in the Party and had given political consciousness to the working class. In his words:

> *"For the factory, which seems only a bogey to some, represents that highest form of capitalist co-operation which has united and disciplined the proletariat, taught it to organise … And it is Marxism, the ideology of the proletariat trained by capitalism, has been and is teaching … unstable intellectuals to distinguish between the factory as a means of exploitation (discipline based on fear of starvation) and the factory as a means of organisation (discipline based on collective work …). The discipline and organisation which come so hard to the bourgeois intellectual are very easily acquired by the proletariat just because of this factory 'schooling.'"*
> [**Op. Cit.**, pp. 392-3]

Lenin's analogy is, of course, flawed. The factory is a *"means of exploitation"* because its *"means of organisation"* is top-down and hierarchical. The *"collective work"* which the workers are subjected to is organised by the boss and the *"discipline"* is that of the barracks, not that of free individuals. In fact, the *"schooling"* for revolutionaries is **not** the factory, but the class struggle - healthy and positive self-discipline is generated by the struggle against the way the workplace is organised under capitalism. Factory discipline, in other words, is completely different from the discipline required for social struggle or revolution. Workers become revolutionary in so far as they reject the hierarchical discipline of the workplace and develop the self-discipline required to fight it.

A key task of anarchism is to encourage working class revolt against this type of discipline, particularly in the capitalist workplace. The *"discipline"* Lenin praises simply replaces human thought and association with the following of orders and hierarchy. Thus anarchism aims to undermine capitalist (imposed and brutalising) discipline in favour of solidarity, the *"discipline"* of free association and agreement based on the community of struggle and the political consciousness and revolutionary enthusiasm that struggle creates. Thus, for anarchists, the model of the factory can never be the model for a revolutionary organisation any more than Lenin's vision of society as *"one big workplace"* could be our vision of socialism (see section H.3.1). Ultimately, the factory exists to reproduce hierarchical social relationships and class society just as much as it

exists to produce goods.

It should be noted that Lenin's argument does not contradict his earlier ones. The proletarian and intellectual have complementary jobs in the party. The proletariat is to give lessons in political discipline to the intellectuals as they have been through the process of factory (i.e. hierarchical) discipline. The role of the intellectuals as providers of *"political consciousness"* is the same and so they give political lessons to the workers. Moreover, his vision of the vanguard party is basically the same as in **What is to Be Done?**. This can be seen from his comments that the leading Menshevik Martov **"lumps together** in the party organised and unorganised elements, those who lend themselves to direction and those who do not, the advanced and the incorrigibly backward."* He stressed that the *"division of labour under the direction of a centre evokes from him [the intellectual] a tragicomical outcry against transforming people into 'cogs and wheels.'"* [**Op. Cit.**, p. 258 and p. 392] Thus there is the same division of labour as in the capitalist factory, with the boss (the *"centre"*) having the power to direct the workers (who submit to *"direction"*). Thus we have a "revolutionary" party organised in a **capitalist** manner, with the same *"division of labour"* between order givers and order takers.

H.5.3 Why does vanguardism imply party power?

As we discussed in section H.5.1, anarchists argue that the assumptions of vanguardism lead to party rule over the working class. Needless to say, followers of Lenin disagree. For example, Chris Harman of the British **Socialist Workers Party** argues the opposite case in his essay *"Party and Class."* However, his own argument suggests the elitist conclusions libertarians point to in Lenin's work.

Harman argues that there are two ways to look at the revolutionary party, the Leninist way and the traditional social-democratic way (as represented by the likes of Trotsky and Rosa Luxemburg in 1903-5). *"The latter,"* he argues, *"was thought of as a party of the whole [working] class … All the tendencies within the class had to be represented within it. Any split within it was to be conceived of as a split within the class. Centralisation, although recognised as necessary, was feared as a centralisation over and against the spontaneous activity of the class. Yet it was precisely in this kind of party that the 'autocratic' tendencies warned against by Luxemburg were to develop most. For within it the confusion of member and sympathiser, the massive apparatus needed to hold together a mass of only half-politicised members in a series of social activities, led to a toning down of political debate, a lack of political seriousness, which in turn reduced the ability of the members to make independent political evaluations and increased the need for apparatus-induced involvement."* [**Party and Class**, p. 32]

Thus, the lumping together into one organisation all those who consider themselves as *"socialist"* and agree with the party's aims creates in a mass which results in *"autocratic"* tendencies within the party organisation. As such, it is important to remember that *"the Party, as the vanguard of the working class, must not be confused* with the entire class." [**Op. Cit.**, p. 22] For this reason, the party must be organised in a specific manner which reflect his Leninist assumptions:

> "The alternative [to the vanguard party] is the 'marsh' - where elements motivated by scientific precision are so mixed up with those who are irremediably confused as to prevent any decisive action, effectively allowing the most backward to lead." [**Op. Cit.**, p. 30]

The problem for Harman is to explain how the proletariat can become the ruling class if this were true. He argues that "the party is not the embryo of the workers' state - the workers' council is. The working class as a whole will be involved in the organisations that constitute the state, the most backward as well as the most progressive elements." The "function of the party is not to be the state." [**Op. Cit.**, p. 33] The implication is that the working class will take an active part in the decision making process during the revolution (although the level of this "involvement" is unspecified, probably for good reasons as we explain). If this **is** the case, then the problem of the mass party reappears, but in a new form (we must also note that this problem must have also appeared in 1917, when the Bolshevik party opened its doors to become a mass party).

As the "organisations that constitute the state" are made up of the working class "as a whole," then, obviously, they cannot be expected to wield power (i.e. directly manage the revolution from below). If they did, then the party would be "mixed up" with the "irremediably confused" and so could not lead (as we discuss in section H.5.5, Lenin linked "opportunism" to "primitive" democracy, i.e. self-management, within the party). Hence the need for party power. Which, of course, explains Lenin's 1920 comments that an organisation embracing the whole working class cannot exercise the "dictatorship of the proletariat" and that a "vanguard" is required to do so (see section H.1.2 for details). Of course, Harman does not explain how the "irremediably confused" are able to judge that the party is the best representative of its interests. Surely if someone is competent enough to pick their ruler, they must also be competent enough to manage their own affairs directly? Equally, if the "irremediably confused" vote against the party once it is in power, what happens? Will the party submit to the "leadership" of what it considers "the most backward"? If the Bolsheviks are anything to go by, the answer has to be no.

Significantly, this substitution of the rule of the party for working class self-government and the party apparatus for the party membership does not happen by accident. In order to have a socialist revolution, the working class as a whole must participate in the process so the decision making organisations will be based on the party being "mixed up" with the "irremediably confused" as if they were part of a non-Leninist party. So from Harman's own assumptions, this by necessity results in an "autocratic" regime within the new "workers' state."

This was implicitly recognised by the Bolsheviks when they stressed that the function of the party was to become the government, the head of the state, to "assume power", (see section H.3.3). Thus, while the working class "as a whole" will be "involved in the organisations that constitute the state," the party (in practice, its leadership) will hold power. And for Trotsky, this substitution of the party for the class was inevitable:

> "We have more than once been accused of having substituted for the dictatorship of the Soviets the dictatorship of our party. Yet it can be said with complete justice that the dictatorship of the Soviets became possible only by means of the dictatorship of the party. It is thanks to the clarity of its theoretical vision and its strong revolutionary organisation that the party has afforded to the Soviets the possibility of becoming transformed from shapeless parliaments of labour into the apparatus of the supremacy of labour. In this 'substitution' of the power of the party for the power of the working class there is nothing accidental, and in reality there is no substitution at all. The Communists express the fundamental interests of the working class. It is quite natural that, in the period in which history brings up those interests … the Communists have become the recognised representatives of the working class as a whole." [**Terrorism and Communism**, p. 109]

He noted that within the state, "the last word belongs to the Central Committee of the party." [**Op. Cit.**, p. 107] As we discuss in section H.3.8, he held this position into the 1930s.

This means that given Harman's own assumptions, autocratic rule by the party is inevitable. Ironically, he argues that "to be a 'vanguard' is not the same as to substitute one's own desires, or policies or interests, for those of the class." He stresses that an "organisation that is concerned with participating in the revolutionary overthrow of capitalism by the working class cannot conceive of substituting itself for the organs of the direct rule of that class." [**Op. Cit.**, p. 33 and p. 34] However, the logic of his argument suggests otherwise. Simply put, his arguments against a broad party organisation are also applicable to self-management during the class struggle and revolution. The rank and file party members are "mixed up" in the class. This leads to party members becoming subject to bourgeois influences. This necessitates the power of the higher bodies over the lower (see section H.5.5). The highest party organ, the central committee, must rule over the party machine, which in turn rules over the party members, who, in turn, rule over the workers. This logical chain was, ironically enough, recognised by Trotsky in 1904 in his polemic against Lenin:

> "The organisation of the party substitutes itself for the party as a whole; then the central committee substitutes itself for the organisation; and finally the 'dictator' substitutes himself for the central committee." [quoted by Harman, **Op. Cit.**, p. 22]

Obviously once in power this substitution was less of a concern for him! Which, however, does not deny the insight Trotsky had previously showed about the dangers inherent in the Bolshevik assumptions on working class spontaneity and how revolutionary ideas develop. Dangers which he, ironically, helped provide empirical evidence for.

This false picture of the party (and its role) explains the progression of the Bolshevik party after 1917. As the soviets organised all workers, we have the problem that the party (with its *"scientific"* knowledge) is swamped by the class. The task of the party is to *"persuade, not coerce these [workers] into accepting its lead"* and, as Lenin made clear, for it to take political power. [Harman, **Op. Cit.**, p. 34] Once in power, the decisions of the party are in constant danger of being overthrown by the working class, which necessitates a state run with *"iron discipline"* (and the necessary means of coercion) by the party. With the disempowering of the mass organisations by the party, the party itself becomes a substitute for popular democracy as being a party member is the only way to influence policy. As the party grows, the influx of new members *"dilutes"* the organisation, necessitating a similar growth of centralised power at the top of the organisation. This eliminated the substitute for proletarian democracy which had developed within the party (which explains the banning of factions within the Bolshevik party in 1921). Slowly but surely, power concentrates into fewer and fewer hands, which, ironically enough, necessitates a bureaucracy to feed the party leaders information and execute its will. Isolated from all, the party inevitably degenerates and Stalinism results.

We are sure that many Trotskyists will object to our analysis, arguing that we ignore the problems facing the Russian Revolution in our discussion. Harman argues that it was *"not the form of the party that produces party as opposed to soviet rule, but the decimation of the working class"* that occurred during the Russian Revolution. [**Op. Cit.**, p. 37] This is false. As noted, Lenin was always explicit about the fact that the Bolshevik's sought party rule (*"full state power"*) and that their rule **was** working class rule. As such, we have the first, most basic, substitution of party power for workers power. Secondly, as we discuss in section H.6.1, the Bolshevik party had been gerrymandering and disbanding soviets before the start of the Civil War, so proving that the war cannot be held accountable for this process of substitution. Thirdly, Leninists are meant to know that civil war is inevitable during a revolution. To blame the inevitable for the degeneration of the revolution is hardly convincing (particularly as the degeneration started before the civil war broke out).

Unsurprisingly, anarchists reject the underlying basis of this progression, the idea that the working class, by its own efforts, is incapable of developing beyond a *"trade union consciousness."* The actions of the working class itself condemned these attitudes as outdated and simply wrong long before Lenin's infamous comments were put on paper. In every struggle, the working class has created its own organisations to co-ordinate its struggle. In the process of struggle, the working class changes its perspectives. This process is uneven in both quantity and quality, but it does happen. However, anarchists do not think that **all** working class people will, at the same time, spontaneously become anarchists. If they did, we would be in an anarchist society today! As we argue in section J.3, anarchists acknowledge that political development within the working class is uneven. The difference between anarchism and Leninism is how we see socialist ideas developing and how revolutionaries influence that process.

In every class struggle there is a radical minority which takes the lead and many of this minority develop revolutionary conclusions from their experiences. As such, members of the working class develop their own revolutionary theory and it does not need bourgeois intellectuals to inject it into them. Anarchists go on to argue that this minority (along with any members of other classes who have broken with their background and become libertarians) should organise and work together. The role of this revolutionary organisation is to spread, discuss and revise its ideas and help others draw the same conclusions as they have from their own, and others, experiences. The aim of such a group is, by word and deed, to assist the working class in its struggles and to draw out and clarify the libertarian aspects of this struggle. It seeks to abolish the rigid division between leaders and led which is the hallmark of class society by drawing the vast majority of the working class into social struggle and revolutionary politics by encouraging their direct management of the struggle. Only this participation and the political discussion it generates will allow revolutionary ideas to become widespread.

In other words, anarchists argue that precisely **because** of political differences ("unevenness") we need the fullest possible democracy and freedom to discuss issues and reach agreements. Only by discussion and self-activity can the political perspectives of those in struggle develop and change. In other words, the fact Bolshevism uses to justify its support for party power is the strongest argument against it.

Our differences with vanguardism could not be more clear.

H.5.4 Did Lenin abandon vanguardism?

Vanguardism rests on the premise that the working class cannot emancipate itself. As such, the ideas of Lenin as expounded in **What is to be Done?** (**WITBD**) contradict the key idea of Marx that the emancipation of the working class is the task of the working class itself. Thus the paradox of Leninism. On the one hand, it subscribes to an ideology allegedly based on working class self-liberation. On the other, the founder of that school wrote an obviously influential work whose premise not only logically implies that they cannot, it also provides the perfect rationale for party dictatorship over the working class (and as the history of Leninism in power shows, this underlying premise was much stronger than any democratic-sounding rhetoric).

It is for this reason that many Leninists are somewhat embarrassed by Lenin's argument in that key text. Some go to even more extreme lengths, denying that Lenin even held such a position. For example, Hal Draper argued at length that Lenin did not, in fact, hold the opinions he actually expressed in his book! While Draper covers many aspects of what he called the *"Myth of Lenin's 'Concept of The Party'"* in his essay of the same name, we will concentrate on the key idea, namely that socialist ideas are developed outside the class struggle by the radical intelligentsia and introduced into the working class from without. Here, as argued in section H.5.1, is the root of the anti-socialist basis of Leninism.

So what did Draper say? On the one hand, he denied that Lenin held this theory (he states that it is a *"virtually non-existent theory"* and *"non-existent after **WITBD**"*). He argued that those who hold the position that Lenin actually meant what he said in his book *"never quote anything other than **WITBD**,"* and stated that this is a *"curious fact"* (a fact we will disprove shortly). Draper argued as follows: *"Did Lenin put this theory forward even in **WITBD**? Not exactly."* He then noted that Lenin *"had just read this theory in the most prestigious theoretical organ of Marxism of the whole international socialist movement"* and it had been *"put forward in an important article by the leading Marxist authority,"* Karl Kautsky and so *"Lenin first paraphrased Kautsky"* before *"quot[ing] a long passage from Kautsky's article."*

This much, of course, is well known by anyone who has read Lenin's book. By paraphrasing and quoting Kautsky as he does, Lenin is showing his agreement with Kautsky's argument. Indeed, Lenin states before quoting Kautsky that his comments are *"profoundly true and important"*. [**Essential Works of Lenin**, p. 79] By explicitly agreeing with Kautsky, it can be said that it also becomes Lenin's theory as well! Over time, particularly after Kautsky had been labelled a *"renegade"* by Lenin, Kautsky's star waned and Lenin's rose. Little wonder the argument became associated with Lenin rather than the discredited Kautsky. Draper then speculated that *"it is curious … that no one has sought to prove that by launching this theory … Kautsky was laying the basis for the demon of totalitarianism."* A simply reason exists for this, namely the fact that Kautsky, unlike Lenin, was never the head of a one-party dictatorship and justified this system politically. Indeed, Kautsky attacked the Bolsheviks for this, which caused Lenin to label him a *"renegade."* Kautsky, in this sense, can be considered as being inconsistent with his political assumptions, unlike Lenin who took these assumptions to their logical conclusions.

How, after showing the obvious fact that *"the crucial 'Leninist' theory was really Kautsky's,"* he then wondered: *"Did Lenin, in **WITBD**, adopt Kautsky's theory?"* He answered his own question with an astounding *"Again, not exactly"*! Clearly, quoting approvingly of a theory and stating it is *"profoundly true"* does not, in fact, make you a supporter of it! What evidence does Draper present for his amazing answer? Well, Draper argued that Lenin *"tried to get maximum mileage out of it against the right wing; this was the point of his quoting it. If it did something for Kautsky's polemic, he no doubt figured that it would do something for his."* Or, to present a more simple and obvious explanation, Lenin **agreed** with Kautsky's *"profoundly true"* argument!

Aware of this possibility, Draper tried to combat it. *"Certainly,"* he argued, *"this young man Lenin was not (yet) so brash as to attack his 'pope' or correct him overtly. But there was obviously a feeling of discomfort. While showing some modesty and attempting to avoid the appearance of a head-on criticism, the fact is that Lenin inserted two longish footnotes rejecting (or if you wish, amending) precisely what was worst about the Kautsky theory on the role of the proletariat."* So, here we have Lenin quoting Kautsky to prove his own argument (and noting that Kautsky's words were *"profoundly true and important"*!) but *"feeling discomfort"* over what he has just approvingly quoted! Incredible!

So how does Lenin *"amend"* Kautsky's *"profoundly true and important"* argument? In two ways, according to Draper. Firstly, in a footnote which *"was appended right after the Kautsky passage"* Lenin quoted. Draper argued that it *"was specifically formulated to undermine and weaken the theoretical content of Kautsky's position. It began: 'This does not mean, of course, that the workers*

have no part in creating such an ideology.' But this was exactly what Kautsky did mean and say. In the guise of offering a caution, Lenin was proposing a modified view. 'They [the workers] take part, however,' Lenin's footnote continued, 'not as workers, but as socialist theoreticians, as Proudhons and Weitlings; in other words, they take part only when they are able …' In short, Lenin was reminding the reader that Kautsky's sweeping statements were not even 100% true historically; he pointed to exceptions."* Yes, Lenin **did** point to exceptions **in order to refute objections to Kautsky's argument before they were raised**! It is clear that Lenin was **not** refuting Kautsky. Thus Proudhon adds to socialist ideology in so far as he is a *"socialist theoretician"* and not a worker! How clear can you be? This can be seen from the rest of the sentence Draper truncates. Lenin continued by noting that people like Proudhon *"take part only to the extent that they are able, more or less, to acquire the knowledge of their age and advance that knowledge."* [**Op. Cit.**, p. 82f] In other words, insofar as they learn from the *"vehicles of science."* Neither Kautsky or Lenin denied that it was possible for workers to acquire such knowledge and pass it on (sometimes even develop it). However this does **not** mean that they thought workers, as part of their daily life and struggle **as workers,** could develop *"socialist theory."* Thus Lenin's footnote reiterated Kautsky's argument rather than, as Draper hoped, refute it.

Draper turns to another footnote, which he noted *"was not directly tied to the Kautsky article, but discussed the 'spontaneity' of the socialist idea. 'It is often said,' Lenin began, 'that the working class **spontaneously** gravitates towards socialism. This is perfectly true in the sense that socialist theory reveals the causes of the misery of the working class … and for that reason the workers are able to assimilate it so easily,' but he reminded that this process itself was not subordinated to mere spontaneity. 'The working class spontaneously gravitates towards socialism; nevertheless, … bourgeois ideology spontaneously imposes itself upon the working class to a still greater degree.'"* Draper argued that this *"was obviously written to modify and recast the Kautsky theory, without coming out and saying that the Master was wrong."* So, here we have Lenin approvingly quoting Kautsky in the main text while, at the same time, providing a footnote to show that, in fact, he did not agree with what he has just quoted! Truly amazing - and easily refuted.

Lenin's footnote stressed, in a part Draper did not consider it wise to quote, that workers appreciate socialist theory *"**provided,** however, that this theory does not step aside for spontaneity and **provided** it subordinates spontaneity to itself."* [**Op. Cit.**, p. 84f] In other words, workers *"assimilate"* socialist theory only when socialist theory does not adjust itself to the *"spontaneous"* forces at work in the class struggle. The workers adjust to socialist theory, they do not create it. Thus, rather than refuting Kautsky by the backdoor, Lenin in this footnote still agreed with him. Socialism does not develop, as Kautsky stressed, from the class struggle but rather has to be injected into it. This means, by necessity, the party *"subordinates spontaneity to itself."*

Draper argued that this *"modification"* simply meant that there *"are several things that happen 'spontaneously,' and what will win out is not decided only by spontaneity"* but as can be seen, this is not the case. Only when *"spontaneity"* is subordinated to the theory (i.e. the party) can socialism be won, a totally different position. As such, when Draper asserted that *"[a]ll that was clear at this point was that Lenin was justifiably dissatisfied with the formulation of Kautsky's theory,"* he was simply expressing wishful thinking. This footnote, like the first one, continued the argument developed by Lenin in the main text and in no way is in contradiction to it. As is obvious.

Draper as final evidence of his case asserted that it *"is a curious fact that no one has ever found this alleged theory anywhere else in Lenin's voluminous writings, not before and not after [**WITBD**]. It never appeared in Lenin again. No Leninologist has ever quoted such a theory from any other place in Lenin."* However, as this theory was the orthodox Marxist position, Lenin had no real need to reiterate this argument continuously. After all, he had quoted the acknowledged leader of Marxism on the subject explicitly to show the orthodoxy of his argument and the non-Marxist base of those he argued against. Once the debate had been won and orthodox Marxism triumphant, why repeat the argument again? This, as we will see, was exactly the position Lenin **did** take in 1907 when he wrote an introduction to a book which contained **What is to Be Done?**.

In contradiction to Draper's claim, Lenin **did** return to this matter. In October 1905 he wrote a short article in praise of an article by Stalin on this very subject. Stalin had sought to explain Lenin's ideas to the Georgian Social-Democracy and, like Lenin, had sought to root the argument in Marxist orthodoxy (partly to justify the argument, partly to expose the Menshevik opposition as being non-Marxists). Stalin argued along similar lines to Lenin:

> *"the question now is: who works out, who is able to work out this socialist consciousness (i.e. scientific socialism)? Kautsky says, and I repeat his idea, that the masses of proletarians, as long as they remain proletarians, have neither the time nor the opportunity to work out socialist consciousness … The vehicles of science are the intellectuals … who have both the time and opportunity to put themselves in the van of science and workout socialist consciousness. Clearly, socialist consciousness is worked out by a few Social-Democratic intellectuals who posses the time and opportunity to do so."* [**Collected Works**, vol. 1, p. 164]

Stalin stressed the Marxist orthodoxy by stating Social-Democracy *"comes in and introduces socialist consciousness into the working class movement. This is what Kautsky has in mind when he says 'socialist consciousness is something introduced into the proletarian class struggle from without.'"* [**Op. Cit.**, pp. 164-5] That Stalin was simply repeating Lenin's and Kautsky's arguments is clear, as is the fact it was considered the orthodox position within social-democracy.

If Draper were right, then Lenin would have taken the opportunity to attack Stalin's article and express the alternative viewpoint Draper was convinced he held. Lenin, however, put pen to paper to **praise** Stalin's work, noting *"the splendid way in which the problem of the celebrated 'introduction of a consciousness from without' had been posed."* Lenin explicitly agreed with Stalin's summary of his

argument, writing that *"social being determines consciousness … Socialist consciousness corresponds to the position of the proletariat"* before quoting Stalin: *"'Who can and does evolve this consciousness (scientific socialism)?'"* He answers by again approvingly quoting Stalin: *"its 'evolution' is a matter for a few Social-Democratic intellectuals who posses the necessary means and time.'"* Lenin did argue that Social-Democracy meets *"an instinctive **urge** towards socialism"* when it *"comes to the proletariat with the message of socialism,"* but this does not counter the main argument that the working class cannot develop socialist consciousness by it own efforts and the, by necessity, elitist and hierarchical politics that flow from this position. [Lenin, **Collected Works**, vol. 9, p. 388]

That Lenin did not reject his early formulations can also be seen from his introduction to the pamphlet *"Twelve Years"* which contained **What is to be Done?**. Rather than explaining the false nature of that work's more infamous arguments, Lenin in fact defended them. For example, as regards the question of professional revolutionaries, he argued that the statements of his opponents now *"look ridiculous"* as **"today** the idea of an organisation of professional revolutionaries has **already** scored a complete victory,"* a victory which *"would have been impossible if this idea had not been pushed to the **forefront** at the time."* He noted that his work had *"vanquished Economism … and finally **created** this organisation."* On the question of socialist consciousness, he simply reiterated the Marxist orthodoxy of his position, noting that its *"formulation of the relationship between spontaneity and political consciousness was agreed upon by all the **Iskra** editors … Consequently, there could be no question of any difference in principle between the draft Party programme and **What is to be Done?** on this issue."* So while Lenin argued that his book *"straightens out what had been twisted by the Economists,"* (who had *"gone to one extreme"*) he did not correct his earlier arguments. [**Collected Works**, vol. 13, p. 101, p. 102 and p. 107]

Looking at Lenin's arguments at the Communist International on the question of the party we see an obvious return to the ideas of **WITBD** (see section H.5.5). Here we have a similar legal/illegal duality, strict centralism, strong hierarchy and the vision of the party as the *"head"* of the working class (i.e. its consciousness). In **Left-Wing Communism**, Lenin mocks those who reject the idea that dictatorship by the party is the same as that of the class (see section H.3.3).

For Draper, the key problem was that critics of Lenin *"run two different questions together: (a) What was, historically, the **initial** role of intellectuals in the beginnings of the socialist movement, and (b) what **is** - and above all, what should be - the role of bourgeois intellectuals in a working-class party today."* He argued that Kautsky did not believe that *"**if** it can be shown that intellectuals historically played a certain initiatory role, they **must** and **should** continue to play the same role now and forever. It does not follow; as the working class matured, it tended to throw off leading strings."* However, this is unconvincing. If socialist consciousness cannot be generated by the working class by its own struggles then this is applicable now and in the future. Thus workers who join the socialist movement will be repeating the party ideology, as developed by intellectuals in the past. If they **do** develop new theory, it would be, as Lenin stressed, *"not as workers, but as socialist theoreticians"* and so socialist consciousness still does not derive from their own class experiences. This places the party in a privileged position vis-à-vis the working class and so the elitism remains.

Somewhat ironically given how much Draper is at pains to distance his hero Lenin from claims of elitism, he himself **agreed** with the arguments of Kautsky and Lenin. For Draper socialism did **not** develop out of the class struggle: *"As a matter of fact, in the International of 1902 no one really had any doubts about the historical facts concerning the beginnings of the movement."* This was true. Plekhanov, the father of Russian Marxism, made similar arguments to Kautsky's before Lenin put pen to paper. For Plekhanov, the socialist intelligentsia *"will bring **consciousness** into the working class."* It must *"become the leader of the working class"* and *"explain to it its political and economic interests."* This would *"prepare them to play an independent role in the social life of Russia."* [quoted by Neil Harding, **Lenin's Political Thought**, vol. 1, p. 50 and p. 51]

As one expert notes, *"Lenin's position ... did not differ in any essentials"* from those *"Plekhanov had himself expressed."* Its *"basic theses were his own"*, namely that it is *"clear from Plekhanov's writing that it was the intelligentsia which virtually created the working class movement in its conscious form. It brought it science, revolutionary theory and organisation."* In summary, *"Lenin's views of the Party ... are not to be regarded as extraordinary, innovatory, perverse, essentially Jacobin or unorthodox. On the contrary"* they were *"the touchstone of orthodoxy"* and so *"what it [**What is to be Done?**] presented at the time"* was *"a restatement of the principles of Russian Marxist orthodoxy."* By quoting Kautsky, Lenin also proved that he was simply repeating the general Marxist orthodoxy: *"Those who dispute Lenin's conclusions on the genesis of socialist consciousness must it seems, also dispute Kautsky's claim to represent Social-Democratic orthodoxy."* [Harding, **Op. Cit.**, p. 170, p. 172, pp. 50-1, p. 187, p. 188, p. 189 and p. 169]

Moreover, Engels wrote some interesting words in the 1840s on this issue which places the subsequent development of Marxism into sharper light. He noted that *"it is evident that the working-men's movement is divided into two sections, the Chartists and the Socialists. The Chartists are theoretically the more backward, the less developed, but they are genuine proletarians ... The Socialists are more far-seeing ... but proceeding originally from the bourgeoisie, are for this reason unable to amalgamate completely with the working class. The union of Socialism with Chartism ... will be the next step ... Then, only when this has been achieved, will the working class be the true intellectual leader of England."* Thus socialist ideas have to be introduced into the proletariat, as they are *"more backward"* and cannot be expected to develop theory for themselves! In the same year, he expounded on what this *"union"* would entail, writing in an Owenite paper that *"the union between the German philosophers ... and the German working men ... is all but accomplished. With the philosophers to think, and the working mean to fight for us, will any earthly power be strong enough to resist our progress?"* [**Collected Works**, vol. 4, pp. 526-7 and p. 236] This, of course, fits in with the **Communist Manifesto**'s assertion that *"a small section of the ruling class cuts itself adrift, and joins the revolutionary class."* Today, this *"portion of the bourgeois ideologists"* have *"raised themselves to the level of comprehending theoretically the historical movement as a whole."* [**The Marx-Engels Reader**, p. 481] This, needless to say, places *"bourgeois ideologists"* (like Marx, Engels, Kautsky and Lenin) in a privileged position within the movement and has distinctly vanguardist undercurrents.

Seemingly unaware how this admission destroyed his case, Draper went on to ask: *"But what followed from those facts?"* To which he argued that Marx and Engels *"concluded, from the same facts and subsequent experiences, that the movement had to be sternly warned against the influence of bourgeois intellectuals inside the party."* (We wonder if Marx and Engels included themselves in the list of *"bourgeois intellectuals"* the workers had to be *"sternly warned"* about?) Thus, amusingly enough, Draper argued that Marx, Engels, Kautsky and Lenin all held to the *"same facts"* that socialist consciousness developed outside the experiences of the working classes!

Ultimately, the whole rationale for the kind of wishful thinking that Draper inflicted on us is flawed. You do not combat what you think is an incorrect position with one which you consider as also being wrong or do not agree with! You counter what you consider as an incorrect position with one you consider correct and agree with. As Lenin, in **WITBD**, explicitly did. This means that later attempts by his followers to downplay the ideas raised in Lenin's book are unconvincing. Moreover, as he was simply repeating Social-Democratic orthodoxy it seems doubly unconvincing.

Clearly, Draper was wrong. Lenin did, as indicated above, actually meant what he said in **WITBD**. The fact that Lenin quoted Kautsky simply shows, as Lenin intended, that this position was the orthodox Social Democratic one, held by the mainstream of the party (one with roots in Marx and Engels). Given that Leninism was (and still is) a "radical" offshoot of this movement, this should come as no surprise. However, Draper's comments remind us how religious many forms of Marxism are - why do we need facts when we have the true faith?

H.5.5 What is "democratic centralism"?

Anarchists oppose vanguardism for three reasons, one of which is the way it recommends how revolutionaries should organise to influence the class struggle.

So how is a "vanguard" party organised? To quote the Communist International's 1920 resolution on the role of the Communist Party in the revolution, the party must have a *"centralised political apparatus"* and *"must be organised on the basis of iron proletarian centralism."* This, of course, suggests a top-down structure internally, which the resolution explicitly calls for. In its words, *"Communist cells of every kind must be subordinate to one another as precisely as possible in a strict hierarchy."* [**Proceedings and Documents of the Second Congress 1920**, vol. 1, p. 193, p. 198 and p. 199] Therefore, the vanguard party is organised in a centralised, top-down way. However, this is not all, as well as being *"centralised,"* the party is also meant to be democratic, hence the expression *"democratic centralism."* On this the resolution states:

"The Communist Party must be organised on the basis of democratic centralism. The most important principle of democratic centralism is election of the higher party organs by the lowest, the fact that all instructions by a superior body are unconditionally and necessarily binding on lower ones, and existence of a strong central party leadership whose authority over all leading party comrades in the period between one party congress and the next is universally accepted." [**Op. Cit.**, p. 198]

For Lenin, speaking in the same year, democratic centralism meant *"only that representatives from the localities meet and elect a responsible body which must then govern … Democratic centralism consists in the Congress checking on the Central Committee, removing it and electing a new one."* [quoted by Robert Service, **The Bolshevik Party in Revolution**, p. 131] Thus, *"democratic centralism"* is inherently top-down, although the *"higher"* party organs are, in principle, elected by the *"lower."* However, the key point is that the central committee is the active element, the one whose decisions are implemented and so the focus of the structure is in the *"centralism"* rather than the *"democratic"* part of the formula.

The Communist Party was expected to have a dual structure, one legal and the other illegal. It was the *"duty"* of these parties *"to create everywhere a parallel illegal organisational apparatus."* [**Proceedings and Documents of the Second Congress 1920**, vol. 2, p. 767] This would be the real controlling body as the *"legal work must be placed under the actual control of the illegal party at all times."* [**Op. Cit.**, vol. 1, pp. 198-9] So the illegal structure is the real power in the party and it cannot be expected to be as democratic as the legal party, which in turn would be less than democratic as the illegal would have the real power within the organisation.

All this has clear parallels with Lenin's **What is to be done?**, where he argued for *"a powerful and strictly secret organisation, which concentrates in its hands all the threads of secret activities, an organisation which of necessity must be a centralised organisation."* This call for centralisation is not totally dependent on secrecy, though. As he noted, *"specialisation necessarily presupposes centralisation, and in its turn imperatively calls for it."* Such a centralised organisation would need leaders and Lenin argued that *"no movement can be durable without a stable organisation of leaders to maintain continuity."* As such, *"the organisation must consist chiefly of persons engaged in revolutionary activities as a profession."* Thus, we have a centralised organisation which is managed by specialists, by *"professional revolutionaries."* This does not mean that these all come from the bourgeoisie or petit bourgeoisie. According to Lenin a *"workingman agitator who is at all talented and 'promising' must not be left to work eleven hours a day in a factory. We must arrange that he be maintained by the Party, that he may in due time go underground."* [**Essential Works of Lenin**, p. 158, p. 153, p. 147, p. 148 and p. 155]

Thus the full time professional revolutionaries are drawn from all classes into the party apparatus. However, in practice the majority of such full-timers were/are middle class. Trotsky noted that *"just as in the Bolshevik committees, so at the [1905] Congress itself,*

there were almost no workingmen. The intellectuals predominated." [**Stalin**, vol. 1, p. 101] This did not change, even after the influx of working class members in 1917 the *"incidence of middle-class activists increases at the highest echelons of the hierarchy of executive committees."* [Robert Service, **Op. Cit.**, p. 47] An ex-worker was a rare sight in the Bolshevik Central Committee, an actual worker non-existent. However, regardless of their original class background what unites the full-timers is not their origin but rather their current relationship with the working class, one of separation and hierarchy.

The organisational structure of this system was made clear at around the same time as **What is to be Done?**, with Lenin arguing that the factory group (or cell) of the party *"must consist of a small number of **revolutionaries,** receiving **direct from the [central] committee** orders and power to conduct the whole social-democratic work in the factory. All members of the factory committee must regard themselves as agents of the [central] committee, bound to submit to all its directions, bound to observe all 'laws and customs' of this 'army in the field' in which they have entered and which they cannot leave without permission of the commander."* [quoted by E.H. Carr, **The Bolshevik Revolution**, vol. 1, p. 33] The similarities to the structure proposed by Lenin and agreed to by the Comintern in 1920 is obvious. Thus we have a highly centralised party, one run by *"professional revolutionaries"* from the top down.

It will be objected that Lenin was discussing the means of party building under Tsarism and advocated wider democracy under legality. However, given that in 1920 he universalised the Bolshevik experience and urged the creation of a dual party structure (based on legal and illegal structures), his comments on centralisation are applicable to vanguardism in general. Moreover, in 1902 he based his argument on experiences drawn from democratic capitalist regimes. As he argued, *"no revolutionary organisation has ever practised **broad** democracy, nor could it, however much it desired to do so."* This was not considered as just applicable in Russia under the Tsar as Lenin then goes on to quote the Webb's *"book on trade unionism"* in order to clarify what he calls *"the confusion of ideas concerning the meaning of democracy."* He noted that *"in the first period of existence in their unions, the British workers thought it was an indispensable sign of democracy for all members to do all the work of managing the unions."* This involved *"all questions [being] decided by the votes of all the members"* and all *"official duties"* being *"fulfilled by all the members in turn."* He dismissed *"such a conception of democracy"* as *"absurd"* and *"historical experience"* made them *"understand the necessity for representative institutions"* and *"full-time professional officials."* [**Essential Works of Lenin**, p. 161 and pp. 162-3]

Needless to say, Lenin linked this to Kautsky, who *"shows the need for **professional** journalists, parliamentarians, etc., for the Social-Democratic leadership of the proletarian class struggle"* and who *"attacks the 'socialism of anarchists and **litterateurs'** who … proclaim the principle that laws should be passed directly by the whole people, completely failing to understand that in modern society this principle can have only a relative application."* The universal nature of his dismissal of self-management within the revolutionary organisation in favour of representative forms is thus stressed. Significantly, Lenin stated that this *"'primitive' conception* of democracy" exists in two groups, the "*masses of the students and workers*" and the "*Economists of the Bernstein persuasion*" (i.e. reformists). Thus the idea of directly democratic working class organisations is associated with opportunism. He was generous, noting that he "*would not, of course, … condemn practical workers who have had too few opportunities for studying the theory and practice of real democratic [sic!] organisation*" but individuals "*play[ing] a leading role*" in the movement should be so condemned! [**Op. Cit.**, p. 163] These people should know better! Thus "*real*" democratic organisation implies the restriction of democracy to that of electing leaders and any attempt to widen the input of ordinary members is simply an expression of workers who need educating from their "*primitive*" failings!

In summary, we have a model of a "*revolutionary*" party which is based on full-time "*professional revolutionaries*" in which the concept of direct democracy is replaced by a system of, at best, representative democracy. It is highly centralised, as befitting a specialised organisation. As noted in section H.3.3, the "*organisational principle of revolutionary Social-Democracy*" was "*to proceed from the top downward*" rather than "*from the bottom upward.*" [Lenin, **Collected Works**, vol. 7, pp. 396-7] Rather than being only applicable in Tsarist Russia, Lenin drew on examples from advanced, democratic capitalist countries to justify his model in 1902 and in 1920 he advocated a similar hierarchical and top-down organisation with a dual secret and public organisation in the **Communist International**. The continuity of ideas is clear.

H.5.6 Why do anarchists oppose "democratic centralism"?

What to make of Lenin's suggested model of "*democratic centralism*" discussed in the last section? It is, to use Cornelius Castoriadis's term, a "*revolutionary party organised in a capitalist manner*" and so in practice the "*democratic centralist*" party, while being centralised, will not be very democratic. In fact, the level of democracy would reflect that in a capitalist republic rather than a socialist society:

> "*The dividing up of tasks, which is indispensable wherever there is a need for co-operation, becomes a real division of labour, the labour of giving orders being separate from that of carrying them out … this division between directors and executants tends to broaden and deepen by itself. The leaders specialise in their role and become indispensable while those who carry out orders become absorbed in their concrete tasks. Deprived of information, of the general view of the situation, and of the problems of organisation, arrested in their development by their lack of participation in the overall life of the Party, the organisation's rank-and-file militants less and less have the means or the possibility of having any control over those at the top.*
>
> "*This division of labour is supposed to be limited by 'democracy.' But democracy, which should mean that the*

majority rules, is reduced to meaning that the majority *designates its rulers;* copied in this way from the model of bourgeois parliamentary democracy, drained of any real meaning, it quickly becomes a veil thrown over the unlimited power of the rulers. The base does not run the organisation just because once a year it elects delegates who designate the central committee, no more than the people are sovereign in a parliamentary-type republic because they periodically elect deputies who designate the government.

> "*Let us consider, for example, 'democratic centralism' as it is supposed to function in an ideal Leninist party. That the central committee is designated by a 'democratically elected' congress makes no difference since, once it is elected, it has complete (statutory) control over the body of the Party (and can dissolve the base organisations, kick out militants, etc.) or that, under such conditions, it can determine the composition of the next congress. The central committee could use its powers in an honourable way, these powers could be reduced; the members of the Party might enjoy 'political rights' such as being able to form factions, etc. Fundamentally this would not change the situation, for the central committee would still remain the organ that defines the political line of the organisation and controls its application from top to bottom, that, in a word, has permanent monopoly on the job of leadership. The expression of opinions only has a limited value once the way the group functions prevents this opinion from forming on solid bases, i.e. permanent* **participation** *in the organisation's activities and in the solution of problems that arise. If the way the organisation is run makes the solution of general problems the specific task and permanent work of a separate category of militants, only their opinion will, or will appear, to count to the others.*" [Castoriadis, **Social and Political Writings**, vol. 2, pp. 204-5]

Castoriadis' insight is important and strikes at the heart of the problem with vanguard parties. They simply reflect the capitalist society they claim to oppose. As such, Lenin's argument against "*primitive*" democracy in the revolutionary and labour movements is significant. When he asserts that those who argue for direct democracy "*completely*" fail to "*understand that in modern society this principle can have only a relative application,*" he is letting the cat out of the bag. [Lenin, **Op. Cit.**, p. 163] After all, "*modern society*" is capitalism, a class society. In such a society, it is understandable that self-management should not be applied as it strikes at the heart of class society and how it operates. That Lenin can appeal to "*modern society*" without recognising its class basis says a lot. The question becomes, if such a "*principle*" is valid for a class system, is it applicable in a socialist society and in the movement aiming to create such a society? Can we postpone the application of our ideas until "*after the revolution*" or can the revolution only occur when we apply our socialist principles in resisting class society?

In a nutshell, can the same set of organisational structures be used for the different ends? Can bourgeois structures be considered neutral or have they, in fact, evolved to ensure and protect minority rule? Ultimately, form and content are not independent of each other. Form and content adapt to fit each other and they cannot be divorced in reality. Thus, if the bourgeoisie embrace centralisation and representation they have done so because they fit perfectly with their specific form of class society. Neither centralisation nor representation can undermine minority rule and, if they did, they would quickly be eliminated.

Surely we can expect decisive structural differences to exist between capitalism and socialism if these societies are to have different aims. Where one is centralised to facilitate minority rule, the other must be decentralised and federal to facilitate mass participation. Where one is top-down, the other must be from the bottom-up. If a "socialism" exists which uses bourgeois organisational elements then we should not be surprised if it turns out to be socialist in name only. The same applies to revolutionary organisations. As the anarchists of **Trotwatch** explain:

> "In reality, a Leninist Party simply reproduces and institutionalises existing capitalist power relations inside a supposedly 'revolutionary' organisation: between leaders and led; order givers and order takers; between specialists and the acquiescent and largely powerless party workers. And that elitist power relation is extended to include the relationship between the party and class." [**Carry on Recruiting!**, p. 41]

If you have an organisation which celebrates centralisation, having an institutionalised "leadership" separate from the mass of members becomes inevitable. Thus the division of labour which exists in the capitalist workplace or state is created. Forms cannot and do not exist independently of people and so imply specific forms of social relationships within them. These social relationships shape those subject to them. Can we expect the same forms of authority to have different impacts simply because the organisation has "socialist" or "revolutionary" in its name? Of course not. It is for this reason that anarchists argue that only in a "libertarian socialist movement the workers learn about non-dominating forms of association through creating and experimenting with forms such as libertarian labour organisations, which put into practice, through struggle against exploitation, principles of equality and free association." [John Clark, **The Anarchist Moment**, p. 79]

As noted above, a "democratic centralist" party requires that the "lower" party bodies (cells, branches, etc.) should be subordinate to the higher ones (e.g. the central committee). The higher bodies are elected at the (usually) annual conference. As it is impossible to mandate for future developments, the higher bodies therefore are given carte blanche to determine policy which is binding on the whole party (hence the "from top-down" principle). In between conferences, the job of full time (ideally elected, but not always) officers is to lead the party and carry out the policy decided by the central committee. At the next conference, the party membership can show its approval of the leadership by electing another. The problems with this scheme are numerous:

> "The first problem is the issue of hierarchy. Why should 'higher' party organs interpret party policy any more accurately than 'lower' ones? The pat answer is that the 'higher' bodies compromise the most capable and experienced members and are (from their lofty heights) in a better position to take an overall view on a given issue. In fact what may well happen is that, for example, central committee members may be more isolated from the outside world than mere branch members. This might ordinarily be the case because given the fact than many central committee members are full timers and therefore detached from more real issues such as making a living ..." [ACF, **Marxism and its Failures**, p. 8]

Equally, in order that the "higher" bodies can evaluate the situation they need effective information from the "lower" bodies. If the "lower" bodies are deemed incapable of formulating their own policies, how can they be wise enough, firstly, to select the right leaders and, secondly, determine the appropriate information to communicate to the "higher" bodies? Given the assumptions for centralised power in the party, can we not see that "democratic centralised" parties will be extremely inefficient in practice as information and knowledge is lost in the party machine and whatever decisions are reached at the top are made in ignorance of the real situation on the ground? As we discuss in section H.5.8, this is usually the fate of such parties. Within the party, as noted, the role of "professional revolutionaries" (or "full timers") is stressed. As Lenin argued, any worker who showed any talent must be removed from the workplace and become a party functionary. Is it surprising that the few Bolshevik cadres (i.e. professional revolutionaries) of working class origin soon lost real contact with the working class? Equally, what will their role **within** the party be? As we discuss in section H.5.12, their role in the Bolshevik party was essentially conservative in nature and aimed to maintain their own position.

That the anarchist critique of "democratic centralism" is valid, we need only point to the comments and analysis of numerous members (and often soon to be ex-members) of such parties. Thus we get a continual stream of articles discussing why specific parties are, in fact, "bureaucratic centralist" rather than "democratic centralist" and what is required to reform them. That every "democratic centralist" party in existence is not that democratic does not hinder their attempts to create one which is. In a way, the truly "democratic centralist" party is the Holy Grail of modern Leninism. As we discuss in section H.5.10, their goal may be as mythical as that of the Arthurian legends.

H.5.7 Is the way revolutionaries organise important?

As we discussed in the last section, anarchists argue that the way revolutionaries organise today is important. However, according to some of Lenin's followers, the fact that the "revolutionary" party is organised in a non-revolutionary manner does not matter. In the words of Chris Harman, a leading member of the British **Socialist Workers Party**, *"[e]xisting under capitalism, the revolutionary organisation [i.e. the vanguard party] will of necessity have a quite different structure to that of the workers' state that will arise in the process of overthrowing capitalism."* [**Party and Class**, p. 34] However, in practice this distinction is impossible to make. If the party is organised in specific ways then it is so because this is conceived to be *"efficient,"* *"practical"* and so on. Hence we find Lenin arguing against *"backwardness in organisation"* and that the *"point at issue is whether our ideological struggle is to have **forms of a higher type** to clothe it, forms of Party organisation binding on all."* Why would the "workers' state" be based on "backward" or "lower" kinds of organisational forms? If, as Lenin remarked, *"the organisational principle of revolutionary Social-Democracy"* was *"to proceed from the top downward"*, why would the party, once in power, reject its *"organisational principle"* in favour of one it thinks is *"opportunist,"* *"primitive"* and so on? [**Collected Works**, vol. 7, p. 389, p. 388 and pp. 396-7]

Therefore, as the **vanguard** the party represents the level to which the working class is supposed to reach then its organisational principles must, similarly, be those which the class must reach. As such, Harman's comments are incredulous. How we organise today is hardly irrelevant, particularly if the revolutionary organisation in question seeks (to use Lenin's words) to *"tak[e] full state power alone."* [**Op. Cit.**, vol. 26, p. 94] These prejudices (and the political and organisational habits they generate) will influence the shaping of the *"workers' state"* by the party once it has taken power. This decisive influence of the party and its ideological as well as organisational assumptions can be seen when Trotsky argued in 1923 that *"the party created the state apparatus and can rebuild it anew … from the party you get the state, but not the party from the state."* [**Leon Trotsky Speaks**, p. 161] This is to be expected, after all the aim of the party is to take, hold and execute power. Given that the vanguard party is organised as it is to ensure effectiveness and efficiency, why should we assume that the ruling party will not seek to recreate these organisational principles once in power? As the Russian Revolution proves, this is the case (see section H.6)

To claim how we organise under capitalism is not important to a revolutionary movement is simply not true. The way revolutionaries organise have an impact both on themselves and how they will view the revolution developing. An ideological prejudice for centralisation and "top-down" organisation will not disappear once the revolution starts. Rather, it will influence the way the party acts within it and, if it aims to seize power, how it will exercise that power once it has.

For these reasons anarchists stress the importance of building the new world in the shell of the old (see section H.1.6). All organisations create social relationships which shape their memberships. As the members of these parties will be part of the revolutionary process, they will influence how that revolution will develop and any "transitional" institutions which are created. As the aim of such organisations is to facilitate the creation of socialism, the obvious implication is that the revolutionary organisation must, itself, reflect the society it is trying to create. Clearly, then, the idea that how we organise as revolutionaries today can be considered somehow independent of the revolutionary process and the nature of post-capitalist society and its institutions cannot be maintained (particularly if the aim of the *"revolutionary"* organisation is to seize power on behalf of the working class).

H.5.8 Are vanguard parties effective?

In a word, no. Vanguard parties have rarely been proven to be effective organs for fermenting revolutionary change which is, let us not forget, their stated purpose. Indeed, rather than being in the vanguard of social struggle, the Leninist parties are often the last to recognise, let alone understand, the initial stirrings of important social movements and events. It is only once these movements have exploded in the streets that the self-proclaimed "vanguards" notice them and decide they require the party's leadership.

Part of this process are constant attempts to install their political program onto movements that they do not understand, movements that have proven to be successful using different tactics and methods of organisation. Rather than learn from the experiences of others, social movements are seen as raw material, as a source of new party members, to be used in order to advance the party rather than the autonomy and combativeness of the working class. This process was seen in the *"anti-globalisation"* or *"anti-capitalist"* movement at the end of the 20th century. This started without the help of these self-appointed vanguards, who once it appeared spent a lot of time trying to catch up with the movement while criticising its proven organisational principles and tactics.

The reasons for such behaviour are not too difficult to find. They lie in the organisational structure favoured by these parties and the mentality lying behind them. As anarchists have long argued, a centralised, top-down structure will simply be unresponsive to the needs of those in struggle. The inertia associated with the party hierarchy will ensure that it responds slowly to new developments and its centralised structure means that the leadership is isolated from what is happening on the ground and cannot respond appropriately. The underlying assumption of the vanguard party, namely that the party represents the interests of the working class, makes it unresponsive to new developments within the class struggle. As Lenin argued that spontaneous working class struggle tends to reformism, the leaders of a vanguard party automatically are suspicious of new developments which, by their very nature, rarely fit into previously agreed models of *"proletarian"* struggle. The example of Bolshevik hostility to the soviets spontaneously formed by workers during the 1905 Russian revolution is one of the best known examples of this tendency.

Murray Bookchin is worth quoting at length on this subject:

"The 'glorious party,' when there is one, almost invariably lags behind the events … In the beginning … it tends to have an inhibitory function, not a 'vanguard' role. Where it exercises influence, it tends to slow down the flow of events, not 'co-ordinate' the revolutionary forces. This is not accidental. The party is structured along hierarchical lines **that reflect the very society it professes to oppose.** Despite its theoretical pretensions, it is a bourgeois organism, a miniature state, with an apparatus and a cadre whose function it is to **seize** power, not **dissolve** power. Rooted in the pre-revolutionary period, it assimilates all the forms, techniques and mentality of bureaucracy. Its membership is schooled in obedience and in the preconceptions of a rigid dogma and is taught to revere the leadership. The party's leadership, in turn, is schooled in habits born of command, authority, manipulation and egomania. This situation is worsened when the party participates in parliamentary elections. In election campaigns, the vanguard party models itself completely on existing bourgeois forms and even acquires the paraphernalia of the electoral party…

"As the party expands, the distance between the leadership and the ranks inevitably increases. Its leaders not only become 'personages,' they lose contact with the living situation below. The local groups, which know their own immediate situation better than any remote leaders, are obliged to subordinate their insights to directives from above. The leadership, lacking any direct knowledge of local problems, responds sluggishly and prudently. Although it stakes out a claim to the 'larger view,' to greater 'theoretical competence,' the competence of the leadership tends to diminish as one ascends the hierarchy of command. The more one approaches the level where the real decisions are made, the more conservative is the nature of the decision-making process, the more bureaucratic and extraneous are the factors which come into play, the more considerations of prestige and retrenchment supplant creativity, imagination, and a disinterested dedication to revolutionary goals.

"The party becomes less efficient from a revolutionary point of view the more it seeks efficiency by means of hierarchy, cadres and centralisation. Although everyone marches in step, the orders are usually wrong, especially when events begin to move rapidly and take unexpected turns - as they do in all revolutions…

"On the other hand, this kind of party is extremely vulnerable in periods of repression. The bourgeoisie has only to grab its leadership to destroy virtually the entire movement. With its leaders in prison or in hiding, the party becomes paralysed; the obedient membership has no one to obey and tends to flounder. Demoralisation sets in rapidly. The party decomposes not only because of the repressive atmosphere but also because of its poverty of inner resources.

"The foregoing account is not a series of hypothetical inferences, it is a composite sketch of all the mass Marxian parties of the past century - the Social Democrats, the Communists and the Trotskyist party of Ceylon (the only mass party of its kind). To claim that these parties failed to take their Marxian principles seriously merely conceals another question: why did this failure happen in the first place? The fact is, these parties were co-opted into bourgeois society because they were structured along bourgeois lines. The germ of treachery existed in them from birth." [**Post-Scarcity Anarchism**, pp. 123-6]

The evidence Bookchin summarises suggests that vanguard parties are less than efficient in promoting revolutionary change. Sluggish, unresponsive, undemocratic, they simply cannot adjust to the dynamic nature of social struggle, never mind revolution. This is to be expected:

"For the state centralisation is the appropriate form of organisation, since it aims at the greatest possible uniformity in social life for the maintenance of political and social equilibrium. But for a movement whose very existence depends on prompt action at any favourable moment and on the independent thought and action of its supporters, centralism could but be a curse by weakening its power of decision and systematically repressing all immediate action. If, for example, as was the case in Germany, every local strike had first to be approved by the Central, which was often hundreds of miles away and was not usually in a position to pass a correct judgement on the local conditions, one cannot wonder that the inertia of the apparatus of organisation renders a quick attack quite impossible, and there thus arises a state of affairs where the energetic and intellectually alert groups no longer serve as patterns for the less active, but are condemned by these to inactivity, inevitably bringing the whole movement to stagnation. Organisation is, after all, only a means to an end. When it becomes an end in itself, it kills the spirit and the vital initiative of its members and sets up that domination by mediocrity which is the characteristic of all bureaucracies." [Rudolf Rocker, **Anarcho-Syndicalism**, p. 61]

As we discuss in section H.5.12, the example of the Bolshevik party during the Russian Revolution amply proves Rocker's point. Rather than being a highly centralised, disciplined vanguard party, the Bolshevik party was marked by extensive autonomy throughout its ranks. Party discipline was regularly ignored, including by Lenin in his attempts to get the central party bureaucracy to catch up with the spontaneous revolutionary actions and ideas of the Russian working class. As Bookchin summarised, the "Bolshevik leadership was ordinarily extremely conservative, a trait that Lenin had to fight throughout 1917 - first in his efforts to reorient the Central Committee against the provisional government (the famous conflict over the 'April Theses'), later in driving the Central Committee toward insurrection in October. In both cases he threatened to resign from the Central Committee and bring his views to 'the lower ranks of the party.'" Once in power, however, "the Bolsheviks tended to centralise their party to the degree that they became isolated from the working class." [**Op. Cit.**, pp. 126 and p. 127]

The "vanguard" model of organising is not only inefficient and ineffective from a revolutionary perspective, it generates bureaucratic and elitist tendencies which undermine any revolution unfortunate enough to be dominated by such a party. For these extremely practical and sensible reasons anarchists reject it wholeheartedly. As we discuss in the next section, the only thing vanguard parties **are** effective at is to supplant the diversity produced and required by revolutionary movements with the drab conformity produced by centralisation and to replace popular power and freedom with party power and tyranny.

H.5.9 What are vanguard parties effective at?

As we discussed the last section, vanguard parties are not efficient as agents of revolutionary change. So, it may be asked, what **are** vanguard parties effective at? If they are harmful to revolutionary struggle, what are they good at? The answer to this is simple. No anarchist would deny that vanguard parties are extremely efficient and effective at certain things, most notably reproducing hierarchy and bourgeois values into so-called "revolutionary" organisations and movements. As Murray Bookchin put it, the party "is efficient in only one respect - in moulding society in its own hierarchical image if the revolution is successful. It recreates bureaucracy, centralisation and the state. It fosters the very social conditions which justify this kind of society. Hence, instead of 'withering away,' the state controlled by the 'glorious party' preserves the very conditions which 'necessitate' the existence of a state - and a party to 'guard' it." [**Post-Scarcity Anarchism**, pp. 125-6]

By being structured along hierarchical lines that reflect the very system that it professes to oppose, the vanguard party very "effectively" reproduces that system within both the current radical social movements **and** any revolutionary society that may be created. This means that once in power, it shapes society in its own image. Ironically, this tendency towards conservatism and bureaucracy was noted by Trotsky:

> "As often happens, a sharp cleavage developed between the classes in motion and the interests of the party machines. Even the Bolshevik Party cadres, who enjoyed the benefit of exceptional revolutionary training, were definitely inclined to disregard the masses and to identify their own special interests and the interests of the machine on the very day after the monarchy was overthrown. What, then, could be expected of these cadres when they became an all-powerful state bureaucracy?" [**Stalin**, vol. 1, p. 298]

In such circumstances, it is unsurprising that urging party power and identifying it with working class power would have less than revolutionary results. Discussing the Bolsheviks in 1905 Trotsky points out this tendency existed from the start:

> "The habits peculiar to a political machine were already forming in the underground. The young revolutionary bureaucrat was already emerging as a type. The conditions of conspiracy, true enough, offered rather meagre scope for such formalities of democracy as electiveness, accountability and control. Yet, undoubtedly the committeemen narrowed these limitations considerably more than necessity demanded and were far more intransigent and severe with the revolutionary workingmen than with themselves, preferring to domineer even on occasions that called for lending an attentive ear to the voice of the masses." [**Op. Cit.**, p. 101]

He quoted Krupskaya, a party member, on these party bureaucrats, the "committeemen," and how "as a rule" they "did not recognise any party democracy" and "did not want any innovations. The 'committeeman' did not desire, and did not know how to, adapt himself to rapidly changing conditions." [quoted by Trotsky, **Op. Cit.**, p. 101] This conservatism played havoc in the party during 1917, incidentally. It would be no exaggeration to argue that the Russian revolution occurred in spite of, rather than because of, Bolshevik organisational principles (see section H.5.12). These principles, however, came into their own once the party had seized power, ensuring the consolidation of bureaucratic rule by an elite. That a vanguard party helps to produces a bureaucratic regime once in power should not come as a surprise. If the party, to use Trotsky's expression, exhibits a "caste tendency of the committeemen" can we be surprised if once in power it reproduces such a tendency in the state it is now the master of? [**Op. Cit.**, p. 102] And this "tendency" can be seen today in the multitude of Leninist sects that exist.

H.5.10 Why does "democratic centralism" produce "bureaucratic centralism"?

In spite of the almost ritualistic assertions that vanguard parties are "the most democratic the world has seen," an army of ex-members, expelled dissidents and disgruntled members testify that they do not live up to the hype. They argue that most, if not all, "vanguard" parties are not "democratic centralist" but are, in fact, "bureaucratic centralist." Within the party, in other words, a bureaucratic clique controls it from the top-down with little democratic control, never mind participation. For anarchists, this is hardly surprising. The reasons why this continually happens are rooted in the nature of "democratic centralism" itself.

Firstly, the assumption of "democratic centralism" is that the membership elect a leadership and give them the power to decide policy between conferences and congresses. This has a subtle impact on the membership, as it is assumed that the leadership has a special insight into social problems above and beyond that of anyone else, otherwise they would not have been elected to such an important position. Thus many in the membership come to believe that disagreements with the leadership's analysis, even before they had been clearly articulated, are liable to be wrong. Doubt dares not speak its name. Unquestioning belief in the party leadership has been an all too common recurring theme in many accounts of vanguard parties. The hierarchical structure of the party promotes a hierarchical mentality in its members.

Conformity within such parties is also reinforced by the intense activism expected by members, particularly leading activists and full-time members. Paradoxically, the more deeply people participate in activism, the harder it becomes to reflect on what they are doing. The unrelenting pace often induces exhaustion and depression, while making it harder to *"think your way out"* - too many commitments have been made and too little time is left over from party activity for reflection. Moreover, high levels of activism prevent many, particularly the most committed, from having a personal life outside their role as party members. This high-speed political existence means that rival social networks atrophy through neglect, so ensuring that the party line is the only perspective which members get exposed to. Members tend to leave, typically, because of exhaustion, crisis, even despair rather than as the result of rational reflection and conscious decision.

Secondly, given that vanguard parties are based on the belief that they are the guardians of *"scientific socialism,"* this means that there is a tendency to squeeze all of social life into the confines of the party's ideology. Moreover, as the party's ideology is a "science" it is expected to explain everything (hence the tendency of Leninists to expound on every subject imaginable, regardless of whether the author knows enough about the subject to discuss it in an informed way). The view that the party's ideology explains everything eliminates the need for fresh or independent thought, precludes the possibility of critically appraising past practice or acknowledging mistakes, and removes the need to seek meaningful intellectual input outside the party's own ideological fortress. As Victor Serge, anarchist turned Bolshevik, admitted in his memoirs: *"Bolshevik thinking is grounded in the possession of the truth. The Party is the repository of truth, and any form of thinking which differs from it is a dangerous or reactionary error. Here lies the spiritual source of its intolerance. The absolute conviction of its lofty mission assures it of a moral energy quite astonishing in its intensity - and, at the same time, a clerical mentality which is quick to become Inquisitorial."* [**Memoirs of a Revolutionary**, p. 134]

The intense level of activism means that members are bombarded with party propaganda, are in endless party meetings, or spend time reading party literature and so, by virtue of the fact that there is not enough time to read everything, members end up reading nothing but party publications. Most points of contact with the external world are eliminated or drastically curtailed. Indeed, such alternative sources of information and such thinking is regularly dismissed as being contaminated by bourgeois influences. This often goes so far as to label those who question any aspect of the party's analysis revisionists or deviationists, bending to the *"pressures of capitalism,"* and they are usually driven from the ranks as heretics. All this is almost always combined with contempt for all other organisations on the Left (indeed, the closer they are to the party's own ideological position the more likely they are to be the targets of abuse).

Thirdly, the practice of *"democratic centralism"* also aids this process towards conformity. Based on the idea that the party must be a highly disciplined fighting force, the party is endowed with a powerful central committee and a rule that all members must publicly defend the agreed-upon positions of the party and the decisions of the central committee, whatever opinions they might hold to the contrary in private. Between conferences, the party's leading bodies usually have extensive authority to govern the party's affairs, including updating party doctrine and deciding the party's response to current political events.

As unity is the key, there is a tendency to view any opposition as a potential threat. It is not at all clear when *"full freedom to criticise"* policy internally can be said to disturb the unity of a defined action. The norms of democratic centralism confer all power between conferences onto a central committee, allowing it to become the arbiter of when a dissident viewpoint is in danger of weakening unity. The evidence from numerous vanguard parties suggest that their leaderships usually view **any** dissent as precisely such a disruption and demand that dissidents cease their action or face expulsion from the party.

It should also be borne in mind that Leninist parties also view themselves as vitally important to the success of any future revolution. This cannot help but reinforce the tendency to view dissent as something which automatically imperils the future of the planet and, therefore, something which must be combated at all costs. As Lenin stressed an a polemic directed to the international communist movement in 1920, *"[w]hoever brings about even the slightest weakening of the iron discipline of the party of the proletariat (especially during its dictatorship) is actually aiding the bourgeoisie against the proletariat."* [**Collected Works**, vol. 31, p. 45] As can be seen, Lenin stresses the importance of *"iron discipline"* at all times, not only during the revolution when *"the party"* is applying *"its dictatorship"* (see section H.3.8 for more on this aspect of Leninism). This provides a justification of whatever measures are required to restore the illusion of unanimity, including the trampling underfoot of whatever rights the membership may have on paper and the imposition of any decisions the leadership considers as essential between conferences.

Fourthly, and more subtly, it is well known that when people take a public position in defence of a proposition, there is a strong tendency for their private attitudes to shift so that they harmonise with their public behaviour. It is difficult to say one thing in public and hold to a set of private beliefs at variance with what is publicly expressed. In short, if people tell others that they support X (for whatever reason), they will slowly begin to change their own opinions and, indeed, internally come to support X. The more public such declarations have been, the more likely it is that such a shift will take place. This has been confirmed by empirical research (see R. Cialdini's **Influence: Science and Practice**). This suggests that if, in the name of democratic centralism, party members publicly uphold the party line, it becomes increasingly difficult to hold a private belief at variance with publicly expressed opinions. The evidence suggests that it is not possible to have a group of people presenting a conformist image to society at large while maintaining an inner party regime characterised by frank and full discussion. Conformity in public tends to produce conformity in private. So given what is now known of social influence, *"democratic centralism"* is almost certainly destined to prevent genuine internal discussion. This is sadly all too often confirmed in the internal regimes of vanguard parties, where debate is often narrowly focused on a few minor issues of emphasis rather than fundamental issues of policy and theory.

It has already been noted (in section H.5.5) that the organisational norms of democratic centralism imply a concentration of power at the top. There is abundant evidence that such a concentration has been a vital feature of every vanguard party and that such a concentration limits party democracy. An authoritarian inner party regime is maintained, which ensures that decision making is concentrated in elite hands. This regime gradually dismantles or ignores all formal controls on its activities. Members are excluded from participation in determining policy, calling leaders to account, or expressing dissent. This is usually combined with persistent assurances about the essentially democratic nature of the organisation, and the existence of exemplary democratic controls - on paper. Correlated with this inner authoritarianism is a growing tendency toward the abuse of power by the leaders, who act in arbitrary ways, accrue personal power and so on (as noted by Trotsky with regards to the Bolshevik party machine). Indeed, it is often the case that activities that would provoke outrage if engaged in by rank-and-file members are tolerated when their leaders do it. As one group of Scottish libertarians noted:

> *"Further, in so far as our Bolshevik friends reject and defy capitalist and orthodox labourist conceptions, they also are as much 'individualistic' as the anarchist. Is it not boasted, for example, that on many occasions Marx, Lenin and Trotsky were prepared to be in a minority of one - if they thought they were more correct than all others on the question at issue? In this, like Galileo, they were quite in order. Where they and their followers, obsessed by the importance of their own judgement go wrong, is in their tendency to refuse this inalienable right to other protagonists and fighters for the working class."* [APCF, *"Our Reply,"* **Class War on the Home Front**, p. 70]

As in any hierarchical structure, the tendency is for those in power to encourage and promote those who agree with them. This means that members usually find their influence and position in the party dependent on their willingness to conform to the hierarchy and its leadership. Dissenters will rarely find their contribution valued and advancement is limited, which produces a strong tendency not to make waves. As Miasnikov, a working class Bolshevik dissident, argued in 1921, *"the regime within the party"* meant that *"if someone dares to have the courage of his convictions,"* they are called either a self-seeker or, worse, a counter-revolutionary, a Menshevik or an SR. Moreover, within the party, favouritism and corruption were rife. In Miasnikov's eyes a new type of Communist was emerging, the toadying careerist who *"knows how to please his superiors."* [quoted by Paul Avrich, **Bolshevik Opposition to Lenin**, p. 8 and p. 7] At the last party congress Lenin attended, Miasnikov was expelled. Only one delegate, V. V. Kosior, *"argued that Lenin had taken the wrong approach to the question of dissent. If someone … had the courage to point out deficiencies in party work, he was marked down as an oppositionist, relieved of authority, placed under surveillance, and - a reference to Miasnikov - even expelled from the party."* [Paul Avrich, **Op. Cit.**, p. 15] Serge noted about the same period that Lenin *"proclaimed a purge of the Party, aimed at those revolutionaries who had come in from other parties - i.e. those who were not saturated with the Bolshevik mentality. This meant the establishment within the Party of a dictatorship of the old Bolsheviks, and the direction of disciplinary measures, not against the unprincipled careerists and conformist late-comers, but against those sections with a critical outlook."* [**Op. Cit.**, p. 135]

This, of course, also applies to the party congress, on paper the sovereign body of the organisation. All too often resolutions at party conferences will either come from the leadership or be completely supportive of its position. If branches or members submit resolutions which are critical of the leadership, enormous pressure is exerted to ensure that they are withdrawn. Moreover, often delegates to the congress are not mandated by their branches, so ensuring that rank and file opinions are not raised, never mind discussed. Other, more drastic measures have been known to occur. Victor Serge saw what he termed the *"Party steamroller"* at work in early 1921 when *"the voting [was] rigged for Lenin's and Zinoviev's 'majority'"* in one of the districts of Petrograd. [**Op. Cit.**, p.123]

All to often, such parties have "elected" bodies which have, in practice, usurped the normal democratic rights of members and become increasingly removed from formal controls. All practical accountability of the leaders to the membership for their actions is eliminated. Usually this authoritarian structure is combined with militaristic sounding rhetoric and the argument that the "revolutionary" movement needs to be organised in a more centralised way than the current class system, with references to the state's forces of repression (notably the army). As Murray Bookchin argued, the Leninist *"has always had a grudging admiration and respect for that most inhuman of all hierarchical institutions, the military."* [**Toward an Ecological Society**, p. 254f]

Our account of the workings of vanguard parties explains, in part, why many anarchists and other libertarians voice concern about them and their underlying ideology. We do so because their practices are disruptive and alienate new activists, hindering the very goal (socialism/revolution) they claim to be aiming for. As anyone familiar with the numerous groupings and parties in the Leninist left will attest, the anarchist critique of vanguardism seems to be confirmed in reality while the Leninist defence seems sadly lacking (unless, of course, the person is a member of such a party and then their organisation is the exception to the rule!).

H.5.11 Can you provide an example of the negative nature of vanguard parties?

Yes. Our theoretical critique of vanguardism we have presented in the last few sections is more than proved by the empirical evidence of such parties in operation today. Rarely do "vanguard" parties reach in practice the high hopes their supporters like to claim for them. Such parties are usually small, prone to splitting as well as leadership cults, and usually play a negative role in social struggle. A long line of ex-members complain that such parties are elitist, hierarchical and bureaucratic.

Obviously we cannot hope to discuss all such parties. As such, we will take just one example, namely the arguments of one group of dissidents of the biggest British Leninist party, the **Socialist Workers Party**. It is worth quoting their account of the internal workings of the SWP at length:

> "The SWP is not democratic centralist but bureaucratic centralist. The leadership's control of the party is unchecked by the members. New perspectives are initiated exclusively by the central committee (CC), who then implement their perspective against all party opposition, implicit or explicit, legitimate or otherwise.

> "Once a new perspective is declared, a new cadre is selected from the top down. The CC select the organisers, who select the district and branch committees - any elections that take place are carried out on the basis of 'slates' so that it is virtually impossible for members to vote against the slate proposed by the leadership. Any members who have doubts or disagreements are written off as 'burnt out' and, depending on their reaction to this, may be marginalised within the party and even expelled.

> "These methods have been disastrous for the SWP in a number of ways: Each new perspective requires a new cadre (below the level of the CC), so the existing cadre are actively marginalised in the party. In this way, the SWP has failed to build a stable and experienced cadre capable of acting independently of the leadership. Successive layers of cadres have been driven into passivity, and even out of the revolutionary movement altogether. The result is the loss of hundreds of potential cadres. Instead of appraising the real, uneven development of individual cadres, the history of the party is written in terms of a star system (comrades currently favoured by the party) and a demonology (the 'renegades' who are brushed aside with each turn of the party). As a result of this systematic dissolution of the cadre, the CC grows ever more remote from the membership and increasingly bureaucratic in its methods. In recent years the national committee has been abolished (it obediently voted for its own dissolution, on the recommendation of the CC), to be replaced by party councils made up of those

comrades active at any one time (i.e. those who already agree with current perspectives); district committees are appointed rather than elected; the CC monopolise all information concerning the party, so that it is impossible for members to know much about what happens in the party outside their own branch; the CC give a distorted account of events rather than admit their mistakes ... history is rewritten to reinforce the prestige of the CC ... The outcome is a party whose conferences have no democratic function, but serve only to orientate party activists to carry out perspectives drawn up before the delegates even set out from their branches. At every level of the party, strategy and tactics are presented from the top down, as pre-digested instructions for action. At every level, the comrades 'below' are seen only as a passive mass to be shifted into action, rather than as a source of new initiatives ...

> "The only exception is when a branch thinks up a new tactic to carry out the CC's perspective. In this case, the CC may take up this tactic and apply it across the party. In no way do rank and file members play an active role in determining the strategy and theory of the party - except in the negative sense that if they refuse to implement a perspective eventually even the CC notice, and will modify the line to suit. A political culture has been created in which the leadership outside of the CC consists almost solely of comrades loyal to the CC, willing to follow every turn of the perspective without criticism ... Increasingly, the bureaucratic methods used by the CC to enforce their control over the political direction of the party have been extended to other areas of party life. In debates over questions of philosophy, culture and even anthropology an informal party 'line' emerged (i.e. concerning matters in which there can be no question of the party taking a 'line'). Often behind these positions lay nothing more substantial than the opinions of this or that CC member, but adherence to the line quickly became a badge of party loyalty, disagreement became a stigma, and the effect was to close down the democracy of the party yet further by placing even questions of theory beyond debate. Many militants, especially working class militants with some experience of trade union democracy, etc., are often repelled by the undemocratic norms in the party and refuse to join, or keep their distance despite accepting our formal politics." [ISG, **Discussion Document of Ex-SWP Comrades**]

The dissidents argue that a "democratic" party would involve the "[r]egular election of all party full-timers, branch and district leadership, conference delegates, etc. with the right of recall," which means that in the SWP appointment of full-timers, leaders and so on is the norm. They argue for the "right of branches to propose motions to the party conference" and for the "right for members to communicate horizontally in the party, to produce and distribute their own documents." They stress the need for "an independent

Control Commission to review all disciplinary cases (independent of the leadership bodies that exercise discipline), and the right of any disciplined comrades to appeal directly to party conference." They argue that in a democratic party "no section of the party would have a monopoly of information" which indicates that the SWP's leadership is essentially secretive, withholding information from the party membership. Even more significantly, given our discussion on the influence of the party structure on post-revolutionary society in section H.5.7, they argue that "[w]orst of all, the SWP are training a layer of revolutionaries to believe that the organisational norms of the SWP are a shining example of proletarian democracy, applicable to a future socialist society. Not surprisingly, many people are instinctively repelled by this idea."

Some of these critics of specific Leninist parties do not give up hope and still look for a truly democratic centralist party rather than the bureaucratic centralist ones which seem so common. For example, our group of ex-SWP dissidents argue that "[a]nybody who has spent time involved in 'Leninist' organisations will have come across workers who agree with Marxist politics but refuse to join the party because they believe it to be undemocratic and authoritarian. Many draw the conclusion that Leninism itself is at fault, as every organisation that proclaims itself Leninist appears to follow the same pattern." [ISG, **Lenin vs. the SWP: Bureaucratic Centralism Or Democratic Centralism?**] This is a common refrain with Leninists - when reality says one thing and the theory another, it must be reality that is at fault. Yes, every Leninist organisation may be bureaucratic and authoritarian but it is not the theory's fault that those who apply it are not capable of actually doing so successfully. Such an application of scientific principles by the followers of "scientific socialism" is worthy of note - obviously the usual scientific method of generalising from facts to produce a theory is inapplicable when evaluating "scientific socialism" itself. However, rather than ponder the possibility that "democratic centralism" does not actually work and automatically generates the "bureaucratic centralism," they point to the example of the Russian revolution and the original Bolshevik party as proof of the validity of their hopes.

Indeed, it would be no exaggeration to argue that the only reason people take the vanguard party organisational structure seriously is the apparent success of the Bolsheviks in the Russian revolution. However, as noted above, even the Bolshevik party was subject to bureaucratic tendencies and as we discuss in the next section, the experience of the 1917 Russian Revolutions disprove the effectiveness of "vanguard" style parties. The Bolshevik party of 1917 was a totally different form of organisation than the ideal "democratic centralist" type argued for by Lenin in 1902 and 1920. As a model of revolutionary organisation, the "vanguardist" one has been proven false rather than confirmed by the experience of the Russian revolution. Insofar as the Bolshevik party was effective, it operated in a non-vanguardist way and insofar as it did operate in such a manner, it held back the struggle.

H.5.12 Surely the Russian Revolution proves that vanguard parties work?

No, far from it. Looking at the history of vanguardism we are struck by its failures, not its successes. Indeed, the proponents of "democratic centralism" can point to only one apparent success of their model, namely the Russian Revolution. Strangely, though, we are warned by Leninists that failure to use the vanguard party will inevitably condemn future revolutions to failure:

> "The proletariat can take power only through its vanguard... Without the confidence of the class in the vanguard, without support of the vanguard by the class, there can be no talk of the conquest of power ... The Soviets are the only organised form of the tie between the vanguard and the class. A revolutionary content can be given to this form only by the party. This is proved by the positive experience of the October Revolution and by the negative experience of other countries (Germany, Austria, finally, Spain). No one has either shown in practice or tried to explain articulately on paper how the proletariat can seize power without the political leadership of a party that knows what it wants." [Trotsky, **Writings 1936-37**, p. 490]

To anarchist ears, such claims seem out of place. After all, did the Russian Revolution actually result in socialism or even a viable form of soviet democracy? Far from it. Unless you picture revolution as simply the changing of the party in power, you have to acknowledge that while the Bolshevik party **did** take power in Russian in November 1917, the net effect of this was **not** the stated goals that justified that action. Thus, if we take the term "effective" to mean "an efficient means to achieve the desired goals" then vanguardism has not been proven to be effective, quite the reverse. Needless to say, Trotsky blames the failure of the Russian Revolution on "objective" factors rather than Bolshevik policies and practice, an argument we address in section H.6 and will not do so here.

So while Leninists make great claims for the effectiveness of their chosen kind of party, the hard facts of history are against their positive evaluation of vanguard parties. Ironically, even the Russian Revolution disproves the claims of Leninists. The fact is that the Bolshevik party in 1917 was very far from the "democratic centralist" organisation which supporters of vanguardism like to claim it as. As such, its success in 1917 lies more in its divergence from the principles of "democratic centralism" than in their application. The subsequent degeneration of the revolution and the party is marked by the increasing **application** of those principles in the life of the party.

Thus, to refute the claims of the "effectiveness" and "efficiency" of vanguardism, we need to look at its one and only success, namely the Russian Revolution. As the Cohen-Bendit brothers argued, "far from leading the Russian Revolution forwards, the Bolsheviks were responsible for holding back the struggle of the masses between February and October 1917, and later for turning the revolution into a bureaucratic counter-revolution - in both cases because of the party's very nature, structure and ideology." Indeed, "[f]rom April to October, Lenin had to fight a constant battle to keep the Party leadership in tune with the masses." [**Obsolete Communism**, p. 183 and p. 187] It was only by continually violating its own "nature, structure and ideology" that the Bolshevik party played an important role in the revolution. Whenever the principles of "democratic centralism" were applied, the Bolshevik party played the role the Cohen-Bendit brothers subscribed to it (and once in power, the party's negative features came to the fore).

Even Leninists acknowledge that, to quote Tony Cliff, throughout the history of Bolshevism, "a certain conservatism arose." Indeed, "[a]t practically all sharp turning points, Lenin had to rely on the lower strata of the party machine against the higher, or on the rank and file against the machine as a whole." [**Lenin**, vol. 2, p. 135] This fact, incidentally, refutes the basic assumptions of Lenin's party schema, namely that the broad party membership, like the working class, was subject to bourgeois influences so necessitating central leadership and control from above.

Looking at both the 1905 and 1917 revolutions, we are struck by how often this "conservatism" arose and how often the higher bodies lagged behind the spontaneous actions of the masses and the party membership. Looking at the 1905 revolution, we discover a classic example of the inefficiency of "democratic centralism." Facing the rise of the soviets, councils of workers' delegates elected to co-ordinate strikes and other forms of struggle, the Bolsheviks did not know what to do. "The Petersburg Committee of the Bolsheviks," noted Trotsky, "was frightened at first by such an innovation as a non-partisan representation of the embattled masses, and could find nothing better to do than to present the Soviet with an ultimatum: immediately adopt a Social-Democratic program or disband. The Petersburg Soviet as a whole, including the contingent of Bolshevik workingmen as well ignored this ultimatum without batting an eyelash." [**Stalin**, vol. 1, p. 106] More than that, "[t]he party's Central Committee published the resolution on October 27, thereby making it the binding directive for all other Bolshevik organisations." [Oskar Anweiler, **The Soviets**, p. 77] It was only the return of Lenin which stopped the Bolshevik's open attacks against the Soviet. As we discuss in section H.6.2, the rationale for these attacks is significant as they were based on arguing that the soviets could not reflect workers' interests because they were elected by the workers! The implications of this perspective came clear in 1918, when the Bolsheviks gerrymandered and disbanded soviets to remain in power (see section H.6.1). That the Bolshevik's position flowed naturally from Lenin's arguments in **What is to be Done?** is clear. Thus the underlying logic of Lenin's vanguardism ensured that the Bolsheviks played a negative role with regards the soviets which, combined with "democratic centralism" ensured that it was spread far and wide. Only by ignoring their own party's principles and staying in the Soviet did rank and file Bolsheviks play a positive role in the revolution. This divergence of top and bottom would be repeated in 1917.

Given this, perhaps it is unsurprising that Leninists started to rewrite the history of the 1905 revolution. Victor Serge, an anti-Stalinist Leninist, asserted in the late 1920s that in 1905 the Petrograd Soviet was "led by Trotsky and inspired by the Bolsheviks." [**Year One of the Russian Revolution**, p. 36]. While the former claim is partially correct, the latter is not. As noted, the Bolsheviks initially opposed the soviets and systematically worked to undermine them. Unsurprisingly, Trotsky at that time was a Menshevik, not a Bolshevik. After all, how could the most revolutionary party that ever existed have messed up so badly? How could democratic centralism fare so badly in practice? Best, then, to suggest that it did not and give the Bolsheviks a role better suited to the rhetoric of Bolshevism than its reality.

Trotsky was no different. He, needless to say, denied the obvious implications of these events in 1905. While admitting that the Bolsheviks "adjusted themselves more slowly to the sweep of the movement" and that the Mensheviks "were preponderant in the Soviet," he tries to save vanguardism by asserting that "the general direction of the Soviet's policy proceeded in the main along Bolshevik lines." So, in spite of the lack of Bolshevik influence, in spite of the slowness in adjusting to the revolution, Bolshevism was, in fact, the leading set of ideas in the revolution! Ironically, a few pages later, he mocks the claims of Stalinists that Stalin had "isolated the Mensheviks from the masses" by noting that the "figures hardly bear [the claims] out." [**Op. Cit.**, p. 112 and p. 117] Shame he did not apply this criteria to his own assertions.

Of course, every party makes mistakes. The question is, how did the "most revolutionary party of all time" fare in 1917. Surely that revolution proves the validity of vanguardism and "democratic centralism"? After all, there was a successful revolution, the Bolshevik party did seize power. However, the apparent success of 1917 was not due to the application of "democratic centralism," quite the reverse. While the myth of 1917 is that a highly efficient, democratic centralist vanguard party ensured the overthrow of the Provisional Government in November 1917 in favour of the Soviets (or so it seemed at the time) the facts are somewhat different. Rather, the Bolshevik party throughout 1917 was a fairly loose collection of local organisations (each more than willing to ignore central commands and express their autonomy), with much internal dissent and infighting and no discipline beyond what was created by common loyalty. The "democratic centralist" party, as desired by Lenin, was only created in the course of the Civil War and the tightening of the party dictatorship. In other words, the party became more like a "democratic centralist" one as the revolution degenerated. As such, the various followers of Lenin (Stalinists, Trotskyists and their multitude of offshoots) subscribe to a myth, which probably explains their lack of success in reproducing a similar organisation since. So assuming that the Bolsheviks did play an important role in the Russian revolution, it was because it was **not** the centralised, disciplined Bolshevik party of Leninist myth. Indeed, when the party **did** operate in a vanguardist manner, failure was soon to follow.

This claim can be proven by looking at the history of the 1917 revolution. The February revolution started with spontaneous protests and strikes yet "the Petrograd organisation of the Bolsheviks opposed the calling of strikes precisely on the eve of the revolution which was destined to overthrow the Tsar. Fortunately, the workers ignored the Bolshevik 'directives' and went on strike anyway. In the events which followed, no one was more surprised by the revolution than the 'revolutionary' parties, including the Bolsheviks." [Murray

Bookchin, **Post-Scarcity Anarchism**, p. 123] Trotsky quoted one of the Bolshevik leaders at the time:

> *"Absolutely no guiding initiative from the party centres was felt … the Petrograd Committee had been arrested and the representative of the Central Committee … was unable to give any directives for the coming day."* [**History of the Russian Revolution**, vol. 1, p. 147]

Not the best of starts. Of course rank and file Bolsheviks took part in the demonstrations, street fights and strikes and so violated the principles their party was meant to be based on. As the revolution progressed, so did the dual nature of the Bolshevik party (i.e. its practical divergence from "democratic centralism" in order to be effective and attempts to force it back into that schema which handicapped the revolution). However, during 1917, "democratic centralism" was ignored in order to ensure the Bolsheviks played any role at all in the revolution. As one historian of the party makes clear, in 1917 and until the outbreak of the Civil War, the party operated in ways that few modern "vanguard" parties would tolerate:

> *"The committees were a law unto themselves when it came to accepting orders from above. Democratic centralism, as vague a principle of internal administration as there ever has been, was commonly held at least to enjoin lower executive bodies that they should obey the behests of all higher bodies in the organisational hierarchy. But town committees in practice had the devil's own job in imposing firm leadership … Insubordination was the rule of the day whenever lower party bodies thought questions of importance were at stake.*
>
> *"Suburb committees too faced difficulties in imposing discipline. Many a party cell saw fit to thumb its nose at higher authority and to pursue policies which it felt to be more suited to local circumstances or more desirable in general. No great secret was made of this. In fact, it was openly admitted that hardly a party committee existed which did not encounter problems in enforcing its will even upon individual activists."* [Robert Service, **The Bolshevik Party in Revolution 1917-1923**, pp. 51-2]

So while Lenin's ideal model of a disciplined, centralised and top-down party had been expounded since 1902, the operation of the party never matched his desire. As Service notes, *"a disciplined hierarchy of command stretching down from the regional committees to party cells"* had *"never existed in Bolshevik history."* In the heady days of the revolution, when the party was flooded by new members, Bolshevik party life was the exact opposite of that usually considered (by both opponents and supporters of Bolshevism) as it normal mode of operation. *"Anarchist attitudes to higher authority,"* he argues, *"were the rule of the day"* and *"no Bolshevik leader in his right mind could have contemplated a regular insistence upon rigid standards of hierarchical control and discipline unless he had abandoned all hope of establishing a mass socialist party."* This meant that *"in the Russia of 1917 it was the easiest thing in the world for lower party bodies to rebut the demands and pleas by*

higher authority." He stresses that *"[s]uburb and town committees … often refused to go along with official policies … they also … sometimes took it into their heads to engage in active obstruction."* [**Op. Cit.**, p. 80, p. 62 p. 56 and p. 60]

This worked both ways, of course. Town committees did *"snub their nose at lower-echelon viewpoints in the time before the next election. Try as hard as they might, suburb committees and ordinary cells could meanwhile do little to rectify matters beyond telling their own representative on their town committee to speak on their behalf. Or, if this too failed, they could resort to disruptive tactics by criticising it in public and refusing it all collaboration."* [**Op. Cit.**, pp. 52-3] Even by early 1918, the Bolshevik party bore little resemblance to the "democratic centralist" model desired by Lenin:

> *"The image of a disciplined hierarchy of party committees was therefore but a thin, artificial veneer which was used by Bolshevik leaders to cover up the cracked surface of the real picture underneath. Cells and suburb committees saw no reason to kow-tow to town committees; nor did town committees feel under compulsion to show any greater respect to their provincial and regional committees than before."* [**Op. Cit.**, p. 74]

It is this insubordination, this local autonomy and action in spite of central orders which explains the success of the Bolsheviks in 1917. Rather than a highly centralised and disciplined body of "professional" revolutionaries, the party saw a *"significant change … within the membership of the party at local level … From the time of the February revolution requirements for party membership had been all but suspended, and now Bolshevik ranks swelled with impetuous recruits who knew next to nothing about Marxism and who were united by little more than overwhelming impatience for revolutionary action."* [Alexander Rabinowitch, **Prelude to Revolution**, p. 41]

This mass of new members (many of whom were peasants who had just recently joined the industrial workforce) had a radicalising effect on the party's policies and structures. As even Leninist commentators argue, it was this influx of members who allowed Lenin to gain support for his radical revision of party aims in April. However, in spite of this radicalisation of the party base, the party machine still was at odds with the desires of the party. As Trotsky acknowledged, the situation *"called for resolute confrontation of the sluggish Party machine with masses and ideas in motion."* He stressed that *"the masses were incomparably more revolutionary than the Party, which in turn was more revolutionary than its committeemen."* Ironically, given the role Trotsky usually gave the party, he admits that *"[w]ithout Lenin, no one had known what to make of the unprecedented situation."* [**Stalin**, vol. 1, p. 301, p. 305 and p. 297]

Which is significant in itself. The Bolshevik party is usually claimed as being the most "revolutionary" that ever existed, yet here is Trotsky admitting that its leading members did not have a clue what to do. He even argued that *"[e]very time the Bolshevik leaders had to act without Lenin they fell into error, usually inclining to the Right."* [**Op. Cit.**, p. 299] This negative opinion of the Bolsheviks applied even to the *"left Bolsheviks, especially the workers"* whom we are informed *"tried with all their force to break through this quarantine"* created by the Bolshevik leaders policy *"of waiting, of accommodation, and of actual retreat before the Compromisers"* after the February revolution and before the arrival of Lenin. Trotsky argued that *"they did not know how to refute the premise about the bourgeois character of the revolution and the danger of an isolation of the proletariat. They submitted, gritting their teeth, to the directions of their leaders."* [**History of the Russian Revolution**, vol. 1, p. 273] It seems strange, to say the least, that without one person the whole of the party was reduced to such a level given that the aim of the "revolutionary" party was to develop the political awareness of its members.

Lenin's arrival, according to Trotsky, allowed the influence of the more radical rank and file to defeat the conservatism of the party machine. By the end of April, Lenin had managed to win over the majority of the party leadership to his position. However, this *"April conflict between Lenin and the general staff of the party was not the only one of its kind. Throughout the whole history of Bolshevism ... all the leaders of the party at all the most important moments stood to the **right** of Lenin."* [**Op. Cit.**, p. 305] As such, if "democratic centralism" had worked as intended, the whole party would have been arguing for incorrect positions the bulk of its existence (assuming, of course, that Lenin was correct most of the time).

For Trotsky, *"Lenin exerted influence not so much as an individual but because he embodied the influence of the class on the Party and of the Party on its machine."* Yet, this was the machine which Lenin had forged, which embodied his vision of how a "revolutionary" party should operate and was headed by him. To argue that the party machine was behind the party membership and the membership behind the class shows the bankruptcy of Lenin's organisational scheme. This "backwardness", moreover, indicates an independence of the party bureaucracy from the membership and the membership from the masses. As Lenin's constantly repeated aim was for the party to seize power (based on the dubious assumption that class power would only be expressed, indeed was identical to, party power) this independence held serious dangers, dangers which became apparent once this goal was achieved. This is confirmed when Trotsky asked the question *"by what miracle did Lenin manage in a few short weeks to turn the Party's course into a new channel?"* Significantly, he answers as follows: *"Lenin's personal attributes and the objective situation."* [**Stalin**, vol. 1, p. 299] No mention is made of the democratic features of the party organisation, which suggests that without Lenin the rank and file party members would not have been able to shift the weight of the party machine in their favour. Trotsky seemed close to admitting this:

> *"As often happens, a sharp cleavage developed between the classes in motion and the interests of the party machines. Even the Bolshevik Party cadres, who enjoyed the benefit of exceptional revolutionary training, were definitely inclined to disregard the masses and to identify their own special interests and the interests of the machine on the very day after the monarchy was overthrown."* [**Op. Cit.**, p. 298]

Thus the party machine, which embodied the principles of "democratic centralism" proved less than able to the task assigned it

in practice. Without Lenin, it is doubtful that the party membership would have overcome the party machine:

> *"Lenin was strong not only because he understood the laws of the class struggle but also because his ear was faultlessly attuned to the stirrings of the masses in motion. He represented not so much the Party machine as the vanguard of the proletariat. He was definitely convinced that thousands from among those workers who had borne the brunt of supporting the underground Party would now support him. The masses at the moment were more revolutionary than the Party, and the Party more revolutionary than its machine. As early as March the actual attitude of the workers and soldiers had in many cases become stormily apparent, and it was widely at variance with the instructions issued by all the parties, including the Bolsheviks."* [**Op. Cit.**, p. 299]

Little wonder the local party groupings ignored the party machine, practising autonomy and initiative in the face of a party machine inclined to conservatism, inertia, bureaucracy and remoteness. This conflict between the party machine and the principles it was based on and the needs of the revolution and party membership was expressed continually throughout 1917:

> *"In short, the success of the revolution called for action against the 'highest circles of the party,' who, from February to October, utterly failed to play the revolutionary role they ought to have taken in theory. The masses themselves made the revolution, with or even against the party - this much at least was clear to Trotsky the historian. But far from drawing the correct conclusion, Trotsky the theorist continued to argue that the masses are incapable of making a revolution without a leader."* [Daniel & Gabriel Cohn-Bendit, **Op. Cit.**, p. 188]

Looking at the development of the revolution from April onwards, we are struck by the sluggishness of the party hierarchy. At every revolutionary upsurge, the party simply was not up to the task of responding to the needs of masses and the local party groupings closest to them. The can be seen in June, July and October itself. At each turn, the rank and file groupings or Lenin had to constantly violate the principles of their own party in order to be effective.

For example, when discussing the cancellation by the central committee of a demonstration planned for June 10th by the Petrograd Bolsheviks, the unresponsiveness of the party hierarchy can be seen. The *"speeches by Lenin and Zinoviev [justifying their actions] by no means satisfied the Petersburg Committee. If anything, it appears that their explanations served to strengthen the feeling that at best the party leadership had acted irresponsibly and incompetently and was seriously out of touch with reality."* Indeed, many *"blamed the Central Committee for taking so long to respond to Military Organisation appeals for a demonstration."* During the discussions in late June, 1917, on whether to take direct action against the Provisional Government there was a *"wide gulf"* between lower organs evaluations of the current situation and that of the Central Committee. [Rabinowitch, **Op. Cit.**, p. 88, p. 92 and p. 129] Indeed, among the delegates from the Bolshevik military groups, only Lashevich (an old Bolshevik) spoke in favour of the Central Committee position and he noted that *"[f]requently it is impossible to make out where the Bolshevik ends and the Anarchist begins."* [quoted by Rabinowitch, **Op. Cit.**, p. 129]

In the July days, the breach between the local party groups and the central committee increased. This spontaneous uprising was opposed to by the Bolshevik leadership, in spite of the leading role of their own militants (along with anarchists) in fermenting it. While calling on their own activists to restrain the masses, the party leadership was ignored by the rank and file membership who played an active role in the event. Sickened by being asked to play the role of *"fireman"*, the party militants rejected party discipline in order to maintain their credibility with the working class. Rank and file activists, pointing to the snowballing of the movement, showed clear dissatisfaction with the Central Committee. One argued that it *"was not aware of the latest developments when it made its decision to oppose the movement into the streets."* Ultimately, the Central Committee appeal *"for restraining the masses ... was removed from"* **Pravda** *"and so the party's indecision was reflected by a large blank space on page one."* [Rabinowitch, **Op. Cit.**, p. 150, p. 159 and p. 175] Ultimately, the indecisive nature of the leadership can be explained by the fact it did not think it could seize state power for itself (*"the state of popular consciousness ... made impossible the seizure of power by the Bolsheviks in July."* [Trotsky, **History of the Russian Revolution**, vol. 2, p. 81]).

Significantly, one of the main Bolshevik groupings which helped organise and support the July uprising, the Military Organisation, started their own paper after the Central Committee had decreed after the failed revolt that neither it, nor the Petersburg Committee, should be allowed to have one. It *"angrily insisted on what it considered its just prerogatives"* and in *"no uncertain terms it affirmed its right to publish an independent newspaper and formally protested what is referred to as 'a system of persecution and repression of an extremely peculiar character which had begun with the election of the new Central Committee.'"* [Rabinowitch, **Op. Cit.**, p. 227] The Central Committee backed down, undoubtedly due to the fact it could not enforce its decision.

Even by October, the party machine still lagged behind the needs of the revolution. In fact, Lenin could only impose his view by going over the head of the Central Committee. According to Trotsky's account, *"this time he [wa]s not satisfied with furious criticism"* of the *"ruinous Fabianism of the Petrograd leadership"* and *"by way of protest he resign[ed] from the Central Committee."* [**History of the Russian Revolution**, vol. 3, p. 131] Trotsky quoted Lenin as follows:

> *"I am compelled to request permission to withdraw from the Central Committee, which I hereby do, and leave myself freedom of agitation in the lower ranks of the party and at the party congress."* [**Op. Cit.**, p. 131]

Thus the October revolution was precipitated by a blatant violation of the principles Lenin spent his life advocating. Indeed, if someone else other than Lenin had done this we are sure that Lenin, and his numerous followers, would have dismissed it as the action of a *"petty-bourgeois intellectual"* who cannot handle party *"discipline."* This is itself significant, as is the fact that he decided to appeal to

the *"lower ranks"* of the party - rather than being "democratic" the party machine effectively blocked communication and control from the bottom-up. Looking to the more radical party membership, he *"could only impose his view by going over the head of his Central Committee."* [Daniel and Gabriel Cohn-Bendit, **Op. Cit.**, p. 187] He made sure to send his letter of protest to *"the Petrograd and Moscow committees"* and also made sure that *"copies fell into the hands of the more reliable party workers of the district locals."* By early October (and *"over the heads of the Central Committee"*) he wrote *"directly to the Petrograd and Moscow committees"* calling for insurrection. He also *"appealed to a Petrograd party conference to speak a firm word in favour of insurrection."* [Trotsky, **Op. Cit.**, p. 131 and p. 132]

In October, Lenin had to fight what he called *"a wavering"* in the *"upper circles of the party"* which lead to a *"sort of dread of the struggle for power, an inclination to replace this struggle with resolutions, protests and conferences."* [quoted by Trotsky, **Op. Cit.**, p. 132] For Trotsky, this represented *"almost a direct pitting of the party against the Central Committee,"* required because *"it was a question of the fate of the revolution"* and so *"all other considerations fell away."* On October 8th, when Lenin addressed the Bolshevik delegates of the forthcoming Northern Congress of Soviets on this subject, he did so *"personally"* as there *"was no party decision"* and the *"higher institutions of the party had not yet expressed themselves."* [Trotsky, **Op. Cit.**, pp. 132-3 and p. 133] Ultimately, the Central Committee came round to Lenin's position but they did so under pressure of means at odds with the principles of the party.

This divergence between the image and reality of the Bolsheviks explains their success. If the party had applied or had remained true to the principles of "democratic centralism" it is doubtful that it would have played an important role in the movement. As Alexander Rabinowitch argues, Bolshevik organisational unity and discipline is *"vastly exaggerated"* and, in fact, Bolshevik success in 1917 was down to *"the party's internally relatively democratic, tolerant, and decentralised structure and method of operation, as well as its essentially open and mass character - in striking contrast to the traditional Leninist model."* In 1917, he goes on, *"subordinate party bodies like the Petersburg Committee and the Military Organisation were permitted considerable independence and initiative ... Most importantly, these lower bodies were able to tailor their tactics and appeals to suit their own particular constituencies amid rapidly changing conditions. Vast numbers of new members were recruited into the party ... The newcomers included tens of thousands of workers and soldiers ... who knew little, if anything, about Marxism and cared nothing about party discipline."* For example, while the slogan *"All Power to the Soviets"* was *"officially withdrawn by the Sixth [Party] Congress in late July, this change did not take hold at the local level."* [**The Bolsheviks Come to Power**, p. 311, p. 312 and p. 313]

It is no exaggeration to argue that if any member of a current vanguard party acted as the Bolshevik rank and file did in 1917, they would quickly be expelled (this probably explains why no such party has been remotely successful since). However, this ferment from below was quickly undermined within the party with the start of the Civil War. It is from this period when "democratic centralism" was actually applied within the party and clarified as an organisational principle:

> "It was quite a turnabout since the anarchic days before the Civil War. The Central Committee had always advocated the virtues of obedience and co-operation; but the rank-and-filers of 1917 had cared little about such entreaties as they did about appeals made by other higher authorities. The wartime emergency now supplied an opportunity to expatiate on this theme at will." [Service, **Op. Cit.**, p. 91]

Service stresses that *"it appears quite remarkable how quickly the Bolsheviks, who for years had talked idly about a strict hierarchy of command inside the party, at last began to put ideas into practice."* [**Op. Cit.**, p. 96]

In other words, the conversion of the Bolshevik party into a fully fledged *"democratic centralist"* party occurred during the degeneration of the Revolution. This was both a consequence of the rising authoritarianism within the party, state and society as well as one of its causes so it is quite ironic that the model used by modern day followers of Lenin is that of the party during the decline of the revolution, not its peak. This is not surprising. Once in power, the Bolshevik party imposed a state capitalist regime onto the Russian people. Can it be surprising that the party structure which it developed to aid this process was also based on bourgeois attitudes and organisation? The party model advocated by Lenin may not have been very effective during a revolution but it was exceedingly effective at promoting hierarchy and authority in the post-revolutionary regime. It simply replaced the old ruling elite with another, made up of members of the radical intelligentsia and the odd ex-worker or ex-peasant.

This was due to the hierarchical and top-down nature of the party Lenin had created. While the party base was largely working class, the leadership was not. Full-time revolutionaries, they were either middle-class intellectuals or (occasionally) ex-workers and (even rarer) ex-peasants who had left their class to become part of the party machine. Even the delegates at party congresses did not truly reflect the class basis of the party membership. For example, the number of delegates was still dominated by white-collar or others (59.1% to 40.9%) at the sixth party congress at the end of July 1917. [Cliff, **Lenin**, vol. 2, p. 160] So while the party gathered more working class members in 1917, it cannot be said that this was reflected in the party leadership which remained dominated by non-working class elements. Rather than being a genuine working class organisation, the Bolshevik party was a hierarchical group headed by non-working class elements whose working class base could not effectively control them even during the revolution in 1917. It was only effective because these newly joined and radicalised working class members ignored their own party structure and its defining ideology.

After the revolution, the Bolsheviks saw their membership start to decrease. Significantly, *"the decline in numbers which occurred from early 1918 onwards"* started happening *"contrary to what is usually assumed, some months before the Central Committee's decree in midsummer that the party should be purged of its 'undesirable' elements."* These lost members reflected two things. Firstly, the general decline in the size of the industrial working class. This meant that the radicalised new elements from the countryside which had flocked to the Bolsheviks in 1917 returned home. Secondly, the loss of popular support due to the realities of the Bolshevik regime. This can be seen from the fact that while the Bolsheviks were losing members, the Left SRs almost doubled in size to 100,000 (the Mensheviks claimed to have a similar number). Rather than non-proletarians leaving, *"[i]t is more probable by far that it was industrial workers who were leaving in droves. After all, it would have been strange if the growing unpopularity of Sovnarkom in factory milieu had been confined exclusively to non-Bolsheviks."* Unsurprisingly, given its position in power, *"[a]s the proportion of working-class members declined, so that of entrants from the middle-class rose; the steady drift towards a party in which industrial workers no longer numerically predominated was under way."* By late 1918 membership started to increase again but *"[m]ost newcomers were not of working-class origin … the proportion of Bolsheviks of working-class origin fell from 57 per cent at the year's beginning to 48 per cent at the end."* It should be noted that it was not specified how many classed as having working-class origin were still employed in working-class jobs. [Robert Service, **Op. Cit.**, p. 70, pp. 70-1 and p. 90] A new ruling elite was thus born, thanks to the way vanguard parties are structured and the application of vanguardist principles which had previously been ignored.

In summary, the experience of the Russian Revolution does not, in fact, show the validity of the "vanguard" model. The Bolshevik party in 1917 played a leading role in the revolution only insofar as its members violated its own organisational principles (Lenin included). Faced with a real revolution and an influx of more radical new members, the party had to practice anarchist ideas of autonomy, local initiative and the ignoring of central orders which had no bearing to reality on the ground. When the party did try to apply the top-down and hierarchical principles of "democratic centralism" it failed to adjust to the needs of the moment. Moreover, when these principles were finally applied they helped ensure the degeneration of the revolution. This was to be expected, given the nature of vanguardism and the Bolshevik vision of socialism.

H.6

Why did the Russian Revolution fail?

The greatest myth of Marxism must surely be the idea that the Russian Revolution failed solely due to the impact of objective factors. While the date Leninists consider the revolution to have become beyond reform varies (over time it has moved backwards towards 1917 as the authoritarianism under Lenin and Trotsky has become better known), the actual reasons are common. For Leninists, the failure of the revolution was the product of such things as civil war, foreign intervention, economic collapse and the isolation and backwardness of Russia and **not** Bolshevik ideology. Bolshevik authoritarianism, then, was forced upon the party by difficult objective circumstances. It follows that there are no fundamental problems with Leninism and so it is a case of simply applying it again, hopefully in more fortuitous circumstances.

Anarchists are not impressed by this argument and we will show why by refuting common Leninist explanations for the failure of the revolution. For anarchists, Bolshevik ideology played its part, creating social structures (a new state and centralised economic organisations) which not only disempowered the masses but also made the objective circumstances being faced much worse. Moreover, we argue, vanguardism could not help turn the rebels of 1917 into the ruling elite of 1918. We explore these arguments and the evidence for them in this section.

For those who argue that the civil war provoked Bolshevik policies, the awkward fact is that many of the features of war communism, such as the imposition of one-man management and centralised state control of the economy, were already apparent before war communism. As one historian argues, *"[f]rom the first days of Bolshevik power there was only a weak correlation between the extent of 'peace' and the mildness or severity of Bolshevik rule, between the intensity of the war and the intensity of proto-war communist measures ... Considered in ideological terms there was little to distinguish the 'breathing space' (April-May 1918) from the war communism that followed."* Unsurprisingly, then, *"the breathing space of the first months of 1920 after the victories over Kolchak and Denikin ... saw their intensification and the militarisation of labour"* and, in fact, *"no serious attempt was made to review the aptness of war communist policies."* Ideology *"constantly impinged on the choices made at various points of the civil war ... Bolshevik authoritarianism cannot be ascribed simply to the Tsarist legacy or to adverse circumstances."* [Richard Sakwa, **Soviet Communists in Power**, p. 24, p. 27 and p. 30] The inherent tendencies of Bolshevism were revealed by the civil war, a war which only accelerated the development of what was implicit (and, often, not so implicit) in Bolshevik ideology and its vision of socialism, the state and the role of the party.

Thus *"the effective conclusion of the Civil War at the beginning of 1920 was followed by a more determined and comprehensive attempt to apply these so-called War Communism policies rather than their relaxation"* and so the *"apogee of the War Communism economy occurred after the Civil War was effectively over."* With the fighting over Lenin *"forcefully raised the introduction of one-man management ... Often commissars fresh from the Red Army were drafted into management positions in the factories."* By the autumn of 1920, one-man management was in 82% of surveyed workplaces. This *"intensification of War Communism labour policies would not have been a significant development if they had continued to be applied in the same haphazard manner as in 1919, but in early 1920 the Communist Party leadership was no longer distracted by the Civil War from concentrating its thoughts and efforts on the formulation and implementation of its labour policies."* While the *" experience of the Civil War was one factor predisposing communists towards applying military methods"* to the economy in early 1920, *"ideological considerations were also important."* [Jonathan Aves, **Workers Against Lenin**, p. 2, p. 17, p. 15, p. 30, p. 17 and p. 11]

So it seems incredulous for Leninist John Rees to assert, for example, that *"[w]ith the civil war came the need for stricter labour*

discipline and for ... 'one man management'. Both these processes developed lock step with the war." [*"In Defence of October,"* pp. 3-82, **International Socialism**, no. 52, p. 43] As we discuss in the next section, Lenin was advocating both of these **before** the outbreak of civil war in May 1918 **and** after it was effectively over. Indeed he explicitly, both before and after the civil war, stressed that these policies were being implemented because the lack of fighting meant that the Bolsheviks could turn their full attention to building socialism. How these facts can be reconciled with claims of policies being in *"lock step"* with the civil war is hard to fathom.

Part of the problem is the rampant confusion within Leninist circles as to when the practices condemned as Stalinism actually started. For example, Chris Harman (of the UK's SWP) in his summary of the rise of Stalinism asserted that after *"Lenin's illness and subsequent death"* the *"principles of October were abandoned one by one."* Yet the practice of, and ideological commitment to, party dictatorship, one-man management in industry, banning opposition groups/parties (as well as factions within the Communist Party), censorship, state repression of strikes and protests, piece-work, Taylorism, the end of independent trade unions and a host of other crimes against socialism were all implemented under Lenin and normal practice at the time of his death. In other words, the *"principles of October"* were abandoned under, and by, Lenin. Which, incidentally, explains why, Trotsky *"continued to his death to harbour the illusion that somehow, despite the lack of workers' democracy, Russia was a 'workers' state.'"* [**Bureaucracy and Revolution in Eastern Europe**, p. 14 and p. 20] Simply put, there had been no workers' democracy when Trotsky held state power and he considered that regime a *"workers' state"*. The question arises why Harman thinks Lenin's Russia was some kind of "workers' state" if workers' democracy is the criteria by which such things are to be judged.

From this it follows that, unlike Leninists, anarchists do not judge a regime by who happens to be in office. A capitalist state does not become less capitalist just because a social democrat happens to be prime minister or president. Similarly, a regime does not become state capitalist just because Stalin is in power rather than Lenin. While the Marxist analysis concentrates on the transfer of state power from one regime to another, the anarchist one focuses on the transfer of power from the state and bosses to working class people. What makes a regime socialist is the social relationships it has, not the personal opinions of those in power. Thus if the social relationships under Lenin are similar to those under Stalin, then the nature of the regime is similar. That Stalin's regime was far more brutal, oppressive and exploitative than Lenin's does not change the underlying nature of the regime. As such, Chomsky is right to point to *"the techniques of use of terminology to delude"* with respect to the Bolshevik revolution. Under Lenin and Trotsky, *"a popular revolution was taken over by a managerial elite who immediately dismantled all the socialist institutions."* They used state power to *"create a properly managed society, run by smart intellectuals, where everybody does his job and does what he's told ... That's Leninism. That's **the exact opposite of socialism**. If socialism means anything, it means workers' control of production and then on from there. That's the first thing they destroyed. So why do we call it socialism?"* [**Language and Politics**, p. 537]

To refute in advance one obvious objection to our argument, the anarchist criticism of the Bolsheviks is **not** based on the utopian notion that they did not create a fully functioning (libertarian) communist society. As we discussed section H.2.5, anarchists have never thought a revolution would immediately produce such an outcome. As Emma Goldman argued, she had not come to Russia *"expecting to find Anarchism realised"* nor did she *"expect Anarchism to follow in the immediate footsteps of centuries of despotism and submission."* Rather, she *"hope[d] to find in Russia at least the beginnings of the social changes for which the Revolution had been fought"* and that *"the Russian workers and peasants as a whole had derived essential social betterment as a result of the Bolshevik regime."* Both hopes were dashed. [**My Disillusionment in Russia**, p. xlvii] Equally, anarchists were, and are, well aware of the problems facing the revolution, the impact of the civil war and economic blockade. Indeed, both Goldman and Berkman used these (as Leninists still do) to rationalise their support for the Bolsheviks, in spite of their authoritarianism (for Berkman's account see **The Bolshevik Myth** [pp. 328-31]). Their experiences in Russia, particularly after the end of the civil war, opened their eyes to the impact of Bolshevik ideology on its outcome.

Nor is it a case that anarchists have no solutions to the problems facing the Russian Revolution. As well as the negative critique that statist structures are unsuitable for creating socialism, particularly in the difficult economic circumstances that affect every revolution, anarchists stressed that genuine social construction had to be based on the people's own organisations and self-activity. This was because, as Goldman concluded, the state is a *"menace to the constructive development of the new social structure"* and *"would become a dead weight upon the growth of the new forms of life."* Therefore, she argued, the *"industrial power of the masses, expressed through their libertarian associations - Anarchosyndicalism - is alone able to organise successfully the economic life and carry on production"* If the revolution had been made a la Bakunin rather than a la Marx *"the result would have been different and more satisfactory"* as (echoing Kropotkin) Bolshevik methods *"conclusively demonstrated how a revolution should **not** be made."* [**Op. Cit.**, pp. 253-4 and p. liv]

It should also be mentioned that the standard Leninist justification for party dictatorship is that the opposition groups supported the counter-revolution or took part in armed rebellions against "soviet power" (i.e., the Bolsheviks). Rees, for example, asserts that some Mensheviks *"joined the Whites. The rest alternated between accepting the legitimacy of the government and agitating for its overthrow. The Bolsheviks treated them accordingly."* [**Op. Cit.**, p. 65] However, this is far from the truth. As one historian noted, while the *"charge of violent opposition would be made again and again"* by the Bolsheviks, along with being *"active supporters of intervention and of counter-revolution"*, in fact this *"charge was untrue in relation to the Mensheviks, and the Communists, if they ever believed it, never succeeded in establishing it."* A few individuals did reject the Menshevik *"official policy of confining opposition to strictly constitutional means"* and they were *"expelled from the party, for they had acted without its knowledge."* [Leonard Schapiro, **The Origin of the Communist Autocracy**, p. 193] Significantly, the Bolsheviks annulled their June 14th expulsion of the Mensheviks from the soviets on the 30th of November of the same year, 1918. [E. H. Carr, **The Bolshevik Revolution**, vol. 1, p. 180]

By *"agitating"* for the *"overthrow"* of the Bolshevik government, Rees is referring to the Menshevik tactic of standing for election to soviets with the aim of securing a majority and so forming a new government! Unsurprisingly, the sole piece of evidence presented by Rees is a quote from historian E.H. Carr: *"If it was true that the Bolshevik regime was not prepared after the first few months to tolerate an organised opposition, it was equally true that no opposition party was prepared to remain within legal limits. The premise of dictatorship was common to both sides of the argument."* [**Op. Cit.**, p. 190] Yet this *"judgment ignores"* the Mensheviks whose policy of legal opposition: *"The charge that the Mensheviks were not prepared to remain within legal limits is part of the Bolsheviks' case; it does not survive an examination of the facts."* [Schapiro, **Op. Cit.**, p. 355fn]

As regards the SRs, this issue is more complicated. The right-SRs welcomed and utilised the rebellion of the Czech Legion in May 1918 to reconvene the Constituent Assembly (within which they had an overwhelming majority and which the Bolsheviks had dissolved). After the White General Kolchak overthrew this government in November 1918 (and so turned the civil war into a Red against White one), most right-SRs sided with the Bolsheviks and, in return, the Bolsheviks reinstated them to the soviets in February 1919. [Carr, **Op. Cit.**, p. 356 and p. 180] It must be stressed that, contra Carr, the SRs aimed for a democratically elected government, not a dictatorship (and definitely not a White one). With the Left-SRs, it was the Bolsheviks who denied them their majority at the Fifth All-Congress of Soviets. Their rebellion was **not** an attempted coup but rather an attempt to force the end of the Brest-Litovsk treaty with the Germans by restarting the war (as Alexander Rabinowitch proves beyond doubt in his **The Bolsheviks in Power**). It would be fair to say that the anarchists, most SRs, the Left SRs and Mensheviks were not opposed to the revolution, they were opposed to Bolshevik policy.

Ultimately, as Emma Goldman came to conclude, *"what [the Bolsheviks] called 'defence of the Revolution' was really only the defence of [their] party in power."* [**Op. Cit.**, p. 57]

At best it could be argued that the Bolsheviks had no alternative but to impose their dictatorship, as the other socialist parties would have succumbed to the Whites and so, eventually, a White dictatorship would have replaced the Red one. This was why, for example, Victor Serge claimed he sided with the Communists against the Kronstadt sailors even though the latter had right on their side for *"the country was exhausted, and production practically at a standstill; there was no reserves of any kind … The working-class **elite** that had been moulded in the struggle against the old regime was literally decimated… . If the Bolshevik dictatorship fell, it was only a short step to chaos … and in the end, through the sheer force of events, another dictatorship, this time anti-proletarian."* [**Memoirs of a Revolutionary**, pp. 128-9]

This, however, is sheer elitism and utterly violates the notion that socialism is the self-emancipation of the working class. Moreover, it places immense faith on the goodwill of those in power - a utopian position. Equally, it should not be forgotten that both the Reds and Whites were anti-working class. At best it could be argued that the Red repression of working class protests and strikes as well as opposition socialists would not have been as terrible as that of the Whites, but that is hardly a good rationale for betraying the principles of socialism. Yes, libertarians can agree with Serge that embracing socialist principles may not work. Every revolution is a gamble and may fail. As libertarian socialist Ante Ciliga correctly argued:

> "Let us consider, finally, one last accusation which is commonly circulated: that action such as that at Kronstadt could have **indirectly** let loose the forces of the counter-revolution. It is **possible** indeed that even by placing itself on a footing of workers' democracy the revolution might have been overthrown; but what is **certain** is that it has perished, and that it has perished on account of the policy of its leaders. The repression of Kronstadt, the suppression of the democracy of workers and soviets by the Russian Communist party, the elimination of the proletariat from the management of industry, and the introduction of the NEP, already signified the death of the Revolution." ["*The Kronstadt Revolt*", pp. 330-7, **The Raven**, no, 8, p. 333 p. 335]

So it should be stressed that no anarchist would argue that if an anarchist path had been followed then success would have automatically followed. It is possible that the revolution would have failed but one thing is sure: by following the Bolshevik path it **did** fail. While the Bolsheviks may have remained in power at the end of the civil war, the regime was a party dictatorship presiding over a state capitalist economy. In such circumstances, there could no further development towards socialism and, unsurprisingly, there was none. Ultimately, as the rise of Stalin showed, the notion that socialism could be constructed without basic working class freedom and self-government was a baseless illusion.

As we will show, the notion that objective circumstances (civil war, economic collapse, and so on) cannot fully explain the failure of the Russian Revolution. This becomes clear once the awkward fact that Bolshevik authoritarianism and state capitalist policies started before the outbreak of civil war is recognised (see section H.6.1); that their ideology inspired and shaped the policies they implemented and these policies themselves made the objective circumstances worse (see section H.6.2); and that the Bolsheviks had to repress working class protest and strikes against them throughout the civil war, so suggesting a social base existed for a genuinely socialist approach (see section H.6.3).

Finally, there is a counter-example which, anarchists argue, shows the impact of Bolshevik ideology on the fate of the revolution. This is the anarchist influenced Makhnovist movement (see Peter Arshinov's **The History of the Makhnovist Movement** or Alexandre Skirda's **Nestor Makhno Anarchy's Cossack** for more details). Defending the revolution in the Ukraine against all groups aiming to impose their will on the masses, the Makhnovists were operating in the same objective conditions facing the Bolsheviks - civil war, economic disruption, isolation and so forth. However, the policies the Makhnovists implemented were radically different than those of the Bolsheviks. While the Makhnovists called soviet congresses, the Bolsheviks disbanded them. The former encouraged

free speech and organisation, the latter crushed both. While the Bolsheviks raised party dictatorship and one-man management to ideological truisms, the Makhnovists stood for and implemented workplace, army, village and soviet self-management. As one historian suggests, far from being necessary or even functional, Bolshevik policies "*might even have made the war more difficult and more costly. If the counter-example of Makhno is anything to go by then [they] certainly did.*" [Christopher Read, **From Tsar to Soviets**, p. 265] Anarchists argue that it shows the failure of Bolshevism cannot be put down to purely objective factors like the civil war: the politics of Leninism played their part.

H.6.1 Can objective factors explain the failure of the Russian Revolution?

Leninist John Rees recounts the standard argument, namely that the objective conditions in Russia meant that the "*subjective factor*" of Bolshevik ideology "*was reduced to a choice between capitulation to the Whites or defending the revolution with whatever means were at hands. Within these limits Bolshevik policy was decisive. But it could not wish away the limits and start with a clean sheet.*" From this perspective, the key factor was the "*vice-like pressure of the civil war*" which "*transformed the state*" as well as the "*Bolshevik Party itself.*" Industry was "*reduced ... to rubble*" and the "*bureaucracy of the workers' state was left suspended in mid-air, its class based eroded and demoralised.*" ["*In Defence of October,*" pp. 3-82, **International Socialism**, no. 52, p. 30, p. 70, p. 66 and p. 65] Due to these factors, argue Leninists, the Bolsheviks became dictators **over** the working class and **not** due to their political ideas. Anarchists are not convinced by this analysis, arguing that is factually and logically flawed.

The first problem is factual. Bolshevik authoritarianism started **before** the start of the civil war and major economic collapse. Whether it is soviet democracy, workers' economic self-management, democracy in the armed forces or working class power and freedom generally, the fact is the Bolsheviks had systematically attacked and undermined it from the start. They also, as we indicate in section H.6.3 repressed working class protests and strikes along with opposition groups and parties. As such, it is difficult to blame something which had not started yet for causing Bolshevik policies.

Although the Bolsheviks had seized power under the slogan "*All Power to the Soviets,*" as we noted in section H.3.11 the facts are the Bolsheviks aimed for party power and only supported soviets as long as they controlled them. To maintain party power, they had to undermine the soviets and they did. This onslaught on the soviets started quickly, in fact overnight when the first act of the Bolsheviks was to create an executive body, the Council of People's Commissars (or Sovnarkon), over and above the soviets. This was in direct contradiction to Lenin's **The State and Revolution**, where he had used the example of the Paris Commune to argue for the merging of executive and legislative powers. Then, a mere four days after this seizure of power by the Bolsheviks, the Sovnarkom unilaterally took for itself legislative power simply by issuing a decree to this effect: *"This was, effectively, a Bolshevik coup d'état that made clear the government's (and party's) pre-eminence over the soviets and their executive organ. Increasingly, the Bolsheviks relied upon the appointment from above of commissars with plenipotentiary powers, and they split up and reconstituted fractious Soviets and intimidated political opponents."* [Neil Harding, **Leninism**, p. 253] The highest organ of soviet power, the Central Executive Committee (VTsIK) was turned into little more than a rubber stamp, with its Bolshevik dominated presidium using its power to control the body. Under the Bolsheviks, the presidium was converted *"into the **de facto** centre of power within VTsIK."* It *"began to award representations to groups and factions which supported the government. With the VTsIK becoming ever more unwieldy in size by the day, the presidium began to expand its activities"* and was used *"to circumvent general meetings."* Thus the Bolsheviks were able *"to increase the power of the presidium, postpone regular sessions, and present VTsIK with policies which had already been implemented by the Sovnarkon. Even in the presidium itself very few people determined policy."* [Charles Duval, *"Yakov M. Sverdlov and the All-Russian Central Executive Committee of Soviets (VTsIK)"*, pp. 3-22, **Soviet Studies**, vol. XXXI, no. 1, p.7, p. 8 and p. 18]

At the grassroots, a similar process was at work with oligarchic tendencies in the soviets increasing post-October and *"[e]ffective power in the local soviets relentlessly gravitated to the executive committees, and especially their presidia. Plenary sessions became increasingly symbolic and ineffectual."* The party was *"successful in gaining control of soviet executives in the cities and at **uezd** [district] and **guberniya** [province] levels. These executive bodies were usually able to control soviet congresses, though the party often disbanded congresses that opposed major aspects of current policies."* Local soviets *"had little input into the formation of national policy"* and *"[e]ven at higher levels, institutional power shifted away from the soviets."* [Carmen Sirianni, **Workers' Control and Socialist Democracy**, p. 204 and p. 203] In Moscow, for example, power in the soviet *"moved away from the plenum to ever smaller groups at the apex."* The presidium, created in November 1917, *"rapidly accrued massive powers."* [Richard Sakwa, **Soviet Communists in Power**, p. 166]

The Bolshevik dominated soviet executives used this power to maintain a Bolshevik majority, by any means possible, in the face of popular disillusionment with their regime. While the influence of the Mensheviks *"had sunk to insignificance by October 1917"*, the *"unpopularity of government policy"* changed that and by the *"middle of 1918 the Mensheviks could claim with some justification that large numbers of the industrial working class were now behind them, and that but for the systematic dispersal and packing of the soviets, and the mass arrests at workers' meeting and congresses, their party could have won power by its policy of constitutional opposition."* The soviet elections in the spring of 1918 across Russia saw *"arrests, military dispersal, even shootings"* whenever Mensheviks *"succeeded in winning majorities or a substantial representation."* [Leonard Schapiro, **The Origin of the Communist Autocracy**, p. 191]

One such technique to maintain power was to postpone new soviet elections, another was to gerrymander the soviets to ensure their majority. The Bolsheviks in Petrograd, for example, faced *"demands from below for the immediate re-election"* of the Soviet. However, before the election, the Bolshevik Soviet confirmed new regulations *"to help offset possible weaknesses"* in their *"electoral strength in factories."* The *"most significant change in the makeup of the new soviet was that numerically decisive representation was given to agencies in which the Bolsheviks had overwhelming strength, among them the Petrograd Trade Union Council, individual trade unions, factory committees in closed enterprises, district soviets, and district non-party workers' conferences."* This ensured that *"[o]nly 260 of roughly 700 deputies in the new soviet were to be elected in factories, which guaranteed a large Bolshevik majority in advance"* and so the Bolsheviks *"contrived a majority"* in the new Soviet long before gaining 127 of the 260 factory delegates. Then there is *"the nagging question of how many Bolshevik deputies from factories were elected instead of the opposition because of press restrictions, voter intimidation, vote fraud, or the short duration of the campaign."* The SR and Menshevik press, for example, were reopened *"only a couple of days before the start of voting."* Moreover, *"Factory Committees from closed factories could and did elect soviet deputies (the so-called dead souls), one deputy for each factory with more than one thousand workers at the time of shutdown"* while the electoral assemblies for unemployed workers *"were organised through Bolshevik-dominated trade union election commissions."* Overall, then, the Bolshevik election victory *"was highly suspect, even on the shop floor."* [Alexander Rabinowitch, **The Bolsheviks in Power**, pp. 248-9, p. 251 and p. 252] This meant that it was *"possible for one worker to be represented in the soviet five times ... without voting once."* Thus the soviet *"was no longer a popularly elected assembly: it had been turned into an assembly of Bolshevik functionaries."* [Vladimir N. Brovkin, **The Mensheviks After October**, p. 240]

When postponing and gerrymandering failed, the Bolsheviks turned to state repression to remain in power. For all the provincial soviet elections in the spring and summer of 1918 for which data is available, there was an *"impressive success of the Menshevik-SR block"* followed by *"the Bolshevik practice of disbanding soviets that came under Menshevik-SR control."* The *"subsequent wave of anti-Bolshevik uprisings"* were repressed by force. [Brovkin, **Op. Cit.**, p. 159] Another historian also notes that by the spring of 1918 *"Menshevik newspapers and activists in the trade unions, the Soviets, and the factories had made a considerable impact on a working class which was becoming increasingly disillusioned with the Bolshevik regime, so much so that in many places the Bolsheviks felt constrained to dissolve Soviets or prevent re-elections where Mensheviks and Socialist Revolutionaries had gained majorities."* [Israel Getzler, **Martov**, p. 179]

When the opposition parties raised such issues at the VTsIK, it had no impact. In April 1918, one deputy *"protested that non-Bolshevik controlled soviets were being dispersed by armed force, and wanted to discuss the issue."* The chairman *"refus[ed] to include it in the agenda because of lack of supporting material"* and requested such information be submitted to the presidium of the soviet. The majority (i.e. the Bolsheviks) *"supported their chairman"* and the facts were *"submitted ... to the presidium, where they apparently remained."* [Charles Duval, **Op. Cit.**, pp. 13-14] Given that the

VTsIK was meant to be the highest soviet body between congresses, this lack of concern clearly shows the Bolshevik contempt for soviet democracy.

The Bolsheviks also organised rural poor committees, opposed to by all other parties (particularly the Left-SRs). The Bolshevik leadership *"was well aware that the **labouring peasantry**, largely represented in the countryside by the Left Socialist-Revolutionary party, would be excluded from participation."* These committees were *"subordinated to central policy and thus willing to implement a policy opposing the interests of the mass of the peasants"* and were also used for the *"disbandment of the peasants' soviets in which Bolshevik representation was low or nil"*. It should be noted that between March and August 1918 *"the Bolsheviks were losing power not only in favour of the Left Socialist-Revolutionaries"* but also *"in favour of non-party people."* [Silvana Malle, **The Economic Organisation of War Communism, 1918-1921**, pp. 366-7]

Unsurprisingly, the same contempt was expressed at the fifth All-Russian Soviet Congress in July 1918 when the Bolsheviks gerrymandered it to maintain their majority. They banned the Mensheviks in the context of political losses **before** the Civil War, which gave the Bolsheviks an excuse and they *"drove them underground, just on the eve of the elections to the Fifth Congress of Soviets in which the Mensheviks were expected to make significant gains"*. While the Bolsheviks *"offered some formidable fictions to justify the expulsions"* there was *"of course no substance in the charge that the Mensheviks had been mixed in counter-revolutionary activities on the Don, in the Urals, in Siberia, with the Czechoslovaks, or that they had joined the worst Black Hundreds."* [Getzler, **Op. Cit.**, p. 181]

With the Mensheviks and Right-SRs banned from the soviets, popular disenchantment with Bolshevik rule was expressed by voting Left-SR. The Bolsheviks ensured their majority in the congress and, therefore, a Bolshevik government by gerrymandering it as they had the Petrograd soviet. Thus *"electoral fraud gave the Bolsheviks a huge majority of congress delegates"*. In reality, *"the number of legitimately elected Left SR delegates was roughly equal to that of the Bolsheviks."* The Left-SRs expected a majority but did not include *"roughly 399 Bolsheviks delegates whose right to be seated was challenged by the Left SR minority in the congress's credentials commission."* Without these dubious delegates, the Left SRs and SR Maximalists would have outnumbered the Bolsheviks by around 30 delegates. This ensured *"the Bolshevik's successful fabrication of a large majority in the Fifth All-Russian Congress of Soviets."* [Rabinowitch, **Op. Cit.**, p. 396, p. 288, p. 442 and p. 308] Moreover, the Bolsheviks also *"allowed so-called committees of poor peasants to be represented at the congress... This blatant gerrymandering ensured a Bolshevik majority ... Deprived of their democratic majority the Left SRs resorted to terror and assassinated the German ambassador Mirbach."* [Geoffrey Swain, **The Origins of the Russian Civil War**, p. 176] The Bolsheviks falsely labelled this an uprising against the soviets and the Left-SRs joined the Mensheviks and Right-SRs in being made illegal. It is hard not to agree with Rabinowitch when he comments that *"however understandable framed against the fraudulent composition of the Fifth All-Russian Congress of Soviets and the ominous developments at the congresses's start"* this act *"offered Lenin a better excuse*

than he could possibly have hoped for to eliminate the Left SRs as a significant political rival." [**Op. Cit.**, p. 308]

So before the start of the civil war all opposition groups, bar the Left-SRs, had suffered some form of state repression by the hands of the Bolshevik regime (the Bolsheviks had attacked the anarchist movement in April, 1918 [Paul Avrich, **The Russian Anarchists**, pp. 184-5]). Within six weeks of it starting **every** opposition group had been excluded from the soviets. Significantly, in spite of being, effectively, a one-party state Lenin later proclaimed that soviet power *"is a million times more democratic than the most democratic bourgeois republic"* and pointed to the 6th Congress of Soviets in November with its 97% of Bolsheviks! [**Collected Works**, vol. 28, p. 248 and p. 303]

A similar authoritarian agenda was aimed at the armed forces and industry. Trotsky simply abolished the soldier's committees and elected officers, stating that *"the principle of election is politically purposeless and technically inexpedient, and it has been, in practice, abolished by decree."* [**How the Revolution Armed**, vol. 1, p. 47] The death penalty for disobedience was restored, along with, more gradually, saluting, special forms of address, separate living quarters and other privileges for officers. Somewhat ironically, nearly 20 years later, Trotsky himself lamented how the *"demobilisation of the Red Army of five million played no small role in the formation of the bureaucracy. The victorious commanders assumed leading posts in the local Soviets, in economy, in education, and they persistently introduced everywhere that regime which had ensured success in the civil war."* For some reason he failed to mention who had introduced that very regime, although he felt able to state, without shame, that the *"commanding staff needs democratic control. The organisers of the Red Army were aware of this from the beginning, and considered it necessary to prepare for such a measure as the election of commanding staff."* [**The Revolution Betrayed**, p. 90 and p. 211] So it would be churlish to note that *"the root of the problem lay in the very organisation of the army on traditional lines, for which Trotsky himself had been responsible, and against which the Left Communists in 1918 had warned."* [Richard Sakwa, **Soviet Communists in Power**, p. 231]

In industry, Lenin, as we discussed in section H.3.14, started to champion one-man management armed with *"dictatorial"* powers in April, 1918. Significantly, he argued that his new policies were **not** driven by the civil war for *"[i]n the main ... the task of suppressing the resistance of the exploiters was fulfilled"* (since *"(approximately) February 1918."*). The task *"now coming to the fore"* was that of *"organising [the] **administration** of Russia."* It *"has become the main and central task"* precisely **because** of *"the peace which has been achieved - despite its extremely onerous character and extreme instability"* and so *"the Russian Soviet Republic has gained an opportunity to concentrate its efforts for a while on the most important and most difficult aspect of the socialist revolution, namely, the task of organisation."* This would involve imposing one-man management, that is *"individual executives"* with *"dictatorial powers (or 'unlimited' powers)"* as there was *"absolutely no contradiction in principle between Soviet (**that is**, socialist) democracy and the exercise of dictatorial powers by individuals."* [**Op. Cit.**, vol. 27, p. 242, p. 237, p. 267 and p. 268]

Trotsky concurred, arguing in the same speech which announced the destruction of military democracy that workplace democracy *"is not the last word in the economic constructive work of the proletariat"*. The *"next step must consist in self-limitation of the collegiate principle"* and its replacement by *"[p]olitical collegiate control by the Soviets"*, i.e. the state control Lenin had repeatedly advocated in 1917. However *"for executive functions we must appoint technical specialists."* He ironically called this the working class *"throwing off the one-man management principles of its masters of yesterday"* and failed to recognise it was imposing the one-man management principles of new masters. As with Lenin, the destruction of workers' power at the point of production was of little concern for what mattered was that *"with power in our hands, we, the representatives of the working class"* would introduce socialism. [**How the Revolution Armed**, vol. 1, p. 37 and p. 38]

In reality, the Bolshevik vision of socialism simply replaced private capitalism with state capitalism, taking control of the economy out of the hands of the workers and placing it into the hands of the state bureaucracy. As one historian correctly summarises the so-called workers' state *"oversaw the reimposition of alienated labour and hierarchical social relations. It carried out this function in the absence of a ruling class, and then played a central role in ushering that class into existence - a class which subsequently ruled not through its ownership of private property but through its 'ownership' of the state. That state was antagonistic to the forces that could have best resisted the retreat of the revolution, i.e. the working class."* [Simon Pirani, **The Russian Revolution in Retreat, 1920-24**, p. 240]

Whether it is in regards to soviet, workplace or army democracy or the rights of the opposition to organise freely and gather support, the facts are the Bolsheviks had systematically eliminated them **before** the start of the civil war. So when Trotsky asserted that *"[i]n the beginning, the party had wished and hoped to preserve freedom of political struggle within the framework of the Soviets"* but that it was civil war which *"introduced stern amendments into this calculation,"* he was rewriting history. Rather than being *"regarded not as a principle, but as an episodic act of self-defence"* the opposite is the case. As we note in section H.3.8 from roughly October 1918 onwards, the Bolsheviks **did** raise party dictatorship to a *"principle"* and did not care that this was *"obviously in conflict with the spirit of Soviet democracy."* Trotsky was right to state that *"on all sides the masses were pushed away gradually from actual participation in the leadership of the country."* [**The Revolution Betrayed**, p. 96 and p. 90] He was just utterly wrong to imply that this process happened **after** the end of the civil war rather than before its start and that the Bolsheviks did not play a key role in so doing. Thus, *"in the soviets and in economic management the embryo of centralised and bureaucratic state forms had already emerged by mid-1918."* [Sakwa, **Op. Cit.**, pp. 96-7]

It may be argued in objection to this analysis that the Bolsheviks faced resistance from the start and, consequently, civil war existed from the moment Lenin seized power and to focus attention on the events of late May 1918 gives a misleading picture of the pressures they were facing. After all, the Bolsheviks had the threat of German Imperialism and there were a few (small) White Armies in existence as well as conspiracies to combat. However, this is unconvincing as Lenin himself pointed to the ease of Bolshevik success post-

October. On March 14th, 1918, Lenin had proclaimed that *"the civil war was one continuous triumph for Soviet power"* and in June argued that *"the Russian bourgeoisie was defeated in open conflict … in the period from October 1917 to February and March 1918"*. [**Collected Works**, vol. 27, p. 174 and p. 428] It can be concluded that the period up until March 1918 was not considered by the Bolsheviks themselves as being so bad as requiring the adjustment of their politics. This explains why, as one historian notes, that the *"revolt of the Czechoslovak Legion on 25 May 1918 is often considered to be the beginning of full-scale military activity. There followed a succession of campaigns."* This is reflected in Bolshevik policy as well, with war communism *"lasting from about mid-1918 to March 1921."* [Sakwa, **Op. Cit.**, p. 22 and p. 19]

Significantly, the introduction of one-man management was seen not as an emergency measure forced upon the Bolsheviks by dire circumstances of civil war but rather as a natural aspect of building socialism itself. In March, 1918, for example, Lenin argued that civil war *"became a fact"* on October, 25, 1917 and *"[i]n this civil war … victory was achieved with … extraordinary ease … The Russian revolution was a continuous triumphal march in the first months."* [**Op. Cit.**, pp. 88-9] Looking back at this time from April 1920, Lenin reiterated his position (*"Dictatorial powers and one-man management are not contradictory to socialist democracy."*) while also stressing that this was not forced upon the Bolsheviks by civil war. Discussing how, again, the civil war was ended and it was time to build socialism he argued that the *"whole attention of the Communist Party and the Soviet government is centred on peaceful economic development, on problems of the dictatorship and of one-man management … When we tackled them for the first time in 1918, there was no civil war and no experience to speak of."* So it was *"not only experience"* of civil war, argued Lenin *"but something more profound … that has induced us now, as it did two years ago, to concentrate all our attention on labour discipline."* [**Op. Cit.**, vol. 30, p. 503 and p. 504] Trotsky also argued that Bolshevik policy was not conditioned by the civil war (see section H.3.14).

As historian Jonathan Aves notes, *"the Communist Party took victory as a sign of the correctness of its ideological approach and set about the task of economic construction on the basis of an intensification of War Communism policies."* [**Workers Against Lenin**, p. 37] In addition, this perspective flowed, as we argue in the next section, from the Bolshevik ideology, from its vision of socialism, rather than some alien system imposed upon an otherwise healthy set of ideas.

Then there is the logical problem. Leninists say that they are revolutionaries. As we noted in section H.2.1, they inaccurately mock anarchists for not believing that a revolution needs to defend itself. Yet, ironically, their whole defence of Bolshevism rests on the *"exceptional circumstances"* produced by the civil war they claim is inevitable. If Leninism cannot handle the problems associated with actually conducting a revolution then, surely, it should be avoided at all costs. This is particularly the case as leading Bolsheviks all argued that the specific problems their latter day followers blame for their authoritarianism were natural results of any revolution and, consequently, unavoidable. Lenin, for example, in 1917 mocked those who opposed revolution because *"the situation is exceptionally complicated."* He noted *"the development of the revolution itself always* creates an **exceptionally** complicated situation" and that it was an *"incredibly complicated and painful process."* In fact, it was *"the most intense, furious, desperate class war and civil war. Not a single great revolution in history has taken place without civil war. And only a 'man in a muffler' can think that civil war is conceivable without an 'exceptionally complicated situation.'" "If the situation were not exceptionally complicated there would be no revolution."* [**Op. Cit.**, vol. 26, pp. 118-9]

He reiterated this in 1918, arguing that *"every great revolution, and a socialist revolution in particular, even if there is no external war, is inconceivable without internal war, i.e., civil war, which is even more devastating than external war, and involves thousands and millions of cases of wavering and desertion from one side to another, implies a state of extreme indefiniteness, lack of equilibrium and chaos."* [**Op. Cit.**, vol. 27, p. 264] He even argued that revolution in an advanced capitalist nations would be far more devastating and ruinous than in Russia. [**Op. Cit.**, vol. 28, p. 298]

Therefore, Lenin stressed, *"it will never be possible to build socialism at a time when everything is running smoothly and tranquilly; it will never be possible to realise socialism without the landowners and capitalists putting up a furious resistance."* Those *"who believe that socialism can be built at a time of peace and tranquillity are profoundly mistaken: it will be everywhere built at a time of disruption, at a time of famine. That is how it must be."* Moreover, *"not one of the great revolutions of history has taken place"* without civil war and *"without which not a single serious Marxist has conceived the transition from capitalism to socialism."* Obviously, *"there can be no civil war - the inevitable condition and concomitant of socialist revolution - without disruption."* [**Op. Cit.**, vol. 27, p. 520, p. 517, p. 496 and p. 497]

Moreover, anarchists had long argued that a revolution would be associated with economic disruption, isolation and civil war and, consequently, had developed their ideas to take these into account. For example, Kropotkin was *"certain that the coming Revolution ... will burst upon us in the middle of a great industrial crisis ... There are millions of unemployed workers in Europe at this moment. It will be worse when Revolution has burst upon us ... The number of the out-of-works will be doubled as soon as barricades are erected in Europe and the United States ... we know that in time of Revolution exchange and industry suffer most from the general upheaval ... A Revolution in Europe means, then, the unavoidable stoppage of at least half the factories and workshops."* The *"smallest attack upon property will bring in its train the complete disorganisation"* of the capitalist economy. This meant that society *"itself will be forced to take production in hand ... and to reorganise it to meet the needs of the whole people."* [**The Conquest of Bread**, pp. 69-70] This prediction was a common feature of Kropotkin's politics (as can be seen from, say, his *"The First Work of the Revolution"* [**Act for Yourselves**, pp. 56-60]).

Revolutionary anarchism, then, is based on a clear understanding of the nature of a social revolution, the objective problems it will face and the need for mass participation and free initiative to solve them. So it must, therefore, be stressed that the very *"objective factors"* supporters of Bolshevism use to justify the actions of Lenin and Trotsky were predicted correctly by anarchists decades beforehand and integrated into our politics. Moreover, anarchists had

developed their ideas on social revolution to make sure that these inevitable disruptions would be minimised. By stressing the need for self-management, mass participation, self-organisation and free federation, anarchism showed how a free people could deal with the difficult problems they would face (as we discuss in the section H.6.2 there is substantial evidence to show that Bolshevik ideology and practice made the problems facing the Russian revolution much worse than they had to be).

It should also be noted that every revolution has confirmed the anarchist analysis. For example, the German Revolution after 1918 faced an economic collapse which was, relatively, just as bad as that facing Russia the year before. The near revolution produced extensive political conflict, including civil war, which was matched by economic turmoil. Taking 1928 as the base year, the index of industrial production in Germany was slightly lower in 1913, namely 98 in 1913 to 100 in 1928. In 1917, the index was 63 and by 1918, it was 61 (i.e. industrial production had dropped by nearly 40%). In 1919, it fell again to 37, rising to 54 in 1920 and 65 in 1921. Thus, in 1919, the *"industrial production reached an all-time low"* and it *"took until the late 1920s for [food] production to recover its 1912 level."* [V. R. Berghahn, **Modern Germany**, p. 258, pp. 67-8 and p. 71] In Russia, the index for large scale industry fell to 77 in 1917 from 100 in 1913, falling again to 35 in 1918, 26 in 1919 and 18 in 1920. [Tony Cliff, **Lenin**, vol. 3, p. 86]

Strangely, Leninists do not doubt that the spread of the Russian Revolution to Germany would have allowed the Bolsheviks more leeway to avoid authoritarianism and so save the Revolution. Yet this does not seem likely given the state of the German economy. Comparing the two countries, there is a similar picture of economic collapse. In the year the revolution started, production had fallen by 23% in Russia (from 1913 to 1917) and by 43% in Germany (from 1913 to 1918). Once revolution had effectively started, production fell even more. In Russia, it fell to 65% of its pre-war level in 1918, in Germany it fell to 62% of its pre-war level in 1919. However, no Leninist argues that the German Revolution was impossible or doomed to failure. Similarly, no Leninist denies that a socialist revolution was possible during the depths of the Great Depression of the 1930s or to post-world war two Europe, marked as it was by economic collapse. This was the case in 1917 as well, when economic crisis had been a fact of Russian life throughout the year. This did not stop the Bolsheviks calling for revolution and seizing power. Nor did this crisis stop the creation of democratic working class organisations, such as soviets, trade unions and factory committees being formed nor did it stop mass collective action. It appears, therefore, that while the economic crisis of 1917 did not stop the development of socialist tendencies to combat it, the seizure of power by a socialist party did.

To conclude, it seems hypocritical in the extreme for Leninists to blame difficult circumstances for the failure of the Russian Revolution. As Lenin himself argued, the Bolsheviks *"never said that the transition from capitalism to socialism would be easy. It will invoke a whole period of violent civil war, it will involve painful measures."* They knew *"that the transition from capitalism to socialism is a struggle of an extremely difficult kind"* and so *"[i]f there ever existed a revolutionary who hoped that we could pass to the socialist system without difficulties, such a revolutionary, such a* socialist, would not be worth a brass farthing." [**Op. Cit.**, p. 431, p. 433 and pp. 432-3] He would have been surprised to discover that many of his own followers would be *"such a socialist"*!

Consequently, it is not hard to conclude that for Leninists difficult objective circumstances place socialism off the agenda only when they are holding power. So even if we ignore the extensive evidence that Bolshevik authoritarianism started before the civil war, the logic of the Leninist argument is hardly convincing. Yet it does have advantages, for by focusing attention on the civil war, Leninists also draw attention away from Bolshevik ideology and tactics. As Peter Kropotkin recounted to Emma Goldman this simply cannot be done:

> *"the Communists are a political party firmly adhering to the idea of a centralised State, and that as such they were bound to misdirect the course of the Revolution … [Their policies] have paralysed the energies of the masses and have terrorised the people. Yet without the direct participation of the masses in the reconstruction of the country, nothing essential could be accomplished … They created a bureaucracy and officialdom … [which were] parasites on the social body … It was not the fault of any particular individual: rather it was the State they had created, which discredits every revolutionary ideal, stifles all initiative, and sets a premium on incompetence and waste … Intervention and blockade were bleeding Russia to death, and were preventing the people from understanding the real nature of the Bolshevik regime."*
> [**My Disillusionment in Russia**, p. 99]

Obviously, if the "objective" factors do not explain Bolshevik authoritarianism and the failure of the revolution we are left with the question of which aspects of Bolshevik ideology impacted negatively on the revolution. As Kropotkin's comments indicate, anarchists have good reason to argue that one of the greatest myths of state socialism is the idea that Bolshevik ideology played no role in the fate of the Russian Revolution. We turn to this in the next section.

H.6.2 Did Bolshevik ideology influence the outcome of the Russian Revolution?

As we discussed in the last section, anarchists reject the Leninist argument that the failure of Bolshevism in the Russian Revolution can be blamed purely on the difficult objective circumstances they faced. As Noam Chomsky summarises:

> *"In the stages leading up to the Bolshevik coup in October 1917, there **were** incipient socialist institutions developing in Russia - workers' councils, collectives, things like that. And they survived to an extent once the Bolsheviks took over - but not for very long; Lenin and Trotsky pretty much eliminated them as they consolidated their power. I mean, you can argue about the **justification** for eliminating them, but the fact is that the socialist initiatives were pretty quickly eliminated.*

> *"Now, people who want to justify it say, 'The Bolsheviks had to do it' - that's the standard justification: Lenin and Trotsky had to do it, because of the contingencies of the civil war, for survival, there wouldn't have been food otherwise, this and that. Well, obviously the question is, was that true. To answer that, you've got to look at the historical facts: I don't think it was true. In fact, I think the incipient socialist structures in Russia were dismantled **before** the really dire conditions arose … But reading their own writings, my feeling is that Lenin and Trotsky knew what they were doing, it was conscious and understandable."* [**Understanding Power**, p. 226]

Chomsky is right on both counts. The attack on the basic building blocks of genuine socialism started before the civil war. Moreover, it did not happen by accident. The attacks were rooted in the Bolshevik vision of socialism. As Maurice Brinton concluded:

> *"there is a clear-cut and incontrovertible link between what happened under Lenin and Trotsky and the later practices of Stalinism … The more one unearths about this period the more difficult it becomes to define - or even to see - the 'gulf' allegedly separating what happened in Lenin's time from what happened later. Real knowledge of the facts also makes it impossible to accept … that the whole course of events was 'historically inevitable' and 'objectively determined'. Bolshevik ideology and practice were themselves important and sometimes decisive factors in the equation, at every critical stage of this critical period."* [**The Bolsheviks and Workers' Control**, p. 84]

This is not to suggest that the circumstances played no role in the development of the revolution. It is simply to indicate that Bolshevik ideology played its part as well by not only shaping the policies implemented but also how the results of those policies themselves contributed to the circumstances being faced. This is to be expected, given that the Bolsheviks were the ruling party and, consequently, state power was utilised to implement their policies, policies which, in turn, were influenced by their ideological preferences and prejudices. Ultimately, to maintain (as Leninists do) that the ideology of the ruling party played no (or, at best, a minor) part hardly makes sense logically nor, equally importantly, can it be supported once even a basic awareness of the development of the Russian Revolution is known.

A key issue is the Bolsheviks support for centralisation. Long before the revolution, Lenin had argued that within the party it was a case of *"the transformation of the power of ideas into the power of authority, the subordination of lower Party bodies to higher ones."* [**Collected Works**, vol. 7, p. 367] Such visions of centralised organisation were the model for the revolutionary state and, once in power, they did not disappoint. Thus, *"for the leadership, the principle of maximum centralisation of authority served more than expedience. It consistently resurfaced as the image of a peacetime political system as well."* [Thomas F. Remington, **Building Socialism in Bolshevik Russia**, p. 91]

However, by its very nature centralism places power into a few hands and effectively eliminates the popular participation required for any successful revolution to develop. The power placed into the hands of the Bolshevik government was automatically no longer in the hands of the working class. So when Leninists argue that "objective" circumstances forced the Bolsheviks to substitute their power for that of the masses, anarchists reply that this substitution had occurred the moment the Bolsheviks centralised power and placed it into their own hands. As a result, popular participation and institutions began to wither and die. Moreover, once in power, the Bolsheviks were shaped by their new position and the social relationships it created and, consequently, implemented policies influenced and constrained by the hierarchical and centralised structures they had created.

This was not the only negative impact of Bolshevik centralism. It also spawned a bureaucracy. As we noted in section H.1.7, the rise of a state bureaucracy started immediately with the seizure of power. Thus "red tape and vast administrative offices typified Soviet reality" as the Bolsheviks "rapidly created their own [state] apparatus to wage the political and economic offensive against the bourgeoisie and capitalism. As the functions of the state expanded, so did the bureaucracy" and so "following the revolution the process of institutional proliferation reached unprecedented heights ... a mass of economic organisations [were] created or expanded." [Richard Sakwa, **Soviet Communists in Power**, p. 190 and p. 191] This was a striking confirmation of the anarchist analysis which argued that a new bureaucratic class develops around any centralised body. This body would soon become riddled with personal influences and favours, so ensuring that members could be sheltered from popular control while, at the same time, exploiting its power to feather their own nest. Over time, this permanent collection of bodies would become the real power in the state, with the party members nominally in charge really under the control of an unelected and uncontrolled officialdom. This was recognised by Lenin in 1922:

> "If we take Moscow with its 4,700 Communists in responsible positions, and if we take that huge bureaucratic machine, that gigantic heap, we must ask: who is directing whom? I doubt very much whether it can truthfully be said that the Communists are directing that heap. To tell the truth, they are not directing, they are being directed." [**The Lenin Anthology**, p. 527]

By the end of 1920, there were five times more state officials than industrial workers (5,880,000 were members of the state bureaucracy). However, the bureaucracy had existed since the start. In Moscow, in August 1918, state officials represented 30 per cent of the workforce there and by 1920 the general number of office workers "still represented about a third of those employed in the city" (200,000 in November, 1920, rising to 228,000 in July, 1921 and, by October 1922, to 243,000). [Sakwa, **Op. Cit.**, pp. 191-3] And with bureaucracy came the abuse of it simply because it held **real** power:

> "The prevalence of bureaucracy, of committees and commissions ... permitted, and indeed encouraged, endless permutations of corrupt practices. These raged from the style of living of communist functionaries to

> bribe-taking by officials. With the power of allocation of scare resources, such as housing, there was an inordinate potential for corruption." [**Op. Cit.**, p. 193]

The growth in **power** of the bureaucracy should not, therefore, come as a major surprise given that it had existed from the start in sizeable numbers. Yet, for the Bolsheviks "the development of a bureaucracy" was a puzzle, "whose emergence and properties mystified them." It should be noted that, "[f]or the Bolsheviks, bureaucratism signified the escape of this bureaucracy from the will of the party as it took on a life of its own." [**Op. Cit.**, p. 182 and p. 190] This was the key. They did not object to the usurpation of power by the party (indeed they placed party dictatorship at the core of their politics and universalised it to a general principle for **all** "socialist" revolutions). Nor did they object to the centralisation of power and activity (and so the bureaucratisation of life). As such, the Bolsheviks failed to understand how their own politics helped the rise of this new ruling class. They failed to understand the links between centralism and bureaucracy. Bolshevik nationalisation and centralism (as well as being extremely inefficient) also ensured that the control of society, economic activity and its product would be in the hands of the state and, so, class society would continue. Unsurprisingly, complaints by working class people about the privileges enjoyed by Communist Party and state officials were widespread.

Another problem was the Bolshevik vision of (centralised) democracy. Trotsky is typical. In April 1918 he argued that once elected the government was to be given total power to make decisions and appoint people as required as it is "better able to judge in the matter than" the masses. The sovereign people were expected to simply obey their public servants until such time as they "dismiss that government and appoint another." Trotsky raised the question of whether it was possible for the government to act "against the interests of the labouring and peasant masses?" And answered no! Yet it is obvious that Trotsky's claim that "there can be no antagonism between the government and the mass of the workers, just as there is no antagonism between the administration of the union and the general assembly of its members" is just nonsense. [**Leon Trotsky Speaks**, p. 113] The history of trade unionism is full of examples of committees betraying their membership. Needless to say, the subsequent history of Lenin's government shows that there can be "antagonism" between rulers and ruled and that appointments are always a key way to further elite interests.

This vision of top-down "democracy" can, of course, be traced back to Marx (section H.3.2) and Lenin (section H.3.3). By equating centralised, top-down decision making by an elected government with "democracy," the Bolsheviks had the ideological justification to eliminate the functional democracy associated with the soviets, factory committees and soldiers committees. The Bolshevik vision of democracy became the means by which real democracy was eliminated in area after area of Russian working class life. Needless to say, a state which eliminates functional democracy in the grassroots will not stay democratic in any meaningful sense for long.

Nor does it come as too great a surprise to discover that a government which considers itself as "better able to judge" things than the people finally decides to annul any election results it dislikes. As we discussed in section H.5, this perspective is at the heart of vanguardism, for in Bolshevik ideology the party, not the class, is in the final analysis the repository of class consciousness. This means that once in power it has a built-in tendency to override the decisions of the masses it claimed to represent and justify this in terms of the advanced position of the party (as historian Richard Sakwa notes a *"lack of identification with the Bolshevik party was treated as the absence of political consciousness altogether"* [**Op. Cit.**, p. 94]). Combine this with a vision of "democracy" which is highly centralised and which undermines local participation then we have the necessary foundations for the turning of party power into party dictatorship.

Which brings us to the next issue, namely the Bolshevik idea that the party should seize power, not the working class as a whole, equating party power with popular power. The question instantly arises of what happens if the masses turn against the party? The gerrymandering, disbanding and marginalisation of the soviets in the spring and summer of 1918 answers that question (see last section). It is not a great step to party dictatorship **over** the proletariat from the premises of Bolshevism. In a clash between soviet democracy and party power, the Bolsheviks consistently favoured the latter - as would be expected given their ideology.

This can be seen from the Bolsheviks' negative response to the soviets of 1905. At one stage the Bolsheviks demanded the St. Petersburg soviet accept the Bolshevik political programme and then disband. The rationale for these attacks is significant. The St. Petersburg Bolsheviks were convinced that *"only a strong party along class lines can guide the proletarian political movement and preserve the integrity of its program, rather than a political mixture of this kind, an indeterminate and vacillating political organisation such as the workers council represents and cannot help but represent."* [quoted by Anweiler, **The Soviets**, p. 77] In other words, the soviets could not reflect workers' interests because they were elected by the workers! The implications of this perspective became clear in 1918, as are its obvious roots in Lenin's arguments in **What is to be Done?**. As one historian argues, the 1905 position on the soviets *"is of particular significance in understanding the Bolshevik's mentality, political ambitions and modus operandi."* The Bolshevik campaign *"was repeated in a number of provincial soviets"* and *"reveals that from the outset the Bolsheviks were distrustful of, if not hostile towards the Soviets, to which they had at best an instrumental and always party-minded attitude."* The Bolsheviks actions showed an *"ultimate aim of controlling [the soviets] and turning them into one-party organisations, or, failing that, of destroying them."* [Israel Getzler, *"The Bolshevik Onslaught on the Non-Party 'Political Profile' of the Petersburg Soviet of Workers' Deputies October-November 1905"*, **Revolutionary History**, pp. 123-146, vol. 5, no. 2, pp. 124-5]

That the mainstream of Bolshevism expressed this perspective once in power goes without saying, but even dissident Communists expressed identical views. Left-Communist V. Sorin argued in 1918 that the *"party is in every case and everywhere superior to the soviets ... The soviets represent labouring democracy in general; and its interest, and in particular the interests of the petty bourgeois peasantry, do not always coincide with the interests of the proletariat."* [quoted by Sakwa, **Op. Cit.**, p. 182] As one

historian notes, *"[a]ccording to the Left Communists ... the party was the custodian of an interest higher than that of the soviets."* Unsurprisingly, in the party there was *"a general consensus over the principles of party dictatorship for the greater part of the [civil] war. But the way in which these principles were applied roused increasing opposition."* [Sakwa, **Op. Cit.**, p. 182 and p. 30] This consensus existed in all the so-called opposition (including the **Workers' Opposition** and Trotsky's **Left Opposition** in the 1920s). The ease with which the Bolsheviks embraced party dictatorship is suggestive of a fundamental flaw in their political perspective which the problems of the revolution, combined with loss of popular support, simply exposed.

Then there is the Bolshevik vision of socialism. As we discussed in section H.3.12, the Bolsheviks, like other Marxists at the time, saw the socialist economy as being built upon the centralised organisations created by capitalism. They confused state capitalism with socialism. The former, Lenin wrote in May 1917, *"is a complete **material** preparation for socialism, the threshold of socialism"* and so socialism *"is nothing but the next step forward from state capitalist monopoly."* It is *"merely state-capitalist monopoly **which is made to serve the interests of the whole people** and has to that extent **ceased** to be capitalist monopoly."* [**Collected Works**, vol. 25, p. 359 and p. 358] A few months later, he was talking about how the institutions of state capitalism could be taken over and used to create socialism. Unsurprisingly, when defending the need for state capitalism in the spring of 1918 against the "Left Communists," Lenin stressed that he gave his *"'high' appreciation of state capitalism ... **before** the Bolsheviks seized power."* And, as Lenin noted, his praise for state capitalism can be found in his **State and Revolution** and so it was *"significant that [his opponents] did **not** emphasise **this**"* aspect of his 1917 ideas. [**Op. Cit.**, vol. 27, p. 341 and p. 354] Unsurprisingly, modern-day Leninists do not emphasise that element of Lenin's ideas either.

Given this perspective, it is unsurprising that workers' control was not given a high priority once the Bolsheviks seized power. While in order to gain support the Bolsheviks **had** paid lip-service to the idea of workers' control, as we noted in section H.3.14 the party had always given that slogan a radically different interpretation than the factory committees had. While the factory committees had seen workers' control as being exercised directly by the workers and their class organisations, the Bolshevik leadership saw it in terms of state control in which the factory committees would play, at best, a minor role. Given who held actual power in the new regime, it is unsurprising to discover which vision was actually introduced:

> *"On three occasions in the first months of Soviet power, the [factory] committee leaders sought to bring their model into being. At each point the party leadership overruled them. The result was to vest both managerial **and** control powers in organs of the state which were subordinate to the central authorities, and formed by them."* [Thomas F. Remington, **Building Socialism in Bolshevik Russia**, p. 38]

Given his vision of socialism, Lenin's rejection of the factory committee's model comes as no surprise. As Lenin put it in 1920, the *"domination of the proletariat consists in the fact that the* landowners and capitalists have been deprived of their property ... The victorious proletariat has abolished property ... and therein lies its domination as a class. The prime thing is the question of property." [**Op. Cit.**, vol. 30, p. 456] As we proved in section H.3.13, the Bolsheviks had no notion that socialism required workers' self-management of production and, unsurprisingly, they, as Lenin had promised, built from the top-down their system of unified administration based on the Tsarist system of central bodies which governed and regulated certain industries during the war. The **Supreme Economic Council** (Vesenka) was set up in December of 1917, and "was widely acknowledged by the Bolsheviks as a move towards 'statisation' (ogosudarstvleniye) of economic authority." During the early months of 1918, the Bolsheviks began implementing their vision of "socialism" and the Vesenka began "to build, from the top, its 'unified administration' of particular industries. The pattern is informative" as it "gradually took over" the Tsarist state agencies such as the **Glakvi** (as Lenin had promised) "and converted them ... into administrative organs subject to [its] direction and control." The Bolsheviks "clearly opted" for the taking over of "the institutions of bourgeois economic power and use[d] them to their own ends." This system "necessarily implies the perpetuation of hierarchical relations within production itself, and therefore the perpetuation of class society." [Brinton, **Op. Cit.**, p. 22, p. 36 and p. 22] Thus the Supreme Council of the National Economy "was an expression of the principle of centralisation and control from above which was peculiar to the Marxist ideology." In fact, it is "likely that the arguments for centralisation in economic policy, which were prevalent among Marxists, determined the short life of the All-Russian Council of Workers' Control." [Silvana Malle, **The Economic Organisation of War Communism, 1918-1921**, p. 95 and p. 94]

Moreover, the Bolsheviks had systematically stopped the factory committees organising together, using their controlled unions to come "out firmly against the attempt of the Factory Committees to form a national organisation." The unions "prevented the convocation of a planned All-Russian Congress of Factory Committees. [I. Deutscher, quoted by Brinton, **Op. Cit.**, p. 19] Given that one of the key criticisms of the factory committees by leading Bolsheviks was their "localism", this blocking of co-ordination is doubly damning.

At this time Lenin "envisaged a period during which, in a workers' state, the bourgeoisie would still retain the formal ownership and effective management of most of the productive apparatus" and workers' control "was seen as the instrument" by which the "capitalists would be coerced into co-operation." [Brinton, **Op. Cit.**, p. 13] The Bolsheviks turned to one-management in April, 1918 (it was applied first on the railway workers). As the capitalists refused to co-operate, with many closing down their workplaces, the Bolsheviks were forced to nationalise industry and place it fully under state control in late June 1918. This saw state-appointed "dictatorial" managers replacing the remaining capitalists (when it was not simply a case of the old boss being turned into a state manager). The Bolshevik vision of socialism as nationalised property replacing capitalist property was at the root of the creation of state capitalism within Russia. This was very centralised and very inefficient:

"it seems apparent that many workers themselves ... had now come to believe ... that confusion and anarchy [sic!] **at the top** were the major causes of their difficulties, and with some justification. The fact was that Bolshevik administration was chaotic ... Scores of competitive and conflicting Bolshevik and Soviet authorities issued contradictory orders, often brought to factories by armed Chekists. The Supreme Economic Council... issu[ed] dozens of orders and pass[ed] countless directives with virtually no real knowledge of affairs." [William G. Rosenberg, **Russian Labour and Bolshevik Power**, p. 116]

Faced with the chaos that their own politics, in part, had created, like all bosses, the Bolsheviks blamed the workers. Yet abolishing the workers' committees resulted in "a terrifying proliferation of competitive and contradictory Bolshevik authorities, each with a claim of life or death importance ... Railroad journals argued plaintively about the correlation between failing labour productivity and the proliferation of competing Bolshevik authorities." Rather than improving things, Lenin's one-man management did the opposite, "leading in many places ... to a greater degree of confusion and indecision" and "this problem of contradictory authorities clearly intensified, rather than lessened." Indeed, the "result of replacing workers' committees with one man rule ... on the railways ... was not directiveness, but distance, and increasing inability to make decisions appropriate to local conditions. Despite coercion, orders on the railroads were often ignored as unworkable." It got so bad that "a number of local Bolshevik officials ... began in the fall of 1918 to call for the restoration of workers' control, not for ideological reasons, but because workers themselves knew best how to run the line efficiently, and might obey their own central committee's directives if they were not being constantly countermanded." [William G. Rosenberg, **Workers' Control on the Railroads**, p. D1208, p. D1207, p. D1213 and pp. D1208-9]

That it was Bolshevik policies and not workers' control which was to blame for the state of the economy can be seen from what happened **after** Lenin's one-man management was imposed. The centralised Bolshevik economic system quickly demonstrated how to **really** mismanage an economy. The Bolshevik onslaught against workers' control in favour of a centralised, top-down economic regime ensured that the economy was handicapped by an unresponsive system which wasted the local knowledge in the grassroots in favour of orders from above which were issued in ignorance of local conditions. Thus the **glavki** "did not know the true number of enterprises in their branch" of industry. To ensure centralism, customers had to go via a central orders committee, which would then pass the details to the appropriate **glavki** and, unsurprisingly, it was "unable to cope with these enormous tasks". As a result, workplaces often "endeavoured to find less bureaucratic channels" to get resources and, in fact, the "comparative efficiency of factories remaining outside the **glavki** sphere increased." In summary, the "shortcomings of the central administrations and **glavki** increased together with the number of enterprises under their control". [Malle, **Op. Cit.**, p. 232, p. 233 and p. 250] In summary:

"The most evident shortcoming ... was that it did not ensure central allocation of resources and central distribution of output, in accordance with any priority ranking ... materials were provided to factories in arbitrary proportions: in some places they accumulated, whereas in others there was a shortage. Moreover, the length of the procedure needed to release the products increased scarcity at given moments, since products remained stored until the centre issued a purchase order on behalf of a centrally defined customer. Unused stock coexisted with acute scarcity. The centre was unable to determine the correct proportions among necessary materials and eventually to enforce implementation of the orders for their total quantity. The gap between theory and practice was significant." [**Op. Cit.**, p. 233]

Thus there was a clear *"gulf between the abstraction of the principles on centralisation and its reality."* This was recognised at the time and, unsuccessfully, challenged. Provincial delegates argued that *"[w]aste of time was ... the effect of strict compliance of vertical administration ... semi-finished products [were] transferred to other provinces for further processing, while local factories operating in the field were shut down"* (and given the state of the transport network, this was a doubly inefficient). The local bodies, knowing the grassroots situation, *"had proved to be more far-sighted than the centre."* For example, flax had been substituted for cotton long before the centre had issued instructions for this. Arguments reversing the logic of centralisation were raised: *"there was a lot of talk about scarcity of raw materials, while small factories and mills were stuffed with them in some provinces: what's better, to let work go on, or to make plans?"* These *"expressed feelings ... about the inefficiency of the **glavk** system and the waste which was visible locally."* Indeed, *"the inefficiency of central financing seriously jeopardised local activity."* While *"the centre had displayed a great deal of conservatism and routine thinking,"* the localities *"had already found ways of rationing raw materials, a measure which had not yet been decided upon at the centre."* [**Op. Cit.**, p.269, p. 270 and pp. 272-3]

This did not result in changes as such demands *"challenged ... the central directives of the party"* which *"approved the principles on which the **glavk** system was based"* and *"the maximum centralisation of production."* Even the *"admission that some of the largest works had been closed down, owning to the scarcity of raw materials and fuel, did not induce the economists of the party to question the validity of concentration, although in Russia at the time impediments due to lack of transport jeopardised the whole idea of convergence of all productive activity in a few centres."* The party leadership *"decided to concentrate the tasks of economic reconstruction in the hands of the higher organs of the state."* Sadly, *"the **glavk** system in Russia did not work ... Confronted with production problems, the central managers needed the collaboration of local organs, which they could not obtain both because of reciprocal suspicion and because of a lack of an efficient system of information, communications and transport. But the failure of **glavkism** did not bring about a reconsideration of the problems of economic organisation ... On the contrary, the ideology*

of centralisation was reinforced." [**Op. Cit.**, p. 271 and p. 275]

The failings of centralisation can be seen from the fact that in September 1918, the Supreme Economic Council (SEC) chairman reported that *"approximately eight hundred enterprises were known to have been nationalised and another two hundred or so were presumed to be nationalised but were not registered as such. In fact, well over two thousand enterprises had been taken over by this time."* The *"centre's information was sketchy at best"* and *"efforts by the centre to exert its power more effectively would provoke resistance from local authorities."* [Thomas F. Remington, **Op. Cit.**, pp. 58-9] This kind of clashing could not help but occur when the centre had no real knowledge nor understanding of local conditions:

"Organisations with independent claims to power frequently ignored it. It was deluged with work of an ad hoc character ... Demands for fuel and supplies piled up. Factories demanded instructions on demobilisation and conversion. Its presidium ... scarcely knew what its tasks were, other than to direct the nationalisation of industry. Control over nationalisation was hard to obtain, however. Although the SEC intended to plan branch-wide nationalisations, it was overwhelmed with requests to order the nationalisation of individual enterprises. Generally it resorted to the method, for want of a better one, of appointing a commissar to carry out each act of nationalisation. These commissars, who worked closely with the Cheka, had almost unlimited powers over both workers and owners, and acted largely on their own discretion." [**Op. Cit.**, p. 61-2]

Unsurprisingly, *"[r]esentment of the **glavki** was strongest where local authorities had attained a high level of competence in co-ordinating local production. They were understandably distressed when orders from central organs disrupted local production plans."* Particularly given that the centre *"drew up plans for developing or reorganising the economy of a region, either in ignorance, or against the will, of the local authorities."* "Hypercentralisation", ironically, *"multiplied the lines of command and accountability, which ultimately reduced central control."* For example, one small condensed milk plan, employing fewer than 15 workers, *"became the object of a months-long competition among six organisations."* Moreover, the **glavki** *"were filled with former owners."* Yet *"throughout 1919, as the economic crisis grew worse and the war emergency sharper the leadership strengthened the powers of the **glavki** in the interests of centralisation."* [**Op. Cit.**, p. 68, p. 69, p. 70 and p. 69]

A clearer example of the impact of Bolshevik ideology on the fate of the revolution would be hard to find. While the situation was pretty chaotic in early 1918, this does not prove that the factory committees' socialism was not the most efficient way of running things under the (difficult) circumstances. Unless of course, like the Bolsheviks, you have a dogmatic belief that centralisation is always more efficient. That favouring the factory committees, as anarchists stressed then and now, could have been a possible solution to the economic problems being faced is not utopian. After all rates of *"output and productivity began to climb steadily after"*

January 1918 and *"[i]n some factories, production doubled or tripled in the early months of 1918 ... Many of the reports explicitly credited the factory committees for these increases."* [Carmen Sirianni, **Workers' Control and Socialist Democracy**, p. 109] Another expert notes that there is *"evidence that until late 1919, some factory committees performed managerial tasks successfully. In some regions factories were still active thanks to their workers' initiatives in securing raw materials."* [Malle, **Op. Cit.**, p. 101]

Moreover, given how inefficient the Bolshevik system was, it was only the autonomous self-activity at the base which keep it going. Thus the Commissariat of Finance was *"not only bureaucratically cumbersome, but [it] involved mountainous accounting problems"* and *"with the various offices of the Sovnarkhoz and commissariat structure literally swamped with 'urgent' delegations and submerged in paperwork, even the most committed supporters of the revolution - perhaps one should say **especially** the most committed - felt impelled to act independently to get what workers and factories needed, even if this circumvented party directives."* [William G. Rosenberg, *"The Social Background to Tsektran,"* pp. 349-373, **Party, State, and Society in the Russian Civil War**, Diane P. Koenker, William G. Rosenberg and Ronald Grigor Suny (eds.), p. 357] *"Requisition and confiscation of resources,"* as Malle notes, *"largely undertaken by the **glavki**, worked against any possible territorial network of complementary industries which might have been more efficient in reducing delays resulting from central financing, central ordering, central supply and delivery."* By integrating the factory committees into a centralised state structure, this kind of activity became harder to do and, moreover, came up against official resistance and opposition. Significantly, due to *"the run-down of large-scale industry and the bureaucratic methods applied to production orders"* the Red Army turned to small-scale workplaces to supply personal equipment. These workplaces *"largely escaped the **glavk** administration"* and *"allowed the Bolsheviks to support a well equipped army amidst general distress and disorganisation."* [**Op. Cit.**, p. 251, p. 477 and p. 502]

Needless to say, Lenin never wavered in his support for one-man management nor in his belief in the efficiency of centralism to solve all problems, particularly the problems it itself created in abundance. Nor did his explicit call to reproduce capitalist social relations in production cause him any concern for, if the primary issue were property and not who **manages** the means of production, then factory committees are irrelevant in determining the socialist nature of the economy. Equally, if (as with Engels) all forms of organisation are inherently authoritarian then it does not fundamentally matter whether that authority is exercised by an elected factory committee or an appointed dictatorial manager (see section H.4). And it must be noted that the politics of the leading members of the factory committee movement also played its part. While the committees expressed a spontaneous anarchism, almost instinctively moving towards libertarian ideas, the actual influence of conscious anarchists was limited. Most of the leaders of the movement were, or became, Bolsheviks and, as such, shared many of the statist and centralistic assumptions of the party leadership as well as accepting party discipline. As such, they did not have the theoretical accruement to resist their leadership's assault on the factory committees and, as a result, did integrate them into the

trade unions when demanded.

As well as advocating one-man management, Lenin's proposals also struck at the heart of workers' power in other ways. For example, he argued that *"we must raise the question of piece-work and apply it and test in practice; we must raise the question of applying much of what is scientific and progressive in the Taylor system"*. [**Op. Cit.**, vol. 27, p. 258] As Leninist Tony Cliff noted, *"the employers have at their disposal a number of effective methods of disrupting th[e] unity [of workers as a class]. One of the most important of these is the fostering of competition between workers by means of piece-work systems."* He added that these were used by the Nazis and the Stalinists *"for the same purpose."* [**State Capitalism in Russia**, pp. 18-9] Obviously piece-work is different when Lenin introduces it!

Other policies undermined working class collectivity. Banning trade helped undermine a collective response to the problems of exchange between city and country. For example, a delegation of workers from the Main Workshops of the Nikolaev Railroad to Moscow reported to a well-attended meeting that *"the government had rejected their request [to obtain permission to buy food collectively] arguing that to permit the free purchase of food would destroy its efforts to come to grips with hunger by establishing a 'food dictatorship.'"* [David Mandel, **The Petrograd Workers and the Soviet Seizure of Power**, p. 392] Bolshevik ideology replaced collective working class action with an abstract "collective" response via the state, which turned the workers into isolated and atomised individuals. As such, the Bolsheviks provided a good example to support Malatesta's argument that *"if ... one means government action when one talks of social action, then this is still the resultant of individual forces, but only of those individuals who form the government ... it follows... that far from resulting in an increase in the productive, organising and protective forces in society, it would greatly reduce them, limiting initiative to a few, and giving them the right to do everything without, of course, being able to provide them with the gift of being all-knowing."* [**Anarchy**, pp. 38-9] Can it be surprising, then, that Bolshevik policies aided the atomisation of the working class by replacing collective organisation and action by state bureaucracy?

The negative impact of Bolshevik ideology showed up in other areas of the economy as well. For example, the Leninist fetish that bigger was better resulted in the *"waste of scare resources"* as the *"general shortage of fuel and materials in the city took its greatest toll on the largest enterprises, whose overhead expenditures for heating the plant and firing the furnaces were proportionately greater than those for smaller enterprises. This point ... was recognised later. Not until 1919 were the regime's leaders prepared to acknowledge that small enterprises, under the conditions of the time, might be more efficient in using resources; and not until 1921 did a few Bolsheviks theorists grasp the economic reasons for this apparent violation of their standing assumption that larger units were inherently more productive."* [Remington, **Op. Cit.**, p. 106] Given how disrupted transport was and how scare supplies were, this kind of ideologically generated mistake could not fail to have substantial impact.

Post-October Bolshevik policy is a striking confirmation of the anarchist argument that a centralised structure would stifle the initiative of the masses and their own organs of self-management.

Not only was it disastrous from a revolutionary perspective, it was hopelessly inefficient. The constructive self-activity of the people was replaced by the bureaucratic machinery of the state. The Bolshevik onslaught on workers' control, like their attacks on soviet democracy and workers' protest, undoubtedly engendered apathy and cynicism in the workforce, alienating even more the positive participation required for building socialism which the Bolshevik mania for centralisation had already marginalised. The negative results of Bolshevik economic policy confirmed Kropotkin's prediction that a revolution which *"establish[ed] a strongly centralised Government"*, leaving it to *"draw up a statement of all the produce"* in a country and *"then* **command** *that a prescribed quantity"* of some good *"be sent to such a place on such a day"* and *"stored in particular warehouses"* would *"not merely"* be *"undesirable, but it never could by any possibility be put into practice."* *"In any case,"* Kropotkin stressed, *"a system which springs up spontaneously, under stress of immediate need, will be infinitely preferable to anything invented between four-walls by hide-bound theorists sitting on any number of committees."* [**The Conquest of Bread**, pp. 82-3 and p. 75]

Some Bolsheviks were aware of the problems. One left-wing Communist, Osinskii, concluded that *"his six weeks in the provinces had taught him that the centre must rely on strong regional and provincial councils, since they were more capable than was the centre of managing the nationalised sector."* [Remington, **Op. Cit.**, p. 71] However, Marxist ideology seemed to preclude even finding the words to describe a possible solution to the problems faced by the regime: *"I stand not for a local point of view and not for bureaucratic centralism, but for organised centralism, - I cannot seem to find the actual word just now, - a more balanced centralism."* [Osinskii, quoted by Remington, **Op. Cit.**, p. 71] Any anarchist would know that the word he was struggling to find was federalism! Little wonder Goldman concluded that anarcho-syndicalism, not nationalisation, could solve the problems facing Russia:

> *"Only free initiative and popular participation in the affairs of the revolution can prevent the terrible blunders committed in Russia. For instance, with fuel only a hundred versts [about sixty-six miles] from Petrograd there would have been no necessity for that city to suffer from cold had the workers' economic organisations of Petrograd been free to exercise their initiative for the common good. The peasants of the Ukraina would not have been hampered in the cultivation of their land had they had access to the farm implements stacked up in the warehouses of Kharkov and other industrial centres awaiting orders from Moscow for their distribution. These are characteristic examples of Bolshevik governmentalism and centralisation, which should serve as a warning to the workers of Europe and America of the destructive effects of Statism."* [**My Disillusionment in Russia**, p. 253]

If Bolshevik industrial policy reflected a basic ignorance of local conditions and the nature of industry, their agricultural policies were even worse. Part of the problem was that the Bolsheviks were simply ignorant of peasant life (as one historian put it, *"the deeply held views of the party on class struggle had overcome the need*

for evidence." [Christopher Read, **From Tsar to Soviets**, p. 225]). Lenin, for example, thought that inequality in the villages was much, much higher than it actually was, a mistaken assumption which drove the unpopular and counter-productive "Committees of Poor Peasants" (kombedy) policy of 1918. Rather than a countryside dominated by a few rich kulaks (peasants who employed wage labour), Russian villages were predominantly pre-capitalist and based on actual peasant farming (i.e., people who worked their land themselves). While the Bolsheviks attacked kulaks, they, at best, numbered only 5 to 7 per cent of the peasantry and even this is high as only 1 per cent of the total of peasant households employed more than one labourer. The revolution itself had an equalising effect on peasant life, and during 1917 *"average size of landholding fell, the extremes of riches and poverty diminished."* [Alec Nove, **An economic history of the USSR: 1917-1991**, p. 103 and p. 102]

By 1919, even Lenin had to admit that the policies pursued in 1918, against the advice and protest of the Left-SRs, were failures and had alienated the peasantry. While admitting to errors, it remains the case that it was Lenin himself, more than anyone, who was responsible for them. Still, there was no fundamental change in policy for another two years. Defenders of the Bolsheviks argue that they had no alternative but to use violence to seize food from the peasants to feed the starving cities. However, this fails to acknowledge two key facts. Firstly, Bolshevik industrial policy made the collapse of industry worse and so the lack of goods to trade for grain was, in part, a result of the government. It is likely that if the factory committees had been fully supported then the lack of goods to trade may have been reduced. Secondly, it cannot be said that the peasants did not wish to trade with the cities. They were willing, but at a fair price as can be seen from the fact that throughout Russia peasants with bags of grain on their backs went to the city to exchange them for goods. In fact, in the Volga region official state sources indicate *"that grain-hoarding and the black market did not become a major problem until the beginning of 1919, and that during the autumn the peasants, in general, were 'wildly enthusiastic to sell as much grain as possible' to the government."* This changed when the state reduced its fixed prices by 25% and *"it became apparent that the new government would be unable to pay for grain procurements in industrial goods."* [Orlando Figes, **Peasant Russia, Civil War**, p. 253 and p. 254] Thus, in that region at least, it was **after** the introduction of central state food requisition in January 1919 that peasants started to hoard food. Thus Bolshevik policy made the situation worse. And as Alec Nove noted *"at certain moments even the government itself was compelled to 'legalise' illegal trade. For example, in September 1918 the wicked speculators and meshochniki [bag-men] were authorised to take sacks weighing up to 1.5 poods (54 lbs.) to Petrograd and Moscow, and in this month … they supplied four times more than did the official supply organisation."* [**Op. Cit.**, p. 55]

Yet rather than encourage this kind of self-activity, the Bolsheviks denounced it as speculation and did all in their power to suppress it (this included armed pickets around the towns and cities). This, of course, drove the prices on the black market higher due to the risk of arrest and imprisonment this entailed and so the regime made the situation worse: *"it was in fact quite impossible to live on the official rations, and the majority of the supplies even of bread* come through the black market. *The government was never able to prevent this market from functioning, but did sufficiently disrupt it to make food shortages worse."* By January 1919, only 19% of all food came through official channels and rose to around 30% subsequently. Official sources, however, announced an increase in grain, with total procurements amounting to 30 million poods in the agricultural year 1917-18 to 110 million poods in 1918-19. [Nove, **Op. Cit.**, p. 55 and p. 54] Needless to say, the average worker in the towns saw nothing of this improvement in official statistics (and this in spite of dropping urban populations!).

In the face of repression (up to and including torture and the destruction of whole villages), the peasantry responded by both cutting back on the amount of grain planted (something compounded by the state often taking peasant reserves for next season) and rising in insurrection. Unsurprisingly, opposition groups called for free trade in an attempt to both feed the cities and stop the alienation of the peasantry from the revolution. The Bolsheviks denounced the call, before being forced to accept it in 1921 due to mass pressure from below. Three years of bad policies had made a bad situation worse. Moreover, if the Bolsheviks had not ignored and alienated the Left-SRs, gerrymandered the Fifth All-Russian Congress of Soviets and pushed them into revolt then their links with the countryside would not have been so weak and sensible policies which reflected the reality of village life may have been implemented.

Nor did it help that the Bolsheviks undermined Russia's extensive network of consumer co-operatives because they were associated with the moderate socialists. It should also be noted that the peasants (or "kulaks") were blamed for food shortages when problems on the transport network or general bureaucratic mismanagement was the real reason. That there is *is little evidence to support the Leninist view"* that kulaks were behind the peasant resistance and revolts resulting from the Bolshevik food requisition policies should go without saying. [Figes, **Op. Cit.**, p. 155]

Given all this, it is not hard to conclude that alternatives existed to Bolshevik policies - particularly as even the Bolsheviks had to admit in 1919 their decisions of the previous year were wrong! The New Economic Policy (NEP) was introduced in 1921 (under immense popular pressure) in conditions even worse than those in 1918, for example. Since NEP allowed wage labour, it was a step backwards from the ideas of the peasantry itself, peasant based parties like the SRs and Left-SRs as well as such rebels as the Kronstadt sailors. A more socialistic policy, recognising that peasants exchanging the product of their labour was **not** capitalism, could have been implemented much earlier but Bolshevik ignorance and disdain for the peasantry combined with a false belief that centralised state control was more efficient and more socialist ensured that this option was unlikely to be pursued, particularly given the collapse of industrial production Bolshevik state capitalist policies helped deepen.

The pre-revolution Bolshevik vision of a socialist system was fundamentally centralised and, consequently, top-down. This was what was implemented post-October, with disastrous results. At each turning point, the Bolsheviks tended to implement policies which reflected their prejudices in favour of centralism, nationalisation and party power. Unsurprisingly, this also undermined the genuine

socialist tendencies which existed at the time and so the Bolshevik vision of socialism and democracy played a key role in the failure of the revolution. Therefore, the Leninist idea that politics of the Bolsheviks had no influence on the outcome of the revolution, that their policies during the revolution were a product purely of objective forces, is unconvincing. This is enforced by the awkward fact that the Bolshevik leaders *justified what they were doing in theoretical terms, e.g. in whole books by Bukharin and Trotsky."* [Pirani, **The Russian Revolution in Retreat, 1920-24**, p. 9] Remember, we are talking about the ideology of a ruling party and so it is more than just ideas for after the seizure of power, they became a part of the real social situation within Russia. Individually, party members assumed leadership posts in all spheres of social life and started to make decisions influenced by that ideology and its prejudices in favour of centralisation, the privileged role of the party, the top-down nature of decision making, the notion that socialism built upon state capitalism, amongst others. Then there is the hierarchical position which the party leaders found themselves. *"If it is true that people's real social existence determines their consciousness,"* argued Cornelius Castoriadis, *"it is from that moment illusory to expect the Bolshevik party to act in any other fashion than according to its real social position. The real social situation of the Party is that of a directorial organ, and its point of view toward this society henceforth is not necessarily the same as the one this society has toward itself."* [**Political and Social Writings**, vol. 3, p. 97]

Ultimately, the Bolshevik's acted as if they were trying to prove Bakunin's critique of Marxism was right (see section H.1.1). Implementing a dictatorship of the proletariat in a country where the majority were not proletarians failed while, for the proletariat, it quickly became a dictatorship **over** the proletariat by the party (and in practice, a few party leaders and justified by the privileged access they had to socialist ideology). Moreover, centralisation proved to be as disempowering and inefficient as Bakunin argued.

Sadly, far too many Marxists seem keen on repeating rather than learning from history while, at the same time, ignoring the awkward fact that anarchism's predictions were confirmed by the Bolshevik experience. It is not hard to conclude that another form of socialism was essential for the Russian revolution to have any chance of success. A decentralised socialism based on workers running their workplaces and the peasants controlling the land was not only possible but was being implemented by the people themselves. For the Bolsheviks, only a centralised planned economy was true socialism and, as a result, fought this alternative socialism and replaced it with a system reflecting that perspective. Yet socialism needs the mass participation of all in order to be created. Centralisation, by its very nature, limits that participation (which is precisely **why** ruling classes have always centralised power into states). As Russian Anarchist Voline argued, state power *"seeks more or less to take in its hands the reins of social life. It* ***predisposes the masses to passivity,*** *and all spirit of initiative is stifled by the very existence of power"* and so under state socialism the *"tremendous new creative forces which are latent in the masses thus remain unused."* [**The Unknown Revolution**, p. 250] This cannot help have a negative impact on the development of the revolution and, as anarchists had long feared and predicted, it did.

H.6.3 Were the Russian workers "declassed" and "atomised"?

A standard Leninist explanation for the dictatorship of the Bolshevik party (and subsequent rise of Stalinism) is based on the "atomisation" or "declassing" of the proletariat. Leninist John Rees summarised this argument:

> "The civil war had reduced industry to rubble. The working class base of the workers' state, mobilised time and again to defeat the Whites, the rock on which Bolshevik power stood, had disintegrated. The Bolsheviks survived three years of civil war and wars in intervention, but only at the cost of reducing the working class to an atomised, individualised mass, a fraction of its former size, and no longer able to exercise the collective power that it had done in 1917 ... The bureaucracy of the workers' state was left suspended in mid-air, its class base eroded and demoralised. Such conditions could not help but have an effect on the machinery of the state and organisation of the Bolshevik Party." ["In Defence of October," pp. 3-82, **International Socialism**, no. 52, p. 65]

It should be noted that this perspective originated in Lenin's arguments that the Russian proletariat had become "declassed." In 1921 it was the case that the proletariat, "owning to the war and to the desperate poverty and ruin, has become declassed, i.e. dislodged from its class groove, and had ceased to exist as proletariat ... the proletariat has disappeared." [**Collected Works**, vol. 33, p. 66] However, unlike his later-day followers, Lenin was sure that while it "would be absurd and ridiculous to deny that the fact that the proletariat is declassed is a handicap" it could still "fulfil its task of winning and holding state power." [**Op. Cit.**, vol. 32, p. 412] Since Lenin, this argument has been utilised repeatedly by Leninists to justify his regime as well as explaining both its authoritarianism and the rise of Stalinism.

It does, of course, contain an element of truth. The numbers of industrial workers **did** decrease dramatically between 1918 and 1921, particularly in Petrograd and Moscow (although the drop in both cities was exceptional, with most towns seeing much smaller reductions). As one historian summarises, the "social turmoil at this time undeniably reduced the size of Russia's working class ... . Yet a substantial core of urban workers remained in the factories, and their attitudes towards the Bolsheviks were indeed transformed." [Donald J. Raleigh, **Experiencing Russia's Civil War**, p. 348] This core was those with the least ties with the countryside - the genuine industrial worker.

Nor can it be maintained that the Russian working class was incapable of collective action during the civil war. Throughout that period, as well as before and after, the Russian workers proved themselves quite capable of taking collective action - against the Bolshevik state. Simply put, an "atomised, individualised mass" does not need extensive state repression to control it. So while the working class **was** "a fraction of its former size" it **was** able "to exercise the collective power it had done in 1917." Significantly,

rather than decrease over the civil war period, the mass protests **grew** in militancy. By 1921 these protests and strikes were threatening the very existence of the Bolshevik dictatorship, forcing it to abandon key aspects of its economic policies.

This process of collective action by workers and Bolshevik repression started before the Civil War began, continued throughout and after it. For example, "[t]hroughout the civil war there was an undercurrent of labour militancy in Moscow ... both the introduction and the phasing out of war communism were marked by particularly active periods of labour unrest." In the Moscow area, while it is "impossible to say what proportion of workers were involved in the various disturbances," following the lull after the defeat of the protest movement in mid-1918 "each wave of unrest was more powerful than the last, culminating in the mass movement from late 1920." [Richard Sakwa, **Soviet Communists in Power**, p. 94 and p. 93] This was the case across Russia, with "periodic swings in the workers' political temper. When Soviet rule stood in peril" this "spared the regime the defection of its proletarian base. During lulls in the fighting, strikes and demonstrations broke out." [Thomas F. Remington, **Building Socialism in Bolshevik Russia**, p. 101] Workers' resistance and protests against the Bolsheviks shows not only that a "workers' state" is a contradiction in terms but also that there was a social base for possible alternatives to Leninism.

The early months of Bolshevik rule were marked by "worker protests, which then precipitated violent repressions against hostile workers. Such treatment further intensified the disenchantment of significant segments of Petrograd labour with Bolshevik-dominated Soviet rule." [Alexander Rabinowitch, **Early Disenchantment with Bolshevik Rule**, p. 37] The first major act of state repression was an attack on a march in Petrograd in support of the Constituent Assembly when it opened in January 1918. Early May saw "the shooting of protesting housewives and workers in the suburb of Kolpino", the "arbitrary arrest and abuse of workers" in Sestroretsk, the "closure of newspapers and arrests of individuals who protested the Kolpino and Sestroretsk events" and "the resumption of labour unrest and conflict with authorities in other Petrograd factories." This was no isolated event, as "violent incidents against hungry workers and their family demanding bread occurred with increasing regularity." [Alexander Rabinowitch, **The Bolsheviks in Power**, pp. 229-30] The shooting at Kolpino "triggered a massive wave of indignation ... Work temporarily stopped at a number of plants." In Moscow, Tula, Kolomna, Nizhnii-Novoprod, Rybinsk, Orel, Tver' and elsewhere "workers gathered to issue new protests." In Petrograd, "textile workers went on strike for increased food rations and a wave of demonstrations spread in response to still more Bolshevik arrests." This movement was the "first major wave of labour protest" against the regime, with "protests against some form of Bolshevik repression" being common. [William Rosenberg, **Russian Labor and Bolshevik Power**, pp. 123-4]

This general workers' opposition generated the Menshevik inspired, but independent, Extraordinary Assembly of Delegates (EAD). "The emergence of the EAD", Rabinowitch notes, "was also stimulated by the widespread view that trade unions, factory committees, and soviets ... were no longer representative, democratically run working-class institutions; instead they had been transformed into arbitrary, bureaucratic government agencies. There was ample reason for this concern." To counter the EAD, the Bolsheviks organised non-party conferences which, in itself, shows that the soviets had become as distant from the masses as the opposition argued. District soviets *"were deeply concerned about their increasing isolation ... At the end of March ... they resolved to convene successive nonparty workers' conferences ... in part to undercut the EAD by strengthening ties between district soviets and workers."* This was done amidst *"unmistakable signs of the widening rift between Bolshevik-dominated political institutions and ordinary factory workers."* The EAD, argues Rabinowitch, was an expression of the *"growing disenchantment of Petrograd workers with economic conditions and the evolving structure and operation of Soviet political institutions".* [**Op. Cit.**, p. 224, p. 232 and p. 231]

Anarchists should be not too surprised that the turning of popular organisations into parts of a state soon resulted in their growing isolation from the masses. The state, with its centralised structures, is simply not designed for mass participation - and this does doubly for the highly centralised Leninist state.

These protests and repression continued after the start of the civil war. *"At the end of May and beginning of June, a wave of strikes to protest the lack of bread swept Nivskii district factories"* and *"strikes followed by bloody clashes between workers and Soviet authorities had erupted in scattered parts of central Russia."* On June 21, a general meeting of Obukhov workers *"seized control of the plant"* and the next day the assembled workers *"resolved to demand that the EAD should declare political strikes ... to protest the political repression of workers."* Orders were issued by the authorities *"to shut down Obukhov plant"* and *"the neighbourhood surrounding the plant was placed under martial law."* [Rabinowitch, **Op. Cit.**, p. 231 and pp. 246-7] However *"workers were not so readily pacified. In scores of additional factories and shops protests mounted and rapidly spread along the railways."* [Rosenberg, **Op. Cit.**, pp. 126-7]

Faced with this mounting pressure of spontaneous strikes, the EAD declared a general strike for the 2nd of July. The Bolshevik authorities acted quickly: *"Any sign of sympathy for the strike was declared a criminal act. More arrests were made. In Moscow, Bolsheviks raided the Aleksandrovsk railroad shops, not without bloodshed. Dissidence spread."* On July 1st, *"machine guns were set up at main points throughout the Petrograd and Moscow railroad junctions, and elsewhere in both cities as well. Controls were tightened in factories. Meetings were forcefully dispersed."* [Rosenberg, **Op. Cit.**, p. 127] Factories were warned *"that if they participated in the general strike they would face immediate shutdown, and individual strikes were threatened with fines or loss of work. Agitators and members of strike committees were subject to immediate arrest."* Opposition printing presses *"were sealed, the offices of hostile trade unions were raided, martial law on lines in the Petrograd rail hub was declared, and armed patrols with authority to prevent work stoppages were formed and put on twenty-four hour duty at key points around the city."* Perhaps unsurprisingly, given *"the brutal suppression of the EAD's general strike"*, it was not successful. [Rabinowitch, **Op. Cit.**, p. 254 and p. 259]

Thus *"[b]y the early summer of 1918"* there were *"widespread anti-Bolshevik protests. Armed clashes occurred in the factory districts of Petrograd and other industrial centres."* [Rosenberg, **Op. Cit.**, p.

107] It should also be noted that at the end of September of that year, there was a revolt by Baltic Fleet sailors demanding (as they did again in 1921) a *"return to government by liberated, democratic soviets - that is, 1917-type soviets."* As after the more famous 1921 revolt, the Left-SR controlled Kronstadt soviet had been disbanded and replaced by a Bolshevik revolutionary committee in July 1918, during the repression after the Left-SR assassination of the German ambassador. [Rabinowitch, **Op. Cit.**, p. 352 and p. 302]

As well as state repression, the politics of the opposition played a role in its defeat. Before October 1918, both the Mensheviks and SRs were in favour of the Constituent Assembly and Dumas as the main organs of power, with the soviets playing a minor role. This allowed the Bolsheviks to portray themselves as defenders of "soviet power" (a position which still held popular support). Understandably, many workers were unhappy to support an opposition which aimed to replace the soviets with typically bourgeois institutions. Many also considered the Bolshevik government as a "soviet power" and so, to some degree, their own regime. With the civil war starting, many working class people would also have been uneasy in protesting against a regime which proclaimed its soviet and socialist credentials. After October 1918, the Mensheviks supported the idea of (a democratically elected) soviet power, joining the Left-SRs (who were now effectively illegal after their revolt of July - see section H.6.1). However, by then it was far too late as Bolshevik ideology had adjusted to Bolshevik practice and the party was now advocating party dictatorship. Thus, we find Victor Serge in the 1930s noting that *"the degeneration of Bolshevism"* was apparent by that time, *"since at the start of 1919 I was horrified to read an article by Zinoviev ... on the monopoly of the party in power."* [**The Serge-Trotsky Papers**, p. 188] It should be noted, though, that Serge kept his horror well hidden throughout this period - and well into the 1930s (see section H.1.2 for his public support for this monopoly).

As noted above, this cycle of resistance and repression was not limited to Petrograd. In July 1918, a leading Bolshevik insisted *"that severe measures were needed to deal with strikes"* in Petrograd while in other cities *"harsher forms of repression"* were used. For example, in Tula, in June 1918, the regime declared *"martial law and arrested the protestors. Strikes followed and were suppressed by violence"*. In Sormovo, 5,000 workers went on strike after a Menshevik-SR paper was closed. Violence was *"used to break the strike."* [Remington, **Op. Cit.**, p. 105]

Similar waves of protests and strikes as those in 1918 took place the following year with 1919 seeing a *"new outbreak of strikes in March"*, with the *"pattern of repression ... repeated."* One strike saw *"closing of the factory, the firing of a number of workers, and the supervised re-election of its factory committee."* In Astrakhan, a mass meeting of 10,000 workers was fired on by Red Army troops, killing 2,000 (another 2,000 were taken prisoner and subsequently executed). [Remington, **Op. Cit.**, p. 109] Moscow, at the end of June, saw a *"committee of defence (KOM) [being] formed to deal with the rising tide of disturbances."* The KOM *"concentrated emergency power in its hands, overriding the Moscow Soviet, and demanding obedience from the population. The disturbances died down under the pressure of repression."* [Sakwa, **Op. Cit.**, pp. 94-5] In the Volga region, delegates to a conference of railroad workers "protested the Cheka's arrest of union members, which the delegates insisted further disrupted transport. It certainly curbed the number of strikes." [Raleigh, **Op. Cit.**, p. 371] In Tula "after strikes in the spring of 1919" local Menshevik party activists had been arrested while Petrograd saw "violent strikes" at around the same time. [Jonathan Aves, **Workers Against Lenin**, p. 19 and p. 23] As Vladimir Brovkin argues in his account of the strikes and protests of 1919:

"Data on one strike in one city may be dismissed as incidental. When, however, evidence is available from various sources on simultaneous independent strikes in different cities an overall picture begins to emerge. All strikes developed along a similar timetable: February, brewing discontent; March and April, peak of strikes: May, slackening in strikes; and June and July, a new wave of strikes ...

"Workers' unrest took place in Russia's biggest and most important industrial centres ... Strikes affected the largest industries, primarily those involving metal: metallurgical, locomotive, and armaments plants ... In some cities ... textile and other workers were active protesters as well. In at least five cities ... the protests resembled general strikes." ["Workers' Unrest and the Bolsheviks' Response in 1919", pp. 350-373, **Slavic Review**, Vol. 49, No. 3, p. 370]

These strikes raised both economic and political demands, such as "free and fair elections to the soviets." Unsurprisingly, in all known cases the Bolsheviks' "initial response to strikes was to ban public meetings and rallies" as well as "occup[ying] the striking plant and dismiss[ing] the strikers en masse." They also "arrested strikers" and executed some. [**Op. Cit.**, p. 371 and p. 372]

1920 saw similar waves of strikes and protests. In fact, strike action "remained endemic in the first nine months of 1920." Soviet figures report a total of 146 strikes, involving 135,442 workers for the 26 provinces covered. In Petrograd province, there were 73 strikes with 85,642 participants. "This is a high figure indeed, since at this time ... there were 109,100 workers" in the province. Overall, "the geographical extent of the February-March strike wave is impressive" and the "harsh discipline that went with labour militarisation led to an increase in industrial unrest in 1920." [Aves, **Op. Cit.**, p. 69, p. 70 and p. 80]

Saratov, for example, saw a wave of factory occupations break out in June and mill workers went out in July while in August, strikes and walkouts occurred in its mills and other factories and these "prompted a spate of arrests and repression." In September railroad workers went out on strike, with arrests making "the situation worse, forcing the administration to accept the workers' demands." [Raleigh, **Op. Cit.**, p. 375] In January 1920, a strike followed a mass meeting at a railway repair shop in Moscow. Attempts to spread were foiled by arrests. The workshop was closed, depriving workers of their rations and 103 workers of the 1,600 employed were imprisoned. "In late March 1920 there were strikes in some factories" in Moscow and "[a]t the height of the Polish war the protests and strikes, usually provoked by economic issues but not

restricted to them, became particularly frequent ... The assault on non-Bolshevik trade unionism launched at this time was probably associated with the wave of unrest since there was a clear danger that they would provide a focus for opposition." [Sakwa, **Op. Cit.**, p. 95] The "largest strike in Moscow in the summer of 1920" was by tram workers over the equalisation of rations. It began on August 12th, when one tram depot went on strike, quickly followed by others while workers "in other industries joined in to." The tram workers "stayed out a further two days before being driven back by arrests and threats of mass sackings." In the textile manufacturing towns around Moscow "there were large-scale strikes" in November 1920, with 1000 workers striking for four days in one district and a strike of 500 mill workers saw 3,000 workers from another mill joining in. [Simon Pirani, **The Russian Revolution in Retreat, 1920-24**, p. 32 and p. 43]

In Petrograd the Aleksandrovskii locomotive building works "had seen strikes in 1918 and 1919" and in August 1920 it again stopped work. The Bolsheviks locked the workers out and placed guards outside it. The Cheka then arrested the SRs elected to the soviet from that workplace as well as about 30 workers. After the arrests, the workers refused to co-operate with elections for new soviet delegates. The "opportunity was taken to carry out a general round-up, and arrests were made" at three other works. The enormous Briansk works "experienced two major strikes in 1920", and second one saw the introduction of martial law on both the works and the settlement it was situated in. A strike in Tula saw the Bolsheviks declare a "state of siege", although the repression "did not prevent further unrest and the workers put forward new demands" while, in Moscow, a strike in May by printers resulted in their works "closed and the strikers sent to concentration camps." [Aves, **Op. Cit.**, p. 41, p. 45, p. 47, pp. 48-9, pp. 53-4 and p. 59]

These expressions of mass protest and collective action continued in 1921, unsurprisingly as the civil war was effectively over in the previous autumn. Even John Rees had to acknowledge the general strike in Russia at the time, stating that the Kronstadt revolt was "preceded by a wave of serious but quickly resolved strikes." [**Op. Cit.**, p. 61] Significantly, he failed to note that the Kronstadt sailors rebelled in solidarity with those strikes and how it was state repression which "resolved" the strikes. Moreover, he seriously downplays the scale and importance of these strikes, perhaps unsurprisingly as "[b]y the beginning of 1921 a revolutionary situation with workers in the vanguard had emerged in Soviet Russia" with "the simultaneous outbreak of strikes in Petrograd and Moscow and in other industrial regions." In February and March 1921, "industrial unrest broke out in a nation-wide wave of discontent or **volynka**. General strikes, or very widespread unrest" hit all but one of the country's major industrial regions and "workers protest consisted not just of strikes but also of factory occupations, 'Italian strikes', demonstrations, mass meetings, the beating up of communists and so on." Faced with this massive strike wave, the Bolsheviks did what many ruling elites do: they called it something else. Rather than admit it was a strike, they "usually employed the word **volynka**, which means only a 'go-slow'". [Aves, **Op. Cit.**, p. 3, p. 109, p. 112, pp. 111-2] Mid-February 1921 saw workers in Moscow striking and "massive city-wide protest spread through Petrograd ... Strikes and demonstrations spread. The regime responded as it had done in the past, with lock-outs, mass arrests, heavy show of force - and concessions." [Remington, **Op. Cit.**, p. 111] As Paul Avrich recounts, in Petrograd these "street demonstrations were heralded by a rash of protest meetings" in workplaces. On the 24th of February, the day after a workplace meeting, the Trubochny factory workforce downed tools and walked out the factory. Additional workers from nearby factories joined in. The crowd of 2,000 was dispersed by armed military cadets. The next day, the Trubochny workers again took to the streets and visited other workplaces, bringing them out on strike too. In the face of a near general strike, a three-man Defence Committee was formed. Zinoviev "proclaimed martial law" and "[o]vernight Petrograd became an armed camp." Strikers were locked out and the "application of military force and the widespread arrests, not to speak of the tireless propaganda waged by the authorities" was "indispensable in restoring order" (as were economic concessions). [**Kronstadt 1921**, pp. 37-8, p. 39, pp. 46-7 and p. 50]

In Moscow, "industrial unrest ... turned into open confrontation and protest spilled on to the streets", starting with a "wave of strikes that had its centre in the heart of industrial Moscow." Strikes were "also spreading outside Moscow city itself into the surrounding provinces" and so "Moscow and Moscow province were put under martial law". [Aves, **Op. Cit.**, p. 130, p. 138, p. 143 and p. 144] This strike wave started when "[m]eetings in factories and plants gathered and criticised government policies, beginning with supply and developing into general political criticism." As was typical, the "first response of the civil authorities to the disturbances was increased repression" although as "the number of striking factories increased some concessions were introduced." Military units called in against striking workers "refused to open fire, and they were replaced by the armed communist detachments" which did. "That evening mass protest meetings were held ... The following day several factories went on strike" and troops were "disarmed and locked in as a precaution" by the government against possible fraternising. February 23rd saw a 10,000 strong street demonstration and "Moscow was placed under martial law with a 24-hour watch on factories by the communist detachments and trustworthy army units." The disturbances were accompanied by factory occupations and on the 1st of March the soviet called on workers "not to go on strike." However, "wide-scale arrests deprived the movement of its leadership." March 5th saw disturbances at the Bromlei works, "resulting in the now customary arrest of workers. A general meeting at the plant on 25 March called for new elections to the Moscow Soviet. The management dispersed the meeting but the workers called on other plants to support the calls for new elections. As usual, the ringleaders were arrested." [Sakwa, **Op. Cit.**, pp. 242-3, p. 245 and p. 246]

The events at the Bromlei works were significant in that the March 25th mass meeting passed an anarchist and Left-SR initiated resolution supporting the Kronstadt rebels. The party "responded by having them sacked en masse". The workers "demonstrated through" their district "and inspired some brief solidarity strikes." Over 3000 workers joined the strikes and about 1000 of these joined the flying picket (managers at one print shop locked their workers in to stop them joining the protest). While the party was willing to negotiate economic issues, "it had no wish to discuss politics with workers" and so arrested those who initiated the resolution,

sacked the rest of the workforce and selectively re-employed them. Two more strikes were conducted "to defend the political activists in their midst" and two mass meetings demanded the release of arrested ones. Workers also struck on supply issues in May, July and August. [Pirani, **Op. Cit.**, pp. 83-4]

While the Kronstadt revolt took place too late to help the Petrograd strikes, it did inspire a strike wave in Ekaterinoslavl (in the Ukraine) in May, 1921. It started in the railway workshops and became "quickly politicised," with the strike committee raising a "series of political ultimatums that were very similar in content to the demands of the Kronstadt rebels" (many of the resolutions put to the meeting almost completely coincided with them). The strike "spread to the other workshops" and on June 1st the main large Ekaterinoslavl factories joined the strike. The strike was spread via the use of trains and telegraph and soon an area up to fifty miles around the town was affected. The strike was finally ended by the use of the Cheka, using mass arrests and shootings. Unsurprisingly, the local communists called the revolt a "little Kronstadt." [Aves, **Op. Cit.**, pp. 171-3]

Saratov also saw a mass revolt in March 1921, when a strike by railroad workers over a reduction in food rations spread to the metallurgical plants and other large factories "as workers and non-workers sent representatives to the railroad shops." They forced the Communists to allow the setting up of a commission to re-examine the activities of all economic organs and the Cheka. During the next two days, "the assemblies held at factories to elect delegates to the commission bitterly denounced the Communists." The "unrest spilled over into Pokrovsk." The commission of 270 had less than ten Communists and "demanded the freeing of political prisoners, new elections to the soviets and to all labour organisations, independent unions, and freedom of speech, the press, and assembly." The Communists "resolved to shut down the commission before it could issue a public statement" and set up a Provincial Revolutionary Committee which "introduced martial law both in the city and the garrison" as well as arresting "the ringleaders of the workers' movement." The near general strike was broken by a "wave of repression" but "railroad workers and dockworkers and some printers refused to resume work." [Raleigh, **Op. Cit.**, pp. 388-9]

Post-**volynka**, workplaces "that had been prominent in unrest were particularly hit by ... purges ... The effect on the willingness of workers to support opposition parties was predictable." However, "the ability to organise strikes did not disappear" and they continued to take place throughout 1921. The spring of 1922 saw "a new strike wave." [Aves, **Op. Cit.**, p. 182 and p. 183] For example, in early March, "long strikes" hit the textile towns around Moscow. At the Glukhovskaia mills 5000 workers struck for 5 days, 1000 at a nearby factory for 2 days and 4000 at the Voskresenskaia mills for 6 days. In May, 1921, workers in the city of Moscow reacted to supply problems "with a wave of strikes. Party officials reckoned that in a 24-day period in May there were stoppages at 66 large enterprises." These included a sit-down strike at one of Moscow's largest plants, while "workers at engineering factories in Krasnopresnia followed suit, and Cheka agents reported 'dissent, culminating in strikes and occupation' in Bauman." August 1922 saw 19,000 workers strike in textile mills in Moscow region for several days. Tram workers also struck that year, while teachers *"organised strikes and mass meetings"*. Workers usually elected delegates to negotiate with their trade unions as well as their bosses as both were Communist Party members. Strike organisers, needless to say, were sacked. [Pirani, **Op. Cit.**, p. 82, pp. 111-2 and p. 157]

While the strike wave of early 1921 is the most famous, due to the Kronstadt sailors rebelling in solidarity with it, the fact is that this was just one of many strike waves during the 1918 and 1921 period. In response to protests, *"the government had combined concessions with severe repression to restore order"* as well as *"commonly resort[ing] to the lock out as a means of punishing and purging the work force."* Yet, *"as the strike waves show, the regime's sanctions were not sufficient to prevent all anti-Bolshevik political action."* [Remington, **Op. Cit.**, p. 111, p. 107, and p. 109] In fact, repression *"did not prevent strikes and other forms of protest by workers becoming endemic in 1919 and 1920"* while in early 1921 the Communist Party *"faced what amounted to a revolutionary situation. Industrial unrest was only one aspect of a more general crisis that encompassed the Kronstadt revolt and the peasant rising in Tambov and Western Siberia."* This *"industrial unrest represented a serious political threat to the Soviet regime ... From Ekaterinburg to Moscow, from Petrograd to Ekaterinoslavl, workers took to the streets, often in support of political slogans that called for the end of Communist Party rule ... soldiers in many of the strike areas showed themselves to be unreliable [but] the regime was able to muster enough forces to master the situation. Soldiers could be replaced by Chekists, officer cadets and other special units where Party members predominated."* [Aves, **Op. Cit.**, p. 187, p. 155 and p. 186]

Yet, an *"atomised"* and powerless working class does not need martial law, lockouts, mass arrests and the purging of the workforce to control it. As Russian anarchist Ida Mett succinctly put it: *"And if the proletariat was that exhausted how come it was still capable of waging virtually total general strikes in the largest and most heavily industrialised cities?"* [**The Kronstadt Rebellion**, p. 81] The end of the civil war also saw the Bolsheviks finally destroy what was left of non-Bolshevik trade unionism. In Moscow, this took place against fierce resistance of the union members. As one historian concludes:

> *"Reflecting on the determined struggle mounted by printers, bakers and chemical workers in Moscow during 1920-1, in spite of appalling economic conditions, being represented by organisations weakened by constant repression ... to retain their independent labour organisations it is difficult not to feel that the social basis for a political alternative existed."* [Jonathan Aves, *"The Demise of Non-Bolshevik Trade Unionism in Moscow: 1920-21"*, pp. 101- 33, **Revolutionary Russia**, vol. 2, no. 1, p. 130]

Elsewhere, Aves argues that an *"examination of industrial unrest after the Bolshevik seizure of power ... shows that the Revolution had brought to the surface resilient traditions of organisation in society and had released tremendous forces in favour of greater popular participation ... The survival of the popular movement through the political repression and economic devastation of the Civil War testifies to its strength."* [**Workers Against Lenin**, p. 186] The idea that the Russian working class was incapable of collective struggle is hard to defend given this series of struggles (and state repression). The class struggle in Bolshevik Russia did not stop, it continued except the ruling class had changed. All the popular energy and organisation this expressed, which could have been used to combat the problems facing the revolution and create the foundations of a genuine socialist society, were wasted in fighting the Bolshevik regime. Ultimately, the *"sustained, though ultimately futile, attempts to revive an autonomous workers' movement, especially in mid-1918 and from late 1920, failed owing to repression."* [Sakwa, **Op. Cit.**, p. 269] Another historian notes that *"immediately after the civil war"* there was *"a revival of working class collective action that culminated in February-March 1921 in a widespread strike movement and the revolt at the Kronstadt naval base."* As such, the position expounded by Rees and other Leninists *"is so one-sided as to be misleading."* [Pirani, **Op. Cit.**, p. 7 and p. 23]

Nor is this commonplace Leninist rationale for Bolshevik rule particularly original, as it dates back to Lenin and was first formulated *"to justify a political clamp-down."* Indeed, this argument was developed in response to rising working class protest rather than its lack: *"As discontent amongst workers became more and more difficult to ignore, Lenin ... began to argue that the consciousness of the working class had deteriorated ... workers had become 'declassed.'"* However, there *"is little evidence to suggest that the demands that workers made at the end of 1920 ... represented a fundamental change in aspirations since 1917."* [Aves, **Op. Cit.**, p. 18, p. 90 and p. 91] So while the *"working class had decreased in size and changed in composition,... the protest movement from late 1920 made clear that it was not a negligible force and that in an inchoate way it retained a vision of socialism which was not identified entirely with Bolshevik power ... Lenin's arguments on the declassing of the proletariat was more a way of avoiding this unpleasant truth than a real reflection of what remained, in Moscow at least, a substantial physical and ideological force."* [Sakwa, **Op. Cit.**, p. 261]

Nor can it be suggested, as the Bolsheviks did at the time, that these strikes were conducted by newly arrived workers, semi-peasants without an awareness of proletarian socialism or traditions. Links between the events in 1917 and those during the civil war are clear. Jonathan Aves writes that there were *"distinct elements of continuity between the industrial unrest in 1920 and 1917 ... As might be anticipated, the leaders of unrest were often to be found amongst the skilled male workers who enjoyed positions of authority in the informal shop-floor hierarchies."* Looking at the strike wave of early 1921 in Petrograd, the *"strongest reason for accepting the idea that it was established workers who were behind the **volynka** is the form and course of protest. Traditions of protest reaching back through the spring of 1918 to 1917 and beyond were an important factor in the organisation of the **volynka"**. In fact, *"an analysis of the industrial unrest of early 1921 shows that long-standing workers were prominent in protest."* [Aves, **Op. Cit.**, p. 39, p. 126 and p. 91] As another example, *"although the ferment touched all strata of Saratov workers, it must be emphasised that the skilled metalworkers, railroad workers, and printers - the most 'conscious'* workers - demonstrated the most determined resistance." They "contested repression and the Communists' violation of fair play and workplace democracy." [Raleigh, **Op. Cit.**, p. 376] As Ida Mett argued in relation to the strikes in early 1921:

> "The population was drifting away from the capital. All who had relatives in the country had rejoined them. The authentic proletariat remained till the end, having the most slender connections with the countryside.
>
> "This fact must be emphasised, in order to nail the official lies seeking to attribute the Petrograd strikes ... to peasant elements, 'insufficiently steeled in proletarian ideas.' The real situation was the very opposite ... There was certainly no exodus of peasants into the starving towns! ... It was the famous Petrograd proletariat, the proletariat which had played such a leading role in both previous revolutions, that was finally to resort to the classical weapon of the class struggle: the strike." [**The Kronstadt Uprising**, p. 36]

As one expert on this issue argues, while the number of workers did drop "a sizeable core of veteran urban proletarians remained in the city; they did not all disappear." In fact, "it was the loss of young activists rather than of all skilled and class-conscious urban workers that caused the level of Bolshevik support to decline during the Civil War. Older workers had tended to support the Menshevik Party in 1917". Given this, "it appears that the Bolshevik Party made deurbanisation and declassing the scapegoats for its political difficulties when the party's own policies and its unwillingness to accept changing proletarian attitudes were also to blame." It should also be noted that the notion of declassing to rationalise the party's misfortunes was used long before the civil war: "This was the same argument used to explain the Bolsheviks' lack of success among workers in the early months of 1917 - that the cadres of conscious proletarians were diluted by nonproletarian elements." [Diane P. Koenker, "Urbanisation and Deurbanisation in the Russian Revolution and Civil War", pp. 81-104, **Party, State, and Society in the Russian Civil War**, Diane P. Koenker, William G. Rosenberg and Ronald Grigor Suny (eds.), p. 96, p. 95, p. 100 and p. 84]

While there is still much research required, what facts that are available suggest that throughout the time of Lenin's regime the Russian workers took collective action in defence of their interests. This is not to say that workers did not also respond to the problems they faced in an individualistic manner, often they did. However, such responses were, in part (as we noted in the last section), because Bolshevik policy **itself** gave them little choice as it limited their ability to respond collectively. Yet in the face of difficult economic circumstances, workers turned to mass meetings and strikes. In response, the Bolsheviks used state repression to break resistance and protest against their regime. In such circumstances it is easy to see how the Bolshevik party became isolated from the masses they claimed to be leading but were, in fact, ruling. This transformation of rebels into a ruling elite comes as no great surprise given that Bolsheviks aimed to seize power themselves in a centralised and hierarchical institution, a state, which has always been the method by which ruling classes secured their position (as we argued in

section H.3.7, this perspective flowed from the flawed Marxist theory of the state). Just as they had to, first, gerrymander and disband soviets to regime in power in the spring and summer of 1918, so the Bolsheviks had to clamp down on any form of collective action by the masses. As such, it is incredulous that latter day Leninists justify Bolshevik authoritarianism on a lack of collective action by workers when that authoritarianism was often driven precisely to break it!

So the claim by John Rees that the "dialectical relationship between the Bolsheviks and the working class was broken, shattered because the working class itself was broke-backed after the civil war" leaves a lot to be desired. [**Op. Cit.**, p. 22] The Bolsheviks did more than their fair share of breaking the back of the working class. This is unsurprising for a government which grants to the working class the greatest freedom undermines its own power by so doing. Even a limited relaxation of its authority will allow people to organise themselves, listen to alternative points of view and to act on them. That could not but undermine the rule of the party and so could not be supported - nor was it.

For example, in his 1920 diatribe against Left-wing Communism, Lenin pointed to "non-Party workers' and peasants' conferences" and Soviet Congresses as means by which the party secured its rule. Yet, **if** the congresses of soviets were "**democratic** institutions, the like of which even the best democratic republics of the bourgeois have never known", the Bolsheviks would have no need to "support, develop and extend" non-Party conferences "to be able to observe the temper of the masses, come closer to them, meet their requirements, promote the best among them to state posts". [**The Lenin Anthology**, p. 573] How the Bolsheviks met "their requirements" is extremely significant - they disbanded them, just as they had with soviets with non-Bolshevik majorities in 1918. This was because "[d]uring the disturbances" of late 1920, "they provided an effective platform for criticism of Bolshevik policies." Their frequency was decreased and they "were discontinued soon afterward." [Sakwa, **Op. Cit.**, p. 203]

In the soviets themselves, workers turned to non-partyism, with non-party groups winning majorities in soviet delegates from industrial workers' constituencies in many places. This was the case in Moscow, where Bolshevik support among "industrial workers collapsed" in favour of non-party people. Due to support among the state bureaucracy and the usual packing of the soviet with representatives from Bolshevik controlled organisations, the party had, in spite of this, a massive majority. Thus the Moscow soviet elections of April-May 1921 "provided an opportunity to revive working-class participation. The Bolsheviks turned it down." [Pirani, **Op. Cit.**, pp. 97-100 and p. 23] Indeed, one Moscow Communist leader stated that these soviet elections had seen "a high level of activity by the masses and a striving to be in power themselves." [quoted by Pirani, **Op. Cit.**, p. 101]

1921 also saw the Bolsheviks disperse provincial trade unions conferences in Vologda and Vitebsk "because they had anti-communist majorities." [Aves, **Op. Cit.**, p. 176] At the All-Russian Congress of Metalworkers' Union in May, the delegates voted down the party-list of recommended candidates for union leadership. The Central Committee of the Party "disregarded every one of the votes and appointed a Metalworkers' Committee of its own. So much for 'elected and revocable delegates'. Elected by the union rank and file and revocable by the Party leadership!" [Brinton, **Op. Cit.**, p. 83] Another telling example is provided in August 1920 by Moscow's striking tram workers who, in addition to economic demands, called for a general meeting of all depots. This was *"significant: here the workers' movement was trying to get on the first rung of the ladder of organisation, and being knocked off by the Bolsheviks."* The party *"responded to the strike in such a way as to undermine workers' organisation and consciousness"* and *"throttl[ed] independent action"* by *"repression of the strike by means reminiscent of tsarism."* The Bolshevik's *"dismissive rejection"* of the demand for a city-wide meeting *"spoke volumes about their hostility to the development of the workers' movement, and landed a blow at the type of collective democracy that might have better able to confront supply problems."* This, along with the other strikes that took place, showed that *"the workers' movement in Moscow was, despite its numerical weakness and the burdens of civil war, engaged with political as well as industrial issues ... the working class was far from non-existent, and when, in 1921, it began to resuscitate soviet democracy, the party's decision to make the Moscow soviet its 'creature' was not effect but cause."* [Pirani, **Op. Cit.**, p. 32, p. 33, p. 37 and p. 8]

When such things happen, we can conclude that Bolshevik desire to remain in power had a significant impact on whether workers were able to exercise collective power or not. As Pirani concludes:

> *"one of the most important choices the Bolsheviks made ... was to turn their backs on forms of collective, participatory democracy that workers briefly attempted to revive [post civil war]. [Available evidence] challenges the notion ... that political power was forced on the Bolsheviks because the working class was so weakened by the civil war that it was incapable of wielding it. In reality, non-party workers were willing and able to participate in political processes, but in the Moscow soviet and elsewhere, were pushed out of them by the Bolsheviks. The party's vanguardism, i.e. its conviction that it had the right, and the duty, to make political decisions on the workers' behalf, was now reinforced by its control of the state apparatus. The working class was politically expropriated: power was progressively concentrated in the party, specifically in the party elite."* [**Op. Cit.**, p. 4]

It should also be stressed that fear of arrest limited participation. A sadly typical example of this occurred in April 1920, which saw the first conference of railway workers on the Perm-Ekaterinburg line. The meeting of 160 delegates elected a non-Party chairman who *"demanded that delegates be guaranteed freedom of debate and immunity from arrest."* [Aves, **Op. Cit.**, p. 44] A Moscow Metalworkers' Union conference in early February 1921 saw the first speakers calling *"for the personal safety of the delegates to be guaranteed"* before criticisms would be aired. [Sakwa, **Op. Cit.**, p. 244] Later that year dissidents in the Moscow soviet demanded *"that delegates be given immunity from arrest unless sanctioned by plenary session of the soviet."* Immediately afterwards two of them, including an anarcho-syndicalist, were detained. It was also proposed that delegates' freedom of speech *"included immunity*

from administrative or judicial punishment" along with the right of any number of delegates *"to meet and discuss their work as they chose."* [Pirani, **Op. Cit.** p. 104] Worse, *"[b]y the end of 1920 workers not only had to deal with the imposition of harsh forms of labour discipline, they also had to face the Cheka in their workplace."* This could not help hinder working class collective action, as did the use of the Cheka and other troops to repress strikes. While it is impossible to accurately measure how many workers were shot by the Cheka for participation in labour protest, looking at individual cases *"suggests that shootings were employed to inspire terror and were not simply used in the occasional extreme case."* [Aves, **Op. Cit.**, p. 35] Which means, ironically, those who had seized power in 1917 in the name of the politically conscious proletariat were in fact ensuring their silence by fear of the Cheka or weeding them out, by means of workplace purges and shooting.

Perhaps unsurprisingly, but definitely significantly, of the 17,000 camp detainees on whom statistical information was available on 1 November 1920, peasants and workers constituted the largest groups, at 39% and 34% respectively. Similarly, of the 40,913 prisoners held in December 1921 (of whom 44% had been committed by the Cheka) nearly 84% were illiterate or minimally educated, clearly, therefore, either peasants or workers. [George Leggett, **The Cheka: Lenin's Political Police**, p. 178] Needless to say, Lenin failed to mention this aspect of his system in **The State and Revolution** (a failure shared by later Leninists). Ultimately, the contradictions between Bolshevik rhetoric and the realities of working class life under their rule was closed by coercion.

Such forms of repression could not help ensure both economic chaos and push the revolution away from socialism. As such, it is hard to think of a more incorrect assertion than Lenin's 1921 one that *"[i]ndustry is indispensable, democracy is not. Industrial democracy breeds some utterly false ideas."* [**Collected Works**, vol. 32, p. 27] Yet without industrial democracy, any development towards socialism is aborted and the problems of a revolution cannot be solved in the interests of the working masses.

This account of workers' protest being crushed by the so-called workers' state raises an important theoretical question. Following Marx and Engels, Lenin asserted that the *"state is nothing but a machine for the suppression of one class by another"* [**Collected Works**, vol. 28, p. 259] Yet here is the working class being suppressed by "its" state. If the state is breaking strikes, including general strikes, by what stretch of the imagination can it be considered a "workers' state"? Particularly as the workers, like the Kronstadt sailors, demanded free soviet elections, **not**, as the Leninists then and now claim, "soviets without Communists" (although one soviet historian noted with regards the 1921 revolt that *"taking account of the mood of the workers, the demand for free elections to the soviets meant the implementation in practice of the infamous slogan of soviets without communists."* [quoted by Aves, **Op. Cit.**, p. 123]). If the workers are being repressed and denied any real say in the state, how can they be considered the ruling class? And what class is doing the *"suppression"*? As we discussed in section H.3.8, Bolshevik ideology adjusted to this reality by integrating the need for party dictatorship to combat the "wavering" within the working class into its theory of the state. Yet it is the party (i.e., the state) which determines what is and is not wavering. This suggests that the state apparatus has to be separate from the working class in order to repress it (as always, in its own interests).

So anarchists argue that the actual experience of the Bolshevik state shows that the state is no mere *"machine"* of class rule but has interests of its own. Which confirms the anarchist theory of the state rather than the Marxist (see section H.3.7). It should be stressed that it was **after** the regular breaking of working class protest and strikes that the notion of the dictatorship of the party became Bolshevik orthodoxy. This makes sense, as protests and strikes express "wavering" within the working class which needs to be solved by state repression. This, however, necessitates a normal state power, one which is isolated from the working class and which, in order to enforce its will, **must** (like any state) atomise the working class people and render them unable, or unwilling, to take collective action in defence of their interests. For the defenders of Bolshevism to turn round and blame Bolshevik authoritarianism on the atomisation required for the party to remain in power and enforce its will is staggering.

Finally, it should be noted that Zinoviev, a leading Bolshevik, tried to justify the hierarchical position of the Bolshevik party arguing that *"[i]n time of strike every worker knows that there must be a Strike Committee - a centralised organ to conduct the strike, whose orders must be obeyed - although this Committee is elected and controlled by the rank and file. **Soviet Russia is on strike against the whole capitalist world. The social Revolution is a general strike against the whole capitalist system. The dictatorship of the proletariat is the strike committee of the social Revolution.**"* [**Proceedings and Documents of the Second Congress 1920**, vol. 2, p. 929]

In strikes, however, the decisions which are to be obeyed are those of the strikers. They should make the decisions and the strike committees should carry them out. The actual decisions of the Strike Committee should be accountable to the assembled strikers who have the real power (and so power is **decentralised** in the hands of the strikers and not in the hands of the committee). A far better analogy for what happened in Russia was provided by Emma Goldman:

> *"There is another objection to my criticism on the part of the Communists. Russia is on strike, they say, and it is unethical for a revolutionist to side against the workers when they are striking against their masters. That is pure demagoguery practised by the Bolsheviki to silence criticism.*
>
> *"It is not true that the Russian people are on strike. On the contrary, the truth of the matter is that the Russian people have been **locked out** and that the Bolshevik State - even as the bourgeois industrial master - uses the sword and the gun to keep the people out. In the case of the Bolsheviki this tyranny is masked by a world-stirring slogan: thus they have succeeded in blinding the masses. Just because I am a revolutionist I refuse to side with the master class, which in Russia is called the Communist Party."* [**My Disillusionment in Russia**, p. xlix]

The isolation of the Bolsheviks from the working class was, in large part, required to ensure their power and, moreover, a natural result of utilising state structures. *"The struggle against oppression - political, economic, and social, against the exploitation of man by man"* argued Alexander Berkman, *"is always simultaneously a struggle against government as such. The political State, whatever its form, and constructive revolutionary effort are irreconcilable. They are mutually exclusive."* Every revolution *"faces this alternative: to build freely, independently and despite of the government, or to choose government with all the limitation and stagnation it involves ... Not by the order of some central authority, but organically from life itself, must grow up the closely knit federation of the industrial, agrarian, and other associations; by the workers themselves must they be organised and managed."* The *"very essence and nature"* of the socialist state *"excludes such an evolution. Its economic and political centralisation, its governmentalism and bureaucratisation of every sphere of activity and effort, its inevitable militarisation and degradation of the human spirit mechanically destroy every germ of new life and extinguish the stimuli of creative, constructive work."* [**The Bolshevik Myth**, pp. 340-1] By creating a new state, the Bolsheviks ensured that the mass participation required to create a genuine socialist society could not be expressed and, moreover, came into conflict with the Bolshevik authorities and their attempts to impose their (essentially state capitalist) vision of "socialism".

It need not have been that way. As can be seen from our discussion of labour protest under the Bolsheviks, even in extremely hard circumstances the Russian people were able to organise themselves to conduct protest meetings, demonstrations and strikes. The social base for an alternative to Bolshevik power and policies existed. Sadly Bolshevik politics, policies and the repression they required ensured that it could not be used constructively during the revolution to create a genuine socialist revolution.

Section I
What would an anarchist society look like?

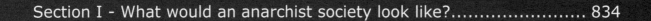

Section I - What would an anarchist society look like?........................ 834

I.1 Isn't libertarian socialism an oxymoron? 837
I.1.1 Is socialism impossible? 839
I.1.2 Is libertarian communism impossible? 845
I.1.3 What is wrong with markets anyway? 852
I.1.4 If capitalism is exploitative, then isn't communism as well? 855
I.1.5 Does capitalism efficiently allocate resources? 857

I.2 Is this a blueprint for an anarchist society? 863
I.2.1 Why discuss what an anarchist society would be like at all? 866
I.2.2 Will it be possible to go straight to an anarchist society from capitalism? 867
I.2.3 How is the framework of an anarchist society created? 869

I.3 What could the economic structure of anarchy look like? 872
I.3.1 What is a "syndicate"? 875
I.3.2 What is workers' self-management? 878
I.3.3 What does socialisation mean? 882
I.3.4 What relations would exist between individual syndicates? 885
I.3.5 What would confederations of syndicates do? 888
I.3.6 What about competition between syndicates? 891
I.3.7 What about people who do not want to join a syndicate? 894
I.3.8 Do anarchists seek "small autonomous communities, devoted to small scale production"? 895

I.4 How could an anarchist economy function? 897
I.4.1 What is the point of economic activity in anarchy? 899
I.4.2 Why do anarchists desire to abolish work? 900
I.4.3 How do anarchists intend to abolish work? 902
I.4.4 What economic decision making criteria could be used in anarchy? 906
I.4.5 What about "supply and demand"? 909
I.4.6 Surely anarchist-communism would just lead to demand exceeding supply? 912
I.4.7 What will stop producers ignoring consumers? 914
I.4.8 What about investment decisions? 916
I.4.9 Should technological advance be seen as anti-anarchistic? 918
I.4.10 What would be the advantage of a wide basis of surplus distribution? 920
I.4.11 If socialism eliminates the profit motive, won't performance suffer? 924
I.4.12 Won't there be a tendency for capitalist enterprise to reappear? 926
I.4.13 Who will do the dirty or unpleasant work? 930
I.4.14 What about the person who will not work? 932
I.4.15 What will the workplace of tomorrow look like? 933
I.4.16 Won't a libertarian communist society be inefficient? 935

I.5 What could the social structure of anarchy look like? 936
I.5.1 What are participatory communities? 938
I.5.2 Why are confederations of participatory communities needed? 941
I.5.3 Would confederations produce bureaucrats and politicians? 943
I.5.4 How will anything ever be decided by all these meetings? 944
I.5.5 Aren't participatory communities and confederations just new states? 947
I.5.6 Won't there be a danger of a "tyranny of the majority" under libertarian socialism? 948
I.5.7 What if I don't want to join a commune? 952
I.5.8 What about crime? 953
I.5.9 What about Freedom of Speech under Anarchism? 957
I.5.10 What about political parties, interest groups and professional bodies? 959
I.5.11 How will an anarchist society defend itself against the power hungry? 961
I.5.12 Would an anarchist society provide health care and other public services? 963

I.6 What about the "Tragedy of the Commons"? 965
I.6.1 How can property "owned by everyone in the world" be used? 968
I.6.2 Doesn't communal ownership involve restricting individual liberty? 969

I.7 Won't Libertarian Socialism destroy individuality? 972

I.8 Does revolutionary Spain show that libertarian socialism can work in practice? 974
I.8.1 Is the Spanish Revolution inapplicable as a model for modern societies? 976
I.8.2 How were the anarchists able to obtain mass popular support in Spain? 977
I.8.3 How were Spanish industrial collectives organised? 980
I.8.4 How were the Spanish industrial collectives co-ordinated? 981
I.8.5 How were the Spanish agricultural co-operatives organised and co-ordinated? 982
I.8.6 What did the agricultural collectives accomplish? 984
I.8.7 Were the rural collectives created by force? 985
I.8.8 But did the Spanish collectives innovate? 990
I.8.9 Why, if it was so good, did it not survive? 991
I.8.10 Why did the CNT collaborate with the state? 991
I.8.11 Was the decision to collaborate a product of anarchist theory? 993
I.8.12 Was the decision to collaborate imposed on the CNT's membership? 999
I.8.13 What political lessons were learned from the revolution? 1001
I.8.14 What economic lessons were learned from the revolution? 1004

Section I
What would an anarchist society look like?

So far this FAQ has been largely critical, focusing on hierarchy, capitalism, the state and so on, and the problems to which they have led, as well as refuting some bogus "solutions" that have been offered by authoritarians of both the right and the left. It is now time to examine the constructive side of anarchism — the libertarian-socialist society that anarchists envision. This is important because anarchism is essentially a **constructive** theory, in stark contradiction to the picture usually painted of anarchism as chaos or mindless destruction.

In this section of the FAQ we will give an outline of what an anarchist society might look like. Such a society has basic features — such as being non-hierarchical, decentralised and, above all else, spontaneous like life itself. This type of development implies that anarchist society would be organised from the simple to the complex, from the individual upwards to the community, the bio-region and, ultimately, the planet. The resulting society, which would be the outcome of nature freely unfolding toward greater diversity and complexity, is ethically preferable to any other sort of order simply because it allows for the highest degree of organic solidarity and freedom. Kropotkin described this vision of a truly free society as follows:

> "We foresee millions and millions of groups freely constituting themselves for the satisfaction of all the varied needs of human beings ... All these will be composed of human beings who will combine freely ... 'Take pebbles,' said Fourier, 'put them in a box and shake them, and they will arrange themselves in a mosaic that you could never get by instructing to anyone the work of arranging them harmoniously.'" [**The Place of Anarchism in Socialistic Evolution**, pp. 11-12]

Anarchist opposition to hierarchy is an essential part of a spontaneously ordered society, for authority stops the free development and growth of the individual. From this natural growth of individuals, groups and society as a whole anarchists expect a society which meets the needs of all — for individual and social freedom, material goods to meet physical needs and free and equal social relationships that meet what could be termed "spiritual needs" (i.e., mental and emotional wellbeing, creativity, ethical development and so on). Any attempt to force society or individuals into a pre-determined structure which restricts their liberty will produce **dis**-order as natural balances and development is hindered and distorted in anti-social and destructive directions. Thus an anarchist society must be a free society of free individuals, associating within libertarian structures, rather than a series of competing hierarchies (be they political or economical). Only in freedom can society and individuals develop and create a just and fair world. In Proudhon's words, "liberty is the mother of order, not its daughter."

As the individual does not exist in a social vacuum, appropriate social conditions are required for individual freedom to develop and blossom according to its full potential. The theory of anarchism is built around the central assertion that individuals and their organisations **cannot** be considered in isolation from each other. That is, social structures shape us, "that there is an interrelationship between the authority structures of institutions and the psychological qualities and attitudes of individuals" and that "the major function of participation is an educative one." [Carole Pateman, **Participation and Democratic Theory**, p. 27] Anarchism presents this position in its most coherent and libertarian form. In other words, freedom is only sustained and protected by activity under conditions of freedom, namely self-government. Freedom is the only precondition for acquiring the maturity required for continued freedom: "Only in freedom can man grow to his full stature. Only in freedom will he learn to think and move, and give the very best in him." [Emma Goldman, **Red Emma Speaks**, p. 72]

As individual freedom can only be created, developed and defended by self-government and free association, a system which encourages individuality must be decentralised and participatory in order for people to develop a psychology that allows them to accept the responsibilities of self-management. Living under the state or any other authoritarian system produces a servile character, as the individual is constantly placed under hierarchical authority, which blunts their critical and self-governing abilities by lack of use. Such a situation cannot promote freedom, and so anarchists "realise that power and authority corrupt those who exercise them as much as those who are compelled to submit to them." [Bakunin, **The Political Philosophy of Bakunin**, p. 249]

Looking at capitalism, we find that under wage labour people sell their creative energy and control over their activity for a given period. The boss does not just take surplus value from the time employees sell, but the time itself — their liberty, their ability to make their own decisions, express themselves through work and with their fellow workers. Wage labour equals wage slavery as you sell your time and skills (i.e. liberty) everyday at work and you will never be able to buy that time back for yourself. Once it is gone; it is gone for good. It also generates, to quote Godwin, a "sense of dependence" and a "servile and truckling spirit", so ensuring that the "feudal spirit still survives that reduced the great mass of mankind to the rank of slaves and cattle for the service of the few." [**The Anarchist Writings of William Godwin**, pp. 125-6] This is why anarchists see the need to "create the situation where each person may live by working freely, without being forced to sell his [or her] work and his [or her] liberty to others who accumulate wealth by the labour of their serfs." [Kropotkin, **Words of a Rebel**, p. 208]

Thus the aim of anarchism is to create a society in which every person "should have the material and moral means to develop his humanity" and so to **organise society in such a way that every individual ... should find ... approximately equal means for the development of [their] various faculties and for their utilisation in [their] work**; to create a society which would place every individual ... in such a position that it would be impossible for [them] to exploit the labour of anyone else" and be "enabled to participate in the enjoyment of social wealth" as long as they *"contributed directly toward the production of that wealth."* [Bakunin, **Op. Cit.**, p. 409] As such, anarchists would agree with George Orwell: *"The question is very simple. Shall people ... be allowed to live the decent, fully human life which is now technically achievable, or shan't they? Shall the common man be pushed back into the mud, or shall he not?"* [**Orwell on Spain**, p. 361]

Anarchism, in summary, is about changing society and abolishing all forms of authoritarian social relationship, putting life before the soul-destroying "efficiency" needed to survive under capitalism; for the anarchist *"takes his stand on his positive right to life and all its pleasures, both intellectual, moral and physical. He loves life, and intends to enjoy it to the full."* [Bakunin, **Michael Bakunin: Selected Writings**, p. 101] Thus, to quote Emma Goldman, *"all human-beings, irrespective of race, colour, or sex, are born with the equal right to share at the table of life; that to secure this right, there must be established among men economic, social, and political freedom."* [**A Documentary History of the American Years**, vol. 2, p. 450] This would be a classless and non-hierarchical society, one without masters and servants, one based on the free association of free individuals which encourages and celebrates individuality and freedom:

> *"The phrase, 'a classless society', no doubt has terrors for any thoughtful person. It calls up immediately the image of dull mediocrity ... all one uniform scale of self-sufficient individuals, living in model-houses, travelling in uniform Fords along endless uniform roads ... But ... the sharing of this wealth would not produce a uniformity of life, simply because there is no uniformity of desire. Uniformity is an unintelligent nightmare; there can be no uniformity in a free human society. Uniformity can only be created by the tyranny of a totalitarian regime."* [Herbert Read, **Anarchy and Order**, pp. 87-8]

Anarchists think that the essential social values are human values, and that society is a complex of associations which express the wills of their members, whose well-being is its purpose. We consider that it is not enough that the forms of association should have the passive or "implied" consent of their members, but that the society, and the individuals who make it up, will be healthy only if it is in the full sense libertarian, i.e. self-governing, self-managed, and egalitarian. This implies not only that all the members should have a right to influence its policy if they so desire, but that the greatest possible opportunity should be afforded for every person to exercise this right. Anarchism involves an active, not merely passive, citizenship on the part of society's members and holds that this principle is not only applied to some "special" sphere of social action called "politics" but to any and every form of social action, including economic activity.

So, as will be seen, the key concept underlying both the social/political and the economic structure of libertarian socialism is *"self-management,"* a term that implies not only workers control of their workplaces but also citizens' control of their communities (where it becomes *"self-government"*), through direct democracy and voluntary federation. Thus self-management is the positive implication of anarchism's "negative" principle of opposition to hierarchical authority. For through self-management, hierarchical authority is dissolved as self-managing workplace and community assemblies/councils are decentralised, "horizontal" organisations in which each participant has an equal voice in the decisions that affect his or her life, instead of merely following orders and being governed by others. Self-management, therefore, is the essential condition for a world in which individuals will be free to follow their own dreams, in their own ways, co-operating together as equals without interference from any form of authoritarian power (such as government or boss).

Perhaps needless to say, this section is intended as a heuristic device **only**, as a way of helping readers envision how anarchist principles might be embodied in practice. It is not (nor is it intended to be, nor is it desired to be) a definitive statement of how they **must** be embodied. The idea that a few people could determine exactly what a free society would look like is contrary to the anarchist principles of free growth and thought, and is far from our intention. Here we simply try to indicate some of the structures that an anarchist society may contain, based on the ideals and ideas anarchists hold, informed by the few examples of anarchy in action that have existed and our critical evaluation of their limitations and successes. As Herbert Read once put it, *"it is always a mistake to build **a priori** constitutions. The main thing is to establish your principles — the principles of equity, of individual freedom, of workers' control. The community then aims at the establishment of these principles from the starting-point of local needs and local conditions."* [**Op. Cit.**, p. 51]

Moreover, we must remember that the state has changed over time and has not always existed. Thus it is possible to have a social organisation which is not a state and to confuse the two would be a *"confusion"* made by those *"who cannot visualise Society without a concentration of the State."* Yet this *"is to overlook the fact that Man lived in Societies for thousands of years before the State had been heard of"* and that *"large numbers of people [have] lived in communes and free federations."* These were not states as the state *"is only one of the forms assumed by society in the course of history. Why then make no distinction between what is permanent and what is accidental?"* [Kropotkin, **The State: Its Historic Role**, pp. 9-10] Similarly, the axioms of capitalist economics **not** withstanding, capitalism is but latest of a series of economies. Just as serfdom replaced slavery and capitalism replaced serfdom, so free (associated) labour can replace hired labour. As Proudhon noted, the *"period through which we are now passing"* is *"distinguished by a special characteristic: WAGE-LABOUR."* Capitalism has not always existed nor need it continue. So while *"the radical vice of political economy"* is *"affirming as a definitive state a transitory condition - namely, the division of society into patricians and proletarians"* in reality, *"in its present form, the organisation [of labour] is inadequate and transitory."* [**Property Is Theft!**, p. 190, p. 174 and p. 170] Anarchists seek to make that transitory condition shorter rather than longer.

Ultimately, a free society based on self-managed communities and associated labour is, in many ways, a natural evolution of tendencies **within** existing society. For example, the means of production can only be used collectively, so suggesting that relations of equality and freedom based on associations of workers are a sensible alternative to ones based on the hierarchy, exploitation and oppression of masters and servants. It is the struggle against those oppressive social relationships which creates the very associations (workplace strike assemblies) which could expropriate the workplaces and make that possibility a reality.

So an anarchist society will not be created overnight nor without links to the past, and so it will initially be based on structures created in social struggle (i.e. created **within** but **against** capitalism and the state) and will be marked with the ideas that inspired and developed within that struggle. For example, the anarchist collectives in Spain were organised in a bottom-up manner, similar to the way the C.N.T. (the anarcho-syndicalist labour union) was organised before the revolution. In this sense, anarchy is not some distant goal but rather an expression of working class struggle. The creation of alternatives to the current hierarchical, oppressive, exploitative and alienated society is a necessary part of the struggle and the maintaining of your liberty and humanity in the insane world of hierarchical society. As such, an anarchist society will be the generalisation of the various types of **"anarchy in action"** created in the various struggles against all forms of oppression and exploitation (see section I.2.3).

This means that how an anarchist society would look like and work is not independent of the specific societies it is created from nor the means used to create it. In other words, an anarchist society will reflect the economic conditions inherited from capitalism, the social struggles which preceded it and the ideas which existed within that struggle as modified by the practical needs of any given situation. Therefore the vision of a free society indicated in this section of the FAQ is not some sort of abstraction which will be created overnight. If anarchists did think that then we would rightly be called utopian. No, an anarchist society is the outcome of social struggle, self-activity which helps to create a mass movement which contains individuals who can think for themselves and are willing and able to take responsibility for their own lives.

So, when reading this section please remember that this is not a blueprint but only possible suggestions of what anarchy would look like. It is designed to provoke thought and indicate that an anarchist society is possible. We hope that our arguments and ideas presented in this section will inspire more debate and discussion of how a free society could work and, equally as important, help to inspire the struggle which will create that society.

We must stress, however, that anarchists do not want a "perfect" society (as is often associated with the term *"utopia"*). This would be as impossible as the neo-classical economic vision of perfect competition. Rather we want a free society and so one based on real human beings and so one with its own problems and difficulties. No society has ever been perfect and no society ever will be. All we argue is that an anarchist society will have fewer problems than those before and be better to live within. Anyone looking for perfection should look elsewhere. Anyone looking for a better, but still human and so imperfect, world may find in anarchism a potential end for their quest.

So anarchists are realistic in their hopes and dreams. We do not conjure up hopes that cannot achieved but rather base our visions in an analysis of what is wrong with society today and a means of changing the world for the better. And even if some people call us utopians, we shrug off the accusation with a smile. After all, dreams are important, not only because they are often the source of change in reality but because of the hope they express:

> *"People may ... call us dreamers ... They fail to see that dreams are also a part of the reality of life, that life without dreams would be unbearable. No change in our way of life would be possible without dreams and dreamers. The only people who are never disappointed are those who never hope and never try to realise their hope."* [Rudolf Rocker, **The London Years**, p. 95]

One last point. We must point out here that we are discussing the social and economic structures of areas within which the inhabitants are predominately anarchists. It is obviously the case that areas in which the inhabitants are not anarchists will take on different forms depending upon the ideas that dominate there. Hence, assuming the end of the current state structure, we could see anarchist communities along with statist ones (capitalist or socialist) and these communities taking different forms depending on what their inhabitants want — communist to individualist communities in the case of anarchist ones, state socialist to private state communities in the statist areas, ones based on religious sects and so on. As Malatesta argued, anarchists *"must be intransigent in our opposition to all capitalist imposition and exploitation, and tolerant of all social concepts which prevail in different human groupings, so long as they do not threaten the equal rights and freedom of others."* [**Errico Malatesta: His Life and Ideas**, p. 174] Thus we respect the wishes of others to experiment and live their own lives as they see fit, while encouraging those in capitalist and other statist communities to rise in revolution against their masters and join the free federation of the anarchist community. Needless to say, we do not discuss non-anarchist communities here as it is up to non-anarchists to present their arguments in favour of their kind of statism.

However, it would be a mistake to assume that just because there are many choices of community available that it automatically makes a society an anarchist one. For example, the modern world boasts over 200 different states. For most of them, individuals can leave and join another if it will let them. There is no world government as such. This does not make this series of states an anarchy. Similarly, a system based on different corporations is not an anarchy either, nor would be one based on a series of company towns and neither would a (quasi-feudal or neo-feudal?) system based on a multitude of landlords who hire their land and workplaces to workers in return for rent. The nature of the associations is just as important as their voluntary nature. As Kropotkin argued, the *"communes of the next revolution will not only break down the state and substitute free federation for parliamentary rule; they will part with parliamentary rule within the commune itself ... They will be anarchist within the commune as they will be anarchist outside it."* [**Selected Writings on Anarchism and Revolution**, p. 132] Hence an anarchist society is one that is freely joined and left, is internally non-hierarchical and non-oppressive and non-exploitative. Thus anarchist communities may co-exist with non-anarchist ones but this does **not** mean the non-anarchist ones are in any way anarchistic or libertarian.

To conclude. Anarchists, to state the blindly obvious, do not aim for chaos, anarchy in the popular sense of the word (George

Orwell once noted how one right-wing author *"use[d] 'Anarchism' indifferently with 'anarchy', which is a hardly more correct use of words than saying that a Conservative is one who makes jam."* [**Op. Cit.**, p. 298]). Nor do anarchists reject any discussion of what a free society would be like (such a rejection is usually based on the somewhat spurious grounds that you cannot prescribe what free people would do). In fact, anarchists have quite strong opinions on the basic outlines of a free society, always premised on the assumption that these are guidelines only. These suggestions are based on libertarian principles, developments in the class struggle and a keen awareness of what is wrong with class and hierarchical systems (and so what **not** to do!).

When reading this section of the FAQ remember that an anarchist society will be created by the autonomous actions of the mass of the population, not by anarchists writing books about it. This means any real anarchist society will make many mistakes and develop in ways we cannot predict. This implies that this is only a series of suggestions on how things **could** work in an anarchist society — it is **not** a blueprint of any kind. All anarchists can do is present what we believe and why we think such a vision is both desirable **and** viable. We hope that our arguments and ideas presented in this section of the FAQ will inspire more debate and discussion of how a free society would work. In addition, and equally as important, we hope it will help inspire the struggle that will create that society.

I.1

Isn't libertarian socialism an oxymoron?

In a word, no. This question is often asked by those who have come across the so-called "libertarian" right. As discussed in section A.1.3, the word libertarian has been used by anarchists for far longer than the pro-free market right have been using it. In fact, anarchists have been using it as a synonym for anarchist for over 150 years, since 1858. In comparison, widespread use of the term by the so-called "libertarian" right dates from the 1970s in America (with, from the 1940s onwards, limited use by a few individuals). Indeed, outside of North America libertarian is still essentially used as an equivalent of anarchist and as a shortened version of libertarian socialist. As Noam Chomsky notes:

> *"Let me just say regarding the terminology, since we happen to be in the United States, we have to be rather careful. Libertarian in the United States has a meaning which is almost the opposite of what it has in the rest of the world traditionally. Here, libertarian means ultra right-wing capitalist. In the European tradition, libertarian meant socialist. So, anarchism was sometimes called libertarian socialism, a large wing of anarchism, so we have to be a little careful about terminology."*
> [**Reluctant Icon**]

This in itself does not prove that the term libertarian socialist is free of contradiction. However, as we will show below, the claim that the term is self-contradictory rests on the assumption that socialism requires the state in order to exist and that socialism is incompatible with liberty (and the equally fallacious claim that capitalism is libertarian and does not need the state). This assumption, as is often true of many objections to socialism, is based on a misconception of what socialism is, a misconception that many authoritarian socialists and the state capitalism of Soviet Russia have helped to foster. In reality it is the term "state socialism" which is the true oxymoron.

Sadly many people take for granted the assertion of many on the right and left that socialism equals Leninism or Marxism and ignore the rich and diverse history of socialist ideas, ideas that spread from communist and individualist-anarchism to Leninism. As Benjamin Tucker once noted, *"the fact that State Socialism … has overshadowed other forms of Socialism gives it no right to a monopoly of the Socialistic idea."* [**Instead of a Book**, pp. 363-4] Unfortunately, many on the left combine with the right to do exactly that. Indeed, the right (and, of course, many on the left) consider that, by definition, "socialism" **is** state ownership and control of the means of production, along with centrally planned determination of the national economy (and so social life).

Yet even a quick glance at the history of the socialist movement indicates that the identification of socialism with state ownership and control is not common. For example, Anarchists, many Guild Socialists, council communists (and other libertarian Marxists), as well as followers of Robert Owen, all rejected state ownership. Indeed, anarchists recognised that the means of production did not change their form as capital when the state took over their ownership nor did wage-labour change its nature when it is the state employing labour (for example, see section H.3.13). For anarchists state ownership of capital is not socialistic in the slightest as it turned **everyone** into a proletarian (bar the state bureaucracy) — hardly a desirable thing for a political theory aiming for the end of wage slavery!

So what **does** socialism mean? Is it compatible with libertarian ideals? What do the words libertarian and socialism actually mean? It is temping to use dictionary definitions as a starting point, although we should stress that such a method holds problems as different dictionaries have different definitions and the fact that dictionaries are rarely politically sophisticated. Use one definition, and someone else will counter with one more to their liking. For example, socialism is often defined as *"state ownership of wealth"* and anarchy as *"disorder."* Neither of these definitions are useful when discussing political ideas, particularly anarchism as, obviously, no form of anarchism would be socialist by such a definition nor do anarchists seek disorder. Therefore, the use of dictionaries is not the end of a discussion and often misleading when applied to politics.

Libertarian, though, is generally defined to mean someone who upholds the principles of liberty, especially individual liberty of thought and action. Such a situation cannot but be encouraged by socialism, by free access to the means of life. This is because in such a situation people associate as equals and so, as John Most and Emma Goldman once argued, the *"system of communism logically excludes any and every relation between master and servant, and means really Anarchism."* [*"Talking about Anarchy"*,

p. 28, **Black Flag**, no. 228, p. 28] In other words, by basing itself on free association and self-management in every aspect of life the anarchist form of socialism cannot but be libertarian.

In other words, there is a reason why anarchists have used the term libertarian for over 150 years! More to the point, why assume that the right's recent appropriation of the word be considered the base point? That implies that private property defends individual liberty rather than suppresses it. Such an assumption, as anarchists have argued from the start of anarchism as a distinct socio-political theory, is wrong. As we discussed earlier (see section B.4, for example), capitalism denies liberty of thought and action within the workplace (unless one is the boss, of course). As one staunch defender of capitalism (and a classical liberal often listed as a forefather of right-wing "libertarianism") glibly noted, the capitalist *"of course exercises power over the workers"*, although *"he cannot exercise it arbitrarily"* thanks to the market but within this limit *"the entrepreneur is free to give full rein to his whims"* and *"to dismiss workers offhand."* [Ludwig von Mises, **Socialism**, p. 443 and p. 444] Right-wing "libertarians" are utterly blind to the liberty-destroying hierarchies associated with private property, perhaps unsurprisingly as they are fundamentally pro-capitalist and anti-socialist (equally unsurprisingly, genuine libertarians tend to call them "propertarians"). As left-wing economist Geoffrey M. Hodgson correctly notes:

> *"By their own logic, [such] market individualists are forced to disregard the organisational structure of the firm, or to falsely imagine that markets exist inside it. To do otherwise would be to admit that a system as dynamic as capitalism depends upon a mode of organisation from which markets are excluded … This … allows market individualists to ignore the reality of non-market organisations in the private sector … They can thus ignore the reality of control and authority within the private capitalist corporation but remain critical of public sector bureaucracy and state planning."* [**Economics and Utopia**, pp. 85-6]

The propertarian perspective inevitably generates massive contradictions, such as admitting that both the state and private property share a common monopoly of decision making over a given area yet opposing only the former (see section F.1). As anarchists have long pointed out, the hierarchical social relations associated with private property have nothing to do with individual liberty. Removing the state but keeping private property would, therefore, not be a step forward: *"A fine business we would make if we destroyed the State and replaced it with a mass of little States! killing a monster with one head and keeping a monster with a thousand heads!"* [Carlo Cafiero, *"Anarchy and Communism"*, pp. 179-86, **The Raven**, No. 6, p. 181]

This is why we argue that anarchism is more than just a stateless society, for while a society without a state is a necessary condition for anarchy it is not sufficient — private hierarchies also limit freedom. Hence Chomsky:

> *"It's all generally based on the idea that hierarchic and authoritarian structures are not self-justifying. They have*

to have a justification … For example, your workplace is one point of contact and association. So, workplaces ought to be democratically controlled by participants … there are all kinds of ways in which people interact with one another. The forms of organisation and association that grow out of those should be, to the extent possible, non-authoritarian, non-hierarchic, managed and directed by the participants." [**Reluctant Icon**]

Therefore, anarchists argue, **real** libertarian ideas **must** be based on workers self-management, i.e. workers must control and manage the work they do, determining where and how they do it and what happens to the fruit of their labour, which in turn means the elimination of wage labour. Unless this is done then the majority of people will become subject to the authoritarian social relationships the likes of Mises and other right-wing "libertarians" support. As one communist-anarchist put it:

> *"It is because the individual does not own himself, and is not permitted to be his true self. He has become a mere market commodity, an instrument for the accumulation of property — for others … Individuality is stretched on the Procrustes bed of business … If our individuality were to be made the price of breathing, what ado there would be about the violence done to the personality! And yet our very right to food, drink and shelter is only too often conditioned upon our loss of individuality. These things are granted to the propertyless millions (and how scantily!) only in exchange for their individuality — they become the mere instruments of industry."* [Max Baginski, *"Stirner: The Ego and His Own"*, pp. 142-151, **Mother Earth**, Vol. II, No. 3, p. 150]

Socialism, anarchists argue, can only mean a classless and anti-authoritarian (i.e. libertarian) society in which people manage their own affairs, either as individuals or as part of a group (depending on the situation). In other words, it implies self-management in all aspects of life — including work. It has always struck anarchists as somewhat strange and paradoxical (to say the least) that a system of *"natural"* liberty (Adam Smith's term, misappropriated by supporters of capitalism) involves the vast majority having to sell that liberty in order to survive. Thus to be consistently libertarian is, logically, to advocate self-management, and so socialism (see section G.4.2). This explains the long standing anarchist opposition to the phoney "individualism" associated with classical liberalism (so-called right-wing "libertarian" ideology, although better termed "propertarian" to avoid confusion). Thus we find Emma Goldman dismissing *"this kind of individualism"* in *"whose name … social oppression are defended and held up as virtues."* [**Red Emma Speaks**, p. 112]

As we will discuss in section I.3.3, socialisation is advocated to ensure the elimination of wage labour and is a common theme of all genuine forms of socialism. Anarchists argue that state socialism does not eliminate wage labour, rather it universalises it. In fact, state socialism shows that socialism is **necessarily** libertarian, not statist. For if the state owns the workplace, then the producers do not, and so they will not be at liberty to manage their own work but will instead be subject to the state as the boss. Moreover, replacing the capitalist owning class by state officials in no way eliminates wage labour; in fact it makes it worse in many cases. Therefore "socialists" who argue for nationalisation of the means of production are **not** socialists (which means that the Soviet Union and the other so-called "socialist" countries were/are **not** socialist nor are parties which advocate nationalisation socialist).

Indeed, attempts to associate socialism with the state misunderstands the nature of socialism. It is an essential principle of socialism that (social) inequalities between individuals must be abolished to ensure liberty for all (**natural** inequalities cannot be abolished, nor do anarchists desire to do so). Socialism, as Proudhon put it, *"is egalitarian above all else."* [**No Gods, No Masters**, vol. 1, p. 57] This applies to inequalities of power as well, especially to **political** power. And any hierarchical system (particularly the state) is marked by inequalities of power — those at the top (elected or not) have more power than those at the bottom. Hence the following comments provoked by the expulsion of anarchists from the social democratic Second International:

> *"It could be argued with much more reason that we are the most logical and most complete socialists, since we demand for every person not just his [or her] entire measure of the wealth of society but also his [or her] portion of social power, which is to say, the real ability to make his [or her] influence felt, along with that of everybody else, in the administration of public affairs."* [Malatesta and Hamon, **Op. Cit.**, vol. 2, p. 20]

The election of someone to administer public affairs **for you** is not having a portion of social power. It is, to use the words of leading French anarcho-syndicalist Emile Pouget, *"an act of abdication,"* the delegating of power into the hands of a few. [**Op. Cit.**, p. 67] This means that *"[a]ll political power inevitably creates a* ***privileged situation*** *for the men who exercise it. Thus it violates, from the beginning, the equalitarian principle."* [Voline, **The Unknown Revolution**, p. 249]

From this short discussion we see the links between libertarian and socialism. To be a true libertarian requires you to support workers' control otherwise you support authoritarian social relationships. To support workers' control, by necessity, means that you must ensure that the producers own (and so control) the means of producing and distributing the goods they create. Without ownership, they cannot truly control their own activity or the product of their labour. The situation where workers possess the means of producing and distributing goods is socialism. Thus to be a true libertarian requires you to be a socialist.

Similarly, a true socialist must also support individual liberty of thought and action, otherwise the producers "possess" the means of production and distribution in name only. If the state owns the means of life, then the producers do not and so are in no position to manage their own activity. As the experience of Russia under Lenin shows, state ownership soon produces state control and the creation of a bureaucratic class which exploits and oppresses the workers even more so than their old bosses. Since it is an essential principle of socialism that inequalities between people must be abolished in order to ensure liberty, it makes no sense for a genuine socialist to support any institution based on inequalities of power (and as we discussed in section B.2, the state is just such an institution). To oppose inequality and not extend that opposition to inequalities in power, especially **political** power, suggests a lack of clear thinking. Thus to be a true socialist requires you to be a libertarian, to be for individual liberty and opposed to inequalities of power which restrict that liberty.

Therefore, rather than being an oxymoron, libertarian socialism indicates that true socialism must be libertarian and that a libertarian who is not a socialist is a phoney. As true socialists oppose wage labour, they must also oppose the state for the same reasons. Similarly, consistent libertarians must oppose wage labour for the same reasons they must oppose the state. So, libertarian socialism rejects the idea of state ownership and control of the economy, along with the state as such. Through workers' self-management it proposes to bring an end to authority, exploitation, and hierarchy in production. This in itself will increase, not reduce, liberty. Those who argue otherwise rarely claim that political democracy results in less freedom than political dictatorship. As Bakunin put it in 1867:

> *"We are convinced that freedom without Socialism is privilege and injustice, and that Socialism without freedom is slavery and brutality."* [**Bakunin on Anarchism**, p. 127]

History has proven him correct. Rather than libertarian socialism being the oxymoron, it is state socialism and libertarian capitalism that are. Both historically (in terms of who first used the word) and logically (in terms of opposing all hierarchical organisations) it is anarchists who should be called libertarians, **not** the propertarian right.

I.1.1
Is socialism impossible?

In 1920, the right-wing economist Ludwig von Mises declared socialism to be impossible. A leading member of the "Austrian" school of economics, he argued this on the grounds that without private ownership of the means of production, there cannot be a competitive market for production goods and without a market for production goods, it is impossible to determine their values. Without knowing their values, economic rationality is impossible and so a socialist economy would simply be chaos: *"the absurd output of a senseless apparatus."* For Mises, socialism meant central planning with the economy *"subject to the control of a supreme authority."* [*"Economic Calculation in the Socialist Commonwealth"*, pp. 87-130, **Collectivist Economic Planning**, F.A von Hayek (ed.), p. 104 and p. 106] While applying his *"economic calculation argument"* to Marxist ideas of a future socialist society, his argument, it is claimed, is applicable to **all** schools of socialist thought, including libertarian ones. It is on the basis of his arguments that many right-wingers claim that libertarian (or any other kind of) socialism is impossible in principle.

Yet as David Schweickart observes it *"has long been recognised that Mises's argument is logically defective. Even without a market* in production goods, their monetary values can be determined." [**Against Capitalism**, p. 88] In other words, economic calculation based on prices is perfectly possible in a libertarian socialist system. After all, to build a workplace requires so many tonnes of steel, so many bricks, so many hours of work and so on. If we assume a mutualist society, then the prices of these goods can be easily found as the co-operatives in question would be offering their services on the market. These commodities would be the inputs for the construction of production goods and so the latter's monetary values can be found.

Ironically enough, Mises **did** mention the idea of such a mutualist system in his initial essay. "*Exchange relations between production-goods can only be established on the basis of private ownership of the means of production*" he asserted. "*When the 'coal syndicate' provides the 'iron syndicate' with coal, no price can be formed, except when both syndicates are the owners of the means of production employed in their business. This would not be socialisation but workers' capitalism and syndicalism.*" [**Op. Cit.**, p. 112] However, his argument is flawed for numerous reasons.

First, and most obvious, socialisation (as we discuss in section I.3.3) simply means free access to the means of life. As long as those who join a workplace have the same rights and liberties as existing members then there is socialisation. A market system of co-operatives, in other words, is **not** capitalist as there is no wage labour involved as a new workers become full members of the syndicate, with the same rights and freedoms as existing members. Thus there are no hierarchical relationships between owners and wage slaves (even if these owners also happen to work there). As all workers' control the means of production they use, it is not capitalism.

Second, nor is such a system usually called, as Mises suggests, "*syndicalism*" but rather mutualism and he obviously considered its most famous advocate, Proudhon and his "*fantastic dreams*" of a mutual bank, as a socialist. [**Op. Cit.**, p. 88] Significantly, Mises subsequently admitted that it was "*misleading*" to call syndicalism workers' capitalism, although "*the workers are the owners of the means of production*" it was "*not genuine socialism, that is, centralised socialism*", as it "*must withdraw productive goods from the market. Individual citizens must not dispose of the shares in the means of production which are allotted to them.*" Syndicalism, i.e., having those who do the work control it, was "*the ideal of plundering hordes*"! [**Socialism**, p. 274fn, p. 270, p. 273 and p. 275]

His followers, likewise, concluded that "syndicalism" was not capitalism with Hayek stating that there were "*many types of socialism*" including "*communism, syndicalism, guild socialism*". Significantly, he indicated that Mises argument was aimed at systems based on the "*central direction of all economic activity*" and so "*earlier systems of more decentralised socialism, like guild-socialism or syndicalism, need not concern us here since it seems now to be fairly generally admitted that they provide no mechanism whatever for a rational direction of economic activity.*" ["*The Nature and History of the Problem*", pp. 1-40, **Collectivist Economic Planning**, F.A von Hayek (ed.),p. 17, p. 36 and p. 19] Sadly he failed to indicate who "*generally admitted*" such a conclusion. More recently, Murray Rothbard urged the state to impose private shares onto the workers in the former Stalinist regimes of Eastern Europe

as ownership was "*not to be granted to collectives or co-operatives or workers or peasants holistically, which would only bring back the ills of socialism in a decentralised and chaotic syndicalist form.*" [**The Logic of Action II**, p. 210]

More importantly, the whole premise of his critique of mutualism is flawed. "*Exchange relations in productive goods*" he asserted, "*can only be established on the basis of private property in the means of production. If the Coal Syndicate delivers coal to the Iron Syndicate a price can be fixed only if both syndicates own the means of production in industry.*" [**Socialism**, p. 132] This may come as a surprise to the many companies whose different workplaces sell each other their products! In other words, capitalism itself shows that workplaces owned by the same body (in this case, a large company) can exchange goods via the market. That Mises makes such a statement indicates well the firm basis of his argument in reality. Thus a socialist society can have extensive autonomy for its co-operatives, just as a large capitalist firm can:

> "*the entrepreneur is in a position to separate the calculation of each part of his total enterprise in such a way that he can determine the role it plays within his whole enterprise. Thus he can look at each section as if it were a separate entity and can appraise it according to the share it contributes to the success of the total enterprise. Within this system of business calculation each section of a firm represents an integral entity, a hypothetical independent business, as it were. It is assumed that this section 'owns' a definite part of the whole capital employed in the enterprise, that it buys from other sections and sells to them, that it has its own expenses and its own revenues, that its dealings result either in a profit or in a loss which is imputed to its own conduct of affairs as distinguished from the result of the other sections. Thus the entrepreneur can assign to each section's management a great deal of independence … Every manager and submanager is responsible for the working of his section or subsection. It is to his credit if the accounts show a profit, and it is to his disadvantage if they show a loss. His own interests impel him toward the utmost care and exertion in the conduct of his section's affairs.*" [**Human Action**, pp. 301-2]

So much, then, for the notion that common ownership makes it impossible for market socialism to work. After all, the libertarian community can just as easily separate the calculation of each part of its enterprise in such a way as to determine the role each co-operative plays in its economy. It can look at each section as if it were a separate entity and appraise it according to the share it contributes as it is assumed that each section "owns" (i.e., has use rights over) its definite part. It can then buy from, and sell to, other co-operatives and a profit or loss can be imputed to evaluate the independent action of each co-operative and so their own interests impel the co-operative workers toward the utmost care and exertion in the conduct of their co-operative's affairs.

So to refute Mises, we need only repeat what he himself argued about large corporations! Thus there can be extensive autonomy for workplaces under socialism and this does not in any way contradict the fact that *"all the means of production are the property of the community."* [*"Economic Calculation in the Socialist Commonwealth"*, **Op. Cit.**, p. 89] Socialisation, in other words, does **not** imply central planning but rather free access and free association. In summary, then, Mises confused property rights with use rights, possession with property, and failed to see how a mutualist system of socialised co-operatives exchanging products can be a viable alternative to the current exploitative and oppressive economic regime.

Such a mutualist economy also strikes at the heart of Mises' claims that socialism was *"impossible."* Given that he accepted that there may be markets, and hence market prices, for consumer goods in a socialist economy his claims of the impossibility of socialism seems unfounded. For Mises, the problem for socialism was that *"because no production-good will ever become the object of exchange, it will be impossible to determine its monetary value."* [**Op. Cit.**, p. 92] The flaw in his argument is clear. Taking, for example, coal, we find that it is both a means of production and of consumption. If a market in consumer goods is possible for a socialist system, then competitive prices for production goods is also possible as syndicates producing production-goods would also sell the product of their labour to other syndicates or communes. As Mises admitted when discussing one scheme of guild socialism, *"associations and sub-associations maintain a mutual exchange-relationship; they receive and give as if they were owners. Thus a market and market-prices are formed."* Thus, when deciding upon a new workplace, railway or house, the designers in question do have access to competitive prices with which to make their decisions. Nor does Mises' argument work against communal ownership in such a system as the commune would be buying products from syndicates in the same way as one part of a company can buy products from another part of the same company under capitalism. That goods produced by self-managed syndicates have market-prices does not imply capitalism for, as they abolish wage labour and are based on free-access (socialisation), it is a form of socialism (as socialists define it, Mises' protestations that *"this is incompatible with socialism"* not-with-standing!). [**Socialism**, p. 518]

Murray Rothbard suggested that a self-managed system would fail, and a system *"composed exclusively of self-managed enterprises is impossible, and would lead ... to calculative chaos and complete breakdown."* When *"each firm is owned jointly by all factor-owners"* then *"there is no separation at all between workers, landowners, capitalists, and entrepreneurs. There would be no way, then, of separating the wage incomes received from the interest or rent incomes or profits received. And now we finally arrive at the real reason why the economy cannot consist completely of such firms (called 'producers' co-operatives'). For, without an external market for wage rates, rents, and interest, there would be no rational way for entrepreneurs to allocate factors in accordance with the wishes of the consumers. No one would know where he could allocate his land or his labour to provide the maximum monetary gains. No entrepreneur would know how to arrange factors in their most value-productive combination to earn greatest profit. There could be no efficiency in production because the requisite knowledge would be lacking."* [quoted by David L. Prychitko, **Markets, Planning and Democracy**, p. 135 and p. 136]

It is hard to take this argument seriously. Consider, for example, a pre-capitalist society of farmers and artisans. Both groups of people own their own means of production (the land and the tools they use). The farmers grow crops for the artisans who, in turn, provide the farmers with the tools they use. According to Rothbard, the farmers would have no idea what to grow nor would the artisans know which tools to buy to meet the demand of the farmers nor which to use to reduce their working time. Presumably, both the farmers and artisans would stay awake at night worrying what to produce, wishing they had a landlord and boss to tell them how best to use their labour and resources.

Let us add the landlord class to this society. Now the landlord can tell the farmer what to grow as their rent income indicates how to allocate the land to its most productive use. Except, of course, it is still the farmers who decide what to produce. Knowing that they will need to pay rent (for access to the land) they will decide to devote their (rented) land to the most profitable use in order to both pay the rent and have enough to live on. Why they do not seek the most profitable use without the need for rent is not explored by Rothbard. Much the same can be said of artisans subject to a boss, for the worker can evaluate whether an investment in a specific new tool will result in more income or reduced time labouring or whether a new product will likely meet the needs of consumers. Moving from a pre-capitalist society to a post-capitalist one, it is clear that a system of self-managed co-operatives can make the same decisions without requiring economic masters. This is unsurprising, given that Mises' asserted that the boss *"of course exercises power over the workers"* but that the *"lord of production is the consumer."* [**Socialism**, p. 443] In which case, the boss need not be an intermediary between the real "lord" and those who do the production!

All in all, Rothbard confirms Kropotkin's comments that economics (*"that pseudo-science of the bourgeoisie"*) *"does not cease to give praise in every way to the benefits of individual property"* yet *"the economists do not conclude, 'The land to him who cultivates it.' On the contrary, they hasten to deduce from the situation, 'The land to the lord who will get it cultivated by wage earners!"* [**Words of a Rebel**, pp. 209-10] In addition, Rothbard implicitly places "efficiency" above liberty, preferring dubious "efficiency" gains to the actual gains in freedom which the abolition of workplace autocracy would create. Given a choice between liberty and "efficiency", the genuine anarchist would prefer liberty. Luckily, though, workplace liberty increases efficiency so Rothbard's decision is a wrong one. It should also be noted that Rothbard's position (as is usually the case) is directly opposite that of Proudhon, who considered it *"inevitable"* that in a free society *"the two functions of* **Wage-Worker** *on the one hand, and of* **Proprietor-Capitalist-Entrepreneur** *on the other, become equal and inseparable in the person of every worker"*. This was the *"first principle of the new economy, a principle full of hope and of consolation for the worker without capital, but a principle full of terror for the parasite and for the tools of parasitism, who see reduced to naught their celebrated formula:* **Capital, labour, talent***!"* [**Property is Theft!**, p. 535 and p. 289]

And it does seem a strange co-incidence that someone born into a capitalist economy, ideologically supporting it with a passion and seeking to justify its class system just happens to deduce from a given set of axioms that landlords and capitalists happen to play a vital role in the economy! It would not take too much time to determine if someone in a society without landlords or capitalists would also logically deduce from the same axioms the pressing economic necessity for such classes. Nor would it take long to ponder why Greek philosophers, like Aristotle, concluded that slavery was natural. And it does seem strange that centuries of coercion, authority, statism, classes and hierarchies all had absolutely no impact on how society evolved, as the end product of real history (the capitalist economy) just happens to be the same as Rothbard's deductions from a few assumptions predict. Little wonder, then, that "Austrian" economics seems more like rationalisations for some ideologically desired result than a serious economic analysis.

Even some dissident "Austrian" economists recognise the weakness of Rothbard's position. Thus *"Rothbard clearly misunderstands the general principle behind producer co-operatives and self-management in general."* In reality, *"[a]s a democratic method of enterprise organisation, workers' self-management is, in principle, fully compatible with a market system"* and so *"a market economy comprised of self-managed enterprises is consistent with Austrian School theory ... It is fundamentally a* **market-based system** *... that doesn't seem to face the epistemological hurdles ... that prohibit rational economic calculation"* under state socialism. Sadly, socialism is still equated with central planning, for such a system *"is certainly not socialism. Nor, however, is it capitalism in the conventional sense of the term."* In fact, it is not capitalism at all and if we assume that free access to resources such as workplaces and credit, then it most definitely **is** socialism (*"Legal ownership is not the chief issue in defining workers' self-management — management is. Worker-managers, though not necessarily the legal owners of all the factors of production collected within the firm, are free to experiment and establish enterprise policy as they see fit."*). [David L. Prychitko, **Op. Cit.**, p. 136, p. 135, pp. 4-5, p. 4 and p. 135] This suggests that non-labour factors can be purchased from other co-operatives, credit provided by mutual banks (credit co-operatives) at cost and so forth. As such, a mutualist system is perfectly feasible.

Thus economic calculation based on competitive market prices is possible under a socialist system. Indeed, we see examples of this even under capitalism. For example, the Mondragon co-operative complex in the Basque Country indicate that a libertarian socialist economy can exist and flourish. Perhaps it will be suggested that an economy needs stock markets to price companies, as Mises did. Thus investment is *"not a matter for the mangers of joint stock companies, it is essentially a matter of the capitalists"* in the *"stock exchanges"*. Investment, he asserted, was *"not a matter of wages"* of managers but of *"the capitalist who buys and sell stocks and shares, who make loans and recover them, who make deposits in the banks."* [**Socialism**, p. 139]

It would be churlish to note that the members of co-operatives under capitalism, like most working class people, are more than able to make deposits in banks and arrange loans. In a mutualist economy, workers will not loose this ability just because the banks are themselves co-operatives. Similarly, it would be equally churlish but essential to note that the stock market is hardly the means by which capital is actually raised within capitalism. As David Engler points out, *"[s]upporters of the system ... claim that stock exchanges mobilise funds for business. Do they? When people*

buy and sell shares, 'no investment goes into company treasuries ... Shares simply change hands for cash in endless repetition.' Company treasuries get funds only from new equity issues. These accounted for an average of a mere 0.5 per cent of shares trading in the US during the 1980s."* [**Apostles of Greed**, pp. 157-158] This is echoed by David Ellerman:

> *"In spite of the stock market's large symbolic value, it is notorious that it has relatively little to do with the production of goods and services in the economy (the gambling industry aside). The overwhelming bulk of stock transactions are in second-hand shares so that the capital paid for shares usually goes to other stock traders, not to productive enterprises issuing new shares."* [**The Democratic Worker-Owned Firm**, p. 199]

This suggests that the *"efficient allocation of capital in production does not require a stock market (witness the small business sector [under capitalism])."* *"Socialist firms,"* he notes, *"are routinely attacked as being inherently inefficient because they have no equity shares exposed to market valuation. If this argument had any merit, it would imply that the whole sector of unquoted closely-held small and medium-sized firms in the West was 'inherently inefficient' — a conclusion that must be viewed with some scepticism. Indeed, in the comparison to large corporations with publicly-traded shares, the closely-held firms are probably* **more** *efficient users of capital."* [**Op. Cit.**, p. 200 and p. 199]

In terms of the impact of the stock market on the economy there is good reason to think that this **hinders** economic efficiency by generating a perverse set of incentives and misleading information flows and so their abolition would actually **aid** production and productive efficiency).

Taking the first issue, the existence of a stock market has serious (negative) effects on investment. As Doug Henwood notes, there *"are serious communication problems between managers and shareholders."* This is because *"[e]ven if participants are aware of an upward bias to earnings estimates [of companies], and even if they correct for it, managers would still have an incentive to try to fool the market. If you tell the truth, your accurate estimate will be marked down by a sceptical market. So, it's entirely rational for managers to boost profits in the short term, either through accounting gimmickry or by making only investments with quick paybacks."* So, managers *"facing a market [the stock market] that is famous for its preference for quick profits today rather than patient long-term growth have little choice but to do its bidding. Otherwise, their stock will be marked down, and the firm ripe for take-over."* While *"[f]irms and economies can't get richer by starving themselves"* stock market investors *"can get richer when the companies they own go hungry — at least in the short term. As for the long term, well, that's someone else's problem the week after next."* [**Wall Street**, p. 171]

Ironically, this situation has a parallel with Stalinist central planning. Under that system the managers of State workplaces had an incentive to lie about their capacity to the planning bureaucracy. The planner would, in turn, assume higher capacity, so harming honest managers and encouraging them to lie. This, of course, had a seriously bad impact on the economy. Unsurprisingly, the similar effects caused by capital markets on economies subject to them are as bad as well as downplaying long term issues and investment. In addition, it should be noted that stock-markets regularly experiences bubbles and subsequent bursts. Stock markets may reflect the collective judgements of investors, but it says little about the quality of those judgements. What use are stock prices if they simply reflect herd mentality, the delusions of people ignorant of the real economy or who fail to see a bubble? Particularly when the real-world impact when such bubbles burst can be devastating to those uninvolved with the stock market?

In summary, then, firms are *"over-whelmingly self-financing — that is, most of their investment expenditures are funded through profits (about 90%, on longer-term averages)"* The stock markets provide *"only a sliver of investment funds."* There are, of course, some *"periods like the 1990s, during which the stock market serves as a conduit for shovelling huge amounts of cash into speculative venues, most of which have evaporated ... Much, maybe most, of what was financed in the 1990s didn't deserve the money."* Such booms do not last forever and are *"no advertisement for the efficiency of our capital markets."* [Henwood, **After the New Economy**, p. 187 and p. 188]

Thus there is substantial reason to question the suggestion that a stock market is necessary for the efficient allocation of capital. There is no need for capital markets in a system based on mutual banks and networks of co-operatives. As Henwood concludes, *"the signals emitted by the stock market are either irrelevant or harmful to real economic activity, and that the stock market itself counts little or nothing as a source of finance. Shareholders ... have no useful role."* [**Wall Street**, p. 292]

Then there is also the ironic nature of Rothbard's assertion that self-management would ensure there *"could be no efficiency in production because the requisite knowledge would be lacking."* This is because capitalist firms are hierarchies, based on top-down central planning, and this hinders the free flow of knowledge and information. As with Stalinism, within the capitalist firm information passes up the organisational hierarchy and becomes increasingly simplified and important local knowledge and details lost (when not deliberately falsified to ensure continual employment by suppressing bad news). The top-management takes decisions based on highly aggregated data, the quality of which is hard to know. The management, then, suffers from information and knowledge deficiencies while the workers below lack sufficient autonomy to act to correct inefficiencies as well as incentive to communicate accurate information and act to improve the production process. As Cornelius Castoriadis correctly noted:

> *"Bureaucratic planning is nothing but the extension to the economy as a whole of the methods created and applied by capitalism in the 'rational' direction of large production units. If we consider the most profound feature of the economy, the concrete situation in which people are placed, we see that bureaucratic planning is the most highly perfected realisation of the spirit of capitalism; it pushes to the limit its most significant tendencies. Just as in the management of a large capitalist production unit, this type of planning is carried out by a separate*

*stratum of managers ... Its essence, like that of capitalist production, lies in an effort to reduce the direct producers to the role of pure and simple executants of received orders, orders formulated by a particular stratum that pursues its own interests. This stratum cannot run things well, just as the management apparatus ... [in capitalist] factories cannot run things well. The myth of capitalism's productive efficiency at the level of the individual factory, a myth shared by bourgeois and Stalinist ideologues alike, cannot stand up to the most elemental examination of the facts, and any industrial worker could draw up a devastating indictment against capitalist 'rationalisation' **judged on its own terms.***

*"First of all, the managerial bureaucracy does not **know** what it is supposed to be managing. The reality of production escapes it, for this reality is nothing but the activity of the producers, and the producers do not inform the managers ... about what is really taking place. Quite often they organise themselves in such a way that the managers won't be informed (in order to avoid increased exploitation, because they feel antagonistic, or quite simply because they have no interest: It isn't **their** business).*

"In the second place, the way in which production is organised is set up entirely against the workers. They always are being asked, one way or another, to do more work without getting paid for it. Management's orders, therefore, inevitably meet with fierce resistance on the part of those who have to carry them out." [**Political and Social Writings**, vol. 2, pp. 62-3]

This is *"the same objection as that Hayek raises against the possibility of a planned economy. Indeed, the epistemological problems that Hayek raised against centralised planned economies have been echoed within the socialist tradition as a problem within the capitalist firm."* There is *"a real conflict within the firm that parallels that which Hayek makes about any centralised economy."* [John O'Neill, **The Market**, p. 142] This is because workers have knowledge about their work and workplace that their bosses lack and a self-managed co-operative workplace would motivate workers to use such information to improve the firm's performance. In a capitalist workplace, as in a Stalinist economy, the workers have no incentive to communicate this information as *"improvements in the organisation and methods of production initiated by workers essentially profit capital, which often then seizes hold of them and turns them against the workers. The workers know it and consequently they restrict their participation in production ... They restrict their output; they keep their ideas to themselves ... They organise among themselves to carry out their work, all the while keeping up a facade of respect for the official way they are supposed to organise their work."* [Castoriadis, **Op. Cit.**, pp. 181-2] An obvious example would be concerns that management would seek to monopolise the workers' knowledge in order to accumulate more profits, better control the workforce or replace them (using the higher productivity as an excuse). Thus self-management rather than hierarchy enhances the flow and use of information in complex organisations and so improves efficiency.

This conclusion, it should be stressed, is not idle speculation and Mises was utterly wrong in his assertions related to self-management. People, he stated, *"err"* in thinking that profit-sharing *"would spur the worker on to a more zealous fulfilment of his duties"* (indeed, it *"must lead straight to Syndicalism"*) and it was *"nonsensical to give 'labour' … a share in management. The realisation of such a postulate would result in syndicalism."* [**Socialism**, p. 268, p. 269 and p. 305] Yet, as we note in section I.3.2, the empirical evidence is overwhelmingly against Mises (which suggests why "Austrians" are so dismissive of empirical evidence, as it exposes flaws in the great chains of deductive reasoning they so love). In fact, workers' participation in management and profit sharing enhance productivity. In one sense, though, Mises is right, in that capitalist firms will tend not to encourage participation or even profit sharing as it shows to workers the awkward fact that while the bosses may need them, they do not need the bosses. As discussed in section J.5.12, bosses are fearful that such schemes **will** lead to "syndicalism" and so quickly stop them in order to remain in power — in spite (or, more accurately, because) of the efficiency and productivity gains they result in.

"Both capitalism and state socialism," summarises Ellerman, *"suffer from the motivational inefficiency of the employment relation."* **Op. Cit.**, pp. 210-1] Mutualism would be **more** efficient as well as freer for, once the stock market and workplace hierarchies are removed, serious blocks and distortions to information flow will be eliminated.

Unfortunately, the state socialists who replied to Mises in the 1920s and 1930s did not have such a libertarian economy in mind. In response to Mises initial challenge, a number of economists pointed out that Pareto's disciple, Enrico Barone, had already, 13 years earlier, demonstrated the theoretical possibility of a *"market-simulated socialism."* However, the principal attack on Mises's argument came from Fred Taylor and Oscar Lange (for a collection of their main papers, see **On the Economic Theory of Socialism**). In light of their work, Hayek shifted the question from theoretical impossibility to whether the theoretical solution could be approximated in practice. Which raises an interesting question, for if (state) socialism is *"impossible"* (as Mises assured us) then what **did** collapse in Eastern Europe? If the "Austrians" claim it **was** "socialism" then they are in the somewhat awkward position that something they assure us is *"impossible"* existed for decades. Moreover, it should be noted that both sides of the argument accepted the idea of central planning of some kind or another. This means that most of the arguments of Mises and Hayek did not apply to libertarian socialism, which rejects central planning along with every other form of centralisation.

Nor was the response by Taylor and Lange particularly convincing in the first place. This was because it was based far more on neo-classical capitalist economic theory than on an appreciation of reality. In place of the Walrasian *"Auctioneer"* (the "god in the machine" of general equilibrium theory which ensures that all markets clear) Taylor and Lange presented the *"Central Planning Board"* whose job it was to adjust prices so that all markets cleared. Neo-classical economists who are inclined to accept Walrasian theory as an adequate account of a working capitalist economy will be forced to accept the validity of their model of "socialism." Little wonder Taylor and Lange were considered, at the time, the victors in the "socialist calculation" debate by most of the economics profession (with the collapse of the Soviet Union, this decision has been revised somewhat — although we must point out that Taylor and Lange's model was not the same as the Soviet system, a fact conveniently ignored by commentators).

Unfortunately, given that Walrasian theory has little bearing to reality, we must also come to the conclusion that the Taylor-Lange "solution" has about the same relevance (even ignoring its non-libertarian aspects, such as its basis in state-ownership, its centralisation, its lack of workers' self-management and so on). Many people consider Taylor and Lange as fore-runners of *"market socialism."* This is incorrect — rather than being market socialists, they are in fact "neo-classical" socialists, building a "socialist" system which mimics capitalist economic **theory** rather than its **reality**. Replacing Walrus's mythical creation of the *"Auctioneer"* with a planning board does not really get to the heart of the problem! Nor does their vision of "socialism" have much appeal — a re-production of capitalism with a planning board and a more equal distribution of money income. Anarchists reject such "socialism" as little more than a nicer version of capitalism, if that.

Thus the *"calculation argument"* does not prove that socialism is impossible. Mises was wrong in asserting that *"a socialist system with a market and market prices is as self-contradictory as is the notion of a triangular square."* [**Human Action**, p. 706] This is because capitalism is not defined by markets as such but rather by wage labour, a situation where working class people do not have free access to the means of production and so have to sell their labour (and so liberty) to those who do. If quoting Engels is not **too** out of place, the *"object of production — to produce commodities — **does not import** to the instrument the character of capital"* as the *"production of commodities is one of the preconditions for the existence of capital … as long as the producer sells only **what he himself** produces, he is not a capitalist; he becomes so only from the moment he makes use of his instrument **to exploit the wage labour of others**."* [**Collected Works**, Vol. 47, pp. 179-80] In this, as noted in section C.2.1, Engels was merely echoing Marx (who, in turn, was simply repeating Proudhon's distinction between property and possession). As mutualism eliminates wage labour by self-management and free access to the means of production, its use of markets and prices (both of which pre-date capitalism) does not mean it is not socialist (and as we note in section G.1.1 Marx, Engels, Bakunin and Kropotkin, like Mises, acknowledged Proudhon as being a socialist). This focus on the market, as David Schweickart suggests, is no accident:

> *"The identification of capitalism with the market is a pernicious error of both conservative defenders of **laissez-faire** [capitalism] and most left opponents … If one looks at the works of the major apologists for capitalism … one finds the focus of the apology always on the virtues of the market and on the vices of central planning. Rhetorically this is an effective strategy, for it is much easier to defend the market than to defend the other two defining*

institutions of capitalism. Proponents of capitalism know well that it is better to keep attention toward the market and away from wage labour or private ownership of the means of production. ["*Market Socialism: A Defense*", pp. 7-22, **Market Socialism: the debate among socialists**, Bertell Ollman (ed.), p. 11]

Dissident economist Geoffrey M. Hodgson is right to suggest that Proudhon's system, in which "*each co-operative association would be able to enter into contractual relations with others*", could be "*described as an early form of 'market socialism'*". In fact, "*instead of Lange-type models, the term 'market socialism' is more appropriately used to refer to such systems. Market socialism, in this more appropriate and meaningful sense, involves producer co-operatives that are owned by the workers within them. Such co-operatives sell their products on markets, with genuine exchanges of property rights*" (somewhat annoyingly, Hodgson incorrectly asserts that "*Proudhon described himself as an anarchist, not a socialist*" when, in reality, the French anarchist repeatedly referred to himself and his mutualist system as socialist). [**Economics and Utopia**, p. 20, p. 37 and p. 20]

Thus it is possible for a socialist economy to allocate resources using markets. By suppressing capital markets and workplace hierarchies, a mutualist system will improve upon capitalism by removing an important source of perverse incentives which hinder efficient use of resources as well as long term investment and social responsibility in addition to reducing inequalities and increasing freedom. As David Ellerman once noted, many "*still look at the world in bipolar terms: capitalism or (state) socialism.*" Yet there "*are two broad traditions of socialism: **state socialism** and **self-management socialism**. State socialism is based on government ownership of major industry, while self-management socialism envisions firms being worker self-managed and not owned or managed by the government.*" [**Op. Cit.**, p. 147] Mutualism is a version of the second vision and anarchists reject the cosy agreement between mainstream Marxists and their ideological opponents on the propertarian right that only state socialism is "real" socialism.

Finally, it should be noted that most anarchists are not mutualists but rather aim for (libertarian) communism, the abolition of money. Many do see a mutualist-like system as an inevitable stage in a social revolution, the transitional form imposed by the objective conditions facing a transformation of a society marked by thousands of years of oppression and exploitation (collectivist-anarchism contains elements of both mutualism and communism, with most of its supporters seeing it as a transitional system). This is discussed in section I.2.2, while section I.1.3 indicates why most anarchists reject even non-capitalist markets. So does Mises's argument mean that a socialism that abolishes the market (such as libertarian communism) is impossible? Given that the vast majority of anarchists seek a libertarian communist society, this is an important question. We address it in the next section.

<table>
<tr><td>

I.1.2 Is libertarian communism impossible?

</td></tr>
</table>

In a word, no. While the "*calculation argument*" (see last section) is often used by propertarians (so-called right-wing "libertarians") as **the** basis for the argument that communism (a moneyless society) is impossible, it is based on certain false ideas of what prices do, the nature of the market and how a communist-anarchist society would function. This is hardly surprising, as Mises based his theory on a variation of neo-classical economics and the Marxist social-democratic (and so Leninist) ideas of what a "socialist" economy would look like. So there has been little discussion of what a true (i.e. libertarian) communist society would be like, one that utterly transformed the existing conditions of production by workers' self-management and the abolition of both wage-labour **and** money. However, it is useful here to indicate exactly why communism would work and why the "*calculation argument*" is flawed as an objection to it.

Mises argued that without money there was no way a socialist economy would make "rational" production decisions. Not even Mises denied that a moneyless society could estimate what is likely to be needed over a given period of time (as expressed as physical quantities of definite types and sorts of objects). As he argued, "*calculation **in natura** in an economy without exchange can embrace consumption-goods only.*" His argument was that the next step, working out which productive methods to employ, would not be possible, or at least would not be able to be done "rationally," i.e. avoiding waste and inefficiency. The evaluation of producer goods "*can only be done with some kind of economic calculation. The human mind cannot orient itself properly among the bewildering mass of intermediate products and potentialities without such aid. It would simply stand perplexed before the problems of management and location.*" Thus we would quickly see "*the spectacle of a socialist economic order floundering in the ocean of possible and conceivable economic combinations without the compass of economic calculation.*" ["*Economic Calculation in the Socialist Commonwealth*", pp. 87-130, **Collectivist Economic Planning**, F.A. von Hayek (ed.), p. 104, p. 103 and p. 110] Hence the claim that monetary calculation based on market prices is the only solution.

This argument is not without its force. How can a producer be expected to know if tin is a better use of resources than iron when creating a product if all they know is that iron and tin are available and suitable for their purpose? Or, if we have a consumer good which can be made with A + 2B or 2A + B (where A and B are both input factors such as steel, oil electricity, etc.) how can we tell which method is more efficient (i.e. which one used least resources and so left the most over for other uses)? With market prices, Mises' argued, it is simple. If A cost $10 and B $5, then clearly method one would be the most efficient ($20 versus $25). Without the market, Mises argued, such a decision would be impossible and so every decision would be "*groping in the dark.*" [**Op. Cit.**, p. 110]

Mises' argument rests on three flawed assumptions, two against communism and one for capitalism. The first two negative assumptions are that communism entails central planning and that it is impossible to make investment decisions without money values. We discuss why each is wrong in this section. Mises' positive assumption for capitalism, namely that markets allow exact and efficient allocation of resources, is discussed in section I.1.5.

Firstly, Mises assumes a centralised planned economy. As Hayek summarised, the crux of the matter was *"the impossibility of a rational calculation in a centrally directed economy from which prices are necessarily absent"*, one which *"involves planning on a most extensive scale — minute direction of practically all productive activity by one central authority"*. Thus the *"one central authority has to solve the economic problem of distributing a limited amount of resources between a practically infinite number of competing purposes"* with *"a reasonable degree of accuracy, with a degree of success equally or approaching the results of competitive capitalism"* is what *"constitutes the problem of socialism as a method."* [*"The Nature and History of the Problem"*, pp. 1-40, **Op. Cit.**, p. 35, p. 19 and pp. 16-7]

While this was a common idea in Marxian social democracy (and the Leninism that came from it), centralised organisations are rejected by anarchism. As Bakunin argued, *"where are the intellects powerful enough to embrace the infinite multiplicity and diversity of real interests, aspirations, wishes, and needs which sum up the collective will of the people? And to invent a social organisation that will not be a Procrustean bed upon which the violence of the State will more or less overtly force unhappy society to stretch out?"* Moreover, a socialist government, *"unless it were endowed with omniscience, omnipresence, and the omnipotence which the theologians attribute to God, could not possibly know and foresee the needs of its people, or satisfy with an even justice those interests which are most legitimate and pressing."* [**Bakunin on Anarchism**, pp. 268-9 and p. 318] For Malatesta, such a system would require *"immense centralisation"* and would either be *"an impossible thing to achieve, or, if possible, would end up as a colossal and very complex tyranny."* [**At the Café**, p. 65]

Kropotkin, likewise, dismissed the notion of central planning as the *"economic changes that will result from the social revolution will be so immense and so profound … that it will be impossible for one or even a number of individuals to elaborate the social forms to which a further society must give birth. The elaboration of new social forms can only be the collective work of the masses."* [**Words of a Rebel**, p. 175] The notion that a *"strongly centralised Government"* could *"**command** that a prescribed quantity"* of a good *"be sent to such a place on such a day"* and be *"received on a given day by a specified official and stored in particular warehouses"* was not only *"undesirable"* but also *"wildly Utopian."* During his discussion of the benefits of free agreement against state tutelage, Kropotkin noted that only the former allowed the utilisation of *"the co-operation, the enthusiasm, the local knowledge"* of the people. [**The Conquest of Bread**, pp. 82-3 and p. 137]

Kropotkin's own experience had shown how the *"high functionaries"* of the Tsarist bureaucracy *"were simply charming in their innocent ignorance"* of the areas they were meant to be administrating and how, thanks to Marxism, the socialist ideal had *"lost the character of something that had to be worked out by the labour organisations themselves, and became state management of industries — in fact,*

state socialism; that is, state capitalism." As an anarchist, he knew that governments become *"isolated from the masses"* and so *"the very success of socialism"* required *"the ideas of no-government, of self-reliance, of free initiative of the individual"* to be *"preached side by side with those of socialised ownership and production."* Thus it was essential that socialism was decentralised, federal and participatory, that the *"structure of the society which we longed for"* was *"worked out, in theory and practice, from beneath"* in by *"all labour unions"* with *"a full knowledge of local needs of each trade and each locality."* [**Memoirs of a Revolutionist**, p. 184, p. 360, p. 374-5 and p. 376] He reiterated this as the Bolsheviks confirmed his warnings:

> *"The immense constructive work demanded by a social revolution cannot be accomplished by a central government … It has need of knowledge, of brains and of the voluntary collaboration of a host of local and specialised forces which alone can attack the diversity of economic problems in their local aspects … Socialism will certainly make considerable progress, and new forms of more independent life will be created based on local autonomy and free initiative … But the success of this reconstruction will depend in great part on the possibility of direct cooperation between the different peoples. To achieve that, it is necessary that … there should be a union of all the workers' organisations of the world, federated to deliver world production from its present subjection to capitalism."* [**Anarchism**, pp. 255-6]

As John O'Neill summarises, the *"argument against centralised planning is one that has been articulated within the history of socialist planning as an argument for democratic and decentralised decision making."* [**The Market**, p. 132] So, for good economic and political reasons, anarchists reject central planning. This central libertarian socialist position feeds directly into refuting Mises' argument, for while a **centralised** system would need to compare a large (*"infinite"*) number of possible alternatives to a large number of possible needs, this is not the case in a **decentralised** system. Rather than a vast multitude of alternatives which would swamp a centralised planning agency, one workplace comparing different alternatives to meet a specific need faces a much lower number of possibilities as the objective technical requirements (use-values) of a project are known and so local knowledge will eliminate most of the options available to a small number which can be directly compared.

As such, removing the assumption of a central planning body automatically drains Mises' critique of much of its force — rather than an *"the ocean of possible and conceivable economic combinations"* faced by a central body, a specific workplace or community has a more limited number of possible solutions for a limited number of requirements. Moreover, any complex machine is a product of less complex goods, meaning that the workplace is a consumer of other workplace's goods. If, as Mises admitted, a customer can decide between consumption goods without the need for money then the user and producer of a *"higher order"* good can decide between consumption goods required to meet their needs.

Mises' other assumption is equally flawed. This is that without the market, no information is passed between producers beyond the final outcome of production. In other words, he assumed that the final product is all that counts in evaluating its use. Needless to say, it is true that without more information than the name of a given product it is impossible to determine whether using it would be an efficient utilisation of resources. Yet more information can be provided which can be used to inform decision making. As socialists Adam Buick and John Crump point out, *"at the level of the individual production unit or industry, the only calculations that would be necessary in socialism would be calculations in kind. On the one side would be recorded the resources (materials, energy, equipment, labour) used up in production and on the other the amount of good produced, together with any by-products... . Socialist production is simply the production of use values from use values, and nothing more."* [**State Capitalism: The Wages System Under New Management**, p. 137] Thus any good used as an input into a production process would require the communication of this kind of information.

The generation and communication of such information implies a decentralised, horizontal network between producers and consumers. This is because what counts as a use-value can only be determined by those directly using it. Thus the production of use-values from use-values cannot be achieved via central planning, as the central planners have no notion of the use-value of the goods being used or produced. Such knowledge lies in many hands, dispersed throughout society, and so socialist production implies decentralisation. Capitalist ideologues claim that the market allows the utilisation of such dispersed knowledge, but as John O'Neill notes, *"the market may be one way in which dispersed knowledge can be put to good effect. It is not ... the only way"*. *"The strength of the epistemological argument for the market depends in part on the implausibility of assuming that all knowledge could be centralised upon some particular planning agency"* he stresses, but Mises' *"argument ignores, however, the existence of the decentralised but predominantly non-market institutions for the distribution of knowledge ... The assumption that only the market can co-ordinate dispersed non-vocalisable knowledge is false."* [**Op. Cit.**, p. 118 and p. 132]

So, in order to determine if a specific good is useful to a person, that person needs to know its "cost." Under capitalism, the notion of cost has been so associated with **price** that we have to put the word "cost" in quotation marks. However, the real cost of, say, writing a book, is not a sum of money but so much paper, so much energy, so much ink, so much human labour. In order to make a rational decision on whether a given good is better for meeting a given need than another, the would-be consumer requires this information. However, under capitalism this information is **hidden** by the price. Somewhat ironically, given how "Austrian" economics tends to stress that the informational limitations are at the root of its *"impossibility"* of socialism, the fact is that the market hides a significant amount of essential information required to make a sensible investment decision. This can be seen from an analysis of Mises' discussion on why labour-time cannot replace money as a decision-making tool. Using labour, he argued, *"leaves the employment of material factors of production out of account"* and presents an example of two goods, P and Q, which take 10 hours to produce. P takes 8

hours of labour, plus 2 units of raw material A (which is produced by an hour's socially necessary labour). Q takes 9 hours of labour and one unit of A. He asserts that in terms of labour P and Q *"are equivalent, but in value terms P is more valuable than Q. The former is false, and only the later corresponds to the nature and purpose of calculation."* [*"Economic Calculation in the Socialist Commonwealth"*, **Op. Cit.**, p. 113]

The flaw in his argument is clear. Assuming that an hour of socially necessary labour is £10 then, in price terms, P would have £80 of direct labour costs, with £20 of raw material A while Q would have £90 of direct labour and £10 of A. Both cost £100 so it hard to see how this *"corresponds to the nature and purpose of calculation"*! Using less of raw material A is a judgement made **in addition** to *"calculation"* in this example. The question of whether to economise on the use of A simply cannot be made using prices. If P, for example, can only be produced via a more ecologically destructive process than Q or if the work process by which P is created is marked by dull, mindless work but Q's is more satisfying for the people involved than Q may be considered a better decision. Sadly, that kind of information is **not** communicated by the price mechanism.

As John O'Neill points out, *"Mises' earlier arguments against socialist planning turned on an assumption about commensurability. His central argument was that rational economic decision-making required a single measure on the basis of which the worth of alternative states of affairs could be calculated and compared."* [**Ecology, Policy and Politics**, p. 115] Anarchists question whether using prices means basing all decision making on one criterion and ignoring all others is a rational thing to do. As O'Neill suggests, *"the relative scarcity of items ... hardly exhaust the full gamut of information that is distributed throughout society which might be relevant to the co-ordination of economic activities and plans."* [**The Market**, p. 196] Saying that a good costs £10 does not tell you much about the amount of pollution its production or use generates, under what conditions of labour it was produced, whether its price is affected by the market power of the firm producing it, whether it is produced in an ecologically sustainable way, and so forth. Similarly, saying that another, similar, good costs £9 does not tell you whether that £1 difference is due to a more efficient use of inputs or whether it is caused by imposing pollution onto the planet.

And do prices **actually** reflect costs? The question of profit, the reward for owning capital and allowing others to use it, is hardly a cost in the same way as labour, resources and so on (attempts to explain profits as an equivalent sacrifice as labour have always been ridiculous and quickly dropped). When looking at prices to evaluate efficient use for goods, you cannot actually tell by the price if this is so. Two goods may have the same price, but profit levels (perhaps under the influence of market power) may be such that one has a higher cost price than another. The price mechanism fails to indicate which uses least resources as it is influenced by market power. Indeed, as Takis Fotopoulos notes, *"[i]f ... both central planning and the market economy inevitably lead to concentrations of power, then neither the former nor the latter can produce the sort of information flows and incentives which are necessary for the best functioning of any economic system."* [**Towards an Inclusive Democracy**, p. 252] Moreover, a good produced under a authoritarian state which represses its workforce could have a lower price than one produced in a country which allowed unions to organise and has basic human rights. The repression would force down the cost of labour, so making the good in question appear as a more "efficient" use of resources. In other words, the market can mask inhumanity as "efficiency" and actually reward that behaviour by market share.

In other words, market prices can be horribly distorted in that they ignore quality issues. Exchanges therefore occur in light of false information and, moreover, with anti-social motivations — to maximise short-term surplus for the capitalists regardless of losses to others. Thus they distort valuations and impose a crass, narrow and ultimately self-defeating individualism. Prices are shaped by more than costs, with, for example, market power increasing market prices far higher than actual costs. Market prices also fail to take into account public goods and so bias allocation choices against them not to mention ignoring the effects on the wider society, i.e. beyond the direct buyers and sellers. Similarly, in order to make rational decisions relating to using a good, you need to know **why** the price has changed for if a change is permanent or transient implies different responses. Thus the current price is not enough in itself. Has the good become more expensive temporarily, due, say, to a strike? Or is it because the supply of the resource has been exhausted? Actions that are sensible in the former situation will be wrong in the other. As O'Neill suggests, *"the information [in the market] is passed back without dialogue. The market informs by 'exit' — some products find a market, others do not. 'Voice' is not exercised. This failure of dialogue ... represents an informational failure of the market, not a virtue ... The market ... does distribute information ... it also blocks a great deal."* [**Op. Cit.**, p. 99]

So a purely market-based system leaves out information on which to base rational resource allocations (or, at the very least, hides it). The reason for this is that a market system measures, at best, preferences of **individual** buyers among the **available** options. This assumes that all the pertinent use-values that are to be outcomes of production are things that are to be consumed by the individual, rather than use-values that are collectively enjoyed (like clean air). Prices in the market do not measure social costs or externalities, meaning that such costs are not reflected in the price and so you cannot have a rational price system. Similarly, if the market measures only preferences amongst things that can be monopolised and sold to individuals, as distinguished from values that are enjoyed collectively, then it follows that information necessary for rational decision-making in production is not provided by the market. In other words, capitalist "calculation" fails because private firms are oblivious to the social cost of their labour and raw materials inputs.

Indeed, prices often **mis**-value goods as companies can gain a competitive advantage by passing costs onto society (in the form of pollution, for example, or de-skilling workers, increasing job insecurity, and so on). This externalisation of costs is actually rewarded in the market as consumers seek the lowest prices, unaware of the reasons **why** it is lower (such information cannot be gathered from looking at the price). Even if we assume that such activity is penalised by fines later, the damage is still done and cannot be undone. Indeed, the company may be able to weather

the fines due to the profits it originally made by externalising costs (see section E.3). Thus the market creates a perverse incentive to subsidise their input costs through off-the-book social and environmental externalities. As Chomsky suggests:

"it is by now widely realised that the economist's 'externalities' can no longer be consigned to footnotes. No one who gives a moment's thought to the problems of contemporary society can fail to be aware of the social costs of consumption and production, the progressive destruction of the environment, the utter irrationality of the utilisation of contemporary technology, the inability of a system based on profit or growth-maximisation to deal with needs that can only be expressed collectively, and the enormous bias this system imposes towards maximisation of commodities for personal use in place of the general improvement of the quality of life." [**Radical Priorities**, pp. 190-1]

Prices hide the actual costs that production involved for the individual, society, and the environment, and instead boils everything down into **one** factor, namely price. There is a lack of dialogue and information between producer and consumer.

Moreover, without using another means of cost accounting instead of prices how can supporters of capitalism know there is a correlation between actual and price costs? One can determine whether such a correlation exists by measuring one against the other. If this cannot be done, then the claim that prices measure costs is a tautology (in that a price represents a cost and we know that it is a cost because it has a price). If it can be done, then we can calculate costs in some other sense than in market prices and so the argument that only market prices represent costs falls. Equally, there may be costs (in terms of quality of life issues) which **cannot** be reflected in price terms.

Simply put, the market fails to distribute all relevant information and, particularly when prices are at disequilibrium, can communicate distinctly **misleading** information. As *"prices in capitalism provided at best incomplete and partial information that obscured the workings of capitalism, and would generate and reproduce economic and social inequalities. Ignoring the social character of the economy with their methodological individualism, economic liberals also ignored the social costs of particular choices and the question of externalities."* [Michael Schmidt and Lucien van der Walt, **Black Flame**, p. 92] This suggests that prices cannot be taken to reflect real costs any more that they can reflect the social expression of the valuation of goods. They are the result of a conflict waged over these goods and those that acted as their inputs (including, of course, labour). Market and social power, much more than need or resource usage, decides the issue. The inequality in the means of purchasers, in the market power of firms and in the bargaining position of labour and capital all play their part, so distorting any relationship a price may have to its costs in terms of resource use. Prices are misshapen.

Little wonder Kropotkin asked whether *"are we not yet bound to analyse that compound result we call price rather than to accept it as a supreme and blind ruler of our actions?"* [**Fields, Factories and Workshops Tomorrow**, p. 71] It is precisely these **real** costs, hidden by price, which need to be communicated to producers and consumers for them to make informed and rational decisions concerning their economic activity.

It is useful to remember that Mises argued that it is the **complexity** of a modern economy that ensures money is required: *"Within the narrow confines of household economy, for instance, where the father can supervise the entire economic management, it is possible to determine the significance of changes in the processes of production, without such aids to the mind [as monetary calculation], and yet with more or less of accuracy."* However, *"the mind of one man alone — be it ever so cunning, is too weak to grasp the importance of any single one among the countlessly many goods of higher order. No single man can ever master all the possibilities of production, innumerable as they are, as to be in a position to make straightway evident judgements of value without the aid of some system of computation."* [**Op. Cit.**, p. 102]

A libertarian communist society would, it must be stressed, use various *"aids to the mind"* to help individuals and groups to make economic decisions. This would reduce the complexity of economic decision making, by allowing different options and resources to be compared to each other. Hence the complexity of economic decision making in an economy with a multitude of goods can be reduced by the use of rational algorithmic procedures and methods to aid the process. Such tools would aid decision making, not dominate it as these decisions affect humans and the planet and should never be made automatically.

That being the case, a libertarian communist society would quickly develop the means of comparing the real impact of specific *"higher order"* goods in terms of their real costs (i.e. the amount of labour, energy and raw materials used plus any social and ecological costs). Moreover, it should be remembered that production goods are made up on inputs of other goods, that is, higher goods are made up of consumption goods of a lower order. If, as Mises admits, calculation without money is possible for consumption goods then the creation of *"higher order"* goods can be also achieved and a record of its costs made and communicated to those who seek to use it.

While the specific *"aids to the mind"* as well as "costs" and their relative weight would be determined by the people of a free society, we can speculate that it would include direct and indirect labour, externalities (such as pollution), energy use and materials, and so forth. As such, it must be stressed that a libertarian communist society would seek to communicate the "costs" associated with any specific product as well as its relative scarcity. In other words, it needs a means of determining the objective or absolute costs associated with different alternatives as well as an indication of how much of a given good is available at a given it (i.e., its scarcity). Both of these can be determined without the use of money and markets.

Section I.4 discusses possible frameworks for an anarchist economy, including suggestions for libertarian communist economic decision-making processes. In terms of *"aids to the mind"*, these include methods to compare goods for resource allocation by indicating the absolute costs involved in producing a good and the relative scarcity of a specific good, among other things. Such a framework is necessary because *"an appeal to a necessary role for practical judgements in decision making is **not** to deny any role to general*

*principles. Neither ... does it deny any place for the use of technical rules and algorithmic procedures ... Moreover, there is a necessary role for rules of thumb, standard procedures, the default procedures and institutional arrangements that can be followed unreflectively and which **reduce** the scope for **explicit** judgements comparing different states of affairs. There are limits in time, efficient use of resources and the dispersal of knowledge which require rules and institutions. Such rules and institutions can free us for space and time for reflective judgements where they matter most."* [John O'Neill, **Ecology, Policy and Politics**, pp. 117-8] It is these *"rules and institutions need themselves to be open to critical and reflective appraisal."* [O'Neill, **The Market**, p. 118]

Economic decisions, in other words, cannot be reduced down to one factor yet Mises argued that anyone *"who wished to make calculations in regard to a complicated process of production will immediately notice whether he has worked more economically than others or not; if he finds, from reference to the exchange values obtaining in the market, that he will not be able to produce profitably, this shows that others understand how to make better use of the higher-order goods in question."* [**Op. Cit.**, pp. 97-8] However, this only shows whether someone has worked more **profitably** than others, not whether it is more economical. Market power automatically muddles this issue, as does the possibility of reducing the monetary cost of production by recklessly exploiting natural resources and labour, polluting, or otherwise passing costs onto others. Similarly, the issue of wealth inequality is important, for if the production of luxury goods proves more profitable than basic essentials for the poor does this show that producing the former is a better use of resources? And, of course, the key issue of the relative strength of market power between workers and capitalists plays a key role in determining "profitably."

Basing your economic decision making on a single criteria, namely profitability, can, and does, lead to perverse results. Most obviously, the tendency for capitalists to save money by not introducing safety equipment (*"To save a dollar the capitalist build their railroads poorly, and along comes a train, and loads of people are killed. What are their lives to him, if by their sacrifice he has saved money?"* [Emma Goldman, **A Documentary History of the American Years**, vol. 1, p. 157]). Similarly, it is considered a more "efficient" use of resources to condemn workers to deskilling and degrading work than "waste" resources in developing machines to eliminate or reduce it (*"How many machines remain unused solely because they do not return an immediate profit to the capitalist! ... How many discoveries, how many applications of science remain a dead letter solely because they don't bring the capitalist enough!"* [Carlo Cafiero, *"Anarchy and Communism"*, pp. 179-86, **The Raven**, No. 6, p. 182]). Similarly, those investments which have a higher initial cost but which, in the long run, would have, say, a smaller environmental impact would not be selected in a profit-driven system.

This has seriously irrational effects, because the managers of capitalist enterprises are obliged to choose technical means of production which produce the cheapest results. All other considerations are subordinate, in particular the health and welfare of the producers and the effects on the environment. The harmful effects resulting from "rational" capitalist production methods have long been pointed out. For example, speed-ups, pain, stress, accidents, boredom, overwork, long hours and so on all harm the physical and mental health of those involved, while pollution, the destruction of the environment, and the exhaustion of non-renewable resources all have serious effects on both the planet and those who live on it. As green economist E. F. Schumacher argued:

> "But what does it **mean** when we say that something is uneconomic? ... [S]omething is uneconomic when it fails to earn an adequate profit in terms of money. The method of economics does not, and cannot, produce any other meaning ... The judgement of economics ... is an extremely **fragmentary** judgement; out of the large number of aspects which in real life have to be seen and judged together before a decision can be taken, economics supplies only one — whether a money profit accrues **to those who undertake it** or not." [**Small is Beautiful**, pp. 27-8]

Schumacher stressed that "about the **fragmentary** nature of the judgements of economics there can be no doubt whatever. Even with the narrow compass of the economic calculus, these judgements are necessarily and **methodically** narrow. For one thing, they give vastly more weight to the short than to the long term... [S]econd, they are based on a definition of cost which excludes all 'free goods' ... [such as the] environment, except for those parts that have been privately appropriated. This means that an activity can be economic although it plays hell with the environment, and that a competing activity, if at some cost it protects and conserves the environment, will be uneconomic." Moreover, "[d]o not overlook the words 'to those who undertake it.' It is a great error to assume, for instance, that the methodology of economics is normally applied to determine whether an activity carried out by a group within society yields a profit to society as a whole." [**Op. Cit.**, p. 29]

To claim that prices include all these "externalities" is nonsense. If they did, we would not see capital moving to third-world countries with few or no anti-pollution or labour laws. At best, the "cost" of pollution would only be included in a price if the company was sued successfully in court for damages — in other words, once the damage is done. Ultimately, companies have a strong interest in buying inputs with the lowest prices, regardless of **how** they are produced. In fact, the market rewards such behaviour as a company which was socially responsible would be penalised by higher costs, and so market prices. It is reductionist accounting and its accompanying "ethics of mathematics" that produces the "irrationality of rationality" which plagues capitalism's exclusive reliance on prices (i.e. profits) to measure "efficiency."

Ironically enough, Mises also pointed to the irrational nature of the price mechanism. He stated (correctly) that there are "extra-economic" elements which "monetary calculation cannot embrace" because of "its very nature." He acknowledged that these "considerations themselves can scarcely be termed irrational" and, as examples, listed "[i]n any place where men regard as significant the beauty of a neighbourhood or a building, the health, happiness and contentment of mankind, the honour of individuals or nations." He also noted that "they are just as much motive forces of rational conduct as are economic factors" but they "do not enter into exchange relationships." How rational is an economic system which ignores the "health, happiness and contentment" of people? Or the beauty of their surroundings? Which, moreover, penalises those who take these factors into consideration? For anarchists, Mises comments indicate well the inverted logic of capitalism. That Mises can support a system which ignores the needs of individuals, their happiness, health, surroundings, environment and so on by "its very nature" says a lot. His suggestion that we assign monetary values to such dimensions begs the question and has plausibility only if it assumes what it is supposed to prove. [**Op. Cit.**, p. 99-100] Indeed, the person who would put a price on friendship would have no friends as they simply do not understand what friendship is and are thereby excluded from much which is best in human life. Likewise for other "extra-economic" goods that individuals value, such as beautiful places, happiness, the environment and so on.

So essential information required for sensible decision making would have to be recorded and communicated in a communist society and used to evaluate different options using agreed methods of comparison. This differs drastically from the price mechanism as it recognises that mindless, automatic calculation is impossible in social choices. Such choices have an unavoidable ethical and social dimension simply because they involve other human beings and the environment. As Mises himself acknowledged, monetary calculation does not capture such dimensions.

We, therefore, need to employ practical judgement in making choices aided by a full understanding of the **real** social and ecological costs involved using, of course, the appropriate "aids to the mind." Given that an anarchist society would be complex and integrated, such aids would be essential but, due to its decentralised nature, it need not embrace the price mechanism. It can evaluate the efficiency of its decisions by looking at the **real** costs involved to society rather than embrace the distorted system of costing explicit in the price mechanism (as Kropotkin once put it, "if we analyse **price**" we must "make a distinction between its different elements". [**Op. Cit.**, p. 72]).

In summary, then, Mises considered only central planning as genuine socialism, meaning that a decentralised communism was not addressed. Weighting up the pros and cons of how to use millions of different goods in the millions of potential situations they could be used would be impossible in a centralised system, yet in decentralised communism this is not an issue. Each individual commune and syndicate would be choosing from the few alternatives required to meet their needs. With the needs known, the alternatives can be compared — particularly if agreed criteria ("aids to the mind") are utilised and the appropriate agreed information communicated.

Efficient economic decision making in a moneyless "economy" is possible, assuming that sufficient information is passed between syndicates and communes to evaluate the relative and absolute costs of a good. Thus, decisions can be reached which aimed to reduce the use of goods in short supply or which take large amounts of resources to produce (or which produce large externalities to create). While a **centralised** system would be swamped by the large number of different uses and combinations of goods, a **decentralised** communist system would not be.

Thus, anarchists argue that Mises was wrong. Communism **is** viable, but only if it is **libertarian** communism. Ultimately, though, the real charge is not that socialism is *"impossible"* but rather that it would be inefficient, i.e., it would allocate resources such that too much is used to achieve specified goals and that there would be no way to check that the allocated resources were valued sufficiently to warrant their use in the first place. While some may portray this as a case of planning against markets (no-planning), this is false. Planning occurs in capitalism (as can be seen from any business), it is a question of whether capitalism ensures that more plans can be co-ordinated and needs met by means of relative prices and profit-loss accounting than by communism (free access and distribution according to need). As such, the question is does the capitalist system add additional problems to the efficient co-ordination of plans? Libertarian communists argue, yes, it does (as we discuss at length in section I.1.5).

All choices involve lost possibilities, so the efficient use of resources is required to increase the possibilities for creating other goods. At best, all you can say is that by picking options which cost the least a market economy will make more resources available for other activities. Yet this assumption crucially depends equating "efficient" with profitable, a situation which cannot be predicted beforehand and which easily leads to inefficient allocation of resources (particularly if we are looking at meeting human needs). Then there are the costs of using money for if we are talking of opportunity costs, of the freeing up of resources for other uses, then the labour and other resources used to process money related activities should be included. While these activities (banking, advertising, defending property, and so forth) are essential to a capitalist economy, they are not needed and unproductive from the standpoint of producing use values or meeting human need. This would suggest that a libertarian communist economy would have a productive advantage over a capitalist economy as the elimination of this structural waste intrinsic to capitalism will free up a vast amount of labour and materials for socially useful production. This is not to mention the so-called "costs" which are no such thing, but relate to capitalist property rights. Thus "rent" may be considered a cost under capitalism, but would disappear if those who used a resource controlled it rather than pay a tribute to gain access to it. As Kropotkin argued, *"the capitalist system makes us pay for everything three or four times its labour value"* thanks to rent, profit, interest and the actions of middle men. Such system specific "costs" hide the actual costs (in terms of labour and resource use) by increasing the price compared to if we *"reckon our expenses in labour"*. [**Op. Cit.**, p. 68]

Finally, it should be noted that most anarchists would question the criteria Hayek and Mises used to judge the relative merits of communism and capitalism. As the former put it, the issue was *"a distribution of income independent of private property in the means of production and a volume of output which was at least approximately the same or even greater than that procured under free competition."* [*"The Nature and History of the Problem"*, **Op. Cit.**, p. 37] Thus the issue is reduced to that of output (quantity), not issues of freedom (quality). If slavery or Stalinism **had** produced more output than free market capitalism, that would not make either system desirable This was, in fact, a common argument against Stalinism during the 1950s and 1960s when it **did** appear that central planning was producing more goods. Similarly, that

capitalism produces more alcohol and Prozac to meet the higher demand for dulling the minds of those trying to survive under it would **not** be an argument against libertarian communism! As we discuss in section I.4, while anarchists seek to meet material human needs we do not aim, as under capitalism, to sacrifice all other goals to that aim as capitalism does. Thus, to state the obvious, the aim for maximum volume of output only makes sense under capitalism as the maximum of human happiness and liberty may occur with a lower volume of output in a free society. The people of a society without oppression, exploitation and alienation will hardly act in identical ways, nor seek the same volume of output, as those in one, like capitalism, marked by those traits!

Moreover, the volume of output is a somewhat misleading criteria as it totally ignores its distribution. If the bulk of that volume goes to a few, then that is hardly a good use of resources. This is hardly an academic concern as can be seen from the Hayek influenced neo-liberalism of the 1980s onwards. As economist Paul Krugman notes, the value of the output of an average worker *"has risen almost 50 percent since 1973. Yet the growing concentration of income in the hands of a small minority had proceeded so rapidly that we're not sure whether the typical American has gained anything from rising productivity."* This means that wealth has flooded upwards, and *"the lion's share of economic growth in America over the past thirty years has gone to a small, wealthy minority."* [**The Conscience of a Liberal**, p. 124 and p. 244]

To conclude. Capitalist "efficiency" is hardly rational and for a fully human and ecological efficiency libertarian communism is required. As Buick and Crump point out, *"socialist society still has to be concerned with using resources efficiently and rationally, but the criteria of 'efficiency' and 'rationality' are not the same as they are under capitalism."* [**Op. Cit.**, p. 137] Under communist-anarchism, the decision-making system used to determine the best use of resources is not more or less "efficient" than market allocation, because it goes beyond the market-based concept of "efficiency." It does not seek to mimic the market but to do what the market fails to do. This is important, because the market is not the rational system its defenders often claim. While reducing all decisions to one common factor is, without a doubt, an easy method of decision making, it also has serious side-effects **because** of its reductionistic basis. The market makes decision making simplistic and generates a host of irrationalities and dehumanising effects as a result. So, to claim that communism will be "more" efficient than capitalism or vice versa misses the point. Libertarian communism will be "efficient" in a totally different way and people will act in ways considered "irrational" only under the narrow logic of capitalism.

For another critique of Mises, see Robin Cox's *"The 'Economic Calculation' controversy: unravelling of a myth"* [**Common Voice**, Issue 3]

I.1.3 What is wrong with markets anyway?

A lot. Markets soon result in what are termed *"market forces,"* impersonal forces which ensure that the people in the economy do what is required of them in order for the economy to function. The market system, in capitalist apologetics, is presented to appear as a regime of freedom where no one forces anyone to do anything, where we "freely" exchange with others as we see fit. However, the facts of the matter are somewhat different, since the market often ensures that people act in ways **opposite** to what they desire or forces them to accept "free agreements" which they may not actually desire. Wage labour is the most obvious example of this, for, as we indicated in section B.4, most people have little option but to agree to work for others.

We must stress here that not all anarchists are opposed to the market. Individualist anarchists favour it while Proudhon wanted to modify it while retaining competition. For many, the market equals capitalism but this is not the case as it ignores the fundamental issue of (economic) class, namely who owns the means of production. Capitalism is unique in that it is based on wage labour, i.e. a market for labour as workers do not own their own means of production and have to sell themselves to those who do. Thus it is entirely possible for a market to exist within a society and for that society **not** to be capitalist. For example, a society of independent artisans and peasants selling their product on the market would not be capitalist as workers would own and control their means of production. Similarly, Proudhon's competitive system of self-managed co-operatives and mutual banks would be non-capitalist (and socialist) for the same reason. Anarchists object to capitalism due to the quality of the social relationships it generates between people (i.e. it generates authoritarian ones). If these relationships are eliminated then the kinds of ownership which do so are anarchistic. Thus the issue of ownership matters only in-so-far it generates relationships of the desired kind (i.e. those based on liberty, equality and solidarity). To concentrate purely on "markets" or "property" means to ignore social relationships and the key aspect of capitalism, namely wage labour. That right-wingers do this is understandable (to hide the authoritarian core of capitalism) but why (libertarian or other) socialists should do so is less clear.

In this section of the FAQ we discuss anarchist objections to the market **as such** rather than the capitalist market. The workings of the market do have problems with them which are independent of, or made worse by, the existence of wage-labour. It is these problems which make most anarchists hostile to the market and so desire a (libertarian) communist society. So, even if we assume a mutualist (a libertarian market-socialist) system of competing self-managed workplaces, then communist anarchists would argue that market forces would soon result in many irrationalities occurring.

Most obviously, operating in a market means submitting to the profit criterion. This means that however much workers might want to employ social criteria in their decision making, they cannot. To ignore profitability would cause their firm to go bankrupt. Markets, therefore, create conditions that compel producers to decide things

which are not be in their, or others, interest, such as introducing deskilling or polluting technology, working longer hours, and so on, in order to survive on the market. For example, a self-managed workplace will be more likely to invest in safe equipment and working practices, this would still be dependent on finding the money to do so and may still increase the price of their finished product. This tendency for self-managed firms to adjust to market forces by increasing hours, working more intensely, allocating resources to accumulating equipment rather than leisure time or consumption can be seen in co-operatives under capitalism. While lacking bosses may reduce this tendency in a post-capitalist economy, it will not eliminate it. This is why many socialists, including anarchists, call the way markets force unwilling members of co-operatives to make such unpleasant decisions a form of "self-exploitation" (although this is somewhat misleading, as there no exploitation in the capitalist sense of owners appropriating unpaid labour). For communist-anarchists, a market system of co-operatives *"has serious limitations"* as *"a collective enterprise is not necessarily a commune — nor is it necessarily communistic in its outlook."* This is because it can end up *"competing with like concerns for resources, customers, privileges, and even profits"* as they *"become a particularistic interest"* and *"are subjected to the same social pressures by the market in which they must function."* This *"tends increasingly to encroach on their higher ethical goals — generally, in the name of 'efficiency', and the need to 'grow' if they are to survive, and the overwhelming temptation to acquire larger earnings."* [Murray Bookchin, **Remaking Society**, pp. 193-4]

Similarly, a market of self-managed firms would still suffer from booms and slumps as the co-operatives response to changes in prices would still result in over-production (see section C.7.2) and over-investment (see section C.7.3). While the lack of non-labour income would help reduce the severity of the business cycle, it seems unlikely to eliminate it totally. Equally, many of the problems of market-increased uncertainty and the destabilising aspects of price signals discussed in section I.1.5 are just as applicable to all markets, including post-capitalist ones.

As we noted in section E.3, markets tend to reward those who act in anti-social ways and externalise costs (in terms of pollution and so on). In a market economy, it is impossible to determine whether a low cost reflects actual efficiency or a willingness to externalise, i.e., impose costs on others. Markets rarely internalise external costs. Two economic agents who strike a market-rational bargain between themselves need not consider the consequences of their bargain for other people outside their bargain, nor the consequences for the earth. In reality, then, market exchanges are never bilateral agreements as their effects impact on the wider society (in terms of, say, pollution, inequality and so on). This awkward fact is ignored in the market. As the left-wing economist Joan Robinson put it: *"In what industry, in what line of business, are the true social costs of the activity registered in its accounts? Where is the pricing system that offers the consumer a fair choice between air to breath and motor cars to drive about in?"* [**Contribution to Modern Economics**, p. 10]

While, to be fair, there will be a reduced likelihood for a workplace of self-employed workers to pollute their own neighbourhoods in a free society, the competitive pressures and rewards would still be there and it seems unlikely that they will be ignored, particularly if survival on the market is at stake so communist-anarchists fear that while not having bosses, capitalists and landlords would mitigate some of the irrationalities associated with markets under capitalism, it will not totally remove them. While the market may be free, people would not be.

Even if we assume that self-managed firms resist the temptations and pressures of the market, any market system is also marked by a continuing need to expand production and consumption. In terms of environmental impact, a self-managed firm must still make profits in order to survive and so the economy must grow. As such, every market system will tend to expand into an environment which is of fixed size. As well as placing pressure on the planet's ecology, this need to grow impacts on human activity as it also means that market forces ensure that work continually has to expand. Competition means that we can never take it easy, for as Max Stirner argued, *"[r]estless acquisition does not let us take breath, take a calm **enjoyment**. We do not get the comfort of our possessions … Hence it is at any rate helpful that we come to an agreement about **human** labours that they may not, as under competition, claim all our time and toil."* [**The Ego and Its Own**, p. 268] Value needs to be created, and that can only be done by labour and so even a non-capitalist market system will see work dominate people's lives. Thus the need to survive on the market can impact on broader (non-monetary) measures of welfare, with quality of life falling as a higher GDP is created as the result of longer working hours with fewer holidays. Such a regime may, perhaps, be good for material wealth but it is not great for people.

The market can also block the efficient use of resources. For example, for a long time energy efficient light-bulbs were much more expensive than normal ones. Over the long period, however, they used far less energy than normal ones, meaning less need to produce more energy (and so burn coal and oil, for example). However, the high initial price ensured that most people continued to use the less efficient bulbs and so waste resources. Much the same can be said of alternative forms of energy, with investment in (say) wind energy ignored in favour of one-use and polluting energy sources. A purely market system would not allow decisions which benefit the long-term interests of people to be made (for example, by distributing energy-efficient light-bulbs freely or at a reduced cost) as these would harm the profits of those co-operatives which tried to do so.

Also, markets do not reflect the values of things we do not put a price upon (as we argued in section B.5). It cannot protect wilderness, for example, simply because it requires people to turn it into property and sell it as a commodity. If you cannot afford to visit the new commodity, the market turns it into something else, no matter how much you value it. The market also ignores the needs of future generations as they always discount the value of the long term future. A payment to be made 1,000 years from now (a mere speck in geological time) has a market value of virtually zero according to any commonly used discount rate. Even 50 years in the future cannot be adequately considered as competitive pressures force a short term perspective on people harmful to present and future generations, plus the ecology of the planet.

Then there are corrosive effects of the market on human personalities.

As we have argued elsewhere (see section B.1.3), competition in a free market creates numerous problems — for example, the creation of an *"ethics of mathematics"* and the strange inversion of values in which things (property/money) become more important than people. This can have a de-humanising effect, with people becoming cold-hearted calculators who put profits before people. This can be seen in capitalism, where economic decisions are far more important than ethical ones — particularly as such an inhuman mentality can be rewarded on the market. Merit does not necessarily breed success, and the successful do not necessarily have merit. The truth is that, in the words of Noam Chomsky, *"wealth and power tend to accrue to those who are ruthless, cunning, avaricious, self-seeking, lacking in sympathy and compassion, subservient to authority and willing to abandon principle for material gain, and so on … Such qualities might be just the valuable ones for a war of all against all."* [**For Reasons of State**, pp. 139-140]

Needless to be said, if the market does reward such people with success it can hardly be considered as a **good** thing. A system which elevates making money to the position of the most important individual activity will obviously result in the degrading of human values and an increase in neurotic and psychotic behaviour. Little wonder, as Alfie Kohn has argued, competition can have serious negative effects on us outside of work, with it damaging both our personal psychology and our interpersonal relationships. Thus competition *"itself is responsible for the development of a lower moral standard"* which places winning at any cost above fairness and justice. Kohn quotes Nathan Ackerman, the father of family therapy, who noted that the *"strife of competition reduces empathic sympathy, distorts communication, impairs the mutuality of support and sharing, and decreases the satisfaction of personal need."* [**No Contest**, p. 163 and pp. 142-3] Thus, the market can impoverish us as individuals, sabotaging self-esteem, promoting conformity, ruining relationships and making us less than what we could be. This is a problem of markets as such, not only capitalist ones and so non-capitalist markets could make us less human and more a robot.

All market decisions are crucially conditioned by the purchasing power of those income groups that can back their demands with money. Not everyone can work (the sick, the very old, children and so forth) and for those who can, personal circumstances may impact on their income. Moreover, production has become so interwoven that it *"is utterly impossible to draw a distinction between the work of each"* and so we should *"put the **needs** above the **works**, and first of all to recognise **the right to live**, and later on **the right to well-being** for all those who took their share in production."* This is particularly the case as *"the needs of the individual, do not always correspond to his **works**"* — for example, *"a man of forty, father of three children, has other needs than a young man of twenty"* and *"the woman who suckles her infant and spends sleepless nights at its bedside, cannot do as much **work** as the man who has slept peacefully."* [Kropotkin, **Conquest of Bread**, p. 170 and p. 171] This was why communist-anarchists like Kropotkin stressed the need not only to abolish wage-labour but also money, the wages system.

So it goes without saying that purchasing power (demand) and need are not related, with people often suffering simply because they do not have the money required to purchase, say, health care, housing or food for themselves or their families. While economic distress may be less in a non-capitalist market system, it still would exist as would the fear of it. The market is a continuous bidding for goods, resources, and services, with those who have the most purchasing power the winners. This means that the market system is the worst one for allocating resources when purchasing power is unequally distributed (this is why orthodox economists make the convenient assumption of a *"given distribution of income"* when they try to show that a capitalist allocation of resources is the best one via *"Pareto optimality"*). While a mutualist system should reduce inequality drastically, it cannot be assumed that inequalities will not increase over time. This is because inequalities in resources leads to inequalities of power on the market and, assuming self-interest, any trade or contract will benefit the powerful more than the powerless, so re-enforcing and potentially increasing the inequalities and power between the parties. Similarly, while an anarchist society would be created with people driven by a sense of solidarity and desire for equality, markets tend to erode those feelings and syndicates or communes which, thanks to the resources they control (such as rare raw materials or simply the size of their investments reducing competitive pressures) have an advantage on the market may be tempted to use their monopoly power vis-à-vis other groups in society to accrue more income for themselves at the expense of less fortunate syndicates and communes. This could degenerate back into capitalism as any inequalities that exist between co-operatives would be increased by competition, forcing weaker co-operatives to fail and so creating a pool of workers with nothing to sell but their labour. The successful co-operatives could then hire those workers and so re-introduce wage labour. So these possibilities could, over time, return a post-capitalist market system to capitalism if the inequalities become so great that the new rich become so alienated from the rest of society they recreate wage-labour and, by necessity, a state to enforce a desire for property in land and the means of production against public opinion.

All this ensures that the market cannot really provide the information necessary for rational-decision making in terms of ecological impact as well as human activity and so resources are inefficiently allocated. We all suffer from the consequences of that, with market forces impoverishing our environment and quality of life. Thus are plenty of reasons for concluding that efficiency and the market not only do not necessarily coincide, but, indeed, necessarily do not coincide. Indeed, rather than respond to individual needs, the market responds to money (more correctly, profit), which by its very nature provides a distorted indication of individual preferences (and does not take into account values which are enjoyed collectively, such as clean air, or **potentially** enjoyed, such as the wilderness a person may never visit but desires to see exist and protected).

This does not mean that social anarchists propose to "ban" the market — far from it. This would be impossible. What we do propose is to convince people that a profit-based market system has distinctly **bad** effects on individuals, society and the planet's ecology, and that we can organise our common activity to replace it with libertarian communism. As Max Stirner argued, competition *"has a continued existence"* because *"all do not attend to **their affair** and come to an **understanding** with each other about it ... .*

*Abolishing competition is not equivalent to favouring the guild. The difference is this: In the **guild** baking, etc., is the affair of the guild-brothers; in **competition**, the affair of chance competitors; in the **union**, of those who require baked goods, and therefore my affair, yours, the affair of neither guildic nor the concessionary baker, but the affair of the **united.**"* [**Op. Cit.**, p. 275]

Therefore, social anarchists do not appeal purely to altruism in their struggle against the de-humanising effects of the market, but also to egoism: the simple fact that co-operation and mutual aid is in our best interests as individuals. By co-operating and controlling *"the affairs of the united,"* we can ensure a free society which is worth living in, one in which the individual is not crushed by market forces and has time to fully develop his or her individuality and uniqueness:

> *"Solidarity is therefore the state of being in which Man attains the greatest degree of security and wellbeing; and therefore egoism itself, that is the exclusive consideration of one's own interests, impels Man and human society towards solidarity."* [Errico Malatesta, **Anarchy**, p. 30]

In conclusion then, communist-anarchists argue that even non-capitalist markets would result in everyone being so busy competing to further their "self-interest" that they would loose sight of what makes life worth living and so harm their **actual** interests. Ultimately, what counts as self-interest is shaped by the surrounding social system. The pressures of competing may easily result in short-term and narrow interests taking precedence over richer, deeper needs and aspirations which a communal system could allow to flourish by providing the social institutions by which individuals can discuss their joint interests, formulate them and act to achieve them. That is, even non-capitalist markets would result in people simply working long and hard to survive on the market rather than **living**. If one paradox of authoritarian socialism is that it makes everyone miserable by forcing them to altruistically look out for the happiness of others, market-based libertarian socialism could produce the potential paradox of making everyone miserable by the market forcing them to pursue a limited notion of self-interest which ensures that they do not have the time or opportunity to really be happy and at one with themselves and others.

In other words, bosses act as they do under capitalism in part because markets force them to. Getting rid of bosses need not eliminate all the economic pressures which influence the bosses' decisions and, in turn, could force groups of workers to act in similar ways. Thus a competitive system would undermine many of the benefits which people sought when they ended capitalism. This is why some socialists inaccurately call socialist schemes of competing co-operatives "self-managed capitalism" or "self-exploitation" — they are simply drawing attention to the negative aspects of markets which getting rid of the boss cannot solve. Significantly, Proudhon was well aware of the negative aspect of market forces and suggested various institutional structures, such as the agricultural-industrial federation, to combat them (so while in favour of competition he was, unlike the individualist anarchists, against the free market). Communist anarchists, unsurprisingly, argue that individualist anarchists tend to stress the positive aspects of competition while ignoring or downplaying its negative sides. While, undoubtedly, capitalism makes the negative side of competition worse than it could be it does not automatically follow that a non-capitalist market would not have similar, if smaller, negative aspects to it.

I.1.4 If capitalism is exploitative, then isn't communism as well?

Some libertarian Marxists (as well as Leninists) claim that non-communist forms of socialism are just "self-managed" capitalism. Strangely, propertarians (the so-called "libertarian" right) also say yes to this question, arguing that socialist opposition to exploitation does not imply socialism but what they also call "self-managed" capitalism. Thus some on the left proclaim anything short of communism is a form of capitalism while, on the right, some proclaim that communism is exploitative and only a market system (which they erroneously equate to capitalism) is non-exploitative. Both are wrong. First, and most obviously, socialism does not equal communism (and vice versa). While there is a tendency on both right and left to equate socialism with communism (particularly Marxism), in reality, as Proudhon once noted, socialism *"was not founded as a sect or church; it has seen a number of different schools."* [**Property is Theft!**, p. 23] Only a few of these schools are communist, just as only a few of them are libertarian. Second, not all socialist schools aim to abolish the market and payment by deed. Proudhon, for example, opposed communism and state socialism just as much as he opposed capitalism. Third, capitalism does not equal the market. The market predates capitalism and, for some libertarian socialists, will survive it. The defining feature of capitalism is **wage labour**, not the market.

So opposition to capitalism can imply both socialism (distribution according to deed, or selling the product of ones labour) and communism (distribution according to need, or a moneyless economy). The theory is a critique of capitalism, based on an analysis of that system as being rooted in the exploitation of labour (as we discussed in section C.2), i.e., it is marked by workers not being paid the full-value of the goods they create. This analysis, however, is not necessarily the basis of a socialist economy although it **can** be considered this as well. As noted, Proudhon used his critique of capitalism as an exploitative system as the foundation of his proposals for mutual banking and co-operatives. Marx, on the other hand, used a similar analysis as Proudhon's purely as a critique of capitalism while hoping for communism. Robert Owen used it as the basis of his system of labour notes while Kropotkin argued that such a system was just the wages-system under another form and a free society *"having taken possession of all social wealth, having boldly proclaimed the right of all to this wealth ... will be compelled to abandon any system of wages, whether in currency or labour-notes."* [**The Conquest of Bread**, p. 167]

In other words, though a system of co-operative selling on the market or exchanging labour-time values would not be communism, it is **not** capitalism. This is because the workers are not separated from the means of production. Therefore, the attempts by propertarians to claim that it is capitalism are false. However, it could be argued

that communism (based on free access and communal ownership of all resources including the product of labour) would mean that workers are exploited by non-workers (the young, the sick, the elderly and so on). As communism abolishes the link between performance and payment, it could be argued that the workers under communism would be just as exploited as under capitalism, although (of course) not by a class of capitalists and landlords but by the community. As Proudhon put it, while the *"members of a community, it is true, have no private property"* the community itself *"is proprietor"* and so communism *"is inequality, but not as property is. Property is the exploitation of the weak by the strong. Communism is the exploitation of the strong by the weak."* [**What is Property?**, p. 250]

Needless to say, subsequent anarchists rejected Proudhon's blanket opposition to all forms of communism, rejecting this position as only applicable to authoritarian, not libertarian, communism. Which, it must be remembered, was the only kind around when this was written in 1840 (as we noted in section H.1, what was known as communism in Proudhon's time was authoritarian). Suffice to say, Proudhon's opposition to communism shares little with that of the Propertarian-right. However, the notion that communism (distribution according to need) rather than socialism (distribution according to deed) is exploitative misses the point as far as communist anarchism goes. This is because of two reasons.

Firstly, Anarchist Communism *"means voluntary Communism, Communism from free choice."* [Alexander Berkman, **What is Anarchism**, p. 148] This means it is not imposed on anyone but is created and practised only by those who believe in it.

Therefore it would be up to the communities and syndicates to decide how they wish to distribute the products of their labour and individuals to join, or create, those that meet their ideas of right and wrong. Some may decide on equal pay, others on payment in terms of labour time, yet others on communistic associations. The important thing to realise is that individuals and the co-operatives they join will decide what to do with their output, whether to exchange it or to distribute it freely. Hence, because it is based on free agreement, communist-anarchism cannot be exploitative. Members of a commune or co-operative which is communistic are free to leave, after all. Needless to say, the co-operatives will usually distribute their product to others within their confederation and exchange with the non-communist ones in a different manner. We say "usually" for in the case of emergencies like earthquakes and so forth the situation would call for, and produce, mutual aid just as it does today to a large degree, even under capitalism.

The reason why capitalism is exploitative is that workers **have** to agree to give the product of their labour to another (the boss, the landlord) in order to be employed in the first place (see section B.4). While they can choose who to be exploited by (and, to varying degrees, pick the best of the limited options available to them) they cannot avoid selling their liberty to property owners (a handful do become self-employed and some manage to join the exploiting class, but not enough to make either a meaningful option for the bulk of the working class). In libertarian communism, by contrast, the workers themselves agree to distribute part of their product to others (i.e. society as a whole, their neighbours, friends, and so forth). It is based on free agreement, while capitalism is marked by power, authority, and the firm (invisible) hand of market forces (supplemented, as necessary, by the visible fist of the state). As resources are held in common under anarchism, people always have the option of working alone if they so desire (see section I.3.7). Secondly, unlike under capitalism, there is no separate class which is appropriating the goods produced. The so-called "non-workers" in a libertarian communist society have been, or will be, workers. As the noted Spanish anarchist De Santillan pointed out, "[n]aturally, children, the aged and the sick are not considered parasites. The children will be productive when they grow up. The aged have already made their contribution to social wealth and the sick are only temporarily unproductive." [**After the Revolution**, p. 20] In other words, over their life time, everyone contributes to society and so using the "account book" mentality of capitalism misses the point. As Kropotkin put it:

> "Services rendered to society, be they work in factory or field, or mental services, **cannot be** valued in money. There can be no exact measure of value (of what has been wrongly-termed exchange value), nor of use value, with regard to production. If two individuals work for the community five hours a day, year in year out, at different work which is equally agreeable to them, we may say that on the whole their labour is equivalent. But we cannot divide their work, and say that the result of any particular day, hour, or minute of work of the one is worth the result of a minute or hour of the other." [**Conquest of Bread**, p. 168]

So it is difficult to evaluate how much an individual worker or group of workers actually contribute to society. This can be seen whenever workers strike, particularly so-called "key" areas like transport. Then the media is full of accounts of how much the strike is costing "the economy" and it is always far more than that of the wages lost in strike action. Yet, according to capitalist economics, the wages of a worker are equal to their contribution to production — no more, no less. Striking workers, in other words, should only harm the economy to the value of their wages yet, of course, this is obviously not the case. This is because of the interconnected nature of any advanced economy, where contributions of individuals are so bound together.

Needless to say, this does not imply that a free people would tolerate the able-bodied simply taking without contributing towards the mass of products and services society. As we discuss in section I.4.14, such people will be asked to leave the community and be in the same situation as those who do not wish to be communists.

Ultimately, the focus on calculating exact amounts and on the evaluation of contributions down to the last penny is exactly the kind of narrow-minded account-book mentality which makes most people socialists in the first place. It would be ironic if, in the name of non-exploitation, a similar accounting mentality to that which records how much surplus value is extracted from workers under capitalism is continued into a free society. It makes life easier not to have to worry whether you can afford to visit the doctors or dentists, not to have to pay for use of roads and bridges, know that you can visit a public library for a book and so forth. For those who wish to spend their time calculating such activities and seeking to

pay the community for them simply because they hate the idea of being "exploited" by the "less" productive, the ill, the young or the old then we are sure that a libertarian communist society will accommodate them (although we are sure that emergencies will be an exception and they will be given free access to communal hospitals, fire services and so forth).

Thus the notion that communism would be exploitative like capitalism misses the point. While all socialists accuse capitalism for failing to live up to its own standards, of not paying workers the full product of their labour, most do not think that a socialist society should seek to make that full payment a reality. Life, for libertarian communists, is just too complex and fleeting to waste time and energy calculating exactly the contribution of each to society. As Malatesta put it:

> "I say that **the worker has the right to the entire product of his work**: but I recognise that this right is only a formula of abstract justice; and means, in practice, that there should be no exploitation, that everyone must work and enjoy the fruits of their labour, according to the custom agreed among them.

> "Workers are not isolated beings that live by themselves and for themselves, but social beings ... Moreover, it is impossible, the more so with modern production methods, to determine the exact labour that each worker contributed, just as it is impossible to determine the differences in productivity of each worker or each group of workers, how much is due to the fertility of the soil, the quality of the implements used, the advantages or difficulties flowing from the geographical situation or the social environment. Hence, the solution cannot be found in respect to the strict rights of each person, but must be sought in fraternal agreement, in solidarity." [**At the Café**, pp. 56-7]

All in all, most anarchists reject the notion that people sharing the world (which is all communism really means) equates to them being exploited by others. Rather than waste time trying to record the minutiae of who contributed exactly what to society, most anarchists are happy if people contribute to society roughly equal amounts of time and energy and take what they need in return. To consider such a situation of free co-operation as exploitative is simply ridiculous (just as well consider the family as the exploitation of its working members by their non-working partners and children). Those who do are free to leave such an association and pay their own way in everything (a task which would soon drive home the simplicity and utility of communism, most anarchists would suggest).

I.1.5 Does capitalism efficiently allocate resources?

We have discussed, in section I.1.1, the negative effects of workplace hierarchy and stock markets and, in section I.1.2, the informational problems of prices and the limitations in using profit as the sole criteria for decision making for the efficient allocation of resources. As such, anarchists have reason to doubt the arguments of the "Austrian" school of economics that (libertarian) socialism is impossible, as first suggested by Ludwig Von Mises in 1920. ["*Economic Calculation in the Socialist Commonwealth*", **Collectivist Economic Planning**, F.A von Hayek (ed.), pp. 87-130] Here, we discuss why anarchists also have strong reason to question the underlying assumption that capitalism efficiently allocates resources and how this impacts on claims that "socialism" is impossible. This is based on an awareness of the flaws in any (implicit) assumption that all prices are at equilibrium, the issue of uncertainty, the assumption that human well-being is best served by market forces and, lastly, the problem of periodic economic crisis under capitalism.

The first issue is that prices provide adequate knowledge for rational decision making only if they are at their equilibrium values as this equates supply and demand. Sadly, for the "Austrian" school and its arguments against socialism, it rejects the notion that prices could be at equilibrium. While modern "Austrian" economics is keen to stress its (somewhat underdeveloped) disequilibrium analysis of capitalism, this was not always the case. When Mises wrote his 1920 essay on socialism his school of economics was considered a branch of the neo-classicalism and this can be seen from Mises' critique of central planning. In fact, it would be fair to say that the neo-"Austrian" focus of prices as information and (lip-service to) disequilibrium flowed from the Economic Calculation debate, specifically the awkward fact that their more orthodox neo-classical peers viewed Lange's "solution" as answering Mises and Hayek.

Thus there is a fundamental inconsistency in Mises' argument, namely that while Austrian economics reject the notion of equilibrium and the perfect competition of neo-classical economics he nonetheless maintains that market prices are the correct prices and can be used to make rational decisions. Yet, in any real market, these correct prices must be ever changing so making the possibility that "*precise*" economic decisions by price can go wrong on a large scale (i.e., in slumps). In other words, Mises effectively assumed away uncertainty and, moreover, failed to mention that this uncertainty is increased dramatically within capitalism.

This can be seen from modern "Austrian" economics which, after the Economic Calculation debates of the 1920s and 1930s, moved increasingly away from neo-classical equilibrium theory. However, this opened up a whole new can of worms which, ironically, weakened the "Austrian" case against socialism. For the modern "Austrian" economist, the economy is considered not to be in equilibrium, with the entrepreneur being seen as the means by which it is brought towards it. Thus "*this approach postulates a tendency for profit opportunities to be **discovered** and **grasped** by routine-resisting entrepreneurial market participants*", with this "*tending to nudge the market in the equilibrative direction.*" Lip-service is paid to the obvious fact that entrepreneurs can make errors but "***there is no tendency for entrepreneurial errors to be made.** The tendency which the market generates toward greater mutual awareness, is not offset by any equal but opposite tendency in the direction of diminishing awareness*" and so the "*entrepreneurial market process may indeed reflect a systematically equilibrative **tendency**, but this by no means constitutes a **guaranteed** unidirectional, flawlessly converging trajectory.*" All this results on the "*speculative actions of entrepreneurs who see opportunities for pure profit in the conditions of disequilibrium.*" [Israel M. Kirzner, "*Entrepreneurial Discovery and the Competitive Market Process: An Austrian Approach*", pp. 60-85, **Journal of Economic Literature**, Vol. 35, No. 1, p. 71, p. 73, p. 82, p. 72 and p. 68]

When evaluating this argument, it is useful to remember that "*postulate*" means **"to assume without proof to be true"** or **"to take as self-evident."** At its most simple, this argument ignores how entrepreneurial activity pushes an economy **away** from equilibrium (unlike radical economists, only a few "Austrian" economists, such as those who follow Ludwig Lachmann, recognise that market forces have both equilibrating **and** disequilibrium effects, acknowledged in passing by Kirzner: "*In a world of incessant change, they argue, it is precisely those acts of entrepreneurial boldness which must frustrate any discovery efforts made by fellow entrepreneurs.*" [**Op. Cit.**, p. 79]). In other words, market activity can lead to economic crisis and inefficient allocation decisions. A successful entrepreneur will, by their actions, frustrate the plans of others, most obviously those of his competitors but also those who require the goods they used to produce their commodities and those whose incomes are reduced by the new products being available. It staggers belief to think that **every** action by a firm will be step towards equilibrium or a better co-ordination of plans, particularly if you include **unsuccessful** entrepreneurs into the process. In other words, the market can be as discoordinating as it can be co-ordinating and it cannot be "postulated" beforehand which will predominate at any given time.

There is an obvious example of entrepreneurial activity which leads to increasing disequilibrium, one (ironically) drawn straight from "Austrian" economics itself. This is the actions of bankers extending credit and so deviating from the "natural" (equilibrium) rate of interest. As one post-Keynesian economist notes, this, the "Austrian" theory of the business cycle, "*not only proved to be vulnerable to the Cambridge capital critique … , but also appeared to reply upon concepts of equilibrium (the 'natural rate of interest', for example) that were inconsistent with the broader principles of Austrian economic theory.*" [J.E. King, **A history of post Keynesian economics since 1936**, p. 230] As we discussed in section C.8, this kind of activity is to be expected of entrepreneurs seeking to make money from meeting market demand. The net result of this activity is a tendency **away** from equilibrium. This can be generalised for all markets, with the profit seeking activities of some businesses frustrating the plans of others. Ultimately, the implication that all entrepreneurial activity is stabilising, virtuous arbitrage that removes disequilibria is as unconvincing as is the suggestion that the misinformation conveyed by disequilibrium prices can cause very substantial macroeconomic distortions for only one good (credit). Surely, the argument as regards interest rates can apply to other disequilibrium prices, with responses to unsustainable prices for other goods being equally capable of generating mal-investment (which only becomes apparent when the prices adjust towards their "natural" levels). After all, any single price distortion leads to all other prices becoming distorted because of the ramifications for exchange ratios throughout the economy.

One of the reasons why neo-classical economists stress equilibrium is that prices provide the basis for rational calculation only in that state, for disequilibrium prices can convey extremely misleading information. When people trade at disequilibrium prices, it has serious impacts on the economy (which is why neo-classical economics abstracts from it). As one economist notes, if people *were to buy and sell at prices which did not clear the market*" then once "*such trading has taken place, there can be no guarantee that, even if an equilibrium exists, the economy will ever converge to it. In fact, it is likely to move in cycles around the equilibrium.*" This "*is more than a mere supposition. It is an accurate description of what does happen in the real world.*" [Paul Ormerod, **The Death of Economics**, pp. 87-8] Once we dismiss the ideologically driven "*postulate*" of "Austrian" economics, we can see how these opportunities for "pure profit" (and, of course, a corresponding pure loss for the buyer) impacts on the economy and how the market system adds to uncertainty. As dissident economist Steve Keen puts it:

> "*However, a change in prices in one market will affect consumer demand in all other markets. This implies that a move towards equilibrium by one market could cause some or all others to move away from equilibrium. Clearly it is possible that this ... might never settle down to equilibrium.*
>
> "*This will be especially so if trades actually occur at disequilibrium — as in practice they must ... A disequilibrium trade will mean that the people on the winning side of the bargain — sellers if the price is higher than equilibrium — will gain real income at the expense of the losers, compared to the alleged standard of equilibrium. This shift in income distribution will then affect all other markets, making the dance of many markets even more chaotic.*"
> [**Debunking Economics**, p. 169]

That prices can, and do, convey extremely misleading information is something which "Austrians" have a tendency to downplay. Yet in economies closer to their ideal (for example, nineteenth century America) there were many more recessions (usually triggered by financial crises arising from the collapse of speculative bubbles) than in the twentieth and so the economy was fundamentally more unstable, resulting in the market "precisely" investing in the "wrong" areas. Of course, it could be argued that there was not really free market capitalism then (e.g., protectionism, no true free banking due to regulation by state governments and so on) yet this would be question begging in the extreme (particularly since the end of the 20th and dawn of the 21st centuries saw speculative crises precisely in those areas which were regulated least).

Thus, the notion that prices can ensure the efficient allocation of resources is question begging. If prices are in disequilibrium, as "Austrians" suggest, then the market does not automatically ensure that they move towards equilibrium. Without equilibrium, we cannot say that prices provide companies sufficient information to make rational investment decisions. They may act on price information which is misleading, in that it reflects temporary highs or lows in the market or which is a result of speculative bubbles. An investment decision made on the **mis**-information implied in disequilibrium prices is as likely to produce mal-investment and subsequent macro-economic distortions as decisions made in light of the interest rate not being at its "natural" (equilibrium) value. So unless it is assumed that the market is in equilibrium when an investment decision is made then prices can reflect misinformation as much as information. These, the obvious implications of disequilibrium, help undermine Mises' arguments against socialism.

Even if we assume that prices are at or, at best, near equilibrium when investment decisions are made, the awkward fact is that these prices do not tell you prices in the future nor what will be bought when production is finished. Rather, they tell you what was **thought** to be profitable before **investment began**. There are always differences between the prices used to cost various investments and the prices which prevail on the market when the finished goods are finally sold, suggesting that the market presents systematically misleading signals. In addition, rival companies respond to the same price signals by undertaking long term investments at the same time, so creating the possibility of a general crisis of over-accumulation and over-production when they are complete. As we discussed in section C.7.2, this is a key factor in the business cycle. Hence the recurring possibility of over-production, when the aggregate response to a specific market's rising price results in the market being swamped by goods, so driving the market price down. Thus the market is marked by uncertainty, the future is not known. So it seems ironic to read Mises asserting that "*in the socialist commonwealth every economic change becomes an undertaking whose success can be neither appraised in advance nor later retrospectively determined. There is only groping in the dark.*" [**Op. Cit.**, p. 110]

In terms of "*appraised in advance*", Mises is essentially assuming that capitalists can see the future. In the real world, rather than in the unreal world of capitalist economics, the future is unknown and, as a result, success can only be guessed at. This means that any investment decision under **real** capitalism is, equally, "*groping in the dark*" because there is no way to know, before hand, whether the expectations driving the investment decisions will come to be. As Mises himself noted as part of his attack on socialism, "*a static state is impossible in real life, as our economic data are for ever changing*" and so, needless to say, the success of an investment **cannot** be appraised beforehand with any real degree of certainty. Somewhat ironically, Mises noted that "*the static nature of economic activity is only a theoretical assumption corresponding to no real state of affairs, however necessary it may be for our thinking and for the perfection of our knowledge of economics.*" [**Op. Cit.**, p. 109] Or, for that matter, our critique of socialism! This can be seen from one of his examples against socialism:

> "*Picture the building of a new railroad. Should it be built at all, and if so, which out of a number of conceivable roads*

should be built? In a competitive and monetary economy, this question would be answered by monetary calculation. The new road will render less expensive the transport of some goods, and it may be possible to calculate whether this reduction of expense transcends that involved in the building and upkeep of the next line. That can only be calculated in money." [**Op. Cit.**, p. 108]

It *"may be possible"*? Not before hand. At best, an investor could **estimate** the willingness of firms to swap to the new railroad and whether those expected costs will result in a profit on both fixed and running costs. The construction costs can be estimated, although unexpected price rises in the future may make a mockery of these too, but the amount of future income cannot. Equally, the impact of building the new railroad will change the distribution of income as well, which in turn affects prices across the market and people's consumption decisions which, in turn, affects the profitability of new railroad investment. Yet all this is ignored in order to attack socialism.

In other words, Mises assumes that the future can be accurately predicted in order to attack socialism. Thus he asserts that a socialist society *"would issue an edict and decide for or against the projected building. Yet this decision would depend at best upon vague estimates; it would never be based upon the foundation of an exact calculation of value."* [**Op. Cit.**, p. 109] Yet any investment decision in a **real** capitalist economy depends *"at best upon vague estimates"* of future market conditions and expected returns on the investment. This is because accounting is backward looking, while investment depends on the unknowable future.

In other words, *"people recognise that their economic future is uncertain (nonergodic) and cannot be reliably predicted from existing market information. Consequently, investment expenditures on production facilities and people's desire to save are typically based on differing expectations of an unknowable, uncertain future."* This means that in an uncertain world future profits *"can neither be reliably forecasted from existing market information, nor endogenously determined via today's planned saving propensity of income earners ... Thus, unless one assumes that entrepreneurs can accurately predict the future from here to eternity, current expectations of prospective yield must depend on the animal optimism or pessimism of entrepreneurs."* [Paul Davidson, **John Maynard Keynes**, pp. 62-3] So, yes, under capitalism you can determine the money cost (price) of a building but the decision to build is based on estimates and guesses of the future, to use Mises' words *"vague estimates."* A change in the market can mean that even a building which is constructed exactly to expected costs does not produce a profit and so sits empty. Even in terms of *"exact calculation"* of inputs these can change, so undermining the projected final cost and so its profit margin.

For a good explanation of the problems of uncertainty, we must turn to Keynes who placed it at the heart of his analysis of capitalism. *"The actual results of an investment over a long term of years,"* argued Keynes, *"very seldom agree with the initial expectation"* since *"our existing knowledge does not provide a sufficient basis for a calculated mathematical expectation. In point of fact, all sorts of considerations enter into the market valuation which are in no*

way relevant to the prospective yield." He stressed that *"human decisions affecting the future, whether personal or political or economic, cannot depend on strict mathematical expectation, since the basis for making such calculations does not exist."* He also suggested that the *"chief result"* of wage flexibility *"would be to cause a great instability of prices, so violent perhaps as to make business calculations futile."* [**The General Theory**, p. 152, pp. 162-3 and p. 269]

Much the same can be said of other prices as well. So under capitalism **all** decisions are *"groping in the dark"*. Which can, and does, lead to inefficient allocations of resources:

> *"It leads, that is to say, to **misdirected** investment. But over and above this it is an essential characteristic of the boom that investments which will in fact yield, say, 2 per cent. in conditions of full employment are made in the expectation of a yield of, say, 6 per cent., and are valued accordingly. When the disillusion comes, this expectation is replaced by a contrary 'error of pessimism', with the result that the investments, which would in fact yield 2 per cent. in conditions of full employment, are expected to yield less than nothing; and the resulting collapse of new investment then leads to a state of unemployment in which the investments, which would have yielded 2 per cent. in conditions of full employment, in fact yield less than nothing. We reach a condition where there is a shortage of houses, but where nevertheless no one can afford to live in the houses that there are."* [Keynes, **Op. Cit.**, pp. 321-2]

Thus uncertainty and expectations of profit can lead to massive allocation inefficiencies and waste. Of course Mises pays lip-service to this uncertainty of markets. He noted that there are *"ceaseless alternations in other economic data"* and that exchange relations are *"subject to constant ... fluctuations"* but those *"fluctuations disturb value calculations only in the slightest degree"*! He admitted that *"some mistakes are inevitable in such a calculation"* but rest assured *"[w]hat remains of uncertainty comes into the calculation of the uncertainty of future conditions, which is an inevitable concomitant of the dynamic nature of economic life."* [**Op. Cit.**, p. 98, p. 110 and p. 111] So, somewhat ironically, Mises assumed that, when attacking socialism, that prices are so fluid that no central planning agency could ever compute their correct price and so allocated resources inefficiently yet, when it comes to capitalism, prices are not so fluid that they make investment decisions difficult!

The question is, does capitalism reduce or increase these uncertainties? We can suggest that capitalism adds two extra layers of uncertainty. As with any economy, there is the uncertainty that produced goods will meet an actual need of others (i.e., that it has a use-value). The market adds another layer of uncertainty by adding the need for its price to exceed costs. Finally, capitalism adds another level of uncertainty in that the capitalist class must make sufficient profits as well. Thus, regardless of how much people need a specific good if capitalists cannot make a profit from it then it will not be produced.

Uncertainty will, of course, afflict a communist-anarchist society. Mistakes in resource allocation will happen, with some goods over produced at times and under-produced at others. However, a communist society removes the added uncertainty associated with a capitalist economy as such mistakes do **not** lead to general slumps as losses result in the failure of firms and rising unemployment. In other words, without Mises' precise economic calculation society will no longer be afflicted by the uncertainty associated with the profit system.

Significantly, there are developments within capitalism which point to the benefits of communism in reducing uncertainty. This is the rise of the large-scale corporation. In fact, many capitalist firms expand precisely to reduce the uncertainties associated with market prices and their (negative) impact on the plans they make. Thus companies integrate horizontally by take-over to gain more control over investment and supply decisions as well as vertically to stabilise costs and secure demand for necessary inputs.

As economist John Kenneth Galbraith noted, when investment is large, *"[n]o form of market uncertainty is so serious as that involving the terms and conditions on which capital is obtained."* As a result internal funds are used as *"the firm has a secure source of capital"* and *"no longer faces the risks of the market."* This applies to other inputs, for a *"firm cannot satisfactorily foresee and schedule future action or prepare for contingencies if it does not know what its prices will be, what its sales will be, what its costs, including labour and capital costs, will be and what will be available at these costs. If the market is uncontrolled, it will not know these things … Much of what the firm regards as planning consists in minimising uncontrolled market influences."* This partly explains why firms grow (the other reason is to dominate the market and reap oligopolistic profits). The *"market is superseded by vertical integration"* as the firm *"takes over the source of supply or the outlet"*. This *"does not eliminate market uncertainty"* but rather replaces *"the large and unmanageable uncertainty as to the price"* of inputs with *"smaller, more diffuse and more manageable uncertainties"* such as the costs of labour. A large firm can only control the market, by *"reducing or eliminating the independence of action"* of those it sells to or buys from. This means the behaviour of others can be controlled, so that *"uncertainty as to that behaviour is reduced."* Finally, advertising is used to influence the amount sold. Firms also *"eliminate market uncertainty"* by *"entering into contracts specifying prices and amounts to be provided or bought for substantial periods of time."* Thus *"one of the strategies of eliminating market uncertainty is to eliminate the market."* [**The New Industrial State** p. 47, pp. 30-6 and p. 47]

Of course, such attempts to reduce uncertainty within capitalism are incomplete and subject to breakdown. Such planning systems can come into conflict with others (for example, the rise of Japanese corporations in the 1970s and 1980s and subsequent decline of American industrial power). They are centralised, hierarchically structured and based on top-down central planning (and so subject to the informational problems we highlighted in section I.1.2). Market forces can reassert themselves, making a mockery of even the best organised plans. However, these attempts at transcending the market within capitalism, as incomplete as they are, show a major problem with relying on markets and market prices to allocate resources. They add an extra layer of uncertainty which ensure that investors and firms are as much in the dark about their decisions as

Mises argued central planners would be. As such, to state as Mises does that production in socialism can *"never be based upon the foundation of an exact calculation of value"* is somewhat begging the question. [**Op. Cit.**, p. 109] This is because knowing the *"exact"* price of an investment is meaningless as the key question is whether it makes a profit or not — and that is unknown when it is made and if it makes a loss, it is still a waste of resources! So it does not follow that a knowledge of current prices allows efficient allocation of resources (assuming, of course, that profitability equates to social usefulness).

So in terms of Mises' claim that only capitalism ensures that success can be *"appraised in advance"*, it is clear that in reality that system is as marked by *"groping in the dark"* as any other. What of the claim that only markets can ensure that a project's success is *"later retrospectively determined"*? By this, Mises makes a flawed assumption — namely the dubious notion that what is profitable is right. Thus economically is identified with profitably. So even if we assume prices provide enough information for rational decision making, that the economy jumps from one state of equilibrium to another and that capitalists can predict the future, the awkward fact is that maximising profit does not equal maximising human well-being.

Neither well-being nor efficiency equals profitability as the latter does not take into account **need**. Meeting needs is not *"retrospectively determined"* under capitalism, only profit and loss. An investment may fail not because it is not needed but because there is no effective demand for it due to income inequalities. So it is important to remember that the distribution of income determines whether something is an "efficient" use of resources or not. As Thomas Balogh noted, real income *"is measured in terms of a certain set of prices ruling in a given period and that these prices will reflect the prevailing distribution of income. (With no Texan oil millionaires there would be little chance of selling a baby blue Roll-Royce … at a price ten times the yearly income of a small farmer or sharecropper)."* [**The Irrelevance of Conventional Economics**, pp. 98-9] The market demand for commodities, which allocates resources between uses, is based not on the tastes of consumers but on the distribution of purchasing power between them. This, ironically, was mentioned by Mises as part of his attack on socialism, arguing that the central planners could not use current prices for *"the transition to socialism must, as a consequence of the levelling out of the differences in income and the resultant re-adjustments in consumption, and therefore production, change all economic data."* [**Op. Cit.**, p. 109] He did not mention the impact this has in terms of "efficiency" or profitability! After all, what is and is not profitable ("efficient") depends on effective demand, which in turn depends of a specific income distribution. Identical production processes become efficient and inefficient simply by a redistribution of income from the rich to the poor, and vice versa. Similarly, changes in market prices may make once profitably investments unprofitable, without affecting the needs they were satisfying. And this, needless to say, can have serious impacts on human well-being.

As discussed in section C.1.5, this becomes most obvious during famines. As Allan Engler points out, *"[w]hen people are denied access to the means of livelihood, the invisible hand of market forces does not intervene on their behalf. Equilibrium between supply* *and demand has no necessary connection with human need. For example, assume a country of one million people in which 900,000 are without means of livelihood. One million bushels of wheat are produced. The entire crop is sold to 100,000 people at $10 a bushel. Supply and demand are in equilibrium, yet 900 000 people will face starvation."* [**Apostles of Greed**, pp. 50-51] In case anyone thinks that this just happens in theory, the example of numerous famines (from the Irish famine of the 1840s to those in African countries in 1980s) gives a classic example of this occurring in practice, with rich landowners exporting food to the other nations while millions starve in their own.

So the distributional consequences of the market system play havoc with any attempt to define what is and is not an "efficient" use of resources. As markets inform by 'exit' only — some products find a market, others do not — 'voice' is absent. The operation of 'exit' rather than 'voice' leaves behind those without power in the marketplace. This means a division grows between two environments: one inhabited by those with wealth and one inhabited by those without it. One dissident economist states the blindingly obvious, namely that the *"market and democracy clash at a fundamental level. Democracy runs on the principle of 'one man (one person), one vote.' The market runs on the principle of 'one dollar, one vote.' Naturally, the former gives equal weight to each person, regardless of the money she/he has. The latter gives greater weight to richer people."* This means that the market is automatically skewed in favour of the wealthy and so *"[l]eaving everything to the market means that the rich may be able to realise even the most frivolous element of their desires, while the poor may not be able even to survive — thus the world spends twenty times more research money on slimming drugs than on malaria, which claims more than a million lives and debilitates millions more in developing countries every year."* [Ha-Joon Chang, **Bad Samaritans**, p. 172 and p. 174]

In other words, markets are always biased in favour of effective demand, i.e. in favour of the demands of people with money, and so can never (except in the imaginary abstractions of neo-classical economics) allocate the necessities of life to those who need them the most. Thus a simple redistribution of wealth (via militant unions or the welfare state, for example) could make previously "bad" investments good simply because the new income allows those who had previously needed, but could not afford, the good or service in question to purchase it. So just because something makes a loss under one distribution of income does not mean that it is an inefficient use of resources in the sense of meeting human needs (and could make a profit under another, more equal, distribution of wealth). So the "efficient" allocation of resources in terms of price (i.e., profit) is often no such thing as the wealthy few skew market decisions in their favour.

It is important to remember that, for the "Austrians", preferences are demonstrated through action in the market and they are not interested in opinions, thus any preference which is not expressed by action is irrelevant to them. So any attempt to collectively prioritise, say, building decent housing for all, provide health care for everyone, and so forth are all considered "inefficient" uses of resources as those who receive them would not, normally, be able to afford them and, consequently, do not really desire them anyway

(as they, needless to say, do not express that desire by market exchanges!). Yet this ignores the awkward fact that in the market, people can only act if they have money to make their preferences known. Thus those who have a need but no money do not count when determining if the market is efficient or not. There is simply no room for the real people who can be harmed by real markets. As economist Amartya Sen argues, the workings of a "pure" capitalist market, as desired by "Austrian" economists and other propertarians, *"can be problematic since the actual consequences of the operation of these entitlements can, quite possibly, include rather terrible results. It can, in particular, lead to the violation of the substantive freedom of individuals to achieve those things to which they have reason to attach great importance, including escaping avoidable mortality, being well nourished and healthy, being able to read, write and count and so on."* In fact, *"even gigantic famines can result without anyone's [right] libertarian rights (including property rights) being violated. The destitutes such as the unemployed or the impoverished may starve precisely because their 'entitlements' ... do not give them enough food."* Similarly, *"deprivation"* such as *"regular undernourishment"*, the *"lack of medical care for curable illnesses"* can *"coexist with all [right] libertarian rights (including rights of property ownership) being fully satisfied."* [**Development as Freedom**, p. 66]

All of which, it must be stressed, is ignored in the "Austrian" case against socialism. In other words, if a person loses their job and, as a consequence, loses their home then, according to this logic, they do not "need" a home as their "demonstrated preference" (i.e., their actual choices in action) shows that they genuinely value living under a bridge (assuming they gain the bridge owners agreement, of course).

As an aside, this obvious fact shows that the "Austrian" assertion that intervention in the market **always** reduces social utility cannot be supported. The argument that the market maximises utility is based on assuming a given allocation of resources before the process of free exchange begins. If someone does not have sufficient income to, say, buy food or essential medical treatment then this is not reflected in the market. If wealth is redistributed and they then they get access to the goods in question, then (obviously) their utility has increased and it is a moot point whether social utility has decreased as the disutility of the millionaire who was taxed to achieve it cannot be compared to it. Significantly, those "Austrians" who have sought to prove that all intervention in the market reduces social utility have failed. For example, as one dissident "Austrian" economist notes, while Murray Rothbard *"claimed he offered a purely deductive"* argument that state intervention always reduced social utility *"his case [was] logically flawed."* He simply assumed that social utility was reduced although he gave no reason for such an assumption as he admitted that interpersonal comparisons of utility were impossible. For someone *"who asks that his claims be tested only by their logic"*, his ultimate conclusions about state intervention *"do not follow"* and exhibit *"a careless self-contradiction"* [David L. Prychitko, **Markets, Planning and Democracy**, p. 189, p. 111 and p. 110]

As such, Mises was wrong to assert that *"[b]etween production for profit and production for need, there is no contrast."* [**Socialism**, p. 143] In fact, it seems incredible that anyone claiming to be an economist could make such a comment. As Proudhon and Marx (like Smith and Ricardo before them) made clear, a commodity in order to be exchanged must first have a use-value (utility) to others. Thus production for profit, by definition, means production for "use" — otherwise exchange would not happen. What socialists were highlighting by contrasting production for profit to need was, firstly, that need comes after profit and so without profit a good will not be produced no matter how many people need it. Secondly, it highlights the fact that during crises capitalism is marked by an over-production of goods reducing profits, so stopping production, while people who need those goods go without them. Thus capitalism is marked by homeless people living next to empty housing and hungry people seeing food exported or destroyed in order to maximise profit. Ultimately, if the capitalist does not make a profit then it is a bad investment — regardless of whether it could be used to meet people's needs and so make their lives better. In other words, Mises ignores the very basis of capitalism (production for profit) and depicts it as production aiming at the direct satisfaction of consumers.

Equally, that something makes a profit does not mean that it is an efficient use of resources. If, for example, that profit is achieved by imposing pollution externalities or by market power then it cannot be said that society as a whole, rather than the capitalist, has benefited. Similarly, non-market based systems can be seen to be more efficient than market based ones in terms of outcome. For example, making health care available to all who need it rather than those who can afford it is economically "inefficient" in "Austrian" eyes but only an ideologue would claim that we should not do so because of this particularly as we can point to the awkward fact that the more privatised health care systems in the USA and Chile are more inefficient than the nationalised systems elsewhere in the world. Administration costs are higher and the societies in question pay far more for an equivalent level of treatment.

In addition, in a highly unequal society costs are externalised to those at the bottom of the social hierarchy. The consequences are harmful, as suggested by the newspeak used to disguise this reality. For example, there is what is called "increasing flexibility of the labour market." "Flexibility" sounds great: rigid structures are unappealing and hardly suitable for human growth. In reality, as Noam Chomsky points out *"[f]lexibility means insecurity. It means you go to bed at night and don't know if you have a job tomorrow morning. That's called flexibility of the labour market, and any economist can explain that's a good thing for the economy, where by 'the economy' now we understand profit-making. We don't mean by 'the economy' the way people live. That's good for the economy, and temporary jobs increase flexibility. Low wages also increase job insecurity. They keep inflation low. That's good for people who have money, say, bondholders. So these all contribute to what's called a 'healthy economy,' meaning one with very high profits. Profits are doing fine. Corporate profits are zooming. But for most of the population, very grim circumstances. And grim circumstances, without much prospect of a future, may lead to constructive social action, but where that's lacking they express themselves in violence."* [**Keeping the Rabble in Line**, pp. 283-4] So it simply cannot be assumed that what is good for the economy (profits) equates to what is good for people (at least the working class).

Thus the "Austrians" prize profitability above all and this assumption is at the root of the "Calculation Argument" against socialism, but this makes sense only insofar as efficiency is confused with profit. The market will invest in coal if profits are higher and, in so doing, contribute to global warming. It will deny medical care to the sick (no profits and so it is inefficient) while contributing to, say, a housing bubble because it makes short-term profits by providing loans to people who really cannot afford them. It will support all kinds of economic activity, regardless of the wider impact, and so "efficiency" (i.e., profits) can, and does, contradict both wisdom and ethics and so, ultimately, an efficient allocation of resources to meet people's needs.

Lastly, our critique has so far ignored the periodic crises that hit capitalist economies which produce massive unemployment and social disruption — crises that are due to subjective and objective pressures on the operation of the price mechanism (see section C.7 for details). In the upswing, when expectations are buoyant, firms will invest and produce a mutually reinforcing expansion. However, the net effect of such decisions eventually leads to over-investment, excess capacity and over-production — mal-investment and the waste of the embodied resources. This leads to lower than expected profits, expectations change for the worse and the boom turns into bust, capital equipment is scrapped, workers are unemployed and resources are either wasted or left idle.

In a crisis we see the contradiction between use value and exchange value come to a head. Workers are no less productive than when the crisis started, the goods and services they create are no less needed than before. The means of production are just as productive as they were. Both are just as capable as before of affording for everyone a decent standard of living. Even though people are homeless, housing stands empty. Even though people need goods, production is stopped. Even though people want jobs, workplaces are closed. Yet, according to the logic of *"exact"* "economic calculation", production is now "inefficient" and should be closed-down, workers made unemployed and expected to find work by forcing down the wages of those lucky enough to remain employed in the hope that the owners of the means of life will find it profitable to exploit them as much as before (for when hard times arrive it is never long until somebody suggests that the return of prosperity requires sacrifices at the bottom of the heap and, needless to say, the "Austrian" economists are usually the first to do so).

This suggests that the efficient allocation of resources becomes meaningless if its reality is a cycle where consumers go without essential goods due to scarcity and high prices followed by businesses going bust because of over-production and low prices. This process ruins large numbers of people's lives, not to mention wasting vast stocks of productive equipment and goods. There are always people who need the over-produced goods and so the market adds to uncertainty as there is a difference between the over-production of goods and the over-production of commodities. If more goods were produced in a communist society this may signify a waste of resources but it would not, as under capitalism, produce a crisis situation as well!

So in a real capitalist economy, there are numerous reasons for apparently rational investment decisions going wrong. Not that these investments produce goods which people do not need, simply that "exact" "economic calculation" indicates that they are not making a profit and so are an "inefficient" use of resources. However, it is question begging in the extreme to argue that if (thanks to a recession) workers can no longer buy food then is it an "efficient" allocation of resources that they starve. Similarly, during the Great Depression, the American government (under the New Deal) hired about 60% of the unemployed in public works and conservation projects. These saw a billion trees planted, the whooping crane saved, the modernisation of rural America, and the building of (among others) the Cathedral of Learning in Pittsburgh, the Montana state capitol, New York's Lincoln Tunnel and Triborough Bridge complex, the Tennessee Valley Authority as well as building or renovating 2,500 hospitals, 45,000 schools, 13,000 parks and playgrounds, 7,800 bridges, 700,000 miles of roads, 1,000 airfields as well as employing 50,000 teachers and rebuilding the country's entire rural school system. Can all these schemes really be considered a waste of resources simply because they would never have made a capitalist a profit?

Of course, our discussion is affected by the fact that "actually existing" capitalism has various forms of state-intervention. Some of these "socialise" costs and risks, such as publicly funded creation of an infrastructure and Research and Development (R&D). Given that much R&D is conducted via state funding (via universities, military procurements, and so on) and (of course!) the profits of such research are then privatised, question arises would the initial research have gone ahead if the costs had not been "socialised"? Would Mises' "exact" calculation have resulted in, say, the internet being developed? If, as seems likely, not, does it not mean our current use of the World Wide Web is an inefficient use of resources? Then there are the numerous state interventions which exist to ensure that certain activities become "efficient" (i.e., profitable) such as specifying and defending intellectual property rights, the limited liability of corporations and enforcing capitalist property rights (in land, for example). While we take this activity for granted when evaluating capitalism, they are serious imperfections in the market and so what counts as an "efficient" use of resources. Other state interventions aim to reduce uncertainty and stabilise the market, such as welfare maintaining aggregate demand.

Removing these "imperfections" in the market would substantially affect the persuasiveness of Mises' case. "What data we do have," notes Doug Henwood, "don't lend any support to the notion that the nineteenth century was more 'stable' than the twentieth … the price level bounced all over the place, with periods of inflation alternating with periods of deflation, and GDP growth in the last three decades … was similarly volatile. The busts were savage, resulting in massive bank failures and very lean times for workers and farmers." [**After the New Economy**, p. 242] Looking at business cycle data for America, what becomes clear is that some of those regular nineteenth century slumps were extremely long: the Panic of 1873, for example, was followed by a recession that lasted 5 1/2 years. The New York Stock Exchange closed for ten days and 89 of the country's 364 railroads went bankrupt. A total of 18,000 businesses failed between 1873 and 1875. Unemployment reached 14% by 1876, during a time which became known as the Long Depression. Construction work lagged, wages were cut, real estate values fell and corporate profits vanished.

Given this, given the tendency of capitalism to crisis and to ignore real needs in favour of effective demand, it is far better to be roughly right than precisely wrong. In other words, the economic calculation that Mises celebrates regularly leads to situations where people suffer because it precisely shows that workplaces should shut because, although nothing had changed in their productivity and the need of their products, they can no longer make a profit. Saying, in the middle of a crisis, that people should be without work, be homeless and go hungry because economic calculation proves they have no need for employment, homes and food shows the irrationality of glorifying "economic calculation" as the be all and end all of resource allocation.

In summary, then, not only is libertarian communism possible, capitalism itself makes economic calculation problematic and resource allocation inefficient. Given the systematic uncertainty which market dynamics imply and the tendencies to crisis inherent in the system, "economic calculation" ensures that resources are wasted. Using the profit criteria as the measure of "efficiency" is also problematic as it ensures that real needs are ignored and places society in frequent situations (crises) where "economic calculation" ensures that industries close, so ensuring that goods and services people need are no longer produced. As Proudhon put it, under capitalism there is "a miserable oscillation between usury and bankruptcy." [**Property is Theft!**, p. 285] For anarchists, these drawbacks to capitalist allocation are obvious. Equally obvious is the reason why Mises failed to discuss them: ultimately, like neo-classical economics, the "Austrian" school seeks to eulogise capitalism rather than to understand it.

I.2
Is this a blueprint for an anarchist society?

No, far from it. There can be no such thing as a "blueprint" for a free society. "Anarchism", as Rocker correctly stressed, "is no patent solution for all human problems, no Utopia of a perfect social order, as it has so often been called, since on principle it rejects all absolute schemes and concepts. It does not believe in any absolute truth, or in definite final goals for human development, but in an unlimited perfectibility of social arrangements and human living conditions, which are always straining after higher forms of expression, and to which for this reason one can assign no definite terminus nor set any fixed goal." [**Anarcho-Syndicalism**, p. 15]

All we can do here is indicate those general features that we believe a free society **must** have in order to qualify as truly libertarian. For example, a society based on hierarchical management in the workplace (like capitalism) would not be libertarian and would soon see private or public states developing to protect the power of those at the top. Beyond such general considerations, however, the specifics of how to structure a non-hierarchical society must remain open for discussion and experimentation:

"Anarchism, meaning Liberty, is compatible with the most diverse economic [and social] conditions, on the premise *that these cannot imply, as under capitalist monopoly, the negation of liberty."* [D. A. de Santillan, **After the Revolution**, p. 95]

So, our comments should not be regarded as a detailed plan but rather a series of suggestions based on what anarchists have traditionally advocated as an alternative to capitalism combined with what has been tried in various social revolutions. Anarchists have always been reticent about spelling out their vision of the future in too much detail for it would be contrary to anarchist principles to be dogmatic about the precise forms the new society must take. Free people will create their own alternative institutions in response to conditions specific to their area as well as their needs, desires and hopes and it would be presumptuous of us to attempt to set forth universal policies in advance. As Kropotkin argued, once expropriation of social wealth by the masses has been achieved *"then, after a period of groping, there will necessarily arise a new system of organising production and exchange ... and that system will be a lot more attuned to popular aspirations and the requirements of co-existence and mutual relations than any theory, however splendid, devised by the thinking and imagination of reformers"*. This, however, did not stop him *"predicting right now that"* in some areas influenced by anarchists *"the foundations of the new organisation will be the free federation of producers' groups and the free federation of Communes and groups in independent Communes."* [**No Gods, No Masters**, vol. 1, p. 232]

This is because what we think now will influence the future just as real experience will influence and change what we think. Given the libertarian critique of the state and capitalism, certain kinds of social organisation are implied. Thus, our recognition that wage-labour creates authoritarian social relationships and exploitation suggests a workplace in a free society can only be based on associated and co-operative labour (i.e., self-management). Similarly, given that the state is a top-down centralised body it is not hard to imagine that a free society would have communal institutions which were federal and organised from the bottom-up.

Moreover, given the ways in which our own unfree society has shaped our ways of thinking, it is probably impossible for us to imagine what new forms will arise once humanity's ingenuity and creativity is unleashed by the removal of its present authoritarian fetters. Thus any attempts to paint a detailed picture of the future will be doomed to failure. Ultimately, anarchists think that *"the new society should be organised with the direct participation of all concerned, from the periphery to the centre, freely and spontaneously, at the prompting of the sentiment of solidarity and under pressure of the natural needs of society."* [E. Malatesta and A. Hamon, **Op. Cit.**, vol. 2, p. 20]

Nevertheless, anarchists have been willing to specify some broad principles indicating the general framework within which they expect the institutions of the new society to grow. It is important to emphasise that these principles are not the arbitrary creations of intellectuals in ivory towers. Rather, they are based on the actual political, social and economic structures that have arisen **spontaneously** whenever working class people have attempted to throw off their chains during eras of heightened revolutionary activity, such as the Paris Commune, the Russian Revolution, the Spanish Revolution, and the Hungarian uprising of 1956, France in 1968, the Argentinean revolt against neo-liberalism in 2001, to name just a few. It is clear, from these examples, that federations of self-managed workers' councils and community assemblies appear repeatedly in such popular revolts as people attempt to manage their own destinies directly, both economically and socially. While their names and specific organisational structures differ, these can be considered basic libertarian socialist forms, since they have appeared during all revolutionary periods. Ultimately, such organisations are the only alternatives to political, social and economic authority — unless we make our own decisions ourselves, someone else will.

So, when reading these sections, please remember that this is just an attempt to sketch the outline of a possible future. It is in no way an attempt to determine **exactly** what a free society would be like, for such a free society will be the result of the actions of all of society, not just anarchists. As Malatesta argued:

> *"it is a question of freedom for everybody, freedom for each individual so long as he [or she] respects the equal freedom of others."*

> *"None can judge with certainty who is right and who is wrong, who is nearest to the truth, or which is the best way to achieve the greatest good for each and everyone. Freedom, coupled by experience, is the only way of discovering the truth and what is best; and there is no freedom if there is a denial of the freedom to err."* [**Errico Malatesta: His Life and Ideas**, p. 49]

And, of course, real life has a habit of over-turning even the most realistic sounding theories, ideas and ideologies. Marxism, Leninism, Monetarism, laissez-faire capitalism (among others) have proven time and time again that ideology applied to real life has effects not predicted by the theory before hand (although in all four cases, their negative effects were predicted by others; in the case of Marxism and Leninism by anarchists). Anarchists are aware of this, which is why we reject ideology in favour of theory and why we are hesitant to create blue-prints for the future. History has repeatedly proven Proudhon right when he stated that *"every society declines the moment it falls into the hands of the ideologists."* [**System of Economical Contradictions**, p. 115]

Only life, as Bakunin stressed, can create and so life must inform theory — and so if the theory is producing adverse results it is better to revise the theory than deny reality or justify the evil effects it creates on real people. Thus this section of the FAQ is not a blue print, rather it is a series of suggestions (suggestions drawn, we stress, from actual experiences of working class revolt and organisation). These suggestions may be right or wrong and informed by Malatesta's comments that:

> *"We do not boast that we possess absolute truth, on the contrary, we believe that **social truth** is not a fixed quantity, good for all times, universally applicable or determinable in advance, but that instead, once freedom has been secured, mankind will go forward discovering and acting gradually with the least number of upheavals and with a minimum of friction. Thus our solutions always*

leave the door open to different and, one hopes, better solutions." [**Op. Cit.**, p.21]

It is for this reason that anarchists, to quote Bakunin, think that the *"revolution should not only be made for the people's sake; it should also be made by the people."* [**No Gods, No Masters**, vol. 1, p. 141] Social problems will be solved in the interests of the working class only if working class people solve them themselves. This applies to a social revolution — it will only liberate the working class if working class people make it themselves, using their own organisations and power. Indeed, it is the course of struggling for social change, to correct social problems, by, say, strikes, occupations, demonstrations and other forms of direct action, that people can transform their assumptions about what is possible, necessary and desirable. The necessity of organising their struggles and their actions ensures the development of assemblies and other organs of popular power in order to manage their activity. These create, potentially, an alternative means by which society can be organised. As Kropotkin argued, *"[a]ny strike trains the participants for a common management of affairs."* [quoted by Caroline Cahm, **Kropotkin and the Rise of Revolutionary Anarchism**, p. 233] The ability of people to manage their own lives, and so society, becomes increasingly apparent and the existence of hierarchical authority, the state, the boss or a ruling class, becomes clearly undesirable and unnecessary. Thus the framework of the free society will be created by the very process of class struggle, as working class people create the organisations required to fight for improvements and change within capitalism (see section I.2.3).

Thus, the **actual** framework of an anarchist society and how it develops and shapes itself is dependent on the needs and desires of those who live in such a society or are trying to create one. This is why anarchists stress the need for mass assemblies in both the community and workplace and their federation from the bottom up to manage common affairs. Anarchy can only be created by the active participation of the mass of people. In the words of Malatesta, an anarchist society would be based on *"decisions taken at popular assemblies and carried out by groups and individuals who have volunteered or are duly delegated."* The *"success of the revolution"* depends on *"a large number of individuals with initiative and the ability to tackle practical tasks: by accustoming the masses not to leave the common cause in the hands of a few, and to delegate, when delegation is necessary, only for specific missions and for limited duration."* [**Op. Cit.**, p. 129] This self-management would be the basis on which an anarchist society would change and develop, with the new society created by those who live within it. Thus Bakunin:

> *"revolution everywhere must be created by the people, and supreme control must always belong to people organised into a free federation of agricultural and industrial associations ... organised from the bottom upwards by means of revolutionary delegation."* [**Michael Bakunin: Selected Writings**, p. 172]

And, we must not forget that while we may be able to roughly guess the way an anarchist society could start initially, we cannot pretend to predict how it will develop in the long term. A social revolution is just the beginning of a process of social transformation. Unfortunately, we have to start where we are now, not where we hope to end up! Therefore our discussion will, by necessity, reflect the current society as this is the society we will be transforming. While, for some, this outlook may not be of a sufficient qualitative break with the world we now inhabit, it is essential. We need to offer and discuss suggestions for action in the **here and now**, not for some future pie in the sky world which can only possibly exist years, even decades, **after** a successful revolution.

For example, the ultimate goal of anarchism, we stress, is **not** the self-management of existing workplaces or industries within the same industrial structure produced by capitalism. However, a revolution will undoubtedly see the occupation and placing under self-management much of existing industry and we start our discussion assuming a similar set-up as exists today. This does not mean that an anarchist society will continue to be like this, we simply present the initial stages using examples we are all familiar with. It is simply the first stage of transforming industry into something more ecologically safe, socially integrated and individually and collectively empowering for people.

Some people **seriously** seem to think that after a social revolution working people will continue using the same technology, in the same old workplaces, in the same old ways and not change a single thing (except, perhaps, electing their managers). They simply transfer their own lack of imagination onto the rest of humanity. For anarchists, it is *"certain, however, that, when they [the workers] find themselves their own masters, they will modify the old system to suit their convenience in a variety of ways ... as common sense is likely to suggest to free men [and women]."* [Charlotte M. Wilson, **Anarchist Essays**, p. 23] So we have little doubt that working people will quickly transform their work, workplaces and society into one suitable for human beings, rejecting the legacy of capitalism and creating a society we simply cannot predict. The occupying of workplaces is, we stress, simply the first stage of the process of transforming them and the rest of society. These words of the strikers just before the 1919 Seattle General Strike expresses this perspective well:

> *"Labour will not only SHUT DOWN the industries, but Labour will REOPEN, under the management of the appropriate trades, such activities as are needed to preserve public health and public peace. If the strike continues, Labour may feel led to avoid public suffering by reopening more and more activities,*
>
> *"UNDER ITS OWN MANAGEMENT.*
>
> *"And that is why we say that we are starting on a road that leads — NO ONE KNOWS WHERE!"* [quoted by Jeremy Brecher, **Strike!**, p. 110]

People's lives in a post-revolutionary society will not centre around fixed jobs and workplaces as they do now. Productive activity will go on, but not in the alienated way it does today. Similarly, in their communities people will apply their imaginations, skills and hopes to transform them into better places to live (the beautification of the commune, as the CNT put it). The first stage, of course, will be to take over their existing communities and place them under community control. Therefore, it is essential to remember that our discussion can only provide an indication on how an anarchist society will operate in the months and years after a successful revolution, an anarchist society still marked by the legacy of capitalism. However, it would be a great mistake to think that anarchists do not seek to transform all aspects of society to eliminate that legacy and create a society fit for unique individuals to live in. As an anarchist society develops it will, we stress, transform society in ways we cannot guess at now, based on the talents, hopes, dreams and imaginations of those living in it.

I.2.1 Why discuss what an anarchist society would be like at all?

Partly, in order to indicate why people should become anarchists. Most people do not like making jumps in the dark, so an indication of what anarchists think a desirable society could look like may help those people who are attracted to anarchism, inspiring them to become committed to its practical realisation. Partly, it's a case of learning from past mistakes. There have been numerous anarchistic social experiments on varying scales, and its useful to understand what happened, what worked and what did not. In that way, hopefully, we will not make the same mistakes twice.

However, the most important reason for discussing what an anarchist society would look like is to ensure that the creation of such a society is the action of as many people as possible. As Errico Malatesta indicated in the middle of the Italian revolutionary *"Two Red Years"* (see section A.5.5), *"either we all apply our minds to thinking about social reorganisation, and right away, at the very same moment that the old structures are being swept away, and we shall have a more humane and more just society, open to future advances, or we shall leave such matters to the 'leaders' and we shall have a new government."* [**The Anarchist Revolution**, p. 69]

Hence the importance of discussing what the future will be like in the here and now. The more people who have a fairly clear idea of what a free society would look like the easier it will be to create that society and ensure that no important matters are left to others to decide for us. The example of the Spanish Revolution comes to mind. For many years before 1936, the C.N.T. and F.A.I. put out publications discussing what an anarchist society would look like (for example, **After the Revolution** by Diego Abel de Santillan and **Libertarian Communism** by Isaac Puente), the end product of libertarians organising and educating in Spain for almost seventy years before the revolution. When it finally occurred, the millions of people who participated already shared a similar vision and started to build a society based on it, thus learning firsthand where their books were wrong and which areas of life they did not adequately cover.

So, this discussion of what an anarchist society might look like is not a drawing up of blueprints, nor is it an attempt to force the future into the shapes created in past revolts. It is purely and simply an attempt to start people discussing what a free society would be like and to learn from previous experiments. However, as anarchists recognise the importance of building the new world in the shell of the old, our ideas of what a free society would be like can feed into how we organise and struggle today. And vice versa; for how we organise and struggle today will have an impact on the future.

As Malatesta pointed out, such discussions are necessary and essential, for it is *"absurd to believe that, once government has been destroyed and the capitalists expropriated, 'things will look after themselves' without the intervention of those who already have an idea on what has to be done and who immediately set about doing it"* for *"social life, as the life of individuals, does not permit of interruption."* He stressed that to *"neglect all the problems of reconstruction or to pre-arrange complete and uniform plans are both errors, excesses which, by different routes, would led to our defeat as anarchists and to the victory of new or old authoritarian regime. The truth lies in the middle."* [**Op. Cit.**, p. 121]

Moreover, the importance of discussing the future can help indicate whether our activities are actually creating a better world. After all, if Karl Marx had been more willing to discuss his vision of a socialist society then the Stalinists would have found it much harder to claim that their hellish system was, in fact, socialism. Given that anarchists like Proudhon and Bakunin gave a broad outline of their vision of a free society it would have been impossible for anarchism to be twisted as Marxism was. Most anarchists would agree with Chomsky's evaluation of the issue:

> *"A movement of the left should distinguish with clarity between its long-range revolutionary aims and certain more immediate effects it can hope to achieve …*

> *"But in the long run, a movement of the left has no chance of success, and deserves none, unless it develops an understanding of contemporary society and a vision of a future social order that is persuasive to a large majority of the population. Its goals and organisational forms must take shape through their active participation in political struggle [in its widest sense] and social reconstruction. A genuine radical culture can be created only through the spiritual transformation of great masses of people the essential feature of any social revolution that is to extend the possibilities for human creativity and freedom … The cultural and intellectual level of any serious radical movement will have to be far higher than in the past … It will not be able to satisfy itself with a litany of forms of oppression and injustice. It will need to provide compelling answers to the question of how these evils can be overcome by revolution or large-scale reform. To accomplish this aim, the left will have to achieve and maintain a position of honesty and commitment to libertarian values."* [**Radical Priorities**, pp. 189-90]

We hope that this section of the FAQ, in its own small way, will encourage as many people as possible to discuss what a libertarian society would be like and use that discussion to bring it closer.

I.2.2 Will it be possible to go straight to an anarchist society from capitalism?

Possibly, it depends what is meant by an anarchist society.

If it is meant a fully classless society (what some people, inaccurately, would call a "utopia") then the answer is a clear *"no, that would be impossible."* Anarchists are well aware that *"class difference do not vanish at the stroke of a pen whether that pen belongs to the theoreticians or to the pen-pushers who set out laws or decrees. Only action, that is to say direct action (not through government) expropriation by the proletarians, directed against the privileged class, can wipe out class difference."* [Luigi Fabbri, *"Anarchy and 'Scientific' Communism"*, pp. 13-49, **The Poverty of Statism**, pp. 13-49, Albert Meltzer (ed.), p. 30]

As we discussed in section H.2.5, few anarchists consider it likely that a perfectly functioning libertarian communist society would be the immediate effect of a social revolution. For anarchists a social revolution is a **process** and not an event (although, of course, a process marked by such events as general strikes, uprisings, insurrections and so on). As Kropotkin argued:

> *"It is a whole insurrectionary period of three, four, perhaps five years that we must traverse to accomplish our revolution in the property system and in social organisation."* [**Words of a Rebel**, p. 72]

His famous work **The Conquest of Bread** aimed, to use his words, at *"prov[ing] that communism — at least partial — has more chance of being established than collectivism, especially in communes taking the lead"* and tried *"to indicate how, during a revolutionary period, a large city — if its inhabitants have accepted the idea — could organise itself on the lines of free communism."* [**Anarchism**, p. 298] The revolution, in other words, would progress towards communism after the initial revolt:

> *"we know that an **uprising** can overthrow and change a government in one day, while a **revolution** needs three or four years of revolutionary convulsion to arrive at tangible results ... if we should expect the revolution, from its **earliest** insurrections, to have a communist character, we would have to relinquish the possibility of a revolution, since in that case there would be need of a strong majority to agree on carrying through a change in the direction of communism."* [Kropotkin, quoted by Max Nettlau, **A Short History of Anarchism**, pp. 282-3]

In addition, different areas will develop in different speeds and in different ways, depending on the influences dominant in the area. *"Side by side with the revolutionised communes,"* argued Kropotkin, other areas *"would remain in an expectant attitude, and would go on living on the Individualist system ... revolution would break out everywhere, but revolution under different aspects; in one country State Socialism, in another Federation; everywhere more or less Socialism, not conforming to any particular rule."* Thus *"the Revolution will take a different character in each of the different*

European nations; the point attained in the socialisation of wealth will not be everywhere the same."* [**The Conquest of Bread**, pp. 81-2 and p. 81]

Kropotkin was also aware that a revolution would face many problems, including the disruption of economic activity, civil war and isolation. He argued that it was *"certain that the coming Revolution ... will burst upon us in the middle of a great industrial crisis ... There are millions of unemployed workers in Europe at this moment. It will be worse when Revolution has burst upon us ... The number of the out-of-works will be doubled as soon as barricades are erected in Europe and the United States ... we know that in time of Revolution exchange and industry suffer most from the general upheaval ... A Revolution in Europe means, then, the unavoidable stoppage of at least half the factories and workshops."* He stressed that there would be *"the complete disorganisation"* of the capitalist economy and that during a revolution *"[i]nternational commerce will come to a standstill"* and *"the circulation of commodities and of provisions will be paralysed."* This would, of course, have an impact on the development of a revolution and so the *"circumstances will dictate the measures."* [**Op. Cit.**, pp. 69-70, p. 191 and p. 79]

Thus we have anarcho-communism being introduced *"during a revolutionary period"* rather than instantly and the possibility that it will be *"partial"* in many, if not all areas, depending on the *"circumstances"* encountered. Therefore the (Marxist inspired) claim that anarchists think a fully communist society is possible overnight is simply false — we recognise that a social revolution takes time to develop after it starts. As Malatesta put it, *"after the revolution, that is after the defeat of the existing powers and the overwhelming victory of the forces of insurrection"* then *"gradualism really comes into operation. We shall have to study all the practical problems of life: production, exchange, the means of communication, relations between anarchist groupings and those living under some kind of authority, between communist collectives and those living in an individualistic way; relations between town and country ... and so on."* [**Errico Malatesta: His Life and Ideas**, p. 173] In other words, *"each community will decide for itself during the transition period the method they deem best for the distribution of the products of associated labour."* [James Guillaume, *"On Building the New Social Order"*, pp. 356-79, **Bakunin on Anarchism**, p. 362]

However, if by "anarchist society" it is meant a society that has abolished the state and started the process of transforming society from below then anarchists argue that such a society is not only possible after a successful revolution, it is essential. Thus the anarchist social revolution would be political (abolition of the state), economic (abolition of capitalism) and social (abolition of hierarchical social relationships). Or, more positively, the introduction of self-management into every aspect of life. In other words, *"political transformation"* and *"economic transformation"* must be *"accomplished together and simultaneously."* [Bakunin, **The Basic Bakunin**, p. 106] This transformation would be based upon the organisations created by working class people in their struggle against capitalism and the state (see next section). Thus the framework of a free society would be created by the struggle for freedom itself, by the class struggle **within** but **against** hierarchical society. This revolution would come ***"from below"*** and would expropriate capital as well as smash the state (see section

H.2.4). Such a society, as Bakunin argued, will not be "perfect" by any means:

> "I do not say that the peasants [and workers], freely organised from the bottom up, will miraculously create an ideal organisation, conforming in all respects to our dreams. But I am convinced that what they construct will be living and vibrant, a thousands times better and more just than any existing organisation. Moreover, this ... organisation, being on the one hand open to revolutionary propaganda ... , and on the other, not petrified by the intervention of the State ... will develop and perfect itself through free experimentation as fully as one can reasonably expect in our times.

> "With the abolition of the State, the spontaneous self-organisation of popular life ... will revert to the communes. The development of each commune will take its point of departure the actual condition of its civilisation." [**Bakunin on Anarchism**, p. 207]

How far such a new social organisation will meet all the ideals and hopes of communist-anarchists will vary according to objective circumstances and the influence of libertarian theory. As people start to liberate themselves they will under go an ethical and psychological transformation as they act to end specific hierarchical social structures and relationships. It does not imply that people need to be "perfect" nor that a perfect anarchist society will come about "overnight. Rather, it means that while an anarchist society (i.e., one without a state or private property) would be created by revolution, it will be one initially marked by the society it came from and would require a period of self-activity by which individuals reshape and change themselves as they are reshaping and changing the world about them. Thus Malatesta:

> "And even after a successful insurrection, could we overnight realise all desires and pass from a governmental and capitalist hell to a libertarian-communist heaven which is the complete freedom of man within the wished-for community of interests with all men?

> "These are illusions which can take root among authoritarians who look upon the masses as the raw material which those who have power can, by decrees, supported by bullets and handcuffs, mould to their will. But these illusions have not taken among anarchists. We need the people's consensus, and therefore we must persuade by means of propaganda and example ... to win over to our ideas an ever greater number of people." [**Op. Cit.**, pp. 82-3]

So, clearly, the idea of a "one-day revolution" is one rejected as a harmful fallacy by anarchists. We are aware that revolutions are a **process** and not an event (or series of events). We should mention here that some anarchists, like the individualists and mutualists, do not support the idea of revolution and instead see anarchist alternatives growing within capitalism and slowly replacing it. In other words anarchists agree that an anarchist society cannot be created overnight, for to assume so would be to imagine that anarchists could enforce their ideas on a pliable population. Libertarian socialism can only be created from below, by people who want it and understand it, organising and liberating themselves. "Communist organisations," argued Kropotkin, "must be the work of all, a natural growth, a product of the constructive genius of the great mass. Communism cannot be imposed from above; it could not live even for a few months if the constant and daily co-operation of all did not uphold it. It must be free." [**Anarchism**, p. 140] The results of the Russian Revolution should have cleared away long ago any contrary illusions about how to create "socialist" societies. The lesson from every revolution is that the mistakes made by people in liberating themselves and transforming society are always minor compared to the results of creating authorities, who eliminate such "ideological errors" by destroying the freedom to make mistakes (and so freedom as such). Freedom is the only real basis on which socialism can be built ("Experience through freedom is the only means to arrive at the truth and the best solutions; and there is no freedom if there is not the freedom to be wrong." [Malatesta, **Op. Cit.**, p. 72]). Therefore, most anarchists would agree with Malatesta:

> "To organise a [libertarian] communist society on a large scale it would be necessary to transform all economic life radically, such as methods of production, of exchange and consumption; and all this could not be achieved other than gradually, as the objective circumstances permitted and to the extent that the masses understood what advantages could be gained and were able to act for themselves." [**Op. Cit.**, p. 36]

This means that while the conditions necessary of a free society would be created in a broad way by a social revolution, it would be utopian to imagine everything will be perfect immediately. Few anarchists have argued that such a jump would be possible — rather they have argued that revolutions create the conditions for the evolution towards an anarchist society by abolishing state and capitalism. "Besides," argued Alexander Berkman, "you must not confuse the social revolution with anarchy. Revolution, in some of its stages, is a violent upheaval; anarchy is a social condition of freedom and peace. The revolution is the **means** of bringing anarchy about but it is not anarchy itself. It is to pave the road to anarchy, to establish conditions which will make a life of liberty possible." However, "to achieve its purpose the revolution must be imbued with and directed by the anarchist spirit and ideas. The end shapes the means ... the social revolution must be anarchist in method as in aim." [**What is Anarchism?**, p. 231]

This means that while acknowledging the possibility of a transitional **society**, anarchists reject the notion of a transitional **state** as confused in the extreme (and, as can be seen from the experience of Marxism, dangerous as well). An anarchist society can only be achieved by anarchist means. Hence French Syndicalist Fernand Pelloutier's comments:

> "Nobody believes or expects that the coming revolution ... will realise unadulterated anarchist-communism... it will erupt, no doubt, before the work of anarchist education

has been completed … [and as] a result … , while we do preach perfect communism, it is not in the certainty or expectation of [libertarian] communism's being the social form of the future: it is in order to further men's [and women's] education … so that, by the time of the day of conflagration comes, they will have attained maximum emancipation. But must the transitional state to be endured necessarily or inevitability be the collectivist [i.e. state socialist/capitalist] jail? Might it not consist of libertarian organisation confined to the needs of production and consumption alone, with all political institutions having been done away with?" [**No Gods, No Masters**, vol. 2, p. 55]

One thing **is** certain: an anarchist social revolution or mass movement will need to defend itself against attempts by statists and capitalists to defeat it. Every popular movement, revolt, or revolution has had to face a backlash from the supporters of the status quo. An anarchist revolution or mass movement will face (and indeed has faced) such counter-revolutionary movements. However, this does not mean that the destruction of the state and capitalism need be put off until after the forces of reaction are defeated. For anarchists, a social revolution and free society can only be defended by anti-statist means (for more discussion of this important subject see section J.7.6).

I.2.3 How is the framework of an anarchist society created?

Anarchists do not abstractly compare a free society with the current one. Rather, we see an **organic** connection between what is and what could be. In other words, anarchists see the initial framework of an anarchist society as being created under statism and capitalism when working class people organise themselves to resist hierarchy. As Kropotkin argued:

> "To make a revolution it is not … enough that there should be … [popular] risings … It is necessary that after the risings there should be something new in the institutions [that make up society], which would permit new forms of life to be elaborated and established." [**The Great French Revolution**, vol. 1, p. 200]

Anarchists have seen these new institutions as being linked with the need of working class people to resist the evils of hierarchy, capitalism and statism, as being the product of the class struggle and attempts by working class people to resist authority, oppression and exploitation. Thus the struggle of working class people to protect and enhance their liberty under hierarchical society will be the basis for a society **without** hierarchy. This basic insight allowed anarchists like Bakunin and Proudhon to predict future developments in the class struggle such as workers' councils (such as those which developed during the 1905 and 1917 Russian Revolutions). As Oskar Anweiler notes in his definitive work on the Russian Soviets (Workers' Councils):

"Proudhon's views are often directly associated with the Russian councils … Bakunin …, much more than Proudhon, linked anarchist principles directly to revolutionary action, thus arriving at remarkable insights into the revolutionary process that contribute to an understanding of later events in Russia …

"In 1863 Proudhon declared … 'All my economic ideas as developed over twenty-five years can be summed up in the words: agricultural-industrial federation. All my political ideas boil down to a similar formula: political federation or decentralisation.' … Proudhon's conception of a self-governing state [sic!] founded on producers' corporations [i.e. federations of co-operatives], is certainly related to the idea of 'a democracy of producers' which emerged in the factory soviets. To this extent Proudhon can be regarded as an ideological precursor of the councils …

"Bakunin … suggested the formation of revolutionary committees with representatives from the barricades, the streets, and the city districts, who would be given binding mandates, held accountable to the masses, and subject to recall. These revolutionary deputies were to form the 'federation of the barricades,' organising a revolutionary commune to immediately unite with other centres of rebellion …

"Bakunin proposed the formation of revolutionary committees to elect communal councils, and a pyramidal organisation of society 'through free federation from the bottom upward, the association of workers in industry and agriculture — first in the communities, then through federation of communities into districts, districts into nations, and nations into international brotherhood.' These proposals are indeed strikingly similar to the structure of the subsequent Russian system of councils …

"Bakunin's ideas about spontaneous development of the revolution and the masses' capacity for elementary organisation undoubtedly were echoed in part by the subsequent soviet movement… Because Bakunin … was always very close to the reality of social struggle, he was able to foresee concrete aspects of the revolution. The council movement during the Russian Revolution, though not a result of Bakunin's theories, often corresponded in form and progress to his revolutionary concepts and predictions." [**The Soviets**, pp. 8-11]

"As early as the 1860's and 1870's," Paul Avrich also noted, "the followers of Proudhon and Bakunin in the First International were proposing the formation of workers' councils designed both as a weapon of class struggle against capitalists and as the structural basis of the future libertarian society." [**The Russian Anarchists**, p. 73]

In this sense, anarchy is not some distant goal but rather an aspect of the current struggles against domination, oppression and exploitation (i.e. the class struggle, to use an all-embracing term, although we must stress that anarchists use this term to cover all struggles against domination). *"Anarchism,"* argued Kropotkin, *"is not a mere insight into a remote future. Already now, whatever the sphere of action of the individual, he [or she] can act, either in accordance with anarchist principles or on an opposite line."* It was *"born among the people — in the struggles of real life"* and *"owes its origin to the constructive, creative activity of the people."* [**Anarchism**, p. 75, p. 150 and p. 149] Thus, *"Anarchism is not ... a theory of the future to be realised by divine inspiration. It is a living force in the affairs of our life, constantly creating new conditions."* It *"stands for the spirit of revolt"* and so *"[d]irect action against the authority in the shop, direct action against the authority of the law, of direct action against the invasive, meddlesome authority of our moral code, is the logical, consistent method of Anarchism."* [Emma Goldman, **Anarchism and Other Essays**, p. 63 and p. 66]

Anarchism draws upon the autonomous self-activity and spontaneity of working class people in struggle to inform both its political theory and its vision of a free society. The struggle against hierarchy teaches us not only how to be anarchists but also gives us a glimpse of what an anarchist society would be like, what its initial framework could be and the experience of managing our own activities which is required for such a society to function successfully. It would, therefore, be useful to give a quick summary of anarchist views on this subject.

Proudhon, for example, looked to the self-activity of French workers, artisans and peasants and used that as the basis of his ideas on anarchism. While seeing such activity as essentially reformist in nature, like subsequent revolutionary anarchists he saw the germs of anarchy *"generating from the bowels of the people, from the depths of labour, a greater authority, a more potent fact, which shall envelop capital and the State and subjugate them"* as *"it is of no use to change the holders of power or introduce some variation into its workings: an agricultural and industrial combination must be found by means of which power, today the ruler of society, shall become its slave."* [**Property is Theft!**, p. 226 and p. 225] Workers should follow the example of those already creating co-operatives:

> *"Do not the worker's societies at this moment serve as the cradle for the social revolution ... ? Are they not always the open school, both theoretical and practical, where the worker learns the science of the production and distribution of wealth, where he studies, without masters and without books, by his own experience solely, the laws of ... industrial organisation ... ?"* [**Op. Cit.**, pp. 552-3]

Attempts to form workers associations, therefore, *"should be judged, not by the more or less successful results which they obtain, but only according to their silent tendency to assert and establish the social republic."* The *"importance of their work lies, not in the petty interests of their company, but in the negation of the capitalist regime."* They will *" take over the great departments of industry, which are their natural prerogative."* [**Op. Cit.**, pp. 558-9]

This linking of the present and the future through the self-activity and self-organisation of working class people is also found in Bakunin. Unlike Proudhon, Bakunin stressed **revolutionary** activity and so he saw the militant labour movement, and the revolution itself, as providing the basic structure of a free society. As he put

it, *"the organisation of the trade sections and their representation in the Chambers of Labour ... bear in themselves the living seeds of the new society which is to replace the old one. They are creating not only the ideas, but also the facts of the future itself."* [**Bakunin on Anarchism**, p. 255]

The needs of the class struggle would create the framework of a new society, a federation of workers councils, as *"strikes indicate a certain collective strength already, a certain understanding among the workers ... each strike becomes the point of departure for the formation of new groups."* [**The Basic Bakunin**, pp. 149-50] This pre-revolutionary development would be accelerated by the revolution itself:

> *"the revolution must set out from the first to radically and totally destroy the State ... The natural and necessary consequence of this destruction will be ... [among others, the] dissolution of army, magistracy, bureaucracy, police and priesthood... confiscation of all productive capital and means of production on behalf of workers' associations, who are to put them to use ... the federative Alliance of all working men's associations ... [will] constitute the Commune ... [the] Communal Council [will be] composed of ... delegates ... vested with plenary but accountable and removable mandates... all provinces, communes and associations ... by first reorganising on revolutionary lines ... [will] constitute the federation of insurgent associations, communes and provinces ... [and] organise a revolutionary force capable defeating reaction ... [and for] self-defence ... [The] revolution everywhere must be created by the people, and supreme control must always belong to the people organised into a free federation of agricultural and industrial associations ... organised from the bottom upwards by means of revolutionary delegation."* [**Michael Bakunin: Selected Writings**, pp. 170-2]

Like Bakunin, Kropotkin stressed that revolution transformed those taking part in it. As he noted in his classic account of the French Revolution, *"by degrees, the revolutionary education of the people was being accomplished by the revolution itself."* Part of this process involved creating new organisations which allowed the mass of people to take part in the decision making of the revolution. He pointed to *"the popular Commune,"* arguing that *"the Revolution began by creating the Commune ... and through this institution it gained ... immense power."* He stressed that it was *"by means of the 'districts' [of the Communes] that ... the masses, accustoming themselves to act without receiving orders from the national representatives, were practising what was to be described later as Direct Self-Government."* Such a system did not imply isolation, for while *"the districts strove to maintain their own independence"* they also *"sought for unity of action, not in subjection to a Central Committee, but in a federative union."* The Commune *"was thus made **from below upward**, by the federation of the district organisations; it spring up in a revolutionary way, from popular initiative."* Thus the process of class struggle, of the needs of the fighting against the existing system, generated the framework of an anarchist society for *"the districts of Paris laid the foundations of a new, free, social organisation."* Little wonder he argued that *"the* *principles of anarchism … already dated from 1789, and that they had their origin, not in theoretical speculations, but in the **deeds** of the Great French Revolution"* and that *"the libertarians would no doubt do the same to-day."* [**The Great French Revolution**, vol. 1, p. 261, p. 200, p. 203, p. 206, p. 204 and p. 206]

Similarly, as we noted in section H.2.6 we discover him arguing in **Mutual Aid** that strikes and labour unions were an expression of mutual aid in capitalist society. Elsewhere, Kropotkin argued that *"labour combinations"* like the *"Sections"* of French revolution were one of the *"main popular anarchist currents"* in history, expressing the *"same popular resistance to the growing power of the few."* [**Anarchism**, p. 159] For Kropotkin, like Bakunin, libertarian labour unions were *"natural organs for the direct struggle with capitalism and for the composition of the future social order."* [quoted by Paul Avrich, **The Russian Anarchists**, p. 81]

As can be seen, the major anarchist thinkers pointed to forms of organisation autonomously created and managed by the working class as the framework of an anarchist society. Both Bakunin and Kropotkin pointed to militant, direct action based labour unions while Proudhon pointed towards workers' experiments in co-operative production and mutual credit. Later anarchists followed them. The anarcho-syndicalists, like Bakunin and Kropotkin, pointed to the developing labour movement as the framework of an anarchist society, as providing the basis for the free federation of workers' associations which would constitute the commune. Others, such as the Russians Maximov, Arshinov, Voline and Makhno, saw the spontaneously created workers' councils (soviets) of 1905 and 1917 as the basis of a free society, as another example of Bakunin's federation of workers' associations.

Thus, for all anarchists, the structural framework of an anarchist society was created by the class struggle, by the needs of working class people to resist oppression, exploitation and hierarchy. As Kropotkin stressed, *"[d]uring a revolution new forms of life will always germinate on the ruins of the old forms … It is impossible to legislate for the future. All we can do is vaguely guess its essential tendencies and clear the road for it."* [**Evolution and Environment**, pp. 101-2] These essential tendencies were discovered, in practice, by the needs of the class struggle. The necessity of practising mutual aid and solidarity to survive under capitalism (as in any other hostile environment) makes working people and other oppressed groups organise together to fight their oppressors and exploiters. Thus the co-operation necessary for a libertarian socialist society, like its organisational framework, would be generated by the need to resist oppression and exploitation under capitalism. The process of resistance produces organisation on a wider and wider scale which, in turn, can become the framework of a free society as the needs of the struggle promote libertarian forms of organisation such as decision making from the bottom up, autonomy, federalism, mandated delegates subject to instant recall and so on.

For example, a strikers' assembly would be the basic decision-making forum in a struggle for improved wages and working conditions. It would create a strike committee to implement its decisions and send delegates to spread the strike. These delegates inspire other strikes, requiring a new organisation to co-ordinate the struggle. This results in delegates from all the strikes meeting and forming a federation (a workers' council). The strikers decide

to occupy the workplace and the strike assemblies take over the means of production. The strike committees become the basis for factory committees which could administer the workplaces, based on workers' self-management via workplace assemblies (the former strikers' assemblies). The federation of strikers' delegates becomes the local communal council, replacing the existing state with a self-managed federation of workers' associations. In this way, the class struggle creates the framework of a free society.

This, obviously, means that any suggestions of how an anarchist society would look like are based on the fact that the **actual** framework of a free society will be the product of **actual** struggles. This means that the form of the free society will be shaped by the process of social change and the organs it creates. This is an important point and worth repeating.

So, as well as changing themselves while they change the world, a people in struggle also create the means by which they can manage society. By having to organise and manage their struggles, they become accustomed to self-management and self-activity and create the possibility of a free society and the organisations which will exist within it. Anarchy is not a jump into the dark but rather a natural progression of the struggle for freedom in an unfree society. The contours of a free society will be shaped by the process of creating it and, therefore, will not be an artificial construction imposed on society. Rather, it will be created from below up by society itself as working class people start to break free of hierarchy. The class struggle thus transforms those involved as well as society **and** creates the organisational structure and people required for a libertarian society.

This clearly suggests that the **means** anarchists support are important as they are have a direct impact on the ends they create. In other words, means influence ends and so our means must reflect the ends we seek and empower those who use them. As the present state of affairs is based on the oppression, exploitation and alienation of the working class, any tactics used in the pursuit of a free society must be based on resisting and destroying those evils. This is why anarchists stress tactics and organisations which increase the power, confidence, autonomy, initiative, participation and self-activity of oppressed people. As we indicate in section J (*"What Do Anarchists Do?"*) this means supporting direct action, solidarity and self-managed organisations built and run from the bottom-up. Only by fighting our own battles, relying on ourselves and our own abilities and power, in organisations we create and run ourselves, can we gain the power and confidence and experience needed to change society for the better and, hopefully, create a new society in place of the current one.

Needless to say, a revolutionary movement will never, at its start, be purely anarchist:

> *"All of the workers' and peasants' movements which have taken place … have been movements within the limits of the capitalist regime, and have been more or less tinged with anarchism. This is perfectly natural and understandable. The working class do not act within a world of wishes, but in the real world where they are daily subjected to the physical and psychological blows of hostile forces … the workers continually feel the influence*

of all the real conditions of the capitalist regime and of intermediate groups ... Consequently it is natural that the struggle which they undertake inevitably carries the stamp of various conditions and characteristics of contemporary society. The struggle can never be born in the finished and perfected anarchist form which would correspond to all the requirements of the ideas ... When the popular masses engage in a struggle of large dimensions, they inevitably start by committing errors, they allow contradictions and deviations, and only through the process of this struggle do they direct their efforts in the direction of the ideal for which they are struggling." [Peter Arshinov, **The History of the Makhnovist Movement**, pp. 239-40]

The role of anarchists is *"to help the masses to take the right road in the struggle and in the construction of the new society"* and *"support their first constructive efforts, assist them intellectually."* However, the working class *"once it has mastered the struggle and begins its social construction, will no longer surrender to anyone the initiative in creative work. The working class will then direct itself by its own thought; it will create its society according to its own plans."* [Arshinov, **Op. Cit.**, pp. 240-1] All anarchists can do is help this process by being part of it, arguing our case and winning people over to anarchist ideas (see section J.3 for more details). Thus the process of struggle and debate will, hopefully, turn a struggle **against** capitalism and statism into one **for** anarchism. In other words, anarchists seek to preserve and extend the anarchistic elements that exist in every struggle and to help them become consciously libertarian by discussion and debate as members of those struggles.

Lastly, we must stress that it is only the **initial** framework of a free society which is created in the class struggle. As an anarchist society develops, it will start to change and develop in ways we cannot predict. The forms in which people express their freedom and their control over their own lives will, by necessity, change as these requirements and needs change. As Bakunin argued:

*"Even the most rational and profound science cannot divine the form social life will take in the future. It can only determine the **negative** conditions, which follow logically from a rigorous critique of existing society. Thus, by means of such a critique, social and economic science rejected hereditary individual property and, consequently, took the abstract and, so to speak, **negative** position of collective property as a necessary condition of the future social order. In the same way, it rejected the very idea of the state or statism, meaning government of society from above downward ... Therefore, it took the opposite, or negative, position: anarchy, meaning the free and independent organisation of all the units and parts of the community and their voluntary federation from below upward, not by the orders of any authority, even an elected one, and not by the dictates of any scientific theory, but as the natural development of all the varied demands put forth by life itself.*

"Therefore no scholar can teach the people or even define

for himself how they will and must live on the morrow of the social revolution. That will be determined first by the situation of each people, and secondly by the desires that manifest themselves and operate most strongly within them." [**Statism and Anarchy**, pp. 198-9]

So while it will be reasonable to conclude that, for example, the federation of strike/factory assemblies and their councils/committees will be the framework by which production will initially be organised, this framework will mutate to take into account changing production and social needs. The actual structures created will, by necessity, be transformed as industry is transformed from below upwards to meet the real needs of society and producers as both the structure and nature of work and industry developed under capitalism bears the marks of its economic class, hierarchies and power (*"a radical social ecology not only raises traditional issues such as the reunion of agriculture with industry, but also questions the very structure of industry itself."* [Murray Bookchin, **The Ecology of Freedom**, p. 408]). Therefore, under workers' self-management industry, work and the whole structure and organisation of production will be transformed in ways we can only guess at today. We can point the general direction (i.e. self-managed, ecologically balanced, decentralised, federal, empowering, creative and so on) but that is all. Similarly, as cities and towns are transformed into ecologically integrated communes, the initial community assemblies and their federations will transform along with the transformation of our surroundings. What they will evolve into we cannot predict, but their fundamentals of instant recall, delegation over representation, decision making from the bottom up, and so on will remain.

So, while anarchists see *"the future in the present"* as the initial framework of a free society, we recognise that such a society will evolve and change. However, the fundamental principles of a free society will not change and so it is useful to present a summary of how such a society could work, based on these principles.

I.3
What could the economic structure of anarchy look like?

Here we will examine possible frameworks of a libertarian socialist economy. We stress that it is **frameworks** rather than framework because it is likely that any anarchist society will see a diverse number of economic systems co-existing in different areas, depending on what people in those areas want. *"In each locality,"* argued Diego Abad de Santillan, *"the degree of communism, collectivism or mutualism will depend on the conditions prevailing. Why dictate rules? We who make freedom our banner, cannot deny it in economy. Therefore there must be free experimentation, free show of initiative and suggestions, as well as the freedom of organisation."* As such, anarchism *"can be realised in a multiformity of economic arrangements, individual and collective. Proudhon advocated mutualism; Bakunin, collectivism; Kropotkin, communism. Malatesta has conceived the possibility of* *mixed agreements, especially during the first period."* [**After the Revolution**, p. 97 and p. 96]

Here, we will highlight and discuss the four major schools of anarchist economic thought: Individualist anarchism, mutualism, collectivism and communism. It is up to the reader to evaluate which school best maximises individual liberty and the good life (as individualist anarchist Joseph LaBadie wisely said, *"Anarchism will not dictate to them any explicit rules as to what they must do, but that it opens to them the opportunities of putting into practice their own ideas of enhancing their own happiness."* [**The Individualist Anarchists**, pp. 260-1]). *"Nothing is more contrary to the real spirit of Anarchy than uniformity and intolerance,"* argued Kropotkin. *"Freedom of development implies difference of development, hence difference of ideas and actions."* Experience, then, is *"the best teacher, and the necessary experience can only be gained by entire freedom of action."* [quoted by Ruth Kinna, *"Fields of Vision: Kropotkin and Revolutionary Change"*, pp. 67-86, **SubStance**, Vol. 36, No. 2, p. 81] There may, of course, be other economic practices but these may not be libertarian. In Malatesta's words:

> *"Admitted the basic principle of anarchism — which is that no-one should wish or have the opportunity to reduce others to a state of subjection and oblige them to work for him — it is clear that all, and only, those ways of life which respect freedom, and recognise that each individual has an equal right to the means of production and to the full enjoyment of the product of his own labour, have anything in common with anarchism."* [**Errico Malatesta: His Life and Ideas**, p. 33]

In addition, it should be kept in mind that in practice it is impossible to separate the economic realm from the social and political realms, as there are numerous interconnections between them: anarchist thinkers like Bakunin argued that the "political" institutions of a free society would be based upon workplace associations while Kropotkin placed the commune at the heart of his vision of a communist-anarchist economy **and** society. Thus the division between social and economic forms is not clear cut in anarchist theory — as it should be as society is not, and cannot be, considered as separate from or inferior to the economy. An anarchist society will try to integrate the social and economic, embedding the latter in the former in order to stop any harmful externalities associated economic activity being passed onto society. As Karl Polanyi argued, capitalism *"means no less than the running of society as an adjunct to the market. Instead of the economy being being embedded in social relations, social relations are embedded in the economic system."* [**The Great Transformation**, p. 57] Given the negative effects of such an arrangement, little wonder that anarchism seeks to reverse it.

Also, by discussing the economy first we are not implying that dealing with economic domination or exploitation is more important than dealing with other aspects of the total system of domination, e.g. social hierarchies, patriarchal values, racism, etc. We follow this order of exposition because of the need to present one thing at a time, but it would have been equally easy to start with the social and political structure of anarchy. However, Rudolf Rocker is correct to argue that an economic transformation in the economy is an essential aspect of a social revolution:

> *"[A] social development in this direction [i.e. a stateless society] was not possible without a fundamental revolution in existing economic arrangements; for tyranny and exploitation grow on the same tree and are inseparably bound together. The freedom of the individual is secure only when it rests on the economic and social well-being of all ... The personality of the individual stands the higher, the more deeply it is rooted in the community, from which arise the richest sources of its moral strength. Only in freedom does there arise in man the consciousness of responsibility for his acts and regard for the rights of others; only in freedom can there unfold in its full strength that most precious of social instinct: man's sympathy for the joys and sorrows of his fellow men and the resultant impulse toward mutual aid and in which are rooted all social ethics, all ideas of social justice."* [**Nationalism and Culture**, pp. 147-8]

The aim of any anarchist society would be to maximise freedom and so creative work:

> *"If it is correct, as I believe it is, that a fundamental element of human nature is the need for creative work or creative inquiry, for free creation without the arbitrary limiting effects of coercive institutions, then of course it will follow that a decent society should maximise the possibilities for this fundamental human characteristic to be realised. Now, a federated, decentralised system of free associations incorporating economic as well as social institutions would be what I refer to as anarcho-syndicalism. And it seems to me that it is the appropriate form of social organisation for an advanced technological society, in which human beings do not have to be forced into the position of tools, of cogs in a machine."* [Noam Chomsky, **Manufacturing Consent: Noam Chomsky and the Media**, p. 31]

So, as one might expect, since the essence of anarchism is opposition to hierarchical authority, anarchists totally oppose the way the current economy is organised. This is because authority in the economic sphere is embodied in centralised, hierarchical workplaces that give an elite class (capitalists) dictatorial control over privately owned means of production, turning the majority of the population into order takers (i.e. wage slaves). In contrast, the libertarian-socialist economy will be based on decentralised, egalitarian workplaces in which workers democratically self-manage their productive activity in **socially** owned means of production.

The key principles of libertarian socialism are decentralisation, self-management, socialisation, voluntary association, and free federation. These principles determine the form and function of both the economic and political systems. In this section we will consider just the economic system. Bakunin gives an excellent overview of such an economy when he wrote that in a free society the *"land belongs to only those who cultivate it with their own hands; to the agricultural communes. The capital and all the tools of production belong to the workers; to the workers' associations."* These associations are often called *"co-operatives"* and *"syndicates"* (see section I.3.1). This feeds into an essential economic concept for libertarian socialists, *"workers' self-management"* This refers to those who do the work managing it, where the land and workplaces are *"owned and operated by the workers themselves: by their freely organised federations of industrial and agricultural workers"* (see section I.3.2). For most anarchists, *"socialisation"* is the necessary foundation for a free society, as only this ensures universal self-management by allowing free access to the means of production (see section I.3.3). Thus an anarchist economy would be based on *"the land, tools of production and all other capital"* being *"converted into collective property of the whole of society and utilised only by the workers, i.e., by their agricultural and industrial associations."* [**Bakunin on Anarchy**, p. 247, p. 400 and p. 427] As Berkman summarised:

> *"The revolution abolishes private ownership of the means of production, distribution, and with it goes capitalistic business. Personal possession remains only in the things you use. Thus, your watch is your own, but the watch factory belongs to the people. Land, machinery, and all other public utilities will be collective property, neither to be bought nor sold. Actual use will be considered the only title [in communist anarchism] — not to ownership but to possession. The organisation of the coal miners, for example, will be in charge of the coal mines, not as owners but as the operating agency. Similarly will the railroad brotherhoods run the railroads, and so on. Collective possession, co-operatively managed in the interests of the community, will take the place of personal ownership privately conducted for profit."* [**What is Anarchism?**, p. 217]

So the solution proposed by social anarchists is **society-wide** ownership of the means of production and distribution, with each workplace run co-operatively by its members. However, no workplace exists in isolation and would seek to associate with others to ensure it gets the raw materials it needs for production and to see what it produces goes to those who need it. These links would be based on the anarchist principles of free agreement and voluntary federation (see section I.3.4). For social anarchists, this would be supplemented by confederal bodies or co-ordinating councils at two levels: first, between all firms in a particular industry; and second, between all industries (including agriculture) throughout the society (section I.3.5). Such federations may, depending on the type of anarchism in question, also include people's financial institutions.

While, for some anarcho-syndicalists, this structure is seen as enough, most communist-anarchists consider that the economic federation should be held accountable to society as a whole (i.e. the economy must be communalised). This is because not everyone in society is a worker (e.g. the young, the old and infirm) nor will everyone belong to a syndicate (e.g. the self-employed), but as they also have to live with the results of economic decisions, they should have a say in what happens. In other words, in communist-anarchism, workers make the day-to-day decisions concerning their work and workplaces, while the social criteria behind these decisions are made by everyone. As anarchist society is based on free access and a resource is controlled by those who use it. It

is a decentralised, participatory, self-managed, organisation whose members can secede at any time and in which all power and initiative arises from and flows back to the grassroots level. Such a society combines free association, federalism and self-management with communalised ownership. Free labour is its basis and socialisation exists to complement and protect it. Such a society-wide economic federation of this sort is **not** the same thing as a centralised state agency, as in the concept of nationalised or state-owned industry. The exact dynamics of a socialised self-managed system varies between anarchist schools. Most obviously, as discussed in section I.3.6, while individualists view competition between workplaces as unproblematic and mutualists see its negative aspects but consider it necessary, collectivists and communists oppose it and argue that a free society can do without it. Moreover, socialisation should not be confused with forced collectivisation — individuals and groups will be free **not** to join a syndicate and to experiment in different forms of economy (see section I.3.7). Lastly, anarchists argue that such a system would be applicable to all economies, regardless of size and development, and aim for an economy based on appropriately sized technology (Marxist assertions **not** withstanding — see section I.3.8).

Regardless of the kind of anarchy desired, anarchists all agree on the importance of decentralisation, free agreement and free association. Kropotkin's summary of what anarchy would look like gives an excellent feel of what sort of society anarchists desire:

> *"harmony in such a society being obtained, not by submission to law, or by obedience to any authority, but by free agreements concluded between the various groups, territorial and professional, freely constituted for the sake of production and consumption, as also for the satisfaction of the infinite variety of needs and aspirations of a civilised being.*

> *"In a society developed on these lines ... voluntary associations ... would represent an interwoven network, composed of an infinite variety of groups and federations of all sizes and degrees, local, regional, national and international temporary or more or less permanent — for all possible purposes: production, consumption and exchange, communications, sanitary arrangements, education, mutual protection, defence of the territory, and so on; and, on the other side, for the satisfaction of an ever-increasing number of scientific, artistic, literary and sociable needs.*

> *"Moreover, such a society would represent nothing immutable. On the contrary — as is seen in organic life at large - harmony would (it is contended) result from an ever-changing adjustment and readjustment of equilibrium between the multitudes of forces and influences, and this adjustment would be the easier to obtain as none of the forces would enjoy a special protection from the State."* [**Anarchism**, p. 284]

If this type of system sounds "utopian" it should be kept in mind that it was actually implemented and worked quite well in the collectivist economy organised during the Spanish Revolution of 1936, despite the enormous obstacles presented by an ongoing civil war as well as the relentless (and eventually successful) efforts of Republicans, Stalinists and Fascists to crush it (see section I.8 for an introduction).

I.3.1
What is a "syndicate"?

As we will use the term, a *"syndicate"* (also called a *"producer co-operative"*, or *"co-operative"*, for short, sometimes a *"collective"*, *"producers' commune"*, *"association of producers"*, *"guild factory"* or *"guild workplace"*) is a democratically self-managed productive enterprise whose assets are controlled by its workers. It is a useful generic term to describe the situation aimed at by anarchists where *"associations of men and women who ... work on the land, in the factories, in the mines, and so on, [are] themselves the managers of production."* [Kropotkin, **Evolution and Environment**, p. 78] This means that where labour is collective, *"the ownership of production should also be collective."* *"Each workshop, each factory,"* correctly suggested James Guillaume, *"will organise itself into an association of workers who will be free to administer production and organise their work as they think best, provided that the rights of each worker are safeguarded and the principles of equality and justice are observed."* This applies to the land as well, for anarchism aims to answer *"the question of how best to work the land and what form of possession is best."* It does not matter whether peasants *"keep their plots of land and continue to cultivate it with the help of their families"* or whether they *"take collective possession of the vast tracts of land and work them in common"* as *"the main purpose of the Revolution"* has been achieved, namely that *"the land is now the property of those who cultivate it, and the peasants no longer work for the profit of an idle exploiter who lives by their sweat."* Any *"former hired hands"* will become *"partners and share ... the products which their common labour extracts from the land"* as *"the Revolution will have abolished agricultural wage slavery and peonage and the agricultural proletariat will consist only of free workers living in peace and plenty."* As with industrial workplaces, the *"internal organisation ... need not necessarily be identical; organisational forms and procedures will vary greatly according to the preferences of the associated workers."* The *"administration of the community"* could be *"entrusted either to an individual or to a commission of many members,"* for example, but would always be *"elected by all the members."* [*"On Building the New Social Order"*, pp. 356-79, **Bakunin on Anarchism**, p. 363, p. 359, p. 360 and p. 361]

It must be noted that this libertarian goal of abolishing the hierarchical capitalist workplace and ending wage labour by associating and democratising industry is as old as anarchism itself. Thus we find Proudhon arguing in 1840 that the aim was a society of *"possessors without masters"* (rather than wage-labourers and tenants *"controlled by proprietors"*) with *"leaders, instructors, superintendents"* and so forth being *"chosen from the workers by the workers themselves."* *"Workers' Associations are*

the locus of a new principle and model of production," Proudhon argued 18 years later. *"There is mutuality,"* he went in, *"when in an industry, all the workers, instead of working for an owner who pays them and keeps their product, work for one another and thereby contribute to a common product from which they share the profit ... extend the principle of mutuality that unites the workers of each group to all the Workers' Associations as a unit, and you will have created a form of civilisation that, from all points of view — political, economic, aesthetic — differs completely from previous civilisations."* In summary: *"All associated and all free."* [**Property is Theft!**, p. 122, p. 119, p. 616 and p. 12]

Nor was this idea invented by Proudhon and other anarchists. Rather, it was first raised by workers themselves and subsequently taken up by the likes of Proudhon and Bakunin. So working class people came up with this fundamental libertarian socialist idea by themselves. The idea that wage labour would be replaced by associated labour was raised in many different countries in the 19th century. In France, it was during the wave of strikes and protests unleashed by the 1830 revolution. That year saw Parisian printers, for example, producing a newspaper (**L'Artisan: Journal de la classes ouvriere**) which suggested that the only way to stop being exploited by a master was for workers to form co-operatives. During the strikes of 1833, this was echoed by other skilled workers and so co-operatives were seen by many workers as a method of emancipation from wage labour. Proudhon even picked up the term **Mutualisme** from the workers in Lyon in the early 1840s and their ideas of co-operative credit, exchange and production influenced him as surely as he influenced them. In America, as Chomsky notes, *"[i]f we go back to the labour activism from the early days of the industrial revolution, to the working class press in 1850s, and so on, it's got a real anarchist strain to it. They never heard of European anarchism ... It was spontaneous. They took for granted wage labour is little different from slavery, that workers should own the mills"* [**Anarchism Interview**] As we noted in section F.8.6, this was a commonplace response for working class people facing the rise of capitalism.

In many ways a syndicate is similar to a co-operative under capitalism. Indeed, Proudhon pointed to such experiments as examples of what he desired, with *"co-operative associations"* being a key part of his *"general liquidation"* of capitalist society. [**General Idea of the Revolution**, p. 203] Bakunin, likewise, argued that anarchists are *"convinced that the co-operative will be the preponderant form of social organisation in the future, in every branch of labour and science."* [**Basic Bakunin**, p. 153] Therefore, even from the limited examples of co-operatives functioning in the capitalist market, the essential features of a libertarian socialist economy can be seen. The basic economic element, the workplace, will be a free association of individuals who will organise their joint work as equals: *"Only associated labour, that is, labour organised upon the principles of reciprocity and co-operation, is adequate to the task of maintaining ... civilised society."* [Bakunin, **The Political Philosophy of Bakunin**, p. 341]

Co-operation in this context means that the policy decisions related to their association will be based on the principle of "one member, one vote," with administrative staff elected and held accountable to the workplace as a whole. In the words of economist

David Ellerman: *"Every enterprise should be legally reconstructured as a partnership of all who work in the enterprise. Every enterprise should be a democratic worker-owned firm."* [**The Democratic Worker-Owned Firm**, p. 43] Anarchists, unsurprisingly, reject the Leninist idea that state property means the end of capitalism as simplistic and confused. Ownership is a juridical relationship. The **real** issue is one of management. Do the users of a resource manage it? If so, then we have a real (i.e. libertarian) socialist society. If not, we have some form of class society (for example, in the Soviet Union the state replaced the capitalist class but workers still had no control over their labour or the product of that labour). Workplace self-management does not mean, as some apologists of capitalism suggest, that knowledge and skill will be ignored and **all** decisions made by everyone. This is an obvious fallacy, since engineers, for example, have a greater understanding of their work than non-engineers and under workers' self-management will control it directly:

> *"we must understand clearly wherein this Guild democracy consists, and especially how it bears on relations between different classes of workers included in a single Guild. For since a Guild includes* **all** *the workers by hand and brain engaged in a common service, it is clear that there will be among its members very wide divergences of function, of technical skill, and of administrative authority. Neither the Guild as a whole nor the Guild factory can determine all issues by the expedient of the mass vote, nor can Guild democracy mean that, on all questions, each member is to count as one and none more than one. A mass vote on a matter of technique understood only by a few experts would be a manifest absurdity, and, even if the element of technique is left out of account, a factory administered by constant mass votes would be neither efficient nor at all a pleasant place to work in. There will be in the Guilds technicians occupying special positions by virtue of their knowledge, and there will be administrators possessing special authority by virtue both of skill and ability and of personal qualifications."* [G.D.H. Cole, **Guild Socialism Restated**, pp. 50-51]

The fact that some decision-making has been delegated in this manner sometimes leads people to ask whether a syndicate would not just be another form of hierarchy. The answer is that it would not be hierarchical because the workers' assemblies and their councils, open to all workers, would decide what types of decision-making to delegate, thus ensuring that ultimate power rests at the base. Moreover, **power** would not be delegated. Malatesta clearly indicates the difference between administrative decisions and policy decisions:

> *"Of course in every large collective undertaking, a division of labour, technical management, administration, etc. is necessary. But authoritarians clumsily play on words to produce a* **raison d'être** *for government out of the very real need for the organisation of work. Government, it is well to repeat, is the concourse of individuals who have had, or seized, the right and the means to make laws and to oblige people to obey; the administrator, the engineer, etc., instead are people who are appointed or assume the responsibility to carry out a particular job and so on. Government means the delegation of power, that is the abdication of initiative and sovereignty of all into the hands of a few; administration means the delegation of work, that is tasks given and received, free exchange of services based on free agreement … Let one not confuse the function of government with that of an administration, for they are essentially different, and if today the two are often confused, it is only because of economic and political privilege."* [**Anarchy**, pp. 41-2]

Given that power remains in the hands of the workplace assembly, it is clear that the organisation required for every collective endeavour cannot be equated with government. Also, never forget that administrative staff are elected by and accountable to the rest of an association. If, for example, it turned out that a certain type of delegated decision-making activity was being abused, it could be revoked by the whole workforce. Because of this grassroots control, there is every reason to think that crucial types of decision-making activity which could become a source of power (and so with the potential for seriously affecting all workers' lives) would not be delegated but would remain with the workers' assemblies. For example, powers that are now exercised in an authoritarian manner by managers under capitalism, such as those of hiring and firing, introducing new production methods or technologies, changing product lines, relocating production facilities, determining the nature, pace and rhythm of productive activity and so on would remain in the hands of the associated producers and **not** be delegated to anyone.

New syndicates will be created upon the initiative of individuals within communities. These may be the initiative of workers in an existing syndicate who desire to expand production, or members of the local community who see that the current syndicates are not providing adequately in a specific area of life. Either way, the syndicate will be a voluntary association for producing useful goods or services and would spring up and disappear as required. Therefore, an anarchist society would see syndicates developing spontaneously as individuals freely associate to meet their needs, with both local and confederal initiatives taking place.

While having a common basis in co-operative workplaces, different forms of anarchism see them work in different ways. Under mutualism, workers organise themselves into syndicates and share in its gains and losses. This means that in *"the labour-managed firm there is no profit, only income to be divided among members. Without employees the labour-managed firm does not have a wage bill, and labour costs are not counted among the expenses to the subtracted from profit, as they are in the capitalist firm."* The *"labour-managed firm does not hire labour. It is a collective of workers that hires capital and necessary materials."* [Christopher Eaton Gunn, **Workers' Self-Management in the United States**, pp. 41-2] In this way, Proudhon and his followers argued, exploitation would end and workers would receive the full-product of their labour. This, it should be noted, does not mean that workers consume all the proceeds of sales in personal consumption (i.e., no investment). It means that labour **controls** what to do with the sales income, i.e., how much to invest and how much to allocate to consumption:

"If Labour appropriated the whole product, that would include appropriating the liabilities for the property used up in the production process in addition to appropriating the produced outputs. Present Labour would have to pay input suppliers (e.g., past labour) to satisfy those liabilities." [Ellerman, **Op. Cit.**, p. 24]

So under mutualism, surpluses (profits) would be either equally divided between all members of the co-operative or divided unequally on the basis of the type of work done, with the percentages allotted to each type being decided by democratic vote, on the principle of one worker, one vote. Worker co-operatives of this type do have the virtue of preventing the exploitation and oppression of labour by capital, since workers are not hired for wages but, in effect, become partners in the firm. This means that the workers control both the product of their labour (so that the value-added that they produce is not appropriated by a privileged elite) and the work process itself (and so they no longer sell their liberty to others). However, such a limited form of co-operation is rejected by most anarchists. Non-mutualist anarchists argue that this, at best, is but a step in the right direction and the ultimate aim is distribution according to need.

Production for use rather than profit/money is the key concept that distinguishes collectivist and communist forms of anarchism from the competitive mutualism advocated by Proudhon. This is for two reasons. First, because of the harmful effects of markets we indicated in section I.1.3 could make co-operatives become, in effect, "collective capitalists" and compete against each other in the market as ferociously as actual capitalists. As Kropotkin put it, while co-operation had "at its origin" an "essentially mutual aid character", it "is often described as 'joint-stock individualism'" and "such as it is now, it undoubtedly tends to breed a co-operative egotism, not only towards the community at large, but also among the co-operators themselves." [**Mutual Aid**, p. 214] While he was discussing co-operatives under capitalism, his worries are equally applicable to a mutualist system of competing syndicates. This would also lead to a situation where market forces ensured that the workers involved made irrational decisions (from both a social and individual point of view) in order to survive in the market. For mutualists, this "irrationality of rationality" is the price to be paid to ensure workers receive the full product of their labour and, moreover, any attempt to overcome this problem holds numerous dangers to freedom. Other social anarchists disagree. They think co-operation between workplaces can increase, not reduce, freedom. Second, as discussed in section I.1.4, distribution according to work does not take into account the different needs of the workers (nor non-workers like the ill, the young and the old). As such, mutualism does not produce what most anarchists would consider a decent society, one where people co-operate to make a decent life for all.

What about entry into a syndicate? In the words of Cole, guilds (syndicates) are "open associations which any man [or woman] may join" but "this does not mean, of course, that any person will be able to claim admission, as an absolute right, into the guild of his choice." This means that there may be training requirements (for example) and obviously "a man [or woman] clearly cannot get into a Guild unless it needs fresh recruits for its work. [The worker] will have free choice, but only of the available openings." [**Op. Cit.**, p. 75] As David Ellerman notes, it is important to remember that "the labour market would not exist" in a self-managed economy as labour would "always be the residual claimant." This means that capital would not be hiring labour as under capitalism, rather workers would be seeking out associations to join. "There would be a job market in the sense of people looking for firms they could join," Ellerman continues, "but it would not be a labour market in the sense of the selling of labour in the employment contract." [**Op. Cit.**, p. 91]

All schools of social anarchism, therefore, are based on the use rights resting in the specific syndicate while ownership would be socialised rather than limited to the syndicate's workers. This would ensure free access to the means of production as new members of a syndicate would have the same rights and power as existing members. If this were not the case, then the new members would be the wage slaves of existing ones and it is **precisely** to avoid this that anarchists argue for socialisation (see section I.3.3). With socialisation, free access is guaranteed and so all workers are in the same position so ensuring self-management and no return to workplace hierarchy.

Obviously, as in any society, an individual may not be able to pursue the work they are most interested in (although given the nature of an anarchist society they would have the free time to pursue it as a hobby). However, we can imagine that an anarchist society would take an interest in ensuring a fair distribution of work and so would try to arrange work sharing if a given work placement is popular (see section I.4.13 on the question of who will do unpleasant work, and for more on work allocation generally, in an anarchist society). Of course there may be the danger of a syndicate or guild trying to restrict entry from an ulterior motive, as such the exploitation of monopoly power vis-à-vis other groups in society. However, in an anarchist society individuals would be free to form their own syndicates and this would ensure that such activity is self-defeating. In addition, in a non-individualist anarchist system, syndicates would be part of a confederation (see section I.3.4). It is a responsibility of the inter-syndicate congresses to assure that membership and employment in the syndicates is not restricted in any anti-social way. If an individual or group of individuals felt that they had been unfairly excluded from a syndicate then an investigation into the case would be organised at the congress. In this way any attempts to restrict entry would be reduced (assuming they occurred to begin with). And, of course, individuals are free to form new syndicates or leave the confederation if they so desire.

With the question of entry into syndicates comes the question of whether there would be enough places for those seeking to work (what could be termed "unemployment"). Ultimately, there are always an objective number of places available in a workplace: there is little point having people join a syndicate if there are no machines or materials for them to work on! Would a self-managed economy ensure that there are enough places available for those who seek them?

Perhaps unsurprisingly, neo-classical economics says no and equally unsurprisingly this conclusion is based not on empirical evidence of real co-operatives but rather on an abstract model developed in 1958. The model is based on deducing the implications of assuming that a labour-managed ("*Illyrian*") firm will seek to maximise net income per worker rather than, in a capitalist firm, maximising net profit. This results in various perverse results compared to a capitalist firm. This makes a co-operative-based economy extremely unstable and inefficient, as well as leading to co-operatives firing workers when prices rise as this maximises income per (remaining) worker. Thus a co-operative system ends in *"producing less output and using less labour than its capitalist counterpart."* [Benjamin Ward, *"The Firm in Illyria: Market Syndicalism"*, pp. 566-589, **The American Economic Review**, Vol. 48, No. 4, p. 580]

Of course, it would be churlish to note that, unlike the theory, actual capitalism is marked by extensive unemployment (as noted in section C.1.5, this is not surprising as it is required to secure bosses' power over their wage slaves). It would be equally churlish to note that, to quote one Yugoslav economist, this is *"a theory whose predictions have absolutely nothing to do with the observed facts."* [Branko Horvat, *"The Theory of the Worker-Managed Firm Revisited"*, pp. 9-25, **Journal of Comparative Economics**, vol. 10, no. 1, p. 9] As David Ellerman summarises:

> *"It might be noted parenthetically that there is a whole academic literature on what is called the 'Illyrian firm' … The main peculiarity of this model is that it assumes the firm would expel members when that would increase the net income of the surviving members. The resulting short-run perversities have endeared the model to capitalist economists. Yet the Illyrian model had been an academic toy in the grand tradition of much of modern economics. The predicted short-run behaviour has not been observed in Yugoslavia or elsewhere, and worker-managed firms such as the Mondragon co-operatives take membership as a short-run fixed factor … Hence we will continue to treat the Illyrian model with its much-deserved neglect."* [**Op. Cit.**, p. 150]

The experience of self-managed collectives during the Spanish Revolution also confirms this, with collectives sharing work equitably in order to avoid laying people off during the harsh economic conditions caused by the Civil War (for example, one collective *"adopted a three-day workweek, dividing available work among all those who had worked at the plant — thereby avoiding unemployment — and continued to pay everyone his or her basic salary"* [Martha A. Ackelsberg, **Free Women of Spain**, p. 101]).

We need, therefore, to *"appeal to empirical reality and common sense"* when evaluating the claim of neo-classical economics on the issue of co-operatives. The *"empirical evidence supports"* the argument that this model is flawed. There *"has been no tendency for workers to lay off co-workers when times are good, neither in Mondragon nor in Yugoslavia. Even in bad times, layoffs are rare."* Unsurprisingly, *"in the short run, a worker-managed firm responds in the same fashion as a capitalist firm"* and workers are added to the collective to meet increases in demand. [David Schweickart, **Against Capitalism**, p. 91, p. 92 and p. 93] A conclusion shared by economist Geoffrey M. Hodgson:

"Much of the evidence we do have about the behaviour of real-world worker co-operatives is that they respond to changes in market prices in a similar manner to the capitalist firm … Accordingly, the basic assumptions in the model are questioned by the evidence." [**Economics and Utopia**, pp. 223-4]

So, as Branko Horvat observes, in spite of the neo-classical analysis producing specific predictions the *"mere fact that nothing of the kind has ever been observed in real-world economies leaves them undisturbed."* At most they would say that a *"self-managed firm may not behave as the theory predicts, but this is because it behaves irrationally. If something is wrong, it is not the theory but the reality."* Interestingly, though, if you assume that capitalist firms *"maximise the rate of profit, profit per unit invested"* rather than total profit then neo-classical theory *"generates equally absurd results."* That is why the distinction between short and long runs was invented, so that in the short run the amount of capital is fixed. If this is applied to a co-operative, so that *"in the short run, the work force is fixed"* then the alleged problems with labour-managed workplaces disappear. Needless to say, a real co-operative acts on the assumption that the work force is fixed and as *"the workers are no longer hired"* this means that the worker-managers *"do not fire their colleagues when business is slack; they reduce work time or work for inventories. When the demand temporarily increases, they work overtime or contract outside work."* [**Op. Cit.**, pp. 11-13]

To sum up, syndicates are voluntary associations of workers who manage their workplace and their own work. Within the syndicate, the decisions which affect how the workplace develops and changes are in the hands of those who work there. In addition, it means that each section of the workforce manages its own activity and sections and that all workers placed in administration tasks (i.e. *"management"*) are subject to election and recall by those who are affected by their decisions. The workers' self-management is discussed in the next section.

I.3.2 What is workers' self-management?

Quite simply, workers' self-management (sometimes called *"workers' control"*) means that all workers affected by a decision have an equal voice in making it, on the principle of "one worker, one vote." Thus *"revolution has launched us on the path of industrial democracy."* [**Property is Theft!**, p. 12] That is, workers *"ought to be the real managers of industries."* [Peter Kropotkin, **Fields, Factories and Workshops Tomorrow**, p. 157] This is essential to ensure *"a society of equals, who will not be compelled to sell their hands and their brains to those who choose to employ them … but who will be able to apply their knowledge and capacities to production, in an organism so constructed as to combine all the efforts for procuring the greatest possible well-being for all, while full, free scope will be left for every individual initiative."* [Kropotkin, **Memoirs of a Revolutionist**, p. 372] As Chomsky put it:

"Compassion, solidarity, friendship are also human needs. They are driving needs, no less than the desire to increase one's share of commodities or to improve working conditions. Beyond this, I do not doubt that it is a fundamental human need to take an active part in the democratic control of social institutions. If this is so, then the demand for industrial democracy should become a central goal of any revitalised left with a working-class base." [**Radical Priorities**, p. 191]

As noted earlier, however, we need to be careful when using the term *"workers' control,"* as others use it and give it an entirely different meaning from the one intended by anarchists. Like the terms anarchist and libertarian, it has been co-opted by others to describe less than libertarian schemes.

The first to do so were the Leninists, starting with Lenin, who have used the term "workers' control" to describe a situation were workers have limited supervision over either the capitalists or the appointed managers of the so-called workers' state. These do not equate to what anarchists aim for and, moreover, such limited experiments have not lasted long (see section H.3.14). More recently, "workers' control" has been used by capitalists to describe schemes in which workers' have more say in how their workplaces are run while maintaining wage slavery (i.e. capitalist ownership, power and ultimate control). So, in the hands of capitalists, "workers' control" is now referred to by such terms as "participation", "co-determination", "consensus", "empowerment", "Japanese-style management," etc. *"For those whose function it is to solve the new problems of boredom and alienation in the workplace in advanced industrial capitalism, workers' control is seen as a hopeful solution"*, Sam Dolgoff noted, *"a solution in which workers are given a modicum of influence, a strictly limited area of decision-making power, a voice at best secondary in the control of conditions of the workplace. Workers' control, in a limited form sanctioned by the capitalists, is held to be the answer to the growing non-economic demands of the workers."* [**The Anarchist Collectives**, p. 81]

Hence anarchists prefer the term **workers' self-management**, a concept which refers to the exercise of workers' power through collectivisation and federation. It means *"a transition from private to collective ownership"* which, in turn, *"call[s] for new relationships among the members of the working community."* [Abel Paz, **The Spanish Civil War**, p. 55] Self-management in this sense *"is not a new form of mediation between the workers and their capitalist bosses, but instead refers to the very process by which the workers themselves* **overthrow** *their managers and take on their own management and the management of production in their own workplace. Self-management means the organisation of all workers … into a workers' council or factory committee (or agricultural syndicate), which makes all the decisions formerly made by the owners and managers."* [Dolgoff, **Op. Cit.**, p. 81] Self-management means the end of hierarchy and authoritarian social relationships in the workplace and their replacement by free agreement, collective decision-making, direct democracy, social equality and libertarian social relationships.

As anarchists use the term, workers' self-management means collective worker ownership, control and direction of all aspects of production, distribution and investment. This is achieved through participatory-democratic workers' assemblies, councils and federations, in both agriculture and industry. These bodies would perform all the functions formerly reserved for capitalist owners, managers, executives and financiers where these activities actually relate to productive activity rather than the needs to maximise minority profits and power (in which case they would disappear along with hierarchical management). These workplace assemblies will be complemented by people's financial institutions or federations of syndicates which perform all functions formerly reserved for capitalist owners, executives, and financiers in terms of allocating investment funds or resources.

Workers' self-management is based around general meetings of the whole workforce, held regularly in every industrial or agricultural syndicate. These are the source of and final authority over decisions affecting policy within the workplace as well as relations with other syndicates. These meetings elect workplace councils whose job is to implement the decisions of these assemblies and to make the day to day administration decisions that will crop up. These councils are directly accountable to the workforce and its members subject to re-election and instant recall. It is also likely that membership of these councils will be rotated between all members of the syndicate to ensure that no one monopolises an administrative position. In addition, smaller councils and assemblies would be organised for divisions, units and work teams as circumstances dictate.

In this way, workers would manage their own collective affairs together, as free and equal individuals. They would associate together to co-operate without subjecting themselves to an authority over themselves. Their collective decisions would remain under their control and power. This means that self-management creates *"an organisation so constituted that by affording everyone the fullest enjoyment of his [or her] liberty, it does not permit anyone to rise above the others nor dominate them in any way but through the natural influence of the intellectual and moral qualities which he [or she] possesses,* **without this influence ever being imposed as a right and without leaning upon any political institution whatever.**" [**The Political Philosophy of Bakunin**, p. 271] Only by convincing your fellow associates of the soundness of your ideas can those ideas become the agreed plan of the syndicate. No one is in a position to impose their ideas simply because of the post they hold or the work they do.

Most anarchists think that it is likely that purely administrative tasks and decisions would be delegated to elected individuals in this way, freeing workers and assemblies to concentrate on important activities and decisions rather than being bogged down in trivial details. As Bakunin put it:

"Is not administrative work just as necessary to production as is manual labour — if not more so? Of course, production would be badly crippled, if not altogether suspended, without efficient and intelligent management. But from the standpoint of elementary justice and even efficiency, the management of production need not be exclusively monopolised by one or several individuals. And managers are not at all entitled to more pay. The co-operative workers associations have demonstrated

that the workers themselves, choosing administrators from their own ranks, receiving the same pay, can efficiently control and operate industry. The monopoly of administration, far from promoting the efficiency of production, on the contrary only enhances the power and privileges of the owners and their managers." [**Bakunin on Anarchism**, p. 424]

What is important is that what is considered as important or trivial, policy or administration rests with the people affected by the decisions and subject to their continual approval. Anarchists do not make a fetish of direct democracy and recognise that there are more important things in life than meetings and voting! While workers' assemblies play the key role in self-management, they are not the focal point of **all** decisions. Rather it is the place where all the important policy decisions are made, administrative decisions are ratified or rejected and what counts as a major decision determined. Needless to say, what are considered as important issues will be decided upon by the workers themselves in their assemblies.

Unsurprisingly, anarchists argue that, as well as being more free, workers self-management is more efficient and productive than the hierarchical capitalist firm (efficiency here means accomplishing goals without wasting valued assets). Capitalist firms fail to tap humanity's vast reservoir of practical knowledge, indeed they block it as any application of that knowledge is used to enrich the owners rather than those who generate and use it. Thus the hierarchical firm disenfranchises employees and reduces them to the level of order-takers with an obvious loss of information, knowledge and insight (as discussed in section I.1.1). With self-management, that vast source of knowledge and creativity can be expressed. Thus, self-management and worker ownership *"should also reap other rewards through the greater motivation and productivity of the workers."* [David Ellerman, **The Democratic Worker-Owned Firm**, p. 139]

This explains why some firms try to simulate workers' control (by profit-sharing or "participation" schemes). For, as market socialist David Schweickart notes, *"the empirical evidence is overwhelming"* and supports those who argue for workers' participation. The *"evidence is strong that both worker participation in management and profit sharing tend to enhance productivity and that worker-run enterprises often are more productive than their capitalist counterparts."* [**Against Capitalism**, p. 100] In fact, 94% of 226 studies into this issue showed a positive impact, with 60% being statistically significant, and so the empirical evidence is *"generally supportive of a positive link between profit sharing and productivity."* This applies to co-operatives as well. [Martin L. Weitzman and Douglas L. Kruse, *"Profit Sharing and Productivity"*, pp. 95-140, **Paying for Productivity**, Alan S. Blinder (ed.), p. 137, p. 139 and pp. 131-2] Another study concludes that the *"available evidence is strongly suggestive that for employee ownership … to have a strong impact on performance, it needs to be accompanied by provisions for worker participation in decision making."* In addition, *"narrow differences in wages and status"*, as anarchists have long argued, *"increase productivity"*. [David I. Levine and Laura D'Andrea Tyson, *"Participation, Productivity, and the Firm's Environment"*, pp. 183-237, **Op. Cit.**, p. 210 and p. 211]

This should be unsurprising, for as Geoffrey M. Hodgson notes, the neo-classical model of co-operatives *"wrongly assume[s] that social relations and technology are separable … Yet we have much evidence … to support the contention that participation and co-operation can increase technological efficiency. Production involves people — their ideas and aspirations — and not simply machines operating under the laws of physics. It seems that, in their search for pretty diagrams and tractable mathematical models, mainstream economists often forget this."* [**Economics and Utopia**, p. 223] Therefore anarchists have strong evidence to support Herbert Read's comment that libertarian socialism would *"provide a standard of living far higher than that realised under any previous form of social organisation."* [**Anarchy and Order**, p. 49] It confirms Cole's comment that the *"key to real efficiency is self-government; and any system that is not based upon self-government is not only servile, but also inefficient. Just as the labour of the wage-slave is better than the labour of the chattel-slave, so … will the labour of the free man [and woman] be better than either."* [**Self-Government in Industry**, p. 157] Yet it is important to remember, as important as this evidence is, real social change comes not from "efficiency" concerns but from ideals and principles. While anarchists are confident that workers' self-management will be more efficient and productive than capitalism, this is a welcome side-effect of the deeper goal of increasing freedom. The evidence confirms that freedom is the best solution for social problems but if, for example, slavery or wage-labour proved to be more productive than free, associated, labour it does not make them more desirable!

A self-managed workplace, like a self-managed society in general, does not mean that specialised knowledge (where it is meaningful) will be neglected or not taken into account. Quite the opposite. Specialists (i.e. workers who are interested in a given area of work and gain an extensive understanding of it) are part of the assembly of the workplace, just like other workers. They can and have to be listened to, like anyone else, and their expert advice included in the decision making process. Anarchists do not reject the idea of expertise nor the rational authority associated with it. As we indicated in section B.1, anarchists recognise the difference between being **an** authority (i.e. having knowledge of a given subject) and being **in** authority (i.e. having power over someone else). As discussed in section H.4, we reject the latter and respect the former.

Such specialisation does not imply the end of self-management, but rather the opposite. *"The greatest intelligence,"* Bakunin argued, *"would not be equal to a comprehension of the whole. Thence results, for science as well as industry, the necessity of the division and association of labour."* [**God and the State**, p. 33] Thus specialised knowledge is part of the associated workers and not placed above them in positions of power. The other workers in a syndicate can compliment the knowledge of the specialists with the knowledge of the work process they have gained by working and so enrich the decision. Knowledge is distributed throughout society and only a society of free individuals associated as equals and managing their own activity can ensure that it is applied effectively (part of the inefficiency of capitalism results from the barriers to knowledge and information flow created by its hierarchical workplace).

A workplace assembly is perfectly able to listen to an engineer, for example, who suggests various ways of reaching various goals (i.e. if you want X, you would have to do A or B. If you do A, then C, D and E is required. If B is decided upon, then F, G, H and I are entailed). But it is the assembly, **not** the engineer, that decides the goals and methods to be implemented. As Cornelius Castoriadis put it: "*We are not saying: people will have to decide **what** to do, and then technicians will tell them **how** to do it. We say: after listening to technicians, people will decide what to do **and** how to do it. For the **how** is not neutral — and the **what** is not disembodied. What and how are neither **identical**, nor **external** to each other. A 'neutral' technique is, of course, an illusion. A conveyor belt is linked to a type of product **and** a type of producer — and vice versa.*" [**Social and Political Writings**, vol. 3, p. 265]

However, we must stress that while an anarchist society would "inherit" a diverse level of expertise and specialisation from class society, it would not take this as unchangeable. Anarchists argue for **"all-round"** (or integral) education as a means of ensuring that everyone has a basic knowledge or understanding of science, engineering and other specialised tasks. As Bakunin argued, "*in the interests of both labour and science ... there should no longer be either workers or scholars but only human beings.*" Education must "*prepare every child of each sex for the life of thought as well as for the life of labour.*" [**The Basic Bakunin**, p. 116 and p. 119] This does not imply the end of all specialisation (individuals will, of course, express their individuality and know more about certain subjects than others) but it does imply the end of the artificial specialisation developed under capitalism which tries to deskill and disempower the wage worker by concentrating knowledge into hands of management.

And, just to state the obvious, self-management does not imply that the mass of workers decide on the application of specialised tasks. Self-management implies the autonomy of those who do the work as well as collective decision making on collective issues. For example, in a self-managed hospital the cleaning staff would not have a say in the doctors' treatment of patients just as the doctors would not tell the cleaners how to do their work (of course, it is likely that an anarchist society will **not** have people whose work is simply to clean and nothing else, we just use this as an example people will understand). All members of a syndicate would have a say in what happens in the workplace as it affects them collectively, but individual workers and groups of workers would manage their own activity within that collective.

Needless to say, self-management abolishes the division of labour inherent in capitalism between order takers and order givers. It integrates (to use Kropotkin's words) brain work and manual work by ensuring that those who do the work also manage it and that a workplace is managed by those who use it. Such an integration of labour will, undoubtedly, have a massive impact in terms of productivity, innovation and efficiency. As Kropotkin argued, the capitalist firm has a negative impact on those subject to its hierarchical and alienating structures:

> "*The worker whose task has been specialised by the permanent division of labour has lost the intellectual interest in his [or her] labour, and it is especially so in the great industries; he has lost his inventive powers.*

> *Formerly, he [or she] invented very much ... But since the great factory has been enthroned, the worker, depressed by the monotony of his [or her] work, invents no more.*" [**Fields, Factories and Workshops Tomorrow**, p. 171]

Must all the skills, experience and intelligence that every one has be swept away or crushed by hierarchy? Or could it not become a new fertile source of progress under a better organisation of production? Self-management would ensure that the independence, initiative and inventiveness of workers (which disappears under wage slavery) comes to the fore and is applied. Combined with the principles of "all-round" (or integral) education (see section J.5.13) who can deny that working people could transform the current economic system to ensure "*well-being for all*"? And we must stress that by "*well-being*" we mean well-being in terms of meaningful, productive activity in humane surroundings and using appropriate technology, in terms of goods of utility and beauty to help create strong, healthy bodies and in terms of surroundings which are inspiring to live in and ecologically integrated.

Little wonder Kropotkin argued that self-management and the "*erasing [of] the present distinction between the brain workers and manual worker*" would see "*social benefits*" arising from "*the concordance of interest and harmony so much wanted in our times of social struggles*" and "*the fullness of life which would result for each separate individual, if he [or she] were enabled to enjoy the use of both ... mental and bodily powers.*" This is in addition to the "*increase of wealth which would result from having ... educated and well-trained producers.*" [**Op. Cit.**, p. 180]

Let us not forget that today workers **do** manage their own working time to a considerable extent. The capitalist may buy an hour of a workers' time but they have to ensure that the worker follows their orders during that time. Workers resist this imposition and this results in considerable shop-floor conflict. Frederick Taylor, for example, introduced his system of "*scientific management*" in part to try and stop workers managing their own working activity. As David Noble notes, workers "*paced themselves for many reason: to keep time for themselves, to avoid exhaustion, to exercise authority over their work, to avoid killing so-called gravy piece-rate jobs by overproducing and risking a pay cut, to stretch out available work for fear of layoffs, to exercise their creativity, and, last but not least, to express their solidarity and their hostility to management.*" These were "*[c]oupled with collective co-operation with their fellows on the floor*" and "*labour-prescribed norms of behaviour*" to achieve "*shop floor control over production.*" [**Forces of Production**, p. 33] This is why *working to rule*" is such an efficient weapon in the class struggle (see section H.4.4) In other words, workers naturally tend towards self-management anyway and it is this natural movement towards liberty during work hours which is combated by bosses (who wins, of course, depends on objective and subjective pressures which swing the balance of power towards labour or capital).

Self-management will build upon this already existing unofficial workers control over production and, of course, our knowledge of the working process which actually doing it creates. The conflict over who controls the shop floor — either those who do the work or those who give the orders — not only shows that self-management is **possible** but also show how it can come about as it brings to the fore the awkward fact that while the bosses need us, we do not need them!

I.3.3 What does socialisation mean?

A key aspect of anarchism is the socialisation of the means of life. This means that the land, housing, workplaces and so forth become common property, usable by all who need them. Thus Emma Goldman's summary:

> "That each and every individual is and ought to be free to own himself and to enjoy the full fruit of his labour; that man is absolved from all allegiance to the kings of authority and capital; that he has, by the very fact of his being, free access to the land and all means of production, and entire liberty of disposing of the fruits of his efforts; that each and every individual has the unquestionable right of free and voluntary association with other equally sovereign individuals for economic, political, social, and other purposes, and that to achieve this end man must emancipate himself from the sacredness of property, the respect for man-made law, the fear of the Church, the cowardice of public opinion, the stupid arrogance of national, racial, religious, and sex superiority, and from the narrow puritanical conception of human life." [**A Documentary History of the American Years**, vol. 2, pp. 450-1]

This is required because private ownership of collectively used "property" (such as workplaces and land) results in a situation where the many have to sell their labour (i.e., liberty) to the few who own it. This creates hierarchical and authoritarian social relationships as well as economic classes. For anarchists, society cannot be divided into "a possessing and a non-possessing" class system as this is "a condition of social injustice" as well as making the state "indispensable to the possessing minority for the protection of its privileges." [Rudolf Rocker, **Anarcho-Syndicalism**, p. 11] In other words, "as long as land and capital are unappropriated, the workers are free, and that, when these have a master, the workers also are slaves." [Charlotte M. Wilson, **Anarchist Essays**, p. 21]

While there is a tendency by state socialists and the right to equate socialisation with nationalisation, there are key differences which the different names signify. Nationalisation, in practice and usually in theory, means that the means of life become state property. This means that rather than those who need and use a specific part of the co-operative commonwealth deciding what to do with it, the government does. As we discussed in section B.3.5 this would just be state capitalism, with the state replacing the current capitalist and landlords.

As Emma Goldman argued, there is a clear difference between socialisation and nationalisation. "The first requirement of Communism," she argued, "is the socialisation of the land and of the machinery of production and distribution. Socialised land and machinery belong to the people, to be settled upon and used by individuals and groups according to their needs." Nationalisation, on the other hand, means that a resource "belongs to the state; that is, the government has control of it and may dispose of it according to its wishes and views." She stressed that "when a thing is socialised, every individual has free access to it and may use it without interference from anyone." When the state owned property, "[s]uch a state of affairs may be called state capitalism, but it would be fantastic to consider it in any sense communistic." [**Red Emma Speaks**, pp. 406-7]

Socialisation aims at replacing property rights by use rights. The key to understanding socialisation is to remember that it is about **free access**. In other words, that every one has the same rights to the means of life as everyone else, that no one is exploited or oppressed by those who own the means of life. In the words of Herbert Read:

> "The essential principle of anarchism is that mankind has reached a stage of development at which it is possible to abolish the old relationship of master-man (capitalist-proletarian) and substitute a relationship of egalitarian co-operation. This principle is based, not only on ethical ground, but also on economic grounds." [**Anarchy and Order**, p. 92]

This implies two things. Firstly, that the means of life are common property, without an owning class. Secondly, there is free association between equals within any association and so industrial democracy (or self-management).

This has been an anarchist position as long as anarchism has been called anarchism. Thus we find Proudhon arguing in 1840 that "the land is indispensable to our existence" and "consequently a common thing, consequently insusceptible of appropriation" and that "all accumulated capital being social property, no one can be its exclusive proprietor." This means that "all property" must become "collective and undivided." Without this there is inequality and a restriction of freedom as the worker lives on the "benevolence" proprietor "to whom he has sold and surrendered his liberty." The "civilised labourer who bakes a loaf that he may eat a slice of bread ... is not free. His employer ... is his enemy." In fact, "neither a commercial, nor an industrial, nor an agricultural association can be conceived of in the absence of equality." The aim was a society of "possessors without masters" rather than wage-labourers and tenants "controlled by proprietors." Within any economic association there would be democracy, with "leaders, instructors, superintendents" and so forth being "chosen from the labourers by the labourers themselves, and must fulfil the conditions of eligibility. It is the same with all public functions, whether of administration or instruction." [**Property is Theft!**, p. 105, p. 118, p. 137, p. 117, p. 7, p. 129, p. 122 and p. 119]

So "under universal association, ownership of the land and of the instruments of labour is **social** ownership" with "democratically organised workers associations." Workplaces "are the common and undivided property of all those who take part therein" rather than "companies of stockholders who plunder the bodies and souls of the wage workers." This meant free access, with "every individual employed in the association" having "an undivided share in the property of the company" and has "a right to fill any position" as "all positions are elective, and the by-laws subject to the approval of the members." Each member "shall participate in the gains and in the losses of the company, in proportion to his [or her] services." [**Op. Cit**, p. 377 and pp. 584-5] Proudhon's idea of free credit from a People's Bank, it should be noted, is another example of free access, of socialisation. Needless to say, anarchists like Bakunin and Kropotkin based their arguments for socialisation on this vision of self-managed workplaces and free access to the means of life. For Bakunin, for example, "the land, the instruments of work and all other capital may become the collective property of the whole of society and be utilised only by the workers, in other words, by the agricultural and industrial associations." [**Michael Bakunin: Selected Writings**, p. 174]

So the means of production are socialised in mutualism, collectivism and communism and all rest on the same principle of equal access. So when someone joins an existing workers association they become full members of the co-operative, with the same rights and duties as existing members. In other words, they participate in the decisions on a basis of one person, one vote. How the products of that association are distributed vary in different types of anarchism, but the associations that create them are rooted in the free association of equals. In contrast, a capitalist society places the owner in the dominant position and new members of the workforce are employees and so subordinate members of an organisation which they have no say in (see section B.1).

Socialisation would mean that workplaces would become "small worker republics." [Proudhon, **Property is Theft!**, p. 780] As economist David Ellerman explains, the democratic workplace "is a social community, a community of work rather than a community residence. It is a republic, or **res publica** of the workplace. The ultimate governance rights are assigned as personal rights … to the people who work in the firm … This analysis shows how a firm can be socialised and yet remain 'private' in the sense of not being government-owned." As noted in section I.3.1, this means the end of the labour market as there would be free access to workplaces and so workers would not be wage-labourers employed by bosses. Instead, there would be a people seeking associations to join and associations seeking new associates to work with. "Instead of abolishing the employment relation," Ellerman argues, "state socialism nationalised it … Only the democratic firm — where the workers are jointly self-employed — is a genuine alternative to private or public employment." [**The Democratic Worker-Owned Firm**, p. 76 and p. 209]

So libertarian socialism is based on decentralised decision making within the framework of socially-owned but independently-run and worker-self-managed syndicates. The importance of socialisation should not be downplayed. This is because the self-management of work is not sufficient in and of itself to ensure an anarchist society. Under feudalism, the peasants managed their own labour but such a regime was hardly libertarian for, at a minimum, the peasants paid the landlord rent. An industrial equivalent can be imagined, where workers hire workplaces and land from capitalists and landlords. As left-wing economist Geoffrey M. Hodgson suggests:

"Assume that the workers are self-employed but do not own all the means of production. In this case there still may be powerful owners of factories, offices and machines … the owners of the means of production would still receive an income, emanating from that ownership. In bargaining with these owners, the workers would be required to concede the claim of these owners to an income, as they would be unable to produce without making use of the means of production owned by others. Hence the workers would still be deprived of … 'surplus value'. Profits would still derive from ownership of the means of production." [**Economics and Utopia**, p. 168]

This would not be (libertarian) socialism (as workers would still be exploited) nor would it be capitalism (as there is no wage labour as such, although there would be a proletariat). Thus genuine anarchism requires socialisation of the means of life, which ensures free access (no usury). In other words, self-management (while an essential part of anarchism) is not sufficient to make a society anarchistic. Without socialism (free access to the means of life) it would be yet another class system and rooted in exploitation. To eliminate all exploitation, social anarchists propose that productive assets such as workplaces and land be owned by society as a whole and run by syndicates and self-employed individuals. Thus Kropotkin: "Free workers, on free land, with free machinery, and freely using all the powers given to man by science." [**Act for Yourselves**, p. 102]

This vision of socialisation, of free access, also applies to housing. Proudhon, for example, suggested that payments of rent in housing under capitalism would be "carried over to the account of the purchase of the property" and once paid for the house "shall pass under the control of the communal administration … in the name of all the tenants, and shall guarantee them all a domicile, in perpetuity, at the cost of the building." Rented farm land would be the same and would, once paid for, "revert immediately to the commune, which shall take the place of the former proprietor." Provision "shall be made for the supervision of the communes, for the installation of cultivators, and for the fixing of the boundaries of possessions." [**Op. Cit.**, p. 576 and p. 578] Kropotkin had a similar end in mind, namely "the abolition of rent", but by different means, namely by "the expropriation of houses" during a social revolution. This would be "the communalising of houses and the right of each family to a decent dwelling." [**The Conquest of Bread**, p. 91 and p. 95]

It is important to note here that while anarchists tend to stress communes (see section I.5) this does **not** imply communal living in the sense of one-big family. As Kropotkin, for example, was at pains to stress such continual communal living is "repugnant to millions of human beings. The most reserved man [and woman] certainly feels the necessity of meeting his [or her] fellows for the pursue of common work … But it is not so for the hours of leisure, reserved for rest and intimacy." Communal living in the sense of a human bee-hive "can please some, and even all at a certain period of their life, but the great mass prefers family life (family life of the future, be it understood). They prefer isolated apartments." A community living together under one roof "would be hateful, were it the general rule. Isolation, alternating with time spent in society, is the normal desire of human nature." [**Op. Cit.**, pp. 123-4] Thus the aim is "*Communism, but not the monastic or barrack-room Communism formerly advocated [by state socialists], but the free Communism which places the products reaped or manufactured at the disposal of all, leaving to each the liberty to consume them as he pleases in his [or her] own home.*" [**The Place of Anarchism in the Evolution of Socialist Thought**, p. 7] Needless to say, each household, like each workplace, would be under the control of its users and socialisation exists to ensure that remains the case (i.e., that people cannot become tenants/subjects of landlords).

See section I.6 for a discussion of how socialisation and free access could work.

Beyond this basic vision of self-management and socialisation, the schools of anarchism vary. Mutualism eliminates wage labour and unites workers with the means of production they use. Such a system is socialist as it is based on self-management and workers' control/ownership of the means of production. However, other social anarchists argue that such a system is little more than "petit-bourgeois co-operativism" in which the worker-owners of the co-operatives compete in the marketplace with other co-operatives for customers, profits, raw materials, etc. — a situation that could result in many of the same problems that arise under capitalism or even a return to capitalism (see section I.1.3). Some Mutualists recognise this danger. Proudhon, as discussed in section I.3.5, advocated an agro-industrial federation to combat the effects of market forces in generating inequality and wage labour. In addition, supporters of mutualism can point to the fact that existing co-operatives rarely fire their members and are far more egalitarian in nature than corresponding capitalist firms. This they argue will ensure that mutualism will remain socialist, with easy credit available to those who are made unemployed to start their own co-operatives again.

In contrast, within anarcho-collectivism and anarcho-communism society as a whole owns the means of life, which allows for the elimination of both competition for survival and the tendency for workers to develop a proprietary interest in the enterprises in which they work. As Kropotkin argued, "*[t]here is no reason why the factory ... should not belong to the community ... It is evident that now, under the capitalist system, the factory is the curse of the village, as it comes to overwork children and to make paupers of its male inhabitants; and it is quite natural that it should be opposed by all means by the workers ... But under a more rational social organisation, the factory would find no such obstacles; it would be a boon to the village.*" Needless to say, such a workplace would be based on workers' self-management, as "*the workers ... ought to be the real managers of industries.*" [**Fields, Factories and Workshops Tomorrow**, p. 152 and p. 157] This "*socially organised industrial production*" (to use Kropotkin's term) would ensure a decent standard of living without the problems associated with a market, even a non-capitalist one.

In other words, the economy is communalised, with land and the means of production being turned into common "property". The community determines the social and ecological framework for production while the workforce makes the day-to-day decisions about what to produce and how to do it. This is because a system based purely on workplace assemblies effectively disenfranchises those individuals who do not work but live with the effects of production (e.g., ecological disruption). In Murray Bookchin's words, the aim would be to advance "*a holistic approach to an ecologically oriented economy*" with key policy decisions "*made by citizens in face-to-face assemblies — as **citizens**, not simply as workers, farmers, or professionals ... As citizens, they would function in such assemblies by their highest level — their **human** level — rather than as socially ghettoised beings. They would express their general human interests, not their particular status interests.*" These communalised economies would join with others "*into a regional confederal system. Land, factories, and workshops would be controlled by the popular assemblies of free communities, not by a nation-state or by worker-producers who might very well develop a proprietary interest in them.*" [**Remaking Society**, p. 194]

An important difference between workplace and community assemblies is that the former can be narrow in focus while the latter can give a hearing to solutions that bring out the common ground of people as people rather than as workers in a specific workplace or industry. This would be in the context of communal participation, through face-to-face voting of the whole community in local neighbourhood and confederal assemblies, which will be linked together through voluntary federations. It does **not** mean that the state owns the means of production, as under Marxism-Leninism or social democracy, because there is no state under libertarian socialism (for more on community assemblies, see section I.5).

This means that when a workplace is communalised workers' self-management is placed within the broader context of the community, becoming an aspect of community control. This does not mean that workers' do not control what they do or how they do it. Rather, it means that the framework within which they make their decisions is determined by the community. For example, the local community may decide that production should maximise recycling and minimise pollution, and workers informed of this decision make investment and production decisions accordingly. In addition, consumer groups and co-operatives may be given a voice in the confederal congresses of syndicates or even in the individual workplaces (although it would be up to local communities to decide whether this would be practical or not). In these ways, consumers could have a say in the administration of production and the type and quality of the product, adding their voice and interests in the creation as well as the consumption of a product.

Given the general principle of social ownership and the absence of a state, there is considerable leeway regarding the specific forms that collectivisation might take — for example, in regard to methods of distribution, the use or non-use of money, etc. — as can be seen by the different systems worked out in various areas of Spain during the Revolution of 1936-39. Nevertheless, freedom is undermined when some communities are poor while others are wealthy. Therefore the method of surplus distribution must insure that all communities have an adequate share of pooled revenues and resources held at higher levels of confederation as well as guaranteed minimum levels of public services and provisions to meet basic human needs. That is why anarchists have supported the need for syndicates and communities to federate (see next section)

Finally, one key area of disagreement between anarchist schools is how far socialisation should go. Mutualists think that it should only include the means of production while communist-anarchists argue that socialisation, to be consistent, must embrace what is produced as well as what produced it. Collectivist-anarchists tend to agree with mutualists on this, although many think that, over time, the economy would evolve into communism as the legacies of capitalism and scarcity are overcome. Proudhon spoke for the mutualists:

> "This, then, is the first point settled: property in product, if we grant so much, does not carry with it property in the means of production; that seems to me to need no further demonstration ... all ... are proprietors of their products — not one is proprietor of the means of production. The right to product is exclusive — **jus in re**; the right to means is common — **jus ad rem**." [**Property is Theft!**, p. 112]

For libertarian communists, socialisation should be extended to the products of labour as well. This means that as well as having free access to the means of production, people would also have free access to the goods and services produced by them. Again, this does not imply people having to share the possessions they use. Rather it means that instead of having to buy the goods in question they are distributed freely, according to need. To maintain socialisation of the means of product but not in goods means basing society *"on two absolutely opposed principles, two principles that contradict one another continually."* [Kropotkin, **The Conquest of Bread**, p. 163] The need is to go beyond the abolition of wage labour into the abolition of money (the wages system). This is because any attempt at measuring a person's contribution to society will be flawed and, more importantly, people *"differ from one another by the amount of their* **needs**. *There is the young unmarried woman and the mother of a family of five or six children. For the employer of our days there is no consideration of the needs of"* each and *"the labour cheque ... acts in the same way."* [Kropotkin, **Act For Yourselves**, pp. 108-9]

Regardless of precisely which mode of distribution specific individuals, workplaces, communes or areas picks, socialisation would be underlying all. Free access to the means of production will ensure free individuals, including the freedom to experiment with different anarchistic economic systems.

I.3.4 What relations would exist between individual syndicates?

Just as individuals associate together to work on and overcome common problems, so would syndicates. Few, if any, workplaces are totally independent of others. They require raw materials as inputs and consumers for their products. Therefore there will be links between different syndicates. These links are twofold: firstly, free agreements between individual syndicates; secondly, confederations of syndicates (within branches of industry and regionally).

Combined with this desire for free co-operation is a desire to end centralised systems. The opposition to centralisation is often framed in a distinctly false manner. This can be seen when Alex Nove, a leading market socialist, argued that *"there are horizontal links (market), there are vertical links (hierarchy). What other dimension is there?"* [**The Economics of Feasible Socialism**, p. 226] In other words, to oppose central planning means to embrace the market. This is not true: horizontal links need not be market based any more than vertical links need be hierarchical. An anarchist society must be based essentially on horizontal links between individuals and associations, freely co-operating together as they (not a central body) sees fit. This co-operation will be source of many links in an anarchist economy. When a group of individuals or associations meet together and discuss common interests and make common decisions they will be bound by their own decisions. This is radically different from a central body giving out orders because those affected will determine the content of these decisions. In other words, instead of decisions being handed down from the top, they will be created from the bottom up.

Let us consider free agreement. Anarchists recognise the importance of letting people organise their own lives. This means that they reject central planning and instead urge direct links between workers' associations. In the words of Kropotkin, *"[f]ree workers would require a free organisation, and this cannot have any other basis than free agreement and free co-operation, without sacrificing the autonomy of the individual."* Those directly involved in production (and in consumption) know their needs far better than any bureaucrat. Thus voluntary agreement is the basis of a free economy, such agreements being *"entered by free consent, as a free choice between different courses equally open to each of the agreeing parties."* [**Anarchism**, p. 52 and p. 69] Without the concentration of wealth and power associated with capitalism, free agreement will become real and no longer a mask for hierarchy.

The anarchist economy *"starts from below, not from above. Like an organism, this free society grows into being from the simple unit up to the complex structure. The need for ... the individual struggle for life"* is *"sufficient to set the whole complex social machinery in motion. Society is the result of the individual struggle for existence; it is not, as many suppose, opposed to it."* So anarchists think that *"[i]n the same way that each free individual has associated with his brothers [and sisters!] to produce ... all that was necessary for life, driven by no other force than his [or her] desire for the full enjoyment of life, so each institution is free and self-contained, and co-operates and enters into agreements with others because by so doing it extends its own possibilities."* This suggests a decentralised economy — even more decentralised than capitalism (which is decentralised only in capitalist mythology, as shown by big business and transnational corporations, for example) — one *"growing ever more closely bound together and interwoven by free and mutual agreements."* [George Barrett, **The Anarchist Revolution**, p. 18] An anarchist economy would be based on spontaneous order as workers practised mutual aid and free association. For communist anarchists, this would take the form of *"free exchange without the medium of money and without profit, on the basis of requirement and the supply at hand."* [Alexander Berkman, **What is Anarchism?**, p. 217] *"Anarchists"*, summarised Rocker, *"desire a federation of free communities which shall be bound to one another by their common economic and social interest and shall arrange their affairs* by mutual agreement and free contract." [**Anarcho-Syndicalism**, p. 1] An example of one such agreement would be orders for products and services:

> "This factory of ours is, then, to the fullest extent consistent with the character of its service, a self-governing unit, managing its own productive operations, and free to experiment to the heart's content in new methods, to develop new styles and products... This autonomy of the factory is the safeguard... against the dead level of mediocrity, the more than adequate substitute for the variety which the competitive motive was once supposed to stimulate, the guarantee of liveliness, and of individual work and workmanship." [G.D.H. Cole, **Guild Socialism Restated**, p. 59]

This means that free agreement will ensure that customers would be able to choose their own suppliers, meaning that production units would know whether they were producing what their customers wanted, when they wanted it (i.e., whether they were meeting individual and social needs). If they were not, customers would go elsewhere, to other production units within the same branch of production. We should stress that in addition to this negative check (i.e. "exit" by consumers) it is likely, via consumer groups and co-operatives as well as communes, that workplaces will be subject to positive checks on what they produced. Consumer groups, by formulating and communicating needs to producer groups, will have a key role in ensuring the quality of production and goods and that it satisfies their needs (see section I.4.7 for more details of this).

These direct horizontal links between syndicates are essential to ensure that goods are produced which meet the needs of those who requested them. Without specific syndicates requesting specific goods at specific times to meet specific requirements, an economy will not meet people's needs. A central plan, for example, which states that 1 million tonnes of steel or 25 million shirts need to be produced in a year says nothing about what specifically needs to be produced and when, which depends on how it will be used and the needs of those using it. As Malatesta argued, *"it would be an absurd waste of energy to produce blindly for all possible needs, rather than calculating the actual needs and organising to satisfy them with as little effort as possible ... the solution lies in accord between people and in the agreements ... that will come about"* between them. [**At the Café**, pp. 62-3] Hence the pressing need for the classic anarchist ideas on free association, free agreement and mutual aid! These direct links between producer and consumer can communicate the information required to produce the right thing at the right time! As Kropotkin argued (based on his firsthand experience of state capitalism in Russia under Lenin):

> "production and exchange represent an undertaking so complicated that the plans of the state socialists ... would prove to be absolutely ineffective as soon as they were applied to life. No government would be able to organise production if the workers themselves through their unions did not do it in each branch of industry; for in all production there arise daily thousands of difficulties which no government can solve or foresee. It is certainly

impossible to foresee everything. Only the efforts of thousands of intelligences working on the problems can co-operate in the development of a new social system and find the best solutions for the thousands of local needs." [**Anarchism**, pp. 76-77]

This brings us to the second form of relationships between syndicates, namely confederations of syndicates in the same industry or geographical area. It should be noted that inter-workplace federations are not limited to collectivist, syndicalist and communist anarchists. The idea of federations of syndicates goes back to Proudhon's agro-industrial federation, first raised during the 1848 revolution and named as such in his 1863 book, **The Federative Principle**. This is the structural support organisation for his system of self-managed co-operatives. These confederations of syndicates, are necessary to aid communication between workplaces. No syndicate exists in isolation, and so there is a real need for a means by which syndicates can meet together to discuss common interests and act on them. Thus confederations are complementary to free agreement and also reflect anarchist ideas of free association and decentralised organisation as well as concern for practical needs:

> "Anarchists are strenuously opposed to the authoritarian, centralist spirit ... So they picture a future social life in the basis of federalism, from the individual to the municipality, to the commune, to the region, to the nation, to the international, on the basis of solidarity and free agreement. And it is natural that this ideal should be reflected also in the organisation of production, giving preference as far as possible, to a decentralised sort of organisation; but this does not take the form of an absolute rule to be applied in every instance. A libertarian order would be in itself ... rule out the possibility of imposing such a unilateral solution." [Luigi Fabbri, "Anarchy and 'Scientific Communism", pp. 13-49, **The Poverty of Statism**, Albert Meltzer (ed.), p. 23]

A confederation of syndicates (called a *"guild"* by some libertarian socialists, or *"industrial union"* by others) works on two levels: within an industry and across industries. The basic operating principle of these confederations is the same as that of the syndicate itself — voluntary co-operation between equals in order to meet common needs. In other words, each syndicate in the confederation is linked by horizontal agreements with the others, and none owe any obligations to a separate entity above the group (see section A.2.11 for more on the nature of anarchist confederation). As Herbert Read summarised:

> "The general principle is clear: each industry forms itself into a federation of self-governing collectives; the control of each industry is wholly in the hands of the workers in that industry, and these collectives administer the whole economic life of the country." [**Anarchy and Order**, p. 49]

Kropotkin's comments on federalism between communes indicate this (a syndicate can be considered as a producers' commune). *"The Commune of tomorrow,"* he argued *"will know that it cannot admit any higher authority; above it there can only be the interests of the*

Federation, freely accepted by itself as well as other communes." So federalism need not conflict with autonomy, as each member would have extensive freedom of action within its boundaries and so each *"Commune will be absolutely free to adopt all the institutions it wishes and to make all the reforms and revolutions it finds necessary."* [**Words of a Rebel**, p. 83] Moreover, these federations would be diverse and functional. Economic federation would produce a complex inter-networking between associations and federations:

> *"Our needs are in fact so various, and they emerge with such rapidity, that soon a single federation will not be sufficient to satisfy them all. The Commune will then feel the need to contract other alliances, to enter into other federations. Belonging to one group for the acquisition of food supplies, it will have to join a second group to obtain other goods, such as metals, and then a third and a fourth group for textiles and works of art."* [**Op. Cit.**, p. 87]

Therefore, a confederation of syndicates would be adaptive to its members needs. As Tom Brown argued, the *"syndicalist mode of organisation is extremely elastic, therein is its chief strength, and the regional confederations can be formed, modified, added to or reformed according to local conditions and changing circumstances."* [**Syndicalism**, p. 58] As would be imagined, these confederations are voluntary associations and *"[j]ust as factory autonomy is vital in order to keep the Guild system alive and vigorous, the existence of varying democratic types of factories in independence of the National Guilds may also be a means of valuable experiment and fruitful initiative of individual minds. In insistently refusing to carry their theory to its last 'logical' conclusion, the Guildsmen [and anarchists] are true to their love of freedom and varied social enterprise."* [G.D.H. Cole, **Op. Cit.**, p. 65] This, it must be stressed does not mean centralised control from the top:

> *"But when we say that ownership of the tools of production, including the factory itself, should revert to the corporation [i.e. confederation] we do not mean that the workers in the individual workshops will be ruled by any kind of industrial government having power to do what it pleases with the tools of production. No, the workers in the various factories have not the slightest intention of handing over their hard-won control … to a superior power … What they will do is … to guarantee reciprocal use of their tools of production and accord their fellow workers in other factories the right to share their facilities, receiving in exchange the same right to share the facilities of the fellow workers with whom they have contracted the pact of solidarity."* [James Guillaume, *"On Building the New Social Order"*, pp. 356-79, **Bakunin on Anarchism**, pp. 363-364]

So collectivist and communist anarchism, like mutualism, is rooted in self-management in the workplace. This implies the ability of workers to pick the kinds of productive tasks they want to do. It would not be the case of workplaces simply being allocated tasks by some central body and expected to fulfil them (a task which,

ignoring the real issues of bureaucracy and freedom, would be difficult to implement in any large and complex economy). Rather, workplaces would have the power to select tasks submitted to them by other associations (economic and communal) and control how the work required to achieve them was done. In this type of economic system, workers' assemblies and councils would be the focal point, formulating policies for their individual workplaces and deliberating on industry-wide or economy-wide issues through general meetings of the whole workforce in which everyone would participate in decision making. Voting in the councils would be direct, whereas in larger confederal bodies, voting would be carried out by temporary, unpaid, mandated, and instantly recallable delegates, who would resume their status as ordinary workers as soon as their mandate had been carried out.

Mandated here means that the delegates from workers' assemblies and councils to meetings of higher confederal bodies would be instructed, at every level of confederation, by the workers who elected them on how to deal with any issue. They would be delegates, not representatives, and so would attend any confederal meeting with specific instructions on how to vote on a particular issue. **Recallable** means that if they do not vote according to that mandate they will be replaced and the results of the vote nullified. The delegates, in other words, would be given imperative mandates (binding instructions) that committed them to a framework of policies within which they would have to act, and they could be recalled and their decisions revoked at any time for failing to carry out the mandates they were given (this support for mandated delegates has existed in anarchist theory since at least 1848, when Proudhon argued that it was *"a consequence of universal suffrage"* to ensure that *"the people … do not … abjure their sovereignty."* [**Property is Theft!**, p. 379]). Because of this right of mandating and recalling their delegates, the workers' assemblies at the base would be the source of, and final "authority" (so to speak) over, policy for all higher levels of confederal co-ordination of the economy. Delegates will be ordinary workers rather than paid full-time representatives or union leaders, and they will return to their usual jobs as soon as the mandate for which they have been elected has been carried out. In this way, decision-making power remains with the workers' councils and does not become concentrated at the top of a bureaucratic hierarchy in an elite class of professional administrators or union leaders. What these confederations could do is discussed in the next section.

In summary, a free society *"is freely organised, from the bottom to top, staring from individuals that unite in associations which slowly grow bit by bit into ever more complex federations of associations"*. [Malatesta, **At the Cafe**, p. 65]

I.3.5 What would confederations of syndicates do?

Voluntary confederation among syndicates is considered necessary by social anarchists for numerous reasons but mostly in order to decide on the policies governing relations between syndicates and to co-ordinate their activities. This could vary from agreeing technical standards, to producing guidelines and policies on specific issues, to agreeing major investment decisions or prioritising certain large-scale economic projects or areas of research. In addition, they would be the means by which disputes could be solved and any tendencies back towards capitalism or some other class society identified and acted upon.

This can be seen from Proudhon, who was the first to suggest the need for such federations. *"All my economic ideas, elaborated for twenty-five years,"* he stated, *"can be summarised in these three words: Agricultural-Industrial Federation"* This was required because *"[h]owever irreproachable the federal constitution may be in its logic ... it can only last as long as it does not encounter constant causes of dissolution in public economy. In other words, political right must have the buttress of economic right."* A free society could not survive *"divided in two classes, one of owners-capitalists-entrepreneurs, the other of wage-earning proletarians; one rich, the other poor."* Thus *"from an economic standpoint, one can federate for a mutual protection in commerce and industry ... The aim of these particular federations is to shield the citizens ... from bankocratic and capitalist exploitation, as much from the inside as from the outside; they form by their ensemble ... an agricultural-industrial federation"* [**Property is Theft!**, p. 714, p. 709 and p. 711]

While capitalism results in *"interest on capital"* and *"economic serfdom or wage-labour, in a word, the inequality of conditions and fortunes"*, the *"agricultural-industrial federation ... tends to approximate equality more and more ... by mutual credit and insurance ... guaranteeing work and education, by a combination of work to allow each worker to evolve from a mere labourer to a skilled worker or even an artist, and from a wage-earner to their own master."* The *"industrial federation"* will apply *"on the highest scale"* the *"principles of mutuality"* and *"economic solidarity"*. As *"industries are sisters"*, they *"are parts of the same body"* and *"one cannot suffer without the others suffering because of it. "* They should therefore *"federate, not to absorb one another and merge, but to mutually guarantee the conditions of prosperity that are common to them all and on which none can claim a monopoly."* [**Op. Cit.**, pp. 712-3]

Later anarchists took up, built upon and clarified these ideas of economic federation. There are two basic kinds of confederation: an industrial one (i.e., a federation of all workplaces of a certain type) and a regional one (i.e. a federation of all syndicates within a given economic area). Thus there would be a federation for each industry and a federation of all syndicates in a geographical area. Both would operate at different levels, meaning there would be confederations for both industrial and inter-industrial associations at the local and regional levels and beyond. The basic aim of this inter-industry and cross-industry networking is to ensure that the relevant information is spread across the various parts of the economy so that each can effectively co-ordinate its plans with the others in a way which minimises ecological and social harm. Thus there would be a railway workers confederation to manage the rail network but the local, regional and national depots and stations would send a delegate to meet regularly with the other syndicates in the same geographical area to discuss general economic issues.

However, it is essential to remember that each syndicate within the confederation is autonomous. The confederations seek to co-ordinate activities of joint interest (in particular investment decisions for new plant and the rationalisation of existing plant in light of reduced demand). They do not determine what work a syndicate does or how they do it:

> *"With the factory thus largely conducting its own concerns, the duties of the larger Guild organisations [i.e. confederations] would be mainly those of co-ordination, or regulation, and of representing the Guild in its external relations. They would, where it was necessary, co-ordinate the production of various factories, so as to make supply coincide with demand... they would organise research ... This large Guild organisation... must be based directly on the various factories included in the Guild."* [Cole, **Guild Socialism Restated**, pp. 59-60]

So it is important to note that the lowest units of confederation — the workers' assemblies — will control the higher levels, through their power to elect mandated and recallable delegates to meetings of higher confederal units. It would be fair to make the assumption that the "higher" up the federation a decision is made, the more general it will be. Due to the complexity of life it would be difficult for federations which cover wide areas to plan large-scale projects in any detail and so would be, in practice, more forums for agreeing guidelines and priorities than planning actual specific projects or economies. As Russian anarcho-syndicalist G.P. Maximov put it, the aim *"was to co-ordinate all activity, all local interest, to create a centre but not a centre of decrees and ordinances but a centre of regulation, of guidance — and only through such a centre to organise the industrial life of the country."* [quoted by M. Brinton, **For Workers' Power**, p. 330]

So this is a decentralised system, with the workers' assemblies and councils at the base having the final say on **all** policy decisions, being able to revoke policies made by those with delegated decision-making power and to recall those who made them:

> *"When it comes to the material and technical method of production, anarchists have no preconceived solutions or absolute prescriptions, and bow to what experience and conditions in a free society recommend and prescribe. What matters is that, whatever the type of production adopted, it should be the free choice of the producers themselves, and cannot possibly be imposed, any more than any form is possible of exploitations of another's labour... Anarchists do not **a priori** exclude any practical solution and likewise concede that there may be a number of different solutions at different times."* [Luigi Fabbri,

Confederations would exist for specific reasons. Mutualists, as can be seen from Proudhon, are aware of the dangers associated with even a self-managed, socialistic market and create support structures to defend workers' self-management. Moreover, it is likely that industrial syndicates would be linked to mutual banks (a credit syndicate). Such syndicates would exist to provide interest-free credit for self-management, new syndicate expansion and so on. And if the experience of capitalism is anything to go by, mutual banks will also reduce the business cycle as *"[c]ountries like Japan and Germany that are usually classified as bank-centred — because banks provide more outside finance than markets, and because more firms have long-term relationships with their banks — show greater growth in and stability of investment over time than the market-centred ones, like the US and Britain ... Further, studies comparing German and Japanese firms with tight bank ties to those without them also show that firms with bank ties exhibit greater stability in investment over the business cycle."* [Doug Henwood, **Wall Street**, pp. 174-5]

One argument against co-operatives is that they do not allow the diversification of risk (all the worker's eggs are in one basket). Ignoring the obvious point that most workers today do not have shares and are dependent on their job to survive, this objection can be addressed by means of *"the **horizontal association** or grouping of enterprises to pool their business risk. The Mondragon co-operatives are associated together in a number of regional groups that pool their profits in varying degrees. Instead of a worker diversifying his or her capital in six companies, six companies partially pool their profits in a group or federation and accomplish the same risk-reduction purpose without transferable equity capital."* Thus *"risk-pooling in federations of co-operatives"* ensure that *"transferable equity capital is not necessary to obtain risk diversification in the flow of annual worker income."* [David Ellerman, **The Democratic Worker-Owned Firm**, p. 104] Moreover, as the example of many isolated co-operatives under capitalism have shown, support networks are essential for co-operatives to survive. It is no co-incidence that the Mondragon co-operative complex in the Basque region of Spain has a credit union and mutual support networks between its co-operatives and is by far the most successful co-operative system in the world. The *"agro-industrial federation"* exists precisely for these reasons.

Under collectivist and communist anarchism, the federations would have addition tasks. There are two key roles. Firstly, the sharing and co-ordination of information produced by the syndicates and, secondly, determining the response to the changes in production and consumption indicated by this information.

Confederations (negotiated-co-ordination bodies) would be responsible for clearly defined branches of production, and in general, production units would operate in only one branch of production. These confederations would have direct links to other confederations and the relevant communal confederations, which supply the syndicates with guidelines for decision making (see section I.4.4) and ensure that common problems can be highlighted and discussed. These confederations exist to ensure that information is spread between workplaces and to ensure that the industry responds to changes in social demand. In other words, these confederations exist to co-ordinate major new investment decisions (i.e. if demand exceeds supply) and to determine how to respond if there is excess capacity (i.e. if supply exceeds demand).

It should be pointed out that these confederated investment decisions will exist along with the investments associated with the creation of new syndicates, plus internal syndicate investment decisions. We are not suggesting that **every** investment decision is to be made by the confederations. (This would be particularly impossible for **new** industries, for which a confederation would not exist!) Therefore, in addition to co-ordinated production units, an anarchist society would see numerous small-scale, local activities which would ensure creativity, diversity, and flexibility. Only after these activities had spread across society would confederal co-ordination become necessary. So while production will be based on autonomous networking, the investment response to consumer actions would, to some degree, be co-ordinated by a confederation of syndicates in that branch of production. By such means, the confederation can ensure that resources are not wasted by individual syndicates over-producing goods or over-investing in response to changes in production. By communicating across workplaces, people can overcome the barriers to co-ordinating their plans which one finds in market systems (see section C.7.2) and so avoid the economic and social disruptions associated with them.

Thus, major investment decisions would be made at congresses and plenums of the industry's syndicates, by a process of horizontal, negotiated co-ordination. Major investment decisions are co-ordinated at an appropriate level, with each unit in the confederation being autonomous, deciding what to do with its own productive capacity in order to meet social demand. Thus we have self-governing production units co-ordinated by confederations (horizontal negotiation), which ensures local initiative (a vital source of flexibility, creativity, and diversity) and a rational response to changes in social demand. As links between syndicates are non-hierarchical, each syndicate remains self-governing. This ensures decentralisation of power and direct control, initiative, and experimentation by those involved in doing the work.

It should be noted that during the Spanish Revolution the self-managed workplaces successfully federated in many different ways. Gaston Leval noted that these forms of confederation did not harm the libertarian nature of self-management:

> *"Everything was controlled by the syndicates. But it must not therefore be assumed that everything was decided by a few higher bureaucratic committees without consulting the rank and file members of the union. Here libertarian democracy was practised. As in the C.N.T. there was a reciprocal double structure; from the grass roots at the base ... upwards, and in the other direction a reciprocal influence from the federation of these same local units at all levels downwards, from the source back to the source."*
> [**The Anarchist Collectives**, p. 105]

The exact nature of any confederal responsibilities will vary, although we *"prefer decentralised management; but ultimately, in practical and technical problems, we defer to free experience."* [Luigi Fabbri,

Op. Cit., p. 24] The specific form of organisation will obviously vary as required from industry to industry, area to area, but the underlying ideas of self-management and free association will be the same. Moreover, the *"essential thing … is that its [the confederation or guild] function should be kept down to the minimum possible for each industry."* [Cole, **Op. Cit.**, p. 61]

Another important role for inter-syndicate federations is to even-out inequalities. After all, each area will not be identical in terms of natural resources, quality of land, situation, accessibility, and so on. Simply put, social anarchists *"believe that because of natural differences in fertility, health and location of the soil it would be impossible to ensure that every individual enjoyed equal working conditions."* Under such circumstances, it would be *"impossible to achieve a state of equality from the beginning"* and so *"justice and equity are, for natural reasons, impossible to achieve … and that freedom would thus also be unachievable."* [Malatesta, **The Anarchist Revolution**, p. 16 and p. 21]

This was recognised by Proudhon, who saw the need for economic federation due to differences in raw materials, quality of land and so on, and as such argued that a portion of income from agricultural produce be paid into a central fund which would be used to make equalisation payments to compensate farmers with less favourably situated or less fertile land. As he put it, economic rent *"in agriculture has no other cause than the inequality in the quality of land … if anyone has a claim on account of this inequality … [it is] the other land workers who hold inferior land. That is why in our scheme for liquidation [of capitalism] we stipulated that every variety of cultivation should pay a proportional contribution, destined to accomplish a balancing of returns among farm workers and an assurance of products."* In addition, *"all the communes of the Republic shall come to an understanding for equalising among them the quality of tracts of land, as well as accidents of culture."* [**Property is Theft!**, p. 582 and p. 578]

By federating together, workers can ensure that *"the earth will … be an economic domain available to everyone, the riches of which will be enjoyed by all human beings."* [Malatesta, **Errico Malatesta: His Life and Ideas**, p. 93] Local deficiencies of raw materials, in the quality of land, and, therefore, supplies would be compensated from outside, by the socialisation of production and consumption. This would allow all of humanity to share and benefit from economic activity, so ensuring that well-being for all is possible.

Federation would eliminate the possibility of rich and poor collectives and syndicates co-existing side by side. As Kropotkin argued, *"[c]ommon possession of the necessities for production implies the common enjoyment of the fruits of common production … when everybody, contributing for the common well-being to the full extent of his [or her] capacities, shall enjoy also from the common stock of society to the fullest possible extent of his [or her] needs."* [**Anarchism**, p. 59] Hence we find the CNT arguing in its 1936 resolution on libertarian communism that *"[a]s far as the interchange of produce between communes is concerned, the communal councils are to liase with the regional federations of communes and with the confederal council of production and distribution, applying for whatever they may need and [giving] any available surplus stocks."* [quoted by Jose Peirats, **The CNT in the Spanish Revolution**, vol. 1, p. 107] This clearly followed Kropotkin's comments that the

"socialising of production, consumption, and exchange" would be based on workplaces *"belong[ing] to federated Communes."* [**The Conquest of Bread**, p. 136]

> The legacy of capitalism, with its rich and poor areas, its rich and poor workplaces, will be a problem any revolution will face. The inequalities produced by centuries of class society will take time to change. This is one of the tasks of the confederation, to ensure the socialisation of both production and consumption so that people are not penalised for the accidents of history and that each commune can develop itself to an adequate level.

Workers' self-management does not automatically mean that all forms of economic domination and exploitation would be eliminated. After all, in a market economy firms can accrue super-profits simply because of their size or control over a specific technology or resource. Hence Proudhon's suggestion that *"advocates of mutualism"* would *"regulate the market"* to ensure *"an honest breakdown of cost prices"*, fix *"after amicable discussion of a **maximum** and **minimum** profit margin"* and *"the organising of regulating societies."* [**Op. Cit.**, pp. 33-4] It seems likely that the agro-industrial federation would be the body which ensures that. Similarly, the federation would be the means by which to air, and deal with, suggestions that syndicates are monopolising their resources, i.e., treating them as private property rather than socialised possessions. Thus the federation would unite workers *"to guarantee the mutual use of the tools of production"* which are, *"by a reciprocal contract"*, the *"collective property of the whole."* [James Guillaume, *"On Building the New Social Order"*, pp. 356-79, **Bakunin on Anarchism**, p. 376]

The inter-industry confederations help ensure that when the members of a syndicate change work to another syndicate in another (or the same) branch of industry, they have the same rights as the members of their new syndicate. In other words, by being part of the confederation, a worker ensures that s/he has the same rights and an equal say in whatever workplace is joined. This is essential to ensure that a co-operative society remains co-operative, as the system is based on the principle of *"one person, one vote"* by all those involved the work process. If specific syndicates **are** restricting access and so producing wage-labour, monopolising resources and so charging monopoly prices, the federation would be a forum to publicly shame such syndicates and organise boycotts of them. Such anti-social activity is unlikely to be tolerated by a free people seeking to protect that freedom.

However, it could again be argued that these confederations are still centralised and that workers would still be following orders coming from above. This is incorrect, for any decisions concerning an industry or plant are under the direct control of those involved. For example, the steel industry confederation may decide to rationalise itself at one of its congresses. Murray Bookchin sketches the response to this situation as follows:

> *"let us suppose that a board of highly qualified technicians is established [by this congress] to propose changes in the steel industry. This board … advances proposals to rationalise the industry by closing down some plants and*

*expanding the operation of others ... Is this a 'centralised' body or not? The answer is both yes and no. Yes, only in the sense that the board is dealing with problems that concern the country as a whole; no, because it can make no decision that **must** be executed for the country as a whole. The board's plan must be examined by all the workers in the plants [that are affected] ... The board itself has no power to enforce 'decisions'; it merely makes recommendations. Additionally, its personnel are controlled by the plant in which they work and the locality in which they live ... they would have no decision-making powers. The adoption, modification or rejection of their plans would rest entirely with ... [those] involved."* [**Post Scarcity Anarchism**, p. 180]

Therefore, confederations would not be in positions of power over the individual syndicates. No attempt is made to determine which plants produce which steel for which customers in which manner. Thus, the confederations of syndicates ensure a decentralised, spontaneous economic order without the negative side-effects of capitalism (namely power concentrations within firms and in the market, periodic crises, etc.).

As one can imagine, an essential feature of these confederations will be the collection and processing of information in order to determine how an industry is developing. This does not imply bureaucracy or centralised control at the top. Taking the issue of centralisation first, the confederation is run by delegate assemblies, meaning that any officers elected at a congress only implement the decisions made by the delegates of the relevant syndicates. It is in the congresses and plenums of the confederation that new investment decisions, for example, are made. The key point to remember is that the confederation exists purely to co-ordinate joint activity and share information, it does not take an interest in how a workplace is run or what orders from consumers it fills. (Of course, if a given workplace introduces policies which other syndicates disapprove of, it can be expelled). As the delegates to these congresses and plenums are mandated and their decisions subject to rejection and modification by each productive unit, the confederation is not centralised.

As far as bureaucracy goes, the collecting and processing of information does necessitate an administrative staff to do the work. However, this problem affects capitalist firms as well; and since syndicates are based on bottom-up decision making, its clear that, unlike a centralised capitalist corporation, administration would be smaller. In fact, it is likely that a fixed administration staff for the confederation would not exist in the first place! At the regular congresses, a particular syndicate may be selected to do the confederation's information processing, with this job being rotated regularly around different syndicates. In this way, a specific administrative body and equipment can be avoided and the task of collating information placed directly in the hands of ordinary workers. Further, it prevents the development of a bureaucratic elite by ensuring that **all** participants are versed in information-processing procedures.

Lastly, what information would be collected? That depends on the context. Individual syndicates would record inputs and outputs, producing summary sheets of information. For example, total energy input, in kilowatts and by type, raw material inputs, labour hours spent, orders received, orders accepted, output, and so forth. This information can be processed into energy use and labour time per product (for example), in order to give an idea of how efficient production is and how it is changing over time. For confederations, the output of individual syndicates can be aggregated and local and other averages can be calculated. In addition, changes in demand can be identified by this aggregation process and used to identify when investment will be needed or plants closed down. In this way the chronic slumps and booms of capitalism can be avoided without creating a system which is even more centralised than capitalism.

I.3.6 What about competition between syndicates?

This is a common question, particularly from defenders of capitalism. They argue that syndicates will not co-operate together unless forced to do so, and will compete against each other for raw materials, skilled workers, and so on. The result of this process, it is claimed, will be rich and poor syndicates, inequality within society and within the workplace, and (possibly) a class of unemployed workers from unsuccessful syndicates who are hired by successful ones. In other words, they argue that libertarian socialism will need to become authoritarian to prevent competition, and that if it does not do so it will become capitalist very quickly.

For individualist anarchists and mutualists, competition is not viewed as a problem. They think that competition, based around co-operatives and mutual banks, would minimise economic inequality, as the new economic structure based around free credit and co-operation would eliminate non-labour (i.e. unearned) income such as profit, interest and rent and give workers enough bargaining power to eliminate exploitation. For these anarchists it is a case of capitalism perverting competition and so are not against competition itself. Other anarchists think that whatever gains might accrue from competition (assuming there are, in fact, any) would be more than offset by its negative effects, which are outlined in section I.1.3. It is to these anarchists that the question is usually asked.

Before continuing, we would like to point out that individuals trying to improve their lot in life is not against anarchist principles. How could it be? Being selfish *"is not a crime,"* John Most and Emma Goldman noted, *"it only becomes a crime when conditions are such as to give an individual the opportunity to satisfy his selfishness to the detriment of others. In an anarchistic society everyone will seek to satisfy his ego"* but in order to do so he *"will extend his aid to those who will aid him, and then selfishness will no more be a curse but a blessing."* [*"Talking about Anarchy"*, **Black Flag**, no. 228, p. 28] Thus anarchists see co-operation and mutual aid as an expression of "self-interest", in that working with people as equals is in our joint benefit. In the words of John O'Neill:

> *"for it is the institutions themselves that define what counts as one's interests. In particular, the market encourages egoism, not primarily because it encourages an individual to be 'self-interested' — it would be unrealistic not to*

expect individuals to act for the greater part in a 'self-interested' manner — but rather because it defines an individual's interests in a particularly narrow fashion, most notably in terms of possession of certain material goods. In consequence, where market mechanism enter a particular sphere of life, the pursuit of goods outside this narrow range of market goods is institutionally defined as an act of altruism." [**The Market**, p. 158]

As such, anarchists would suggest that we should not confuse competition with self-interest and that a co-operative society would tend to promote institutions and customs which would ensure that people recognised that co-operation between equals maximises individual freedom and self-interest far more than individualistic pursuit to material wealth at the expense of all other goals. Ultimately, what use would it be to gain the world and loose what makes life worth living?

Of course, such a society would not be based on exactly equal shares of everything. Rather, it would mean equal opportunity and free, or equal, access to resources (for example, that only ill people use medical resources is unproblematic for egalitarians!). So a society with unequal distributions of resources is not automatically a non-anarchist one. What **is** against anarchist principles is centralised power, oppression, and exploitation, all of which flow from large inequalities of income and private property. This is the source of anarchist concern about equality — concern that is not based on some sort of *"politics of envy."* Anarchists oppose inequality because it soon leads to the few oppressing the many (a relationship which distorts the individuality and liberty of all involved as well as the health and very lives of the oppressed).

Anarchists desire to create a society in which such relationships are impossible, believing that the most effective way to do this is by empowering all, by creating an egoistic concern for liberty and equality among the oppressed, and by developing social organisations which encourage self-management. As for individuals' trying to improve their lot, anarchists maintain that co-operation is the best means to do so, **not** competition. And there is substantial evidence to support this claim (for example, Alfie Kohn's **No Contest: The Case Against Competition** and Robert Axelrod's **The Evolution of Co-operation** present abundant evidence that co-operation is in our long term interests and provides better results than short term competition). This suggests that, as Kropotkin argued, mutual aid, not mutual struggle, will be in an individual's self-interest and so competition in a free, sane society would be minimised and reduced to sports and other individual pastimes. As Stirner argued, co-operation is just as egoistic as competition (a fact sometimes lost on many due to the obvious ethical superiority of co-operation):

> *"But should competition some day disappear, because concerted effort will have been acknowledged as more beneficial than isolation, then will not every single individual inside the associations be equally egoistic and out for his own interests?"* [**No Gods, No Masters**, vol. 1, p. 22]

Now to the "competition" objection, which we'll begin to answer by noting that it ignores a few key points.

Firstly, the assumption that a libertarian society would "become capitalist" in the absence of a **state** is obviously false. If competition did occur between collectives and did lead to massive wealth inequalities, then the newly rich would have to create a state to protect their private property against the dispossessed. So inequality, not equality, leads to the creation of states. It is no co-incidence that the anarchic communities that existed for millennia were also egalitarian.

Secondly, as noted in section A.2.5, anarchists do not consider *"equal"* to mean *"identical."* Therefore, to claim that wage differences mean the end of anarchism makes sense only if one thinks that *"equality"* means everyone getting **exactly** equal shares. As anarchists do not hold such an idea, wage differences in an otherwise anarchistically organised syndicate do not indicate a lack of equality. How the syndicate is **run** is of far more importance, because the most pernicious type of inequality from the anarchist standpoint is inequality of **power,** i.e. unequal influence on political and economic decision making.

Under capitalism, wealth inequality translates into such an inequality of power, and vice versa, because wealth can buy private property (and state protection of it), which gives owners authority over that property and those hired to produce with it; but under libertarian socialism, minor or even moderate differences in income among otherwise equal workers would not lead to this kind of power inequality, because self-management and socialisation severs the link between wealth and power. Moreover, when labour becomes free in a society of rebels (and, surely, an anarchist society could be nothing but) few would tolerate relatively minor income inequalities becoming a source of power.

Thirdly, anarchists do not pretend that an anarchist society will be perfect. Hence there may be periods, particularly just after capitalism has been replaced by self-management, when differences in skill, etc., leads to some people exploiting their position and getting more wages, better hours and conditions, and so forth. This problem existed in the industrial collectives in the Spanish Revolution. As Kropotkin pointed out, *"[b]ut, when all is said and done, some inequalities, some inevitable injustice, undoubtedly will remain. There are individuals in our societies whom no great crisis can lift out of the deep mire of egoism in which they are sunk. The question, however, is not whether there will be injustices or no, but rather how to limit the number of them."* [**The Conquest of Bread**, p. 94]

In other words, these problems will exist, but there are a number of things that anarchists can do to minimise their impact. There will be a *"gestation period"* before the birth of an anarchist society, in which social struggle, new forms of education and child-rearing, and other methods of consciousness-raising increase the number of anarchists and decrease the number of authoritarians.

The most important element in this gestation period is social struggle. Such self-activity will have a major impact on those involved in it (see section J.2). By direct action and solidarity, those involved develop bounds of friendship and support with others, develop new forms of ethics and new ideas and ideal. This radicalisation process will help to ensure that any differences in education and skill do not develop into differences in power in an anarchist society by making people less likely to exploit their advantages nor, more importantly, for others to tolerate them doing so!

In addition, education within the anarchist movement should aim, among other things, to give its members familiarity with technological skills so that they are not dependent on "experts" and can thus increase the pool of skilled workers who will be happy working in conditions of liberty and equality. This will ensure that differentials between workers can be minimised. In the long run, however, popularisation of non-authoritarian methods of child-rearing and education (see section J.6) are particularly important because, as we suggested in section B.1.5, secondary drives such as greed and the desire the exercise power over others are products of authoritarian upbringing based on punishments and fear. Only if the prevalence of such drives is reduced among the general population can we be sure that an anarchist revolution will not degenerate into some new form of domination and exploitation.

However, there are other reasons why economic inequality — say, in differences of income levels or working conditions, which may arise from competition for "better" workers — would be far less severe under any form of anarchist society than it is under capitalism.

Firstly, the syndicates would be democratically managed. This would result in much smaller wage differentials, because there is no board of wealthy directors setting wage levels for their own gain. So without hierarchies in the workplace no one would be in a position to monopolise the work of others and grow rich as a result:

> "Poverty is the symptom: slavery the disease. The extremes of riches and destitution follow inevitably upon the extremes of license and bondage. The many are not enslaved because they are poor, they are poor because they are enslaved. Yet Socialists have all too often fixed their eyes upon the material misery of the poor without realising that it rests upon the spiritual degradation of the slave." [G.D.H. Cole, **Self-Government in Industry**, p. 41]

Empirical evidence supports anarchist claims as co-operatives have a far more egalitarian wage structure than capitalist firms. This can be seen from the experience of the Mondragon co-operatives, where the wage difference between the highest paid and lowest paid worker was 4 to 1. This was only increased when they had to compete with large capitalist companies, and even then the new ratio of 9 to 1 is **far** smaller than those in capitalist companies (in America the ratio is 200 to 1 and beyond!). Thus, even under capitalism, there "is evidence that the methods of distribution chosen by worker-controlled or self-managed firms are more egalitarian than distribution according to market precepts." [Christopher Eaton Gunn, **Workers' Self-Management in the United States**, p. 45] Given that market precepts fail to take into account power differences, this is unsurprising. Thus we can predict that a fully self-managed economy would be just as, if not, more egalitarian as differences in power would be eliminated, as would unemployment (James K. Galbraith, in his book **Created Unequal**, has presented extensive evidence that unemployment increases inequality, as would be expected).

It is a common myth that managers, executives and so on are paid so highly because of their unique abilities. Actually, they are so highly paid because they are bureaucrats in command of large hierarchical institutions. It is the hierarchical nature of the capitalist firm that ensures inequality, **not** exceptional skills. Even enthusiastic supporters of capitalism provide evidence to support this claim. In the 1940s Peter Drucker, a supporter of capitalism, brushed away the claim that corporate organisation brings managers with exceptional ability to the top when he noted that "[n]o institution can possibly survive if it needs geniuses or supermen to manage it. It must be organised in such a way as to be able to get along under a leadership of average human beings." For Drucker, "the things that really count are not the individual members but the relations of command and responsibility among them." [**Concept of the Corporation**, p. 35 and p. 34] Little has changed, beyond the power of PR to personalise the bureaucratic structures of corporations.

Secondly, having no means of unearned income (such as rent, interest and intellectual property rights), anarchism will reduce income differentials substantially.

Thirdly, management positions would be rotated, ensuring that everyone gets experience of the work, thus reducing the artificial scarcity created by the division of labour. Also, education would be extensive, ensuring that engineers, doctors, and other skilled workers would do the work because they **enjoyed** doing it and not for financial reward.

Fourthly, we should like to point out that people work for many reasons, not just for high wages. Feelings of solidarity, empathy, friendship with their fellow workers would also help reduce competition between syndicates.

Of course, the "competition" objection assumes that syndicates and members of syndicates will place financial considerations above all else. This is not the case, and few individuals are the economic robots assumed in capitalist dogma. Indeed, the evidence from co-operatives refutes such claims (ignoring, for the moment, the vast evidence of our own senses and experiences with real people rather than the insane "economic man" of capitalist economic ideology). As noted in section I.3.1 neo-classical economic theory, deducing from its basic assumptions, argues that members of co-operatives will aim to maximise profit per worker and so, perversely, fire their members during good times. Reality contradicts these claims. In other words, the underlying assumption that people are economic robots cannot be maintained — there is extensive evidence pointing to the fact that different forms of social organisation produce different considerations which motivate people accordingly.

So, while recognising that competition could exist, anarchists think there are plenty of reasons not to worry about massive economic inequality being created, which in turn would re-create the state. The apologists for capitalism who put forward this argument forget that the pursuit of self-interest is universal, meaning that everyone would be interested in maximising his or her liberty, and so would be unlikely to allow inequalities to develop which threatened that liberty. It would be in the interests of communes and syndicates to share with others instead of charging high prices for them as they may find themselves boycotted by others, and so denied the advantages of social co-operation. Moreover, they may be subject to such activities themselves and so it would wise for them to remember to "treat others as you would like them to treat you under similar circumstances." As anarchism will never come about unless people desire it and start to organise their own lives, it is clear that an anarchist society would be inhabited by individuals who followed that ethical principle.

So it is doubtful that people inspired by anarchist ideas would start to charge each other high prices, particularly since the syndicates and community assemblies are likely to vote for a wide basis of surplus distribution, precisely to avoid this problem and to ensure that production will be for use rather than profit. In addition, as other communities and syndicates would likely boycott any syndicate or commune that was acting in non-co-operative ways, it is likely that social pressure would soon result in those willing to exploit others rethinking their position. Co-operation does not imply a willingness to tolerate those who desire to take advantage of you. In other words, neither mutual aid nor anarchist theory implies people are naive indiscriminate altruists but rather people who, while willing to work with others co-operatively, will act to stop others taking advantage of them. Mutual aid, in other words is based on reciprocal relationships. If someone or a syndicate does not co-operate but rather seeks to take advantage of others, then the others are well within their rights to boycott them and otherwise protest against them. A free society is based on **all** people pursuing their self-interest, not just the few. This suggests that anarchists reject the assumption that those who lose by competition should be altruistic and let competition ruin their lives.

Moreover, given the experience of the neo-liberal period from the 1980s onwards (with rising inequality marked by falling growth, lower wage growth, rising unemployment and increased economic instability) the impact of increased competition and inequality harms the vast majority. It is doubtful that people aware of these tendencies (and that, as we argued in section F.3, "free exchange" in an unequal society tends to **increase**, not decrease, inequality) would create such a regime.

Unsurprisingly, examples of anarchism in action show that there are ways of working together to reduce the dangers of isolation and competition. One thing to remember is that anarchy will not be created "overnight" and so potential problems will be worked out over time. Underlying all these kinds of objections is the assumption that co-operation will **not** be more beneficial to all involved than competition. However, in terms of quality of life, co-operation will soon be seen to be the better system, even by the most highly paid workers. There is far more to life than the size of one's pay packet, and anarchism exists in order to ensure that life is far more than the weekly grind of boring work and the few hours of hectic consumption in which people attempt to fill the "spiritual hole" created by a way of life which places profits above people.

I.3.7 What about people who do not want to join a syndicate?

In this case, they are free to work alone, by their own labour. Anarchists have no desire to force people to join a syndicate. Emma Goldman spoke for all anarchists when she stated that "[w]e believe in every person living his own life in his own way and not in coercing others to follow any one's dictation." [**A Documentary History of the American Years**, vol. 2, p. 324]

Therefore, the decision to join a syndicate will be a free one, with the potential for living outside it guaranteed for non-exploitative and non-oppressive individuals and groups. Malatesta stressed this when he argued that in an anarchist revolution "what has to be destroyed at once … is **capitalistic property,** that is, the fact that a few control the natural wealth and the instruments of production and can thus oblige others to work for them" but one must have a "right and the possibility to live in a different regime, collectivist, mutualist, individualist — as one wishes, always on the condition that there is no oppression or exploitation of others." [**Errico Malatesta: Life and Ideas**, p. 102] In other words, different forms of social life will be experimented with, depending on what people desire.

Of course some people ask how anarchists can reconcile individual freedom with expropriation of capital. All we can say is that these critics subscribe to the idea that one should not interfere with the "individual freedom" of those in positions of authority to oppress others, and that this premise turns the concept of individual freedom on its head, making oppression a "right" and the denial of freedom a form of it!

However, it is a valid question to ask if anarchism would result in self-employed people being forced into syndicates as the result of a popular movement. The answer is no. This is because the destruction of title deeds would not harm the independent worker, whose real title is possession and the work done. What anarchists want to eliminate is not possession but capitalist **property**. Thus such workers "may prefer to work alone in his own small shop" rather than join an association or a federation. [James Guillaume, "On Building the New Social Order", pp. 356-79, **Bakunin on Anarchism**, p. 362]

This means that independent producers will still exist within an anarchist society, and some workplaces — perhaps whole areas — will not be part of a confederation. This is natural in a free society for different people to have different ideas and ideals. Nor do such independent producers imply a contradiction with libertarian socialism, for "[w]hat we concerned with is the destruction of the titles of proprietors who exploit the labour of others and, above all, of expropriating them in fact in order to put … all the means of production at the disposal of those who do the work." [Malatesta, **Op. Cit.**, p. 103] Such freedom to work independently or associate as desired does **not** imply any support for private property (as discussed in section I.6.2). Thus any individual in a libertarian socialist economy "always has the liberty to isolate himself and work alone, without being considered a bad citizen or a suspect." [Proudhon, quoted by K. Steven Vincent, **Pierre-Joseph Proudhon and the Rise of French Republican Socialism**, p. 145]

In summary, in a free society people need not join syndicates nor does a co-operative need to confederate with others. Given we have discussed the issue of freedom of economic arrangements at length in section G.2.1 we will leave this discussion here.

I.3.8 Do anarchists seek "small autonomous communities, devoted to small scale production"?

No. The idea that anarchism aims for small, self-sufficient, communes is a Leninist slander. They misrepresent anarchist ideas on this matter, suggesting that anarchists seriously want society based on *"small autonomous communities, devoted to small scale production."* In particular, they point to Kropotkin, arguing that he *"looked backwards for change"* and *"witnessed such communities among Siberian peasants and watchmakers in the Swiss mountains."* [Pat Stack, *"Anarchy in the UK?"*, **Socialist Review**, no. 246] Another Leninist, Donny Gluckstein, makes a similar assertion about Proudhon wanting a federation of *"tiny economic units"*. [**The Paris Commune**, p. 75]

So what do anarchists make of the assertion that we aim for *"small autonomous communities, devoted to small scale production"*? Simply put, we think it is nonsense (as would be quickly obvious from reading anarchist theory). Indeed, it is hard to know where this particular anarchist "vision" comes from. As Luigi Fabbri noted, in his reply to an identical assertion by the leading Bolshevik Nikolai Bukharin, *"[i]t would be interesting to learn in what anarchist book, pamphlet or programme such an 'ideal' is set out, or even such a hard and fast rule!"* [*"Anarchy and 'Scientific' Communism"*, pp. 13-49, **The Poverty of Statism**, Albert Meltzer (ed.), p. 21] If we look at, say, Proudhon, we soon see no such argument for "small scale" production: *"Large industry and high culture come to us by big monopoly and big property: it is necessary in the future to make them rise from the [workers] association."* In fact, he **explicitly** rejected the position Stack inflicts on him by arguing that it *"would be to retrograde"* and *"impossible"* to wish *"the division of labour, with machinery and manufactures, to be abandoned, and each family to return to the system of primitive indivision, - that is, to **each one by himself, each one for himself**, in the most literal meaning of the words."* [**Property is Theft!**, p. 11 and p. 194] As historian K. Steven Vincent correctly summarises:

> *"On this issue, it is necessary to emphasise that, contrary to the general image given in the secondary literature, Proudhon was not hostile to large industry. Clearly, he objected to many aspects of what these large enterprises had introduced into society. For example, Proudhon strenuously opposed the degrading character of ... work which required an individual to repeat one minor function continuously. But he was not opposed in principle to large-scale production. What he desired was to humanise such production, to socialise it so that the worker would not be the mere appendage to a machine. Such a humanisation of large industries would result, according to Proudhon, from the introduction of strong workers' associations. These associations would enable the workers to determine jointly by election how the enterprise was to be directed and operated on a day-to-day basis."* [**Proudhon and the Rise of French Republican Socialism,** p. 156]

Moreover, Proudhon did not see an anarchist society as one of isolated communities or workplaces. Like other anarchists, as we discussed in section I.3.4, Proudhon saw a free society's productive activity centred around federations of syndicates.

This vision of a federation of workplaces can also be found in Bakunin's writings: *"The future organisation of society must proceed from the bottom up only, through free association or federations of the workers, into their associations to begin with, then into communes, regions, nations and, finally, into a great international and universal federation."* [**No Gods, No Masters**, vol. 1, p. 176] Like Proudhon, Bakunin also explicitly rejected the idea of seeking small-scale production, arguing that *"if [the workers] tried to divide among themselves the capital that exists, they would ... reduce to a large decree its productive power."* Therefore the need was for *"the collective property of capital"* to ensure *"the emancipation **of** labour and of the workers."* [**The Basic Bakunin**, p. 91] Bakunin, again like Proudhon, considered that *"[i]ntelligent free labour will necessarily be associated labour"* as under capitalism the worker *"works for others"* and her labour is *"bereft of liberty, leisure and intelligence."* Under anarchism, *"the free productive associations"* would become *"their own masters and the owners of the necessary capital"* and *"amalgamate among themselves"* and *"sooner or later"* will *"expand beyond national frontiers"* and *"form one vast economic federation."* [**Michael Bakunin: Selected Writings**, pp. 81-3]

Nor can such a vision be attributed to Kropotkin. While, of course, supporting decentralisation of power and decision making as did Proudhon and Bakunin, he did not reject the necessity of federations to co-ordinate activity. As he put it, the *"commune of tomorrow will know that it cannot admit any higher authority; above it there can only be the interests of the Federation, freely accepted by itself as well as the other communes"*. For anarchists the commune *"no longer means a territorial agglomeration; it is rather a generic name, a synonym for the grouping of equals which knows neither frontiers nor walls ... Each group in the Commune will necessarily be drawn towards similar groups in other communes; they will come together and the links that federate them will be as solid as those that attach them to their fellow citizens."* [**Words of a Rebel**, p. 83 and p. 88] Nor did he reject industry or machinery, stating he *"understood the poetry of machinery"* and that while in *"our present factories, machinery work is killing for the worker"* this was *"a matter of bad organisation, and has nothing to do with the machine itself."* [**Memiors of a Revolutionist**, p. 111]

Kropotkin's vision was one of federations of decentralised communities in which production would be based on the *"scattering of industries over the country — so as to bring the factory amidst the fields ... agriculture ... combined with industry ... to produce a combination of industrial with agricultural work."* He considered this as *"surely the next step to be made, as soon as a reorganisation of our present conditions is possible"* and *"is imposed by the very necessity of **producing for the producers themselves.**"* [**Fields, Factories and Workshops Tomorrow**, pp. 157-8] He based this vision on a detailed analysis of current economic statistics and trends.

Kropotkin did not see such an anarchist economy as being based around the small community, taking the basic unit of a free society as one *"large enough to dispose of a certain variety* of natural resources — it may be a nation, or rather a region — produces and itself consumes most of its own agricultural and manufactured produce." Such a region would "find the best means of combining agriculture with manufacture — the work in the field with a decentralised industry." Moreover, he recognised that the "geographical distribution of industries in a given country depends ... to a great extent upon a complexus of natural conditions; it is obvious that there are spots which are best suited for the development of certain industries ... The[se] industries always find some advantages in being grouped, to some extent, according to the natural features of separate regions." [**Op. Cit.**, p. 26, p. 27 and pp. 154-5]

He stressed that agriculture "cannot develop without the aid of machinery and the use of a perfect machinery cannot be generalised without industrial surroundings ... The village smith would not do." He supported the integration of agriculture and industry, with "the factory and workshop at the gates of your fields and gardens" in which a "variety of agricultural, industrial and intellectual pursuits are combined in each community" to ensure "the greatest sum total of well-being." He thought that "large establishments" would still exist, but these would be "better placed at certain spots indicated by Nature." He stressed that it "would be a great mistake to imagine industry ought to return to its hand-work stage in order to be combined with agriculture. Whenever a saving of human labour can be obtained by means of a machine, the machine is welcome and will be resorted to; and there is hardly one single branch of industry into which machinery work could not be introduced with great advantage, at least at some of the stages of the manufacture." [**Op. Cit.**, p. 156, p. 197, p. 18, pp. 154-5 and pp. 151-2]

Clearly Kropotkin was **not** opposed to large-scale industry for "if we analyse the modern industries, we soon discover that for some of them the co-operation of hundred, even thousands, of workers gathered at the same spot is really necessary. The great iron works and mining enterprises decidedly belong to that category; oceanic steamers cannot be built in village factories." However, he stressed that this objective necessity was not the case in many other industries and centralised production existed in these purely to allow capitalists "to hold command of the market" and "to suit the temporary interests of the few — by no means those of the nation." Kropotkin made a clear division between economic tendencies which existed to aid the capitalist to dominate the market and enhance their profits and power and those which indicated a different kind of future. Once we consider the "moral and physical advantages which man would derive from dividing his work between field and the workshop" we must automatically evaluate the structure of modern industry with the criteria of what is best for the worker (and society and the environment) rather than what was best for capitalist profits and power. [**Op. Cit.**, p. 153, p. 147 and p. 153]

Clearly, Leninist summaries of Kropotkin's ideas on this subject are nonsense. Rather than seeing "small-scale" production as the basis of his vision of a free society, he saw production as being geared around the economic unit of a nation or region: "Each region will become its own producer and its own consumer of manufactured goods ... [and] its own producer and consumer of agricultural produce." Industry would come to the village "not in its present shape of a capitalist factory" but "in the shape of a socially organised

industrial production, with the full aid of machinery and technical knowledge." [**Op. Cit.**, p. 40 and p. 151]

Industry would be decentralised and integrated with agriculture and based around communes, but these communes would be part of a federation and so production would be based around meeting the needs of these federations. A system of rational decentralisation would be the basis of Kropotkin's communist-anarchism, with productive activity and a free society's workplaces geared to the appropriate level. For those forms of industry which would be best organised on a large-scale would continue to be so organised, but for those whose current (i.e., capitalist) structure had no objective need to be centralised would be broken up to allow the transformation of work for the benefit of both workers and society. Thus we would see a system of workplaces geared to local and district needs complementing larger factories which would meet regional and wider needs.

Anarchism rejects the idea of small-scale production and isolated communes and, as we discussed in section H.2.3, it does **not** look backwards for its ideal. The same applies to other forms of libertarian socialism with, for example, G.D.H. Cole arguing that we "cannot go back to 'town economy', a general regime of handicraft and master-craftmanship, tiny-scale production. We can neither pull up our railways, fill our mines, and dismantle our factories nor conduct our large-scale enterprises under a system developed to fit the needs of a local market and a narrowly-restricted production." The aim is "to reintroduce into industry the communal spirit, by re-fashioning industrialism in such a way as to set the communal motives free to co-operate." [**Guild Socialism Restated**, pp. 45-6 and p. 46]

The obvious implication of Leninist arguments against anarchist ideas on industrial transformation after a revolution is that they think that a socialist society will basically be the same as capitalism, using the technology, industry and industrial structure developed under class society without change (as noted in section H.3.12, Lenin did suggest that was the case). Needless to say, capitalist industry, as Kropotkin was aware, has not developed neutrally nor purely because of technical needs. Rather it has been distorted by the twin requirements to maintain capitalist profits and power. One of the first tasks of a social revolution will be to transform the industrial structure, not keep it as it is. You cannot use capitalist means for socialist ends. So while we will "inherit" an industrial structure from capitalism it would be the greatest possible error to leave it unchanged and an even worse one to accelerate the processes by which capitalists maintain and increase their power (i.e. centralisation and concentration) in the name of "socialism."

We are sorry to have laboured this point, but this issue is one which arises with depressing frequency in Marxist accounts of anarchism. It is best that we indicate that those who make the claim that anarchists seek "small scale" production geared for "small autonomous communities" simply show their ignorance. In actuality, anarchists see production as being geared to whatever makes most social, economic and ecological sense. Some production and workplaces will be geared to the local commune, some will be geared to the district federation, some to the regional federation, and so on. It is for this reason anarchists support the federation of workers' associations as the means of combining local autonomy with the needs for co-ordination and joint activity. To claim otherwise is simply to misrepresent anarchist theory.

Finally, it must be psychologically significant that Leninists continually go on about anarchists advocating "small" and "tiny" workplaces. Apparently size **does** matter and Leninists think their productive units are much, much bigger than anarchist ones. As has been proven, anarchists advocate **appropriately sized** workplaces and are not hung-up about their size. Why Leninists are could be a fruitful area of research...

I.4

How could an anarchist economy function?

This is an important question facing all opponents of a given system — what will you replace it with? We can say, of course, that it is pointless to make blueprints of how a future anarchist society will work as the future will be created by everyone, not just the few anarchists and libertarian socialists who write books and FAQs. This is very true, we cannot predict what a free society will actually be like or develop and we have no intention to do so here. However, this reply (whatever its other merits) ignores a key point, people need to have some idea of what anarchism aims for before they decide to spend their lives trying to create it.

So, how would an anarchist system function? That depends on the economic ideas people have. A mutualist economy will function differently than a communist one, for example, but they will have similar features. As Rudolf Rocker put it:

> "Common to all Anarchists is the desire to free society of all political and social coercive institutions which stand in the way of development of a free humanity. In this sense Mutualism, Collectivism and Communism are not to be regarded as closed systems permitting no further development, but merely as economic assumptions as to the means of safeguarding a free community. There will even probably be in society of the future different forms of economic co-operation operating side by side, since any social progress must be associated with that free experiment and practical testing out for which in a society of free communities there will be afforded every opportunity." [**Anarcho-Syndicalism**, p. 9]

So given the common ideals and aims of anarchists, it is unsurprising that the economic systems we suggest have common features such as workers' self-management, federation, free agreement and so on (as discussed in last section). For all anarchists, the "task for a modern industrial society is to achieve what is now technically realisable, namely, a society which is really based on free voluntary participation of people who produce and create, live their lives freely within institutions they control, and with limited hierarchical structures, possibly none at all." [Noam Chomsky, quoted by Albert and Hahnel, **Looking Forward**, p. 62]

This is achieved by means of "voluntary association that will organise labour, and be the manufacturer and distributor of necessary commodities" and this "is to make what is useful. The individual is to make what is beautiful." [Oscar Wilde, **The Soul of Man Under Socialism**, p. 1183] For example, the machine "will supersede hand-work in the manufacture of plain goods. But at the same time, hand-work very probably will extend its domain in the artistic finishing of many things which are made entirely in the factory." [Peter Kropotkin, **Fields, Factories and Workplaces Tomorrow**, p. 152] Murray Bookchin, decades later, argued for the same idea: "the machine will remove the toil from the productive process, leaving its artistic completion to man." [**Post-Scarcity Anarchism**, p. 134]

The aim would be to maximise the time available for individuals to express and develop their individuality, including in production. As Stirner put it, the "organisation of labour touches only such labours as others can do for us... the rest remain egoistic, because no one can in your stead elaborate your musical compositions, carry out your projects of painting, etc.; nobody can replace Raphael's labours. The latter are labours of a unique person, which only he is competent to achieve." Criticising the authoritarian socialists of his time, Stirner went on to ask "for whom is time to be gained [by association]? For what does man require more time than is necessary to refresh his wearied powers of labour? Here Communism is silent." He then answers his own question by arguing it is gained for the individual "[t]o take comfort in himself as unique, after he has done his part as man!" [**The Ego and Its Own**, p. 268 and p. 269] Which is exactly what libertarian communists argue:

> "[We] recognise that man [sic!] has other needs besides food, and as the strength of Anarchy lies precisely in that it understands **all** human faculties and **all** passions, and ignores none, we shall ... contrive to satisfy all his intellectual and artistic needs ... the man [or woman] who will have done the four or five hours of ... work that are necessary for his existence, will have before him five or six hours which his will seek to employ according to tastes ...
>
> "He will discharge his task in the field, the factory, and so on, which he owes to society as his contribution to the general production. And he will employ the second half of his day, his week, or his year, to satisfy his artistic or scientific needs, or his hobbies." [Kropotkin, **Conquest of Bread**, pp. 110-1]

Thus, while **authoritarian** Communism ignores the unique individual (and that was the only kind of Communism existing when Stirner wrote his classic book) **libertarian** communists agree with Stirner and are not silent. Like him, they consider the whole point of organising labour is to provide the means of providing the individual with the time and resources required to express their individuality. In other words, to pursue "labours of a unique person." Thus all anarchists base their arguments for a free society on how it will benefit actual individuals, rather than abstracts or amorphous collectives (such as "society"). Hence chapter 9 of **The Conquest of Bread**, "The Need for Luxury" and, for that matter, chapter 10, "Agreeable Work."

In other words, anarchists desire to organise voluntary workers associations which will try to ensure a minimisation of mindless labour in order to maximise the time available for creative activity both inside and outside "work." This is to be achieved by free co-operation between equals, which is seen as being based on self-interest. After all, while capitalist ideology may proclaim that competition is an expression of self-interest it, in fact, results in the majority of people sacrificing themselves for the benefits of the few who own and control society. The time you sell to a boss in return for them ordering you about and keeping the product of your labour is time you never get back. Anarchists aim to end a system which crushes individuality and create one in which solidarity and co-operation allow us time to enjoy life and to gain the benefits of our labour ourselves. Mutual Aid, in other words, results in a better life than mutual struggle and so "the **association for struggle** will be a much more effective support for civilisation, progress, and evolution than is the **struggle for existence** with its savage daily competitions." [Luigi Geallani, **The End of Anarchism**, p. 26]

> In the place of the rat race of capitalism, economic activity in an anarchist society would be one of the means to humanise and individualise ourselves and society, to move from **surviving** to **living.** Productive activity should become a means of self-expression, of joy, of art, rather than something we have to do to survive. Ultimately, "work" should become more akin to play or a hobby than the current alienated activity. The priorities of life should be towards individual self-fulfilment and humanising society rather than "running society as an adjunct to the market," to use Polanyi's expression, and turning ourselves into commodities on the labour market.

The aim of anarchism is far more than the end of inequality. Hence Proudhon's comment that socialism's "underlying dogma" is that the "objective of socialism is the liberation of the proletariat and the eradication of poverty." This emancipation would be achieved by ending "wage-labour" via "democratically organised workers' associations." [**Property is Theft!**, p. 372 and p. 377] Or, to use Kropotkin's expression, "well-being for all" — physical, mental, emotional and ethical! Indeed, by concentrating on just poverty and ignoring the emancipation of the proletariat, the real aims of socialism are obscured:

> "The 'right to well-being' means the possibility of living like human beings, and of bringing up children to be members of a society better than ours, whilst the 'right to work' only means the right to be a wage-slave, a drudge, ruled over and exploited by the middle class of the future. The right to well-being is the Social Revolution, the right to work means nothing but the Treadmill of Commercialism. It is high time for the worker to assert his right to the common inheritance, and to enter into possession of it."
> [Kropotkin, **Op. Cit.**, p. 44]

So, while refusing to define exactly how an anarchist system will work, we will explore the implications of how the anarchist principles and ideals outlined above could be put into practice. Bear in mind that this is just a possible framework for a system which

has few historical examples to draw upon. This means that we can only indicate the general outlines of what an anarchist society could be like. Those seeking blue-prints and exactness should look elsewhere. In all likelihood, the framework we present will be modified and changed (even ignored) in light of the real experiences and problems people will face when creating a new society.

We should point out that there may be a tendency for some to compare this framework with the **theory** of capitalism (i.e. perfectly functioning "free" markets or quasi-perfect ones) as opposed to its reality. A perfectly working capitalist system only exists in text books and in the heads of ideologues who take the theory as reality. No system is perfect, particularly capitalism, and to compare "perfect" text-book capitalism with any real system is a pointless task. As we discussed in depth in section C, capitalist economics does not even describe the reality of capitalism so why think it would enlighten discussion of post-capitalist systems? What hope does it have of understanding post-capitalist systems which reject its proprietary despotism and inequalities? As anarchists aim for a qualitative change in our economic relationships, we can safely say that its economic dynamics will reflect the specific forms it will develop rather than those produced by a class-ridden hierarchical system like capitalism and the a-historic individualistic abstractions invented to defend it!

So any attempt to apply the notions developed from theorising about (or, more correctly, justifying and rationalising) capitalism to anarchism will fail to capture the dynamics of a non-capitalist system. John Crump stressed this point in his discussion of Japanese anarchism between the World Wars:

> "When considering the feasibility of the social system advocated by the pure anarchists, we need to be clear about the criteria against which it should be measured. It would, for example, be unreasonable to demand that it be assessed against such yardsticks of a capitalist economy as annual rate of growth, balance of trade and so forth … evaluating anarchist communism by means of the criteria which have been devised to measure capitalism's performance does not make sense … capitalism would be … baffled if it were demanded that it assess its operations against the performance indicators to which pure anarchists attached most importance, such as personal liberty, communal solidarity and the individual's unconditional right to free consumption. Faced with such demands, capitalism would either admit that these were not yardsticks against which it could sensibly measure itself or it would have to resort to the type of grotesque ideological subterfuges which it often employs, such as identifying human liberty with the market and therefore with wage slavery … The pure anarchists' confidence in the alternative society they advocated derived not from an expectation that it would **quantitatively** outperform capitalism in terms of GNP, productivity or similar capitalist criteria. On the contrary, their enthusiasm for anarchist communism flowed from their understanding that it would be **qualitatively** different from capitalism. Of course, this is not to say that the pure anarchists were

indifferent to questions of production and distribution ... they certainly believed that anarchist communism would provide economic well-being for all. But neither were they prepared to give priority to narrowly conceived economic expansion, to neglect individual liberty and communal solidarity, as capitalism regularly does." [**Hatta Shuzo and Pure Anarchism in Interwar Japan**, pp. 191-3]

Finally, anarchists are well aware that transforming how an economy works does not happen overnight. As discussed in section I.2.2, we have long rejected the idea of instantaneous social transformation and argued that revolution will take time to develop and change the legacy of centuries of class and hierarchical society. This transformation and the resulting changes in people and surroundings can only be achieved by the full participation of all in overcoming the (many) problems a free society will face and the new ways of relating to each other liberation implies. A free people will find their own practical solutions to their problems, for *"there will be all sorts of practical difficulties to overcome, but the [libertarian socialist] system is simplicity itself compared with the monster of centralised State control, which sets such an inhuman distance between the worker and the administrator that there is room for a thousand difficulties to intervene."* [Herbert Read, **Anarchy and Order**, p. 49] Thus, for anarchists, the *"enthusiasm generated by the revolution, the energies liberated, and the inventiveness stimulated by it must be given full freedom and scope to find creative channels."* [Alexander Berkman, **What is Anarchism?**, p. 223] As such, the ideas within this section of our FAQ are merely suggestions, possibilities.

I.4.1 What is the point of economic activity in anarchy?

The basic point of economic activity in an anarchist society is to ensure, to use Kropotkin's expression, ***"well-being for all"***. Rather than toil to make the rich richer, people in a free society would work together to *"ensure to society as a whole its life and further development."* Such an economy would be based upon *"giving society the greatest amount of useful products with the least waste of human energy"*, to meet *"the needs of mankind"*. [**The Conquest of Bread**, p. 43, p. 144 and p. 175] Needless to say, today we must also add: with the least disruption of nature.

In terms of needs, it should be stressed that these are not limited to just material goods (important as they may be, particularly to those currently living in poverty). Needs also extend to having meaningful work which you control, pleasant and ecologically viable surroundings, the ability to express oneself freely within and outwith work, and a host of other things associated with the quality of life rather than merely survival. Anarchism seeks to transform economic activity rather than merely liberate it by self-management (important as that is).

Therefore, for anarchists, *"[r]eal wealth consists of things of utility and beauty, in things that help create strong, beautiful bodies and surroundings inspiring to live in."* Anarchism's *"goal is the freest*

possible expression of all the latent powers of the individual" and this *"is only possible in a state of society where man [sic!] is free to choose the mode of work, the conditions of work, and the freedom to work. One whom making a table, the building of a house, or the tilling of the soil is what the painting is to the artist and the discovery to the scientist — the result of inspiration, of intense longing, and deep interest in work as a creative force."* [Emma Goldman, **Red Emma Speaks**, p. 67 and p. 68]

So the point of economic activity in an anarchist society is to produce as and when required and not, as under capitalism, to organise production for the sake of production in order to make profits for the few. Production, to use Kropotkin's words, is to become *"the mere servant of consumption; it must mould itself on the wants of the consumer, not dictate to him [or her] conditions."* [**Act For Yourselves**, p. 57] This should **not** be taken to imply that anarchism seeks production for the sake of production in order to meet all the needs of all. Far from it, as such a regime would, to quote Malatesta, involve *"employing **all** of one's strength in producing things, because taken literally, this would mean working until one is exhausted, which would mean that by maximising the satisfaction of human needs we destroy humanity."* In other words, a free society would take into account the wants of the producers (and the planet we live on) when meeting the wants of consumers. Thus, there would be a balance sought. *"What we would like,"* continued Malatesta, *"is for everybody to live in the best possible way: so that everybody with a minimum amount of effort will obtain maximum satisfaction."* [**At the Café**, p. 61]

So while the basic aim of economic activity in an anarchist society is, obviously, producing wealth — i.e., satisfying individual needs — without enriching capitalists or other parasites in the process, it is far more than that. Yes, an anarchist society will aim to create society in which everyone will have a standard of living suitable for a fully human life. Yes, it will aim to eliminate poverty, inequality, individual want and social waste and squalor, but it aims for far more than that. It aims to create free individuals who express their individuality within and outwith "work." After all, what is the most important thing that comes out of a workplace? Pro-capitalists may say profits, others the finished commodity or good. In fact, the most important thing that comes out of a workplace is the **worker.** What happens to us in the workplace will have an impact on all aspects of our life and so cannot be ignored.

To value "efficiency" above all else, as capitalism says it does (it, in fact, values **profits** above all else and hinders developments like workers' control which increase efficiency but harm power and profits), is to deny our own humanity and individuality. Without an appreciation for grace and beauty there is no pleasure in creating things and no pleasure in having them. Our lives are made drearier rather than richer by "progress." How can a person take pride in their work when skill and care are considered luxuries (if not harmful to "efficiency" and, under capitalism, the profits and power of the capitalist and manager)? We are not machines. We have a need for craftspersonship and anarchism recognises this and takes it into account in its vision of a free society. This means that, in an anarchist society, economic activity is the process by which we produce what is useful but, in addition, is also beautiful (to use Oscar Wilde's words) in a way that empowers the individual. We anarchists charge capitalism with wasting human energy and time due to its irrational nature and workings, energy that could be spent creating what is beautiful (both in terms of individualities and products of labour). Under capitalism we are *"toiling to live, that we may live to toil."* [William Morris, **Useful Work Versus Useless Toil**, p. 37]

In addition, we must stress that the aim of economic activity within an anarchist society is **not** to create equality of outcome — i.e. everyone getting exactly the same goods. As we noted in section A.2.5, such a "vision" of "equality" attributed to socialists by pro-capitalists indicates more the poverty of imagination and ethics of the critics of socialism than a true account of socialist ideas. Anarchists, like other genuine socialists, support **social** equality in order to maximise freedom, including the freedom to choose between options to satisfy ones needs. To treat people equally, as equals, means to respect their desires and interests, to acknowledge their right to equal liberty. To make people consume the same as everyone else does not respect the equality of all to develop ones abilities as one sees fit. Socialism means equality of opportunity to satisfy desires and interests, not the imposition of an abstract minimum (or maximum) on unique individuals. To treat unique individuals equally means to acknowledge that uniqueness, not to deny it.

Thus the **real** aim of economic activity within an anarchy is to ensure *"that every human being should have the material and moral means to develop his humanity."* [Michael Bakunin, **The Political Philosophy of Bakunin**, p. 295] And you cannot develop your humanity if you cannot express yourself freely. Needless to say, to treat unique people "equally" (i.e. identically) is simply evil. You cannot, say, have a 70 year old woman do the same work in order to receive the same income as a 20 year old man. No, anarchists do not subscribe to such "equality," which is a product of the *"ethics of mathematics"* of capitalism and **not** of anarchist ideals. Such a scheme is alien to a free society. The equality anarchists desire is a social equality, based on control over the decisions that affect you. The aim of anarchist economic activity, therefore, is to provide the goods required for *"equal freedom for all, an equality of conditions such as to allow everyone to do as they wish."* [Errico Malatesta, **Errico Malatesta: His Life and Ideas**, p. 49] Thus anarchists *"demand not natural but social equality of individuals as the condition for justice and the foundations of morality."* [Bakunin, **Op. Cit.**, p. 249]

I.4.2 Why do anarchists desire to abolish work?

Anarchists desire to see humanity liberate itself from work. This may come as a shock for many people and will do much to "prove" that anarchism is essentially utopian. However, we think that such an abolition is not only necessary, it is possible. This is because work as we know it today is one of the major dangers to freedom we face.

If by freedom we mean self-government, then it is clear that being subjected to hierarchy in the workplace subverts our abilities to

think and judge for ourselves. Like any skill, critical analysis and independent thought have to be practised continually in order to remain at their full potential. So a workplace environment with power structures undermines these abilities. This was recognised by Adam Smith who argued that the *"understandings of the greater part of men are necessarily formed by their ordinary employments."* That being so, *"the man whose life is spent in performing a few simple operations, of which the effects too are, perhaps, always the same, or nearly the same, has no occasion to extend his understanding … and generally becomes as stupid and ignorant as it is possible for a human creature to be … But in every improved and civilised society this is the state into which the labouring poor, that is the great body of the people, must necessarily fall, unless government takes pains to prevent it."* [quoted by Noam Chomsky, **Year 501**, p. 18]

Smith's argument (usually ignored by those who claim to follow his ideas) is backed up by extensive evidence. Different types of authority structures and different technologies have different effects on those who work within them. Carole Pateman notes that the evidence suggests that *"[o]nly certain work situations were found to be conducive to the development of the psychological characteristics"* suitable for freedom, such as *"the feelings of personal confidence and efficacy that underlay the sense of political efficacy."* [**Participation and Democratic Theory**, p. 51] She quotes one expert who argues that within capitalist companies based upon a highly rationalised work environment and extensive division of labour, the worker has no control over the pace or technique of his work, no room to exercise skill or leadership and so they *"have practically no opportunity to solve problems and contribute their own ideas."* The worker, according to a psychological study, is *"resigned to his lot … more dependent than independent … he lacks confidence in himself … he is humble … the most prevalent feeling states … seem to be fear and anxiety."* [quoted by Pateman, **Op. Cit.**, p. 51 and p. 52]

The evidence Pateman summarises shows that an individual's *"attitudes will depend to a large degree on the authority structure of his [or her] work environment"*, with workplaces which are more autocratic and with a higher division of labour being worse for an individual's sense of self-esteem, feelings of self-worth and autonomy. In workplaces where *"the worker has a high degree of personal control over his [or her] work … and a very large degree of freedom from external control"* or is based on the *"collective responsibility of a crew of employees"* who *"had control over the pace and method of getting the work done, and the work crews were largely internally self-disciplining"* a different social character is seen. [Pateman, **Op. Cit.**, pp. 52-3] This was characterised by *"a strong sense of individualism and autonomy, and a solid acceptance of citizenship in the large society"* and *"a highly developed feeling of self-esteem and a sense of self-worth and is therefore ready to participate in the social and political institutions of the community."* Thus the *"nature of a man's work affects his social character and personality"* and that an *"industrial environment tends to breed a distinct social type."* [R. Blauner, quoted by Pateman, **Op. Cit.**, p. 52]

Thus, to quote Bob Black (who notes that Smith's comments against the division of labour are his *"critique of work"*), the capitalist workplace turns us into *"stultified submissives"* and places us *"under the sort of surveillance that ensures servility."* For this reason anarchists desire, to use Bob Black's phrase, *"the abolition of work."* [**The Abolition of Work and other essays**, p. 26, p. 22 and p. 19]

Work, in this context, does not mean any form of productive activity. Far from it. Work (in the sense of doing necessary things or productive activity) will always be with us. There is no getting away from it; crops need to be grown, schools built, homes fixed, and so on. No, work in this context means any form of labour in which the worker does not control his or her own activity. In other words, **wage labour** in all its many forms.

A society based upon hierarchical relations in production will result in a society within which the typical worker uses few of their abilities, exercise little or no control over their work because they are governed by a boss during working hours. This has been proved to lower the individual's self-esteem and feelings of self-worth, as would be expected in any social relationship that denied self-government. Capitalism is marked by an extreme division of labour, particularly between mental and physical labour. It reduces the worker to a mere machine operator, following the orders of his or her boss. Therefore, a libertarian that does not support economic liberty (i.e. self-management) is no libertarian at all.

Capitalism bases its rationale for itself on consumption and this results in a viewpoint which minimises the importance of the time we spend in productive activity. Anarchists consider that it is essential for individuals to use and develop their unique attributes and capacities in all walks of life, to maximise their powers. Therefore, the idea that "work" should be ignored in favour of consumption is totally mad. Productive activity is an important way of developing our inner-powers and expressing ourselves; in other words, be creative. Capitalism's emphasis on consumption shows the poverty of that system. As Alexander Berkman argued:

> *"We do not live by bread alone. True, existence is not possible without opportunity to satisfy our physical needs. But the gratification of these by no means constitutes all of life. Our present system of disinheriting millions, made the belly the centre of the universe, so to speak. But in a sensible society … [t]he feelings of human sympathy, of justice and right would have a chance to develop, to be satisfied, to broaden and grow."* [**What is Anarchism?**, pp. 152-3]

Therefore, capitalism is based on a constant process of alienated consumption, as workers try to find the happiness associated within productive, creative, self-managed activity in a place it does not exist — on the shop shelves. This can partly explain the rise of both mindless consumerism and the continuation of religions, as individuals try to find meaning for their lives and happiness, a meaning and happiness frustrated in wage labour and other hierarchies.

Capitalism's impoverishment of the individual's spirit is hardly surprising. As William Godwin argued, *"[t]he spirit of oppression, the spirit of servility, and the spirit of fraud, these are the immediate growth of the established administration of property. They are alike hostile to intellectual and moral improvement."* [**The Anarchist Reader**, p. 131] Any system based on hierarchical relationships in

work will result in a deadening of the individual and in a willingness to defer to economic masters. Which is why Anarchists desire to change this and create a society based upon freedom in all aspects of life. Hence anarchists desire to abolish work, simply because it restricts the liberty and distorts the individuality of those who have to do it. To quote Emma Goldman:

> *"Anarchism aims to strip labour of its deadening, dulling aspect, of its gloom and compulsion. It aims to make work an instrument of joy, of strength, of colour, of real harmony, so that the poorest sort of a man should find in work both recreation and hope."* [**Anarchism and Other Essays**, p. 61]

Anarchists do not think that by getting rid of work we will not have to produce necessary goods. Far from it. An anarchist society *"doesn't mean we have to stop doing things. It does mean creating a new way of life based on play; in other words, a ludic revolution … a collective adventure in generalised joy and freely interdependent exuberance. Play isn't passive."* The aim is *"to abolish work and replace it, insofar as it serves useful purposes, with a multitude of new kinds of free activities. To abolish work requires going at it from two directions, quantitative and qualitative."* In terms of the first, *"we need to cut down massively the amount of working being done"* (luckily, *"most work is useless or worse and we should simply get rid of it"*). For the second, *"we have to take what useful work remains and transform it into a pleasing variety of game-like and craft-like pastimes, indistinguishable from other pleasurable pastimes, except that they happen to yield useful end-products."* [Bob Black, **Op. Cit.**, p. 17 and p. 28]

This means that in an anarchist society every effort would be made to reduce boring, unpleasant activity to a minimum and ensure that whatever productive activity is required to be done is as pleasant as possible and based upon voluntary labour. However, it is important to remember Cornelius Castoriadis point: *"Socialist society will be able to reduce the length of the working day, and will have to do so, but this will not be the fundamental preoccupation. Its first task will be to … transform the very nature of work. The problem is not to leave more and more 'free' time to individuals — which might well be* **empty** *time — so that they may fill it at will with 'poetry' or the carving of wood. The problem is to make all time a time of liberty and to allow concrete freedom to find expression in creative activity."* Essentially, the *"problem is to put poetry into work."* [**Political and Social Writings**, vol. 2, p. 107]

This is why anarchists desire to abolish "work" (i.e., productive activity not under control of the people doing it), to ensure that whatever productive economic activity is required to be done is managed by those who do it. In this way it can be liberated, transformed, and so become a means of self-realisation and not a form of self-negation. In other words, anarchists want to abolish work because *"[l]ife, the art of living, has become a dull formula, flat and inert."* [Berkman, **Op. Cit.**, p. 166] Anarchists want to bring the spontaneity and joy of life back into productive activity and save humanity from the dead hand of capital. Anarchists consider economic activity as an expression of the human spirit, an expression of the innate human need to express ourselves and to create. Capitalism distorts these needs and makes economic activity a deadening experience by the division of labour and hierarchy. We think that *"industry is not an end in itself, but should only be a means to ensure to man his material subsistence and to make accessible to him the blessings of a higher intellectual culture. Where industry is everything and man is nothing begins the realm of a ruthless economic despotism whose workings are no less disastrous than those of any political despotism. The two mutually augment one another, and they are fed from the same source."* [Rudolph Rocker, **Anarcho-Syndicalism**, p. 2]

One last point on the abolition of work. May 1st — International Workers' Day — was, as we discussed in section A.5.2, created to commemorate the Chicago Anarchist Martyrs. Anarchists then, as now, think that it should be celebrated by strike action and mass demonstrations. In other words, for anarchists, International Workers' Day should be a non-work day! That sums up the anarchist position to work nicely — that the celebration of workers' day should be based on the rejection of work.

The collection of articles in **Why Work? Arguments for the Leisure Society** (edited by Vernon Richards) is a useful starting place for libertarian socialist perspectives on work.

I.4.3 How do anarchists intend to abolish work?

Basically by workers' self-management of production and common ownership of the means of production. It is hardly in the interests of those who do the actual "work" to have bad working conditions, boring, repetitive labour, and so on. Therefore, a key aspect of the liberation from work is to create a self-managed society, *"a society in which everyone has equal means to develop and that all are or can be at the same time intellectual and manual workers, and the only differences remaining between men [and women] are those which stem from the natural diversity of aptitudes, and that all jobs, all functions, give an equal right to the enjoyment of social possibilities."* [Errico Malatesta, **Anarchy**, p. 42]

Essential to this task is decentralisation and the use of appropriate technology. Decentralisation is important to ensure that those who do work can determine how to liberate it. A decentralised system will ensure that ordinary people can identify areas for technological innovation and so understand the need to get rid of certain kinds of work. Unless ordinary people understand and control the introduction of technology, then they will never be fully aware of the benefits of technology and resist advances which may be in their best interests to introduce. This is the full meaning of appropriate technology, namely the use of technology which those most affected feel to be best in a given situation. Such technology may or may not be technologically "advanced" but it will be of the kind which ordinary people can understand and, most importantly, control.

The potential for rational use of technology can be seen from capitalism. Under capitalism, technology is used to increase profits, to expand the economy, not to liberate **all** individuals from useless toil (it does, of course, liberate a few from such "activity"). As economist Juliet B. Schor points out, productivity *"measures the goods and services that result from each hour worked. When productivity rises, a worker can either produce the current output*

in less time, or remain at work the same number of hours and produce more." With rising productivity, we are presented with the possibility of more free time. For example, since 1948 the level of productivity of the American worker *"has more than doubled. In other words, we could now produce our 1948 standard of living … . in less than half the time it took that year. We could actually have chosen the four-hour day. Or a working year of six months."* [**The Overworked American**, p. 2]

And, remember, these figures include production in many areas of the economy that would not exist in a free society — state and capitalist bureaucracy, weapons production for the military, property defence, the finance sector, and so on. As Alexander Berkman argued, millions are *"engaged in trade, … advertisers, and various other middlemen of the present system"* along with the armed forces and *"the great numbers employed in unnecessary and harmful occupations, such as building warships, the manufacture of ammunition and other military equipment"* would be *"released for useful work by a revolution."* [**What is Anarchism**, pp. 224-5]

So the working week will be reduced simply because more people will be available for doing essential work. Moreover, goods will be built to last and so much production will become sensible and not governed by an insane desire to maximise profits at the expense of everything else. In addition, this is not taking into account the impact of a more just distribution of consumption in terms of living standards and production, meaning that a standard of living produced by working half the time would be far higher than that implied by Schor's 1948 baseline (not to mention the advances in technology since then either!). In short, do not take the 1948 date as implying a literal return to that period!

Moreover, a lower working week would see productivity rising. *"Thus,"* as one economist summarises, *"when the hours of labour were reduced, the better-rested workers were often able to produce as much or more in the shorter hours than they had previously in longer hours."* Yet *"competition between employers would make it unlikely that a working day of optimal length would be established"* under capitalism. In addition, *"more disposable time might better contribute to people's well-being — that is, to things such as trust, health, learning, family life, self-reliance and citizenship"*. While this may reduce such conventional economic measures as GDP, the fact is that such measures are flawed. After all, *"an increase in GDP could represent a diminution of free time accompanied by an increased output of goods and services whose sole utility was either facilitating labour-market participation or repairing some of the social damage that resulted from the stress of overwork or neglect of non-market activity."* [Tom Walker, *"Why Economists dislike a Lump of Labor"*, pp. 279-91, **Review of Social Economy**, vol. 65, No. 3, p. 286, pp. 287-8 and p. 288]

All this suggests the level of production for useful goods with a four-hour working day would be much higher than the 1948 level or, of course, the working day could be made even shorter. As such, we can easily combine a decent standard of living with a significant reduction of the necessary working time required to produce it. Once we realise that much work under capitalism exists to manage aspects of the profit system or are produced as a result of that system and the damage it does, we can see how a self-managed society can give us more time for ourselves in addition to producing useful goods (rather than working long and hard to produce surplus value for the few).

However, anarchists do not see it as simply a case of reducing the hours of work while keeping the remaining work as it is. That would be silly. We aim to transform what useful productive activity is left. When self-management becomes universal we will see the end of division of labour as mental and physical work becomes unified and those who do the work also manage it. This will allow *"the free exercise of all the faculties of man"* both inside and outside "work." [Peter Kropotkin, **The Conquest of Bread**, p. 148] The aim of such a development would be to turn productive activity, as far as possible, into an enjoyable experience. In the words of Murray Bookchin it is the **quality** and **nature** of the work process that counts:

> *"If workers' councils and workers' management of production do not transform the work into a joyful activity, free time into a marvellous experience, and the workplace into a community, then they remain merely formal structures, in fact, class structures. They perpetuate the limitations of the proletariat as a product of bourgeois social conditions. Indeed, no movement that raises the demand for workers' councils can be regarded as revolutionary unless it tries to promote sweeping transformations in the environment of the work place."*
> [**Post-Scarcity Anarchism**, p. 88]

Work will become, primarily, the expression of a person's pleasure in what they are doing and become like an art — an expression of their creativity and individuality. Work as an art will become expressed in the workplace as well as the work process, with workplaces transformed and integrated into the local community and environment (see section I.4.15). This will obviously apply to work conducted in the home as well, otherwise the *"revolution, intoxicated with the beautiful words, Liberty, Equality, Solidarity, would not be a revolution if it maintained slavery at home. Half [of] humanity subjected to the slavery of the hearth would still have to rebel against the other half."* [Kropotkin, **Op. Cit.**, p. 128]

In other words, anarchists desire *"to combine the best part (in fact, the only good part) of work — the production of use-values — with the best of play ... its freedom and its fun, its voluntariness and its intrinsic gratification"*. In short, the transformation of production (creating *"what seems needful"'*) into *"**productive play**"*. [Bob Black, *"Smokestack Lightning"*, **Friendly Fire**, p. 48 and p. 49]

Workers' self-management of production (see section I.3.2) would be the means of achieving this. Only those subject to a specific mode of working can be in a position to transform it and their workplace into something fit for free individuals to create in. Only those who know a workplace which would only exist in a hierarchical system like capitalism can be in a position to decommission it safely and quickly. The very basis of free association will ensure the abolition of work, as individuals will apply for "work" they enjoy doing and so would be interested in reducing "work" they did not want to do to a minimum. Therefore, an anarchist society would abolish work by ensuring that those who do it actually control it. *"Personal initiative will be encouraged and every tendency to uniformity and centralisation combated."* [Kropotkin, quoted by Martin Buber, **Paths in Utopia**, p. 42]

All this does not imply that anarchists think that individuals will not seek to "specialise" in one form of productive activity rather than another. Far from it, people in a free society will pick activities which interest them as the main focal point of their means of self-expression (after all, not everyone enjoys the same games and pastimes so why expect the same of productive play?). *"It is evident,"* noted Kropotkin, *"that all men and women cannot equally enjoy the pursuit of scientific work. The variety of inclinations is such that some will find more pleasure in science, some others in art, and others again in some of the numberless branches of the production of wealth."* This "division of work" is commonplace in humanity, this natural desire to do what interests you and what you are good at will be encouraged in an anarchist society. As Kropotkin argued, anarchists *"fully recognise the necessity of specialisation of knowledge, but we maintain that specialisation must follow general education, and that general education must be given in science and handicraft alike. To the division of society into brain workers and manual workers we oppose the combination of both kinds of activities ... we advocate the **education integrale** [integral education], or complete education, which means the disappearance of that pernicious division."* Anarchists are, needless to say, aware that training and study are required to qualify you to do some tasks and a free society would ensure that individuals would achieve the necessary recognised levels before undertaking them (by means of, say, professional bodies who organise a certification process). Kropotkin was aware, however, that both individuals and society would benefit from a diversity of activities and a strong general knowledge: *"But whatever the occupations preferred by everyone, everyone will be the more useful in his [or her] branch if he [or she] is in possession of a serious scientific knowledge. And, whosoever he might be ... he would be the gainer if he spent a part of his life in the workshop or the farm (the workshop **and** the farm), if he were in contact with humanity in its daily work, and had the satisfaction of knowing that he himself discharges his duties as an unprivileged producer of wealth."* [**Fields, Factories and Workshops Tomorrow**, p. 186, p. 172 and p. 186]

However, while specialisation would continue, the permanent division of individuals into manual or brain workers would be eliminated. Individuals will manage all aspects of the "work" required (for example, engineers will also take part in self-managing their workplaces), a variety of activities would be encouraged and the strict division of labour of capitalism will be abolished. In other words, anarchists want to replace the division of labour by the division of work. We must stress that we are not playing with words here. John Crump presents a good summary of the ideas of the Japanese anarchist Hatta Shuzo on this difference:

> *"[We must] recognise the distinction which Hatta made between the 'division of labour' ... and the 'division of work' ... while Hatta believed that the division of labour ... was the cause of class divisions and exploitation, he did not see anything sinister in the division of work ... On the contrary, Hatta believed that the division of work was a benign and unavoidable feature of any productive process: 'it goes without saying that within society, whatever the kind of production, there has to be a division*

of work.' ... [For] the dangers [of division of labour] to which Hatta [like other anarchists like Proudhon and Kropotkin] drew attention did not arise from a situation where, at any one time, different people were engaged in different productive activities ... What did spell danger, however, was when, either individually or collectively, people permanently divided along occupational lines ... and gave rise to the disastrous consequences ... . [of] the degrading of labour to a mechanical function; the lack of responsibility for, understanding of, or interest in other branches of production; and the need for a superior administrative organ to co-ordinate the various branches of production." [**Hatta Shuzo and Pure Anarchism in Interwar Japan**, pp. 146-7]

As Kropotkin argued:

"while a **temporary** division of functions remains the surest guarantee of success in each separate undertaking, the **permanent** division is doomed to disappear, and to be substituted by a variety of pursuits — intellectual, industrial, and agricultural — corresponding to the different capacities of the individual, as well as to the variety of capacities within every human aggregate." [**Op. Cit.**, p. 26]

As an aside, supporters of capitalism argue that **integrated** labour must be more inefficient than **divided** labour as capitalist firms have not introduced it. This is false for numerous reasons.

Firstly, we have to point out the inhuman logic of the assertion. After all, few would argue in favour of slavery if it were, in fact, **more** productive than wage labour but such is the logical conclusion of this argument. If someone did argue that the only reason slavery was not the dominant mode of labour simply because it was inefficient we would consider them as less than human. Simply put, it is a sick ideology which happily sacrifices individuals for the sake of slightly more products. Sadly, that is what many defenders of capitalism do, ultimately, argue for.

Secondly, capitalist firms are not neutral structures but rather a system of hierarchies, with entrenched interests and needs. Managers will only introduce a work technique that maintains their power (and so their profits). As we argue in section J.5.12, while experiments in workers' participation see a rise in efficiency and productivity, managers stop them simply because they recognise that workers' control undercuts their power by empowering workers who then can fight for a greater slice of the value they produce (not to mention come to the conclusion that while the boss needs them to work, they don't need to boss to manage them!). So the lack of integrated labour under capitalism simply means that it does not empower management nor secure their profits and power, **not** that it is less efficient.

Thirdly, the attempts by managers and bosses to introduce "flexibility" by eliminating unions suggests that integration **is** more efficient. After all, one of the major complaints directed towards union contracts are that they explicitly documented what workers could and could not do (for example, union members would refuse to do work which was outside their agreed job descriptions). This is

usually classed as an example of the evil of regulations. However, if we look at it from the viewpoint of contract and division of labour, it exposes the inefficiency and inflexibility of both as a means of co-operation. After all, what does this refusal actually mean? It means that the worker refuses to do work that is not specified in his or her contract! Their job description indicates what they have been contracted to do and anything else has not been agreed upon in advance. The contract specifies a clear, specified and agreed division of labour in a workplace between worker and boss.

While being a wonderful example of a well-designed contract, managers discovered that they could not operate their workplaces because of them. Rather, they needed a general "do what you are told" contract (which of course is hardly an example of contract reducing authority) and such a contract **integrates** numerous work tasks into one. The managers diatribe against union contracts suggests that production needs some form of integrated labour to actually work (as well as showing the hypocrisy of the labour contract under capitalism as labour "flexibility" simply means labour "commodification" — a machine does not question what its used for, the ideal under capitalism is a similar unquestioning nature for labour). The union job description indicates that production needs the integration of labour while demanding a division of work. As Cornelius Castoriadis argued:

"Modern production has destroyed many traditional professional qualifications. It has created automatic or semi-automatic machines. It has thereby itself demolished its own traditional framework for the industrial division of labour. It has given birth to a universal worker who is capable, after a relatively short apprenticeship, of using most machines. Once one gets beyond its class aspects, the 'posting' of workers to particular jobs in a big modern factory corresponds less and less to a genuine division of **labour** and more and more to a simple division of tasks. Workers are not allocated to given areas of the productive process and then riveted to them because their 'occupational skills' invariably correspond to the 'skills required' by management. They are placed there ... just because a particular vacancy happened to exist." [**Political and Economic Writings**, vol. 2, p. 117]

By replacing the division of labour with the division of work, a free society will ensure that productive activity can be transformed into an enjoyable task (or series of tasks). By integrating labour, all the capacities of the producer can be expressed so eliminating a major source of alienation and unhappiness in society. "The main subject of social economy," argued Kropotkin, is "the **economy of energy required for the satisfaction of human needs.**" These needs obviously expressed both the needs of the producers for empowering and interesting work and their need for a healthy and balanced environment. Thus Kropotkin discussed the "advantages" which could be "derive[d] from a combination of industrial pursuits with intensive agriculture, and of brain work with manual work." The "greatest sum total of well-being can be obtained when a variety of agricultural, industrial and intellectual pursuits are combined in each community; and that man [and woman] shows his best when he is in a position to apply his usually-varied capacities to several *pursuits in the farm, the workshop, the factory, the study or the studio, instead of being riveted for life to one of these pursuits only."* [**Op. Cit.**, pp. 17-8] This means that *"[u]nder socialism, factories would have no reason to accept the artificially rigid division of labour now prevailing. There will be every reason to encourage a rotation of workers **between shops and departments** and between production and office areas."* The *"residues of capitalism's division of labour gradually will have to be eliminated"* as *"socialist society cannot survive unless it demolishes this division."* [Castoriadis, **Op. Cit.**, p. 117]

Anarchists think that a decentralised social system will allow "work" to be abolished and economic activity humanised and made a means to an end (namely producing useful things and liberated individuals). This would be achieved by, as Rudolf Rocker puts it, the *"alliance of free groups of men and women based on co-operative labour and a planned administration of things in the interest of the community."* However, as things are produced by people, it could be suggested that this implies a *"planned administration of people"* (although few who suggest this danger apply it to capitalist firms which are like mini-centrally planned states). This objection is false simply because anarchism aims *"to reconstruct the economic life of the peoples from the ground up and build it up anew in the spirit of Socialism"* and, moreover, *"only the producers themselves are fitted for this task, since they are the only value-creating element in society out of which a new future can arise."* Such a reconstructed economic life would be based on anarchist principles, that is *"based on the principles of federalism, a free combination from below upwards, putting the right of self-determination of every member above everything else and recognising only the organic agreement of all on the basis of like interests and common convictions."* [**Anarcho-Syndicalism**, p. 72, p. 62 and p. 60]

In other words, those who produce also administer and so govern themselves in free association (and it should be pointed out that any group of individuals in association will make "plans" and "plan", the important question is who does the planning and who does the work. Only in anarchy are both functions united into the same people). The *"planned administration of things"* would be done by the producers **themselves,** in their independent groupings. This would likely take the form (as we indicated in section I.3) of confederations of syndicates who communicate information between themselves and respond to changes in the production and distribution of products by increasing or decreasing the required means of production in a co-operative (i.e. *"planned"*) fashion. No "central planning" or "central planners" governing the economy, just workers co-operating together as equals (as Kropotkin argued, free socialism *"must result from thousands of separate local actions, all directed towards the same aim. It cannot be dictated by a central body: it must result from the numberless local needs and wants."* [**Act for Yourselves**, p. 54]).

Now, any form of association requires agreement. Therefore, even a society based on the communist-anarchist maxim *"from each according to their ability, to each according to their need"* will need to make agreements in order to ensure co-operative ventures succeed. In other words, members of a co-operative commonwealth would have to make and keep to their agreements between themselves. This means that the members of a syndicate would agree joint starting and finishing times, require notice if individuals want to change "jobs" and so on within and between syndicates. Any joint effort requires some degree of co-operation and agreement. Moreover, between syndicates, an agreement would be reached (in all likelihood) that determined the minimum working hours required by all members of society able to work. As Kropotkin argued, a communist anarchist society would be based upon the such a minimum-hour "contract" between its members:

> *"We undertake to give you the use of our houses, stores, streets, means of transport, schools, museums, etc., on condition that, from twenty to forty-five or fifty years of age, you consecrate four or five hours a day to some work recognised as necessary to existence. Choose yourself the producing group which you wish to join, or organise a new group, provided that it will undertake to produce necessaries. And as for the remainder of your time, combine together with whomsoever you like, for recreation, art, or science, according to the bent of your taste … Twelve or fifteen hundred hours of work a year … is all we ask of you. For that amount of work we guarantee to you the free use of all that these groups produce, or will produce."* [**The Conquest of Bread**, pp. 153-4]

With such work *"necessary to existence"* being recognised by individuals and expressed by demand for labour from productive syndicates. It is, of course, up to the individual to decide which work he or she desires to perform from the positions available in the various associations in existence. A union card could be the means by which work hours would be recorded and access to the common wealth of society ensured. And, of course, individuals and groups are free to work alone and exchange the produce of their labour with others, including the confederated syndicates, if they so desired. An anarchist society will be as flexible as possible.

Therefore, we can imagine a social anarchist society being based on two basic arrangements — firstly, an agreed minimum working week of, say, 16 hours, in a syndicate of your choice, plus any amount of hours doing "work" which you feel like doing — for example, art, scientific experimentation, DIY, playing music, composing, gardening and so on. How that minimum working week was actually organised would vary between workplace and commune, with work times, flexi-time, job rotation and so on determined by each syndicate (for example, one syndicate may work 8 hours a day for 2 days, another 4 hours a day for 4 days, one may use flexi-time, another more rigid starting and stopping times). Needless to say, in response to consumption patterns, syndicates will have to expand or reduce production and will have to attract volunteers to do the necessary work as would syndicates whose work was considered dangerous or unwanted. In such circumstances, volunteers could arrange doing a few hours of such activity for more free time or it could be agreed that one hour of such unwanted positions equals more hours in a more desired one (see section I.4.13 for more on this). Needless to say, the aim of technological progress would be to eliminate unpleasant and unwanted tasks and to reduce the basic working week more and more until the very concept of necessary "work" and free time enjoyments is abolished. Anarchists are convinced that the decentralisation of power within a free society would unleash a wealth of innovation and ensure that unpleasant tasks are minimised and fairly shared while required productive activity is made as pleasant and enjoyable as possible.

Therefore, free agreement between free and equal individuals is considered the key to abolishing work, based upon decentralisation of power and the use of appropriate technology.

I.4.4 What economic decision making criteria could be used in anarchy?

Firstly, it should be noted that anarchists do not have any set idea about the answer to this question. Most anarchists are communists, desiring to see the end of money, but that does not mean they want to impose communism onto people. Far from it, communism can only be truly libertarian if it is organised from the bottom up. So, anarchists would agree with Kropotkin that it is a case of not *"determining in advance what form of distribution the producers should accept in their different groups — whether the communist solution, or labour checks, or equal salaries, or any other method"* while considering a given solution best in their opinion. [**Anarchism**, p. 166] Free experimentation is a key aspect of anarchism.

While certain anarchists have certain preferences on the social system they want to live in and so argue for that, they are aware that objective circumstances and social desires will determine what is introduced during a revolution. However, we will outline some possible means of economic decision making criteria as this question is an important one and so we will indicate what possible solutions exist in different forms of anarchism.

In a mutualist or collectivist system, the answer is easy. Prices will exist and be used as a means of making decisions (although, as Malatesta suggested, such non-communist anarchies would *"seek a way to ensure that money truly represents the useful work performed by its possessors"* rather than, as today, *"the means for living on the labour of others"* [**Errico Malatesta: His Life and Ideas**, p. 101 and p. 100]). Mutualism will be more market orientated than collectivism, with collectivism being based on confederations of collectives to respond to changes in demand (i.e. to determine investment decisions and ensure that supply is kept in line with demand). Mutualism, with its system of market based distribution around a network of co-operatives and mutual banks, does not really need a further discussion as its basic operations are the same as in any non-capitalist market system. Collectivism and communism will have to be discussed in more detail. However, all systems are based on workers' self-management and so the individuals directly affected make the decisions concerning what to produce, when to do it, and how to do it. In this way workers retain control of the product of their labour. It is the social context of these decisions and what criteria workers use to make their decisions that differ between anarchist schools of thought.

Although collectivism promotes the greatest autonomy for worker associations, it should not be confused with a market economy as advocated by supporters of mutualism or Individualist anarchism. The goods produced by the collectivised factories and workshops

are exchanged not according to highest price that can be wrung from consumers, but according to their actual production costs. The determination of these honest prices would be made by a *"Bank of Exchange"* in each community (obviously an idea borrowed from Proudhon). These Banks would represent the various producer confederations and consumer/citizen groups in the community and would seek to negotiate these "honest" prices (which would, in all likelihood, include "hidden" costs like pollution). These agreements would be subject to ratification by the assemblies of those involved.

As James Guillaume put it *"the value of the commodities having been established in advance by a contractual agreement between the regional co-operative federations and the various communes, who will also furnish statistics to the Banks of Exchange. The Bank of Exchange will remit to the producers negotiable vouchers representing the value of their products; these vouchers will be accepted throughout the territory included in the federation of communes."* These vouchers would be related to hours worked, for example, and when used as a guide for investment decisions could be supplemented with cost-benefit analysis of the kind possibly used in a communist-anarchist society (see below). Although this scheme bears a strong resemblance to Proudhonian *"People's Banks,"* it should be noted that the Banks of Exchange, along with a *"Communal Statistical Commission,"* are intended to have a planning function as well to ensure that supply meets demand. This does not imply a Stalinist-like command economy, but simple book keeping for *"each Bank of Exchange makes sure in advance that these products are in demand [in order to risk] nothing by immediately issuing payment vouchers to the producers."* [*"On Building the New Social Order"*, pp. 356-79, **Bakunin on Anarchism**, p. 366 and p. 367] The workers syndicates would still determine what orders to produce and each commune would be free to choose its suppliers.

As will be discussed in more depth later (see section I.4.8) information about consumption patterns will be recorded and used by workers to inform their production and investment decisions. In addition, we can imagine that production syndicates would encourage communes as well as consumer groups and co-operatives to participate in making these decisions. This would ensure that produced goods reflect consumer needs. Moreover, as conditions permit, the exchange functions of the communal "banks" would (in all likelihood) be gradually replaced by the distribution of goods in accordance with the needs of the consumers. In other words, most supporters of collectivist anarchism see it as a temporary measure before anarcho-communism could develop.

Communist anarchism would be similar to collectivism, i.e. a system of confederations of collectives, communes and distribution centres (Communal stores). However, in an anarcho-communist system, prices are not used. How will economic decision making be done? One possible solution is as follows:

> *"As to decisions involving choices of a general nature, such as what forms of energy to use, which of two or more materials to employ to produce a particular good, whether to build a new factory, there is a ... technique ... that could be [used] ... 'cost-benefit analysis' ... [I]n socialism a points scheme for attributing relative*

importance to the various relevant considerations could be used … The points attributed to these considerations would be subjective, in the sense that this would depend on a deliberate social decision rather than some objective standard, but this is the case even under capitalism when a monetary value has to be attributed to some such 'cost' or 'benefit' … In the sense that one of the aims of socialism is precisely to rescue humankind from the capitalist fixation with production time/money, cost-benefit analyses, as a means of taking into account other factors, could therefore be said to be more appropriate for use in socialism than under capitalism. Using points systems to attribute relative importance in this way … [is] simply to employ a technique to facilitate decision-making in particular concrete cases." [Adam Buick and John Crump, **State Capitalism: The Wages System Under New Management**, pp. 138-139]

This points system would be the means by which producers and consumers would be able to determine whether the use of a particular good is efficient or not. Unlike prices, this cost-benefit analysis system would ensure that production and consumption reflects social and ecological costs, awareness and priorities. Moreover, this analysis would be a **guide** to decision making and not a replacement of human decision making and evaluation. As Lewis Mumford argued:

"it is plain that in the decision as to whether to build a bridge or a tunnel there is a human question that should outweigh the question of cheapness or mechanical feasibility: namely the number of lives that will be lost in the actual building or the advisability of condemning a certain number of men [and women] to spend their entire working days underground supervising tunnel traffic … Similarly the social choice between silk and rayon is not one that can be made simply on the different costs of production, or the difference in quality between the fibres themselves: there also remains, to be integrated in the decision, the question as to difference in working-pleasure between tending silkworms and assisting in rayon production. What the product contributes to the labourer is just as important as what the worker contributes to the product. A well-managed society might alter the process of motor car assemblage, at some loss of speed and cheapness, in order to produce a more interesting routine for the worker: similarly, it would either go to the expense of equipping dry-process cement making plants with dust removers — or replace the product itself with a less noxious substitute. When none of these alternatives was available, it would drastically reduce the demand itself to the lowest possible level." [**The Future of Technics and Civilisation**, pp. 160-1]

Obviously, today, we would include ecological issues as well as human ones. Any decision making process which disregards the quality of work or the effect on the human and natural environment is a deranged one. However, this is how capitalism operates, with

the market rewarding capitalists and managers who introduce de-humanising and ecologically harmful practices. Indeed, so biased against labour and the environment is capitalism that many economists and pro-capitalists argue that reducing "efficiency" by such social concerns (as expressed by the passing laws related to labour rights and environmental protection) is actually **harmful** to an economy, which is a total reversal of common sense and human feelings (after all, surely the economy should satisfy human needs and not sacrifice those needs to the economy?). The argument is that consumption would suffer as resources (human and material) would be diverted from more "efficient" productive activities and so reduce, over all, our economic well-being. What this argument ignores is that consumption does not exist in isolation from the rest of the economy. What we want to consume is conditioned, in part, by the sort of person we are and that is influenced by the kind of work we do, the kinds of social relationships we have, whether we are happy with our work and life, and so on. If our work is alienating and of low quality, then so will our consumption decisions. If our work is subject to hierarchical control and servile in nature then we cannot expect our consumption decisions to be totally rational — indeed they may become an attempt to find happiness via shopping, a self-defeating activity as consumption cannot solve a problem created in production. Thus rampant consumerism may be the result of capitalist "efficiency" and so the objection against socially aware production is question begging.

Of course, as well as absolute scarcity, prices under capitalism also reflect relative scarcity (while in the long term, market prices tend towards their production price plus a mark-up based on the degree of monopoly in a market, in the short term prices can change as a result of changes in supply and demand). How a communist society could take into account such short term changes and communicate them through out the economy is discussed in section I.4.5. Moreover, it is likely that they will factor in the desirability of the work performed to indicate the potential waste in human time involved in production (see section I.4.13 for a discussion of how this could be done). The logic behind this is simple, a resource which people **like** to produce will be a better use of the scare resource of an individual's time than one people hate producing. Another key factor in making sensible decisions would be the relative scarcity of a good. After all, it would make little sense when making a decision to use a good which is in short supply over one which is much more abundant. Thus, while the cost-benefit points system would show absolute costs (number of hours work required, energy use, pollution, etc.) this would be complemented by information about how scare a specific good is and the desirability of the work required to produce it.

Therefore, a communist-anarchist society would be based around a network of syndicates who communicate information between each other. Instead of the price being communicated between workplaces as in capitalism, actual physical data will be sent (the cost). This data is a summary of these (negative) use values of the good (for example resources, labour time and energy used to produce it, pollution details) as well as relative scarcity. With this information a cost-benefit analysis will be conducted to determine which good will be best to use in a given situation based upon mutually agreed common values. These will be used to inform the decision on which goods to use, with how well goods meet the requirements of production (the positive use-value) being compared to their impact in terms of labour, resource use, pollution and so forth (the negative use-values) along with their relative availability.

The data for a given workplace could be compared to the industry as a whole (as confederations of syndicates would gather and produce such information — see section I.3.5) in order to determine whether a specific workplace will efficiently produce the required goods (this system has the additional advantage of indicating which workplaces require investment to bring them in line, or improve upon, the industrial average in terms of working conditions, hours worked and so on). In addition, common rules of thumb would possibly be agreed, such as agreements not to use scarce materials unless there is no alternative (either ones that use a lot of labour, energy and time to produce or those whose demand is currently exceeding supply capacity).

Similarly, when ordering goods, the syndicate, commune or individual involved will have to inform the syndicate why it is required in order to allow the syndicate to determine if they desire to produce the good and to enable them to prioritise the orders they receive. In this way, resource use can be guided by social considerations and "unreasonable" requests ignored (for example, if an individual states they "need" a ship-builders syndicate to build a ship for their personal use, the ship-builders may not "need" to build it and instead build ships for communal use, freely available for all to use in turn — see section I.4.6). However, in almost all cases of individual consumption, no such information will be needed as communal stores would order consumer goods in bulk as they do now. Hence the economy would be a vast network of co-operating individuals and workplaces and the dispersed knowledge which exists within any society can be put to good effect (**better** effect than under capitalism because it does not hide social and ecological costs in the way market prices do and co-operation will eliminate the business cycle and its resulting social problems).

Therefore, production units in a social anarchist society, by virtue of their autonomy within association, are aware of what is socially useful for them to produce and, by virtue of their links with communes, also aware of the social (human and ecological) cost of the resources they need to produce it. They can combine this knowledge, reflecting overall social priorities, with their local knowledge of the detailed circumstances of their workplaces and communities to decide how they can best use their productive capacity. In this way the division of knowledge within society can be used by the syndicates effectively as well as overcoming the restrictions within knowledge communication imposed by the price mechanism (see section I.1.2) and workplaces hierarchies within capitalism (see section I.1.1).

Moreover, production units, by their association within confederations ensure that there is effective communication between them. This results in a process of negotiated co-ordination between equals (i.e. horizontal links and agreements) for major investment decisions, thus bringing together supply and demand and allowing the plans of the various units to be co-ordinated. By this process of co-operation, production units can reduce duplicating effort and so reduce the waste associated with over-investment (and so the irrationalities of booms and slumps associated with the price mechanism, which does not provide sufficient information to allow workplaces to efficiently co-ordinate their plans).

When evaluating production methods we need to take into account as many social and ecological costs as possible and these have to be evaluated. Which costs will be taken into account, of course, be decided by those involved, as will how important they are relative to each other (i.e. how they are weighted). What factors to take into account and how to weigh them in the decision making process will be evaluated and reviewed regularly so to ensure that it reflects real costs and social concerns. As communist-anarchists consider it important to encourage all to participate in the decisions that affect their lives, it would be the role of communal confederations to determine the relative points value of given inputs and outputs. In this way, **all** individuals in a community determine how their society develops, so ensuring that economic activity is responsible to social needs and takes into account the desires of everyone affected by production. In this way consumption and production can be harmonised with the needs of individuals as members of society and the environment they live in. The industrial confederations would seek to ensure that this information is recorded and communicated and (perhaps) formulating industry-wide averages to aid decision-making by allowing syndicates and communes to compare specific goods points to the typical value.

So which factors are to be used to inform decision-making would be agreed and the information communicated between workplaces and communes so that consumers of goods can evaluate their costs in terms of ecological impact, use of resources and human labour. Any agreed values for the Cost-Benefit analysis for inputs can be incorporated in the information associated with the outputs. As such, a communist society would seek to base decisions on more than one criteria, whether it is profits or (say) labour. The reasons for this should be obvious, as one criteria rarely allows sensible decisions. Of course, to some degree people already do this under capitalism but market forces and inequality limit this ability (people will tend to buy cheaper products if they need to make ends meet) while both the price mechanism and the self-interest of companies ensure information about costs are hidden (for example, few companies publically acknowledge their externalities and most spend vast sums on advertising to greenwash their products).

In order to process the information on costs communicated in a libertarian communist economy accounting tools can be created (such as a spreadsheet or computer programme). These could take the decided factors as inputs and returns a cost benefit analysis of the choices available. So while these algorithmic procedures and guidelines can, and indeed should be, able to be calculated by hand, it is likely that computers will be extensively used to take input data and process it into a suitable format. Indeed, many capitalist companies have software which records raw material inputs and finished product into databases and spreadsheets. Such software could be the basis of a libertarian communist decision making algorithm. Of course, currently such data is submerged beneath money and does not take into account externalities and the nature of the work involved (as would be the case in an anarchist society). However, this does not limit their potential or deny that communist use of such software can be used to inform decisions.

Therefore, the claim that communism cannot evaluate different production methods due to lack of prices is inaccurate. Indeed, a look at the actual capitalist market — marked as it is by differences in bargaining and market power, externalities and wage labour — soon shows that the claims that prices accurately reflect costs is simply not accurate. However, it may be such that objective circumstances preclude the immediate introduction of libertarian communism (as discussed in section I.2.2, many communist anarchists consider this likely). As such, there could be a transitional period in which elements of mutualism, collectivism and communism co-exist within a specific economy. It can easily be seen how a mutualist economy (the usual initial product of a social revolution) could evolve into a collectivist and then communist one. The market generated prices could initially be complemented by the non-market information decided upon (for objective costs and the scarcity index) and, overtime, replaced by this data as the main decision making criteria by syndicates and communes.

One final point on this subject. What methods are used, which criteria picked, which information is communicated and how it is processed, will be the decision of a free people. This section was merely a suggestion of one possibility of how a libertarian communist economy could make informed decisions about production. It is not meant as a blue-print nor is it set-in-stone.

I.4.5 What about "supply and demand"?

Anarchists do not ignore the facts of life, namely that at a given moment there is so much a certain good produced and so much of it is desired to be consumed or used. Neither do we deny that different individuals have different interests and tastes. However, this is not what is usually meant by "supply and demand." Often in general economic debate, this formula is given a certain mythical quality which ignores its underlying realities as well as some unwholesome implications of the theory (for example, as discussed in section C.1.5 the market can very efficiently create famines by exporting food to areas where there is demand for it). At the very least, the *"the law of supply and demand"* is not the "most efficient" means of distribution in an unequal society as decisions are skewed in favour of the rich.

As far as "supply and demand" in terms of allocating scare resources is concerned, anarchists are well aware of the need to create and distribute necessary goods to those who require them. The question is, in an anarchist society, how do you know that valuable labour and materials are not being wasted? How do people judge which tools are most appropriate? How do they decide among different materials if they all meet the technical specifications? How important are some goods than others? How important is cellophane compared to vacuum-cleaner bags and so which one should be produced?

It is answers like this that the supporters of the market claim that their system answers. For individualist and mutualist anarchists, their non-capitalist market would indicate such information by differences between market price and cost price and individuals and co-operatives would react accordingly. For communist and collectivist anarchists, who reject even non-capitalist markets, the answer is less simple. As discussed in section I.1.3, these anarchists

argue that although the market does answer such questions it does so in irrational and dehumanising ways (while this is particularly the case under capitalism, it cannot be assumed this will disappear in a post-capitalist market). The question is: can collectivist and communist anarchism answer such questions? Yes, they reply.

So collectivist and communist anarchists reject the market. This rejection often implies, to some, central planning. As the market socialist David Schweickart puts it, *"[i]f profit considerations do not dictate resource usage and production techniques, then central direction must do so. If profit is not the goal of a productive organisation, then physical output (use values) must be."* [**Against Capitalism**, p. 86] However, Schweickart is wrong. Horizontal links need not be market based and co-operation between individuals and groups need not be hierarchical. What is implied in this comment is that there is just two ways to relate to others — either by prostitution (purely by cash) or by hierarchy (the way of the state, the army or capitalist workplace). But people relate to each other in other ways, such as friendship, love, solidarity, mutual aid and so on. Thus you can help or associate with others without having to be ordered to do so or by being paid cash to do so — we do so all the time. You can work together because by so doing you benefit yourself and the other person. This is the **real** communist way, that of mutual aid and free agreement.

So Schweickart is ignoring the vast majority of relations in any society. For example, love/attraction is a horizontal link between two autonomous individuals and profit considerations do not enter into the relationship. Thus anarchists argue that Schweickart's argument is flawed as it fails to recognise that resource usage and production techniques can be organised in terms of human need and free agreement between economic actors, without profits or central command. This system does not mean that we all have to love each other (an impossible wish). Rather, it means that we recognise that by voluntarily co-operating as equals we ensure that we remain free individuals and that we can gain the advantages of sharing resources and work (for example, a reduced working day and week, self-managed work in safe and hygienic working conditions and a free selection of the product of a whole society). In other words, a self-interest which exceeds the narrow and impoverished egotism of capitalist society.

Thus free agreement and horizontal links are not limited to market transactions — they develop for numerous reasons and anarchists recognise this. As George Barrett argued:

> *"Let us imagine now that the great revolt of the workers has taken place, that their direct action has made them masters of the situation. It is not easy to see that some man in a street that grew hungry would soon draw a list of the loaves that were needed, and take it to the bakery where the strikers were in possession? Is there any difficulty in supposing that the necessary amount would then be baked according to this list? By this time the bakers would know what carts and delivery vans were needed to send the bread out to the people, and if they let the carters and vanmen know of this, would these not do their utmost to supply the vehicles … If … [the bakers needed] more benches [to make bread] … the carpenters*

*would supply them [and so on] … So the endless continuity goes on — a well-balanced interdependence of parts guaranteed, because **need** is the motive force behind it all … In the same way that each free individual has associated with his brothers [and sisters] to produce bread, machinery, and all that is necessary for life, driven by no other force than his desire for the full enjoyment of life, so each institution is free and self-contained, and co-operates and enters into agreements with other because by so doing it extends its own possibilities. There is no centralised State exploiting or dictating, but the complete structure is supported because each part is dependent on the whole … It will be a society responsive to the wants of the people; it will supply their everyday needs as quickly as it will respond to their highest aspirations. Its changing forms will be the passing expressions of humanity."* [**The Anarchist Revolution**, pp. 17-19]

To make productive decisions we need to know what others need and information in order to evaluate the alternative options available to us to satisfy that need. Therefore, it is a question of distributing information between producers and consumers, information which the market often hides (or actively blocks) or distorts due to inequalities in resources (i.e. need does not count in the market, *"effective demand"* does and this skews the market in favour of the wealthy). This information network has partly been discussed in the last section where a method of comparison between different materials, techniques and resources based upon use value was discussed. In addition, the need to indicate the current fluctuations in stocks, production and consumption has also to be factored in when making decisions.

To indicate the relative changes in scarcity of a given good it will be necessary to calculate what could be termed its *"scarcity index."* This would inform potential users of this good whether its demand is outstripping its supply so that they may effectively adjust their decisions in light of the decisions of others. This index could be, for example, a percentage figure which indicates the relation of orders placed for a good to the amount actually produced. For example, a good which has a demand higher than its supply would have an index value of 101% or higher. This value would inform potential users to start looking for substitutes for it or to economise on its use. Such a scarcity figure would exist for each syndicate as well as (possibly) a generalised figure for the industry as a whole on a regional, "national", etc. level.

In this way, a specific good could be seen to be in high demand and so only those producers who **really** required it would place orders for it (so ensuring effective use of resources). Needless to say, stock levels and other basic book-keeping techniques would be utilised in order to ensure a suitable buffer level of a specific good existed. This may result in some excess supply of goods being produced and used as stock to handle unexpected changes in the aggregate demand for a good. Such a buffer system would work on an individual workplace level and at a communal level. Syndicates would obviously have their inventories, stores of raw materials and finished goods "on the shelf" which can be used to meet unexpected increases in demand. Communal stores, hospitals and so on would

have their stores of supplies in case of unexpected disruptions in supply.

This is a common practice even in capitalism, with differences between actual demand and expected demand being absorbed by unintended stock changes. Firms today also have spare capacity in order to meet such upsurges in demand. Such policies of maintaining stocks and spare capacity will continue to the case under anarchism. It is assumed that syndicates and their confederations will wish to adjust capacity if they are aware of the need to do so. Hence, price changes in response to changes in demand would not be necessary to provide the information that such adjustments are required. This is because a *"change in demand first becomes apparent as a change in the quantity being sold at existing prices [or being consumed in a moneyless system] and is therefore reflected in changes in stocks or orders. Such changes are perfectly good indicators or signals that an imbalance between demand and current output has developed. If a change in demand for its products proved to be permanent, a production unit would find its stocks being run down and its order book lengthening, or its stocks increasing and orders falling … Price changes in response to changes in demand are therefore not necessary for the purpose of providing information about the need to adjust capacity."* [Pat Devine, **Democracy and Economic Planning**, p. 242]

So syndicates, communes and their confederations will create buffer stocks of goods to handle unforeseen changes in demand and supply. This sort of inventory has also been used by capitalist countries like the USA to prevent changes in market conditions for agricultural products and other strategic raw materials producing wild spot-price movements and inflation. Post-Keynesian economist Paul Davidson argued that the stability of commodity prices this produced *"was an essential aspect of the unprecedented prosperous economic growth of the world's economy"* between 1945 and 1972. US President Nixon dismantled these buffer zone programmes, resulting in *"violent commodity price fluctuations"* which had serious negative economic effects. [**Controversies in Post-Keynesian Economics**, p. 114 and p. 115] Again, an anarchist society is likely to utilise this sort of buffer system to iron out short-term changes in supply and demand. By reducing short-term fluctuations of the supply of commodities, bad investment decisions would be reduced as syndicates would not be mislead, as is the case under capitalism, by market prices being too high or too low at the time when the decisions where being made (as discussed in section I.1.5 such disequilibrium prices convey misinformation which causes very substantial economic distortions).

This, combined with cost-benefit analysis described in section I.4.4, would allow information about changes within a moneyless economy to rapidly spread throughout the whole system and influence all decision makers without the great majority knowing anything about the original causes of these changes. This would allow a syndicate to ascertain which good used up least resources and therefore left the most over for other uses (i.e., relative costs or scarcity) as well as giving them information on what resources were used to create it (i.e., the absolute costs involved) The relevant information is communicated to all involved, without having to be ordered by an "all-knowing" central body as in a Leninist centrally planned economy. As argued in section I.1.2, anarchists have long realised that no centralised body could possibly be able to possess all the information dispersed throughout the economy to organise production and if such a body attempted to do so, the resulting bureaucracy would effectively reduce and impoverish the amount of information available to decision makers and so cause shortages and inefficiencies.

To get an idea how this system could work, let us take the example of a change in the copper industry. Let us assume that a source of copper unexpectedly fails or that the demand for copper increases. What would happen?

First, the initial difference would be a diminishing of stocks of copper which each syndicate maintains to take into account unexpected changes in requests. This would help buffer out short lived, changes in supply or requests. Second, naturally, there is an increase in demand for copper for those syndicates which are producing it. This immediately increases the **scarcity index** of those firms and their product. For example, the index may rise from 95% (indicating a slight over-production in respect to current demand) to 115% (indicating that the demand for copper has risen in respect to the current level of production). This change in the **scarcity index** (combined with difficulties in finding copper producing syndicates which will accept their orders) enters into the decision making algorithms of other syndicates. This, in turn, results in changes in their plans. For example, the syndicates can seek out other suppliers who have a lower scarcity index or substitutes for copper may be used as they have become a more efficient resource to use.

In this way, requests for copper products fall and soon only reflect those requests that really need copper (i.e., do not have realistic substitutes available for it). This would result in the demand falling with respect to the current supply (as indicated by requests from other syndicates and to maintain buffer stock levels). Thus a general message has been sent across the economy that copper has become (relatively) scarce and syndicate plans have changed in light of this information. No central planner made these decisions nor was money required to facilitate them. We have a decentralised, non-market system based on the free distribution of products between self-governing associations.

Looking at the wider picture, the question of how to respond to this change in supply/requests for copper presents itself. The copper syndicate federation and cross-industry syndicate federations have regular meetings and the question of the changes in the copper situation present themselves and they must consider how to response to these changes. Part of this is to determine whether this change is likely to be short term or long term. A short term change (say caused by a mine accident, for example) would not need new investments to be planned. However, long term changes (say the new requests are due to a new product being created by another syndicate or an existing mine becoming exhausted) may need co-ordinated investment (we can expect syndicates to make their own plans in light of changes, for example, by investing in new machinery to produce copper more efficiently or to increase production). If the expected changes of these plans approximately equal the predicted long term changes, then the federation need not act. However, if they do then investment in new copper mines or large scale new investment across the industry may be required. The federation would propose such plans.

Needless to say, the future can be guessed, it cannot be accurately predicted. Thus there may be over-investment in certain industries as expected changes do not materialise. However, unlike capitalism, this would not result in an economic crisis (with over-investment within capitalism, workplaces close due to lack of profits, regardless of social need). All that would happen is that some of the goods produced would not be used, some labour and resources would be wasted and the syndicates would rationalise production, close down relatively inefficient plant and concentrate production in the more efficient ones. The sweeping economic crises of capitalism would be a thing of the past.

In summary, each syndicate receives its own orders and supplies and sends its own produce out to specific consumers. Similarly, communal distribution centres would order required goods from syndicates it determines. In this way consumers can change to syndicates which respond to their needs and so production units are aware of what it is socially useful for them to produce as well as the social cost of the resources they need to produce it. In this way a network of horizontal relations spread across society, with co-ordination achieved by equality of association and not the hierarchy of the corporate structure.

While anarchists are aware of the "isolation paradox" (see section B.6) this does not mean that we think the commune should make decisions **for** people on what they are to consume. That would be a prison. No, all anarchists agree that is up to the individual to determine their own needs and for the collectives they join to determine social requirements like parks, infrastructure improvements and so on. However, social anarchists think that it would be beneficial to discuss the framework around which these decisions would be made. This would mean, for example, that communes would agree to produce eco-friendly products, reduce waste and generally make decisions enriched by social interaction. Individuals would still decide which sort goods they desire, based on what the collectives produce but these goods would be based on a socially agreed agenda. In this way waste, pollution and other "externalities" of atomised consumption could be reduced. For example, while it is rational for individuals to drive a car to work, collectively this results in massive **irrationality** (for example, traffic jams, pollution, illness, unpleasant social infrastructures). A sane society would discuss the problems associated with car use and would agree to produce a fully integrated public transport network which would reduce pollution, stress, illness, and so on.

Therefore, while anarchists recognise individual tastes and desires, they are also aware of the social impact of them and so try to create a social environment where individuals can enrich their personal decisions with the input of other people's ideas.

On a related subject, it is obvious that different syndicates would produce slightly different goods, so ensuring that people have a choice. It is doubtful that the current waste implied in multiple products from different companies (sometimes the same multi-national corporation!) all doing the same job would be continued in an anarchist society. However, production will be "variations on a theme" in order to ensure consumer choice and to allow the producers to know what features consumers prefer. It would be impossible to sit down beforehand and make a list of what features a good should have — that assumes perfect knowledge and that technology is fairly constant. Both these assumptions are of limited use in real life. Therefore, co-operatives would produce goods with different features and production would change to meet the demand these differences suggest (for example, factory A produces a new CD player, and consumption patterns indicate that this is popular and so the rest of the factories convert). This is in addition to R&D experiments and test populations. In this way consumer choice would be maintained, and enhanced as people would be able to influence the decisions of the syndicates as producers (in some cases) and through syndicate/commune dialogue.

Finally, it would be churlish, but essential, to note that capitalism only equates supply and demand in the fantasy world of neo-classical economics. Any **real** capitalist economy, as we discussed in section I.1.5 is marked by uncertainty and a tendency to over-produce in the response to the higher profits caused by previously under-producing goods, with resulting periods of crisis in which falling effective demand sees a corresponding fall in supply. Not to mention the awkward fact that real needs (demand) are not met simply because people are too poor to pay for the goods (i.e., no effective demand). As such, to suggest that only non-market systems have a problem ensuring demand and supply meet is mistaken.

To conclude, anarchists do not ignore *"supply and demand."* Instead, they recognise the limitations of the capitalist version of this truism and point out that capitalism is based on **effective** demand which has no necessary basis with efficient use of resources. Instead of the market, social anarchists advocate a system based on horizontal links between producers which effectively communicates information across society about the relative changes in supply and demand which reflect actual needs of society and not bank balances. The investment response to changes in supply and demand will be discussed in section I.4.8 while section I.4.13 will discuss the allocation of work tasks.

I.4.6 Surely anarchist-communism would just lead to demand exceeding supply?

While non-communist forms of anarchism relate consumption to work done, so automatically relating demand to production, this is not the case in communist-anarchism. In that system, distribution is according to need, not deed. Given this, it is a common objection that libertarian communism would lead to people wasting resources by taking more than they need.

Kropotkin, for example, stated that *"free communism ... places the product reaped or manufactured at the disposal of all, leaving to each the liberty to consume them as he pleases in his own home."* [**The Place of Anarchism in the Evolution of Socialist Thought**, p. 7] But, some argue, what if an individual says they "need" a luxury house or a personal yacht? Simply put, workers may not "need" to produce it. As Tom Brown put it, *"such things are the product of social labour ... Under syndicalism ... it is improbable that any greedy, selfish person would be able to kid a shipyard full of workers to build him a ship all for his own hoggish self. There would*

be steam luxury yachts, but they would be enjoyed in common." [**Syndicalism**, p. 51]

Therefore, communist-anarchists are not blind to the fact that free access to products is based upon the actual work of real individuals — "society" provides nothing, individuals working together do. This is reflected in the classic statement of communism: *"From each according to their ability, to each according to their needs."* This must be considered as a whole as those producing have needs and those receiving have abilities. The needs of both consumer **and** producer have to be taken into account, and this suggests that those producing have to feel the need to do so. This means that if no syndicate or individual desires to produce a specific order then this order can be classed as an "unreasonable" demand — "unreasonable" in this context meaning that no one freely agrees to produce it. Of course, individuals may agree to barter services in order to get what they want produced if they **really** want something but such acts in no way undermine a communist society.

This also applies to the demand for goods which are scarce and, as a result, require substantial labour and resources to produce. In such circumstances, the producers (either as a specific syndicate or in their confederations) would refuse to supply such a "need" or communes and their confederations would suggest that this would be waste of resources. Ultimately, a free society would seek to avoid the irrationalities of capitalism where the drive for profits results in production for the sake of production and consumption for the sake of consumption and the many work longer and harder to meet the demands of a (wealthy) few. A free people would evaluate the pros and cons of any activity before doing it. As Malatesta put it:

> *"[A] communist society ... is not, obviously, about an absolute right to satisfy **all** of one's needs, because needs are infinite ... so their satisfaction is always limited by productive capacity; nor would it be useful or just that the community in order to satisfy excessive needs, otherwise called caprices, of a few individuals, should undertake work, out of proportion to the utility being produced ... What we would like is for everybody to live in the best possible way: so that everybody with a minimum amount of effort will obtain maximum satisfaction."* [**At the Café**, pp. 60-1]

Communist-anarchists recognise that production, like consumption, must be based on freedom. However, it has been argued that free access would lead to waste as people take more than they would if they had to pay for it. This objection is not as serious as it first appears. There are plenty of examples within current society to indicate that free access will not lead to abuses. Let us take a few examples. In public libraries people are free to sit and read books all day but few, if any, actually do so. Neither do people always take the maximum number of books out at a time. No, they use the library as they need to and feel no need to maximise their use of the institution. Some people never use the library, although it is free. In the case of water supplies, it is clear that people do not leave taps on all day because water is often supplied freely or for a fixed charge. Similarly with pavements, people do not walk everywhere because to do so is free. In such cases individuals use the resource as and when they need to. Equally, vegetarians do not start eating meat when they visit their friend's parties just because the buffet is free.

We can expect similar results as other resources become freely available. In effect, this argument makes as much sense as arguing that individuals will travel to stops **beyond** their destination if public transport is based on a fixed charge! Obviously only an idiot would travel further than required in order to get "value for money." However, for many the world seems to be made up of such fools. Perhaps it would be advisable for such critics to hand out political leaflets in the street. Even though the leaflets are free, crowds rarely form around the person handing them out demanding as many copies of the leaflet as possible. Rather, those interested in what the leaflets have to say take them, the rest ignore them. If free access automatically resulted in people taking more than they need then critics of free communism would be puzzled by the lack of demand for what they were handing out!

Communist Anarchists also argue that we cannot judge people's buying habits under capitalism with their actions in a free society. After all, advertising does not exist to meet people's needs but rather to create needs by making people insecure about themselves. Simply put, advertising does not amplify existing needs or sell the goods and services that people already want. Advertising would not need to stoop to the level of manipulative adverts that create false personalities for products and provide solutions for problems that the advertisers themselves create if this were the case. Crude it may be, but advertising is based on the creation of insecurities, preying on fears and obscuring rational thought. In an alienated society in which people are subject to hierarchical controls, feelings of insecurity and lack of control and influence would be natural. It is these fears that advertising multiplies — if you cannot have real freedom, then at least you can buy something new. Advertising is the key means of making people unhappy with what they have and who they are. It is naive to claim that advertising has no effect on the psyche of the receiver or that the market merely responds to the populace and makes no attempt to shape their thoughts. If advertising did not work, firms would not spend so much money on it! Advertising creates insecurities about such matter-of-course things and so generates irrational urges to buy which would not exist in a libertarian communist society.

However, there is a deeper point to be made here about consumerism. Capitalism is based on hierarchy, not liberty. This leads to a weakening of individuality as well as a loss of self-identity and sense of community. Both these senses are a deep human need and consumerism is often a means by which people overcome their alienation from their selves and others (religion, ideology and drugs are other means of escape). Therefore the consumption within capitalism reflects **its** values, not some abstract "human nature." As such, because a firm or industry is making a profit satisfying "needs" within capitalism, it does not follow that people in a free society would have similar wants (i.e., "demand" often does not exist independently of the surrounding society). As Bob Black argues:

"*what we want, what we are capable of wanting is relative to the forms of social organisation. People 'want' fast food because they have to hurry back to work, because*

processed supermarket food doesn't taste much better anyway, because the nuclear family (for the dwindling minority who have even that to go home to) is too small and too stressed to sustain much festivity in cooking and eating — and so forth. It is only people who can't get what they want who resign themselves to want more of what they can get. Since we cannot be friends and lovers, we wail for more candy." [**Friendly Fire**, p. 57]

Therefore, most anarchists think that consumerism is a product of a hierarchical society within which people are alienated from themselves and the means by which they can make themselves **really** happy (i.e. meaningful relationships, liberty, self-managed productive activity, and so on). Consumerism is a means of filling the spiritual hole capitalism creates within us by denying our freedom and violating equality. This means that capitalism produces individuals who define themselves by what they have, not who they are. This leads to consumption for the sake of consumption, as people try to make themselves happy by consuming more commodities. But, as Erich Fromm pointed out, this cannot work for long and only leads to even more insecurity (and so even more consumption):

"*If I am what I have and if what I have is lost, who then am I?* Nobody but a defeated, deflated, pathetic testimony to a wrong way of living. Because I **can** lose what I have, I am necessarily constantly worried that I **shall** lose what I have.*" [**To Have Or To Be**, p. 111]

Such insecurity easily makes consumerism seem a "natural" way of life and so make communism seem impossible. However, rampant consumerism is far more a product of lack of meaningful freedom within an alienated society than a "natural law" of human existence. In a society that encouraged and protected individuality by non-hierarchical social relationships and organisations, individuals would have a strong sense of self and so be less inclined to mindlessly consume. As Fromm put it: "*If **I am what I am** and not what I have, nobody can deprive me of or threaten my security and my sense of identity. My centre is within myself.*" [**Op. Cit.**, p. 112] Such self-centred individuals do not have to consume endlessly to build a sense of security or happiness within themselves.

In other words, the well-developed individuality that an anarchist society would develop would have less need to consume than the average person in a capitalist one. This is not to suggest that life will be bare and without luxuries in an anarchist society, far from it. A society based on the free expression of individuality could be nothing but rich in wealth and diverse in goods and experiences. What we are arguing here is that an anarchist-communist society would not have to fear rampant consumerism making demand outstrip supply constantly and always precisely because freedom will result in a non-alienated society of well developed individuals.

It should not be forgotten that communism has two conditions, distribution according to need **and** production according to ability. If the latter condition is not met, if someone does not contribute to the goods available in the libertarian communist society, then the former condition is not likely to be tolerated and they would be asked to leave so reducing demand for goods. The freedom to associate means being free **not** to associate. Thus a free communist society would see goods being supplied as well as demanded. As Malatesta argued:

> "Basic to the anarchist system, before communism or any other forms of social conviviality is the principle of the free compact; the rule of integral communism — 'from each according to his [or her] ability, to each according to his [or her] need' — applies only to those who accept it, including naturally the conditions which make it practicable." [quoted by Camillo Berneri, "The Problem of Work", pp. 59-82, **Why Work?**, Vernon Richards (ed.), p. 74]

So, as Malatesta suggested, it should be noted that communist-anarchists are well aware that it is likely that free access to all goods and services cannot be done immediately (see section H.2.5 for details). As Alexander Berkman summarised, "when the social revolution attains the stage where it can produce sufficient for all, then is adopted the Anarchist principle of 'to each according to his [or her] needs' ... But until it is reached, the system of equal sharing ... is imperative as the only just method. It goes without saying, of course, that special consideration must be given to the sick and the old, to children, and to women during and after pregnancy." [**What is Anarchism?**, p. 216] Another possibility was suggested by James Guillaume who argued that as long as a product was "in short supply it will to a certain extent have to be rationed. And the easiest way to do this would be to **sell** these scarce products" but as production grows then "it will not be necessary to ration consumption. The practice of selling, which was adopted as a sort of deterrent to immoderate consumption, will be abolished" and goods "will be distribute[d] ... in accordance with the needs of the consumers." ["On Building the New Social Order", pp. 356-79, **Bakunin on Anarchism**, p. 368] Other possibilities may include communes deciding that certain scarce goods are only available to those who do the unpleasant work (such as collecting the rubbish) or that people have equal access but the actual goods are shared and used for short periods of time (as is currently the case with public libraries). As Situationist Ken Knabb suggests after usefully discussing "just some of the possibilities": "Experimenting with different methods, people will find out for themselves what forms of ownership, exchange and reckoning are necessary." [**Public Secrets**, p. 73]

Whether or not full communism **can** be introduced instantly is a moot point amongst collectivist and communist anarchists, although most would like to see society develop towards a communist goal eventually. Of course, for people used to capitalism this may sound totally utopian. Possibly it is. However, as Oscar Wilde said, a map of the world without Utopia on it is not worth having. One thing is sure, if the developments we have outlined above fail to appear and attempts at communism fail due to waste and demand exceeding supply then a free society would make the necessary decisions and introduce some means of limiting supply (such as, for example, labour notes, equal wages, and so on). Rest assured, though, "the difficulty will be solved and obstacles in the shape of making necessary changes in the detailed working of the system of production and its relation to consumption, will vanish before

the ingenuity of the myriad minds vitally concerned in overcoming them." [Charlotte M. Wilson, **Anarchist Essays**, p. 21]

I.4.7 What will stop producers ignoring consumers?

It is often claimed that without a market producers would ignore the needs of consumers. Without the threat (and fear) of unemployment and destitution and the promise of higher profits, producers would turn out shoddy goods. The holders of this argument point to the example of the Soviet Union which was notorious for terrible goods and a lack of consumer commodities.

Capitalism, in comparison to the old Soviet block, does, to some degree, make the producers accountable to the consumers. If the producer ignores the desires of the consumer then they will loose business to those who do not and be forced, perhaps, out of business (large companies, of course, due to their resources can hold out far longer than smaller ones). Thus we have the carrot (profits) and the stick (fear of poverty) — although, of course, the carrot can be used as a stick against the consumer (no profit, no sale, no matter how much the consumer may need it). Ignoring the obvious objection to this analogy (namely we are human beings, **not** donkeys!) it does contain an important point. What will ensure that consumer needs are meet in an anarchist society?

In an Individualist or Mutualist anarchist system, as it is based on a market, producers would be subject to market forces and so have to meet consumers needs. Collectivist-anarchism meets consumer needs in a similar way, as producers would be accountable to consumers by the process of buying and selling between co-operatives. As James Guillaume put it, the workers associations would "deposit their unconsumed commodities in the facilities provided by the [communal] Bank of Exchange ... The Bank of Exchange would remit to the producers negotiable **vouchers** representing the value of their products" (this value "having been established in advance by a contractual agreement between the regional co-operative federations and the various communes"). ["On Building the New Social Order", pp. 356-79, **Bakunin on Anarchism**, pp. 366] If the goods are not in demand then the producer associations would not be able to sell the product of their labour to the Bank of Exchange (or directly to other syndicates or communes) and so they would adjust their output accordingly. Of course, there are problems with these systems due to their basis in the market (as discussed in section I.1.3), although these problems were recognised by Proudhon who argued for an agricultural-industrial federation to protect self-management from the negative effects of market forces (as noted in section I.3.5).

While mutualist and collectivist anarchists can argue that producers would respond to consumer needs otherwise they would not get an income, communist-anarchists (as they seek a moneyless society) cannot argue their system would reward producers in this way. So what mechanism exists to ensure that "the wants of all" are, in fact, met? How does anarcho-communism ensure that production becomes "the mere servant of consumption" and "mould itself on the wants of the consumer, not dictate to him conditions"? [Peter

Kropotkin, **Act for Yourselves**, p. 57] Libertarian communists argue that in a **free** communist society consumers' needs would be met. This is because of the decentralised and federal nature of such a society.

So what is the mechanism which makes producers accountable to consumers in a libertarian communist society? Firstly, communes would practice their power of **"exit"** in the distributive network. If a syndicate was producing sub-standard goods or refusing to change their output in the face of changing consumer needs, then the communal stores would turn to those syndicates which **were** producing the goods desired. The original syndicates would then be producing for their own stocks, a pointless task and one few, if any, would do. After all, people generally desire their work to have meaning, to be useful. To just work, producing something no-one wanted would be such a demoralising task that few, if any, sane people would do it (under capitalism people put up with spirit destroying work as some income is better than none, such an "incentive" would not exist in a free society).

As can be seen, **"exit"** would still exist in libertarian communism. However, it could be argued that unresponsive or inefficient syndicates would still exist, exploiting the rest of society by producing rubbish (or goods which are of less than average quality) and consuming the products of other people's labour, confident that without the fear of poverty and unemployment they can continue to do this indefinitely. Without the market, it is argued, some form of bureaucracy would be required (or develop) which would have the power to punish such syndicates. Thus the state would continue in "libertarian" communism, with the "higher" bodies using coercion against the lower ones to ensure they meet consumer needs or produced enough.

While, at first glance, this appears to be a possible problem on closer inspection it is flawed. This is because anarchism is based not only on **"exit"** but also **"voice"**. Unlike capitalism, libertarian communism is based on association and communication. Each syndicate and commune is in free agreement and confederation with all the others. Thus, if a specific syndicate was producing bad goods or not pulling its weight, then those in contact with them would soon realise this. First, those unhappy with a syndicate's work would appeal to them directly to get their act together. If this did not work, then they would notify their disapproval by refusing to associate with them in the future (i.e. they would use their power of **"exit"** as well as refusing to provide the syndicate with any goods **it** requires). They would also let society as a whole know (via the media) as well as contacting consumer groups and co-operatives and the relevant producer and communal confederations which they and the other syndicates are members of, who would, in turn, inform their members of the problems (the relevant confederations could include local and regional communal confederations, the general cross-industry confederation, its own industrial/communal confederation and the confederation of the syndicate not pulling its weight). In today's society, a similar process of "word of mouth" warnings and recommendations goes on, along with consumer groups and media. Our suggestions here are an extension of this common practice (that this process exists suggests that the price mechanism does not, in fact, provide consumers with all the relevant information they need to make decisions, but this is an aside).

If the syndicate in question, after a certain number of complaints had been lodged against it, still did not change its ways, then it would suffer non-violent direct action. This would involve the boycotting of the syndicate and (perhaps) its local commune (such as denying it products and investment), so resulting in the syndicate being excluded from the benefits of association. The syndicate would face the fact that no one else wanted to associate with it and suffer a drop in the goods coming its way, including consumption products for its members. In effect, a similar process would occur to that of a firm under capitalism that looses its customers and so its income. However, we doubt that a free society would subject any person to the evils of destitution or starvation (as capitalism does). Rather, a bare minimum of goods required for survival would still be available.

In the unlikely event this general boycott did not result in a change of heart, then two options are left available. These are either the break-up of the syndicate and the finding of its members new work places or the giving/selling of the syndicate to its current users (i.e. to exclude them from the society they obviously do not want to be part off). The decision of which option to go for would depend on the importance of the workplace in question and the desires of the syndicates' members. If the syndicate refused to disband, then option two would be the most logical choice (unless the syndicate controlled a scare resource). The second option would, perhaps, be best as this would drive home the benefits of association as the expelled syndicate would have to survive on its own, subject to survival by selling the product of its labour and would soon return to the fold.

Kropotkin argued in these terms over 100 years ago:

> "When a railway company, federated with other companies, fails to fulfil its engagements, when its trains are late and goods lie neglected at the stations, the other companies threaten to cancel the contract, and that threat usually suffices.
>
> "It is generally believed ... that commerce only keeps to its engagements from fear of lawsuits. Nothing of the sort; nine times in ten the trader who has not kept his word will not appear before a judge ... the sole fact of having driven a creditor to bring a lawsuit suffices for the vast majority of merchants to refuse for good to have any dealings with a man who has compelled one of them to go to law.
>
> "This being so, why should means that are used today among ... traders in the trade, and railway companies in the organisation of transport, not be made use of in a society based on voluntary work?" [**The Conquest of Bread**, p. 153]

Thus, to ensure producer accountability of production to consumption, no bureaucratic body is required in libertarian communism (or any other form of anarchism). Rather, communication and direct action by those affected by unresponsive producers would be an effective and efficient means of ensuring the accountability of production to consumption.

I.4.8 What about investment decisions?

Obviously, a given society needs to take into account changes in consumption and so invest in new means of production. An anarchist society is no different. As Guild Socialist G.D.H Cole points out, *"it is essential at all times, and in accordance with considerations which vary from time to time, for a community to preserve a balance between production for ultimate use and production for use in further production. And this balance is a matter which ought to be determined by and on behalf of the whole community."* [**Guild Socialism Restated**, p. 144]

How this balance is determined varies according to the school of anarchist thought considered. All agree, however, that such an important task should be under effective community control.

The mutualists see the solution to the problems of investment as creating a system of mutual banks, which reduce interest rates to zero. This would be achieved by *"the organisation of credit, on the principle of reciprocity or mutualism ... In such an organisation credit is raised to the dignity of a social function, managed by the community; and, as society never speculates upon its members, it will lend its credit ... at the actual cost of transaction."* [Charles A. Dana, **Proudhon and his "Bank of the People"**, p. 36] Loans would be allocated to projects which the mutual banks considered likely to succeed and repay the original loan. In this way, the increase in the money supply implied by these acts of credit providing does not generate inflation for money is **not** created wantonly but rather is aimed at projects which are considered likely to **increase** the supply of goods and services in the economy (see section G.3.6). Another key source of investment would be internal funds (i.e., retained savings) as is the case with co-operatives today: *"Worker-managers finance their new investments partly out of internal funds and partly from external loans ... Entrepreneurial activity of worker-managers ... generates profits and losses, i.e., higher or lower income per worker."* [Branko Horvat, *"The Theory of the Worker-Managed Firm Revisited"*, pp. 9-25, **Journal of Comparative Economics**, vol. 10, no. 1, p. 21] As discussed in section I.1.1, eliminating the stock market will not harm investment (almost all investment funds are from other sources) and will remove an important negative influence in economic activity.

Collectivist and communist anarchists recognise that credit is based on human activity, which is represented as money. As Cole pointed out, the *"understanding of this point [on investment] depends on a clear appreciation of the fact that all real additions to capital take the form of directing a part of the productive power of labour and using certain materials not for the manufacture of products and the rendering of services incidental to such manufacture for purposes of purposes of further production."* [**Op. Cit.**, p. 143] So collectivist and communist anarchists agree with their Mutualist cousins when they state that *"[a]ll credit presupposes labour, and, if labour were to cease, credit would be impossible"* and that the *"legitimate source of credit"* was *"the labouring classes"* who *"ought to control it"* and for *"whose benefit [it should] be used"*. [Dana, **Op. Cit.**, p. 35] Therefore, in collectivism, investment funds would exist for

syndicates, communes and their in community (*"People's"*) banks. These would be used to store depreciation funds and as well as other funds agreed to by the syndicates for investment projects (for example, confederations of syndicates may agree to allocate a certain percentage of their labour notes to a common account in order to have the necessary funds available for major investment projects). Similarly, individual syndicates and communes would also create a store of funds for their own investment projects. Moreover, the confederations of syndicates to which these *"People's Banks"* would be linked would also have a defined role in investment decisions to ensure that production meets demand by being the forum which decides which investment plans should be given funding (this, we stress, is hardly "central planning" as capitalist firms also plan future investments to meet expected demand). In this, collectivist anarchism is like mutualism and so we would also expect interest-free credit being arranged to facilitate investment.

In a communist-anarchist society, things would be slightly different as this would not have the labour notes used in mutualism and collectivism. This means that the productive syndicates would agree that a certain part of their total output and activity will be directed to investment projects. In effect, each syndicate is able to draw upon the resources approved of by the co-operative commonwealth in the form of an agreed claim on the labour power of society (investment *"is essentially an allocation of material and labour, and fundamentally, an allocation of human productive power."* [Cole, **Op. Cit.**, pp. 144-5]). In this way, mutual aid ensures a suitable pool of resources for the future from which all benefit.

It should be remembered that savings are not required before credit can be issued. Under capitalism, for example, banks regularly issue credit in excess of their actual reserves of cash (if they did not then, one, they would not be very good capitalists and, two, the economy would grind to a halt). Nor does the interest rate reflect a preference for future goods (as discussed in section C.2.6 interest rates reflect market power, the degree of monopoly in the credit industry, the social and class position of individuals and a host of other factors). Moreover, a developed economy replaces a process in time with a process in space. In peasant and tribal societies, individuals usually did have to spend time and energy making their own tools (the hunter had to stop hunting in order to create a new improved bow or spear). However, with a reasonably developed division of work then different people produce the tools others use and can do so at the same time as the others produce. If workers producing investment goods had to wait until sufficient savings had been gathered before starting work then it is doubtful that any developed economy could function. Thus the notion that "investment" needs saving is somewhat inappropriate, as different workplaces produce consumption goods and others produce investment goods. The issue becomes one of ensuring that enough people and resources go towards both activities.

How would this work? Obviously investment decisions have implications for society as a whole. The implementation of these decisions require the use of **existing** capacity and so must be the responsibility of the appropriate level of the confederation in question. Investment decisions taken at levels above the production unit become effective in the form of demand for the current output of the syndicates which have the capacity to produce the goods required. This would require each syndicate to *"prepare a budget, showing its estimate of requirements both of goods or services for immediate use, and of extensions and improvements."* [Cole, **Op. Cit.**, p. 145] These budgets and investment projects would be discussed at the appropriate level of the confederation (in this, communist-anarchism would be similar to collectivist anarchism).

The confederation of syndicates/communes would be the ideal forum to discuss the various investment plans required — and to allocate scarce resources between different ends. This would involve, possibly, dividing investment into two groups — necessary and optional — and using statistical techniques to consider the impact of an investment decision (for example, the use of input-output tables could be used to see if a given investment decision in, say, the steel industry would require investment in energy production). In this way social needs **and** social costs would be taken into account and ensure that investment decisions are not taken in isolation from one another, so causing bottle-necks and insufficient production due to lack of inputs from other industries.

Necessary investments are those which have been agreed upon by the appropriate confederation. It means that resources and productive capacity are prioritised towards them, as indicated in the agreed investment project. It will not be required to determine precisely **which** syndicates will provide the necessary goods for a given investment project, just that it has priority over other requests. Under capitalism, when a bank gives a company credit, it rarely asks exactly which companies will be contracted with when the money is spent but, rather, it gives the company the power to command the labour of other workers by supplying them with credit/money. Similarly in an anarcho-communist society, except that the other workers have agreed to supply their labour for the project in question by designating it a ***"necessary investment"***. This means when a request arrives at a syndicate for a ***"necessary investment"*** a syndicate must try and meet it (i.e. it must place the request into its production schedule before *"optional"* requests, assuming that it has the capacity to meet it). A list of necessary investment projects, including what they require and if they have been ordered, will be available to all syndicates to ensure such a request is a real one.

Optional investment is simply investment projects which have not been agreed to by a confederation. This means that when a syndicate or commune places orders with a syndicate they may not be met or take longer to arrive. The project may go ahead, but it depends on whether the syndicate or commune can find workers willing to do that work. This would be applicable for small scale investment decisions or those which other communes/syndicates do not think of as essential.

Thus we have two inter-related investment strategies. A communist-anarchist society would prioritise certain forms of investment by the use of ***"necessary"*** and ***"optional"*** investment projects. This socialisation of investment will allow a free society to ensure that social needs are meet while maintaining a decentralised and dynamic economy. Major projects to meet social needs will be organised effectively, but with diversity for minor projects. The tasks of ensuring investment production, making orders for specific goods and so forth, would be as decentralised as other aspects of a free economy and so anarchism *"proposes … [t]hat usufruct of instruments of production — land included — should be free to all workers, or groups of workers"*, that *"workers should group themselves, and arrange their work as their reason and inclination prompt"* and that *"the necessary connections between the various industries … should be managed on the same voluntary principle."* [Charlotte M. Wilson, **Anarchist Essays**, p. 21]

As for when investment is needed, it is clear that this will be based on the changes in demand for goods in both collectivist and communist anarchism. As Guilliaume put it: *"By means of statistics gathered from all the communes in a region, it will be possible to scientifically balance production and consumption. In line with these statistics, it will also be possible to add more help in industries where production is insufficient and reduce the number of men where there is a surplus of production."* [*"On Building the New Social Order"*, pp. 356-79, **Bakunin on Anarchism**, p. 370] Obviously, investment in branches of production with a high demand would be essential and this would be easily seen from the statistics generated by the collectives and communes. Tom Brown made this obvious point:

> *"Goods, as now, will be produced in greater variety, for workers like producing different kinds, and new models, of goods. Now if some goods are unpopular, they will be left on the shelves … Of other goods more popular, the shops will be emptied. Surely it is obvious that the [shop] assistant will decrease his order of the unpopular line and increase his order of the popular."* [**Syndicalism**, p. 55]

As a rule of thumb, syndicates that produce investment goods would be inclined to supply other syndicates who are experiencing excess demand before others, all other things being equal. Because of such guidelines and communication between producers, investment would go to those industries that actually required them. In other words, customer choice (as indicated by individuals choosing between the output of different syndicates) would generate information that is relevant to investment decisions.

As production would be decentralised as far as it is sensible and rational to do so, each locality/region would be able to understand its own requirements and apply them as it sees fit. This means that large-scale planning would not be conducted (assuming that it could work in practice, of course) simply because it would not be needed. This, combined with an extensive communications network, would ensure that investment not only did not duplicate unused plant within the economy but that investments take into account the specific problems and opportunities each locality has. Of course, collectives would experiment with new lines and technology as well as existing lines and so invest in new technologies and products. As occurs under capitalism, extensive consumer testing would occur before dedicating major investment decisions to new products.

In addition, investment decisions would also require information which showed the different outcomes of different options. By this we simply mean an analysis of how different investment projects relate to each other in terms of inputs and outputs, compared to the existing techniques. This would be in the form of cost-benefit analysis (as outlined in section I.4.4) and would show when it would make economic, social and ecological sense to switch industrial techniques to more efficient and/or more empowering and/or more ecologically sound methods. Such an evaluation would indicate levels of inputs and compare them to the likely outputs. For example, if a new production technique reduced the number of hours worked in total (comparing the hours worked to produce the machinery with that reduced in using it) as well as reducing waste products for a similar output, then such a technique would be implemented.

Similarly with communities. A commune will obviously have to decide upon and plan civic investment (e.g. new parks, housing and so forth). They will also have the deciding say in industrial developments in their area as it would be unfair for syndicate to just decide to build a cement factory next to a housing co-operative if they did not want it. There is a case for arguing that the local commune will decide on investment decisions for syndicates in its area (for example, a syndicate may produce X plans which will be discussed in the local commune and one plan finalised from the debate). Regional decisions (for example, a new hospital) could be decided at the appropriate level, with information fed from the health syndicate and consumer co-operatives. The actual location for investment decisions will be worked out by those involved. However, local syndicates must be the focal point for developing new products and investment plans in order to encourage innovation.

Therefore, under anarchism no capital market is required to determine whether investment is required and what form it would take. The work that apologists for capitalism claim currently is done by the stock market can be replaced by co-operation and communication between workplaces in a decentralised, confederated network. The relative needs of different consumers of a product can be evaluated by the producers and an informed decision reached on where it would best be used. Without private property, housing, schools, hospitals, workplaces and so on will no longer be cramped into the smallest space possible. Instead, they will be built within a "green" environment. This means that human constructions will be placed within a natural setting and no longer stand apart from nature. In this way human life can be enriched and the evils of cramping as many humans and things into a small a space as is "economical" can be overcome.

Only by taking investment decisions away from "experts" and placing it in the hands of ordinary people will current generations be able to invest according to their, and future generations', benefit. It is hardly in our best interests to have a system whose aim is to make the wealthy even wealthier and on whose whims are dependent the lives of millions of people.

I.4.9 Should technological advance be seen as anti-anarchistic?

Not necessarily. This is because technology can allow us to "do more with less," technological progress can improve standards of living for all people, and technologies can be used to increase personal freedom: medical technology, for instance, can free people from the scourges of pain, illness, and a "naturally" short life span; technology can be used to free labour from mundane chores associated with production; advanced communications technology can enhance our ability to freely associate. The list is endless. So the vast majority of anarchists agree with Kropotkin's comment that the *"development*

of [the industrial] technique at last gives man [sic!] the opportunity to free himself from slavish toil." [**Ethics**, p. 2]

For example, increased productivity under capitalism usually leads to further exploitation and domination, displaced workers, economic crisis, etc. However, it does not have to so in an anarchist world. By way of example, consider a commune in which 5 people desire to be bakers (or 5 people are needed to work the communal bakery) and 20 hours of production per person, per week is spent on baking bread. Now, what happens if the introduction of automation, **as desired, planned and organised by the workers themselves**, reduces the amount of labour required for bread production to 15 person-hours per week? Clearly, no one stands to lose — even if someone's work is "displaced" that person will continue to receive the same access to the means of life as before — and they might even gain. This last is due to the fact that 5 person-hours have been freed up from the task of bread production, and those person-hours may now be used elsewhere or converted to leisure, either way increasing each person's standard of living.

Obviously, this happy outcome derives not only from the technology used, but also (and critically) from its use in an equitable economic and social system: in the end, there is no reason why the use of technology cannot be used to empower people and increase their freedom!

Of course technology can be used for oppressive ends. Human knowledge, like all things, can be used to increase freedom or to decrease it, to promote inequality or reduce it, to aid the worker or to subjugate them, and so on. Technology, as we argued in section D.10, cannot be considered in isolation from the society it is created and used in. In a hierarchical society, technology will be introduced that serves the interests of the powerful and helps marginalise and disempower the majority. It does not evolve in isolation from human beings and the social relationships and power structures between them. Vernon Richards stated the obvious:

"We maintain that the term 'productivity' has meaning, or is socially important, only when all production serves a public need ...

"Productivity has meaning if it results both in a raising of living standards and an increase of leisure for all.

"'Productivity' in the society we live in, because it is not a means to a social end, but is the means whereby industrialists hope to make greater profits for themselves and their shareholders, should be resolutely resisted by the working people, for it brings them neither greater leisure nor liberation from wage-slavery. Indeed for many it means unemployment ...

*"The attempts by managers and the technocrats to streamline industry are resisted intuitively by most work people even if they haven't two political ideas in their heads to knock together, not because they are resistant to change **per se** but because they cannot see that 'change' will do them any good. And of course they are right! Such an attitude is nevertheless a negative one, and the task of anarchist propagandists should be to make them*

aware of this and point to the only alternative, which, in broad terms, is that the producers of wealth must control it for the benefit of all." [**Why Work?**, Vernon Richards (ed.), p. 206]

This means that in an anarchist society, technology would have to be transformed and/or developed which empowered those who used it, so reducing any oppressive aspects associated with it. As Kropotkin argued, we are (potentially) in a good position, because *"[f]or the first time in the history of civilisation, mankind has reached a point where the means of satisfying its needs are in excess of the needs themselves. To impose, therefore, as hitherto been done, the curse of misery and degradation upon vast divisions of mankind, in order to secure well-being and further development for the few, is needed no more: well-being can be secured for all, without placing on anyone the burden of oppressive, degrading toil and humanity can at last build its entire social life on the basis of justice."* [**Op. Cit.**, p. 2] The question is, for most anarchists, how can we humanise and modify this technology and make it socially and individually liberatory, rather than destroying it (where applicable, of course, certain forms of technology and industry will be eliminated due to their inherently destructive nature).

For Kropotkin, like most anarchists, the way to humanise technology and industry was for *"the workers [to] lay hands on factories, houses and banks"* and so *"present production would be completely revolutionised by this simple fact."* This would be the start of a process which would **integrate** industry and agriculture, as it was *"essential that work-shops, foundries and factories develop within the reach of the fields."* [**The Conquest of Bread**, p. 190] Such a process would obviously involve the transformation of both the structure and technology of capitalism rather than its simple and unthinking application. As discussed in section A.3.9, while a few anarchists do seek to eliminate all forms of technology, most would agree with Bakunin when he argued that *"to destroy ... all the instruments of labour ... would be to condemn all humanity — which is infinitely too numerous today to exist ... on the simple gifts of nature ... — to ... death by starvation."* His solution to the question of technology was, like Kropotkin's, to place it at the service of those who use it, to create *"the intimate and complete union of capital and labour"* so that it would *"not ... remain concentrated in the hands of a separate, exploiting class."* Only this could *"smash the tyranny of capital."* [**The Basic Bakunin**, pp. 90-1] So most anarchists seek to transform rather then eliminate technology and to do that we need to be in possession of the means of production before we can decide what to keep, what to change and what to throw away as inhuman. In other words, it is not enough to get rid of the boss, although this is a necessary first step!

Anarchists of all types recognise the importance of critically evaluating technology, industry and so on. The first step of any revolution will be the seizing of the means of production. The second **immediate** step will be the start of their radical transformation by those who use them and are affected by them (i.e. communities, those who use the products they produce and so on). Few, if any, anarchists seek to maintain the current industrial set-up or apply, unchanged, capitalist technology. We doubt that many of the workers who use that technology and work in industry will leave either unchanged.

Rather, they will seek to liberate the technology they use from the influences of capitalism, just as they liberated themselves.

This will, of course, involve the shutting down (perhaps instantly or over a period of time) of many branches of industry and the abandonment of such technology which cannot be transformed into something more suitable for use by free individuals. And, of course, many workplaces will be transformed to produce new goods required to meet the needs of the revolutionary people or close due to necessity as a social revolution will disrupt the market for their goods — such as producers of luxury export goods or suppliers of repressive equipment for state security forces. Altogether, a social revolution implies the transformation of technology and industry, just as it implies the transformation of society.

This process of transforming work can be seen from the Spanish Revolution. Immediately after taking over the means of production, the Spanish workers started to transform it. They eliminated unsafe and unhygienic working conditions and workplaces and created new workplaces based on safe and hygienic working conditions. Working practices were transformed as those who did the work (and so understood it) managed it. Many workplaces were transformed to create products required by the war effort (such as weapons, ammunition, tanks and so on) and to produce consumer goods to meet the needs of the local population as the normal sources of such goods, as Kropotkin predicted, were unavailable due to economic disruption and isolation. Needless to say, these were only the beginnings of the process but they clearly point the way any libertarian social revolution would progress, namely the total transformation of work, industry and technology. Technological change would develop along new lines, ones which will take into account human and ecological needs rather the power and profits of a minority.

Explicit in anarchism is the belief that capitalist and statist methods cannot be used for socialist and libertarian ends. In our struggle for workers' and community self-management is the awareness that workplaces are not merely sites of production — they are also sites of **re**production, the reproduction of certain social relationships based on specific relations of authority between those who give orders and those who take them. The battle to democratise the workplace, to place the collective initiative of the direct producers at the centre of any productive activity, is clearly a battle to transform the workplace, the nature of work and, by necessity, technology as well. As Kropotkin argued:

> *"revolution is more than a mere change of the prevailing political system. It implies the awakening of human intelligence, the increasing of the inventive spirit tenfold, a hundredfold; it is the dawn of a new science ... It is a revolution in the minds of men, as deep, and deeper still, than in their institutions ... the sole fact of having laid hands on middle-class property will imply the necessity of completely re-organising the whole of economic life in the workplaces, the dockyards, the factories."* [**Op. Cit.**, p. 192]

And some think that industry and technology will remain unchanged by such a process and that workers will continue doing the same sort of work, in the same way, using the same methods!

For Kropotkin *"all production has taken a wrong direction, as it is not carried on with a view to securing well-being for all"* under capitalism. [**Op. Cit.**, p. 101] Well-being for all obviously includes those who do the producing and so covers the structure of industry and the technological processes used. Similarly, well-being also includes a person's environment and surroundings and so technology and industry must be evaluated on an ecological basis. Technological progress in an anarchist society, needless to say, will have to take into account these factors as well as others people think are relevant, otherwise the ideal of *"well-being for all"* is rejected (see section I.4.15 for a discussion of what the workplace of the future could look like).

So, technology always partakes of and expresses the basic values of the social system in which it is embedded. If you have a system (capitalism) that alienates everything, it will naturally produce alienated forms of technology and it will orient those technologies so as to reinforce itself. Capitalists will select technology which re-enforces their power and profits and skew technological change in that direction rather than in those which empower individuals and make the workplace more egalitarian.

All this suggests that technological progress is not neutral but dependent on who makes the decisions. As David Noble argues, *"[t]echnological determinism, the view that machines make history rather than people, is not correct … If social changes now upon us seem necessary, it is because they follow not from any disembodied technological logic, but form a social logic."* Technology conforms to *"the interests of power"* but as *"technological process is a social process"* then *"it is, like all social processes, marked by conflict and struggle, and the outcome, therefore, is always ultimately indeterminate."* Viewing technological development *"as a social process rather than as an autonomous, transcendent, and deterministic force can be liberating … because it opens up a realm of freedom too long denied. It restores people once again to their proper role as subjects of the story, rather than mere pawns of technology … And technological development itself, now seen as a social construct, becomes a new variable rather than a first cause, consisting of a range of possibilities and promising a multiplicity of futures."* [**Forces of Production**, pp. 324-5]

This does not mean that we have to reject all technology and industry because it has been shaped by, or developed within, class society. Certain technologies are, of course, so insanely dangerous that they will no doubt be brought to a prompt halt in any sane society. Similarly, certain forms of technology and industrial process will be impossible to transform as they are inherently designed for oppressive ends. Many other industries which produce absurd, obsolete or superfluous commodities will, of course, cease automatically with the disappearance of their commercial or social rationales. But many technologies, however they may presently be misused, have few if any inherent drawbacks. They could be easily adapted to other uses. When people free themselves from domination, they will have no trouble rejecting those technologies that are harmful while adapting others to beneficial uses.

Change society and the technology introduced and utilised will likewise change. By viewing technological progress as a new variable, dependent on those who make the decisions and the type of society they live in, allows us to see that technological development is not inherently anti-anarchist. A non-oppressive, non-exploitative, ecological society will develop non-oppressive, non-exploitative, ecological technology just as capitalism has developed technology which facilitates exploitation, oppression and environmental destruction. Thus an anarchist questions technology: The best technology? Best for whom? Best for what? Best according to what criteria, what visions, according to whose criteria and whose visions?

Needless to say, different communities and different regions would choose different priorities and different lifestyles. As the CNT's Zaragoza resolution on libertarian communism made clear, *"those communes which reject industrialisation … may agree upon a different model of co-existence."* Using the example of *"naturists and nudists,"* it argued that they *"will be entitled to an autonomous administration released from the general commitments"* agreed by the communes and their federations and *"their delegates to congresses of the … Confederation of Autonomous Libertarian Communes will be empowered to enter into economic contacts with other agricultural and industrial Communes."* [quoted by Jose Peirats, **The CNT in the Spanish Revolution**, vol. 1, p. 106]

For most anarchists, though, technological advancement is important in a free society in order to maximise the free time available for everyone and replace mindless toil with meaningful work. The means of doing so is the use of **appropriate** technology (and **not** the worship of technology as such). Only by critically evaluating technology and introducing such forms which empower, are understandable and are controllable by individuals and communities as well as minimising ecological distribution can this be achieved. Only this critical approach to technology can do justice to the power of the human mind and reflect the creative powers which developed the technology in the first place. Unquestioning acceptance of technological progress is just as bad as being unquestioningly anti-technology.

I.4.10 What would be the advantage of a wide basis of surplus distribution?

We noted earlier (in section I.3.1) that competition between syndicates could lead to *"co-operative egotism"* (to use Kropotkin's term) and that to eliminate this problem, the basis of collectivisation needs to be widened so that production is based on need and, as a result, surpluses are distributed society-wide. The advantage of a wide surplus distribution is that it allows all to have a decent life and stop market forces making people work harder and longer to survive in the economy (see section I.1.3). The consolidation of syndicates that would otherwise compete will, it is hoped, lead to a more efficient allocation of resources and technical improvements so allowing the transformation of work and reduction of the time we need to spend in production. We will back up this claim with illustrations from the Spanish Revolution as well as from today's system.

Collectivisation in Catalonia embraced not only major industries like municipal transportation and utilities, but smaller establishments as well: small factories, artisan workshops, service and repair shops, etc. Augustin Souchy describes the process as follows:

> "The artisans and small workshop owners, together with their employees and apprentices, often joined the union of their trade. By consolidating their efforts and pooling their resources on a fraternal basis, the shops were able to undertake very big projects and provide services on a much wider scale ... The collectivisation of the hairdressing shops provides an excellent example of how the transition of a small-scale manufacturing and service industry from capitalism to socialism was achieved ...

> "Before July 19th, 1936 [the date of the Revolution], there were 1,100 hairdressing parlours in Barcelona, most of them owned by poor wretches living from hand to mouth. The shops were often dirty and ill-maintained. The 5,000 hairdressing assistants were among the most poorly paid workers ... Both owners and assistants therefore voluntarily decided to socialise all their shops.

> "How was this done? All the shops simply joined the union. At a general meeting they decided to shut down all the unprofitable shops. The 1,100 shops were reduced to 235 establishments, a saving of 135,000 pesetas per month in rent, lighting, and taxes. The remaining 235 shops were modernised and elegantly outfitted. From the money saved, wages were increased by 40%. Everyone having the right to work and everyone received the same wages. The former owners were not adversely affected by socialisation. They were employed at a steady income. All worked together under equal conditions and equal pay. The distinction between employers and employees was obliterated and they were transformed into a working community of equals — socialism from the bottom up." [**The Anarchist Collectives**, Sam Dolgoff (ed.), pp. 93-94]

The collectives, as well as improving working conditions, also ensured access to other goods and services which market forces had previously denied working class people. Across Republican Spain collectives in towns and villages organised health care. For example, in the village of Magdalena de Pulpis housing "*was free and completely socialised, as was medical care ... Medicines, supplies, transfer to hospitals in Barcelona or Castellon, surgery, services of specialists — all was paid for by the collective.*" This was also done for education, with collectives forming and running schools, colleges and universities. For example, Regional Peasant Federation of Levant saw each collective organise "*one or two free schools for the children*" and "*almost wiped out illiteracy*" (over 70% of rural Spain was illiterate before the Civil War). It also organised a "*University of Moncada*" which "*gave courses in animal husbandry, poultry raising. animal breeding, agriculture, tree science, etc.*" [Gaston Leval, **Op. Cit.**, p. 156 and p. 125]

These examples, social anarchists argue, show that co-operation ensures that resources are efficiently allocated and waste is minimised by cutting down needless competition. It also ensures

that necessary goods and services which meet vital areas for human well-being and development are available for all rather than the few. Rather than reduce choice, such co-operation increased it by making such things available to all (and as consumers have choices in which syndicate to consume from as well as having direct communication between consumer co-operatives and productive units, there is little danger that rationalisation in production will hurt the interests of the consumer).

Another way in which wide distribution of surplus can be advantageous is in Research and Development (R&D). By creating a fund for research and development which is independent of the fortunes of individual syndicates, society as a whole can be improved by access to useful new technologies and processes. Therefore, in a libertarian socialist society, people (both within the workplace and in communities) are likely to decide to allocate significant amounts of resources for basic research from the available social output. This is because the results of this research would be freely available to all and so would aid everyone in the long term. In addition, because workers directly control their workplace and the local community effectively "owns" it, all affected would have an interest in exploring research which would reduce labour, pollution, waste and so on or increase output with little or no social impact.

It should also be mentioned here that research would be pursued more and more as people take an increased interest in both their own work and education. As people become liberated from the grind of everyday life, they will explore possibilities as their interests take them and so research will take place on many levels within society - in the workplace, in the community, in education and so on.

This means that research and innovation would be in the direct interests of everyone involved and that all would have the means to do it. Under capitalism, this is not the case. Most research is conducted in order to get an edge in the market by increasing productivity or expanding production into new (previously unwanted) areas. Any increased productivity often leads to unemployment, deskilling and other negative effects for those involved. Libertarian socialism will not face this problem. Moreover, it should be stressed that basic research is not something which free-market capitalism does well. As Doug Henwood notes, basic science research "*is heavily funded by the public sector and non-profit institutions like universities.*" The internet and computer, for example, were both projects for the Pentagon and "*the government picked up the basic R&D tab for decades, when neither Wall Street nor private industry showed any interest. In fact, capital only became interested when the start-up costs had all been borne by the public sector and there were finally profits to be made ... good American individualists don't like to talk about the public sector, since their hero is the plucky entrepreneur.*" [**After the New Economy**, p. 196 and p. 6] The rise of such systems across the world indicates that basic research often needs public support in order to be done. Even such a leading neo-classical economist as Kenneth Arrow had to admit in the 1960s that market forces are insufficient:

> "*basic research, the output of which is only used as an informational input into other inventive activities, is especially unlikely to be rewarded. In fact, it is likely to be of commercial value to the firm undertaking it only*

if other firms are prevented from using the information. But such restriction reduces the efficiency of inventive activity in general, and will therefore reduce its quantity also." [quoted by David Schweickart, **Against capitalism**, p. 132]

Nothing has changed since. Would modern society have produced so many innovations if it had not been for the Pentagon system, the space race and so on? Take the Internet, for example — it is unlikely that this would have got off the ground if it had not been for public funding. Needless to say, of course, much of this technology has been developed for evil reasons and purposes and would be in need of drastic change (or in some cases abolition) before it could be used in a libertarian society. However, the fact remains that it is unlikely that a pure market based system could have generated most of the technology we take for granted. As Noam Chomsky argues:

"*[Alan] Greenspan [then head of the US Federal Reserve] gave a talk to newspaper editors in the US. He spoke passionately about the miracles of the market, the wonders brought by consumer choice, and so on. He also gave examples: the Internet, computers, information processing, lasers, satellites, transistors. It's an interesting list: these are textbook examples of creativity and production in the public sector. In the case of the Internet, for 30 years it was designed, developed and funded primarily in the public sector, mostly the Pentagon, then the National Science Foundation — that's most of the hardware, the software, new ideas, technology, and so on. In just the last couple of years it has been handed over to people like Bill Gates … In the case of the Internet, consumer choice was close to zero, and during the crucial development stages that same was true of computers, information processing, and all the rest …*

"*In fact, of all the examples that Greenspan gives, the only one that maybe rises above the level of a joke is transistors, and they are an interesting case. Transistors, in fact, were developed in a private laboratory — Bell Telephone Laboratories of AT&T — which also made major contributions to solar cells, radio astronomy, information theory, and lots of other important things. But what is the role of markets and consumer choice in that? Well, again, it turns out, zero. AT&T was a government supported monopoly, so there was no consumer choice, and as a monopoly they could charge high prices: in effect a tax on the public which they could use for institutions like Bell Laboratories … So again, it's publicly subsidised. As if to demonstrate the point, as soon as the industry was deregulated, Bell Labs went out of existence, because the public wasn't paying for it any more … But that's only the beginning of the story. True, Bell invented transistors, but they used wartime technology, which, again, was publicly subsidised and state-initiated. Furthermore, there was nobody to buy transistors at that time, because they were very expensive to produce. So,*

for ten years the government was the major procurer … Government procurement provided entrepreneurial initiatives and guided the development of the technology, which could then be disseminated to industry." [**Rogue States**, pp. 192-3]

The free market can also have a negative impact on innovation. This is because, in order to please shareholders with higher share prices, companies may reduce funds available for real investment as well as R&D which would also depress growth and employment in the long term. What shareholders might condemn as "uneconomic" (investment projects and R&D) can, and does, make society as a whole better off. However, these gains are over the long term and, within capitalism, it is short-term gains which count. Higher share prices in the here and now are essential in order to survive and so see the long-run.

A socialised economy with a wide-scale sharing of surpluses and resources could easily allocate resources for R&D, long term investment, innovation and so on. Via the use of mutual banks or confederations of syndicates and communes, resources could be allocated which take into account the importance of long-term priorities, as well as social costs, which are not taken into account (indeed, are beneficial to ignore) under capitalism. Rather than penalise long term investment and research and development, a socialised economy would ensure that adequate resources are available, something which would benefit everyone in society in some way.

If we look at vocational training and education, a wide basis of surplus distribution would aid this no end. Under free market capitalism, vocational training suffers for profit seeking firms will not incur costs that will be enjoyed by others. This means that firms will be reluctant to spend money on training if they fear that the trained workers will soon be poached by other firms which can offer more money because they had not incurred the cost of providing training. As a result few firms will provide the required training as they could not be sure that the trained workers will not leave for their competitors (and, of course, a trained work force also, due to their skill, have more workplace power and are less replaceable). So as well as technological developments, a wide basis of surplus distribution would help improve the skills and knowledge of the members of a community. As Keynesian economist Michael Stewart points out, "*[t]here are both theoretical and empirical reasons to suppose that market forces under-provide research and development expenditures, as well as both education and training.*" [**Keynes in the 1990s**, p. 77]

By socialising training via confederations of workplaces, syndicates could increase productivity via increasing the skill levels of their members. Higher skill levels will also tend to increase innovation and enjoyment at "work" when combined with workers' self-management. This is because an educated workforce in control of their own time will be unlikely to tolerate mundane, boring, machine-like work and seek ways to eliminate it, improve the working environment and increase productivity to give them more free time.

In addition to work conducted by syndicates, education establishments, communes and so on, it would be essential to provide resources for individuals and small groups to pursue "pet projects." Of course, syndicates and confederations will have their own research institutions but the innovatory role of the interested "amateur" cannot be over-rated. As Kropotkin argued:

> "What is needed to promote the spirit of innovation is ... the awakening of thought, the boldness of conception, which our entire education causes to languish; it is the spreading of a scientific education, which would increase the numbers of inquirers a hundred-fold; it is faith that humanity is going to take a step forward, because it is enthusiasm, the hope of doing good, that has inspired all the great inventors. The Social Revolution alone can give this impulse to thought, this boldness, this knowledge, this conviction of working for all.

> "Then we shall have vast institutes ... immense industrial laboratories open to all inquirers, where men will be able to work out their dreams, after having acquitted themselves of their duty towards society; ... where they will make their experiments; where they will find other comrades, experts in other branches of industry, likewise coming to study some difficult problem, and therefore able to help and enlighten each other — the encounter of their ideas and experiences causing the longed-for solution to be found." [**The Conquest of Bread**, p. 117]

The example of free software (operating systems, programming languages, specific packages and code) today shows the potential of this. Thus socialisation would aid innovation and scientific development by providing the necessary resources (including free time) for such work. Moreover, it would also provide the community spirit required to push the boundaries of science forward. As John O'Neil argues:

> "There is, in a competitive market economy, a disincentive to communicate information. The market encourages secrecy, which is inimical to openness in science. It presupposes a view of property in which the owner has rights to exclude others. In the sphere of science, such rights of exclusion place limits on the communication of information and theories which are incompatible with the growth of knowledge ... science tends to grow when communication is open... [In addition a] necessary condition for the acceptability of a theory or experimental result is that it pass the public, critical scrutiny of competent scientific judges. A private theory or result is one that is shielded from the criteria of scientific acceptability." [**The Market**, p. 153]

Today inventors often "carefully hide their inventions from each other, as they are hampered by patents and Capitalism — that bane of present society, that stumbling-block in the path of intellectual and moral progress." In a free society, socialisation would ensure that inventors will be able to build upon the knowledge of everyone, including past generations. Rather than hide knowledge from others, in case they get a competitive advantage, knowledge would be shared, enriching all involved as well as the rest of society. Thus

the "spreading of a scientific education, which would increase the number of inquirers", "faith that humanity is going to take a step forward" and the "enthusiasm, the hope of doing good, that has inspired all the great inventors" will be maximised and innovation increased. [Kropotkin, **Op. Cit.**, p. 117 and pp. 116-7]

Social anarchists would also suggest that socialisation would produce more benefits by looking at existing societies. The evidence from the UK, USA, Australia, New Zealand and China shows that privatisation of nationalised industries associated with neo-liberalism failed in its stated aims of cheaper and better services while more than succeeding in their unstated aim of redistributing wealth upwards (for details see **In Government we Trust: Market Failure and the delusions of privatisation** by Warrick Funnell, Robert Jupe and Jane Andrew). The examples of railway and utility privatisation, the energy crisis in California (with companies like Enron reaping huge speculative profits while consumers faced blackouts) and the Sydney water treatment scandal in Australia are sadly all too typical. Ironically, in the UK after 30 years of Thatcherite policies (first under the Tories and then New Labour) the readers of the right-wing press who supported it are subjected to article after article complaining about "Rip off Britain" and yet more increases in the prices charged for privatised utilities, services and goods. This, it must be stressed, is not to suggest that anarchists aim for nationalisation (we do not, we aim for socialisation and workers' self-management) but rather to indicate that privatising resources does not benefit the majority of people in a given society.

It should also be noted that more unequal societies are bad for almost everyone within them. Richard Wilkinson and Kate Pickett in their book **The Spirit Level: Why More Equal Societies Almost Always Do Better** show that almost every modern social and environmental problem (including ill-health, lack of community life, violence, drugs, obesity, mental illness, long working hours, big prison populations) is more likely to occur in an unequal society than a more equal one. Based on thirty years of research, it shows that inequality, as anarchists have long argued, is bad for us. As such, socialisation of wealth would benefit us all.

Lastly, there is the issue of those who cannot work and the general provision of public goods. With a wide distribution of surplus, communal hospitals, schools, universities and so on can be created. The simple fact is that any society has members who cannot (indeed, should not) work unless they want to, such as the young, the old and the sick. In an Individualist Anarchist society, there is no real provision for these individuals unless someone (a family member, friend or charity) provides them with the money required for hospital fees and so on. For most anarchists, such a situation seems far too much like the system we are currently fighting against to be appealing. As such, social anarchists argue that everyone deserves an education, health care and so on as a right and so be able live a fully human life as a right, rather than a privilege to be paid for. A communal basis for distribution would ensure that every member of the commune can receive such things automatically, as and when required. The removal of the worry that, for example, privatised health care produces can be seen as a benefit of socialisation which cannot be reflected in, say, GDP or similar economic measures (not to mention the ethical statement it makes).

Significantly, though, non-privatised systems of health care are more efficient. Competition as well as denying people treatment also leads to inefficiencies as prices are inflated to pay for advertising, competition related administration costs, paying dividends to share-holders and so on. This drives up the cost for those lucky enough to be covered, not to mention the stress produced by the constant fear of losing insurance or being denied payment due to the insurance company deciding against the patient and their doctor. For example, in 1993, Canada's health plans devoted 0.9% of spending to overhead, compared to U.S. figures of 3.2% for Medicare and 12% for private insurers. In addition, when Canada adopted its publicly financed system in 1971, it and the U.S. both spent just over 7% of GDP on health care. By 1990, the U.S. was up to 12.3%, verses Canada's 9%. Since then costs have continued to rise and rise, making health-care reform of key interest to the public who are suffering under it (assuming they are lucky enough to have private insurance, of course).

The madness of private health-care shows the benefits of a society-wide distribution of surpluses. Competition harms health-care provision and, as a result, people. According to Alfie Kohn:

> "More hospitals and clinics are being run by for-profit corporations; many institutions, forced to battle for 'customers,' seem to value a skilled director of marketing more highly than a skilled caregiver. As in any other economic sector, the race for profits translates into pressure to reduce costs, and the easiest way to do it here is to cut back on services to unprofitable patients, that is, those who are more sick than rich … The result: hospital costs are actually **higher** in areas where there is more competition for patients." [**No Contest**, p. 240]

American Liberal Robert Kuttner concurs:

> "The American health-care system is a tangle of inequity and inefficiency — and getting worse as private-market forces seek to rationalise it. A shift to a universal system of health coverage would cut this Gordian knot at a stroke. It would not only deliver the explicitly medical aspects of health more efficiently and fairly, but, by socialising costs of poor health, it would also create a powerful financial incentive for society as a whole to stress primary prevention… every nation with a universal system spends less of its GDP on health care than the United States … And nearly every other nation with a universal system has longer life spans from birth (though roughly equivalent life spans from adulthood) … most nations with universal systems also have greater patient satisfaction.

> "The reasons … should be obvious. By their nature, universal systems spend less money on wasteful overhead, and more on primary prevention. Health-insurance overhead in the United States alone consumes about 1 percent of the GDP, compared to 0.1 percent in Canada. Though medical inflation is a problem everywhere, the universal systems have had far lower rates of cost inflation … In the years between 1980 and 1987, total health costs in the United States increased by 2.4 times the rate of GDP growth. In nations with universal systems, they increased

far more slowly. The figures for Sweden, France, West Germany, and Britain were 1.2, 1.6, 1.8, and 1.7 percent, respectively …

> "Remarkably enough, the United States spends most money on health care, but has the fewest beds per thousand in population, the lowest admission rate, and the lowest occupancy rate — coupled with the highest daily cost, highest technology-intensiveness, and greatest number of employees per bed." [**Everything for Sale**, pp. 155-6]

Significantly, we should note that the use of surplus for communal services (such as hospitals and education) can be seen from the Spanish Revolution. Many collectives funded new hospitals and colleges for their members, providing hundreds of thousands with services they could never have afforded by their own labour. This is a classic example of co-operation helping the co-operators achieve far more than they could by their own isolated activities. How this libertarian health system was run and how other public services would be organised in a free society are discussed in section I.5.12.

So we can generalise from our experiences of different kinds of capitalism. If you want to live in a society of well-educated people, working today as equals in pleasant surroundings with more than ample leisure time to pursue your own projects and activities, then a wide sharing of the social surplus is required. Otherwise, you could live in a society where people work long and hard to survive on the market, without the time or opportunity for education and leisure, and be bossed about for most of your waking hours to enrich the wealthy few so that they can live a life of leisure (which, in turn, will apparently inspire you to work harder in spite of the fact that such high inequality produces low social mobility). The first society, according to some, would be one of self-sacrificing altruism and "collectivism" while the latter is, apparently, one based on "individualism" and self-interest…

I.4.11 If socialism eliminates the profit motive, won't performance suffer?

Firstly, just to be totally clear, by the profit motive we mean money profit. As anarchists consider co-operation to be in our self-interest — i.e. we will "profit" from it in the widest sense possible — we are **not** dismissing the fact people usually act to improve their own situation. However, money profit is a **very** narrow form of "self-interest," indeed so narrow as to be positively harmful to the individual in many ways (in terms of personal development, interpersonal relationships, economic and social well-being, and so on). In other words, do not take our discussion here on the "profit motive" to imply a denial of self-interest, quite the reverse. Anarchists simply reject the "narrow concept of life which consist[s] in thinking that **profits** are the only leading motive of human society." [Peter Kropotkin, **Fields, Factories and Workshops Tomorrow**, p. 25]

Secondly, we cannot hope to deal fully with the harmful effects of competition and the profit motive. For more information, we recommend Alfie Kohn's **No Contest: The Case Against Competition** and **Punished by Rewards: The Trouble with Gold Stars, Incentive Plans, A's, Praise and Other Bribes**. He documents the extensive evidence accumulated that disproves the "common sense" of capitalism that competition and profits are the best way to organise a society.

According to Kohn, a growing body of psychological research suggests that rewards can lower performance levels, especially when the performance involves creativity. His books summarise the related series of studies which show that intrinsic interest in a task — the sense that something is worth doing for its own sake — typically declines when someone is rewarded for doing it. Much of the research on creativity and motivation has been performed by Theresa Amabile, associate professor of psychology at Brandeis University. She has consistently found that those promised rewards did the least creative work: *"rewards killed creativity, and this was true regardless of the type of task, the type of reward, the timing of the reward or the age of the people involved."* [**Punished by Rewards**, p. 45] Such research casts doubt on the claim that financial reward is the only effective way — or even the best way — to motivate people. They challenge the behaviourist assumption that any activity is more likely to occur or be better in terms of outcome if it is rewarded.

These findings re-enforce the findings of other scientific fields. Biology, social psychology, ethnology and anthropology all present evidence that support co-operation as the natural basis for human interaction. For example, ethnological studies indicate that virtually all indigenous cultures operate on the basis of highly co-operative relationships and anthropologists have presented evidence to show that the predominant force driving early human evolution was co-operative social interaction, leading to the capacity of hominids to develop culture. This is even sinking into capitalism, with industrial psychology now promoting "worker participation" and team functioning because it is decisively more productive than hierarchical management. More importantly, the evidence shows that co-operative workplaces are more productive than those organised on other principles. All other things equal, producers' co-operatives will be more efficient than capitalist or state enterprises, on average. Co-operatives can often achieve higher productivity even when their equipment and conditions are worse. Furthermore, the better the organisation approximates the co-operative ideal, the better the productivity.

All this is unsurprising to social anarchists (and it should make individualist anarchists reconsider their position). Peter Kropotkin argued that, *"[i]f we ... ask Nature: 'Who are the fittest: those who are continually at war with each other, or those who support one another?' we at once see that those animals which acquire habits of mutual aid are undoubtedly the fittest. They have more chances to survive, and they attain, in their respective classes, the highest development of intelligence and bodily organisation."* [**Mutual Aid**, p. 24]

It should be noted that, as one biologist points out, *"Kropotkin's ideas, though unorthodox, were scientifically respectable, and indeed the contention that mutual aid can be a means of increasing fitness*

had become a standard part of modern sociobiology." [Douglas H. Boucher, *"The Idea of Mutualism, Past and Future"*, pp. 1-28, **The Biology of Mutualism: Biology and Evolution**, Douglas H. Boucher (ed.), p. 17] Frans de Waal (a leading primatologist) and Jessica C. Flack argue that Kropotkin is part of a wider tradition *"in which the view has been that animals assist each other precisely because by doing so they achieve long term, collective benefits of greater value than the short term benefits derived from straightforward competition."* They summarise that the *"basic tenet of [Kropotkin's] ideas was on the mark. Almost seventy years later, in an article entitled 'The Evolution of Reciprocal Altruism', [Robert] Trivers refined the concepts Kropotkin advanced and explained how co-operation and, more importantly, a system of reciprocity (called 'reciprocal altruism' by Trivers) could have evolved."* [*"'Any Animal Whatever': Darwinian Building Blocks of Morality in Monkeys and Apes"*, pp. 1-29, **Journal of Consciousness Studies**, Vol. 7, No. 1-2, p. 4]

So modern research has reinforced Kropotkin's argument. This applies to both human and non-human animals. For the former, the evidence is strong that we have intrinsic abilities and needs to co-operate as well as an intrinsic senses of fairness and ethics. This suggests that co-operation is part of "human nature" and so studies which show that such behaviour is more productive than competition should come as no surprise — and the evidence is impressive. As noted, Alfie Kohn is also the author of **No Contest: The Case Against Competition** and he spent seven years reviewing more than 400 research studies dealing with competition and co-operation. According to Kohn, there are three principle consequences of competition:

Firstly, it has a negative effect on productivity and excellence. This is due to increased anxiety, inefficiency (as compared to co-operative sharing of resources and knowledge), and the undermining of inner motivation. Competition shifts the focus to victory over others, and away from intrinsic motivators such as curiosity, interest, excellence, and social interaction. Studies show that co-operative behaviour, by contrast, consistently produces good performance — a finding which holds true under a wide range of subject variables. Interestingly, the positive benefits of co-operation become more significant as tasks become more complex, or where greater creativity and problem-solving ability is required.

Secondly, competition lowers self-esteem and hampers the development of sound, self-directed individuals. A strong sense of self is difficult to attain when self-evaluation is dependent on seeing how we measure up to others. On the other hand, those whose identity is formed in relation to how they contribute to group efforts generally possess greater self-confidence and higher self-esteem.

Thirdly, competition undermines human relationships. Humans are social beings; we best express our humanness in interaction with others. By creating winners and losers, competition is destructive to human unity and prevents close social feeling.

Social Anarchists have long argued these points. In the competitive mode, people work at cross purposes, or purely for (material) personal gain. This leads to an impoverishment of society as well as hierarchy, with a lack of communal relations that result in an impoverishment of all the individuals involved (mentally, spiritually, ethically and, ultimately, materially). This not only leads to a weakening of individuality and social disruption, but also to economic inefficiency as energy is wasted in class conflict and invested in building bigger and better cages to protect the haves from the have-nots. Instead of creating useful things, human activity is spent in useless toil reproducing an injust and authoritarian system.

All in all, the results of competition (as documented by a host of scientific disciplines) show its poverty as well as indicating that co-operation is the means by which the fittest survive.

Moreover, the notion that material rewards result in better work is simply not true. Basing itself on simple behaviourist psychology, such arguments fail to meet the test of long-term success (and, in fact, can be counter-productive). Indeed, it means treating human beings as little better than pets or other animals (Kohn argues that it is *"not an accident that the theory behind 'Do this and you'll get that' derives from work with other species, or that behaviour management is frequently described in words better suited to animals."*) In other words, it *"is by its very nature dehumanising."* Rather than simply being motivated by outside stimuli like mindless robots, people are not passive. We are *"beings who possess natural curiosity about ourselves and our environment, who search for and overcome challenges, who try and master skills and attain competence, and who seek new levels of complexity in what we learn and do ... in general we act on the environment as much as we are acted on by it, and we do not do so simply in order to receive a reward."* [**Punished by Rewards**, p. 24 and p. 25]

Kohn presents extensive evidence to back up his case that rewards harm activity and individuals. We cannot do justice to it here so we will present a few examples. One study with college students showed that those paid to work on a puzzle *"spent less time on it than those who hadn't been paid"* when they were given a choice of whether to work on it or not. *"It appeared that working for a reward made people less interested in the task."* Another study with children showed that *"extrinsic rewards reduce intrinsic motivation."* [**Op. Cit.**, p. 70 and p. 71] Scores of other studies confirmed this. This is because a reward is effectively saying that a given activity is not worth doing for its own sake — and why would anyone wish to do something they have to be bribed to do?

In the workplace, a similar process goes on. Kohn presents extensive evidence to show that extrinsic motivation also fails even there. Indeed, he argues that *"economists have it wrong if they think of work as a 'disutility' — something unpleasant we must do in order to be able to buy what we need, merely a means to an end."* Kohn stresses that *"to assume that money is what drives people is to adopt an impoverished understanding of human motivation."* Moreover, *"the risk of **any** incentive or pay-for-performance system is that it will make people less interested in their work and therefore less likely to approach it with enthusiasm and a commitment to excellence. Furthermore, **the more closely we tie compensation (or other rewards) to performance, the most damage we do.**"* [**Op. Cit.**, p. 131, p. 134 and p. 140]

Kohn argues that the idea that humans will only work for profit or rewards *"can be fairly described as dehumanising"* if *"the capacity for responsible action, the natural love of learning, and the desire to do good work are already part of who we are."* Also, it is *"a way of trying to control people"* and so to *"anyone who is troubled by a model of human relationships founded principally on the idea of one person controlling another must ponder whether rewards are as innocuous as they are sometimes made out to be"*. So *"there is no getting around the fact that 'the basic purpose of merit pay is manipulative.' One observer more bluntly characterises incentives as 'demeaning' since the message they really convey is, 'Please big daddy boss and you will receive the rewards that the boss deems appropriate.'"* [**Op. Cit.**, p. 26]

Given that much work is controlled by others and can be a hateful experience under capitalism does not mean that it has to be that way. Clearly, even under wage slavery most workers can and do find work interesting and seek to do it well — not because of possible rewards or punishment but because we seek meaning in our activities and try and do them well. Given that research shows that reward orientated work structures harm productivity and excellence, social anarchists have more than just hope to base their ideas. Such research confirms Kropotkin's comments:

> *"Wage-work is serf-work; it cannot, it must not, produce all it could produce. And it is high time to disbelieve the legend which presents wagedom as the best incentive to productive work. If industry nowadays brings in a hundred times more than it did in the days of our grandfathers, it is due to the sudden awakening of physical and chemical sciences towards the end of the [18th] century; not to the capitalist organisation of wagedom, but **in spite** of that organisation."* [**The Conquest of Bread**, p. 150]

For these reasons, social anarchists are confident that the elimination of the profit motive within the context of self-management will not harm productivity and creativity, but rather **enhance** them (within an authoritarian system in which workers enhance the power and income of bureaucrats, we can expect different results). With the control of their own work and workplaces ensured, all working people can express their abilities to the full. This will see an explosion of creativity and initiative, not a reduction.

I.4.12 Won't there be a tendency for capitalist enterprise to reappear?

This is a common right-wing "libertarian" objection. Robert Nozick, for example, imagined the following scenario:

> *"small factories would spring up in a socialist society, unless forbidden. I melt some of my personal possessions and build a machine out of the material. I offer you and others a philosophy lecture once a week in exchange for yet other things, and so on ... some persons might even want to leave their jobs in socialist industry and work full time in this private sector ... [This is] how private property even in means of production would occur in a socialist society ... [and so] the socialist society will have to forbid capitalist acts between consenting adults."* [**Anarchy, State and Utopia**, pp. 162-3]

There are numerous flawed assumptions in this argument and we will discuss them here. The key flaws are the confusion of exchange with capitalism and the typically impoverished propertarian vision that freedom is, essentially, the freedom to sell your liberty, to become a wage slave and so unfree. Looking at history, we can say that both these assumptions are wrong. Firstly, while markets and exchange have existed for thousands of years capitalism has not. Wage-labour is a relatively recent development and has been the dominant mode of production for, at best, a couple of hundred years. Secondly, few people (when given the choice) have freely become wage-slaves. Just as the children of slaves often viewed slavery as the "natural" order, so do current workers. Yet, as with chattel slavery, substantial state coercion was required to achieve such a "natural" system.

As discussed in section F.8, actually existing capitalism was **not** created by Nozick's process — it required substantial state intervention to separate workers from the means of production they used and to ensure, eventually, that the situation in which they sold their liberty to the property owner was considered "natural." Without that coercion, people do **not** seek to sell their liberty to others. Murray Bookchin summarised the historical record by noting that in *"every precapitalist society, countervailing forces … existed to restrict the market economy. No less significantly, many precapitalist societies raised what they thought were insuperable obstacles to the penetration of the State into social life."* He pointed to *"the power of village communities to resist the invasion of trade and despotic political forms into society's abiding communal substrate."* [**The Ecology of Freedom**, pp. 207-8] Anarchist anthropologist David Graeber notes that in the ancient Mediterranean world *"[w]hile one does periodically run into evidence of arrangements which to the modern eye look like wage-labour contracts, on closer examination they almost always actually turn out to be contracts to rent slaves … Free men and women thus avoided anything remotely like wage-labour, seeing it as a matter, effectively, of slavery, renting themselves out."* This means that wage labour *"(as opposed to, say, receiving fees for professional services) involves a degree of subordination: a labourer has to be to some degree at the command of his or her employer. This is exactly why, through most of history, free men and women tended to avoid wage-labour, and why, for most of history, capitalism … never emerged."* [**Possibilities**, p. 92]

Thus while the idea that people will happily become wage slaves may be somewhat common place today (particularly with supporters of capitalism) the evidence of history is that people, given a choice, will prefer self-employment and **resist** wage labour (often to the death). As E. P. Thompson noted, for workers at the end of the 18th and beginning of the 19th centuries, the *"gap in status between a 'servant,' a hired wage-labourer subject to the orders and discipline of the master, and an artisan, who might 'come and go' as he pleased, was wide enough for men to shed blood rather than allow themselves to be pushed from one side to the other. And, in the value system of the community, those who resisted degradation were in the right."* [**The Making of the English Working Class**, p. 599] Over one hundred years later, the rural working class of Aragon showed the same dislike of wage slavery. After Communist troops destroyed their self-managed collectives, the *"[d]ispossessed peasants, intransigent collectivists, refused to work in a system of private property, and were even less willing to rent out their labour."* [Jose Peirats, **Anarchists in the Spanish Revolution**, p. 258] The rural economy collapsed as the former collectivists refused to be the servants of the few.

People who have tasted freedom are unlikely to go back to oppression. Therefore, any perception that people will become wage-slaves through choice in a free society is based on the assumption what people accept through necessity under capitalism will pass over, without change, into a free one. This assumption is unfounded and anarchists expect that once people struggle for freedom and taste the pleasures of freedom they will not freely accept a degradation back to having a master — and as history shows, we have some evidence to support our argument. It seems a strangely debased perspective on freedom to ponder whether people will be "free" to alienate their freedom — it is a bit like proclaiming it a restriction of freedom to *"forbid"* owning slaves (and, as noted in section F.2.2, Nozick did support voluntary slave contracts).

So anarchists think Nozick's vision of unfreedom developing from freedom is unlikely. As anarcho-syndicalist Jeff Stein points out *"the only reason workers want to be employed by capitalists is because they have no other means for making a living, no access to the means of production other than by selling themselves. For a capitalist sector to exist there must be some form of private ownership of productive resources, and a scarcity of alternatives. The workers must be in a condition of economic desperation for them to be willing to give up an equal voice in the management of their daily affairs and accept a boss."* ["Market Anarchism? Caveat Emptor!", **Libertarian Labour Review**, no. 13]

In an anarchist society, there is no need for anyone to *"forbid"* capitalist acts. All people have to do is **refrain** from helping would-be capitalists set up monopolies of productive assets. This is because, as we have noted in section B.3.2, capitalism cannot exist without some form of state to protect such monopolies. In a libertarian-socialist society, of course, there would be no state to begin with, and so there would be no question of it "refraining" people from doing anything, including protecting would-be capitalists' monopolies of the means of production. In other words, would-be capitalists would face stiff competition for workers in an anarchist society. This is because self-managed workplaces would be able to offer workers more benefits (such as self-government, better working conditions, etc.) than the would-be capitalist ones. The would-be capitalists would have to offer not only excellent wages and conditions but also, in all likelihood, workers' control and hire-purchase on capital used. The chances of making a profit once the various monopolies associated with capitalism are abolished are slim.

Thus the would-be capitalist would *"not [be] able to obtain assistance or people to exploit"* and *"would find none because nobody, having a right to the means of production and being free to work on his own or as an equal with others in the large organisations of production would want to be exploited by a small employer"*. [Malatesta, **Errico Malatesta: His Life and Ideas**, pp. 102-103] So where would the capitalist wannabe find people to work for him? As Kropotkin argued:

> *"Everywhere you will find that the wealth of the wealthy springs from the poverty of the poor. That is*

why an anarchist society need not fear the advent of a [millionaire] who would settle in its midst. If every member of the community knows that after a few hours of productive toil he [or she] will have a right to all the pleasures that civilisation procures, and to those deeper sources of enjoyment which art and science offer to all who seek them, he [or she] will not sell his strength ... No one will volunteer to work for the enrichment of your [millionaire]." [**Conquest of Bread**, p. 61]

However, let us suppose there is a self-employed inventor, Ferguson, who comes up with a new innovation without the help of the socialised sector. Would anarchists steal his idea? Not at all. The syndicates, which by hypothesis have been organised by people who believe in giving producers the full value of their product, would pay Ferguson an equitable amount for his idea, which would then become common across society. However, if he refused to sell his invention and instead tried to claim a patent monopoly on it in order to gather a group of wage slaves to exploit, no one would agree to work for him unless they got the full control over both the product of their labour and the labour process itself. And, assuming that he did find someone willing to work for him (and so be governed by him), the would-be capitalist would have to provide such excellent conditions and pay such good wages as to reduce his profits to near zero. Moreover, he would have to face workers whose neighbours would be encouraging them to form a union and strike for even **better** conditions and pay, including workers' control and so on. Such a militant workforce would be the last thing a capitalist would desire. In addition, we would imagine they would also refuse to work for someone unless they also got the capital they used at the end of their contract (i.e. a system of "hire-purchase" on the means of production used). In other words, by removing the statist supports of capitalism, would-be capitalists would find it hard to "compete" with the co-operative sector and would not be in a position to exploit others' labour.

With a system of communal production (in social anarchism) and mutual banks (in individualist anarchism), **usury** — i.e. charging a use-fee for a monopolised item, of which patents are an instance — would no longer be possible and the inventor would be like any other worker, exchanging the product of his or her labour. As Benjamin Tucker argued, *"the patent monopoly ... consists in protecting inventors and authors against competition for a period of time long enough for them to extort from the people a reward enormously in excess of the labour measure of their services — in other words, in giving certain people a right of property for a term of years in laws and facts of nature, and the power to extract tribute from others for the use of this natural wealth, which should be open to all. The abolition of this monopoly would fill its beneficiaries with a wholesome fear of competition which should cause them to be satisfied with pay for their services equal to that which other labourers get for theirs, and secure it by placing their products and works on the market at the outset at prices so low that their lines of business would be no more tempting to competitors than any other lines."* [**The Anarchist Reader**, pp. 150-1]

So, if someone has labour to sell then they deserve a free society to do it in — as Tucker once pointed out. Such an environment would make the numbers seeking employment so low as to ensure that the rate of exploitation would be zero. Little wonder that, when faced with a self-employed, artisan workforce, capitalists have continually turned to the state to create the "correct" market forces. So without statism to back up various class-based monopolies of capitalist privilege, capitalism would not have become dominant.

It should also be noted that Nozick makes a serious error in his case. He assumes that the "use rights" associated with an anarchist (i.e. socialist) society are identical to the "property rights" of a capitalist one. This is **not** the case, and so his argument is weakened and loses its force. Simply put, there is no such thing as an absolute or *"natural"* law of property. As John Stuart Mill pointed out, *"powers of exclusive use and control are very various, and differ greatly in different countries and in different states of society."* Therefore, Nozick slips an ideological ringer into his example by erroneously interpreting socialism (or any other society for that matter) as specifying a distribution of capitalist property rights along with the wealth. As Mill argued: *"One of the mistakes oftenest committed, and which are the sources of the greatest practical errors in human affairs, is that of supposing that the same name always stands for the same aggregation of ideas. No word has been subject of more of this kind of misunderstanding that the word property."* [*"Chapters on Socialism,"* **Principles of Political Economy**, p. 432]

In other words, Nozick assumes that in **all** societies capitalist property rights are distributed along with consumption **and** production goods. As Cheyney C. Ryan comments *"[d]ifferent conceptions of justice differ not only in how they would apportion society's holdings but in what rights individuals have over their holdings once they have been apportioned."* [*"Property Rights and Individual Liberty"*, pp. 323-43, **Reading Nozick**, Jeffrey Paul (Ed.), p. 331] This means that when goods are distributed in a libertarian socialist society the people who receive or take them have specific (use) rights to them. As long as an individual remained a member of a commune and abided by the rules they helped create in that commune then they would have full use of the resources of that commune and could use their possessions as they saw fit (even *"melt them down"* to create a new machine, or whatever). If they used those goods to create an enterprise to employ (i.e., exploit and oppress) others then they have, in effect, announced their withdrawal from civilised society and, as a result, would be denied the benefits of co-operation. They would, in effect, place themselves in the same situation as someone who does not wish to join a syndicate (see section I.3.7). If an individual did desire to use resources to employ wage labour then they would have effectively removed themselves from *"socialist society"* and so that society would bar them from using **its** resources (i.e. they would have to buy access to all the resources they currently took for granted).

Would this be a restriction of freedom? While it may be considered so by the impoverished definitions of capitalism, it is not. In fact, it mirrors the situation within capitalism as what possessions someone holds are **not** his or her property (in the capitalist sense) any more than a company car is currently the property of the employee under capitalism. While the employee can use the car outside of work, they lack the "freedom" to sell it or melt it down and turn it into machines. Such lack of **absolute** "ownership" in a free society does not reduce liberty any more than in this case.

This point highlights another flaw in Nozick's argument. If his argument were true, then it applies equally to capitalist society. For 40 hours plus a week, workers are employed by a boss. In that time they are given resources to use and they are most definitely **not** allowed to melt down these resources to create a machine or use the resources they have been given access to further their own plans. This can apply equally to rented accommodation as well, for example when landlords ban working from home or selling off the furniture that is provided. Thus, ironically, *"capitalist society will have to forbid capitalist acts between consenting adults"* — and does so all the time.

Moreover, it must be stressed that as well as banning capitalist acts between consenting adults, capitalism involves the continual banning of socialist acts between consenting adults. For example, if workers agree to form a union, then the boss can fire them. If they decide to control their own work, the boss can fire them for not obeying orders. Thus capitalism forbids such elemental freedoms as association and speech — at least for the majority, for the wage slaves. Why would people seek such "freedom" in a free society?

Of course, Nozick's reply to this point would be that the individuals involved have "consented" to these rules when they signed their contract. Yet the same can be said of an anarchist society — it is freely joined and freely left. To join a communist-anarchist society it would simply be a case of agreeing to "exchange" the product of ones labour freely with the other members of that society and not to create oppressive or exploitative social relationships within it. If this is "authoritarian" then so is capitalism — and we must stress that at least anarchist associations are based on self-management and so the individuals involved have an equal say in the obligations they live under.

Notice also that Nozick confused exchange with capitalism (*"I offer you a lecture once a week in exchange for other things"*). This is a telling mistake by someone who claims to be an expert on capitalism, because the defining feature of capitalism is not exchange (which obviously took place long before capitalism existed) but labour contracts involving wage labour. Nozick's example is merely a direct labour contract between the producer and the consumer. It does not involve wage labour, what makes capitalism capitalism. It is only this latter type of transaction that libertarian socialism prevents — and not by "forbidding" it but simply by refusing to maintain the conditions necessary for it to occur, i.e. protection of capitalist property.

In addition, we must note that Nozick also confused *"private property in the means of production"* with capitalism. Libertarian socialism can be easily compatible with *"private property in the means of production"* when that *"private property"* is limited to what a self-employed worker uses rather than capitalistic property (see section G.2.1). Nozick, in other words, confused pre-capitalist forms of production with capitalist ones (see section G.1.2). Thus possession of the means of production by people outside of the free commune is perfectly acceptable to social anarchists (see section I.6.2).

Thus an anarchist society would have a flexible approach to Nozick's (flawed) argument. Individuals, in their free time, could *"exchange"* their time and possessions as they saw fit. These are **not** *"capitalist acts"* regardless of Nozick's claims. However, the moment an individual employs wage labour then, by this act, they have broken their agreements with their fellows and are, therefore, no longer part of *"socialist society."* This would involve them no longer having access to the benefits of communal life and to communal possessions. They have, in effect, placed themselves outside of their community and must fend for themselves. After all, if they desire to create *"private property"* (in the capitalist sense) then they have no right of access to communal possessions without paying for that right. For those who become wage slaves, a socialist society would, probably, be less strict. As Bakunin argued:

> *"Since the freedom of every individual is inalienable, society shall never allow any individual whatsoever legally to alienate his [or her] freedom or engage upon any contract with another on any footing but the utmost equality and reciprocity. It shall not, however, have the power to disbar a man or woman so devoid of any sense of personal dignity as to contract a relationship of voluntary servitude with another individual, but it will consider them as living off private charity and therefore unfit to enjoy political rights **throughout the duration of that servitude.**"* [**Michael Bakunin: Selected Writings**, pp. 68-9]

Lastly, we must also note that Nozick also ignored the fact that acquisition **must** come before transfer, meaning that before "consenting" capitalist acts occur, individual ones must precede it. As argued in section B.3.4, Nozick provided no convincing arguments why natural resources held in common can be appropriated by individuals. This means that his defence of transferring absolute capitalist property rights in goods is without foundations. Moreover, his argument in favour of such appropriations ignore that liberties are very definitely restricted by private property (and it should be kept in mind that the destruction of commonly held resources, such as village commons, was imposed by the state — see section F.8.3). As pointed out in section F.2, right-wing "libertarians" would better be termed *"Propertarians"* (why is liberty accorded a primary importance when arguing against socialism but not when private property restricts liberty?). As Cheyney C. Ryan points out, Nozick *"invoke[s] personal liberty as the decisive ground for rejecting patterned principles of justice [such as socialism] and restrictions on the ownership of capital ... [b]ut where the rights of private property admittedly restrict the liberties of the average person, he seems perfectly happy to **trade off** such liberties against material gain for society as a whole."* [**Op. Cit.**, p. 339] This can be seen by his lack of comment on how capitalism forbids socialist acts between consenting adults, not to mention quite a few numerous capitalist acts for good measure.

Thus Nozick's acquisition of resources is based on the would-be capitalist stealing communally owned resources and barring others from using them. This obviously would restrict the liberty of those who currently used them and so be hotly opposed by members of a community. As Murray Bookchin noted, a free society is based on *"the practice of **usufruct**, the freedom of individuals in a community to appropriate resources merely by virtue of the fact that they are using them. Such resources belong to the user as long as they are being used."* [**The Ecology of Freedom**, p. 116] As the would-be capitalist is not actually using the machines they have created, they would be in constant worry that their wage-slaves would simply expropriate them — with the full backing of the local commune and its federations.

So, to conclude, this question involves some strange logic (and many question begging assumptions) and ultimately fails in its attempt to prove libertarian socialism must *"forbid capitalistic acts between individuals."* In addition, Nozick cannot support the creation of private property out of communal property in the first place. It also undermines capitalism because that system must forbid socialistic acts by and between individuals. Thus Nozick's society would forbid squatting unused property or trespassing on private property as well as, say, the formation of unions against the wishes of the property owner (who is sovereign over their property and those who use it) or the use of workplace resources to meet the needs of the producer rather than the owner. As such, Nozick exposes how capitalism's hierarchical nature means that capitalist society *"forbids socialist acts between consenting adults."*

I.4.13 Who will do the dirty or unpleasant work?

This problem affects every society, including capitalism of course. Under capitalism, this problem is "solved" by ensuring that such jobs are done by those at the bottom of the social pile. In other words, it does not really solve the problem at all — it just ensures that some people are subject to this work the bulk of their working lives. Most anarchists reject this flawed solution in favour of something better, one that shares the good with the bad and so ensure everyone's life is better. How this would be done depends on the kind of libertarian community you are a member of.

Obviously, few would argue against the idea that individuals will voluntarily work at things they enjoyed doing. However there are some jobs that few, if any, would enjoy (for example, collecting rubbish, processing sewage, dangerous work, etc.). So how would an anarchist society deal with it?

It is obvious that not all "jobs" are equal in interest or enjoyment. It is sometimes argued that people would start to join or form syndicates which are involved in more fun activities. By this process excess workers would be found in the more enjoyable "jobs" while the boring and dangerous ones would suffer from a scarcity of willing workers. Hence, so the argument goes, a socialist society would have to force people to do certain jobs and that requires a state. Obviously, this argument ignores the fact that under capitalism usually it is the boring, dangerous work which is the least well paid with the worst working conditions. In addition, this argument ignores the fact that under workers self-management boring, dangerous work would be minimised and transformed as much as possible. Only under capitalist hierarchy are people in no position to improve the quality of their work and working environment. As George Barrett argued:

> *"Now things are so strangely organised at present that it is just the dirty and disagreeable work that men will*

do cheaply, and consequently there is no great rush to invent machines to take their place. In a free society, on the other hand, it is clear that the disagreeable work will be one of the first things that machinery will be called upon to eliminate. It is quite fair to argue, therefore, that the disagreeable work will, to a large extent, disappear in a state of anarchism." [**Objections to Anarchism**, p. 361]

Moreover, most anarchists would think that the argument that there would be a flood of workers taking up "easy" work placements is abstract and ignores the dynamics of a real society. While many individuals would try to create new productive syndicates in order to express themselves in innovative work outwith the existing research and development going on within existing syndicates, the idea that the majority of individuals would leave their current work at a drop of a hat is crazy. A workplace is a community and part of a community and people would value the links they have with their fellow workers. As such they would be aware of the impacts of their decisions on both themselves and society as a whole. So, while we would expect a turnover of workers between syndicates, the mass transfers claimed in this argument are unlikely. Most workers who did want to try their hand at new work would apply for work places at syndicates that required new people, not create their own ones. Because of this, work transfers would be moderate and easily handled.

However, the possibility of mass desertions does exist and so must be addressed. So how would a libertarian socialist society deal with a majority of its workers deciding to all do interesting work, leaving the boring and/or dangerous work undone? It, of course, depends on the type of anarchism in question and each offers alternative ways to ensure that individual preference for certain types of work matches the requirements of social demand for labour.

Under individualist anarchism and mutualism, those who desired a certain form of work done would reach an agreement with workers or a co-operative and pay them to do the work in question. Within a co-operative, as Proudhon argued, a person's *"education, instruction, and apprenticeship should ... be so directed that, while permitting him to do his share of unpleasant and disagreeable tasks, they may also give variety of work and knowledge, and may assure him ... an encyclopaedic attitude and a sufficient income."* [**Property is Theft!**, pp.585-6] In terms of unpleasant tasks for other people (for example, collecting and processing a community's rubbish) then individuals would form co-operatives which would have to find their place on the market and this would ensure that such work was done as they would contract with others to provide the appropriate services. However, this could lead to some people doing unpleasant work all the time and so is hardly a solution. As in capitalism, we may see some people doing terrible work because it is better than no work at all. This is a solution few anarchists would support.

In a collectivist or communist anarchist society, such an outcome would be avoided as far as possible. Noam Chomsky points to two possible alternatives, one *"in which the undesired work, after the best efforts to make it meaningful, is shared"* and another one *"where the undesired work receives high extra pay, so that individuals voluntarily choose to do it.*" Such schemes are "*consistent with ... anarchist principles*" unlike the current situation where "*the undesired work is given to wage-slaves.*" [**Radical Priorities**, p. 220] Another way, somewhat complementary to these two, would be to take a leaf from "*peasant attitudes toward labour*" and their "*most striking feature*", the extent "*to which any kind of communal toil, however onerous, can be transformed by the workers themselves into festive occasions that serve to reinforce community ties.*" [Murray Bookchin, **The Ecology of Freedom**, p. 342]

It would be easy to imagine a free community sharing such tasks as fairly as possible between a community's members by, for example, allocating a few days a month to all fit members of a community to do work which no one volunteers to do. This would soon ensure that it would be done, particularly if it were part of a festival or before a party. In this way, every one shares in the unpleasant as well as pleasant tasks (and, of course, minimises the time any one individual has to spend on it). Or, for tasks which are very popular, individuals would also have to do unpleasant tasks as well. In this way, popular and unpopular tasks could balance each other out. Or such tasks could be rotated randomly by lottery. The possibilities are many and, undoubtedly, a free people will try many different ones in different areas.

Another possible solution could be to follow the ideas of Josiah Warren and take into account the undesirability of the work when considering the level of labour notes received or communal hours worked. In other words, in a collectivist society the individuals who do unpleasant work may be "rewarded" (along with social esteem) with a slightly higher pay — the number of labour notes, for example, for such work would be a multiple of the standard amount, the actual figure being related to how much supply exceeds demand (in a communist society, a similar solution could be possible, with the number of necessary hours required by an individual being reduced by an amount that corresponds to the undesirability of the work involved). The actual levels of "reward" would be determined by agreements between the syndicates. For example, if a given type of work has 50% more people wanting to do it than actually required, then the labour value for one hours work in this industry would correspondingly be less than one hour. If fewer people applied than required, then the labour value would increase, as would holiday time, etc. For "work" placements in which supply exceeded demand, it would be easy to arrange a work share scheme to ensure that most people get a chance to do that kind of work (along with such methods as increasing the value of an hour's labour, reducing holiday allocations and such like).

In this way, "supply and demand" for workers would soon approximate each other. In addition, a collectivist society would be better placed than the current system to ensure work-sharing and other methods to spread unpleasant and pleasant tasks equally around society due to its organs of self-management and the rising social awareness via participation and debate within those organs.

A communist-anarchist society's solution would be similar to the collectivist one. There would still be basic agreements between its members for work done and so for work placements with excess supply of workers the amount of hours necessary to meet the agreed minimum would correspondingly increase. For example,

an industry with 100% excess supply of volunteers would see its minimum requirement increase from (say) 20 hours a week to 30 hours. An industry with less applicants than required would see the number of required hours decrease, plus increases in holiday time and so on. As G.D.H. Cole argued in respect of this point:

> "*Let us first by the fullest application of machinery and scientific methods eliminate or reduce ... 'dirty work' that admit to such treatment. This has never been tried ... under capitalism ... It is cheaper to exploit and ruin human beings ... Secondly, let us see what forms of 'dirty work' we can do without ... [and] if any form of work is not only unpleasant but degrading, we will do without it, whatever the cost. No human being ought to be allowed or compelled to do work that degrades. Thirdly, for what dull or unpleasant work remains, let us offer whatever special conditions are required to attract the necessary workers, not in higher pay, but in shorter hours, holidays extending over six months in the year, conditions attractive enough to men who have other uses for their time or attention to being the requisite number to undertake it voluntarily.*" [**Guild Socialism Restated**, p. 76]

By these methods a balance between industrial sectors would be achieved as individuals would balance their desire for interesting work with their desires for free time. Over time, by using the power of appropriate technology, even such time keeping would be minimised or even got eliminated as society developed freely. Until such time as it can be automated away, a free society will have to encourage people to volunteer for "work" placements they do not particularly want to do by these and other methods.

It will be clear what is considered unpleasant work in any society — few people (if any) will volunteer to do it. As in any advanced society, communities and syndicates who required extra help would inform others of their need by the various form of media that existed. In addition, it would be likely that each community would have a "division of activity" syndicate whose work would be to distribute information about these posts and to which members of a community would go to discover what placements existed for the line of "work" they were interested in. So we have a means by which syndicates and communes can ask for new associates and the means by which individuals can discover these placements. Obviously, some tasks will still require qualifications and that will be taken into account when syndicates and communes "advertise" for help.

And it is important to remember that the means of production required by new syndicates do not fall from the sky. Other members of society will have to work to produce the required goods. Therefore it is likely that the syndicates and communes would agree that only a certain (maximum) percentage of production would be allocated to start-up syndicates (as opposed to increasing the resources of existing confederations). Such a figure would obviously be revised periodically in order to take into account changing circumstances. Members of the community who decide to form syndicates for new productive tasks or syndicates which do the same work but are independent of existing confederations would have to get the agreement of other workers to supply them with the necessary means of production (just as today they have to get the agreement of a bank to receive the necessary credit to start a new business). By budgeting the amounts available, a free society can ensure that individual desires for specific kinds of work can be matched with the requirements of society for useful production.

And we must point out (just to make sure we are not misunderstood) that there will be no group of "planners" deciding which applications for resources get accepted. Instead, individuals and associations would apply to different production units for resources, whose workers in turn decide whether to produce the goods requested. If it is within the syndicate's agreed budget then it is likely that they will produce the required materials. In this way, a communist-anarchist society will ensure the maximum amount of economic freedom to start new syndicates and join existing ones plus ensure that social production does not suffer in the process.

Of course, no system is perfect — we are sure that not everyone will be able to do the work they enjoy the most (this is also the case under capitalism, we may add). In an anarchist society every method of ensuring that individuals pursue the work they are interested in would be investigated. If a possible solution can be found, we are sure that it will. What a free society would make sure of was that neither the capitalist market redeveloped (which ensures that the majority are marginalised into wage slavery) or a state socialist "labour army" type allocation process developed (which would ensure that free socialism did not remain free or socialist for long).

> In this manner, anarchism will be able to ensure the principle of voluntary labour and free association as well as making sure that unpleasant and unwanted "work" is done. Moreover, most anarchists are sure that in a free society such requirements to encourage people to volunteer for unpleasant work will disappear over time as feelings of mutual aid and solidarity become more and more common place. Indeed, it is likely that people will gain respect for doing jobs that others might find unpleasant and so it might become "glamorous" to do such activity. Showing off to friends can be a powerful stimulus in doing any activity.

We should note here that the education syndicates would obviously take into account the trends in "work" placement requirements when deciding upon the structure of their classes. In this way, education would respond to the needs of society as well as the needs of the individual (as would any productive syndicate).

I.4.14 What about the person who will not work?

Anarchism is based on voluntary labour. If people do not desire to work then they cannot (must not) be forced to by means of physical coercion. This makes some wonder what happens if someone refuses to work in a libertarian society.

In terms of a mutualist or collectivist anarchy, this question is easy to answer for goods are distributed according to work done and so if people do not work then they are left dependent on the charity of those who do (exceptions for the young, old and ill would apply, of course).

So this question is directed towards communist-anarchists, with many people arguing that communism is impossible because people simply would not work unless they get paid. This ignores the many people who do volunteer work (often in addition to their "real jobs"). It also ignores those who spend their time contributing to projects they are interested in (such as fan journals) which would be considered work in other contexts. A classic example of this is the internet, particularly webpages like Wikipedia and software projects like php. Then there is the activity of the pro-capitalists themselves, often fanatical anti-communists (which they almost always equate to Stalinism), who spend their free time working on wikipedia, newsgroups, webpages and journals explaining how communism could not work because people would never voluntarily contribute to society! It is one of the great ironies of life that those who hate communism the most often, by their actions, prove its viability.

So, communist-anarchists argue, in a society based on self-managed work in pleasant surroundings and a reduction of the working week to a minimum, there would be few people who refuse to do any kind of productive activity. The question arises of what to do with those (a small minority, to be sure) who refuse to work.

On this question there is some disagreement. Some anarchists argue that the lazy should not be deprived of the means of life. Social pressure, they argue, would ensure those who take from, but do not contribute, to the community listen to their conscience and start producing for the community that supports them. If this did not happen, then the person who refused to contribute would be asked to leave (freedom of association means the freedom **not** to associate). As Kropotkin argued;

> "First of all, is it not evident that if a society, founded on the principle of free work, were really menaced by loafers, it could protect itself without the authoritarian organisation we have nowadays, and without having recourse to wagedom [i.e., payment by deeds]?

> "Let us take a group of volunteers, combining for some particular enterprise. Having its success at heart, they all work with a will, save one of the associates, who is frequently absent from his post … some day the comrade who imperils their enterprise will be told: 'Friend, we should like to work with you; but as you are often absent from your post, and you do your work negligently, we must part. Go and find other comrades who will put up with your indifference!'

> "This is so natural that it is practised everywhere, even nowadays, in all industries … [I]f [a worker] does his work badly, if he hinders his comrades by his laziness or other defects, if he is quarrelsome, there is an end of it; he is compelled to leave the workshop.

> "Authoritarians pretend that it is the almighty employer and his overseers who maintain regularity and quality of

work in factories. In reality ... it is the factory itself, the workmen [and women] who see to the good quality of the work." [**The Conquest of Bread**, pp. 152-3]

Most anarchists agree with Camillo Berneri when he argued that anarchism should be based upon *"no compulsion to work, but no duty towards those who do not want to work."* [*"The Problem of Work"*, pp. 59-82, **Why Work?**, Vernon Richards (ed.), p. 74] This means that an anarchist society will not continue to feed, clothe, house someone who can produce but refuses to. Anarchists have had enough of the wealthy under capitalism consuming but not producing and do not see why they should support a new group of parasites after the revolution.

Obviously, there is a difference between not wanting to work and being unable to work. The sick, children, the old, pregnant women and so on will be looked after in libertarian communism. As child rearing would be considered "work" along with other more obviously economic tasks, mothers and fathers will not have to leave their children unattended and work to make ends meet. Instead, consideration will be given to the needs of both parents and children as well as the creation of community nurseries and child care centres.

We have to stress here that an anarchist society will not deny anyone the means of life. This would violate the voluntary labour which is at the heart of all schools of anarchism. Unlike capitalism, the means of life will not be monopolised by any group — including the commune. This means that someone who does not wish to join a commune or who does not pull their weight within a commune and are expelled or choose to leave will have access to the means of making a living.

We stated that we stress this fact as many supporters of capitalism seem to be unable to understand this point (or prefer to ignore it and so misrepresent the anarchist position). In an anarchist society, no one will be forced to join a commune simply because they do not have access to the means of production and/or land required to work alone. Unlike capitalism, where access to these essentials of life is dependent on buying access to them from the capitalist class (and so, effectively, denied to the vast majority), an anarchist society will ensure that all have access and have a real choice between living in a commune and working independently. This access is based on the fundamental difference between possession and property — the commune possesses as much land as it needs, as do non-members. The resources used by them are subject to the usual possession rationale — they possess it only as long as they use it and cannot bar others using it if they do not (i.e., it is not property).

Thus an anarchist commune remains a voluntary association and ensures the end of all forms of domination. The member of the commune has the choice of working as part of a community, giving according to their abilities and taking according to their needs (or some other means of organising production and consumption such as equal income or receiving labour notes, and so on), or working independently and so free of communal benefits as well as any commitments (bar those associated with using communal resources such as roads and so on).

So, in most, if not all, anarchist communities, individuals have two options, either they can join a commune and work together

as equals, or they can work as an individual or independent co-operative and exchange the product of their labour with others. If an individual joins a commune and does not carry their weight, even after their fellow workers ask them to, then that person will possibly be expelled and given enough land, tools or means of production to work alone. Of course, if a person is depressed, run down or otherwise finding it hard to join in communal responsibilities then their friends and fellow workers would do everything in their power to help and be flexible in their approach to the problem. What method a community would use would depend on what people in that community thought was best.

However, most social anarchists think that the problem of people trying not to work would be a very minor one in a free society. This is because productive activity is part of human life and an essential way to express oneself. With work being voluntary and self-managed, it will become like current day hobbies and many people work harder at their hobbies than they do at "real" work (this FAQ can be considered as an example of this!). How long this takes to organise fully is, of course, unknown but one of the most important tasks of a free society will be to ensure work is transformed and the burden of what remains is shared in order to reduce toil to a minimum.

It is the nature of employment under capitalism, the hierarchical nature of its workplace, that makes it "work" instead of pleasure. Work need not be a part of the day that we wish would end. It is **not** work that people hate. Rather it is **over**-work, in unpleasant circumstances and under the control of others that people hate. Reduce the hours of labour, improve the working conditions and place the work under self-management and work will stop being a hated thing. All these will help ensure that only an idiot would desire to work alone for, as Malatesta argued, the *"individual who wished to supply his own material needs by working alone would be the slave of his labours."* [**The Anarchist Revolution**, p. 15]

So, enlightened self-interest would secure the voluntary labour and egalitarian distribution anarchists favour in the vast majority of the population. The parasitism associated with capitalism would be a thing of the past. Thus the problem of the "lazy" person fails to understand the nature of humanity or the revolutionising effects of freedom on the nature and content of work.

I.4.15 What will the workplace of tomorrow look like?

Given the anarchist desire to liberate the artist in all of us, we can easily imagine that a free society would totally transform the working environment. No longer would workers be indifferent to their workplaces, but they would express themselves in transforming them into pleasant places, integrated into both the life of the local community and into the local environment. After all, *"no movement that raises the demand for workers' councils can be regarded as revolutionary unless it tries to promote sweeping transformations in the environment of the work place."* [Murray Bookchin, **Post-Scarcity Anarchism**, p. 88]

A glimpse of the future workplace can been seen from the actual class struggle. In the 40 day sit-down strike at Fisher Body plant #1 in Flint, Michigan in 1936, *"there was a community of two thousand strikers ... Committees organised recreation, information, classes, a postal service, sanitation ... There were classes in parliamentary procedure, public speaking, history of the labour movement. Graduate students at the University of Michigan gave courses in journalism and creative writing."* [Howard Zinn, **A People's History of the United States**, p. 391] In the same year, during the Spanish Revolution, collectivised workplaces also created libraries and education facilities as well as funding schools, health care and other social necessities (a practice, we must note, that had started before the revolution when anarchist unions had funded schools, social centres, libraries and so on).

The future workplace would be expanded to include education and classes in individual development. This follows Proudhon's suggestion made during the 1848 revolution that we should *"[o]rganise association, and by the same token, every workshop becoming a school, every worker becomes a master, every student an apprentice."* [**Property is Theft!**, p. 378] This means that in a free society *"Workers' associations have a very important role to play ... Linked to the system of public education, they will become both centres of production and centres for education ... The working masses will be in daily contact with the youthful army of agricultural and industrial workers. Labour and study, which have for so long and so foolishly been kept apart, will finally emerge side by side in their natural state of union. Instead of being confined to narrow, specialised fields, vocational education will include a variety of different types of work which, taken as a whole, will insure that each student becomes an all-round worker."* [Proudhon, **Selected Writings of Pierre-Joseph Proudhon**, p. 87]

This would allow work to become part of a wider community, drawing in people from different areas to share their knowledge and learn new insights and ideas. In addition, children would have part of their school studies with workplaces, getting them aware of the practicalities of many different forms of work and so allowing them to make informed decisions in what sort of activity they would be interested in pursuing when they were older.

Obviously, a workplace managed by its workers would also take care to make the working environment as pleasant as possible. No more "sick building syndrome" or unhealthy and stressful work areas for *"can we doubt that work will become a pleasure and a relaxation in a society of equals, in which 'hands' will not be compelled to sell themselves to toil, and to accept work under any conditions Repugnant tasks will disappear, because it is evident that these unhealthy conditions are harmful to society as a whole. Slaves can submit to them, but free men [and women] will create new conditions, and their work will be pleasant and infinitely more productive."* [Kropotkin, **The Conquest of Bread**, p. 123] Workplaces would be designed to maximise space and allow individual expression within them. We can imagine such places surrounded by gardens and allotments which were tended by workers themselves, giving a pleasant surrounding to the workplace. There would, in effect, be a break down of the city/rural divide — workplaces would be placed next to fields and integrated into the surroundings:

"Have the factory and the workshop at the gates of your

fields and gardens, and work in them. Not those large establishments, of course, in which huge masses of metals have to be dealt with and which are better placed at certain spots indicated by Nature, but the countless variety of workshops and factories which are required to satisfy the infinite diversity of tastes among civilised men [and women] ... factories and workshops which men, women and children will not be driven by hunger, but will be attracted by the desire of finding an activity suited to their tastes, and where, aided by the motor and the machine, they will choose the branch of activity which best suits their inclinations." [Kropotkin, **Fields, Factories and Workshops Tomorrow**, p. 197]

This vision of rural and urban integration is just part of the future anarchists see for the workplace. As Kropotkin argued, *"[w]e proclaim **integration**... a society of integrated, combined labour. A society where each individual is a producer of both manual and intellectual work; where each able-bodied human being is a worker, and where each worker works both in the field and the industrial workshop; where every aggregation of individuals, large enough to dispose of a certain variety of natural resources — it may be a nation, or rather a region — produces and itself consumes most of its own agricultural and manufactured produce."* [**Op. Cit.**, p. 26]

The future workplace would be an expression of the desires of those who worked there. It would be based around a pleasant working environment, within gardens and with an extensive library, resources for education classes and other leisure activities. All this, and more, will be possible in a society based upon self-realisation and self-expression and one in which individuality is not crushed by authority and capitalism. To quote Kropotkin, the future workplace would be *"airy and hygienic, and consequently economical, factories in which human life is of more account than machinery and the making of extra profits."* [**Op. Cit.**, p. 197] For, obviously, *"if most of the workshops we know are foul and unhealthy, it is because the workers are of no account in the organisation of factories"*. [**The Conquest of Bread**, p. 121]

"So in brief," argued William Morris, *"our buildings will be beautiful with their own beauty of simplicity as workshops"* and *"besides the mere workshops, our factory will have other buildings which may carry ornament further than that, for it will need dinning-hall, library, school, places for study of different kinds, and other such structures."* [**A Factory as It Might Be**, p. 9] This is possible and is only held back by capitalism which denounces such visions of freedom as "uneconomic." Yet such claims ignore the distribution of income in class society:

*"Impossible I hear an anti-Socialist say. My friend, please to remember that most factories sustain today large and handsome gardens, and not seldom parks ... **only** the said gardens, etc. are twenty miles away from the factory, **out of the smoke,** and are kept up for **one member of the factory only,** the sleeping partner to wit."* [Morris, **Op. Cit.**, pp. 7-8]

Pleasant working conditions based upon the self-management of work can produce a workplace within which economic "efficiency" can be achieved without disrupting and destroying individuality and the environment (also see section I.4.9 for a fuller discussion of anarchism and technology).

I.4.16 Won't a libertarian communist society be inefficient?

It is often argued that anarcho-communism and other forms of non-market libertarian-socialism would promote inefficiency and unproductive work. The basis of this argument is that without market forces to discipline workers and the profit motive to reward them, workers would have no incentive to work in a way which minimises time or resources. The net effect of this would be inefficient use of recourses, particularly an individual's time.

This is a valid point in some ways; for example, a society can (potentially) benefit from increasing productivity as the less time and resources it takes to produce a certain good, the more of both it gains for other activities (although, of course, in a class society the benefits of increased productivity generally accrue to, first and foremost, those at the top and, for the rest, the "other activities" mean more work). Indeed, for an individual, a decent society depends on people having time available for them to do what they want, to develop themselves in whatever way they want, to enjoy themselves. In addition, doing more with less can have a positive environment impact as well. It is for these reasons that an anarchist society would be interested in promoting efficiency and productiveness during production.

A free society will undoubtedly create new criteria for what counts as an efficient use of resources and time. What passes for "efficient" use under capitalism often means what is efficient in increasing the power and profits of the few, without regard to the wasteful use of individual time, energy and potential as well as environmental and social costs. Such a narrow criteria for decision making or evaluating efficient production will not exist in an anarchist society (see our discussion of the irrational nature of the price mechanism in section I.1.2, for example). When we use the term efficiency we mean the dictionary definition of efficiency (i.e. reducing waste, maximising use of resources) rather than what the capitalist market distorts this into (i.e. what creates most profits for the boss).

While capitalism has turned improvements in productivity as a means of increasing work, enriching the few and generally proletarianising the working class, a free society would take a different approach to the problem. As argued in section I.4.3, a communist-anarchist society would be based upon the principle of *"for some much per day (in money today, in labour tomorrow) you are entitled to satisfy — luxury excepted — this or the other of your wants."* [Peter Kropotkin, **Small Communal Experiments and why the fail**, p. 8] Building upon this, we can imagine a situation where the average output for a given industry in a given amount of time is used to encourage efficiency and productivity. If a given syndicate can produce this average output with at least average quality in less time than the agreed average/minimum (and without causing ecological or social externalities, of course) then the members of that syndicate can and should have that time off.

This would be a powerful incentive to innovate, improve productivity, introduce new machinery and processes as well as work efficiently without reintroducing the profit motive and material inequality. With the possibility of having more time available for themselves and their own projects, people involved in productive activities would have a strong interest in being efficient. Of course, if the work in question is something they enjoy then any increases in efficiency would **enhance** what makes their work enjoyable and not eliminate it.

Rewarding efficiency with free time would also be an important means to ensure efficient use of resources as well as a means of reducing time spent in productive activity which was considered as boring or otherwise undesirable. The incentive of getting unpleasant tasks over with as quickly as possible would ensure that the tasks were done efficiently and that innovation was directed towards them. Moreover, when it came to major investment decisions, a syndicate would be more likely to get others to agree to its plans if the syndicate had a reputation of excellence. This, again, would encourage efficiency as people would know that they could gain resources for their communities and workplaces (i.e. themselves) more easily if their work is efficient and reliable. This would be a key means of encouraging efficient and effective use of resources.

Similarly, an inefficient or wasteful syndicate would have negative reactions from their fellow workers. As we argued in section I.4.7, a libertarian communist economy would be based on free association. If a syndicate or community got a reputation for being inefficient with resources then others would not associate with them (i.e. they would not supply them with materials, or place them at the end of the queue when deciding which production requests to supply, and so on). As with a syndicate which produced shoddy goods, the inefficient syndicate would also face the judgement of its peers. This will produce an environment which will encourage efficient use of resources and time.

All these factors, the possibility of increased free time, the respect and resources gained for efficient and excellent work and the possibility of a lack of co-operation with others for inefficient use of resources, would ensure that an anarchist-communist or anarchist-collectivist society would have no need to fear inefficiency. Indeed, by placing the benefits of increased efficiency into the hands of those who do the work, efficiency will no doubt increase.

With self-management, we can soon see time and resources being used efficiently and productively simply because those doing the work would have a direct and real interest in it. Rather than alienate their liberty, as under capitalism, they would apply their creativity and minds to transforming their productive activity in such a way as to make it enjoyable and not a waste of their time.

Little wonder Kropotkin argued that modern knowledge could be applied to a society in which people, *"with the work of their own hands and intelligence, and by the aid of the machinery already invented and to be invented, should themselves create all imaginable riches. Technics and science will not be lagging behind if production takes such a direction. Guided by observation, analysis and experiment, they will answer all possible demands. They will reduce the time required for producing wealth to any desired amount, so as to leave to everyone as much leisure as he or she may ask for … they guarantee … the happiness that can be found in the full and varied exercise of the different capacities of the human being, in work that need not be overwork."* [**Fields, Factories and Workshops Tomorrow**, pp. 198-9]

The social and political structure of anarchy is similar to that of the economic structure, i.e., it is based on a voluntary federation of decentralised, directly democratic policy-making bodies. These are the neighbourhood and community assemblies and their confederations. In these grassroots political units, the concept of ***"self-management"*** becomes that of ***"self-government"***, a form of municipal organisation in which people take back control of their living places from the bureaucratic state and the capitalist class whose interests it serves. Bakunin's comments are very applicable here:

> *"[A] truly popular organisation begins from below, from the association, from the commune. Thus starting out with the organisation of the lowest nucleus and proceeding upward, federalism becomes a political institution of socialism, the free and spontaneous organisation of popular life."* [**The Political Philosophy of Bakunin**, pp. 273-4]

"A new economic phase demands a new political phase," argued Kropotkin, *"A revolution as profound as that dreamed of by the socialists cannot accept the mould of an out-dated political life. A new society based on equality of condition, on the collective possession of the instruments of work, cannot tolerate for a week … the representative system … if we want the social revolution, we must seek a form of political organisation that will correspond to the new method of economic organisation … The future belongs to the free groupings of interests and not to governmental centralisation; it belongs to freedom and not to authority."* [**Words of a Rebel**, pp. 143-4]

Thus the social structure of an anarchist society will be the opposite of the current system. Instead of being centralised and top-down as in the state, it will be decentralised and organised from the bottom up. As Kropotkin argued, *"socialism must become **more popular**, more communalistic, and less dependent upon indirect government through elected representatives. It must become more **self-governing.**"* [**Anarchism**, p. 185] In this, Kropotkin (like Bakunin) followed Proudhon who argued that *"[u]nless democracy is a fraud, and the sovereignty of the People a joke, it must be admitted that each citizen in the sphere of his [or her] industry, each municipal, district or provincial council within its own territory, is the only natural and legitimate representative of the Sovereign, and that therefore each locality should act direct and by itself in administering the interests which it includes, and should exercise full sovereignty in relation to them."* [**Propert is Theft!**, p. 595] While anarchists have various different conceptions of how this

communal system would be constituted (as we will see), there is total agreement on these basic visions and principles.

The aim is *"to found an order of things wherein the principle of the sovereignty of the people, of man and of the citizen, would be implemented to the letter"* and *"where every member"* of a society *"retaining his independence and continuing to act as sovereign, would be self-governing"* and any social organisation *"would concern itself solely with collective matters; where as a consequence, there would be certain common matters but no centralisation."* This means that the *"federative, mutualist republican sentiment"* (as summarised these days by the expression self-management) will *"bring about the victory of Labour Democracy right around the world."* [Proudhon, **Op. Cit.**, p. 574 and p. 763]

This empowerment of ordinary citizens through decentralisation and direct democracy will eliminate the alienation and apathy that are now rampant in the modern city and town, and (as always happens when people are free) unleash a flood of innovation in dealing with the social breakdown now afflicting our urban wastelands. The gigantic metropolis with its hierarchical and impersonal administration, its atomised and isolated "residents," will be transformed into a network of humanly scaled participatory communities (usually called "communes"), each with its own unique character and forms of self-government, which will be co-operatively linked through federation with other communities at several levels, from the municipal through the bioregional to the global.

This means that the social perspective of libertarian socialism is as distinctive as its economic vision. While mainstream socialism is marked by support for centralised states, anarchists stay true to socialism as equality and argue that means decentralisation. Thus socialism *"wears two distinct faces. When it is said that a man is a Socialist, it is implied that he regards the monopoly of private property in the means of production as the cause of the existing unequal distribution of wealth and its attendant ills … Socialists are divided into the centralising and decentralising parties, the party of the State and the party of the federatic commune."* [Charlotte M. Wilson, **Anarchist Essays**, p. 37] Only such a federal, bottom-up, system can ensure people can manage their own fates and ensure genuine freedom and equality through mass participation and self-management.

Of course, it can (and has) been argued that people are just not interested in "politics." Further, some claim that this disinterest is why governments exist — people delegate their responsibilities and power to others because they have better things to do. Such an argument, however, is flawed on empirical grounds. As we indicated in section B.2.6, centralisation of power in both the French and American revolutions occurred **because** working people were taking **too much** interest in politics and social issues, not the reverse (*"To attack the central power, to strip it of its prerogatives, to decentralise, to dissolve authority, would have been to abandon to the people the control of its affairs, to run the risk of a truly popular revolution. That is why the bourgeoisie sought to reinforce the central government even more…"* [Kropotkin, **Words of a Rebel**, p. 143]).

Simply put, the state is centralised to facilitate **minority rule** by excluding the mass of people from taking part in the decision making processes within society. This is to be expected as social structures do not evolve by chance — rather they develop to meet specific needs and requirements. The specific need of the ruling class is to rule and that means marginalising the bulk of the population. Its requirement is for minority power and this is transformed into the structure of the state.

Even if we ignore the historical evidence on this issue, anarchists do not draw this conclusion from the current apathy that surrounds us. In fact, we argue that this apathy is not the cause of government but its result. Government is an inherently hierarchical system in which ordinary people are deliberately marginalised. The powerlessness people feel due to the workings of the system ensures that they are apathetic about it, thus guaranteeing that wealthy and powerful elites govern society without hindrance from the oppressed and exploited majority.

Moreover, government usually sticks its nose into areas that most people have no real interest in. Some things, as in the regulation of industry or workers' safety and rights, a free society could leave to those affected to make their own decisions (we doubt that workers would subject themselves to unsafe working conditions, for example). In others, such as the question of personal morality and acts, a free people would have no interest in (unless it harmed others, of course). This, again, would reduce the number of issues that would be discussed in a free commune.

Also, via decentralisation, a free people would be mainly discussing local issues, so reducing the complexity of many questions and solutions. Wider issues would, of course, be discussed but these would be on specific issues and so more focused in their nature than those raised in the legislative bodies of the state. So, a combination of centralisation and an irrational desire to discuss every and all questions also helps make "politics" seem boring and irrelevant.

As noted above, this result is not an accident and the marginalisation of "ordinary" people is actually celebrated in bourgeois "democratic" theory. As Noam Chomsky notes:

> "Twentieth century democratic theorists advise that 'The public must be put in its place,' so that the 'responsible men' may 'live free of the trampling and roar of a bewildered herd,' 'ignorant and meddlesome outsiders' whose 'function' is to be 'interested spectators of action,' not participants, lending their weight periodically to one or another of the leadership class (elections), then returning to their private concerns. (Walter Lippman). The great mass of the population, 'ignorant and mentally deficient,' must be kept in their place for the common good, fed with 'necessary illusion' and 'emotionally potent oversimplifications' (Wilson's Secretary of State Robert Lansing, Reinhold Niebuhr). Their 'conservative' counterparts are only more extreme in their adulation of the Wise Men who are the rightful rulers — in the service of the rich and powerful, a minor footnote regularly forgotten." [**Year 501**, p. 18]

This marginalisation of the public from political life ensures that the wealthy can be "left alone" to use their power as they see fit. In other words, such marginalisation is a necessary part of a fully functioning capitalist society. Hence, under capitalism, libertarian social structures have to be discouraged. Or as Chomsky puts it,

the "rabble must be instructed in the values of subordination and a narrow quest for personal gain within the parameters set by the institutions of the masters; meaningful democracy, with popular association and action, is a threat to be overcome." [**Op. Cit.**, p. 18] This philosophy can be seen in the statement of a US Banker in Venezuela under the murderous Jimenez dictatorship:

> "You have the freedom here to do whatever you want to do with your money, and to me, that is worth all the political freedom in the world." [quoted by Chomsky, **Op. Cit.**, p. 99]

Deterring libertarian alternatives to statism is a common feature of our current system. By marginalising and disempowering people, the ability of individuals to manage their own social activities is undermined and weakened. They develop a "fear of freedom" and embrace authoritarian institutions and "strong leaders", which in turn reinforces their marginalisation.

This consequence is hardly surprising. Anarchists maintain that the desire to participate and the ability to participate are in a symbiotic relationship: participation builds on itself. By creating the social structures that allow participation, participation will increase. As people increasingly take control of their lives, so their ability to do so also increases. The challenge of having to take responsibility for decisions that make a difference is at the same time an opportunity for personal development. To begin to feel power, having previously felt powerless, to win access to the resources required for effective participation and learn how to use them, is a liberating experience. Once people become active subjects, making things happen in one aspect of their lives, they are less likely to remain passive objects, allowing things to happen to them, in other aspects.

All in all, "politics" is far too important a subject to leave to politicians, the wealthy and bureaucrats. After all, it is (or, at least, it should be) what affects, your friends, community, and, ultimately, the planet you live on. Such issues cannot be left to anyone but you.

Hence a meaningful communal life based on self-empowered individuals is a distinct possibility (indeed, it has repeatedly appeared throughout history). It is the hierarchical structures in statism and capitalism, marginalising and disempowering the majority, which are at the root of the current wide scale apathy in the face of increasing social and ecological disruption. Libertarian socialists therefore call for a radically new form of political system to replace the centralised nation-state, a form that would be based around confederations of self-governing communities. In other words, in anarchism "**[s]ociety is a society of societies; a league of leagues of leagues; a commonwealth of commonwealths of commonwealths; a republic of republics of republics.** Only there is freedom and order, only there is spirit, a spirit which is self-sufficiency and community, unity and independence." [Gustav Landauer, **For Socialism**, pp. 125-126]

To create such a system would require dismantling the nation-state and reconstituting relations between communities on the basis of self-determination and free and equal confederation from below. In the following subsections we will examine in more detail why this new system is needed and what it might look like. As we have stressed repeatedly, these are just suggestions of possible anarchist solutions to social organisation. Most anarchists recognise that anarchist communities will co-exist with non-anarchist ones after the destruction of the existing state. As we are anarchists we are discussing anarchist visions. We will leave it up to non-anarchists to paint their own pictures of a possible future.

I.5.1 What are participatory communities?

A key concept in anarchist thought is that of the participatory community. Traditionally, these participatory communities were called **communes** in anarchist theory (*"The basic social and economic cell of the anarchist society is the free, independent commune"* [A. Grachev, quoted by Paul Avrich, **The Anarchists in the Russian Revolution**, p. 64]). These are seen as the way people participate in the decisions that affect them and their neighbourhoods, regions and, ultimately, planet. These are the means for transforming our social environment from one disfigured by economic and political power and its needs to one fit for human beings to live and flourish in.

The creation of a network of participatory communities ("communes") based on self-government through direct, face-to-face democracy in grassroots neighbourhood assemblies is the means to that end. As we argued in section I.2.3 such assemblies will be born in social struggle and so reflect the needs of the struggle and those within it so our comments here must be considered as generalisations of the salient features of such communities and **not** blue-prints.

The reason for the use of the term commune is due to anarchism's roots in France where it refers to a organisation unit of the state which can be of any size, from the smallest hamlet to the biggest city (hence the Paris Commune). Proudhon used the term to describe the social units of a non-statist society and subsequent anarchists like Bakunin and Kropotkin followed his lead. As the term "commune" has, since the 1960s, often referred to "intentional communities" where people drop out of society and form their own counter-cultural groups and living spaces we have, in order to avoid confusion, decided to use "participatory community" as well (other anarchists have used other terms, including *"free municipality"*).

Within anarchist thought, there are two main conceptions of the free commune. One vision is based on workplace delegates, the other on neighbourhood assemblies. We will sketch each in turn.

The first type of participatory community (in which *"the federative Alliance of all working men's associations … will constitute the commune"*) is most associated with Bakunin. He argued that the *"future social organisation must be made solely from the bottom upwards, by the free association or federation of workers, firstly in their unions, then in communes, regions, nations and finally in a great federation, international and universal."* [**Michael Bakunin: Selected Writings**, p. 170 and p. 206] This vision was stressed by later anarchist thinkers. For example, Spanish anarchist Issac Puente thought that in towns and cities *"the part of the free municipality is played by local federation … Ultimate sovereignty in the local federation of industrial unions lies with the general assembly of all local producers."* [**Libertarian Communism**, p. 27] The Russian

anarchist G. P. Maximoff saw the *"communal confederation"* as being *"constituted by thousands of freely acting labour organisations."* [**The Program of Anarcho-Syndicalism**, p. 43]

This vision of the commune was created during many later revolutions (such as in Russia in 1905 and 1917 as well as Hungary in 1956). Being based on workplaces, this form of commune has the advantage of being based on groups of people who are naturally associated during most of the day (Bakunin considered workplace bodies as *"the natural organisation of the masses"* as they were *"based on the various types of work"* which *"define their actual day-to-day life"* [**The Basic Bakunin**, p. 139]). This would facilitate the organisation of assemblies, discussion on social, economic and political issues and the mandating and recalling of delegates. Moreover, it combines political and economic power in one organisation, so ensuring that the working class actually manages society.

Other anarchists counterpoise neighbourhood assemblies to workers' councils. These assemblies will be general meetings open to all citizens in every neighbourhood, town, and village, and will be the source of and final *"authority"* over public policy for all levels of confederal co-ordination. Such *"town meetings"* will bring ordinary people directly into the political process and give them an equal voice in the decisions that affect their lives. Such anarchists point to the experience of the French Revolution of 1789 and the *"sections"* of the Paris Commune as the key example of *"a people governing itself directly — when possible — without intermediaries, without masters."* It is argued, based on this experience, that *"the principles of anarchism … dated from 1789, and that they had their origin, not in theoretical speculations, but in the **deeds** of the Great French Revolution."* [Peter Kropotkin, **The Great French Revolution**, vol. 1, p. 210 and p. 204]

Critics of workers' councils point out that not all working class people work in factories or workplaces. Many are parents who look after children, for example. By basing the commune around the workplace, such people are automatically excluded. Moreover, in most modern cities many people do not live near where they work. It would mean that local affairs could not be effectively discussed in a system of workers' councils as many who take part in the debate are unaffected by the decisions reached (this is something which the supporters of workers' councils **have** noticed and some argue for councils which are delegates from both the inhabitants **and** the enterprises of an area). In addition, some anarchists argue that workplace based systems automatically generate "special interests" and so exclude community issues. Only community assemblies can *"transcend the traditional special interests of work, workplace, status, and property relations, and create a **general** interest based on shared community problems."* [Murray Bookchin, **From Urbanisation to Cities**, p. 254]

However, such community assemblies can only be valid if they can be organised rapidly in order to make decisions and to mandate and recall delegates. In the capitalist city, many people work far from where they live and so such meetings have to be called for after work or at weekends. Thus the key need is to reduce the working day/week and to communalise industry. For this reason, many anarchists continue to support the workers' council vision of the commune, complemented by community assemblies for those who live in an area but do not work in a traditional workplace (e.g. parents bring up small children, the old, the sick and so on).

These positions are not hard and fast divisions, far from it. Puente, for example, thought that in the countryside the dominant commune would be *"all the residents of a village or hamlet meeting in an assembly (council) with full powers to administer local affairs."* [**Op. Cit.**, p. 25] Kropotkin supported the soviets of the Russian Revolution, arguing that the *"idea of soviets ... of councils of workers and peasants ... controlling the economic and political life of the country is a great idea. All the more so, since it necessarily follows that these councils should be composed of all who take part in the production of natural wealth by their own efforts."* [**Anarchism**, p. 254]

Which method, workers' councils or community assemblies, will be used in a given community will depend on local conditions, needs and aspirations and it is useless to draw hard and fast rules. It is likely that some sort of combination of the two approaches will be used, with workers' councils being complemented by community assemblies until such time as a reduced working week and decentralisation of urban centres will make purely community assemblies the more realistic option. It is likely that in a fully libertarian society, community assemblies will be the dominant communal organisation but in the period immediately after a revolution this may not be immediately possible. Objective conditions, rather than predictions, will be the deciding factor. Under capitalism, anarchists pursue both forms of organisation, arguing for community **and** industrial unionism in the class struggle (see sections J.5.1 and J.5.2).

Regardless of the exact make up of the commune, it has certain key features. It would be a free association, based upon the self-assumed obligation of those who join. In free association, participation is essential simply because it is the **only** means by which individuals can collectively govern themselves (and unless they govern themselves, someone else will). *"As a unique individual,"* Stirner argued, *"you can assert yourself alone in association, because the association does not own you, because you are one who owns it or who turns it to your own advantage."* The rules governing the association are determined by the associated and can be changed by them (and so a vast improvement over "love it or leave") as are the policies the association follows. Thus, the association *"does not impose itself as a spiritual power superior to my spirit. I have no wish to become a slave to my maxims, but would rather subject them to my ongoing criticism."* [Max Stirner, **No Gods, No Masters**, vol. 1, p. 17]

Thus participatory communities are freely joined and self-managed by their members with no division between order givers and order takers as exists within the state. Rather the associated govern themselves and while the assembled people collectively decide the rules governing their association, and are bound by them as individuals, they are also superior to them in the sense that these rules can always be modified or repealed (see section A.2.11 for more details). As can be seen, a participatory commune is new form of social life, radically different from the state as it is decentralised, self-governing and based upon individual autonomy and free agreement. Thus Kropotkin:

"The representative system was organised by the bourgeoisie to ensure their domination, and it will disappear with them. For the new economic phase that is about to begin we must seek a new form of political organisation, based on a principle quite different from that of representation. The logic of events imposes it." [**Words of a Rebel**, p. 125]

This *"new form of political organisation has to be worked out the moment that socialistic principles shall enter our life. And it is self-evident that this new form will have to be **more popular, more decentralised, and nearer to the folk-mote self-government** than representative government can ever be."* Kropotkin, like all anarchists, considered the idea that socialism could be created by taking over the current state or creating a new one as doomed to failure. Instead, he recognised that socialism would only be built using new organisations that reflect the spirit of socialism (such as freedom, self-government and so on). He, like Proudhon and Bakunin before him, therefore argued that *"**was the form that the social revolution must take** — the independent commune"* whose *"inhabitants have decided that they **will** communalise the consumption of commodities, their exchange and their production."* [**Anarchism**, p. 184 and p. 163]

In a nutshell, a participatory community is a free association, based upon the mass assembly of people who live in a common area, the means by which they make the decisions that affect them, their communities, bio-regions and the planet. Their essential task is to provide a forum for raising public issues and deciding them. Moreover, these assemblies will be a key way of generating a community (and community spirit) and building and enriching social relationships between individuals and, equally important, of developing and enriching individuals by the very process of participation in communal affairs. By discussing, thinking and listening to others, individuals develop their own abilities and powers while at the same time managing their own affairs, so ensuring that no one else does (i.e. they govern themselves and are no longer governed from above by others). As Kropotkin argued, self-management has an educational effect on those who practice it:

"The 'permanence' of the general assemblies of the sections — that is, the possibility of calling the general assembly whenever it was wanted by the members of the section and of discussing everything in the general assembly... will educate every citizen politically... The section in permanence — the forum always open — is the only way ... to assure an honest and intelligent administration." [**The Great French Revolution**, vol. 1, pp. 210-1]

As well as integrating the social life of a community and encouraging the political and social development of its members, these free communes will also be integrated into the local ecology. Humanity would live in harmony with nature as well as with itself — as discussed in section E.2, these would be **eco**-communities part of their local eco-systems with a balanced mix of agriculture and industry (as described by Kropotkin in his classic work **Fields, Factories and Workshops**). Thus a free commune would aim to integrate the individual into social and communal life, rural and urban life into a balanced whole and human life into the wider ecology. In this way the free commune would make human habitation fully ecological, ending the sharp and needless (and dehumanising and de-individualising) division of human life from the rest of the planet. The commune will be a key means of expressing diversity within humanity and the planet as well as improving the quality of life in society:

> "The Commune … will be entirely devoted to improving the communal life of the locality. Making their requests to the appropriate Syndicates, Builders', Public Health, Transport or Power, the inhabitants of each Commune will be able to gain all reasonable living amenities, town planning, parks, play-grounds, trees in the street, clinics, museums and art galleries. Giving, like the medieval city assembly, an opportunity for any interested person to take part in, and influence, his town's affairs and appearance, the Commune will be a very different body from the borough council …

> "In ancient and medieval times cities and villages expressed the different characters of different localities and their inhabitants. In redstone, Portland or granite, in plaster or brick, in pitch of roof, arrangements of related buildings or patterns of slate and thatch each locality added to the interests of travellers … each expressed itself in castle, home or cathedral.

> "How different is the dull, drab, or flashy ostentatious monotony of modern England. Each town is the same. The same Woolworth's, Odeon Cinemas, and multiple shops, the same 'council houses' or 'semi-detached villas' … North, South, East or West, what's the difference, where is the change?

> "With the Commune the ugliness and monotony of present town and country life will be swept away, and each locality and region, each person will be able to express the joy of living, by living together." [Tom Brown, **Syndicalism**, p. 59]

The size of the neighbourhood assemblies will vary, but it will probably fluctuate around some ideal size, discoverable in practice, that will provide a viable scale of face-to-face interaction and allow for both a variety of personal contacts and the opportunity to know and form a personal estimation of everyone in the neighbourhood. This suggests that any town or city would itself be a confederation of assemblies — as was, of course, practised very effectively in Paris during the Great French Revolution.

Such assemblies would meet regularly, at the very least monthly (probably more often, particularly during periods which require fast and often decision making, like a revolution), and deal with a variety of issues. In the words of the CNT's resolution on libertarian communism:

> "the foundation of this administration will be the commune. These communes are to be autonomous and

will be federated at regional and national levels to achieve their general goals. The right to autonomy does not preclude the duty to implement agreements regarding collective benefits … [A] commune without any voluntary restrictions will undertake to adhere to whatever general norms may be agreed by majority vote after free debate … the commune is to be autonomous and confederated with the other communes … the commune will have the duty to concern itself with whatever may be of interest to the individual.

> "It will have to oversee organising, running and beautification of the settlement. It will see that its inhabitants; are housed and that items and products be made available to them by the producers' unions or associations.

> "Similarly, it is to concern itself with hygiene, the keeping of communal statistics and with collective requirements such as education, health services and with the maintenance and improvement of local means of communication.

> "It will orchestrate relations with other communes and will take care to stimulate all artistic and cultural pursuits.

> "So that this mission may be properly fulfilled, a communal council is to be appointed … None of these posts will carry any executive or bureaucratic powers … [its members] will perform their role as producers coming together in session at the close of the day's work to discuss the detailed items which may not require the endorsement of communal assemblies.

> "Assemblies are to be summoned as often as required by communal interests, upon the request of the communal council or according to the wishes of the inhabitants of each commune … The inhabitants of a commune are to debate among themselves their internal problems." [quoted by Jose Peirats, **The CNT in the Spanish Revolution**, vol. 1, pp. 106-7]

Thus the communal assembly discusses that which affects the community and those within it. As these local community associations, will be members of larger communal bodies, the communal assembly will also discuss issues which affect wider areas, as indicated, and mandate their delegates to discuss them at confederation assemblies. This system, we must note, was applied with great success during the Spanish revolution (see section I.8) and so cannot be dismissed as wishful thinking.

However, of course, the actual framework of a free society will be worked out in practice. As Bakunin correctly argued, society "can, and must, organise itself in a different fashion [than what came before], but not from top to bottom and according to an ideal plan" [**Michael Bakunin: Selected Writings**, p. 205] What does seem likely is that confederations of communes will be required. We turn to this in the next section.

I.5.2 Why are confederations of participatory communities needed?

Since not all issues are local, the neighbourhood and community assemblies will also elect mandated and recallable delegates to the larger-scale units of self-government in order to address issues affecting larger areas, such as urban districts, the city or town as a whole, the county, the bio-region, and ultimately the entire planet. Thus the assemblies will confederate at several levels in order to develop and co-ordinate common policies to deal with common problems. In the words of the CNT's resolution on libertarian communism:

> "The inhabitants of a commune are to debate among themselves their internal problems … Federations are to deliberate over major problems affecting a country or province and all communes are to be represented at their reunions and assemblies, thereby enabling their delegates to convey the democratic viewpoint of their respective communes.

> "If, say, roads have to be built to link villages of a county or any matter arises to do with transportation and exchange of produce between agricultural and industrial counties, then naturally every commune which is implicated will have its right to have its say.

> "On matters of a regional nature, it is the duty of the regional federation to implement agreements which will represent the sovereign will of all the region's inhabitants. So the starting point is the individual, moving on through the commune, to the federation and right on up finally to the confederation.

> "Similarly, discussion of all problems of a national nature shall follow a like pattern … " [quoted by Jose Peirats, **The CNT in the Spanish Revolution**, p. 107]

In other words, the commune "cannot any longer acknowledge any superior: that, above it, there cannot be anything, save the interests of the Federation, freely embraced by itself in concert with other Communes." [Kropotkin, **No Gods, No Masters**, vol. 1, p. 259]

Federalism is applicable at all levels of society. As Kropotkin pointed out, anarchists "understand that if no central government was needed to rule the independent communes, if national government is thrown overboard and national unity is obtained by free federation, then a central **municipal** government becomes equally useless and noxious. The same federative principle would do within the commune." [**Anarchism**, pp. 163-164] Thus the whole of society would be a free federation, from the local community right up to the global level. And this free federation would be based squarely on the autonomy and self-government of local groups. With federalism, co-operation replaces coercion.

This need for co-operation does not imply a centralised body. To exercise your autonomy by joining self-managing organisations and, therefore, agreeing to abide by the decisions you help make is not a denial of that autonomy (unlike joining a hierarchical structure, where you forsake autonomy **within** the organisation). In a **centralised** system, we must stress, **power** rests at the top and the role of those below is simply to obey (it matters not if those with the power are elected or not, the principle is the same). In a **federal** system, power is **not** delegated into the hands of a few (obviously a "federal" government or state is a centralised system). Decisions in a federal system are made at the base of the organisation and flow upwards so ensuring that power remains decentralised in the hands of all. Working together to solve common problems and organise common efforts to reach common goals is not centralisation and those who confuse the two make a serious error — they fail to understand the different relations of authority each generates and confuse obedience with co-operation.

As in the economic federation of collectives, the lower levels will control the higher, thus eliminating the current pre-emptive powers of centralised government hierarchies. Delegates to higher-level co-ordinating councils or conferences will be instructed, at every level of confederation, by the assemblies they represent, on how to deal with any issue. As Proudhon argued in March 1848:

> "In the end, we are all voters; we can choose the most worthy.

> "We can do more; we can follow them step-by-step in their legislative acts and their votes; we will make them transmit our arguments and our documents; we will suggest our will to them, and when we are discontented, we will recall and dismiss them.

> "The choice of talents, the imperative mandate [**mandate impertif**], and permanent revocability are the most immediate and incontestable consequences of the electoral principle. It is the inevitable program of all democracy." [**Property is Theft!**, p. 273]

So these instructions will be binding, committing delegates to a framework of policies within which they must act and providing for their recall and the nullification of their decisions if they fail to carry out their mandates. Delegates may be selected by election and/or sortition (i.e. random selection by lot, as for jury duty currently). As Murray Bookchin argued:

> "A confederalist view involves a clear distinction between policy making and the co-ordination and execution of adopted policies. Policy making is exclusively the right of popular community assemblies based on the practices of participatory democracy. Administration and co-ordination are the responsibility of confederal councils, which become the means for interlinking villages, towns, neighbourhoods, and cities into confederal networks. Power flows from the bottom up instead of from the top down, and in confederations, the flow of power from the bottom up diminishes with the scope of the federal council ranging territorially from localities to regions and from regions to ever-broader territorial areas." [**From Urbanisation to Cities**, p. 253]

Thus the people will have the final word on policy, which is the essence of self-government, and each citizen will have his or her turn to participate in the co-ordination of public affairs. In other words, self-government will be the people themselves organised in their community assemblies and their confederal co-ordinating councils, with any delegates limited to implementing policy formulated by the people.

In such a system there will, undoubtedly, be the need for certain individuals to be allocated certain tasks to do. We stress the word "tasks" because their work is essentially administrative in nature, without power. For example, an individual or a group of individuals may be elected to look into alternative power supplies for a community and report back on what they discover. They cannot impose their decision **onto** the community as they do not have the power to do so. They simply present their findings to the body which had mandated them. These findings are **not** a law which the electors are required to follow, but a series of suggestions and information from which the assembled people chose what they think is best. Or, to use another example, someone may be elected to overlook the installation of a selected power supply but the decision on what power supply to use and which specific project to implement has been decided upon by the whole community. Similarly with any delegate elected to a confederal council.

The scales and levels of confederation can only be worked out in practice. In general, it would be safe to say that confederations would be needed on a wide scale, starting with towns and cities and then moving onto regional and other levels. No village, town or city could be self-sufficient nor would desire to be — communication and links with other places are part and parcel of life and anarchists have no desire to retreat back into an isolated form of localism:

> "No community can hope to achieve economic autarchy, nor should it try to do so. Economically, the wide range of resources that are needed to make many of our widely used goods preclude self-enclosed insularity and parochialism. Far from being a liability, this interdependence among communities and regions can well be regarded as an asset — culturally as well as politically ... Divested of the cultural cross-fertilisation that is often a product of economic intercourse, the municipality tends to shrink into itself and disappear into its own civic privatism. Shared needs and resources imply the existence of sharing and, with sharing, communication, rejuvenation by new ideas, and a wider social horizon that yields a wider sensibility to new experiences." [Bookchin, **Op. Cit.**, p. 237]

This means that the scale and level of the confederations created by the communes will be varied and extensive. It would be hard to generalise about them, particularly as different confederations will exist for different tasks and interests. Moreover, any system of communes would start off based on the existing villages, towns and cities of capitalism. That is unavoidable and will, of course, help determine the initial scale and level of confederations.

It seems likely that the scale of the confederation will be dependent on the inhabited area in question. A village, for example, would be based on one assembly and (minimally) be part of a local confederation covering all the villages nearby. In turn, this local confederation would be part of a district confederation, and so on up to (ultimately) a continental and world scale. Needless to say, the higher the confederation the less often it would meet and the less it would have to consider in terms of issues to decide. On such a level, only the most general issues and decisions could be reached (in effect, only guidelines which the member confederations would apply as they saw fit).

In urban areas, the town or city would have to be broken down into confederations and these confederations would constitute the town or city assembly of delegates. Given a huge city like London, New York or Mexico City it would be impossible to organise in any other way. Smaller towns would probably be able to have simpler confederations. We must stress that few, if any, anarchists consider it desirable to have huge cities in a free society and one of the major tasks of social transformation will be to break the metropolis into smaller units, integrated with the local environment. However, a social revolution will take place in these vast metropolises and so we have to take them into account in our discussion.

Thus the issue of size would determine when a new level of confederation would be needed. A town or village of several thousand people could be organised around the basic level of the commune and it may be that a libertarian socialist society would probably form another level of confederation once this level has been reached. Such units of confederation would, as noted above, include urban districts within today's large cities, small cities, and rural districts composed of several nearby towns. The next level of confederation would, we can imagine, be dependent on the number of delegates required. After a certain number, the confederation assembly may became difficult to manage, so implying that another level of confederation is required. This would, undoubtedly, be the base for determining the scale and level of confederation, ensuring that any confederal assembly can actually manage its activities and remain under the control of lower levels.

Combined with this consideration, we must also raise the issue of economies of scale. A given level of confederation may be required to make certain social and economic services efficient (we are thinking of economies of scale for such social needs as universities, hospitals, and cultural institutions). While every commune may have a doctor, nursery, local communal stores and small-scale workplaces, not all can have a university, hospital, factories and so forth. These would be organised on a wider level, so necessitating the appropriate confederation to exist to manage them.

Moreover, face-to-face meetings of the whole population are impractical at this size. Therefore, the decision making body at this level would be the **confederal council,** which would consist of mandated, recallable, and rotating delegates from the neighbourhood assemblies. These delegates would co-ordinate policies which have been discussed and voted on by the neighbourhood assemblies, with the votes being summed across the district to determine district policy. The issues to be discussed by these confederal meetings/ assemblies would be proposed by local communes, the confederal council would collate these proposals and submit them to the other communes in the confederation for discussion. Thus the flow of decision making would be from the bottom up, with the "lowest" bodies having the most power, particularly the power to formulate, suggest, correct and, if need be, reject decisions made at "higher" levels in the confederation.

Ties between bioregions or larger territories based on the distribution of such things as geographically concentrated mineral deposits, climate dependent crops, and production facilities that are most efficient when concentrated in one area will unite communities confederally on the basis of common material needs as well as values. At the bioregional and higher levels of confederation, councils of mandated, recallable, and rotating delegates will co-ordinate policies at those levels, but such policies will still be subject to approval by the neighbourhood and community assemblies through their right to recall their delegates and revoke their decisions.

In summary, the size and scale of confederations will depend on practical considerations, based on what people found were optimal sizes for their neighbourhood assemblies and the needs of co-operation between them, towns, cities, regions and so on. We cannot, and have no wish, to predict the development of a free society. Therefore the scale and levels of confederation will be decided by those actually creating an anarchist world. All we can do is make a few suggestions of what seems likely.

Thus confederations of communes are required to co-ordinate joint activity and discuss common issues and interests. Confederation is also required to protect individual, community and social freedom, allow social experimentation and protect the distinctiveness, dignity, freedom and self-management of communities and so society as a whole. This is why *"socialism is federalist"* and *"true federalism, the political organisation of socialism, will be attained only"* when *"popular grass-roots institutions"* like *"communes, industrial and agricultural associations"* are *"organised in progressive stages from the bottom up."* [**Bakunin on Anarchism**, p. 402]

I.5.3 Would confederations produce bureaucrats and politicians?

Of course, **any** organisation holds the danger that the few who have been given tasks to perform could misuse their position for personal benefit or, over time, evolve into a bureaucracy with power over the rest of society. As such, some critics of social anarchism suggest that a system of communes and confederation would simply be a breeding ground for politicians and bureaucrats. This is obviously the case with the state and many generalise from this experience for **all** forms of social organisation, including the anarchist commune.

While recognising that this **is** a danger, anarchists are sure that such developments are unlikely in an anarchy. This is because, based on our analysis and critique of the state, we have long argued for various institutional arrangements which, we think, reduce the danger of such things developing. These include electing delegates rather than representatives, giving these delegates a binding mandate and subjecting them to instant recall by their electors. They would **not**, in general, be paid and so delegates are expected, as far as possible, to remain in their current communities, conducting their communal tasks after their usual work. For the few exceptions to this that may occur, delegates would receive the average pay of their commune, in mutualism and collectivism or, in communism,

no special access to communal resources. Moreover, it seems likely that regular rotation of delegates would be utilised and, perhaps random selection as happens in jury duty today in many countries. Lastly, communes could leave any confederation if its structure was becoming obviously misshapen and bureaucratic.

By these methods, delegates to communal bodies would remain under the control of their electors and not, as in the state, become their masters. Moreover, anarchists have stressed that any communal body must be a working organisation. This will reduce bureaucratic tendencies as implementing tasks will be done by elected delegates rather than faceless (and usually unelected) bureaucrats. This means, as Bakunin put it in 1868, that *"the Communal Council"* (made up of delegates *"with binding mandates and accountable and revocable at all times"*) would create *"separate executive committees from among its membership for each branch of the Commune's revolutionary administration."* [Bakunin, **No Gods, No Masters**, vol. 1, p. 155] This would no longer be a body of people, a government, separate from the delegates of the people. This, it should be noted, repeats Proudhon's comments from 1848:

> *"It is up to the National Assembly, through organisation of its committees, to exercise executive power, just the way it exercises legislative power … Besides universal suffrage and as a consequence of universal suffrage, we want implementation of the binding mandate. Politicians balk at it! Which means that in their eyes, the people, in electing representatives, do not appoint mandatories but rather abjure their sovereignty! That is assuredly not socialism: it is not even democracy."* [**Op. Cit.**, p. 63]

Due to mandating and recall, any delegate who starts to abuse their position or even vote in ways opposed to by the communal assembly would quickly be recalled and replaced. As such a person may be an elected delegate of the community but that does not mean that they have power or authority (i.e., they are **not** a representative but rather a delegate). Essentially they are an agent of the local community who is controlled by, and accountable to, that community. Clearly, such people are unlike politicians. They do not, and cannot, make policy decisions on behalf of (i.e., govern) those who elected them — they are not given power to make decisions for people. In addition, people in specific organisations or with specific tasks will be rotated frequently to prevent a professionalisation of politics and the problem of politicians being largely on their own once elected. And, of course, they will continue to work and live with those who elected them and receive no special privileges due to their election (in terms of more income, better housing, and so on). This means that such delegates would be extremely unlikely to turn into representatives or bureaucrats as they would be under the strict control of the organisations that elected them to such posts. As Kropotkin argued, the general assembly of the community *"in permanence - the forum always open — is the only way … to assure an honest and intelligent administration"* as it is based upon *"distrust of all executive powers."* [**The Great French Revolution**, Vol. 1, p. 211]

The current means of co-ordinating wide scale activity — centralism via the state — is a threat to freedom as, to quote Proudhon, *"the citizens resign their sovereignty"* and the commune, the department and province *"are absorbed into the central authority, becoming mere agencies under the immediate direction of the ministry."* The consequences are obvious: *"the citizen and the commune being deprived of all dignity, the invasions of the State increase ... It is no longer the government that is made for the people, it is the people that is made for the government. Power invades everything, seizes everything, claims everything."* [**Property is Theft!**, p. 706] In such a regime, the generation of a specific caste of politicians and bureaucrats is inevitable.

Moreover, *"[t]he principle of political centralism is openly opposed to all laws of social progress and of natural evolution. It lies in the nature of things that every cultural advance is first achieved within a small group and only gradually finds adoption by society as a whole. Therefore, political decentralisation is the best guaranty for the unrestricted possibilities of new experiments. For such an environment each community is given the opportunity to carry through the things which it is capable of accomplishing itself without imposing them on others. Practical experimentation is the parent of every development in society. So long as each district is capable of effecting the changes within its own sphere which its citizens deem necessary, the example of each becomes a fructifying influence on the other parts of the community since they will have the chance to weigh the advantages accruing from them without being forced to adopt them if they are not convinced of their usefulness. The result is that progressive communities serve the others as models, a result justified by the natural evolution of things."* [Rudolf Rocker, **Pioneers of American Freedom**, pp. 16-7] The contrast with centralisation of the state could not be more clear. Rocker continued:

> *"In a strongly centralised state, the situation is entirely reversed and the best system of representation can do nothing to change that. The representatives of a certain district may have the overwhelming majority of a certain district on his [or her] side, but in the legislative assembly of the central state, he [or she] will remain in the minority, for it lies in the nature of things that in such a body not the intellectually most active but the most backward districts represent the majority. Since the individual district has indeed the right to give expression of its opinion, but can effect no changes without the consent of the central government, the most progressive districts will be condemned to stagnate while the most backward districts will set the norm."* [**Op. Cit.**, p. 17]

Little wonder anarchists have always stressed what Kropotkin termed *"local action"* and argued that the libertarian social revolution would *"proceed by proclaiming independent Communes"* which *"will endeavour to accomplish the economic transformation within ... their respective surroundings."* [**Act For Yourselves**, p. 43] Thus the advanced communities will inspire the rest to follow them by showing them a practical example of what is possible. Only decentralisation and confederation can promote the freedom and resulting social experimentation which will ensure social progress and make society a good place to live.

Moreover, confederation is required to maximise self-management and reduce the possibility that delegates will become isolated from the people who mandated them. As Rocker explained:

> *"In a smaller community, it is far easier for individuals to observe the political scene and become acquainted with the issues which have to be resolved. This is quite impossible for a representative in a centralised government. Neither the single citizen nor his [or her] representative is completely or even approximately to supervise the huge clockwork of the central state machine. The deputy is forced daily to make decisions about things of which he [or she] has no personal knowledge and for the appraisal of which he must therefore depend on others [i.e. bureaucrats and lobbyists]. That such a system necessarily leads to serious errors and mistakes is self-evident. And since the citizen for the same reason is not able to inspect and criticise the conduct of his representative, the class of professional politicians is given added opportunity to fish in troubled waters."* [**Op. Cit.**, p. 17-18]

These principles, it must be stressed, have been successfully applied on a mass scale. For example, this is how anarcho-syndicalist unions operate and, as was the case with the CNT in Spain in the 1930s, worked well with over one million members. They were also successfully applied during the Spanish Revolution and the federations of collectives produced by it.

So the way communes and confederations are organised protect society and the individual against the dangers of centralisation, from the turning of delegates into representatives and bureaucrats. As Bakunin stressed, there are two ways of organising society, *"as it is today, from high to low and from the centre to circumference by means of enforced unity and concentration"* and the way of the future, by federalism *"starting with the free individual, the free association and the autonomous commune, from low to high and from circumference to centre, by means of free federation."* [**Michael Bakunin: Selected Writings**, p. 88] In other words, *"the organisation of society from the bottom up."* [**The Basic Bakunin**, p. 131] This suggests that a free society will have little to fear in way of its delegates turning into politicians or bureaucrats as it includes the necessary safeguards (election, mandates, recall, decentralisation, federalism, etc.) which will reduce such developments to a small, and so manageable, level (if not eliminate it totally).

I.5.4 How will anything ever be decided by all these meetings?

Anarchists have little doubt that the confederal structure will be an efficient means of decision making and will not be bogged down in endless meetings. We have various reasons for thinking this. As Murray Bookchin once noted: *"History does provide us with a number of working examples of forms that are largely libertarian. It also provides us with examples of confederations and leagues that made the coordination of self-governing communities feasible without impinging on their autonomy and freedom."* [**The Ecology of Freedom**, p. 436]

Firstly, we doubt that a free society will spend all its time in assemblies or organising confederal conferences. Certain questions are more important than others and few anarchists desire to spend all their time in meetings. The aim of a free society is to allow individuals to express their desires and wants freely — they cannot do that if they are continually at meetings (or preparing for them). So while communal and confederal assemblies will play an important role in a free society, do not think that they will be occurring all the time or that anarchists desire to make meetings the focal point of individual life. Far from it!

Thus communal assemblies may occur, say, once a week, or fortnightly or monthly in order to discuss truly important issues. There would be no real desire to meet continuously to discuss every issue under the sun and few people would tolerate this occurring. This would mean that such meetings would occur regularly and when important issues needed to be discussed, **not** continuously (although, if required, continuous assembly or daily meetings may have to be organised in emergency situations but this would be rare). Nor is it expected that everyone will attend every meeting for *"[w]hat is decisive, here, is the principle itself: the freedom of the individual to participate, not the compulsive need to do so."* [**Op. Cit.**, p. 435] This suggests that meetings will be attended by those with a specific interest in an issue being discussed and so would be focused as a result.

Secondly, it is extremely doubtful that a free people would desire to waste vast amounts of time at such meetings. While important and essential, communal and confederal meetings would be functional in the extreme and not forums for hot air. It would be the case that those involved in such meetings would quickly make their feelings known to time wasters and those who like the sound of their own voices. Thus Cornelius Castoriadis:

> *"It might be claimed that the problem of numbers remains and that people never would be able to express themselves in a reasonable amount of time. This is not a valid argument. There would rarely be an assembly over twenty people where everyone would want to speak, for the very good reason that when there is something to be decided upon there are not an infinite number of options or an infinite number of arguments. In unhampered rank-and-file workers' gatherings (convened, for instance, to decide on a strike) there have never been 'too many' speeches. The two or three fundamental opinions having been voiced, and various arguments exchanged, a decision is soon reached.*

> *"The length of speeches, moreover, often varies inversely with the weight of their content. Russian leaders sometimes talk on for four hours at Party Congresses without saying anything … For an account of the laconicism of revolutionary assemblies, see Trotsky's account of the Petrograd soviet of 1905 — or accounts of the meetings of factory representatives in Budapest in 1956."* [**Political and Social Writings**, vol. 2, pp. 144-5]

As we shall see below, this was definitely the case during the Spanish Revolution as well.

Thirdly, as these assemblies and congresses are concerned purely with joint activity and co-ordination, it is likely that they will not be called very often. Different associations, syndicates and co-operatives have a functional need for co-operation and so would meet more regularly and take action on practical activity which affects a specific section of a community or group of communities. Not every issue that a member of a community is interested in is necessarily best discussed at a meeting of all members of a community or at a confederal conference. As Herbert Read suggested, anarchism *"proposes to liquidate the bureaucracy first by federal devolution"* and so *"hands over to the syndicates all … administrative functions"* related to such things as *"transport, and distribution, health and education."* [**Anarchy and Order**, p. 101] Such issues will be mainly discussed in the syndicates involved and so community discussion would be focused on important issues and themes of general policy rather than the specific and detailed laws discussed and implemented by politicians who know nothing about the issues or industries at hand.

In other words, communal assemblies and conferences will have specific, well-defined agendas, and so there is little danger of "politics" (for want of a better word!) taking up everyone's time. Hence, far from discussing abstract laws and pointless motions on everything under the sun and which no one actually knows much about, the issues discussed in these conferences will be on specific issues which are important to those involved. In addition, the standard procedure may be to elect a sub-group to investigate an issue and report back at a later stage with recommendations. The conference can change, accept, or reject any proposals.

As Kropotkin argued, anarchy would be based on *"free agreement, by exchange of letters and proposals, and by congresses at which delegates met to discuss well specified points, and to come to an agreement about them, but not to make laws. After the congress was over, the delegates"* would return *"not with a law, but with the draft of a contract to be accepted or rejected."* [**Conquest of Bread**, p. 131]

By reducing conferences to functional bodies based on concrete issues, the problems of endless discussions can be reduced, if not totally eliminated. In addition, as functional groups would exist outside of these communal confederations (for example, industrial collectives would organise conferences about their industry with invited participants from consumer groups), there would be a limited agenda in most communal get-togethers.

The most important issues would be to agree on the guidelines for industrial activity, communal investment (e.g. houses, hospitals, etc.) and overall co-ordination of large scale communal activities. In this way everyone would be part of the commonwealth, deciding on how resources would be used to maximise human well-being and ecological survival. The problems associated with *"the tyranny of small decisions"* would be overcome without undermining individual freedom. (In fact, a healthy community would enrich and develop individuality by encouraging independent and critical thought, social interaction, and empowering social institutions based on self-management).

Is such a system fantasy? Given that such a system has existed and worked at various times, we can safely argue that it is not. Obviously we cannot cover **every** example, so we point to just two — revolutionary Paris and Spain.

As Murray Bookchin points out, Paris "*in the late eighteenth century was, by the standards of that time, one of the largest and economically most complex cities in Europe: its population approximated a million people ... Yet in 1793, at the height of the French Revolution, the city was managed* **institutionally** *almost entirely by [48] citizen assemblies... and its affairs were co-ordinated by the* **Commune** *.. . and often, in fact, by the assemblies themselves, or sections as they were called, which established their own interconnections without recourse to the* **Commune.**" ["Transition to the Ecological Society", pp. 92-105, **Society and Nature**, no. 3, p. 96]

Here is his account of how communal self-government worked in practice:

> "*What, then, were these little-known forty-eight sections of Paris ... How were they organised? And how did they function?*
>
> "*Ideologically, the* **sectionnaires** *(as their members were called) believed primarily in sovereignty of the people. This concept of popular sovereignty, as Albert Soboul observes, was for them 'not an abstraction, but the concrete reality of the people united in sectional assemblies and exercising all their rights.' It was in their eyes an inalienable right, or, as the section de la Cite declared in November 1792, 'every man who assumes to have sovereignty [over others] will be regarded as a tyrant, usurper of public liberty and worthy of death.'*
>
> "*Sovereignty, in effect, was to be enjoyed by* **all** *citizens, not pre-empted by 'representatives' ... The radical democrats of 1793 thus assumed that every adult was, to one degree or another, competent to participate in management public affairs. Thus, each section ... was structured around a* **face-to-face democracy**: *basically a general assembly of the people that formed the most important deliberative body of a section, and served as the incarnation of popular power in a given part of the city ... each elected six deputies to the Commune, presumably for the purpose merely of co-ordinating all the sections in the city of Paris.*
>
> "*Each section also had its own various administrative committees, whose members were also recruited from the general assembly.*" [**The Third Revolution**, vol. 1, p. 319]

Little wonder Kropotkin argued that these "sections" showed "*the principles of anarchism*" had "*their origin, not in theoretical speculations, but in the* **deeds** *of the Great French Revolution*" [**The Great French Revolution**, vol. 1, p. 204]

Communal self-government was also practised, and on a far wider scale, in revolutionary Spain. All across Republican Spain, workers and peasants formed communes and federations of communes (see section I.8 for fuller details). Gaston Leval summarised the experience:

> "*There was, in the organisation set in motion by the Spanish Revolution and by the libertarian movement,* which was its mainspring, a structuring from the bottom to the top, which corresponds to a real federation and true democracy ... the controlling and co-ordinating **Comités** [Committees], clearly indispensable, do not go outside the organisation that has chosen them, **they remain in their midst**, always controllable by and accessible to the members. If any individuals contradict by their actions their mandates, it is possible to call them to order, to reprimand them, to replace them. It is only by and in such a system that the 'majority lays down the law.'*
>
> "*The syndical assemblies were the expression and the practice of libertarian democracy, a democracy having nothing in common with the democracy of Athens where the citizens discussed and disputed for days on end on the Agora; where factions, clan rivalries, ambitions, personalities conflicted, where, in view of the social inequalities precious time was lost in interminable wrangles ...*
>
> "*Normally those periodic meetings would not last more than a few hours. They dealt with concrete, precise subjects concretely and precisely. And all who had something to say could express themselves. The Comite presented the new problems that had arisen since the previous assembly, the results obtained by the application of such and such a resolution ... relations with other syndicates, production returns from the various workshops or factories. All this was the subject of reports and discussion. Then the assembly would nominate the commissions, the members of these commissions discussed between themselves what solutions to adopt, if there was disagreement, a majority report and a minority report would be prepared.*
>
> "*This took place in* **all** *the syndicates* **throughout Spain**, *in* **all** *trades and* **all** *industries, in assemblies which, in Barcelona, from the very beginnings of our movement brought together hundreds or thousands of workers depending on the strength of the organisations. So much so that the awareness of the duties, responsibilities of each spread all the time to a determining and decisive degree ...*
>
> "*The practice of this democracy also extended to the agricultural regions ... the decision to nominate a local management* **Comité** *for the villages was taken by general meetings of the inhabitants of villages, how the delegates in the different essential tasks which demanded an indispensable co-ordination of activities were proposed and elected by the whole assembled population. But it is worth adding and underlining that in all the collectivised villages and all the partially collectivised villages, in the 400 Collectives in Aragon, in the 900 in the Levante region, in the 300 in the Castilian region, to mention only the large groupings ... the population was called together weekly, fortnightly or monthly and kept fully informed of everything concerning the commonweal.*

"This writer was present at a number of these assemblies in Aragon, where the reports on the various questions making up the agenda allowed the inhabitants to know, to so understand, and to feel so mentally integrated in society, to so participate in the management of public affairs, in the responsibilities, that the recriminations, the tensions which always occur when the power of decision is entrusted to a few individuals, be they democratically elected without the possibility of objecting, did not happen there. The assemblies were public, the objections, the proposals publicly discussed, everybody being free, as in the syndical assemblies, to participate in the discussions, to criticise, propose, etc. Democracy extended to the whole of social life." [**Collectives in the Spanish Revolution**, pp. 204-7]

These collectives organised federations embracing thousands of communes and workplaces, whole branches of industry, hundreds of thousands of people and whole regions of Spain. As such, it was a striking confirmation of Proudhon's argument that under federalism *"the sovereignty of the contracting parties ... serves as a positive guarantee of the liberty of ... communes and individuals. So, no longer do we have the abstraction of people's sovereignty ... but an effective sovereignty of the labouring masses"* and *"the labouring masses are actually, positively and effectively sovereign: how could they not be when the economic organism — labour, capital, property and assets — belongs to them entirely."* [**Property is Theft!**, pp. 760-1]

In other words, it **is** possible. It **has** worked. With the massive improvements in communication technology it is even more viable than before. Whether or not we reach such a self-managed society depends on whether we desire to be free or not.

I.5.5 Aren't participatory communities and confederations just new states?

No. As we have seen in section B.2, a state can be defined both by its structure and its function. As far as structure is concerned, a state involves the politico-military and economic domination of a certain geographical territory by a ruling elite, based on the delegation of power into the hands of the few, resulting in hierarchy (centralised authority). As such, it would be a massive theoretical error to confuse any form of social organisation with the specific form which is the state.

As we have discussed in section H.3.7, the state has evolved its specific characteristics as a result of its role as an instrument of class rule. If a social organisation does not have these characteristics then it is not a state. Thus, for anarchists, *"the essence of the state"* is *"centralised power* **or to put it another way the coercive authority** *of which the state enjoys the monopoly, in that organisation of violence known as 'government'; in the hierarchical despotism, juridical, police and military despotism that imposes laws on everyone."* [Luigi Fabbri, *"Anarchy and 'Scientific'*

Communism", in **The Poverty of Statism**, pp. 13-49, Albert Meltzer (ed.), pp. 24-5] This is why Malatesta stressed that the state *"means the delegation of power, that is the abdication of initiative and sovereignty of all into the hands of a few."* [**Anarchy**, p. 41] If a social organisation is **not** centralised and top-down then it is not a state.

In a system of federated participatory communities there is no ruling elite, and thus no hierarchy, because power is retained by the lowest-level units of confederation through their use of direct democracy and mandated, rotating, and recallable delegates to meetings of higher-level confederal bodies. This eliminates the problem in "representative" democratic systems of the delegation of power leading to the elected officials becoming isolated from and beyond the control of the mass of people who elected them. As Kropotkin pointed out, an anarchist society would make decisions by *"means of congresses, composed of delegates, who discuss among themselves, and submit* **proposals**, *not* **laws**, *to their constituents"* [**The Conquest of Bread**, p. 135] So it is based on **self**-government, **not** representative government (and its inevitable bureaucracy). As Proudhon put it, *"the federative system is the opposite of administrative and governmental hierarchy or centralisation"* and so *"a confederation is not precisely a state ... What we call a federative Authority, finally, is not a government; it is an agency created ... for the common running of some services".* [**Property is Theft!**, pp. 697-8]

Perhaps it will be objected that communal decision making is just a form of "statism" based on direct, as opposed to representative, democracy — "statist" because the individual is still being subject to the rules of the majority and so is not free. This objection, however, confuses statism with free agreement (i.e. co-operation). Since participatory communities, like productive syndicates, are voluntary associations, the decisions they make are based on self-assumed obligations (see section A.2.11), and dissenters can leave the association if they so desire. Thus communes are no more "statist" than the act of promising and keeping ones word.

In addition, in a free society, dissent and direct action can be used by minorities to press their case (or defend their freedom) as well as debate. As Carole Pateman argues, *"[p]olitical disobedience is merely one possible expression of the active citizenship on which a self-managing democracy is based."* [**The Problem of Political Obligation**, p. 162] In this way, individual liberty can be protected in a communal system and society enriched by opposition, confrontation and dissent. Without self-management and minority dissent, society would become an ideological cemetery which would stifle ideas and individuals as these thrive on discussion (*"those who will be able to create in their mutual relations a movement and a life based on the principles of free understanding ... will understand that* **variety, conflict even, is life and that uniformity is death**" [Kropotkin, **Anarchism**, p. 143]). So a society based on voluntary agreements and self-management would, out of interpersonal empathy and self-interest, create a society that encouraged individuality and respect for minorities.

Therefore, a commune's participatory nature is the opposite of statism. April Carter agrees, stating that *"commitment to direct democracy or anarchy in the socio-political sphere is incompatible with political authority"* and that the *"only authority that can exist* in a direct democracy is the collective 'authority' vested in the body politic ... it is doubtful if authority can be created by a group of equals who reach decisions by a process of mutual persuasion." [**Authority and Democracy**, p. 69 and p. 380] Which echoes, we must note, Proudhon's comment that *"the true meaning of the word 'democracy'"* was the *"dismissal of government."* [**No Gods, No Masters**, vol. 1, p. 42] Bakunin argued that when the *"whole people govern"* then *"there will be no one to be governed. It means that there will be no government, no State."* [**The Political Philosophy of Bakunin**, p. 287] Malatesta, decades later, made the same point: *"government by everybody is no longer government in the authoritarian, historical and practical sense of the word."* [**No Gods, No Masters**, vol. 2, p. 38] And, of course, Kropotkin argued that by means of the directly democratic sections of the French Revolution the masses *"practic[ed] what was to be described later as Direct Self-Government"* and expressed *"the principles of anarchism."* [**The Great French Revolution**, vol. 1, p. 200 and p. 204]

Anarchists argue that individuals and the institutions they create cannot be considered in isolation. Authoritarian institutions will create individuals who have a servile nature, who cannot govern themselves. Anarchists, therefore, consider it common sense that individuals, in order to be free, **must** take part in determining the general agreements they make with their neighbours which give form to their communities. Otherwise, a free society could not exist and individuals would be subject to rules others make **for** them (following orders is hardly libertarian). Somewhat ironically, those who stress "individualism" and denounce communes as new "states" advocate a social system which produces extremely hierarchical social relationships based on the authority of the property owner. In other words, abstract individualism produces authoritarian (i.e., state-like) social relationships (see section F.1). Therefore, anarchists recognise the social nature of humanity and the fact any society based on an abstract individualism (like capitalism) will be marked by authority, injustice and inequality, **not** freedom. As Bookchin pointed out: *"To speak of 'The Individual' apart from its social roots is as meaningless as to speak of a society that contains no people or institutions."* [**Anarchism, Marxism, and the Future of the Left**, p. 154]

Society cannot be avoided and *"[u]nless everyone is to be psychologically homogeneous and society's interests so uniform in character that dissent is simply meaningless, there must be room for conflicting proposals, discussion, rational explication and majority decisions - in short, democracy."* [Bookchin, **Op. Cit.**, p. 155] Those who reject democracy in the name of liberty (such as many supporters of capitalism claim to do) usually also see the need for laws and hierarchical authority (particularly in the workplace). This is unsurprising, as such authority is the only means left by which collective activity can be co-ordinated if self-management is rejected (usually as "statist", which is ironic as the resulting institutions, such as a capitalist company, are far more statist than self-managed ones).

So, far from being new states by which one section of a community (historically, almost always a wealthy ruling minority) imposes its ethical standards on another, the anarchist commune is just a public forum. In this forum, issues of community interest (for example, management of the commons, control of communalised

economic activity, and so forth) are discussed and policy agreed upon. In addition, interests beyond a local area are also discussed and delegates for confederal conferences are mandated with the wishes of the community. Hence, administration of things replaces government of people, with the community of communities existing to ensure that the interests of all are managed by all and that liberty, justice and equality for all are more than just ideals. Moreover, a free society would be one without professional bodies of armed people (i.e., there would be no armed forces or police). It would not have the means of enforcing the decisions of conferences and communes which reflected the interests of a few (would-be politicians or bureaucrats) rather than popular opinion.

Of course, it could be argued that popular opinion can be as oppressive as any state, a possibility anarchists are aware of and take steps to combat. Remember, the communities and confederations of a free society would be made up of free people. They would **not** be too concerned with the personal behaviour of others unless it impacted on their own lives. As such, they would not be seeking to restrict the liberty of those who live with them. A community, therefore, is unlikely to make decisions like, for example, outlawing homosexuality or censoring the press. This is not to say that there is no danger of majorities abusing minorities. As we discuss in the next section, anarchists are aware of this possibility and suggest means of reducing it, even eliminating it. Suffice to say, a free society would seek to encourage diversity and so leave minorities free to live their own lives (assuming they are not oppressing or exploiting others, of course).

For these reasons, a libertarian-socialist society would not have a state. Structurally, it would be based on egalitarian and decentralised institutions, the direct opposite of the hierarchical and centralised state. Functionally, it would be based on mass participation of all to ensure they manage their own affairs rather than, in a state, exclusion of the many to ensure the rule by an elite (usually the wealthy). The communes and confederations of a libertarian system are not just states with new names but rather the forums by which free people manage their own affairs rather than being ruled by a state and its politicians and bureaucrats.

This is why Proudhon, for example, argued that *"under the democratic constitution ... the political and the economic are ... one and the same system ... based upon a single principle, mutuality ... and form this vast humanitarian organism of which nothing previously could give the idea."* And so *"is this not the system of the old society turned upside down"*? [**Property is Theft!**, p. 760 and p. 761]

I.5.6 Won't there be a danger of a "tyranny of the majority" under libertarian socialism?

While the *"tyranny of the majority"* objection does contain an important point, it is often raised for self-serving reasons. This is because those who have historically raised the issue (for example, and as discussed in section B.2.5, creators of the 1789 American constitution like Hamilton and Madison) saw the minority to be protected as the rich. In other words, the objection is not opposed to majority tyranny as such (they have no objections when the majority support their right to their riches and powers) but rather attempts of the majority to change their society to a fairer and freer one. Such concerns can easily be dismissed as an ingenious argument in favour of rule by the few — particularly as its proponents (such as the propertarian right and other defenders of capitalism) have no problem with the autocratic rule of property owners over their wage-slaves!

However, as noted, the objection to majority rule **does** contain a valid point and one which anarchists have addressed — namely, what about minority freedom within a self-managed society? So this is a danger, one raised by people who are most definitely **not** seeking minority rule. For example, someone who was sympathetic to anarchism, George Orwell, expressed this fear:

> "the totalitarian tendency which is explicit in the anarchist ... vision of Society. In a Society in which there is no law, and in theory no compulsion, the only arbiter of behaviour is public opinion. But pubic opinion, because of the tremendous urge to conformity in gregarious animals, is less tolerant than any system of law. When human beings are governed by 'thou shalt not', the individual can practise a certain amount of eccentricity: when they are supposedly governed by 'love' or 'reason', he is under continuous pressure to make him behave and think in exactly the same way as everyone else." [**Inside the Whale and Other Essays**, p. 132]

There is, of course, this danger in **any** society, be its decision making structure direct (anarchy) or indirect (by some form of government). However, this does not really address the issue to point out this obvious fact. Anarchists are at the forefront in expressing concern about it, recognising that the majority is often a threat to freedom by its fear of change (see, for example, Emma Goldman's classic essay *"Minorities versus Majorities"*). We are well aware that the mass, as long as the individuals within it do not free themselves, can be a dead-weight on others, resisting change and enforcing conformity. As Goldman argued, *"even more than constituted authority, it is social uniformity and sameness that harass the individual the most."* [**Red Emma Speaks**, p. 116] Hence Malatesta's comment that anarchists *"have the special mission of being vigilant custodians of freedom, against all aspirants to power and against the possible tyranny of the majority."* [**Errico Malatesta: His Life and Ideas**, p. 161]

However, rather than draw elitist conclusions from this fact of life under capitalism and urge forms of government and organisation which restrict popular participation (and promote rule, and tyranny, by the few) — as classical liberals do — libertarians argue that only a process of self-liberation through struggle and participation can break up the mass into free, self-managing individuals (as discussed in section H.2.11 attempts by Leninists to portray anarchists as elitists are both hypocritical and wrong). Moreover, we also argue that participation and self-management is the only way that majorities can come to see the point of minority ideas and for seeing the importance of protecting minority freedoms. This means that any attempt to restrict participation in the name of

minority rights actually enforces the herd mentality, undermining minority and individual freedom rather than protecting it. As Carole Pateman argues:

> "the evidence supports the arguments ... that we do learn to participate by participating and that feelings of political efficacy are more likely to be developed in a participatory environment. Furthermore, the evidence indicates that experience of a participatory authority structure might also be effective in diminishing tendencies towards non-democratic attitudes in the individual." [**Participation and Democratic Theory**, p. 105]

However, while there is cause for concern (and anarchists are at the forefront in expressing it), the *"tyranny of the majority"* objection fails to take note of the vast difference between direct and representative forms of democracy.

In the current system, as we pointed out in section B.5, voters are mere passive spectators of occasional, staged, and highly rehearsed debates among candidates pre-selected by the corporate elite, who pay for campaign expenses. More often the public is expected to choose simply on the basis of political ads and news sound bites. Once the choice is made, cumbersome and ineffective recall procedures insure that elected representatives can act more or less as they (or rather, their wealthy sponsors) please. The function, then, of the electorate in bourgeois "representative government" is ratification of "choices" that have been **already made for them**! This is also the case in referenda, where the people *"are not to* **propose** *the questions: the government is to do that. Only to questions* **proposed** *by the government, the people may answer* **Yes** *or* **No***, like a child in the catechism. The people will not even have a chance to make amendments."* [Proudhon, **General Idea of the Revolution**, p. 148]

By contrast, in a direct, libertarian democracy, decisions are made following public discussion in community assemblies open to all. After decisions have been reached, outvoted minorities — even minorities of one — still have ample opportunity to present reasoned and persuasive counter-arguments to try to change the decision. This process of debate, disagreement, challenge, and counter-challenge, which goes on even after the defeated minority has temporarily acquiesced in the decision of the majority, is virtually absent in the representative system, where *"tyranny of the majority"* is truly a problem. In addition, minorities can secede from an association if the decision reached by it are truly offensive to them.

And let us not forget that in all likelihood, issues of personal conduct or activity will not be discussed in the neighbourhood assemblies. Why? Because we are talking about a society in which most people consider themselves to be unique, free individuals, who would thus recognise and act to protect the uniqueness and freedom of others. Unless people are indoctrinated by religion or some other form of ideology, they can be tolerant of others and their individuality. If this is not the case now, then it has more to do with the existence of authoritarian social relationships — relationships that will be dismantled under libertarian socialism — and the type of person they create rather than some innate human flaw.

Thus there will be vast areas of life in a libertarian socialist community which are none of other people's business. Anarchists have always stressed the importance of personal space and "private" areas. Indeed, for Kropotkin, the failure of many "utopian" communities directly flowed from a lack personal space. One of the mistakes made by such intentional communities within capitalism was *"the desire to manage the community after the model of a family, to make it 'the great family.' They lived all in the same house and were thus forced to continuously meet the same 'brethren and sisters.' It is already difficult often for two real brothers to live together in the same house, and family life is not always harmonious; so it was a fundamental error to impose on all the 'great family' instead of trying, on the contrary, to guarantee as much freedom and home life to each individual."* Thus in an anarchist society, continual agreement on all issues is not desired. The members of a free society *"need only agree as to some advantageous method of common work, and are free otherwise to live in their own way."* [**Small Communal Experiments and Why they Fail**, pp. 8-9 and p. 22]

Which brings us to another key point. When anarchists talk of democratising or communalising the household or any other association, we do not mean that it should be stripped of its private status and become open to the "tyranny of the majority" or regulation by general voting in a single, universal public sphere. Rather, we mean that households and other relationships should take in libertarian characteristics and be consistent with the liberty of all its members. Thus a society based on self-management does not imply the destruction of private spheres of activity — it implies the extension of anarchist principles into all spheres of life, both private and public. It does not mean the subordination of the private by the public, or vice versa.

As an example, we can point to inter-personal relationships. Anarchists are opposed to the patriarchy implicit (and, in the past, explicit) in marriage and suggest free love as an alternative. As discussed in section H.4.2 , free love means that both people in a relationship have equal decision making power rather than, as in marriage, the woman becoming the property of the husband. Thus, self-management in this context does not mean the end of interpersonal relationships by the imposition of the commune onto all spheres of life but, obviously, the creation of interpersonal relationships based on equality and liberty within them.

So, in other words, it is highly unlikely that the "tyranny of the majority" will exert itself where most rightly fear it — in their homes, how they act with friends, their personal space, and so on. As long as individual freedom and rights are protected, it is of little concern what people get up to (including the rights of children, who are also individuals and **not** the property of their parents). Direct democracy in anarchist theory is purely concerned with common resources and their use and management. It is highly unlikely that a free society would debate issues of personal behaviour or morality and instead would leave them to those directly affected by them — as it should be, as we all need personal space and experimentation to find the way of life that best suits us.

Today an authoritarian worldview, characterised by an inability to think beyond the categories of domination and submission, is imparted by conditioning in the family, schools, religious institutions, clubs, fraternities, the army, etc., and produces a type of personality that is intolerant of any individual or group perceived as threatening to the perpetuation of that worldview and its corresponding

institutions and values. Thus, as Bakunin argued, *"public opinion"* is potentially intolerant *"simply because hitherto this power has not been humanised itself; it has not been humanised because the social life of which it is ever the faithful expression is based … in the worship of divinity, not on respect for humanity; in authority, not on liberty; on privilege, not on equality; in the exploitation, not on the brotherhood, of men; on iniquity and falsehood, not on justice and truth. Consequently its real action, always in contradiction of the humanitarian theories which it professes, has constantly exercised a disastrous and depraving influence."* [**God and the State**, p. 43f] In other words, *"if society is ever to become free, it will be so through liberated individuals, whose free efforts make society."* [Emma Goldman, **Anarchism and Other Essays**, p. 44] In an anarchist society a conscious effort will be made to dissolve the institutional and traditional sources of the authoritarian/submissive type of personality, and thus to free "public opinion" of its current potential for intolerance.

This is not to suggest that such a society of free individuals will not become stuck in routine and, over time, become oppressive to minorities who question certain aspects of public opinion or how it works. Public opinion and social organisations can evolve over generations in ways which no one expects. The best known, albeit fictional, example is in Ursula Le Guin's classic science-fiction book **The Dispossessed** where the anarchist society of Anarres has developed something of a weak informal bureaucracy due to the routine of everyday life and the unconscious pressures of public opinion. When the protagonist, Shevek, and his friends try to point this out and do something about (including Shevek leaving Anarres for the capitalist world of Urras), most on the planet are extremely hostile to this activity (precisely because it is going against the normal routine). Significantly, though, a large minority end up supporting their activities, activities which can occur precisely **because** the society is still fundamentally communist-anarchist and so the dissenters have a rich libertarian tradition and sensibility to base their direct action on as well having use-rights over the resources they need to propagate their ideas and practice their protest.

In the real world, the best example would be **Mujeres Libres** in the Spanish anarchist movement in the 1930s (see Martha A. Ackelsberg's classic **Free Women Of Spain: Anarchism And The Struggle For The Emancipation Of Women** for more on this important movement). This organisation arose in response to the fact that many male anarchists, while expressing a theoretical commitment to sexual equality, were as sexist as the system they were fighting against. In other words, they subconsciously reflected the oppressive public opinion of what a woman's position should be. Unsurprisingly, many anarchist women were (rightly) angry at this and their marginalised status within a libertarian movement that ostensibly sought to abolish all forms of domination and hierarchy. In response, and often in the face of the hostility or indifference of their male comrades, they organised themselves to change this situation, to combat and transform public opinion both within and outwith the anarchist movement. Their activities met with some success before, like the rest of the libertarian revolution, it was crushed by Franco's victory in the civil war.

We can, therefore, suggest that a free society is unlikely to see public opinion becoming authoritarian. This is because, as the example of the **Mujeres Libres** shows, members of that society would organise to combat such developments and use various means to raise the problem to public awareness and to combat it. Once a free society has been gained, the task of anarchists would be to ensure it remained free and that would mean keeping a constant watch on possible sources of authority, including those associated with organisations developing informal bureaucracies and public opinion. While a free society would place numerous safeguards against such developments, no system would be perfect and so the actions of dissident minorities would be essential to point out and protest if such dangers appeared to be developing.

As such, it should be noted that anarchists recognise that the practice of self-assumed political obligation implied in free association also implies the right to practice dissent and disobedience as well. As Carole Pateman notes:

> "Even if it is impossible to be unjust to myself, I do not vote for myself alone, but alone with everyone else. Questions about injustice are always appropriate in political life, for there is no guarantee that participatory voting will actually result in decisions in accord with the principles of political morality." [**The Problem of Political Obligation**, p. 160]

If an individual or group of individuals feel that a specific decision threatens their freedom (which is the basic principle of political morality in an anarchist society) they can (and must) act to defend that freedom:

> "The political practice of participatory voting rests in a collective self-consciousness about the meaning and implication of citizenship. The members of the political association understand that to vote is simultaneously to commit oneself, to commit one's fellow citizens, and also to commit oneself to them in a mutual undertaking ... a refusal to vote on a particular occasion indicates that the refusers believe ... [that] the proposal ... infringes the principle of political morality on which the political association is based ... A refusal to vote [or the use of direct action] could be seen as an appeal to the 'sense of justice' of their fellow citizens." [Pateman, **Op. Cit.**, p. 161]

As they no longer consent to the decisions made by their community they can appeal to the "sense of justice" of their fellow citizens by direct action and indicate that a given decision may have impacts which the majority were not aware. Hence direct action and dissent is a key aspect of an anarchist society and help ensure against the tyranny of the majority. Anarchism rejects the "love it or leave it" attitude that marks classical liberalism as well as Rousseau (this aspect of his work being inconsistent with its foundations in participation).

This vision of self-assumed obligation, with its basis in individual liberty, indicates the basic flaw of Joseph Schumpeter's argument against democracy as anything bar a political **method** of arriving at decisions (in his case who will be the leaders of a society). Schumpeter proposed *"A Mental Experiment"* of imagining a country which, using a democratic process, *"reached the decision to persecute religious dissent"* (such as Jews and witches). He argued that we should not approve of these practices just because they have been decided upon by a majority or using a democratic method and, therefore, democracy cannot be an end in itself. [**Capitalism, Socialism and Democracy**, pp. 240-3]

However, such systematic persecution would conflict with the rules of procedure required if a country's or community's political method is to be called "democratic." This is because, in order to be democratic, the minority must be in a position for its ideas to become the majority's via argument and convincing the majority (and that requires freedom of discussion and association). A country or community in which the majority persecutes or represses a minority automatically ensures that the minority can never be in a position to become the majority (as the minority is barred by force from becoming so) or convince the majority of the errors of its way (even if it cannot become the majority physically, it can become so morally by convincing the majority to change its position). Schumpeter's example utterly violates democratic principles and so cannot be squared with the rules of democratic procedure. Thus majority tyranny is an outrage against both democratic theory **and** individual liberty (unsurprisingly, as the former has its roots in the latter). Unsurprisingly, then, the *"freedom of the collectivity to crush the individual is not, however, true Liberty in the eyes of Anarchists. It is one of those shams, which the Revolution is to destroy."* [Charlotte M. Wilson, **Anarchist Essays**, p. 25]

This argument applies with even more force to a self-managed community too and so any system in which the majority tyrannises over a minority is, by definition, **not** self-managed as one part of the community is excluded from convincing the other (*"the enslaving of part of the nation is the very negation of the federative principal."* [Proudhon, **Property is Theft!**, p. 698f]). Thus individual freedom and minority rights are essential to direct democracy and self-management. As Proudhon argued, *"a new spirit has dawned on the world. Freedom has opposed itself to the State, and since the idea of freedom has become universal people have realised that it is not a concern of the individual merely, but rather that it must exist in the group also."* [quoted by Martin Buber, **Paths in Utopia**, p. 28]

It should be stressed, however, that most anarchists do not think that the way to guard against possible tyranny by the majority is to resort to decision-making by consensus (where no action can be taken until every person in the group agrees) or a property system (based in contracts). Both consensus (see section A.2.12) and contracts (see section A.2.14) soon result in authoritarian social relationships developing in the name of "liberty." Rather, we seek new forms of free agreement to replace contract and new forms of decision making which do not replace the possible tyranny of the majority with the real tyranny of a minority.

As Malatesta argued, *"for if it is unjust that the majority should oppress the minority, the contrary would be quite as unjust; and if the minority has a right to rebel, the majority has a right to defend itself ... it is true that this solution is not completely satisfactory. The individuals put out of the association would be deprived of many social advantages, which an isolated person or group must do without, because they can only be procured by the co-operation of a great number of human beings. But what would you have? These malcontents cannot fairly demand that the wishes of many others should be sacrificed for their sakes."* [**A Talk about Anarchist-Communism**, p. 29] In other words, freedom of association means the freedom **not** to associate and so communities can expel individuals or groups of individuals who constantly hinder community decisions — assuming they do not leave voluntarily and seek a community more in tune with their needs. This is a very important freedom for both the majority and the minority, and must be defended.

So while minorities have significant rights in a free society, so does the majority. We can imagine that there will be ethical reasons why participants will not act in ways to oppose joint activity — as they took part in the decision making process they would be considered childish if they reject the final decision because it did not go in their favour. Moreover, they would also have to face the reaction of those who also took part in the decision making process. It would be likely that those who ignored such decisions (or actively hindered them) would soon face non-violent direct action in the form of non-co-operation, shunning, boycotting and so on. Anarchists think that such occurrences would be rare.

However, as an isolated life is impossible, the need for communal associations is essential. It is only by living together in a supportive community that individuality can be encouraged and developed along with individual freedom. However, anarchists are aware that not everyone is a social animal and that there are times that people like to withdraw into their own personal space. Thus our support for free association and federalism along with solidarity, community and self-management. Hence most anarchists have recognised that majority decision making, though not perfect, is the best way to reach decisions in a political system based on maximising individual (and so social) freedom. Direct democracy in grassroots confederal assemblies and workers' councils ensures that decision making is "horizontal" in nature (i.e. between **equals**) and not hierarchical (i.e. governmental, between order giver and order taker). In other words, anarchists support self-management because it ensures liberty — **not** because we subscribe to the flawed assumption that the majority is always right.

I.5.7 What if I don't want to join a commune?

As would be expected, no one would be **forced** to join a commune nor take part in its assemblies. To suggest otherwise would be contrary to anarchist principles. Thus a commune would be a free society, in which individual liberty would be respected and encouraged.

However, what about individuals who live within the boundaries of a commune but decide not to join? For example, a local neighbourhood may include households that desire to associate and a few that do not (this actually happened during the Spanish Revolution). What happens to the minority of dissenters?

Obviously individuals can leave to find communities more in line with their own concepts of right and wrong if they cannot convince their neighbours of the validity of their ideas. And, equally obviously,

not everyone will want to leave an area they like. So we must discuss those who decide not to find a more suitable community. Are the communal decisions binding on non-members? Obviously not. If an individual or family desire **not** to join a commune (for whatever reason), their freedoms must be respected. However, this also means that they cannot benefit from communal activity and resources (such a free housing, hospitals, and so forth) and, possibly, have to pay for their use. As long as they do not exploit or oppress others, an anarchist community would respect their decision (as discussed in section G.2.1, for example).

Many who oppose anarchist self-management in the name of freedom often do so because they desire to oppress and exploit others. In other words, they oppose participatory communities because they (rightly) fear that this would restrict their ability to oppress, exploit and grow rich off the labour of others (this type of opposition can be seen from history, when rich elites, in the name of liberty, have replaced democratic forms of social decision making with representative or authoritarian ones — see section B.2.6). So it goes without saying that the minority, as in any society, will exist within the ethical norms of the surrounding society and they will be have to adhere to them in the same sense that they have to adhere to not murdering people (few sane people would say that forcing people not to commit murder is a restriction of their liberty). Therefore, while allowing the maximum of individual freedom of dissent, an anarchist community would still have to apply its ethical standards to those beyond that community. Individuals would not be allowed to murder, harm or enslave others and claim that they are allowed to do so because they are not part of the local community (see section I.5.8 on crime in an anarchist society).

Similarly, individuals would not be allowed to develop private property (as opposed to possession) simply because they wanted to. This rejection of private property would not be a restriction on liberty simply because stopping the development of authority hardly counts as an authoritarian act (for an analogy, supporters of capitalism do not think that banning theft is a restriction of liberty and because this view is — currently — accepted by the majority, it is enforced on the minority). Regardless of what defenders of capitalism claim, "voluntary bilateral exchanges" affect third parties and can harm others indirectly. This can easily be seen from examples like concentrations of wealth which have effects across society or the ecological impacts of consumption and production. This means that an anarchist society would be aware that inequality, and so statism, could develop again and take precautions against it. As Malatesta put it, some *"seem almost to believe that after having brought down government and private property we would allow both to be quietly built up again, because of respect for the **freedom** of those who might feel the need to be rulers and property owners. A truly curious way of interpreting our ideas."* [**Anarchy**, p. 43]

The suggestion that denying property ownership is a restriction in freedom is wrong, as it is the would-be capitalist who is trying to ban freedom for others on their property. Members of a free society would simply refuse to recognise the claims of private property — they would simply ignore the would-be capitalist's pretensions and *"keep out"* signs. Without a state, or hired thugs, to back up their claims, they would just end up looking silly.

This means that Anarchists do not support the liberty of being a boss (anarchists will happily work **with** someone but not **for** someone). Of course, those who desire to create private property against the wishes of others expect those others to respect their wishes. So, when would-be propertarians happily fence off their "property" and exclude others from it, could not these others remember these words from Woody Guthrie's **This Land is Your Land**, and act accordingly?

> **"As I went rumbling that dusty highway**
> **I saw a sign that said private property**
> **But on the other side it didn't say nothing**
> **This land was made for you and me"**

While happy to exclude others from "their" property, such owners seem more than happy to use the resources held in common by others. They are the ultimate "free riders," desiring the benefits of society but rejecting the responsibilities that go with it. In the end, such "individualists" usually end up supporting the state (an institution they claim to hate) precisely because it is the only means by which private property and their "freedom" to exercise authority can be defended.

This means, it should be stressed, the freedom to live your life as you see fit, using the resources you need to do so. It simply means not being able to proclaim ownership over more than you could reasonably use. In other words, *"Occupancy and use"* would be the limits of possession — and so property would become *"that control of a thing by a person which will receive either social sanction, or else unanimous individual sanction, when the laws of social expediency shall have been fully discovered."* [Benjamin Tucker, **Instead of a Book**, p. 131] As we discuss in section I.6.2, this perspective on use rights is shared by both individualist and social anarchists.

Therefore anarchists support the maximum of experiments while ensuring that the social conditions that allow this experimentation are protected against concentrations of wealth and power. As Malatesta put it: *"Anarchism involves all and only those forms of life that respect liberty and recognise that every person has an equal right to enjoy the good things of nature and the products of their own activity."* [**The Anarchist Revolution**, p. 14]

So, as a way to eliminate the problem of minorities seeking power and property for themselves, an anarchist revolution places social wealth (starting with the land) in the hands of all and promises to protect only those uses of it which are considered just by society as a whole. In other words, by recognising that "property" is a product of society, an anarchist society will ensure that an individual's "property" is protected by his or her fellows when it is based purely upon actual occupancy and use. Thus attempts to transform minority dissent into, say, property rights would be fought by simply ignoring the "keep out" signs of property owned, but not used, by an individual or group.

In summary, individuals will be free not to join a participatory community, and hence free to place themselves outside its decisions and activities on most issues that do not apply to the fundamental ethical standards of a society. Hence individuals who desire to live outside of anarchist communities would be free to live as they see fit but would not be able to commit murder, rape, create private property or other activities that harmed individuals. It should be noted, moreover, that this does not mean that their possessions will be taken from them by "society" or that "society" will tell them what to do with them. Freedom, in a complex world, means that such individuals will not be in a position to turn their possessions into **property** and thus recreate capitalism (for the distinction between "property" and "possessions," see section B.3.1). This will not be done by "anarchist police" or by "banning" voluntary agreements, but purely by recognising that "property" is a social creation and by creating a social system that will encourage individuals to stand up for their rights and co-operate with each other to protect their freedom against those seeking to reduce others to the conditions of servants working their property for them.

I.5.8
What about crime?

For anarchists, "crime" can best be described as anti-social acts, or behaviour which harms someone else or which invades their personal space. Anarchists, in other words, *"believe that to act criminally means to violate the liberty of others"* and so criminals in a free society would be *"those who would encroach on personal integrity, liberty and the well being of others."* [Malatesta, **At the Café**, p. 100 and p. 132]

This definition of crime is similar, of course, to that used in capitalist society but libertarians note that the state defines as "crime" many things which a sane society would not (such as, say, consensual acts of adults in private or expropriation of private property). Similarly, a free society would consider as anti-social many acts which the state allows under capitalism (such as the appropriation of resources or exploitation of others labour). This is to be expected, as social customs evolve and reflect the socio-economic basis of a given society. Hence Malatesta:

> *"Naturally the crimes we are talking about are anti-social acts, that is those which offend human feelings and which infringe the right of others to equality in freedom, and not the many actions which the penal code punishes simply because they offend against the privileges of the dominant classes."* [**Errico Malatesta: His Life and Ideas**, pp. 105-6]

Anarchists argue that the root cause for crime is not some perversity of human nature or "original sin" but is due to the type of society by which people are moulded. For example, anarchists point out that by eliminating private property, crime could be reduced significantly, since most crime today is currently motivated by evils stemming from private property such as poverty, homelessness, unemployment, and alienation. Moreover, by adopting anarchist methods of non-authoritarian child rearing and education, most of the remaining crimes could also be eliminated, because they are largely due to the anti-social, perverse, and cruel "secondary drives" that develop because of authoritarian child-rearing practices (see section J.6). However, as long as the few *"violates the equal freedom of others … we must defend ourselves."* [Malatesta, **Op. Cit.**, p. 106]

Nor can it be said that governments are required to protect people from crime and criminals. Rather, as Alexander Berkman argued, "[d]oes not government itself create and uphold conditions which make for crime? Does not the invasion and violence upon which all governments rest cultivate the spirit of intolerance and persecution, of hatred and more violence?" Crime, then, "is the result of economic conditions, of social inequality, of wrongs and evils of which government and monopoly are parents. Government and law can only punish the criminal. They neither cure nor prevent crime. The only real cure for crime is to abolish its causes, and this the government can never do because it is there to preserve those very causes." This suggests that crimes "resulting from government, from its oppression and injustice, from inequality and poverty, will disappear under Anarchy. These constitute by far the greatest percentage of crime." [**What is Anarchism?**, p. 151] Nor should we forget that today we are subject to rule by the anti-social, for the "owners and rulers" are "criminals" who are "powerful and have organised their dominance on a stable basis" ("Who is more of a thief than the owners who get wealthy stealing the produce of the workers' labour?"). [Malatesta, **At the Café**, p. 100 and p. 130]

"Crime", therefore, cannot be divorced from the society within which it occurs. Society, in Emma Goldman's words, gets the criminals it deserves. For example, anarchists do not think it unusual nor unexpected that crime exploded under the pro-free market capitalist regimes of Thatcher and Reagan. Crime, the most obvious symptom of social crisis, took 30 years to double in Britain (from 1 million incidents in 1950 to 2.2 million in 1979). However, between 1979 and 1992 the crime rate more than doubled, exceeding the 5 million mark in 1992. These 13 years were marked by a government firmly committed to the "free market" and "individual responsibility." It was entirely predictable that the social disruption, atomisation of individuals, and increased poverty caused by freeing capitalism from social controls would rip society apart and increase criminal activity. Also unsurprisingly (from an anarchist viewpoint), under these pro-market governments we also saw a reduction in civil liberties, increased state centralisation, and the destruction of local government. As Malatesta put it, the classical liberalism which these governments represented could have had no other effect, for "the government's powers of repression must perforce increase as free competition results in more discord and inequality." [**Anarchy**, p. 47]

Hence the apparent paradox of governments with flowing rhetoric about "individual rights," the "free market" and "getting the state off our backs" increasing state power and reducing rights while holding office during a crime explosion is no paradox at all. "The conjuncture of the rhetoric of individual freedom and a vast increase in state power," argues Carole Pateman, "is not unexpected at a time when the influence of contract doctrine is extending into the last, most intimate nooks and crannies of social life. Taken to a conclusion, contract undermines the conditions of its own existence. Hobbes showed long ago that contract — all the way down — requires absolutism and the sword to keep war at bay." [**The Sexual Contract**, p. 232]

Capitalism, and the contract theory on which it is built, will inevitably rip apart society. Capitalism is based upon a vision of humanity as isolated individuals with no connection other than that of money and contract. Such a vision cannot help but institutionalise anti-social acts. As Kropotkin argued "it is not love and not even sympathy upon which Society is based in mankind. It is the conscience — be it only at the stage of an instinct — of human solidarity. It is the unconscious recognition of the force that is borrowed by each man [and woman] from the practice of mutual aid; of the close dependency of every one's happiness upon the happiness of all; and of the sense of justice, or equity, which brings the individual to consider the rights of every other individual as equal to his [or her] own." [**Mutual Aid**, p. 16] The social atomisation required and created by capitalism destroys the basic bonds of society - namely human solidarity - and hierarchy crushes the individuality required to understand that we share a common humanity with others and so understand **why** we must be ethical and respect others rights. Significantly, as Richard Wilkinson and Kate Pickett note in **The Spirit Level: Why More Equal Societies Almost Always Do Better**, more unequal societies have more crime and bigger prison populations (equality, as well as reducing crime, consistently delivers other advantages for people).

We should also point out that prisons have numerous negative affects on society as well as often re-enforcing criminal (i.e. anti-social) behaviour. Anarchists use the all-to-accurate description of prisons as "Universities of Crime" wherein the first-time criminal learns new techniques and has to adapt to the prevailing ethical standards within them. Hence, prisons would have the effect of increasing the criminal tendencies of those sent there and so prove to be counter-productive. In addition, prisons do not affect the social conditions which promote many forms of crime.

We are not saying, however, that anarchists reject the concept of individual responsibility. While recognising that rape, for example, is the result of a social system which represses sexuality and is based on patriarchy (i.e. rape has more to do with power than sex), anarchists do not "sit back" and say "it's society's fault." Individuals have to take responsibility for their own actions and recognise the consequences of those actions.

Therefore, while anarchists reject the ideas of law and a specialised justice system, they are not blind to the fact that anti-social action may not totally disappear in a free society. Nor are they blind to the fact that, regardless of our hopes about a free society reducing crime, we will not create it over-night ("all the bad passions ... will not disappear at a stroke. There will still be for a long time those who will feel tempted to impose their will on others with violence, who will wish to exploit favourable circumstances to create privileges for themselves" [Malatesta, **At the Café**, p. 131]). Therefore, some sort of justice system would still be necessary to deal with the remaining crimes and to adjudicate disputes between citizens.

This does not, it must be stressed, signify some sort of contradiction within anarchism. Anarchists have never advocated the kind of "freedom" which assumes that people can do what they want. When people object to anarchy, they often raise the question as to those who would steal, murder, rape and so forth and seem to assume that such people would be free to act as they like. This is, needless to say, an utter misunderstanding of both our ideas and freedom in general. Simply put, if people impose themselves by force on others then "they will be the government" and "we will oppose them with force" for "if today we want to make a revolution against the government, it is not in order to submit ourselves supinely to new oppressors." [Malatesta, **Op. Cit**, p. 99] This applies equally to the need to defend a free society against organised counter-revolution and against those within it conducting anti-social ("criminal") activities. The principle is the same, it is just the scale which is different.

It should be remembered that just because the state monopolises or organises a (public) service, it does not mean that the abolition of the state means the abolition of what useful things it provided. For example, many states own and run the train network but the abolition of the state does not mean that there will no longer be any trains! In a free society management of the railways would be done by the rail workers themselves, in association with the community. The same applies to anti-social behaviour and so we find Kropotkin, for example, pointing to how *"voluntary associations"* would *"substitute themselves for the State in all its functions,"* including for *"mutual protection"* and *"defence of the territory."* [**Anarchism**, p. 284]

This applies to what is termed justice, namely the resolution of disputes and anti-social acts ("crime"). This means that anarchists argue that *"people would not allow their wellbeing and their freedom to be attacked with impunity, and if the necessity arose, they would take measures to defend themselves against the anti-social activities of a few. But to do so, what purpose is served by people whose profession is the making of laws; while other people spend their lives seeking out and inventing law-breakers?"* [**Anarchy**, pp. 43-4] This means that in a free society the resolution of anti-social behaviour would rest in the hands of all, **not** in a specialised body separate from and above the masses. As Proudhon put it, an anarchy would see the *"police, judiciary, administration, everywhere committed to the hands of the workers"* [**Property is Theft!**, p. 596] And so:

> *"Let each household, each factory, each association, each municipality, each district, attend to its own police, and administer carefully its own affairs, and the nation will be policed and administered. What need have we to be watched and ruled, and to pay, year in and year out, ... millions? Let us abolish prefects, commissioners, and policemen too."* [**Op. Cit.**, p. 593]

Precisely how this will work will be determined by free people based on the circumstances they face. All we can do is sketch out likely possibilities and make suggestions.

In terms of resolving disputes between people, it is likely that some form of arbitration system would develop. The parties involved could agree to hand their case to a third party (for example, a communal jury or a mutually agreed individual or set of individuals). There is the possibility that the parties cannot agree (or if the victim were dead). Then the issue could be raised at a communal assembly and a "court" appointed to look into the issue. These "courts" would be independent from the commune, their independence strengthened by popular election instead of executive appointment of judges, by protecting the jury system of selection of random citizens by lot, and so *"all disputes ... will be submitted to juries which will judge not only the facts but the law, the justice of the law [or social custom], its applicability to the given circumstances, and the penalty or damage to be inflicted because of its infraction"*. [Benjamin Tucker, **The Individualist Anarchists**, p. 160] For Tucker, the jury was a

"splendid institution, the principal safeguard against oppression." [**Liberty**, vol. 1, no. 16, p. 1]

As Malatesta suggested, *"when differences were to arise between men [sic!], would not arbitration voluntarily accepted, or pressure of public opinion, be perhaps more likely to establish where the right lies than through an irresponsible magistrate which has the right to adjudicate on everything and everybody and is inevitably incompetent and therefore unjust?"* [**Anarchy**, p. 45] It is in the arbitration system and communal assemblies that what constitutes anti-social behaviour will be discussed and agreed.

In terms of anti-social events when they happen, *"when there remains a residue of criminals, the collective directly concerned should think of placing them in a position where they can do no harm, without delegating to anyone the specific function of persecuting criminals"* [Malatesta, **At the Café**, p. 101] In the case of a "police force", this would not exist either as a public or private specialised body or company. If a local community did consider that public safety required a body of people who could be called upon for help, we imagine that a new system would be created. Such a system would *"not be entrusted to, as it is today, to a special, official body: all able-bodied inhabitants will be called upon to take turns in the security measures instituted by the commune."* [James Guillaume, "On Building the New Social Order", pp. 356-79, **Bakunin on Anarchism**, p. 371]

This system could be based around a voluntary militia, in which all members of the community could serve if they so desired. Those who served would not constitute a professional body; instead the service would be made up of local people who would join for short periods of time and be replaced if they abused their position. Hence the likelihood that a communal militia would become corrupted by power, like the current police force or a private security firm exercising a policing function, would be vastly reduced. Moreover, by accustoming a population to intervene in anti-social acts as part of the militia, they would be empowered to do so when not an active part of it, so reducing the need for its services even more. In this way *"we will defend ourselves ... without delegating to anyone the special function of the defence of society"* and this is *"the only effective method"* of stopping and reducing anti-social activity. [Malatesta, **Op. Cit.**, p. 132]

Such a body would not have a monopoly on protecting others, but would simply be on call if others required it. It would no more be a monopoly of defence (i.e. a "police force") than the current fire service is a monopoly. Individuals are not banned from putting out fires today because the fire service exists, similarly individuals will be free to help stop anti-social crime by themselves, or in association with others, in an anarchist society.

Of course there are anti-social acts which occur without witnesses and so the "guilty" party cannot be readily identified. If such acts did occur we can imagine an anarchist community taking two courses of action. The injured party may look into the facts themselves or appoint an agent to do so or, more likely, an ad hoc group would be elected at a community assembly to investigate specific crimes of this sort. Such a group would be given the necessary "authority" to investigate the crime and be subject to recall by the community if they start trying to abuse whatever authority they had. Once the investigating body thought it had enough evidence it would inform the community as well as the affected parties and then organise a court. Of course, a free society will produce different solutions to such problems, solutions no-one has considered yet and so these suggestions are just that, suggestions.

As is often stated, prevention is better than cure. This is as true of crime as of disease. In other words, crime is best fought by rooting out its **causes** as opposed to punishing those who act in response to these causes. For example, it is hardly surprising that a culture that promotes individual profit and consumerism would produce individuals who do not respect other people (or themselves) and see them as purely means to an end (usually increased consumption). And, like everything else in a capitalist system, such as honour and pride, conscience is also available at the right price — hardly an environment which encourages consideration for others, or even for oneself.

In addition, a society based on hierarchical authority will also tend to produce anti-social activity because the free development and expression it suppresses. Thus, authority (which is often claimed to be the only cure for crime) actually helps produce it. As Emma Goldman argued, crime *"is naught but misdirected energy. So long as every institution of today, economic, political, social, moral conspires to misdirect human energy into wrong channels; so long as most people are out of place doing things they hate to do, living a life they loathe to live, crime will be inevitable, and all the laws on the statues can only increase, but never do away with, crime"* [**Red Emma Speaks**, p. 71] Erich Fromm, decades later, made the same point:

> *"It would seem that the amount of destructiveness to be found in individuals is proportionate to the amount to which expansiveness of life is curtailed. By this we do not refer to individual frustrations of this or that instinctive desire but to the thwarting of the whole of life, the blockage of spontaneity of the growth and expression of man's sensuous, emotional, and intellectual capacities. Life has an inner dynamism of its own; it tends to grow, to be expressed, to be lived ... the drive for life and the drive for destruction are not mutually interdependent factors but are in a reversed interdependence. The more the drive towards life is thwarted, the stronger is the drive towards destruction; the more life is realised, the less is the strength of destructiveness. **Destructiveness is the outcome of unlived life.** Those individual and social conditions that make for suppression of life produce the passion for destruction that forms, so to speak, the reservoir from which particular hostile tendencies — either against others or against oneself — are nourished."* [**The Fear of Freedom**, p. 158]

Therefore, by reorganising society so that it empowers everyone and actively encourages the use of all our intellectual, emotional and sensuous abilities, crime would soon cease to be the huge problem that it is now. As for the anti-social behaviour or clashes between individuals that might still exist in such a society, it would be dealt with in a system based on respect for the individual and a recognition of the social roots of the problem. Restraint would be kept to a minimum. Anarchists think that public opinion and social pressure would be the main means of preventing anti-social acts in an anarchist society, with such actions as boycotting and ostracising used as powerful sanctions to convince those attempting them of the errors of their way. Extensive non-co-operation by neighbours, friends and work mates would be the best means of stopping acts which harmed others. Thus Malatesta:

> *"In order for crime to be treated rationally, in order to seek for its causes and really do everything possible to eliminate it, it is necessary for this task to be entrusted to those who are exposed to and suffer the consequences of crime, in other words the whole public, and not those to whom the existence of crime is a source of power and earnings."* [**At the Café**, p. 135]

An anarchist system of justice, we should note, would have a lot to learn from aboriginal societies simply because they are examples of social order without the state. Indeed many of the ideas we consider as essential to justice today can be found in such societies. As Kropotkin argued, *"when we imagine that we have made great advances in introducing, for instance, the jury, all we have done is to return to the institutions of the so-called 'barbarians' after having changed it to the advantage of the ruling classes."* [**The State: Its Historic Role**, p. 18]

Like aboriginal justice (as documented by Rupert Ross in **Returning to the Teachings: Exploring Aboriginal Justice**) anarchists contend that offenders should not be punished but justice achieved by the teaching and healing of all involved. Public condemnation of the wrongdoing would be a key aspect of this process, but the wrong doer would remain part of the community and so see the effects of their actions on others in terms of grief and pain caused. It would be likely that wrong doers would be expected to try to make amends for their act by community service or helping victims and their families.

So, from a practical viewpoint, almost all anarchists oppose prisons on both practical grounds and ethical grounds. Simply put, prison *"does not improve the prisoner ... it does not prevent him from committing more crimes. It does not then achieve any of the ends it has set itself"* [Kropotkin, **Anarchism**, p. 228] Moreover, they are a failure in terms of their impact on those subject to them: *"We know what prisons mean — they mean broken down body and spirit, degradation, consumption, insanity"*. [Voltairine de Cleyre, quoted by Paul Avrich, **An American Anarchist**, p. 146] The Makhnovists took the usual anarchist position on prisons:

> *"Prisons are the symbol of the servitude of the people, they are always built only to subjugate the people, the workers and peasants ... Free people have no use for prisons. Wherever prisons exist, the people are not free... In keeping with this attitude, [the Makhnovists] demolished prisons wherever they went."* [Peter Arshinov, **The History of the Makhnovist Movement**, p. 153]

With the exception of Benjamin Tucker, no major anarchist writer has supported the institution. Few anarchists think that private prisons (like private policemen) are compatible with their notions of freedom. However, all anarchists are against the current "justice" system which seems to them to be organised around **revenge** and punishing effects and not fixing causes.

However, there are psychopaths and other people in any society who are too dangerous to be allowed to walk freely. Restraint in this case would be the only option and such people may have to be isolated from others for their own, and others, safety. Perhaps mental hospitals would be used, or an area quarantined for their use. However, such cases (we hope) would be rare and *"should be cared for according to the most humane methods of treating the mentally afflicted."* [Voltairine de Cleyre, **The Voltairine de Cleyre Reader**, p. 160]

The one thing that needs to be avoided is the creation of a professional and specialised "justice" system as this would be a key means by which the state could reconstitute itself. As Malatesta explained, *"the major damage caused by crime is not so much the single and transitory instance of the violation of the rights of a few individuals, but the danger that it will serve as an opportunity and pretext for the constitution of an authority that, with the outward appearance of defending society will subdue and oppress it."* In other words, it *"would truly be a great piece of foolishness to protect oneself from a few violent people, a few idlers and some degenerates, by opening a school for idleness and violence"* [**Op. Cit.**, p. 101 and p. 132] The libertarian perspective on crime does not rest on an idealised vision of people. *"We do not believe"*, as Malatesta suggested, *in the infallibility, nor even the general goodness of the masses"*, rather *"we believe even less in the infallibility and goodness of those who seize power and legislate"* and so we must *"avoid the creation of bodies specialising in police work"*. [**Errico Malatesta: His Life and Ideas**, p. 109 and p. 108] After all, as George Barrett argued:

> *"All that we can say is that ... disputes are very much better settled without the interference of authority. If the two [parties] were reasonable, they would probably mutually agree to allow their dispute to be settled by some mutual friend whose judgement they could trust. But if instead of taking this sane course they decide to set up a fixed authority, disaster will be the inevitable result. In the first place, this authority will have to be given power wherewith to enforce its judgement in such matters. What will then take place? The answer is quite simple. Feeling it is a superior force, it will naturally in each case take to itself the best of what is disputed, and allot the rest to its friends.*

> *"What a strange question is this. It supposes that two people who meet on terms of equality and disagree could not be reasonable or just. But, on the other hand, it supposes that a third party, starting with an unfair advantage, and backed up by violence, will be the incarnation of justice itself. Commonsense should certainly warn us against such a supposition, and if we are lacking in this commodity, then we may learn the lesson by turning to the facts of life. There we see everywhere Authority standing by, and in the name of justice and fair play using its organised violence in order to take the lion's share of the world's wealth for the governmental class."*
> [**Objections to Anarchism**, pp. 349-50]

So instead of prisons and a legal code based on the concept of punishment and revenge, anarchists support the use of pubic opinion and pressure to stop anti-social acts and the need to therapeutically rehabilitate those who commit anti-social acts. Rather than a parasitic legal system which creates and defends inequality and privilege, anarchists agree with Kropotkin: *"Liberty, equality, and practical human sympathy are the most effective barriers we can oppose to the anti-social instinct of certain among us"*. [**Op. Cit.**, p. 218] *"We want justice, not rigid, but elastic"*, argued Tucker, *"we want justice, not stern, but tempered with mercy, with eyes sharp enough to detect causes, conditions, and circumstances; we want justice, not superficial, but profound."* The current system of rigid law imposed by the state and implemented by a judge was false and *"no such justice is wanted in any civilised community."* [**Op. Cit.**, Vol. 13, No. 5, p. 4]

In summary, then, anarchists have spent considerable time discussing the issue and how it could (and should not) be dealt with in a free society. Somewhat ironically, given that many think the issue of crime is the weakest point of the anarchist case, the outlines of a solution to this problem are well established in anarchist theory, both in terms of what **not** to do and in terms of combating both crime and its causes. Anarchy is based on people being free but freedom does **not** mean the "freedom" to violate the equal freedom of others. That is oppression, that is exploitation, that is the embryo of the state and capitalism.

Unsurprisingly, most anarchist thinkers have discussed the issue of anti-social activity. We can recommend the section *"Crime and Punishment"* by Malatesta (**Errico Malatesta: His Life and Ideas**) as well as Kropotkin's essays *"Law and Authority"* and *"Prisons and their moral influence on prisoners"* (both within the **Anarchism** collection). Emma Goldman's *"Prisons: A social crime and Failure"* (**Red Emma Speaks**), de Cleyre's *"Crime and Punishment"* (**The Voltairine de Cleyre Reader**) and Colin Ward's *"How Deviant Dare you get?"* (**Anarchy in Action**) are also worth reading. A useful collection of writings on this issue are found in **Under the Yoke of the State: Selected Anarchist Responses to Prisons and Crime** (edited by the Dawn Collective).

I.5.9 What about Freedom of Speech under Anarchism?

Free speech in an anarchist society would be far greater than under capitalism. This is obvious, anarchists argue, because we *"fight against oppression and tyranny for a future in which they will be neither masters nor slaves, neither rich nor poor, neither oppressors nor oppressed ... the freedom of each is rooted in the freedom of all, and that in this universal freedom is the guarantee of liberty, self-development, autonomy, and free speech for each and everyone."* [Emma Goldman, **A Documentary History of the American Years**, p. 104] As such, libertarian socialism would be marked by extensive freedom of speech but also freedom of the press, of the media and so forth.

Some, however, express the idea that **all** forms of socialism would endanger freedom of speech, press, and so forth. The usual formulation of this argument is in relation to state socialism and goes as follows: if the state (or "society") owned all the means of communication, then only the views which the government supported would get access to the media.

This is an important point and it needs to be addressed. However, before doing so, we should point out that under capitalism the major media are effectively controlled by the wealthy. As we argued in section D.3, the media are **not** the independent defenders of freedom that they like to portray themselves as. This is hardly surprising, since newspapers, television companies, and so forth are capitalist enterprises owned by the wealthy and with managing directors and editors who are also wealthy individuals with a vested interest in the status quo. Hence there are institutional factors which ensure that the "free press" reflects the interests of capitalist elites.

However, in democratic capitalist states there is little overt censorship. Radical and independent publishers can still print their papers and books without state intervention (although market forces ensure that this activity can be difficult and financially unrewarding). Under socialism, it is argued, because "society" owns the means of communication and production, this liberty will not exist. Instead, as can be seen from all examples of "actually existing socialism," such liberty is crushed in favour of the ruling elites' point of view.

As anarchism rejects the state, we can say that this danger does not exist under libertarian socialism. However, since social anarchists argue for the communalisation of production, could not restrictions on free speech still exist? We argue no, for three reasons.

Firstly, publishing houses, radio and TV stations, newspapers, internet sites and so on will be run by their workers directly. They will be supplied by other syndicates, with whom they will make agreements, and **not** by "central planning" officials, who would not exist. In other words, there is no bureaucracy of officials allocating (and so controlling) resources (and so the means of communication). Hence, anarchist self-management will ensure that there is a wide range of opinions in different magazines and papers. There would be community papers, radio and TV stations, internet sites, etc., and obviously they would play an increased role in a free society. But they would not be the only media. Associations, political parties, industrial syndicates, and so on would have their own media and/or would have access to the resources of communication workers' syndicates, so ensuring that a wide range of opinions can be expressed.

Secondly, the "ultimate" power in a free society will be the individuals of which it is composed. This power will be expressed in communal and workplace assemblies that can recall delegates and revoke their decisions. It is doubtful that these assemblies would tolerate a set of would-be bureaucrats determining what they can or cannot read, see, or hear.

Thirdly, individuals in a free society would be interested in hearing different viewpoints and discussing them. This is the natural side-effect of critical thought (which self-management would encourage), and so they would have a vested interest in defending the widest possible access to different forms of media for different views. Having no vested interests to defend, a free society would hardly encourage or tolerate the censorship associated with the capitalist media ("*I listen to criticism because I am* **greedy.** *I listen to criticism*

because I am **selfish.** *I would not deny myself another's insights*" [For Ourselves, **The Right to be Greedy**, Thesis 113]).

Therefore, anarchism will **increase** freedom of speech in many important ways, particularly in the workplace (where it is currently denied under capitalism). This will be a natural result of a society based on maximising freedom and the desire to enjoy life: "*We claim the right of discussing ... whatever subject interests us. If free speech and free press mean anything, they mean freedom of discussion.*" [Goldman, **Op. Cit.**, p. 203]

We would also like to point out that during both the Spanish and Russian revolutions, freedom of speech was protected within anarchist areas. For example, the Makhnovists in the Ukraine "*fully applied the revolutionary principles of freedom of speech, of thought, of the Press, and of political association. In all the cities and towns occupied ... Complete freedom of speech, Press, assembly, and association of any kind and for everyone was immediately proclaimed.*" [Peter Arshinov, **The History of the Makhnovist Movement**, p. 153] This is confirmed by Michael Malet who notes that "*[o]ne of the most remarkable achievements of the Makhnovists was to preserve a freedom of speech more extensive than any of their opponents.*" [**Nestor Makhno in the Russian Civil War**, p. 175] In revolutionary Spain republicans, liberals, communists, Trotskyites and many different anarchist groups all had freedom to express their views. Emma Goldman wrote that "*[o]n my first visit to Spain in September 1936, nothing surprised me so much as the amount of political freedom I found everywhere. True, it did not extend to Fascists*" but "*everyone of the anti-Fascist front enjoyed political freedom which hardly existed in any of the so-called European democracies.*" As for the few restrictions that were in place, remember that there was a war on so it was "*childish to expect the CNT-FAI to include Fascists and other forces engaged in their destruction in the extension of complete political freedom.*" [**Vision on Fire**, p.147 and p. 228] The freedom of speech in anarchist areas is confirmed in a host of other eye-witnesses, including George Orwell in **Homage to Catalonia** (in fact, it was the rise of the pro-capitalist republicans and communists that introduced censorship).

Both movements were fighting a life-and-death struggle against communist, fascist and pro-capitalist armies and so this defence of freedom of expression, given the circumstances, is particularly noteworthy. Freedom of speech, like freedom of association, applies to all groups (including, of course, religious ones). The only exception would be, as Goldman noted, for organisations which are actively fighting to enslave a free society. In other words, during a social revolution it is unlikely that freedom of speech and organisation would apply to those supporting the counter-revolutionary forces. As the threat of violence by these forces decreases, so the freedom of their supporters would increase.

In summary, then, a free society would have substantial freedom of speech along with other fundamental freedoms (including freedom of worship and of religious association). Such freedoms would be respected, supported and encouraged for all shades of political opinion, from the left through to the right. The only exception would be if an organisation were **actively** supporting those seeking to impose their rule on a free people and in such cases some restrictions may be decided upon (their nature would depend on the state of the struggle, with them decreasing as the danger decreased).

To those who claim that refusing freedom of speech to counter-revolutionaries equates to statism or implies a contradiction in libertarian ideas anarchists would reply that such arguments are flawed. In terms of the former, it is equating state imposed censorship with the active disobedience of a free people. Rather than the government imposing a ban, members of a free society would simply discuss the issue at hand and, if considered appropriate, actively and collectively boycott those supporting attempts to enslave them. Without electricity, paper, distribution networks and so on, reactionaries would find it hard to publish or broadcast. As for the latter, there is no contradiction as it is hardly contradictory to support and encourage freedom while, at the same time, resisting attempts to enslave you! As such, this argument makes the same logical error Engels did in his diatribe against anarchism, namely considering it "authoritarian" to destroy authority (see section H.4.7). Similarly, it is hardly authoritarian to resist those seeking to impose their authority on you or their supporters! This perspective seems to assume that the true 'libertarian' approach is to let others impose their rule on you as stopping them is 'authoritarian'! A truly strange way of understanding our ideas....

To conclude, based upon both theory and practice, we can say that anarchism will not endanger freedom of expression. Indeed, by breaking up the capitalist oligopoly which currently exists and introducing workers' self-management of the media, a far wider range of opinions will become available in a free society. Rather than reflect the interests of a wealthy elite, the media would reflect the interests of society as a whole and the individuals and groups within it.

I.5.10 What about political parties, interest groups and professional bodies?

Political parties and other interest groups will exist in an anarchist society as long as people feel the need to join them. They will not be banned in any way, and their members will have the same rights as everyone else. Individuals who are members of political parties or associations can take part in communal and other assemblies and try to convince others of the soundness of their ideas.

However, there is a key difference between such activity and politics under a capitalist democracy. This is because the elections to positions of responsibility in an anarchist society will not be based on party tickets nor will they involve the delegation of power. Emile Pouget's description of the difference between the syndicalist trade union and elections drives this difference home:

"The constituent part of the trade union is the individual. Except that the union member is spared the depressing phenomenon manifest in democratic circles where, thanks to the veneration of universal suffrage, the trend is towards the crushing and diminution of the human personality. In a democratic setting, the elector can avail of his [or her] will only in order to perform an act of abdication: his role

is to 'award' his 'vote' to the candidate whom he [or she] wishes to have as his [or her] 'representative.'

"Affiliation to the trade union has no such implication ... In joining the union, the worker merely enters into a contract — which he may at any time abjure — with comrades who are his equals in will and potential ... In the union, say, should it come to the appointment of a trade union council to take charge of administrative matters, such 'selection' is not to be compared with 'election': the form of voting customarily employed in such circumstances is merely a means whereby the labour can be divided and is not accompanied by any delegation of authority. The strictly prescribed duties of the trade union council are merely administrative. The council performs the task entrusted to it, without ever overruling its principals, without supplanting them or acting in their place.

"The same might be said of all decisions reached in the union: all are restricted to a definite and specific act, whereas in democracy, election implies that the elected candidate has been issued by his [or her] elector with a carte blanche empowering him [or her] to decide and do as he [or she] pleases, in and on everything, without even the hindrance of the quite possibly contrary views of his [or her] principals, whose opposition, in any case, no matter how pronounced, is of no consequence until such time as the elected candidate's mandate has run its course.

"So there cannot be any possible parallels, let alone confusion, between trade union activity and participation in the disappointing chores of politics." [**No Gods, No Masters**, vol. 2, pp. 67-68]

In other words, when individuals are elected to administrative posts they are elected to carry out their mandate, **not** to carry out their party's programme. Of course, if the individuals in question had convinced their fellow workers and citizens that their programme was correct, then this mandate and the programme would be identical. However this is unlikely in practice. We would imagine that the decisions of collectives and communes would reflect the complex social interactions and diverse political opinions their members and of the various groupings within the association.

This freedom of political association has existed in every anarchist revolution. During the Russian Revolution, the Makhnovists organised soviets and regional congresses at every opportunity and these saw delegates elected who were members of different political parties. For example, members of the peasant-socialist Left-SR party were active in the Makhnovist movement and attended soviet congresses (for example, the resolution of the February 1919 congress *"was written by the anarchists, left Socialist Revolutionaries, and the chairman."* [Michael Palij, **The Anarchism of Nestor Makhno, 1918-1921**, p. 155]). The Makhnovist Revolutionary Military Soviet created at the Aleksandrovsk congress in late 1919 had three Communists elected to it while there were 18 delegates from workers at that congress, six being Mensheviks and the remaining

12 included Communists [Malet, **Op. Cit.**, p. 111, p. 124] Clearly, members of political parties were elected to both the congresses and the Revolutionary Military Soviet. As such, the idea that libertarian socialism excludes members of political parties standing for election is false. In the words of the Makhnovist reply to a Bolshevik attempt to ban one of their congresses:

> "The Revolutionary Military Council ... holds itself above the pressure and influence of all parties and only recognises the people who elected it. Its duty is to accomplish what the people have instructed it to do, and to create no obstacles to any left socialist party in the propagation of ideas. Consequently, if one day the Bolshevik idea succeeds among the workers, the Revolutionary Military Council ... will necessarily be replaced by another organisation, 'more revolutionary' and more Bolshevik." [quoted by Peter Arshinov, **The History of the Makhnovist Movement**, pp. 103-4]

As such, the Makhnovists supported the right of working-class self-determination, as expressed by one delegate to a conference in February 1919:

> "No party has a right to usurp governmental power into its hands ... We want life, all problems, to be decided locally, not by order from any authority above; and all peasants and workers should decide their own fate, while those elected should only carry out the toilers' wish." [quoted by Palij, **Op. Cit.**, p. 154]

It should be mentioned that a myth has sprung up fostered by some Leninists that parties were banned from election to these bodies (for example, Jason Yanowitz's terrible "On the Makhno Myth" [**International Socialist Review**, no. 53]). These claims flow from basic ignorance of how the soviets were organised during the revolution combined with a misunderstanding of this Makhnovist proclamation from January 1920::

> "Only workers participating in work vital to the people's economy should be elected to these soviets. The representatives of political organisations have no place in the soviets of workers and peasants given that their participation in a soviet could turn it into a soviet of party political deputies, thereby leading the soviet order to perdition." [quoted by Alexandre Skirda, **Nestor Makhno: Anarchy's Cossack**, p. 164]

When the soviets were formed in Petrograd and other Russian cities in 1917 the initiative had come (unlike in 1905) from political parties and these ensured that they had members who were representatives from political parties within their executive committees (as distinct from elected delegates who happened to be members of a political party). This was how, for example, "high party leaders became voting delegates" in the soviets, by being "selected by the leadership of each political organisation, and not by the soviet assembly itself." [Samuel Farber, **Before Stalinism**, p. 31] Thus the Makhnovists were rejecting the means by which many soviet members were not directly elected by actual workers.

In addition, the Makhnovists were following the Russian Anarcho-Syndicalists who argued for "effective soviets organised on collective lines with the direct delegation of workers and peasants ... and not political chatterboxes gaining entry through party lists and turning the soviets into talking-shops". [**The Anarchists in the Russian Revolution**, Paul Avrich (ed.), p. 118] This use of party lists meant that soviet delegates could be anyone. For example, the leading left-wing Menshevik Martov recounts that in early 1920 a chemical factory "put up Lenin against me as a candidate [to the Moscow soviet]. I received seventy-six votes he - eight (in an open vote)." [quoted by Israel Getzler, **Martov**, p. 202] How would either of these two intellectuals actually know and reflect the concerns and interests of the workers they would be "delegates" of? If the soviets were meant to be the delegates of working people, then why should non-working class members of political parties be elected as mandated and recallable delegates to a soviet from a workplace they have never visited except, perhaps, to gather votes?

Hence anarchism will likely contain many different political groupings and ideas. The relative influence of these within collectives and communes would reflect the strength of their arguments and the relevance of their ideas, as would be expected in a free society. As Bakunin argued: "The abolition of this mutual influence would be death. And when we vindicate the freedom of the masses, we are by no means suggesting the abolition of any of the natural influences that individuals or groups of individuals exert on them. What we want is the abolition of influences which are artificial, privileged, legal, official." [quoted by Malatesta, **Anarchy**, p. 51]

It is only when representative government replaces self-management that political debate results in "elected dictatorship" and centralisation of power into the hands of one party which claims to speak for the whole of society, as if the latter had one mind.

This applies, needless to say, to other areas of life. Anarchists do not think that social life can be reduced to political and economic associations alone. Individuals have many different interests and desires which they must express in order to have a truly free and interesting life. Therefore an anarchist society will see the development of numerous voluntary associations and groups to express these interests. For example, there would be consumer groups, musical groups, scientific associations, art associations, clubs, housing co-operatives and associations, craft and hobby guilds, fan clubs, animal rights associations, groups based around gender, sexuality, creed and colour and so forth. Associations will be created for all human interests and activities. As Kropotkin argued:

> "He who wishes for a grand piano will enter the association of musical instrument makers. And by giving the association part of his half-days' leisure, he will soon possess the piano of his dreams. If he is fond of astronomical studies he will join the association of astronomers ... and he will have the telescope he desires by taking his share of the associated work ... In short, the five or seven hours a day which each will have at his disposal, after having consecrated several hours to the production of necessities, would amply suffice to satisfy all longings for luxury, however varied. Thousands of associations would undertake to supply them." [**The Conquest of Bread**, p. 120]

We can imagine, therefore, an anarchist society being based around associations and interest groups on every subject which fires the imagination of individuals and for which individuals want to meet in order to express and further their interests. Housing associations, for example, would exist to allow inhabitants to manage their local areas, design and maintain their homes and local parks and gardens. Animal rights and other interest groups would produce information on issues they consider important, trying to convince others of the errors of eating meat or whatever. Consumer groups would be in dialogue with syndicates about improving products and services, ensuring that syndicates produce what is required by consumers. Environment groups would exist to watch production and make sure that it is not creating damaging side effects and informing both syndicates and communes of their findings. Feminist, homosexual, bisexual and anti-racist groups would exist to put their ideas across, highlighting areas in which social hierarchies and prejudice still existed. All across society, people would be associating together to express themselves and convince others of their ideas on many different issues.

This applies to professional groupings who would seek to ensure that those work tasks that require qualifications to do (for example, medicine and such like) have recognised standards and certifications. In this way, others in society would know whether a fellow worker is a recognised expert in their field and has the appropriate qualifications to do the work required or give advice. While a free society would break down the line between intellectual and manual work, the fact remains that people will wish to be happy that the doctor or nurse they are visiting knows what they are doing. This is where professional groupings would come into play, organising training and certification based on mutually agreed standards and qualifications. This would not stop others seeking to practice such tasks, of course, but it will mean that few, if any, would frequent someone without the basic professional standards.

Hence in a anarchist society, free association would take on a stronger and more positive role than under capitalism. In this way, social life would take on many dimensions, and the individual would have the choice of thousands of societies to join to meet his or her interests or create new ones with other like-minded people. Anarchists would be the last to deny that there is more to life than work!

I.5.11 How will an anarchist society defend itself against the power hungry?

A common objection to anarchism is that an anarchist society will be vulnerable to be taken over by thugs or those who seek power. A similar argument is that a group without a leadership structure becomes open to charismatic leaders so anarchy would just lead to tyranny.

For anarchists, such arguments are strange. Society already **is** run by thugs and/or the off-spring of thugs. Kings were originally just successful thugs who succeeded in imposing their domination over a given territorial area. The modern state has evolved from the

structure created to impose this domination. Similarly with property, with most legal titles to land being traced back to its violent seizure by thugs who then passed it on to their children who then sold it or gave it to their offspring. The origins of the current system in violence can be seen by the continued use of violence by the state and capitalists to enforce and protect their domination over society. When push comes to shove, the dominant class will happily re-discover their thug past and employ extreme violence to maintain their privileges. The descent of large parts of Europe into Fascism in the 1920s and 1930s, or Pinochet's coup in Chile in 1973 indicates how far they will go. As Peter Arshinov argued (in a slightly different context):

"Statists fear free people. They claim that without authority people will lose the anchor of sociability, will dissipate themselves, and will return to savagery. This is obviously rubbish. It is taken seriously by idlers, lovers of authority and of the labour of others, or by blind thinkers of bourgeois society. The liberation of the people in reality leads to the degeneration and return to savagery, not of the people, but of those who, thanks to power and privilege, live from the labour of the people's arms and from the blood of the people's veins ... The liberation of the people leads to the savagery of those who live from its enslavement." [**The History of the Makhnovist Movement**, p. 85]

Anarchists are not impressed with the argument that anarchy would be unable to stop thugs seizing power. It ignores the fact that we live in a society where the power-hungry already hold power. As an argument against anarchism it fails and is, in fact, an argument against hierarchical societies.

Moreover, it also ignores the fact that people in an anarchist society would have gained their freedom by overthrowing every existing and would-be thug who had or desired power over others. They would have defended that freedom against those who desired to re-impose it. They would have organised themselves to manage their own affairs and, therefore, to abolish all hierarchical power. And we are to believe that these people, after struggling to become free, would quietly let a new set of thugs impose themselves? As Kropotkin argued:

"The only way in which a state of Anarchy can be obtained is for each man [or woman] who is oppressed to act as if he [or she] were at liberty, in defiance of all authority to the contrary ... In practical fact, territorial extension is necessary to ensure permanency to any given individual revolution. In speaking of the Revolution, we signify the aggregate of so many successful individual and group revolts as will enable every person within the revolutionised territory to act in perfect freedom ... without having to constantly dread the prevention or the vengeance of an opposing power upholding the former system ... Under these circumstance it is obvious that any visible reprisal could and would be met by a resumption of the same revolutionary action on the part of the individuals or groups affected, and that the **maintenance** *of a state of Anarchy in this manner would be far easier than the gaining of a state of Anarchy by the same methods and in the face of hitherto unshaken opposition ... They have it in their power to apply a prompt check by boycotting such a person and refusing to help him with their labour or to willingly supply him with any articles in their possession. They have it in their power to use force against him. They have these powers individually as well as collectively. Being either past rebels who have been inspired with the spirit of liberty, or else habituated to enjoy freedom from their infancy, they are hardly to rest passive in view of what they feel to be wrong."* [**Act for Yourselves**, pp. 87-8]

Thus a free society would use direct action to resist the would-be ruler just as it had used direct action to free itself from existing rulers. An anarchist society would be organised in a way which would facilitate this direct action as it would be based on networks of solidarity and mutual aid. An injury to one is an injury to all and a would-be ruler would face a whole liberated society acting against him or her. Faced with the direct action of the population (which would express itself in non-co-operation, strikes, demonstrations, occupations, insurrections and so on) a would be power seeker would find it difficult to impose themselves. Unlike those accustomed to rulership in existing society, an anarchist people would be a society of rebels and so difficult to dominate and conquer: *"In the future society, Anarchy will be defence, the prevention of the re-establishment of any authority, any power, any State."* [Carlo Cafiero, *"Anarchy and Communism"*, pp. 179-86, **The Raven**, No. 6, p. 180]

Anarchists point to the example of the rise of Fascism in Italy, Spain and Germany to prove their point. In areas with strong anarchist movements the fascists were resisted most strongly. While in Germany Hitler took power with little or no opposition, in Italy and Spain the fascists had to fight long and hard to gain power. The anarchist and anarcho-syndicalist organisations fought the fascists tooth and nail, with some success before betrayal by the Republicans and Marxists. From this historical experience anarchists argue that an anarchist society would quickly and easily defeat would-be thugs as people would be used to practising direct action and self-management and would have no desire to stop practising them. A free people would quickly organise itself in self-managed militias for self-defence (just as they would during a social revolution to defend it — section J.7.6).

As for self-management resulting in "charismatic" leaders, well the logic is astounding. As if hierarchical structures are **not** based on leadership structures and do not require a charismatic leader! Such an argument is inherently self-contradictory — as well as ignoring the nature of modern society and its leadership structures. Rather than mass assemblies being dominated by leaders, it is the case that hierarchical structures are the natural breeding ground for dictators. All the great dictators the world has seen have come to the forefront in **hierarchical** organisations, **not** libertarian structured ones. Hitler, for example, did not come to power via a libertarian organisation. Rather he used a highly centralised and hierarchically organised party to take control of a centralised, hierarchical state. The very disempowerment of the population in capitalist society results in them looking to leaders to act for them and so "charismatic" leaders are a natural result. An anarchist society, by empowering all, would make it more difficult, not less, for a would-be leader to gain power — few people, if any, would be willing to sacrifice and negate themselves for the benefit of another.

Our discussion on the power hungry obviously relates to the more general question of whether ethical behaviour will be rewarded in an anarchist society. In other words, could an anarchist society be stable or would the unethical take over?

One of the most disturbing aspects of living in a world where the rush to acquire wealth is the single most important aspect of living is what happens to people who follow an ethical path in life. Under capitalism, the ethical generally do not succeed as well as those who stab their fellows in the back, those who cut corners, indulge in sharp business practises, drive competitors into the ground and live their lives with an eye on the bottom line but they do survive. Loyalty to a firm or a group, bending over backwards to provide a service, giving a helping hand to somebody in need, placing friendship above money, count for nothing when the bills come in. People who act ethically in a capitalist society are usually punished and penalised for their ethical, moral and principled behaviour. Indeed, the capitalist market rewards unethical behaviour as it generally reduces costs and so gives those who do it a competitive edge.

It is different in a free society. Anarchism is based on two principles of association, equal access to power and wealth. Everybody in an anarchist society irrespective of what they do, or who they are or what type of work they perform is entitled to share in society's wealth. Whether a community survives or prospers depends on the combined efforts of the people in that community. Ethical behaviour would become the norm in an anarchist community; those people who act ethically would be rewarded by the standing they achieve in the community and by others being more than happy to work with and aid them. People who cut corners, try to exercise power over others, refuse to co-operate as equals or otherwise act in an unethical manner would lose their standing in an anarchist society. Their neighbours and work mates would refuse to co-operate with them (or reduce co-operation to a minimum) and take other forms of non-violent direct action to point out that certain forms of activity were inappropriate. They would discuss the issue with the unethical person and try to convince them of the errors of their way. In a society where the necessities are guaranteed, people would tend to act ethically because ethical behaviour raises an individuals profile and standing within such a community. Capitalism and ethical behaviour are mutually exclusive concepts; anarchism encourages and rewards ethical behaviour. Needless to say, as we discussed in section I.5.8, anarchists are aware that a free society would need to defend itself against whatever anti-social behaviour remains in a free and equal society and seeking to impose your will on others defines unethical and anti-social!

Therefore, as can be seen, anarchists argue that a free society would not have to fear would-be thugs, "charismatic" leaders or the unethical. An anarchist society would be based on the co-operation of free individuals. It is unlikely that they would tolerate such behaviour and would use their own direct action as well as social and economic organisations to combat it. Moreover, the nature of free co-operation would reward ethical behaviour as those who practice it would have it reciprocated by their fellows, and, if worse came to worse, they would defend their liberty!

One last point. Some people seem to think that anarchism is about the powerful being appealed to **not** to oppress and dominate others. Far from it. Anarchism is about the oppressed and exploited refusing to let others dominate them. It is **not** an appeal to the "better side" of the boss or would-be boss; it is about the solidarity and direct action of those subject to a boss **getting rid of the boss** — whether the boss agrees to it or not! Once this is clearly understood the idea that an anarchist society is vulnerable to the power-hungry is clearly nonsense — anarchy is based on resisting power and so is, by its very nature, more resistant to would-be rulers than a hierarchical one.

So, to summarise, anarchists are well aware that an anarchist society will have to defend itself from both inside and outside attempts to re-impose capitalism and the state. Indeed, every revolutionary anarchist has argued that a revolution will have to defend itself (as proven in section H.2.1, Marxist assertions otherwise have always been myths).

I.5.12 Would an anarchist society provide health care and other public services?

It depends on the type of anarchist society you are talking about. Different anarchists propose different solutions.

In an individualist-mutualist society, for example, health care and other public services would be provided by individuals or co-operatives on a pay-for-use basis. It would be likely that individuals or co-operatives/associations would subscribe to various insurance providers or enter into direct contracts with health care providers. Thus the system would be similar to privatised health care but without the profit margins as competition, it is hoped, would drive prices down to cost.

Other anarchists reject such a system. They are in favour of socialising health care and other public services. They argue that a privatised system would only be able to meet the requirements of those who can afford to pay for it and so would be unjust and unfair. In addition, such systems would have higher overheads (the need to pay share-holders and the wages of management, most obviously) as well as charge more (privatised public utilities under capitalism have tended to charge consumers more, unsurprisingly as by their very nature they are natural monopolies).

Looking at health care, for example, the need for medical attention is not dependent on income and so a civilised society would recognise this fact. Under capitalism, profit-maximising medical insurance sets premiums according to the risks of the insured getting ill or injured, with the riskiest not being able to find insurance at any price. Private insurers shun entire industries as too dangerous for their profits due to the likelihood of accidents or illness. They review contracts regularly and drop people who get sick for the slightest reason (understandably, given that they make profits by minimising payouts for treatment). Hardly a vision to inspire a free society or

one compatible with equality and mutual respect.

Therefore, most anarchists are in favour of a socialised and universal health-care system for both ethical and efficiency reasons (see section I.4.10 for more details). Needless to say, an anarchist system of socialised health care would differ in many ways to the current systems of universal health-care provided by the state (which, while called socialised medicine by its enemies is better described as nationalised medicine — although it should be stressed that this is better than the privatised system). Such a system of socialised health-care will be built from the bottom-up and based around the local commune. In a social anarchist society, *"medical services ... will be free of charge to all inhabitants of the commune. The doctors will not be like capitalists, trying to extract the greatest profit from their unfortunate patients. They will be employed by the commune and expected to treat all who need their services."* Moreover, prevention will play an important part, as *"medical treatment is only the* **curative** *side of the science of health care; it is not enough to treat the sick, it is also necessary to prevent disease. That is the true function of hygiene."* [James Guillaume, *"On Building the New Social Order"*, pp. 356-79, **Bakunin on Anarchism**, p. 371] The same would go for other public services and works.

While rejecting privatisation, anarchists also reject nationalisation in favour of socialisation and worker's self-management. In this we follow Proudhon, who argued that there was a series of industries and services which were *"public works"* which he thought best handled by communes and their federations. Thus *"the control undertaking such works will belong to the municipalities, and to districts within their jurisdiction"* while *"the control of carrying them out will rest with the workmen's associations."* This was due to both their nature and libertarian values and so the *"direct, sovereign initiative of localities, in arranging for public works that belong to them, is a consequence of the democratic principle and the free contract: their subordination to the State is ... a return to feudalism."* Workers' self-management of such public workers is, again, a matter of libertarian principles for *"it becomes necessary for the workers to form themselves into democratic societies, with equal conditions for all members, on pain of a relapse into feudalism."* Railways should be given *"to responsible companies, not of capitalists, but of WORKMEN."* [**General Idea of the Revolution**, p. 276, p. 277 and p. 151]

This was applied during the Spanish Revolution. Gaston Leval discussed *"Achievements in the Public Sector"* and a whole chapter of his account of the collectives is concerned with this. Syndicates organised water, gas and electricity utilities in Catalonia, while the Trams and railways were run more efficiently and cheaper than under capitalist management. All across Spain, the workers in the health service re-organised their industry in libertarian lines and in association with the local collective or commune and the unions of the CNT. As Leval summarised:

> *"For the socialisation of medicine was not just an initiative of militant libertarian doctors. Wherever we were able to make a study of villages and small towns transformed by the Revolution, medicine and existing hospitals had been municipalised, expanded, placed*

under the aegis of the Collective. When there were none, they were improvised. The socialisation of medicine was becoming everyone's concern, for the benefit of all. It constituted one of the most remarkable achievements of the Spanish Revolution." [**Collectives in the Spanish Revolution**, p. 278]

So the Spanish Revolution indicates how an anarchist health service would operate. In rural areas local doctors would usually join the village collective and provide their services like any other worker. Where local doctors were not available, *"arrangements were made by the collectives for treatment of their members by hospitals in nearby localities. In a few cases, collectives themselves build hospitals; in many they acquired equipment and other things needed by their local physicians."* For example, the Monzon comercal (district) federation of collectives in Aragon established maintained a hospital in Binefar, the Casa de Salud Durruti. By April 1937 it had 40 beds, in sections which included general medicine, prophylaxis and gynaecology. It saw about 25 outpatients a day and was open to anyone in the 32 villages of the comarca. [Robert Alexander, **The Anarchists in the Spanish Civil War**, vol. 1, p. 331 and pp. 366-7]

In the Levante, the CNT built upon its existing **Sociedad de Socorros Mutuos de Levante** (a health service institution founded by the union as a kind of mutual benefit society which had numerous doctors and specialists). During the revolution, the Mutua had 50 doctors and was available to all affiliated workers and their families. The socialisation of the health care took on a slightly different form in Catalonia but on the same libertarian principles. Gaston Leval provided us with an excellent summary:

"The socialisation of health services was one of the greatest achievements of the revolution. To appreciate the efforts of our comrades it must be borne in mind that they rehabilitated the health service in all of Catalonia in so short a time after July 19th. The revolution could count on the co-operation of a number of dedicated doctors whose ambition was not to accumulate wealth but to serve the afflicted and the underprivileged.

"The Health Workers' Union was founded in September, 1936. In line with the tendency to unite all the different classifications, trades, and services serving a given industry, all health workers, from porters to doctors and administrators, were organised into one big union of health workers ...

"Our comrades laid the foundations of a new health service ... The new medical service embraced all of Catalonia. It constituted a great apparatus whose parts were distributed according to different needs, all in accord with an overall plan. Catalonia was divided into nine zones ... In turn, all the surrounding villages and towns were served from these centres.

"Distributed throughout Catalonia were twenty-seven towns with a total of thirty-six health centres conducting services so thoroughly that every village, every hamlet, every isolated peasant in the mountains, every woman, every child, anywhere, received adequate, up-to-date medical care. In each of the nine zones there was a central syndicate and a Control Committee located in Barcelona. Every department was autonomous within its own sphere. But this autonomy was not synonymous with isolation. The Central Committee in Barcelona, chosen by all the sections, met once a week with one delegate from each section to deal with common problems and to implement the general plan ...

"The people immediately benefited from the projects of the health syndicate. The syndicate managed all hospitals and clinics. Six hospitals were opened in Barcelona... Eight new sanatoriums were installed in converted luxurious homes ideally situated amidst mountains and pine forests. It was no easy task to convert these homes into efficient hospitals with all new facilities." [**The Anarchist Collectives**, Sam Dolgoff (ed.), pp. 99-100]

People were no longer required to pay for medical services. Each collective, if it could afford it, would pay a contribution to its health centre. Building and facilities were improved and modern equipment introduced. Like other self-managed industries, the health service was run at all levels by general assemblies of workers who elected delegates and hospital administration.

We can expect a similar process to occur in the future anarchist society. It would be based on self-management, of course, with close links to the local commune and federations of communes. Each hospital or health centre would be autonomous but linked in a federation with the others, allowing resources to be shared as and when required while allowing the health service to adjust to local needs and requirements as quickly as possible. Workers in the health industry will organise their workplaces, federate together to share resources and information, to formulate plans and improve the quality of service to the public in a system of generalised self-management and socialisation. The communes and their federations, the syndicates and federations of syndicates will provide resources and effectively own the health system, ensuring access for all.

Similar systems would operate in other public services. For example, in education we expect the members of communes to organise a system of free schools. This can be seen from the Spanish revolution. Indeed, the Spanish anarchists organised Modern Schools before the outbreak of the revolution, with 50 to 100 schools in various parts funded by local anarchist groups and CNT unions. During the revolution everywhere across Spain, syndicates, collectives and federations of collectives formed and founded schools. Indeed, education *"advanced at an unprecedented pace. Most of the partly or wholly socialised collectives and municipalities built at least one school. By 1938, for example, every collective in the Levant Federation had its own school."* [Gaston Leval, quoted by Sam Dolgoff, **Op. Cit.**, p. 168] These schools aimed, to quote the CNT's resolution on Libertarian Communism, to *"help mould men with minds of their own — and let it be clear that when we use the word 'men' we use it in the generic sense — to which end it will* be necessary for the teacher to cultivate every one of the child's faculties so that the child may develop every one of its capacities to the full." [quoted by Jose Periats, **The CNT in the Spanish Revolution**, p. 70] Libertarian education, of encouraging freedom instead of authority in the school, was applied on vast scale (see section J.5.13 for more details on Modern Schools and libertarian education).

This educational revolution was not confined to collectives or children. For example, the **Federacion Regional de Campesinos de Levante** formed institutes in each of its five provinces. The first was set up in October 1937 in an old convent with 100 students. The Federation also set up two *"universities"* in Valencia and Madrid which taught a wide variety of agricultural subjects and combined learning with practical experience in an experimental form attached to each university. The Aragon collectives formed a similar specialised school in Binefar. The CNT was heavily involved in transforming education in Catalonia. In addition, the local federation of the CNT in Barcelona established a school to train women workers to replace male ones being taken into the army. The school was run by the anarchist-feminist group the **Mujeres Libres**. [Robert Alexander, **Op. Cit.**, p. 406, p. 670 and pp. 665-8 and p. 670]

Ultimately, the public services that exist in a social anarchist society will be dependent on what members of that society desire. If, for example, a commune or federation of communes desires a system of communal health-care or schools then they will allocate resources to implement it. They will allocate the task of creating such a system to, say, a special commission based on volunteers from the interested parties such as the relevant syndicates, professional associations, consumer groups and so on. For example, for communal education a commission or working group would include delegates from the teachers union, from parent associations, from student unions and so on. The running of such a system would be based, like any other industry, on those who work in it. Functional self-management would be the rule, with doctors managing their work, nurses theirs and so on, while the general running of, say, a hospital would be based on a general assembly of all workers there who would elect and mandate delegates, the administration staff and decide the policy the hospital would follow. Needless to say, other interested parties would have a say, including patients in the health system and students in the education system. As Malatesta argued:

> "And is it difficult to understand why there should be people who believe that the carrying out and the normal functioning of public services vital to our daily lives would be more reliable if carried out under the instructions of a government rather by the workers themselves who, by direct election or through agreements made with others, have chosen to do that kind of work and carry it out under the direct control of all the interested parties."
> [**Anarchy**, p. 41]

Needless to say, any system of public services would not be imposed on those who did not desire it. They would be organised for and by members of the communes. Therefore, individuals who were not part of a local commune or syndicate would have to pay to gain access to the communal resources. However, it is unlikely that an anarchist society would be as barbaric as a capitalist one and

refuse entry to cases who were ill and could not pay, nor turn away emergencies because they did not have enough money to pay. And just as other workers need not join a syndicate or commune, so doctors, teachers and so on could practice their trade outside the communal system as either individual artisans or as part of a co-operative. However, given the availability of free medical services it is doubtful they would grow rich doing so. Medicine, teaching and so on would revert back to what usually initially motivates people to take these up professions — the desire to help others and make a positive impact in peoples lives.

Thus, as would be expected, public services would be organised by the public, organised in their syndicates and communes. They would be based on workers' self-management of their daily work and of the system as a whole. Non-workers who took part in the system (patients, students) would not be ignored and would also play a role in providing essential feedback to assure quality control of services and to ensure that the service is responsive to users needs. The resources required to maintain and expand the system would be provided by the communes, syndicates and their federations. For the first time, public services would truly be public and not a statist system imposed upon the public from above nor a system by which the few fleece the many by exploiting natural monopolies for their own interests. Public Services in a free society will be organised by those who do the work and under the effective control of those who use them.

Finally, this vision of public services being run by workers' associations could be raised as a valid libertarian reform under capitalism (not to mention raising the demand to turn firms into co-operatives when they are bailed out during economic crisis). Equally, rather than nationalisation or privatisation, public utilities could be organised as a consumer co-operative (i.e., owned by those who use it) while the day-to-day running could be in the hands of a producer co-operative.

I.6
What about the "Tragedy of the Commons"?

The term *"Tragedy of the Commons"* is a phrase which is used to describe why, according to some, commonly owned resources will be destructively overused. The term was first coined by Garret Hardin in December 1968. [*"The Tragedy of the Commons"*, **Science**, Vol. 162, No. 3859, pp. 1243-1248] It quickly became popular with those arguing against any form of collective ownership or socialism and would be the basis for many arguments for privatisation.

Unsurprisingly, given its popularity with defenders of capitalism and neo-classical economists, Hardin's argument was a pure thought experiment with absolutely no empirical evidence to support it. He suggested a scenario in which commonly owned pasture was open to all local herdsmen to feed their cattle on. Hardin complemented this assumption with the standard ones of neo-classical economics, arguing that each herdsman would try to keep as many cattle as possible on the commons to maximise their income. This would result in overgrazing and environmental destruction as the cost of each feeding additional animals is shouldered by all who use the commons while the benefits accrue to the individual herdsman. However, what is individually rational becomes collectively irrational when each herdsman, acting in isolation, does the same thing. The net result of the individual's actions is the ending of the livelihood of **every** herdsman as the land becomes overused.

His article was used to justify both nationalisation and privatisation of communal resources (the former often a precursor for the latter). As state ownership fell out of favour, the lesson of this experiment in logic was as uniform as it was simple: only privatisation of common resources could ensure their efficient use and stop them being overused and destroyed. Coming as it did before the rise of neo-liberalism in the 1970s, Hardin's essay was much referenced by those seeking to privatise nationalised industries and eliminate communal institutions in tribal societies in the Third World. That these resulted in wealth being concentrated in a few hands should come as no surprise.

Needless to say, there are numerous problems with Hardin's analysis. Most fundamentally, it was a pure thought experiment and, as such, was not informed by historical or current practice. In other words, it did not reflect the reality of the commons as a social institution. The so-called *"Tragedy of the Commons"* was no such thing. It is actually an imposition of the *"tragedy of the free-for-all"* to communally owned resources (in this case, land). In reality, commons were **never** *"free for all"* resources and while the latter may see overuse and destruction the former managed to survive thousands of years. So, unfortunately for the supporters of private property who so regularly invoke the *"Tragedy of the Commons"*, they simply show their ignorance of what true commons are. As socialist Allan Engler points out:

> *"Supporters of capitalism cite what they call the tragedy of the commons to explain the wanton plundering of forests, fish and waterways, but common property is not the problem. When property was held in common by tribes, clans and villages, people took no more than their share and respected the rights of others. They cared for common property and when necessary acted together to protect it against those who would damage it. Under capitalism, there is no common property. (Public property is a form of private property, property owned by the government as a corporate person.) Capitalism recognises only private property and free-for-all property. Nobody is responsible for free-for-all property until someone claims it as his own. He then has a right to do as he pleases with it, a right that is uniquely capitalist. Unlike common or personal property, capitalist property is not valued for itself or for its utility. It is valued for the revenue it produces for its owner. If the capitalist owner can maximise his revenue by liquidating it, he has the right to do that."* [**Apostles of Greed**, pp. 58-59]

Therefore, as Colin Ward argues, *"[l]ocal, popular, control is the surest way of avoiding the tragedy of the commons."* [**Reflected in Water**, p. 20] Given that a social anarchist society is a communal, decentralised one, it will have little to fear from irrational overuse

or abuse of communally owned and used resources.

So, the **real** problem is that a lot of economists and sociologists conflate Hardin's scenario, in which **unmanaged** resources are free for all, with the situation that prevailed in the use of commons which were communally **managed** resources in village and tribal communities. Historian E.P. Thompson, for example, noted that Hardin was *"historically uninformed"* when he assumed that commons were pastures open to all. The commons, in reality, **were** managed by common agreements between those who used them. In an extensive investigation on this subject, Thompson showed that the *"argument [is] that since resources held in common are not owned and protected by anyone, there is an inexorable economic logic that dooms them to over-exploitation ... Despite its common sense air, what it overlooks is that commoners themselves were not without common sense. Over time and over space the users of commons have developed a rich variety of institutions and community sanctions which have effected restraints and stints upon use ... As the old ... institutions lapsed, so they fed into a vacuum in which political influence, market forces, and popular assertion contested with each other without common rules."* [**Customs in Common**, p. 108fn and p. 107] Colin Ward points to a more recent example, that of Spain after the victory of Franco:

> *"The water history of Spain demonstrates that the tragedy of the commons is not the one identified by Garrett Hardin. Communal control developed an elaborate and sophisticated system of fair shares for all. The private property recommended by Hardin resulted in the selfish individualism that he thought was inevitable with common access, or in the lofty indifference of the big landowners."* [**Op. Cit.**, p. 27]

So, for a while, Hardin's essay *"was taken to provide an argument for the privatisation of the commons. It is now a well-developed point that Hardin's argument is not a tragedy of common ownership at all ... Hardin's argument is a problem not of common ownership, but of open access in a context of private ownership of particular assets."* [John O'Neill, **Markets, Deliberation and Environment**, p. 54] Significantly, Hardin later admitted his mistake and noted that *"it is clear to me that the title of my original contribution should have been **The Tragedy of the** Unmanaged **Commons** ... I can understand how I might have misled others."* [quoted by O'Neill, **Op. Cit.**, p. 199] But, of course, by then the damage had been done.

There is something quite arrogant about Hardin's assertions, as he basically assumed that peasant farmers are unable to recognise certain disaster and change their behaviour accordingly. This, apparently, is where enlightened elites (governmental and economic) step in. However, in the real world, small farmers (and others) have created their own institutions and rules for preserving resources and ensuring that their community has the resources it needed to survive. Hardin, in other words, ignored what actually happens in a real commons, namely communal control and self-regulation by the communities involved who develop the appropriate communal institutions to do so.

Surely, the very obvious fact that humans have lived in societies with commons for centuries and did not overuse them disproves

Hardin's most fundamental assumptions. "*If we misunderstand the true nature of the commons,*" argues scientist Susan Jane Buck Cox "*we also misunderstand the implications of the demise of the traditional, commons system. Perhaps what existed in fact was not a 'tragedy of the commons' but rather a triumph: that for hundreds of years — and perhaps thousands, although written records do not exist to prove the longer era — land was managed successfully by communities.*" This suggests that it is a case of "*the myth of the tragedy of the commons*", rooted in an argument which is "*historically false*" as the "*commons were carefully and painstakingly regulated.*" She points to a wider issue, namely whether "*our perceptions of the nature of humankind are awry*" for "*it seems quite likely if 'economic man' had been managing the commons that tragedy really would have occurred,*" so "*perhaps someone else was running the common.*" ["*No Tragedy on the Commons*", pp. 49-61, **Environmental Ethics**, vol. 7, p. 60, p. 53, p. 56 and p. 61]

One economist has noted that the "tragedy of the commons" only makes sense once the assumption of neo-classical economics are taken for granted. If we assume atomised individuals accessing unmanaged lands then Hardin's conclusions automatically flow. However, "*if the property were **really** common, this would imply the necessary existence of institutional agreements … between the co-owners to establish the rules for decisions governing the management of the resource. To put it more clearly, for common property to be truly common property implies its existence as an institution.*" It is precisely these kinds of human institutions which neo-classical economics ignores and so "*the so-called 'tragedy of the commons' is more accurately considered 'the tragedy of a methodological individualism'*". As many critics note, there are numerous "*conceptual errors*" contained in the article and these "*have been repeated systematically by economists.*" In summary, "*the so-called tragedy of the commons has nothing to do with common property, but with unrestricted and unregulated access.*" [F. Aguilera-Klink, "*Some Notes on the Misuse of Classic Writings in Economics on the Subject of Common Property*", pp. 221-8, **Ecological Economics**, No. 9, p. 223, p. 221, p. 224 and p. 226]

Much the same can be said against those who argue that the experience of Stalinism in the Eastern Block and elsewhere shows that public property leads to pollution and destruction of natural resources. Such arguments also show a lack of awareness of what common property actually is (it is no co-incidence that the propertarian-right use such an argument). This is because the resources in question, as we discussed in section B.3.5, were **not** owned or managed in common — the fact that these countries were dictatorships excluded popular control of resources. Thus Stalinism does not, in fact, show the dangers of having commons or public ownership. Rather it shows the danger of not subjecting those who manage a resource to public control (and it is no co-incidence that the USA is far more polluted than Western Europe — in the USA, like in the USSR, the controllers of resources are not subject to popular control and so pass pollution on to the public). Stalinism shows the danger of state owned resource use (nationalisation) rather than commonly owned resource use (socialisation), particularly when the state in question is not under even the limited control of its subjects implied in representative democracy.

This confusion of public and state owned resources has, of course, been used to justify the stealing of communal property by the rich and the state. The continued acceptance of this "confusion" in political debate, like the continued use of Hardin's original and flawed "Tragedy of the Commons", is due to the utility of the theory for the rich and powerful, who have a vested interest in undermining pre-capitalist social forms and stealing communal resources. Most examples used to justify the "*tragedy of the commons*" are **false** examples, based on situations in which the underlying social context is assumed to be radically different from that involved in using true commons.

In reality, the "*tragedy of the commons*" comes about only after wealth and private property, backed by the state, starts to eat into and destroy communal life. This is well indicated by the fact that commons existed for thousands of years and only disappeared after the rise of capitalism — and the powerful central state it requires — had eroded communal values and traditions. Without the influence of wealth concentrations and the state, people get together and come to agreements over how to use communal resources and have been doing so for millennia. That was how the commons were successfully managed before the wealthy sought to increase their holdings and deny the poor access to land in order to make them fully dependent on the power and whims of the owning class.

Thus, as Kropotkin stressed, the state "*systematically weeded out all institutions in which the mutual-aid tendency had formerly found its expression. The village communities were bereft of their folkmotes, their courts and independent administration; their lands were confiscated.*" [**Mutual Aid**, p. 182] The possibilities of free discussion and agreement were destroyed in the name of "absolute" property rights and the power and authority which goes with them. Both political influence and market forces were, and are, dominated by wealth: "*There were two occasions that dictated absolute precision: a trial at law and a process of enclosure. And both occasions favoured those with power and purses against the little users.*" Popular assertion meant little when the state enforces property rights in the interests of the wealthy. Ultimately, "*Parliament and law imposed capitalist definitions to exclusive property in land.*" [Thompson, **Op. Cit.**, p. 134 and p. 163] As Cox suggested, many tenants were "*denied [their] remedy at law for the illegal abuses of the more powerful landowners*" and "*[s]ponsored by wealthy landowners, the land reform was frequently no more than a sophisticated land-grab.*" [**Op. Cit.**, p. 58 and p. 59] Gerrard Winstanley, the Digger (and proto-anarchist), was only expressing a widespread popular sentiment when he complained that "*in Parishes where Commons lie the rich Norman Freeholders, or the new (more covetous) Gentry overstock the Commons with sheep and cattle, so that the inferior Tenants and poor labourers can hardly keep a cow but half starve her.*" [quoted by Maurice Dobb, **Studies in the Development of Capitalism**, p. 173] The working class is only "left alone" to starve.

As discussed in section F.8, the enclosures were part of a wider state-imposition of capitalism onto society. Of course, enclosure was often justified by supporters of capitalism by the increased productivity which, they claim, resulted from it (in effect, repeating Locke's earlier, and flawed, argument — see section B.3.4). There are three objections to this. First, it cannot be assumed that increased productivity could not be achieved by keeping the commons and by the commoners applying the improved techniques and technologies that contributed to any post-enclosure increased productivity. Second, it ignores the key issue of liberty and replaces it with property (increases in wealth being considered more important than reducing the freedom of the working class). Third, and more importantly, this paternalistic rationale for coercion and state action does not fit well with such apologist's opposition to (certain forms of) state intervention today (such as taxation or popular land reform). If the "ends justify the means" (which is what their arguments boil down to) when applied to the rural working class, then they have little basis for opposing taxation of the wealthy elite or pro-worker land-reform in a democracy or a popular social revolution.

To conclude. The "tragedy of the commons" argument is conceptually flawed and empirically wrong (unsurprising, given that no actual empirical evidence was presented to support the argument). Sadly, this has not stopped Hardin, or those inspired by his arguments, from suggesting policies based on a somewhat dubious understanding of history and humanity. Perhaps this is not that surprising, given that Hardin's assumptions (which drive his conclusions) are based not on actual people nor historical evidence but rather by fundamental components of capitalist economic theory. While under capitalism, and the short-termism imposed by market forces, you could easily imagine that a desire for profit would outweigh a person's interest in the long-term survival of their community, such a perspective is relatively recent in human history.

In fact, communal ownership produces a strong incentive to protect such resources for people are aware that their offspring will need them and so be inclined to look after them. By having more resources available, they would be able to resist the pressures of short-termism and so resist maximising current production without regard for the future. Capitalist owners have the opposite incentive for, as argued in section E.3, unless they maximise short-term profits then they will not be around in the long-term (so if wood means more profits than centuries-old forests then the trees will be chopped down). By combining common ownership with decentralised and federated communal self-management, anarchism will be more than able to manage resources effectively, avoiding the pitfalls of both privatisation and nationalisation.

I.6.1 How can property "owned by everyone in the world" be used?

First, we need to point out the fallacy normally lying behind this objection. It is assumed that because everyone owns something, then everyone has to be consulted in what it is used for. This, however, applies the logic of private property to non-capitalist social forms. While it is true that everyone owns collective "property" in an anarchist society, it does not mean that everyone **uses** it. Carlo Cafiero, one of the founders of communist-anarchism, stated the obvious:

> "The common wealth being scattered right across the planet, while belonging by right to the whole of humanity, those who happen to be within reach of that wealth and in

a position to make use of it will utilise it in common. The folk from a given country will use the land, the machines, the workshops, the houses, etc., of that country and they will all make common use of them. As part of humanity, they will exercise here, in fact and directly, their rights over a portion of mankind's wealth. But should an inhabitant of Peking visit this country, he [or she] would enjoy the same rights as the rest: in common with the others, he would enjoy all the wealth of the country, just as he [or she] would have in Peking." [**No Gods, No Masters**, vol. 1, p. 250]

Anarchists, therefore, think that those who **use** a part of society's wealth have the most say in what happens to it (e.g., workers control the means of production they use and the work they do when using it). This does not mean that those using it can do what they like to it. Users would be subject to recall by local communities if they are abusing their position (for example, if a workplace were polluting the environment, then the local community could act to stop or, if need be, close down the workplace). Thus use rights (or usufruct) replace property rights in a free society, combined with a strong dose of *"think globally, act locally."*

It is no coincidence that societies that are stateless are also without private property. As Murray Bookchin pointed out *"an individual appropriation of goods, a personal claim to tools, land, and other resources … is fairly common in organic [i.e. aboriginal] societies … By the same token, co-operative work and the sharing of resources on a scale that could be called communistic is also fairly common … But primary to both of these seemingly contrasting relationships is the practice of* **usufruct.**" Such stateless societies are based upon *"the principle of* **usufruct**, *the freedom of individuals in a community to appropriate resources merely by the virtue of the fact they are using them … Such resources belong to the user as long as they are being used. Function, in effect, replaces our hallowed concept of possession."* [**The Ecology of Freedom**, p. 116] The future stateless society anarchists hope for would also be based upon such a principle.

In effect, critics of social anarchism confuse property with possession and think that abolishing property automatically abolishes possession and use rights. However, as argued in section B.3, property and possession are distinctly different. In the words of Charlotte Wilson:

> "**Property** is the **domination** of an individual, or a coalition of individuals, over things; it is not the claim of any person or persons to the use of things — this is, usufruct, a very different matter. Property means the monopoly of wealth, the right to prevent others using it, whether the owner needs it or not. Usufruct implies the claim to the use of such wealth as supplies the users needs. If any individual shuts of a portion of it (which he is not using, and does not need for his own use) from his fellows, he is defrauding the whole community." [**Anarchist Essays**, p. 40]

Thus an anarchist society has a simple and effective means of deciding how communally owned resources are used, one based on possession and usufruct. The key thing to remember, as discussed in section I.3.3, is that socialisation means that **access** is free: users of a resource are not subjected to hierarchical social relationships in order to use it. Socialisation does not mean that people can, say, wander into someone's workplace and simply take away a machine or computer. Rather, it means that when someone joins a workplace they are sharing in the use of a common resource and do so as a free and equal associate rather than as an obedient wage-slave. If a resource is not being used, then they have free access to use it. If it is being used then it will be managed by those who use it, with access granted in agreed ways which ensure egalitarian, and so free, relationships and outcomes.

As for deciding what a given area of commons is used for, that falls to the local communities who live next to them. If, for example, a local self-managed factory wants to expand and eat into the commons, then the local community who uses (and so controls) the local commons would discuss it and come to an agreement concerning it. If a minority **really** objects, they can use direct action to put their point across. But anarchists argue that rational debate among equals will not result in too much of that. Or suppose an individual wanted to set up an allotment in a given area, which had not been allocated as a park. Then he or she would notify the community assembly by appropriate means (e.g. on a notice board or newspaper), and if no one objected at the next assembly or in a set time-span, the allotment would go ahead, as no one else desired to use the resource in question.

Other communities would be confederated with this one, and joint activity would also be discussed by debate, with a community (like an individual) being free **not** to associate if they so desire. Other communities could and would object to ecologically and individually destructive practices. The interrelationship of ecosystems and freedom is well known, and it is doubtful that free individuals would sit back and let some amongst them destroy **their** planet.

Therefore, those who use something control it. This means that "users groups" would be created to manage resources used by more than one person. For workplaces this would (essentially) be those who worked there (with, possibly, the input of consumer groups and co-operatives). Housing associations made up of tenants would manage housing and repairs. Resources that are used by associations within society, such as communally owned schools, workshops, computer networks, and so forth, would be managed on a day-to-day basis by those who use them. User groups would decide access rules (for example, time-tables and booking rules) and how they are used, making repairs and improvements. Such groups would be accountable to their local community. Hence, if that community thought that any activities by a group within it was destroying communal resources or restricting access to them, the matter would be discussed at the relevant assembly. In this way, interested parties manage their own activities and the resources they use (and so would be very likely to have an interest in ensuring their proper and effective use), but without private property and its resulting hierarchies and restrictions on freedom.

Lastly, let us examine clashes of use rights, i.e. cases where two or more people, communes or syndicates desire to use the same resource. In general, such problems can be resolved by discussion and decision making by those involved. This process would be roughly as follows: if the contesting parties are reasonable, they would probably mutually agree to allow their dispute to be settled by some mutual friend whose judgement they could trust, or they would place it in the hands of a jury, randomly selected from the community or communities in question. This would take place only if they could not come to an agreement between themselves to share the resource in question.

On thing is certain, however, such disputes are much better settled without the interference of authority or the re-creation of private property. If those involved do not take the sane course described above and instead decide to set up an authority, disaster will be the inevitable result. In the first place, this authority will have to be given power to enforce its judgement in such matters. If this happens, the new authority will undoubtedly keep for itself the best of what is disputed (as payment for services rendered, of course!). If private property were re-introduced, such authoritarian bodies would develop sooner, rather than later, with two new classes of oppressors being created — the property owners and the enforcers of "justice." Ultimately, it is strange to think that two parties who meet on terms of equality and disagree could not be reasonable or just, and that a third party with power backed up by violence will be the incarnation of justice itself. Common sense should warn us against such an illusion and, if common sense is lacking, then history shows that using authority or property to solve disputes is not wise!

And, we should note, it is equally as fallacious, as Leninists suggest, that only centralisation can ensure common access and common use. Centralisation, by removing control from the users into a body claiming to represent "society", replaces the dangers of abuse by a small group of workers with the dangers of abuse by a bureaucracy invested with power and authority over **all**. If members of a commune or syndicate can abuse their position and restrict access for their own benefit, so can the individuals who make up the bureaucracy gathered round a centralised body (whether that body is, in theory, accountable by election or not). Indeed, it is far more likely to occur as the experience of Leninism shows beyond doubt. Thus **decentralisation** is the key to common ownership and access, **not** centralisation.

Communal ownership needs communal structures in order to function. Use rights, and discussion among equals, replace property rights in a free society. Freedom cannot survive if it is caged behind laws enforced by public or private states.

I.6.2 Doesn't communal ownership involve restricting individual liberty?

This point is expressed in many different forms. John Henry MacKay (an individualist anarchist) put the point as follows:

> "*Would you [the social anarchist], in the system of society which you call 'free Communism' prevent individuals from exchanging their labour among themselves by means of their own medium of exchange? And further: Would*

you prevent them from occupying land for the purpose of personal use?' ... [The] question was not to be escaped. If he answered 'Yes!' he admitted that society had the right of control over the individual and threw overboard the autonomy of the individual which he had always zealously defended; if on the other hand he answered 'No!' he admitted the right of private property which he had just denied so emphatically." [**Patterns of Anarchy**, p. 31]

However, anarchist theory has a simple and clear answer to this question. To see what this answer is, it simply a case of remembering that use rights replace property rights in an anarchist society. In other words, individuals can exchange their labour as they see fit and occupy land for their own use. This in no way contradicts the abolition of private property, because occupancy and use is directly opposed to private property (see section B.3). Socialisation is rooted in this concept of *"occupancy and use"* and this means that in a free communist society individuals can occupy and use whatever land and such tools and equipment as they need — they do not have to join the free communist society (see section I.5.7). If they do not, however, they cannot place claims on the benefits others receive from co-operation and communal life.

This can be seen from Charlotte Wilson's discussions on anarchism written a few years before MacKay published his *"inescapable"* question. She asks the question: *"Does Anarchism ... then ... acknowledge ... no personal property?"* She answers by noting that *"every man [or woman] is free to take what he [or she] requires"* and so *"it is hardly conceivable that personal necessaries and conveniences will not be appropriated"* by individual's for their personal consumption and use. For *"[w]hen property is protected by no legal enactments, backed by armed force, and is unable to buy personal service, its resuscitation on such a scale as to be dangerous to society is little to be dreaded. The amount appropriated by each individual ... must be left to his [or her] own conscience, and the pressure exercised upon him [or her] by the moral sense and distinct interests of his [or her] neighbours."* This system of *"usufruct"* would also apply to the *"instruments of production — land included"*, being *"free to all workers, or groups of workers"* for *"as long as land and capital are unappropriated, the workers are free, and that, when these have a master, the workers also are slaves."* [**Anarchist Essays**, p. 24 and p. 21] This is because, as with all forms of anarchism, communist-anarchism bases itself on the distinction between property and possession.

In other words, **possession** replaces private property in a free society. This applies to those who decide to join a free communist society and those who desire to remain outside. This is clear from the works of many leading theorists of free communism (as indicated in section G.2.1), none of whom thought the occupying of land for personal use (or a house or the means of production) entailed the *"right of private property."* For example, looking at land we find both Kropotkin and Proudhon arguing along the same lines. For the former: *"Who, then, can appropriate for himself the tiniest plot of ground ... without committing a flagrant injustice?"* [**Conquest of Bread**, p. 90] For the latter: *"The land cannot be appropriated"*. Neither denied that individuals could **use** the land or other resources, simply that it could not be turned into private property.

Thus Proudhon: *"Every occupant is, then, necessarily a possessor or usufructuary, — a function that excludes proprietorship."* [**Property is Theft!**, p. 103 and p. 100] Obviously John Henry MacKay, unlike Kropotkin, had not read his Proudhon! As Wilson argued:

> *"Proudhon's famous dictum, 'Property is theft', is the key to the equally famous enigma ... 'From each according to his capacities, to each according to his needs'. When the workers clearly understand that in taking possession of railways and ships, mines and fields, farm buildings and factories, raw material and machinery, and all else they need for their labour, they are claiming the right to use freely for the benefit of society, what social labour has created, or utilised in the past, and that, in return for their work, they have a just right to take from the finished product whatever they personally require."* [**Op. Cit.**, pp. 20-1]

This can be seen from libertarian communist William Morris and his account of Proudhon. Morris classed the French anarchist as *"the most noteworthy figure"* of a group of *"Socialist thinkers who serve as a kind of link between the Utopians and the school of ... scientific Socialists."* As far as his critique of property went, Morris argued that in **What is Property?** Proudhon's *"position is that of a Communist pure and simple."* [**Political Writings**, p. 569 and p. 570]

Unsurprisingly, then, we find Kropotkin arguing that *"[a]ll things belong to all, and provided that men and women contribute their share of labour for the production of necessary objects, they are entitled to their share of all that is produced by the community at large."* He went on to state that *"free Communism ... places the products reaped or manufactured in common at the disposal of all, leaving to each the liberty to consume them as he [or she] pleases in his [or her] own home."* [**The Place of Anarchism in Socialistic Evolution,**, p. 6 and p. 7] This obviously implies a situation of *"occupancy and use"* (with those who are actually using a resource controlling it).

This support for possession does not, of course, imply any contradiction with communism as MacKay suggested. The aim of communism is to place the fruits of society at the disposal of society, to be used and consumed as the members of that society desire. As such, individuals are **not** stopped from taking and using the goods produced and, obviously, this automatically means "excluding" others from using and consuming them. This in no way implies the recreation of private property in any meaningful sense. Significantly, this perspective has been pretty commonplace in human society and numerous authors have pointed out *"how many languages lack any verb for unilateral ownership."* [David Graeber, **Possibilities**, p. 23]

For example, a group of friends go on a picnic and share the food stuffs they bring. If someone takes an apple from the common bounty and eats it, then obviously it is no longer available for others to eat. However, this does not change the common ownership of foodstuffs the picnic is based on. Similarly, in a communist society people would still have their own homes and, of course, would have the right to restrict entry to just those whom they have invited. People would not come in from the street and take up residence in the main bedroom on the dubious rationale that it is not being used as the inhabitant is watching TV in the lounge, is on holiday or visiting friends.

Thus communism is based on the obvious fact that individuals will "appropriate" (use) the products of society to satisfy their own needs (assuming they can find someone who needs to produce it). What it does, though, is to deprive individuals of the ability to turn possession into private property and, as a result, subjugate others to their will by means of wage labour or landlordism.

In other words, possession (personal "property") is not transformed into social property. Hence the communist support for individuals **not** joining the commune, working their land or tools and living by their own hands. Being based on **possession**, this is utterly compatible with communist principles and the abolition of private property. This is because people are **using** the resources in question and for that simple reason are exercising the same rights as the rest of communist society. Thus the case of the non-member of free communism is clear — they would also have access to what they possessed and used such as the land, housing and means of production. The difference is that the non-communists would have to barter with the rest of society for goods rather than take what they need from the communal stores.

To re-iterate, the resources non-communists use do **not** become private property because they are being used and they revert back into common ownership once they are no longer occupied and used. In other words, **possession** replaces **property.** Thus communist-anarchists agree with Individualist Anarchist John Beverley Robinson when he wrote:

> "There are two kinds of land ownership, proprietorship or property, by which the owner is absolute lord of the land to use it or hold it out of use, as it may please him; and possession, by which he is secure in the tenure of land which he uses and occupies, but has no claim on it at all if he ceases to use it. For the secure possession of his crops or buildings or other products, he needs nothing but the possession of the land he uses." [**Patterns of Anarchy**, p. 273]

This system, we must note, was used in the rural collectives during the Spanish Revolution, with people free to remain outside the collective working only as much land and equipment as they could "occupy and use" by their own labour. Similarly, the individuals within the collective worked in common and took what they needed from the communal stores (see section I.8).

MacKay's comments raise another interesting point. Given that Individualist Anarchists oppose the current system of private property in land, **their** system entails that "society ha[s] the right of control over the individual." If we look at the "occupancy and use" land system favoured by the likes of Tucker, we discover that it is based on restricting property in land (and so the owners of land). As discussed in section G.1.2, the likes of Tucker looked forward to a time when public opinion (i.e., society) would limit the amount of land which individuals could acquire and so, from MacKay's perspective, controlling their actions and violating their autonomy. Which, we must say, is not surprising as individualism requires the supremacy of the rest of society over the individual in terms of rules relating to the ownership and use of possessions (or "property") — as the Individualist Anarchists themselves implicitly acknowledge.

MacKay goes on to state that "every serious man must declare himself: for Socialism, and thereby for force and against liberty, or for Anarchism, and thereby for liberty and against force." [**Op. Cit.**, p. 32] Which, we must note, is a strange statement for, as indicated in section G.1, individualist anarchists like Benjamin Tucker considered themselves socialists and opposed capitalist private property (while, confusingly, many of them calling their system of possession "property").

However, MacKay's statement begs the question: does private property support liberty? He does not address or even acknowledge the fact that private property will inevitably lead to the owners of such property gaining control over the individuals who use, but do not own, it and so denying them liberty (see section B.4). As Proudhon argued:

> "The purchaser draws boundaries, fences himself in, and says, 'This is mine; each one by himself, each one for himself.' Here, then, is a piece of land upon which, henceforth, no one has right to step, save the proprietor and his friends; which can benefit nobody, save the proprietor and his servants. Let these multiply, and soon the people … will have nowhere to rest, no place of shelter, no ground to till. They will die of hunger at the proprietor's door, on the edge of that property which was their birth-right; and the proprietor, watching them die, will exclaim, 'So perish idlers and vagrants.'" [**Op. Cit.**, p. 111]

Of course, as Proudhon suggested, the non-owner can gain access to the property by becoming a servant, by selling their liberty to the owner and agreeing to submit to the owner's authority. Little wonder that he argued that the "second effect of property is despotism." [**Op. Cit.**, p. 259] As discussed in section G.4.1, this points to a massive contradiction in any form of individualist anarchism which defends private property which goes beyond possession and generates wage-labour. This is because both the state and the property owner **both** assume sole authority over a given area and all within it. Little wonder Emile Pouget, echoing Proudhon, argued that:

> "Property and authority are merely differing manifestations and expressions of one and the same 'principle' which boils down to the enforcement and enshrinement of the servitude of man. Consequently, the only difference between them is one of vantage point: viewed from one angle, slavery appears as a **property crime**, whereas, viewed from a different angle, it constitutes an **authority crime.**" [**No Gods, No Masters**, vol. 2, p. 66]

So the issue changes if someone claims more resources than they can use as individuals or as a co-operative group. If they are attempting to restrict access to others of resources they are not using then the others are entitled to simply ignore the pretensions of the would-be monopoliser. Without a state to enforce capitalist property rights, attempts to recreate private property will flounder in the laughter of their neighbours as these free people defend their liberty by ignoring the would-be capitalist's attempts to subjugate the labour of others for their own benefit by monopolising the means of life. Unsurprisingly, MacKay does not address the fact that private property requires extensive force (i.e. a state) to protect it against those who use it or could use it but do not own it.

So MacKay ignores two important aspects of private property. Firstly, that private property is based upon force, which must be used to ensure the owner's right to exclude others (the main reason for the existence of the state). And secondly, he ignores the anti-libertarian nature of "property" when it creates wage labour — the other side of "private property" — in which the liberty of employees is obviously restricted by the owners whose property they are hired to use. Unlike in a free communist society, in which members of a commune have equal rights, power and say within a self-managed association, under "private property" the owner of the property governs those who use it. When the owner and the user is identical, this is not a problem (i.e. when possession replaces property) but once possession becomes property then despotism, as Proudhon noted, is created. As Charlotte Wilson put it:

> "Property — not the claim to use, but to a right to prevent others from using — enables individuals who have appropriated the means of production, to hold in subjection all those who possess nothing ... and who must work that they may live. No work is possible without land, materials, and tools or machinery; thus the masters of those things are the masters also of the destitute workers, and can live in idleness upon their labour... We look for th[e] socialisation of wealth, not to restraints imposed by authority upon property, but to the removal, by direct personal action of the people themselves, of the restraints which secure property against the claims of popular justice. For authority and property are both manifestations of the egoistical spirit of domination".
> [**Op. Cit.**, pp. 57-8]

Therefore, it seems that in the name of "liberty" John Henry MacKay and a host of other "individualists" end up supporting authority and (effectively) some kind of state. This is hardly surprising as private property is the opposite of personal possession, not its base. In summary, then, far from communal property restricting individual liberty (or even personal use of resources) it is in fact its only defence. That is why all anarchists would agree with Emma Goldman that "it is our endeavour to abolish private property, State ... we aim to free men from tyrants and government." [**A Documentary History of the American Years**, vol. 1, p. 181]

I.7
Won't Libertarian Socialism destroy individuality?

No. Libertarian socialism only suppresses individuality for those who are so shallow that they cannot separate their identity from what they own. However, be that as it may, this is an important objection to any form of socialism and, given the example of "socialist" Russia, needs to be discussed more.

The basic assumption behind this question is that capitalism encourages individuality, but this assumption can be faulted on many levels. As Kropotkin noted, "individual freedom [has] remained, both in theory and in practice, more illusory than real" and that the "want of development of the personality (leading to herd-psychology) and the lack of individual creative power and initiative are certainly one of the chief defects of our time. Economical individualism has not kept its promise: it did not result in any striking development of individuality." [**Ethics**, p. 27 and p. 28] In effect, modern capitalism has reduced individuality to a parody of what it could and should be (see section I.7.4). Little wonder Emma Goldman argued that:

> "The oft repeated slogan of our time is ... that ours is an era of individualism ... Only those who do not probe beneath the surface might be led to entertain this view. Have not the few accumulated the wealth of the world? Are they not the masters, the absolute kings of the situation? Their success, however, is due not to individualism, but the inertia, the cravenness, the utter submission of the mass. The latter wants but to be dominated, to be led, to be coerced. As to individualism, at no time in human history did it have less chance of expression, less opportunity to assert itself in a normal, healthy manner." [**Anarchism and Other Essays**, pp. 70-1]

So we see a system which is apparently based on "egotism" and "individualism" but whose members are free to be standardised individuals, who hardly express their individuality at all. Far from increasing individuality, capitalism standardises it and so restricts it — that it survives at all is more an expression of the strength of humanity than any benefits of the capitalist system. This impoverishment of individuality is hardly surprising in a society based on hierarchical institutions which are designed to assure obedience and subordination. Given this, it comes as no surprise to find libertarian communists like Kropotkin suggesting that "as for knowing what will be the essence of **individual** development, I do not think it **could** be along individualist lines. Individual — yes, without doubt, but individ**ualist** — I have my doubts. That would mean: **narrow egoism** — regressive evolution and even that would be limited to a certain number." [quoted by Ruth Kinna, "Kropotkin's theory of Mutual Aid in Historical Context", pp. 259-283, **International Review of Social History**, No. 40, p. 268] Anarchist organisations and tactics are designed to promote individuality. They are decentralised, participatory organisations and so they give those involved the "social space" required to express themselves and develop their abilities and potential in ways restricted under capitalism. As Gaston Leval noted in his book on the anarchist collectives during the Spanish Revolution, *"so far as collective life is concerned, the freedom of each is the right to participate spontaneously with one's thought, one's will, one's initiative to the full extent of one's capacities. A negative liberty is not liberty; it is nothingness."* [**Collectives in the Spanish Revolution**, p. 346]

By being able to take part in and manage the decision making processes which directly affect you, your ability to think for yourself is increased and so you are constantly developing your abilities and personality. The spontaneous activity described by Leval has important psychological impacts. Thus Erich Fromm: *"In all spontaneous activity, the individual embraces the world. Not only does his [sic] individual self remain intact; it becomes stronger and more solidified.* ***For the self is as strong as it is active.***" [**Escape from Freedom**, p. 225]

Therefore, individuality does not atrophy within an anarchist organisation as it does under capitalism. It will become stronger as people participate and act within the social organisation. In other words, individuality requires community. As German philosopher and sociologist Max Horkheimer once observed, *"individuality is impaired when each man decides to fend for himself … The absolutely isolated individual has always been an illusion. The most esteemed personal qualities, such as independence, will to freedom, sympathy, and the sense of justice, are social as well as individual virtues. The fully developed individual is the consummation of a fully developed society."* [**The Eclipse of Reason**, p. 135]

The sovereign, self-sufficient individual is as much a product of a healthy community as it is of individual self-realisation and the fulfilment of desire. There is a tendency for **community** to enrich and develop **individuality**, with this tendency being seen throughout human history. This suggests that the abstract individualism of capitalism is more the exception than the rule in social life. In other words, history indicates that by working together with others as equals individuality is strengthened far more than in the so-called "individualism" associated with capitalism. Hence the need, as Murray Bookchin put it, to *"arrest the ravaging and simplification of the human spirit, of human personality, of human community, of humanity's idea of the good."* [**The Ecology of Freedom**, p. 409]

Communal support for individuality is hardly surprising as individuality is a product of the interaction between **social** forces and individual attributes. The more an individual cuts themselves off from social life, the more likely their individuality will suffer. This can be seen from the 1980s when neo-liberal governments supporting the individualism associated with free market capitalism were elected in both Britain and the USA. The promotion of market forces lead to social atomisation, social disruption and a more centralised state. As this swept across society, the resulting disruption of social life ensured that many individuals became impoverished ethically and culturally as society became increasingly privatised. Two decades later, David Cameron, the leader of the Conservative party, complained of a broken society in Britain while, of course, skilfully avoiding discussing the neo-liberal reforms imposed by his predecessor Thatcher which made it so.

In other words, many of the characteristics which we associate with

a developed individuality (namely ability to think, to act, to hold your own opinions and standards and so forth) are (essentially) **social** skills and are encouraged by a well developed community. Remove that social background and these valued aspects of individuality are undermined by lack of use, fear of authority, atomisation and limited social interaction. Taking the case of workplaces, for example, surely it is an obvious truism that a hierarchical working environment will marginalise the individual and ensure that they cannot express their opinions, exercise their thinking capacities to the full or manage their own activity. This will have in impact in all aspects of an individual's life.

Hierarchy in all its forms produces oppression and a crushing of individuality (see section B.1). In such a system, as left-wing classical liberal John Stuart Mill argued, the *"business"* side of group activities would be *"properly carried out"* but at the expense of the individuals involved. Anarchists agree with Mill when he called it *"benevolent dictatorship"* and asked *"what sort of human beings can be formed under such a regimen? What development can either their thinking or their active faculties attain under it? … Their moral capacities are equally stunted. Wherever the sphere of action of human beings is artificially circumscribed, their sentiments are narrowed and dwarfed."* [**Representative Government**, pp. 203-4] Like anarchists, he extended his critique of political organisations into all forms of associations and stated that if *"mankind is to continue to improve"* then in the end one form of association will predominate, *"not that which can exist between a capitalist as chief, and workpeople without a voice in the management, but the association of labourers themselves on terms of equality, collectively owning the capital with which they carry on their operations, and working under managers elected and removable by themselves."* [**The Principles of Political Economy**, p. 147]

Hence, anarchism will protect and develop individuality by creating the means by which all individuals can participate in the decisions that affect them, in all aspects of their lives. Anarchism is built upon the central assertion that individuals and their institutions cannot be considered in isolation from one another. Authoritarian organisations will create a servile personality, one that feels safest conforming to authority and what is considered normal. A libertarian organisation, one that is based upon participation and self-management will encourage a strong personality, one that knows its own mind, thinks for itself and feels confident in its own powers.

Therefore, as Bakunin argued, liberty *"is not a fact springing from isolation but from reciprocal action, a fact not of exclusion, but, on the contrary, of social interaction — for freedom of every individual is simply the reflection of his humanity or his human right in the consciousness of all free men, his brothers, his equals."* Freedom *"is something very positive, very complex, and above all eminently social, since it can be realised only by society and only under conditions of strict equality and solidarity."* Hierarchical power, by necessity, kills individual freedom as it is *"characteristic of privilege and of every privileged position to kill the minds and hearts of men"* and *"power and authority corrupt those who exercise them as much as those who are compelled to submit to them."* [**The Political Philosophy of Bakunin**, p. 266, p. 268, p. 269 and p. 249]

A libertarian re-organisation of society will be based upon, and encourage, a self-empowerment and self-liberation of the individual and by participation within self-managed organisations individuals will educate themselves for the responsibilities and joys of freedom. As Carole Pateman points out, *"participation develops and fosters the very qualities necessary for it; the more individuals participate the better able they become to do so."* [**Participation and Democratic Theory**, pp. 42-43] This, of course, implies a mutually interactive transformation of individuals, their social relationships and organisations (in the words of Spanish anarchist Garcia Oliver: *"Who hasn't been changed by the revolution? It wouldn't be worth making it just to continue being the same."* [quoted by Abel Paz, **Durruti in the Spanish Revolution**, p. 498]).

Such a re-organisation (as we will see in section J.2) is based upon the tactic of **direct action.** This tactic also encourages individuality by encouraging the individual to fight for themselves, by their own self-activity, that which they consider to be wrong. As Voltairine de Cleyre put it:

> *"Every person who ever thought he had a right to assert, and went boldly and asserted it, himself, or jointly with others that shared his convictions, was a direct actionist ...*
>
> *Every person who ever had a plan to do anything, and went and did it, or who laid his plan before others, and won their co-operation to do it with him, without going to external authorities to please do the thing for them, was a direct actionist. All co-operative experiments are essentially direct action.*
>
> *"Every person who ever in his life had a difference with anyone to settle, and want straight to the other persons involved to settle it ... was a direct actionist. Examples of such action are strikes and boycotts ...*
>
> *"These actions ... are the spontaneous retorts of those who feel oppressed by a situation."* [**The Voltairine de Cleyre Reader**, pp. 47-8]

Therefore, anarchist tactics base themselves upon self-assertion and this can only develop individuality. Self-activity can only occur when there is a independent, free-thinking self. As self-management is based upon the principle of direct action (*"all co-operative experiments are essentially direct action"*) we can suggest that individuality will have little to fear from an anarchist society. Indeed, anarchists strongly stress the importance of individuality within a society. To quote communist-anarchist J. Burns-Gibson:

> *"to destroy individuality is to destroy society. For society is only realised and alive in the individual members. Society has no motive that does not issue from its individual members, no end that does not centre in them, no mind that is not theirs. 'Spirit of the age,' 'public opinion,' 'commonweal or good,' and like phrases have no meaning if they are thought of as features of something that hovers or floats between man and woman. They name what resides in and proceeds from individuals. Individuality and community, therefore, are equally constitutive of our idea of human life."* [quoted by William R. McKercher, **Freedom and Authority**, p. 31]

Little wonder, then, that anarchism *"recognises and values individuality which means character, conduct and the springs of conduct, free initiative, creativeness, spontaneity, autonomy."* [J. Burns-Gibson, quoted by McKercher, **Op. Cit.**, p. 31f] As Kropotkin put it, anarchism *"seeks the most complete development of individuality combined with the highest development of voluntary association in all its aspects … ever changing, ever modified"*. [**Anarchism**, p. 123]

For anarchists real liberty requires social equality: *"If individuals are to exercise the maximum amount of control over their own lives and environment then authority structures in these areas most be so organised that they can participate in decision making."* [Pateman, **Op. Cit.**, p. 43] Hence individuality will be protected, encouraged and developed in an anarchist society far more than in a class ridden, hierarchical society like capitalism. As Kropotkin argued:

> *"[Libertarian] Communism is the best basis for individual development and freedom; not that individualism which drives men to the war of each against all … but that which represents the full expansion of man's [and woman's] faculties, the superior development of what is original in him [or her], the greatest fruitfulness of intelligence, feeling and will."* [**Op. Cit.**, p. 141]

It is because wonders are so enriching to life, and none is more wonderful than individuality, that anarchists oppose capitalism in the name of socialism — libertarian socialism, the free association of free individuals.

I.8

Does revolutionary Spain show that libertarian socialism can work in practice?

Yes. Revolutionary Spain *"shows you what human beings are like when they are trying to behave as human beings and not as cogs in the capitalist machine."* [George Orwell, **Orwell in Spain**, p. 254] At the heart of the transformation were the CNT (the National Confederation of Labour, an anarcho-syndicalist union) and the FAI (Iberian Anarchist Federation). As Murray Bookchin put it:

> *"In Spain, millions of people took large segments of the economy into their own hands, collectivised them, administered them, even abolished money and lived by communistic principles of work and distribution — all of this in the midst of a terrible civil war, yet without producing the chaos or even the serious dislocations that were and still are predicted by authoritarian 'radicals.' Indeed, in many collectivised areas, the efficiency with which an enterprise worked by far exceeded that of a comparable one in nationalised or private sectors. This 'green shoot' of revolutionary reality has more meaning for us than the most persuasive theoretical arguments to the contrary. On this score it is not the anarchists who are*

the 'unrealistic day-dreamers,' but their opponents who have turned their backs to the facts or have shamelessly concealed them." ["Introductory Essay," **The Anarchist Collectives**, Sam Dolgoff (ed.), p. xxxix]

Anarchist and CNT activist Gaston Leval comments that in those areas which defeated the fascist uprising on the 19th of July 1936 a profound social revolution took place based, mostly, on anarchist ideas:

> "In Spain, during almost three years, despite a civil war that took a million lives, despite the opposition of the political parties ... this idea of libertarian communism was put into effect. Very quickly more than 60% of the land was collectively cultivated by the peasants themselves, without landlords, without bosses, and without instituting capitalist competition to spur production. In almost all the industries, factories, mills, workshops, transportation services, public services, and utilities, the rank and file workers, their revolutionary committees, and their syndicates reorganised and administered production, distribution, and public services without capitalists, high-salaried managers, or the authority of the state.
>
> "Even more: the various agrarian and industrial collectives immediately instituted economic equality in accordance with the essential principle of communism, 'From each according to his ability and to each according to his needs.' They co-ordinated their efforts through free association in whole regions, created new wealth, increased production (especially in agriculture), built more schools, and bettered public services. They instituted not bourgeois formal democracy but genuine grass roots functional libertarian democracy, where each individual participated directly in the revolutionary reorganisation of social life. They replaced the war between men, 'survival of the fittest,' by the universal practice of mutual aid, and replaced rivalry by the principle of solidarity ...
>
> "This experience, in which about eight million people directly or indirectly participated, opened a new way of life to those who sought an alternative to anti-social capitalism on the one hand, and totalitarian state bogus socialism on the other." [**Op. Cit.**, pp. 6-7]

Thus about eight million people directly or indirectly participated in the libertarian based new economy during the short time it was able to survive the military assaults of the fascists and the attacks and sabotage of the Communists and Republican state. This in itself suggests that libertarian socialist ideas are of a practical nature.

Lest the reader think that Leval and Bookchin are exaggerating the accomplishments and ignoring the failures of the Spanish collectives, in the following subsections we will present specific details and answer some objections often raised by misinformed critics. We will try to present an objective analysis of the revolution, its many successes, its strong and weak points, the mistakes made and possible lessons to be drawn from the experience, both from the successes and the failures. However, this will hardly do justice

to the collectivisation as it "assumed an infinite diversity of forms from village to village, and even in the different firms collectivised in the cities ... there was an element of improvisation and of the exceptional wartime conditions experienced by the country (i.e., the war against fascism) and the arrangements had their flaws as well as their good points." [Jose Peirats, **The CNT in the Spanish Revolution**, vol. 1, p. 223]

This libertarian influenced revolution has (generally) been ignored by historians, or its existence mentioned in passing. Some so-called historians and "objective investigators" have slandered it and lied about (when not ignoring) the role anarchists played in it. Communist histories are particularly unreliable (to use a polite word for their activities) but it seems that almost **every** political perspective has done this (including liberal, so-called right-wing "libertarian", Stalinist, Trotskyist, Marxist, and so on). So any attempt to investigate what actually occurred in Spain and the anarchists' role in it is subject to a great deal of difficulty. Moreover, the positive role that Anarchists played in the revolution and the positive results of our ideas when applied in practice are also downplayed, if not ignored. Indeed, the misrepresentations of the Spanish Anarchist movement are downright amazing (see Jerome R. Mintz's wonderful book **The Anarchists of Casa Viejas** and J. Romero Maura's article "The Spanish case" [**Anarchism Today**, J. Joll and D. Apter (eds.)] for a refutation of many of the standard assertions and distortions about the Spanish anarchist movement by historians). The myths generated by Marxists of various shades are, perhaps needless to say, the most extensive.

All we can do here is present a summary of the social revolution that took place and attempt to explode a few of the myths that have been created around the work of the CNT and FAI during those years. We must stress that this can be nothing but a short introduction to the Spanish Revolution. We concentrate on the economic and political aspects of the revolution as we cannot cover everything. However, we must mention the social transformations that occurred all across non-fascist Spain. The revolution saw the traditional social relationships between men and women, adults and children, individual and individual transformed, revolutionised in a libertarian way. CNT militant Abel Paz gave a good idea of what happened:

> "Industry is in the hands of the workers and all the production centres conspicuously fly the red and black flags as well as inscriptions announcing that they have really become collectives. The revolution seems to be universal. Changes are also evident in social relations. The former barriers which used to separate men and woman arbitrarily have been destroyed. In the cafes and other public places there is a mingling of the sexes which would have been completely unimaginable before. The revolution has introduced a fraternal character to social relations which has deepened with practice and show clearly that the old world is dead." [**Durruti: The People Armed**, p. 243]

The social transformation empowered individuals and these, in turn, transformed society. Anarchist militant Enriqueta Rovira presents a vivid picture of the self-liberation the revolution generated:

*"The atmosphere then, the feelings were very special. It was beautiful. A feeling of — how shall I say it — of power, not in the sense of domination, but in the sense of things being under **our** control, of under anyone's. Of **possibility**. We **had** everything. We had Barcelona: It was ours. You'd walk out in the streets, and they were ours — here, CNT; there, **comite** this or that. It was totally different. Full of possibility. A feeling that we could, together, really **do** something. That we could make things different."* [quoted by Martha A. Ackelsberg and Myrna Margulies Breithart, *"Terrains of Protest: Striking City Women"*, pp. 151-176, **Our Generation**, vol. 19, No. 1, pp. 164-5]

Moreover, the transformation of society that occurred during the revolution extended to all areas of life and work. For example, the revolution saw *"the creation of a health workers' union, a true experiment in socialised medicine. They provided medical assistance and opened hospitals and clinics."* [Juan Gomez Casas, **Anarchist Organisation: The History of the FAI**, p. 192] We discuss this example in some detail in section I.5.12 and so will not do so here. We simply stress that this section of the FAQ is just an introduction to what happened and does not (indeed, cannot) discuss all aspects of the revolution. We just present an overview, bringing out the libertarian aspects of the revolution, the ways workers' self-management was organised, how the collectives organised and what they did.

Needless to say, many mistakes were made during the revolution. We point out and discuss some of them in what follows. Moreover, much of what happened did not correspond exactly with what many people consider as the essential steps in a communist (libertarian or otherwise) revolution. Nor, it must be stressed, did much of it reflect the pre-revolution stated aims of the CNT itself. Economically, for example, the collectives themselves were an unexpected development, one which was based on libertarian principles but also reflected the reality of the situation the CNT militants found themselves in. Much the same can be said of the fact that few collectives reached beyond mutualism or collectivism in spite of the CNT seeking a libertarian communist economy. Politically, the fear of a fascist victory made many anarchists accept collaboration with the state as a lesser evil. However, to dismiss the Spanish Revolution because it did not meet the ideals laid out by a handful of revolutionaries beforehand would be sectarian and elitist nonsense. No working class revolution is pure, no mass struggle is without its contradictions, no attempt to change society is perfect. *"It is only those who do nothing who make no mistakes,"* as Kropotkin so correctly pointed out. [**Anarchism**, p. 143] The question is whether the revolution creates a system of institutions which will allow those involved to discuss the problems they face, change the decisions reached and correct any mistakes they make. In this, the Spanish Revolution clearly succeeded, creating organisations based on the initiative, autonomy and power of working class people.

For more information about the social revolution, Sam Dolgoff's anthology **The Anarchist Collectives** is an excellent starting place. Gaston Leval's **Collectives in the Spanish Revolution** is another essential text. Jose Peirats' **Anarchists in the Spanish Revolution** and his three volume quasi-official history **The CNT in the Spanish Revolution** are key works. Vernon Richards' **Lessons of the Spanish Revolution** is an excellent critical anarchist work on the revolution and the role of the anarchists. **Spain 1936-1939: Social Revolution and Counter-Revolution** (edited by Vernon Richards) is a useful collection of articles from the time. Abel Paz's **Durruti in the Spanish Revolution** is a classic biography of Spanish anarchism's most famous militant (this is an expanded version of his earlier **Durruti: The People Armed**). Emma Goldman's opinions on the Spanish Revolution are collected in **Vision on Fire**.

Robert Alexander's **The Anarchists in the Spanish Civil War** is a good general overview of the anarchist's role in the revolution and civil war, as is Burnett Bolloten's **The Spanish Civil War**. Daniel Guérin's anthology **No Gods, No Masters** has two sections on the Spanish Revolution, one specifically on the collectives. Noam Chomsky's excellent essay *"Objectivity and Liberal Scholarship"* indicates how liberal books on the Spanish Civil War can be misleading, unfair and essentially ideological in nature (this classic essay can be found in **Chomsky on Anarchism**, **The Chomsky Reader**, and **American Power and the New Mandarins**). George Orwell's **Homage to Catalonia** cannot be bettered as an introduction to the subject (Orwell was in the POUM militia at the Aragón Front and was in Barcelona during the May Days of 1937). This classic account is contained along with other works by Orwell about the conflict in the anthology **Orwell in Spain**. Murray Bookchin's **The Spanish Anarchists** is a useful history, but ends just as the revolution breaks out and so needs to be completed by his **To Remember Spain** and the essay *"Looking Back at Spain"*. Stuart Christie's **We, The Anarchists!** is an important history of the Iberian Anarchist Federation.

I.8.1 Is the Spanish Revolution inapplicable as a model for modern societies?

Quite the reverse. More urban workers took part in the revolution than in the countryside. So while it is true that collectivisation was extensive in rural areas, the revolution also made its mark in urban areas and in industry.

In total, the *"regions most affected"* by collectivisation *"were Catalonia and Aragón, where about 70 per cent of the workforce was involved. The total for the whole of Republican territory was nearly 800,000 on the land and a little more than a million in industry. In Barcelona workers' committees took over all the services, the oil monopoly, the shipping companies, heavy engineering firms such as Volcano, the Ford motor company, chemical companies, the textile industry and a host of smaller enterprises … Services such as water, gas and electricity were working under new management within hours of the storming of the Atarazanas barracks … a conversion of appropriate factories to war production meant that metallurgical concerns had started to produce armed cars by 22 July … The industrial workers of Catalonia were the most skilled in Spain … One of the most impressive feats of those early days was the resurrection of the public transport system at a time when the streets were still littered and barricaded."* Five days after the fighting had stopped, 700 tramcars rather than the usual 600, all painted in the black-and-red colours of the CNT-FAI, were operating in Barcelona. [Antony Beevor, **The Spanish Civil War**, pp. 91-2] About 75% of Spanish industry was concentrated in Catalonia, the stronghold of the anarchist labour movement, and widespread collectivisation of factories took place there. As Sam Dolgoff rightly observed, this *"refutes decisively the allegation that anarchist organisational principles are not applicable to industrial areas, and if at all, only in primitive agrarian societies or in isolated experimental communities."* [**The Anarchist Collectives**, pp. 7-8] According to Augustin Souchy:

> *"It is no simple matter to collectivise and place on firm foundations an industry employing almost a quarter of a million textile workers in scores of factories scattered in numerous cities. But the Barcelona syndicalist textile union accomplished this feat in a short time. It was a tremendously significant experiment. The dictatorship of the bosses was toppled, and wages, working conditions and production were determined by the workers and their elected delegates. All functionaries had to carry out the instructions of the membership and report back directly to the men on the job and union meetings. The collectivisation of the textile industry shatters once and for all the legend that the workers are incapable of administrating a great and complex corporation."*
> [**Op. Cit.**, p. 94]

Moreover, Spain in the 1930s was **not** a backward, peasant country, as is sometimes supposed. Between 1910 and 1930, the industrial working class more than doubled to over 2,500,000. This represented just over 26% of the working population (compared to 16% twenty years previously). In 1930, only 45% of the working population were engaged in agriculture. [Ronald Fraser, **The Blood of Spain**, p. 38] In Catalonia alone, 200,000 workers were employed in the textile industry and 70,000 in metal-working and machinery manufacturing. This was very different than the situation in Russia at the end of World War I, where the urban working class made up only 10% of the population.

Capitalist social relations had also penetrated the rural economy by the 1930s with agriculture oriented to the world market and approximately 90% of farmland in the hands of the bourgeoisie. [Fraser, **Op. Cit.**, p. 37] So by 1936 agriculture was predominately capitalist, with Spanish agribusiness employing large numbers of labourers who either did not own enough land to support themselves or were landless. The labour movement in the Spanish countryside in the 1930s was precisely based on this large population of rural wage-earners (the socialist UGT land workers union had 451,000 members in 1933, 40% of its total membership, for example). In Russia at the time of the revolution of 1917, agriculture mostly consisted of small farms on which peasant families worked mainly for their own subsistence, bartering or selling their surplus.

Therefore the Spanish Revolution cannot be dismissed as a product of a pre-industrial society. The urban collectivisations occurred predominately in the most heavily industrialised part of Spain and indicate that anarchist ideas are applicable to modern societies. Indeed, comforting Marxist myths aside, the CNT organised most of the unionised urban working class and agricultural workers were a minority of its membership (by 1936, the CNT was making inroads in Madrid, previously a socialist stronghold while the UGT main area of growth in the 1930s was with, ironically, rural workers). The revolution in Spain was the work (mostly) of rural and urban wage labourers (joined with poor peasants) fighting a well developed capitalist system.

In summary, then, the anarchist revolution in Spain has many lessons for revolutionaries in developed capitalist countries and cannot be dismissed as a product of industrial backwardness. The main strength of the anarchist movement was in urban areas and unsurprisingly, the social revolution took place in the most heavily industrialised areas as well as on the land.

I.8.2 How were the anarchists able to obtain mass popular support in Spain?

Revolutionary anarchism was introduced in Spain in 1868 by Giuseppi Fanelli, an associate of Michael Bakunin, and found fertile soil among both the workers and the peasants. Those historians who gleefully note that Bakunin sent someone who did not speak Spanish to spread his message in Spain forget how close the Latin languages are to each other. Fanelli was more than able to be understood by his Spanish and Catalan speaking hosts who, it should be noted, were already familiar with Proudhon's ideas.

The key reason why Bakunin's ideas gained such ready support in Spain was that they reflected ideas that they had already developed themselves. The peasants supported anarchism because of the rural tradition of Iberian collectivism which had existed for generations. The urban workers supported it because its ideas of direct action, solidarity and free federation of unions corresponded to their needs in their struggle against capitalism and the state. Neither needed to be told that capitalism was oppressive and exploitative or that the state existed to defend this class system. In addition, many Spanish workers were well aware of the dangers of centralisation and the republican tradition in Spain was very much influenced by federalist ideas (coming, in part, from Proudhon's work as popularised by Pi y Margall, soon to become the President of the first Republic). The movement spread back and forth between countryside and cities as urban based union organisers and anarchist militants visited villages and peasants and landless agricultural workers came to industrial cities, like Barcelona, looking for work.

Therefore, from the start anarchism in Spain was associated with the labour movement (as Bakunin desired) and so anarchists had a practical area to apply their ideas and spread the anarchist message. By applying their principles in everyday life, the anarchists in Spain ensured that anarchist ideas became commonplace and accepted in a large section of the population.

This acceptance of anarchism cannot be separated from the structure and tactics of the CNT and its forerunners. The practice of direct action and solidarity encouraged workers to rely on themselves, to identify and solve their own problems. The decentralised structure of the anarchist unions had an educational effect on their members. By discussing issues, struggles, tactics, ideals and politics in their union assemblies, the members of the union educated themselves and, by the process of self-management in the struggle, prepared themselves for a free society. The very organisational structure of the CNT ensured the dominance of anarchist ideas and the political evolution of the union membership. As one CNT militant from Casas Viejas put it, new members *"asked for too much, because they lacked education. They thought they could reach the sky without a ladder ... they were beginning to learn ... There was good faith but lack of education. For that reason we would submit ideas to the assembly, and the bad ideas would be thrown out."* [quoted by Jerome R. Mintz, **The Anarchists of Casas Viejas**, p. 27]

It was by working in the union meetings that anarchists influenced their fellow workers. The idea that the anarchists, through the FAI, controlled the CNT is a myth. Not all anarchists in the CNT were members of the FAI, for example, while FAI members were also rank-and-file members of the CNT who took part in union meetings as equals. Anarchists who were not members of the FAI indicate this. Jose Borras Casacarosa confirmed that *"[o]ne has to recognise that the FAI did not intervene in the CNT from above or in an authoritarian manner as did other political parties in the unions. It did so from the base through militants ... the decisions which determined the course taken by the CNT were taken under constant pressure from these militants."* Jose Campos noted that FAI militants *"tended to reject control of confederal committees and only accepted them on specific occasions ... if someone proposed a motion in assembly, the other FAI members would support it, usually successfully. It was the individual standing of the **faista** in open assembly."* [quoted by Stuart Christie, **We, the Anarchists**, p. 62]

This explains the success of anarchism in the CNT. Anarchist ideas, principles and tactics, submitted to the union assemblies, proved to be good ideas and were not thrown out. The structure of the organisation, in other words, decisively influenced the **content** of the decisions reached as ideas, tactics, union policy and so on were discussed by the membership and those which best applied to the members' lives were accepted and implemented. The CNT assemblies showed the validity of Bakunin's arguments for self-managed unions as a means of ensuring workers' control of their own destinies and organisations. As he put it, the union *"sections could defend their rights and their autonomy [against union bureaucracy] in only one way: the workers called general membership meetings ... In these great meetings of the sections, the items on the agenda were amply discussed and the most progressive opinion prevailed."* [**Bakunin on Anarchism**, p. 247] The CNT was built on such *"popular assemblies,"* with the same radicalising effect. It showed, in practice, that bosses (capitalist as well as union ones) were not needed — workers can manage their own affairs directly. As a school for anarchism it could not be bettered as it showed that anarchist principles were not utopian. The CNT, by being based on workers' self-management of the class struggle, prepared its members for self-management of the revolution and the new society.

The Spanish Revolution also shows the importance of anarchist education and media. In a country with a very high illiteracy rate,

huge quantities of literature on social revolution were disseminated and read out at meetings for those who could not read. Anarchist ideas were widely discussed: *"There were tens of thousands of books, pamphlets and tracts, vast and daring cultural and popular educational experiments (the Ferrer schools) that reached into almost every village and hamlet throughout Spain."* [Sam Dolgoff, **The Anarchist Collectives**, p. 27] The discussion of political, economic and social ideas was continuous, and *"the centro [local union hall] became the gathering place to discuss social issues and to dream and plan for the future. Those who aspired to learn to read and write would sit around ... studying."* [Mintz, **Op. Cit.**, p. 160] One anarchist militant described it as follows:

> *"With what joy the orators were received whenever a meeting was held ... We spoke that night about everything: of the ruling inequality of the regime and of how one had a right to a life without selfishness, hatred, without wars and suffering. We were called on another occasion and a crowd gathered larger than the first time. That's how the pueblo started to evolve, fighting the present regime to win something by which they could sustain themselves, and dreaming of the day when it would be possible to create that society some depict in books, others by word of mouth. Avid for learning, they read everything, debated, discussed, and chatted about the different modes of perfect social existence."* [Perez Cordon, quoted by Mintz, **Op. Cit.**, p. 158]

Newspapers and periodicals were extremely important. By 1919, more than 50 towns in Andalusia had their own libertarian newspapers. By 1934 the CNT had a membership of around one million and the anarchist press covered all of Spain. In Barcelona the CNT published a daily, **Solidaridad Obrera** (Worker Solidarity), with a circulation of 30,000. The FAI's magazine **Tierra y Libertad** (Land and Liberty) had a circulation of 20,000. In Gijon there was **Vida Obrera** (Working Life), in Seville **El Productor** (The Producer) and in Saragossa **Accion y Cultura** (Action and Culture), each with a large circulation. There were many more.

As well as leading struggles, organising unions, and producing books, papers and periodicals, the anarchists also organised libertarian schools, cultural centres, co-operatives, anarchist groups (the FAI), youth groups (the Libertarian Youth) and women's organisations (the Free Women movement). They applied their ideas in all walks of life and so ensured that ordinary people saw that anarchism was practical and relevant to them.

This was the great strength of the Spanish Anarchist movement. It was a movement *"that, in addition to possessing a revolutionary ideology [sic], was also capable of mobilising action around objectives firmly rooted in the life and conditions of the working class ... It was this ability periodically to identify and express widely felt needs and feelings that, together with its presence at community level, formed the basis of the strength of radical anarchism, and enabled it to build a mass base of support."* [Nick Rider, "The practice of direct action: the Barcelona rent strike of 1931", pp. 79-105, **For Anarchism**, David Goodway (Ed.), p. 99]

Historian Temma Kaplan stressed this in her work on the Andalusian anarchists. She argued that the anarchists were *"rooted in"* social life and created "a movement firmly based in working-class culture." They "formed trade unions, affinity groups such as housewives' sections, and broad cultural associations such as workers' circles, where the anarchist press was read and discussed." Their "great strength ... lay in the merger of communal and militant trade union traditions. In towns where the vast majority worked in agriculture, agricultural workers' unions came to be identified with the community as a whole ... anarchism ... show[ed] that the demands of agricultural workers and proletarians could be combined with community support to create an insurrectionary situation ... It would be a mistake ... to argue that 'village anarchism' in Andalusia was distinct from militant unionism, or that the movement was a surrogate religion." [**Anarchists of Andalusia: 1868-1903**, p. 211, p. 207 and pp. 204-5]

The Spanish anarchists, before and after the CNT was formed, fought in and out of the factory for economic, social and political issues. This refusal of the anarchists to ignore any aspect of life ensured that they found many willing to hear their message, a message based around the ideas of individual liberty. Such a message could do nothing but radicalise workers for "the demands of the CNT went much further than those of any social democrat: with its emphasis on true equality, **autogestion** [self-management] and working class dignity, anarchosyndicalism made demands the capitalist system could not possibly grant to the workers." [J. Romero Maura, "The Spanish case", pp. 60-83, **Anarchism Today**, D. Apter and J. Joll (eds.), p. 79]

Strikes, due to the lack of strike funds, depended on mutual aid to be won, which fostered a strong sense of solidarity and class consciousness in the CNT membership. Strikes did not just involve workers. For example, workers in Jerez responded to bosses importing workers from Malaga "with a weapon of their own — a boycott of those using strike-breakers. The most notable boycotts were against landowners near Jerez who also had commercial establishments in the city. The workers and their wives refused to buy there, and the women stationed themselves nearby to discourage other shoppers." [Mintz, **Op. Cit.**, p. 102]

The structure and tactics of the CNT encouraged the politicisation, initiative and organisational skills of its members. It was a federal, decentralised body, based on direct discussion and decision making from the bottom up ("The CNT tradition was to discuss and examine everything", as one militant put it). In addition, the CNT created a viable and practical example of an alternative method by which society could be organised. A method which was based on the ability of ordinary people to direct society themselves and which showed in practice that special ruling authorities are undesirable and unnecessary. This produced a revolutionary working class the likes of which the world has rarely seen. As Jose Peirats pointed out, "above the union level, the CNT was an eminently political organisation ..., a social and revolutionary organisation for agitation and insurrection." [**Anarchists in the Spanish Revolution**, p. 239] The CNT was organised in such a way as to encourage solidarity and class consciousness. Its organisation was based on the **sindicato unico** (one union) which united all workers of the same workplace in the same union. Instead of organising by trade, and so dividing the workers into numerous different unions, the CNT united all workers in a workplace into the same organisation,

all trades, skilled and unskilled, were in a single organisation and so solidarity was increased and encouraged as well as increasing their fighting power by eliminating divisions within the workforce. All the unions in an area were linked together into a local federation, the local federations into a regional federation and so on. As J. Romero Maura argued, the "territorial basis of organisation linkage brought all the workers from one area together and fomented working-class solidarity over and above corporate [industry or trade] solidarity." [**Op. Cit.**p. 75]

Thus the structure of the CNT encouraged class solidarity and consciousness. In addition, being based on direct action and self-management, the union ensured that working people became accustomed to managing their own struggles and acting for themselves, directly. This prepared them to manage their own personal and collective interests in a free society (as seen by the success of the self-managed collectives created in the revolution). Thus the process of self-managed struggle and direct action prepared people for the necessities of the social revolution and an anarchist society — it built, as Bakunin argued, the seeds of the future in the present.

In other words, "the route to radicalisation ... came from direct involvement in struggle and in the design of alternative social institutions." Every strike and action empowered those involved and created a viable alternative to the existing system. For example, while the strikes and food protests in Barcelona at the end of the First World War "did not topple the government, patterns of organisation established then provided models for the anarchist movement for years to follow." [Martha A. Ackelsberg and Myrna Margulies Breithart, "Terrains of Protest: Striking City Women", pp. 151-176, **Our Generation**, vol. 19, No. 1, p. 164] The same could be said of every strike, which confirmed Bakunin's and Kropotkin's stress on the strike as not only creating class consciousness and confidence but also the structures necessary to not only fight capitalism, but to replace it.

In summary, then, anarchism gained mass support by anarchists participating in mass struggles and movements, showing that its ideas and ideals were applicable to working class experiences. In fact, to even wonder why anarchism gained support in Spain is, to some degree, to implicitly assume, with Marxists of various shades, that only state socialism reflects the needs of working class people. Discussing the question why the social democratic or Communist movements did not replace anarchism in Spain, historian J. Romero Maura correctly pointed out that this "is based on the false assumption that the anarcho-syndicalist conception of the workers' struggle in pre-revolutionary society was completely at odds with what the **real** social process signified (hence the constant reference to 'religious' 'messianic' models as explanations)." After discussing and refuting five common suggestions for the success of anarchism in Spain, he concluded that the "explanation of Spanish anarcho-syndicalism's success in organising a mass movement with a sustained revolutionary **elan** should initially be sought in the very nature of the anarchist conception of society and of how to achieve revolution." [**Op. Cit.** p. 78 and p. 65]

It was the revolutionary nature of the CNT that created a militant membership who were willing and able to use direct action to defend their liberty. Unlike the Marxist led German workers, organised in a centralised fashion and trained in the obedience required by hierarchy, who did nothing to stop Hitler, the Spanish working class (like their comrades in anarchist unions in Italy) took to the streets to stop fascism.

The revolution in Spain did not "just happen"; it was the result of nearly seventy years of persistent anarchist agitation and revolutionary struggle, including a long series of strikes, protests, boycotts, uprisings and other forms of direct action that prepared the peasants and workers to organise popular resistance to the attempted fascist coup in July 1936 and to take control of society when they had defeated it in the streets.

I.8.3 How were Spanish industrial collectives organised?

Martha A. Ackelsberg gives us an excellent short summary of how the industrial collectives were organised:

> "Pre-existing structures of worker organisation made possible a workers' take-over of much of the industrial economy, especially in Catalonia ... Factory committees formed to direct production and co-ordinate with other units within the same industry. Union organisations co-ordinated both the production and distribution of manufactured goods across industries and regions ... In most collectivised industries, general assemblies of workers decided policy, while elected committees managed affairs on a day-to-day basis." [**Free Women of Spain**, p. 100]

The collectives were based on workers' democratic self-management of their workplaces, using productive assets that were under the custodianship of the entire working community and administered through federations of workers' associations:

> "The collectives organised during the Spanish Civil War were workers' economic associations without private property. The fact that collective plants were managed by those who worked in them did not mean that these establishments became their private property. The collective had no right to sell or rent all or any part of the collectivised factory or workshop. The rightful custodian was the CNT, the National Confederation of Workers Associations. But not even the CNT had the right to do as it pleased. Everything had to be decided and ratified by the workers themselves through conferences and congresses." [Augustin Souchy, **The Anarchist Collectives**, p. 67]

In Catalonia "every factory elected its administrative committee composed of its most capable workers. Depending on the size of the factory, the function of these committees included inner plant organisation, statistics, finance, correspondence, and relations with other factories and with the community ... Several months after collectivisation the textile industry of Barcelona was in far better shape than under capitalist management. Here was yet another example to show that grass roots socialism from below does not destroy initiative. Greed is not the only motivation in human relations." [Souchy, **Op. Cit.**, p 95]

Thus the individual collective was based on a mass assembly of those who worked there. This assembly nominated administrative staff who were mandated to implement the decisions of the assembly and who had to report back, and were accountable, to that assembly. For example, in Castellon de la Plana "[e]very month the technical and administrative council presented the general assembly of the Syndicate with a report which was examined and discussed if necessary, and finally introduced when this majority thought it of use. Thus all the activities were known and controlled by all the workers. We find here a practical example of libertarian democracy." [Gaston Leval, **Collectives in the Spanish Revolution**, p. 303] Power rested at the base of the collective, with "all important decisions [being] taken by the general assemblies of the workers" which "were widely attended and regularly held ... if an administrator did something which the general assembly had not authorised, he was likely to be deposed at the next meeting." An example of this process can be seen from the Casa Rivieria company. After the defeat of the army coup "a control committee (Comite de Control) was named by the Barcelona Metal Workers' Union to take over temporary control of the enterprises ... A few weeks after July 19th, there was the first general assembly of the firm's workers ... It elected an enterprise committee (Comite de Empresa) to take control of the firm on a more permanent basis... . Each of the four sections of the firm — the three factories and the office staff — held their own general assemblies at least once a week. There they discussed matters ranging from the most important affairs to the most trivial." [Robert Alexander, **The Anarchists in the Spanish Civil War**, vol. 1, p. 469 and p. 532]

In summary, the collectives in Spain were marked by workplace self-management. They successfully implemented the long-standing libertarian goal of turning industry from an autocracy to a democracy, of replacing wage-labour with free-labour based on the association of equals (see section I.3.1). However, it would be a mistake to assume (as many do, particularly Marxists) that the CNT and FAI considered the creation of self-managed collectives as the end of the revolution. Far from it. While they embodied such key libertarian principles as workers' self-management, they were fundamentally a product of both anarchist ideas **and** the specific situation in which they were created. Rather than seek a market system of producer co-operatives, the CNT was committed to the full socialisation of the economy and the creation of libertarian communism. The collectives were, as a result, seen as development towards that goal rather than as an end in themselves. Moreover, as historian Ronald Fraser notes, it "was doubtful that the CNT had seriously envisaged collectivisation of industry ... before this time." [**The Blood of Spain**, p. 212] CNT policy was opposed to the collectivisation decree of the Catalonian government, for example, which formalised (and controlled) the spontaneous gains of the revolution as expressed by the collectives.

Therefore, the collectives were (initially) a form of "self-management straddling capitalism and socialism, which we maintain would not have occurred had the Revolution been able to extend itself fully under the direction of our syndicates." In other words, the revolution saw the abolition of wage-labour but not of the wages system. Thus capitalism was replaced by mutualism, not the socialism desired by most anarchists (namely libertarian communism). As economic and political development are closely related, the fact that the CNT did not carry out the **political** aspect of the revolution meant that the revolution in the economy was doomed to failure. As Leval stressed, in *"the industrial collectives, especially in the large towns, matters proceeded differently as a consequence of contradictory factors and of opposition created by the co-existence of social currents emanating from different social classes."* [Gaston Leval, **Collectives in the Spanish Revolution**, pp. 227-8 and p. 227]

That the initial forms of the revolution were not as expected should, perhaps, be unsurprising. After all, no social transformation ever exactly matches the hopes of those who had advocated it and the people had more pressing matters to attend to such as re-starting production and fighting Franco. So it is utterly understandable that the collectives only embodied some and not all aspects of aims of the CNT and FAI! Moreover, social change does not produce instant perfect transformations and the workers *"had to build new circuits of consumption and distribution, new types of social relations between the proletariat and the peasantry, and new modes of production."* [Abel Paz, **Durruti in the Spanish Revolution**, p. 451] That process was started, even if it were initially incomplete. That a wider goal was envisioned by these organisations can be seen from the fact that union activists sought to extend the degree of socialisation. So, and again in line with libertarian theory, the collectives also expressed a desire to co-operate within and across industries (see section I.3.5). These attempts at federation and co-ordination will be discussed in next section, along with some of the conclusions that can be drawn from these experiments. For, as would be expected, this attempt to introduce libertarian socialism had its drawbacks as well as successes.

I.8.4 How were the Spanish industrial collectives co-ordinated?

The methods of co-operation tried by the collectives varied considerably. Initially, there were very few attempts to co-ordinate economic activities beyond the workplace. This is hardly surprising, given that the overwhelming need was to restart production, convert a civilian economy to a wartime one and to ensure that the civilian population and militias were supplied with necessary goods. This lead to a situation of anarchist mutualism developing, with many collectives selling the product of their own labour on the market.

This lead to some economic problems as there existed no framework of institutions between collectives to ensure efficient co-ordination of activity and so led to pointless competition between collectives (which led to even more problems). As there were initially no confederations of collectives nor mutual/communal banks this led to the continuation of any inequalities that initially existed between collectives (due to the fact that workers took over rich and poor capitalist firms) and it made the many ad hoc attempts at mutual aid between collectives difficult and often of an ad hoc nature.

Given that the CNT programme of libertarian communism recognised that a fully co-operative society must be based upon production for use, CNT militants fought against this system of mutualism and for inter-workplace co-ordination. They managed to convince their fellow workers of the difficulties of mutualism by free debate and discussion within their unions and collectives. Given this the degree of socialisation varied over time (as would be expected). Initially, after the defeat of Franco's forces, there was little formal co-ordination and organisation. The most important thing was to get production started again. However, the needs of co-ordination soon became obvious (as predicted in anarchist theory and the programme of the CNT). Gaston Leval gives the example of Hospitalet del Llobregat with regards to this process:

> *"Local industries went through stages almost universally adopted in that revolution ... [I]n the first instance, **comités** [committees] nominated by the workers employed in them [were organised]. Production and sales continued in each one. But very soon it was clear that this situation gave rise to competition between the factories ... creating rivalries which were incompatible with the socialist and libertarian outlook. So the CNT launched the watchword: 'All industries must be ramified in the Syndicates, completely socialised, and the regime of solidarity which we have always advocated be established once and for all.'*

> *"The idea won support immediately."* [**Collectives in the Spanish Revolution**, pp. 291-2]

Another example was the woodworkers' union which had a massive debate on socialisation and decided to do so (the shopworkers' union had a similar debate, but the majority of workers rejected socialisation). According to Ronald Fraser a *"union delegate would go round the small shops, point out to the workers that the conditions were unhealthy and dangerous, that the revolution was changing all this, and secure their agreement to close down and move to the union-built Double-X and the 33 EU."* [Ronald Fraser, **Blood of Spain**, p. 222]

A plenum of syndicates met in December of 1936 and formulated norms for socialisation in which the inefficiency of the capitalist industrial system was analysed. The report of the plenum stated:

> *"The major defect of most small manufacturing shops is fragmentation and lack of technical/commercial preparation. This prevents their modernisation and consolidation into better and more efficient units of production, with better facilities and co-ordination ... For us, socialisation must correct these deficiencies and systems of organisation in every industry ... To socialise an industry, we must consolidate the different units of each branch of industry in accordance with a general and organic plan which will avoid competition and other difficulties impeding the good and efficient organisation of production and distribution."* [quoted by Souchy, **Anarchist Collectives**, p. 83]

As Souchy pointed out, this document is very important in the evolution of collectivisation, because it indicates a realisation that "workers must take into account that partial collectivisation will in time degenerate into a kind of bourgeois co-operativism." [**Op. Cit.**, p. 83] Thus many collectives did not compete with each other for profits, as surpluses were pooled and distributed on a wider basis than the individual collective.

This process went on in many different unions and collectives and, unsurprisingly, the forms of co-ordination agreed to led to different forms of organisation in different areas and industries, as would be expected in a free society. However, the two most important forms can be termed syndicalisation and confederationalism (we will ignore the forms created by the collectivisation decree as these were not created by the workers themselves).

Syndicalisation (our term) meant that the CNT's industrial union ran the whole industry. This solution was tried by the woodworkers' union after extensive debate. One section of the union, "*dominated by the FAI, maintained that anarchist self-management meant that the workers should set up and operate autonomous centres of production so as to avoid the threat of bureaucratisation.*" However, those in favour of syndicalisation won the day and production was organised in the hands of the union, with administration posts and delegate meetings elected by the rank and file. However, the "*major failure … (and which supported the original anarchist objection) was that the union became like a large firm*" and its "*structure grew increasingly rigid.*" [Fraser, **Op. Cit.**, p. 222] According to one militant, "*From the outside it began to look like an American or German trust*" and the workers found it difficult to secure any changes and "*felt they weren't particularly involved in decision making.*" [quoted by Fraser, **Op. Cit.**, p. 222 and p. 223] However, this did not stop workers re-electing almost all posts at the first Annual General Assembly.

In the end, the major difference between the union-run industry and a capitalist firm organisationally appeared to be that workers could vote for (and recall) the industry management at relatively regular General Assembly meetings. While a vast improvement on capitalism, it is hardly the best example of participatory self-management in action. However, it must be stressed that the economic problems caused by the Civil War and Stalinist led counter-revolution obviously would have had an effect on the internal structure of any industry and so we cannot say that the form of organisation created was totally responsible for any marginalisation that took place.

The other important form of co-operation was what we will term **confederalisation**. This system was based on horizontal links between workplaces (via the CNT union) and allowed a maximum of self-management **and** mutual aid. This form of co-operation was practised by the Badalona textile industry (and had been defeated in the woodworkers' union). It was based upon each workplace being run by its elected management, selling its own production, getting its own orders and receiving the proceeds. However, "*everything each mill did was reported to the union which charted progress and kept statistics. If the union felt that a particular factory was not acting in the best interests of the collectivised industry as a whole, the enterprise was informed and asked to change course.*" This system ensured that the "*dangers of the big 'union trust' as of the atomised collective were avoided.*" [Fraser, **Op. Cit.**, p. 229] According to one militant, the union "*acted more as a socialist control of collectivised*

industry than as a direct hierarchised executive.*" The federation of collectives created "*the first social security system in Spain*" (which included retirement pay, free medicines, sick and maternity pay) and a compensation fund was organised "*to permit the economically weaker collectives to pay their workers, the amount each collective contributed being in direct proportion to the number of workers employed.*" [quoted by Fraser, **Op. Cit.**, p. 229]

As can be seen, the industrial collectives co-ordinated their activity in many ways, with varying degrees of success. As would be expected, mistakes were made and different solutions found as an anarchist society can hardly be produced "overnight" (as discussed in section H.2.5, anarchists have always been aware that social transformation takes time). So it is hardly surprising that the workers of the CNT faced numerous problems and had to develop their self-management experiment as objective conditions allowed them to. Unfortunately, thanks to fascist aggression and Communist Party and Republican back-stabbing, the experiment did not last long enough to fully answer all the questions we have about the viability of the solutions tried. Given time, however, we are sure they would have solved the problems they faced for the social experimentation which was conducted was not only highly successful but also rich in promise.

I.8.5 How were the Spanish agricultural co-operatives organised and co-ordinated?

Jose Peirats described collectivisation among the peasantry as follows:

"*The expropriated lands were turned over to the peasant syndicates, and it was these syndicates that organised the first collectives. Generally the holdings of small property owners were respected, always on the condition that only they or their families would work the land, without employing wage labour. In areas like Catalonia, where the tradition of petty peasant ownership prevailed, the land holdings were scattered. There were no great estates. Many of these peasants, together with the CNT, organised collectives, pooling their land, animals, tools, chickens, grain, fertiliser, and even their harvested crops.*

"*Privately owned farms located in the midst of collectives interfered with efficient cultivation by splitting up the collectives into disconnected parcels. To induce owners to move, they were given more or even better land located on the perimeter of the collective.*

"*The collectivist who had nothing to contribute to the collective was admitted with the same rights and the same duties as the others. In some collectives, those joining had to contribute their money (Girondella in Catalonia, Lagunarrotta in Aragón, and Cervera del Maestra in Valencia).*" [**The Anarchist Collectives**, p. 112]

Dolgoff observed that *"supreme power was vested in, and actually exercised by, the membership in general assemblies, and all power derived from, and flowed back to, the grass roots organisations of the people."* [**Op. Cit.**, p 119fn] Peirats also noted that the collectives were *"fiercely democratic"* as regards decision-making. For example, in Ademuz *"assemblies were held every Saturday"* while in Alcolea de Cinca *"they were held whenever necessary."* [**Anarchists in the Spanish Revolution**, p. 146] Eyewitness Gaston Leval summarised this explosion in self-management as follows:

> *"Regular general membership meetings were convoked weekly, bi-weekly, or monthly ... and these meetings were completely free of the tensions and recriminations which inevitably emerge when the power of decisions is vested in a few individuals — even if democratically elected. The Assemblies were open for everyone to participate in the proceedings. Democracy embraced all social life. In most cases, even the 'individualists' who were not members of the collective could participate in the discussions, and they were listened to by the collectivists."* [**The Anarchist Collectives**, p 119fn]

Work was *"usually done in groups on a co-operative basis. In smaller collectives, all workers gathered to discuss the work needed to be done and how to allocate it. In larger collectives, representatives of each work group would gather at regular intervals. General assemblies of the collective met on a weekly, biweekly, or monthly basis, and took up issues ranging from hours and wages to the distribution of food and clothing."* [Martha A. Ackelsberg in **Free Women of Spain**, p. 106] It was in these face-to-face assemblies that decisions upon the distribution of resources were decided both within and outwith the collective. Here, when considering the importance of mutual aid, appeals were made to an individual's sense of empathy. As one activist remembered:

> *"There were, of course, those who didn't want to share and who said that each collective should take care of itself. But they were usually convinced in the assemblies. We would try to speak to them in terms they understood. We'd ask, 'Did you think it was fair when the **cacique** [local boss] let people starve if there wasn't enough work?' and they said, 'Of course not.' They would eventually come around. Don't forget, there were three hundred thousand collectivists [in Aragón], but only ten thousand of us had been members of the CNT. We had a lot of educating to do."* [quoted by Ackelsberg, **Op. Cit.**, p. 107]

In addition, regional federations of collectives were formed in many areas of Spain (for example, in Aragón and the Levant). The federations were created at congresses to which the collectives in an area sent delegates. These congresses agreed a series of general rules about how the federation would operate and what commitments the affiliated collectives would have to each other. The congress elected an administration council, which took responsibility for implementing agreed policy. The Levant Federation was organised as follows:

> *"The 900 Collectives were brought together in 54 cantonal federations which grouped themselves and at the same time subdivided into five provincial federations which at the top level ended in the Regional **Comite** ... [This] was nominated directly by the annual congresses answerable to them and to the hundreds of peasant delegates chosen by their comrades ... . It was also on their initiative that the Levante Federation was divided into 26 general sections in accordance with specialisations in work and other activities. Those 26 sections constituted a whole which embraced probably for the first time in history outside the State and governmental structures, the whole of social life."* [Gaston Leval, **Collectives in the Spanish Revolution**, p. 154]

The Aragón Federation statues were agreed at its founding congress in mid-February 1937 by 500 delegates. These stated that there would be *"as many county federations"* as deemed *"necessary for the proper running of the collectives"* and the Federation would *"hold its ordinary congress at intervals of six months, in addition to whatever extraordinary ones ... deemed appropriate."* New collectives could join after *"consent in general assembly of the inhabitants of the collective"*. The federation aimed to *"coordinate the economic potential of the region and ... be geared towards solidarity in accordance with the norms of autonomy and federalism."* [quoted by Jose Peirats, **The CNT in the Spanish Revolution**, vol. 1, p. 240]

These federations had many tasks. They ensured the distribution of surplus produce to the front line and to the cities, cutting out middlemen and ensuring the end of exploitation. They also arranged for exchanges between collectives to take place. In addition, the federations allowed the individual collectives to pool resources together in order to improve the infrastructure of the area (building roads, canals, hospitals and so on) and invest in means of production which no one collective could afford. In this way individual collectives pooled their resources, increased and improved the means of production and the social and economic infrastructure of their regions. All this, combined with an increase of consumption in the villages and towns as well as the feeding of militia men and women fighting the fascists at the front.

Rural collectivisation allowed the potential creative energy that existed among the rural workers and peasants to be unleashed, an energy that had been wasted under private property. The popular assemblies allowed community problems and improvements to be identified and solved directly, drawing upon the ideas and experiences of everyone and enriched by discussion and debate. To quote one participant: *"We were always prepared to adapt our ideas in every area of collective life if things did not work. That was the advantage of our collectives over state-created ones like those in Russia. We were free. Each village could do as it pleased. There was local stimulus, local initiative."* [quoted by Ronald Fraser, **Blood of Spain**, p. 357] As we discuss in the next section, this enabled rural Spain to be transformed from one marked by poverty and fear into one of increased well-being and hope.

I.8.6 What did the agricultural collectives accomplish?

Most basically, self-management in collectives combined with co-operation in rural federations allowed an improvement in quality of rural life. From a purely economic viewpoint, production increased and as historian Benjamin Martin summarises: *"Though it is impossible to generalise about the rural land take-overs, there is little doubt that the quality of life for most peasants who participated in co-operatives and collectives notably improved."* [**The Agony of Modernisation**, p. 394] Another historian, Antony Beevor, notes that *"[i]n terms of production and improved standards for the peasants, the self-managed collectives appear to have been successful. They also seem to have encouraged harmonious community relations."* [**The Spanish Civil War**, p. 95]

More importantly, however, this improvement in the quality of life included an increase in freedom as well as in consumption. To re-quote the member of the Beceite collective in Aragón: *"it was marvellous ... to live in a collective, a free society where one could say what one thought, where if the village committee seemed unsatisfactory one could say. The committee took no big decisions without calling the whole village together in a general assembly. All this was wonderful."* [quoted by Ronald Fraser, **Blood of Spain**, p. 288] As Beevor suggests, *"self-managed collectives were much happier when no better off than before. What mattered was that the labourers ran their own collectives — a distinct contrast to the disasters of state collectivisation in the Soviet Union."* [**Op. Cit.**, p. 95] Here are a few examples provided by Jose Peirats:

> *"In Montblanc the collective dug up the old useless vines and planted new vineyards. The land, improved by modern cultivation with tractors, yielded much bigger and better crops ... Many Aragón collectives built new roads and repaired old ones, installed modern flour mills, and processed agricultural and animal waste into useful industrial products. Many of these improvements were first initiated by the collectives. Some villages, like Calanda, built parks and baths. Almost all collectives established libraries, schools, and cultural centres."* [**The Anarchist Collectives**, p. 116]

Gaston Leval pointed out that *"the Peasant Federation of Levant ... produced more than half of the total orange crop in Spain: almost four million kilos (1 kilo equals about 2 and one-fourth pounds). It then transported and sold through its own commercial organisation (no middlemen) more than 70% of the crop. (The Federation's commercial organisation included its own warehouses, trucks, and boats. Early in 1938 the export section established its own agencies in France: Marseilles, Perpignan, Bordeaux, Cherbourg, and Paris.) Out of a total of 47,000 hectares in all Spain devoted to rice production, the collective in the Province of Valencia cultivated 30,000 hectares."* [**Op. Cit.**, p. 124] To quote Peirats again:

> *"Preoccupation with cultural and pedagogical innovations was an event without precedent in rural Spain. The Amposta collectivists organised classes for semi-literates,*

kindergartens, and even a school of arts and professions. The Seros schools were free to all neighbours, collectivists or not. Grau installed a school named after its most illustrious citizen, Joaquin Costa. The Calanda collective (pop. only 4,500) schooled 1,233 children. The best students were sent to the Lyceum in Caspe, with all expenses paid by the collective. The Alcoriza (pop. 4,000) school was attended by 600 children. Many of the schools were installed in abandoned convents. In Granadella (pop. 2,000), classes were conducted in the abandoned barracks of the Civil Guards. Graus organised a print library and a school of arts and professions, attended by 60 pupils. The same building housed a school of fine arts and high grade museum. In some villages a cinema was installed for the first time. The Penalba cinema was installed in a church. Viladecana built an experimental agricultural laboratory. [**Op. Cit.**, p. 116]

Peirats summed up the accomplishments of the agricultural collectives as follows:

> *"In distribution the collectives' co-operatives eliminated middlemen, small merchants, wholesalers, and profiteers, thus greatly reducing consumer prices. The collectives eliminated most of the parasitic elements from rural life, and would have wiped them out altogether if they were not protected by corrupt officials and by the political parties. Non-collectivised areas benefited indirectly from the lower prices as well as from free services often rendered by the collectives (laundries, cinemas, schools, barber and beauty parlours, etc.)."* [**Op. Cit.**, p. 114]

Leval emphasised the following achievements (among others):

> *"In the agrarian collectives solidarity was practised to the greatest degree. Not only was every person assured of the necessities, but the district federations increasingly adopted the principle of mutual aid on an inter-collective scale. For this purpose they created common reserves to help out villages less favoured by nature. In Castile special institutions for this purpose were created. In industry this practice seems to have begun in Hospitalet, on the Catalan railways, and was applied later in Alcoy. Had the political compromise not impeded open socialisation, the practices of mutual aid would have been much more generalised ... A conquest of enormous importance was the right of women to livelihood, regardless of occupation or function. In about half of the agrarian collectives, the women received the same wages as men; in the rest the women received less, apparently on the principle that they rarely live alone ... In all the agrarian collectives of Aragón, Catalonia, Levant, Castile, Andalusia, and Estremadura, the workers formed groups to divide the labour or the land; usually they were assigned to definite areas. Delegates elected by the work groups met with the collective's delegate for agriculture to plan out the work. This typical organisation arose quite spontaneously, by local initiative ... In addition ... the collective as a whole*

met in weekly, bi-weekly or monthly assembly ... The assembly reviewed the activities of the councillors it named, and discussed special cases and unforeseen problems. All inhabitants — men and women, producers and non-producers — took part in the discussion and decisions ... In land cultivation the most significant advances were: the rapidly increased use of machinery and irrigation; greater diversification; and forestation. In stock raising: the selection and multiplication of breeds; the adaptation of breeds to local conditions; and large-scale construction of collective stock barns." [**Op. Cit.**, pp. 166-167]

Collectivisation, as Graham Kelsey notes, "allowed a rationalisation of village societies and a more efficient use of the economic resources available. Instead of carpenters and bricklayers remaining idle because no wealthy landowner had any use for their services they were put to work constructing agricultural facilities and providing the villages with the kind of social amenities which until then they had scarcely been able to imagine." [**Anarchosyndicalism, Libertarian Communism and the State**, p. 169] Martha A. Ackelsberg sums up the experience well:

"The achievements of these collectives were extensive. In many areas they maintained, if not increased, agricultural production [not forgetting that many young men were at the front line], often introducing new patterns of cultivation and fertilisation ... collectivists built chicken coups, barns, and other facilities for the care and feeding of the community's animals. Federations of collectives co-ordinated the construction of roads, schools, bridges, canals and dams. Some of these remain to this day as lasting contributions of the collectives to the infrastructure of rural Spain. The collectivists also arranged for the transfer of surplus produce from wealthier collectives to those experiencing shortages, either directly from village to village or through mechanisms set up by regional committees." [**The Free Women of Spain**, pp. 106-7]

As well as this inter-collective solidarity, the rural collectives also supplied food to the front-line troops:

"The collectives voluntarily contributed enormous stocks of provisions and other supplies to the fighting troops. Utiel sent 1,490 litres of oil and 300 bushels of potatoes to the Madrid front (in addition to huge stocks of beans, rice, buckwheat, etc.). Porales de Tujana sent great quantities of bread, oil, flour, and potatoes to the front, and eggs, meat, and milk to the military hospital.

"The efforts of the collectives take on added significance when we take into account that their youngest and most vigorous workers were fighting in the trenches. 200 members of the little collective of Vilaboi were at the front; from Viledecans, 60; Amposta, 300; and Calande, 500." [Jose Peirats, **The Anarchist Collectives**, p. 120]

Therefore, as well as significant economic achievements, the collectives ensured social and political ones too. Solidarity was

practised and previously marginalised people took direct and full management of the affairs of their communities, transforming them to meet their own needs and desires.

I.8.7 Were the rural collectives created by force?

No, they were not. The myth that the rural collectives were created by "terror," organised and carried out by the anarchist militia, was started by the Stalinists of the Spanish Communist Party. As Vernon Richards noted: "However discredited Stalinism may appear to be today the fact remains that the Stalinist lies and interpretation of the Spanish Civil War still prevail, presumably because it suits the political prejudices of those historians who are currently interpreting it." ["Introduction", Gaston Leval, **Collectives in the Spanish Revolution**, p. 11] Here we shall present evidence to refute claims that the rural collectives were created by force.

Firstly, we should point out that rural collectives were created in many different areas of Spain, such as the Levant (900 collectives), Castile (300) and Estremadera (30), where the anarchist militia did not exist. In Catalonia, for example, the CNT militia passed through many villages on its way to Aragón and only around 40 collectives were created unlike the 450 in Aragón. In other words, the rural collectivisation process occurred independently of the existence of anarchist troops, with the majority of the 1,700 rural collectives created in areas without a predominance of anarchist militias.

One historian, Ronald Fraser, seems to imply that collectives were imposed upon the Aragón population. As he put it, the "collectivisation, carried out under the general cover, if not necessarily the direct agency, of CNT militia columns, represented a revolutionary minority's attempt to control not only production but consumption for egalitarian purposes and the needs of the war." Notice that he does not suggest that the anarchist militia actually **imposed** the collectives, a claim for which there is little or no evidence. Moreover, Fraser presents a somewhat contradictory narrative to the facts he presents. On the one hand, he suggests that "[o]bligatory collectivisation was justified, in some libertarians' eyes, by a reasoning closer to war communism than to libertarian communism." On the other hand, he presents extensive evidence that the collectives did not have a 100% membership rate. How can collectivisation be obligatory if people remain outside the collectives? Similarly, he talks of how **some** CNT militia leaders justified "[f]orced collectivisation" in terms of the war effort while acknowledging the official CNT policy of opposing forced collectivisation, an opposition expressed in practice as only around 20 (i.e., 5%) of the collectives were total. [**Blood of Spain**, p. 370, p. 349 and p. 366] This is shown in his own book as collectivists interviewed continually note that people remained outside their collectives!

Thus Fraser's attempts to paint the Aragón collectives as a form of "war communism" imposed upon the population by the CNT and obligatory for all fails to co-incide with the evidence he presents.

Fraser states that "[t]here was no need to dragoon them [the peasants] at pistol point [into collectives]: the coercive climate, in which 'fascists' were being shot, was sufficient. 'Spontaneous' and 'forced' collectives existed, as did willing and unwilling collectivists within them." [**Op. Cit.**, p. 349] Therefore, his implied suggestion that the Aragón collectives were imposed upon the rural population is based upon the insight that there was a *"coercive climate"* in Aragón at the time. Of course a civil war against fascism would produce a *"coercive climate"* particularly near the front line. However, the CNT can hardly be blamed for that. As historian Gabriel Jackson summarised, while such executions took place the CNT did not conduct a general wave of terror:

> *"the anarchists made a constant effort to separate active political enemies from those who were simply bourgeois by birth or ideology or economic function. Anarchist political committees wanted to know what the accused monarchists or conservatives had done, not simply what they thought or how they voted ... There is no inherent contradiction involved in recognising both that the revolution included some violence and that its social and economic results ... were approved of by the majority of peasants in an area."* [quoted in Jose Peirats, **The CNT in the Spanish Revolution**, vol. 1, p. 146]

This was a life and death struggle against fascism, in which the fascists were systematically murdering vast numbers of anarchists, socialists and republicans in the areas under their control. It is hardly surprising that some anarchist troops took the law into their own hands and murdered some of those who supported and would help the fascists. Given what was going on in fascist Spain, and the experience of fascism in Germany and Italy, the CNT militia knew exactly what would happen to them and their friends and family if they lost.

The question does arise, however, of whether the climate was made so coercive by the war and the nearness of the anarchist militia that individual choice was impossible. The facts speak for themselves. At its peak, rural collectivisation in Aragón embraced around 70% of the population in the area saved from fascism. Around 30% of the population felt safe enough not to join a collective, a sizeable percentage. If the collectives had been created by anarchist terror or force, we would expect a figure of 100% membership. This was not the case, indicating the basically voluntary nature of the experiment (we should point out that other figures suggest a lower number of collectivists which makes the forced collectivisation argument even less likely). Historian Antony Beevor (while noting that there *"had undoubtedly been pressure, and no doubt force was used on some occasions in the fervour after the rising"*) just stated the obvious when he wrote that *"the very fact that every village was a mixture of collectivists and individualists shows that peasants had not been forced into communal farming at the point of a gun."* [**The Spanish Civil War**, p. 206] In addition, if the CNT militia had forced peasants into collectives we would expect the membership of the collectives to peak almost overnight, not grow slowly over time:

> *"At the regional congress of collectives, held at Caspe in mid-February 1937, nearly 80 000 collectivists were represented from 'almost all the villages of the region.' This, however, was but a beginning. By the end of April the number of collectivists had risen to 140,000; by the*

end of the first week of May to 180,000; and by the end of June to 300,000." [Graham Kelsey, *"Anarchism in Aragón,"* pp. 60-82, **Spain in Conflict 1931-1939**, Martin Blinkhorn (ed.), p. 61]

If the collectives had been created by force, then their membership would have been 300,000 in February, 1937, not increasing steadily to reach that number four months later. Neither can it be claimed that the increase was due to new villages being collectivised, as almost all villages had sent delegates in February. This indicates that many peasants joined the collectives because of the advantages associated with common labour, the increased resources it placed at their hands and the fact that the surplus wealth which had in the previous system been monopolised by the few was used instead to raise the standard of living of the entire community.

The voluntary nature of the collectives is again emphasised by the number of collectives which allowed people to remain outside. There *"were few villages which were completely collectivised."* [Beevor, **Op. Cit.**, p. 94] One eye-witness in Aragón, an anarchist schoolteacher, noted that the forcing of smallholders into a collective *"wasn't a widespread problem, because there weren't more than twenty or so villages where collectivisation was total and no one was allowed to remain outside."* [quoted by Fraser, **Op. Cit.**, p. 366] Instead of forcing the minority in a village to agree with the wishes of the majority, the vast majority (95%) of Aragón collectives stuck to their libertarian principles and allowed those who did not wish to join to remain outside.

So, only around 20 were *"total"* collectives (out of 450) and around 30% of the population felt safe enough **not** to join. In other words, in the vast majority of collectives those joining could see that those who did not were safe. These figures indicate of the basically spontaneous and voluntary nature of the movement as do the composition of the new municipal councils created after July 19th. As Graham Kelsey notes: *"What is immediately noticeable from the results is that although the region has often been branded as one controlled by anarchists to the total exclusion of all other forces, the CNT was far from enjoying the degree of absolute domination often implied and inferred."* [**Anarchosyndicalism, Libertarian Communism and the State**, p. 198]

In his account of the rural revolution, Burnett Bolloten noted that it *"embraced more than 70 percent of the population"* in liberated Aragón and that *"many of the 450 collectives of the region were largely voluntary"* although *"it must be emphasised that this singular development was in some measure due to the presence of militiamen from the neighbouring region of Catalonia, the immense majority of whom were members of the CNT and FAI."* [**The Spanish Civil War**, p. 74] This, it should be noted, was not denied by anarchists. As Gaston Leval pointed out, *"it is true that the presence of these forces ... favoured indirectly these constructive achievements by preventing active resistance by the supporters of the bourgeois republic and of fascism."* [**Collectives in the Spanish Revolution**, p. 90]

So the presence of the militia changed the balance of class forces in Aragón by destroying the capitalist state (i.e. the local bosses — caciques — could not get state aid to protect their property) and many landless workers took over the land. The presence of the militia ensured that land could be taken over by destroying the capitalist "monopoly of force" that existed before the revolution (the power of which will be highlighted below) and so the CNT militia allowed the possibility of experimentation by the Aragónese population. This class war in the countryside is reflected by Bolloten: "If the individual farmer viewed with dismay the swift and widespread collectivisation of agriculture, the farm workers of the Anarchosyndicalist CNT and the Socialist UGT saw it as the commencement of a new era." [**Op. Cit.**, p. 63] Both were mass organisations and supported collectivisation.

Therefore, anarchist militias allowed the rural working class to abolish the artificial scarcity of land created by private property (and enforced by the state). The rural bosses obviously viewed with horror the possibility that they could not exploit day workers' labour (as Bolloten pointed out "the collective system of agriculture threaten[ed] to drain the rural labour market of wage workers." [**Op. Cit.**, p. 62]). Little wonder the richer peasants and landowners hated the collectives. A report on the district of Valderrobes which indicates popular support for the collectives:

> "Collectivisation was nevertheless opposed by opponents on the right and adversaries on the left. If the eternally idle who have been expropriated had been asked what they thought of collectivisation, some would have replied that it was robbery and others a dictatorship. But, for the elderly, the day workers, the tenant farmers and small proprietors who had always been under the thumb of the big landowners and heartless usurers, it appeared as salvation." [quoted by Bolloten, **Op. Cit.**, p. 71]

However, many historians ignore the differences in class that existed in the countryside and explain the rise in collectives in Aragón (and ignore those elsewhere) as the result of the CNT militia. For example, Fraser:

> "Very rapidly collectives ... began to spring up. It did not happen on instructions from the CNT leadership — no more than had the [industrial] collectives in Barcelona. Here, as there, the initiative came from CNT militants; here, as there, the 'climate' for social revolution in the rearguard was created by CNT armed strength: the anarcho-syndicalists' domination of the streets of Barcelona was re-enacted in Aragón as the CNT militia columns, manned mainly by Catalan anarcho-syndicalist workers, poured in. Where a nucleus of anarcho-syndicalists existed in a village, it seized the moment to carry out the long-awaited revolution and collectivised spontaneously. Where there was none, villagers could find themselves under considerable pressure from the militias to collectivise." [**Op. Cit.**, p. 347]

Fraser implies that the revolution was mostly imported into Aragón from Catalonia. However, as he himself notes, the CNT column leaders (except Durruti) "opposed" the creation of the Council of Aragón (a confederation for the collectives). Hardly an example of Catalan CNT imposed social revolution! Moreover, the Aragón CNT was a widespread and popular organisation, suggesting that the idea that the collectives were imported into the region by the Catalan CNT is simply **false**. Fraser states that in "some [of the Aragónese villages] there was a flourishing CNT, in others the UGT was strongest, and in only too many there was no unionisation at all." [**Op. Cit.**, p. 350 and p. 348] The question arises of how extensive was that strength. The evidence shows that the rural CNT in Aragón was extensive, strong and growing, so making the suggestion of imposed collectives a false one. In fact, by the 1930s the "authentic peasant base of the CNT ... lay in Aragón." CNT growth in Zaragoza "provided a springboard for a highly effective libertarian agitation in lower Aragón, particularly among the impoverished labourers and debt-ridden peasantry of the dry steppes region." [Murray Bookchin, **The Spanish Anarchists**, p. 203]

Graham Kelsey, in his social history of the CNT in Aragón between 1930 and 1937, provides more evidence on this matter. He points out that as well as the "spread of libertarian groups and the increasing consciousness among CNT members of libertarian theories ... contribu[ting] to the growth of the anarchosyndicalist movement in Aragón" the existence of "agrarian unrest" also played an important role in that growth. This all lead to the "revitalisation of the CNT network in Aragón". So by 1936, the CNT had built upon the "foundations laid in 1933" and "had finally succeeded in translating the very great strength of the urban trade-union organisation in Zaragoza into a regional network of considerable extent." [**Op. Cit.**, pp. 80-81, p. 82 and p. 134]

Kelsey notes the long history of anarchism in Aragón, dating back to the late 1860s. However, before the 1910s there had been little gains in rural Aragón by the CNT due to the power of local bosses (called **caciques**):

> "Local landowners and small industrialists, the **caciques** of provincial Aragón, made every effort to enforce the closure of these first rural anarchosyndicalist cells [created after 1915]. By the time of the first rural congress of the Aragónese CNT confederation in the summer of 1923, much of the progress achieved through the organisation's considerable propaganda efforts had been countered by repression elsewhere." ["Anarchism in Aragón", **Op. Cit.**, p. 62]

A CNT activist indicated the power of these bosses and how difficult it was to be a union member in Aragón:

> "Repression is not the same in the large cities as it is in the villages where everyone knows everybody else and where the Civil Guards are immediately notified of a comrade's slightest movement. Neither friends nor relatives are spared. All those who do not serve the state's repressive forces unconditionally are pursued, persecuted and on occasions beaten up." [quoted by Kelsey, **Op. Cit.**, p. 74]

However, while there were some successes in organising rural unions, even in 1931 "propaganda campaigns which led to the establishment of scores of village trade-union cells, were followed by a counter-offensive from village **caciques** which forced them to close." [**Op. Cit.** p. 67] Even in the face of this repression the CNT grew and "from the end of 1932" there was "a successful expansion of the anarchosyndicalist movement into several parts of the region where previously it had never penetrated." [Kelsey, **Anarchosyndicalism, Libertarian Communism and the State**, p. 185] This growth was built upon in 1936, with increased rural activism which had slowly eroded the power of the **caciques** (which in part explains their support for the fascist coup). After the election of the Popular Front, years of anarchist propaganda and organisation paid off with *"dramatic growth in rural anarcho-syndicalist support"* in the six weeks after the general election. This *"was emphasised"* in the Aragón CNT's April congress's agenda and it was decided to direct *"attention to rural problems"* while the agreed programme was *"exactly what was to happen four months later in liberated Aragón."* In its aftermath, a series of intensive propaganda campaigns was organised through each of the provinces of the regional confederation. Many meetings were held in villages which had never before heard anarcho-syndicalist propaganda. This was very successful and by the beginning of June, 1936, the number of Aragón unions had topped 400, compared to only 278 one month earlier. [Kelsey, *"Anarchism in Aragón"*, **Op. Cit.**, pp. 75-76]

This increase in union membership reflected increased social struggle by the Aragónese working population and their attempts to improve their standard of living, which was very low for most of the population. A journalist from the conservative Catholic **Heraldo de Aragón** visited lower Aragón in the summer of 1935 and noted *"[t]he hunger in many homes, where the men are not working, is beginning to encourage the youth to subscribe to misleading teachings."* [quoted by Kelsey, **Op. Cit.**, p. 74] Little wonder, then, the growth in CNT membership and social struggle Kelsey indicates:

> *"Evidence of a different kind was also available that militant trade unionism in Aragón was on the increase. In the five months between mid-February and mid-July 1936 the province of Zaragoza experienced over seventy strikes, more than had previously been recorded in any entire year, and things were clearly no different in the other two provinces ... the great majority of these strikes were occurring in provincial towns and villages. Strikes racked the provinces and in at least three instances were actually transformed into general strikes."*
> [**Op. Cit.**, p. 76]

So in the spring and summer of 1936 there was a massive growth in CNT membership which reflected the growing militant struggle by the urban and rural population of Aragón. Years of propaganda and organising had ensured this growth in libertarian influence, a growth which was reflected in the creation of collectives in liberated Aragón during the revolution. Therefore, the construction of a collectivised society was founded directly upon the emergence, during the five years of the Second Republic, of a mass trade-union movement infused by anarchist principles. These collectives were constructed in accordance with the programme agreed at the Aragón CNT conference of April 1936 which reflected the wishes of the rural membership of the unions within Aragón (and due to the rapid growth of the CNT afterwards obviously reflected popular feelings in the area):

"libertarian dominance in post-insurrection Aragón itself reflected the predominance that anarchists had secured before the war; *by the summer of 1936 the CNT had succeeded in establishing throughout Aragón a mass trade-union movement of strictly libertarian orientation, upon which widespread and well-supported network the extensive collective experiment was to be founded."* [Kelsey, **Op. Cit.**, p. 61]

Additional evidence that supports a high level of CNT support in rural Aragón can be provided by the fact that it was Aragón that was the centre of the December 1933 insurrection organised by the CNT. As Bookchin noted, *"only Aragón rose on any significant scale, particularly Saragossa ... many of the villages declared libertarian communism and perhaps the heaviest fighting took place between the vineyard workers in Rioja and the authorities"*. [**Op. Cit.**, p. 238] It is unlikely for the CNT to organise an insurrection in an area within which it had little support or influence. According to Kelsey, *"it was precisely those areas which had most important in December 1933"* which were in 1936 *"seeking to create a new pattern of economic and social organisation, to form the basis of libertarian Aragón."* [**Anarchosyndicalism, Libertarian Communism and the State**, p. 161]

So the majority of collectives in Aragón were the product of CNT (and UGT) influenced workers taking the opportunity to create a new form of social life, a form marked by its voluntary and directly democratic nature. Far from being unknown in rural Aragón, the CNT was well established and growing at a fast rate: *"Spreading out from its urban base ... the CNT, first in 1933 and then more extensively in 1936, succeeded in converting an essentially urban organisation into a truly regional confederation."* [Kelsey, **Op. Cit.**, p. 184]

The evidence suggests that historians like Fraser are wrong to imply that the Aragón collectives were created by the CNT militia and enforced upon a unwilling population. The Aragón collectives were the natural result of years of anarchist activity within rural Aragón and directly related to the massive growth in the CNT between 1930 and 1936. Thus Kelsey is correct to state that libertarian communism and agrarian collectivisation *"were not economic terms or social principles enforced upon a hostile population by special teams of urban anarchosyndicalists."* [**Op. Cit.**, p. 161] This is not to suggest that there were **no** examples of people joining collectives involuntarily because of the *"coercive climate"* of the front line nor that there were villages which did not have a CNT union within them before the war and so created a collective because of the existence of the CNT militia. It is to suggest that these can be considered as exceptions to the rule.

Moreover, the way the CNT handled such a situation is noteworthy. Fraser indicates such a situation in the village of Alloza. In the autumn of 1936, representatives of the CNT district committee had come to suggest that the villagers collectivise (we would like to stress here that the CNT militia which had passed through the village had made no attempt to create a collective there). A village assembly was called and the CNT members explained their ideas and suggested how to organise the collective. However, who would join and how the villagers would organise the collective was left totally up to them (the CNT representatives *"stressed that no one was to be maltreated"*). Within the collective, self-management was the rule and one member recalled that *"[o]nce the work groups were established on a friendly basis and worked their own lands,* everyone got on well enough." "There was no need for coercion, no need for discipline and punishment ... A collective wasn't a bad idea at all." [Fraser, **Op. Cit.**, p. 360] This collective, like the vast majority, was voluntary and democratic: "I couldn't oblige him to join; we weren't living under a dictatorship." [quoted by Fraser, **Op. Cit.**, p. 362] In other words, **no** force was used to create the collective and the collective was organised by local people directly. Of course, as with any public good (to use economic jargon), all members of the community had to pay for the war effort and feed the militia. As Kelsey notes, "[t]he military insurrection had come at a critical moment in the agricultural calendar. Throughout lower Aragón there were fields of grain ready for harvesting ... At the assembly in Albalate de Cinca the opening clause of the agreed programme had required everyone in the district, independent farmers and collectivists alike, to contribute equally to the war effort, thereby emphasising one of the most important considerations in the period immediately following the rebellion." [**Op. Cit.**, p. 164] In addition, the collectives controlled the price of crops in order to ensure that speculation and inflation were controlled. However, these policies as with the equal duties of individualists and collectivists in the war effort were enforced upon the collectives by the war.

Lastly, in support of the popular nature of the rural collectives, we will indicate the effects of the suppression of the collectives in August 1937 by the Communists, namely the collapse of the rural economy. This sheds considerable light on the question of popular attitudes.

In October 1937, the Communist-controlled Regional Delegation of Agrarian Reform acknowledged that "in the majority of villages agricultural work was paralysed causing great harm to our agrarian economy." This is confirmed by Jose Silva, a Communist Party member and general secretary of the Institute of Agrarian Reform, who commented that after Lister had attacked Aragón, "labour in the fields was suspended almost entirely, and a quarter of the land had not been prepared at the time for sowing." At a meeting of the agrarian commission of the Aragónese Communist Party (October 9th, 1937), Silva emphasised "the little incentive to work of the entire peasant population" and that the situation brought about by the dissolution of the collectives was "grave and critical." [quoted by Bolloten, **Op. Cit.**, p. 530] Jose Peirats explained the reasons for this economic collapse as a result of popular boycott:

> "When it came time to prepare for the next harvest, smallholders could not by themselves work the property on which they had been installed [by the communists]. Dispossessed peasants, intransigent collectivists, refused to work in a system of private property, and were even less willing to rent out their labour." [**Anarchists in the Spanish Revolution**, p. 258]

If the collectives were unpopular, created by anarchist force, then why did the economy collapse after the suppression? If Lister had overturned a totalitarian anarchist regime, why did the peasants not reap the benefit of their toil? Could it be because the collectives were essentially a spontaneous Aragónese development and supported by most of the population there? This analysis is supported by historian Yaacov Oved:

> "Those who were responsible for this policy [of attacking the Aragón collectives], were convinced that the farmers would greet it joyfully because they had been coerced into joining the collectives. But they were proven wrong. Except for the rich estate owners who were glad to get their land back, most of the members of the agricultural collectives objected and lacking all motivation they were reluctant to resume the same effort in the agricultural work. This phenomenon was so widespread that the authorities and the communist minister of agriculture were forced to retreat from their hostile policy." [**"Communismo Libertario" and Communalism in the Spanish Collectivisations (1936-1939)**, pp. 53-4]

Even in the face of Communist repression, most of the collectives kept going. This, if nothing else, proves that the collectives were popular institutions. "Through the widespread reluctance of collectivists to co-operate with the new policy," Oved argues, "it became evident that most members had voluntarily joined the collectives and as soon as the policy was changed a new wave of collectives was established. However, the wheel could not be turned back. An atmosphere of distrust prevailed between the collectives and the authorities and every initiative was curtailed" [**Op. Cit.**, p. 54]

Jose Peirats summed up the situation after the communist attack on the collectives and the legalisation of the collectives as follows:

> "It is very possible that this second phase of collectivisation better reflects the sincere convictions of the members. They had undergone a severe test and those who had withstood it were proven collectivists. Yet it would be facile to label as anti-collectivists those who abandoned the collectives in this second phase. Fear, official coercion and insecurity weighed heavily in the decisions of much of the Aragónese peasantry." [**Op. Cit.**, p. 258]

While the collectives had existed, there was a 20% increase in production (and this is compared to the pre-war harvest which had been "a good crop" [Fraser, **Op. Cit.**p. 370]). After the destruction of the collectives, the economy collapsed. Hardly the result that would be expected if the collectives were forced upon an unwilling peasantry (the forced collectivisation by Stalin in Russia resulted in a famine). Only the victory of fascism made it possible to restore the so-called "natural order" of capitalist property in the Spanish countryside. The same land-owners who welcomed the Communist repression of the collectives also, we are sure, welcomed the fascists who ensured a lasting victory of property over liberty.

So, overall, the evidence suggests that the Aragón collectives, like their counterparts in the Levante, Catalonia and so on, were **popular** organisations, created by and for the rural population and, essentially, an expression of a spontaneous and popular social revolution. Claims that the anarchist militia created them by force of arms are **false**. While acts of violence **did** occur and some acts of coercion **did** take place (against CNT policy, we may add) these were the exceptions to the rule. Bolloten's summary best fits the facts:

"But in spite of the cleavages between doctrine and practice that plagued the Spanish Anarchists whenever they collided with the realities of power, it cannot be overemphasised that notwithstanding the many instances of coercion and violence, the revolution of July 1936 distinguished itself from all others by the generally spontaneous and far-reaching character of its collectivist movement and by its promise of moral and spiritual renewal. Nothing like this spontaneous movement had ever occurred before." [**Op. Cit.**, p. 78]

I.8.8 But did the Spanish collectives innovate?

Yes. In contradiction to the old capitalist claim that no one will innovate unless private property exists, the workers and peasants exhibited much more incentive and creativity under libertarian socialism than they had under the private enterprise system. This is apparent from Gaston Leval's description of the results of collectivisation in Cargagente in the southern part of the province of Valencia:

"The climate of the region is particularly suited for the cultivation of oranges ... All of the socialised land, without exception, is cultivated with infinite care. The orchards are thoroughly weeded. To assure that the trees will get all the nourishment needed, the peasants are incessantly cleaning the soil. 'Before,' they told me with pride, 'all this belonged to the rich and was worked by miserably paid labourers. The land was neglected and the owners had to buy immense quantities of chemical fertilisers, although they could have gotten much better yields by cleaning the soil ...' With pride, they showed me trees that had been grafted to produce better fruit.

"In many places I observed plants growing in the shade of the orange trees. 'What is this?,' I asked. I learned that the Levant peasants (famous for their ingenuity) have abundantly planted potatoes among the orange groves. The peasants demonstrate more intelligence than all the bureaucrats in the Ministry of Agriculture combined. They do more than just plant potatoes. Throughout the whole region of the Levant, wherever the soil is suitable, they grow crops. They take advantage of the four month [fallow period] in the rice fields. Had the Minister of Agriculture followed the example of these peasants throughout the Republican zone, the bread shortage problem would have been overcome in a few months." [**Anarchist Collectives**, p. 153]

This is just one from a multitude of examples presented in the accounts of both the industrial and rural collectives. We have already noted some examples of the improvements in efficiency realised by collectivisation during the Spanish Revolution (section I.4.10). Another example was the baking industry. Souchy reported

that, *"[a]s in the rest of Spain, Barcelona's bread and cakes were baked mostly at night in hundreds of small bakeries. Most of them were in damp, gloomy cellars infested with roaches and rodents. All these bakeries were shut down. More and better bread and cake were baked in new bakeries equipped with new modern ovens and other equipment."* [**Op. Cit.**, p. 82] In Granollers, the syndicate *"was at all times a prime-mover. All kinds of initiatives tending to improve the operation and structure of the local economy could be attributed to it."* The collectivised hairdressing, shoe-making, wood-working and engineering industries were all improved, with small, unhealthy and inefficient workplaces closed and replaced by larger, more pleasant and efficient establishments. *"Socialisation went hand in hand with rationalisation."* [Gaston Leval, **Collectives in the Spanish Revolution**, p. 287] For more see sectionI.8.6 as well as section C.2.8 (in which we present more examples when refuting the charge that workers' control would stifle innovation).

The substantial evidence available, of which these examples are but a small number, proves that the membership of the collectives showed a keen awareness of the importance of investment and innovation in order to increase production, to make work both lighter and more interesting **and** that the collectives allowed that awareness to be expressed freely. The collectives indicate that, given the chance, everyone will take an interest in their own affairs and express a desire to use their minds to improve their lives and surroundings. In fact, capitalism distorts what innovation exists under hierarchy by channelling it purely into how to save money and maximise investor profit, ignoring other, more important, issues. As Gaston Leval suggested, self-management encouraged innovation:

"The theoreticians and partisans of the liberal economy affirm that competition stimulates initiative and, consequently, the creative spirit and invention without which it remains dormant. Numerous observations made by the writer in the Collectives, factories and socialised workshops permit him to take quite the opposite view. For in a Collective, in a grouping where each individual is stimulated by the wish to be of service to his fellow beings, research, the desire for technical perfection and so on are also stimulated. But they also have as a consequence that other individuals join those who were first to get together. Furthermore, when, in present society, an individualist inventor discovers something, it is used only by the capitalist or the individual employing him, whereas in the case of an inventor living in a community not only is his discovery taken up and developed by others, but is immediately applied for the common good. I am convinced that this superiority would very soon manifest itself in a socialised society." [**Op. Cit.**, p. 347]

Therefore the actual experiences of self-management in Spain support the points made in section I.4.11. Freed from hierarchy, individuals will creatively interact with the world to improve their circumstances. For the human mind is an active agent and unless crushed by authority it can no more stop thinking and acting than the Earth can stop revolving round the Sun. In addition, the Collectives indicate that self-management allows ideas to be enriched by discussion.

The experience of self-management proved Bakunin's point that society is collectively more intelligent than even the most intelligent individual simply because of the wealth of viewpoints, experience and thoughts contained there. Capitalism impoverishes individuals and society by its artificial boundaries and authority structures.

I.8.9 Why, if it was so good, did it not survive?

Just because something is good does not mean that it will survive. For example, the Warsaw Ghetto uprising against the Nazis failed but that does not mean that the uprising was a bad cause or that the Nazi regime was correct, far from it. Similarly, while the experiment in workers' self-management and free communes undertaken across Republican Spain is one of the most important social experiments in a free society ever undertaken, this cannot change the fact that Franco's forces and the Communists had access to more and better weapons.

Faced with the aggression and terrorism of Franco, and behind him the military might of Fascist Italy and Nazi Germany, the treachery of the Communists, and the aloofness of the Western "democratic" states (whose policy of "non-intervention" was strangely ignored when their citizens aided Franco) it is amazing the revolution lasted as long as it did.

This does not excuse the actions of the anarchists themselves. As is well known, the CNT co-operated with the other anti-fascist parties and trade unions on the Republican side ultimately leading to anarchists joining the government (see next section). This co-operation helped ensure the defeat of the revolution. While much of the blame can be placed at the door of the would-be "leaders" (who like most leaders started to think themselves irreplaceable), it must be stated that the rank-and-file of the movement did little to stop them. Most of the militant anarchists were at the front-line (and so excluded from union and collective meetings) and so could not influence their fellow workers (it is no surprise that the radical "Friends of Durruti" anarchist group were mostly ex-militia men). However, it seems that the mirage of anti-fascist unity proved too much for the majority of CNT members (see section I.8.12).

A few anarchists still maintain that the Spanish anarchist movement had no choice and that collaboration (while having unfortunate effects) was the only choice available. This view was defended by Sam Dolgoff and finds some support in the writings of Gaston Leval, August Souchy and other participants in the revolution. However, most anarchists today oppose collaboration and think it was a terrible mistake (at the time, this position was held by the majority of non-Spanish anarchists plus a large minority of the Spanish movement, becoming a majority as the implications of collaboration became clear). This viewpoint finds its best expression in Vernon Richard's **Lessons of the Spanish Revolution** and, in part, in such works as **Anarchists in the Spanish Revolution** by Jose Peirats, **Anarchist Organisation: The History of the FAI** by Juan Gomaz Casas and **Durruti in the Spanish Revolution** by Abel Paz as well as in a host of pamphlets and articles written by anarchists ever since.

So, regardless of how good a social system is, objective facts will overcome that experiment. Saturnino Carod (a leader of a CNT Militia column at the Aragón Front) summed up the successes of the revolution as well as its objective limitations:

> "Always expecting to be stabbed in the back, always knowing that if we created problems, only the enemy across the lines would stand to gain. It was a tragedy for the anarcho-syndicalist movement; but it was a tragedy for something greater — the Spanish people. For it can never be forgotten that it was the working class and peasantry which, by demonstrating their ability to run industry and agriculture collectively, allowed the republic to continue the struggle for thirty-two months. It was they who created a war industry, who kept agricultural production increasing, who formed militias and later joined the army. Without their creative endeavour, the republic could not have fought the war ..." [quoted by Ronald Fraser, **Blood of Spain**, p. 394]

So, regardless of its benefits, regardless of its increase in liberty and equality, the revolution was defeated. This should not blind us to its achievements or the potential it expressed. Rather, it should be used both as a source of inspiration and lessons.

I.8.10 Why did the CNT collaborate with the state?

As is well known, in September 1936 the CNT joined the Catalan government, followed by the central government in November. This flowed from the decision made on July 21st to not speak of Libertarian Communism until after Franco had been defeated. In other words, to collaborate with other anti-fascist parties and unions in a common front against fascism. This decision, initially, involved the CNT agreeing to join a *"Central Committee of Anti-Fascist Militias"* proposed by the leader of the Catalan government, Louis Companys. This committee was made up of representatives of various anti-fascist parties and groups. From this it was only a matter of time until the CNT joined an official government as no other means of co-ordinating activities existed (see section I.8.13).

The question must arise, **why** did the CNT decide to collaborate with the state, forsake its principles and, in its own way, contribute to the counter-revolution and the loosing of the war. This is an important question. Indeed, it is one Marxists always throw up in arguments with anarchists or in anti-anarchist diatribes. Does the failure of the CNT to implement anarchism after July 19th mean that anarchist politics are flawed? Or, rather, does the experience of the CNT and FAI during the Spanish revolution indicate a failure of **anarchists** rather than of **anarchism,** a mistake made under difficult objective circumstances and one which anarchists have learnt from? Needless to say, anarchists argue that the latter is correct. In other words, as Vernon Richards argued, *"the basis of [this] criticism is not that anarchist ideas were proved to be unworkable by the Spanish experience, but that the Spanish anarchists and syndicalists failed* *to put their theories to the test, adopting instead the tactics of the enemy."* [**Lessons of the Spanish Revolution**, p. 14]

So, why **did** the CNT collaborate with the state during the Spanish Civil War? Simply put, rather than being the fault of anarchist theory (as Marxists like to claim), its roots can be discovered in the situation facing the Catalan anarchists on July 20th. The objective conditions facing the leading militants of the CNT and FAI influenced the decisions they took, decisions which they later justified by **mis**-using anarchist theory.

What was the situation facing the Catalan anarchists on July 20th? Simply put, it was an unknown situation, as the report made by the CNT to the **International Workers Association** made clear:

> *"Levante was defenceless and uncertain ... We were in a minority in Madrid. The situation in Andalusia was unknown ... There was no information from the North, and we assumed the rest of Spain was in the hands of the fascists. The enemy was in Aragón, at the gates of Catalonia. The nervousness of foreign consular officials led to the presence of a great number of war ships around our ports."* [quoted by Jose Peirats, **Anarchists in the Spanish Revolution**, p. 180]

Anarchist historian Jose Peirats noted that according to the report *"the CNT was in absolute control of Catalonia in July 19, 1936, but its strength was less in Levante and still less in central Spain where the central government and the traditional parties were dominant. In the north of Spain the situation was confused. The CNT could have mounted an insurrection on its own 'with probable success' but such a take-over would have led to a struggle on three fronts: against the fascists, the government and foreign capitalism. In view of the difficulty of such an undertaking, collaboration with other antifascist groups was the only alternative."* [**Op. Cit.**, p. 179] In the words of the CNT report itself:

> *"The CNT showed a conscientious scrupulousness in the face of a difficult alternative: to destroy completely the State in Catalonia, to declare war against the Rebels [i.e. the fascists], the government, foreign capitalism, and thus assuming complete control of Catalan society; or collaborating in the responsibilities of government with the other antifascist fractions."* [quoted by Robert Alexander, **The Anarchists in the Spanish Civil War**, vol. 2, p. 1156]

Moreover, as Gaston Leval later argued, given that the *"general preoccupation"* of the majority of the population was *"to defeat the fascists ... the anarchists would, if they came out against the state, provoke the antagonism ... of the majority of the people, who would accuse them of collaborating with Franco."* Implementing an anarchist revolution would, in all likelihood, also result in *"the instant closing of the frontier and the blockade by sea by both fascists and the democratic countries. The supply of arms would be completely cut off, and the anarchists would rightly be held responsible for the disastrous consequences."* [**The Anarchist Collectives**, p. 52 and p. 53]

While the supporters of Lenin and Trotsky will constantly point out the objective circumstances in which their heroes made their decisions during the Russian Revolution, they rarely mention those facing the anarchists in Spain on the 20th of July, 1936. It seems hypocritical to point to the Russian Civil War as the explanation of all of the Bolsheviks' crimes against the working class (indeed, humanity) while remaining silent on the forces facing the CNT-FAI at the start of the Spanish Civil War. The fact that **if** the CNT had decided to implement libertarian communism in Catalonia they would have to face the fascists (commanding the bulk of the Spanish army), the Republican government (commanding the rest) **plus** those sections in Catalonia which supported the republic is rarely mentioned. Moreover, when the decision to collaborate was made it was **immediately after the defeat of the army uprising in Barcelona** — the situation in the rest of the country was uncertain and when the social revolution was in its early days. Stuart Christie indicates the dilemma facing the leadership of the CNT at the time:

> *"The higher committees of the CNT-FAI-FIJL in Catalonia saw themselves caught on the horns of a dilemma: social revolution, fascism or bourgeois democracy. Either they committed themselves to the solutions offered by social revolution, regardless of the difficulties involved in fighting both fascism and international capitalism, or, through fear of fascism (or of the people), they sacrificed their anarchist principles and revolutionary objectives to bolster, to become, part of the bourgeois state ... Faced with an imperfect state of affairs and preferring defeat to a possibly Pyrrhic victory, the Catalan anarchist leadership renounced anarchism in the name of expediency and removed the social transformation of Spain from their agenda.*
>
> *"But what the CNT-FAI leaders failed to grasp was that the decision whether or not to implement Libertarian Communism, was not theirs to make. Anarchism was not something which could be transformed from theory into practice by organisational decree ... [the] spontaneous defensive movement of 19 July had developed a political direction of its own."* [**We, the Anarchists!**, p. 99]

Given that the pro-fascist army still controlled a third or more of Spain (including Aragón) and that the CNT was not the dominant force in the centre and north of Spain, it was decided that a war on three fronts would only aid Franco. Moreover, it was a distinct possibility that by introducing libertarian communism in Catalonia, Aragón and elsewhere, the workers' militias and self-managed industries would have been starved of weapons, resources and credit. That isolation was a real problem can be seen from Abad de Santillán's later comments on why the CNT joined the government:

> *"The Militias Committee guaranteed the supremacy of the people in arms ... but we were told and it was repeated to us endlessly that as long as we persisted in retaining it, that is, as long as we persisted in propping up the power of the people, weapons would not come to Catalonia, nor would we be granted the foreign currency to obtain them from abroad, nor would we be supplied with the raw materials for our industry. And since losing*

the war meant losing everything and returning to a state like that prevailed in the Spain of Ferdinand VII, and in the conviction that the drive given by us and our people could not vanish completely from the new economic life, we quit the Militias Committee to join the Generalidad government." [quoted by Christie, **Op. Cit.**, p. 109]

It was decided to collaborate and reject the basic ideas of anarchism until the war was over. A terrible mistake, but one which can be understood given the circumstances in which it was made. This is not, we stress, to justify the decision but rather to explain it and place it in context. Ultimately, the **experience** of the Civil War saw a blockade of the Republic by both "democratic" and fascist governments, the starving of the militias and self-managed collectives of resources and credit as well as a war on two fronts when the State felt strong enough to try and crush the CNT and the semi-revolution its members had started. Most CNT members did not think that when faced with the danger of fascism, the liberals, the right-wing socialists and communists would prefer to undermine the anti-fascist struggle by attacking the CNT. They were wrong and, in this, history proved Durruti totally correct:

"For us it is a matter of crushing Fascism once and for all. Yes, and in spite of the Government.

"No government in the world fights Fascism to the death. When the bourgeoisie sees power slipping from its grasp, it has recourse to Fascism to maintain itself. The liberal government of Spain could have rendered the fascist elements powerless long ago. Instead it compromised and dallied. Even now at this moment, there are men in this Government who want to go easy on the rebels. You can never tell, you know — he laughed — the present Government might yet need these rebellious forces to crush the workers' movement …

"We know what we want. To us it means nothing that there is a Soviet Union somewhere in the world, for the sake of whose peace and tranquillity the workers of Germany and China were sacrificed to Fascist barbarians by Stalin. We want revolution here in Spain, right now, not maybe after the next European war. We are giving Hitler and Mussolini far more worry to-day with our revolution than the whole Red Army of Russia. We are setting an example to the German and Italian working class on how to deal with fascism.

"I do not expect any help for a libertarian revolution from any Government in the world. Maybe the conflicting interests of the various imperialisms might have some influence in our struggle. That is quite possible … But we expect no help, not even from our own Government, in the last analysis."

"You will be sitting on a pile of ruins if you are victorious," said [the journalist] van Paasen.

Durruti answered: *"We have always lived in slums and holes in the wall. We will know how to accommodate ourselves for a time. For, you must not forget, we can also build. It is we the workers who built these palaces and cities here in Spain and in America and everywhere. We, the workers, can build others to take their place. And better ones! We are not in the least afraid of ruins. We are going to inherit the earth; there is not the slightest doubt about that. The bourgeoisie might blast and ruin its own world before it leaves the stage of history. We carry a new world here, in our hearts. That world is growing this minute."* [quoted by Vernon Richards, **Lessons of the Spanish Revolution**, pp. 193-4f]

This desire to push the revolution further was not limited to Durruti, as can be seen from this communication from the Catalan CNT leadership in August 1936. It also expresses the fears driving the decisions which had been made:

"Reports have also been received from other regions. There has been some talk about the impatience of some comrades who wish to go further than crushing fascism, but for the moment the situation in Spain as a whole is extremely delicate. In revolutionary terms, Catalonia is an oasis within Spain.

"Obviously no one can foresee the changes which may follow the civil war and the conquest of that part of Spain which is still under the control of mutinous reactionaries." [quoted by Jose Peirats, **Op. Cit.**, pp. 151-2]

Isolation, the uneven support for a libertarian revolution across Spain and the dangers of fascism were real problems, but they do not excuse the libertarian movement for its mistakes. The biggest of these mistakes was forgetting basic anarchist ideas and an anarchist approach to the problems facing the Spanish people. If these ideas had been applied in Spain, the outcome of the Civil War and Revolution could have been different.

In summary, while the decision to collaborate is one that can be understood (due to the circumstances under which it was made), it cannot be justified in terms of anarchist theory. Indeed, as we argue in the next section, attempts by the CNT leadership to justify the decision in terms of anarchist principles are not convincing and cannot be done without making a mockery of anarchism.

I.8.11 Was the decision to collaborate a product of anarchist theory?

Marxist critics of Anarchism point to CNT's decision to collaborate with the bourgeois state against Franco as the key proof that libertarian socialism is flawed. Such a claim, anarchists reply, is false for rather than being the product of anarchist ideology, the decision was made in light of the immediate danger of fascism and the situation in other parts of the country. The fact is that the circumstances in which the decision to collaborate was made are rarely mentioned by Marxists. To quote a sadly typical Marxist diatribe:

"This question of state power, and which class holds it, was to prove crucial for revolutionaries during the Spanish Civil War and in particular during the revolutionary upheavals in Catalonia. Here anarchism faced its greatest test and greatest opportunity, yet it failed the former and therefore missed the latter.

"When the government in the region under the leadership of Companys admitted its impotence and offered to dissolve, effectively handing power to the revolutionary forces, the anarchists turned them down. CNT leader and FAI ... militant Garcia Oliver explained, 'The CNT and the FAI decided on collaboration and democracy, renouncing revolutionary totalitarianism which would lead to the strangulation of the revolution by the anarchist and Confederal dictatorship. We had to choose, between Libertarian Communism, which meant anarchist dictatorship, and democracy, which meant collaboration.' The choice was between leaving the state intact and paving the way for Franco's victory or building a workers' government in Catalonia which could act as a focal point for the defeat of Franco and the creation of the structures of a new workers' state. In choosing the former the anarchists were refusing to distinguish between a capitalist state and a workers' state ... The movement that started by refusing to build a workers' state ended up by recognising a capitalist one and betraying the revolution in the process." [Pat Stack, *"Anarchy in the UK?"*, **Socialist Review**, no. 246]

There are four key flaws in this kind of argument. First, there is the actual objective situation in which the decision to collaborate was made in. Strangely, for all his talk of anarchists ignoring *"material conditions"* when we discuss the Russian revolution, Stack fails to mention any when he discusses Spain. As such, his critique is pure idealism, without any attempt to ground it in the objective circumstances facing the CNT and FAI. Second, the quote provided as the only evidence for Stack's analysis dates from a year **after** the decision was made. Rather than reflect the actual concerns of the CNT and FAI at the time, they reflect the attempts of the leaders of an organisation which had significantly departed from its libertarian principles to justify their actions. While this obviously suits Stack's idealist analysis of events, its use is flawed for that reason. Thirdly, clearly the decision of the CNT and FAI **ignored** anarchist theory. As such, it seems ironic to blame anarchism when anarchists ignore its recommendations, yet this is what Stack does. Lastly, there is the counter-example of Aragón, which clearly refutes Stack's case.

To understand why the CNT and FAI made the decisions it did, it is necessary to do what Stack fails to do, namely to provide some context. The decision to ignore anarchist theory, ignore the state rather than smashing it and work with other anti-fascist organisations was made immediately after the army had been defeated on the streets of Barcelona on the 20th of July, 1936. As we indicated in the last section, the decision of the CNT to collaborate with the state was driven by the fear of isolation. The possibility that by declaring libertarian communism it would have had to fight the Republican

government and foreign interventions **as well as** the military coup influenced the decision reached by the militants of Catalan anarchism. They concluded that pursuing implementing anarchism in the situation they faced would only aid Franco and result in a quick defeat.

As such, the **real** choice facing the CNT was not *"between leaving the state intact ... or building a workers' government in Catalonia which could act as a focal point for the defeat of Franco"* but rather something drastically different: Either work with other anti-fascists against Franco so ensuring unity against the common enemy and pursue anarchism after victory **or** immediately implement libertarian communism and possibly face a conflict on two fronts, against Franco **and** the Republic (and, possibly, imperialist intervention against the social revolution). This situation made the CNT-FAI decided to collaborate with other anti-fascist groups in the Catalan **Central Committee of Anti-Fascist Militias**. To downplay these objective factors and the dilemma they provoked and instead simply blame the decision on anarchist politics is a joke.

Similarly, the Garcia Oliver quote provided by Stack dated from July 1937. They were made as justifications of CNT-FAI actions and were designed for political effect. As such, they simply cannot be taken at face value for these two reasons. It is significant, though, that rather than discuss the actual problems facing the CNT Marxists like Stack prefer to ritualistically trot out a quote made over a year later. They argue that it exposes the bankruptcy of anarchist theory. So convinced of this, they rarely bother discussing the problems facing the CNT after the defeat of the military coup nor do they compare these quotes to the anarchist theory they claim inspired them.

There are good reasons for this. Firstly, if they presented the objective circumstances the CNT found itself it then their readers may see that the decision, while wrong, is understandable and had nothing to do with anarchist theory. Secondly, by comparing this quote to anarchist theory their readers would soon see how at odds they are with each other. Indeed, Garcia Oliver invoked anarchism to justify conclusions that were the exact **opposite** to what that theory actually recommends!

So what can be made of Garcia Oliver's argument? As Abel Paz noted: *"It is clear that the explanations given ... were designed for their political effect, hiding the atmosphere in which these decisions were taken. These declarations were made a year later when the CNT were already far removed from their original positions. It is also the period when they had become involved in the policy of collaboration which led to them taking part in the Central Government. But in a certain way they shed light on the unknown factors which weighted so heavily on these who took part in the historic Plenum."* [**Durruti: The People Armed**, p. 215]

For example, when the decision was made, the revolution had not started yet. The street fighting had just ended and the Plenum decided *"not to speak about Libertarian Communism as long as part of Spain was in the hands of the fascists."* [Mariano R. Vesquez, quoted by Paz, **Op. Cit.**, p. 214] The revolution took place **from below** in the days following the decision, independently of the wishes of the Plenum. In the words of Abel Paz:

"When the workers reached their workplaces ... they found them deserted ... The major centres of production

had been abandoned by their owners ... The CNT and its leaders had certainly not foreseen this situation; if they had, they would have given appropriate guidance to the workers when they called off the General Strike and ordered a return to work. What happened next was the result of the workers' spontaneous decision to take matters into their own hands.

"Finding the factories deserted, and no instructions from their unions, they resolved to operate the machines themselves." [**The Spanish Civil War**, pp. 54-5]

The rank and file of the CNT, on their own initiative, took advantage of the collapse of state power to transform the economy and social life of Catalonia. Paz stressed that *"no orders were given for expropriation or collectivisation — which proved that the union, which represented the will of their members until July 18th, had now been overtaken by events"* and the *"union leaders of the CNT committees were confronted with a revolution that they had not foreseen ... the workers and peasants had bypassed their leaders and taken collective action."* [**Op. Cit.**, p. 40 and p. 56] As historian Ronald Fraser summarises the *"revolutionary initiative had sprung not from the CNT's leading committees — how could it when the libertarian revolution had been officially 'postponed'? — but from individual CNT unions impelled by the most advanced syndicalist militants."* So while the Catalan CNT *"had 'put off' libertarian revolution ... daily, the revolution in Barcelona was taking root in CNT collectives and union-run industries."* [**Blood of Spain**, p. 139 and p. 179]

As the revolution had not yet begun and the CNT Plenum had decided **not** to call for its start, it is difficult to see how *"libertarian communism"* (i.e. the revolution) could *"lead to the strangulation of the revolution"* (i.e. libertarian communism). In other words, this particular rationale put forward by Garcia Oliver could not reflect the real thoughts of those present at the CNT plenum and so, obviously, was a later justification for the CNT's actions. Moreover, the decision made then clearly stated that Libertarian Communism would be back on the agenda once Franco was defeated. Oliver's comments were applicable **after** Franco was defeated just as much as on July 20th, 1936.

Similarly, Libertarian Communism is based on self-management, by its nature opposed to dictatorship. According to the CNT's resolution at its congress in Zaragoza in May, 1936, *"the foundation of this administration will be the Commune"* which is *"autonomous"* and *"federated at regional and national levels."* The commune *"will undertake to adhere to whatever general norms [that] may be agreed by majority vote after free debate."* [quoted by Jose Peirats, **The CNT in the Spanish Revolution**, vol. 1, p. 106] It stressed the free nature of society aimed at by the CNT:

"The inhabitants of a commune are to debate among themselves their internal problems ... Federations are to deliberate over major problems affecting a country or province and all communes are to be represented at their reunions and assemblies, thereby enabling their delegates to convey the democratic viewpoint of their respective communes ... every commune which is implicated will have

its right to have its say ... On matters of a regional nature, it is the duty of the regional federation to implement agreements ... So the starting point is the individual, moving on through the commune, to the federation and right on up finally to the confederation." [quoted by Peirats, **Op. Cit.**, p. 107]

Hardly a picture of *"anarchist dictatorship"*! Indeed, it is far more democratic than the capitalist state Oliver described as *"democracy."* So Oliver's arguments from 1937 are totally contradictory. After all, he is arguing that libertarian communism (a society based on self-managed free associations organised and run from the bottom up) is an *"anarchist dictatorship"* and **less** democratic than the capitalist Republic he had been fighting against between 1931 and 1936! Moreover, libertarian communism **inspired** the revolution and so to reject it in favour of capitalist democracy to stop *"the strangulation of the revolution"* makes no sense.

Clearly, these oft quoted words of Garcia Oliver cannot be taken at face value. Made in 1937, they present an attempt to misuse anarchist ideals to defend the anti-anarchist activities of the CNT leadership rather than a meaningful explanation of the decisions made on the 20th of July, 1936. It is safe to take his words with a large pinch of salt. To rely upon them for an analysis of the actions of the Spanish Anarchists or the failings of anarchism suggests an extremely superficial perspective. This is particularly the case when we look at both the history of the CNT and anarchist theory.

This can clearly been seen from the report made by the CNT to the **International Workers Association** to justify the decision to forget anarchist theory and collaborate with bourgeois parties and join the government. The report states that *"the CNT, loyal to its ideals and its purely anarchist nature, did not attack the forms of the State, nor try publicly to penetrate or dominate it ... none of the political or juridical institutions were abolished."* [quoted by Robert Alexander, **The Anarchists in the Spanish Civil War**, vol. 2, p. 1156] In other words, according to this report, "anarchist" ideals do not, in fact, mean the destruction of the state, but rather the **ignoring** of the state. That this is nonsense, concocted to justify the CNT leaderships' betrayal of its ideals, is clear. To prove this we just need to look at Bakunin and Kropotkin and look at the activities of the CNT **before** the start of the war.

According to anarchist ideas, to quote Bakunin, *"the revolution must set out from the first to radically and totally destroy the State"* and that the *"natural and necessary consequence of this destruction"* will include the *"dissolution of army, magistracy, bureaucracy, police and priesthood"* as well as the *"confiscation of all productive capital and means of production on behalf of workers' associations, who are to put them to use"*. The state would be replaced by *"the federative Alliance of all working men's associations"* which *"will constitute the Commune."* These communes, in turn, would *"constitute the federation of insurgent associations ... and organise a revolutionary force capable of defeating reaction."* [**Michael Bakunin: Selected Writings**, pp. 170-1] For Kropotkin, the *"Commune ... must break the State and replace it by the Federation."* [**Words of a Rebel**, p. 83]

Thus anarchism has always been clear on what to do with the state, and it is obviously not what the CNT did to it! The CNT ignored these recommendations and so given that it did **not** destroy the state, nor create a federation of workers' councils, then how can anarchist theory be blamed? It seems strange to point to the failure of anarchists to apply their politics as an example of the failure of those politics, yet this is what the likes of Stack are doing.

Nor had the CNT always taken this perspective. Before the start of the Civil War, the CNT had organised numerous insurrections against the state. For example, in the spontaneous revolt of CNT miners in January 1932, the workers *"seized town halls, raised the black-and-red flags of the CNT, and declared **communismo libertario**."* In Tarassa, the same year, the workers again *"seiz[ed] town halls"* and the town was *"swept by street fighting."* The revolt in January 1933 began with *"assaults by Anarchist action groups … on Barcelona's military barracks … Serious fighting occurred in working-class **barrios** and the outlying areas of Barcelona … Uprising occurred in Tarassa, Sardanola-Ripollet, Lerida, in several **pueblos** in Valencia province, and in Andalusia."* In December 1933, the workers *"reared barricades, attacked public buildings, and engaged in heavy street fighting … many villages declared libertarian communism."* [Murray Bookchin, **The Spanish Anarchists**, p. 225, p. 226, p. 227 and p. 238]

It seems that the CNT leadership's loyalty to *"its ideals and its purely anarchist nature"* which necessitated *"not attack[ing] the forms of the State"* was a very recent development!

As can be seen, the rationales later developed to justify the betrayal of anarchist ideas and the revolutionary workers of Spain have no real relationship to anarchist theory. They were created to justify a non-anarchist approach to the struggle against fascism, an approach based on ignoring struggle from below and instead forging alliances with parties and unions at the top. This had been not always been the case. Throughout the 1930s the UGT and Socialist Party had rejected the CNT's repeated calls for a revolutionary alliance from below in favour of a top-down *"Workers' Alliance"* which, they believed, would be the only way which would allow them to control the labour movement. The CNT, rightly, rejected such a position in favour of an alliance from the bottom up yet, in July 1936, the need for unity was obvious and the UGT was not changing its position. So while in Barcelona the state had been destroyed in all but name, *"in Madrid, thanks to the Socialist Party, bourgeois structures were left intact and even fortified: a semi-dead state received a new lease of life and no dual power was created to neutralise it."* [Abel Paz, **Durruti in the Spanish Revolution**, p. 462]

Rather than trying to cement a unity with other organisations at the top level in July 1936, the leadership of the CNT should have applied their anarchist ideas by inciting the oppressed to enlarge and consolidate their gains (which they did anyway). This would have liberated all the potential energy within the country (and elsewhere), energy that clearly existed as can be seen from the spontaneous collectivisations that occurred after the fateful Plenum of July 20th and the creation of volunteer workers' militia columns sent to liberate those parts of Spain which had fallen to Franco.

The role of anarchists, therefore, was that of *"inciting the people to abolish capitalistic property and the institutions through which it exercises its power for the exploitation of the majority by a minority"* and *"to support, to incite and encourage the development of the social revolution and to frustrate any attempts by the bourgeois* *capitalist state to reorganise itself, which it would seek to do."* This would involve *"seeking to destroy bourgeois institutions through the creation of revolutionary organisms."* [Vernon Richards, **Lessons of the Spanish Revolution**, p. 44, p. 46 and p. 193] In other words, to encourage, the kind of federation of communities and workplaces Bakunin and Kropotkin had called for.

Indeed, such an organisation already existing in embryo in the CNT's **barrios** defence committees which had led and co-ordinated the struggle against the military coup throughout Barcelona. *"The Neighbourhood Committees, which had diverse names but all shared a libertarian outlook, federated and created a revolutionary Local Co-ordination Committee."* They *"became Revolutionary Committees and formed what was called the 'Federation of Barricades.' It was the Committees that held power in Barcelona that evening."* [Paz, **Op. Cit.**, p. 470 and p. 445] Rather than collaborate with political parties and the UGT at the top, in the Central Committee of Anti-Fascist Militias, the CNT should have developed these organs of community self-organisation:

> *"Power lay in the street on July 20, represented by the people in arms … Life took on a new momentum and it both destroyed and created as the people worked to resolve practical necessities born from a collective life that lived — and wanted to continue living — in the street … The street and the people in arms were the living force of the revolution … The Defence Committees, now transformed into Revolutionary Committees, back up this force. They organised what was called the 'Federation of Barricades.' Militants, standing resolutely behind these barricades, represented them in the Revolutionary Committees."* [Paz, **Op. Cit.**, pp. 450-1]

Later, a delegate meeting from the various workplaces (whether previously unionised or not) would have had to been arranged to organise, to re-quote Bakunin, *"the federal Alliance of all working men's associations"* which would *"constitute the Commune"* and complement the *"federation of the barricades."* [**Op. Cit.**, p. 170] In more modern terminology, a federation of workers' councils combined with a federation of workers' militias and community assemblies. Without this, the revolution was doomed as was the war against Franco. A minority of anarchists **did** see this genuinely libertarian solution at the time, but sadly they were a minority. For example, the members of the **Nosotros** Group, which included Durruti, thought *"it was necessary to transcend the alliance between the CNT and the political parties and create an authentic revolutionary organisation. That organisation would rest directly on Barcelona's and Catalonia's unions and Revolutionary Committees. Together, those groups would form a Regional Assembly, which would be the revolution's executive body."* [Paz, **Op. Cit.**, p. 471] Such a development, applying the basic ideas of anarchism (and as expounded in the CNT's May resolution on Libertarian Communism), was not an impossibility. After all, as we will see, the CNT-FAI organised along those lines in Aragón.

Concern that Catalonia would be isolated from the rest of the Republic was foremost in the minds of many in the CNT and FAI. The fear that if libertarian communism was implemented then a civil war within the anti-fascist forces would occur (so aiding Franco) was a real one. Unfortunately, the conclusion drawn from that fear, namely to win the war against Franco before talking about the revolution, was the wrong one. After all, a civil war within the Republican side **did** occur, when the state had recovered enough to start it. Similarly, with the fear of a blockade by foreign governments. This happened anyway, confirming the analysis of activists like Durruti.

Organising a full and proper delegate meeting in the first days of the revolution would have allowed all arguments and suggestions to be discussed by the whole membership of the CNT and, perhaps, a different decision may have been reached on the subject of collaboration. After all, many CNT members were applying anarchist politics by fighting fascism via a revolutionary war. This can be seen by the rank and file of the CNT and FAI ignoring the decision to "postpone" the revolution in favour of an anti-fascist war. All across Republican Spain, workers and peasants started to expropriate capital and the land, placing it under workers' self-management. They did so on their own initiative. It is also possible, as discussed in the next section, that anti-fascist unity would have prevailed and so the some decision would have been reached.

Be that as it may, by thinking they could postpone the revolution until after the war, the CNT leadership made two mistakes. Firstly, they should have known that their members would hardly miss this opportunity to implement libertarian ideas so making their decision redundant (and a statist backlash inevitable). Secondly, they abandoned their anarchist ideas, failing to understand that the struggle against fascism would never be effective without the active participation of the working class. Such participation could never be achieved by placing the war before the revolution and by working in top-down, statist structures or within a state.

Indeed, the mistake made by the CNT, while understandable, cannot be justified given that their consequences had been predicted by numerous anarchists beforehand, including Kropotkin. Decades earlier in an essay on the Paris Commune, the Russian anarchist refuted the two assumptions of the CNT leadership — first, of placing the war before the revolution and, second, that the struggle could be waged by authoritarian structures or a state. He explicitly attacked the mentality and logic of those who argued *"Let us first make sure of victory, and then see what can be done"*:

> *"Make sure of victory! As if there were any way of transforming society into a free commune without laying hands upon property! As if there were any way of defeating the enemy so long as the great mass of the people is not directly interested in the triumph of the revolution, in witnessing the arrival of material, moral and intellectual well-being for all! They sought to consolidate the Commune first of all while postponing the social revolution for later on, while the only effective way of proceeding was* **to consolidate the Commune by the social revolution***!"* [**Words of a Rebel**, p. 97]

Kropotkin's argument was sound, as the CNT discovered. By waiting until victory in the war they were defeated (as Abel Paz suggested, the workers of Spain *"had to build a new world to secure and defend their victory."* [**Op. Cit.**, p. 451]). Kropotkin also indicated the inevitable effects of the CNT's actions in co-operating with the state and joining representative bodies:

> *"Paris … sent her devoted sons to the Hotel-de-Ville [town hall]. Indeed, immobilised there by fetters of red tape, forced to discuss when action was needed, and losing the sensitivity that comes from continual contact with the masses, they saw themselves reduced to impotence. Paralysed by their distancing from the revolutionary centre — the people — they themselves paralysed the popular initiative."* [**Op. Cit.**, pp. 97-8]

Which, in a nutshell, was what happened to the leading militants of the CNT who collaborated with the state. Kropotkin was proved right, as was anarchist theory from Bakunin onwards. As Vernon Richards argued, *"there can be no excuse"* for the CNT's decision, as *"they were not mistakes of judgement but the deliberate abandonment of the principles of the CNT."* [**Op. Cit.**, pp. 41-2] It seems difficult to blame anarchist theory for the decisions of the CNT when that theory argues the opposite position. That enemies of anarchism quote Garcia Oliver's words from 1937 to draw conclusions about anarchist theory says more about their politics than about anarchism!

Moreover, while the experience of Spain confirms anarchist theory **negatively**, it also confirms it **positively** by the creation of the Regional Defence Council of Aragón. The Council of Aragón was created by a meeting of delegates from CNT unions, village collectives and militia columns to protect the new society based on libertarian communism the people of Aragón were building. The meeting also decided to press for the setting up of a National Defence Committee which would link together a series of regional bodies that were organised on principles similar to the one now established in Aragón. Durruti stressed that the collectives *"had to build their own means of self-defence and not rely on the libertarian columns which would leave Aragón as the war evolved. They needed to co-ordinate themselves, although he also warned them against forming an anti-fascist political front like the type existing in other parts of Spain. They needn't make the same error as their compatriots elsewhere … The popular assembly must be sovereign."* After a CNT regional assembly militants decided to *"form the Aragón Defence Council and the Aragón Federation of Collectives."* [Paz, **Op. Cit.**, pp. 540-1] This exposes as false the claim that anarchism failed during the Spanish Civil War. In Aragón, the CNT **did** follow the ideas of anarchism, abolishing both the state and capitalism. If they had done this in Catalonia, the outcome of the Civil War may have been different.

The continuity of what happened in Aragón with the ideas of anarchism and the CNT's 1936 Zaragoza Resolution on Libertarian Communism is obvious. The formation of the Regional Defence Council was an affirmation of commitment to the principles of libertarian communism. This principled stand for revolutionary social and economic change stands at odds with the claims that the Spanish Civil War indicates the failure of anarchism. After all, in Aragón the CNT **did** act in accordance with anarchist theory as well as in its own history and politics. It created a federation of workers' associations as argued by Bakunin. To contrast Catalonia and Aragón shows the weakness of Stack's argument. The same organisation, with the same politics, yet different results. How can anarchist ideas be blamed for what happened in Catalonia when they had been applied in Aragón? Such a position could not be logically argued and, unsurprisingly, Aragón usually fails to get mentioned by Marxists when discussing Anarchism during the Spanish Civil War.

Therefore, the activities of the CNT during the Civil War cannot be used to discredit anarchism although it can be used to show that anarchists, like everyone else, can and do make wrong decisions in difficult circumstances. That Marxists always point to this event in anarchist history is unsurprising, for it **was** a terrible mistake. Yet how could anarchism have "failed" during the Spanish Revolution when it was ignored in Catalonia (for fear of fascism) and applied in Aragón? How can it be argued that anarchist politics were to blame when those very same politics had formed the Council of Aragón? It cannot. Simply put, the Spanish Civil War showed the failure of certain anarchists to apply their ideas in a difficult situation rather than the failure of anarchism. As Emma Goldman argued, the *"contention that there is something wrong with Anarchism … because the leading comrades in Spain failed Anarchism seems to be very faulty reasoning … the failure of one or several individuals can never take away from the depth and truth of an ideal."* [**Vision on Fire**, p. 299]

To use the Catalan CNT to generalise about anarchism is false as it, firstly, requires a dismissal of the objective circumstances the decision was made in and, secondly, it means ignoring anarchist theory and history. It also gives the impression that anarchism as a revolutionary theory must be evaluated purely from one event in its history. The experiences of the Makhnovists in the Ukraine, the USI and UAI in the factory occupations of 1920 and fighting fascism in Italy, the insurrections of the CNT during the 1930s, the Council of Aragón created by the CNT in the Spanish Revolution and so on, are all ignored. Hardly convincing, although handy for Marxists. As is clear from the experiences of the Makhnovists and the Council of Aragón, anarchism has been applied successfully on a large scale, both politically and economically, in revolutionary situations.

Equally flawed are any attempts to suggest that those anarchists who remained true to libertarian theory somehow, by so doing, rejected it and moved towards Marxism. This is usually done to the anarchist group the **Friends of Durruti** (FoD). In the words of Pat Stack:

> *"Interestingly the one Spanish anarchist group that developed the most sophisticated critique of all this was the Friends of Durutti [sic!]. As [Trotskyist] Felix Morrow points out, 'They represented a conscious break with the anti-statism of traditional anarchism. They explicitly declared the need for democratic organs of power, juntas or soviets, in the overthrow of capitalism, and the necessary state measures of repression against the counter-revolution.' The failure of the Spanish anarchists to understand exactly that these were the stark choices, workers' power, or capitalist power followed by reaction."* [**Op. Cit.**]

That Stack could not bother to spell Durruti's name correctly shows how seriously we should take this analysis. The FoD were an anarchist grouping within the CNT and FAI which, like a large minority of others, strongly and consistently opposed the policy of anti-fascist unity. Rather than signify a *"conscious break"* with anarchism, it signified a conscious **return** to it. This can be clearly seen when we compare their arguments to those of Bakunin. As noted by Stack, the FoD argued for *"juntas"* in the overthrow of capitalism and to defend against counter-revolution. Yet this was **exactly** what revolutionary anarchists have argued for since Bakunin (see section H.2.1 for details). The continuity of the ideas of the FoD with the pre-Civil War politics of the CNT and the ideas of revolutionary anarchism are clear. As such, the FoD were simply arguing for a return to the traditional positions of anarchism and cannot be considered to have broken with it. If Stack or Morrow knew anything about anarchism, then they would have known this.

As such, the failure of the Spanish anarchists was not the *"stark choice"* between *"workers' power"* and *"capitalist power"* but rather the making of the wrong choice in the real dilemma of introducing anarchism (which would, by definition, be based on workers' power, organisation and self-management) or collaborating with other anti-fascist groups in the struggle against the greater enemy of Franco (i.e. fascist reaction). That Stack does not see this suggests that he simply has no appreciation of the dynamics of the Spanish Revolution and prefers abstract sloganeering to a serious analysis of the problems facing it. He ends by summarising:

> *"The most important lesson … is that whatever ideals and gut instincts individual anarchists may have, anarchism, both in word and deed, fails to provide a roadworthy vehicle for human liberation. Only Marxism, which sees the centrality of the working class under the leadership of a political party, is capable of leading the working class to victory."* [**Op. Cit.**]

As a useful antidote to these claims, we need simply quote Trotsky on what the Spanish anarchists should have done. In his words: *"Because the leaders of the CNT renounced dictatorship **for themselves** they left the place open for the Stalinist dictatorship."* Hardly an example of "workers' power"! Or, as he put it earlier in the same year, a *"revolutionary party, even having seized power (of which the anarchist leaders were incapable in spite of the heroism of the anarchist workers), is still by no means the sovereign ruler of society."* Ultimately, it was the case that the failure of the Spanish Revolution confirmed for Trotsky the truism that the *"revolutionary dictatorship of a proletarian party … is an objective necessity … The revolutionary party (vanguard) which renounces **its own dictatorship** surrenders the masses to the counter-revolution."* Rather than seeing, as anarchists do, workers' councils as being key, Trotsky considered the party, in fact the *"dictatorship of a party"*, as being the decisive factor. [our emphasis, **Writings of Leon Trotsky 1936-37**, p. 514, p. 488 and pp. 513-4] At best, such organs would be used to achieve party power and would simply be a figleaf for its rule (see section H.3.8).

Clearly, the leading Marxist at the time was not arguing for the *"centrality of the working class under the leadership of a political party."* He was arguing for the dictatorship of a "revolutionary" party **over** the working class. Rather than the working class being "central" to the running of a revolutionary regime, Trotsky saw the party taking that position. What sort of *"victory"* is possible when the party has dictatorial power over the working class and the *"sovereign ruler"* of society? Simply the kind of "victory" that leads to Stalinism. Rather than seeing working class organisations as the means by which working people run society, Leninists see them purely in instrumental terms — the means by which the party can seize power. As the Russian Revolution proved beyond doubt, in a conflict between workers' power and party power Leninists will suppress the former to ensure the latter.

To paraphrase Stack, the most important lesson from both the Russian and Spanish revolutions is that whatever ideals and gut instincts individual Leninists may have, Leninism, both in word and deed, fails to provide a roadworthy vehicle for human liberation. Only Anarchism, which sees the centrality of working class self-management of the class struggle and revolution, is capable of ensuring the creation of a real, free, socialist society.

Lastly, it could be argued that our critique of the standard Leninist attack on Spanish anarchism is similar to that presented by Leninists to justify Bolshevik authoritarianism during the Russian Revolution. After all, Leninists like Stack point to the objective circumstances facing Lenin's regime — its isolation, civil war and economic problems — as explaining its repressive actions. Yet any similarity is superficial as the defeat of the Revolution in Spain was due to anarchists **not** applying all of our ideas, while, in Russia, it was due to the Bolsheviks **applying** their ideology. The difficulties that faced the Russian Revolution pushed the Bolsheviks further down the road they were already travelling down (not to mention that Bolshevik ideology significantly contributed to making many of these problems worse). As we discuss in section H.6, the notion that "objective circumstances" explains Bolshevik tyranny is simply unconvincing, particularly given the role Bolshevik ideology played in this process.

So, to conclude, rather than show the failure of anarchism, the experience of the Spanish Revolution indicates the failure of anarchists to apply their ideas in practice. Faced with extremely difficult circumstances, they compromised their ideas in the name of anti-fascist unity. Their compromises **confirmed** rather than refuted anarchist theory as they led to the defeat of both the revolution **and** the civil war.

I.8.12 Was the decision to collaborate imposed on the CNT's membership?

A few words have to be said about the development of the CNT and FAI after the 19th of July, 1936. It is clear that both changed in nature and were the not same organisations as they were **before** that date. Both organisations became more centralised and bureaucratic, with the membership excluded from many major decisions. As Peirats suggested:

"In the CNT and among militant anarchists there had been a tradition of the most scrupulous respect for the deliberations and decisions of the assemblies, the grassroots of the federalist organisation. Those who held

administrative office had been merely the mandatories of those decisions. The regular motions adopted by the National congresses spelled out to the Confederation and its representative committees ineluctable obligations of a basic and general nature incumbent upon very affiliated member regardless of locality or region. And the forming of such general motions was the direct responsibility of all of the unions by means of motions adopted at their respective general assemblies. Similarly, the Regional or Local Congresses would establish the guidelines of requirement and problems that obtained only at regional or local levels. In both instances, sovereignty resided always with the assemblies of workers whether in their unions or in their groups.

"This sense of rigorous, everyday federalist procedure was abruptly amended from the very outset of the revolutionary phase… This amendment of the norms of the organisation was explained away by reference to the exceptional turn of events, which required a greater agility of decisions and resolutions, which is to say a necessary departure from the circuitous procedures of federalist practice which operated from the bottom upwards." [**The CNT in the Spanish Revolution**, vol. 1, p. 213]

In other words, the CNT had become increasingly hierarchical, with the higher committees becoming transformed into executive bodies rather than administrative ones as *"it is safe to assert that the significant resolutions in the organisation were adopted by the committees, very rarely by the mass constituency. Certainly, circumstances required quick decisions from the organisation, and it was necessary to take precautions to prevent damaging leaks. These necessities tempted the committees to abandon the federalist procedures of the organisation."* [Jose Peirats, **Anarchists in the Spanish Revolution**, p. 188]

Ironically, rather than the *"anarchist leaders"* of the CNT failing to *"seize power"* as Trotsky and his followers lament (see last section), they did — **in their own organisations.** Such a development proved to be a disaster and re-enforced the anarchist critique against hierarchical and centralised organisations. The CNT higher committees became isolated from the membership, pursued their own policies and compromised and paralysed the creative work being done by the rank and file — as predicted in anarchist theory. However, be that as it may, as we will indicate below, it would be false to assert that these higher committees simply imposed the decision to collaborate on their memberships (as, for example, Vernon Richards seems to imply in his **Lessons of the Spanish Revolution**). While it **is** true that the committees presented many decisions as a **fait accompli,** the rank-and-file of the CNT and FAI did not simply follow orders nor ratify all of the decisions blindly.

In any revolutionary situation decisions have to be made quickly and sometimes without consulting the base of the organisation. However, such decisions must be accountable to the membership who must discuss and ratify them (this was the policy within the CNT militias, for example). The experience of the CNT and FAI in countless strikes, insurrections and campaigns had proven the decentralised, federal structure was more than capable of pursuing the class war — revolution is no exception as it is the class war in its most concentrated form. In other words, the organisational principles of the CNT and FAI were more than adequate for a revolutionary situation.

The centralising tendencies, therefore, cannot be blamed on the exceptional circumstances of the war. Rather, it was the policy of collaboration which explains them. Unlike the numerous strikes and revolts that occurred before July 19th, 1936, the CNT higher committees had started to work within the state structure. This, by its very nature, must generate hierarchical and centralising tendencies as those involved must adapt to the states basic structure and form. The violations of CNT policy flowed from the initial decision to compromise in the name of *"anti-fascist unity"* and a vicious circle developed — each compromise pushed the CNT leadership further into the arms of the state, which increased hierarchical tendencies, which in turn isolated these higher committees from the membership, which in turn encouraged a conciliatory policy by those committees.

This centralising and hierarchical tendency did not mean that the higher committees of the CNT simply imposed their will on the rest of the organisation. It is very clear that the decision to collaborate had, initially, the passive support of the majority of the CNT and FAI (probably because they thought the war would be over after a few weeks or months). As visiting French anarchist Sebastian Faure noted, while *"effective participation in central authority has had the approval of the majority within the unions and in the groups affiliated to the FAI, that decision has in many places encountered the opposition of a fairly substantial minority. Thus there has been no unanimity."* [quoted by Jose Peirats, **The CNT in the Spanish Revolution**, vol. 1, p. 183] In the words of Peirats:

> *"Were all of the militants of the same mind? ... Excepting some vocal minorities which expressed their protests in their press organs and through committees, gatherings, plenums and assemblies, the dismal truth is that the bulk of the membership was in thrall to a certain fatalism which was itself a direct consequence of the tragic realities of the war."* [**Op. Cit.**, p. 181]

And:

> *"We have already seen how, on the economic plane, militant anarchism forged ahead, undaunted, with its work of transforming the economy. It is not to be doubted — for to do so would have been to display ignorance of the psychology of the libertarian rank and file of the CNT — that a muffled contest, occasionally erupting at plenums and assemblies and manifest in some press organs broke out as soon as the backsliding began. In this connection, the body of opinion hostile to any possible deviation in tactics and principles was able to count throughout upon spirited champions."* [**Op. Cit.**, p. 210]

Thus, within the libertarian movement, there was a substantial minority who opposed the policy of collaboration and made their opinions known in various publications and meetings. While many (if not most) revolutionary anarchists volunteered for the militias and so

were not active in their unions as before, there were various groups (such as Catalan Libertarian Youth, the Friends of Durruti, other FAI groups, and so on) which were opposed to collaboration and argued their case openly in the streets, collectives, organisational meetings and so on. Moreover, outside the libertarian movement the two tiny Trotskyist groups also argued against collaboration, as did sections of the POUM. Therefore it is impossible to state that the CNT membership were unaware of the arguments against the dominant policy. Also the Catalan CNT's higher committees, for example, after the May Days of 1937 could not get union assemblies or plenums to expel the Friends of Durruti nor to get them to withhold financial support for the Libertarian Youth, who opposed collaboration vigorously in their publications, nor get them to call upon various groups of workers to stop distributing opposition publications in the public transit system or with the daily milk. [Abe Bluestein, *"Translator's Note"*, Juan Gomez Casas, **Anarchist Organisation: The History of the FAI**, p. 10]

This suggests that in spite of centralising tendencies, the higher committees of the CNT were still subject to some degree of popular influence and control and should not be seen as having dictatorial powers over the organisation. While many decisions **were** presented as **fait accompli** to the union plenums (often called by the committees at short notice), in violation of past CNT procedures, the plenums could not be railroaded into ratifying **any** decision the committees wanted. The objective circumstances associated with the war against Franco and fascism convinced most CNT members and libertarian activists that working with other parties and unions within the state was the only feasible option. Also to do otherwise, they thought, was to weaken the war effort by provoking another Civil War in the anti-Franco camp. While such a policy did not work (when it was strong enough the Republican state did start a civil war against the CNT which gutted the struggle against fascism) it cannot be argued that it was imposed upon the membership nor that they did not hear opposing positions. Sadly, the call for anti-fascist unity dominated the minds of the libertarian movement.

In the early stages, the majority of rank-and-file militants believed that the war would be over in a matter of weeks. After all, a few days had been sufficient to rout the army in Barcelona and other industrial centres. This inclined them to, firstly, tolerate (indeed, support) the collaboration of the CNT with the *"Central Committee of Anti-Fascist Militias"* and, secondly, to start expropriating capitalism in the belief that the revolution would soon be back on track (the opportunity to start introducing anarchist ideas was simply too good to waste, regardless of the wishes of the CNT leadership). They believed that the revolution and libertarian communism, as debated and adopted by the CNT's Zaragoza Congress of May that year, was an inseparable aspect of the struggle against fascism and proceeded appropriately. The ignoring of the state, rather than its destruction, was seen as a short-term compromise, soon to be corrected. Sadly, they were wrong — collaboration had a logic all its own, one which got worse as the war dragged on (and soon it was too late).

Which, we must note indicates the superficial nature of most Marxist attacks on anarchism using the CNT as the key evidence. After all, it was the anarchists and anarchist influenced members of the CNT who organised the collectives, militias and started the transformation of Spanish society. They did so inspired by anarchism and in an anarchist way. To praise their actions, while attacking "anarchism", shows a lack of logic. Indeed, these actions have more in common with anarchist ideas than the actions and rationales of the CNT leadership. Thus, to attack "anarchism" by pointing to the anti-anarchist actions of a few leaders while ignoring the anarchist actions of the majority is flawed.

Therefore, to summarise, it is clear that while the internal structure of the CNT was undermined and authoritarian tendencies increased by its collaboration with the state, the CNT was not transformed into a mere appendage to the higher committees of the organisation. The union plenums could and did reject the calls made by the leadership of the CNT. Support for "anti-fascist unity" was widespread among the CNT membership (in spite of the activities and arguments of large minority of anarchists) and was reflected in the policy of collaboration pursued by the organisation. While the CNT higher committees were transformed into a bureaucratic leadership, increasingly isolated from the rank and file, it cannot be argued that their power was absolute nor totally at odds with the wishes of the membership. Ironically, but unsurprisingly, the divergences from the CNT's previous libertarian organisational principles confirmed anarchist theory, becoming a drag on the revolution and a factor in its defeat.

As we argued in section I.8.11, the initial compromise with the state, the initial betrayal of anarchist theory and CNT policy, contained all the rest. Moreover, rather than refute anarchism, the experience of the CNT after it had rejected anarchist theory confirmed it — centralised, hierarchical organisations hindered and ultimately destroyed the revolution. The experience of the CNT and FAI suggests that those, like Leninists, who argue for **more** centralisation and for "democratic" hierarchical structures have refused to understand, let alone learn from, history. The increased centralisation within the CNT aided and empowered the leadership (a minority) and disempowered the membership (the majority). Rather than federalism hindering the revolution, it, as always, was centralism which did so.

Therefore, in spite of a sizeable minority of anarchists **within** the CNT and FAI arguing against the dominant policy of "anti-fascist unity" and political collaboration, this policy was basically agreed to by the CNT membership and was not imposed upon them. The membership of the CNT could, and did, reject suggestions of the leadership and so, in spite of the centralisation of power that occurred in the CNT due to the policy of collaboration, it cannot be argued that this policy was alien to the wishes of the rank-and-file however lamentable the results of that position were.

I.8.13 What political lessons were learned from the revolution?

The most important political lesson learned from the Spanish Revolution is that a revolution cannot compromise with existing power structures. In this, it just confirmed anarchist theory and the basic libertarian position that a social revolution will only succeed if it follows an anarchist path and does not seek to compromise in the name of fighting a "greater evil." As Kropotkin put it, a "revolution that stops half-way is sure to be soon defeated." [**The Great French Revolution**, vol. 2, p. 553]

On the 20th of July, after the fascist coup had been defeated in Barcelona, the CNT sent a delegation of its members to meet the leader of the Catalan Government. A plenum of CNT union shop stewards, in the light of the fascist coup, agreed that libertarian communism would be postponed until Franco had been defeated (the rank and file ignored them and collectivised their workplaces). They organised a delegation to visit the Catalan president to discuss the situation:

> "The delegation ... was intransigent ... Either Companys [the Catalan president] must accept the creation of a Central Committee [of Anti-Fascist Militias] as the ruling organisation or the CNT would **consult the rank and file and expose the real situation to the workers.** Companys backed down." [our emphasis, Abel Paz, **Durruti: The People Armed**, p. 216]

The CNT committee members used their new-found influence in the eyes of Spain to unite with the leaders of other organisations/ parties but not the rank and file. This process lead to the creation of the **Central Committee of Anti-Fascist Militias**, in which political parties as well as labour unions were represented. This committee was not made up of mandated delegates from workplaces, communities or barricades, but of representatives of existing organisations, nominated by committees. Instead of a genuine confederal body (made up of mandated delegates from workplace, militia and neighbourhood assemblies) the CNT created a body which was not accountable to, nor could reflect the ideas of, working class people expressed in their assemblies. The state and government was not abolished by self-management, only ignored. This was a mistake and many soon came "to realise that once they went into the so-called united-front, they could do nothing else but go further. In other words, the one mistake, the one wrong step inevitably led to others as it always does. I am more than ever convinced that if the comrades had remained firm on their own grounds they would have remained stronger than they are now. But I repeat, once they had made common cause for the period of the anti-Fascist war, they were driven by the logic of events to go further." [Emma Goldman, **Vision on Fire**, pp. 100-1]

The most obvious problem, of course, was that collaboration with the state ensured that a federation of workers' associations could not be created to co-ordinate the struggle against fascism and the social revolution. As Stuart Christie argues: "By imposing their leadership from above, these partisan committees suffocated the mushrooming popular autonomous revolutionary centres — the grass-roots factory and local revolutionary committees — and prevented them from proving themselves as an efficient and viable means of co-ordinating communications, defence and provisioning. They also prevented the Local Revolutionary committees from integrating with each other to form a regional, provincial and national federal network which would facilitate the revolutionary task of social and economic reconstruction." [**We, the Anarchists!**, pp. 99-100] Without such a federation, it was only a matter of time before the CNT joined the bourgeois government.

Rather than being "a regime of **dual power**" and the "most important" of the "new organs of power" as many Trotskyists, following Felix Morrow, maintain, the **Central Committee of Anti-Fascist Militias** created on July 20th, 1936, was, in fact, an organ of class collaboration and a handicap to the revolution. [**Revolution and Counter-Revolution in Spain**, p. 85 and p. 83] Stuart Christie was correct to call it an "artificial and hybrid creation," a "compromise, an artificial political solution, an officially sanctioned appendage of the Generalidad government" which "drew the CNT-FAI leadership inexorably into the State apparatus, until then its principal enemy." [**Op. Cit.**, p. 105] Only a true federation of delegates from the fields, factories and workplaces could have been the framework of a true organisation of (to use Bakunin's expression) "the social (and, by consequence, anti-political) power of the working masses." [**Michael Bakunin: Selected Writings**, pp. 197-8]

Therefore, the CNT forgot a basic principle of anarchism, namely "the destruction ... of the States." Instead, like the Paris Commune, the CNT thought that "in order to combat ... reaction, they had to organise themselves in reactionary Jacobin fashion, forgetting or sacrificing what they themselves knew were the first conditions of revolutionary socialism." The real basis of the revolution, the basic principle of anarchism, was that the "future social organisation must be made solely from the bottom upwards, by the free association or federation of workers, firstly in their unions, then in communes, regions, nations and finally in a great federation, international and universal." [Bakunin, **Op. Cit.**, p. 198, p. 202 and p. 204] By not doing this, by working in a top-down compromise body rather than creating a federation of workers' councils, the CNT leadership could not help eventually sacrificing the revolution in favour of the war.

Of course, if a full plenum of CNT unions and **barrios** defence committees, with delegates invited from UGT and unorganised workplaces, had taken place there is no guarantee that the decision reached would have been in line with anarchist theory. The feelings for antifascist unity were strong. However, the decision would have been fully discussed by the rank and file of the union, under the influence of the revolutionary anarchists who were later to join the militias and leave for the front. It is likely, given the wave of collectivisation and what happened in Aragón, that the decision would have been different and the first step would have made to turn this plenum into the basis of a free federation of workers associations — i.e. the framework of a self-managed society — which could have smashed the state and ensured no other appeared to take its place.

So the basic idea of anarchism, the need to create a federation of workers councils, was ignored. In the name of "antifascist" unity, the CNT worked with parties and classes which hated both them and the revolution. In the words of Sam Dolgoff "both before and after July 19th, an unwavering determination to crush the revolutionary movement was the leitmotif behind the policies of the Republican government; irrespective of the party in power." [**The Anarchist Collectives**, p. 40] Without creating a means to organise the "social power" of the working class, the CNT was defenceless against these parties once the state had re-organised itself.

To justify their collaboration, the leaders of the CNT-FAI argued that not to do so would have lead to a civil war within the civil war, so allowing Franco easy victory. In practice, while paying lip service to the revolution, the Communists and republicans attacked the collectives, murdered anarchists, restricted supplies to collectivised industries (even **war** industries) and disbanded the anarchist militias after refusing to give them weapons and ammunition (preferring to arm the Civil Guard in the rearguard in order to crush the CNT and the revolution). By collaborating, a civil war was not avoided. One occurred anyway, with the working class as its victims, as soon as the state felt strong enough.

Garcia Oliver (the first ever, and hopefully last, "anarchist" minister of justice) stated in 1937 that collaboration was necessary and that the CNT had "renounc[ed] revolutionary totalitarianism, which would lead to the strangulation of the revolution by anarchist and Confederal [CNT] dictatorship. We had confidence in the word and in the person of a Catalan democrat" Companys (who had in the past jailed anarchists). [quoted by Vernon Richards, **Lessons of the Spanish Revolution**, p. 34] Which means that only by working with the state, politicians and capitalists can an anarchist revolution be truly libertarian! Furthermore:

"This argument contains ... two fundamental mistakes, which many of the leaders of the CNT-FAI have since recognised, but for which there can be no excuse, since they were not mistakes of judgement but the deliberate abandonment of the principles of the CNT. Firstly, that an armed struggle against fascism or any other form of reaction could be waged more successfully within the framework of the State and subordinating all else, including the transformation of the economic and social structure of the country, to winning the war. Secondly, that it was essential, and possible, to collaborate with political parties — that is politicians — honestly and sincerely, and at a time when power was in the hands of the two workers organisations ...

"All the initiative ... was in the hands of the workers. The politicians were like generals without armies floundering in a desert of futility. Collaboration with them could not, by any stretch of the imagination, strengthen resistance to Franco. On the contrary, it was clear that collaboration with political parties meant the recreation of governmental institutions and the transferring of initiative from the armed workers to a central body with executive powers. By removing the initiative from the workers, the responsibility for the conduct of the struggle and its objectives were also transferred to a governing hierarchy, and this could not have other than an adverse effect on the morale of the revolutionary fighters." [Richards, **Op. Cit.**, p. 42]

The dilemma of "anarchist dictatorship" or "collaboration" raised in 1937 was fundamentally wrong. It was never a case of banning parties, and other organisations under an anarchist system, far from it. Full rights of free speech, organisation and so on should have existed for all but the parties would only have as much influence as they exerted in union, workplace, community and militia assemblies, as should be the case! "Collaboration" yes, but within the rank and file and within organisations organised in an anarchist manner. Anarchism does not respect the "freedom" to be a boss or politician. In his history of the FAI, Juan Gomaz Casas (an active FAI member in 1936) made this clear:

> "How else could libertarian communism be brought about? It would always signify dissolution of the old parties dedicated to the idea of power, or at least make it impossible for them to pursue their politics aimed at seizure of power. There will always be pockets of opposition to new experiences and therefore resistance to joining 'the spontaneity of the unanimous masses.' In addition, the masses would have complete freedom of expression in the unions and in the economic organisations of the revolution as well as their political organisations in the district and communities." [**Anarchist Organisation: the History of the FAI**, p. 188f]

Instead of this "collaboration" from the bottom up, by means of a federation of workers' associations, community assemblies and militia columns as argued for by anarchists from Bakunin onwards, the CNT and FAI committees favoured "collaboration" from the top down. The leaders ignored the state and co-operated with other trade unions officials as well as political parties in the **Central Committee of Anti-Fascist Militias**. In other words, they ignored their political ideas in favour of a united front against what they considered the greater evil, namely fascism. This inevitably lead the way to counter-revolution, the destruction of the militias and collectives, as they was no means by which these groups could co-ordinate their activities independently of the state. The continued existence of the state ensured that economic confederalism between collectives (i.e. extending the revolution under the direction of the syndicates) could not develop naturally nor be developed far enough in all places. Due to the political compromises of the CNT the tendencies to co-ordination and mutual aid could not develop freely (see next section).

It is clear that the defeat in Spain was due to a failure not of anarchist theory and tactics but a failure of anarchists to **apply** their theory and tactics. Instead of destroying the state, the CNT-FAI ignored it. For a revolution to be successful it needs to create organisations which can effectively replace the state and the market; that is, to create a widespread libertarian organisation for social and economic decision-making through which working class people can start to set their own agendas. Only by going down this route can the state and capitalism be effectively smashed.

In building the new world we must destroy the old one. Revolutions may be, as Engels suggested, "authoritarian" by their very nature, but only in respect to institutions, structures and social relations which promote injustice, hierarchy and inequality. As discussed in section H.7.4, it is not "authoritarian" to destroy authority and not tyrannical to dethrone tyrants! Revolutions, above all else, must be libertarian in respect to the oppressed. That is, they must develop structures that involve the great majority of the population, who have previously been excluded from decision-making on social and economic issues. In fact, a revolution is the most **libertarian** thing ever.

As the **Friends of Durruti** argued a "revolution requires the absolute domination of the workers' organisations." ["The Friends of Durruti

accuse", **Class War on the Home Front**, Wildcat Group (ed.), p. 34] Only this, the creation of viable anarchist social organisations, can ensure that the state and capitalism can be destroyed and replaced with a just system based on liberty, equality and solidarity. Just as Bakunin, Kropotkin and a host of other anarchist thinkers had argued decades previously (see section H.1.4). Thus the most important lesson gained from the Spanish Revolution is simply the correctness of anarchist theory on the need to organise the social and economic power of the working class by a free federation of workers associations to destroy the state. Without this, no revolution can be lasting. As Gomez Casas correctly argued, "if instead of condemning that experience [of collaboration], the movement continues to look for excuses for it, the same course will be repeated in the future ... exceptional circumstances will again put ... anarchism on [its] knees before the State." [**Op. Cit.**, p. 251]

The second important lesson is on the nature of anti-fascism. The CNT leadership, along with many (if not most) of the rank-and-file, were totally blinded by the question of anti-fascist unity, leading them to support a "democratic" state against a "fascist" one. While the basis of a new world was being created around them by the working class, inspiring the fight against fascism, the CNT leaders collaborated with the system that spawns fascism. While the anti-fascist feelings of the CNT leadership were sincere, the same cannot be said of their "allies" (who seemed happier attacking the gains of the semi-revolution than fighting fascism). As the Friends of Durruti make clear: "Democracy defeated the Spanish people, not Fascism." [**Op. Cit.**, p. 30] To be opposed to fascism is not enough, you also have to be anti-capitalist. As Durruti stressed, "[n]o government in the world fights fascism to the death. When the bourgeoisie sees power slipping from its grasp, it has recourse to fascism to maintain itself." [quoted by Vernon Richards, **Op. Cit.**, p. 193f] In Spain, anti-fascism destroyed the revolution, not fascism. As the Scottish Anarchist Ethel McDonald argued at the time: "Fascism is not something new, some new force of evil opposed to society, but is only the old enemy, Capitalism, under a new and fearful sounding name ... Anti-Fascism is the new slogan by which the working class is being betrayed." [**Workers Free Press**, October 1937]

Thirdly, the argument of the CNT that Libertarian Communism had to wait until after the war was a false one. Fascism can only be defeated by ending the system that spawned it (i.e. capitalism). In addition, in terms of morale and inspiration, the struggle against fascism could only be effective if it were also a struggle **for** something better — namely a free society. To fight fascism for a capitalist democracy which had repressed the working class would hardly inspire those at the front. Similarly, the only hope for workers' self-management was to push the revolution as far as possible, i.e. to introduce libertarian communism while fighting fascism. The idea of waiting for libertarian communism ultimately meant sacrificing it for the war effort. This would, by necessity, mean the end of the revolutionary spirit and hope which could inspire and sustain the war effort. Why would people fight for a return to the status quo? A status quo that they had rebelled against before the start of the civil war and which had provoked the fascist coup in the first place.

Fourthly, the role of anarchists in a social revolution is to always encourage organisation "from below" (to use one of Bakunin's favourite expressions), revolutionary organisations which can effectively smash the state. Bakunin himself argued (see section I.8.11) in favour of workers' councils, complemented by community assemblies (the federation of the barricades) and a self-managed militia. This model is still applicable today and was successfully applied in Aragón by the CNT.

Therefore, the political lessons gained from the experience of the CNT come as no surprise. They simply repeat long standing positions within anarchist theory. As anarchists have argued since Bakunin, no revolution is possible unless the state is smashed, capital expropriated and a free federation of workers' associations created as the framework of libertarian socialism. Rather than refuting anarchism, the experience of the Spanish Revolution confirms it.

I.8.14 What economic lessons were learned from the revolution?

The most important economic lesson from the revolution is the fact that working class people took over the management of industry and did an amazing job of keeping (and improving!) production in the face of the direst circumstances (a factor often overlooked by the opponents of anarchism and the revolution). Not only did workers create a war industry from almost nothing in Catalonia, they also improved working conditions and innovated with new techniques and processes. The Spanish Revolution shows that self-management is possible and that the constructive powers of people inspired by an ideal can transform society.

Self-management allowed a massive increase in innovation and new ideas. The Spanish Revolution is clear proof of the anarchist case against hierarchy and validates Isaac Puente's words that in *"a free collective each benefits from accumulated knowledge and specialised experiences of all, and vice versa. There is a reciprocal relationship wherein information is in continuous circulation."* [**The Anarchist Collectives**, p. 32] The workers, freed from economic autocracy, started to transform their workplaces and how they produced goods.

From the point of view of individual freedom, it is clear that self-management allowed previously marginalised people to take an active part in the decisions that affected them. Egalitarian organisations provided the framework for a massive increase in participation and individual self-government, which expressed itself in the extensive innovations carried out by the Collectives. The Collectives indicate, in Stirner's words, that *"[o]nly in the union can you assert yourself as unique, because the union does not possess you, but you possess it or make it of use to you."* [**The Ego and Its Own**, p. 312] A fact Emma Goldman confirmed from her visits to collectives and discussions with their members:

> *"I was especially impressed with the replies to my questions as to what actually had the workers gained by the collectivisation … the answer always was, first, greater freedom. And only secondly, more wages and less time of work. In two years in Russia [1920-21] I never heard any workers express this idea of greater freedom."* [**Vision on Fire**, p. 62]

As predicted in anarchist theory, and borne out by actual experience, there exists large untapped reserves of energy and initiative in the ordinary person which self-management can call forth. The collectives proved Kropotkin's argument that co-operative work is more productive and that if the economists wish to prove *"their thesis in favour of **private property** against all other forms of **possession**, should not the economists demonstrate that under the form of communal property land never produces such rich harvests as when the possession is private. But this they could not prove; in fact, it is the contrary that has been observed."* [**The Conquest of Bread**, p. 146]

Beyond this five important lessons can be derived from the actual experience of a libertarian socialist economy:

Firstly, that an anarchist society cannot be created overnight, but is a product of many different influences as well as the objective conditions. In this the anarchist collectives confirmed the ideas of anarchist thinkers like Bakunin and Kropotkin (see section I.2.2). The collectives although, as mentioned in section I.8.3, based on key libertarian principles they were a somewhat unexpected development. They reflected objective circumstances facing the revolution as well as libertarian theory and, with regards the latter, were somewhat limited. However, they were organisations created from below by the revolution and so capable of development and progress.

The lesson from every revolution is that the mistakes made in the process of liberation by people themselves are always minor compared to the results of a self-proclaimed vanguard creating institutions **for** people. The Spanish Revolution is a clear example of this, with the Catalan state's *"collectivisation decree"* causing more harm than good (as intended, it controlled and so limited the economic transformation of the economy). Luckily, the Spanish anarchists recognised the importance of having the freedom to make mistakes, as can be seen by the many different forms of collectives and federations tried. The actual process in Spain towards industrial co-ordination and so socialisation was dependent on the wishes of the workers involved — as would be expected in a true social revolution. As Bakunin argued, the *"revolution should not only be made for the people's sake; it should also be made by the people."* [**No Gods, No Masters**, vol. 1, p. 141] The problems faced by a social revolution will be solved in the interests of the working class only if working class people solve them themselves. For this to happen it requires working class people to manage their own affairs directly — and this implies anarchism, not centralisation or state control/ownership. The experience of the collectives in Spain supports this.

Secondly, the importance of decentralisation of management. As discussed in section I.8.4, different areas and industries tried different forms of federation. The woodworkers' union experience indicates that a collectivised industry can became centralised, with even a democratically elected administration leading to rank-and-file workers becoming marginalised which could soon result in apathy developing within it. This was predicted by Kropotkin and other anarchist theorists (and by many anarchists in Spain at the time). While undoubtedly better than capitalist hierarchy, such democratically run industries are only close approximations to anarchist ideas of self-management. Importantly, however, the collectivisation experiments also indicate that co-operation need not imply centralisation (as can be seen from the Badelona collectives).

Thirdly, the importance of building links of solidarity between workplaces as soon as possible. While the importance of starting production after the fascist uprising made attempts at co-ordination seem of secondary importance to the collectives, the competition that initially occurred between workplaces helped the state to undermine self-management (for example, the state *"was actively using its control of finances to contain and stifle radical change"* [Graham Kelsey, **Anarchosyndicalism, Libertarian Communism and the State**, p. 172]). As there was no People's Bank or federal body to co-ordinate credit and production, state control of credit and the gold reserves made it easier for the Republican state to undermine the revolution by controlling the collectives and (effectively) nationalising them in time (Durruti and a few others planned to seize the gold reserves but were advised not to by Abad de Santillán).

This attack on the revolution started when the Catalan State issued a decree legalising (and so controlling) the collectives in October 1936 (the infamous *"Collectivisation Decree"*). The counter-revolution also withheld funds for collectivised industries, even war industries, until they agreed to come under state control. The industrial organisation created by this decree was a compromise between anarchist ideas and those of other parties (particularly the communists) and in the words of Gaston Leval, *"the decree had the baneful effect of preventing the workers' syndicates from extending their gains. It set back the revolution in industry."* [**The Anarchist Collectives**, p. 54]

And lastly, that an economic revolution can only succeed if the existing state is destroyed. As Kropotkin argued, *"a new form of economic organisation will necessarily require a new form of political structure."* [**Anarchism**, p. 181] Capitalism needs the state, socialism needs anarchy. Without the new political structure, the new economic organisation cannot develop to its full potential. Due to the failure to consolidate the revolution **politically**, it was lost **economically**. The decree *"legalising"* collectivisation *"distorted everything right from the start."* [Leval, **Collectives in the Spanish Revolution**, p. 227] This helped undermine the revolution by ensuring that the mutualism of the collectives did not develop freely into libertarian communism (*"The collectives lost the economic freedom they had won at the beginning"* due to the decree, as one participant put it). Collectives, of course, tried to ignore the state. As an eyewitness pointed out, the CNT's *"policy was thus not the same as that pursued by the decree."* [quoted by Ronald Fraser, **Blood of Spain**, p. 230 and p. 213] Indeed, leading anarchists like Abad de Santillán opposed it:

> *"I was an enemy of the decree because I considered it premature … when I became councillor, I had no intention of taking into account or carrying out the decree: I intended to allow our great people to carry on the task as they best saw fit, according to their own inspiration."* [quoted by Fraser, **Op. Cit.**, p. 212fn]

However, with the revolution lost politically, the CNT was soon forced to compromise and support the decree (the CNT did propose more libertarian forms of co-ordination between workplaces but these were undermined by the state). A lack of effective mutual aid organisations allowed the state to gain power over the collectives and so undermine and destroy self-management. Working class control over the economy (important as it is) does not automatically destroy the state. In other words, the economic aspects of the revolution cannot be considered in isolation from its political ones. Yet these points do not diminish the successes of the Spanish revolution. As Gaston Leval argued, *"in spite of these shortcomings"* caused by lack of complete socialisation *"the important fact is that the factories went on working, the workshops and works produced without the owners, capitalists, shareholders and without high management executives."* [**Collectives in the Spanish Revolution**, p. 228] Beyond doubt, these months of economic liberty in Spain show not only that libertarian socialism **works** and that working class people can manage and run society but also that we can improve the quality of life and increase freedom. Given the time and breathing space, the experiment would undoubtedly have ironed out its problems. Even in the very difficult environment of a civil war (and with resistance of almost all other parties and unions) the workers and peasants of Spain showed that a better society is possible. They gave a concrete example of what was previously just a vision, a world which was more humane, more free, more equitable and more civilised than that run by capitalists, managers, politicians and bureaucrats.

Section J
What do anarchists do?

Section J - What do anarchists do?..1008

J.1 Are anarchists involved in social struggles? 1009
J.1.1 Why are social struggles important? 1011
J.1.2 Are anarchists against reforms? 1012
J.1.3 Why are anarchists against reformism? 1013
J.1.4 What attitude do anarchists take to "single-issue" campaigns? . 1015
J.1.5 Why do anarchists try to generalise social struggles? 1016

J.2 What is direct action? 1017
J.2.1 Why do anarchists favour using direct action to change things? . 1019
J.2.2 Why do anarchists reject voting as a means for change? 1020
J.2.3 What are the political implications of voting? 1023
J.2.4 Surely voting for radical parties will be effective? 1024
J.2.5 Why do anarchists support abstentionism and what are its implications? . 1024
J.2.6 What are the effects of radicals using electioneering? 1025
J.2.7 Surely we should vote for reformist parties in order to expose them? . 1028
J.2.8 Will abstentionism lead to the right winning elections? 1029
J.2.9 What do anarchists do instead of voting? 1030
J.2.10 Does rejecting electioneering mean that anarchists are apolitical? . 1032

J.3 What kinds of organisation do anarchists build? 1034
J.3.1 What are affinity groups? 1036
J.3.2 What are "synthesis" federations? 1037
J.3.3 What is the "Platform"? 1039
J.3.4 Why do many anarchists oppose the "Platform"? 1041
J.3.5 Are there other kinds of anarchist federation? 1044
J.3.6 What role do these groups play in anarchist theory? 1044
J.3.7 Doesn't Bakunin's "Invisible Dictatorship" prove that anarchists are secret authoritarians? ... 1048
J.3.8 What is anarcho-syndicalism? 1051
J.3.9 Why are many anarchists not anarcho-syndicalists? 1054

J.4 What trends in society aid anarchist activity? 1058
J.4.1 Why is social struggle a good sign? 1058
J.4.2 Won't social struggle do more harm than good? 1060

J.5 What alternative social organisations do anarchists create? .. 1065
J.5.1 What is community unionism? 1066
J.5.2 Why do anarchists support industrial unionism? 1069
J.5.3 What attitude do anarchists take to existing unions? 1072
J.5.4 What are industrial networks? 1074
J.5.5 What forms of co-operative credit do anarchists support? ... 1075
J.5.6 Why are mutual credit schemes important? 1076
J.5.7 Do most anarchists think mutual credit is sufficient to abolish capitalism? . 1077
J.5.8 What would a modern system of mutual banking look like? 1078
J.5.9 How does mutual credit work? 1079
J.5.10 Why do anarchists support co-operatives? 1080
J.5.11 If workers really want self-management then why are there so few co-operatives? . 1082
J.5.12 If self-management were more efficient then surely capitalists would introduce it? . 1086
J.5.13 What are Modern Schools? 1090
J.5.14 What is Libertarian Municipalism? 1092
J.5.15 What attitude do anarchists take to the welfare state? 1093
J.5.16 Are there any historical examples of collective self-help? . 1096

J.6 What methods of child rearing do anarchists advocate? 1098
J.6.1 What are the main obstacles to raising free children? 1100
J.6.2. What are some examples of libertarian child-rearing methods? . 1101
J.6.3 If children have nothing to fear, how can they be good? 1102
J.6.4 But how will a free child ever learn unselfishness? 1104
J.6.5 Isn't "libertarian child-rearing" just another name for spoiling the child? . 1104
J.6.6 What is the anarchist position on teenage sexual liberation? . 1106
J.6.7 But isn't this concern with sexual liberation just a distraction from revolution? . 1107

J.7 What do anarchists mean by social revolution? 1108
J.7.1 Why are most anarchists revolutionaries? 1110
J.7.2 Is social revolution possible? 1112
J.7.3 Doesn't revolution mean violence? 1114
J.7.4 What would a social revolution involve? 1115
J.7.5 What is the role of anarchists in a social revolution? 1119
J.7.6 How could an anarchist revolution defend itself? 1120

Section J
What do anarchists do?

This section discusses what anarchists get up to. There is little point thinking about the world unless you also want to change it for the better. And by trying to change it, you change yourself and others, making radical change more of a possibility. Therefore anarchists give their whole-hearted support to attempts by ordinary people to improve their lives by their own actions. We urge *"emancipation through practical action"* recognising that the *"collective experience"* gained in *"the collective struggle of the workers against the bosses"* will transform how they see the world and the world itself. [Bakunin, **The Basic Bakunin**, p. 103] Ultimately, *"[t]he true man does not lie in the future, an object of longing, but lies, existent and real, in the present."* [Stirner, **The Ego and Its Own**, p. 327]

Anarchism is more than just a critique of statism and capitalism or a vision of a freer, better way of life. It is first and foremost a movement, the movement of working class people attempting to change the world. Therefore the kind of activity we discuss in this section of the FAQ forms the bridge between capitalism and anarchy. By self-activity and direct action, people can change both themselves and their surroundings. They develop within themselves the mental, ethical and spiritual qualities which can make an anarchist society a viable option. As Noam Chomsky argues:

> *"Only through their own struggle for liberation will ordinary people come to comprehend their true nature, suppressed and distorted within institutional structures designed to assure obedience and subordination. Only in this way will people develop more humane ethical standards, 'a new sense of right', 'the consciousness of their strength and their importance as a social factor in the life of their time' and their capacity to realise the strivings of their 'inmost nature.' Such direct engagement in the work of social reconstruction is a prerequisite for coming to perceive this 'inmost nature' and is the indispensable foundations upon which it can flourish"* [*"preface"*, Rudolf Rocker, **Anarcho-Syndicalism**, p. iii]

In other words, anarchism is not primarily a vision of a better future, but the actual social movement which is fighting within the current unjust and unfree society for that better future and to improve things in the here and now. Without standing up for yourself and what you believe is right, nothing will change. Thus anarchy can be found *"wherever free thought breaks loose from the chains of dogma; wherever the spirit of inquiry rejects the old formulas, wherever the human will asserts itself through independent actions; wherever honest people, rebelling against all enforced discipline, join freely together in order to educate themselves, and to reclaim, without any master, their share of life, and the complete satisfaction of their needs."* [Elisée Reclus, quoted by John P. Clark and Camille Martin (ed.), **Anarchy, Geography, Modernity**, p. 62]

For anarchists, the future is **already appearing in the present** and is expressed by the creativity of working class self-activity.

Anarchy is not some-day-to-be-achieved utopia, it is a living reality whose growth only needs to be freed from constraint. As such anarchist activity is about discovering and aiding emerging trends of mutual aid which work against capitalist domination, so the Anarchist *"studies society and tries to discover its **tendencies**, past and present, its growing needs, intellectual and economic, and in his [or her] ideal he merely points out in which direction evolution goes."* [Peter Kropotkin, **Anarchism**, p. 47] Indeed, as we discussed in section I.2.3, the future structures of a free society are created in the struggles against oppression today.

The kinds of activity outlined in this section are a general overview of anarchist work. It is by no means exclusive — we are sure to have left something out. However, the key aspect of **real** anarchist activity is ***direct action*** - self-activity, self-help, self-liberation and solidarity (*"We wish,"* as French syndicalist Fernand Pelloutier wrote, *"that the emancipation of the people might be the work of the people themselves."* [quoted by Jeremy Jennings, **Syndicalism in France**, p. 18]). Such activity may be done by individuals (for example, propaganda work), but usually anarchists emphasise collective activity. This is because most of our problems are of a social nature, meaning that their solutions can only be worked on collectively. Individual solutions to social problems are doomed to failure, at best slowing down what they are opposed to (most obviously, ethical consumerism as discussed in section E.5). In addition, collective action gets us used to working together, promoting the experience of self-management and building organisations that will allow us to actively manage our own affairs. Also, and we would like to emphasise this, it can be **fun** to get together with other people and work with them, it can be fulfilling and empowering.

Anarchists do not ask those in power to give up that power. No, we promote forms of activity and organisation by which all the oppressed can liberate themselves by their own hands. In other words, we do not think that those in power will altruistically renounce that power or their privileges. Instead, the oppressed must take the power **back** into their own hands by their own actions. We must free ourselves, no one else can do it for us.

Here we will discuss anarchist ideas on struggle, what anarchists actually (and, almost as importantly, do not) do in the here and now and the sort of alternatives anarchists try to build within statism and capitalism in order to destroy them. As well as a struggle against oppression, anarchist activity is also struggle for freedom. As well as fighting against material poverty, anarchists combat spiritual poverty. By resisting hierarchy we emphasis the importance of **living** and of **life as art.** By proclaiming ***"Neither Master nor Slave"*** we urge an ethical transformation, a transformation that will help create the possibility of a truly free society. This point was stressed by Emma Goldman after she saw the defeat of the Russian Revolution by a combination of Leninist politics and capitalist armed intervention:

> *"revolution is in vain unless inspired by its ultimate ideal. Revolutionary methods must be in tune with revolutionary aims … In short, the ethical values which the revolution is to establish must be initiated with the revolutionary activities … The latter can only serve as a real and dependable bridge to the better life if built of the*

same material as the life to be achieved." [**Red Emma Speaks**, p. 404]

In other words, anarchist activity is more than creating libertarian alternatives and resisting hierarchy, it is about building the new world in the shell of the old not only with regards to organisations and self-activity, but also within the individual. It is about transforming yourself while transforming the world (both processes obviously interacting and supporting each other) for while "*we associate ourselves with others in working for ... social revolution, which for us means the destruction of all monopoly and all government, and the direct seizure by the workers of the means of production*" we do not forget that "*the first aim of Anarchism is to assert and make good the dignity of the individual human being.*" [Charlotte Wilson, **Anarchist Essays**, p. 43 and p. 51]

By direct action, self-management and self-activity we can make the words first heard in Paris, 1968 a living reality: "***All power to the imagination!***" Words, we are sure, previous generations of anarchists would have whole-heartedly agreed with. There is a power in humans, a creative power, a power to alter *what is* into *what should be*. Anarchists try to create alternatives that will allow that power to be expressed, the power of imagination.

Such a social movement will change how we act as individuals, with anarchists seeking to apply our principles in our daily lives as much as our daily struggles. This means that libertarians must change how we relate to our comrades and fellow workers by applying our egalitarian ideals everywhere. Part of the task of anarchists is to challenge social hierarchies everywhere, including in the home. As Durruti put it:

> "*When will you stop thinking like the bourgeoisie, that women are men's servants? It's enough that society is divided into classes. We're not going to make even more classes by creating differences between men and women in our own homes!*" [quoted by Abel Paz, **Durruti in the Spanish Revolution**, p. 341]

So we have a interactive process of struggle and transformation of both society and the individuals within it. In the sections that follow we will discuss the forms of self-activity and self-organisation which anarchists think will stimulate and develop the imagination of those oppressed by hierarchy, build anarchy in action and help create a free society.

J.1

Are anarchists involved in social struggles?

Yes. Anarchism, above all else, is a movement which aims to not only analyse the world but also to change it. Therefore anarchists aim to participate in and encourage social struggle. Social struggle includes strikes, marches, protests, demonstrations, boycotts, occupations and so on. Such activities show that the "***spirit of revolt***" is alive and well, that people are thinking and acting for themselves and against what authorities want them to do. This, in the eyes of anarchists, plays a key role in helping create the seeds of anarchy within capitalism.

Anarchists consider socialistic tendencies to develop within society as people see the benefits of co-operation and particularly when mutual aid develops within the struggle against authority, oppression and exploitation. Anarchism, as Kropotkin argued, "*originated in everyday struggles.*" [**Environment and Revolution**, p. 58] Therefore, anarchists do not place anarchy abstractly against capitalism but see it as a tendency within and against the system — a tendency created by struggle and which can be developed to such a degree that it can **replace** the dominant structures and social relationships with new, more liberatory and humane ones. This perspective indicates why anarchists are involved in social struggles — they are an expression of these tendencies within but against capitalism which can ultimately replace it.

However, there is another reason why anarchists are involved in social struggle — namely the fact that we are part of the oppressed and, like other oppressed people, fight for our freedom and to make our life better in the here and now. It is not in some distant tomorrow that we want to see the end of oppression, exploitation and hierarchy. It is today, in our own life, that the anarchist wants to win our freedom, or at the very least, to improve our situation, reduce oppression, domination and exploitation as well as increasing individual liberty for "*every blow given to the institutions of private property and to the government, every exaltation of the conscience of man, disruption of the present conditions, every lie unmasked, every part of human activity taken away from the control of the authorities, every augmentation of the spirit of solidarity and initiative is a step towards Anarchism.*" [Errico Malatesta, **Towards Anarchism**, p. 75] We are aware that we often fail to do so, but the very process of struggle can help create a more libertarian aspect to society:

> "*Whatever may be the practical results of the struggle for immediate gains, the greatest value lies in the struggle itself. For thereby workers [and other oppressed sections of society] learn that the bosses interests are opposed to theirs and that they cannot improve their conditions, and much less emancipate themselves, except by uniting and becoming stronger than the bosses. If they succeed in getting what they demand, they will be better off: they will earn more, work fewer hours and will have more time and energy to reflect on the things that matter to them, and will immediately make greater demands and have greater needs. If they do not succeed they will be led to study the reasons of their failure and recognise the need for closer unity and greater activity and they will in the end understand that to make victory secure and definite, it is necessary to destroy capitalism. The revolutionary cause, the cause of moral elevation and emancipation of the workers [and other oppressed sections of society] must benefit by the fact that workers [and other oppressed people] unite and struggle for their interests.*" [Malatesta, **Errico Malatesta: His Life and Ideas**, p. 191]

Therefore, "*we as anarchists and workers, must incite and encourage*" workers and other oppressed people "*to struggle, and join them in their struggle."* [Malatesta, **Op. Cit.**, p. 190] This is for three reasons. Firstly, struggle helps generate libertarian ideas and movements which could help make existing society more anarchistic and less oppressive. Secondly, struggle creates people, movements and organisations which are libertarian in nature and which, potentially, can replace capitalism with a more humane society. Thirdly, because anarchists are part of the oppressed and so have an interest in taking part in and showing solidarity with struggles and movements that can improve our life in the here and now (*"an injury to one is an injury to all"*).

As we will see in section J.2 anarchists encourage direct action within social struggles as well as arguing for anarchist ideas and theories. However, what is important to note here is that social struggle is a sign that people are thinking and acting for themselves and working together to change things. Howard Zinn is completely correct:

> *"civil disobedience ... is **not** our problem. Our problem is civil **obedience.** Our problem is that numbers of people all over the world have obeyed the dictates of the leaders of their government and have gone to war, and millions have been killed because of this obedience ... Our problem is that people are obedient all over the world in the face of poverty and starvation and stupidity, and war, and cruelty. Our problem is that people are obedient while the jails are full of petty thieves, and all the while the grand thieves are running the country. That's our problem."*
> [**Failure to Quit**, p. 45]

Therefore, social struggle is an important thing for anarchists and we take part in it as much as we can. Moreover, anarchists do more than just take part. We are fighting to get rid of the system that causes the problems which people fight against. We explain anarchism to those who are involved in struggle with us and seek to show the relevance of anarchism to people's everyday lives through such struggles and the popular organisations which they create. By so doing we try to popularise the ideas and methods of anarchism, namely solidarity, self-management and direct action.

Anarchists do not engage in abstract propaganda (become an anarchist, wait for the revolution — if we did that, in Malatesta's words, *"that day would never come."* [**Op. Cit.**, p. 195]). We know that our ideas will only win a hearing and respect when we can show both their relevance to people's lives in the here and now and show that an anarchist world is both possible and desirable. In other words, social struggle is the "school" of anarchism, the means by which people become anarchists and anarchist ideas are applied in action. Hence the importance of social struggle and anarchist participation within it.

Before discussing issues related to social struggle, it is important to point out here that anarchists are interested in struggles against all forms of oppression and do not limit ourselves to purely economic issues. The hierarchical and exploitative nature of the capitalist economy is only part of the story — other forms of oppression are needed in order to keep it going (not to mention those associated with the state) and have resulted from its workings (in addition to those inherited from previous hierarchical and class systems). Domination, exploitation, hierarchy and oppression do not remain

in the workplace. They infest our homes, our friendships and our communities. They need to be fought everywhere, not just in work.

Therefore, anarchists are convinced that human life and the struggle against oppression cannot be reduced to mere money and, indeed, the *"proclivity for economic reductionism is now actually obscurantist. It not only shares in the bourgeois tendency to render material egotism and class interest the centrepieces of history it also denigrates all attempts to transcend this image of humanity as a mere economic being ... by depicting them as mere 'marginalia' at best, as 'well-intentioned middle-class ideology' at worse, or sneeringly, as 'diversionary,' 'utopian,' and 'unrealistic' ... Capitalism, to be sure, did not create the 'economy' or 'class interest,' but it subverted all human traits — be they speculative thought, love, community, friendship, art, or self-governance — with the authority of economic calculation and the rule of quantity. Its 'bottom line' is the balance sheet's sum and its basic vocabulary consists of simple numbers."* [Murray Bookchin, **The Modern Crisis**, pp. 125-126]

In other words, issues such as freedom, justice, individual dignity, quality of life and so on cannot be reduced to the categories of capitalist economics. Anarchists think that any radical movement which does so fails to understand the nature of the system it is fighting against (indeed, economic reductionism plays into the hands of capitalist ideology). So, when anarchists take part in and encourage social struggle they do not aim to restrict or reduce them to economic issues (however important these are). The anarchist knows that the individual has more interests than just material ones and we consider it essential to take into account the needs of the emotions, mind and spirit just as much as those of the belly:

> *"The class struggle does not centre around material exploitation alone but also around spiritual exploitation. In addition, entirely new issues emerge: coercive attitudes, the quality of work, ecology (or stated in more general terms, psychological and environmental oppression) ... Terms like 'classes' and 'class struggle,' conceived of almost entirely as economic categories and relations, are too one-sided to express the **universalisation** of the struggle. Use these limited expressions if you like (the target is still a ruling class and a class society), but this terminology, with its traditional connotations, does not reflect the sweep and the multi-dimensional nature of the struggle ... [and] fail to encompass the cultural and spiritual revolt that is taking place along with the economic struggle."* [**Post-Scarcity Anarchism**, pp. 151-2]

For anarchists, exploitation and class rule are just part of a wider system of domination and hierarchy. Material gains, therefore, can never completely make-up for oppressive social relationships. As the anarchist character created by science-fiction writer Ursula Le Guin put it, capitalists *"think if people have enough things they will be content to live in prison."* [**The Dispossessed**, p. 120] Anarchists disagree — and the experience of social revolt in the "affluent" 1960s proves their case.

This is unsurprising for, ultimately, the *"antagonism [between classes] is spiritual rather than material. There will never be a sincere understanding between bosses and workers... because the bosses above all want to remain bosses and secure always more power at the expense of the workers, as well as by competition with other bosses, whereas the workers have had their fill of bosses and don't want any more."* [Malatesta, **Op. Cit.**, p. 79]

J.1.1 Why are social struggles important?

Social struggle is an expression of the class struggle, namely the struggle of working class people **against** their exploitation, oppression and alienation and **for** their liberty from capitalist and state. It is what happens when one group of people have hierarchical power over another: where there is oppression, there is resistance and where there is resistance to authority you will see anarchy in action. For this reason anarchists are in favour of, and are involved within, social struggles. Ultimately they are a sign of individuals asserting their autonomy and disgust at an unfair system. As Howard Zinn stresses:

"Both the source and the solution of our civil liberties problems are in the situations of every day: where we live, where we work, where we go to school, where we spend most of our hours. Our actual freedom is not determined by the Constitution or by [the Supreme] Court, but by the power the policeman has over us in the street or that of the local judge behind him; by the authority of our employers [if we are working]; by the power of teachers, principals, university president, and boards of trustees if we are students; by the welfare bureaucracy if we are poor [or unemployed]; by prison guards if we are in jail; by landlords if we are tenants; by the medical profession or hospital administration if we are physically or mentally ill.

"Freedom and justice are local things, at hand, immediate. They are determined by power and money, whose authority over our daily lives is much less ambiguous than decisions of the Supreme Court. Whatever claim we … can make to liberty on the national level … on the local level we live at different times in different feudal fiefdoms where our subordination is clear." [**Failure to Quit**, pp. 53-4]

These realities of wealth and power will remain unshaken unless counter-forces appear on the very ground our liberty is restricted — on the street, in workplaces, at home, at school, in hospitals and so on. For the *"only limit to the oppression of government is the power with which people show themselves capable of opposing it."* [Malatesta, **Errico Malatesta: His Life and Ideas**, p. 196]

Social struggles for improvements are also important indications of the spirit of revolt and of people supporting each other in the continual assertion of their (and our) freedom. They show people standing up for what they consider right and just, building alternative organisations, creating their own solutions to their problems - and are a slap in the face of all the paternal authorities which dare

govern us. Hence their importance to anarchists and all people interested in extending freedom.

In addition, social struggle helps break people from their hierarchical conditioning. Anarchists view people not as fixed objects to be classified and labelled, but as human beings engaged in making their own lives. We live, love, think, feel, hope, dream, and can change ourselves, our environment and social relationships. Social struggle is the way this is done collectively. Such struggle promotes attributes within people which are crushed by hierarchy (attributes such as imagination, organisational skills, self-assertion, self-management, critical thought, self-confidence and so on) as people come up against practical problems in their struggles and have to solve them themselves. This builds self-confidence and an awareness of individual and collective power. By seeing that their boss, the state and so on are against them they begin to realise that they live in a class ridden, hierarchical society that depends upon their submission to work. As such, social struggle is a politicising experience.

Struggle allows those involved to develop their abilities for self-rule through practice and so begins the process by which individuals assert their ability to control their own lives and to participate in social life directly. These are all key elements of anarchism and are required for an anarchist society to work (*"Self-management of the struggle comes first, then comes self-management of work and society"* [Alfredo Bonnano, *"Self-Management"*, pp. 35-37, **Anarchy: A Journal of Desire Armed**, no. 48, p. 35]). So self-activity is a key factor in self-liberation, self-education and the creating of anarchists. In a nutshell, people learn in struggle:

"In our opinion all action which is directed toward the destruction of economic and political oppression, which serves to raise the moral and intellectual level of the people; which gives them an awareness of their individual rights and their power, and persuades them themselves to act on their own behalf … brings us closer to our ends and is therefore a good thing. On the other hand all activity which tends to preserve the present state of affairs, that tends to sacrifice man against his will for the triumph of a principle, is bad because it is a denial of our ends. [Malatesta, **Op. Cit.**, p. 69]

A confident working class is an essential factor in making successful and libertarian improvements within the current system and, ultimately, in making a revolution. Without that self-confidence people tend to just follow "leaders" and we end up changing rulers rather than changing society. So part of our job as anarchists is to encourage people to fight for whatever small reforms are possible at present, to improve our/their conditions, to give people confidence in their ability to start taking control of their lives, and to point out that there is a limit to whatever (sometimes temporary) gains capitalism will or can concede. Hence the need for a revolutionary change.

Only this can ensure that anarchist ideas are the most popular ones for if we think a movement is, all things considered, a positive or progressive one then we should not abstain but should seek to popularise anarchist ideas and strategies within it. In this way we create **"schools of anarchy"** within the current system and lay the foundations of something better. Revolutionary tendencies and movements, in other words, must create the organisations that contain, in embryo, the society of the future (see section H.1.6). These organisations, in turn, further the progress of radical change by providing social spaces for the transformation of individuals (via the use of direct action, practising self-management and solidarity, and so on). Therefore, social struggle aids the creation of a free society by accustoming people to govern themselves within self-managed organisations and empowering the (officially) disempowered via the use of direct action and mutual aid.

Hence the importance of social (or class) struggle for anarchists (which, we may add, goes on all the time and is a two-sided affair). Social struggle is the means of breaking the normality of capitalist and statist life, a means of developing the awareness for social change and the means of making life better under the current system. The moment that people refuse to bow to authority, its days are numbered. Social struggle indicates that some of the oppressed see that by using their power of disobedience they can challenge, perhaps eventually end, hierarchical power.

Ultimately, anarchy is not just something you believe in, it is not a cool label you affix to yourself, it is something you do. You participate. If you stop doing it, anarchy crumbles. Social struggle is the means by which we ensure that anarchy becomes stronger and grows.

J.1.2 Are anarchists against reforms?

No, we are not. While most anarchists are against reformism (namely the notion that we can somehow reform capitalism and the state away) we are most definitely in favour of reforms (i.e. improvements in the here and now). Anarchists are radicals; as such, we seek the root causes of societal problems. Reformists seek to ameliorate the symptoms of societal problems, while anarchists focus on the causes.

This does not mean, however, that we ignore struggles for reforms in the here and now. The claim that anarchists are against such improvements are often put forth by opponents of anarchism in an effort to paint us as irrelevant extremists with no practical outlet for our ideas beyond abstract calls for revolution. This is not true. Libertarians are well aware that we can act to make our lives better while, at the same time, seeking to remove the root causes of the problems we face. (see, for example, Emma Goldman's account of her recognition of how false it was deny the need for short-term reforms in favour of revolution. [**Living My Life**, vol. 1, p. 52]). In the words of the revolutionary syndicalist Emile Pouget:

> *"Trade union endeavour has a double aim: with tireless persistence, it must pursue betterment of the working class's current conditions. But, without letting themselves become obsessed with this passing concern, the workers should take care to make possible and imminent the essential act of comprehensive emancipation: the expropriation of capital.*

> *"At present, trade union action is designed to win partial and gradual improvements which, far from constituting a goal, can only be considered as a means of stepping up demands and wresting further improvements from capitalism …*

> *"This question of partial improvements served as the pretext for attempts to sow discord in the trades associations. Politicians … have tried to … stir up ill-feeling and to split the unions into two camps, by categorising workers as reformists and as revolutionaries. The better to discredit the latter, they have dubbed them 'the advocates of all or nothing' and they have falsely represented them as supposed adversaries of improvements achievable right now.*

> *"The most that can be said about this nonsense is that it is witless. There is not a worker … who, on grounds of principle or for reasons of tactics, would insist upon working ten hours for an employer instead of eight hours, while earning six francs instead of seven …*

> *"What appears to afford some credence to such chicanery is the fact that the unions, cured by the cruel lessons of experience from all hope in government intervention, are justifiably mistrustful of it. They know that the State, whose function is to act as capital's gendarme, is, by its very nature, inclined to tip the scales in favour of the employer side. So, whenever a reform is brought about by legal avenues, they do not fall upon it with the relish of a frog devouring the red rag that conceals the hook, they greet it with all due caution, especially as this reform is made effective only if the workers are organised to insist forcefully upon its implementation.*

> *"The trade unions are even more wary of gifts from the government because they have often found these to be poison gifts … Wanting real improvements … instead of waiting until the government is generous enough to bestow them, they wrest them in open battle, through direct action.*

> *"If, as sometimes is the case, the improvement they seek is subject to the law, the trade unions strive to obtain it through outside pressure brought to bear upon the authorities and not by trying to return specially mandated deputies to Parliament, a puerile pursuit that might drag on for centuries before there was a majority in favour of the yearned-for reform.*

> *"When the desired improvement is to be wrestled directly from the capitalist, the trades associations resort to vigorous pressure to convey their wishes. Their methods may well vary, although the direct action principle underlies them all …*

"But, whatever the improvement won, it must always represent a reduction in capitalist privileges and be a partial expropriation. So ... the fine distinction between 'reformist' and 'revolutionary' evaporates and one is led to the conclusion that the only really reformist workers are the revolutionary syndicalists." [**No Gods, No Masters**, vol. 2, pp. 71-3]

Pouget was referring to revolutionary unions but his argument can be generalised to all social movements.

By seeking improvements from below by direct action, solidarity and the organisation of those who directly suffer the injustice, anarchists can make reforms more substantial, effective and long lasting than "reforms" made from above by reformists. By recognising that the effectiveness of a reform is dependent on the power of the oppressed to resist those who would dominate them, anarchists seek change from the bottom-up and so make reforms real rather than just words gathering dust in the law books.

For example, a reformist sees poverty and looks at ways to lessen the destructive and debilitating effects of it: this produced things like the minimum wage, affirmative action, the projects in the USA and similar reforms in other countries. An anarchist looks at poverty and says, "what causes this?" and attacks that source of poverty, rather than the symptoms. While reformists may succeed in the short run with their institutional panaceas, the festering problems remain untreated, dooming reform to eventual costly, inevitable failure — measured in human lives, no less. Like a quack that treats the symptoms of a disease without getting rid of what causes it, all the reformist can promise is short-term improvements for a condition that never goes away and may ultimately kill the sufferer. The anarchist, like a real doctor, investigates the causes of the illness and treats them while fighting the symptoms.

Therefore, anarchists are of the opinion that *"[w]hile preaching against every kind of government, and demanding complete freedom, we must support all struggles for partial freedom, because we are convinced that one learns through struggle, and that once one begins to enjoy a little freedom one ends by wanting it all. We must always be with the people ... [and] get them to understand ... [what] they may demand should be obtained by their own efforts and that they should despise and detest whoever is part of, or aspires to, government."* [Malatesta, **Errico Malatesta: His Life and Ideas** p. 195]

So, anarchists are not opposed to struggles for reforms and improvements in the here and now. Indeed, few anarchists think that an anarchist society will occur without a long period of anarchist activity encouraging and working within social struggle against injustice. Thus Malatesta's words:

"the subject is not whether we accomplish Anarchism today, tomorrow or within ten centuries, but that we walk towards Anarchism today, tomorrow and always." [**Towards Anarchism**, p. 75]

So, when fighting for improvements anarchists do so in an anarchist way, one that encourages self-management, direct action and the creation of libertarian solutions and alternatives to both capitalism and the state.

J.1.3 Why are anarchists against reformism?

Firstly, it must be pointed out that the struggle for reforms within capitalism is **not** the same as reformism. Reformism is the idea that reforms within capitalism are enough in themselves and attempts to change the system are impossible (and not desirable). As such all anarchists are against this form of reformism — we think that the system can be (and should be) changed and until that happens any reforms, no matter how essential, will not get to the root of social problems.

In addition, particularly in the old social democratic labour movement, reformism also meant the belief that social reforms could be used to **transform** capitalism into socialism. In this sense, only Individualist anarchists and Mutualists can be considered reformist as they think their system of mutual banking can reform capitalism into a free system. However, in contrast to Social Democracy, such anarchists think that such reforms cannot come about via government action, but only by people creating their own alternatives and solutions by their own actions:

"But experience testifies and philosophy demonstrates, contrary to that prejudice, that any revolution, to be effective, must be spontaneous and emanate, not from the heads of the authorities but from the bowels of the people: that government is reactionary rather than revolutionary: that it could not have any expertise in revolutions, given that society, to which that secret is alone revealed, does not show itself through legislative decree but rather through the spontaneity of its manifestations: that, ultimately, the only connection between government and labour is that labour, in organising itself, has the abrogation of government as its mission." [Proudhon, **No Gods, No Master**, vol. 1, p. 52]

So, anarchists oppose reformism because it takes the steam out of revolutionary movements by providing easy, decidedly short-term "solutions" to deep social problems. In this way, reformists can present the public with what they've done and say "look, all is better now. The system worked." Trouble is that over time, the problems will only continue to grow because the reforms did not tackle them in the first place. To use Alexander Berkman's excellent analogy:

"If you should carry out [the reformers'] ideas in your personal life, you would not have a rotten tooth that aches pulled out all at once. You would have it pulled out a little to-day, some more next week, for several months or years, and by then you would be ready to pull it out altogether, so it should not hurt so much. That is the logic of the reformer. Don't be 'too hasty,' don't pull a bad tooth out all at once." [**What is Anarchism?**, p. 64]

Rather than seek to change the root cause of the problems (namely a hierarchical, oppressive and exploitative system), reformists try to make the symptoms better. In the words of Berkman again:

"Suppose a pipe burst in your house. You can put a bucket under the break to catch the escaping water. You can keep on putting buckets there, but as long as you do not mend the broken pipe, the leakage will continue, no matter how much you may swear about it ... until you repair the broken social pipe." [**Op. Cit.**, pp. 67-8]

What reformism fails to do is fix the underlying root causes of the real problems society faces. Therefore, reformists try to pass laws which reduce the level of pollution rather than work to end a system in which it makes economic sense to pollute. Or they pass laws to improve working conditions and safety while failing to get rid of the wage slavery which creates the bosses whose interests are served by them ignoring those laws and regulations. The list is endless. Ultimately, reformism fails because reformists *"believe in good faith that it is possible to eliminate the existing social evils by recognising and respecting, in practice if not in theory, the basic political and economic institutions which are the cause of, as well as the prop that supports these evils."* [Malatesta, **Errico Malatesta: His Life and Ideas**, p. 82]

Revolutionaries, in contrast to reformists, fight both symptoms **and** the root causes. They recognise that as long as the cause of the evil remains, any attempts to fight the symptoms, however necessary, will never get to the root of the problem. There is no doubt that we have to fight the symptoms, however revolutionaries recognise that this struggle is not an end in itself and should be considered purely as a means of increasing working class strength and social power within society until such time as capitalism and the state (i.e. the root causes of most problems) can be abolished.

Reformists also tend to objectify the people whom they are "helping": they envision them as helpless, formless masses who need the wisdom and guidance of the "best and the brightest" to lead them to the Promised Land. Reformists mean well, but this is altruism borne of ignorance, which is destructive over the long run. Freedom cannot be given and so any attempt to impose reforms from above cannot help but ensure that people are treated as children, incapable of making their own decisions and, ultimately, dependent on bureaucrats to govern them. This can be seen from public housing. As Colin Ward argues, the *"whole tragedy of publicly provided non-profit housing for rent and the evolution of this form of tenure in Britain is that the local authorities have simply taken over, though less flexibly, the role of the landlord, together with all the dependency and resentment that it engenders."* [**Housing: An Anarchist Approach**, p. 184] This feature of reformism was skilfully used by the right-wing to undermine publicly supported housing and other aspects of the welfare state. The reformist social-democrats reaped what they had sown.

Reformism often amounts to little more than an altruistic contempt for the masses, who are considered as little more than victims who need to be provided for by state. The idea that we may have our own visions of what we want is ignored and replaced by the vision of the reformists who enact legislation **for** us and make "reforms" from the top-down. Little wonder such reforms can be counter-productive — they cannot grasp the complexity of life and the needs of those subject to them. Reformists effectively say, *"don't do anything, we'll do it for you."* You can see why anarchists would loathe this

sentiment; anarchists are the consummate do-it-yourselfers, and there's nothing reformists hate more than people who can take care of themselves, who will not let them "help" them.

Also, it is funny to hear left-wing "revolutionaries" and "radicals" put forward the reformist line that the capitalist state can help working people (indeed be used to abolish itself!). Despite the fact that leftists blame the state and capitalism for most of the problems we face, they usually turn to the **capitalist** state to remedy the situation, not by leaving people alone, but by becoming more involved in people's lives. They support government housing, government jobs, welfare, government-funded and regulated child care, government-funded drug "treatment," and other government-centred programmes and activities. If a capitalist (and racist/sexist/authoritarian) government is the problem, how can it be depended upon to change things to the benefit of working class people or other oppressed sections of the population? Surely any reforms passed by the state will not solve the problem? As Malatesta suggested:

"Governments and the privileged classes are naturally always guided by instincts of self-preservation, of consolidation and the development of their powers and privileges; and when they consent to reforms it is either because they consider that they will serve their ends or because they do not feel strong enough to resist, and give in, fearing what might otherwise be a worse alternative." [**Op. Cit.**, p. 81]

Therefore, reforms gained by direct action are of a different quality and nature than those passed by reformist politicians — these latter will only serve the interests of the ruling class as they do not threaten their privileges while the former have the potential for real change.

This is not to say that Anarchists oppose **all** state-based reforms nor that we join with the right in seeking to destroy them (or, for that matter, with "left" politicians in seeking to "reform" them, i.e., reduce them). Without a popular social movement creating alternatives to state welfare, so-called "reform" by the state almost always means attacks on the most vulnerable elements in society in the interests of capital. As anarchists are against both state and capitalism, we can oppose such reforms without contradiction while, at the same time, arguing that welfare for the rich should be abolished long before welfare for the many is even thought about. See section J.5.15 for more discussion on the welfare state and anarchist perspectives on it.

Instead of encouraging working class people to organise themselves and create their own alternatives and solutions to their problem (which can supplement, and ultimately replace, whatever welfare state activity which is actually useful), reformists and other radicals urge people to get the state to act for them. However, the state is not the community and so whatever the state does for people you can be sure it will be in **its** interests, not theirs. As Kropotkin put it:

"We maintain that the State organisation, having been the force to which the minorities resorted for establishing and organising their power over the masses, cannot be the force which will serve to destroy these privileges ...

the economic and political liberation of man will have to create new forms for its expression in life, instead of those established by the State.

"Consequently, the chief aim of Anarchism is to awaken those constructive powers of the labouring masses of the people which at all great moments of history came forward to accomplish the necessary changes ...

*"This is also why the Anarchists refuse to accept the functions of legislators or servants of the State. We know that the social revolution will not be accomplished by means of **laws**. Laws only **follow** the accomplished facts ... a law remains a dead letter so long as there are not on the spot the living forces required for making of the **tendencies** expressed in the law an accomplished **fact**.*

*"On the other hand ... the Anarchists have always advised taking an active part in those workers' organisations which carry on the **direct** struggle of Labour against Capital and its protector, — the State.*

"Such a struggle ... better than any other indirect means, permits the worker to obtain some temporary improvements in the present conditions of work [and life in general], while it opens his [or her] eyes to the evil that is done by Capitalism and the State that supports it, and wakes up his [or her] thoughts concerning the possibility of organising consumption, production, and exchange without the intervention of the capitalist and the State." [**Environment and Evolution**, pp. 82-3]

Therefore, while seeking reforms, anarchists are against reformism and reformists. Reforms are not seen as an end in themselves but rather a means of changing society from the bottom-up and a step in that direction:

"Each step towards economic freedom, each victory won over Capitalism will be at the same time a step towards political liberty — towards liberation from the yoke of the State ... And each step towards taking from the State any one of its powers and attributes will be helping the masses to win a victory over Capitalism." [Kropotkin, **Op. Cit.**, p. 95]

However, no matter what, anarchists *"will never recognise the institutions; we will take or win all possible reforms with the same spirit that one tears occupied territory from the enemy's grasp in order to keep advancing, and we will always remain enemies of every government."* Therefore, it is *"not true to say"* that anarchists *"are systematically opposed to improvements, to reforms. They oppose the reformists on the one hand because their methods are less effective for securing reforms from government and employers, who only give in through fear, and because very often the reforms they prefer are those which not only bring doubtful immediate benefits, but also serve to consolidate the existing regime and to give the workers a vested interest in its continued existence."* [Malatesta, **Op. Cit.**, p. 81 and p. 83]

Only working class people, by our own actions and organisations, getting the state and capital out of the way can produce an improvement in our lives, indeed it is the only thing that will lead to **real** changes for the better. Encouraging people to rely on themselves instead of the state or capital can lead to self-sufficient, independent, and, hopefully, more rebellious people. Working class people, despite having fewer options in a number of areas in our lives, due both to hierarchy and restrictive laws, still are capable of making choices about our actions, organising our own lives and are responsible for the consequences of our decisions. We are also more than able to determine what is and is not a good reform to existing institutions and do not need politicians informing us what is in our best interests (particularly when it is the right seeking to abolish those parts of the state not geared purely to defending property). To think otherwise is to infantilise us, to consider us less fully human than other people and reproduce the classic capitalist vision of working class people as means of production, to be used, abused, and discarded as required. Such thinking lays the basis for paternalistic interventions in our lives by the state, ensuring our continued dependence and inequality — and the continued existence of capitalism and the state. Ultimately, there are two options:

"The oppressed either ask for and welcome improvements as a benefit graciously conceded, recognise the legitimacy of the power which is over them, and so do more harm than good by helping to slow down, or divert ... the processes of emancipation. Or instead they demand and impose improvements by their action, and welcome them as partial victories over the class enemy, using them as a spur to greater achievements, and thus a valid help and a preparation to the total overthrow of privilege, that is, for the revolution." [Malatesta, **Op. Cit.**, p. 81]

Reformism encourages the first attitude within people and so ensures the impoverishment of the human spirit. Anarchism encourages the second attitude and so ensures the enrichment of humanity and the possibility of meaningful change. Why think that ordinary people cannot arrange their lives for themselves as well as Government people can arrange it not for themselves but for others?

J.1.4 What attitude do anarchists take to "single-issue" campaigns?

Firstly, we must note that anarchists do take part in "single-issue" campaigns, but do not nourish false hopes in them. This section explains what anarchists think of such campaigns.

A "single-issue" campaign is usually run by a pressure group which concentrates on tackling issues one at a time. For example, C.N.D. (The Campaign for Nuclear Disarmament) is a classic example of "single-issue" campaigning with the aim of getting rid of nuclear weapons as the be-all and end-all of its activity. For anarchists, however, single-issue campaigning can be seen as a source of false hopes. The possibilities of changing one aspect of a totally inter-related system and the belief that pressure groups can compete fairly with transnational corporations, the military and so forth, in their influence over decision making bodies can both be seen to be optimistic at best.

In addition, many "single-issue" campaigns desire to be "apolitical", concentrating purely on the one issue which unites the campaign and so refuse to analyse or discuss wider issues and the root causes of the issue in question (almost always, the system we live under). This means that they end up accepting the system which causes the problems they are fighting against. At best, any changes achieved by the campaign must be acceptable to the establishment or be so watered down in content that no practical long-term good is done. This can be seen from the green movement, where groups like **Greenpeace** and **Friends of the Earth** accept the status quo as a given and limit themselves to working within it. This often leads to them tailoring their "solutions" to be "practical" within a fundamentally anti-ecological political and economic system, so slowing down (at best) ecological disruption.

For anarchists these problems all stem from the fact that social problems cannot be solved as single issues. As Larry Law argued:

> "single issue politics … deals with the issue or problem in isolation. When one problem is separated from all other problems, a solution really is impossible. The more campaigning on an issue there is, the narrower its perspectives become … As the perspective of each issue narrows, the contradictions turn into absurdities … What single issue politics does is attend to 'symptoms' but does not attack the 'disease' itself. It presents such issues as nuclear war, racial and sexual discrimination, poverty, starvation, pornography, etc., as if they were aberrations or faults in the system. In reality such problems are the inevitable consequence of a social order based on exploitation and hierarchical power … single issue campaigns lay their appeal for relief at the feet of the very system which oppresses them. By petitioning they acknowledge the right of those in power to exercise that power as they choose." [**Bigger Cages, Longer Chains**, pp. 17-20].

Single issue politics often prolong the struggle for a free society by fostering illusions that it is just parts of the capitalist system which are wrong, not the whole of it, and that those at the top of the system can, and will, act in our interests. While such campaigns can do some good, practical, work and increase knowledge and education about social problems, they are limited by their very nature and can not lead to extensive improvements in the here and now, never mind a free society.

Therefore, anarchists often support and work within single-issue campaigns, trying to get them to use effective methods of activity (such as direct action), work in an anarchistic manner (i.e. from the bottom up) and to try to "politicise" them into questioning the whole of the system. However, anarchists do not let themselves be limited to such activity as a social revolution or movement is not a group of single-issue campaigns but a mass movement which understands the inter-related nature of social problems and so the need to change every aspect of life.

J.1.5 Why do anarchists try to generalise social struggles?

Basically, we do it in order to encourage and promote solidarity. This is **the** key to winning struggles in the here and now as well as creating the class consciousness necessary to create an anarchist society. At its most simple, generalising different struggles means increasing the chances of winning them. Take, for example, when one trade or one workplace goes on strike while the others continue to work:

> "Consider yourself how foolish and inefficient is the present form of labour organisation in which one trade or craft may be on strike while the other branches of the same industry continue to work. Is it not ridiculous that when the street car workers of New York, for instance, quit work, the employees of the subway, the cab and omnibus drivers remain on the job? … It is clear, then, that you compel compliance [from your bosses] only when you are determined, when your union is strong, when you are well organised, when you are united in such a manner that the boss cannot run his factory against your will. But the employer is usually some big … company that has mills or mines in various places… If it cannot operate … in Pennsylvania because of a strike, it will try to make good its losses by continuing … and increasing production [elsewhere] … In that way the company … breaks the strike." [Alexander Berkman, **What is Anarchism?**, pp. 199-200]

By organising all workers in one union (after all they all have the same boss) it increases the power of each trade considerably. It may be easy for a boss to replace a few workers, but a whole workforce would be far more difficult. By organising all workers in the same industry, the power of each workplace is correspondingly increased. Extending this example to outside the workplace, its clear that by mutual support between different groups increases the chances of each group winning its fight. As the I.W.W. put it: **"An injury to one is an injury to all."** By generalising struggles, by practising mutual aid we can ensure that when we are fighting for our rights and against injustice we will not be isolated and alone. If we don't support each other, groups will be picked off one by one. and if we go into struggle, there will be no one there to support us and we are more likely to be defeated.

Therefore, from an anarchist point of view, the best thing about generalising struggles is that as well as increasing the likelihood of success ("Solidarity is Strength") it leads to an increased spirit of solidarity, responsibility and class consciousness. This is because by working together and showing solidarity those involved get to understand their common interests and that the struggle is not against **this** injustice or **that** boss but against **all** injustice and **all** bosses.

This sense of increased social awareness and solidarity can be seen from the experience of the C.N.T in Spain during the 1930s. The C.N.T. organised all workers in a given area into one big union.

Each workplace was a union branch and were joined together in a local area confederation. The result was that the territorial basis of the unions brought all the workers from one area together and fomented **class** solidarity over and before industry-loyalties and interests. This can also be seen from the experiences of the syndicalist unions in Italy and France as well. The structure of such local federations also situates the workplace in the community where it really belongs.

Also, by uniting struggles together, we can see that there are really no "single issues" — that all various different problems are inter-linked. For example, ecological problems are not just that, but have a political and economic basis and that economic and social domination and exploitation spills into the environment. Inter-linking struggles means that they can be seen to be related to other struggles against capitalist exploitation and oppression and so encourage solidarity and mutual aid. What goes on in the environment, for instance, is directly related to questions of domination and inequality within human society, that pollution is often directly related to companies cutting corners to survive in the market or increase profits. Similarly, struggles against sexism or racism can be seen as part of a wider struggle against hierarchy, exploitation and oppression in all their forms. As such, uniting struggles has an important educational effect above and beyond the benefits in terms of winning struggles.

Murray Bookchin presents a concrete example of this process of linking issues and widening the struggle:

"Assume there is a struggle by welfare mothers to increase their allotments ... Without losing sight of the concrete issues that initially motivated the struggle, revolutionaries would try to catalyse an order of relationships between the mothers entirely different from [existing ones] ... They would try to foster a deep sense of community, a rounded human relationship that would transform the very subjectivity of the people involved ... Personal relationships would be intimate, not merely issue-orientated. People would get to **know** each other, to **confront** each other; they would **explore** each other with a view of achieving the most complete, unalienated relationships. Women would discuss sexism, as well as their welfare allotments, child-rearing as well as harassment by landlords, their dreams and hopes as human beings as well as the cost of living.

"From this intimacy there would grow, hopefully, a supportive system of kinship, mutual aid, sympathy and solidarity in daily life. The women might collaborate to establish a rotating system of baby sitters and child-care attendants, the co-operative buying of good food at greatly reduced prices, the common cooking and partaking of meals, the mutual learning of survival skills and the new social ideas, the fostering of creative talents, and many other shared experiences. Every aspect of life that could be explored and changed would be one part of the kind of relationships ...

"The struggle for increased allotments would expand beyond the welfare system to the schools, the hospitals, the police, the physical, cultural, aesthetic and recreational resources of the neighbourhood, the stores, the houses, the doctors and lawyers in the area, and so on — into the very ecology of the district.

"What I have said on this issue could be applied to every issue — unemployment, bad housing, racism, work conditions — in which an insidious assimilation of bourgeois modes of functioning is masked as 'realism' and 'actuality.' The new order of relationships that could be developed from a welfare struggle ... [can ensure that the] future penetrates the present; it recasts the way people 'organise' and the goals for which they strive."
[**Post-Scarcity Anarchism**, pp. 153-4]

As the anarchist slogan puts it: **"Resistance is Fertile."** Planting the seed of autonomy, direct action and self-liberation can result, potentially, in the blossoming of free individuals due to the nature of struggle itself (see section A.2.7) Therefore, the generalisation of social struggle is not only a key way of winning a specific fight, it can (and should) also spread into different aspects of life and society and play a key part in developing free individuals who reject hierarchy in all aspects of their life.

Social problems are not isolated from each other and so struggles against them cannot be. The nature of struggle is such that once people start questioning one aspect of society, the questioning of the rest soon follows. So, anarchists seek to generalise struggles for these three reasons — firstly, to ensure the solidarity required to win; secondly, to combat the many social problems we face as **people** and to show how they are inter-related; and, thirdly, to encourage the transformation of those involved into unique individuals in touch with their humanity, a humanity eroded by hierarchical society and domination.

J.2

What is direct action?

Direct action, to use Rudolf Rocker's words, is *"every method of immediate warfare by the workers [or other sections of society] against their economic and political oppressors. Among these the outstanding are: the strike, in all its graduations from the simple wage struggle to the general strike; the boycott; sabotage in all its countless forms; anti-militarist propaganda, and in particularly critical cases ... armed resistance of the people for the protection of life and liberty."* [**Anarcho-Syndicalism**, p. 78]

Not that anarchists think that direct action is only applicable within the workplace. Far from it. Direct action must occur everywhere! So, in non-workplace situations, direct action includes rent strikes, consumer boycotts, occupations (which, of course, can include sit-down strikes by workers), eco-tage, individual and collective non-payment of taxes, blocking roads and holding up construction work of an anti-social nature and so forth. Also direct action, in a workplace setting, includes strikes and protests on social issues, not directly related to working conditions and pay. Such activity aims to ensure the *"protection of the community against the most pernicious outgrowths of the present system. The social strike seeks to force upon the employers a responsibility to the public. Primarily it has in view the protection of the customers, of whom the workers themselves [and their families] constitute the great majority"* [**Op. Cit.**, p. 86]

Basically, direct action means that instead of getting someone else to act for you (e.g. a politician), you act for yourself. Its essential feature is an organised protest by ordinary people to make a change by their own efforts. Thus Voltairine De Cleyre's excellent statement on this topic:

> *"Every person who ever thought he had a right to assert, and went boldly and asserted it, himself, or jointly with others that shared his convictions, was a direct actionist. Some thirty years ago I recall that the Salvation Army was vigorously practicing direct action in the maintenance of the freedom of its members to speak, assemble, and pray. Over and over they were arrested, fined, and imprisoned; but they kept right on singing, praying, and marching, till they finally compelled their persecutors to let them alone. The Industrial Workers [of the World] are now conducting the same fight, and have, in a number of cases, compelled the officials to let them alone by the same direct tactics.*
>
> *"Every person who ever had a plan to do anything, and went and did it, or who laid his plan before others, and won their co-operation to do it with him, without going to external authorities to please do the thing for them, was a direct actionist. All co-operative experiments are essentially direct action.*
>
> *"Every person who ever in his life had a difference with anyone to settle, and went straight to the other persons involved to settle it, either by a peaceable plan or otherwise, was a direct actionist. Examples of such action are strikes and boycotts; many persons will recall the action of the housewives of New York who boycotted the butchers, and lowered the price of meat; at the present moment a butter boycott seems looming up, as a direct reply to the price-makers for butter.*
>
> *"These actions are generally not due to any one's reasoning overmuch on the respective merits of directness or indirectness, but are the spontaneous retorts of those who feel oppressed by a situation. In other words, all people are, most of the time, believers in the principle of direct action, and practisers of it."* [**The Voltairine De Cleyre Reader**, pp. 47-8]

So direct action means acting for yourself against injustice and oppression. It can, sometimes, involve putting pressure on politicians or companies, for example, to ensure a change in an oppressive law or destructive practices. However, such appeals are direct action simply because they do not assume that the parties in question will act for us — indeed the assumption is that change only occurs when we act to create it. Regardless of what it is, *"if such actions are to have the desired empowerment effect, they must be largely self-generated, rather than being devised and directed from above"* and be *"ways in which people could take control of their lives"* so that it *"empowered those who participated in it."* [Martha Ackelsberg, **Free Women of Spain**, p. 55]

So, in a nutshell, direct action is any form of activity which people themselves decide upon and organise themselves which is based on their own collective strength and does not involve getting intermediates to act for them. As such direct action is a natural expression of liberty, of self-government, for direct action *"against the authority in the shop, direct action against the authority of the law, direct action against the invasive, meddlesome authority of our moral code, is the logical, consistent method of Anarchism."* [Emma Goldman, **Red Emma Speaks**, pp. 76-7] It is clear that by acting for yourself you are expressing the ability to govern yourself. Thus it is a means by which people can take control of their own lives. It is a means of self-empowerment and self-liberation.

Anarchists reject the view that society is static and that people's consciousness, values, ideas and ideals cannot be changed. Far from it and anarchists support direct action **because** it actively encourages the transformation of those who use it. Direct action is the means of creating a new consciousness, a means of self-liberation from the chains placed around our minds, emotions and spirits by hierarchy and oppression.

As direct action is the expression of liberty, the powers that be are vitally concerned only when the oppressed use direct action to win its demands, for it is a method which is not easy or cheap to combat. Any hierarchical system is placed into danger when those at the bottom start to act for themselves and, historically, people have invariably gained more by acting directly than could have been won by playing ring around the rosy with indirect means. Direct action tore the chains of open slavery from humanity. Over the centuries it has established individual rights and modified the life and death power of the master class. Direct action won political liberties such as the vote and free speech. Used fully, used wisely and well, direct action can forever end injustice and the mastery of humans by other humans.

In the sections that follow, we will indicate why anarchists are in favour of direct action and why they are against electioneering as a means of change.

J.2.1 Why do anarchists favour using direct action to change things?

Simply because it is effective and it has a radicalising impact on those who practice it. As it is based on people acting for themselves, it shatters the dependency and marginalisation created by hierarchy. This is key:

> "What is even more important about direct action is that it forms a decisive step toward recovering the personal power over social life that the centralised, over-bearing bureaucracies have usurped from the people ... we not only gain a sense that we can control the course of social events again; we recover a new sense of selfhood and personality without which a truly free society, based in self-activity and self-management, is utterly impossible." [Murray Bookchin, **Toward an Ecological Society**, p. 47]

By acting for themselves, people gain a sense of their own power and abilities. This is essential if people are to run their own lives. As such, direct action is **the** means by which individuals empower themselves, to assert their individuality, to make themselves count as individuals by organising and acting collectively. It is the opposite of hierarchy, within which individuals are told again and again that they are nothing, are insignificant and must dissolve themselves into a higher power (the state, the company, the party, the people, etc.) and feel proud in participating in the strength and glory of this higher power. Direct action, in contrast, is the means of asserting your individual opinion, interests and happiness, of fighting against self-negation:

> "man has as much liberty as he is willing to take. Anarchism therefore stands for direct action, the open defiance of, and resistance to, all laws and restrictions, economic, social and moral. But defiance and resistance are illegal. Therein lies the salvation of man. Everything illegal necessitates integrity, self-reliance, and courage. In short, it calls for free independent spirits, for men who are men, and who have a bone in their back which you cannot pass your hand through." [Emma Goldman, **Red Emma Speaks**, pp. 75-6]

In addition, because direct action is based around individuals solving their own problems, by their own action, it awakens those aspects of individuals crushed by hierarchy and oppression — such as initiative, solidarity, imagination, self-confidence and a sense of individual and collective power, that what you do matters and that you with others like you **can** change the world. Direct action is the means by which people can liberate themselves and educate themselves in the ways of and skills required for self-management and liberty:

> "Direct action meant that the goal of ... these activities was to provide ways for people to get in touch with their own powers and capacities, to take back the power of naming themselves and their lives ... we learn to think and

act for ourselves by joining together in organisations in which our experience, our perception, and our activity can guide and make the change. Knowledge does not precede experience, it flows from it ... People learn to be free only by exercising freedom. [As one Spanish Anarchist put it] 'We are not going to find ourselves ... with people ready-made for the future ... Without continued exercise of their faculties, there will be no free people ... The external revolution and the internal revolution presuppose one another, and they must be simultaneous in order to be successful.'" [Martha Ackelsberg, **Free Women of Spain**, pp. 54-5]

So direct action, to use Bookchin's words, is "the means whereby each individual awakens to the hidden powers within herself and himself, to a new sense of self-confidence and self-competence; it is the means whereby individuals take control of society directly." [**Op. Cit.**, p. 48]

In addition, direct action creates the need for new forms of social organisation. These new forms of organisation will be informed and shaped by the process of self-liberation, so be more anarchistic and based upon self-management. Direct action, as well as liberating individuals, can also create the free, self-managed organisations which can replace the current hierarchical ones (see section I.2.3). For example, for Kropotkin, unions were "natural organs for the direct struggle with capitalism and for the composition of the future order." [quoted by Paul Avrich, **The Russian Anarchists**, p. 81] In other words, direct action helps create the new world in the shell of the old:

> "direct action not only empowered those who participated in it, it also had effects on others ... [it includes] exemplary action that attracted adherents by the power of the positive example it set ... While such activities empower those who engage in them, they also demonstrate to others that non-hierarchical forms of organisation can and do exist — and that they can function effectively." [Ackelsberg, **Op. Cit.**, p. 55]

Also, direct action such as strikes encourage and promote class consciousness and class solidarity. According to Kropotkin, "the strike develops the sentiment of solidarity" while, for Bakunin, it "is the beginnings of the social war of the proletariat against the bourgeoisie ... Strikes are a valuable instrument from two points of view. Firstly, they electrify the masses, invigorate their moral energy and awaken in them the feeling of the deep antagonism which exists between their interests and those of the bourgeoisie ... secondly they help immensely to provoke and establish between the workers of all trades, localities and countries the consciousness and very fact of solidarity: a twofold action, both negative and positive, which tends to constitute directly the new world of the proletariat, opposing it almost in an absolute way to the bourgeois world." [quoted by Caroline Cahm, **Kropotkin and the Rise of Revolutionary Anarchism 1872-1886**, p. 256 and pp. 216-217] Direct action, therefore, helps to create anarchists and anarchist alternatives within capitalism and statism. As such, it plays an essential role in anarchist theory and activity. For anarchists, direct action *"is not a 'tactic' ... it is a moral principle, an ideal, a sensibility. It should imbue every aspect of our lives and behaviour and outlook."* [Bookchin, **Op. Cit.**, p. 48]

J.2.2 Why do anarchists reject voting as a means for change?

Simply because electioneering does not work. History is littered with examples of radicals being voted into office only to become as, or even more, conservative than the politicians they replaced.

As we have discussed previously (see section B.2) any government is under pressure from two sources of power, the state bureaucracy and big business. This ensures that any attempts at social change would be undermined and made hollow by vested interests, assuming they even reached that level to begin with (the de-radicalising effects of electioneering is discussed in section J.2.6). Here we will highlight the power of vested interests within democratic government.

For anarchists, the general nature of the state and its role within society is to ensure *"the preservation of the economic 'status quo,' the protection of the economic privileges of the ruling class, whose agent and **gendarme** it is"*. [Luigi Galleani, **The End of Anarchism?**, p. 28] As such, the state and capital restrict and control the outcome of political action of the so-called sovereign people as expressed by voting.

Taking capital to begin with, if we assume that a relatively reformist government were elected it would soon find itself facing various economic pressures. Either capital would disinvest, so forcing the government to back down in the face of economic collapse, or the government in question would control capital leaving the country and so would soon be isolated from new investment and its currency would become worthless. Either is an effective weapon to control democratically elected governments as both ensure that the economy would be severely damaged and the promised "reforms" would be dead letters. Far fetched? No, not really. As discussed in section D.2.1 such pressures were inflicted on the 1974 Labour Government in Britain and we see the threat reported everyday when the media reports on what *"the markets"* think of government policies or when loans are given only with the guarantee that the country is structurally adjusted in-line with corporate interests and bourgeois economic dogma.

As far as political pressures go, we must remember that there is a difference between the state and government. The state is the permanent collection of institutions that have entrenched power structures and interests. The government is made up of various politicians. It is the institutions that have power in the state due to their permanence, not the representatives who come and go. In other words, the state bureaucracy has vested interests and elected politicians cannot effectively control them:

> *"Such a bureaucracy consists of armed forces, police forces, and a civil service. These are largely autonomous bodies. Theoretically they are subordinate to a democratically elected Parliament, but the Army, Navy, and Air Forces are controlled by specially trained officers*

who from their schooldays onwards are brought up in a narrow caste tradition, and who always, in dealing with Parliament, can dominate that body by their superior technical knowledge, professional secrecy, and strategic bluff. As for the bureaucracy proper, the Civil Service, anyone who has had any experience of its inner workings knows the extent to which it controls the Cabinet, and through the Cabinet, Parliament itself. We are really ruled by a secret shadow cabinet ... All these worthy servants of the State are completely out of touch with the normal life of the nation."* [Herbert Read, **Anarchy and Order**, p. 100]

As an aside, it should be noted that while *"in a society of rich and poor nothing is more necessary"* than a bureaucracy as it is *"necessary to protect an unfair distribution of property"* it would be wrong to think that it does not have its own class interests: *"Even if you abolish all other classes and distinctions and retain a bureaucracy you are still far from the classless society, for the bureaucracy is itself the nucleus of a class whose interests are totally opposed to the people it supposedly serves."* [**Op. Cit.**, p. 99 and p. 100]

In addition to the official bureaucracies and their power, there is also the network of behind the scenes agencies which are its arm. This can be termed *"the permanent government"* and *"the secret state"*, respectively. The latter, in Britain, is *"the security services, MI5, Special Branch and the secret intelligence service, MI6."* Other states have their equivalents (the FBI, CIA, and so on in the USA). By the former, it is meant *"the secret state plus the Cabinet Office and upper echelons of Home and Foreign and Commonwealth Offices, the Armed Forces and Ministry of Defence ... and the so-called 'Permanent Secretaries Club,' the network of very senior civil servants — the 'Mandarins.'"* In short, the upper-echelons of the bureaucracy and state apparatus. Add to this *"its satellites"*, including M.P.s (particularly right-wing ones), *"agents of influence"* in the media, former security services personnel, think tanks and opinion forming bodies, front companies of the security services, and so on. [Stephen Dorril and Robin Ramsay, **Smear! Wilson and the Secret State**, pp. X-XI]

These bodies, while theoretically under the control of the elected government, can effectively (via disinformation, black operations, bureaucratic slowdowns, media attacks, etc.) ensure that any government trying to introduce policies which the powers that be disagree with will be stopped. In other words the state is **not** a neutral body, somehow rising above vested interests and politics. It is, and always will be, a institution which aims to protect specific sections of society as well as its own.

An example of this "secret state" at work can be seen in the campaign against Harold Wilson, the Labour Prime Minister of Britain in the 1970s, which resulted in his resignation (as documented by Stephen Dorril and Robin Ramsay). Left-wing Labour M.P. Tony Benn was subjected to intense pressure by "his" Whitehall advisers during the same period:

> *"In early 1975, the campaign against Benn by the media was joined by the secret state. The timing is interesting. In January, his Permanent Secretary had 'declared war' and the following month began the most extraordinary*

campaign of harassment any major British politician has experienced. While this is not provable by any means, it does look as though there is a clear causal connection between withdrawal of Prime Ministerial support, the open hostility from the Whitehall mandarins and the onset of covert operations." [Dorril and Ramsay, **Op. Cit.**, p. 279]

This is not to forget the role of the secret state in undermining reformist and radical organisations and movements. This involvement goes from pure information gathering on "subversives", to disruption and repression. Taking the example of the US secret state, Howard Zinn notes that in 1975:

"congressional committees … began investigations of the FBI and CIA.

"The CIA inquiry disclosed that the CIA had gone beyond its original mission of gathering intelligence and was conducting secret operations of all kinds … [for example] the CIA - with the collusion of a secret Committee of Forty headed by Henry Kissinger - had worked to 'destabilize' the [democratically elected, left-wing] Chilean government …

"The investigation of the FBI disclosed many years of illegal actions to disrupt and destroy radical groups and left-wing groups of all kinds. The FBI had sent forged letters, engaged in burglaries … opened mail illegally, and in the case of Black Panther leader Fred Hampton, seems to have conspired in murder …

"The investigations themselves revealed the limits of government willingness to probe into such activities … [and they] submitted its findings on the CIA to the CIA to see if there was material the Agency wanted omitted."
[**A People's History of the United States**, pp. 542-3]

Also, the CIA secretly employs several hundred American academics to write books and other materials to be used for propaganda purposes, an important weapon in the battle for hearts and minds. In other words, the CIA, FBI (and their equivalents in other countries) and other state bodies can hardly be considered neutral bodies, who just follow orders. They are a network of vested interests, with specific ideological viewpoints and aims which usually place the wishes of the voting population below maintaining the state-capital power structure in place.

Therefore we cannot expect a different group of politicians to react in different ways to the same economic and institutional influences and interests. Its no coincidence that left-wing, reformist parties have introduced right-wing, pro-capitalist ("Thatcherite/Reaganite") policies similar to those right-wing, explicitly pro-capitalist parties have. This is to be expected as the basic function of any political system is to manage the existing state and economic structures and a society's power relationships. It is **not** to alter them radically, The great illusion of politics is the notion that politicians have the power to make whatever changes they like. Looking at the international picture, the question obviously arises as to what real control do the politicians have over the international economy and its institutions or the pattern of world trade and investment. These institutions have great power and, moreover, have a driving force (the profit motive) which is essentially out of control (as can be seen by the regular financial crises during the neo-liberal era).

This can be seen most dramatically in the military coup in Chile against the democratically re-elected (left-wing) Allende government by the military, aided by the CIA, US based corporations and the US government to make it harder for the Allende regime. The coup resulted in thousands murdered and years of terror and dictatorship, but the danger of a pro-labour government was ended and the business environment was made healthy for profits (see section C.11). An extreme example, we know, but an important one for any believer in freedom or the idea that the state machine is somehow neutral and can be captured and used by left-wing parties — particularly as the fate of Chile has been suffered by many other reformist governments across the world.

Of course there have been examples of quite extensive reforms which did benefit working class people in major countries. The New Deal in the USA and the 1945-51 Labour Governments spring to mind. Surely these indicate that our claims are false? Simply put, no, they do not. Reforms can be won from the state when the dangers of not giving in outweigh any weakening of ruling class power implied in the reforms. In the face of economic crisis and working class protest, the ruling elite often tolerates changes it would otherwise fight tooth-and-nail in other circumstances. Reforms will be allowed if they can be used to save the capitalist system and the state from its own excesses and even improve their operation or if not bending will mean being broke in the storm of social protest. After all, the possibility of getting rid of the reforms when they are no longer required will always exist as long as class society remains.

This can be seen from the reformist governments of 1930s USA and 1940s UK. Both faced substantial economic problems and both were under pressure from below, by waves of militant working class struggle which could have developed beyond mere reformism. The waves of sit-down strikes in the 1930s ensured the passing of pro-union laws which allowed workers to organise without fear of being fired. This measure also partly integrated the unions into the capitalist-state machine by making them responsible for controlling "unofficial" workplace action (and so ensuring profits). The nationalisation of roughly 20% of the UK economy during the Labour administration of 1945 (the most unprofitable sections of it as well) was also the direct result of ruling class fear. As Conservative M.P. Quintin Hogg acknowledged in the House of Commons on the 17th February 1943: *"If you do not give the people reform they are going to give you revolution"*. Memories of the near revolutions across Europe after the First World War were obviously in many minds, on both sides. Not that nationalisation was particularly feared as "socialism." Indeed it was argued that it was the best means of improving the performance of the British economy. As anarchists at the time noted *"the real opinions of capitalists can be seen from Stock Exchange conditions and statements of industrialists than the Tory Front bench"* and from these it be seen *"that the owning class is not at all displeased with the record and tendency of the Labour Party."* [**Neither Nationalisation nor Privatisation**, Vernon Richards (ed.), p. 9]

History confirms Proudhon's argument that the state *"can only turn into something and do the work of the revolution insofar as it will be* so invited, provoked or compelled by some power outside of itself that seizes the initiative and sets things rolling," namely by "a body representative of the proletariat be formed in Paris ... in opposition to the bourgeoisie's representation." [**Property is Theft!**, p. 325] So, if extensive reforms have implemented by the state, just remember that they were in response to militant pressure from below and that we could have got so much more. In general, things have little changed since this anarchist argument against electioneering was put forward in the 1880s:

> "in the electoral process, the working class will always be cheated and deceived ... if they did manage to send, one, or ten, or fifty of them[selves to Parliament], they would become spoiled and powerless. Furthermore, even if the majority of Parliament were composed of workers, they could do nothing. Not only is there the senate ... the chiefs of the armed forces, the heads of the judiciary and of the police, who would be against the parliamentary bills advanced by such a chamber and would refuse to enforce laws favouring the workers (it has happened); but furthermore laws are not miraculous; no law can prevent the capitalists from exploiting the workers; no law can force them to keep their factories open and employ workers at such and such conditions, nor force shopkeepers to sell as a certain price, and so on." [S. Merlino, quoted by Galleani, **Op. Cit.**, p. 13]

As any worker will tell you, just because there are laws on such things as health and safety, union organising, working hours or whatever, it does not mean that bosses will pay any attention to them. While firing people for joining a union is illegal in America, it does not stop bosses doing so. Similarly, many would be surprised to discover that the 8 hour working day was legally created in many US states by the 1870s but workers had to strike for it in 1886 as it was not enforced. Ultimately, political action is dependent on direct action to be enforced where it counts (in the workplace and streets). And if only direct action can enforce a political decision once it is made, then it can do so beforehand so showing the limitations in waiting for politicians to act.

Anarchists reject voting for other reasons. The fact is that electoral procedures are the opposite of direct action. They are **based** on getting someone else to act on your behalf. Therefore, far from empowering people and giving them a sense of confidence and ability, electioneering **dis**-empowers them by creating a "leader" figure from which changes are expected to flow. As Brian Martin observes:

> "all the historical evidence suggests that parties are more a drag than an impetus to radical change. One obvious problem is that parties can be voted out. All the policy changes they brought in can simply be reversed later.
>
> "More important, though, is the pacifying influence of the radical party itself. On a number of occasions, radical parties have been elected to power as a result of popular upsurges. Time after time, the 'radical' parties have become chains to hold back the process

of radical change." ["Democracy without Elections", pp. 123-36, **Reinventing Anarchy, Again**, Howard J. Ehrlich (ed.), p. 124]

This can easily be seen from the history of various left-wing parties. Labour or socialist parties, elected in periods of social turbulence, have often acted to reassure the ruling elite by dampening popular action that could have threatened capitalist interests. For example, the first action undertaken by the Popular Front elected in France in 1936 was to put an end to strikes and occupations and generally to cool popular militancy, which was the Front's strongest ally in coming to power. The Labour government elected in Britain in 1945 got by with as few reforms as it could, refusing to consider changing basic social structures and simply replaced wage-labour to a boss with wage-labour to the state via nationalisation of certain industries. It did, however, manage to find time within the first days of taking office to send troops in to break a dockers' strike (this was no isolated event: Labour has used troops to break strikes far more often than the Conservatives have).

These points indicate why existing power structures cannot effectively be challenged through elections. For one thing, elected representatives are not **mandated,** which is to say they are not tied in any binding way to particular policies, no matter what promises they have made or what voters may prefer. Around election time, the public's influence on politicians is strongest, but after the election, representatives can do practically whatever they want, because there is no procedure for **instant recall.** In practice it is impossible to recall politicians before the next election, and between elections they are continually exposed to pressure from powerful special-interest groups — especially business lobbyists, state bureaucracies and political party power brokers.

Under such pressure, the tendency of politicians to break campaign promises has become legendary. Generally, such promise breaking is blamed on bad character, leading to periodic "throw-the-bastards-out" fervour — after which a new set of representatives is elected, who also mysteriously turn out to be bastards! In reality it is the system itself that produces "bastards," the sell-outs and shady dealing we have come to expect from politicians. Nevertheless, some voters continue to participate, pinning their hopes on new parties or trying to reform a major party. For anarchists this activity is pointless as it does not get at the root of the problem, it is the system which shapes politicians and parties in its own image and marginalises and alienates people due to its hierarchical and centralised nature. No amount of party politics can change that.

However, we should make it clear that most anarchists recognise there is a difference between voting for a government and voting in a referendum. Here we are discussing the former, electioneering, as a means of social change. Referenda are closer to anarchist ideas of direct democracy and are, while flawed, far better than electing a politician to office once every four years or so. In addition, Anarchists are not necessarily against **all** involvement in electoral politics. Some advocate voting when the possible outcome of an election could be disastrous (for example, if a fascist or quasi-fascist party looks likely to win the election). Some Social Ecologists, following Murray Bookchin's arguments, support actual standing in elections and think anarchists by taking part in local elections can use them to create self-governing community assemblies. However, few anarchists support such means to create community assemblies (see section J.5.14 for a discussion on this).

The problem of elections in a statist system, even on a local scale, means that the vast majority of anarchists reject voting as a means of change. Instead we wholeheartedly support direct action as the means of getting improvements in the here and now as well as the means of creating an alternative to the current system.

J.2.3 What are the political implications of voting?

At its most basic, voting implies agreement with the status quo. It is worth quoting the Scottish libertarian socialist James Kelman at length on this:

> "State propaganda insists that the reason why at least 40 percent of the voting public don't vote at all is because they have no feelings one way or the other. They say the same thing in the USA, where some 85 percent of the population are apparently 'apolitical' since they don't bother registering a vote. Rejection of the political system is inadmissible as far as the state is concerned ... Of course the one thing that does happen when you vote is that someone else has endorsed an unfair political system ... A vote for any party or any individual is always a vote for the political system. You can interpret your vote in whichever way you like but it remains an endorsement of the apparatus ... If there was any possibility that the apparatus could effect a change in the system then they would dismantle it immediately. In other words the political system is an integral state institution, designed and refined to perpetuate its own existence. Ruling authority fixes the agenda by which the public are allowed 'to enter the political arena' and that's the fix they've settled on." [**Some Recent Attacks**, p. 87]

Elections come to be seen as the only legitimate form of political participation, thus making it likely that any revolts by oppressed or marginalised groups will be viewed by the general public as illegitimate. It helps focus attention away from direct action and building new social structures back into institutions which the ruling class can easily control. The general election during the May '68 revolt in France, for example, helped diffuse the revolutionary situation, as did the elections during the Argentine revolt against neo-liberalism in the early 2000s.

So by turning political participation into the "safe" activities of campaigning and voting, elections have reduced the risk of more radical direct action as well as building a false sense of power and sovereignty among the general population. Voting disempowers the grassroots by diverting energy from grassroots action. After all, the goal of electoral politics is to elect a representative who will act **for** us. Therefore, instead of taking direct action to solve problems ourselves, action becomes indirect, though the government. This is an insidiously easy trap to fall into, as we have been conditioned

in hierarchical society from day one into attitudes of passivity and obedience, which gives most of us a deep-seated tendency to leave important matters to the "experts" and "authorities." Kropotkin described well the net effect:

> "Vote! Greater men than you will tell you the moment when the self-annihilation of capital has been accomplished. They will then expropriate the few usurpers left ... and you will be freed without having taken any more trouble than that of writing on a bit of paper the name of the man whom the heads of your faction of the party told you to vote for!" [quoted by Ruth Kinna, "Kropotkin's theory of Mutual Aid in Historical Context", pp. 259-283, **International Review of Social History**, No. 40, pp. 265-6]

Anarchists also criticise elections for giving citizens the false impression that the government serves, or can serve, the people. As Brian Martin reminds us "the founding of the modern state a few centuries ago was met with great resistance: people would refuse to pay taxes, to be conscripted or to obey laws passed by national governments. The introduction of voting and the expanded suffrage have greatly aided the expansion of state power. Rather than seeing the system as one of ruler and ruled, people see at least the possibility of using state power to serve themselves. As electoral participation has increased, the degree of resistance to taxation, military service, and the immense variety of laws regulating behaviour, has been greatly attenuated." ["Democracy without Elections", pp. 123-36, **Reinventing Anarchy, Again**, Howard J. Ehrlich (ed.), p. 126]

Ironically, voting has legitimated the growth of state power to such an extent that the state is now beyond any real popular control by the form of participation that made that growth possible. Nevertheless, the idea that electoral participation means popular control of government is so deeply implanted in people's psyches that even the most overtly sceptical radical often cannot fully free themselves from it.

Therefore, voting has the important political implication of encouraging people to identify with state power and to justify the status quo. In addition, it feeds the illusion that the state is neutral and that electing parties to office means that people have control over their own lives. Moreover, elections have a tendency to make people passive, to look for salvation from above and not from their own self-activity. As such it produces a division between leaders and led, with the voters turned into spectators of activity, not the participants within it.

All this does not mean, obviously, that anarchists prefer dictatorship or an "enlightened" monarchy. Far from it, democratising state power can be an important step towards abolishing it. All anarchists agree with Bakunin when he argued that "the most imperfect republic is a thousand times better that even the most enlightened monarchy." [quoted by Daniel Guerin, **Anarchism**, p. 20] It simply means that anarchists refuse to join in with the farce of electioneering, particularly when there are more effective means available for changing things for the better. Anarchists reject the idea that our problems can be solved by the very institutions that cause them in the first place!

J.2.4 Surely voting for radical parties will be effective?

There is no doubt that voting can lead to changes in policies, which can be a good thing as far as it goes. However, such policies are formulated and implemented within the authoritarian framework of the hierarchical capitalist state — a framework which itself is never open to challenge by voting. On the contrary, voting legitimates the state framework ensuring that social change will be (at best) mild, gradual, and reformist rather than rapid and radical. Indeed, the "democratic" process has resulted in all successful political parties becoming committed to "more of the same" or tinkering with the details at best (which is usually the limits of any policy changes). This seems unlikely to change.

Given the need for radical systemic changes as soon as possible due to the exponentially accelerating crises of modern civilisation, working for gradual reforms within the electoral system must be seen as a potentially deadly tactical error. Electioneering has always been the death of radicalism. Political parties are only radical when they do not stand a chance of election. However, many social activists continue to try to use elections, so participating in the system which disempowers the majority and so helps create the social problems they are protesting against. It should be a widely recognised truism in radical circles that elections empower the politicians and not the voters. Thus elections focus attention to a few leaders, urging them to act **for** rather than acting for ourselves (see section H.1.5). If genuine social change needs mass participation then, by definition, using elections will undermine that. This applies to within the party as well, for working "within the system" disempowers grassroots activists, as can be seen by the Green party in Germany during the early eighties. The coalitions into which the Greens entered with Social Democrats in the German legislature often had the effect of strengthening the status quo by co-opting those whose energies might otherwise have gone into more radical and effective forms of activism. Principles were ignored in favour of having some influence, so producing watered-down legislation which tinkered with the system rather than transforming it.

As discussed in section H.3.9, the state is more complicated than the simple organ of the economically dominant class pictured by Marxists. There are continual struggles both inside and outside the state bureaucracies, struggles that influence policies and empower different groups of people. This can produce clashes within the ruling elite, while the need of the state to defend the system **as a whole** causes conflict with the interests of sections of the capitalist class. Due to this, many radical parties believe that the state is neutral and so it makes sense to work within it — for example, to obtain labour, consumer, and environmental protection laws. However, this reasoning ignores the fact that the organisational structure of the state is not neutral.

It may be argued that if a new political group is radical enough it will be able to use state power for good purposes. We discuss this in more detail in section J.2.6. However, as we argued in the previous section, radical parties are under pressure from economic and state bureaucracies that ensure that even a sincere radical party would be powerless to introduce significant reforms. The only real response to the problems of representative democracy is to urge people not to vote. Such anti-election campaigns can be a valuable way of making others aware of the limitations of the current system, which is a necessary condition for their seriously considering the anarchist alternative of using direct action and building alternative social and economic organisations. The implications of abstentionism are discussed in the next section.

J.2.5 Why do anarchists support abstentionism and what are its implications?

At its most basic, anarchists support abstentionism because *"participation in elections means the transfer of one's will and decisions to another, which is contrary to the fundamental principles of anarchism."* [Emma Goldman, **Vision on Fire**, p. 89] For, as Proudhon stressed, in a statist democracy, the people *"is limited to choosing, every three or four years, its chiefs and its imposters."* [quoted by George Woodcock, **Pierre-Joseph Proudhon**, p. 152] If you reject hierarchy then participating in a system by which you elect those who will govern you is almost like adding insult to injury! For, as Luigi Galleani pointed out, *"whoever has the political competence to choose his own rulers is, by implication, also competent to do without them."* [**The End of Anarchism?**, p. 37] In other words, because anarchists reject the idea of authority, we reject the idea that picking the authority (be it bosses or politicians) makes us free. Therefore, anarchists reject governmental elections in the name of self-government and free association. We refuse to vote as voting is endorsing authoritarian social structures. We are (in effect) being asked to make obligations to the state, not our fellow citizens, and so anarchists reject the symbolic process by which our liberty is alienated from us.

Anarchists are aware that elections serve to legitimate government. We have always warned that since the state is an integral part of the system that perpetuates poverty, inequality, racism, imperialism, sexism, environmental destruction, and war, we should not expect to solve any of these problems by changing a few nominal state leaders every four or five years. Therefore anarchists (usually) advocate abstentionism at election time as a means of exposing the farce of "democracy", the disempowering nature of elections and the real role of the state.

For anarchists then, when you vote, you are choosing between rulers. Instead of urging people to vote we raise the option of choosing to rule yourself, to organise freely with others — in your workplace, in your community, everywhere — as equals. The option of something you cannot vote for, a new society. Instead of waiting for others to make some changes for you, anarchists urge that you do it yourself. In this way, you cannot but build an alternative to the state which can reduce its power now and, in the long run, replace it. This is the core of the anarchist support for abstentionism.

In addition, beyond this basic anarchist rejection of elections from an anti-statist position, anarchists also support abstentionism as it allows us to put across our ideas at election time. It is a fact that at such times people are often more interested in politics than usual. So, by arguing for abstentionism we can get our ideas across about the nature of the current system, how elected politicians do not control the state bureaucracy, now the state acts to protect capitalism and so on. In addition, it allows us to present the ideas of direct action and encourage those disillusioned with political parties and the current system to become anarchists by presenting a viable alternative to the farce of politics. For, after all, a sizeable percentage of non-voters and voters are disillusioned with the current set-up. Many who vote do so simply against the other candidate, seeking the least-worse option. Many who do not vote do so for essentially political reasons, such as being fed up with the political system, failing to see any major differences between the parties, or recognition that the candidates were not interested in people like them. These non-voters are often disproportionately left-leaning, compared with those who did vote. Anarchist abstentionism is a means of turning this negative reaction to an unjust system into positive activity.

So, anarchist opposition to electioneering has deep political implications which Luigi Galleani addressed when he wrote:

"The anarchists' electoral abstentionism implies not only a conception that is opposed to the principle of representation (which is totally rejected by anarchism), it implies above all an absolute lack of confidence in the State … Furthermore, anarchist abstentionism has consequences which are much less superficial than the inert apathy ascribed to it by the sneering careerists of 'scientific socialism' [i.e. Marxism]. It strips the State of the constitutional fraud with which it presents itself to the gullible as the true representative of the whole nation, and, in so doing, exposes its essential character as representative, procurer and policeman of the ruling classes.

"Distrust of reforms, of public power and of delegated authority, can lead to direct action [in the class struggle] … It can determine the revolutionary character of this … action; and, accordingly, anarchists regard it as the best available means for preparing the masses to manage their own personal and collective interests; and, besides, anarchists feel that even now the working people are fully capable of handling their own political and administrative interests." [**Op. Cit.**, pp. 13-14]

Therefore abstentionism stresses the importance of self-activity and self-liberation as well as having an important educational effect in highlighting that the state is not neutral but serves to protect class rule and that meaningful change only comes from below, by direct action. For the dominant ideas within any class society reflect the opinions of the ruling elite of that society and so any campaign at election times which argues for abstentionism and indicates why voting is a farce will obviously challenge them. In other words, abstentionism combined with direct action and the building of libertarian alternatives is a very effective means of changing people's ideas and encouraging a process of self-education and, ultimately, self-liberation.

In summary, anarchists urge abstentionism in order to **encourage** activity, not apathy. Not voting is **not** enough, and anarchists urge people to **organise** and **resist** as well. Abstentionism must be the political counterpart of class struggle, self-activity and self-management in order to be effective — otherwise it is as pointless as voting is.

J.2.6 What are the effects of radicals using electioneering?

While many radicals would be tempted to agree with our analysis of the limitations of electioneering and voting, few would automatically agree with anarchist abstentionist arguments. Instead, they argue that we should combine direct action with electioneering. In that way (it is argued) we can overcome the limitations of electioneering by invigorating it with self-activity. In addition, they suggest, the state is too powerful to leave in the hands of the enemies of the working class. A radical politician will refuse to give the orders to crush social protest that a right-wing, pro-capitalist one would.

While these are important arguments in favour of radicals using elections, they ultimately fail to take into account the nature of the state and the corrupting effect it has on radicals. This reformist idea has met a nasty end. If history is anything to go by, the net effect of radicals using elections is that by the time they are elected to office the radicals will happily do what they claimed the right-wing would have done. In 1899, for example, the Socialist Alexandre Millerand joined the French Government. Nothing changed. During industrial disputes strikers *"appealed to Millerand for help, confident that, with him in the government, the state would be on their side. Much of this confidence was dispelled within a few years. The government did little more for workers than its predecessors had done; soldiers and police were still sent in to repress serious strikes."* [Peter N. Stearns, **Revolutionary Syndicalism and French Labour**, p. 16] Aristide Briand, another socialist politician was the Minister of the Interior in 1910 and *"broke a general strike of railwaymen by use of the most draconian methods. Having declared a military emergency he threatened all strikers with court martial."* [Jeremy Jennings, **Syndicalism in France** p. 36] These events occurred, it should be noted, during the period when social democratic parties were self-proclaimed revolutionaries and arguing against anarcho-syndicalism by using the argument that working people needed their own representatives in office to stop troops being used against them during strikes!

Looking at the British Labour government of 1945 to 1951 we find the same actions. What is often considered the most left-wing Labour government ever used troops to break strikes in every year it was in office, starting with a dockers' strike days after it became the new government. Again, in the 1970s, Labour used troops to break strikes. Indeed, the Labour Party has used troops to break strikes more often than the Conservative Party.

Many blame the individuals elected to office for these betrayals, arguing that we need to elect **better** politicians, select **better** leaders. For anarchists nothing could be more wrong as its the means used, not the individuals involved, which is the problem. Writing of his personal experience as a member of Parliament, Proudhon recounted that "[a]s soon as I set foot in the parliamentary Sinai, I ceased to be in touch with the masses; because I was absorbed by my legislative work, I entirely lost sight of the current events ... One must have lived in that isolator which is called a National Assembly to realise how the men who are most completely ignorant of the state of the country are almost always those who represent it." There was "ignorance of daily facts" and "fear of the people" ("the sickness of all those who belong to authority") for "the people, for those in power, are the enemy." [**Property is Theft!**, p. 19] Ultimately, as syndicalist Emile Pouget argued, this fate was inevitable as any socialist politician "could not break the mould; he is only a cog in the machine of oppression and whether he wishes it or not he must, as minister, participate in the job of crushing the proletariat." [quoted by Jennings, **Op. Cit.**, p. 36]

These days, few enter Parliament as radicals like Proudhon. The notion of using elections for radical change is rare. Such a development in itself shows the correctness of the anarchist critique of electioneering. At its most basic, electioneering results in the party using it becoming more moderate and reformist — it becomes the victim of its own success. In order to gain votes, the party must appear "moderate" and "practical" and that means working within the system:

> "Participation in the politics of the bourgeois States has not brought the labour movement a hair's-breadth nearer to Socialism, but thanks to this method, Socialism has almost been completely crushed and condemned to insignificance ... Participation in parliamentary politics has affected the Socialist Labour movement like an insidious poison. It destroyed the belief in the necessity of constructive Socialist activity, and, worse of all, the impulse to self-help, by inoculating people with the ruinous delusion that salvation always comes from above." [Rudolf Rocker, **Anarcho-Syndicalism**, p. 54]

This corruption does not happen overnight. Alexander Berkman indicated how it slowly developed:

> "In former days the Socialists ... claimed that they meant to use politics only for the purpose of propaganda ... and took part in elections on order to have an opportunity to advocate Socialism
>
> "It may seem a harmless thing but it proved the undoing of Socialism. Because nothing is truer than the means you use to attain your object soon themselves become your object ... Little by little they changed their attitude. Instead of electioneering being merely an educational method, it gradually became their only method to secure political office, to get elected to legislative bodies and other government positions. The change naturally led the Socialists to tone down their revolutionary ardour; it compelled them to soften their criticism of capitalism and government in order to avoid persecution and secure more votes ... they have ceased to be revolutionists; they have become reformers who want to change things by law ... And everywhere, without exception, they have followed

the same course, everywhere they have forsworn their ideals, have duped the masses ... There is a deeper reason for this constant and regular betrayal [than individual scoundrels being elected] ... no man turns scoundrel or traitor overnight.

> "It is **power** which corrupts ... The filth and contamination of politics everywhere proves that. Moreover, even with the best intentions Socialists in legislative bodies or in governments find themselves entirely powerless to accomplishing anything of a socialistic nature ... The demoralisation and vitiation take place little by little, so gradually that one hardly notices it himself ... [The elected Socialist] finds himself in a strange and unfriendly atmosphere ... and he must participate in the business that is being transacted. Most of that business ... has no bearing whatever on the things the Socialist believes in, no connection with the interests of the working class voters who elected him ... when a bill of some bearing upon labour ... comes up ... he is ignored or laughed at for his impractical ideas on the matter ...
>
> "Our Socialist perceives that he is regarded as a laughing stock [by the other politicians] ... and finds more and more difficulty in securing the floor... he knows that neither by his talk nor by his vote can he influence the proceedings ... His speeches don't even reach the public ... He appeals to the voters to elect more comrades... Years pass ... [and a] number ... are elected. Each of them goes through the same experience ... [and] quickly come to the conclusion ... [that they] must show that they are practical men ... that they are doing something for their constituency ... In this manner the situation compels them to take a 'practical' part in the proceedings, to 'talk business,' to fall in line with the matters actually dealt with in the legislative body ... Spending years in that atmosphere, enjoying good jobs and pay, the elected Socialists have themselves become part and parcel of the political machinery ... With growing success in elections and securing political power they turn more and more conservative and content with existing conditions. Removal from the life and suffering of the working class, living in the atmosphere of the bourgeoisie ... they have become what they call 'practical' ... Power and position have gradually stifled their conscience and they have not the strength and honesty to swim against the current ... They have become the strongest bulwark of capitalism." [**What is Anarchism?**, pp. 92-8]

So the "political power which they had wanted to conquer had gradually conquered their Socialism until there was scarcely anything left of it." [Rocker, **Op. Cit.**, p. 55]

Not that these arguments are the result of hindsight, we must add. Bakunin was arguing in the early 1870s that the "inevitable result [of using elections] will be that workers' deputies, transferred to a purely bourgeois environment, and into an atmosphere of purely bourgeois political ideas ... will become middle class in their outlook, perhaps even more so than the bourgeois themselves."

As long as universal suffrage *"is exercised in a society where the people, the mass of workers, are **economically** dominated by a minority holding exclusive possession the property and capital of the country"* elections *"can only be illusory, anti-democratic in their results."* [**The Political Philosophy of Bakunin**, p. 216 and p. 213] This meant that *"the election to the German parliament of one or two workers … from the Social Democratic Party"* was *"not dangerous"* and, in fact, was *"highly useful to the German state as a lightning-rod, or a safety-valve."* Unlike the *"political and social theory"* of the anarchists, which *"leads them directly and inexorably to a complete break with all governments and all forms of bourgeois politics, leaving no alternative but social revolution,"* Marxism, he argued, *"inexorably enmeshes and entangles its adherents, under the pretext of political tactics, in endless accommodation with governments and the various bourgeois political parties - that is, it thrusts them directly into reaction."* [Bakunin, **Statism and Anarchy**, p. 193 and pp. 179-80] In the case of the German Social Democrats, this became obvious in 1914, when they supported their state in the First World war, and after 1918, when they crushed the German Revolution.

So history proved Bakunin's prediction correct (as it did with his prediction that Marxism would result in elite rule). Simply put, for anarchists, the net effect of socialists using bourgeois elections would be to put them (and the movements they represent) into the quagmire of bourgeois politics and influences. In other words, the parties involved will be shaped by the environment they are working within and not vice versa.

History is littered with examples of radical parties becoming a part of the system. From Marxian Social Democracy at the turn of the 19th century to the German Green Party in the 1980s, we have seen radical parties, initially proclaiming the need for direct action and extra-parliamentary activity denouncing these activities once in power. From only using parliament as a means of spreading their message, the parties involved end up considering votes as more important than the message. Janet Biehl sums up the effects on the German Green Party of trying to combine radical electioneering with direct action:

> *"the German Greens, once a flagship for the Green movement worldwide, should now be considered stink normal, as their **de facto** boss himself declares. Now a repository of careerists, the Greens stand out only for the rapidity with which the old cadre of careerism, party politics, and business-as-usual once again played itself out in their saga of compromise and betrayal of principle. Under the superficial veil of their old values — a very thin veil indeed, now — they can seek positions and make compromises to their heart's content … They have become 'practical,' 'realistic' and 'power-orientated.' This former New Left ages badly, not only in Germany but everywhere else. But then, it happened with the S.P.D. [The German Social Democratic Party] in August 1914, then why not with Die Grunen in 1991? So it did."* ["Party or Movement?", **Greenline**, no. 89, p. 14]

This, sadly, is the end result of all such attempts. Ultimately, supporters of using political action can only appeal to the good intentions and character of their candidates. Anarchists, however,

present an analysis of state structures and other influences that will determine how the character of the successful candidates will change. In other words, in contrast to Marxists and other radicals, anarchists present a materialist, scientific analysis of the dynamics of electioneering and its effects on radicals. Like most forms of idealism, the arguments of Marxists and other radicals flounder on the rocks of reality.

However, many radicals refuse to learn this lesson of history and keep trying to create a new party which will not repeat the saga of compromise and betrayal which all other radical parties have suffered. And they say that anarchists are utopian! *"You cannot dive into a swamp and remain clean."* [Berkman, **Op. Cit.**, p. 99] Such is the result of rejecting (or "supplementing" with electioneering) direct action as the means to change things, for any social movement *"to ever surrender their commitment to direct action for 'working within the system' is to destroy their personality as socially innovative movements. It is to dissolve back into the hopeless morass of 'mass organisations' that seek respectability rather than change."* [Murray Bookchin, **Toward an Ecological Society**, p. 47]

Moreover, the use of electioneering has a centralising effect on the movements that use it. Political actions become considered as parliamentary activities made **for** the population by their representatives, with the 'rank and file' left with no other role than that of passive support. Only the leaders are actively involved and the main emphasis falls upon them and it soon becomes taken for granted that they should determine policy. Conferences become little more than rallies with politicians freely admitting that they will ignore any conference decisions as and when required. Not to mention the all-too-common sight of politicians turning round and doing the exact opposite of what they promised. In the end, party conferences become simply like parliamentary elections, with party members supporting this leader against another.

Soon the party reflects the division between manual and mental labour so necessary for the capitalist system. Instead of working class self-activity and self-determination, there is a substitution of a non-working class leadership acting **for** people. This replaces self-management in social struggle and within the party itself. Electoralism strengthens the leaders dominance over the party and the party over the people it claims to represent. The real causes and solutions to the problems we face are mystified by the leadership and rarely discussed in order to concentrate on the popular issues that will get them elected. Ultimately, radicals *"instead of weakening the false and enslaving belief in law and government … actually work to **strengthen** the people's faith in forcible authority and government."* [Berkman, **Op. Cit.**, p. 100] Which has always proved deadly to encouraging a spirit of revolt, self-management and self-help — the very keys to creating change in a society. Thus this 1870 resolution of the Spanish section of the First International seems to have been proven to be correct:

> *"Any participation of the working class in the middle class political government would merely consolidate the present state of affairs and necessarily paralyse the socialist revolutionary action of the proletariat. The Federation [of unions] is the true representative of labour, and should work outside the political system."* [quoted by Jose Pierats, **Anarchists in the Spanish Revolution**, p. 169]

Instead of trying to gain control of the state, for whatever reasons, anarchists try to promote a culture of resistance within society that makes the state subject to pressure from outside (see section J.2.9). And, we feel, history has proven us right time and time again.

J.2.7 Surely we should vote for reformist parties in order to expose them?

Some Leninist socialists (like the British **Socialist Workers Party** and its offshoots) argue that we should urge people to vote for Labour and other social democratic parties. In this they follow Lenin's 1920 argument against the anti-Parliamentarian left that revolutionaries *"help"* elect such parties as many workers still follow their lead so that they will be *"convinced by their own experience that we are right,"* that such parties *"are absolutely good for nothing, that they are petty-bourgeois and treacherous by nature, and that their bankruptcy is inevitable."* If we *"want the masses to follow us"*, we need to *"support"* such parties *"in the same way as the rope supports a hanged man."* In this way, by experiencing the reformists in office, *"the majority will soon become disappointed in their leaders and will begin to support communism."* [**The Lenin Anthology**, p. 603, p. 605 and p. 602]

This tactic is suggested for two reasons. The first is that revolutionaries will be able to reach more people by being seen to support popular, trade union based, parties. If they do not, then they are in danger of alienating sizeable sections of the working class by arguing that such parties will be no better than explicitly pro-capitalist ones. The second, and the more important one, is that by electing reformist parties into office the experience of living under such a government will shatter whatever illusions its supporters had in them. The reformist parties will be given the test of experience and when they betray their supporters to protect the status quo it will radicalise those who voted for them, who will then seek out **real** socialist parties (namely the likes of the SWP).

Libertarians reject these arguments for three reasons.

Firstly, it is deeply dishonest as it hides the true thoughts of those who support the tactic. To tell the truth is a revolutionary act. Radicals should not follow the capitalist media by telling half-truths, distorting the facts, hiding what they believe or supporting a party they are opposed to. If this means being less popular in the short run, then so be it. Attacking nationalism, capitalism, religion, or a host of other things can alienate people but few revolutionaries would be so opportunistic as to hold their tongues on these. In the long run being honest about your ideas is the best way of producing a movement which aims to get rid of a corrupt social system. Starting such a movement with half-truths is doomed to failure.

Secondly, anarchists reject the basis of this argument. The logic underlying it is that by being disillusioned by their reformist leaders and party, voters will look for **new,** "better" leaders and parties. However, this fails to go to the root of the problem, namely the dependence on leaders which hierarchical society creates within people. Anarchists do not want people to follow the "best" leadership, they want them to govern themselves, to be **self**-active,

manage their own affairs and not follow **any** would-be leaders. If you seriously think that the liberation of the oppressed is the task of the oppressed themselves (as Leninists claim to do) then you **must** reject this tactic in favour of ones that promote working class self-activity.

The third reason we reject this tactic is that it has been proven to fail time and time again. What most of its supporters seem to fail to notice is that voters have indeed put reformist parties into office many times. Lenin suggested this tactic in 1920 and there has been no general radicalisation of the voting population by this method, nor even in reformist party militants in spite of the many Labour Party governments in Britain which all attacked the working class. Moreover, the disillusionment associated with the experience of reformist parties often expresses itself as a demoralisation with socialism **as such**, rather than with the reformist's watered down version of it. If Lenin's position could be persuasive to some in 1920 when it was untried, the experience of subsequent decades should show its weakness.

This failure, for anarchists, is not surprising, considering the reasons why we reject this tactic. Given that this tactic does not attack hierarchy or dependence on leaders, does not attack the ideology and process of voting, it will obviously fail to present a real alternative to the voting population (who will turn to other alternatives available at election time and not embrace direct action). Also the sight of a so-called "socialist" or "radical" government managing capitalism, imposing cuts, breaking strikes and generally attacking its supporters will damage the credibility of any form of socialism and discredit all socialist and radical ideas in the eyes of the population. If the experience of the Labour Government in Britain during the 1970s and New Labour after 1997 are anything to go by, it may result in the rise of the far-right who will capitalise on this disillusionment.

By refusing to argue that no government is "on our side," radicals who urge us to vote reformist "without illusions" help to disarm theoretically the people who listen to them. Working class people, surprised, confused and disorientated by the constant "betrayals" of left-wing parties may turn to right wing parties (who can be elected) to stop the attacks rather than turn to direct action as the radical minority within the working class did not attack voting as part of the problem. How many times must we elect the same party, go through the same process, the same betrayals before we realise this tactic does not work? Moreover, if it **is** a case of having to experience something before people reject it, few state socialists take this argument to its logical conclusion. We rarely hear them argue we must experience the hell of fascism or Stalinism or the nightmare of free market capitalism in order to ensure working class people "see through" them.

Anarchists, in contrast, say that we can argue against reformist politics without having to associate ourselves with them by urging people to vote for them. By arguing for abstentionism we can help to theoretically arm the people who will come into conflict with these parties once they are in office. By arguing that all governments will be forced to attack us (due to the pressure from capital and state) and that we have to rely on our own organisations and power to defend ourselves, we can promote working class self-confidence in its own abilities, and encourage the rejection of capitalism, the state and hierarchical leadership as well as the use of direct action. Finally, we must add, it is not required for radicals to associate themselves with the farce of parliamentary propaganda in order to win people over to our ideas. Non-anarchists will see us use **direct action,** see us **act,** see the anarchistic alternatives we create and see our propaganda. Non-anarchists can be reached quite well without taking part in, or associating ourselves with, parliamentary action.

J.2.8 Will abstentionism lead to the right winning elections?

Possibly. However anarchists don't just say "don't vote", we say "organise" as well. Apathy is something anarchists have no interest in encouraging.

The reasons **why** people abstain is more important than the act. The idea that the USA is closer to anarchy because around 50% of people do not vote is nonsense. Abstentionism in this case is the product of apathy and cynicism, not political ideas. So anarchists recognise that apathetic abstentionism is **not** revolutionary or an indication of anarchist sympathies. It is produced by apathy and a general level of cynicism at **all** forms of political ideas and the possibility of change.

That is why anarchist abstentionism always stresses the need for direct action and organising economically and socially to change things, to resist oppression and exploitation. In such circumstances, the effect of an electoral strike would be fundamentally different than an apathy induced lack of voting. *"If the anarchists",* Vernon Richards argued, *"could persuade half the electorate to abstain from voting this would, from an electoral point of view, contribute to the victory of the Right. But it would be a hollow victory, for what government could rule when half the electorate by not voting had expressed its lack of confidence in all governments?"* The party in office would have to rule over a country in which a sizeable minority, even a majority, had rejected government as such. This would mean that the politicians *"would be subjected to real pressures from people who believed in their own power"* and acted accordingly. So anarchists call on people **not** to vote, but instead organise themselves and be conscious of their own power. Only this *"can command the respect of governments, can curb the power of government as millions of crosses on bits of paper never will."* [**The Impossibilities of Social Democracy**, p. 142]

For, as Emma Goldman pointed out, *"if the Anarchists were strong enough to swing the elections to the Left, they must also have been strong enough to rally the workers to a general strike, or even a series of strikes … In the last analysis, the capitalist class knows too well that officials, whether they belong to the Right or the Left, can be bought. Or they are of no consequence to their pledge."* [**Vision on Fire**, p. 90] The mass of the population, however, cannot be bought off and if they are willing and able to resist then they can become a power second to none. Only by organising, fighting back and practicing solidarity where we live and work can we **really** change things. That is where **our** power lies, that is where we can create a **real** alternative. By creating a network of self-managed, pro-active community and workplace organisations we can impose by direct action that which politicians can never give us from Parliament. Only such a movement can stop the attacks upon us by whoever gets into office. A government (left or right) which faces a mass movement based upon direct action and solidarity will always think twice before proposing cuts or introducing authoritarian laws. Howard Zinn expressed it well:

"I think a way to behave is to think not in terms of representative government, not in terms of voting, not in terms of electoral politics, but thinking in terms of organising social movements, organising in the workplace, organising in the neighbourhood, organising collectives that can become strong enough to eventually take over — first to become strong enough to resist what has been done to them by authority, and second, later, to become strong enough to actually take over the institutions … the crucial question is not who is in office, but what kind of social movement do you have. Because we have seen historically that if you have a powerful social movement, it doesn't matter who is in office. Whoever is in office, they could be Republican or Democrat, if you have a powerful social movement, the person in office will have to yield, will have to in some ways respect the power of social movements … voting is not crucial, and organising is the important thing." [**An Interview with Howard Zinn on Anarchism: Rebels Against Tyranny**]

Of course, all the parties claim that they are better than the others and this is the logic of this question — namely, we must vote for the lesser evil as the right-wing in office will be terrible. But what this forgets is that the lesser evil is still an evil. What happens is that instead of the greater evil attacking us, we get the lesser evil doing what the right-wing was going to do. Let us not forget it was the "lesser evil" of the Democrats (in the USA) and Labour (in the UK) who first introduced, in the 1970s, the monetarist and other policies that Reagan and Thatcher made their own in the 1980s.

This is important to remember. The central fallacy in this kind of argument is the underlying assumption that "the left" will **not** implement the same kind of policies as the right. History does not support such a perspective and it is a weak hope to place a political strategy on. As such, when people worry that a right-wing government will come into power and seek to abolish previous social gains (such as abortion rights, welfare programmes, union rights, and so forth) they seem to forget that so-called left-wing administrations have also undermined such reforms. In response to queries by the left on how anarchists would seek to defend such reforms if their abstentionism aided the victory of the right, anarchists reply by asking the left how they seek to defend such reforms when their "left-wing" government starts to attack them.

Ultimately, voting for other politicians will make little difference. The reality is that politicians are puppets. As we argued in section J.2.2, real power in the state does not lie with politicians, but instead within the state bureaucracy and big business. Faced with these powers, we have seen left-wing governments from Spain to New Zealand introduce right-wing policies. So even if we elected a radical party, they would be powerless to change anything important and soon be forced to attack us in the interests of capitalism. Politicians come and go, but the state bureaucracy and big business remain forever! Simply put, we cannot expect a different group of politicians to react that differently to the same economic and political pressures and influences.

Therefore we cannot rely on voting for the lesser evil to save us from the possible dangers of a right-wing election victory. All we can hope for is that no matter who gets in, the population will resist the government because it knows and can use its real power: **direct action**. For the *"only limit to the oppression of government is the power with which the people show themselves capable of opposing it."* [Malatesta, **Errico Malatesta: His Life and Ideas**, p. 196] Hence Vernon Richards:

> *"If the anarchist movement has a role to play in practical politics it is surely that of suggesting to, and persuading, as many people as possible that their freedom from the Hitlers, Francos and the rest, depends not on the right to vote or securing a majority of votes 'for the candidate of ones choice,' but on evolving new forms of political and social organisation which aim at the direct participation of the people, with the consequent weakening of the power, as well of the social role, of government in the life of the community."* ["Anarchists and Voting", pp. 176-87, **The Raven**, no. 14, pp. 177-8]

We discuss what this could involve in the next section.

J.2.9 What do anarchists do instead of voting?

While anarchists reject electioneering and voting, it does not mean that we are politically apathetic. Indeed, part of the reason why anarchists reject voting is because we think that voting is not part of the solution, it is part of the problem. This is because it endorses an unjust and unfree political system and makes us look to others to fight our battles for us. It **blocks** constructive self-activity and direct action. It **stops** the building of alternatives in our communities and workplaces. Voting breeds apathy and apathy is our worse enemy.

Given that we have had universal suffrage for some time in the West and we have seen the rise of Labour and Radical parties aiming to use that system to effect change in a socialistic direction, it seems strange that we are probably further away from socialism than when they started. The simple fact is that these parties have spent so much time trying to win elections that they have stopped even thinking about creating socialist alternatives in our communities and workplaces. That is in itself enough to prove that electioneering, far from eliminating apathy, in fact helps to create it.

So, because of this, anarchists argue that the only way to not waste your vote is to spoil it! We are the only political movement which argues that nothing will change unless you act for yourself, take back the power and fight the system **directly.** Only direct action breaks down apathy and gets results. It is the first steps towards real freedom, towards a free and just society. Unsurprisingly, then,

anarchists are the first to point out that not voting is not enough: we need to actively struggle for an alternative to both voting **and** the current system. Just as the right to vote was won after a long series of struggles, so the creation of a free, decentralised, self-managed, libertarian socialist society will be the product of social struggle.

Anarchists are the last people to deny the importance of political liberties or the importance in wining the right to vote. The question we must ask is whether it is a more a fitting tribute to the millions of people who used direct action, fought and suffered for the right to vote to use that victory to endorse a deeply unfair and undemocratic system or to use other means (indeed the means they used to win the vote) to create a system based upon true popular self-government? If we are true to our (and their) desire for a real, meaningful democracy, we would have to reject political action in favour of direct action.

This obviously gives an idea of what anarchists do instead of voting, we agitate, organise and educate. Or, to quote Proudhon, the *"problem before the labouring classes ... consists not in capturing, but in subduing both power and monopoly, — that is, in generating from the bowels of the people, from the depths of labour, a greater authority, a more potent fact, which shall envelop capital and the state and subjugate them."* For, *"to combat and reduce power, to put it in its proper place in society, it is of no use to change the holders of power or introduce some variation into its workings: an agricultural and industrial combination must be found by means of which power, today the ruler of society, shall become its slave."* [**Property is Theft!**, p. 226 and p. 225]

We do this by organising what Bakunin called *"antipolitical social power of the working classes."* [**Bakunin on Anarchism**, p. 263] This activity which bases itself on the two broad strategies of encouraging direct action and building alternatives where we live and work.

Taking the first strategy, anarchists say that by using direct action we can force politicians to respect the wishes of the people. For example, if a government or boss tries to limit free speech, then anarchists would try to encourage a free speech fight to break the laws in question until such time as they are revoked. If a government or landlord refuses to limit rent increases or improve safety requirements for accommodation, anarchists would organise squats and rent strikes. In the case of environmental destruction, anarchists would support and encourage attempts at halting the damage by mass trespassing on sites, blocking the routes of developments, organising strikes and so on. If a boss refuses to introduce an 8 hour day, then workers should form a union and go on strike or simply stop working after 8 hours. Unlike laws, the boss cannot ignore direct action. Similarly, strikes combined with social protest would be effective means of stopping authoritarian laws being passed. For example, anti-union laws would be best fought by strike action and community boycotts (and given the utterly ineffectual defence pursued by pro-labour parties using political action to stop anti-union laws who can seriously say that the anarchist way would be any worse?). Collective non-payment of taxes would ensure the end of unpopular government decisions. The example of the poll tax rebellion in the UK in the late in 1980s shows the power of such direct action. The government could happily handle hours of speeches by opposition politicians but they could not ignore social protest (and we must add that the Labour Party which claimed to oppose the tax happily let the councils controlled by them introduce the tax and arrest non-payers).

The aim would be to spread struggles and involve as many people as possible, for it is *"merely stupid for a group of workers — even for the workers organised as a national group — to invite the making of a distinction between themselves and the community. The real protagonists in this struggle are the community and the State — the community as an organic and inclusive body and the State as the representatives of a tyrannical minority ... The General Strike of the future must be organised as a strike of the community against the State. The result of that strike will not be in doubt."* [Herbert Read, **Anarchy and Order**, p. 52]

Such a counter-power would focus the attention of those in power far more than a ballot in a few years time (particularly as the state bureaucracy is not subject to even that weak form of accountability). As Noam Chomsky argues, *"[w]ithin the constraints of existing state institutions, policies will be determined by people representing centres of concentrated power in the private economy, people who, in their institutional roles, will not be swayed by moral appeals but by the costs consequent upon the decisions they make — not because they are 'bad people,' but because that is what the institutional roles demands."* He continues: *"Those who own and manage the society want a disciplined, apathetic and submissive public that will not challenge their privilege and the orderly world in which it thrives. The ordinary citizen need not grant them this gift. Enhancing the Crisis of Democracy by organisation and political engagement is itself a threat to power, a reason to undertake it quite apart from its crucial importance in itself as an essential step towards social change."* [**Turning the Tide**, pp. 251-2]

In this way, by encouraging social protest, any government would think twice before pursuing authoritarian, destructive and unpopular policies. In the final analysis, governments can and will ignore the talk of opposition politicians, but they cannot ignore social action for very long. In the words of a Spanish anarchosyndicalist, anarchists *"do not ask for any concessions from the government. Our mission and our duty is to impose from the streets that which ministers and deputies are incapable of realising in parliament."* [quoted by Graham Kelsey, **Anarchosyndicalism, Libertarian Communism and the State**, p. 79] This was seen after the Popular Front was elected February 1936 and the Spanish landless workers, sick and tired of waiting for the politicians to act, started to occupy the land. The government *"resorted to the time-tested procedure of expelling the peasants with the Civil Guard."* The peasants responded with a *"dramatic rebellion"* which forced the politicians to *"legalise the occupied farms. This proved once again that the only effective reforms are those imposed by force from below. Indeed, direct action was infinitely more successful than all the parliamentary debates that took place between 1931 and 1933 about whether to institute the approved Agrarian Reform law."* [Abel Paz, **Durruti in the Spanish Revolution**, p. 391]

The second strategy of building alternatives flows naturally from the first. Any form of campaign requires organisation and by organising in an anarchist manner we build organisations that *"bear in them the living seeds of the new society which is to replace the old world."* [Bakunin, **Op. Cit.**, p. 255] In organising strikes in the workplace and community we can create a network of activists

and union members who can encourage a spirit of revolt against authority. By creating assemblies where we live and work we can create an effective countering power to the state and capital. Such a union, as the anarchists in Spain and Italy proved, can be the focal point for recreating self-managed schools, social centres and so on. In this way the local community can ensure that it has sufficient independent, self-managed resources available to educate its members. Also, combined with credit unions (or mutual banks), cooperative workplaces and stores, a self-managed infrastructure could be created which would ensure that people can directly provide for their own needs without having to rely on capitalists or governments. In the words of a C.N.T. militant:

"We must create that part of libertarian communism which can be created within bourgeois society and do so precisely to combat that society with our own special weapons." [quoted by Kelsey, **Op. Cit.**, p. 79]

So, far from doing nothing, by not voting the anarchist actively encourages alternatives. As the British anarchist John Turner argued, we *"have a line to work upon, to teach the people self-reliance, to urge them to take part in non-political [i.e. non-electoral] movements directly started by themselves for themselves ... as soon as people learn to rely upon themselves they will act for themselves ... We teach the people to place their faith in themselves, we go on the lines of self-help. We teach them to form their own committees of management, to repudiate their masters, to despise the laws of the country."* [quoted by John Quail, **The Slow Burning Fuse**, p. 87] In this way we encourage self-activity, self-organisation and self-help — the opposite of apathy and doing nothing.

Ultimately, what the state and capital gives, they can also take away. What we build by our own self-activity can last as long as we want it to and act to protect it:

"The future belongs to those who continue daringly, consistently, to fight power and governmental authority. The future belongs to us and to our social philosophy. For it is the only social ideal that teaches independent thinking and direct participation of the workers in their economic struggle. For it is only through the organised economic strength of the masses that they can and will do away with the capitalist system and all the wrongs and injustices it contains. Any diversion from this stand will only retard our movement and make it a stepping stone for political climbers." [Emma Goldman, **Vision on Fire**, p. 92]

In short, what happens in our communities, workplaces and environment is too important to be left to politicians — or the ruling elite who control governments. Anarchists need to persuade *"as many people as possible that their freedom ... depends not on the right to vote or securing a majority of votes ... but on evolving new forms of political and social organisation which aim at the direct participation of the people, with the consequent weakening of the power, as well as of the social role, of government in the life of the community."* [*"Anarchists and Voting"*, pp. 176-87, **The Raven**, No. 14, pp. 177-8] We discuss what new forms of economic and social organisations that this could involve in section J.5.

J.2.10 Does rejecting electioneering mean that anarchists are apolitical?

No. Far from it. The "apolitical" nature of anarchism is Marxist nonsense. As it desires to fundamentally change society, anarchism can be nothing but political. However, anarchism does reject (as we have seen) "normal" political activity as ineffectual and corrupting. However, many (particularly Marxists) imply this rejection of the con of capitalist politics means that anarchists concentrate on purely "economic" issues like wages, working conditions and so forth. By so doing, Marxists claim that anarchists leave the political agenda to be dominated by capitalist ideology, with disastrous results for the working class.

This view, however, is **utterly** wrong. Indeed, Bakunin explicitly rejected the idea that working people could ignore politics and actually agreed with the Marxists that political indifference only led to capitalist control of the labour movement:

> "[some of] the workers in Germany … [were organised in] a kind of federation of small associations … 'Self-help' … was its slogan, in the sense that labouring people were persistently advised not to anticipate either deliverance or help from the state and the government, but only from their own efforts. This advice would have been excellent had it not been accompanied by the false assurance that liberation for the labouring people is possible under **current conditions of social organisation** … Under this delusion … the workers subject to [this] influence were supposed to disengage themselves systematically from all political and social concerns and questions about the state, property, and so forth … [This] completely subordinated the proletariat to the bourgeoisie which exploits it and for which it was to remain an obedient and mindless tool." [**Statism and Anarchy**, p. 174]

In addition, Bakunin argued that the labour movement (and so the anarchist movement) would have to take into account political ideas and struggles but to do so in a working class way:

> "The International does not reject politics of a general kind; it will be compelled to intervene in politics so long as it is forced to struggle against the bourgeoisie. It rejects only bourgeois politics." [**The Political Philosophy of Bakunin**, p. 313]

To state the obvious, anarchists only reject working class "*political action*" if you equate (as did the early Marxists) "political action" with electioneering, standing candidates for Parliament, local town councils and so on — what Bakunin termed bourgeois politics. We do not reject "political action" in the sense of direct action to effect political changes and reforms. As two American syndicalists argued, libertarians use "*the term 'political action' … in its ordinary and correct sense. Parliamentary action resulting from the exercise of the franchise is political action. Parliamentary action caused by the influence of direct action tactics … is not political action. It is simply*

a registration of direct action." They also noted that syndicalists "*have proven time and again that they can solve the many so-called political questions by direct action.*" [Earl C. Ford and William Z. Foster, **Syndicalism**, p. 19f and p. 23]

So, anarchists reject capitalist politics (i.e. electioneering), but we do not ignore politics, wider political discussion or political struggles. Anarchists have always recognised the importance of political debate and ideas in social movements. Bakunin asked should a workers organisation "*cease to concern itself with political and philosophical questions? Would [it] … ignore progress in the world of thought as well as the events which accompany or arise from the political struggle in and between states, concerning itself only with the economic problem?*" He rejected such a position: "*We hasten to say that it is absolutely impossible to ignore political and philosophical questions. An exclusive pre-occupation with economic questions would be fatal for the proletariat. Doubtless the defence and organisation of its economic interests … must be the principle task of the proletariat. But is impossible for the workers to stop there without renouncing their humanity and depriving themselves of the intellectual and moral power which is so necessary for the conquest of their economic rights.*" [**Bakunin on Anarchism**, p. 301]

Nor do anarchists ignore elections. As Vernon Richards suggested, anarchists "*cannot be uninterested in … election results, whatever their view about the demerits of the contending Parties. The fact that the anarchist movement has campaigned to persuade people not to use their vote is proof of our commitment and interest. If there is, say, a 60 per cent. poll we will not assume that the 40 per cent. abstentions are anarchists, but we would surely be justified in drawing the conclusion that among the 40 per cent. there are a sizeable minority who have lost faith in political parties and were looking for other instruments, other values.*" [**The Impossibilities of Social Democracy**, p. 141] Nor, needless to say, are anarchists indifferent to struggles for political reforms and the need to stop the state pursuing authoritarian policies, imperialist adventures and such like.

Thus the charge anarchists are apolitical or indifferent to politics (even capitalist politics) is a myth. Rather, "*we are not concerned with choosing between governments but with creating the situation where government can no longer operate, because only then will we organise locally, regionally, nationally and internationally to satisfy real needs and common aspirations.*" For "*so long as we have capitalism and government, the job of anarchists is to fight both, and at the same time encourage people to take what steps they can to run their own lives.*" ["*Anarchists and Voting*", pp. 176-87, **The Raven**, No. 14, p. 179]

Part of this process will be the discussion of political, social and economic issues in whatever self-managed organisations people create in their communities and workplaces (as Bakunin argued) and the use of these organisations to fight for (political, social and economic) improvements and reforms in the here and now using direct action and solidarity. This means, as Rudolf Rocker pointed out, anarchists desire a unification of political and economic struggles as the two are inseparable:

> "*Within the socialist movement itself the Anarchists*

represent the viewpoint that the war against capitalism must be at the same time a war against all institutions of political power, for in history economic exploitation has always gone hand in hand with political and social oppression. The exploitation of man by man and the domination of man over man are inseparable, and each is the condition of the other." [**Anarcho-Syndicalism**, p. 11]

Such a unification must take place on the social and economic field, not the political, as that is where the working class is strongest. So anarchists are well aware of the need to fight for political issues and reforms, and so are "not in any way opposed to the political struggle, but in their opinion this struggle ... must take the form of direct action, in which the instruments of economic [and social] power which the working class has at its command are the most effective. The most trivial wage-fight shows clearly that, whenever the employers find themselves in difficulties, the state steps in with the police, and even in some cases with the militia, to protect the threatened interests of the possessing classes. It would, therefore, be absurd for them to overlook the importance of the political struggle. Every event that affects the life of the community is of a political nature. In this sense every important economic action ... is also a political action and, moreover, one of incomparably greater importance than any parliamentary proceeding." In other words, "just as the worker cannot be indifferent to the economic conditions of his life in existing society, so he cannot remain indifferent to the political structure of his country. Both in the struggle for his daily bread and for every kind of propaganda looking towards his social liberation he needs political rights and liberties, and he must fight for these himself with all his strength whenever the attempt is made to wrest them from him." So the "focal point of the political struggle lies, then, not in the political parties, but in the economic [and social] fighting organisations of the workers." [Rocker, **Op. Cit.**, p. 77, p. 74 and p. 77] Hence the comments in the CNT's newspaper **Solidaridad Obrera**:

"Does anyone not know that we want to participate in public life? Does anyone not know that we have always done so? Yes, we want to participate. With our organisations. With our papers. Without intermediaries, delegates or representatives. No. We will not go to the Town Hall, to the Provincial Capitol, to Parliament." [quoted by Jose Pierats, **Anarchists in the Spanish Revolution**, p. 173]

Indeed, Rudolf Rocker makes the point very clear. "It has often been charged against Anarcho-Syndicalism," he wrote, "that it has no interest in the political structure of the different countries, and consequently no interest in the political struggles of the time, and confines its activities entirely to the fight for purely economic demands. This idea is altogether erroneous and springs either from outright ignorance or wilful distortion of the facts. It is not the political struggle as such which distinguishes the Anarcho-Syndicalist from the modern labour parties, both in principle and tactics, but the form of this struggle and the aims which it has in view ... their efforts are also directed, even today, at restricting the activities of the state ... The attitude of Anarcho-Syndicalism towards the political power of the present-day state is exactly the same as it takes towards the system of capitalist exploitation" and "pursue the same tactics in their fight against ... the state." [**Op. Cit.**, pp. 73-4]

As historian Bob Holton suggests, the notion that syndicalism is apolitical "is certainly a deeply embedded article of faith among those marxists who have taken Lenin's strictures against syndicalism at face value. Yet it bears little relation to the actual nature of revolutionary industrial movements ... Nor did syndicalists neglect politics and the state. Revolutionary industrial movements were on the contrary highly 'political' in that they sought to understand, challenge and destroy the structure of capitalist power in society, They quite clearly perceived the oppressive role of the state whose periodic intervention in industrial unrest could hardly have been missed." For example, the "vigorous campaign against the 'servile state' certainly disproves the notion that syndicalists ignored the role of the state in society. On the contrary, their analysis of bureaucratic state capitalism helped to make considerable inroads into prevailing Labourist and state socialist assumptions that the existing state could be captured by electoral means and used as an agent of through-going social reform." [**British Syndicalism, 1900-1914**, pp. 21-2 and p. 204]

Thus anarchism is not indifferent to or ignores political struggles and issues. Rather, it fights for political change and reforms as it fights for economic ones — by direct action and solidarity. If anarchists "reject any participation in the works of bourgeois parliaments, it is not because they have no sympathy with political struggles in general, but because they are firmly convinced that parliamentary activity is for the workers the very weakest and most hopeless form of the political struggle." [Rocker, **Op. Cit.**, p. 76] Anarchists reject the idea that political and economic struggles can be divided. Such an argument just reproduces the artificially created division of labour between mental and physical activity of capitalism within working class organisations and within anti-capitalist movements. We say that we should not separate out politics into some form of specialised activity that only certain people (i.e. our "representatives") can do. Instead, anarchists argue that political struggles, ideas and debates must be brought into the **social** and **economic** organisations of our class where they must be debated freely by all members as they see fit and that political and economic struggle and change must go hand in hand. Rather than being something other people discuss on behalf of working class people, anarchists, argue that politics must no longer be in the hands of so-called experts (i.e. politicians) but instead lie in the hands of those directly affected by it. Also, in this way the social struggle encourages the political development of its members by the process of participation and self-management.

In other words, political issues must be raised in economic and social organisations and discussed there, where working class people have real power. As Bakunin put it, "the proletariat itself will pose" political and philosophical questions in their own organisations and so the political struggle (in the widest scene) will come from the class struggle, for "[w]ho can entertain any doubt that out of this ever-growing organisation of the militant solidarity of the proletariat against bourgeois exploitation there will issue forth the political struggle of the proletariat against the bourgeoisie?"

Anarchists simply think that the *"policy of the proletariat"* should be *"the destruction of the State"* rather than working within it and we argue for a union of political ideas and social organisation and activity. This is essential for promoting radical politics as it *"digs a chasm between the bourgeoisie and the proletariat and places the proletariat outside the activity and political conniving of all parties within the State … in placing itself outside all bourgeois politics, the proletariat necessarily turns against it."* So, by *"placing the proletariat outside the politics in the State and of the bourgeois world, [the working class movement] thereby constructed a new world, the world of the united proletarians of all lands."* [**Op. Cit.**, p. 302 p. 276, p. 303 and p. 305]

History supports Bakunin's arguments, as it indicates that any attempt at taking social and economic issues into political parties has resulting in wasted energy and their watering down into, at best, reformism and, at worse, the simple ignoring of them by politicians once in office (see section J.2.6). Only by rejecting the artificial divisions of capitalist society can we remain true to our ideals of liberty, equality and solidarity. Every example of radicals using electioneering has resulted in them being changed by the system instead of them changing it. They have become dominated by capitalist ideas and activity (what is usually termed "realistic" and "practical") and by working within capitalist institutions they have, to use Bakunin's words, *"filled in at a single stroke the abyss … between the proletariat and the bourgeoisie"* that economic and social struggle creates and, worse, *"have tied the proletariat to the bourgeois towline."* [**Op. Cit.**, p. 290]

In addition, so-called "economic" struggles do not occur in a vacuum. They take place in a social and political context and so, necessarily, there can exist a separation of political and economic struggles only in the mind. Strikers or eco-warriors, for example, face the power of the state enforcing laws which protect the power of employers and polluters. This necessarily has a "political" impact on those involved in struggle. By channelling any "political" conclusions drawn by those involved in struggle into electoral politics, this development of political ideas and discussion will be distorted into discussions of what is possible in the current system, and so the radical impact of direct action and social struggle is weakened. Given this, is it surprising that anarchists argue that the people *"must organise their powers apart from and against the State."* [Bakunin, **The Political Philosophy of Bakunin**, p. 376]

To conclude, anarchists are only "apolitical" about bourgeois elections and the dubious liberty and benefits associated with picking who will rule us and maintain capitalism for the next four or five years as well as the usefulness of socialists participating in them. We feel that our predictions have been confirmed time and time again. Anarchists reject electioneering not because they are "apolitical" but because they do not desire to see politics remain a thing purely for politicians and bureaucrats. Political issues are far too important to leave to such people. Anarchists desire to see political discussion and change develop from the bottom up, this is hardly "apolitical" — in fact with our desire to see ordinary people directly discuss the issues that affect them, act to change things by their own action and draw their own conclusions from their own activity anarchists are very "political." The process of individual and social liberation is the most political activity we can think of!

J.3

What kinds of organisation do anarchists build?

Anarchists are well aware of the importance of building organisations. Organisations allow those within them to multiply their strength and activity, becoming the means by which an individual can see their ideas, hopes and dreams realised. This is as true for getting the anarchist message across as for building a home, running a hospital or creating some useful product. Anarchists support two types of organisation — organisations of anarchists and popular organisations which are not made up exclusively of anarchists such as industrial unions, co-operatives and community assemblies.

Here we will discuss the kinds, nature and role of the first type of organisation, namely explicitly anarchist organisations. In addition, we discuss anarcho-syndicalism, a revolutionary unionism which aims to create an anarchist society by anarchist tactics, as well as why many anarchists are not anarcho-syndicalists. The second type of organisations, popular ones, are discussed in section J.5. Both forms of organisation, however, share the anarchist commitment to confederalism, decentralisation, self-management and decision making from the bottom up. In such organisations the membership plays the decisive role in running them and ensuring that power remains in their hands. They express the anarchist vision of the power and creative efficacy people have when they are self-reliant, when they act for themselves and manage their own lives directly. Only by organising in this way can we create a new world, a world worthy of human beings and unique individuals.

Anarchist organisation in all its forms reflects our desire to *"build the new world in the shell of the old"* and to empower the individual. We reject the notion that it does not really matter how we organise to change society. Indeed, nothing could be further from the truth. We are all the products of the influences and social relationships in our lives, this is a basic idea of (philosophical) materialism. Thus the way our organisations are structured has an impact on us. If the organisation is centralised and hierarchical (no matter how "democratically" controlled officials or leaders are) then those subject to it will, as in any hierarchical organisation, see their abilities to manage their own lives, their creative thought and imagination eroded under the constant stream of orders from above. This in turn justifies the pretensions to power of those at the top, as the capacity of self-management of the rank and file is weakened by authoritarian social relationships. This means anarchist organisations are structured so that they allow everyone the maximum potential to participate. Such participation is the key for a free organisation. As Malatesta argued:

> *"The real being is man, the individual. Society or the collectivity … if it is not a hollow abstraction, must be made up of individuals. And it is in the organism of every individual that all thoughts and human actions inevitably have their origin, and from being individual they become collective thoughts and acts when they are or become accepted by many individuals. Social action, therefore,*

is neither the negation nor the complement of individual initiative, but is the resultant of initiatives, thoughts and actions of all individuals who make up society." [**Anarchy**, p. 36]

Anarchist organisations exist to allow this development and expression of individual initiatives. This empowering of the individual is an important aspect of creating viable solidarity for sheep cannot express solidarity, they only follow the shepherd. Therefore, *"to achieve their ends, anarchist organisations must, in their constitution and operation, remain in harmony with the principles of anarchism; that is, they must know how to blend the free action of individuals with the necessity and the joy of co-operation which serve to develop the awareness and initiative of their members and a means of education for the environment in which they operate and of a moral and material preparation for the future we desire."* [Malatesta, **The Anarchist Revolution**, p. 95]

As such, anarchist organisations reflect the sort of society anarchists desire. We reject as ridiculous the claim of Leninists that the form of organisation we build is irrelevant and therefore we must create highly centralised parties which aim to become the leadership of the working class. No matter how "democratic" such organisations are, they just reflect the capitalist division of labour between brain and manual work and the Liberal ideology of surrendering our ability to govern ourselves to an elected elite. In other words, they just mirror the very society we are opposed to and so will soon produce the very problems **within** so-called anti-capitalist organisations which originally motivated us to oppose capitalism in the first place (see section H.5). Given this, anarchists regard *"the Marxist party as another statist form that, if it succeeded in 'seizing power,' would preserve the power of one human being over another, the authority of the leader over the led. The Marxist party ... was a mirror image of the very society it professed to oppose, an invasion of the camp of revolutionaries by bourgeois values, methods, and structures."* [**The Spanish Anarchists**, pp. 179-80] As can be seen from the history of the Russian Revolution, this was the case with the Bolsheviks soon taking the lead in undermining workers' self-management, soviet democracy and, finally, democracy within the ruling party itself (see section H.6).

From an anarchist (i.e. materialist) point of view, this was highly predictable — after all, *"facts are before ideas; yes, the ideal, as Proudhon said, is but a flower whose root lies in the material conditions of existence."* [Bakunin, **God and the State**, p. 9] So it is unsurprising that hierarchical parties helped to maintain a hierarchical society. In the words of the famous Sonvillier Circular: *"How could one want an egalitarian and free society to issue from an authoritarian organisation? It is impossible."* [quoted in **Bakunin on Anarchism**, p. 45]

We must stress here that anarchists are **not** opposed to organisation and are **not** opposed to organisations of anarchists (i.e. **political** organisations, although anarchists generally reject the term "party" due to its statist and hierarchical associations). Murray Bookchin made it clear when he wrote that the *"real question at issue here is not organisation versus non-organisation, but rather what **kind** of organisation"* Anarchist organisations are *"organic developments from below ... They are social movements, combing a creative*

revolutionary lifestyle with a creative revolutionary theory ... As much as is humanly possibly, they try to reflect the liberated society they seek to achieve" and *"co-ordination between groups ... discipline, planning, and unity in action ... achieved **voluntarily**, by means of a self-discipline nourished by conviction and understanding."* [**Post-Scarcity Anarchism**, pp. 138-9]

Ultimately, centralised organisations are undemocratic and, equally as important, **ineffective.** Hierarchical organisations kill people's enthusiasm and creativity, where plans and ideas are not adopted because they are the best but simply because they are what a handful of leaders **think** are best for everyone else. Really effective organisations are those which make decisions based frank and open co-operation and debate, where dissent is **not** stifled and ideas are adopted because of their merit and not imposed from the top-down by a few party leaders. This is why anarchists stress federalist organisation. It ensures that co-ordination flows from below and there is no institutionalised leadership. By organising in a way that reflects the kind of society we want, we train ourselves in the skills and decision making processes required to make a free and classless society work. Means and ends are united and this ensures that the means used will result in the desired ends. Simply put, libertarian means must be used if you want libertarian ends (see section H.1.6 for further discussion).

In the sections that follow, we discuss the nature and role of anarchist organisation. Anarchists would agree with Situationist Guy Debord that a *"revolutionary organisation must always remember that its objective is not getting people to listen to speeches by expert leaders, but getting them to speak for themselves."* We organise our groups accordingly. In section J.3.1 we discuss the basic building block of specifically anarchist organisations, the **"affinity group."** Sections J.3.2, J.3.3, J.3.4 and J.3.5, we discuss the main types of federations of **affinity groups** anarchists create to help spread our message and influence. Then section J.3.6 highlights the role these organisations play in our struggles to create an anarchist society. In section J.3.7, we analyse Bakunin's unfortunate expression *"Invisible Dictatorship"* in order to show how many Marxists distort Bakunin's ideas on this matter. Finally, in sections J.3.8 and J.3.9 we discuss anarcho-syndicalism and other anarchists attitudes to it.

Anarchist organisations, therefore, aim to enrich social struggle by their ideas and suggestions but also, far more importantly, enrich the libertarian idea by practical experience and activity. In other words, a two way process by which life informs theory and theory aids life. The means by which this social dynamic is created and developed is the underlying aim of anarchist organisation and is reflected in its theoretical role. The power of ideas cannot be under estimated, for *"if you have an idea you can communicate it to a million people and lose nothing in the process, and the more the idea is propagated the more it acquires in power and effectiveness."* [Malatesta, **Op. Cit.**, p. 46] The right idea at the right time, one that reflects the needs of individuals and of required social change, can have a transforming effect on society. That is why organisations that anarchists create to spread their message are so important and why we devote a whole section to them.

J.3.1
What are affinity groups?

Affinity groups are the basic organisation which anarchists create to spread the anarchist idea. The term *"affinity group"* comes from the Spanish F.A.I. (**Iberian Anarchist Federation**) and refers to the organisational form devised in their struggles for freedom (from *"grupo de afinidad"*). At its most basic, it is a (usually small) group of anarchists who work together to spread their ideas to the wider public, using propaganda, initiating or working with campaigns and spreading their ideas **within** popular organisations (such as unions) and communities. It aims not to be a "leadership" but to give a lead, to act as a catalyst within popular movements. Unsurprisingly it reflects basic anarchist ideas:

> *"Autonomous, communal and directly democratic, the group combines revolutionary theory with revolutionary lifestyle in its everyday behaviour. It creates a free space in which revolutionaries can remake themselves individually, and also as social beings."* [Murray Bookchin, **Post-Scarcity Anarchism**, p. 144]

The reason for this is simple, for a *"movement that sought to promote a liberatory revolution had to develop liberatory and revolutionary forms. This meant ... that it had to mirror the free society it was trying to achieve, not the repressive one it was trying to overthrow. If a movement sought to achieve a world united by solidarity and mutual aid, it had to be guided by these precepts; if it sought to achieve a decentralised, stateless, non-authoritarian society, it had to be structured in accordance with these goals."* [Bookchin, **The Spanish Anarchists**, p. 180]

The aim of an anarchist organisation is to promote a sense of community, of confidence in one's own abilities, to enable all to be involved in the identification, initiation and management of group needs, decisions and activities. They must ensure that individuals are in a position (both physically, as part of a group, and mentally, as an individual) to manage their own lives and take direct action in the pursuit of individual and communal needs and desires. Anarchist organisation is about empowering all, to develop "integral" or whole individuals and a community that encourages individuality (not abstract "individualism") and solidarity. It is about collective decision making from the bottom up, that empowers those at the "base" of the structure and only delegates the work of co-ordinating and implementing the members decisions (and not the power of making decisions for people). In this way the initiative and power of the few (government) is replaced by the initiative and empowerment of all (anarchy). Affinity groups exist to achieve these aims and are structured to encourage them.

The local affinity group is the means by which anarchists co-ordinate their activities in a community, workplace, social movement and so on. Within these groups, anarchists discuss their ideas, politics and hopes, what they plan to do, organise propaganda work, discuss how they are going to work within wider organisations like unions, how their strategies fit into their long term plans and goals and so on. It is the basic way that anarchists work out their ideas, pool their resources and get their message across to others. There can be affinity groups for different interests and activities (for example a workplace affinity group, a community affinity group, an anarcha-feminist affinity group, etc., could all exist within the same area, with overlapping members). Moreover, as well as these more "political" activities, the "affinity group" also stresses the *"importance of education and the need to live by Anarchist precepts — the need ... to create a counter-society that could provide the space for people to begin to remake themselves."* [Bookchin, **Op. Cit.**, p. 180] In other words, "affinity groups" aim to be the *"living germs"* of the new society in **all** aspects, not purely in a structurally way.

So affinity groups are self-managed, autonomous groupings of anarchists who unite and work on specific activities and interests. This means that *"[i]n an anarchist organisation the individual members can express any opinion and use any tactic which is not in contradiction with accepted principles and which does not harm the activities of others."* [Errico Malatesta, **The Anarchist Revolution**, p. 102] Such groups are a key way for anarchists to co-ordinate their activity and spread their message of individual freedom and voluntary co-operation. However, the description of what an "affinity group" is does not explain **why** anarchists organise in that way. Essentially, these affinity groups are the means by which anarchists actually intervene in social movements and struggles in order to win people to the anarchist idea and so help transform them from struggles **against** injustice into struggles **for** a free society. We will discuss the role these groups play in anarchist theory in section J.3.6.

These basic affinity groups are not seen as being enough in themselves. Most anarchists see the need for local groups to work together with others in a confederation. Such co-operation aims to pull resources and expand the options for the individuals and groups who are part of the federation. As with the basic affinity group, the anarchist federation is a self-managed organisation:

> *"Full autonomy, full independence and therefore full responsibility of individuals and groups; free accord between those who believe it is useful to unite in co-operating for a common aim; moral duty to see through commitments undertaken and to do nothing that would contradict the accepted programme. It is on these bases that the practical structures, and the right tools to give life to the organisation should be built and designed. Then the groups, the federations of groups, the federations of federations, the meetings, the congresses, the correspondence committees and so forth. But all this must be done freely, in such a way that the thought and initiative of individuals is not obstructed, and with the sole view of giving greater effect to efforts which, in isolation, would be either impossible or ineffective."* [Malatesta, **Op. Cit.**, p. 101]

To aid in this process of propaganda, agitation, political discussion and development, anarchists organise federations of affinity groups. These take three main forms, **"synthesis"** federations (see section J.3.2), **"Platformist"** federations (see section J.3.3 while section J.3.4 has criticism of this tendency) and **"class struggle"** groups (see section J.3.5). All the various types of federation are based on groups of anarchists organising themselves in a libertarian fashion. This is because anarchists try to live by the values of the future to the extent that this is possible under capitalism and try to develop organisations based upon mutual aid, in which control would be exercised from below upward, not downward from above. We must also note here that these types of federation are not mutually exclusive. Synthesis type federations often have "class struggle" and "Platformist" groups within them (although, as will become clear, Platformist federations do not have synthesis groups within them) and most countries have different federations representing the different perspectives within the movement. Moreover, it should also be noted that no federation will be a totally "pure" expression of each tendency. "Synthesis" groups merge into "class struggle" ones, Platformist groups do not subscribe totally to the Platform and so on. We isolate each tendency to show its essential features. In real life few, if any, federations will exactly fit the types we highlight. It would be more precise to speak of organisations which are descended from a given tendency, for example the French **Anarchist Federation** is mostly influenced by the synthesis tradition but it is not, strictly speaking, 100% synthesis. Lastly, we must also note that the term "class struggle" anarchist group in no way implies that "synthesis" and "Platformist" groups do not support the class struggle or take part in it, they most definitely do — it is simply a technical term to differentiate between types of organisation!

It must be stressed anarchists do not reduce the complex issue of political organisation and ideas into **one** organisation but instead recognise that different threads within anarchism will express themselves in different political organisations (and even within the same organisation). A diversity of anarchist groups and federations is a good sign and expresses the diversity of political and individual thought to be expected in a movement aiming for a society based upon freedom. All we aim to do is to paint a broad picture of the similarities and differences between the various perspectives on organising in the movement and indicate the role these federations play in libertarian theory, namely of an aid in the struggle, not a new leadership seeking power.

J.3.2 What are "synthesis" federations?

The "synthesis" federation acquired its name from the work of Voline (a Russian exile) and leading French anarchist Sebastien Faure in the 1920s. Voline published in 1924 a paper calling for *"the anarchist synthesis"* and was also the author of the article in Faure's **Encyclopedie Anarchiste** on the very same topic. Its roots lie in the Russian revolution and the **Nabat** federation created in the Ukraine during 1918 whose aim was *"organising all of the life forces of anarchism; bringing together through a common endeavour all anarchists seriously desiring of playing an active part in the social revolution which is defined as a process (of greater or lesser duration) giving rise to a new form of social existence for the organised masses."* [**No Gods, No Masters**, vol. 2, p. 117]

The "synthesis" organisation is based on uniting all kinds of anarchists in one federation as there is, to use the words of the **Nabat**, *"validity in all anarchist schools of thought. We must consider all diverse tendencies and accept them."* The synthesis organisation attempts to get different kinds of anarchists *"joined together on a number of basic positions and with the awareness of the need for planned, organised collective effort on the basis of federation."* [quoted in *"The Reply by Several Russian Anarchists"*, pp. 32-6, **Constructive Anarchism**, G. P. Maximoff (ed.), p. 32] These basic positions would be based on a synthesis of the viewpoints of the members of the organisation, but each tendency would be free to agree their own ideas due to the federal nature of the organisation.

An example of this synthesis approach is provided by the differing assertions that anarchism is a theory of classes (as stated by the Platform, among others), that anarchism is a humanitarian ideal for all people and that anarchism is purely about individuals (and so essentially individualist and having nothing to do with humanity or with a class). The synthesis of these positions would be to *"state that anarchism contains class elements as well as humanism and individualist principles ... Its class element is above all its means of fighting for liberation; its humanitarian character is its ethical aspect, the foundation of society; its individualism is the goal of humanity."* [**Op. Cit.**, p. 32]

So, as can be seen, the "synthesis" tendency aims to unite all anarchists (be they individualist, mutualist, syndicalist or communist) into one common federation. Thus the "synthesis" viewpoint is "inclusive" and obviously has affinities with the *"anarchism without adjectives"* approach favoured by many anarchists (see section A.3.8). However, in practice many "synthesis" organisations are more restrictive (for example, they could aim to unite all **social** anarchists) and so there can be a difference between the general idea of the synthesis and how it is concretely applied.

The basic idea behind the synthesis is that the anarchist movement (in most countries, at most times) is divided into three main tendencies: communist anarchism, anarcho-syndicalism, and individualist anarchism. This division can cause severe damage to the movement simply because of the many (and often redundant) arguments and diatribes on why "my anarchism is best" can get in the way of working in common in order to fight our common enemies (state, capitalism and authority). The "synthesis" federations are defined by agreeing what is the common denominator of the various tendencies within anarchism and agreeing a minimum programme based on this for the federation. This would allow a *"certain ideological and tactical unity among organisations"* within the "synthesis" federation. [**Op. Cit.**, p. 35] Moreover, as well as saving time and energy for more important tasks, there are technical and efficiency reasons for unifying into one organisation, namely allowing the movement to have access to more resources and being able to co-ordinate them so as to maximise their use and impact.

The "synthesis" federation, like all anarchist groups, aims to spread anarchist ideas within society as a whole. They believe that their role is to *"assist the masses only when they need such assistance ... the anarchists are part of the membership in the economic and social mass organisations [such as trade unions]. They act and build as part of the whole. An immense field of action is opened to* them for ideological, social and creative activity without assuming a position of superiority over the masses. Above all they must fulfil their ideological and ethical influence in a free and natural manner ... [they] offer ideological assistance, but not in the role of leaders." [**Op. Cit.**, p. 33] This, as we shall see in section J.3.6, is the common anarchist position as regards the role of an anarchist group.

The great strength of "synthesis" federations, obviously, is that they allow a wide and diverse range of viewpoints to be expressed within the organisation which can allow the development of political ideas and theories by constant discussion and debate. They allow the maximum amount of resources to be made available to individuals and groups within the organisation by increasing the number of members. This is why we find the original promoters of the "synthesis" arguing that *that first step toward achieving unity in the anarchist movement which can lead to serious organisation is collective ideological work on a series of important problems that seek the clearest possible collective solution,"* discussing *"concrete questions"* rather than *"philosophical problems and abstract dissertations"* and *"suggest that there be a publication for discussion in every country where the problems in our ideology and tactics can be fully discussed, regardless of how 'acute' or even 'taboo' it may be. The need for such a printed organ, as well as oral discussion, seems to us to be a 'must' because it is the practical way to try to achieve 'ideological unity', 'tactical unity', and possibly organisation ... A full and tolerant discussion of our problems ... will create a basis for understanding, not only among anarchists, but among different conceptions of anarchism."* [**Op. Cit.**, p. 35]

The "synthesis" idea for anarchist organisation was taken up by those who opposed the Platform (see next section). For both Faure and Voline, the basic idea was the same, namely that the various tendencies in anarchism must co-operate and work in the same organisation. However, there are differences between Voline's and Faure's points of view. The latter saw these various tendencies as a wealth in themselves and advocated that each tendency would gain from working together in a common organisation. From Voline's point of view, the emergence of these various tendencies was historically needed to discover the in-depth implications of anarchism in various settings (such as the economical, the social and individual life). However, it was the time to go back to anarchism as a whole, an anarchism considerably empowered by what each tendency could give it, and in which tendencies as such should dissolve. Moreover, these tendencies co-existed in every anarchist at various levels, so all anarchists should aggregate in an organisation where these tendencies would disappear (both individually and organisationally, i.e. there would not be an "anarcho-syndicalist" specific tendency inside the organisation, and so forth).

The "synthesis" federation would be based on complete autonomy (within the basic principles of the Federation and Congress decisions, of course) for groups and individuals, so allowing all the different trends to work together and express their differences in a common front. The various groups would be organised in a federal structure, combining to share resources in the struggle against state, capitalism and other forms of oppression. This federal structure is organised at the local level through a "local union" (i.e. the groups in a town or city), at the regional level (i.e. all groups in, say, Strathclyde are members of the same regional union) up to the "national" level (i.e.

all groups in Scotland, say) and beyond.

As every group in the federation is autonomous, it can discuss, plan and initiate an action (such as campaign for a reform, against a social evil, and so on) without having to wait for others in the federation (or have to wait for instructions). This means that the local groups can respond quickly to issues and developments. This does not mean that each group works in isolation. These initiatives may gain federal support if local groups see the need. The federation can adopt an issue if it is raised at a federal conference and other groups agree to co-operate on that issue. Moreover, each group has the freedom **not** to participate on a specific issue while leaving others to do so. Thus groups can concentrate on what they are interested in most.

The programme and policies of the federation would be agreed at regular delegate meetings and congresses. The "synthesis" federation is managed at the federal level by "relations committees" made up of people elected and mandated at the federation congresses. These committees would have a purely administrative role, spreading information, suggestions and proposals coming from groups and individuals within the organisation, looking after the finances of the federation and so on. They do not have any more rights than any other member of the federation (i.e. they could not make a proposal as a committee, just as members of their local group or as individuals). These administrative committees are accountable to the federation and subject to both mandates and recall.

Most national sections of the **International of Anarchist Federations** (IFA) are good examples of successful federations which are heavily influenced by "synthesis" ideas (such as the French and Italian federations). Obviously, though, how effective a "synthesis" federation is depends upon how tolerant members are of each other and how seriously they take their responsibilities towards their federations and the agreements they make.

Of course, there are problems with most forms of organisation, and the "synthesis" federation is no exception. While diversity can strengthen an organisation by provoking debate, a too diverse grouping can often make it difficult to get things done. Platformist and other critics of the "synthesis" federation argue that it can be turned into a talking shop and any common programme difficult to agree, never mind apply. For example, how can mutualists and communists agree on the ends, never mind the means, their organisation supports? One believes in co-operation within a (modified) market system and reforming capitalism away, while the other believes in the abolition of commodity production and money, seeing revolution as the means of so doing. Ultimately, all they could do would be to agree to disagree and thus any joint programmes and activity would be somewhat limited. It could, indeed, be argued that both Voline and Faure forgot essential points, namely what is this common denominator between the different kinds of anarchism, how do we achieve it and what is in it? For without this agreed common position, many synthesist organisations do end up becoming little more than talking shops, escaping from any social or organisational perspective. This seems to have been the fate of many groups in Britain and America during the 1960s and 1970s, for example.

It is this (potential) disunity that lead the authors of the Platform to argue that *"[s]uch an organisation having incorporated heterogeneous theoretical and practical elements, would only be a mechanical assembly of individuals each having a different conception of all the questions of the anarchist movement, an assembly which would inevitably disintegrate on encountering reality."* [**The Organisational Platform of the Libertarian Communists**, p. 12] The Platform suggested *"Theoretical and Tactical Unity"* as a means of overcoming this problem, but that term provoked massive disagreement in anarchist circles (see section J.3.4). In reply to the Platform, supporters of the "synthesis" counter by pointing to the fact that "Platformist" groups are usually very small, far smaller that "synthesis" federations (for example, compare the size of the **French Anarchist Federation** with, say, the Irish **Workers Solidarity Movement** or the French-language **Alternative Libertaire**). This means, they argue, that the Platform does not, in fact, lead to a more effective organisation, regardless of the claims of its supporters. Moreover, they argue that the requirements for *"Theoretical and Tactical Unity"* help ensure a small organisation as differences would express themselves in splits rather than constructive activity. Needless to say, the discussion continues within the movement on this issue!

What can be said is that this potential problem within "synthesisism" has been the cause of some organisations failing or becoming little more than talking shops, with each group doing its own thing and so making co-ordination pointless as any agreements made would be ignored. Most supporters of the synthesis would argue that this is not what the theory aims for and that the problem lies in misunderstanding it rather than in the theory itself (as can be seen from mainland Europe, "synthesis" inspired federations can be **very** successful). Non-supporters are more critical, with some supporting the "Platform" as a more effective means of organising to spread anarchist ideas and influence (see the next section). Other social anarchists create the "class struggle" type of federation (this is a common organisational form in Britain, for example) as discussed in section J.3.5.

J.3.3
What is the "Platform"?

The Platform is a current within anarcho-communism which has specific suggestions on the nature and form which an anarchist federation should take. Its roots lie in the Russian anarchist movement, a section of which, in 1926, published *"The Organisational Platform of the Libertarian Communists"* when in exile from the Bolshevik dictatorship. The authors of the work included Nestor Makhno, Peter Arshinov and Ida Mett. At the time it provoked intense debate (and still does in many anarchist circles) between supporters of the Platform (usually called "Platformists") and those who oppose it (which includes other communist-anarchists, anarcho-syndicalists and supporters of the "synthesis"). We will discuss why many anarchists oppose the Platform in the next section. Here we discuss what the Platform argued for.

Like the "synthesis" federation (see last section), the Platform was created in response to the experiences of the Russian Revolution.

The authors of the Platform (like Voline and other supporters of the "synthesis") had participated in that Revolution and saw all their work, hopes and dreams fail as the Bolshevik state triumphed and destroyed any chances of socialism by undermining soviet democracy, workers' self-management of production, trade union democracy as well as fundamental individual freedoms and rights (see the section H.6 for details). Moreover, the authors of the Platform had been leading activists in the Makhnovist movement in the Ukraine which had successfully resisted both White and Red armies in the name of working class self-determination and anarchism. Facing the same problems as the Bolshevik government, the Makhnovists had actively encouraged popular self-management and organisation, freedom of speech and of association, and so on, whereas the Bolsheviks had not. Thus they were aware that anarchist ideas not only worked in practice, but that the claims of Leninists who maintained that Bolshevism (and the policies it introduced at the time) was the only "practical" response to the problems facing a revolution were false.

They wrote the pamphlet in order to examine why the anarchist movement had failed to build on its successes in gaining influence within the working class. As can be seen from libertarian participation in the factory committee movement, where workers organised self-management in their workplaces and anarchist ideas had proven to be both popular and practical. While repression by the Bolsheviks did play a part in this failure, it did not explain everything. Also important, in the eyes of the Platform authors, was the lack of anarchist organisation **before** the revolution:

> *"It is very significant that, in spite of the strength and incontestably positive character of libertarian ideas, and in spite of the facing up to the social revolution, and finally the heroism and innumerable sacrifices borne by the anarchists in the struggle for anarchist communism, the anarchist movement remains weak despite everything, and has appeared, very often, in the history of working class struggles as a small event, an episode, and not an important factor."* [**Organisational Platform of the Libertarian Communists**, p. 11]

This weakness in the movement derived, they argued, from a number of causes, the main one being *"the absence of organisational principles and practices"* within the anarchist movement. This resulted in an anarchist movement *"represented by several local organisations advocating contradictory theories and practices, having no perspectives for the future, nor of a continuity in militant work, and habitually disappearing, hardly leaving the slightest trace behind them."* This explained the *"contradiction between the positive and incontestable substance of libertarian ideas, and the miserable state in which the anarchist movement vegetates."* [**Op. Cit.**, p. 11] For anyone familiar with the anarchist movement in many countries, these words will still strike home. Thus the Platform still appears to many anarchists a relevant and important document, even if they are not Platformists.

The author's of the Platform proposed a solution to this problem, namely the creation of a new type of anarchist organisation. This organisation would be based upon communist-anarchist ideas exclusively, while recognising syndicalism as a principal method of struggle. Like most anarchists, the Platform placed class and class struggle at the centre of their analysis, recognising that the *"social and political regime of all states is above all the product of class struggle ... The slightest change in the course of the battle of classes, in the relative locations of the forces of the class struggle, produces continuous modifications in the fabric and structure of society."* Again, like most anarchists, the Platform aimed to *"transform the present bourgeois capitalist society into a society which assures the workers the products of the labours, their liberty, independence, and social and political equality"*, one based on a *"workers organisations of production and consumption, united federatively and self-administering."* The *"birth, the blossoming, and the realisation of anarchist ideas have their roots in the life and the struggle of the working masses and are inseparable bound to their fate."* [**Op. Cit.**, p. 14, p. 15, p. 19 and p. 15] Again, most anarchists (particularly social anarchists) would agree — anarchist ideas will wither when isolated from working class life since only working class people, the vast majority, can create a free society and anarchist ideas are expressions of working class experience (remove the experience and the ideas do not develop as they should).

In order to create such a free society it is necessary, argue the Platformists, *"to work in two directions: on the one hand towards the selection and grouping of revolutionary worker and peasant forces on a libertarian communist theoretical basis (a specifically libertarian communist organisation); on the other hand, towards regrouping revolutionary workers and peasants on an economic base of production and consumption (revolutionary workers and peasants organised around production [i.e. syndicalism]; workers and free peasants co-operatives)."* Again, most anarchists would agree with this along with the argument that *"anarchism should become the leading concept of revolution ... The leading position of anarchist ideas in the revolution suggests an orientation of events after anarchist theory. However, this theoretical driving force should not be confused with the political leadership of the statist parties which leads finally to State Power."* [**Op. Cit.**, p. 20 and p. 21]

This *"leadership of ideas"* (as it has come to be known) would aim at developing and co-ordinating libertarian feelings already existing within social struggle. *"Although the masses,"* explained the Platform, *"express themselves profoundly in social movements in terms of anarchist tendencies and tenets, these ... do however remain dispersed, being uncoordinated, and consequently do not lead to the ... preserving [of] the anarchist orientation of the social revolution."* [**Op. Cit.**, p. 21] The Platform argued that a specific anarchist organisation was required to ensure that the libertarian tendencies initially expressed in any social revolution or movement (for example, free federation, self-management in mass assemblies, mandating of delegates, decentralisation, etc.) do not get undermined by statists and authoritarians who have their own agendas. This would be done by actively working in mass organisation and winning people to libertarian ideas and practices by argument (see section J.3.6).

However, these principles do not, in themselves, determine a Platformist organisation. After all, most anarcho-syndicalists and non-Platformist communist-anarchists would agree with these positions. The main point which distinguishes the Platform is its position on how an anarchist organisation should be structured and work. This is sketched in the *"Organisational Section,"* the shortest

and most contentious part of the whole work. They called this the **General Union of Anarchists** and where they introduced the concepts of ***"Theoretical and Tactical Unity"*** and ***"Collective Responsibility,"*** concepts which are unique to the Platform. Even today within the anarchist movement these are contentious ideas so it is worth exploring them in a little more detail.

By *"Theoretical Unity"* the Platform meant any anarchist organisation must come to an agreement on the theory upon which it is based. In other words, that members of the organisation must agree on a certain number of basic points, such as class struggle, social revolution and libertarian communism, and so on. An organisation in which half the members thought that union struggles were important and the other half that they were a waste of time would not be effective as the membership would spend all their time arguing with themselves. While most Platformists admit that everyone will not agree on everything, they think it is important to reach as much agreement as possible, and to translate this into action. Once a theoretical position is reached, the members have to argue it in public (even if they initially opposed it within the organisation but they do have the right to get the decision of the organisation changed by internal discussion). Which brings us to *"Tactical Unity"* by which the Platform meant that the members of an organisation should struggle together **as an organised force** rather than as individuals. Once a strategy has been agreed by the Union, all members would work towards ensuring its success (even if they initially opposed it). In this way resources and time are concentrated in a common direction, towards an agreed objective.

Thus *"Theoretical and Tactical Unity"* means an anarchist organisation that agrees specific ideas and the means of applying them. The Platform's basic assumption is that there is a link between coherency and efficiency. By increasing the coherency of the organisation by making collective decisions and applying them, the Platform argues that this will increase the influence of anarchist ideas. Without this, they argue, more organised groups (such as Leninist ones) would be in a better position to have their arguments heard and listened to than anarchists would. Anarchists cannot be complacent, and rely on the hope that the obvious strength and rightness of our ideas will shine through and win the day. As history shows, this rarely happens and when it does, the authoritarians are usually in positions of power to crush the emerging anarchist influence (this was the case in Russia, for example). Platformists argue that the world we live in is the product of struggles between competing ideas of how society should be organised and if the anarchist voice is weak, quiet and disorganised it will not be heard and other arguments, other perspectives, will win the day.

Which brings us to *"Collective Responsibility,"* which the Platform defines as *"the entire Union will be responsible for the political and revolutionary activity of each member; in the same way, each member will be responsible for the political and revolutionary activity of the Union."* In short, that each member should support the decisions made by the organisation and that each member should take part in the process of collective decision making process. Without this, argue Platformists, any decisions made will be paper ones as individuals and groups would ignore the agreements made by the federation (the Platform calls this *"the tactic of irresponsible individualism"*). [**Op. Cit.**, p. 32] With *"Collective Responsibility,"* the strength of all the individuals that make up the group is magnified and collectively applied.

The last principle in the *"Organisational Section"* of the Platform is *"Federalism,"* which it defined as *"the free agreement of individuals and organisations to work collectively towards a common objective"* and which *"reconciles the independence and initiative of individuals and the organisation with service to the common cause."* However, the Platform argued that this principle has been *"deformed"* within the movement to mean the *"right"* to *"manifest one's 'ego,' without obligation to account for duties as regards the organisation"* one is a member of. In order to overcome this problem, they stress that *"the federalist type of anarchist organisation, while recognising each member's rights to independence, free opinion, individual liberty and initiative, requires each member to undertake fixed organisation duties, and demands execution of communal decisions."* [**Op. Cit.**, p. 33 and pp. 33-4]

As part of their solution to the problem of anarchist organisation, the Platform suggested that each group would have *"its secretariat, executing and guiding theoretically the political and technical work of the organisation."* Moreover, the Platform urged the creation of an **"executive committee of the Union"** which would *"be in charge"* of *"the execution of decisions taken by the Union with which it is entrusted; the theoretical and organisational orientation of the activity of isolated organisations consistent with the theoretical positions and the general tactical lines of the Union; the monitoring of the general state of the movement; the maintenance of working and organisational links between all the organisations in the Union; and with other organisation."* The rights, responsibilities and practical tasks of the executive committee are fixed by the congress of the Union. [**Op. Cit.**, p. 34]

This suggestion, unsurprisingly, meet with strong disapproval by most anarchists, as we will see in the next section, who argued that this would turn the anarchist movement into a centralised, hierarchical party similar to the Bolsheviks. Needless to say, supporters of the Platform reject this argument and point out that the Platform itself is not written in stone and needs to be discussed fully and modified as required. In fact, few, if any, Platformist groups, do have this *"secretariat"* structure (it could, in fact, be argued that there are no actual "Platformist" groups, rather groups influenced by the Platform, namely on the issues of *"Theoretical and Tactical Unity"* and *"Collective Responsibility"*).

Similarly, most modern day Platformists reject the idea of gathering all anarchists into one organisation. The original Platform seemed to imply that the **General Union** would be an umbrella organisation, made up of different groups and individuals. Most Platformists would argue that not only will there never be one organisation which encompasses everyone, they do not think it necessary. Instead they envisage the existence of a number of organisations, each internally unified, each co-operating with each other where possible, a much more amorphous and fluid entity than a **General Union of Anarchists**.

Alexandre Skirda's book **Facing the Enemy** contains the key documents on the original Platformists (including the original draft Platform, supplementary documents clarifying issues and polemics against critiques). In the next section we discuss the objections that most anarchists have towards the Platform.

J.3.4 Why do many anarchists oppose the "Platform"?

When the "Platform" was published it provoked a massive amount of debate and comment, the majority of it critical. Most famous anarchists rejected the Platform. Indeed, only Nestor Makhno (who co-authored the work) supported its proposals, with (among others) Alexander Berkman, Emma Goldman, Voline, G.P. Maximoff, Luigi Fabbri, Camilo Berneri and Errico Malatesta rejecting its suggestions on how anarchists should organise. Some argued that the Platform was trying to *"Bolshevise"* anarchism (*""They are only one step away from bolshevism."* [*"The Reply by Several Russian Anarchists"*, pp. 32-6, **Constructive Anarchism**, G.P. Maximoff (ed.), pp. 36]). Others, such as Malatesta, suggested that the authors were too impressed by the apparent "success" of the Bolsheviks in Russia. Since then, it has continued to provoke a lot of debate in anarchist circles. So why do so many anarchists oppose the Platform?

While many of the anti-Platformists made points about most parts of the Platform (both Maximoff and Voline pointed out that while the Platform denied the need of a *"Transitional Period"* in theory, it accepted it in practice, for example) the main bone of contention was found in the *"Organisational Section"* with its call for *"Tactical and Theoretical Unity,"* *"Collective Responsibility"* and group and executive *"secretariats"* guiding the organisation. Here most anarchists found ideas they considered incompatible with libertarian ideas. We will concentrate on this issue as it is usually considered as the most important.

Today, in some quarters of the libertarian movement, the Platformists are often dismissed as "would-be leaders." Yet this was not where Malatesta and other critics of the Platform took issue. Malatesta and Maximoff both argued that, to use Maximoff's words, anarchists should *"go into the masses"* and *" work with them, struggle for their soul, and attempt to win it **ideologically** and give it guidance."* So the question was *"not the rejection of **leadership**, but making certain it is **free** and **natural**."* [**Constructive Anarchism**, p. 19] Moreover, as Maximoff noted, the "synthesis" anarchists came to the same conclusion. Thus all sides of the debate accepted that anarchists should take the lead. The question, as Malatesta and the others saw it, was not whether to lead, but rather **how** you should lead - a fairly important distinction.

Malatesta posed two alternatives, either you *"provide leadership by advice and example leaving people themselves to … adopt our methods and solutions if these are, or seem to be, better than those suggested and carried out by others"* or you can *"direct by taking over command, that is by becoming a government."* He asked the Platformists: *"In which manner do you wish to direct?"* While he thought, from his knowledge of Makhno and his work, that the answer would be the first option, he was *"assailed by doubt that [Makhno] would also like to see, within the general movement, a central body that would, in an authoritarian manner, dictate the theoretical and practical programme for the revolution."* This was because of the *"Executive Committee"* in the Platform which would *"give ideological and organisational direction to the association."* [**The Anarchist Revolution**, p. 108 and p. 110]

Maximoff made the same point, arguing that the Platform implied that anarchists in the unions are responsible to the anarchist federation, **not** to the union assemblies that elected them. As he put it, according to the Platform anarchists *"are to join the Trades Unions with ready-made recipes and are to carry out their plans, if necessary, against the will of the Unions themselves."* This was just one example of a general problem, namely that the Platform *"places its Party on the same height as the Bolsheviks do, i.e., it places the interests of the Party above the interests of the masses since the Party has the monopoly of understanding these interests."* [**Constructive Anarchism**, p. 19 and p. 18] This flowed from the Platform arguing that anarchists must *"enter into revolutionary trade unions as an organised force, responsible to accomplish work in the union before the general anarchist organisation and orientated by the latter."* However, Maximoff's argument may be considered harsh as the Platform also argued that anarchism *"aspires neither to political power nor dictatorship"* and so they would hardly be urging the opposite principles within the trade union movement. [**The Organisational Platform of the Libertarian Communists**, p. 25 and p. 21] If we take the Platform's comments within a context informed by the *"leadership of ideas"* concept (see section J.3.6) then what they meant was simply that the anarchist group would convince the union members of the validity of their ideas by argument which was something Maximoff did not disagree with. In short, the disagreement becomes one of unclear (or bad) use of language by the Platform's authors.

Despite many efforts and many letters on the subject (in particular between Malatesta and Makhno) the question of "leadership" could not be clarified to either side's satisfaction, in part because there was an additional issue in dispute. This was the related issue of organisational principles (which in themselves make up the defining part of the original Platform). Malatesta argued that this did not conform with anarchist methods and principles, and so could not *"help bring about the triumph of anarchism."* [**The Anarchist Revolution**, p. 97] This was because of two main reasons, the first being the issue of the Platform's "secretariats" and "executive committee" and the issue of "Collective Responsibility." We will take each in turn.

With a structure based round "secretariats" and "executive committees" the *"will of the [General] Union [of Anarchists] can only mean the will of the majority, expressed through congresses which nominate and control the **Executive Committee** and decide on all important issues. Naturally, the congresses would consist of representatives elected by the majority of member groups … So, in the best of cases, the decisions would be taken by a majority of a majority, and this could easily, especially when the opposing opinions are more than two, represent only a minority."* This, Malatesta argued, *"comes down to a pure majority system, to pure parliamentarianism"* and so non-anarchist in nature. [**Op. Cit.**, p. 100]

As long as a Platformist federation is based on *"secretariats"* and *"executive committees"* directing the activity and development of the organisation, this critique is valid. In such a system, as these bodies control the organisation and members are expected to follow their decisions (due to *"theoretical and tactical unity"* and *"collective responsibility"*) they are, in effect, the government of the association.

While this government may be elected and accountable, it is still a government simply because these bodies have executive power. As Maximoff argued, individual initiative in the Platform *"has a special character … Each organisation (i.e. association of members with the right to individual initiative) has its secretariat which … **directs** the ideological, political and technical activities of the organisation … In what, then, consists the self-reliant activities of the rank-and-file members? Apparently in one thing: initiative to obey the secretariat and carry out its directives."* [**Op. Cit.**, p. 18] This seems to be the logical conclusion of the structure suggested by the Platform. *"The spirit,"* argued Malatesta, *"the tendency remains authoritarian and the educational effect would remain anti-anarchist."* [**Op. Cit.**, p. 98]

Malatesta, in contrast, argued that an anarchist organisation must be based on the *"[f]ull autonomy, full independence and therefore the full responsibility of individuals and groups"* with all organisational work done *"freely, in such a way that the thought and initiative of individuals is not obstructed."* The individual members of such an organisation *"express any opinion and use any tactic which is not in contradiction with accepted principles and which does not harm the activities of others."* Moreover, the administrative bodies such organisations nominate would *"have no executive powers, have no directive powers"* leaving it up to the groups and their federal meetings to decide their own fates. The congresses of such organisations would be *"free from any kind of authoritarianism, because they do not lay down the law; they do not impose their own resolutions on others … and do not become binding and enforceable except on those who accept them."* [**Op. Cit.**, p. 101, p. 102 and p. 101] Such an organisation does not exclude collective decisions and self-assumed obligations, rather it is based upon them.

Most groups inspired by the Platform, however, seem to reject this aspect of its organisational suggestions. Instead of "secretariats" and "executive committees" they have regular conferences and meetings to reach collective decisions on issues and practice unity that way. Thus the **really** important issue is of *"theoretical and tactical unity"* and *"collective responsibility,"* rather than the structure suggested by the Platform. Indeed, this issue was the main topic in Makhno's letter to Malatesta, for example, and so we would be justified in saying that this is the key issue dividing "Platformists" from other anarchists.

So in what way did Malatesta disagree with this concept? As we mentioned in the last section, the Platform defined the idea of "Collective Responsibility" as *"the entire Union will be responsible for the political and revolutionary activity of each member; in the same way, each member will be responsible for the political and revolutionary activity of the Union."* To which Malatesta replied:

> *"But if the Union is responsible for what each member does, how can it leave to its members and to the various groups the freedom to apply the common programme in the way they think best? How can one be responsible for an action if it does not have the means to prevent it? Therefore, the Union and in its name the Executive Committee, would need to monitor the action of the individual member and order them what to do and what not to do; and since disapproval after the event cannot*

put right a previously accepted responsibility, no-one would be able to do anything at all before having obtained the go-ahead, the permission of the committee. And, on the other hand, can an individual accept responsibility for the actions of a collectivity before knowing what it will do and if he cannot prevent it doing what he disapproves of?" [**Op. Cit.**, p. 99]

In other words, the term *"collective responsibility"* (if taken literally) implies a highly inefficient and somewhat authoritarian mode of organisation. Before any action could be undertaken, the organisation would have to be consulted and this would crush individual, group and local initiative. The organisation would respond slowly to developing situations, if at all, and this response would not be informed by first hand knowledge and experience. Moreover, this form of organisation implies a surrendering of individual judgement, as members would have to *"submit to the decisions of the majority before they have even heard what those might be."* [Malatesta, **Op. Cit.**, 101] In the end, all a member could do would be to leave the organisation if they disagree with a tactic or position and could not bring themselves to further it by their actions.

This structure also suggests that the Platform's commitment to federalism is in words only. As most anarchists critical of the Platform argued, while its authors affirm federalist principles they, in fact, *"outline a perfectly centralised organisation with an Executive Committee that has responsibility to give ideological and organisational direction to the different anarchist organisations, which in turn will direct the professional organisations of the workers."* [*"The Reply by Several Russian Anarchists"*, **Op. Cit.**, pp. 35-6]

Thus it is likely that "Collective Responsibility" taken to its logical conclusion would actually **hinder** anarchist work by being too bureaucratic and slow. However, let us assume that by applying collective responsibility as well as tactical and theoretical unity, anarchist resources and time will be more efficiently utilised. What is the point of being "efficient" if the collective decision reached is wrong or is inapplicable to many areas? Rather than local groups applying their knowledge of local conditions and developing theories and policies that reflect these conditions (and co-operating from the bottom up), they may be forced to apply inappropriate policies due to the "Unity" of the Platformist organisation. It is true that Makhno argued that the *"activities of local organisations can be adapted, as far as possible, to suit local conditions"* but only if they are *"consonant with the pattern of the overall organisational practice of the Union of anarchists covering the whole country."* [**The Struggle Against the State and Other Essays**, p. 62] Which still begs the question on the nature of the Platform's unity (however, it does suggest that the Platform's position may be less extreme than might be implied by the text, as we will discuss). That is why anarchists have traditionally supported federalism and free agreement within their organisations, to take into account the real needs of localities.

If we do not take the Platform's definition of "Collective Responsibility" literally or to its logical extreme (as Makhno's comments suggest) then the differences between Platformists and non-Platformists may not be that far. As Malatesta pointed out in his reply to Makhno's letter:

"I accept and support the view that anyone who associates and co-operates with others for a common purpose must feel the need to co-ordinate his [or her] actions with those of his [or her] fellow members and do nothing that harms the work of others ... and respect the agreements that have been made ... [Moreover] I maintain that those who do not feel and do not practice that duty should be thrown out of the association.

"Perhaps, speaking of collective responsibility, you mean precisely that accord and solidarity that must exist among members of an association. And if that is so, your expression amounts ... to an incorrect use of language, but basically it would only be an unimportant question of wording and agreement would soon be reached." [**Op. Cit.**, pp. 107-8]

This, indeed, seems to be the way that most Platformist organisations do operate. They have agreed broad theoretical and tactical positions on various subjects (such as, for example, the nature of trade unions and how anarchists relate to them) while leaving it to local groups to act within these guidelines. Moreover, the local groups do not have to report to the organisation before embarking on an activity. In other words, most Platformist groups do not take the Platform literally and so many differences are, to a large degree, a question of wording. As two supporters of the Platform note:

"The Platform doesn't go into detail about how collective responsibility works in practice. There are issues it leaves untouched such as the question of people who oppose the majority view. We would argue that obviously people who oppose the view of the majority have a right to express their own views, however in doing so they must make clear that they don't represent the view of the organisation. If a group of people within the organisation oppose the majority decision they have the right to organise and distribute information so that their arguments can be heard within the organisation as a whole. Part of our anarchism is the belief that debate and disagreement, freedom and openness strengthens both the individual and the group to which she or he belongs." [Aileen O'Carroll and Alan MacSimoin, *"The Platform"*, pp. 29-31, **Red and Black Revolution**, no. 4, p. 30]

While many anarchists are critical of Platformist groups for being too centralised for their liking, it is the case that the Platform has influenced many anarchist organisations, even non-Platformist ones (this can be seen in the "class struggle" groups discussed in the next section). This influence has been both ways, with the criticism the original Platform was subjected to having had an effect on how Platformist groups have developed. This, of course, does not imply that there is little or no difference between Platformists and other anarchists. Platformist groups tend to stress "collective responsibility" and "theoretical and tactical unity" more than others, which has caused problems when Platformists have worked within "synthesis" organisations (as was the case in France, for example, which resulted in much bad-feeling between Platformists and others).

Constructive Anarchism by the leading Russian anarcho-syndicalist G.P. Maximoff gathers all the relevant documents in one place. As well as Maximoff's critique of the Platform, it includes the "synthesis" reply, Malatesta's review and subsequent exchange of letters between him and Makhno. **The Anarchist Revolution** also contains Malatesta's article and the exchange of letters between him and Makhno.

J.3.5 Are there other kinds of anarchist federation?

Yes. Another type of anarchist federation is what we term the **"class struggle"** group. Many local anarchist groups in Britain, for example, organise in this fashion. They use the term "class struggle" to indicate that their anarchism is based on collective working class resistance as opposed to reforming capitalism via lifestyle changes and the support of, say, co-operatives (many "class struggle" anarchists do these things, of course, but they are aware that they cannot create an anarchist society by so doing). We follow this use of the term here. And just to stress the point again, our use of "class struggle" to describe this type of anarchist group does not imply that "synthesis" or "Platformist" do not support the class struggle. They do!

This kind of group is half-way between the "synthesis" and the "Platform." The "class struggle" group agrees with the "synthesis" in so far as it is important to have a diverse viewpoints within a federation and that it would be a mistake to try to impose a common-line on different groups in different circumstances as the Platform does. However, like the "Platform," the class struggle group recognises that there is little point in creating a forced union between totally different strands of anarchism. Thus the "class struggle" group rejects the idea that individualist or mutualist anarchists should be part of the same organisation as anarchist communists or syndicalists or that anarcho-pacifists should join forces with non-pacifists. Thus the "class struggle" group acknowledges that an organisation which contains viewpoints which are dramatically opposed can lead to pointless debates and paralysis of action due to the impossibilities of overcoming those differences.

Instead, the "class struggle" group agrees a common set of **"aims and principles"** which are the basic terms of agreement within the federation. If an individual or group does not agree with this statement then they cannot join. If they are members and try to change this statement and cannot get the others to agree its modification, then they are morally bound to leave the organisation. In other words, there is a framework within which individuals and groups apply their own ideas and their interpretation of agreed policies. It means that individuals in a group and the groups within a federation have something to base their local activity on, something which has been agreed collectively. There would be a common thread to activities and a guide to action (particularly in situations were a group or federation meeting cannot be called). In this way individual initiative and co-operation can be reconciled, without hindering either. In addition, the **"aims and principles"** shows potential members where the anarchist group was coming from.

In this way the "class struggle" group solves one of the key problems with the "synthesis" grouping, namely that any such basic statement of political ideas would be hard to agree and be so watered down as to be almost useless (for example, a federation combining individualist and communist anarchists would find it impossible to agree on such things as the necessity for revolution, communal ownership, and so on). By clearly stating its ideas, the "class struggle" group ensures a common basis for activity and discussion.

Such a federation, like all anarchist groups, would be based upon regular assemblies locally and in frequent regional, national, etc., conferences to continually re-evaluate policies, tactics, strategies and goals. In addition, such meetings prevent power from collecting in the higher administration committees created to co-ordinate activity. The regular conferences aim to create federation policies on specific topics and agree common strategies. Such policies, once agreed, are morally binding on the membership, who can review and revise them as required at a later stage but cannot take action which would hinder their application (they do not have to apply them, if they consider them as a big mistake).

For example, minorities in such a federation can pursue their own policies as long as they clearly state that theirs is a minority position and does not contradict the federation's aims and principles. In this way the anarchist federation combines united action and dissent, for no general policy will be applicable in all circumstances and it is better for minorities to ignore policies which they know will make even greater problems in their area. As long as their actions and policies do not contradict the federation's basic political ideas, then diversity is an essential means for ensuring that the best tactic and ideas are be identified.

J.3.6 What role do these groups play in anarchist theory?

The aim of anarchist groups and federations is to spread libertarian ideas within society and within social movements. They aim to convince people of the validity of anarchist ideas and analysis, of the need for a libertarian transformation of society and of themselves by working with others as equals. Such groups are convinced that (to use Murray Bookchin's words) *"anarcho-communism cannot remain a mere mood or tendency, wafting in the air like a cultural ambience. It must be organised — indeed **well-organised** — if it is effectively to articulate and spread this new sensibility; it must have a coherent theory and extensive literature; it must be capable of duelling with the authoritarian movements that try to denature the intuitive libertarian impulses of our time and channel social unrest into hierarchical forms of organisation."* [*"Looking Back at Spain,"* pp. 53-96, Dimitrios I. Roussopoulos (ed.), **The Radical Papers**, p. 90]

These groups and federations play a key role in anarchist theory. This is because anarchists are well aware that there are different levels of knowledge and consciousness in society. While people learn through struggle and their own experiences, different people develop at different speeds, that each individual is unique and is subject to different influences. As one pamphlet by the British **Anarchist Federation** puts it, the "*experiences of working class life constantly lead to the development of ideas and actions which question the established order ... At the same time, different sections of the working class reach different degrees of consciousness.*" [**The Role of the Revolutionary Organisation**, p. 13] This can easily be seen from any group of individuals of the same class or even community. Some are anarchists, others Marxists, some social democrats/labourites, others conservatives, others liberals, most "apolitical," some support trade unions, others are against and so on.

Because we are aware that we are one tendency among many, anarchists organise as anarchists to influence social struggle. Only when anarchists ideas are accepted by the vast majority will an anarchist society be possible. We wish, in other words, to win the most widespread understanding and influence for anarchist ideas and methods in the working class and in society, primarily because we believe that these alone will ensure a successful revolutionary transformation of society. Hence Malatesta:

> "*anarchists, convinced of the validity of our programme, must strive to acquire overwhelming influence in order to draw the movement towards the realisation of our ideals. But such influence must be won by doing more and better than others, and will be useful if won in that way ... we must deepen, develop and propagate our ideas and co-ordinate our forces in a common action. We must act within the labour movement to prevent it being limited to and corrupted by the exclusive pursuit of small improvements compatible with the capitalist system ... We must work with ... [all the] masses to awaken the spirit of revolt and the desire for a free and happy life. We must initiate and support all movements that tend to weaken the forces of the State and of capitalism and to raise the mental level and material conditions of the workers.*" [**The Anarchist Revolution**, p. 109]

Anarchist organisation exists to help the process by which people come to anarchist conclusions. It aims to make explicit the feelings and thoughts that people have (such as, wage slavery is hell, that the state exists to oppress people and so on) by exposing as wrong common justifications for existing society and social relationships by a process of debate and providing a vision of something better. In other words, anarchist organisations seek to explain and clarify what is happening in society and show why anarchism is the only real solution to social problems. As part of this, we also have to combat wrong ideas such as Liberalism, Social Democracy, Leninism, right-wing populism and so on, indicating why these proposed solutions are false. In addition, an anarchist organisation must also be a 'collective memory' for the oppressed, keeping alive and developing the traditions of the labour and radical movements as well as anarchism so that new generations of libertarians have a body of experience to build upon and use in their struggles.

Anarchist organisations see themselves in the role of aiders, **not** leaders. As Voline argued, the minority which is politically aware "*should intervene. But, in every place and under all circumstances,*" they "*should freely participate in the common work, as true

collaborators, not as dictators.* It is necessary that they especially create an example, and employ themselves ... without dominating, subjugating, or oppressing anyone ... Accordingly to the libertarian thesis, it is the labouring masses themselves, who, by means of the various class organisations, factory committees, industrial and agricultural unions, co-operatives, et cetera, federated ... should apply themselves everywhere, to solving the problems of waging the Revolution.*" As for the politically aware, "*their role, according to the libertarians, is to **help** the masses, enlighten them, teach them, give them necessary advice, impel them to take initiative, provide them with an example, and support them in their action — **but not to direct them governmentally.**" [**The Unknown Revolution**, pp. 177-8]

This role is usually called providing a **"leadership of ideas"**. Anarchists stress the difference of this concept with authoritarian notions of "leadership" such as Leninist ones. While both anarchist and Leninist organisations exist to overcome the problem of "uneven development" within the working class, the aims, role and structure of these groups could not be more different (as discussed in section H.5, anarchists reject the assumptions and practice of vanguardism as incompatible with genuine socialism).

Anarchist groups are needed for, no matter how much people change through struggle, it is not enough in itself (if it were, we would be living in an anarchist society now!). So anarchists stress, as well as self-organisation, self-liberation and self-education through struggle developing libertarian socialist thought, the need for anarchist groups to work within popular organisations and in the mass of the population in general. These groups would play an important role in helping to clarify the ideas of those in struggle and undermining the internal and external barriers against these ideas. The first of these are what Emma Goldman termed the "*internal tyrants,*" the "*ethical and social conventions*" of existing, hierarchical society which accustom people to authoritarian social relationships, injustice, lack of freedom and so on. [**Red Emma Speaks**, pp. 164-5] External barriers are what Chomsky terms "*the Manufacture of Consent,*" the process by which the population at large are influenced to accept the status quo and the dominant elites viewpoint via the education system and media. It is this "manufacture of consent" which helps explain why, relatively speaking, there are so few anarchists even though we argue that anarchism is the natural product of working class life. While, objectively, the experiences of life drives working class people to resist domination and oppression, they enter that struggle with a history behind them, a history of education in capitalist schools, of consuming capitalist media, and so on.

This means that while social struggle is radicalising, it also has to combat years of pro-state and pro-capitalist influences. So even if an anarchist consciousness springs from the real conditions of working class life, because we live in a class society there are numerous counter-tendencies that **inhibit** the development of that consciousness (such as religion, current morality, the media, pro-business and pro-state propaganda, state and business repression and so on). This explains the differences in political opinion within the working class, as people develop at different speeds and are subject to different influences and experiences. However, the numerous internal and external barriers to the development of anarchist opinions created by our *"internal tyrants"* and by the process of *"manufacturing consent"* can be, and are, weakened by rational discussion as well as social struggle and self-activity. Indeed, until such time as we have *"learned to defy them all [the internal tyrants], to stand firmly on [our] own ground and to insist upon [our] own unrestricted freedom"* we can never be free or successfully combat the "manufacture of consent." [Goldman, **Op. Cit.**, p. 140] And this is where the anarchist group can play a part, for there is an important role to be played by those who have been through this process already, namely to aid those going through it. Of course the activity of an anarchist group does not occur in a vacuum. In periods of low class struggle, where there is little collective action, anarchist ideas will seem utopian and so dismissed by most. In these situations, only a few will become anarchists simply because the experiences of working people do not breed confidence that an alternative to the current system is possible. In addition, if anarchist groups are small, many who are looking for an alternative may join other groups which are more visible and express a libertarian sounding rhetoric (such as Leninist groups, who often talk about workers' control, workers' councils and so on while meaning something distinctly different from what anarchists mean by these terms). However, as the class struggle increases and people become more inclined to take collective action, they can become empowered and radicalised by their own activity and be more open to anarchist ideas and the possibility of changing society. In these situations, anarchist groups grow and the influence in anarchist ideas increases. This explains why anarchist ideas are not as widespread as they could be. It also indicates another important role for the anarchist group, namely to provide an environment and space where those drawn to anarchist ideas can meet and share experiences and ideas during periods of reaction.

The role of the anarchist group, therefore, is **not** to import a foreign ideology into the working class, but rather to help develop and clarify the ideas of those working class people who are moving towards anarchism and so aid those undergoing that development. They would aid this development by providing propaganda which exposes the current social system (and the rationales for it) as bankrupt as well as encouraging resistance to oppression and exploitation. The former, for Bakunin, allowed the *"bringing [of] a more just general expression, a new and more congenial form to the existent instincts of the proletariat"* which *"can sometimes facilitate and precipitate development"* and *"give them an awareness of what they have, of what they feel, of what they already instinctively desire, but never can it give to them what they don't have."* The latter *"is the most popular, the most potent, and the most irresistible form of propaganda"* and *"awake[s] in the masses all the social-revolutionary instincts which reside deeply in the heart of every worker"* so allowing instinct to become transformed into *"reflected socialist thought."* [quoted by Richard B. Saltman, **The Social and Political Thought of Michael Bakunin**, p. 107, p. 108 and p. 141]

To quote the UK **Anarchist Federation**, again *"the [libertarian] organisation is not just a propaganda group: above all it must actively work in all the grassroots organisations of the working class such as rank and file [trade union] groups, tenants associations, squatters and unemployed groups as well as women's, black*

and gay groups." It *"respects the independence of working class movements and (unlike] others) does not try to subordinate them to the revolutionary organisation. This does not mean that it does not seek to spread its ideas in these movements."* [**Op. Cit.**, p. 15 and p. 16] Such an organisation is not vanguardist in the Leninist sense as it recognises that socialist politics derive from working class experience, rather than bourgeois intellectuals (as Lenin and Karl Kautsky argued), and that it does not aim to dominate popular movements but rather work within them as equals.

So while we recognise that "advanced" sections do exist within the working class and that anarchists are one such section, we also recognise that **central** characteristic of anarchism is that its politics are derived from the concrete experience of fighting capitalism and statism directly — that is, from the realities of working class life. This means that anarchists must also learn from working class people in struggle. If we recognise that anarchist ideas are the product of working class experience and self-activity and that these constantly change and develop in light of new experiences and struggles then anarchist theory **must be open to change by learning from non-anarchists.** Not to recognise this fact is to open the door to vanguardism and dogma. Because of this fact, anarchists argue that the relationship between anarchists and non-anarchists must be an egalitarian one, based on mutual interaction and the recognition that no one is infallible or has all the answers — including anarchists! With this in mind, while we recognise the presence of "advanced" groups within the working class (which obviously reflects the uneven development within it), anarchists aim to minimise such unevenness by the way anarchist organisations intervene in social struggle, intervention based on involving **all** in the decision making process (as we discuss below).

Thus the general aim of anarchist groups is to spread ideas — such as general anarchist analysis of society and current events, libertarian forms of organisation, direct action and solidarity and so forth — and win people over to anarchism (i.e. to "make" anarchists). This involves both propaganda and participating as equals in social struggle and popular organisation. Anarchists do not think that changing leaders is a solution to the problem of (bad) leadership. Rather, it is a question of making leaders redundant by empowering all. As Malatesta argued, we *"do not want to **emancipate** the people; we want the people to **emancipate themselves.**"* Thus anarchists *"advocate and practise direct action, decentralisation, autonomy and individual initiative; they should make special efforts to help members [of popular organisations] learn to participate directly in the life of the organisation and to dispense with leaders and full-time functionaries."* [**Errico Malatesta: His Life and Ideas**, p. 90 and p. 125]

This means that anarchists reject the idea that anarchist groups and federations must become the "leaders" of organisations. Rather, we desire anarchist ideas to be commonplace in society and in popular organisations, so that leadership by people from positions of power is replaced by the *"natural influence"* (to use Bakunin's term) of activists within the rank and file on the decisions made **by** the rank and file. While we will discuss Bakunin's ideas in more detail in section J.3.7, the concept of *"natural influence"* can be gathered from this comment of Francisco Ascaso (friend of Durruti and an influential anarchist militant in the CNT and FAI in his own right):

"*There is not a single militant who as a 'FAIista' intervenes in union meetings. I work, therefore I am an exploited person. I pay my dues to the workers' union and when I intervene at union meetings I do it as someone who is exploited, and with the right which is granted me by the card in my possession, as do the other militants, whether they belong to the FAI or not.*" [quoted by Abel Paz, **Durruti: The People Armed**, p. 137]

This shows the nature of the "leadership of ideas." Rather than be elected to a position of power or responsibility, the anarchist presents their ideas at mass meetings and argues his or her case. This obviously implies a two-way learning process, as the anarchist learns from the experiences of others and the others come in contact with anarchist ideas. Moreover, it is an egalitarian relationship, based upon discussion between equals rather than urging people to place someone into power above them. It ensures that everyone in the organisation participates in making, understands and agrees with the decisions reached. This obviously helps the political development of all involved (including, we must stress, the anarchists). As Durruti argued: "*the man [or woman] who alienates his will, can never be free to express himself and follow his own ideas at a union meeting if he feel dominated by the feeblest orator ... As long as a man doesn't think for himself and doesn't assume his own responsibilities, there will be no complete liberation of human beings.*" [quoted by Paz, **Op. Cit.**, p. 184]

Because of our support for the "leadership of ideas", anarchists think that all popular organisations must be open, fully self-managed and free from authoritarianism. Only in this way can ideas and discussion play an important role in the life of the organisation. Since anarchists "*do not believe in the good that comes from above and imposed by force*" and "*want the new way of life to emerge from the body of the people and advance as they advance. It matters to us therefore that all interests and opinions find their expression in a conscious organisation and should influence communal life in proportion to their importance.*" [Malatesta, **Op. Cit.**, p. 90] Bakunin's words with regards the first International Workers Association indicate this clearly:

"*It must be a people's movement, organised from the bottom up by the free, spontaneous action of the masses. There must be no secret governmentalism, the masses must be informed of everything ... All the affairs of the International must be thoroughly and openly discussed without evasions and circumlocutions.*" [**Bakunin on Anarchism**, p. 408]

Given this, anarchists reject the idea of turning the organs created in the class struggle and revolutionary process into hierarchical structures. By turning them from organs of self-management into organs for nominating "leaders," the constructive tasks and political development of the revolution will be aborted before they really begin. The active participation of all will become reduced to the picking of new masters and the revolution will falter. For this reason, anarchists "*differ from the Bolshevik type of party in their belief that genuine revolutionaries must function **within the framework of the forms created by the revolution,** not within forms created by*

the party." This means that "*an organisation is needed to propagate ideas systematically — and not ideas alone, but **ideas which promote the concept of self-management.**" In other words, there "*is a need for a revolutionary organisation — but its function must always be kept clearly in mind. Its first task is propaganda ... In a revolutionary situation, the revolutionary organisation presents the most advanced demands: it is prepared at every turn of events to formulate — in the most concrete fashion — the immediate task that should be performed to advance the revolutionary process. It provides the boldest elements in action and in the decision-making organs of the revolution.*" [Bookchin, **Post-Scarcity Anarchism**, p. 140] What it does **not** do is to supplant those organs or decision-making process by creating institutionalised, hierarchical leadership structures.

Equally as important as **how** anarchists intervene in social struggles and popular organisations and the organisation of those struggles and organisations, there is the question of the nature of that intervention. We would like to quote the following by the British libertarian socialist group **Solidarity** as it sums up the underlying nature of anarchist action and the importance of a libertarian perspective on social struggle and change and how politically aware minorities work within them:

"**Meaningful action,** for revolutionaries, is whatever increases the confidence, the autonomy, the initiative, the participation, the solidarity, the egalitarian tendencies and the self-activity of the masses and whatever assists in their demystification. **Sterile and harmful action** is whatever reinforces the passivity of the masses, their apathy, their cynicism, their differentiation through hierarchy, their alienation, their reliance on others to do things for them and the degree to which they can therefore be manipulated by others — even by those allegedly acting on their behalf.*" [Maurice Brinton, **For Workers' Power**, p. 154]

Part of this "meaningful action" involves encouraging people to "**act for yourselves**" (to use Kropotkin's words). As we noted in section A.2.7, anarchism is based on **self**-liberation and self-activity is key aspect of this. Hence Malatesta's argument:

"*Our task is that of 'pushing' the people to demand and to seize all the freedom they can and to make themselves responsible for providing their own needs without waiting for orders from any kind of authority. Our task is that of demonstrating the uselessness and harmfulness of government, provoking and encouraging by propaganda and action, all kinds of individual and collective activities.

"It is in fact a question of education for freedom, of making people who are accustomed to obedience and passivity consciously aware of their real power and capabilities. One must encourage people to do things for themselves.*" [**Op. Cit.**, pp. 178-9]

This "pushing" people to "do it themselves" is another key role for any anarchist organisation. The encouragement of direct action is just as important as anarchist propaganda and popular participation within social struggle and popular organisations.

As such social struggle develops, the possibility of revolution becomes closer and closer. While we discuss anarchists ideas on social revolution in section J.7, we must note here that the role of the anarchist organisation does not change. As Bookchin argued, anarchists *"seek to persuade the factory committees, assemblies"* and other organisations created by people in struggle *"to make themselves into **genuine organs of popular self-management**, not to dominate them, manipulate them, or hitch them to an all-knowing political party."* [**Op. Cit.**, p. 140] In this way, by encouraging self-management in struggle, anarchists lay the foundations of a self-managed society.

J.3.7 Doesn't Bakunin's "Invisible Dictatorship" prove that anarchists are secret authoritarians?

No. While Bakunin did use the term *"invisible dictatorship"*, it does not prove that Bakunin or anarchists are secret authoritarians. The claim otherwise, often made by Leninists and other Marxists, expresses a distinct, even wilful, misunderstanding of Bakunin's ideas on the role revolutionaries should play in popular movements.

Marxists like Hal Draper quote Bakunin's terms *"invisible dictatorship"* and *"collective dictatorship"* out of context, using it to "prove" that anarchists are secret authoritarians, seeking dictatorship over the masses. The question of setting the record straight about this aspect of Bakunin's theory will help clarify the concept of *"leadership of ideas"* we discussed in the last section. So this section, while initially appearing somewhat redundant and of interest only to academics, is of a far wider interest.

Anarchists have two responses to claims that Bakunin (and, by implication, all anarchists) seek an *"invisible"* dictatorship and so are not true libertarians. Firstly, and this is the point we will concentrate upon in this section, Bakunin's expression is taken out of context and when placed within context it takes on a radically different meaning than that implied by critics of anarchism. Secondly, even **if** the expression means what the critics claim it does, it does not refute anarchism as a political theory. This is because anarchists are **not** Bakuninists (or Proudhonists or Kropotkinites or any other person-ist). We recognise other anarchists for what they are, human beings who said lots of important and useful things but, like any other human being, made mistakes and often do not live up to all of their ideas. For anarchists, it is a question of extracting the useful parts from their works and rejecting the useless (as well as the downright nonsense!). Just because Bakunin said something, it does not make it right! This common-sense approach to politics seems to be lost on Marxists.

However, to return to our main argument, that of the importance of context. Significantly, whenever Bakunin uses the term "invisible" or "collective" dictatorship he also explicitly states his opposition to government power and **in particular** the idea that anarchists should seize it. For example, a Leninist quotes the following passage from *"a Bakuninist document"* to show *"the dictatorial ambitions of*

Bakunin" and that the *"principle of anti-democracy was to leave Bakunin unchallenged at the apex of power"*: *"It is necessary that in the midst of popular anarchy, which will constitute the very life and energy of the revolution, unity of thought and revolutionary action should find an organ. This organ must be the secret and world-wide association of the international brethren."* [Derek Howl, *"The legacy of Hal Draper"*, pp. 137-49, **International Socialist**, no. 52, p. 147]

However, in the sentence **immediately before** those quoted, Bakunin stated that *"[t]his organisation rules out any idea of dictatorship and custodial control."* Strange that this part of the document was not quoted! Nor is Bakunin quoted when he wrote, in the same document, that *"[w]e are the natural enemies of those revolutionaries — future dictators, regimentors and custodians of revolution – who"* want *"to create new revolutionary States just as centralist and despotic as those we already know."* Not mentioned either is Bakunin's opinion that the *"revolution everywhere must be created by the people, and supreme control must always belong to the people organised into a free federation of agricultural and industrial associations … organised from the bottom upwards by means of revolutionary delegations"* who *"will set out to administer public services, not to rule over peoples."* [**Michael Bakunin: Selected Writings**, p. 172, p. 169 and p. 172] Selective quoting is only convincing to those ignorant of the subject.

Similarly, when we look at the situations where Bakunin uses the terms *"invisible"* or *"collective"* dictatorship (usually in letters to comrades) we find the same thing — the explicit denial **in these same letters** that Bakunin thought the revolutionary association should take governmental power. For example, in a letter to Albert Richard (a fellow member of the *"Alliance of Social Democracy"*) Bakunin stated that *"[t]here is only one power and one dictatorship whose organisation is salutary and feasible: it is that collective, invisible dictatorship of those who are allied in the name of our principle."* He then immediately adds that *"this dictatorship will be all the more salutary and effective for not being dressed up in any official power or extrinsic character."* Earlier in the letter he argued that anarchists must be *"like invisible pilots in the thick of the popular tempest… steer[ing] it [the revolution] not by any open power but by the collective dictatorship of all the allies — a dictatorship without insignia, titles or official rights, and all the stronger for having none of the paraphernalia of power."* Explicitly opposing *"Committees of Public Safety and official, overt dictatorship"* he explains his idea of a revolution based on *"workers hav[ing] joined into associations … armed and organised by streets and **quartiers**, the federative commune."* [**Op. Cit.**, p. 181, p. 180 and p. 179] Hardly what would be expected from a would-be dictator. As Sam Dolgoff suggested:

> *"an organisation exercising no overt authority, without a state, without official status, without the machinery of institutionalised power to enforce its policies, cannot be defined as a dictatorship … Moreover, if it is borne in mind that this passage is part of a letter repudiating in the strongest terms the State and the authoritarian statism of the 'Robespierres, the Dantons, and the Saint-Justs of the revolution,' it is reasonable to conclude that Bakunin used the word 'dictatorship' to denote preponderant influence*

or guidance exercised largely by example ... In line with this conclusion, Bakunin used the words 'invisible' and 'collective' to denote the underground movement exerting this influence in an organised manner." [**Bakunin on Anarchism**, p. 182]

This analysis is confirmed by other passages from Bakunin's letters. In a letter to the Nihilist Sergi Nechaev (within which Bakunin indicates exactly how far apart politically they were — which is important as, from Marx onwards, many of Bakunin's opponents quote Nechaev's pamphlets as if they were "Bakuninist," when in fact they were not) we find him arguing that:

"These [revolutionary] groups would not seek anything for themselves, neither privilege nor honour nor power ... [but] would be in a position to direct popular movements ... and lead the people towards the most complete realisation of the social-economic ideal and the organisation of the fullest popular freedom. This is what I call **the collective dictatorship** of a secret organisation.

"The dictatorship ... does not reward any of the members that comprise the groups, or the groups themselves, with any profit or honour or official power. It does not threaten the freedom of the people, because, lacking any official character, it does not take the place of State control over the people, and because its whole aim ... consists of the fullest realisation of the liberty of the people.

"This sort of dictatorship is not in the least contrary to the free development and the self-development of the people, nor its organisation from the bottom upward ... for it influences the people exclusively through the natural, personal influence of its members, who have not the slightest power, ... and ... try ... to direct the spontaneous revolutionary movement of the people towards ... the organisation of popular liberty ... This secret dictatorship would in the first place, and at the present time, carry out a broadly based popular propaganda ... and by the power of this propaganda and also by **organisation among the people themselves** join together separate popular forces into a mighty strength capable of demolishing the State." [**Michael Bakunin: Selected Writings**, pp. 193-4]

The key aspect of this is the notion of "natural" influence. In a letter to a Spanish member of the Alliance we find Bakunin arguing that it "will promote the Revolution only through the **natural but never official influence** of all members of the Alliance." [**Bakunin on Anarchism**, p. 387] This term was also used in his public writings, with Bakunin arguing that the "very freedom of every individual results from th[e] great number of material, intellectual, and moral influences which every individual around him and which society ... continually exercise on him" and that "everything alive ... intervene[s] ... in the life of others ... [so] we hardly wish to abolish the effect of any individual's or any group of individuals' natural influence upon the masses." [**The Basic Bakunin**, p. 140 and p. 141]

Thus "natural influence" simply means the effect of communicating which others, discussing your ideas with them and winning them over to your position, nothing more. This is hardly authoritarian, and so Bakunin contrasts this "natural" influence with "official" influence, which replaced the process of mutual interaction between equals with a fixed hierarchy of command and thereby induced the "transformation of natural influence, and, as such, the perfectly legitimate influence over man, into a right." [quoted by Richard B. Saltman, **The Social and Political Thought of Michael Bakunin**, p. 46]

As an example of this difference, consider the case of a union militant (as will become clear, this is the sort of example Bakunin had in mind). As long as they are part of the rank-and-file, arguing their case at union meetings or being delegated to carry out the decisions of these assemblies then their influence is "natural." However, if this militant is elected into a position with executive power in the union (i.e. becomes a full-time union official, for example, rather than a shop-steward) then their influence becomes "official" and so, potentially, corrupting for both the militant and the rank-and-file who are subject to the rule of the official.

Indeed, this notion of "natural" influence was also termed "invisible" by Bakunin: "It is only necessary that one worker in ten join the [International Working-Men's] Association **earnestly** and **with full understanding of the cause** for the nine-tenths remaining outside its organisation nevertheless to be influenced invisibly by it." [**The Basic Bakunin**, p. 139] So, as can be seen, the terms "invisible" and "collective" dictatorship used by Bakunin in his letters is strongly related to the term "natural influence" used in his public works and seems to be used simply to indicate the effects of an organised political group on the masses. To see this, it is worthwhile to quote Bakunin at length about the nature of this "invisible" influence:

"It may be objected that this ... influence on the popular masses suggests the establishment of a system of authority and a new government ... Such a belief would be a serious blunder. The organised effect of the International on the masses ... is nothing but the entirely natural organisation — neither official nor clothed in any authority or political force whatsoever — of the effect of a rather numerous group of individuals who are inspired by the same thought and headed toward the same goal, first of all on the opinion of the masses and only then, by the intermediary of this opinion (restated by the International's propaganda), on their will and their deeds. But the governments ... impose themselves violently on the masses, who are forced to obey them and to execute their decrees ... The International's influence will never be anything but one of opinion and the International will never be anything but the organisation of the natural effect of individuals on the masses." [**Op. Cit.**, pp. 139-40]

Therefore, from both the fuller context provided by the works and letters selectively quoted by Marxists **and** his other writings, we find that rather than being a secret authoritarian, Bakunin was, in fact, trying to express how anarchists could "naturally influence" the masses and their revolution:

*"We are the most pronounced enemies of every sort of **official power** … We are the enemies of any sort of publicly declared dictatorship, we are social revolutionary anarchists … if we are anarchists, by what right do we want to influence the people, and what methods will we use? Denouncing all power, with what sort of power, or rather by what sort of force, shall we direct a people's revolution? **By a force that is invisible … that is not imposed on anyone … [and] deprived of all official rights and significance.**"* [**Michael Bakunin: Selected Writings**, pp. 191-2]

Continually opposing *"official"* power, authority and influence, Bakunin used the term *"invisible, collective dictatorship"* to describe the *"natural influence"* of organised anarchists on mass movements. Rather than express a desire to become a dictator, it in fact expresses the awareness that there is an "uneven" political development within the working class, an unevenness that can only be undermined by discussion within the mass assemblies of popular organisations. Any attempt to by-pass this "unevenness" by seizing or being elected to positions of power (i.e. by *"official influence"*) would be doomed to failure and result in dictatorship by a party — *"triumph of the Jacobins or the Blanquists [or the Bolsheviks, we must add] would be the death of the Revolution."* [**Op. Cit.**, p. 169]

So rather than seek power, the anarchists would seek **influence** based on the soundness of their ideas, what anarchists today term the *"leadership of ideas"* in other words. Thus the anarchist federation *"unleashes their [the peoples] will and gives wider opportunity for their self-determination and their social-economic organisation, which should be created by them alone from the bottom upwards."* The revolutionary organisation must *"not in any circumstances … ever be their master … What is to be the chief aim and pursue of this organisation? **To help the people towards self-determination on the lines of the most complete equality and fullest human freedom in every direction, without the least interference from any sort of domination … that is without any sort of government control.**"* [**Op. Cit.**, p. 191]

This analysis can be seen from Bakunin's discussion on union bureaucracy and how anarchists should combat it. Taking the Geneva section of the IWMA, Bakunin notes that the construction workers' section *"simply left all decision-making to their committees … In this manner power gravitated to the committees, and by a species of fiction characteristic of all governments the committees substituted their own will and their own ideas for that of the membership."* To combat this bureaucracy, the union *"sections could only defend their rights and their autonomy in only one way: the workers called general membership meetings. Nothing arouses the antipathy of the committees more than these popular assemblies … In these great meetings of the sections, the items on the agenda was amply discussed and the most progressive opinion prevailed."* Given that Bakunin considered *"the federative Alliance of all the workers' associations"* would *"constitute the Commune"* by means of delegates with *"always responsible, and revocable mandates"*, we can easily see that the role of the anarchist federation would be to intervene in general assemblies of these associations and ensure,

through debate, that the most progressive opinion prevailed. [**Bakunin on Anarchism**, p. 246, p. 247 and p. 153]

Having shown that the role of Bakunin's revolutionary organisations is drastically different than that suggested by the selective quotations of Marxists, we need to address two more issues. One, the so-called hierarchical nature of Bakunin's organisations and, two, their secret nature. Taking the issue of hierarchy first, we can do no better than quote Richard B. Saltman's summary of the internal organisation of these groups:

"The association's 'single will,' Bakunin wrote, would be determined by 'laws' that every member 'helped to create,' or at a minimum 'equally approved' by 'mutual agreement.' This 'definite set of rules' was to be 'frequently renewed' in plenary sessions wherein each member had the 'duty to try and make his view prevail,' but then he must accept fully the decision of the majority. Thus the revolutionary association's 'rigorously conceived and prescribed plan,' implemented under the 'strictest discipline,' was in reality to be 'nothing more or less than the expression and direct outcome of the reciprocal commitment contracted by each of the members towards the others.'" [**Op. Cit.**, p. 115]

While many anarchists would not totally agree with this set-up (although we think that most supporters of the "Platform" would) all would agree that it is **not** hierarchical. If anything, it appears quite democratic in nature. Moreover, comments in Bakunin's letters to other Alliance members support the argument that his revolutionary associations were more democratic in nature than Marxists suggest. In a letter to a Spanish comrade we find him suggesting that *"all [Alliance] groups… should… from now on accept new members not by majority vote, but unanimously."* [**Op. Cit.**, p. 386] In a letter to Italian members of the IWMA he argued that in Geneva the Alliance did not resort to *"secret plots and intrigues."* Rather:

"Everything was done in broad daylight, openly, for everyone to see … The Alliance had regular weekly open meetings and everyone was urged to participate in the discussions … The old procedure where members sat and passively listened to speakers talking down to them from their pedestal was discarded.

*"It was established that all meetings be conducted by informal round-table conversational discussions in which everybody felt free to participate: not to be talked **at**, but to exchange views."* [**Op. Cit.**, pp. 405-6]

Moreover, we find Bakunin being out-voted within the Alliance, hardly what we would expect if they **were** top-down dictatorships run by him as Marxists claim. The historian T.R. Ravindranathan indicates that after the Alliance was founded *"Bakunin wanted the Alliance to become a branch of the International [Worker's Association] and at the same time preserve it as a secret society. The Italian and some French members wanted the Alliance to be totally independent of the IWA and objected to Bakunin's secrecy. Bakunin's view prevailed on the first question as he succeeded in convincing the majority of the harmful effects of a rivalry between* the Alliance and the International. On the question of secrecy, he gave way to his opponents." [**Bakunin and the Italians**, p. 83] Moreover, if Bakunin **did** seek to create a centralised, hierarchical organisation, as Marxists claim, he did not do a good job. We find him complaining that the Madrid Alliance was breaking up ("*The news of the dissolution of the Alliance in Spain saddened Bakunin. he intensified his letter-writing to Alliance members whom he trusted ... He tried to get the Spaniards to reverse their decision*" [Juan Gomez Casa, **Anarchist Organisation**, pp. 37-8]). While the "Bakuninist" Spanish and Swiss sections of the IWMA sent delegates to its infamous Hague congress, the "Bakuninist" Italian section did not. Of course, Marxists could argue that these facts show Bakunin's cunning nature, but the more obvious explanation is that Bakunin did not create a hierarchical organisation with himself at the top.

The evidence suggests that the Alliance "*was not a compulsory or authoritarian body.*" In Spain, it "*acted independently and was prompted by purely local situations. The copious correspondence between Bakunin and his friends ... was at all times motivated by the idea of offering advice, persuading, and clarifying. It was never written in a spirit of command, because that was not his style, nor would it have been accepted as such by his associates.*" Moreover, there "*is no trace or shadow or hierarchical organisation in a letter from Bakunin to Mora ... On the contrary, Bakunin advises 'direct' relations between Spanish and Italian Comrades.*" The Spanish comrades also wrote a pamphlet which "*ridiculed the fable of orders from abroad.*" [Casa, **Op. Cit.**, p. 25 and p. 40] This is confirmed by George R. Esenwein who argues that "*[w]hile it is true that Bakunin's direct intervention during the early days of the International's development in Spain had assured the predominance of his influence in the various federations and sections*" of the organisation, "*it cannot be said that he manipulated it or otherwise used the Spanish Alliance as a tool for his own subversive designs.*" Thus, "*though the Alliance did exist in Spain, the society did not bear any resemblance to the nefarious organisation that the Marxists depicted.*" [**Anarchist Ideology and the Working Class Movement in Spain**, p. 42] Indeed, as Max Nettlau points out, those Spaniards who did break with the Alliance were persuaded of its "*hierarchical organisation ... not by their own direct observation, but by what they had been told about the conduct of the organisation*" in other countries. [quoted by Casa, **Op. Cit.**, pp. 39-40]. In addition, if Bakunin **did** run the Alliance under his own personal dictatorship we would expect it to change or dissolve upon his death. However, "*the Spanish Alliance survived Bakunin, who died in 1876, yet with few exceptions it continued to function in much the same way it had during Bakunin's lifetime.*" [Esenwein, **Op. Cit.**, p. 43]

Moving on to the second issue, the question of why Bakunin favoured secret organisation. At the time many states were despotic monarchies, with little or no civil rights. As he argued, "*nothing but a secret society would want to take this [arousing a revolution] on, for the interests of the government and of the government classes would be bitterly opposed to it.*" [**Michael Bakunin: Selected Writings**, p. 188] For survival, Bakunin considered secrecy an essential. As Juan Gomez Casas noted: "*In view of the difficulties of that period, Bakunin believed that secret groups of convinced and absolutely trustworthy men were safer and more effective. They*

would be able to place themselves at the head of developments at critical moments, but only to inspire and to clarify the issues." [**Op. Cit.**, p. 22] Even Marxists, faced with dictatorial states, have organised in secret and as George R. Esenwein points out, the "*claim that Bakunin's organisation scheme was not the product of a 'hard-headed realism' cannot be supported in the light of the experiences of the Spanish Alliancists. It is beyond doubt that their adherence to Bakunin's program greatly contributed to the FRE's [Spanish section of the First International] ability to flourish during the early part of the 1870s and to survive the harsh circumstances of repression in the period 1874-1881.*" [**Op. Cit.**, p. 224f] So Bakunin's personal experiences in Tsarist Russia and other illiberal states shaped his ideas on how revolutionaries should organise (and let us not forget that he had been imprisoned in the Peter and Paul prison for his activities).

This is not to suggest that all of Bakunin's ideas on the role and nature of anarchist groups are accepted by anarchists today. Most anarchists would reject Bakunin's arguments for secrecy, for example (particularly as secrecy cannot help but generate an atmosphere of deceit and, potentially, manipulation). Anarchists remember that anarchism did not spring fully formed and complete from Bakunin's (or any other individual's) head. Rather it was developed over time and by many individuals, inspired by many different experiences and movements. As such, anarchists recognise that Bakunin was inconsistent in some ways, as would be expected from a theorist breaking new ground, and this applies to his ideas on how anarchist groups should work within and the role they should play in popular movements. Most of his ideas are valid, once we place them into context, some are not. Anarchists embrace the valid ones and voice their opposition to the others.

In summary, any apparent contradiction between the "public" and "private" Bakunin disappears once we place his comments into context within both the letters he wrote and his overall political theory. As Brian Morris argues, those who argue that Bakunin was in favour of despotism only come to "*these conclusions by an incredible distortion of the substance of what Bakunin was trying to convey in his letters to Richard and Nechaev*" and "*[o]nly the most jaundiced scholar, or one blinded by extreme antipathy towards Bakunin or anarchism, could interpret these words as indicating that Bakunin's conception of a secret society implied a revolutionary dictatorship in the Jacobin sense, still less a 'despotism'*" [**Bakunin: The Philosophy of Freedom**, p. 144 and p. 149]

J.3.8
What is anarcho-syndicalism?

Anarcho-syndicalism (as mentioned in section A.3.2) is a form of anarchism which applies itself (primarily) to creating industrial unions organised in an anarchist manner, using anarchist tactics (such as direct action) to create a free society. To quote "*The Principles of Revolutionary Syndicalism*" of the **International Workers Association**:

"*Revolutionary Syndicalism is that movement of the working classes founded on the basis of class war, which strives for the union of manual and intellectual workers in economic fighting organisations, in order to prepare for and realise in practice their liberation from the yoke of wage-slavery and state oppression. Its goal is the reorganisation of social life on the basis of free communism through the collective revolutionary action of the working classes themselves. It takes the view that only the economic organisations of the proletariat are appropriate for the realisation of this task and turns therefore to the workers in their capacity as producers and generators of social value, in opposition to the modern political labour parties, which for constructive economic purpose do not come into consideration."* [quoted by Wayne Thorpe, **"The Workers Themselves"**, p. 322]

The word *"syndicalism"* is an English rendering of the French for *"revolutionary trade unionism"* (*"syndicalisme revolutionarie"*). In the 1890s many anarchists in France started to work within the trade union movement, radicalising it from within. As the ideas of autonomy, direct action, the general strike and political independence of unions which where associated with the French **Confederation Generale du Travail** (CGT, or General Confederation of Labour) spread across the world (partly through anarchist contacts, partly through word of mouth by non-anarchists who were impressed by the militancy of the CGT), the word "syndicalism" was used to describe movements inspired by the example of the CGT. Thus "syndicalism," "revolutionary syndicalism" and "anarcho-syndicalism" all basically mean "revolutionary unionism" (the term "industrial unionism" used by the IWW essentially means the same thing).

The main difference is between revolutionary syndicalism and anarcho-syndicalism, with anarcho-syndicalism arguing that revolutionary syndicalism concentrates too much on the workplace and, obviously, stressing the anarchist roots and nature of syndicalism more than the former. In addition, anarcho-syndicalism is often considered compatible with supporting a specific anarchist organisation to complement the work of the revolutionary unions. Revolutionary syndicalism, in contrast, argues that the syndicalist unions are sufficient in themselves to create libertarian socialism and rejects anarchist groups along with political parties. However, the dividing line can be unclear and, just to complicate things even more, **some** syndicalists support political parties and are not anarchists (there have been a few Marxist syndicalists, for example) but we will ignore these in our discussion. We will use the term syndicalism to describe what each branch has in common.

The syndicalist union is a self-managed industrial union (see section J.5.2) which is committed to **direct action** and refuses links with political parties, even labour or "socialist" ones. A key idea of syndicalism is that of union autonomy — the idea that the workers' organisation is capable of changing society by its own efforts, that it must control its own fate and not be controlled by any party or other outside group (including anarchist federations). This is sometimes termed **"workerism"** (from the French **"ouverierisme"**), i.e. workers' control of the class struggle and their own organisations. Rather than being a cross-class organisation like the political party, the union is a **class** organisation and is so uniquely capable of representing working class aspirations, interests and hopes.

*"The **syndicat**,"* Emile Pouget wrote, *"groups together those who work against those who live by human exploitation: it brings together interests and not opinions."* [quoted by Jeremy Jennings, **Syndicalism in France**, pp. 30-1] There is, then, *"no place in it for anybody who was not a worker. Professional middle class intellectuals who provided both the leadership and the ideas of the socialist political movement, were therefore at a discount. As a consequence the syndicalist movement was, and saw itself as, a purely working class form of socialism."* Syndicalism *"appears as the great heroic movement of the proletariat, the first movement which took seriously"* the argument *"that the emancipation of the working class must be the task of labour unaided by middle class intellectuals or by politicians and aimed to establish a genuinely working class socialism and culture, free of all bourgeois taints. For the syndicalists, the workers were to be everything, the rest, nothing."* [Geoffrey Ostergaard, **The Tradition of Workers' Control**, p. 38]

Therefore syndicalism is *"consciously anti-parliamentary and anti-political. It focuses not only on the realities of power but also on the key problem of achieving its disintegration. Real power in syndicalist doctrine is economic power. The way to dissolve economic power is to make every worker powerful, thereby eliminating power as a social privilege. Syndicalism thus ruptures all the ties between the workers and the state. It opposes political action, political parties, and any participant in political elections. Indeed it refuses to operate in the framework of the established order and the state. It "turns to direct action — strikes, sabotage, obstruction, and above all, the revolutionary general strike. Direct action not only perpetuates the militancy of the workers and keeps alive the spirit of revolt, but awakens in them a greater sense of individual initiative. By continual pressure, direct action tests the strength of the capitalist system at all times and presumably in its most important arena — the factory, where ruled and ruler seem to confront each other most directly."* [Murray Bookchin, **The Spanish Anarchists**, p. 121]

This does not mean that syndicalism is "apolitical" in the sense of ignoring totally all political issues. This is a Marxist myth. Syndicalists follow other anarchists by being opposed to all forms of authoritarian/capitalist politics but do take a keen interest in "political" questions as they relate to the interests of working people. Thus they do not "ignore" the state, or the role of the state. Indeed, syndicalists (like all libertarians) are well aware that the state exists to protect capitalist property and power and that we need to combat it as well as fight for economic improvements. In short, syndicalism is deeply political in the widest sense of the word, aiming for a radical change in political, economic and social conditions and institutions. Moreover, it is political in the narrower sense of being aware of political issues and aiming for political reforms along with economic ones. It is only "apolitical" when it comes to supporting political parties and using bourgeois political institutions, a position which is "political" in the wider sense of course! This is obviously identical to the usual anarchist position (see section J.2.10).

Which indicates an important difference between syndicalism and trade unionism. Syndicalism aims at changing society rather than just working within it. Thus syndicalism is revolutionary while trade unionism is reformist. For syndicalists the union *"has a double aim: with tireless persistence, it must pursue betterment of the working* class's current conditions. But, without letting themselves become obsessed with this passing concern, the workers should take care to make possible and imminent the essential act of comprehensive emancipation: the expropriation of capital." Thus syndicalism aims to win reforms by direct action and by this struggle bring the possibilities of a revolution, via the general strike, closer. Indeed any *"desired improvement is to be wrested directly from the capitalist"* and *"must always represent a reduction in capitalist privileges and be a partial expropriation."* [Emile Pouget, **No Gods, No Masters**, vol. 2, p. 71 and p. 73] Thus Emma Goldman:

> *"Of course Syndicalism, like the old trade unions, fights for immediate gains, but it is not stupid enough to pretend that labour can expect humane conditions from inhumane economic arrangements in society. Thus it merely wrests from the enemy what it can force him to yield; on the whole, however, Syndicalism aims at, and concentrates its energies upon, the complete overthrow of the wage system.*

> *"Syndicalism goes further: it aims to liberate labour from every institution that has not for its object the free development of production for the benefit of all humanity. In short, the ultimate purpose of Syndicalism is to reconstruct society from its present centralised, authoritative and brutal state to one based upon the free, federated grouping of the workers along lines of economic and social liberty.*

> *"With this object in view, Syndicalism works in two directions: first, by undermining the existing institutions; secondly, by developing and educating the workers and cultivating their spirit of solidarity, to prepare them for a full, free life, when capitalism shall have been abolished.*

> *"Syndicalism is, in essence, the economic expression of Anarchism."* [**Red Emma Speaks**, p. 91]

Which, in turn, explains why syndicalist unions are structured in such an obviously libertarian way. It reflects the importance of empowering every worker by creating a union which is decentralised and self-managed, a union which every member plays a key role in determining its policy and activities. Participation ensures that the union becomes a *"school for the will"* (to use Pouget's expression) and allows working people to learn how to govern themselves and so do without the state. After the revolution, the union can easily be transformed into the body by which production is organised. The aim of the union is workers' self-management of production and distribution after the revolution, a self-management which the union is based upon in the here and now. The syndicalist union is seen as *"the germ of the Socialist economy of the future, the elementary school of Socialism in general"* and we need to *"plant these germs while there is yet time and bring them to the strongest possible development, so as to make the task of the coming social revolution easier and to insure its permanence."* [Rocker, **Op. Cit.**, p. 59]

Thus, as can be seen, syndicalism differs from trade unionism in its structure, its methods and its aims. Its structure, method and aims are distinctly anarchist. Little wonder leading syndicalist theorist Fernand Pelloutier argued that the trade union, *"governing itself along anarchic lines,"* must become *"a practical schooling in anarchism."* [**No Gods, No Masters**, vol. 2, p. 55 and p. 57] In addition, most anarcho-syndicalists support community organisations and struggle alongside the more traditional industry based approach usually associated within syndicalism. While we have concentrated on the industrial side here (simply because this is a key aspect of syndicalism) we must stress that syndicalism can and does lend itself to community struggles. It is a myth that anarcho-syndicalism ignores community struggles and organisation, as can be seen from the history of the Spanish CNT for example (see section J.5.1).

It must be stressed that a syndicalist union is open to all workers regardless of their political opinions (or lack of them). The union exists to defend workers' interests as workers and is organised in an anarchist manner to ensure that their interests are fully expressed. This means that a syndicalist organisation is different from an organisation of syndicalists. What makes the union syndicalist is its structure, aims and methods. Obviously things can change (that is true of any organisation which has a democratic structure) but that is a test revolutionary and anarcho-syndicalists welcome and do not shirk from. As the union is self-managed from below up, its militancy and political content is determined by its membership. As Pouget put it, the union *"offers employers a degree of resistance in geometric proportion with the resistance put up by its members."* [**Op. Cit.**, p. 71] That is why syndicalists ensure that power rests in the members of the union.

Syndicalists have two main approaches to building revolutionary unions — **"dual unionism"** and **"boring from within."** The former approach involves creating new, syndicalist, unions, in opposition to the existing trade unions. This approach was historically and is currently the favoured way of building syndicalist unions (American, Italian, Spanish, Swedish and numerous other syndicalists built their own union federations in the heyday of syndicalism between 1900 and 1920). "Boring from within" simply means working within the existing trade unions in order to reform them and make them syndicalist. This approach was favoured by French and British syndicalists, plus a few American ones. However, these two approaches are not totally in opposition. Many of the dual unions were created by syndicalists who had first worked within the existing trade unions. Once they got sick of the bureaucratic union machinery and of trying to reform it, they split from the reformist unions and formed new, revolutionary, ones. Similarly, dual unionists will happily support trade unionists in struggle and often be "two carders" (i.e. members of both the trade union and the syndicalist one). See section J.5.3 for more on anarchist perspectives on existing trades unions.

Syndicalists no matter what tactics they prefer, favour autonomous workplace organisations, controlled from below. Both tend to favour syndicalists forming networks of militants to spread anarchist/syndicalist ideas within the workplace. Indeed, such a network (usually called *Industrial Networks* — see section J.5.4 for more details) would be an initial stage and essential means for creating syndicalist unions. These groups would encourage syndicalist tactics and rank and file organisation during struggles and so create the potential for building syndicalist unions as libertarian ideas spread and are seen to work.

Syndicalists think that such an organisation is essential for the successful creation of an anarchist society as it builds the new world in the shell of the old, making a sizeable majority of the population aware of anarchism and the benefits of anarchist forms of organisation and struggle. Moreover, they argue that those who reject syndicalism *"because it believes in a permanent organisation of workers"* and urge *"workers to organise 'spontaneously' at the very moment of revolution"* promote a *"con-trick, designed to leave 'the revolutionary movement,' so called, in the hands of an educated class … [or] so-called 'revolutionary party' … [which] means that the workers are only expected to come in the fray when there's any fighting to be done, and in normal times leave theorising to the specialists or students."* [Albert Meltzer, **Anarchism: Arguments for and Against**, pp. 82-3] A self-managed society can only be created by self-managed means, and as only the practice of self-management can ensure its success, the need for libertarian popular organisations is essential. Syndicalism is seen as the key way working people can prepare themselves for revolution and learn to direct their own lives. In this way syndicalism creates a true politics of the people, one that does not create a parasitic class of politicians and bureaucrats (*"We wish to emancipate ourselves, to free ourselves"*, Pelloutier wrote, *"but we do not wish to carry out a revolution, to risk our skin, to put Pierre the socialist in the place of Paul the radical"* [quoted by Jeremy Jennings, **Syndicalism in France**, p. 17]).

This does not mean that syndicalists do not support organisations spontaneously created by workers' in struggle (such as workers' councils, factory committees and so on). Far from it. Syndicalists have played important roles in these kinds of organisation (as can be seen from the Russian Revolution, the factory occupations in Italy in 1920, the British Shop Steward movement and so on). This is because syndicalism acts as a catalyst to militant labour struggles and serves to counteract class-collaborationist tendencies by union bureaucrats and "socialist" politicians. Part of this activity must involve encouraging self-managed organisations where none exist and so syndicalists support and encourage all such spontaneous movements, hoping that they turn into the basis of a syndicalist union movement or a successful revolution. Moreover, most anarcho-syndicalists recognise that it is unlikely that every worker, nor even the majority, will be in syndicalist unions before a revolutionary period starts. This means **new** organisations, created spontaneously by workers in struggle, would have to be the framework of social struggle and the post-capitalist society rather than the syndicalist union as such. All the syndicalist union can do is provide a practical example of how to organise in a libertarian way within capitalism and statism and support spontaneously created organisations.

It should be noted that while the term "syndicalism" dates from the 1890s in France, the ideas associated with these names have a longer history. Anarcho-syndicalist ideas have developed independently in many different countries and times. Indeed, anyone familiar with Bakunin's work will quickly see that much of his ideas prefigure what was latter to become known by these terms. Similarly, we find that the American **International Working People's Association**

organised by anarchists in the 1880s *"anticipated by some twenty years the doctrine of anarcho-syndicalism"* and *"[m]ore than merely resembling the 'Chicago Idea' [of the IWPA], the IWW's principles of industrial unionism resulted from the conscious efforts of anarchists … who continued to affirm … the principles which the Chicago anarchists gave their lives defending."* [Salvatore Salerno, **Red November, Black November**, p. 51 and p. 79] See section H.2.8 for a discussion of why Marxist claims that syndicalism and anarchism are unrelated are obviously false.

For more information on anarcho-syndicalist ideas, Rudolf Rocker's **Anarcho-Syndicalism** is still the classic introduction to the subject. The collection of articles by British syndicalist Tom Brown entitled **Syndicalism** is also worth reading. Daniel Guerin's **No Gods, No Masters** contains articles by leading French syndicalist thinkers.

J.3.9 Why are many anarchists not anarcho-syndicalists?

Before discussing why many anarchists are not anarcho-syndicalists, we must clarify a few points first. Let us be clear, non-syndicalist anarchists usually support the ideas of workplace organisation and struggle, of direct action, of solidarity and so on. Thus most non-syndicalist anarchists do not disagree with anarcho-syndicalists on these issues. Indeed, many even support the creation of syndicalist unions. Many anarcho-communists like Alexander Berkman, Errico Malatesta and Emma Goldman supported anarcho-syndicalist organisations and even, like Malatesta, helped form such revolutionary union federations (namely, the FORA in Argentina) and urged anarchists to take a leading role in organising unions. So when we use the term "non-syndicalist anarchist" we are not suggesting that these anarchists reject all aspects of anarcho-syndicalism. Rather, they are critical of certain aspects of anarcho-syndicalist ideas while supporting the rest.

In the past, a few communist-anarchists **did** oppose the struggle for improvements within capitalism as "reformist." However, these were few and far between and with the rise of anarcho-syndicalism in the 1890s, the vast majority of communist-anarchists recognised that only by encouraging the struggle for reforms would people take them seriously as this showed the benefits of anarchist tactics and organisation in practice so ensuring anarchist ideas grow in influence. Thus syndicalism was a healthy response to the rise of "abstract revolutionarism" that infected the anarchist movement during the 1880s, particularly in France and Italy. Thus communist-anarchists agree with syndicalists on the importance of struggling for and winning reforms and improvements within capitalism by direct action and solidarity.

Similarly, anarchists like Malatesta also recognised the importance of mass organisations like unions. As he argued, *"to encourage popular organisations of all kinds is the logical consequence of our basic ideas … An authoritarian party, which aims at capturing power to impose its ideas, has an interest in the people remaining an amorphous mass, unable to act for themselves and therefore easily dominated … But we anarchists do not want to **emancipate** the people; we want the people to **emancipate themselves** … we* want the new way of life to emerge from the body of the people and correspond to the state of their development and advance as they advance." [**Errico Malatesta: His Life and Ideas**, p. 90] This can only occur when there are popular organisations, like trade unions, within which people can express themselves, come to common agreements and act. Moreover, these organisations must be autonomous, self-governing, be libertarian in nature **and** be independent of all parties and organisations (including anarchist ones). The similarity with anarcho-syndicalist ideas is striking.

So why, if this is the case, are many anarchists not anarcho-syndicalists? There are two main reasons for this. First, there is the question of whether unions are, by their nature, revolutionary organisations. Second, whether syndicalist unions are sufficient to create anarchy by themselves. We will discuss each in turn.

As can be seen from any country, the vast majority of unions are deeply reformist and bureaucratic in nature. They are centralised, with power resting at the top in the hands of officials. This suggests that in themselves unions are not revolutionary. As Malatesta argued, this is to be expected for "*all movements founded on material and immediate interests (and a mass working class movement cannot be founded on anything else), if the ferment, the drive and the unremitting efforts of men [and women] of ideas struggling and making sacrifices for an ideal future are lacking, tend to adapt themselves to circumstances, foster a conservative spirit, and fear of change in those who manage to improve their conditions, and often end up by creating new privileged classes and serving to support and consolidate the system one would want to destroy.*" [**Op. Cit.**, pp. 113-4]

If we look at the **role** of the union within capitalist society we see that in order for it to work, it must offer a reason for the boss to recognise and negotiate with it. This means that the union must be able to offer the boss something in return for any reforms it gets, namely labour discipline. In return for an improvement in wages or conditions, the union must be able to get workers to agree to submit to the contracts the union signs with their boss. In other words, they must be able to control their members — stop them fighting the boss — if they are to have anything with which to bargain with. This results in the union becoming a third force in industry, with interests separate than the workers which it claims to represent. The role of unionism as a seller of labour power means that it often has to make compromises, compromises it has to make its members agree to. This necessities a tendency for power to be taken from the rank and file of the unions and centralised in the hands of officials at the top of the organisation. This ensures that "*the workers organisation becomes what it must perforce be in a capitalist society — a means not of refusing to recognise and overthrowing the bosses, but simply for hedging round and limiting the bosses' power.*" [Errico Malatesta, **The Anarchist Revolution**, p. 29]

Anarcho-syndicalists are aware of this problem. That is why their unions are decentralised, self-managed and organised from the bottom up in a federal manner. As Durruti argued:

"*No anarchists in the union committees unless at the ground level. In these committees, in case of conflict with the boss, the militant is forced to compromise to arrive at an agreement. The contracts and activities which come from being in this position, push the militant towards bureaucracy. Conscious of this risk, we do not wish to run it. Our role is to analyse from the bottom the different dangers which can beset a union organisation like ours. No militant should prolong his job in committees, beyond the time allotted to him. No permanent and indispensable people.*" [quoted by Abel Paz, **Durruti: The People Armed**, p. 183]

However, structure is rarely enough in itself to undermine the bureaucratic tendencies created by the role of unions in the capitalist economy. While such libertarian structures can slow down the tendency towards bureaucracy, non-syndicalist anarchists argue that they cannot stop it. They point to the example of the French CGT which had become reformist by 1914 (the majority of other syndicalist unions were crushed by fascism or communism before they had a chance to develop fully). Even the Spanish CNT (by far the most successful anarcho-syndicalist union) suffered from the problem of reformism, causing the anarchists in the union to organise the FAI in 1927 to combat it (which it did, very successfully). According to Jose Peirats, the "*participation of the anarchist group in the mass movement CNT helped to ensure the CNT's revolutionary nature.*" This indicates the validity of Malatesta's arguments concerning the need for anarchists to remain distinct of the unions organisationally while working within them — just as Peirat's comment that "*[b]linkered by participation in union committees, the FAI became incapable of a wider vision*" indicates the validity of Malatesta's warnings against anarchists taking positions of responsibility in unions! [**Anarchists in the Spanish Revolution**, p. 241 and pp. 239-40]

Moreover, even the structure of syndicalist unions can cause problems: "*In modelling themselves structurally on the bourgeois economy, the syndicalist unions tended to become the organisational counterparts of the very centralised apparatus they professed to oppose. By pleading the need to deal effectively with the tightly knit bourgeoisie and state machinery, reformist leaders in syndicalist unions often had little difficulty in shifting organisational control from the bottom to the top.*" [Murray Bookchin, **The Spanish Anarchists**, p. 123]

In addition, as the syndicalist unions grow in size and influence their initial radicalism is usually watered-down. This is because, "*since the unions must remain open to all those who desire to win from the masters better conditions of life, whatever their opinions may be …, they are naturally led to moderate their aspirations, first so that they should not frighten away those they wish to have with them, and because, in proportion as numbers increase, those with ideas who have initiated the movement remain buried in a majority that is only occupied with the petty interests of the moment.*" [Errico Malatesta, **Anarchism and Syndicalism**, p. 150] Which, ironically given that increased self-management is seen as a way of reducing tendencies towards bureaucracy, means that syndicalist unions have a tendency towards reformism simply because the majority of their members will be non-revolutionary if the union grows in size in non-revolutionary times (as can be seen from the development of the Swedish syndicalist union the SAC).

So, if the union's militant strategy succeeds in winning reforms, more and more workers will join it. This influx of non-libertarians must, in a self-managed organisation, exert a de-radicalising influence on the unions politics and activities in non-revolutionary times. The syndicalist would argue that the process of struggling for reforms combined with the educational effects of participation and self-management will reduce this influence and, of course, they are right. However, non-syndicalist anarchists would counter this by arguing that the libertarian influences generated by struggle and participation would be strengthened by the work of anarchist groups and, without this work, the de-radicalising influences would outweigh the libertarian ones. In addition, the success of a syndicalist union must be partly determined by the general level of class struggle. In periods of great struggle, the membership will be more radical than in quiet periods and it is quiet periods which cause the most difficulties for syndicalist unions. With a moderate membership the revolutionary aims and tactics of the union will also become moderate. As one academic writer on French syndicalism put it, syndicalism *"was always based on workers acting in the economic arena to better their conditions, build class consciousness, and prepare for revolution. The need to survive and build a working-class movement had always forced syndicalists to adapt themselves to the exigencies of the moment."* [Barbara Mitchell, *"French Syndicalism: An Experiment in Practical Anarchism"*, pp. 25-41, **Revolutionary Syndicalism**, Marcel van der Linden and Wayne Thorpe (eds.), p. 25]

As can be seen from the history of many syndicalist unions (and, obviously, mainstream unions too) this seems to be the case — the libertarian tendencies are outweighed by the de-radicalising ones. This can also be seen from the issue of collective bargaining:

> *"The problem of collective bargaining foreshadowed the difficulty of maintaining syndicalist principles in developed capitalist societies. Many organisations within the international syndicalist movement initially repudiated collective agreements with employers on the grounds that by a collaborative sharing of responsibility for work discipline, such agreements would expand bureaucratisation within the unions, undermine revolutionary spirit, and restrict the freedom of action that workers were always to maintain against the class enemy. From an early date, however, sometimes after a period of suspicion and resistance, many workers gave up this position. In the early decades of the century it became clear that to maintain or gain a mass membership, syndicalist unions had to accept collective bargaining."* [Marcel van der Linden and Wayne Thorpe, **Op. Cit.**, p. 19]

Thus, for most anarchists, *"the Trade Unions are, by their very nature reformist and never revolutionary. The revolutionary spirit must be introduced, developed and maintained by the constant actions of revolutionaries who work from within their ranks as well as from outside, but it cannot be the normal, natural definition of the Trade Unions function."* [Malatesta, **Errico Malatesta: His Life and Ideas**, p. 117]

This does not mean that anarchists should not work within labour organisations. Nor does it mean rejecting anarcho-syndicalist unions as an anarchist tactic. Far from it. Rather it is a case of recognising these organisations for what they are, reformist organisations which are not an end in themselves but one (albeit, important) means of preparing the way for the achievement of anarchism. Neither does it mean that anarchists should not try to make labour organisations as anarchistic as possible or have anarchist objectives. Working within the labour movement (at the rank and file level, of course) is essential to gain influence for anarchist ideas, just as is working with unorganised workers. But this does not mean that the unions are revolutionary by their very nature, as syndicalism implies. As history shows, and as syndicalists themselves are aware, the vast majority of unions are reformist. Non-syndicalist anarchists argue there is a reason for that and syndicalist unions are not immune to these tendencies just because they call themselves revolutionary. Due to these tendencies, non-syndicalist anarchists stress the need to organise as anarchists first and foremost in order to influence the class struggle and encourage the creation of autonomous workplace and community organisations to fight that struggle. Rather than fuse the anarchist and working class movement, non-syndicalist anarchists stress the importance of anarchists organising as anarchists to influence the working class movement.

All this does not mean that purely anarchist organisations or individual anarchists cannot become reformist. Of course they can (just look at the Spanish FAI which along with the CNT co-operated with the state during the Spanish Revolution). However, unlike syndicalist unions, the anarchist organisation is not pushed towards reformism due to its role within society. That is an important difference — the institutional factors are not present for the anarchist federation as they are for the syndicalist union federation.

The second reason why many anarchists are not anarcho-syndicalists is the question of whether syndicalist unions are sufficient in themselves to create anarchy. Pierre Monatte, a French syndicalist, argued that *"Syndicalism, as the [CGT's] Congress of Amiens proclaimed in 1906, is sufficient unto itself"* as *"the working class, having at last attained majority, means to be self-sufficient and to rely on no-one else for its emancipation."* [**The Anarchist Reader**, p. 219]

This idea of self-sufficiency means that the anarchist and the syndicalist movement must be fused into one, with syndicalism taking the role of both anarchist group and labour union. Thus a key difference between anarcho-syndicalists and other anarchists is over the question of the need for a specifically anarchist organisation. While most anarchists are sympathetic to anarcho-syndicalism, few totally subscribe to anarcho-syndicalist ideas in their pure form. This is because, in its pure form, syndicalism rejects the idea of anarchist groups and instead considers the union as **the** focal point of social struggle and anarchist activism. However, an anarcho-syndicalist may support a specific anarchist federation to work within the union and outside.

So anarchists critical of anarcho-syndicalism are also active in the labour movement, working with the rank and file while keeping their own identity as anarchists and organising as anarchists. Thus Malatesta: *"In the past I deplored that the comrades isolated themselves from the working-class movement. Today I deplore that many of us, falling into the contrary extreme, let themselves* be swallowed up in the same movement." [**Op. Cit.**, p. 225] In the eyes of other anarchists anarcho-syndicalism in its "pure" (revolutionary syndicalist) form makes the error of confusing the anarchist and union movement and so ensures that the resulting movement can do neither work well: "*Every fusion or confusion between the anarchist movement and the trade union movement ends, either in rendering the later unable to carry out its specific task or by weakening, distorting, or extinguishing the anarchist spirit.*" [Malatesta, **Errico Malatesta: His Life and Ideas**, p. 123]

Most anarchists agree with Malatesta when he argued that "*anarchists must not want the Trade Unions to be anarchist, but they must act within their ranks in favour of anarchist aims, as individuals, as groups and as federations of groups... [I]n the situation as it is, and recognising that the social development of one's workmates is what it is, the anarchist groups should not expect the workers' organisation to act as if they were anarchist, but should make every effort to induce them to approximate as much as possible to the anarchist method.*" [**Op. Cit.**, pp. 124-5] Given that it appears to be the case that labour unions **are** by nature reformist, they cannot be expected to be enough in themselves when creating a free society. Hence the need for anarchists to organise **as anarchists** as well as alongside their fellow workers as workers in order to spread anarchist ideas on tactics and aims. This activity within existing unions does not necessarily mean attempting to "reform" the union in a libertarian manner (although some anarchists would support this approach). Rather it means working with the rank and file of the unions and trying to create autonomous workplace organisations, independent of the trade union bureaucracy and organised in a libertarian way.

This involves creating anarchist organisations separate from but which (in part) work within the labour movement for anarchist ends. Let us not forget that the syndicalist organisation is the union, it organises all workers regardless of their politics. A "union" which just let anarchists join would not be a union, it would be an anarchist group organised in the workplace. As anarcho-syndicalists themselves are aware, an anarcho-syndicalist union is not the same as a union of anarcho-syndicalists. How can we expect an organisation made up of non-anarchists be totally anarchist? Due to this, tendencies always appeared within syndicalist unions that were reformist and because of this most anarchists, including many anarcho-syndicalists we must note, argue that there is a need for anarchists to work within the rank and file of the unions to spread their anarchist ideals and aims, and this implies anarchist organisations separate from the labour movement, even if that movement is based on syndicalist unions.

As Bakunin argued, the anarchist organisation "*is the necessary complement to the International [i.e. the union federation]. But the International and the Alliance [the anarchist federation], while having the same ultimate aims, perform different functions. The International endeavours to unify the working masses ... regardless of nationality or religious and political beliefs, into one compact body: the Alliance, on the other hand, tries to give these masses a really revolutionary direction.*" This did not mean that the Alliance was imposing a foreign theory onto the members of the unions, because the "*programs of one and the other ... differ only in the degree of their revolutionary development ... The program of the*

Alliance represents the fullest unfolding of the International." [**Bakunin on Anarchism**, p. 157] Nor did it imply that anarchists think that unions and other forms of popular organisations should be controlled by anarchists. Far from it! Anarchists are the strongest supporters of the autonomy of all popular organisations. As we indicated in section J.3.6, anarchists desire to influence popular organisations by the strength of our ideas within the rank and file and **not** by imposing our ideas on them.

In addition to these major points of disagreement, there are minor ones as well. For example, many anarchists dislike the emphasis syndicalists place on the workplace and see "*in syndicalism a shift in focus from the commune to the trade union, from all of the oppressed to the industrial proletariat alone, from the streets to the factories, and, in emphasis at least, from insurrection to the general strike.*" [Bookchin, **Op. Cit.**, p. 123] However, most anarcho-syndicalists are well aware that life exists outside the workplace and so this disagreement is largely one of emphasis. Similarly, many anarchists disagreed with the early syndicalist argument that a general strike was enough to create a revolution. They argued, with Malatesta in the forefront, that while a general strike would be "*an excellent means for starting the social revolution*" it would be wrong to think that it made "*armed insurrection unnecessary*" since the "*first to die of hunger during a general strike would not be the bourgeois, who dispose of all the stores, but the workers.*" In order for this **not** to occur, the workers would need to "*take over production*" which are protected by the police and armed forces and this meant "*insurrection.*" [Malatesta, **The Anarchist Reader**, pp. 223-4] Again, however, most modern syndicalists accept this to be the case and see the "*expropriatory general strike,*" in the words of French syndicalist Pierre Besnard, as "*clearly **insurrectional.***" [quoted by Vernon Richards, **Errico Malatesta: His Life and Ideas**, p. 288] We mention this purely to counter Leninist claims that syndicalists subscribe to the same ideas they did in the 1890s.

Despite our criticisms we should recognise that the difference between anarchists and anarcho-syndicalists are slight and (often) just a case of emphasis. Most anarchists support anarcho-syndicalist unions where they exist and often take a key role in creating and organising them. Similarly, many self-proclaimed anarcho-syndicalists also support specific organisations of anarchists to work within and outwith the syndicalist union. Syndicalist unions, where they exist, are far more progressive than any other union. Not only are they democratic unions and create an atmosphere where anarchist ideas are listened to with respect but they also organise and fight in a way that breaks down the divisions into leaders and led, doers and watchers. On its own this is very good but not good enough. For non-syndicalist anarchists, the missing element is an organisation winning support for anarchist ideas and tactics both within revolutionary unions and everywhere else working class people come together.

J.4

What trends in society aid anarchist activity?

In this section we will examine some modern trends which we regard as being potential openings for anarchists to organise and which point in an anarchist direction. These trends are of a general nature, partly as a product of social struggle, partly as a response to economic and social crisis, partly involving people's attitudes to big government and big business, partly in relation to the communications revolution we are currently living through, and so on.

Of course, looking at modern society we see multiple influences, changes which have certain positive aspects in some directions but negative ones in others. For example, the business-inspired attempts to decentralise or reduce (certain) functions of governments should in the abstract be welcomed by anarchists for they lead to the reduction of government. In practice such a conclusion is deeply suspect simply because these developments are being pursued to increase the power and influence of capital as well as to increase wage-labour to, and exploitation by, the economic master class and to undermine working class power and autonomy. As such, they are as anti-libertarian as the status quo (as Proudhon stressed, anarchism is *the denial of Government and of Property."* [**Property is Theft!**, p. 559]). Similarly, increases in self-employment can be seen, in the abstract, as reducing wage slavery. However, if, in practice, this increase is due to corporations encouraging "independent" contractors in order to cut wages and worsen working conditions, increase job insecurity and undermine paying for health and other employee packages then it is hardly a positive sign. Obviously increases in self-employment would be different if it were the result of an increase in the number of co-operatives, for example.

Thus few anarchists celebrate many apparently "libertarian" developments as they are not the product of social movements and activism, but are the product of elite lobbying for private aid and power. Decreasing the power of the state in (certain) areas while leaving (or increasing) the power of capital is a retrograde step in most, if not all, ways. Needless to say, this "rolling back" of the state does not bring into question its role as defender of property and the interests of the capitalist class — nor could it, as it is the ruling class who introduces and supports these developments.

In this section, we aim to discuss tendencies from **below**, not above — tendencies which can truly "roll back" the state rather than reduce its functions purely to that of the armed thug of property. The tendencies we discuss here are not the be all nor end all of anarchist activism or tendencies. We discuss many of the more traditionally anarchist "openings" in section J.5 (such as industrial and community unionism, mutual credit, co-operatives, modern schools and so on) and so will not do so here. However, it is important to stress here that such "traditional" openings are not being downplayed — indeed, much of what we discuss here can only become fully libertarian in combination with these more "traditional" forms of **"anarchy in action."**

For a lengthy discussion of anarchistic trends in society, we recommend Colin Ward's classic book **Anarchy in Action**. Ward covers many areas in which anarchistic tendencies have been expressed, far more than we can cover here. The libertarian tendencies in society are many. No single work could hope to do them justice.

J.4.1 Why is social struggle a good sign?

Simply because it shows that people are unhappy with the existing society and, more importantly, are trying to change at least some part of it. It suggests that certain parts of the population have reflected on their situation and, potentially at least, seen that **by their own actions** they can influence and change it for the better. Given that the ruling minority draws its strength by the acceptance and acquiescence of the majority, the fact that a part of that majority no longer accepts and acquiesces is a positive sign. After all, if the majority did not accept the status quo and acted to change it, the class and state system could not survive. Any hierarchical society survives because those at the bottom follow the orders of those above it. Social struggle suggests that some people are considering their own interests, thinking for themselves and saying "no" and this, by its very nature, is an important, indeed, the most important, tendency towards anarchism. It suggests that people are rejecting the old ideas which hold the system up, acting upon this rejection and creating new ways of doing things.

"Our social institutions," argued Alexander Berkman, *"are founded on certain ideas; as long as the latter are generally believed, the institutions built upon them are safe. Government remains strong because people think political authority and legal compulsion necessary. Capitalism will continue as long as such an economic system is considered adequate and just. The weakening of the ideas which support the evil and oppressive present-day conditions means the ultimate breakdown of government and capitalism."* [**What is Anarchism?**, p. xii]

Social struggle is the most obvious sign of this change of perspective, this change in ideas, this progress towards freedom.

Social struggle is expressed by direct action. We have discussed both social struggle (section J.1) and direct action (section J.2) before and some readers may wonder why we are covering this again here. We do so as we are discussing what trends in society help anarchist activity, it would be wrong **not** to highlight social struggle and direct action here. This is because these factors are key tendencies towards anarchism as social struggle is the means by which people create the new world in the shell of the old, transforming themselves and society.

So social struggle is a good sign as it suggests that people are thinking for themselves, considering their own interests and working together collectively to change things for the better. As the French syndicalist Emile Pouget argued:

> *"Direct action ... means that the working class, forever*

bridling at the existing state of affairs, expects nothing from outside people, powers or forces, but rather creates its own conditions of struggle and looks to itself for its methodology ... Direct Action thus implies that the working class subscribes to notions of freedom and autonomy instead of genuflecting before the principle of authority. Now, it is thanks to this authority principle, the pivot of the modern world — democracy being its latest incarnation — that the human being, tied down by a thousand ropes, moral as well as material, is bereft of any opportunity to display will and initiative." [**Direct Action**, p. 1]

Social struggle means that people come into opposition with the boss and other authorities such as the state and the dominant morality. This challenge to existing authorities generates two related processes: the tendency of those involved to begin taking over the direction of their own activities and the development of solidarity with each other. Firstly, in the course of a struggle, such as a strike, occupation, boycott, and so on, the ordinary life of people, in which they act under the constant direction of the bosses or state, ceases, and they have to think, act and co-ordinate their actions for themselves. This reinforces the expression towards autonomy that the initial refusal that led to the struggle indicates. Secondly, in the process of struggle those involved learn the importance of solidarity, of working with others in a similar situation, in order to win. This means the building of links of support, of common interests, of organisation. The practical need for solidarity to help win the struggle is the basis for the solidarity required for a free society to be viable.

Therefore the real issue in social struggle is that it is an attempt by people to wrestle at least part of the power over their own lives away from the managers, state officials and so on who currently have it and exercise it themselves. This is, by its very nature, anarchistic and libertarian. Thus we find politicians, managers and property owners denouncing strikes and other forms of direct action. This is logical. As direct action challenges the real power-holders in society and because, if carried to its logical conclusion, it would remove them, social struggle and direct action can be considered in essence a revolutionary process.

Moreover, the very act of using direct action suggests a transformation within the people using it. *"Direct action's very powers to fertilise,"* argued Pouget, *"reside in such exercises in imbuing the individual with a sense of his own worth and in extolling such worth. It marshals human resourcefulness, tempers characters and focuses energies. It teaches self-confidence! And self-reliance! And self-mastery! And shifting for oneself!"* Moreover, *"direct action has an unmatched educational value: It teaches people to reflect, to make decisions and to act. It is characterised by a culture of autonomy, an exaltation of individuality and is a fillip to initiative, to which it is the leaven. And this superabundance of vitality and burgeoning of 'self' in no way conflicts with the economic fellowship that binds the workers one with another and far from being at odds with their common interests, it reconciles and bolsters these: the individual's independence and activity can only erupt into splendour and intensity by sending its roots deep into the fertile soil of common agreement."* [**Op. Cit.**, p. 2 and p. 5]

Social struggle is the beginning of a transformation of the people involved and their relationships to each other. While its external expression lies in contesting the power of existing authorities, its inner expression is the transformation of people from passive and isolated competitors into empowered, self-directing, self-governing co-operators. Moreover, this process widens considerably what people think is "possible." Through struggle, by collective action, the fact people **can** change things is driven home, that **they** have the power to govern themselves and the society they live in. Thus struggle can change people's conception of "what is possible" and encourage them to try and create a better world. As Kropotkin argued:

*"since the times of the [first] International Working Men's Association, the anarchists have always advised taking an active part in those workers' organisations which carry on the **direct** struggle of labour against capital and its protector — the State.*

"Such a struggle ...: permits the worker to obtain some temporary improvements ..., while it opens his [or her] eyes to the evil that is done by capitalism and the State ... , and wakes up his [or her] thoughts concerning the possibility of organising consumption, production, and exchange without the intervention of the capitalist and the State." [**Anarchism**, p. 171]

In other words, social struggle has a **radicalising** and **politicising** effect, an effect which brings into a new light existing society and the possibilities of a better world (direct action, in Pouget's words, *"develops the feeling for human personality as well as the spirit of initiative ... it shakes people out of their torpor and steers them to consciousness."* [**Op. Cit.**, p. 5]). The practical need to unite and resist the boss also helps break down divisions within the working class. Those in struggle start to realise that they need each other to give them the power necessary to get improvements, to change things. Thus solidarity spreads and overcomes divisions between black and white, male and female, heterosexual and homosexual, trades, industries, nationalities and so on. The real need for solidarity to win the fight helps to undermine artificial divisions and show that there are only two groups in society, the oppressed and the oppressors. Moreover, struggle as well as transforming those involved is also the basis for transforming society as a whole simply because, as well as producing transformed individuals, it also produces new forms of organisation, organisations created to co-ordinate their struggle and which can, potentially at least, become the framework of a libertarian socialist society (see section I.2.3).

Thus anarchists argue that social struggle opens the eyes of those involved to self-esteem and a sense of their own strength, and the groupings it forms at its prompting are living, vibrant associations where libertarian principles usually come to the fore. We find almost all struggles developing new forms of organisation, forms which are often based on direct democracy, federalism and decentralisation. If we look at every major revolution, we find people creating mass organisations such as workers' councils, factory committees, neighbourhood assemblies and so on as a means of taking back the power to govern their own lives, communities and workplaces. In this way social struggle and direct action lay the foundations for the future. By actively taking part in social life, people are drawn into creating new forms of organisation, new ways of doing things. In this way they educate themselves in participation, in self-government, in initiative and in asserting themselves. They begin to realise that the only alternative to management by others is self-management and organise to achieve it.

Given that remaking society has to begin at the bottom, this finds its expression in direct action, individuals taking the initiative and using the power they have just generated by collective action and organisation to change things by their own efforts. Social struggle is therefore a two way transformation — the external transformation of society by the creation of new organisations and the changing of the power relations within it and the internal transformation of those who take part in the struggle. This is key:

> "Whatever may be the practical results of the struggle for immediate gains, the greatest value lies in the struggle itself. For thereby workers learn that the bosses interests are opposed to theirs and that they cannot improve their conditions, and much less emancipate themselves, except by uniting and becoming stronger than the bosses. If they succeed in getting what they demand, they will be better off ... and immediately make greater demands and have greater needs. If they do not succeed they will be led to study the causes of their failure and recognise the need for closer unity and greater activism and they will in the end understand that to make their victory secure and definitive, it is necessary to destroy capitalism. The revolutionary cause, the cause of the moral elevation and emancipation of the workers must benefit by the fact that workers unite and struggle for their interests." [Malatesta, **Errico Malatesta: His Life and Ideas**, p. 191]

Hence Nestor Makhno's comment that "*[i]n fact, it is only through that struggle for freedom, equality and solidarity that you reach an understanding of anarchism.*" [**The Struggle Against the State and other Essays**, p. 71] The creation of an anarchist society is a **process** and social struggle is the key anarchistic tendency within society which anarchists look for, encourage and support. Its radicalising and transforming nature is the key to the growth of anarchist ideas, the creation of libertarian structures and alternatives within capitalism (structures which may, one day, replace it) and the creation of anarchists and those sympathetic to anarchist ideas. Its importance cannot be underestimated!

J.4.2 Won't social struggle do more harm than good?

It is often argued that social struggle, resisting the powerful and the wealthy, will just do more harm than good. Employers often use this approach in anti-union propaganda, for example, arguing that creating a union will force the company to close and move to less "militant" areas.

There is some truth in this. Yes, social struggle can lead to bosses moving to more compliant workforces — but this also happens in periods lacking social struggle too! If we look at the down-sizing mania that gripped the U.S. in the 1980s and 1990s, we see companies firing tens of thousands of people during a period when unions were weak, workers scared about losing their jobs and class struggle basically becoming mostly informal, atomised and "underground." Moreover, this argument actually indicates the need for anarchism. It is a damning indictment of any social system that it requires people to kow-tow to their masters otherwise they will suffer economic hardship. It boils down to the argument "*do what you are told, otherwise you will regret it.*" Any system based on that maxim is an affront to human dignity!

It would, in a similar fashion, be easy to "prove" that slave rebellions are against the long term interests of the slaves. After all, by rebelling the slaves will face the anger of their masters. Only by submitting without question can they avoid this fate and, perhaps, be rewarded by better conditions. Of course, the evil of slavery would continue but by submitting to it they can ensure their life can become better. Needless to say, any thinking and feeling person would quickly dismiss this reasoning as missing the point and being little more than apologetics for an evil social system that treated human beings as things. The same can be said for the argument that social struggles within capitalism do more harm than good. It betrays a slave mentality unfitting for human beings (although fitting for those who desire to live off the backs of workers or desire to serve those who do).

Moreover, this kind of argument ignores a few key points.

Firstly, by resistance the conditions of the oppressed can be maintained or even improved. If the boss knows that their decisions will be resisted they may be less inclined to impose speed-ups, longer hours and so on. If, on the other hand, they know that their employees will agree to anything then there is every reason to expect them to impose all kinds of oppressions, just as a state will impose draconian laws if it knows that it can get away with it. History is full of examples of non-resistance producing greater evils in the long term and of resistance producing numerous important reforms and improvements (such as higher wages, shorter hours, the right to vote for working class people and women, freedom of speech, the end of slavery, trade union rights and so on).

So social struggle has been proven time and time again to gain successful reforms. For example, before the 8 hour day movement of 1886 in America most companies argued they could not introduce that reform without going bust. However, after displaying a militant mood and conducting an extensive strike campaign, hundreds of thousands of workers discovered that their bosses had been lying and they got shorter hours. Indeed, the history of the labour movement shows what bosses say they can afford and the reforms workers can get via struggle are somewhat at odds. Given the asymmetry of information between workers and bosses, this is unsurprising as workers can only guess at what is available and bosses like to keep their actual finances hidden. Even the threat of labour struggle can be enough to gain improvements. For example, Henry Ford's $5 day is often used as an example of capitalism rewarding good workers. However, this substantial pay increase was largely motivated by the unionisation drive by the **Industrial Workers of the World** among Ford workers in the summer of 1913. [Harry Braverman, **Labour**

and Monopoly Capitalism, p. 144] More recently, it was the mass non-payment campaign against the poll-tax in Britain during the late 1980s and early 1990s which helped ensure its defeat. In the 1990s, France also saw the usefulness of direct action. Two successive prime ministers (Edouard Balladur and Alain Juppe) tried to impose large scale neo-liberal "reform" programmes that swiftly provoked mass demonstrations and general strikes amongst students, workers, farmers and others. Confronted by crippling disruptions, both governments gave in.

Secondly, and in some ways more importantly, the radicalising effect of social struggle can open new doors for those involved, liberate their minds, empower them and create the potential for deep social change. Without resistance to existing forms of authority a free society cannot be created as people adjust themselves to authoritarian structures and accept "what is" as the only possibility. By resisting, people transform and empower themselves as well as transforming society. New possibilities can be seen (possibilities before dismissed as "utopian") and, via the organisation and action required to win reforms, the framework for these possibilities (i.e. of a new, libertarian, society) created. The transforming and empowering effect of social struggle is expressed well by Nick DiGaetano, a one-time Wobbly who had joined during the 1912 Lawrence strike and then became a UAW-CIO shop floor militant:

> "the workers of my generation from the early days up to now [1958] had what you might call a labour insurrection in changing from a plain, humble, submissive creature into a man. The union made a man out of him … I am not talking about the benefits … I am talking about the working conditions and how they affected the men in the plant … Before they were submissive. Today they are men." [quoted by David Brody, "Workplace Contractualism in comparative perspective", pp. 176-205, Helson Lichtenstein and Howell John Harris (eds.), **Industrial Democracy in America**, p. 204]

Other labour historians note the same radicalising process elsewhere (modern day activists could give more examples!):

> "The contest [over wages and conditions] so pervaded social life that the ideology of acquisitive individualism, which explained and justified a society regulated by market mechanisms and propelled by the accumulation of capital, was challenged by an ideology of mutualism, rooted in working-class bondings and struggles … Contests over pennies on or off existing piece rates had ignited controversies over the nature and purpose of the American republic itself." [David Montgomery, **The Fall of the House of Labour**, p. 171]

This radicalising effect is far more dangerous to authoritarian structures than better pay, more liberal laws and so on as they need submissiveness to work. Little wonder that direct action is usually denounced as pointless or harmful by those in power or their spokespersons for direct action will, taken to its logical conclusion, put them out of a job! Struggle, therefore, holds the possibility of a free society as well as of improvements in the here and now. It also changes the perspectives of those involved, creating new ideas and

values to replace the ones of capitalism.

Thirdly, it ignores the fact that such arguments do not imply the end of social struggle and working class resistance and organisation, but rather its **extension.** If, for example, your boss argues that they will move to Mexico if you do not "shut up and put up" then the obvious solution is to make sure the workers in Mexico are also organised! Bakunin argued this basic point over one hundred years ago, and it is still true: "in the long run the relatively tolerable position of workers in one country can be maintained only on condition that it be more or less the same in other countries." The "conditions of labour cannot get worse or better in any particular industry without immediately affecting the workers in other industries, and that workers of all trades are inter-linked with real and indissoluble ties of solidarity." Ultimately, "in those countries the workers work longer hours for less pay; and the employers there can sell their products cheaper, successfully competing against conditions where workers working less earn more, and thus force the employers in the latter countries to cut wages and increase the hours of their workers." [**The Political Philosophy of Bakunin**, pp. 306-7] Bakunin's solution was to organise internationally, to stop this undercutting of conditions by solidarity between workers. As history shows, his argument was correct. Thus it is **not** social struggle or militancy which perhaps could have negative results, just **isolated** militancy, struggle which ignores the ties of solidarity required to win, extend and keep reforms and improvements. In other words, our resistance must be as transnational as capitalism is.

The idea that social struggle and working class organisation are harmful was expressed constantly in the 1970s and 80s. With the post-war Keynesian consensus crumbling, the "New Right" argued that trade unions (and strikes) hampered growth and that wealth redistribution (i.e. welfare schemes which returned some of the surplus value workers produced back into our own hands) hindered "wealth creation" (i.e. economic growth). Do not struggle over income, they argued, let the market decide and everyone will be better off.

This argument was dressed up in populist clothes. Thus we find the right-wing guru F.A. von Hayek arguing that, in the case of Britain, the "legalised powers of the unions have become the biggest obstacle to raising the standards of the working class as a whole. They are the chief cause of the unnecessarily big differences between the best- and worse-paid workers." He maintained that "the elite of the British working class … derive their relative advantages by keeping workers who are **worse off** from improving their position." Moreover, he "predict[ed] that the average worker's income would rise fastest in a country where relative wages are flexible, and where the exploitation of workers by monopolistic trade union organisations of specialised workers are effectively outlawed." [**1980s Unemployment and the Unions**, p. 107, p. 108 and p. 110]

Now, if von Hayek's claims were true we could expect that in the aftermath of Thatcher government's trade union reforms we would have seen: a rise in economic growth (usually considered as **the** means to improve living standards for workers by the right); that this growth would be more equally distributed; a decrease in the differences between high and low paid workers; a reduction in the percentage of low paid workers as they improved their positions when freed from union "exploitation"; and that wages rise fastest in countries with the highest wage flexibility. Unfortunately for von Hayek, the actual trajectory of the British economy exposed his claims as nonsense.

Looking at each of his claims in turn we discover that rather than "exploit" other workers, trade unions are an essential means to shift income from capital to labour (which is why capital fights labour organisers tooth and nail). And, equally important, labour militancy aids **all** workers by providing a floor under which wages cannot drop (non-unionised firms have to offer similar programs to prevent unionisation and be able to hire workers) and by maintaining aggregate demand. This positive role of unions in aiding **all** workers can be seen by comparing Britain before and after Thatcher's von Hayek inspired trade union and labour market reforms.

There has been a steady fall in growth in the UK since the trade union "reforms". In the "bad old days" of the 1970s, with its strikes and "militant unions" growth was 2.4% in Britain. It fell to 2% in the 1980s and fell again to 1.2% in the 1990s. A similar pattern of slowing growth as wage flexibility and market reform has increased can be seen in the US economy (it was 4.4% in the 1960s, 3.2% in the 1970s, 2.8% in the 1980s and 1.9% in the first half of the 1990s). [Larry Elliot and Dan Atkinson, **The Age of Insecurity**, p. 236] Given that the free-market right proclaims higher economic growth is the only way to make workers better off, growth rates have steadily fallen internationally since the domination of their ideology. Thus growth of output per head in the USA, Europe, Japan and the OECD countries between 1979 to 1990 was lower than in 1973-9, and 1990-2004 lower still. The deregulation, privatisation, anti-union laws and other neo-liberal policies have "failed to bring an increase in the growth rate." [Andrew Glyn, **Capitalism Unleashed**, p. 131] What growth spurts there have been were associated with speculative bubbles (in the American economy, dot. com stocks in the late 1990s and housing in the 2000s) which burst with disastrous consequences.

So the rate of "wealth creation" (economic growth) has steadily fallen as unions were "reformed" in line with von Hayek's ideology (and lower growth means that the living standards of the working class as a whole do not rise as fast as they did under the "exploitation" of the "monopolistic" trade unions).

If we look at the differences between the highest and lowest paid workers, we find that rather than decrease, they have in fact shown "a dramatic widening out of the distribution with the best-workers doing much better" since Thatcher was elected in 1979 [Andrew Glyn and David Miliband (eds.), **Paying for Inequality**, p. 100] This is important, as average figures can hide how badly those in the bottom (80%!) are doing. In an unequal society, the gains of growth are monopolised by the few and we would expect rising inequality over time alongside average growth. In America inequality has dramatically increased since the 1970s, with income and wealth growth in the 1980s going predominantly to the top 20% (and, in fact, mostly to the top 1% of the population). The bottom 80% of the population saw their wealth grow by 1.2% and their income by 23.7% in the 1980s, while for the top 20% the respective figures were 98.2% and 66.3% (the figures for the top 1% were 61.6% and 38.9%, respectively). [Edward N. Wolff, "How the Pie is Sliced", **The American Prospect**, no. 22, Summer 1995]

There has been a "fanning out of the pay distribution" with the gap between the top 10% of wage-earners increasing compared to those in the middle and bottom 10%. Significantly, in the neo-liberal countries the rise in inequality is "considerably higher" than in European ones. In America, for example, "real wages at the top grew by 27.2% between 1979 and 2003 as compared to 10.2% in the middle" while real wages for the bottom 10% "did not grow at all between 1979 and 2003." In fact, most of the gains in the top 10% "occurred amongst the top 5%, and two-thirds of it within the top 1%." Unsurprising, the neo-liberal countries of the UK, USA and New Zealand saw the largest increases in inequality. [Glyn, **Op. Cit.**, pp. 116-8 and p. 168]

Given that inequality has increased, the condition of the average worker must have suffered. For example, Ian Gilmore states that "[i]n the 1980s, for the first time for fifty years ... the poorer half of the population saw its share of total national income shirk." [**Dancing with Dogma**, p. 113] According to Noam Chomsky, "[d]uring the Thatcher decade, the income share of the bottom half of the population fell from one-third to one-fourth" and the between 1979 and 1992, the share of total income of the top 20% grew from 35% to 40% while that of the bottom 20% fell from 10% to 5%. In addition, the number of UK employees with weekly pay below the Council of Europe's "decency threshold" increased from 28.3% in 1979 to 37% in 1994. [**World Orders, Old and New**, p. 144 and p. 145] Moreover, "[b]ack in the early 1960s, the heaviest concentration of incomes fell at 80-90 per cent of the mean ... But by the early 1990s there had been a dramatic change, with the peak of the distribution falling at just 40-50 per cent of the mean. One-quarter of the population had incomes below half the average by the early 1990s as against 7 per cent in 1977 and 11 per cent in 1961." [Elliot and Atkinson, **Op. Cit.**, p. 235] "Overall," notes Takis Fotopoulos, "average incomes increased by 36 per cent during this period [1979-1991/2], but 70 per cent of the population had a below average increase in their income." [**Towards an Inclusive Democracy**, p. 113]

The reason for this rising inequality is not difficult to determine. When workers organise and strike, they can keep more of what they produce in their own hands. The benefits of productivity growth, therefore, can be spread. With unions weakened, such gains will accumulate in fewer hands and flood upwards. This is precisely what happened. Before (approximately) 1980 and the neo-liberal assault on unions, productivity and wages rose hand-in-hand in America, afterward productivity continued to rise while wages flattened. In fact, the value of the output of an average worker "has risen almost 50 percent since 1973. Yet the growing concentration of income in the hands of a small minority had proceeded so rapidly that we're not sure whether the typical American has gained **anything** from rising productivity." Rather than "trickle down" "the lion's share of economic growth in America over the past thirty years has gone to a small, wealthy minority." In short: "The big winners ... have been members of a very narrow elite: the top 1 percent or less of the population." [Paul Krugman, **The Conscience of a Liberal**, p. 124, p. 244 and p. 8]

Looking at America, after the Second World War the real income of the typical family ("exploited" by "monopolistic" trade unions) grew by 2.7% per year, with "incomes all through the income distribution grew at about the same rate." Since 1980 (i.e., after working people were freed from the tyranny of unions), "medium family income has risen only about 0.7 percent a year" Median household income "grew modestly" from 1973 to 2005, the total gain was about 16%. Yet this "modest gain" may "overstate" how well American families were doing, as it was achieved in part through longer working hours. For example, "a gain in family income that occurs because a spouse goes to work isn't the same thing as a wage increase. In particular it may carry hidden costs that offset some of the gains in money." This stagnation is, of course, being denied by the right. Yet, as Krugman memorably puts it: "Modern economists debate whether American median income has risen or fallen since the early 1970s. What's really telling is the fact that we're even having this debate." So while the average values may have gone up, because of "rising inequality, good performance in overall numbers like GDP hasn't translated into gains for ordinary workers." [Op. Cit., p. 55, pp. 126-7, p. 124 and p. 201]

Luckily for American capitalism a poll in 2000 found that 39% of Americans believe they are either in the wealthiest 1% or will be there "soon"! [Glyn, Op. Cit., p. 179] In fact, as we discussed in section B.7.2, social mobility has **fallen** under neo-liberalism — perhaps unsurprisingly as it is easier to climb a hill than a mountain. This is just as important as the explosion in inequality as the "free-market" right argue that dynamic social mobility makes up for wealth and income inequality. As Krugman notes, Americans "may believe that anyone can succeed through hard work and determination, but the facts say otherwise." In reality, mobility is "highest in the Scandinavian countries, and most results suggest that mobility is lower in the United States than it is in France, Canada, and maybe even in Britain. Not only don't Americans have equal opportunity, opportunity is less equal here than elsewhere in the West." Without the blinkers of free market capitalist ideology this should be unsurprising: "A society with highly unequal results is, more or less inevitably, a society with highly unequal opportunity, too." [Op. Cit., p. 247 and p. 249]

Looking at the claim that trade union members gained their "relative advantage by keeping workers who are **worse off** from improving their position" it would be fair to ask whether the percentage of workers in low-paid jobs decreased in Britain after the trade union reforms. In fact, the percentage of workers below the Low Pay Unit's definition of low pay (namely two-thirds of men's median earnings) **increased** — from 16.8% in 1984 to 26.2% in 1991 for men, 44.8% to 44.9% for women. For manual workers it rose by 15% to 38.4%, and for women by 7.7% to 80.7% (for non-manual workers the figures were 5.4% rise to 13.7% for men and a 0.5% rise to 36.6%). [Andrew Glyn and David Miliband (eds.), **Op. Cit.**, p.102] If unions **were** gaining at the expense of the worse off, you would expect a **decrease** in the number in low pay, **not** an increase. An OECD study concluded that "[t]ypically, countries with high rates of collective bargaining and trade unionisation tend to have low incidence of low paid employment." [**OECD Employment Outlook**, 1996, p. 94] Within America, we also discover that higher union density is associated with fewer workers earning around the minimum wage and that "right-to-work" states (i.e., those that pass anti-union laws) "tend to have lower wages, lower standard of living, and more workers earning around the minimum

wage." It is hard not to conclude that states "passed laws aimed at making unionisation more difficult would imply that they sought to maintain the monopoly power of employers at the expense of workers." [Oren M. Levin-Waldman, "The Minimum Wage and Regional Wage Structure: Implications for Income Distribution", pp. 635-57, **Journal of Economic Issues**, Vol. XXXVI, No. 3, p. 639 and p. 655]

As far as von Hayek's prediction on wage flexibility leading to the "average worker's income" rising fastest in a country where relative wages are flexible, it has been proved totally wrong. Between 1967 and 1971, real wages grew (on average) by 2.95% per year in the UK (nominal wages grew by 8.94%) [P. Armstrong, A. Glyn and J. Harrison, **Capitalism Since World War II**, p. 272]. In comparison, real household disposable income grew by just 0.5 percent between June 2006 and 2007. Average weekly earnings rose 2.9% between April 2006 and 2007 while inflation rose by 3.6% (Retail Prices Index) and 2.8% (Consumer Prices Index). [Elliot and Atkinson, **The Gods That Failed**, p. 163] This is part of a general pattern, with UK Real Wages per employee being an average 3.17% per year between 1960 and 1974, falling to 1.8% between 1980 and 1999. In America, the equivalent figures are 2.37% and 1.02%. [Eckhard Hein and Thorsten Schulten, **Unemployment, Wages and Collective Bargaining in the European Union**, p. 9] Looking at the wider picture, during the early 1970s when strikes and union membership increased, "real wage increases rose steadily to reach over 4% per year" in the West. However, after von Hayek's anti-union views were imposed, "real wages have grown very slowly." In anti-union America, the median wage was $13.62 in 2003 compared to $12.36 in 1979 (reckoned in 2003 prices). In Europe and Japan "average wages have done only a little better, having grown around 1% per year." [Glyn, **Op. Cit.**, p. 5 and p. 116] It gets worse as these are average figures. Given that inequality soared during this period the limited gains of the neo-liberal era were not distributed as evenly as before (in the UK, for example, wage growth was concentrated at the top end of society. [Elliot and Atkinson, **Fantasy Island**, p. 99]).

Nor can it be said that breaking the unions and lower real wages translated into lower unemployment in the UK as the average unemployment rate between 1996 and 1997 was 7.1% compared to 4.5% between 1975 and 1979 (the year Thatcher took power). The average between 1960 and 1974 was 1.87% compared to 8.7% over the whole Thatcherite period of 1980 to 1999. Perhaps this is not too surprising, given that (capitalist economic theology aside) unemployment "systematically weakens the bargaining power of trade unions." In short: "Neither on the theoretical nor empirical level can a strictly inverse relation between the real wage rate and the level of unemployment be derived." [Hein and Schulten, **Op. Cit.**, p. 9, p. 3 and p. 2] As we discussed in section C.1.5 this should come as no surprise to anyone with awareness of the real nature of unemployment and the labour market. So unemployment did not fall after the trade union reforms, quite the reverse: "By the time Blair came to power [in 1997], unemployment in Britain was falling, although it still remained higher than it had been when the [last Labour Government of] Callaghan left office in May 1979." [Elliot and Atkinson, **Age of Insecurity**, p. 258] To be fair, von Hayek did argue that falls in unemployment would be "a slow process" but nearly 20 years of far higher unemployment is moving backwards! So we have a stark contrast between the assertions of the right and the reality their ideology helped create. The reason for this difference is not hard to discover. As economist Paul Krugman correctly argues unions *"raise average wages for their membership; they also, indirectly and to a lesser extent, raise wages for similar workers … as nonunionised employers try to diminish the appeal of union drives to their workers … unions tend to narrow income gaps among blue-collar workers, by negotiating bigger wage increases for their worse-paid members … And nonunion employers, seeking to forestall union organisers, tend to echo this effect."* He argues that *"if there's a single reason blue-collar workers did so much better in the fifties than they had in the twenties, it was the rise of unions"* and that unions *"were once an important factor limiting income inequality, both because of their direct effect in raising their members' wages and because the union pattern of wage settlements … was … reflected in the labour market as a whole."* With the smashing of the unions came rising inequality, with the *"sharpest increases in wage inequality in the Western world have taken place in the United States and in Britain, both of which experience sharp declines in union membership."* Unions restrict inequality because *"they act as a countervailing force to management."* [**Op. Cit.**, p. 51, p. 49, p. 149 and p. 263]

So under the neo-liberal regime instigated by Thatcher and Reagan the power, influence and size of the unions were reduced considerably and real wage growth fell considerably — which is the **exact** opposite of von Hayek's predictions. Flexible wages and weaker unions have harmed the position of **all** workers (Proudhon: *"Contrary to all expectation! It takes an economist not to expect these things"* [**Property is Theft!**, p. 193]). So comparing the claims of von Hayek to what actually happened after trade union "reform" and the reduction of class struggle suggests that claims that social struggle is self-defeating are false (and self-serving, considering it is usually bosses, employer supported parties and economists who make these claims). A **lack** of social struggle has been correlated with low economic growth and often stagnant (even declining) wages. So while social struggle **may** make capital flee and other problems, lack of it is no guarantee of prosperity (quite the reverse, if the last quarter of the 20th century is anything to go by). Indeed, a lack of social struggle will make bosses be more likely to cut wages, worsen working conditions and so on — after all, they feel they can get away with it! Which brings home the fact that to make reforms last it is necessary to destroy capitalism.

Of course, no one can **know** that struggle will make things better. It is a guess; no one can predict the future. Not all struggles are successful and many can be very difficult. If the *"military is a role model for the business world"* (in the words of an ex-CEO of Hill & Knowlton Public Relations), and it is, then **any** struggle against it and other concentrations of power may, and often is, difficult and dangerous at times. [quoted by John Stauber and Sheldon Rampton in **Toxic Sludge Is Good For You!**, p. 47] But, as Zapata once said, *"better to die on your feet than live on your knees!"* All we can say is that social struggle can and does improve things and, in terms of its successes and transforming effect on those involved, well worth the potential difficulties it can create. Moreover, without struggle there is little chance of creating a free society, dependent

as it is on individuals who refuse to bow to authority and have the ability and desire to govern themselves. In addition, social struggle is always essential, not only to **win** improvements, but to **keep** them as well. In order to fully secure improvements you have to abolish capitalism and the state. Not to do so means that any reforms can and will be taken away (and if social struggle does not exist, they will be taken away sooner rather than later). Ultimately, most anarchists would argue that social struggle is not an option — we either do it or we put up with the all the petty (and not so petty) impositions of authority. If we do not say "no" then the powers that be will walk all over us.

As the history of neo-liberalism shows, a lack of social struggle is fully compatible with worsening conditions. Ultimately, if you want to be treated as a human being you have to stand up for your dignity — and that means thinking and rebelling. As Bakunin argued in **God and the State**, human freedom and development is based on these. Without rebellion, without social struggle, humanity would stagnate beneath authority forever and never be in a position to be free. So anarchists agree wholeheartedly with the Abolitionist Frederick Douglass:

> *"If there is no struggle, there is no progress. Those who profess to favour freedom, and yet depreciate agitation, are men who want crops without ploughing up the ground. They want rain without thunder and lightning. They want the ocean without the awful roar of its many waters.*
>
> *"This struggle may be a moral one; or it may be a physical one; or it may be both moral and physical; but it must be a struggle. Power concedes nothing without a demand. It never did and it never will. Find out just what a people will submit to, and you have found out the exact amount of injustice and wrong which will be imposed upon them; and these will continue till they are resisted with either words or blows, or with both. The limits of tyrants are prescribed by the endurance of those whom they oppress."* [**The Life and Writings of Frederick Douglass**, vol. 2, p. 437]

Of course, being utterly wrong has not dented von Hayek's reputation with the right nor stopped him being quoted in arguments in favour of flexibility and free market reforms (what can we expect? The right still quote Milton Friedman whose track-record was equally impressive). Still, why let the actual development of the economies influenced by von Hayek's ideology get in the way? Perhaps it is fortunate that he once argued that economic theories can *"never be verified or falsified by reference to facts. All that we can and must verify is the presence of our assumptions in the particular case."* [**Individualism and Economic Order**, p. 73] With such a position all is saved — the obvious problem is that capitalism is still not pure enough and the "reforms" must not only continue but be made deeper... As Kropotkin stressed, *"economists who continue to consider economic forces alone … without taking into account **the ideology of the State**, or the forces that each State necessarily places at the service of the rich … remain completely outside the realities of the economic and social world."* [quoted by Ruth Kinna, *"Fields of Vision: Kropotkin and Revolutionary Change"*, pp. 67-86, **SubStance**, Vol. 36, No. 2, pp. 72-3]

And, needless to say, while three decades of successful capitalist class war goes without mention in polite circles, documenting its results gets you denounced as advocating "class war"! It is more than past the time when working class people *should* wage a class war — particularly given the results of not doing so.

Anarchism is all about **"do it yourself"**: people helping each other out in order to secure a good society to live within and to protect, extend and enrich their personal freedom. As such anarchists are keenly aware of the importance of building alternatives to both capitalism and the state in the here and now. Only by creating practical alternatives can we show that anarchism is a viable possibility and train ourselves in the techniques and responsibilities of freedom:

> "If we put into practice the principles of libertarian communism within our organisations, the more advanced and prepared we will be on that day when we come to adopt it completely." [C.N.T. member, quoted by Graham Kelsey, **Anarchosyndicalism, Libertarian Communism and the State**, p. 79]

This idea (to quote the IWW) of "building a new world in the shell of the old" is a long standing one in anarchism. Proudhon during the 1848 revolution "propose[d] that a provisional committee be set up" in Paris and "liaise with similar committees" elsewhere in France. This would be "a body representative of the proletariat ..., **imperium in imperio** [a state within the state], in opposition to the bourgeois representatives." He proclaimed to working class people that "a new society be founded in the heart of the old society" for "the government can do nothing for you. But you can do everything for yourselves." [**Property is Theft!**, pp. 321-2] This was echoed by Bakunin (see section H.2.8) while for revolutionary syndicalists the aim was "to constitute within the bourgeois State a veritable socialist (economic and anarchic) State." [Fernand Pelloutier, quoted by Jeremy Jennings, **Syndicalism in France**, p. 22] By so doing we help create the environment within which individuals can manage their own affairs and develop their abilities to do so. In other words, we create **"schools of anarchism"** which lay the foundations for a better society as well as promoting and supporting social struggle against the current system. Make no mistake, the alternatives we discuss in this section are not an alternative to direct action and the need for social struggle - they are an expression of social struggle and a form of direct action. They are the framework by which social struggle can build and strengthen the anarchist tendencies within capitalist society which will ultimately replace it.

Therefore it is wrong to think that libertarians are indifferent to making life more bearable, even more enjoyable, under capitalism. A free society will not just appear from nowhere, it will be created by individuals and communities with a long history of social struggle and organisation. For as Wilheim Reich so correctly pointed out:

> "Quite obviously, a society that is to consist of 'free individuals,' to constitute a 'free community' and to administer itself, i.e. to 'govern itself,' cannot be suddenly created by decrees. It has to **evolve** organically." [**The Mass Psychology of Fascism**, p. 241]

It is this organic evolution that anarchists promote when they create libertarian alternatives within capitalist society. These alternatives (be they workplace or community unions, co-operatives, mutual banks, and so on) are marked by certain common features such as being self-managed, being based upon equality, decentralised and working with other groups and associations within a confederal network based upon mutual aid and solidarity. In other words, they are **anarchist** in both spirit and structure and so create a practical bridge between now and the future free society.

Anarchists consider the building of alternatives as a key aspect of their activity under capitalism. This is because they, like all forms of direct action, are **"schools of anarchy"** and also because they make the transition to a free society easier. "Through the organisations set up for the defence of their interests," in Malatesta's words, "the workers develop an awareness of the oppression they suffer and the antagonism that divides them from the bosses and as a result begin to aspire to a better life, become accustomed to collective struggle and solidarity and win those improvements that are possible within the capitalist and state regime." [**The Anarchist Revolution**, p. 95] By creating viable examples of **"anarchy in action"** we can show that our ideas are practical and convince people that they are not utopian. Therefore this section of the FAQ will indicate the alternatives anarchists support and **why** we support them.

The approach anarchists take to this activity could be termed **"social unionism"** — the collective action of groups to change certain aspects (and, ultimately, all aspects) of their lives. This takes many different forms in many different areas (some of which, not all, are discussed here) — but they share the same basic aspects of collective direct action, self-organisation, self-management, solidarity and mutual aid. These are a means "of raising the morale of the workers, accustom them to free initiative and solidarity in a struggle for the good of everyone and render them capable of imagining, desiring and putting into practice an anarchist life." [Malatesta, **Op. Cit.**, p. 28] Kropotkin summed up the anarchist perspective well when he argued that working class people had "to form their own organisations for a direct struggle against capitalism" and to "take possession of the necessaries for production, and to control production." [**Memoirs of a Revolutionist**, p. 359] As historian J. Romero Maura correctly summarised, the "anarchist revolution, when it came, would be essentially brought about by the working class. Revolutionaries needed to gather great strength and must beware of underestimating the strength of reaction" and so anarchists "logically decided that revolutionaries had better organise along the lines of labour organisations." ["The Spanish case", pp. 60-83, **Anarchism Today**, D. Apter and J. Joll (eds.), p. 66]

As will quickly become obvious in this discussion (as if it had not been so before!) anarchists are firm supporters of **"self-help,"** an expression that has been sadly corrupted (like freedom) by the right in recent times. Like freedom, self-help should be saved from the clutches of the right who have no real claim to that expression. Indeed, anarchism was created from and based itself upon working class self-help — for what other interpretation can be gathered from Proudhon's 1848 statement that *"the proletariat must emancipate itself"*? [**Op. Cit.,** p. 306] So Anarchists have great faith in the abilities of working class people to work out for themselves what their problems are and act to solve them.

Anarchist support and promotion of alternatives is a **key** aspect of this process of self-liberation, and so a key aspect of anarchism. While strikes, boycotts, and other forms of high profile direct action may be more "sexy" than the long and hard task of creating and building social alternatives, these are the nuts and bolts of creating a new world as well as the infrastructure which supports the other activities. These alternatives involve both combative organisations (such as community and workplace unions) as well as more defensive and supportive ones (such as co-operatives and mutual banks). Both have their part to play in the class struggle, although the combative ones are the most important in creating the spirit of revolt and the possibility of creating an anarchist society.

We must also stress that anarchists look to organic tendencies within social struggle as the basis of any alternatives we try to create. As Kropotkin put it, anarchism is based *"on an analysis of **tendencies of an evolution that is already going on in society**, and on **induction** therefrom as to the future."* It is *"representative ... of the creative, instructive power of the people themselves who aimed at developing institutions of common law in order to protect them from the power-seeking minority."* Anarchism bases itself on those tendencies that are created by the self-activity of working class people and while developing within capitalism are **in opposition** to it — such tendencies are expressed in organisational form as unions and other forms of workplace struggle, co-operatives (both productive and credit), libertarian schools, and so on. For anarchism was *"born among the people — in the struggles of real life and not in the philosopher's studio"* and owes its *"origin to the constructive, creative activity of the people ... and to a protest — a revolt against the external force which had thrust itself upon"* social institutions. [**Anarchism**, p. 158, p. 147, p. 150 and p. 149] This *"creative activity"* is expressed in the organisations created in the class struggle by working people, some of which we discuss in this section of the FAQ. Therefore, the alternatives anarchists support should not be viewed in isolation of social struggle and working class resistance to hierarchy — the reverse in fact, as these alternatives are almost always expressions of that struggle.

Lastly, we should note we do not list all the forms of organisation anarchists create. For example, we have ignored solidarity groups (for workers on strike or in defence of struggles in other countries) and organisations which are created to campaign against or for certain issues or reforms. Anarchists are in favour of such organisations and work within them to spread anarchist ideas, tactics and organisational forms. However, these interest groups (while very useful) do not provide a framework for lasting change as do the ones we highlight below (see section J.1.4 for more details on anarchist opinions on such "single issue" campaigns). We have also ignored what have been called *"intentional communities."* This is when a group of individuals squat or buy land and other resources

within capitalism and create their own anarchist commune in it. Most anarchists reject this idea as capitalism and the state must be fought, not ignored. In addition, due to their small size, they are rarely viable experiments in communal living and nearly always fail after a short time (for a good summary of Kropotkin's attitude to such communities, which can be taken as typical, see Graham Purchase's **Evolution & Revolution** [pp. 122-125]). Dropping out will not stop capitalism and the state and while such communities may try to ignore the system, they will find that the system will not ignore them — they will come under competitive and ecological pressures from capitalism whether they like it or not assuming they avoid direct political interference.

So the alternatives we discuss here are attempts to create anarchist alternatives within capitalism and which aim to **change** it (either by revolutionary or evolutionary means). They are based upon **challenging** capitalism and the state, not ignoring them by dropping out. Only by a process of direct action and building alternatives which are relevant to our daily lives can we revolutionise and change both ourselves and society.

J.5.1
What is community unionism?

Community unionism is our term for the process of creating participatory communities (called "communes" in classical anarchism) within the current society in order to transform it.

Basically, a community union is the creation of interested members of a community who decide to form an organisation to fight against injustice and for improvements locally. It is a forum by which inhabitants can raise issues that affect themselves and others and provide a means of solving these problems. As such, it is a means of directly involving local people in the life of their own communities and collectively solving the problems facing them as both individuals and as part of a wider society. In this way, local people take part in deciding what affects them and their community and create a self-managed "dual power" to the local and national state. They also, by taking part in self-managed community assemblies, develop their ability to participate and manage their own affairs, so showing that the state is unnecessary and harmful to their interests. Politics, therefore, is not separated into a specialised activity that only certain people do (i.e. politicians). Instead, it becomes communalised and part of everyday life and in the hands of all.

As would be imagined, like the participatory communities that would exist in an anarchist society (see section I.5), the community union would be based upon a mass assembly of its members. Here would be discussed the issues that affect the membership and how to solve them. Thus issues like rent increases, school closures, rising cost of living, taxation, cuts and state-imposed "reforms" to the nature and quality of public services, utilities and resources, repressive laws and so on could be debated and action taken to combat them. Like the communes of a future anarchy, these community unions would be confederated with other unions in different areas in order to co-ordinate joint activity and solve common problems. These confederations would be based upon self-management, mandated and recallable delegates and the creation of administrative action committees to see that the memberships decisions are carried out. The community union could also raise funds for strikes and other social protests, organise pickets, boycotts and generally aid others in struggle. By organising their own forms of direct action (such as tax and rent strikes, environmental protests and so on) they can weaken the state while building a self-managed infrastructure of co-operatives to replace the useful functions the state or capitalist firms currently provide. So, in addition to organising resistance to the state and capitalist firms, these community unions could play an important role in creating an alternative economy within capitalism. For example, such unions could have a mutual bank or credit union associated with them which could allow funds to be gathered for the creation of self-managed co-operatives and social services and centres. In this way a communalised co-operative sector could develop, along with a communal confederation of community unions and their co-operative banks.

Such community unions have been formed in many different countries in recent years to fight against numerous attacks on the working class. In the late 1980s and early 1990s groups were created in neighbourhoods across Britain to organise non-payment of the Conservative government's Community Charge (popularly known as the poll tax, this tax was independent of income and was based on the electoral register). Federations of these groups were created to co-ordinate the struggle and pool resources and, in the end, ensured that the government withdrew the hated tax and helped push Thatcher out of government. In Ireland, groups were formed to defeat the privatisation of the water industry by a similar non-payment campaign in the mid-1990s.

However, few of these groups have been taken as part of a wider strategy to empower the local community but the few that have indicate the potential of such a strategy. This potential can be seen from two examples of libertarian community organising in Europe, one in Italy and another in Spain, while the neighbourhood assemblies in Argentina show that such popular self-government can and does develop spontaneously in struggle.

In Southern Italy, anarchists organised a very successful **Municipal Federation of the Base** (FMB) in Spezzano Albanese. This organisation, in the words of one activist, is *"an alternative to the power of the town hall"* and provides a *"glimpse of what a future libertarian society could be."* Its aim is *"the bringing together of all interests within the district. In intervening at a municipal level, we become involved not only in the world of work but also the life of the community ... the FMB make counter proposals [to Town Hall decisions], which aren't presented to the Council but proposed for discussion in the area to raise people's level of consciousness. Whether they like it or not the Town Hall is obliged to take account of these proposals."* In addition, the FMB also supports co-operatives within it, so creating a communalised, self-managed economic sector within capitalism. Such a development helps to reduce the problems facing isolated co-operatives in a capitalist economy — see section J.5.11 — and was actively done in order to *"seek to bring together all the currents, all the problems and contradictions, to seek solutions"* to such problems facing co-operatives. [*"Community Organising in Southern Italy"*, pp. 16-19, **Black Flag**, no. 210, p. 17 and p. 18]

Elsewhere in Europe, the long, hard work of the C.N.T. in Spain has also resulted in mass village assemblies being created in the Puerto Real area, near Cadiz. These community assemblies came about to support an industrial struggle by shipyard workers. One C.N.T. member explains: *"Every Thursday of every week, in the towns and villages in the area, we had all-village assemblies where anyone connected with the particular issue [of the rationalisation of the shipyards], whether they were actually workers in the shipyard itself, or women or children or grandparents, could go along ... and actually vote and take part in the decision making process of what was going to take place."* With such popular input and support, the shipyard workers won their struggle. However, the assembly continued after the strike and *"managed to link together twelve different organisations within the local area that are all interested in fighting ... various aspects"* of capitalism including health, taxation, economic, ecological and cultural issues. Moreover, the struggle *"created a structure which was very different from the kind of structure of political parties, where the decisions are made at the top and they filter down. What we managed to do in Puerto Real was make decisions at the base and take them upwards."* [**Anarcho-Syndicalism in Puerto Real: from shipyard resistance to direct democracy and community control**, p. 6]

More recently, the December 2001 revolt against neo-liberalism in Argentina saw hundreds of neighbourhood assemblies created across the country. These quickly federated into *inter-barrial* assemblies to co-ordinate struggles. The assemblies occupied buildings, created communal projects like popular kitchens, community centres, day-care centres and built links with occupied workplaces. As one participant put it: *"The initial vocabulary was simply: Let's do things for ourselves, and do them right. Let's decide for ourselves. Let's decide democratically, and if we do, then let's explicitly agree that we're all equals here, that there are no bosses ... We lead ourselves. We lead together. We lead and decide amongst ourselves ... no one invented it ... It just happened. We met one another on the corner and decided, enough! ... Let's invent new organisational forms and reinvent society."* Another notes that this was people who *"begin to solve problems themselves, without turning to the institutions that caused the problems in the first place."* The neighbourhood assemblies ended a system in which *"we elected people to make our decisions for us ... now we will make our own decisions."* While the *"anarchist movement has been talking about these ideas for years"* the movement took them up *"from necessity."* [Marina Sitrin (ed.), **Horizontalism: Voices of Popular Power in Argentina**, p. 41 and pp. 38-9]

The idea of community organising has long existed within anarchism. Kropotkin pointed to the directly democratic assemblies of Paris during the French Revolution These were *"constituted as so many mediums of popular administration, it remained of the people, and this is what made the revolutionary power of these organisations."* This ensured that the local revolutionary councils *"which sprang from the popular movement was not separated from the people."* In this popular self-organisation *"the masses, accustoming themselves to act without receiving orders from the national representatives, were practising what was described later on as Direct Self-Government."* These assemblies federated to co-ordinate joint activity but it was based on their permanence: *"that* is, the possibility of calling the general assembly whenever it was wanted by the members of the section and of discussing everything in the general assembly." In short, "the Commune of Paris was not to be a governed State, but a people governing itself directly — when possible — without intermediaries, without masters" and so "the principles of anarchism ... had their origin, not in theoretic speculations, but in the **deeds** of the Great French Revolution." This "laid the foundations of a new, free, social organisation" and Kropotkin predicted that "the libertarians would no doubt do the same to-day." [**Great French Revolution**, vol. 1, p. 201, p. 203, pp. 210-1, p. 210, p. 204 and p. 206]

In Chile during 1925 "a grass roots movement of great significance emerged," the tenant leagues (ligas do arrendatarios). The movement pledged to pay half their rent beginning the 1st of February, 1925, at huge public rallies (it should also be noted that "Anarchist labour unionists had formed previous ligas do arrendatarios in 1907 and 1914."). The tenants leagues were organised by ward and federated into a city-wide council. It was a vast organisation, with 12,000 tenants in just one ward of Santiago alone. The movement also "press[ed] for a law which would legally recognise the lower rents they had begun paying ... the leagues voted to declare a general strike ... should a rent law not be passed." The government gave in, although the landlords tried to get around it and, in response, on April 8th "the anarchists in Santiago led a general strike in support of the universal rent reduction of 50 percent." Official figures showed that rents "fell sharply during 1915, due in part to the rent strikes" and for the anarchists "the tenant league movement had been the first step toward a new social order in Chile." [Peter DeShazo, **Urban Workers and Labor Unions in Chile 1902-1927**, p. 223, p. 327, p. 223, p. 225 and p. 226] As one Anarchist newspaper put it:

> "This movement since its first moments had been essentially revolutionary. The tactics of direct action were preached by libertarians with highly successful results, because they managed to instil in the working classes the idea that if landlords would not accept the 50 percent lowering of rents, they should pay nothing at all. In libertarian terms, this is the same as taking possession of common property. It completes the first stage of what will become a social revolution." [quoted by DeShazo, **Op. Cit.**, p. 226]

A similar concern for community organising and struggle was expressed in Spain. While the collectives during the revolution are well known, the CNT had long organised in the community and around non-workplace issues. As well as neighbourhood based defence committees to organise and co-ordinate struggles and insurrections, the CNT organised various community based struggles. The most famous example of this must be the rent strikes during the early 1930s in Barcelona. In 1931, the CNT's Construction Union organised a **"Economic Defence Commission"** to organise against high rents and lack of affordable housing. Its basic demand was for a 40% rent decrease but it also addressed unemployment and the cost of food. The campaign was launched by a mass meeting on May 1st, 1931. A series of meetings were held in the various working class neighbourhoods of Barcelona and in surrounding suburbs. This culminated in a mass meeting held at the Palace of Fine Arts on July 5th which raised a series of demands for the movement. By July, 45,000 people were taking part in the rent strike and this rose to over 100,000 by August. As well as refusing to pay rent, families were placed back into their homes from which they had been evicted. The movement spread to a number of the outlying towns which set up their own Economic Defence Commissions. The local groups co-ordinated their actions out of CNT union halls or local libertarian community centres. The movement faced increased state repression but in many parts of Barcelona landlords had been forced to come to terms with their tenants, agreeing to reduced rents rather than facing the prospect of having no income for an extended period or the landlord simply agreed to forget the unpaid rents from the period of the rent strike. [Nick Rider, "The Practice of Direct Action: the Barcelona rent strike of 1931", **For Anarchism**, David Goodway (ed.), pp. 79-105] As Abel Paz summarised:

> "Unemployed workers did not receive or ask for state aid ... The workers' first response to the economic crisis was the rent, gas, and electricity strike in mid-1933, which the CNT and FAI's Economic Defence Committee had been laying the foundations for since 1931. Likewise, house, street, and neighbourhood groups began to turn out en masse to stop evictions and other coercive acts ordered by the landlords (always with police support). The people were constantly mobilised. Women and youngsters were particularly active; it was they who challenged the police and stopped the endless evictions." [**Durruti in the Spanish Revolution**, p. 308]

In Gijon, the CNT "reinforced its populist image by ... its direct consumer campaigns. Some of these were organised through the federation's Anti-Unemployment Committee, which sponsored numerous rallies and marches in favour of 'bread and work.' While they focused on the issue of jobs, they also addressed more general concerns about the cost of living for poor families. In a May 1933 rally, for example, demonstrators asked that families of unemployed workers not be evicted from their homes, even if they fell behind on the rent." The "organisers made the connections between home and work and tried to draw the entire family into the struggle." However, the CNT's "most concerted attempt to bring in the larger community was the formation of a new syndicate, in the spring of 1932, for the Defence of Public Interests (SDIP). In contrast to a conventional union, which comprised groups of workers, the SDIP was organised through neighbourhood committees. Its specific purpose was to enforce a generous renters' rights law of December 1931 that had not been vigorously implemented. Following anarchosyndicalist strategy, the SDIP utilised various forms of direct action, from rent strikes, to mass demonstrations, to the reversal of evictions." This last action involved the local SDIP group going to a home, breaking the judge's official eviction seal and carrying the furniture back in from the street. They left their own sign: **"opened by order of the CNT."** The CNT's direct action strategies "helped keep political discourse in the street, and encouraged people to pursue the same extra-legal channels of activism that they had developed under the monarchy." [Pamela Beth Radcliff, **From mobilization to civil war**, pp. 287-288 and p. 289]

Anarchist support and encouragement of community unionism, by creating the means for communal self-management, helps to enrich the community as well as creating the organisational forms required to resist the state and capitalism. In this way we build the anti-state which will (hopefully) replace the state. Moreover, the combination of community unionism with workplace assemblies (as in Puerto Real), provides a mutual support network which can be very effective in helping winning struggles. For example, in Glasgow, Scotland in 1916, a massive rent strike was finally won when workers came out in strike in support of the rent strikers who been arrested for non-payment. Such developments indicate that Isaac Puente was correct:

> "Libertarian Communism is a society organised without the state and without private ownership. And there is no need to invent anything or conjure up some new organisation for the purpose. The centres about which life in the future will be organised are already with us in the society of today: the free union and the free municipality [or Commune].

> "**The union**: in it combine spontaneously the workers from factories and all places of collective exploitation.

> "And **the free municipality**: an assembly … where, again in spontaneity, inhabitants … combine together, and which points the way to the solution of problems in social life …

> "Both kinds of organisation, run on federal and democratic principles, will be sovereign in their decision making, without being beholden to any higher body, their only obligation being to federate one with another as dictated by the economic requirement for liaison and communications bodies organised in industrial federations.

> "The **union and the free municipality** will assume the collective or common ownership of everything which is under private ownership at present [but collectively used] and will regulate production and consumption (in a word, the economy) in each locality.

> "The very bringing together of the two terms (communism and libertarian) is indicative in itself of the fusion of two ideas: one of them is collectivist, tending to bring about harmony in the whole through the contributions and co-operation of individuals, without undermining their independence in any way; while the other is individualist, seeking to reassure the individual that his independence will be respected." [**Libertarian Communism**, pp. 6-7]

The combination of community unionism, along with industrial unionism (see next section), will be the key to creating an anarchist society. Community unionism, by creating the free commune within the state, allows us to become accustomed to managing our own affairs and seeing that an injury to one is an injury to all. In this way a social power is created in opposition to the state. The town council may still be in the hands of politicians, but neither they nor the

central government would be able to move without worrying about what the people's reaction might be, as expressed and organised in their community assemblies and federations.

J.5.2 Why do anarchists support industrial unionism?

Simply because it is effective in resisting capitalist exploitation and winning reforms, ending capitalist oppression and expresses our ideas on how industry will be organised in an anarchist society. For workers "have the most enormous power in their hands, and, if they once become thoroughly conscious of it and used it, nothing could withstand them; they would only have to stop labour, regard the product of labour as theirs, and enjoy it. This is the sense of the labour disturbances which show themselves here and there." [Max Stirner, **The Ego and Its Own**, p. 116] Industrial unionism is simply libertarian workplace organisation and is the best way of organising and exercising this power.

Before discussing why anarchists support industrial unionism, we must point out that the type of unionism anarchists support has very little in common with that associated with reformist unions like the TUC in Britain or the AFL-CIO in the USA (see next section). In such unions, as Alexander Berkman pointed out, the "rank and file have little say. They have delegated their power to leaders, and these have become the boss … Once you do that, the power you have delegated will be used against you and your interests every time." [**What is Anarchism?**, p. 205] Reformist unions, even if they do organise by industry rather than by trade or craft, are top-heavy and bureaucratic. Thus they are organised in the same manner as capitalist firms or the state — and like both of these, the officials at the top have different interests than those at the bottom. Little wonder anarchists oppose such forms of unionism as being counter to the interests of their members. The long history of union officials betraying their members is proof enough of this.

Anarchists propose a different kind of workplace organisation, one that is organised in a different manner than the mainstream unions. We will call this new kind of organisation **"industrial unionism"** (although perhaps industrial syndicalism, or just syndicalism, might be a better name for it). Some anarchists (particularly communist-anarchists) reject calling these workplace organisations "unions" and instead prefer such terms as workplace resistance groups, workplace assemblies and workers councils. No matter what they are called, all class struggle anarchists support the same organisational structure we are going to outline. It is purely for convenience that we term this industrial unionism.

An industrial union is a union which organises all workers in a given workplace and so regardless of their actual trade everyone would be in the one union. On a building site, for example, brick-layers, plumbers, carpenters and so on would all be a member of the Building Workers Union. Each trade may have its own sections within the union (so that plumbers can discuss issues relating to their trade for example) but the core decision making focus would be an assembly of all workers employed in a workplace. As they all have the same employer, the same exploiter, it is logical for them to have the same union.

It is organised by the guiding principle that workers should directly control their own organisations and struggles. It is based upon workplace assemblies because workers have *"tremendous power"* as the *"creator of all wealth"* but *"the strength of the worker is not in the union meeting-hall; it is in the shop and factory, in the mill and mine. It is **there** that he [or she] must organise; there, on the job."* It is there that workers *"decide the matters at issue and carry their decisions out through the shop committees"* (whose members are *"under the direction and supervision of the workers"* and can be *"recalled at will"*). These committees are *"associated locally, regionally and nationally"* to produce *"a power tremendous in its scope and potentialities."* [Berkman, **Op. Cit.**, pp. 205-6] This confederation is usually organised on two directions, between different workplaces in the same industry as well as between different workplaces in the same locality.

So industrial unionism is different from ordinary trade unionism (usually called business unionism by anarchists and syndicalists as it treats the union's job purely as the seller of its members' labour power). It is based on unions managed directly by the rank and file membership rather than by elected officials and bureaucrats. The industrial union is not based on where the worker lives (as is the case with many trade unions). Instead, the union is based and run from the workplace. It is there that union meetings are held, where workers are exploited and oppressed and where their economic power lies. Industrial unionism is based on local branch autonomy, with each branch managing its own affairs. No union officials have the power to declare strikes "unofficial" as every strike is decided upon by the membership is automatically "official" simply because the branch decided it in a mass meeting.

Power in such an organisation would be decentralised into the hands of the membership, as expressed in local workplace assemblies. To co-ordinate strikes and other forms of action, these autonomous branches are part of a federal structure. The mass meeting in the workplace mandates delegates to express the wishes of the membership at "labour councils" and "industrial federations." The labour council (*"Brouse du Travail"*, in French) is the federation of all workplace branches of all industries in a geographical area (say, for example, in a city or region) and it has the tasks of, among other things, education, propaganda and the promotion of solidarity between the different workplaces in its area. Due to the fact it combines all workers into one organisation, regardless of industry or union, the labour council plays a key role in increasing **class** consciousness and solidarity. The industrial federation organises all workplaces in the same industry so ensuring that workers in one part of the country or world are not producing goods so that the bosses *"can supply the market and lose nothing by the strike"*. So these federations are *"organised not by craft or trade but by industries, so that the whole industry — and if necessary the whole working class — could strike as one man."* If that were done *"would any strike be lost?"* [Berkman, **Op. Cit.**, p. 82] In practice, of course, the activities of these dual federations would overlap: labour councils would support an industry wide strike or action while industrial unions would support action conducted by its member unions called by labour councils.

However, industrial unionism should **not** be confused with a closed shop situation where workers are forced to join a union when they become a wage slave in a workplace. While anarchists do desire to see all workers unite in one organisation, it is vitally important that workers can leave a union and join another. The closed shop only empowers union bureaucrats and gives them even more power to control (and/or ignore) their members. As anarchist unionism has no bureaucrats, there is no need for the closed shop and its voluntary nature is essential in order to ensure that a union be subject to "exit" as well as "voice" for it to be responsive to its members wishes. As Albert Meltzer argued, the closed shop means that *"the [trade union] leadership becomes all-powerful since once it exerts its right to expel a member, that person is not only out of the union, but out of a job."* Anarcho-syndicalism, therefore, *"rejects the closed shop and relies on voluntary membership, and so avoids any leadership or bureaucracy."* [**Anarchism: Arguments for and against**, p. 56] Without voluntary membership even the most libertarian union may become bureaucratic and unresponsive to the needs of its members and the class struggle (also see Tom Wetzel's excellent article *"The Origins of the Union Shop"*, [**Ideas & Action** no. 11]). Needless to say, if the union membership refuses to work with non-union members then that is a different situation. Then this is an issue of free association (as free association clearly implies the right **not** to associate). This issue rarely arises and most syndicalist unions operate in workplaces with other unions (the exceptions arise, as happened frequently in Spanish labour history with the Marxist UGT, when the other union scabs when workers are on strike).

In industrial unionism, the membership, assembled in their place of work, are the ones to decide when to strike, when to pay strike pay, what tactics to use, what demands to make, what issues to fight over and whether an action is "official" or "unofficial". In this way the rank and file is in control of their union and, by confederating with other assemblies, they co-ordinate their forces with their fellow workers. As syndicalist activist Tom Brown made clear:

> *"The basis of the Syndicate is the mass meeting of workers assembled at their place of work ... The meeting elects its factory committee and delegates. The factory Syndicate is federated to all other such committees in the locality ... In the other direction, the factory, let us say engineering factory, is affiliated to the District Federation of Engineers. In turn the District Federation is affiliated to the National Federation of Engineers ... Then, each industrial federation is affiliated to the National Federation of Labour ... how the members of such committees are elected is most important. They are, first of all, not representatives like Members of Parliament who air their own views; they are delegates who carry the message of the workers who elect them. They do not tell the workers what the 'official' policy is; the workers tell them.*
>
> *"Delegates are subject to instant recall by the persons who elected them. None may sit for longer than two successive years, and four years must elapse before his [or her] next nomination. Very few will receive wages as delegates, and then only the district rate of wages for the industry ...*

"It will be seen that in the Syndicate the members control the organisation — not the bureaucrats controlling the members. In a trade union the higher up the pyramid a man is the more power he wields; in a Syndicate the higher he is the less power he has.

"The factory Syndicate has full autonomy over its own affairs." [**Syndicalism**, pp. 35-36]

Such federalism exists to co-ordinate struggle, to ensure that solidarity becomes more than a word written on banners. We are sure that many radicals will argue that such decentralised, confederal organisations would produce confusion and disunity. However, anarchists maintain that the statist, centralised form of organisation of the trades unions would produce indifference instead of involvement, heartlessness instead of solidarity, uniformity instead of unity, and elites instead of equality. The centralised form of organisation has been tried and tried again — it has always failed. This is why the industrial union rejects centralisation, for it *"takes control too far away from the place of struggle to be effective on the workers' side."* [Brown, **Op. Cit.**, p. 34] Centralisation leads to disempowerment, which in turn leads to indifference, **not** solidarity. Rudolf Rocker reminds us of the evil effects of centralism when he wrote:

"For the state centralisation is the appropriate form of organisation, since it aims at the greatest possible uniformity in social life for the maintenance of political and social equilibrium. But for a movement whose very existence depends on prompt action at any favourable moment and on the independent thought and action of its supporters, centralism could but be a curse by weakening its power of decision and systematically repressing all immediate action. If, for example, as was the case in Germany, every local strike had first to be approved by the Central, which was often hundreds of miles away and was not usually in a position to pass a correct judgement on the local conditions, one cannot wonder that the inertia of the apparatus of organisation renders a quick attack quite impossible, and there thus arises a state of affairs where the energetic and intellectually alert groups no longer serve as patterns for the less active, but are condemned by these to inactivity, inevitably bringing the whole movement to stagnation. Organisation is, after all, only a means to an end. When it becomes an end in itself, it kills the spirit and the vital initiative of its members and sets up that domination by mediocrity which is the characteristic of all bureaucracies." [**Anarcho-Syndicalism**, p. 61]

Centralised unions ensure that it is the highest level of union officialdom which decides when workers are allowed to strike. Instead of those affected acting, *"the dispute must be reported to the district office of the union (and in some cases to an area office) then to head office, then back again ... The worker is not allowed any direct approach to, or control of the problem."* [Brown, **Op. Cit.**, p. 34] The end result is that *"through the innate conservatism of officialdom"* officials in centralised unions *"ordinarily use their*

great powers to prevent strikes or to drive their unions' members back to work after they have struck in concert with other workers." The notion that a centralised organisation will be more radical *"has not developed in practice"* and the key problem *"is due not to the autonomy of the unions, but to the lack of it."* [Earl C. Ford and William Z. Foster, **Syndicalism**, p. 38] So the industrial union *"is based on the principles of Federalism, on free combination from below upwards, putting the right of self-determination ... above everything else"* and so rejects centralism as an *"artificial organisation from above downwards which turns over the affairs of everybody in a lump to a small minority"* and is *"always attended by barren official routine"* as well as *"lifeless discipline and bureaucratic ossification."* [Rocker, **Op. Cit.**, p. 60]

This implies that as well as being decentralised and organised from the bottom up, the industrial union differs from the normal trade union by having no full-time officials. All union business is conducted by elected fellow workers who do their union activities after work or, if it has to be done during work hours, they get the wages they lost while on union business. In this way no bureaucracy of well paid officials is created and all union militants remain in direct contact with their fellow workers. Given that it is **their** wages, working conditions and so on that are affected by their union activity they have a real interest in making the union an effective organisation and ensuring that it reflects the interests of the rank and file. In addition, all part-time union "officials" are elected, mandated and recallable delegates. If the fellow worker who is elected to the local labour council or other union committee is not reflecting the opinions of those who mandated him or her then the union assembly can countermand their decision, recall them and replace them with someone who **will** reflect these decisions. In short, *"the Syndicalist stands firmly by these things — mass meetings, delegates not bosses, the right of recall ... Syndicalism is organised from the bottom upwards ... all power comes from below and is controlled from below. This is a revolutionary principle."* [Brown, **Op. Cit.**, p. 85]

As can be seen, industrial unionism reflects anarchist ideas of organisation — it is organised from the bottom up, it is decentralised and based upon federation and it is directly managed by its members in mass assemblies. It is anarchism applied to industry and the needs of the class struggle. By supporting such forms of organisation, anarchists are not only seeing *"anarchy in action"*, they are forming effective tools which can win the class war. By organising in this manner, workers are building the framework of a co-operative society within capitalism:

"the syndicate ... has for its purpose the defence of the interests of the producers within existing society and the preparing for and the practical carrying out of the reconstruction of social life ... It has, therefore, a double purpose: 1. As the fighting organisation of the workers against their employers to enforce the demands of the workers for the safeguarding of their standard of living; 2. As the school for the intellectual training of the workers to make them acquainted with the technical management of production and economic life in general, so that when a revolutionary situation arises they will be capable of

taking the socio-economic organism into their own hands and remaking it according to Socialist principles." [Rocker, **Op. Cit.**, pp. 56-7]

So *"[a]t the same time that syndicalism exerts this unrelenting pressure on capitalism, it tries to build the new social order within the old. The unions and the 'labour councils' are not merely means of struggle and instruments of social revolution; they are also the very structure around which to build a free society. The workers are to be educated in the job of destroying the old propertied order and in the task of reconstructing a stateless, libertarian society. The two go together."* [Murray Bookchin, **The Spanish Anarchists**, p. 121] The industrial union is seen as prefiguring the future society, a society which (like the union) is decentralised and self-managed in all aspects.

Given the fact that workers wages have been stagnating (or, at best, falling behind productivity increases) across the world as the trade unions have been weakened and marginalised (partly because of their own tactics, structure and politics) it is clear that there exists a great need for working people to organise to defend themselves. The centralised, top-down trade unions we are accustomed to have proved themselves incapable of effective struggle (and, indeed, the number of times they have sabotaged such struggle are countless — a result not of "bad" leaders but of the way these unions organise and their role within capitalism). Hence anarchists support industrial unionism as an effective alternative to the malaise of official trade unionism. How anarchists aim to encourage such new forms of workplace organisation and struggle will be discussed in section J.5.4.

One last point. We noted that many anarchists, particularly communist-anarchists, consider unions, even anarchosyndicalist ones, as having a strong reformist tendency (as discussed in section J.3.9). However, all anarchists recognise the importance of autonomous class struggle and the need for organisations to help fight that struggle. Thus anarchist-communists, instead of trying to organise industrial unions, apply the ideas of industrial unionism to workplace struggles. They would agree with the need to organise all workers into a mass assembly and to have elected, recallable administration committees to carry out the strikers wishes. This means that while such anarchists do not call their practical ideas "anarcho-syndicalism" nor the workplace assemblies they desire to create "unions," they are **extremely** similar in nature and so we can discuss both using the term "industrial unionism". The key difference is that many (if not most) anarcho-communists consider that permanent workplace organisations that aim to organise **all** workers would become reformist. Because of this they also see the need for anarchists to organise **as anarchists** in order to spread the anarchist message within them and keep their revolutionary aspects at the forefront.

Spontaneously created organisations of workers in struggle play an important role in both communist-anarchist and anarcho-syndicalist theory. Since both advocate that it is the workers, using their own organisations who will control their own struggles (and, eventually, their own revolution) in their own interests, not a vanguard party of elite political theorists, this is unsurprising. It matters little if the specific organisations are revolutionary industrial unions,

factory committees, workers councils, or other labour formations. The important thing is that they are created and run by workers themselves. Meanwhile, anarchists are industrial guerrillas waging class war at the point of production in order to win improvements in the here and now and strengthen tendencies towards anarchism by showing that direct action and libertarian organisation is effective and can win partial expropriations of capitalist and state power. So while there are slight differences in terminology and practice, all anarchists would support the ideas of industrial organisation and struggle we have outlined above.

J.5.3 What attitude do anarchists take to existing unions?

As noted in the last section, anarchists desire to create organisations in the workplace radically different from the existing unions. The question now arises, what attitude do anarchists take to trade unions?

Before answering that question, we must stress that anarchists, no matter how hostile to trade unions as bureaucratic, reformist institutions, **are** in favour of working class struggle. This means that when trade union members or other workers are on strike anarchists will support them (unless the strike is reactionary — for example, no anarchist would support a strike which is racist in nature). This is because anarchists consider it basic to their politics that you do not scab and you do not crawl. So, when reading anarchist criticisms of trade unions do not for an instant think we do not support industrial struggles — we do, we are just very critical of the unions that are sometimes involved.

So, what do anarchists think of the trade unions?

For the most part, one could call the typical anarchist opinion toward them as one of "hostile support." It is hostile insofar as anarchists are well aware of how bureaucratic these unions are and how they continually betray their members. Given that they are usually little more than "business" organisations, trying to sell their members labour-power for the best deal possible, it is unsurprising that they are bureaucratic and that the interests of the bureaucracy are at odds with those of its membership. However, our attitude is "supportive" in that even the worse trade union represents an attempt at working class solidarity and self-help, even if the organisation is now far removed from the initial protests and ideas that set the union up. For a worker to join a trade union means recognising, to some degree, that he or she has different interests from their boss (*"If the interests of labour and capital are the same, why the union?"* [Alexander Berkman, **What is Anarchism?**, p. 76]).

There is no way to explain the survival of unions other than the fact that there are different class interests and workers have understood that to promote their own interests they have to organise collectively. No amount of conservatism, bureaucracy or backwardness within the unions can obliterate this. The very existence of trade unions testifies to the existence of some level of basic class consciousness and the recognition that workers and capitalists do not have the same interests. Claims by trade union officials that the interests of workers and bosses are the same theoretically disarms both the union and its members and so weakens their struggles (after all, if bosses and workers have similar interests then any conflict is bad and the decisions of the boss must be in workers' interests!). That kind of nonsense is best left to the apologists of capitalism (see section F.3.2).

It is no surprise, then, that *"the existing political and economic power ... not only suspected every labour organisation of aiming to improve the condition of its members within the limits of the wage system, but they also looked upon the trade union as the deadly enemy of wage-slavery — and they were right. Every labour organisation of sincere character must needs wage war upon the existing economic conditions, since the continuation of the same is synonymous with the exploitation and enslavement of labour."* [Max Baginski, *"Aim and Tactics of the Trade-Union Movement"*, pp. 297-306, **Anarchy! An Anthology of Emma Goldman's Mother Earth**, Peter Glassgold (ed.), pp. 302-3] Thus anarchist viewpoints on this issue reflect the contradictory nature of trade unions — on the one hand they are products of workers' struggle, but on the other they are bureaucratic, unresponsive, centralised and their full-time officials have no real interest in fighting against wage labour as it would put them out of a job. Indeed, the very nature of trade unionism ensures that the interests of the union (i.e. the full-time officials) come into conflict with the people they claim to represent.

This occurs because trade unions, in order to get recognition from a company, must be able to promise industrial peace. They need to enforce the contracts they sign with the bosses, even if this goes against the will of their members. Thus trade unions become a third force in industry, somewhere between management and the workers and pursuing its own interests. This need to enforce contracts soon ensures that the union becomes top-down and centralised — otherwise their members would violate the union's agreements. They have to be able to control their members — which usually means stopping them fighting the boss — if they are to have anything to bargain with at the negotiation table. This may sound odd, but the point is that the union official has to sell the employer labour discipline and freedom from unofficial strikes as part of their side of the bargain otherwise the employer will ignore them.

The nature of trade unionism, then, is to take power away from the membership and centralise it into the hands of officials at the top of the organisation. Thus union officials sell out their members because of the role trade unions play within society, not because they are nasty individuals (although some are). They behave as they do because they have too much power and, being full-time and highly paid, are unaccountable, in any real way, to their members. Power — and wealth — corrupts, no matter who you are (see *Chapter XI* of Alexander Berkman's **What is Anarchism?** for an excellent introduction to anarchist viewpoints on trade unions).

While, in normal times, most workers will not really question the nature of the trade union bureaucracy, this changes when workers face some threat. Then they are brought face to face with the fact that the trade union has interests separate from theirs. Hence we see trade unions agreeing to wage cuts, redundancies and so on — after all, the full-time trade union official's job is not on the line! But, of course, while such a policy is in the short term interests of

the officials, in the longer term it goes against their interests — who wants to join a union which rolls over and presents no effective resistance to employers? Little wonder Michael Moore had a chapter entitled *"Why are Union Leaders So F#!@ing Stupid?"* in his book **Downsize This!** — essential reading on how moronic trade union bureaucrats can actually be. Sadly trade union bureaucracy seems to afflict all who enter it with short-sightedness — although the chickens do, finally, come home to roost, as the bureaucrats of the AFL, TUC and other trade unions are finding out in this era of global capital and falling membership. So while the activities of trade union leaders may seem crazy and short-sighted, these activities are forced upon them by their position and role within society — which explains why they are so commonplace and why even radical leaders end up doing exactly the same thing in time.

However, few anarchists would call upon members of a trade union to tear-up their membership cards. While some anarchists have nothing but contempt (and rightly so) for trade unions (and so do not work within them — but will support trade union members in struggle), the majority of anarchists take a more pragmatic viewpoint. If no alternative syndicalist union exists, anarchists will work within the existing unions (perhaps becoming shop-stewards — few anarchists would agree to be elected to positions above this in any trade union, particularly if the post were full-time), spreading the anarchist message and trying to create a libertarian undercurrent which would hopefully blossom into a more anarchistic labour movement. So most anarchists "support" the trade unions only until we have created a viable libertarian alternative. Thus we will become trade union members while trying to spread anarchist ideas within and outwith them. This means that anarchists are flexible in terms of our activity in the unions. For example, many IWW members were "two-carders" which meant they were also in the local AFL branch in their place of work and turned to the IWW when the AFL hierarchy refused to back strikes or other forms of direct action.

Anarchist activity within trade unions reflects our ideas on hierarchy and its corrupting effects. We reject the response of left-wing social democrats, Stalinists and mainstream Trotskyists to the problem of trade union betrayal, which is to try and elect 'better' officials. They see the problem primarily in terms of the individuals who hold the posts so ignoring the fact that individuals are shaped by the environment they live in and the role they play in society. Thus even the most left-wing and progressive individual will become a bureaucrat if they are placed within a bureaucracy.

We must note that the problem of corruption does not spring from the high-wages officials are paid (although this is a factor), but from the power they have over their members (which partly expresses itself in high pay). Any claim that electing "radical" full-time officials who refuse to take the high wages associated with the position will be better, is false. The hierarchical nature of the trade union structure has to be changed, not side-effects of it. As the left has no problem with hierarchy as such, this explains why they support this form of "reform." They do not actually want to undercut whatever dependency the members have on leadership, they want to replace the leaders with "better" ones (i.e. themselves or members of their party) and so endlessly call upon the trade union bureaucracy to act **for** its members. In this way, they hope, trade unionists will see the need to support a "better" leadership — namely themselves. Anarchists, in stark contrast, think that the problem is not that the leadership of the trade unions is weak, right-wing or does not act but that the union's membership follows them. Thus anarchists aim at undercutting reliance on leaders (be they left or right) by encouraging self-activity by the rank and file and awareness that hierarchical leadership as such is bad, not individual leaders. Anarchists encourage rank and file self-activity, **not** endless calls for trade union bureaucrats to act for us (as is unfortunately far too common on the left).

Instead of "reform" from above (which is doomed to failure), anarchists work at the bottom and attempt to empower the rank and file of the trade unions. It is self-evident that the more power, initiative and control that lies on the shop floor, the less the bureaucracy has. Thus anarchists work within and outwith the trade unions in order to increase the power of workers where it actually lies: at the point of production. This is usually done by creating networks of activists who spread anarchist ideas to their fellow workers (see next section). Hence Malatesta:

> "The anarchists within the unions should strive to ensure that they remain open to all workers of whatever opinion or party on the sole condition that there is solidarity in the struggle against the bosses. They should oppose the corporatist spirit and any attempt to monopolise labour or organisation. They should prevent the Unions from becoming the tools of the politicians for electoral or other authoritarian ends; they should preach and practice direct action, decentralisation, autonomy and free initiative. They should strive to help members learn how to participate directly in the life of the organisation and to do without leaders and permanent officials.
>
> "They must, in short, remain anarchists, remain always in close touch with anarchists and remember that the workers' organisation is not the end but just one of the means, however important, of preparing the way for the achievement of anarchism." [**The Anarchist Revolution**, pp. 26-7]

As part of this activity anarchists promote the ideas of Industrial Unionism we highlighted in the last section — namely direct workers control of struggle via workplace assemblies and recallable committees — during times of struggle. However, anarchists are aware that economic struggle (and trade unionism as such) "cannot be an end in itself, since the struggle must also be waged at a political level to distinguish the role of the State." [Malatesta, **Errico Malatesta: His Life and Ideas**, p, 115] Thus, as well as encouraging worker self-organisation and self-activity, anarchist groups also seek to politicise struggles and those involved in them. Only this process of self-activity and political discussion between equals **within** social struggles can ensure the process of working class self-liberation and the creation of new, more libertarian, forms of workplace organisation.

J.5.4
What are industrial networks?

Industrial networks are the means by which revolutionary industrial unions and other forms of libertarian workplace organisation can be created. The idea of Industrial Networks originated with the British section of the anarcho-syndicalist **International Workers Association** in the late 1980s. It was developed as a means of promoting libertarian ideas within the workplace, so creating the basis on which a workplace movement based upon the ideas of industrial unionism (see section J.5.2) could grow and expand.

The idea is very simple. An Industrial Network is a federation of militants in a given industry who support the ideas of anarchism and/or anarcho-syndicalism, namely direct action, solidarity and organisation from the bottom up (the difference between purely anarchist networks and anarcho-syndicalist ones will be highlighted later). It would "initially be a political grouping in the economic sphere, aiming to build a less reactive but positive organisation within the industry. The long term aim … is, obviously, the creation of an anarcho-syndicalist union." [**Winning the Class War**, p. 18] The Industrial Network would be an organisation of groups of libertarians within a workplace united on an industrial basis. They would pull their resources together to fund a regular bulletin and other forms of propaganda which they would distribute within their workplaces. These bulletins and leaflets would raise and discuss issues related to work, how to fight back and win as well as placing workplace issues in a social and political context. This propaganda would present anarchist ideas of workplace organisation and resistance as well as general anarchist ideas and analysis. In this way anarchist ideas and tactics would be able to get a wider hearing and anarchists can have an input **as anarchists** into workplace struggles.

Traditionally, many syndicalists and anarcho-syndicalists advocated the **One Big Union** strategy, the aim of which was to organise all workers into one organisation representing the whole working class. Today, however, most anarcho-syndicalists, like other revolutionary anarchists, advocate workers assemblies for decision making during struggles which are open to all workers (union members or not) as they recognise that they face dual unionism (which means there are more than one union within a given workplace or country). This was the case historically, in all countries with a large syndicalist union movement there were also socialist unions. Therefore most anarcho-syndicalists do not expect to ever get a majority of the working class into a revolutionary union before a revolutionary situation develops. In addition, revolutionary unions do not simply appear, they develop from previous struggles and require a lot of work and experience of which the Industrial Networks are but one aspect. The most significant revolutionary unions (such as the IWW, USI and CNT) were originally formed by unions and union militants with substantial experience of struggle behind them, some of whom were part of existing trade union bodies.

Thus industrial networks are intended to deal with the actual situation that confronts us, and provide a strategy for moving from our present reality toward our ultimate goals. The role of the anarchist group or syndicalist union would be to call workplace assemblies and their federation into councils, argue for direct workers control of struggle by these mass assemblies, promote direct action and solidarity, put across anarchist ideas and politics and keep things on the boil, so to speak. When one has only a handful of anarchists and syndicalists in a workplace or scattered across several workplaces there is a clear need for developing ways for these fellow workers to effectively act in union, rather than be isolated and relegated to more general agitation. A handful of anarchists cannot meaningfully call a general strike but we can agitate around specific industrial issues and organise our fellow workers to do something about them. Through such campaigns we demonstrate the advantages of rank-and-file unionism and direct action, show our fellow workers that our ideas are not mere abstract theory but can be implemented here and now, attract new members and supporters, and further develop our capacity to develop revolutionary unions in our workplaces. Thus the creation of Industrial Networks and the calling for workplace assemblies is a recognition of where we are now — with anarchist ideas very much in the minority. Calling for workers assemblies is not an anarchist tactic per se, we must add, but a working class one developed and used plenty of times by workers in struggle (indeed, it was how the current trade unions were created). It also puts the onus on the reformist unions by appealing directly to their members as workers and exposing their bureaucrat organisations and reformist politics by creating an effective alternative to them.

A few anarchists reject the idea of Industrial Networks and instead support the idea of **"rank and file"** groups which aim to put pressure on the current trade unions to become more militant and democratic. Some even think that such groups can be used to reform the trade-unions into libertarian, revolutionary organisations — called *"boring from within"* — but most reject this as utopian, viewing the trade union bureaucracy as unreformable as the state's (and it is likely that rather than change the trade union, "boring from within" would change the syndicalists by watering down their ideas). Moreover, opponents of "rank and file" groups argue that they direct time and energy **away** from practical and constructive activity and instead waste them *"[b]y constantly arguing for changes to the union structure … the need for the leadership to be more accountable, etc., [and so] they not only [offer] false hope but [channel] energy and discontent away from the real problem — the social democratic nature of reformist trade unions."* [**Op. Cit.**, p. 11]

Supporters of the "rank and file" approach fear that the Industrial Networks will isolate anarchists from the mass of trade union members by creating tiny "pure" syndicalist groups. Such a claim is rejected by supporters of Industrial Networks who argue that rather than being isolated from the majority of trade unionists they would be in contact with them where it counts, in the workplace and in struggle rather than in trade union meetings which many workers do not even attend:

"We have no intention of isolating ourselves from the many workers who make up the rest of the rank and file membership of the unions. We recognise that a large proportion of trade union members are only nominally so as the main activity of social democratic unions is outside the workplace … **We aim to unite and not divide workers.**

"It has been argued that social democratic unions will not tolerate this kind of activity, and that we would be all expelled and thus isolated. So be it. We, however, don't think that this will happen until … workplace militants had found a voice independent of the trade unions and so they become less useful to us anyway. Our aim is not to support social democracy, but to show it up as irrelevant to the working class." [**Op. Cit.**, p. 19]

Whatever the merits and disadvantages of both approaches are, it seems likely that the activity of both will overlap in practice with Industrial Networks operating within trade union branches and "rank and file" groups providing alternative structures for struggle. As noted above, there is a slight difference between anarcho-syndicalist supporters of Industrial Networks and communist-anarchist ones. This is to do with how they see the function and aim of these networks. In the short run, both agree that such networks should agitate in their industry and call mass assemblies to organise resistance to capitalist exploitation and oppression. They disagree on who can join the network groups and what their medium term aims should be. Anarcho-syndicalists aim for the Industrial Networks to be the focal point for the building of permanent syndicalist unions and so aim for the Industrial Networks to be open to all workers who accept the general aims of the organisation. Anarcho-communists, however, view Industrial Networks as a means of increasing anarchist ideas within the working class and are not primarily concerned about building syndicalist unions (while many anarcho-communists would support such a development, some do not). In the long term, they both aim for social revolution and workers' self-management of production.

These anarchists, therefore, see the need for workplace-based branches of an anarchist group along with the need for networks of militant 'rank and file' workers, but reject the idea of something that is one but pretends to be the other. They argue that, far from avoiding the problems of classical anarcho-syndicalism, such networks seem to emphasise one of the worst problems — namely that of how the organisation remains anarchist but is open to non-anarchists. However, the similarities between the two positions are greater than the differences and so can be summarised together, as we have done here.

J.5.5 What forms of co-operative credit do anarchists support?

Anarchists tend to support most forms of co-operation, including those associated with credit and money. This co-operative banking takes many forms, such as credit unions, LETS schemes and so on. In this section we discuss two main forms of co-operative credit, **mutualism** and **LETS**.

Mutualism is the name for the ideas associated with Proudhon and his **Bank of the People**. Essentially, it is a confederation of credit unions in which working class people pool their funds and savings so allowing credit to be supplied at cost (no interest), so increasing the options available to them. LETS stands for **Local**

Exchange Trading Schemes and is a similar idea in many ways (see **Bringing the Economy Home from the Market** by Ross V.G. Dobson on LETS). From its start in Canada, LETS has spread across the world and there are now hundreds of schemes involving hundreds of thousands of people.

Both schemes revolve around creating an alternative form of currency and credit within capitalism in order to allow working class people to work outwith the capitalist money system by creating a new circulating medium. In this way, it is hoped, workers would be able to improve their living and working conditions by having a source of community-based (very low interest) credit and so be less dependent on capitalists and the capitalist banking system. Supporters of mutualism considered it as the ideal way of reforming capitalism away for by making credit available to the ordinary worker at very cheap rates, the end of wage slavery could occur as workers would work for themselves by either purchasing the necessary tools required for their work or by buying the capitalists out.

Mutual credit, in short, is a form of credit co-operation, in which individuals pull their resources together in order to benefit themselves as individuals and as part of a community. It has the following key aspects:

> **Co-operation**: No-one owns the network. It is controlled by its members democratically.

> **Non-exploitative**: No interest is charged on account balances or credit. At most administrative costs are charged, a result of it being commonly owned and managed.

> **Consent**: Nothing happens without it, there is no compulsion to trade.

> **Labour-Notes**: They use their own type of money as a means of aiding "honest exchange."

It is hoped, by organising credit, working class people will be able to work for themselves and slowly but surely replace capitalism with a co-operative system based upon self-management. While LETS schemes do not have such grand schemes, historically mutualism aimed at working within and transforming capitalism to socialism. At the very least, LETS schemes reduce the power and influence of banks and finance capital within society as mutualism ensures that working people have a viable alternative to such parasites.

These ideas have a long history within the socialist movement, originating in Britain in the early 19th century when Robert Owen and other Socialists raised the idea of labour notes and labour-exchanges as both a means of improving working class conditions within capitalism and of reforming capitalism into a society of confederated, self-governing communities. Such *"Equitable Labour Exchanges"* were *"founded at London and Birmingham in 1832"* with *"Labour notes and the exchange of small products."* [E. P. Thompson, **The Making of the English Working Class**, p. 870] Apparently independently of these attempts in Britain at what would later be called mutualism, Proudhon arrived at the same ideas decades later in France: *"The People's Bank quite simply embodies the financial and economic aspects of the principle of modern democracy, that is,*

the sovereignty of the People, and of the republican motto, 'Liberty, Equality, Fraternity.'" [**Selected Writings of P-J Proudhon**, p. 75] Similarly, in the USA (partly as a result of Joshua Warren's activities, who got the idea from Robert Owen) there was extensive discussion on labour notes, exchanges and free credit as a means of protecting workers from the evils of capitalism and ensuring their independence and freedom from wage slavery. When Proudhon's works appeared in North America, the basic arguments were well known and they were quickly adopted by radicals there.

Therefore the idea that mutual banking using labour money as a means to improve working class living conditions, even, perhaps, to achieve industrial democracy, self-management and the end of capitalism has a long history in Socialist thought. Unfortunately this aspect of socialism became less important with the rise of Marxism (which called these early socialists *"utopian"*). Attempts at such credit unions and alternative exchange schemes were generally replaced with attempts to build working class political parties and so constructive socialistic experiments and collective working class self-help was replaced by working within the capitalist state. Fortunately, history has had the last laugh on Marxism with working class people yet again creating anew the ideas of mutualism (as can be seen by the growth of LETS and other schemes of community money).

J.5.6 Why are mutual credit schemes important?

Mutual credit schemes are important because they are a way to improve working class life under capitalism and ensure that what money we do have is used to benefit ourselves rather than the elite. By organising credit, we retain control over it and so rather than being used to invest in capitalist schemes it can be used for socialist alternatives.

For example, rather than allow the poorest to be at the mercy of loan sharks a community, by organising credit, can ensure its members receive cheap credit. Rather than give capitalist banks bundles of cash to invest in capitalist firms seeking to extract profits from a locality, it can be used to fund a co-operative instead. Rather than invest pension schemes into the stock market and so help undermine workers pay and living standards by increasing rentier power, it can be used to invest in schemes to improve the community and its economy. In short, rather than bolster capitalist power and so control, mutual credit aims to undermine the power of capitalist banks and finance by placing as much money as much possible in working class hands.

This point is important, as the banking system is often considered "neutral" (particularly in capitalist economics). However, as Malatesta correctly argued, it would be *"a mistake to believe ... that the banks are, or are in the main, a means to facilitate exchange; they are a means to speculate on exchange and currencies, to invest capital and to make it produce interest, and to fulfil other typically capitalist operations."* [**Errico Malatesta: His Life and Ideas**, p. 100] Within capitalism, money is still to a large degree a commodity which is more than a convenient measure of work done in the production of goods and services. It can and does go anywhere in the world where it can get the best return for its owners, and so it tends to drain out of those communities that need it most (why else would a large company invest in a community unless the money it takes out of the area handsomely exceeds that put in?). It is the means by which capitalists can buy the liberty of working people and get them to produce a surplus for them (wealth is, after all, "a power invested in certain individuals by the institutions of society, to compel others to labour for their benefit." [William Godwin, **The Anarchist Writings of William Godwin**, p. 130]). From this consideration alone, working class control of credit and money is an important part of the class struggle as having access to alternative sources of credit can increase working class options and power.

As we discussed in section B.3.2, credit is also an important form of social control — people who have to pay their mortgage or visa bill are more pliable, less likely to strike or make other forms of political trouble. Credit also expands the consumption of the masses in the face of stagnant or falling wages so blunting the impact of increasing exploitation. Moreover, as an added bonus, there is a profit to be made as the "rich need a place to earn interest on their surplus funds, and the rest of the population makes a juicy lending target." [Doug Henwood, **Wall Street**, p. 65]

Little wonder that the state (and the capitalists who run it) is so concerned to keep control of money in its own hands or the hands of its agents. With an increase in mutual credit, interest rates would drop, wealth would stay more in working class communities, and the social power of working people would increase (for people would be more likely to struggle for higher wages and better conditions — as the fear of debt repayments would be less). By the creation of community-based credit unions that do not put their money into "Capital Markets" or into capitalist Banks working class people can control their own credit, their own retirement funds, and find ways of using money as a means of undermining capitalist power and supporting social struggle and change. In this way working people are controlling more and more of the money supply and using it in ways that will stop capital from using it to oppress and exploit them.

An example of why this can be important can be seen from the existing workers' pension fund system which is invested in the stock market in the hope that workers will receive an adequate pension in their old age. However, the only people actually winning are bankers and big companies. Unsurprisingly, the managers of these pension fund companies are investing in those firms with the highest returns, which are usually those who are downsizing or extracting most surplus value from their workforce (which in turn forces other companies to follow the same strategies to get access to the available funds in order to survive). Basically, if your money is used to downsize your fellow workers or increase the power of capital, then you are not only helping to make things harder for others like you, you are also helping making things worse for yourself. No person is an island, and increasing the clout of capital over the working class is going to affect you directly or indirectly. As such, the whole scheme is counter-productive as it effectively means workers have to experience insecurity, fear of downsizing and stagnating wages during their working lives in order to have slightly more money when they retire (assuming that they are

fortunate enough to retire when the stock market is doing well rather than during one of its regular periods of financial instability, of course).

This highlights one of the tricks the capitalists are using against us, namely to get us to buy into the system through our fear of old age. Whether it is going into lifelong debt to buy a home or putting our money in the stock market, we are being encouraged to buy into the system which exploits us and so put its interests above our own. This makes us more easily controlled. We need to get away from living in fear and stop allowing ourselves to be deceived into behaving like "stakeholders" in a Plutocratic system where most shares really are held by an elite. As can be seen from the use of pension funds to buy out firms, increase the size of transnationals and downsize the workforce, such "stakeholding" amounts to sacrificing both the present and the future while others benefit.

The real enemies are **not** working people who take part in such pension schemes. It is the people in power, those who manage the pension schemes and companies, who are trying to squeeze every last penny out of working people to finance higher profits and stock prices — which the unemployment and impoverishment of workers on a world-wide scale aids. They control the governments of the world. They are making the "rules" of the current system. Hence the importance of limiting the money they have available, of creating community-based credit unions and mutual risk insurance co-operatives to increase our control over our money which can be used to empower ourselves, aid our struggles and create our own alternatives. Money, representing as it does the power of capital and the authority of the boss, is not "neutral" and control over it plays a role in the class struggle. We ignore such issues at our own peril.

J.5.7 Do most anarchists think mutual credit is sufficient to abolish capitalism?

The short answer is no, they do not. While the Individualist and Mutualist Anarchists do think that mutual banking is the only sure way of abolishing capitalism, most anarchists do not see it as an end in itself. Few think that capitalism can be reformed away in the manner assumed by Proudhon or Tucker.

In terms of the latter, increased access to credit does not address the relations of production and market power which exist within the economy and so any move for financial transformation has to be part of a broader attack on all forms of capitalist social power in order to be both useful and effective. In short, assuming that Individualist Anarchists do manage to organise a mutual banking scheme it cannot be assumed that as long as firms use wage-labour that any spurt in economic activity will have a long term effect of eliminating exploitation. What is more likely is that an economic crisis would develop as lowering unemployment results in a profits squeeze (as occurred in, say, the 1970s). Without a transformation in the relations of production, the net effect would be the usual capitalist business cycle.

For the former, for mutualists like Proudhon, mutual credit **was** seen as a means of transforming the relations of production (as discussed in section G.4.1, unlike Proudhon, Tucker did not oppose wage-labour and just sought to make it non-exploitative). For Proudhon, mutual credit was seen as the means by which co-operatives could be created to end wage-labour. The organisation of labour would combine with the organisation of credit to end capitalism as workers would fund co-operative firms and their higher efficiency would soon drive capitalist firms out of business. Thus *"the Exchange Bank is the organisation of labour's greatest asset"* as it allowed *"the new form of society to be defined and created among the workers."* *"To organise credit and circulation is to increase production,"* Proudhon stressed, *"to determine the new shapes of industrial society."* So, overtime, co-operative credit would produce co-operative production while associated labour would increase the funds available to associated credit. For Proudhon the *"organisation of credit and organisation of labour amount to one and the same"* and by recognising this the workers *"would soon have wrested alienated capital back again, through their organisation and competition."* [**Property is Theft!**, pp. 17-8]

Bakunin, while he was *"convinced that the co-operative will be the preponderant form of social organisation in the future"* and could *"hardly oppose the creation of co-operatives associations"* now as *"we find them necessary in many respects,"* argued that Proudhon's hope for gradual change by means of mutual banking and the higher efficiency of workers' co-operatives were unlikely to be realised. This was because such claims *"do not take into account the vast advantage that the bourgeoisie enjoys against the proletariat through its monopoly on wealth, science, and secular custom, as well as through the approval — overt or covert but always active — of States and through the whole organisation of modern society. The fight is too unequal for success reasonably to be expected."* [**The Basic Bakunin**, p. 153 and p. 152] Thus capitalism *"does not fear the competition of workers' associations — neither consumers', producers', nor mutual credit associations — for the simple reason that workers' organisations, left to their own resources, will never be able to accumulate sufficiently strong aggregations of capital capable of waging an effective struggle against bourgeois capital."* [**The Political Philosophy of Bakunin**, p. 293]

So, for most anarchists, it is only in combination with other forms of working class self-activity and self-management that mutualist institutions could play an important role in the class struggle. In other words, few anarchists think that mutualist credit or co-operatives are enough in themselves to end capitalism. Revolutionary action is also required — such as the expropriation of capital by workers associations.

This does not mean anarchists reject co-operation under capitalism. By creating a network of mutual banks to aid in creating co-operatives, union organising drives, supporting strikes (either directly by gifts/loans or funding consumer co-operatives which could supply food and other essentials free or at a reduced cost), mutualism can be used as a means of helping build libertarian alternatives within the capitalist system. Such alternatives, while making life better under the current system, also play a role in overcoming that system by aiding those in struggle. Thus Bakunin:

> *"let us co-operate in our common enterprise to make*

our lives a little bit more supportable and less difficult. Let us, wherever possible, establish producer-consumer co-operatives and mutual credit societies which, though under the present economic conditions they cannot in any real or adequate way free us, are nevertheless important inasmuch they train the workers in the practices of managing the economy and plant the precious seeds for the organisation of the future." [**Bakunin on Anarchism**, p. 173]

So while few anarchists think that mutualism would be enough in itself, it can play a role in the class struggle. As a compliment to direct action and workplace and community struggle and organisation, mutualism has an important role in working class self-liberation. For example, community unions (see section J.5.1) could create their own mutual banks and money which could be used to fund co-operatives and support social struggle. In this way a healthy communalised co-operative sector could develop within capitalism, overcoming the problems of isolation facing workplace co-operatives (see section J.5.11) as well as providing solidarity for those in struggle.

Mutual banking can be a way of building upon and strengthening the anarchistic social relations within capitalism. For even under capitalism and statism, there exists extensive mutual aid and, indeed, anarchistic and communistic ways of living. For example, communistic arrangements exist within families, between friends and lovers and within anarchist organisations. Mutual credit could be a means of creating a bridge between this alternative (gift) "economy" and capitalism. The mutualist alternative economy would help strength communities and bonds of trust between individuals, and this would increase the scope of the communistic sector as more and more people help each other without the medium of exchange. In other words, mutualism will help the gift economy that exists within capitalism to grow and develop.

J.5.8 What would a modern system of mutual banking look like?

One scenario for an updated system of mutual banking would be for a community to begin issuing an alternative currency accepted as money by all individuals within it. Let us call this currency-issuing association a "mutual barter clearinghouse," or just "clearinghouse" for short.

The clearinghouse would have a twofold mandate: first, to extend credit at cost to members; second, to manage the circulation of credit-money within the system, charging only a small service fee (one percent or less) sufficient to cover its costs of operation, including labour costs involved in issuing credit and keeping track of transactions, insuring itself against losses from uncollectable debts, and so forth. Some current experiments in community money use labour time worked as their basis (thus notes would be marked one-hour) while others have notes tied to the value of the state currency (thus, say, a Scottish town would issue pounds assumed to be the same as a British pound note).

The clearinghouse would be organised and function as follows.

People could join the clearinghouse by pledging a certain amount of property (including savings) as collateral. On the basis of this pledge, an account would be opened for the new member and credited with a sum of mutual pounds equivalent to some fraction of the assessed value of the property pledged. The new member would agree to repay this amount plus the service fee into their account by a certain date. The mutual pounds could then be transferred through the clearinghouse to the accounts of other members, who have agreed to receive mutual money in payment for all debts or work done.

The opening of this sort of account is, of course, the same as taking out a "loan" in the sense that a commercial bank "lends" by extending credit to a borrower in return for a signed note pledging a certain amount of property as security. The crucial difference is that the clearinghouse does not purport to be "lending" a sum of money that it **already has,** as is fraudulently claimed by commercial banks. Instead it honestly admits that it is creating new money in the form of credit. New accounts can also be opened simply by telling the clearinghouse that one wants an account and then arranging with other people who already have balances to transfer mutual money into one's account in exchange for goods or services.

Another form of mutual credit are LETS systems. In this a number of people get together to form an association. They create a unit of exchange (which is equal in value to a unit of the national currency usually), choose a name for it and offer each other goods and services priced in these units. These offers and wants are listed in a directory which is circulated periodically to members. Members decide who they wish to trade with and how much trading they wish to do. When a transaction is completed, this is acknowledged with a "cheque" made out by the buyer and given to the seller. These are passed on to the system accounts administration which keeps a record of all transactions and periodically sends members a statement of their accounts. The accounts administration is elected by, and accountable to, the membership and information about balances is available to all members.

Unlike the first system described, members do not have to present property as collateral. Members of a LETS scheme can go into "debt" without it, although "debt" is the wrong word as members are not so much going into debt as committing themselves to do some work within the system in the future and by so doing they are creating spending power. The willingness of members to incur such a commitment could be described as a service to the community as others are free to use the units so created to trade themselves. Indeed, the number of units in existence exactly matches the amount of real wealth being exchanged. The system only works if members are willing to spend. It runs on trust and builds up trust as the system is used.

It is likely that a fully functioning mutual banking system would incorporate aspects of both these systems. The need for collateral may be used when members require very large loans while the LETS system of negative credit as a commitment to future work would be the normal function of the system. If the mutual bank agrees a maximum limit for negative balances, it may agree to take collateral for transactions that exceed this limit. However, it is obvious that any mutual banking system will find the best means of working in the circumstances it finds itself.

J.5.9
How does mutual credit work?

Let us consider an example of how business would be transacted using mutual credit within capitalism. There are two possibilities, depending on whether the mutual credit is based upon whether the creditor can provide collateral or not. We will take the case with collateral first.

Suppose that A, an organic farmer, pledges as collateral a certain plot of land that she owns and on which she wishes to build a house. The land is valued at, say, £40,000 in the capitalist market and by pledging the land, A is able to open a credit account at the clearinghouse for, say, £30,000 in mutual money. She does so knowing that there are many other members of the system who are carpenters, electricians, plumbers, hardware suppliers, and so on who are willing to accept mutual pounds in payment for their products or services.

It is easy to see why other subscriber-members, who have also obtained mutual credit and are therefore in debt to the clearinghouse, would be willing to accept such notes in return for their goods and services. They need to collect mutual currency to repay their debts. Why would someone who is not in debt for mutual currency be willing to accept it as money?

To see why, let us suppose that B, an underemployed carpenter, currently has no account at the clearinghouse but that he knows about it and the people who operate and use it. After examining its list of members and becoming familiar with the policies of the new organisation, he is convinced that it does not extend credit frivolously to untrustworthy recipients who are likely to default. He also knows that if he contracts to do the carpentry on A's new house and agrees to be paid for his work in mutual money, he will then be able to use it to buy groceries, clothes, and other goods and services from various people in the community who already belong to the system.

Thus B will be willing, and perhaps even eager (especially if the economy is in recession and regular money is tight) to work for A and receive payment in mutual credit. For he knows that if he is paid, say, £8,000 in mutual money for his labour on A's house, this payment constitutes, in effect, 20 percent of a mortgage on her land, the value of which is represented by her mutual credit. B also understands that A has promised to repay this mortgage by producing new value — that is, by growing organic fruits and vegetables and selling them to other members of the system — and that it is this promise to produce new wealth which gives her mutual credit its value as a medium of exchange.

To put this point slightly differently, A's mutual credit can be thought of as a lien against goods or services which she will create in the future. As security of this guarantee, she agrees that if she is unable for some reason to fulfil her obligation, the land she has pledged will be sold to other members. In this way, a value sufficient to cancel her debt (and probably then some) will be returned to the system. This provision insures that the clearinghouse is able to balance its books and gives members confidence that mutual money is sound. It should be noticed that since new wealth is continually being created, the basis for new mutual credit is also being created at the same time. Thus, suppose that after A's new house has been built, her daughter, C, along with a group of friends D, E, F, ... , decide that they want to start a co-operative restaurant but that C and her friends do not have enough collateral to obtain a start-up loan. A, however, is willing to co-sign a note for them, pledging her new house (valued at say, £80,000) as security. On this basis, C and her partners are able to obtain £60,000 worth of mutual credit, which they then use to buy equipment, supplies, furniture, advertising, etc. to start their restaurant.

This example illustrates one way in which people without property are able to obtain credit in the new system. Another way — for those who cannot find (or perhaps do not wish to ask) someone with property to co-sign for them — is to make a down payment and then use the property which is to be purchased on credit as security, as in the current method of obtaining a home or other loan. With mutual credit, however, this form of financing can be used to purchase anything, including the means of production and other equipment required for workers to work for themselves instead of a boss.

Which brings us to the case of an individual without means for providing collateral — say, for example Z, a plumber, who currently does not own the land she uses. In such a case, Z, who still desires work done, would contact other members of the mutual bank with the skills she requires. Those members with the appropriate skills and who agree to work with her commit themselves to do the required tasks. In return, Z gives them a check in mutual dollars which is credited to their account and deducted from hers. She does not pay interest on this issue of credit and the sum only represents her willingness to do some work for other members of the bank at some future date.

The mutual bank does not have to worry about the negative balance, as this does not create a loss within the group as the minuses which have been incurred have already created wealth (pluses) within the system and it stays there. It is likely, of course, that the mutual bank would agree an upper limit on negative balances and require some form of collateral for credit greater than this limit, but for most exchanges this would be unlikely to be relevant.

It is important to remember that mutual money has no **intrinsic** value, since they cannot be redeemed (at the mutual bank) in gold or anything else. All they are promises of future labour. They are a mere medium for the facilitation of exchange used to facilitate the increased production of goods and services (as discussed in section G.3.6, it is this increase which ensures that mutual credit is not inflationary). This also ensures enough work for all and, ultimately, the end of exploitation as working people can buy their own means of production and so end wage-labour by self-employment and co-operation.

For more information on how mutual banking is seen to work see the collection of Proudhon's works collected in **Proudhon's Solution to the Social Problem**. William B. Greene's **Mutual Banking** and Benjamin Tucker's **Instead of a Book** should also be consulted.

J.5.10 Why do anarchists support co-operatives?

Support for co-operatives is a common feature in anarchist writings. In fact, support for democratic workplaces is as old as use of the term anarchist to describe our ideas. So why do anarchists support co-operatives? It is because they are the only way to guarantee freedom in production and so *"the co-operative system ... carries within it the germ of the future economic order."* [Bakunin, **The Philosophy of Bakunin**, p. 385]

Anarchists support all kinds of co-operatives: housing, food, consumer, credit and workplace ones. All forms of co-operation are useful as they accustom their members to work together for their common benefit as well as ensuring extensive experience in managing their own affairs. As such, all forms of co-operatives are (to some degree) useful examples of self-management and anarchy in action. Here we will concentrate on producer co-operatives as only these can **replace** the capitalist mode of production. They are examples of a new mode of production, one based upon associated, not wage, labour. As long as wage-labour exists within industry and agriculture then capitalism remains and no amount of other kinds of co-operatives will end it. If wage slavery exists, then so will exploitation and oppression and anarchy will remain but a hope.

Co-operatives are the *"germ of the future"* for two reasons. Firstly, co-operatives are based on one worker, one vote. In other words those who do the work manage the workplace within which they do it (i.e. they are based on workers' self-management). Thus co-operatives are an example of the "horizontal" directly democratic organisation that anarchists support and so are an example of *"anarchy in action"* (even if in an imperfect way) within capitalism. Secondly, they are an example of working class self-help and self-activity. Instead of relying on others to provide work, co-operatives show that production can be carried on without the existence of a class of masters employing a class of order takers.

Workplace co-operatives also present evidence of the viability of an anarchist economy. It is well established that co-operatives are usually more productive and efficient than their capitalist equivalents. This indicates that hierarchical workplaces are **not** required in order to produce useful goods and indeed can be harmful. It also indicates that the capitalist market does not actually allocate resources efficiently nor has any tendency to do so.

So why should co-operatives be more efficient? Firstly, there are the positive effects of increased liberty. Co-operatives, by abolishing wage slavery, obviously increase the liberty of those who work in them. Members take an active part in the management of their working lives and so authoritarian social relations are replaced by libertarian ones. Unsurprisingly, this liberty also leads to an increase in productivity — just as wage labour is more productive than slavery, so associated labour is more productive than wage slavery. As Kropotkin argued: *"the only guarantee not to be robbed of the fruits of your labour is to possess the instruments of labour ... man really produces most when he works in freedom, when he has a certain choice in his occupations, when he has no overseer to impede him, and lastly, when he sees his work bringing profit to* him and to others who work like him, but bringing in little to idlers." [**The Conquest of Bread**, p. 145]

There are also the positive advantages associated with participation (i.e. self-management, liberty in other words). Within a self-managed, co-operative workplace, workers are directly involved in decision making and so these decisions are enriched by the skills, experiences and ideas of all members of the workplace. In the words of Colin Ward:

> "You can be **in** authority, or you can be **an** authority, or you can **have** authority. The first derives from your rank in some chain of command, the second derives from special knowledge, and the third from special wisdom. But knowledge and wisdom are not distributed in order of rank, and they are no one person's monopoly in any undertaking. The fantastic inefficiency of any hierarchical organisation — any factory, office, university, warehouse or hospital — is the outcome of two almost invariable characteristics. One is that the knowledge and wisdom of the people at the bottom of the pyramid finds no place in the decision-making leadership hierarchy of the institution. Frequently it is devoted to making the institution work in spite of the formal leadership structure, or alternatively to sabotaging the ostensible function of the institution, because it is none of their choosing. The other is that they would rather not be there anyway: they are there through economic necessity rather than through identification with a common task which throws up its own shifting and functional leadership.

> "Perhaps the greatest crime of the industrial system is the way it systematically thwarts the investing genius of the majority of its workers." [**Anarchy in Action**, p. 41]

Also, as workers also own their place of work, they have an interest in developing the skills and abilities of their members and, obviously, this also means that there are few conflicts within the workplace. Unlike capitalist firms, there is no conflict between bosses and wage slaves over work loads, conditions or the division of value created between them. All these factors will increase the quality, quantity and efficiency of work, increase efficient utilisation of available resources and aid the introduction of new techniques and technologies.

Secondly, the increased efficiency of co-operatives results from the benefits associated with co-operation itself. Not only does co-operation increase the pool of knowledge and abilities available within the workplace and enriches that source by communication and interaction, it also ensures that the workforce are working together instead of competing and so wasting time and energy. As Alfie Kohn notes (in relation to investigations of in-firm co-operation):

> "Dean Tjosvold ... conducted [studies] at utility companies, manufacturing plants, engineering firms, and many other kinds of organisations. Over and over again, Tjosvold has found that 'co-operation makes a work force motivated' whereas 'serious competition undermines co-ordination' ... Meanwhile, the management guru ... T. Edwards Demming, has declared that the practice of having

employees compete against each other is 'unfair [and] destructive. We cannot afford this nonsense any longer ... [We need to] work together on company problems [but] annual rating of performance, incentive pay, [or] bonuses cannot live with team work ... What takes the joy out of learning ... [or out of] anything? Trying to be number one.'" [**No Contest**, p. 240]

Thirdly, there are the benefits associated with increased equality. Studies prove that business performance deteriorates when pay differentials become excessive. In a study of over 100 businesses (producing everything from kitchen appliances to truck axles), researchers found that the greater the wage gap between managers and workers, the lower their product's quality. [Douglas Cowherd and David Levine, "*Product Quality and Pay Equity,*" **Administrative Science Quarterly**, No. 37, pp. 302-30] Businesses with the greatest inequality were plagued with a high employee turnover rate. Study author David Levine said: "*These organisations weren't able to sustain a workplace of people with shared goals.*" [quoted by John Byrne, "*How high can CEO pay go?*" **Business Week**, April 22, 1996] The negative effects of income inequality can also be seen on a national level as well. Economists Torsten Persson and Guido Tabellini conducted a thorough statistical analysis of historical inequality and growth, and found that nations with more equal incomes generally experience faster productive growth. ["*Is Inequality Harmful for Growth?*", **American Economic Review** no. 84, pp. 600-21] Numerous other studies have also confirmed their findings (the negative impacts of inequality on all aspects of life are summarised by Richard Wilkinson and Kate Pickett in **The Spirit Level: Why More Equal Societies Almost Always Do Better**). Real life yet again disproves the assumptions of capitalism: inequality harms us all, even the capitalist economy which produces it.

This is to be expected. Workers, seeing an increasing amount of the value they create being monopolised by top managers and a wealthy elite and not re-invested into the company to secure their employment prospects, will hardly be inclined to put in that extra effort or care about the quality of their work. Bosses who use the threat of unemployment to extract more effort from their workforce are creating a false economy. While they will postpone decreasing profits in the short term due to this adaptive strategy (and enrich themselves in the process) the pressures placed upon the system will bring harsh long term effects — both in terms of economic crisis (as income becomes so skewed as to create realisation problems and the limits of adaptation are reached in the face of international competition) and social breakdown.

As would be imagined, co-operative workplaces tend to be more egalitarian than capitalist ones. This is because in capitalist firms, the incomes of top management must be justified (in practice) to a small number of individuals (namely, those shareholders with sizeable stock in the firm), who are usually quite wealthy and so not only have little to lose in granting huge salaries but are also predisposed to see top managers as being very much like themselves and so are entitled to comparable incomes (and let us not forget that "*corporate boards, largely selected by the CEO, hire compensation experts, almost always chosen by the CEO, to determine how much the CEO is worth.*" [Paul Krugman, **The Conscience of a Liberal**, p. 144]).

In contrast, the incomes of management in worker controlled firms have to be justified to a workforce whose members experience the relationship between management incomes and their own directly and who, no doubt, are predisposed to see their elected managers as being workers like themselves and accountable to them. Such an egalitarian atmosphere will have a positive impact on production and efficiency as workers will see that the value they create is not being accumulated by others but distributed according to work actually done (and not control over power). In the Mondragon co-operatives, for example, the maximum pay differential is 9 to 1 (increased from 3 to 1 after much debate in a response to outside pressures from capitalist firms hiring away workers) while (in the USA) the average CEO is paid well over 100 times the average worker (up from 41 times in 1960).

Therefore, we see that co-operatives prove the advantages of (and the inter-relationship between) key anarchist principles such as liberty, equality, solidarity and self-management. Their application, whether all together or in part, has a positive impact on efficiency and work — and, as we will discuss in section J.5.12, the capitalist market actively **blocks** the spread of these more egalitarian and efficient productive techniques instead of encouraging them. Even by its own standards, capitalism stands condemned — it does not encourage the efficient use of resources and actively places barriers in their development.

From all this it is clear to see why co-operatives are supported by anarchists. We are *"convinced that the co-operative could, potentially, replace capitalism and carries within it the seeds of economic emancipation ... The workers learn from this precious experience how to organise and themselves conduct the economy without guardian angels, the state or their former employers."* [Bakunin, **Bakunin on Anarchism**, p. 399] Co-operatives give us a useful insight into the possibilities of a free, socialist, economy. Even within the hierarchical capitalist economy, co-operatives show us that a better future is possible and that production can be organised in a co-operative fashion and that by so doing we can reap the individual and social benefits of working together as equals.

However, this does not mean that all aspects of the co-operative movement find favour with anarchists. As Bakunin pointed out, *"there are two kinds of co-operative: bourgeois co-operation, which tends to create a privileged class, a sort of new collective bourgeoisie organised into a stockholding society: and truly Socialist co-operation, the co-operation of the future which for this very reason is virtually impossible of realisation at present."* [**Op. Cit.**, p. 385] In other words, while co-operatives are the germ of the future, in the present they are often limited by the capitalist environment they find themselves in, narrow their vision to just surviving within the current system and so adapt to it.

For most anarchists, the experience of co-operatives has proven without doubt that, however excellent in principle and useful in practice, if they are kept within capitalism they cannot become the dominant mode of production and free the masses (see section J.5.11). In order to fully develop, co-operatives must be part of a wider social movement which includes community and industrial unionism and the creation of a anarchistic social framework which can encourage *"truly Socialist co-operation"* and discourage *"bourgeois co-operation."* As Murray Bookchin correctly argued: *"Removed*

*from a libertarian municipalist [or other anarchist] context and movement focused on achieving revolutionary municipalist goals as a **dual power** against corporations and the state, food [and other forms of] co-ops are little more than benign enterprises that capitalism and the state can easily tolerate with no fear of challenge."* [**Democracy and Nature**, no. 9, p. 175]

So while co-operatives are an important aspect of anarchist ideas and practice, they are not the be all or end all of our activity. Without a wider social movement which creates all (or at least most) of the future society in the shell of the old, co-operatives will never arrest the growth of capitalism or transcend the narrow horizons of the capitalist economy.

J.5.11 If workers really want self-management then why are there so few co-operatives?

Supporters of capitalism suggest that producer co-operatives would spring up spontaneously if workers really wanted them. To quote leading propertarian Robert Nozick, under capitalism *"it is open to any wealthy radical or group of workers to buy an existing factory or establish a new one, and to ... institute worker-controlled, democratically-run firms."* If *"they are superior, by market standards, to their more orthodox competitors"* then *"there should be little difficulty in establishing successful factories of this sort."* Thus there is *"a means of realising the worker-control scheme that can be brought about by the voluntary actions of people in a free [sic!] society."* [**Anarchy, State, and Utopia**, pp. 250-2] So if such co-operatives were really economically viable and desired by workers, they would spread until eventually they undermined capitalism. Propertarians conclude that since this is not happening, it must be because workers' self-management is either economically inefficient or is not really attractive to workers, or both.

David Schweickart has decisively answered this argument by showing that the reason there are not more producer co-operatives is structural:

> *"A worker-managed firm lacks an expansionary dynamic. When a capitalist enterprise is successful, the owner can increase her profits by reproducing her organisation on a larger scale. She lacks neither the means nor the motivation to expand. Not so with a worker-managed firm. Even if the workers have the means, they lack the incentive, because enterprise growth would bring in new workers with whom the increased proceeds would have to be shared. Co-operatives, even when prosperous, do not spontaneously grow. But if this is so, then each new co-operative venture (in a capitalist society) requires a new wealthy radical or a new group of affluent radical workers willing to experiment. Because such people doubtless are in short supply, it follows that the absence of a large and growing co-operative movement proves nothing about the viability of worker self-management, nor about the preferences of workers."* [**Against Capitalism**, p. 239]

This means that in, say, a mutualist economy there would be more firms of a smaller size supplying a given market compared to capitalism. So a free economy, with the appropriate institutional framework, need not worry about unemployment for while individual co-operatives may not expand as fast as capitalist firms, more co-operatives would be set up (see section I.3.1 for why the neo-classical analysis of co-operatives which Nozick implicitly invokes is false). In short, the environment within which a specific workplace operates is just as important as its efficiency.

This is important, as the empirical evidence is strong that self-management **is** more efficient than wage-slavery. As economist Geoffrey M. Hodgson summarises, support for *"the proposition that participatory and co-operative firms enjoy greater productivity and longevity comes from a large amount of ... case study and econometric evidence"* and *"the weight of testimony"* is *"in favour or [indicates] a positive correlation between participation and productivity."* [*"Organizational Form and Economic Evolution: A critique of the Williamsonian hypothesis"*, pp. 98-115, **Democracy and Efficiency in Economic Enterprises**, U. Pagano and R. E. Rowthorn (eds.), p. 100] This is ignored by the likes of Nozick in favour of thought-experiments rooted in the dubious assumptions of bourgeois economics. He implicitly assumed that because most firms are hierarchical today then they must be more efficient. In short, Nozick abused economic selection arguments by simply assuming, without evidence, that the dominant form of organisation is, *ipso facto*, more efficient. In reality, this is not the case.

The question now becomes one of explaining why, if co-operation is more efficient than wage-slavery, does economic liberty not displace capitalism? The awkward fact is that individual efficiency is not the key to survival as such an argument *"ignores the important point that the selection of the 'fitter' in evolution is not simply relative to the less successful but is dependent upon the general circumstances and environment in which selection takes place."* Moreover, an organism survives because its birth rate exceeds its death rate. If more capitalist firms secure funding from capitalist banks then, obviously, it is more likely for them to secure dominance in the economy simply because there are more of them rather than because they are more efficient. As such, large numbers do not imply greater efficiency as the *"rapid flow of new entrants of hierarchical form"* may *"swamp the less hierarchical firms even if other selection processes are working in favour of the latter."* [Hodgson, **Op. Cit.**, p. 100 and p. 103] Thus:

> *"The degree of fitness of any organism can only be meaningfully considered in relation to its environment ... the market may help to select firms that are fit for the market, but these surviving firms needn't be the most 'efficient' in some absolute sense. In fact, the specification of 'the market' as a selection process is incomplete because the market is only one institution of many needed to specify an environment."* [Michael J. Everett and Alanson P. Minkler, *"Evolution and organisational choice in nineteenth-century Britain"*, pp. 51-62, **Cambridge Journal of Economics** vol. 17, No. 1, p. 53]

As an obvious example there are the difficulties co-operatives can face in finding access to credit facilities required by them from capitalist banks and investors. As Tom Cahill notes, co-operatives in the nineteenth century *"had the specific problem of ... **giving credit**"* while *"**competition with price cutting capitalist** firms ... highlighting the inadequate reservoirs of the under-financed co-ops."* [*"Co-operatives and Anarchism: A contemporary Perspective"*, pp 235-58, **For Anarchism**, Paul Goodway (ed.), p. 239] This points to a general issue, namely that there are often difficulties for co-operatives in raising money:

> *"Co-operatives in a capitalist environment are likely to have more difficulty in raising capital. Quite apart from ideological hostility (which may be significant), external investors will be reluctant to put their money into concerns over which they will have little or no control — which tends to be the case with a co-operative. Because co-operatives in a capitalist environment face special difficulties, and because they lack the inherent expansionary dynamic of a capitalist firm, it is hardy surprising that they are far from dominant."* [Schweickart, **Op. Cit.**, p 240]

In addition, the *"return on capital is limited"* in co-operatives. [Tom Cahill, **Op. Cit.**, p. 247] This means that investors are less-likely to invest in co-operatives, and so co-operatives will tend to suffer from a lack of investment. So despite *"the potential efficiency of such [self-managed] workplaces"*, capitalism *"may be systematically biased against participatory workplaces"* and as *"a result the economy can be trapped in a socially suboptimal position."* Capital market issues, amongst others, help explain this as such firms *"face higher transaction costs for raising equity and loans."* [David I. Levine and Laura D'Andrea Tyson, *"Participation, Productivity, and the Firm's Environment"*, pp. 183-237, **Paying for Productivity**, Alan S. Blinder (ed.), pp. 235-6 and p. 221]

Tom Cahill outlines the investment problem when he writes that the *"financial problem"* is a major reason why co-operatives failed in the past, for *"basically the unusual structure and aims of co-operatives have always caused problems for the dominant sources of capital. In general, the finance environment has been hostile to the emergence of the co-operative spirit."* He also notes that they were *"unable to devise structuring to **maintain a boundary** between those who work and those who own or control ... It is understood that when outside investors were allowed to have power within the co-op structure, co-ops lost their distinctive qualities."* [**Op. Cit.**, pp. 238-239] So even **if** co-operatives do attract investors, the cost of so doing may be to transform the co-operatives into capitalist firms. So while all investors experience risk, this *"is even more acute"* in co-operatives *"because investors must simultaneously cede control **and** risk their entire wealth. Under an unlimited liability rule, investors will rationally demand some control over the firm's operations to protect their wealth. Since [co-operatives] cannot cede control without violating one of the organisation's defining tenets, investors will demand an investment premium, a premium not required from equity investments."* [Everett and Minkler, **Op. Cit.**, p. 52] Needless to say, such a premium is a strain on a co-operative and makes it harder to survive simply because it has higher costs for debt repayment. If such external investment is not forthcoming, then the co-operative is dependent on retained earnings and its members' savings which, unsurprisingly, are often insufficient.

All of which suggests that Nozick's assertion that *"don't say that its against the class interest of investors to support the growth of some enterprise that if successful would end or diminish the investment system. Investors are not so altruistic. They act in personal and not their class interests"* is false. [**Op. Cit.**, pp. 252-3] Nozick is correct, to a degree, but he forgets that class interest is a fusion of individual interests. Given a choice between returns from investments in capitalist firms because a management elite has similar interests in maximising unpaid labour and workers in a co-operative which controls any surplus, the investor will select the former. Moreover, lack of control by investors plays its role as they cannot simply replace the management in a co-operative — that power lies in the hands of the workforce. The higher premiums required by investors to forsake such privileges place a burden on the co-operative, so reducing their likelihood of getting funds in the first place or surviving and, needless to say, increasing the risk that investors face. Thus the personal and class interest of investors merge, with the personal desire to make money ensuring that the class position of the individual is secured. This does not reflect the productivity or efficiency of the investment — quite the reverse! — it reflects the social function of wage labour in maximising profits and returns on capital (see next section for more on this). In other words, the personal interests of investors will generally support their class interests (unsurprisingly, as class interests are not independent of personal interests and will tend to reflect them!).

There are other structural problems as well. Co-operatives face the negative externalities generated by the capitalist economy they operate within. For one thing, since their pay levels are set by members' democratic vote, co-operatives tend to be more egalitarian in their income structure. This means that in a capitalist environment, co-operatives are in constant danger of having their most skilled members hired away by capitalist firms who can, due to their resources, out-bid the co-operative. While this may result in exploitation of the worker, the capitalist firm has the resources to pay higher wages and so it makes sense for them to leave (*"As to the employer who pays an engineer twenty times more than a labourer, it is simply due to personal interest; if the engineer can economise $4000 a year on the cost of production; the employer pays him $800 … He parts with an extra $40 when he expects to gain $400 by it; and this is the essence of the Capitalist system."* [Kropotkin, **The Conquest of Bread**, p. 165]). However, in a co-operative system there would not be the inequalities of economic wealth (created by capitalist firms and finance structures) which allows such poaching to happen.

There are cultural issues as well. As Jon Elster points out, it is a *"truism, but an important one, that workers' preferences are to a large extent shaped by their economic environment. Specifically, there is a tendency to adaptive preference formation, by which the actual mode of economic organisation comes to be perceived as superior to all others."* [*"From Here to There"*, pp. 93-111, **Socialism**, Paul, Miller Jr., Paul, and Greenberg (eds.), p. 110] In other words, people view "what is" as given and feel no urge to change to "what could be." In the context of creating alternatives within capitalism, this can have serious effects on the spread of alternatives and indicates the importance of anarchists encouraging the spirit of revolt to break down this mental apathy.

This acceptance of "what is" can be seen, to some degree, by some companies which meet the formal conditions for co-operatives, for example ESOP owned firms in the USA, but lack effective workers' control. ESOP (Employee Stock Ownership Plans) enable a firm's workforce to gain the majority of a company's shares but the unequal distribution of shares amongst employees prevents the great majority of workers from having any effective control or influence on decisions. Unlike real co-operatives (based on "one worker, one vote") these firms are based on "one share, one vote" and so have more in common with capitalist firms than co-operatives.

Finally, there is the question of history, of path dependency. Path dependency is the term used to describe when the set of decisions one faces for any given circumstance is limited by the decisions made in the past, even though past circumstances may no longer be relevant. This is often associated with the economics of technological change in a society which depends quantitatively and/or qualitatively on its own past (the most noted example this is the QWERTY keyboard, which would not be in use today except that it happened to be chosen in the nineteenth century). Evolutionary systems are path dependent, with historical events pushing development in specific directions. Thus, if there were barriers against or encouragement for certain forms of organisational structure in the past then the legacy of this will continue to dominate due to the weight of history rather than automatically being replaced by new, more efficient, forms.

This can be seen from co-operatives, as *"labour managed firms were originally at a substantial disadvantage compared to their capitalist counterparts"* as the law *"imposed additional risks and costs"* on them while *"early financial instruments were ill-suited to the establishment and continuation of worker co-operatives. The subsequent coevolution of firms and supporting institutions involved a path-dependent process where labour-managed firms were at a continual disadvantage, even after many of the earlier impediments were removed."* [Hodgson, **Op. Cit.**, p. 103] *"Historically,"* argue Everett and Minkler *"both company and co-operative law were incompatible with democratic decision-making by workers."* The law ensured that the *"burden was more costly"* to labour-managed firms and these *"obstacles led to an environment dominated by investor-controlled firms (capitalist firms) in which informal constraints (behaviours and routines) emerged to reinforce the existing institutions. A path-dependent process incorporating these informal constraints continued to exclude [their] widespread formation."* When the formal constraints which prevented the formation of co-operatives were finally removed, the *"informal constraints"* produced as a result of these *"continued to prevent the widespread formation"* of co-operatives. So the lack of co-operatives *"can thus be explained quite independently of any of the usual efficiency criteria."* [**Op. Cit.**, p. 58 and p. 60] Nor should we forget that the early industrial system was influenced by the state, particularly by rewarding war related contracts to hierarchical firms modelled on the military and that the state rewarded contracts to run various state services and industries to capitalist firms rather than, as Proudhon urged, to workers associations.

So *"there are several good reasons why more efficient firms need not always be selected in a competitive and 'evolutionary' process."* [Hodgson, **Op. Cit.**, p. 99] So it is not efficiency as such which explains the domination of capitalist firms for *"empirical studies suggest that co-operatives are at least as productive as their capitalist counterparts,"* with many having *"an excellent record, superior to conventionally organised firms over a long period."* [Jon Elster, **Op. Cit.**, p. 96] So all things being equal, co-operatives are more efficient than their capitalist counterparts — but when co-operatives compete in a capitalist economy, all things are **not** equal. As David Schweickart argues:

> *"Even if worker-managed firms are preferred by the vast majority, and even if they are more productive, a market initially dominated by capitalist firms may not select for them. The common-sense neo-classical dictum that only those things that best accord with people's desires will survive the struggle of free competition has never been the whole truth with respect to anything; with respect to workplace organisation it is barely a half-truth."* [**Op. Cit.**, p. 240]

It is illuminating, though, to consider why Nozick ignored the substantial empirical evidence that participation **is** more efficient than hierarchy and, as a result, why *"market criteria"* does not result in the more productive and efficient co-operative production displacing the authoritarian workplace. Far better, it must be supposed, to just assume that the dominant form of workplace is more "efficient" and implicitly invoke a quasi-Darwinian individualistic selection mechanism in an ahistorical and institution-less framework. So people like Nozick who suggest that because worker co-operatives are few in number that this means they are forced out by competition because they are inefficient miss the point. A key reason for this lack of co-operative firms, argues Hodgson, *"is that competitive selection depends on the economic context, and while the institutional context of a capitalist system may be more conducive for the capitalist firm, a different context may favour the co-operative firm."* [**Economics and Utopia**, p. 288]

As discussed in section I.3.5, Proudhon was well aware that for mutualism to prosper and survive an appropriate institutional framework was required (the *"agro-industrial federation"* and mutual banking). So an organisation's survival also depends on the co-evolution of supporting informal constraints. If a co-operative is isolated within a capitalist economy, without co-operative institutions around it, it comes as no great surprise to discover that they find it difficult to survive never mind displace its (usually larger and well-established) capitalist competitors.

Yet in spite of these structural problems and the impact of previous state interventions, co-operatives do exist under capitalism but just because they can survive in such a harsh environment it does not automatically mean that they shall **replace** that economy. Co-operatives face pressures to adjust to the dominant mode of production. The presence of wage labour and investment capital in the wider economy will tempt successful co-operatives to hire workers or issue shares to attract new investment. In so doing, however, they may end up losing their identities as co-operatives by diluting ownership (and so re-introducing exploitation by having to pay non-workers interest) or by making the co-operative someone's boss (which creates *"a new class of workers who exploit and profit from the labour of their employees. And all this fosters a bourgeois*

mentality." [Bakunin, **Bakunin on Anarchism**, p. 399]).

Hence the pressures of working in a capitalist market may result in co-operatives pursuing activities which may result in short term gain or survival, but are sure to result in harm in the long run. Far from co-operatives slowly expanding within and changing a capitalist environment it is more likely that capitalist logic will expand into and change the co-operatives that work in it (this can be seen from the Mondragon co-operatives, where there has been a slight rise in the size of wage labour being used and the fact that the credit union has, since 1992, invested in non-co-operative firms). These externalities imposed upon isolated co-operatives within capitalism (which would not arise within a fully co-operative context) block local moves towards anarchism. The idea that co-operation will simply win out in competition within well developed capitalist economic systems is just wishful thinking. Just because a system is more liberatory, just and efficient does not mean it will survive or prosper in an authoritarian economic and social environment.

So both theory and history suggests that isolated co-operatives will more likely adapt to capitalist realities than remain completely true to their co-operative promise. For most anarchists, therefore, co-operatives can reach their full potential only as part of a social movement aiming to change society. Only as part of a wider movement of community and workplace unionism, with mutualist banks to provide long term financial support and commitment, can co-operatives be communalised into a network of solidarity and support that will reduce the problems of isolation and adaptation. Hence Bakunin:

> *"We want co-operation too ... But at the same time, we know that it prospers, developing itself fully and freely, embracing all human industry, only when it is based on equality, when all capital and every instrument of labour, including the soil, belong to the people by right of collective property ... Once this is acknowledged we hardly oppose the creation of co-operative associations; we find them necessary in many respects ... they accustom the workers to organise, pursue, and manage their interests themselves, without interference either by bourgeois capital or by bourgeois control ... [they must be] founded on the principle of solidarity and collectivity rather than on bourgeois exclusivity, then society will pass from its present situation to one of equality and justice without too many great upheavals."* [**The Basic Bakunin**, p. 153]

Until then, co-operatives will exist within capitalism but not replace it by market forces — only a **social** movement and collective action can fully secure their full development. This means that while anarchists support, create and encourage co-operatives within capitalism, we understand *"the impossibility of putting into practice the co-operative system under the existing conditions of the predominance of bourgeois capital in the process of production and distribution of wealth."* Because of this, most anarchists stress the need for more combative organisations such as industrial and community unions and other bodies *"formed,"* to use Bakunin's words, *"for the organisation of toilers against the privileged world"* in order to help bring about a free society. [**The Political Philosophy of Bakunin**, p. 385]

Finally, we must note an irony with Nozick's argument, namely the notion that capitalism (his *"free society"*) allows a *"voluntary"* path to economic liberty. The irony is two-fold. First, the creation of capitalism was the result of state action (see section F.8). While working class people are expected to play by the rules decreed by capitalism, capitalists have never felt the urge to do so. It is this state coercion which helped create the path-dependency which stops *"the market"* selecting more efficient and productive ways of production. Secondly, Nozick's own theory of (property) rights denies that stolen wealth can be legitimately transferred. In other words, expecting workers to meekly accept previous coercion by seeking investors to fund their attempts at economic liberty, as Nozick did, is implicitly accepting that theft is property. While such intellectual incoherence is to be expected from defenders of capitalism, it does mean that propertarians really have no ground to oppose working class people following the advice of libertarians and expropriating their workplaces. In other words, transforming the environment and breaking the path-dependency which stops economic liberty from flowering to its full potential.

J.5.12 If self-management were more efficient then surely capitalists would introduce it?

Some supporters of capitalism argue that if self-management really were more efficient than hierarchy, then capitalists would be forced to introduce it by the market. As propertarian Robert Nozick argued, if workers' control meant that *"the productivity of the workers in a factory **rises** ... then the individual owners pursuing profits will reorganise the productive process. If the productivity of workers **remains the same** ... then in the process of competing for labourers firms will alter their internal work organisation."* This meant that *"individual owners pursuing profits ... will reorganise the productive process."* [**Anarchy, State, and Utopia**, p. 248] As this has not happened then self-management cannot be more efficient. While such a notion seems plausible in theory, in practice it is flawed as *"there is a vast quantity of empirical evidence demonstrating that participatory workplaces tend to be places of higher morale and greater productivity than authoritarian workplaces."* [David Schweickart , **Against Capitalism**, p. 228] So Nozick's thought experiment is contradicted by reality. Capitalism places innumerable barriers to the spread of worker empowering structures within production, in spite (perhaps, as we will see, **because**) of their (well-documented) higher efficiency and productivity. This can be seen from the fact that while the increased efficiency associated with workers' participation and self-management has attracted the attention of many capitalist firms, the few experiments conducted have failed to spread even though they were extremely successful. This is due to the nature of capitalist production and the social relationships it produces.

As we noted in section D.10, capitalist firms (particularly in the west) made a point of introducing technologies and management structures that aimed to deskill and disempower workers. In this way, it was hoped to make the worker increasingly subject to "market discipline" (i.e. easier to train, so increasing the pool of workers available to replace any specific worker and so reducing workers power by increasing management's power to fire them). Of course, what actually happens is that after a short period of time while management gained the upper hand, the workforce found newer and more effective ways to fight back and assert their productive power again. While for a short time the technological change worked, over the longer period the balance of forces changed, so forcing management to continually try to empower themselves at the expense of the workforce.

It is unsurprising that such attempts to reduce workers to order-takers fail. Workers' experiences and help are required to ensure production actually happens at all. When workers carry out their orders strictly and faithfully (i.e. when they "work to rule") production stops. So most capitalists are aware of the need to get workers to "co-operate" within the workplace to some degree. A few capitalist companies have gone further. Seeing the advantages of fully exploiting (and we do mean exploiting) the experience, skills, abilities and thoughts of their employees which the traditional authoritarian capitalist workplace denies them, some have introduced various schemes to "enrich" and "enlarge" work, increase "co-operation" between workers and their bosses, to encourage workers to "participate" in their own exploitation by introducing *"a modicum of influence, a strictly limited area of decision-making power, a voice — at best secondary — in the control of conditions of the workplace."* [Sam Dolgoff, **The Anarchist Collectives**, p. 81] The management and owners still have the power and still reap unpaid labour from the productive activity of the workforce.

David Noble provides a good summary of the problems associated with experiments in workers' self-management within capitalist firms:

> *"Participation in such programs can indeed be a liberating and exhilarating experience, awakening people to their own untapped potential and also to the real possibilities of collective worker control of production. As one manager described the former pilots [workers in a General Electric program]: 'These people will never be the same again. They have seen that things can be different.' But the excitement and enthusiasm engendered by such programs, as well as the heightened sense of commitment to a common purpose, can easily be used against the interests of the work force. First, that purpose is not really 'common' but is still determined by management alone, which continues to decide what will be produced, when, and where. Participation in production does not include participation in decisions on investment, which remains the prerogative of ownership. Thus participation is, in reality, just a variation of business as usual — taking orders — but one which encourages obedience in the name of co-operation.*

> *"Second, participation programs can contribute to the creation of an elite, and reduced, work force, with special privileges and more 'co-operative' attitudes toward management — thus at once undermining the adversary stance of unions and reducing membership ...*

"Third, such programs enable management to learn from workers — who are now encouraged by their co-operative spirit to share what they know — and, then, in Taylorist tradition, to use this knowledge against the workers. As one former pilot reflected, 'They learned from the guys on the floor, got their knowledge about how to optimise the technology and then, once they had it, they eliminated the Pilot Program, put that knowledge into the machines, and got people without any knowledge to run them — on the Company's terms and without adequate compensation. They kept all the gains for themselves.' ...

"Fourth, such programs could provide management with a way to circumvent union rules and grievance procedures or eliminate unions altogether." [**Forces of Production**, pp. 318-9]

Capitalist introduced and supported "workers' control" is very like the situation when a worker receives stock in the company they work for. If it goes a little way toward redressing the gap between the value produced by that person's labour and the wage they receive for it, that in itself cannot be a totally bad thing (although this does not address the issue of workplace hierarchy and its social relations). The real downside of this is the "carrot on a stick" enticement to work harder — if you work extra hard for the company, your stock will be worth more. Obviously, though, the bosses get rich off you, so the more you work, the richer they get, the more you are getting ripped off. It is a choice that anarchists feel many workers cannot afford to make — they need or at least want the money — but we believe that it does not work as workers simply end up working harder, for less. After all, stocks do not represent all profits (large amounts of which end up in the hands of top management) nor are they divided just among those who labour. Moreover, workers may be less inclined to take direct action, for fear that they will damage the value of "their" company's stock, and so they may find themselves putting up with longer, more intense work in worse conditions.

Be that as it may, the results of such capitalist experiments in "workers' control" are interesting and show **why** self-management will not spread by market forces. According to one expert: *"There is scarcely a study in the entire literature which fails to demonstrate that satisfaction in work is enhanced or ... productivity increases occur from a genuine increase in worker's decision-making power. Findings of such consistency ... are rare in social research."* [Paul B. Lumberg, quoted by Herbert Gintis, *"The nature of Labour Exchange and the Theory of Capitalist Production"*, **Radical Political Economy**, vol. 1, Samuel Bowles and Richard Edwards (eds.), p. 252] In spite of these findings, a *"shift toward participatory relationships is scarcely apparent in capitalist production"* and this is *"not compatible with the neo-classical assertion as to the efficiency of the internal organisation of capitalist production."* [Gintz, **Op. Cit.**, p. 252] Economist William Lazonick indicates the reason when he writes that *"[m]any attempts at job enrichment and job enlargement in the first half of the 1970s resulted in the supply of more and better effort by workers. Yet many 'successful' experiments were cut short when the workers whose work*

had been enriched and enlarged began questioning traditional management prerogatives inherent in the existing hierarchical structure of the enterprise." [**Competitive Advantage on the Shop Floor**, p. 282]

This is an important result, as it indicates that the ruling sections within capitalist firms have a vested interest in **not** introducing such schemes, even though they are more efficient methods of production. As can easily be imagined, managers have a clear incentive to resist participatory schemes (as David Schweickart notes, such resistance, *"often bordering on sabotage, is well known and widely documented"* [**Op. Cit.**, p. 229]). As an example of this David Noble discusses a scheme ran by General Electric in the late 1960s:

"After considerable conflict, GE introduced a quality of work life program ... which gave workers much more control over the machines and the production process and eliminated foremen. Before long, by all indicators, the program was succeeding — machine use, output and product quality went up; scrap rate, machine downtime, worker absenteeism and turnover went down, and conflict on the floor dropped off considerably. Yet, little more than a year into the program — following a union demand that it be extended throughout the shop and into other GE locations — top management abolished the program out of fear of losing control over the workforce. Clearly, the company was willing to sacrifice gains in technical and economic efficiency in order to regain and insure management control." [**Progress Without People**, p. 65f]

Simply put, managers and capitalists can see that workers' control experiments expose the awkward fact that they are not needed, that their role is not related to organising production but exploiting workers. They have no urge to introduce reforms which will ultimately make themselves redundant. Moreover, most enjoy the power that comes with their position and have no desire to see it ended. This also places a large barrier in the way of workers' control.

However, it could be claimed that owners of stock, being concerned by the bottom-line of profits, could **force** management to introduce participation. By this method, competitive market forces would ultimately prevail as individual owners, pursuing profits, reorganise production and participation spreads across the economy. Indeed, there are a few firms that **have** introduced such schemes but there has been no tendency for them to spread. This contradicts "free market" capitalist economic theory which states that those firms which introduce more efficient techniques will prosper and competitive market forces will ensure that other firms will introduce the technique.

This has not happened for three reasons.

Firstly, the fact is that within "free market" capitalism **keeping** (indeed strengthening) skills and power in the hands of the workers makes it harder for a capitalist firm to maximise profits (i.e. unpaid labour). It strengthens the power of workers, who can use that power to gain increased wages (i.e. reduce the amount of surplus value they produce for their bosses). Workers' control also leads to a usurpation of capitalist prerogatives — including their share of revenues and their ability to extract more unpaid labour during the working day. While in the short run workers' control may lead to higher productivity (and so may be toyed with), in the long run, it leads to difficulties for capitalists to maximise their profits:

> "given that profits depend on the integrity of the labour exchange, a strongly centralised structure of control not only serves the interests of the employer, but dictates a minute division of labour irrespective of considerations of productivity. For this reason, the evidence for the superior productivity of 'workers control' represents the most dramatic of anomalies to the neo-classical theory of the firm: worker control increases the effective amount of work elicited from each worker and improves the co-ordination of work activities, while increasing the solidarity and delegitimising the hierarchical structure of ultimate authority at its root; hence it threatens to increase the power of workers in the struggle over the share of total value." [Gintz, **Op. Cit.**, p. 264]

A workplace which had extensive workers participation would hardly see the workers agreeing to reduce their skill levels, take a pay cut or increase their pace of work simply to enhance the profits of capitalists. Simply put, profit maximisation is not equivalent to efficiency. Getting workers to work longer, more intensely or in more unpleasant conditions can increase profits but it does not yield more output for the **same** inputs. Workers' control would curtail capitalist means of enhancing profits by changing the quality and quantity of work. It is **this** requirement which also aids in understanding why capitalists will not support workers' control — even though it is more efficient, it reduces capitalist power in production. Moreover, demands to change the nature of workers' inputs into the production process in order to maximise profits for capitalists would provoke a struggle over the intensity of work, working hours, and over the share of value added going to workers, management and owners and so destroy the benefits of participation.

Thus power within the workplace plays a key role in explaining why workers' control does not spread — it reduces the ability of bosses to extract more unpaid labour from workers.

The second reason is related to the first. It too is based on the power structure within the company but the power is related to control over the surplus produced by the workers rather than the ability to control how much surplus is produced in the first place (i.e. power over workers). Hierarchical management is the way to ensure that profits are channelled into the hands of a few. By centralising power, the surplus value produced by workers can be distributed in a way which benefits those at the top (i.e. management and capitalists). This explains the strange paradox of workers' control experiments being successful but being cancelled by management. This is easily explained once the hierarchical nature of capitalist production (i.e. of wage labour) is acknowledged. Workers' control, by placing (some) power in the hands of workers, undermines the authority of management and, ultimately, their power to control the surplus produced by workers and allocate it as they see fit. Thus, while workers' control does reduce costs, increase efficiency and productivity (i.e. maximise the difference between prices and costs) it (potentially) reduces the power of management and owners

to allocate that surplus as they see fit. Indeed, it can be argued that hierarchical control of production exists solely to provide for the accumulation of capital in a few hands, **not** for efficiency or productivity (see Stephan A. Margin, "What do Bosses do? The Origins and Functions of Hierarchy in Capitalist Production", **Op. Cit.**, pp. 178-248).

As David Noble argues, power is the key to understanding capitalism, **not** the drive for profits as such:

> "In opting for control [over the increased efficiency of workers' control] ... management ... knowingly and, it must be assumed, willingly, sacrificed profitable production... . [This] illustrates not only the ultimate management priority of power over both production and profit within the firm, but also the larger contradiction between the preservation of private power and prerogatives, on the one hand, and the social goals of efficient, quality, and useful production, on the other ...

> "It is a common confusion, especially on the part of those trained in or unduly influenced by formal economics (liberal and Marxist alike), that capitalism is a system of profit-motivated, efficient production. This is not true, nor has it ever been. If the drive to maximise profits, through private ownership and control over the process of production, has served historically as the primary means of capitalist development, it has never been the end of that development. The goal has always been domination (and the power and privileges that go with it) and the preservation of domination. There is little historical evidence to support the view that, in the final analysis, capitalists play by the rules of the economic game imagined by theorists. There is ample evidence to suggest, on the other hand, that when the goals of profit-making and efficient production fail to coincide with the requirements of continued dominance, capital will resort to more ancient means: legal, political, and, if need be, military. Always, behind all the careful accounting, lies the threat of force. This system of domination has been legitimated in the past by the ideological invention that private ownership of the means of production and the pursuit of profit via production are always ultimately beneficial to society. Capitalism delivers the goods, it is argued, better, more cheaply, and in larger quantity, and in so doing, fosters economic growth ... The story of the Pilot Program — and it is but one among thousands like it in U.S. industry — raises troublesome questions about the adequacy of this mythology as a description of reality." [**Forces of Production**, pp. 321-2]

Hierarchical organisation (domination) is essential to ensure that profits are controlled by a few and can, therefore, be allocated by them in such a way to ensure their power and privileges. By undermining such authority, workers' control also undermines that power to maximise profits in a certain direction even though it increases "profits" (the difference between prices and costs) in the abstract. As workers' control starts to extend (or management sees its potential to spread) into wider areas such as investment decisions, how to allocate the surplus (i.e. profits) between wages, investment, dividends, management pay and so on, then they will seek to end the project in order to ensure their power over both the workers and the surplus they, the workers, produce (this is, of course, related to the issue of lack of control by investors in co-operatives raised in the last section).

As such, the opposition by managers to workers' control will be reflected by those who actually own the company who obviously would not support a regime which will not ensure the maximum return on their investment. This would be endangered by workers' control, even though it is more efficient and productive, as control over the surplus rests with the workers and not a management elite with similar interests and aims as the owners — an egalitarian workplace would produce an egalitarian distribution of surplus, in other words (as proven by the experience of workers' co-operatives). In the words of one participant of the GE workers' control project: *"If we're all one, for manufacturing reasons, we must share in the fruits equitably, just like a co-op business."* [quoted by Noble, **Op. Cit.**, p. 295] Such a possibility is one few owners would agree to.

Thirdly, to survive within the "free" market means to concentrate on the short term. Long terms benefits, although greater, are irrelevant. A free market requires profits **now** and so a firm is under considerable pressure to maximise short-term profits by market forces. Participation requires trust, investment in people and technology and a willingness to share the increased value added that result from workers' participation with the workers who made it possible. All these factors would eat into short term profits in order to return richer rewards in the future. Encouraging participation thus tends to increase long term gains at the expense of short-term ones (to ensure that workers do not consider participation as a con, they must experience **real** benefits in terms of power, conditions and wage rises). For firms within a free market environment, they are under pressure from share-holders and their financiers for high returns as soon as possible. If a company does not produce high dividends then it will see its stock fall as shareholders move to those companies that do. Thus the market **forces** companies to act in such ways as to maximise short term profits.

If faced with a competitor which is not making such investments (and which is investing directly into deskilling technology or intensifying work loads which lowers their costs) and so wins them market share, or a downturn in the business cycle which shrinks their profit margins and makes it difficult for the firm to meet its commitments to its financiers and workers, a company that intends to invest in people and trust will usually be rendered unable to do so. Faced with the option of empowering people in work or deskilling them and/or using the fear of unemployment to get workers to work harder and follow orders, capitalist firms have consistently chosen (and probably preferred) the latter option (as occurred in the 1970s).

Thus, workers' control is unlikely to spread through capitalism because it entails a level of working class consciousness and power that is incompatible with capitalist control: *"If the hierarchical division of labour is necessary for the extraction of surplus value, then worker preferences for jobs threatening capitalist control will not be implemented."* [Gintis, **Op. Cit.**, p. 253] The reason why it is more efficient, ironically, ensures that a capitalist economy will not select it. The "free market" will discourage empowerment and democratic workplaces, at best reducing "co-operation" and "participation" to marginal issues (and management will still have the power of veto).

The failure of moves towards democratic workplaces within capitalism are an example of that system in conflict with itself — pursuing its objectives by methods which constantly defeat those same objectives. As Paul Carden argued, the *"capitalist system can only maintain itself by trying to reduce workers into mere order-takers … At the same time the system can only function as long as this reduction is never achieved … [for] the system would soon grind to a halt … [However] capitalism constantly has to **limit** this **participation** (if it didn't the workers would soon start deciding themselves and would show in practice how superfluous the ruling class really is)."* [**Modern Capitalism and Revolution**, pp. 45-46] Thus "workers' control" within a capitalist firm is a contradictory thing — too little power and it is meaningless, too much and workplace authority structures and capitalist share of, and control over, value added can be harmed. Attempts to make oppressed, exploited and alienated workers work as if they were neither oppressed, exploited nor alienated will always fail.

Therefore, "participation" within capitalist firms will have little or no tendency to spread due to the actions of market forces. In spite of such schemes almost always being more efficient, capitalism will not select them because they empower workers and make it hard for capitalists to generate and control their profits. Hence capitalism, by itself, will have no tendency to produce more libertarian organisational forms within industry. Those firms that do introduce such schemes will be the exception rather than the rule (and the schemes themselves will be marginal in most respects and subject to veto from above). For such schemes to spread, collective action is required (such as state intervention to create the right environment and support network or — from an anarchist point of view — union and community direct action).

Such schemes, as noted above, are just forms of self-exploitation, getting workers to help their robbers and so **not** a development anarchists seek to encourage. We have discussed this here just to be clear that, firstly, such forms of structural reforms are **not** self-management, as managers and owners still have the real power, and, secondly, even if such forms are somewhat liberatory and more efficient, market forces will not select them precisely **because** the latter is dependent on the former. Thirdly, they would still be organised for exploitation as workers would not be controlling all the goods they produced. As with an existing capitalist firm, part of their product would be used to pay interest, rent and profit. For anarchists *"self-management is not a new form of mediation between workers and their bosses … [it] refers to the very process by which the workers themselves **overthrow** their managers and take on their own management and the management of production in their own workplace."* [Dolgoff, **Op. Cit.**, p. 81] Hence our support for co-operatives, unions and other self-managed structures created and organised from below by and for working class people by their own collective action.

J.5.13
What are Modern Schools?

Modern schools are alternative schools, self-managed by students, teachers and parents which reject the authoritarian schooling methods of the contemporary "education" system. Such schools have been a feature of the anarchist movement since the turn of the 20th century while interest in libertarian forms of education has existed in anarchist theory from the beginning. All the major anarchist thinkers, from Godwin through Proudhon, Bakunin and Kropotkin to modern activists like Colin Ward, have stressed the importance of libertarian (or rational) education, education that develops all aspects of the student (mental and physical — and so termed integral education) as well as encouraging critical thought and mental freedom. The aim of such education is ensure that the "industrial worker, the man [sic!] of action and the intellectual would all be rolled into one." [Proudhon, quoted by Steward Edward, **The Paris Commune**, p. 274]

Anyone involved in radical politics, constantly and consistently challenges the role of the state's institutions and their representatives within our lives. The role of bosses, the police, social workers, the secret service, managers, doctors and priests are all seen as part of a hierarchy which exists to keep us, the working class, subdued. It is relatively rare, though, for the left-wing to call into question the role of teachers. Most left wing activists and a large number of libertarians believe that education is always good.

Those involved in libertarian education believe the contrary. They believe that national education systems exist only to produce citizens who will be blindly obedient to the dictates of the state, citizens who will uphold the authority of government even when it runs counter to personal interest and reason, wage slaves who will obey the orders of their boss most of the time and consider being able to change bosses as freedom. They agree with William Godwin (one of the earliest critics of national education systems) when he wrote that "the project of a national education ought to be discouraged on account of its obvious alliance with national government ... Government will not fail to employ it to strengthen its hand and perpetuate its institutions ... Their views as instigator of a system will not fail to be analogous to their views in their political capacity." [quoted by Colin Ward, **Anarchy in Action**, p. 81]

With the growth of industrialism in the 19th century state schools triumphed, not through a desire to reform but as an economic necessity. Industry did not want free thinking individuals, it wanted workers, instruments of labour, and it wanted them punctual, obedient, passive and willing to accept their disadvantaged position. According to Nigel Thrift, many employers and social reformers became convinced that the earliest generations of workers were almost impossible to discipline (i.e. to get accustomed to wage labour and workplace authority). They looked to children, hoping that "the elementary school could be used to break the labouring classes into those habits of work discipline now necessary for factory production ... Putting little children to work at school for very long hours at very dull subjects was seen as a positive virtue, for it made them habituated, not to say naturalised, to labour and fatigue."

[quoted by Juliet B. Schor, **The Overworked American**, p. 61] Thus supporters of Modern Schools recognise that the role of education is an important one in maintaining hierarchical society — for government and other forms of hierarchy (such as wage labour) must always depend on the opinion of the governed. Francisco Ferrer (the most famous libertarian educator) argued that:

"Rulers have always taken care to control the education of the people. They know their power is based almost entirely on the school and they insist on retaining their monopoly. The school is an instrument of domination in the hands of the ruling class." [quoted by Clifford Harper, **Anarchy: A Graphic Guide**, p. 100]

Little wonder, then, that Emma Goldman argued that "modern methods of education" have "little regard for personal liberty and originality of thought. Uniformity and imitation is [its] motto." The school "is for the child what the prison is for the convict and the barracks for the solder — a place where everything is being used to break the will of the child, and then to pound, knead, and shape it into a being utterly foreign to itself." Hence the importance of Modern Schools. The are a means of spreading libertarian education within a hierarchical society and undercut one of the key supports for that society — the education system. Instead of hierarchical education, Modern schools exist to "develop the individual through knowledge and the free play of characteristic traits, so that [the child] may become a social being, because he had learned to know himself, to know his relation to his fellow[s]." [**Red Emma Speaks**, pp. 141-2, p. 140 and p. 145] It would be an education for freedom, not for subservience:

"Should the notion of freedom but awaken in man, free men dream only of freeing themselves now and for all time: but instead, all we do is churn out learned men who adapt in the most refined manner to every circumstance and fall to the level of slavish, submissive souls. For the most part, what are our fine gentlemen brimful of intellect and culture? Sneering slavers and slaves themselves." [Max Stirner, **No Gods, No Masters**, vol. 1, p. 12]

The Modern School Movement (also known as the Free School Movement) over the past century has been an attempt to represent part of this concern about the dangers of state and church schools and the need for libertarian education. The idea of libertarian education is that knowledge and learning should be linked to real life processes as well as personal usefulness and should not be the preserve of a special institution. Thus Modern Schools are an attempt to establish an environment for self development in an overly structured and rationalised world. An oasis from authoritarian control and as a means of passing on the knowledge to be free:

"The underlying principle of the Modern School is this: education is a process of drawing out, not driving in; it aims at the possibility that the child should be left free to develop spontaneously, directing his own efforts and choosing the branches of knowledge which he desires to study ... the teacher ... should be a sensitive instrument responding to the needs of the child ... a channel through which the child may attain so much of the ordered *knowledge of the world as he shows himself ready to receive and assimilate.*" [Goldman, **Op. Cit.**, p. 146]

The Modern School bases itself on libertarian education techniques. Libertarian education, very broadly, seeks to produce children who will demand greater personal control and choice, who think for themselves and question all forms of authority:

"We don't hesitate to say we want people who will continue to develop. People constantly capable of destroying and renewing their surroundings and themselves: whose intellectual independence is their supreme power, which they will yield to none; always disposed for better things, eager for the triumph of new ideas, anxious to crowd many lives into the life they have. It must be the aim of the school to show the children that there will be tyranny as long as one person depends on another." [Ferrer, quoted by Harper, **Op. Cit.**, p. 100]

Thus the Modern School insists that the child is the centre of gravity in the education process — and that education is just that, **not** indoctrination:

"I want to form a school of emancipation, concerned with banning from the mind whatever divides people, the false concepts of property, country and family so as to attain the liberty and well-being which all desire. I will teach only simple truth. I will not ram dogma into their heads. I will not conceal one iota of fact. I will teach not what to think but how to think." [Ferrer, quoted by Harper, **Op. Cit.**, pp. 99-100]

The Modern School has no rewards or punishments, exams or mark — the everyday tortures of conventional schooling. And because practical knowledge is more useful than theory, lessons were often held in factories, museums or the countryside. The school was also used by parents, and Ferrer planned a Popular University.

"Higher education, for the privileged few, should be for the general public, as every human has a right to know; and science, which is produced by observers and workers of all countries and ages, ought not be restricted to class." [Ferrer, quoted by Harper, **Op. Cit.**, p. 100]

Thus Modern Schools are based on encouraging self-education in a co-operative, egalitarian and libertarian atmosphere in which the pupil (regardless of age) can develop themselves and their interests to the fullest of their abilities. In this way Modern Schools seek to create anarchists by a process of education which respects the individual and gets them to develop their own abilities in a conducive setting.

Modern Schools have been a constant aspect of the anarchist movement since the late 1890s. The movement was started in France by Louise Michel and Sebastien Faure, where Francisco Ferrer became acquainted with them. He founded his Modern School in Barcelona in 1901, and by 1905 there were 50 similar schools in Spain (many of them funded by anarchist groups and trade unions and, from 1919 onward, by the C.N.T. — in all cases the autonomy of the schools was respected). In 1909, Ferrer was falsely accused by the Spanish government of leading an insurrection and executed

in spite of world-wide protest and overwhelming proof of his innocence. His execution, however, gained him and his educational ideas international recognition and inspired a Modern School progressive education movement across the globe.

However, for most anarchists, Modern Schools are not enough in themselves to produce a libertarian society. They agree with Bakunin:

*"For individuals to be moralised and become fully human … three things are necessary: a hygienic birth, all-round education, accompanied by an upbringing based on respect for labour, reason, equality, and freedom and a social environment wherein each human individual will enjoy full freedom and really by, **de jure** and **de facto**, the equal of every other.*

"Does this environment exist? No. Then it must be established… [otherwise] in the existing social environment … on leaving [libertarian] schools they [the student] would enter a society governed by totally opposite principles, and, because society is always stronger than individuals, it would prevail over them … [and] demoralise them." [**The Basic Bakunin**, p, 174]

Because of this, Modern Schools must be part of a mass working class revolutionary movement which aims to build as many aspects of the new world as possible in the old one before, ultimately, replacing it. Otherwise they are just useful as social experiments and their impact on society marginal. Thus, for anarchists, this process of education is **part of** the class struggle, not in place of it and so *"the workers [must] do everything possible to obtain all the education they can in the material circumstances in which they currently find themselves"* while *"concentrat[ing] their efforts on the great question of their economic emancipation, the mother of all other emancipations."* [Bakunin, **Op. Cit.**, p. 175]

Before finishing, we must stress that hierarchical education (like the media), cannot remove the effects of actual life and activity in shaping/changing people and their ideas, opinions and attitudes. While education is an essential part of maintaining the status quo and accustoming people to accept hierarchy, the state and wage slavery, it cannot stop individuals from learning from their experiences, trusting their sense of right and wrong, recognising the injustices of the current system and the ideas that it is based upon. This means that even the best state (or private) education system will still produce rebels — for the **experience** of wage slavery and state oppression (and, most importantly, **struggle**) is shattering to the **ideology** spoon-fed children during their "education" and reinforced by the media.

For more information on Modern Schools see Paul Avrich's **The Modern School Movement: Anarchism and education in the United States**, Emma Goldman's essays *"Francisco Ferrer and the Modern School"* (in **Anarchism and Other Essays**) and *"The Social Importance of the Modern School"* (in **Red Emma Speaks**) as well as A.S Neil's **Summerhill**. For a good introduction to anarchist viewpoints on education see *"Kropotkin and technical education: an anarchist voice"* by Michael Smith (in **For Anarchism**, David Goodway (ed.),) and Michael Bakunin's *"All-Round Education"* (in

The Basic Bakunin). For an excellent summary of the advantages and benefits of co-operative learning, see Alfie Kohn's **No Contest**.

J.5.14 What is Libertarian Municipalism?

As we noted in section J.2, most anarchists reject participating in electoral politics. A notable exception was Murray Bookchin who not only proposed voting but also a non-parliamentary electoral strategy for anarchists. He repeated this proposal in many of his later works, such as **From Urbanisation to Cities**, and has made it — at least in the USA — one of the many alternatives anarchists are involved in.

According to Bookchin, "*the proletariat, as do all oppressed sectors of society, comes to life when it sheds its industrial habits in the free and spontaneous activity of **communising,** or taking part in the political life of the community.*" In other words, Bookchin thought that democratisation of local communities may be as strategically important, or perhaps more important, to anarchists than workplace struggles. Since local politics is humanly scaled, Bookchin argued that it can be participatory rather than parliamentary. Or, as he put it, the "*anarchic ideal of decentralised, stateless, collectively managed, and directly democratic communities — of confederated municipalities or 'communes' — speaks almost intuitively, and in the best works of Proudhon and Kropotkin, consciously, to the transforming role of libertarian municipalism as the framework of a liberatory society.*" "*Theses on Libertarian Municipalism*", pp. 9-22, **The Anarchist Papers**, Dimitrios I. Roussopoulos (ed.),p. 10] He also pointed out that, historically, the city has been the principle countervailing force to imperial and national states, haunting them as a potential challenge to centralised power and continuing to do so today, as can be seen in the conflicts between national government and municipalities in many countries.

Despite the libertarian potential of urban politics, "urbanisation" — the growth of the modern megalopolis as a vast wasteland of suburbs, shopping malls, industrial parks, and slums that foster political apathy and isolation in realms of alienated production and private consumption — is antithetical to the continued existence of those aspects of the city that might serve as the framework for a libertarian municipalism: "*When urbanisation will have effaced city life so completely that the city no longer has its own identity, culture, and spaces for consociation, the bases for democracy — in whatever way the word in defined — will have disappeared and the question of revolutionary forms will be a shadow game of abstractions.*" Despite this danger Bookchin argued that a libertarian politics of local government is still possible, provided anarchists get our act together: "*The Commune still lies buried in the city council; the sections still lie buried in the neighbourhood; the town meeting still lies buried in the township; confederal forms of municipal association still lie buried in regional networks of towns and cities.*" [**Op. Cit.**, p. 16 and p. 21]

What would anarchists do electorally at the local level? Bookchin proposed that libertarians stand in local elections in order to change city and town charters to make them participatory: "*An organic politics based on such radical participatory forms of civic association does not exclude the right of anarchists to alter city and town charters such that they validate the existence of directly democratic institutions. And if this kind of activity brings anarchists into city councils, there is no reason why such a politics should be construed as parliamentary, particularly if it is confined to the civic level and is consciously posed against the state.*" [**Op. Cit.**, p. 21]

In short, Libertarian Municipalism "*depends upon libertarian leftists running candidates at the local level, calling for the division of municipalities into wards, where popular assemblies can be created that bring people into full and direct participation in political life … municipalities would [then] confederate into a dual power to oppose the nation-state and ultimately dispense with it and with the economic forces that underpin statism as such.*" [**Democracy and Nature** no. 9, p. 158] This would be part of a social wide transformation, whose "*[m]inimal steps … include initiating Left Green municipalist movements that propose neighbourhood and town assemblies — even if they have only moral functions at first — and electing town and city councillors that advance the cause of these assemblies and other popular institutions. These minimal steps can lead step-by-step to the formation of confederal bodies … Civic banks to fund municipal enterprises and land purchases; the fostering of new ecologically-orientated enterprises that are owned by the community.*" Thus Bookchin saw Libertarian Municipalism as a process by which the state can be undermined by using elections as the means of creating popular assemblies. Part of this would be the "*municipalisation of property*" which would "*bring the economy **as a whole** into the orbit of the public sphere, where economic policy could be formulated by the **entire** community.*" [**From Urbanisation to Cities**, p. 266 and p. 235]

In evaluating Bookchin's proposal, several points come to mind.

Firstly, it is clear that Libertarian Municipalism's arguments in favour of community assemblies is important and cannot be ignored. Bookchin was right to note that, in the past, many anarchists placed far too much stress on workplace struggles and workers' councils as the framework of a free society. Many of the really important issues that affect us cannot be reduced to workplace organisations, which by their very nature disenfranchise those who do not work in industry (such as housewives, the old, and so on). And, of course, there is far more to life than work and so any future society organised purely around workplace organisations is reproducing capitalism's insane glorification of economic activity, at least to some degree. So, in this sense, Libertarian Municipalism has a very valid point — a free society will be created and maintained within the community as well as in the workplace. However, this perspective was hardly alien to such anarchist thinkers as Proudhon, Bakunin and Kropotkin who all placed communes at the centre of their vision of a free society.

Secondly, Bookchin and other Libertarian Municipalists are correct to argue that anarchists should work in their local communities. Many anarchists are doing just that and are being very successful as well. However, most anarchists reject the idea of a "*confederal municipalist movement run[ning] candidates for municipal councils with demands for the institution of public assemblies*" as viable means of "*struggle toward creating new civic institutions out of old ones (or replacing the old ones altogether).*" [Bookchin, **Op. Cit.**, p. 229 and p. 267]

The most serious objection to this has to do with whether politics in most cities has already become too centralised, bureaucratic, inhumanly scaled, and dominated by capitalist interests to have any possibility of being taken over by anarchists running on platforms of participatory democratisation. Merely to pose the question seems enough to answer it. There is no such possibility in the vast majority of cities, and hence it would be a waste of time and energy for anarchists to support libertarian municipalist candidates in local elections — time and energy that could be more profitably spent in direct action. If the central governments are too bureaucratic and unresponsive to be used by Libertarian Municipalists, the same can be said of local ones too — particularly as the local state has become increasingly controlled by the central authorities (in the UK, for example, the Conservative government of the 1980s successfully centralised power away from local councils to undercut their ability to resist the imposition of its neo-liberal policies).

The counter-argument to this is that even if there is no chance of such candidates being elected, their standing for elections would serve a valuable educational function. The answer to this is: perhaps, but would it be more valuable than direct action? Would its educational value, if any, outweigh the disadvantages of electioneering discussed in section J.2? Given the ability of major media to marginalise alternative candidates, we doubt that such campaigns would have enough educational value to outweigh these disadvantages. Moreover, being an anarchist does not make one immune to the corrupting effects of electioneering. History is littered with radical, politically aware movements using elections and ending up becoming part of the system they aimed to transform. Most anarchists doubt that Libertarian Municipalism will be any different — after all, it is the circumstances the parties find themselves in which are decisive, not the theory they hold. Why would libertarians be immune to this but not Marxists or Greens?

Lastly, most anarchists question the whole process on which Libertarian Municipalism bases itself on. The idea of communes is a key one of anarchism and so strategies to create them in the here and now are important. However, to think that we can use alienated, representative institutions to abolish these institutions is wrong. As Italian activists who organised a neighbourhood assembly by non-electoral means argue *"[t]o accept power and to say that the others were acting in bad faith and that we would be better, would force non-anarchists towards direct democracy. We reject this logic and believe that organisations must come from the grassroots."* ["*Community Organising in Southern Italy*", pp. 16-19, **Black Flag** no. 210, p. 18]

Thus Libertarian Municipalism reverses the process by which community assemblies will be created. Instead of anarchists using elections to build such bodies, they must work in their communities directly to create them (see section J.5.1 for more details). Using the catalyst of specific issues of local interest, anarchists could propose the creation of a community assembly to discuss the issues in question and organise action to solve them. Rather than stand in local elections, anarchists should encourage people to create these institutions themselves and empower themselves by collective self-activity. As Kropotkin argued, *"Laws can only **follow** the accomplished facts; and even if they do honestly follow them — which is usually **not** the case — a law remains a dead letter*

*so long as there are not on the spot the living forces required for making the **tendencies** expressed in the law an accomplished fact."* [**Anarchism**, p. 171] Most anarchists, therefore, think it is far more important to create the *"living forces"* within our communities directly than waste energy in electioneering and the passing of laws creating or "legalising" community assemblies. In other words, community assemblies can only be created from the bottom up, by non-electoral means, a process which Libertarian Municipalism confuses with electioneering.

So, while Libertarian Municipalism **does** raise many important issues and correctly stresses the importance of community activity and self-management, its emphasis on electoral activity undercuts its liberatory promise. For most anarchists, community assemblies can only be created from below, by direct action, and (because of its electoral strategy) a Libertarian Municipalist movement will end up being transformed into a copy of the system it aims to abolish.

J.5.15 What attitude do anarchists take to the welfare state?

The period of neo-liberalism since the 1980s has seen a rollback of the state within society by the right-wing in the name of "freedom," "individual responsibility" and "efficiency." The position of anarchists to this process is mixed. On the one hand, we are all in favour of reducing the size of the state and increasing individual responsibility and freedom but, on the other, we are well aware that this rollback is part of an attack on the working class and tends to increase the power of the capitalists over us as the state's (direct) influence is reduced. Thus anarchists appear to be on the horns of a dilemma — or, at least, apparently.

So what attitude **do** anarchists take to the welfare state and attacks on it?

First we must note that this attack on "welfare" is somewhat selective. While using the rhetoric of "self-reliance" and "individualism," the practitioners of these "tough love" programmes have made sure that the major corporations continue to get state hand-outs and aid while attacking social welfare. In other words, the current attack on the welfare state is an attempt to impose market discipline on the working class while increasing state protection for the ruling class. Therefore, most anarchists have no problem defending social welfare programmes as these can be considered as only fair considering the aid the capitalist class has always received from the state (both direct subsidies and protection and indirect support via laws that protect property and so on). And, for all their talk of increasing individual choice, the right-wing remain silent about the lack of choice and individual freedom during working hours within capitalism.

Secondly, most of the right-wing inspired attacks on the welfare state are inaccurate. For example, Noam Chomsky notes that the *"correlation between welfare payments and family life is real, though it is the reverse of what is claimed [by the right]. As support for the poor has declined, unwed birth-rates, which had risen steadily from the 1940s through the mid-1970s, markedly increased. 'Over the last three decades, the rate of poverty among children almost* perfectly correlates with the birth-rates among teenage mothers a decade later,' Mike Males points out: 'That is, child poverty seems to lead to teenage childbearing, not the other way around.'" ["Rollback III", **Z Magazine**, April, 1995] The same charge of inaccurate scare-mongering can be laid at the claims about the evil effects of welfare which the rich and large corporations wish to save others (but not themselves) from. Such altruism is truly heart warming. For those in the United States or familiar with it, the same can be said of the hysterical attacks on "socialised medicine" and health-care reform funded by insurance companies and parroted by right-wing ideologues and politicians.

Thirdly, anarchists are just as opposed to capitalism as they are the state. This means that privatising state functions is no more libertarian than nationalising them. In fact, less so as such a process **reduces** the limited public say state control implies in favour of more private tyranny and wage-labour. As such, attempts to erode the welfare state without other, pro-working class, social reforms violates the anti-capitalist part of anarchism. Similarly, the introduction of a state supported welfare system rather than a for-profit capitalist run system (as in America) would hardly be considered any more a violation of libertarian principles as the reverse happening. In terms of reducing human suffering, though, most anarchists would oppose the latter and be in favour of the former while aiming to create a third (self-managed) alternative.

Fourthly, we must note that while most anarchists **are** in favour of collective self-help and welfare, we are opposed to the state. Part of the alternatives anarchists try and create are self-managed and community welfare projects (see next section). Moreover, in the past, anarchists and syndicalists were at the forefront in opposing state welfare schemes. This was because they were introduced **not** by socialists but by liberals and other supporters of capitalism to undercut support for radical alternatives and to aid long term economic development by creating the educated and healthy population required to use advanced technology and fight wars. Thus we find that:

> "Liberal social welfare legislation … were seen by many [British syndicalists] not as genuine welfare reforms, but as mechanisms of social control. Syndicalists took a leading part in resisting such legislation on the grounds that it would increase capitalist discipline over labour, thereby undermining working class independence and self-reliance." [Bob Holton, **British Syndicalism: 1900-1914**, p. 137]

Anarchists view the welfare state much as some feminists do. While they note, to quote Carole Pateman, the "patriarchal structure of the welfare state" they are also aware that it has "also brought challenges to patriarchal power and helped provide a basis for women's autonomous citizenship." She goes on to note that "for women to look at the welfare state is merely to exchange dependence on individual men for dependence on the state. The power and capriciousness of husbands is replaced by the arbitrariness, bureaucracy and power of the state, the very state that has upheld patriarchal power." This "will not in itself do anything to challenge patriarchal power relations." [**The Disorder of Women**, p. 195 and p. 200]

Thus while the welfare state does give working people more options than having to take **any** job or put up with **any** conditions, this relative independence from the market and individual capitalists comes at the price of dependence on the state — the very institution that protects and supports capitalism in the first place. And we have became painfully aware in recent years, it is the ruling class who has most influence in the state — and so, when it comes to deciding what state budgets to cut, social welfare ones are first in line. Given that such programmes are controlled by the state, **not** working class people, such an outcome is hardly surprising. Not only this, we also find that state control reproduces the same hierarchical structures that the capitalist firm creates.

Unsurprisingly, anarchists have no great love of such state welfare schemes and desire their replacement by self-managed alternatives. For example, taking municipal housing, Colin Ward writes:

> "The municipal tenant is trapped in a syndrome of dependence and resentment, which is an accurate reflection of his housing situation. People care about what is theirs, what they can modify, alter, adapt to changing needs and improve themselves. They must have a direct responsibility for it … The tenant take-over of the municipal estate is one of those obviously sensible ideas which is dormant because our approach to municipal affairs is still stuck in the groves of nineteenth-century paternalism."
> [**Anarchy in Action**, p. 73]

Looking at state supported education, Ward argues that the "universal education system turns out to be yet another way in which the poor subsidise the rich." Which is the least of its problems, for "it is in the **nature** of public authorities to run coercive and hierarchical institutions whose ultimate function is to perpetuate social inequality and to brainwash the young into the acceptance of their particular slot in the organised system." [**Op. Cit.**, p. 83 and p. 81] The role of state education as a means of systematically indoctrinating the working class is reflected in William Lazonick's words:

> "The Education Act of 1870 … [gave the] state … the facilities … to make education compulsory for all children from the age of five to the age of ten. It had also erected a powerful system of ideological control over the next generation of workers … [It] was to function as a prime ideological mechanism in the attempt by the capitalist class through the medium of the state, to continually **reproduce** a labour force which would passively accept [the] subjection [of labour to the domination of capital]. At the same time it had set up a public institution which could potentially be used by the working class for just the contrary purpose." ["The Subjection of Labour to Capital: The rise of the Capitalist System", **Radical Political Economy** Vol. 2, p. 363]

Lazonick, as did Pateman, indicates the contradictory nature of welfare provisions within capitalism. On the one hand, they are introduced to help control the working class (and to improve long term economic development). On the other hand, these provisions can be used by working class people as weapons against capitalism and give themselves more options than "work or starve" (the fact that the attacks on welfare in the UK during the 1990s — called, ironically enough, **welfare to work** — involves losing benefits if you refuse a job is not a surprising development). Thus we find that welfare acts as a kind of floor under wages. In the US, the two have followed a common trajectory (rising together and falling together). And it is **this**, the potential benefits welfare can have for working people, that is the **real** cause for the current capitalist attacks upon it. As Noam Chomsky summarises:

> "State authority is now under severe attack in the more democratic societies, but not because it conflicts with the libertarian vision. Rather the opposite: because it offers (weak) protection to some aspects of that vision. Governments have a fatal flaw: unlike the private tyrannies, the institutions of state power and authority offer to the public an opportunity to play some role, however limited, in managing their own affairs."
> [**Chomsky on Anarchism**, p. 193]

Because of this contradictory nature of welfare, we find anarchists like Noam Chomsky arguing that (using an expression popularised by South American rural workers unions) *"we should 'expand the floor of the cage.' We know we're in a cage. We know we're trapped. We're going to expand the floor, meaning we will extend to the limits what the cage will allow. And we intend to destroy the cage. But not by attacking the cage when we're vulnerable, so they'll murder us ... You have to protect the cage when it's under attack from even worse predators from outside, like private power. And you have to expand the floor of the cage, recognising that it's a cage. These are all preliminaries to dismantling it. Unless people are willing to tolerate that level of complexity, they're going to be of no use to people who are suffering and who need help, or, for that matter, to themselves."* [**Expanding the Floor of the Cage**]

Thus, even though we know the welfare state is a cage and part of an instrument of class power, we have to defend it from a worse possibility — namely, the state as "pure" defender of capitalism with working people with few or no rights. At least the welfare state does have a contradictory nature, the tensions of which can be used to increase our options. And one of these options is its abolition **from below**!

For example, with regards to municipal housing, anarchists will be the first to agree that it is paternalistic, bureaucratic and hardly a wonderful living experience. However, in stark contrast with the right who desire to privatise such estates, anarchists think that *"tenants control"* is the best solution as it gives us the benefits of individual ownership **along with** community (and so without the negative points of property, such as social atomisation). The demand for *"tenant control"* must come from below, by the *"collective resistance"* of the tenants themselves, perhaps as a result of struggles against *"continuous rent increases"* leading to *"the demand ... for a change in the status of the tenant."* Such a *"tenant take-over of the municipal estate is one of those sensible ideas which is dormant because our approach to municipal affairs is still stuck in the grooves of nineteenth century paternalism."* [Ward, **Op. Cit.**, p. 73]

And it is here that we find the ultimate irony of the right-wing, "free market" attempts to abolish the welfare state — neo-liberalism

wants to end welfare **from above,** by means of the state (which is the instigator of this individualistic "reform"). It does not seek the end of dependency by self-liberation, but the shifting of dependency from state to charity and the market. In contrast, anarchists desire to abolish welfare from **below**. This the libertarian attitude to those government policies which actually do help people. While anarchists would *"hesitate to condemn those measures taken by governments which obviously benefited the people, unless we saw the immediate possibility of people carrying them out for themselves. This would not inhibit us from declaring at the same time that what initiatives governments take would be more successfully taken by the people themselves if they put their minds to the same problems ... to build up a hospital service or a transport system, for instance, from local needs into a national organisation, by agreement and consent at all levels is surely more economical as well as efficient than one which is conceived at top level [by the state] ... where Treasury, political and other pressures, not necessarily connected with what we would describe as **needs**, influence the shaping of policies."* So *"as long as we have capitalism and government the job of anarchists is to fight both, and at the same time encourage people to take what steps they can to run their own lives."* [*"Anarchists and Voting"*, pp. 176-87, **The Raven**, No. 14, p. 179]

Ultimately, unlike the state socialist/liberal left, anarchists reject the idea that the cause of socialism, of a free society, can be helped by using the state. Like the right, the left see political action in terms of the state. All its favourite policies have been statist — state intervention in the economy, nationalisation, state welfare, state education and so on. Whatever the problem, the left see the solution as lying in the extension of the power of the state. They continually push people in relying on **others** to solve their problems for them. Moreover, such state-based "aid" does not get to the core of the problem. All it does is fight the symptoms of capitalism and statism without attacking their root causes — the system itself.

Invariably, this support for the state is a move away from working class people, from trusting and empowering them to sort out their own problems. Indeed, the left seem to forget that the state exists to defend the collective interests of the ruling class and so could hardly be considered a neutral body. And, worst of all, they have presented the right with the opportunity of stating that freedom from the state means the same thing as the freedom of the market (so ignoring the awkward fact that capitalism is based upon domination — wage labour — and needs many repressive measures in order to exist and survive). Anarchists are of the opinion that changing the boss for the state (or vice versa) is only a step sideways, **not** forward! After all, it is **not** working people who control how the welfare state is run, it is politicians, "experts", bureaucrats and managers who do so (*"Welfare is administered by a top-heavy governmental machine which ensures that when economies in public expenditure are imposed by its political masters, they are made in reducing the service to the public, not by reducing the cost of administration."* [Ward, **Op. Cit.** p. 10]). Little wonder we have seen elements of the welfare state used as a weapon in the class war **against** those in struggle (for example, in Britain during the miners strike in 1980s the Conservative Government made it illegal to claim benefits while on strike, so reducing the funds available to workers in struggle and helping bosses force strikers back to work faster).

Anarchists consider it far better to encourage those who suffer injustice to organise themselves and in that way they can change what **they** think is actually wrong, as opposed to what politicians and "experts" claim is wrong. If sometimes part of this struggle involves protecting aspects of the welfare state (*"expanding the floor of the cage"*) so be it — but we will never stop there and will use such struggles as a stepping stone in abolishing the welfare state **from below** by creating self-managed, working class, alternatives. As part of this process anarchists also seek to **transform** those aspects of the welfare state we may be trying to "protect". We do not defend an institution which **is** paternalistic, bureaucratic and unresponsive. For example, if we are involved in trying to stop a local state-run hospital or school from closing, anarchists would try to raise the issue of self-management and local community control into the struggle in the hope of going beyond the status quo.

In this, we follow the suggestion made by Proudhon that rather than *"fatten certain contractors,"* libertarians should be aiming to create *"a new kind of property"* by *"granting the privilege of running"* public utilities, industries and services, *"under fixed conditions, to responsible companies, not of capitalists, but of* **workmen.**" Municipalities would take the initiative in setting up public works but actual control would rest with workers' co-operatives for *"it becomes necessary for the workers to form themselves into democratic societies, with equal conditions for all members, on pain of a relapse into feudalism."* Thus, for example, rather than nationalise or privatise railways, they should be handed over workers' co-operatives to run. The same with welfare services and such like: *"the abolition of the State is the last term of a series, which consists of an incessant diminution, by political and administrative simplification the number of public functionaries and to put into the care of responsible workers societies the works and services confided to the state."* [**Property is Theft!**, p. 25]

Not only does this mean that we can get accustomed to managing our own affairs collectively, it also means that we can ensure that whatever "safety-nets" we have do what we want and not what capital wants. In the end, what we create and run by ourselves will be more responsive to our needs, and the needs of the class struggle, than reformist aspects of the capitalist state. This much, we think, is obvious. And it is ironic to see elements of the "radical" and "revolutionary" left argue against this working class self-help (and so ignore the **long** tradition of such activity in working class movements) and instead select for the agent of their protection a state run by and for capitalists!

There are two traditions of welfare within society, one of *"fraternal and autonomous associations springing from below, the other that of authoritarian institutions directed from above."* [Ward, **Op. Cit.**, p. 123] While sometimes anarchists are forced to defend the latter against the greater evil of "free market" capitalism, we never forget the importance of creating and strengthening the former. As Chomsky suggests, libertarians have to *"defend some state institutions from the attack against them [by private power], while trying at the same time to pry them open to meaningful public participation — and ultimately, to dismantle them in a much more free society, if the appropriate circumstances can be achieved."* [**Chomsky on Anarchism**, p. 194] A point we will discuss more in the next section when we highlight the historical examples of self-managed communal welfare and self-help organisations.

Yes, in all societies we see working class people joining together to practice mutual aid and solidarity. This takes many forms, such as trade and industrial unions, credit unions and friendly societies, co-operatives and so on, but the natural response of working class people to the injustices of capitalism was to practice collective "self-help" in order to improve their lives and protect their friends, communities and fellow workers.

There are, as Colin Ward stresses, *"in fact several quite separate traditions of social welfare: the product of totally different attitudes to social needs ... One of these traditions is that of a service given grudgingly and punitively by authority, another is the expression of social responsibility, or of mutual aid and self-help. One is embodied in* **institutions**, *the other in* **associations**." [**Anarchy in Action**, p. 112] Anarchists, needless to say, favour the latter. Unfortunately, this *"great tradition of working class self-help and mutual aid was written off, not just as irrelevant, but as an actual impediment, by the political and professional architects of the welfare state ... The contribution that the recipients had to make to all this theoretical bounty was ignored as a mere embarrassment — apart, of course, for paying for it ... The socialist ideal was rewritten as a world in which everyone was entitled to everything, but where nobody except the providers had any actual say about anything. We have been learning for years, in the anti-welfare backlash, what a vulnerable utopia that was."* This self-managed working class self-help was the *"welfare road we failed to take."* [Ward, **Social Policy: an anarchist response**, p. 11-2 and p. 9]

Anarchists would argue that self-help is the natural side effect of freedom. There is no possibility of radical social change unless people are free to decide for themselves what their problems are, where their interests lie and are free to organise for themselves what they want to do about them. Self-help is a natural expression of people taking control of their own lives and acting for themselves. Anyone who urges state action on behalf of people is no socialist and any one arguing against self-help as "bourgeois" is no anti-capitalist. It is somewhat ironic that it is the right who have monopolised the rhetoric of "self-help" and turned it into yet another ideological weapon against working class direct action and self-liberation (although, saying that, the right generally likes individualised self-help — given a strike, squatting or any other form of **collective** self-help movement they will be the first to denounce it):

> *"The political Left has, over the years, committed an enormous psychological error in allowing this kind of language ["self-help", "mutual aid", "standing on your own two feet" and so on] to be appropriated by the political Right. If you look at the exhibitions of trade union banners from the last century, you will see slogans like Self Help embroidered all over them. It was those clever Fabians and academic Marxists who ridiculed out of existence the values by which ordinary citizens govern their own lives in favour of bureaucratic paternalising, leaving those values around to be picked up by their political opponents."* [Ward, **Talking Houses**, p. 58]

We cannot be expected to provide an extensive list of working class collective self-help and social welfare activity here, all we can do is present an overview of collective welfare in action (for a discussion of working class self-help and co-operation through the centuries we can suggest no better source than Kropotkin's **Mutual Aid**). In the case of Britain, we find that the *"newly created working class built up from nothing a vast network of social and economic initiatives based on self-help and mutual aid. The list is endless: friendly societies, building societies, sick clubs, coffin clubs, clothing clubs, up to enormous federated enterprises like the trade union movement and the Co-operative movement."* [Ward, **Social Policy**, pp. 10-1] The historian E.P. Thompson confirmed this picture of a wide network of working class self-help organisations. *"Small tradesmen, artisans, labourers"* he summarised, *"all sought to insure themselves against sickness, unemployment, or funeral expenses through membership of ... friendly societies."* These were *"authentic evidence of independent working-class culture and institutions ... out of which ... trade unions grew, and in which trade union officers were trained."* Friendly societies *"did not 'proceed from' an idea: both the ideas and institutions arose from a certain common experience ... In the simple cellular structure of the friendly society, with its workaday ethos of mutual aid, we see many features which were reproduced in more sophisticated and complex form in trade unions, co-operatives, Hampden clubs, Political Unions, and Chartist lodges ... Every kind of witness in the first half of the nineteenth century — clergymen, factory inspectors, Radical publicists — remarked upon the extent of mutual aid in the poorest districts. In times of emergency, unemployment, strikes, sickness, childbirth, then it was the poor who 'helped every one his neighbour.'"* [**The Making of the English Working Class**, p. 458, pp. 460-1 and p. 462] Sam Dolgoff gave an excellent summary of similar self-help activities by the American working class:

> *"Long before the labour movement got corrupted and the state stepped in, the workers organised a network of co-operative institutions of all kinds: schools, summer camps for children and adults, homes for the aged, health and cultural centres, credit associations, fire, life, and health insurance, technical education, housing, etc."* [**The American Labour Movement: A New Beginning**, p. 74]

Dolgoff, like all anarchists, urged workers to *"finance the establishment of independent co-operative societies of all types, which will respond adequately to their needs"* and that such a movement *"could constitute a realistic alternative to the horrendous abuses of the 'establishment' at a fraction of the cost."* [**Op. Cit.**, p. 74 and pp. 74-75] In this way a network of self-managed, communal, welfare associations and co-operatives could be built — paid for, run by and run for working class people. Such a system *"would not ... become a plaything of central government financial policy."* [Ward, **Op. Cit.**, p. 16] Such a network could be initially built upon, and be an aspect of, the struggles of both workers in and claimants, patients, tenants, and other users of the current welfare state. So a *"multiplicity of mutual aid organisations among claimants, patients, victims, represents the most potent lever for change in transforming the welfare state into a genuine welfare society, in turning community care into a caring community."* [Ward, **Anarchy in Action**, p. 125]

The creation of such a co-operative, community-based, welfare system will not occur over night, nor will it be easy. But it **is** possible, as history shows. It will, of course, have its problems, but as Colin Ward notes, *"the standard argument against a localist and decentralised point of view, is that of universalism: an equal service to all citizens, which it is thought that central control achieves. The short answer to this is that it doesn't!"* [Colin Ward, **Social Policy**, p. 16] He notes that richer areas generally get a better service from the welfare state than poorer ones, thus violating the claims of equal service. A centralised system (be it state or private) will most likely allocate resources which reflect the interests and (lack of) knowledge of bureaucrats and experts, **not** on where they are best used or the needs of the users.

Anarchists are sure that a **confederal** network of mutual aid organisations and co-operatives, based upon local input and control, can overcome problems of localism far better than a centralised one — which, due to its lack of local input and participation will more likely **encourage** parochialism and indifference than a wider vision and solidarity. If you have no real say in what affects you, why should you be concerned with what affects others? This is unsurprising, for what else is global action other than the product of thousands of local actions? Solidarity within our class is the flower that grows from the soil of our local self-activity, direct action and self-organisation. Unless we act and organise locally, any wider organisation and action will be hollow. Thus **local** organisation and empowerment is essential to create and maintain wider organisations and mutual aid.

To take another example of the benefits of a self-managed welfare system, we find that it *"was a continual complaint of the authorities"* in the late eighteenth and early nineteenth century *"that friendly societies allowed members to withdraw funds when on strike."* [Thompson, **Op. Cit.**, p. 461f] The same complaints were voiced in Britain about the welfare state allowing strikers to claim benefit while on strike. The Conservative Government of the 1980s changed that by passing a law barring those in industrial dispute to claim benefits — and so removing a potential support for those in struggle. Such a restriction would have been far harder (if not impossible) to impose on a network of self-managed mutual aid co-operatives. Such institutions would have not become the plaything of central government financial policy as the welfare state and the taxes working class people have to pay have become.

All this means that anarchists reject the phoney choice between private and state capitalism we are usually offered. We reject both privatisation **and** nationalisation, both right and left wings (of capitalism). Neither state nor private health care are user-controlled — one is subject to the requirements of politics and the other places profits before people. As we have discussed the welfare state in the last section, it is worthwhile to quickly discuss privatised welfare and why anarchists reject this option even more than state welfare.

Firstly, all forms of private healthcare/welfare have to pay dividends to capitalists, fund advertising, reduce costs to maximise profits by standardising the "caring" process - i.e. McDonaldisation - and so on, all of which inflates prices and produces substandard service across the industry as a whole. According to Alfie Kohn, *"[m]ore* hospitals and clinics are being run by for-profit corporations; many institutions, forced to battle for 'customers,' seem to value a skilled director of marketing more highly than a skilled caregiver. As in any other economic sector, the race for profits translates into pressure to reduce costs, and the easiest way to do it here is to cut back on services to unprofitable patients, that is, those who are more sick than rich ... The result: hospital costs are actually **higher** in areas where there is more competition for patients." [**No Contest**, p. 240] In the UK, attempts to introduce "market forces" into the National Health Service has also lead to increased costs as well as inflating the size and cost of its bureaucracy.

Looking at Chile, hyped by those who desire to privatise Social Security, we find similar disappointing results (well, disappointing for the working class at least, as we will see). Seemingly, Chile's private system has achieved impressive average returns on investment. However, once commissions are factored in, the real return for individual workers is considerably lower. For example, although the average rate of return on funds from 1982 through 1986 was 15.9 percent, the real return after commissions was a mere 0.3 percent! Between 1991 and 1995, the pre-commission return was 12.9 percent, but with commissions it fell to 2.1 percent. According to Doug Henwood, the "*competing mutual funds have vast sales forces, and the portfolio managers all have their vast fees. All in all, administrative costs ... are almost 30% of revenues, compared to well under 1% for the U.S. Social Security system.*" [**Wall Street**, p. 305] In addition, the private pension fund market is dominated by a handful of companies.

Even if commission costs were lowered (by regulation), the impressive returns on capital seen between 1982 and 1995 (when the real annual return on investment averaged 12.7 percent) are likely not to be sustained. These average returns coincided with boom years in Chile, complemented by government's high borrowing costs. Because of the debt crisis of the 1980s, Latin governments were paying double-digit real interest rates on their bonds — the main investment vehicle of social security funds. In effect, government was subsidising the "private" system by paying astronomical rates on government bonds. Another failing of the system is that only a little over half of Chilean workers make regular social security contributions. While many believe that a private system would reduce evasion because workers have a greater incentive to contribute to their own personal retirement accounts, 43.4 percent of those affiliated with the new system in June of 1995 did not contribute regularly. [Stephen J. Kay, "*The Chile Con: Privatizing Social Security in South America*," **The American Prospect** no. 33, pp. 48-52] All in all, privatisation seems to be beneficial only to middle-men and capitalists, if Chile is anything to go by. As Henwood argues, while the "*infusion of money*" resulting from privatising social security "*has done wonders for the Chilean stock market*" "*projections are that as many as half of future retirees will draw a poverty-level pension.*" [Henwood, **Op. Cit.**, pp. 304-5] Suffice to say, all you really need to know about privatisation of pensions and healthcare in Chile is that the military dictatorship which imposed it excluded the military from its dubious benefits. Such altruism is truly touching.

So, anarchists reject private welfare as a con (and an even bigger one than state welfare). As Colin Ward suggests, it "*is the question

of how we get back on the mutual aid road **instead of** commercial health insurance and private pension schemes.*" [**Social Policy**, p. 17] As anarchists are both anti-state and anti-capitalist, swapping private power for the state power is, at best, a step sideways. Usually, it is worse for capitalist companies are accountable only to their owners and the profit criteria. This means, as Chomsky suggests, "*protecting the state sector today is a step towards abolishing the state because it maintains a public arena in which people can participate and organise, and affect policy, and so on, though in limited ways. If that's removed, we'd go back to a ... private dictatorship, but that's hardly a step towards liberation.*" [**Chomsky on Anarchism**, p. 213] Instead anarchists try to create **real** alternatives to hierarchy, be it state or capitalist, in the here and now which reflect our ideas of a free and just society. For, when it boils down to it, freedom cannot be given, only taken and this process of **self**-liberation is reflected in the alternatives we build to help win the class war.

The struggle **against** capitalism and statism requires that we build **for** the future and, moreover, we should remember that "*he who has no confidence in the creative capacity of the masses and in their capability to revolt doesn't belong in the revolutionary movement. He should go to a monastery and get on his knees and start praying. Because he is no revolutionist. He is a son of a bitch.*" [Sam Dolgoff, quoted by Ulrike Heider, **Anarchism: left, right, and green**, p. 12]

J.6

What methods of child rearing do anarchists advocate?

Anarchists have long been aware of the importance of child rearing and education. We are aware that child rearing should aim to develop "*a well-rounded individuality*" and not "*a patient work slave, professional automaton, tax-paying citizen, or righteous moralist.*" In this section of the FAQ we will discuss anarchist approaches to child rearing bearing in mind "*that it is through the channel of the child that the development of the mature man [or woman] must go, and that the present ideas of ... educating or training ... are such as to stifle the natural growth of the child.*" [Emma Goldman, **Red Emma Speaks**, p. 132 and p. 131]

If one accepts the thesis that the authoritarian family is the breeding ground for both individual psychological problems and political reaction, it follows that anarchists should try to develop ways of raising children that will not psychologically cripple them but instead enable them to accept freedom and responsibility while developing natural self-regulation. We will refer to children raised in such a way as **"free children."**

Work in this field is still in its infancy (no pun intended). Wilhelm Reich was the main pioneer in this field (an excellent, short introduction to his ideas can be found in Maurice Brinton's **The Irrational in Politics**). In **Children of the Future**, Reich made numerous suggestions, based on his research and clinical experience, for parents, psychologists, and educators striving to develop libertarian methods of child rearing (although he did not use the term "libertarian").

In this and the following sections we will summarise Reich's main ideas as well as those of other libertarian psychologists and educators who have been influenced by him, such as A.S. Neill and Alexander Lowen. We will examine the theoretical principles involved in raising free children and will illustrate their practical application with concrete examples. Finally, we will examine the anarchist approach to the problems of adolescence.

Such an approach to child rearing is based upon the insight that children "*do not constitute anyone's property: they are neither the property of the parents nor even of society. They belong only to their own future freedom.*" [Michael Bakunin, **The Political Philosophy of Bakunin**, p. 327] As such, what happens to a child when they are growing up **shapes** the person they become and the society they live in. The key question for people interested in freedom is whether "*the child [is] to be considered as an individuality, or as an object to be moulded according to the whims and fancies of those about it?*" [Emma Goldman, **Op. Cit.**, p. 131] Libertarian child rearing is the means by which the individuality of the child is respected and developed.

This is in stark contrast to standard capitalist claims that children are the **property** of their parents. If we accept that children **are** the property of their parents then we are implicitly stating that a child's formative years are spent in slavery, hardly a relationship which will promote the individuality and freedom of the child or the wider society. Little wonder that most anarchists reject such assertions. Instead we argue that the "*rights of the parents shall be confined to loving their children and exercising over them … authority [that] does not run counter to their morality, their mental development, or their future freedom.*" Being someone's property (i.e. slave) runs counter to all these and "*it follows that society, the whole future of which depends upon adequate education and upbringing of children … has not only the right but also the duty to watch over them.*" Hence child rearing should be **part** of society, a communal process by which children learn what it means to be an individual by being respected as one by others: "*real freedom — that is, the full awareness and the realisation thereof in every individual, pre-eminently based upon a feeling of one's dignity and upon the genuine respect for someone else's freedom and dignity, i.e. upon justice — such freedom can develop in children only through the rational development of their minds, character and will.*" [Bakunin, **Op. Cit.**, p. 327]

We wish to re-iterate again that a great deal of work remains to be done in this field. Therefore our comments should be regarded merely as tentative bases for further reflection and research by those involved with raising and educating children. There is, and cannot be, any "rule book" for raising free children, because to follow an inflexible rule book is to ignore the fact that each child and their environment is unique and therefore demands unique responses from their parents. Hence the principles of libertarian child rearing to which we will refer should not be thought of as rules, but rather, as experimental hypotheses to be tested by parents within their own situation by applying their intelligence and deriving their own individual conclusions.

Bringing up children must be like education, and based on similar principles, namely "*upon the free growth and development of the innate forces and tendencies of the child. In this way alone can we hope for the free individual and eventually also for a free community, which shall make interference and coercion of human growth impossible.*" [Goldman, **Op. Cit.**, p. 139] Indeed, child rearing and education **cannot** be separated as life itself is an education and so must share the same principles and be viewed as a process of "*development and exploration, rather than as one of repressing a child's instincts and inculcating obedience and discipline.*" [Martha A. Ackelsberg, **Free Women of Spain**, p. 166]

Moreover, the role of parental example is very important to raising free children. Children often learn by mimicking their parents — children do what their parents do, not as they say. If their mother and father lie to each other, scream, fight and so on, then the child will probably do so as well. Children's behaviour does not come out of thin air, they are a product of the environment they are brought up in. Children can only be encouraged by example, not by threats and commands. So how parents act can be an obstacle to the development of a free child. Parents must do more than just **say** the right things, but also act as anarchists in order to produce free children.

The sad fact is that most modern people have lost the ability to raise free children, and regaining this ability will be a long process of trial and error as well as **parent** education in which it is to be hoped that each succeeding generation will learn from the failures and successes of their predecessors and so improve. In the best-case scenario, over the course of a few generations the number of progressive parents will continue to grow and raise ever freer children, who in turn will become even more progressive parents themselves, thus gradually changing mass psychology in a libertarian direction. Such changes **can** come about very fast, as can be seen from various communes all over the world where society is organised according to libertarian principles. As Reich put it:

> "*We have learned that instead of a jump into the realm of the Children of the Future, we can hope for no more than a steady advance, in which the healthy new overlaps the sick old structure, with the new slowly outgrowing the old.*" [**Children of the Future**, pp. 38-39]

By means of freedom-based child rearing and education, along with other methods of consciousness raising, as well as encouraging resistance to the existing social order anarchists hope to prepare the psychological foundation for a social paradigm shift, from authoritarian to libertarian institutions and values. And indeed, a gradual cultural evolution toward increasing freedom does seem to exist. Most anarchists believe that we must practice what we preach and so the anarchist revolution begins at home. As anarchists raise their own children in capitalist society and/or are involved in the raising and education of the children of other parents, we can practice in part libertarian principles even before the revolution. As such, we think it is important to discuss libertarian child rearing.

J.6.1 What are the main obstacles to raising free children?

The biggest obstacle is the training and character of most parents, physicians, and educators. Individuals within a hierarchical society create psychological walls/defences around themselves and these will obviously have an effect both on the mental and physical state of the individual and so their capacity for living a free life and experiencing pleasure. Such parents then try (often unconsciously) to stifle the life-energy in children. There are, for example, the child's natural vocal expressions (shouting, screaming, bellowing, crying, etc.) and natural body motility. As Reich noted:

> "Small children go through a phase of development characterised by vigorous activity of the voice musculature. The joy the infant derives from loud noises (crying, shrieking, and forming a variety of sounds) is regarded by many parents as pathological aggressiveness. The children are accordingly admonished not to scream, to be 'still,' etc. The impulses of the voice apparatus are inhibited, its musculature becomes chronically contracted, and the child becomes quiet, 'well-brought-up,' and withdrawn. The effect of such mistreatment is soon manifested in eating disturbances, general apathy, pallor of the face, etc. Speech disturbances and retardation of speech development are presumably caused in this manner. In the adult we see the effects of such mistreatment in the form of spasms of the throat. The automatic constrictions of the glottis and the deep throat musculature, with subsequent inhibition of the aggressive impulses of the head and neck, seems to be particularly characteristic."
> [**Children of the Future**, p. 128]

"Clinical experience has taught us," Reich concluded, "that small children must be allowed to 'shout themselves out' when the shouting is inspired by pleasure. This might be disagreeable to some parents, but questions of education must be decided **exclusively in the interests of the child,** not in those of the adults." [**Op. Cit.**, p. 128]

Besides deadening life energy in the body, such stifling also inhibits the anxiety generated by the presence of anti-social, cruel, and perverse impulses within the psyche — for example, destructiveness, sadism, greed, power hunger, brutality, etc. (impulses referred to by Reich as "secondary" drives). In other words, this reduces our ability to empathise with others and so the internal ethical guidelines we all develop are blunted, making us more likely to express such secondary, anti-social, drives. So, ironically, these secondary drives result from the **suppression of the primary drives** and the sensations of pleasure associated with them. These secondary drives develop because the only emotional expressions that can get through a person's defences are distorted, harsh, and/or mechanical. In other words, compulsive morality (i.e. acting according to externally imposed rules) becomes necessary to control the secondary drives **which compulsion itself creates.** By such processes, authoritarian child-rearing becomes self-justifying:

> "Psychoanalysts have failed to distinguish between primary natural and secondary perverse, cruel drives, and they are continuously killing nature in the new-born while they try to extinguish the 'brutish little animal.' They are completely ignorant of the fact that it is **exactly this killing of the natural principle which creates the secondary perverse and cruel nature,** human nature so called, and that these artificial cultural creations in turn make compulsive moralism and brutal laws necessary."
> [Reich, **Op. Cit.**, p. 17-18]

Moralism, however, can never get at the root of the problem of secondary drives, but in fact only increases the pressure of crime and guilt. The real solution is to let children develop what Reich calls **natural self-regulation.** This can be done only by not subjecting them to punishment, coercion, threats, moralistic lectures and admonitions, withdrawal of love, etc. in an attempt to inhibit their spontaneous expression of natural life-impulses. The systematic development of the emphatic tendencies of the young infant is the best way to "socialise" and restrict activities that are harmful to the others. As A.S. Neill pointed out "self-regulation implies a belief in the goodness of human nature; a belief that there is not, and never was, original sin." [**Summerhill**, p. 103]

According to Neill, children who are given freedom from birth and not forced to conform to parental expectations spontaneously learn how to keep themselves clean and develop social qualities like courtesy, common sense, an interest in learning, respect for the rights of others, and so forth. However, once the child has been armoured through authoritarian methods intended to **force** it to develop such qualities, it becomes out of touch with its living core and therefore no longer able to develop self-regulation. In this stage it becomes harder and harder for the pro-social emotions to shape the developing mode of life of the new member of society. At that point, when the secondary drives develop, parental authoritarianism becomes a **necessity.**

This oppression produces an inability to tolerate freedom. The vast majority of people develop this **automatically** from the way they are raised and is what makes the whole subject of bringing up children of crucial importance to anarchists. Reich concluded that if parents do not suppress nature in the first place, then no anti-social drives will be created and no authoritarianism will be required to suppress them: "**What you so desperately and vainly try to achieve by way of compulsion and admonition is there in the new-born infant ready to live and function. Let it grow as nature requires, and change our institutions accordingly.**" [**Op. Cit.**, p. 47] So in order to raise psychologically healthy children, parents need to acquire self-knowledge, particularly of how internal conflicts develop in family relationships, and to free themselves as much as possible from neurotic forms of behaviour. The difficulty of parents acquiring such self-knowledge and sufficiently de-conditioning themselves is obviously another obstacle to raising self-regulated children.

J.6.2. What are some examples of libertarian child-rearing methods?

According to Reich, the problems of parenting a free child actually begin before conception, with the need for a prospective mother to free herself as much as possible from chronic muscular tensions. It has been found in many studies that not only the physical health of the mother can influence the foetus. Various psychological stresses influence the chemical and hormonal environment, affecting the foetus.

Immediately after birth it is important for the mother to establish contact with her child. This means, basically, constant loving attention to the baby, expressed by plenty of holding, cuddling, playing, etc., and especially by breast feeding. By such *"orgonotic"* contact (to use Reich's term), the mother is able to establish the initial emotional bonding with the new born, and a non-verbal understanding of the child's needs. This is only possible, however, if she is in touch with her own emotional and cognitive internal processes: ***"Orgonotic contact is the most essential experiential and emotional element in the interrelationship between mother and child,*** *particularly prenatally and during the first days and weeks of life. The future fate of the child depends on it. It seems to be the core of the new-born infant's emotional development."* [**Children of the Future**, p. 99] It is important for the father to establish orgonotic contact as well.

Reich maintained that the practice of bottle feeding is harmful, particularly if it completely replaces breast feeding from the day of birth, because it eliminates one of the most important forms of establishing physical and emotional contact between mother and child. Another harmful practice is allowing the baby to "cry itself out." Thus: *"Parking a baby in a baby carriage in the garden, perhaps for hours at a time, is a dangerous practice. No one can know what agonising feelings of fear and loneliness a baby can experience on waking up suddenly to find himself alone in a strange place. Those who have heard a baby's screams on such occasions have some idea of the cruelty of this stupid custom."* [Neill, **Summerhill**, p. 336] Indeed, in **The Physical Dynamics of Character Structure**, Alexander Lowen has traced specific neuroses, particularly depression, to this practice. Hospitals also have been guilty of psychologically damaging sick infants by isolating them from their mothers, a practice that has undoubtedly produced untold numbers of neurotics and psychopaths.

Neill summed up the libertarian attitude toward the care of infants as follows: ***"Self-regulation means the right of a baby to live freely without outside authority in things psychic and somatic.*** *It means that the baby feeds when it is hungry; that it becomes clean in habits only when it wants to; that it is never stormed at nor spanked; that it is always loved and protected."* Obviously self-regulation does not mean leaving the baby alone when it heads toward a cliff or starts playing with an electrical socket. Libertarians do not advocate a lack of common sense. We recognise that adults must override an infant's will when it is a question of protecting their physical safety: *"Only a fool in charge of young children would allow unbarred bedroom windows or an unprotected fire in the nursery. Yet, too often, young enthusiasts for self-regulation come to my school as visitors, and exclaim at our lack of freedom in locking poison in a lab closet, or our prohibition about playing on the fire escape. The whole freedom movement is marred and despised because so many advocates of freedom have not got their feet on the ground."* [**Op. Cit.**, p. 105 and p. 106]

Nevertheless, the libertarian position does not imply that a child should be **punished** for getting into a dangerous situation. Nor is the best thing to do in such a case to shout in alarm (unless that is the only way to warn the child before it is too late), but simply to remove the danger without any fuss: *"Unless a child is mentally defective, he will soon discover what interests him. Left free from excited cries and angry voices, he will be unbelievably sensible in his dealing with material of all kinds."* [Neil, **Op. Cit.**, p. 108] Provided, of course, that he or she has been allowed self-regulation from the beginning, and thus has not developed any irrational, secondary drives.

The way to raise a free child becomes clear when one considers how an **un**free child is raised. Thus imagine the typical infant whose upbringing A.S. Neill described:

> *"His natural functions were left alone during the diaper period. But when he began to crawl and perform on the floor, words like **naughty** and **dirty** began to float about the house, and a grim beginning was made in teaching him to be clean.*
>
> *"Before this, his hand had been taken away every time it touched his genitals; and he soon came to associate the genital prohibition with the acquired disgust about faeces. Thus, years later, when he became a travelling salesman, his story repertoire consisted of a balanced number of sex and toilet jokes.*
>
> *"Much of his training was conditioned by relatives and neighbours. Mother and father were most anxious to be correct — to do the proper thing — so that when relatives or next-door neighbours came, John had to show himself as a well-trained child. He had to say **Thank you** when Auntie gave him a piece of chocolate; and he had to be most careful about his table manners; and especially, he had to refrain from speaking when adults were speaking …*
>
> *"All his curiosity about the origins of life were met with clumsy lies, lies so effective that his curiosity about life and birth disappeared. The lies about life became combined with fears when at the age of five his mother found him having genital play with his sister of four and the girl next door. The severe spanking that followed (Father added to it when he came home from work) forever conveyed to John the lesson that sex is filthy and sinful, something one must not even think of."* [**Op. Cit.**, p. 96-7]

Of course, parents' ways of imparting negative messages about sex are not necessarily this severe, especially in our allegedly enlightened age. However, it is not necessary for a child to be spanked or even scolded or lectured in order to acquire a sex-negative attitude. Children are very intuitive and will receive the message "sex is bad" from subtle parental cues like facial expressions, tone of voice, embarrassed silence, avoidance of certain topics, etc. Mere "toleration" of sexual curiosity and play is far different in its psychological effects from positive affirmation.

Along the same lines, to prevent the formation of sex-negative attitudes means that nakedness should never be discouraged: "*The baby should see its parents naked from the beginning. However, the child should be told when he is ready to understand that some people don't like to see children naked and that, in the presence of such people, he should wear clothes.*" Neill maintains that not only should parents never spank or punish a child for genital play, but that spanking and other forms of punishment should never be used in **any** circumstances, because they instil fear, turning children into cowards and often leading to phobias. "*Fear must be entirely eliminated — fear of adults, fear of punishment, fear of disapproval, fear of God. Only hate can flourish in an atmosphere of fear.*" Punishment also turns children into sadists: "*The cruelty of many children springs from the cruelty that has been practised on them by adults. You cannot be beaten without wishing to beat someone else. Every beating makes a child sadistic in desire or practice.*" [Neil **Op. Cit.**, p. 229, p. 124, p. 269 and p. 271] This is obviously an important consideration to anarchists, as sadistic drives provide the psychological ground for militarism, war, police brutality, and so on. Such drives are undoubtedly also part of the desire to exercise hierarchical authority, with its possibilities for using negative sanctions against subordinates as an outlet for sadistic impulses.

Child beating is particularly cowardly because it is a way for adults to vent their hatred, frustration, and sadism on those who are unable to defend themselves. Such cruelty is, of course, always rationalised with excuse like "it hurts me more than it does you," etc., or explained in moral terms, like "I don't want my boy to be soft" or "I want him to prepare him for a harsh world" or "I spank my children because my parents spanked me, and it did me a hell of a lot of good." But despite such rationalisations, the fact remains that punishment is always an act of hate. To this hate the child responds in kind by hating the parents, followed by fantasy, guilt, and repression. For example, the child may fantasise the father's death, which immediately causes guilt, and so is repressed. Often the hatred induced by punishment emerges in fantasies that are seemingly remote from the parents, such as stories of giant killing — always popular with children because the giant represents the father. Obviously, the sense of guilt produced by such fantasies is very advantageous to organised religions that promise redemption from "sin." It is surely no coincidence that such religions are enthusiastic promoters of the sex-negative morality and disciplinarian child rearing practices that keep supplying them with recruits.

What is worse, however, is that punishment actually **creates** "problem children." This is so because the parent arouses more and more hatred (and diminishing trust in other human beings) in the child with each spanking, which is expressed in still worse behaviour, calling for more spankings, and so on, in a vicious circle. In contrast, the "*self-regulated child does not need any punishment,*" Neill argued, "*and he does not go through this hate cycle. He is never punished and he does not need to behave badly. He has no use for lying and for breaking things. His body has never been called filthy*

or wicked. He has not needed to rebel against authority or to fear his parents. Tantrums he will usually have, but they will be short-lived and not tend toward neurosis." [**Op. Cit.**, p. 166]

We could cite many further examples of how libertarian principles of child-rearing can be applied in practice, but we must limit ourselves to these few. The basic principles can be summed up as follows: Get rid of authority, moralising, and the desire to "improve" and "civilise" children. Allow them to be themselves, without pushing them around, bribing, threatening, admonishing, lecturing, or otherwise forcing them to do anything. Refrain from action unless the child, by expressing their "freedom" restricts the freedom of others and **explain** what is wrong about such actions and never mechanically punish.

This is, of course, a radical philosophy, which few parents are willing to follow. It is quite amazing how people who call themselves libertarians in political and economic matters draw the line when it comes to their behaviour within the family — as if such behaviour had no wider social consequences!

J.6.3 If children have nothing to fear, how can they be good?

Obedience that is based on fear of punishment, this-worldly or other-worldly, is not really goodness, it is merely cowardice. True morality (i.e. respect for others and one-self) comes from inner conviction based on experience, it cannot be imposed from without by fear. Nor can it be inspired by hope of reward, such as praise or the promise of heaven, which is simply bribery. If children are given as much freedom as possible from the day of birth, if parents respect them as individuals and give a positive example as well as not being forced to conform to parental expectations, they will spontaneously learn the basic principles of social behaviour, such as cleanliness, courtesy, and so forth. But they must be allowed to develop them **at their own speed,** at the natural stage of their growth, not when parents think they should develop them. What is "natural" timing must be discovered by observation, not by defining it a priori based on one's own expectations.

Can a child really be taught to keep themselves clean without being punished for getting dirty? According to many psychologists, it is not only possible but **vitally important** for the child's mental health to do so, since punishment will give the child a fixed and repressed interest in their bodily functions. As Reich and Lowen have shown various forms of compulsive and obsessive neuroses can be traced back to the punishments used in toilet training. As Neill observed: "*When the mother says **naughty** or **dirty** or even **tut tut**, the element of right and wrong arises. The question becomes a **moral** one — when it should remain a **physical** one.*" He suggested that the **wrong** way to deal with a child who likes to play with faeces is to tell him he is being dirty. The right way "*is to allow him to live out his interest in excrement by providing him with mud or clay. In this way, he will sublimate his interest without repression. He will live through his interest; and in doing so, kill it.*" [**Summerhill**, p. 174]

Similarly, sceptics will probably question how children can be induced to eat a healthy diet without threats of punishment. The answer can be discovered by a simple experiment: set out on the table all kinds of foods, from sweets and ice cream to whole wheat bread, lettuce, sprouts, and so on, and allow the child complete freedom to choose what is desired or to eat nothing at all if he or she is not hungry. Parents will find that the average child will begin choosing a balanced diet after about a week, after the desire for prohibited or restricted foods has been satisfied. This is an example of what can be called "trusting nature." That the question of how to "train" a child to eat properly should even be an issue says volumes about how little the concept of freedom for children is accepted or even understood, in our society. Unfortunately, the concept of "training" still holds the field in this and most other areas.

The disciplinarian argument that that children must be **forced** to respect possessions is also defective, because it always requires some sacrifice of a child's play life (and childhood should be devoted to play, not to "preparing for adulthood," because playing is what children spontaneously do). The libertarian view is that a child should arrive at a sense of value out of his or her own free choice. This means not scolding or punishing them for breaking or damaging things. As they grow out of the stage of preadolescent indifference to possessions, they learn to respect it naturally.

"But shouldn't a child at least be punished for stealing?" it will be asked. Once again, the answer lies in the idea of trusting nature. The concept of "mine" and "yours" is adult, and children naturally develop it as they become mature, but not before. This means that normal children will "steal" — though that is not how they regard it. They are simply trying to satisfy their acquisitive impulses; or, if they are with friends, their desire for adventure. In a society so thoroughly steeped in the idea of respect for property as ours, it is no doubt difficult for parents to resist societal pressure to punish children for "stealing." The reward for such trust, however, will be a child who grows into a healthy adolescent who respects the possessions of others, not out of a cowardly fear of punishment but from his or her own self-nature.

Most parents believe that, besides taking care of their child's physical needs, the teaching of ethical/moral values is their main responsibility and that without such teaching the child will grow up to be a "little wild animal" who acts on every whim, with no consideration for others. This idea arises mainly from the fact that most people in our society believe, at least passively, that human beings are naturally bad and that unless they are "trained" to be good they will be lazy, mean, violent, or even murderous. This, of course, is essentially the idea of "original sin" and because of its widespread acceptance, nearly all adults believe that it is their job to "improve" children. Yet according to libertarian psychologists there is no original sin. In fact, it would be more accurate to say that there is "original virtue." Wilhelm Reich found that externally imposed, compulsive morality actually **causes** immoral behaviour by creating cruel and perverse *"secondary drives."* Neill put it this way: *"I find that when I smash the moral instruction a bad boy has received, he becomes a good boy."* [**Op. Cit.**, p. 250]

Unconscious acceptance of some form of the idea of original sin is the main recruiting tool of organised religions, as people who believe they are born "sinners" feel a strong sense of guilt and need for redemption. Parents to should eliminate any need for redemption,

by telling the child that he is born good, not born bad. This will help keep them from falling under the influence of life-denying religions, which are inimical to the growth of a healthy character structure. Citing ethnological studies, Reich argued the following:

> *"Among those primitive peoples who lead satisfactory, unimpaired sexual lives, there is no sexual crime, no sexual perversion, no sexual brutality between man and woman; rape is unthinkable because it is unnecessary in their society. Their sexual activity flows in normal, well-ordered channels which would fill any cleric with indignation and fear … They love the human body and take pleasure in their sexuality. They do not understand why young men and women should not enjoy their sexuality. But when their lives are invaded by the ascetic, hypocritical morass and by the Church, which bring them 'culture' along with exploitation, alcohol, and syphilis, they begin to suffer the same wretchedness as ourselves. They begin to lead 'moral' lives, i.e. to suppress their sexuality, and from then on they decline more and more into a state of sexual distress, which is the result of sexual suppression. At the same time, they become sexually dangerous; murders of spouses, sexual diseases, and crimes of all sorts start to appear."* [**Children of the Future**, p. 193]

Such crimes in our society would be greatly reduced if libertarian child rearing practices were widely followed. These are obviously important considerations for anarchists, who are frequently asked to explain how crime can be prevented in an anarchist society. The answer is that if people are not suppressed during childhood there will be far less anti-social behaviour, because the secondary-drive structure that leads to it will not be created in the first place. In other words, the solution to the so-called crime problem is not more police, more laws, or a return to the disciplinarianism of "traditional family values," as conservatives claim, but depends mainly on **getting rid** of such values.

There are other problems as well with the moralism taught by organised religions. One danger is making the child a hater: *"If a child is taught that certain things are sinful, his love of life must be changed to hate. When children are free, they never think of another child as being a sinner."* [Neill, **Op. Cit.**, p. 245] From the idea that certain people are sinners, it is a short step to the idea that certain classes or races of people are more "sinful" than others, leading to prejudice, discrimination, and persecution of minorities as an outlet for repressed anger and sadistic drives — drives that are created in the first place by moralistic training during early childhood. Once again, the relevance for anarchism is obvious.

A further danger of religious instruction is the development of a fear of life: *"Religion to a child most always means only fear. God is a mighty man with holes in his eyelids: He can see you wherever you are. To a child, this often means that God can see what is being done under the bedclothes. And to introduce fear into a child's life is the worst of all crimes. Forever the child says nay to life; forever he is an inferior; forever a coward."* [Neill, **Op. Cit.**, p. 246] People who have been threatened with fear of an afterlife in hell can never be entirely free of neurotic anxiety about security in **this** life. In turn, such people become easy targets of ruling-class propaganda that plays upon their material and emotional insecurity, e.g. the rationalisation of imperialist wars, the Military-Industrial Complex, increased state powers, and so on as necessary to "preserve jobs", for security against external threats and so forth.

J.6.4 But how will a free child ever learn unselfishness?

Another common objection to self-regulation is that children can only be taught to be **"unselfish"** through punishment and admonition. Again, however, such a view comes from a distrust of nature and is part of the common attitude that nature is mere "raw material" to be shaped by human beings according to their own wishes. The libertarian attitude is that empathy for others develops at the proper time:

> "To ask a child to be unselfish is wrong. Every child is an egoist and the world belongs to him. When he has an apple, his one wish is to eat that apple. The chief result of mother's encouraging him to share it with his little brother is to make him hate the little brother. Altruism comes later — comes naturally — **if the child is not taught to be unselfish.** It probably never comes at all if the child has been forced to be unselfish. By suppressing the child's selfishness, the mother is fixing that selfishness forever." [Neill, **Summerhill**, pp. 250-251]

Unfulfilled wishes live on in the unconscious so children who are pressured too hard — "taught" — to be unselfish will, while conforming outwardly with parental demands, unconsciously repress part of their real, selfish wishes, and these repressed infantile desires will make the person selfish (and possibly neurotic) throughout life. Moreover, telling children that what they want to do is "wrong" or "bad" is equivalent to teaching them to hate themselves, and it is a well-known principle of psychology that people who do not love themselves cannot love others. Thus moral instruction, although it aims to develop altruism and love for others, is actually self-defeating, having just the opposite result. Moreover, such attempts to produce "unselfish" children (and so adults) actually works **against** developing the individuality of the child and they developing their own abilities (in particular their ability of critical thought). As Erich Fromm put it:

> "Not to be selfish implies not to do what one wishes, to give up one's own wishes for the sake of those in authority … Aside from its obvious implication, it means 'don't love yourself,' 'don't be yourself', but submit yourself to something more important than yourself, to an outside power or its internalisation, 'duty.' 'Don't be selfish' becomes one of the most powerful ideological tools in suppressing spontaneity and the free development of personality. Under the pressure of this slogan one is asked for every sacrifice and for complete submission: only those acts are 'unselfish' which do not serve the individual but somebody or something outside himself." [**Man for Himself**, p. 127]

While such "unselfishness" is ideal for creating "model citizens" and willing wage slaves, it is not conducive for creating anarchists or even developing individuality. Little wonder Bakunin celebrated the urge to rebel and saw it as the key to human progress! Fromm goes on to note that selfishness and self-love, "far from being identical, are actually opposites" and that "selfish persons are incapable of loving others … [or] loving themselves." [**Op. Cit.**, p. 131] Individuals who do not love themselves, and so others, will be more willing to submit themselves to hierarchy than those who do love themselves and are concerned for their own, and others, welfare. Thus the contradictory nature of capitalism, with its contradictory appeals to selfish and unselfish behaviour, can be understood as being based upon lack of self-love, a lack which is promoted in childhood and one which libertarians should be aware of and combat.

Indeed, much of the urge to "teach children unselfishness" is actually an expression of adults' will to power. Whenever parents feel the urge to impose directives on their children, they would be wise to ask themselves whether the impulse comes from their own power drive or their own selfishness. For, since our culture strongly conditions us to seek power over others, what could be more convenient than having a small, weak person at hand who cannot resist one's will to power? Instead of issuing directives, libertarians believe in letting social behaviour develop naturally, which it will do after other people's opinions becomes important **to the child.** As Neill pointed out:

> "Everyone seeks the good opinion of his neighbours. Unless other forces push him into unsocial behaviour, a child will naturally want to do that which will cause him to be well-regarded, but this desire to please others develops at a certain stage in his growth. The attempt by parents and teachers to artificially accelerate this stage does the child irreparable damage." [**Op. Cit.**, p. 256]

Therefore, parents should allow children to be "selfish" and "ungiving", free to follow their own childish interests throughout their childhood. Every interpersonal conflict of interest should be grounds for a lesson in dignity on one side and consideration on the other. Only by this process can a child develop their individuality. By so doing they will come to recognise the individuality of others and this is the first step in developing ethical concepts (which rest upon mutual respect for others and their individuality).

J.6.5 Isn't "libertarian child-rearing" just another name for spoiling the child?

No. This objection confuses the distinction between freedom and license. To raise a child in freedom does not mean letting him or her walk all over you or others; it does not mean never saying "no." It is true that free children are not subjected to punishment, irrational authority, or moralistic admonitions, but they are not "free" to violate the rights of others. As Neill put it: "in the disciplined home, the children have **no** rights. In the spoiled home, they have **all** the rights. The proper home is one in which children and adults have *equal rights."* Or again: *"To let a child have his own way, or do what he wants to **at another's expense,** is bad for the child. It creates a spoiled child, and the spoiled child is a bad citizen."* [**Summerhill**, p. 107 and 167]

There will inevitably be conflicts of will between parents and children, and the healthy way to resolve them is discussion and coming to an agreement. The unhealthy ways are either to resort to authoritarian discipline or to spoil the child by allowing them to have all the social rights. Libertarian psychologists argue that no harm is done to children by insisting on one's individual rights, but that the harm comes from moralism, i.e. when one introduces the concepts of right and wrong or words like "naughty," "bad," or "dirty," which produce guilt.

Therefore it should not be thought that free children are free to "do as they please." Freedom means doing what one likes so long as it does not infringe on the freedom of others. Thus there is a big difference between compelling a child to stop throwing stones at others and compelling him or her to learn geometry. Throwing stones infringes on others' rights, but learning geometry involves only the child. The same goes for forcing children to eat with a fork instead of their fingers; to say "please" and "thank you"; to tidy up their rooms, and so on. Bad manners and untidiness may be annoying to adults, but they are not a violation of adults' rights. One could, of course, define an adult "right" to be free of annoyance from **anything** one's child does, but this would simply be a license for authoritarianism, emptying the concept of children's rights of all content.

As mentioned, giving children freedom does not mean allowing them to endanger themselves physically. For example, a sick child should not be asked to decide whether he wants to go outdoors or take his prescribed medicine, nor a run-down and overtired child whether she wants to go to bed. But the imposition of such forms of necessary authority is compatible with the idea that children should be given as much responsibility as they can handle at their particular age. Only in this way can they develop self-assurance. And, again, it is important for parents to examine their own motives when deciding how much responsibility to give their child. Parents who insist on choosing their children's clothes for them, for example, are generally worried that the child might select clothes that would reflect badly on their parents' social standing.

As for those who equate "discipline" in the home with "obedience," the latter is usually required of a child to satisfy the adults' desire for power. Self-regulation means that there are no power games being played with children, no loud voice saying "You'll do it because I say so, or else!" But, although this irrational, power-seeking kind of authority is absent in the libertarian home, there still remains what can be called a kind of "authority," namely adult protection, care, and responsibility, as well as the insistence on one's own rights. As Neill observed: *"Such authority sometimes demands obedience but at other times gives obedience. Thus I can say to my daughter, 'You can't bring that mud and water into our parlour.' That's no more than her saying to me, 'Get out of my room, Daddy. I don't want you here now,' a wish that I, of course, obey without a word."* [**Op. Cit.**, p. 156]. So there will still be "discipline" in the libertarian home, but it will be of the kind that protects the individual rights of each family member.

Raising children in freedom also does not imply giving them a lot of toys, money, and so on. Reich's followers have argued that children should not be given everything they ask for and that it is better to give them too little than too much. Under constant bombardment by commercial advertising campaigns, parents today generally tend to give their children far too much, with the result that the children stop appreciating gifts and rarely value any of their possessions. This same applies to money, which, if given in excess, can be detrimental to children's' creativity and play life. If children are not given too many toys, they will derive creative joy out of making their own toys out of whatever free materials are at hand — a joy of which they are robbed by overindulgence. Psychologists point out that parents who give too many presents are often trying to compensate for giving too little love.

There is less danger in rewarding children than there is in punishing them, but rewards can still undermine a child's morale. This is because, firstly, rewards are superfluous and in fact often **decrease** motivation and creativity, as several psychological studies have shown (see section I.4.11). Creative people work for the pleasure of creating; monetary interests are not central (or necessary) to the creative process. Secondly, rewards send the wrong message, namely, that doing the deed for which the reward is offered is not worth doing for its own sake and the pleasure associated with productive, creative activity. Thirdly, rewards tend to reinforce the worst aspects of the competitive system, leading to the attitude that money is the only thing which can motivate people to do the work that needs doing in society.

These are just a few of the considerations that enter into the distinction between spoiling children and raising them in freedom. In reality, it is the punishment and fear of a disciplinarian home that **spoils** children in the most literal sense, by destroying their childhood happiness and creating warped personalities. As adults, the victims of disciplinarianism will generally be burdened with one or more anti-social secondary drives such as sadism, destructive urges, greed, sexual perversions, etc., as well as repressed rage and fear. The presence of such impulses just below the surface of consciousness causes anxiety, which is automatically defended against by psychological walls which leave the person stiff, frustrated, bitter and burdened with feelings of inner emptiness. In such a condition people easily fall victim to the capitalist gospel of super-consumption, which promises that money will enable them to fill the inner void by purchasing commodities — a promise that, of course, is hollow.

The neurotically enclosed person also tends to look for scapegoats on whom to blame his or her frustration and anxiety and against whom repressed rage can be vented. Reactionary politicians know very well how to direct such impulses against minorities or "hostile nations" with propaganda designed to serve the interests of the ruling elite. Most importantly, however, the respect for authority combined with sadistic impulses which is acquired from a disciplinarian upbringing typically produces a submissive/authoritarian personality — a man or woman who blindly follows the orders of "superiors" while at the same time desiring to exercise authority on "subordinates," whether in the family, the state bureaucracy, or the company. Ervin Staub's **Roots of Evil** includes interviews of imprisoned SS men, who, in the course of extensive interviews (meant to determine how ostensibly "normal" people could perform acts of untold ruthlessness and violence) revealed that they overwhelmingly came from authoritarian, disciplinarian homes.

In this way, the "traditional" (e.g., authoritarian, disciplinarian, patriarchal) family is the necessary foundation for authoritarian civilisation, reproducing it and its attendant social evils from generation to generation.

J.6.6 What is the anarchist position on teenage sexual liberation?

One of the biggest problems of adolescence is sexual suppression by parents and society in general. The teenage years are the time when sexual energy is at its height. Why, then, the absurd demand that teenagers "wait until marriage," or at least until leaving home, before becoming sexually active? Why are there laws in "advanced" countries like the United States that allow a 19-year-old "boy" who makes love with his 17-year-old girlfriend, with her full consent, to be **arrested** by the girl's parents (!) for "statutory rape"?

To answer such questions, let us recall that the ruling class is not interested in encouraging mass tendencies toward liberty, independence and pleasure not derived from commodities but instead supports whatever contributes to mass submissiveness, docility, dependence, helplessness, and respect for authority — traits that perpetuate the hierarchies on which ruling-class power and privileges depend.

As sex is one of the most intense forms of pleasure and one of the most prominent contributors for intimacy and bonding with people emotionally, repression of sexuality is the most powerful means of psychologically crippling people and giving them a submissive/authoritarian character structure (as well as alienating people from each other). As Reich observed, such a character is composed of a mixture of *"sexual impotence, helplessness, a need for attachments, a nostalgia for a leader, fear of authority, timidity, and mysticism"* and *"people structured in this manner are incapable of democracy. All attempts to build up or maintain genuine democratically directed organisations come to grief when they encounter these character structures. They form the psychological soil of the masses in which dictatorial strivings and bureaucratic tendencies of democratically elected leaders can develop."* Sexual suppression *"produces the authority-fearing, life-fearing vassal, and thus constantly creates new possibilities whereby a handful of men in power can rule the masses."* [**The Sexual Revolution**, p. 82]

No doubt most members of the ruling elite are not fully conscious that their own power and privileges depend on the mass perpetuation of sex-negative attitudes. Nevertheless, they unconsciously sense it. Sexual freedom is the most basic and powerful kind, and every conservative or reactionary instinctively shudders at the thought of the "social chaos" it would unleash — that is, the rebellious, authority-defying type of character it would nourish. This is why "family values," and "religion" (i.e. discipline and compulsive sexual morality) are the mainstays of the conservative/reactionary agenda. Thus it is crucially important for anarchists to address every aspect of sexual suppression in society. This means affirming the right of

adolescents to an unrestricted sex life.

There are numerous arguments for teenage sexual liberation. For example, many teen suicides could be prevented by removing the restrictions on adolescent sexuality. This becomes clear from ethnological studies of sexually unrepressive tribal peoples:

> *"All reports, whether by missionaries or scholars, with or without the proper indignation about the 'moral depravity' of 'savages,' state that the puberty rites of adolescents lead them immediately into a sexual life; that some of these primitive societies lay great emphasis on sexual pleasure; that the puberty rite is an important social event; that some primitive peoples not only do not hinder the sexual life of adolescents but encourage it is every way, as, for instance, by arranging for community houses in which the adolescents settle at the start of puberty in order to be able to enjoy sexual intercourse. Even in those primitive societies in which the institution of strict monogamous marriage exists, adolescents are given complete freedom to enjoy sexual intercourse from the beginning of puberty to marriage. None of these reports contains any indication of sexual misery or suicide by adolescents suffering from unrequited love (although the latter does of course occur). The contradiction between sexual maturity and the absence of genital sexual gratification is non-existent."* [Reich, **Op. Cit.**, p. 85]

Teenage sexual repression is also closely connected with crime. If there are teenagers in a neighbourhood who have no place to pursue intimate sexual relationships, they will do it in dark corners, in cars or vans, etc., always on the alert and anxious lest someone discover them. Under such conditions, full gratification is impossible, leading to a build-up of tension and frustration. Thus they feel unsatisfied, disturb each other, become jealous and angry, get into fights, turn to drugs as a substitute for a satisfying sex life, vandalise property to let off "steam" (repressed rage), or even murder someone. As Reich noted, *"juvenile delinquency is the visible expression of the subterranean sexual crisis in the lives of children and adolescents. And it may be predicted that no society will ever succeed in solving this problem, the problem of juvenile psychopathology, unless that society can muster the courage and acquire the knowledge to regulate the sexual life of its children and adolescents in a sex-affirmative manner."* [**Op. Cit.**, p. 271]

For these reasons, it is clear that a solution to the "gang problem" also depends on adolescent sexual liberation. We are not suggesting, of course, that gangs themselves suppress sexual activity. Indeed, one of their main attractions to teens is undoubtedly the hope of more opportunities for sex as a gang member. However, gangs' typical obsessiveness with the promiscuous, pornographic, sadistic, and other "dark" aspects of sex shows that by the time children reach gang age they have already developed unhealthy secondary drives due to the generally sex-negative and repressive environment in which they have grown up. The expression of such drives is **not** what anarchists mean by "sexual freedom." Rather, anarchist proposals for teenage liberation are based on the premise that a libertarian childhood is the necessary condition for a **healthy** sexual freedom in adolescence.

Applying these insights to our own society, it is clear that teenagers should have ample access to a private room where they can be undisturbed with their sexual partners. Parents should also encourage the knowledge and use of contraceptives and safe sex in general as well as respect for the other person involved in the relationship. This does not mean encouraging promiscuity or sex for the sake of it. Rather, it means encouraging teenagers to know their own minds and desires, refusing to be pressured by anyone into anything. As can be seen from experience of this anarchist activist during the 1930s:

> "One time, a companero from the Juventudes [libertarian youth organisation] came over to me and said, 'You, who say you're so liberated. You're not so liberated.' (I'm telling you this so you'll see the mentality of these men.) 'Because if I ask you to give me a kiss, you wouldn't.

> "I just stood there staring at him, and thinking to myself, 'How do I get out of this one?" And then I said to him, 'Listen, when I want to go to bed with a guy, I'm the one that has to choose him. I don't go to bed with just anyone. You don't interest me as a man. I don't feel anything for you... Why should you want me to 'liberate myself,' as you put it, by going to bed with you? That's no liberation for me. That's just making love simply for the sake of making love.' 'No,' I said to him, 'love is something that has to be like eating: if you're hungry, you eat, and if you want to go to bed with a guy, then... Besides, I'm going to tell you something else ... Your mouth doesn't appeal to me... And I don't like to make love with a guy without kissing him.'

> "He was left speechless! But I did it with a dual purpose in mind... because I wanted to show him that that's not the way to educate companeros... That's what the struggle of women was like in Spain — even with men from our own group — and I'm not even talking about what it was like with other guys." [quoted by Martha A. Ackelsberg, **Free Women of Spain**, pp. 116-7]

So respecting yourself and others, it must be stressed, is essential. As Maurice Brinton pointed out, attempts at sexual liberation will encounter two kinds of responses from established society — direct opposition and attempts at recuperation. The second response takes the form of *"first alienating and reifying sexuality, and then of frenetically exploiting this empty shell for commercial ends. As modern youth breaks out of the dual stranglehold of repressive traditional morality and of the authoritarian patriarchal family it encounters a projected image of free sexuality which is in fact a manipulative distortion of it."* This can be seen from the use of sex in advertising to the successful development of sex into a major consumer industry. However, such a development is the opposite of the healthy sexuality desired by anarchists. This is because *"sex is presented as something to be consumed. But the sexual instinct differs from certain other instincts"* as it can be satisfied only by *"another human being, capable of thinking, acting, suffering. The alienation of sexuality under the conditions of modern capitalism is*

very much part of the general alienating process, in which people are converted into objects (in this case, objects of sexual consumption) and relationships are drained of human content. Undiscriminating, compulsive sexual activity, is not sexual freedom — although it may sometimes be a preparation for it (which repressive morality can never be). The illusion that alienated sex is sexual freedom constitutes yet another obstacle on the road to total emancipation. Sexual freedom implies a realisation and understanding of the autonomy of others." ["The Irrational in Politics", pp. 257-92, **For Workers' Power**, p. 277]

Therefore, anarchists see teenage sexual liberation as a means of developing free individuals **as well as** reducing the evil effects of sexual repression (which, we must note, also helps dehumanise individuals by encouraging the objectification of others, and in a patriarchal society particularly of women).

J.6.7 But isn't this concern with sexual liberation just a distraction from revolution?

It would be insulting to teenagers to suggest that sexual freedom is, or should be, their **only** concern. Many teens have a well-developed social conscience and are keenly interested in problems of economic exploitation, poverty, social breakdown, environmental degradation, and the like. The same can be said of people of any age!

It is essential for anarchists to guard against the attitude typically found in Marxist-Leninist parties that spontaneous discussions about sexual problems are a "diversion from the class struggle." Such an attitude is economistic (not to mention covertly ascetic), because it is based on the premise that economic class must be the focus of all revolutionary efforts toward social change. No doubt transforming the economy is important, but without mass sexual liberation no working class revolution can be complete as there will not be enough people around with the character structures necessary to create a **lasting** self-managed society and economy (i.e., people who are capable of accepting freedom with responsibility). Instead, the attempt to force the creation of such a system without preparing the necessary psychological soil for its growth will lead to a reversion to some new form of hierarchy and exploitation. Equally, society would be "free" in name only if repressive social morals existed and people were not able to express themselves as they so desire.

Moreover, for many people breaking free from the sexual suppression that threatens to cripple them psychologically is a major issue in their lives. For this reason, few of them are likely to be attracted to the anarchist "freedom" movement if its exponents limit themselves to dry discussions of surplus value, alienated labour, and so forth. Instead, addressing sexual questions and problems must be integrated into a multi-faceted attack on the total system of domination. People should feel confident that anarchists are on the side of sexual pleasure and are not revolutionary ascetics demanding self-denial for the "sake of the revolution." Rather, it should be stressed that the capacity for full sexual enjoyment is an essential part of the revolution. Indeed, *"incessant questioning and challenge to authority on the subject of sex and of the compulsive* family can only complement the questioning and challenge to authority in other areas (for instance on the subject of who is to dominate the work process — or the purpose of work itself). Both challenges stress the autonomy of individuals and their domination over important aspects of their lives. Both expose the alienated concepts which pass for rationality and which govern so much of our thinking and behaviour. The task of the conscious revolutionary is to make both challenges explicit, to point out their deeply subversive content, and to explain their inter-relation." [Maurice Brinton, "The Irrational in Politics", pp. 257-92, **For Workers' Power**, p. 278]

We noted previously that in pre-patriarchal society, which rests on a communistic/communal social order, children have complete sexual freedom and that the idea of childhood asceticism develops as such societies turn toward patriarchy in the economic and social structure (see section B.1.5). This sea-change in social attitudes toward sexuality allows the authority-oriented character structure to develop instead of the formerly non-authoritarian ones. Ethnological research has shown that in pre-patriarchal societies the general nature of work life in the community corresponds with the free development of children and adolescents — that is, there are no rules coercing children and adolescents into specific forms of sexual life, and this creates the psychological basis for voluntary integration into the community and voluntary discipline in all forms of collective activity. This supports the premise that widespread sex-positive attitudes are a necessary condition of a viable libertarian socialism.

Psychology also clearly shows that every impediment to free expression of children by parents, teachers, or administrative authorities must be stopped. As anarchists, our preferred way of doing so is by direct action. Thus we should encourage all to feel that they have every chance of building their own personal lives. This will certainly not be an obstacle to or a distraction from their involvement in the anarchist movement. On the contrary, if they can gradually solve the problems facing their private lives, they will work on other social projects with greatly increased pleasure and concentration.

Besides engaging in direct action, anarchists can also support legal protection for free expression and sexuality (repeal of the insane statutory rape laws and equal rights for gays, for example), just as they support legislation that protects workers' right to strike, family leave, and so forth. However, as Reich observed, "under no circumstances will the new order of sexual life be established by the decree of a central authority." [**The Sexual Revolution**, p. 279] That was a Leninist illusion. Rather, it will be established from the bottom up, by the gradual process of ever more widespread dissemination of knowledge about the adverse personal and social effects of sexual repression, and the benefits of libertarian child-rearing and educational methods.

A society in which people are capable of sexual happiness will be one where they prefer to "make love, not war," and so will provide the best guarantee for the general security. Then the anarchist project of restructuring the economic and political systems will proceed spontaneously, based on a spirit of joy rather than hatred and revenge. Only then can it be defended against reactionary threats, because the majority will be on the side of freedom and capable of using it responsibly, rather than unconsciously longing

for an authoritarian father-figure to tell them what to do. Therefore, concern and action upon sexual liberation, libertarian child rearing and libertarian education are **key** parts of social struggle and change. In no way can they be considered as "distractions" from "important" political and economic issues as some "serious" revolutionaries like to claim. As Martha A. Ackelsberg notes in relation to the practical work done by the **Mujeres Libres** group during the Spanish Revolution:

> "Respecting children and educating them well was vitally important to the process of revolutionary change. Ignorance made people particularly vulnerable to oppression and suffering. More importantly, education prepared people for social life. Authoritarian schools (or families), based upon fear, prepared people to be submissive to an authoritarian government [or within a capitalist workplace]. Different schools and families would be necessary to prepare people to live in a society without domination." [**Free Women of Spain**, p. 133]

The personal **is** political and there is little point in producing a free economy if the people in it are not free to lead a full and pleasurable life! As such, the issue of sexual freedom is as important as economic and social freedom for anarchists. This can be seen when Emma Goldman recounted meeting Kropotkin who praised a paper she was involved with but proclaimed "it would do more if it would not waste so much space discussing sex." She disagreed and a heated argument ensued about "the place of the sex problem in anarchist propaganda." Finally, she remarked "All right, dear comrade, when I have reached your age, the sex question may no longer be of importance to me. But it is now, and it is a tremendous factor for thousands, millions even, of young people." This, Goldman recalled, made Kropotkin stop short with "an amused smile lighting up his kindly face. 'Fancy, I didn't think of that,' he replied. 'Perhaps you are right, after all.' He beamed affectionately upon me, with a humorous twinkle in his eye." [**Living My Life**, vol. 1, p. 253]

J.7
What do anarchists mean by social revolution?

In anarchist theory, **social revolution** means far more than just revolution. For anarchists, a true revolution is far more than just a change in the political makeup, structure or form of a society. It must transform all aspects of a society — political, economic, social, interpersonal relationships, and so on — and the individuals who comprise it. Indeed, these two transformations go hand in hand, complementing each other and supporting each other. People, while transforming society, transform themselves. As Alexander Berkman put it:

> "there are revolutions and revolutions. Some revolutions change only the governmental form by putting a new set of rulers in place of the old. These are political revolutions, and as such they often meet with little resistance. But

a revolution that aims to abolish the entire system of wage slavery must also do away with the power of one class to oppress another. That is, it is not any more a mere change of rulers, of government, not a political revolution, but one that seeks to alter the whole character of society. That would be a **social** *revolution."* [**What is Anarchism?**, p. 176]

It means two related things. First, it means transforming all parts of society and not just tinkering with certain aspects of the current system. Where political revolution means, in essence, changing bosses, social revolution means changing society, a transformation in the way society is organised and run. Social revolution, in other words, does not aim to change one form of subjection for another, but to do away with everything that can enslave and oppress the individual. Second, it means bringing about this fundamental change **directly** by the mass of people in society, rather than relying on political means of achieving this end, in the style of Marxist-Leninists and other authoritarian socialists. For anarchists, such an approach is a political revolution only and doomed to failure. The *"actual, positive work of the social revolution must ... be carried out by the toilers themselves, by the labouring people"* as *"the worse victims of present institutions, it is to their own interest to abolish them."* [Berkman, **Op. Cit.**, p. 189 and p. 187]

That is not to say that an anarchist social revolution is not political in content — far from it; it should be obvious to anyone familiar with anarchist theory that there are political theories and goals at work within anarchism. With an analysis of the state which proclaims it to be an instrument of minority class rule, designed to exclude participation by the many, it should be obvious that we aim to abolish it. What we **are** saying, however, is that anarchists do not seek to seize power and attempt, through control of law enforcement and the military (in the style of governments) to bring change about from the top-down. Rather, we seek to bring change upward from below, and in so doing, make such a revolution inevitable and not contingent on the machinations of a political vanguard (unsurprisingly, as we noted in section H.3.3, Lenin dismissed talk of change exclusively from below as anarchist and saw the need for change from above by government). As Durruti argued: *"We never believed that the revolution consisted of the seizure of power by a minority which would impose a dictatorship on the people ... We want a revolution by and for the people. Without this no revolution is possible. It would be a Coup d'Etat, nothing more."* [quoted by Abel Paz, **Durruti: The People Armed**, pp. 135-7]

For anarchists, a social revolution is a movement from below, of the oppressed and exploited struggling for their own freedom. Moreover, such a revolution does not appear as if by magic. Rather, it is the case that revolutions *"are not improvised. They are not made at will by individuals nor even by the most powerful associations. They come independently of all will and all conspiracies, and are always brought on by the natural force of circumstance."* [Bakunin, **The Political Philosophy of Bakunin**, p. 323] Revolutions break-out when the conditions are ripe and cannot be artificially produced (by, say, a union leadership proclaiming out of the blue such-and-such a day for a general strike). However, the actions of individuals and associations can make revolution more likely by their propaganda,

struggles and organising so that when the circumstances change, people are able and willing to act in a revolutionary manner (by, say, spontaneously going on strike and their unions expanding the struggle into a general strike). This means that there is no mechanical, objective, process at work but rather something which we can influence but not command. Revolutions are a product of social evolution and of the social struggle which is an inevitable part of it:

"the oppressed masses ... have never completely resigned themselves to oppression and poverty, and who today more than ever show themselves thirsting for justice, freedom and wellbeing, are beginning to understand that they will not be able to achieve their emancipation except by union and solidarity with all the oppressed, with the exploited everywhere in the world. And they also understand that the indispensable condition for their emancipation which cannot be neglected is the possession of the means of production, of the land and of the instruments of labour." [Malatesta, **Anarchy**, p. 33]

Thus any social revolution proceeds from the daily struggles of working class people (just as anarchism does). It is not an event, rather it is a **process** — a process which is occurring at this moment. So a social revolution is not something in the future which we wait for but an process which is occurring in the here and now which we influence along side other tendencies as well as objective factors. This means that *"evolution and revolution are not two separate and different things. Still less are they opposites ... Revolution is merely the boiling point of evolution."* [Berkman, **Op. Cit.**, p. 179] This means how we act **now** matters as we shape the future by our struggles today. As German Anarchist Gustav Landauer put it:

"The State is not something that can be destroyed by a revolution, but it is a condition, a certain relationship between human beings, a mode of human behaviour; we destroy it by contracting other relationships, by behaving differently." [quoted by George Woodcock, **Anarchism**, p. 421]

This does not mean that anarchists do not recognise that a revolution will be marked by, say, specific events (such as a general strike, wide scale occupations of land, housing, workplaces, actual insurrections and so on). Of course not. It means that we place these events in a process, within social movements recognising that they do not occur in isolation from history nor the evolution of ideas and movements within society.

Berkman echoed this point when he argued that while *"a social revolution is one that entirely changes the foundation of society, its political, economic and social character"* such a change *"must* **first** *take place in the ideas and opinions of the people, in the minds of men [and women]."* This means that *"the social revolution must be prepared. Prepared in the sense of furthering the evolutionary process, of enlightening the people about the evils of present-day society and convincing them of the desirability and possibility, of the justice and practicability of a social life based on liberty."* [**Op. Cit.**, p. 180-1] Such preparation would be the result of social struggle in the here and now, social struggle based on direct action, solidarity and self-managed organisations. While Berkman concentrated on the labour movement, his comments are applicable to all social movements:

> "In the daily struggle of the proletariat such an organisation [a syndicalist union] would be able to achieve victories about which the conservative union, as at present built, cannot even dream ... Such a union would soon become something more than a mere defender and protector of the worker. It would gain a vital realisation of the meaning of unity and consequent power, of labour solidarity. The factory and shop would serve as a training camp to develop the worker's understanding of his [or her] proper role in life, to cultivate his [or her] self-reliance and independence, teach him [or her] mutual help and co-operation, and make him [or her] conscious of his [or her] responsibility. He [or she] will learn to decide and act on his [or her] own judgement, not leaving it to leaders or politicians to attend to his [or her] affairs and look out for his [or her] welfare ... He [or she] will grow to understand that present economic and social arrangements are wrong and criminal, and he [or she] will determine to change them. The shop committee and union will become the field of preparation for a new economic system, for a new social life." [**Op. Cit.**, pp. 206-7]

In other words, the struggle against authority, exploitation, oppression and domination in the here and now is the start of the social revolution. It is this daily struggle, Bakunin stressed, which creates free people and the organisations it generates *"bear ... the living seed of the new society which is to replace the old one. They are creating not only the ideas, but also the facts of the future itself."* Therefore (libertarian) socialism will be attained only *"through the development and organisation of the non-political or anti-political social power of the working classes in city and country."* [**Bakunin On Anarchism**, p. 255 and p. 263] Such social power is expressed in economic and community organisations such as self-managed unions and workplace/community assemblies (see section J.5) and these form the organisational framework of a free society (see section I.2.3).

Anarchists try and follow the example of our Spanish comrades in the C.N.T. and F.A.I. who, when *"faced with the conventional opposition between reformism and revolution, they appear, in effect, to have put forward a third alternative, seeking to obtain immediate practical improvements through the actual development, in practice, of autonomous, libertarian forms of self-organisation."* [Nick Rider, "The Practice of Direct Action: The Barcelona Rent Strike of 1931", pp. 79-105, **For Anarchism**, David Goodway (ed.), p. 99] While doing this, anarchists must also *"beware of ourselves becoming less anarchist because the masses are not ready for anarchy."* [Malatesta, **Errico Malatesta: His Life and Ideas**, p. 162]

So revolution and anarchism is the product of struggle, a social process in which anarchist ideas spread and develop. *"This does not mean,"* argued Malatesta, *"that to achieve anarchy we must wait till **everyone** becomes an anarchist. On the contrary ... under present conditions only a small minority, favoured by specific circumstances, can manage to conceive what anarchy is. It would be wishful thinking to hope for a general conversion before a change actually took place in the kind of environment in which authoritarianism and privilege now flourish. It is precisely for this reason that [we] ... need to organise for the bringing about of anarchy, or at any rate that degree of anarchy which could become gradually feasible, as soon as a sufficient amount of freedom has been won and a nucleus of anarchists somewhere exists that is both numerically strong enough and able to be self-sufficient and to spread its influence locally."* [**The Anarchist Revolution**, pp. 83-4]

Thus anarchists influence social struggle, the revolutionary process, by encouraging anarchistic tendencies within those who are not yet anarchists but are instinctively acting in a libertarian manner. Anarchists spread our message to those in struggle and support libertarian tendencies in it as far as we can. In this way, more and more people will become anarchists and anarchy will become increasingly possible (we discuss the role of anarchists in a social revolution in section J.7.4). For anarchists, a social revolution is the end product of years of struggle. It is marked by the transformation of a given society, the breaking down of all forms of oppression and the creation of new ways of living, new forms of self-managed organisation, a new attitude to life itself. Moreover, we do not wait for the future to introduce such transformations in our daily life. Rather, we try and create as many anarchistic tendencies in today's society as possible in the firm belief that in so doing we are pushing the creation of a free society nearer.

So anarchists, including revolutionary ones, try to make the world today more libertarian and so bring us closer to freedom. Few anarchists think of anarchy as something in (or for) the distant future, rather it is something we try and create in the here and now by living and struggling in a libertarian manner. Once enough people do this, then a more extensive change towards anarchy (i.e. a revolution) is possible.

J.7.1 Why are most anarchists revolutionaries?

While most anarchists do believe that a social revolution is required to create a free society, some reject the idea. This is because they think that revolutions are by their very nature coercive and so are against anarchist principles. In the words of Proudhon (in reply to Marx):

> "Perhaps you still hold the opinion that no reform is possible without a helping **coup de main,** without what used to be called a revolution but which is quite simply a jolt. I confess that my most recent studies have led me to abandon this view, which I understand and would willingly discuss, since for a long time I held it myself. I do not think that this is what we need in order to succeed, and consequently we must not suggest **revolutionary** action as the means of social reform because this supposed means would simply be an appeal to force and to arbitrariness. In brief, it would be a contradiction." [**Selected Writings of Pierre-Joseph Proudhon**, p. 151]

Also they point to the fact that the state is far better armed than the general population, better trained and (as history proves) more than willing to slaughter as many people as required to restore "order." In face of this power, they argue, revolution is doomed to failure.

Those opposed to revolution come from all tendencies of the movement. Traditionally, Individualist anarchists are usually against the idea of revolution, as was Proudhon. However, with the failure of the Russian Revolution and the defeat of the CNT-FAI in Spain, some social anarchists have rethought support for revolution. Rather than seeing revolution as the key way of creating a free society they consider it doomed to failure as the state is too strong a force to be overcome by insurrection. Instead of revolution, such anarchists support the creation of alternatives, such as co-operatives, mutual banks and so on, which will help transform capitalism into libertarian socialism by *"burn[ing] Property little by little"* via *"some system of economics"* which will *"put back into society ... the wealth which has been taken out of society by another system of economics."* [Proudhon, **Op. Cit.**, p. 151] Such alternative building, combined with pressurising the state to, say, use co-operatives to run public services and industries as well as civil disobedience and non-payment of taxes, is seen as the best way to creating anarchy. This may take time, they argue, but such gradual change will be more successful in the long run.

Most revolutionary anarchists agree on the importance of building libertarian alternatives in the here and now. They would agree with Bakunin when he argued that such organisations as libertarian unions, co-operatives and so on are essential *"so that when the Revolution, brought about by the natural force of circumstances, breaks out, there will be a real force at hand which knows what to do and by virtue thereof is capable of taking the Revolution into its own hands and imparting to it a direction salutary for the people: a serious, international organisation of worker's organisations of all countries, capable of replacing the departing political world of the States and the bourgeoisie."* [**The Political Philosophy of Bakunin**, p. 323] Thus, for most anarchists, the difference between evolution and revolution is one of little import — anarchists should support libertarian tendencies within society as they support revolutionary situations when they occur.

However, revolutionary anarchists argue that, ultimately, capitalism cannot be reformed away nor will the state wither away under the onslaught of libertarian institutions and attitudes. Neither mutual banking (see section J.5.7) nor co-operatives (see section J.5.11) can out-compete capitalist institutions. This means that these alternatives, while important, are insufficient to the task of creating a free society. This suggests that while libertarian tendencies within capitalism may make life better under that system, they cannot get rid of it. This requires a social revolution. Such anarchists agree with Alexander Berkman that there *"is no record of any government or authority, of any group or class in power having given up its mastery voluntarily. In every instance it required the use of force, or at least the threat of it."* [**What is Anarchism?**, p. 174] Even the end of State capitalism ("Communism") in Eastern Europe did not contradict this argument. Without the mass action of the population, the regime would have continued. Faced with a massive popular revolt, the Commissars realised that it was better

to renounce (some) power than have it all taken from them (and they were right, as this allowed many of them to become part of the new, private capitalist, ruling class). Thus mass rebellion, the start of any true revolution, was required.

The argument that the state is too powerful to be defeated has been proven wrong time and time again. Every revolution has defeated a military machine which previously had been proclaimed to be unbeatable (most obviously, the people armed in Spain defeated the military in two-thirds of the country). Ultimately, the power of the state rests on its troops following orders. If those troops rebel, then the state is powerless. That is why anarchists have always produced anti-militarist propaganda urging troops to join strikers and other people in revolt. Revolutionary anarchists argue that any state can be defeated, if the circumstances are right and the work of anarchists is to encourage those circumstances.

In addition, revolutionary anarchists argue that even if anarchists did not support revolutionary change, this would not stop such events happening. Revolutions are the product of developments in human society and occur whether we desire them or not. They start with small rebellions, small acts of refusal by individuals, groups, workplaces and communities, then grow. These acts of rebellion are inevitable in any hierarchical society, as is their spreading wider and wider. Revolutionary anarchists argue that anarchists must, by the nature of our politics and our desire for freedom, support such acts of rebellion and, ultimately, social revolution. Not to do so means ignoring people in struggle against our common enemy and ignoring the means by which anarchist ideas and attitudes will grow within existing society. Thus Alexander Berkman was right when he wrote:

> *"That is why it is no prophecy to foresee that some day it must come to decisive struggle between the masters of life and the dispossessed masses.*

> *"As a matter if fact, that struggle is going on all the time.*

> *"There is a continuous warfare between capital and labour. That warfare generally proceeds within so-called legal forms. But even these erupt now and then in violence, as during strikes and lockouts, because the armed fist of government is always at the service of the masters, and that fist gets into action the moment capital feels its profits threatened: then it drops the mask of 'mutual interests' and 'partnership' with labour and resorts to the final argument of every master, to coercion and force.*

> *"It is therefore certain that government and capital will not allow themselves to be quietly abolished if they can help it; nor will they miraculously 'disappear' of themselves, as some people pretend to believe. It will require a revolution to get rid of them."* [**Op. Cit.**, p. 174]

However, all anarchists are agreed that any revolution should be as non-violent as possible. Violence is the tool of oppression and, for anarchists, violence is only legitimate as a means of self-defence against authority. Therefore revolutionary anarchists do not seek "violent revolution" — they are just aware that when people refuse to kow-tow to authority then that authority will use violence against them. This use of violence has been directed against non-violent forms of direct action and so those anarchists who reject revolution will not avoid state violence directed against them unless they renounce **all** forms of resistance to state and capitalist authority. So when it comes to effective action by the subjects of an authority, the relevant question quickly becomes how much does our freedom depend on us **not** exercising it?

Nor do revolutionary anarchists think that revolution is in contradiction to the principles of anarchism. As Malatesta put it, *"[f]or two people to live in peace they must both want peace; if one insists on using force to oblige the other to work for him and serve him, then the other, if he wishes to retain his dignity as a man and not be reduced to abject slavery, will be obliged, in spite of his love of peace, to resist force with adequate means."* [**Errico Malatesta: His Life and Ideas**, p. 54] Under any hierarchical system, those in authority do not leave those subject to them in peace. The boss does not treat his/her workers as equals, working together by free agreement without differences in power. Rather, the boss orders the worker about and uses the threat of sanctions to get compliance. Similarly with the state. Under these conditions, revolution cannot be authoritarian — for it is not authoritarian to destroy authority! To quote Rudolf Rocker:

> *"We ... know that a revolution cannot be made with rosewater. And we know, too, that the owning classes will never yield up their privileges spontaneously. On the day of victorious revolution the workers will have to impose their will on the present owners of the soil, of the subsoil and of the means of production, which cannot be done — let us be clear on this — without the workers taking the capital of society into their own hands, and, above all, without their having demolished the authoritarian structure which is, and will continue to be, the fortress keeping the masses of the people under dominion. Such an action is, without doubt, an act of liberation; a proclamation of social justice; the very essence of social revolution, which has nothing in common with the utterly bourgeois principle of dictatorship."* ["*Anarchism and Sovietism*", pp. 53-74, **The Poverty of Statism**, Albert Meltzer (ed.), p. 73]

It should also be noted that those who proclaim that a revolution is inherently authoritarian like, say, Engels (see section H.4.7) are confused. They fail to see that it is hardly "authoritarian" to stop someone ruling you! It is an act of liberation to free oneself from those oppressing you. Malatesta comments reflect well the position of revolutionary anarchists with regards to the use of force:

> *"We neither seek to impose anything by force nor do we wish to submit to a violent imposition.*
>
> *"We intend to use force against government, because it is by force that we are kept in subjection by government.*
>
> *"We intend to expropriate the owners of property because it is by force that they withhold the raw materials and*

wealth, which is the fruit of human labour, and use it to oblige others to work in their interest.

> *"We shall resist with force whoever would wish by force, to retain or regain the means to impose his will and exploit the labour of others ...*
>
> *"With the exception of these cases, in which the use of violence is justified as a defence against force, we are always against violence, and for self-determination."* [**Op. Cit.**, p. 56]

This is the reason why most anarchists are revolutionaries. They do not think it against the principles of anarchism and consider it the only real means of creating a free society — a society in which the far greater, and permanent, violence which keeps the majority of humanity in servitude can be ended once and for all.

J.7.2
Is social revolution possible?

One objection to the possibility of social revolution is based on what we might call "the paradox of social change." This argument goes as follows: authoritarian institutions reward and select people with an authoritarian type of personality for the most influential positions in society; such types of people have both (a) an interest in perpetuating authoritarian institutions (from which they benefit) and (b) the power to perpetuate them; hence they create a self-sustaining and tightly closed system which is virtually impervious to the influence of non-authoritarian types. Therefore, institutional change presupposes individual change, which presupposes institutional change, and so on. Unless it can be shown, then, that institutions and human psychology can both be changed **at the same time**, hope for a genuine social revolution (instead of just another rotation of elites) appears to be unrealistic.

Connected with this problem is the fact that the psychological root of the hierarchical society is addiction to power — over other people, over nature, over the body and human emotions — and that this addiction is highly contagious. That is, as soon as any group of people anywhere in the world becomes addicted to power, those within range of their aggression also feel compelled to embrace the structures of power, including centralised control over the use of deadly force, in order to protect themselves from their neighbours. Once these structures of power are adopted, authoritarian institutions become self-perpetuating.

In this situation, fear becomes the underlying emotion behind the conservatism, conformity, and mental inertia of the majority, who in that state become vulnerable to the self-serving propaganda of authoritarian elites alleging the necessity of the state, strong leaders, militarism, "law and order," capitalists, rulers, etc. The simultaneous transformation of institutions and individual psychology becomes even more difficult to imagine.

Serious as these obstacles may be, they do not warrant despair. To see why, let us note first that "paradigm shifts" in science have not generally derived from new developments in one field alone but from a convergence of cumulative developments in several different fields at once. For example, the Einsteinian revolution which resulted in the overthrow of the Newtonian paradigm was due to simultaneous progress in mathematics, physics, astronomy and other sciences that all influenced, reacted on, and cross-fertilised each other (see Thomas Kuhn's **The Structure of Scientific Revolutions**). Similarly, if there is going to be a "paradigm shift" in the social realm, i.e. from hierarchical to non-hierarchical institutions, it is likely to emerge from the convergence of a number of different socio-economic and political developments at the same time. In a hierarchical society, the oppression authority produces also generates resistance, and so hope. The *"instinct for freedom"* cannot be repressed forever.

That is why anarchists stress the importance of direct action (section J.2) and self-help (section J.5). By the very process of struggle, by practising self-management, direct action and solidarity, people create the necessary "paradigm shift" in both themselves and society as a whole. Thus the struggle against authority is the school of anarchy — it encourages libertarian tendencies in society and the transformation of individuals into anarchists (*"Only freedom or the struggle for freedom can be the school for freedom."* [Malatesta, **Errico Malatesta: His Life and Ideas**, p. 59]). In a revolutionary situation, this process is accelerated. It is worth quoting Murray Bookchin at length on this subject:

> *"Revolutions are profoundly educational processes, indeed veritable cauldrons in which all kinds of conflicting ideas and tendencies are sifted out in the minds of a revolutionary people …*

> *"Individuals who enter into a revolutionary process are by no means the same after the revolution as they were before it began. Those who encounter a modicum of success in revolutionary times learn more within a span of a few weeks or months than they might have learned over their lifetime in non-revolutionary times. Conventional ideas fall away with extraordinary rapidity; values and prejudices that were centuries in the making disappear almost overnight. Strikingly innovative ideas are quickly adopted, tested, and, where necessary, discarded. Even newer ideas, often flagrantly radical in character, are adopted with an elan that frightens ruling elites — however radical the latter may profess to be — and they soon become deeply rooted in the popular consciousness. Authorities hallowed by age-old tradition are suddenly divested of their prestige, legitimacy, and power to govern …*

> *"So tumultuous socially and psychologically are revolutions in general that they constitute a standing challenge to ideologues, including sociobiologists, who assert that human behaviour is fixed and human nature predetermined. Revolutionary changes reveal a remarkable flexibility in 'human nature,' yet few psychologists have elected to study the social and psychological tumult of revolution as well as the institutional changes it so often produces. Thus much must be said with fervent emphasis: **to continue**

> *to judge the behaviour of a people during and after a revolution by the same standards one judged them by beforehand is completely myopic.*

> *"I wish to argue that the capacity of a revolution to produce far-reaching ideological and moral changes in a people stems primarily from the opportunity it affords ordinary, indeed oppressed, people to exercise popular self-management — to enter directly, rapidly, and exhilaratingly into control over most aspects of their social and personal lives. To the extent that an insurrectionary people takes over the reins of power from the formerly hallowed elites who oppressed them and begins to restructure society along radically populist lines, individuals grow aware of latent powers within themselves that nourish their previously suppressed creativity, sense of self-worth, and solidarity. They learn that society is neither immutable nor sanctified, as inflexible custom had previously taught them; rather, it is malleable and subject, within certain limits, to change according to human will and desire."* [**The Third Revolution**, vol. 1, pp. 6-7]

In short, *"it is only through th[e] struggle for freedom, equality and solidarity that you will reach an understanding of anarchism."* [Nestor Makhno, **The Struggle Against the State and Other Essays**, p. 71]

So, social revolutions are possible. Anarchists anticipate successful revolts within certain circumstance. People who are in the habit of taking orders from bosses are not capable of creating a new society. Tendencies towards freedom, self-management, co-operation and solidarity are not simply an act of ethical will which overcomes the competitive and hierarchical behaviour capitalism generates within those who live in it. Capitalism is, as Malatesta noted, based on competition — and this includes **within** the working class. However, **co-operation** is stimulated within our class by our struggles to survive in and resist the system. This tendency for co-operation generated by struggle against capitalism also produces the habits required for a free society — by struggling to change the world (even a small part of it), people also change themselves. Direct action produces empowered and self-reliant people who can manage their own affairs themselves. It is on the liberating effects of struggle, the tendencies towards individual and collective self-management and direct action it generates, the needs and feelings for solidarity and creative solutions to pressing problems it produces that anarchists base their positive answer on whether social revolution is possible. History has shown that we are right. It will do so again.

J.7.3 Doesn't revolution mean violence?

While many try and paint revolutions (and anarchists) as being violent by their very nature, the social revolution desired by anarchists is essentially non-violent. This is because, to quote Bakunin, *"[i]n order to launch a radical revolution, it is … necessary to attack positions and things and to destroy property and the State, but there will be no need to destroy men and to condemn ourselves to the inevitable reaction which is unfailingly produced in every society by the slaughter of men."* [**Michael Bakunin: Selected Writings**, pp. 168-9] Equally, to destroy the institution of private property there is no need to destroy the actual useful things monopolised by the few:

> *"How to smash the tyranny of capital? Destroy capital? But that would be to destroy all the riches accumulated on earth, all primary materials, all the instruments of labour, all the means of labour … Thus capital cannot and must not be destroyed. It must be preserved … there is but a single solution — **the intimate and complete union of capital and labour** … the workers must obtain not individual but **collective** property in capital … the collective property of capital … [is] the absolutely necessary conditions of the emancipation **of labour and of the workers.**"* [**The Basic Bakunin**, pp. 90-1]

The essentially non-violent nature of anarchist ideas of social revolution can be seen from the Seattle General Strike of 1919. Here is a quote from the Mayor of Seattle (we do not think we need to say that he was not on the side of the strikers):

> *"The so-called sympathetic Seattle strike was an attempted revolution. That there was no violence does not alter the fact … The intent, openly and covertly announced, was for the overthrow of the industrial system; here first, then everywhere … True, there were no flashing guns, no bombs, no killings. Revolution, I repeat, doesn't need violence. The general strike, as practised in Seattle, is of itself the weapon of revolution, all the more dangerous because quiet. To succeed, it must suspend everything; stop the entire life stream of a community … That is to say, it puts the government out of operation. And that is all there is to revolt — no matter how achieved."* [quoted by Howard Zinn, **A People's History of the United States**, pp. 370-1]

If the strikers had occupied their workplaces and local communities and created popular assemblies then the attempted revolution would have become an actual one without any use of violence at all. In Italy, a year later, the occupations of the factories and land started. As Malatesta pointed out, *"in **Umanita Nova** [the daily anarchist newspaper] we … said that if the movement spread to all sectors of industry, that is workers and peasants followed the example of the metallurgists, of getting rid of the bosses and taking over the means of production, the revolution would succeed without shedding a single drop of blood."* Thus the *"occupation of the factories and the land suited perfectly our programme of action."* [**Errico Malatesta: His Life and Ideas**, p. 135] Sadly the workers followed their socialist trade union leaders and stopped the occupations rather than spreading them.

These events indicate the strength of ordinary people and the relative weakness of government and capitalism — they only work when they can force people to respect them. After all, a government is *"only a handful of men"* and is strong *"when the people are with it. Then they supply the government with money, with an army and navy, obey it, and enable it to function."* Remove that support and *"no government can accomplish anything."* The same can be said of capitalists, whose wealth *"would do them no good but for the willingness of the people to work for them and pay tribute to them."* Both would *"find out that all their boasted power and strength disappear when the people refuse to acknowledge them as masters, refuse to let them lord it over them."* In contrast, *"the people's power"* is *"**actual**: it cannot be taken away … It cannot be taken away because it does not consist of possessions but in ability. It is the ability to create, to produce."* To achieve a free society we need to *"be conscious of its tremendous power."* [Alexander Berkman, **What is Anarchism?**, p. 84, p. 86, p. 87 and p. 83]

Therefore the notion that a social revolution is necessarily violent is a false one. For anarchists, social revolution is essentially an act of self-liberation (of both the individuals involved and society as a whole). It has nothing to do with violence, quite the reverse, as anarchists see it as the means to end the rule and use of violence in society. Anarchists hope that any revolution is essentially non-violent, with any violence being defensive in nature. As Malatesta stressed, *"Anarchists are opposed to violence"* and it *"is justifiable only when it is necessary to defend oneself and others from violence."* [**Errico Malatesta: His Life and Ideas**, p. 53]

Of course, many revolutions are marked by violence. It has two sources. First, and most obviously, the violent resistance of those protecting their power and wealth against those seeking liberty. Unsurprisingly, this violence is usually downplayed in history books and the media. Second, acts of revenge resulting from the domination and repression of the system the revolution seeks to end. Such violence is not desired nor the aim of anarchism nor of the revolution. As Berkman argued:

> *"We know that revolution begins with street disturbances and outbreaks; it is the initial phase which involves force and violence. But that is merely the spectacular prologue of the real revolution. The age long misery and indignity suffered by the masses burst into disorder and tumult, the humiliation and injustice meekly borne for decades find vents in acts of fury and destruction. That is inevitable, and it is solely the master class which is responsible for this preliminary character of revolution. For it is even more true socially than individually that 'whoever sows the wind will reap the whirlwind'; the greater the oppression and wretchedness to which the masses had been made to submit, the fiercer will rage the social storm. All history proves it, but the lords of life have never harkened to its warning voice."* [**Op. Cit.**, p. 195]

"*Most people have very confused notions about revolution,*" Berkman suggested. "*To them it means just fighting, smashing things, destroying. It is the same as if rolling up your sleeves for work should be considered the work itself that you have to do. The fighting bit of the revolution is merely the rolling up of your sleeves.*" The task of the revolution is the "*destruction of the existing conditions*" and "**conditions** *are not destroyed [by] breaking and smashing things. You can't destroy wage slavery by wrecking the machinery in the mills and factories ... You won't destroy government by setting fire to the White House.*" To think of revolution "*in terms of violence and destruction is to misinterpret and falsify the whole idea of it. In practical application such a conception is bound to lead to disastrous results.*" For what is there to destroy? "*The wealth of the rich? Nay, that is something we want the whole of society to enjoy.*" The means of production are to be made "*useful to the entire people*" and "*serve the needs of all.*" Thus the aim of revolution is "*to* **take over** *things for the general benefit, not to destroy them. It is to reorganise conditions for public welfare ... to reconstruct and rebuild.*" [**Op. Cit.**, pp. 183-4]

Thus when anarchists like Bakunin speak of revolution as "destruction" they mean that the idea of authority and obedience must be destroyed, along with the institutions that are based on such ideas. We do not mean, as can be clearly seen, the destruction of people or wealth. Nor do we imply the glorification of violence — quite the reverse, as anarchists seek to limit violence to that required for self-defence against oppression and authority.

Therefore a social revolution **may** involve some violence. It may also mean no violence at all. It depends on the revolution and how widely anarchist ideas are spread. One thing is sure, for anarchists social revolution is **not** synonymous with violence. Indeed, violence usually occurs when the ruling class resists the action of the oppressed — that is, when those in authority act to protect their social position.

The wealthy and their state will do anything in their power to prevent having a large enough percentage of anarchists in the population to simply "ignore" the government and property out of existence. If things got that far, the government would suspend the legal rights, elections and round up influential subversives. The question is, what do anarchists do in response to these actions? If anarchists are in the majority or near it, then defensive violence would likely succeed. For example, "*the people armed*" crushed the fascist coup of July 19th, 1936 in Spain and resulted in one of the most important experiments in anarchism the world has ever seen (see section A.5.6). This should be contrasted with the aftermath of the factory occupations in Italy in 1920 and the fascist terror which crushed the labour movement (see section A.5.5). In other words, you cannot just ignore the state even if the majority are acting, you need to abolish it and organise self-defence against attempts to re-impose it or capitalism.

We discuss the question of self-defence and the protection of the revolution in section J.7.6.

J.7.4 What would a social revolution involve?

Social revolution necessitates putting anarchist ideas into daily practice. Therefore it implies that direct action, solidarity and self-management become increasingly the dominant form of living in a society. It implies the transformation of society from top to bottom. We can do no better than quote Errico Malatesta on what revolution means:

"*The Revolution is the creation of new living institutions, new groupings, new social relationships; it is the destruction of privileges and monopolies; it is the new spirit of justice, of brotherhood, of freedom which must renew the whole of social life, raise the moral level and the material conditions of the masses by calling on them to provide, through their direct and conscious action, for their own futures. Revolution is the organisation of all public services by those who work in them in their own interest as well as the public's; Revolution is the destruction of all of coercive ties; it is the autonomy of groups, of communes, of regions; Revolution is the free federation brought about by a desire for brotherhood, by individual and collective interests, by the needs of production and defence; Revolution is the constitution of innumerable free groupings based on ideas, wishes, and tastes of all kinds that exist among the people; Revolution is the forming and disbanding of thousands of representative, district, communal, regional, national bodies which, without having any legislative power, serve to make known and to co-ordinate the desires and interests of people near and far and which act through information, advice and example. Revolution is freedom proved in the crucible of facts — and lasts so long as freedom lasts.*" [**Errico Malatesta: His Life and Ideas**, p. 153]

This, of course, presents a somewhat wide vision of the revolutionary process. We will need to give some more concrete examples of what a social revolution would involve. However, before so doing, we stress that these are purely examples drawn from previous revolutions and are not written in stone. Every revolution creates its own forms of organisation and struggle. The next one will be no different. As we argued in section I.2, an anarchist revolution will create its own forms of freedom, forms which will share features with organisations generated in previous revolutions, but which are unique to this one. Thus the Paris Commune of 1871 had mandated and recallable delegates as did the Russian soviets of 1905 and 1917, but the first was based on geographical delegation and the later on workplaces. All we do here is give a rough overview of what we expect (based on previous revolutions) to see occur in a future social revolution. We are not predicting the future. As Kropotkin put it:

"*A question which we are often asked is: 'How will you organise the future society on Anarchist principles?' If*

*the question were put to ... someone who fancies that a group of men [or women] is able to organise society as they like, it would seem natural. But in the ears of an Anarchist, it sounds very strangely, and the only answer we can give to it is: 'We cannot organise you. It will depend upon **you** what sort of organisation you choose.'"*
[**Act for Yourselves**, p. 32]

And organise themselves they have. In every social revolution, the oppressed have created many different self-managed organisations. These bodies include the directly democratic neighbourhood Sections of the Great French Revolution, the neighbourhood clubs of the 1848 French Revolution and the Paris Commune, the workers councils and factory committees of the Russian and German revolutions, the industrial and rural collectives of the Spanish Revolution, the workers councils of the Hungarian revolution of 1956, assemblies and action committees of the 1968 revolt in France, the neighbourhood assemblies and occupied workplaces of the 2001 revolt in Argentina, and so on. These bodies were hardly uniform in structure and some were more anarchistic than others, but the tendency towards self-management and federation existed in them all. This tendency towards anarchistic solutions and organisation is not unsurprising, for, as Nestor Makhno argued, *"[i]n carrying through the revolution, under the impulsion of the anarchism that is innate in them, the masses of humanity search for free associations. Free assemblies always command their sympathy. The revolutionary anarchist must help them to formulate this approach as best they can."* [**The Struggle Against the State and Other Essays**, p. 85]

In addition, we must stress that we are discussing an **anarchist** social revolution in this section. As we noted in section I.2.2, anarchists recognise that any revolution will take on different forms in different areas and develop in different ways and at different speeds. We leave it up to others to describe their vision of revolution (for Marxists, the creation of a "workers' state" and the seizure of power by the "proletarian" vanguard or party, and so on).

So what would a libertarian revolution involve?

Firstly, a revolution *"is not the work of one day. It means a whole period, mostly lasting for several years, during which the country is in a state of effervescence; when thousands of formerly indifferent spectators take a lively part in public affairs."* It *"criticises and repudiates the institutions which are a hindrance to free development ... it boldly enters upon problems which formerly seemed insoluble."* [Kropotkin, **Op. Cit.**, pp. 25-6] Thus, it would be a **process** in which revolutionary attitudes, ideas, actions and organisations spread in society until the existing system is overthrown and a new one takes its place. It does not come overnight. Rather it is an accumulative development, marked by specific events of course, but fundamentally it goes on in the fabric of society.

So the **real** Russian revolution occurred during the period between the 1917 February and October insurrections when workers took over their workplaces, peasants seized their land, new forms of social life (soviets, factory committees, co-operatives, etc.) were formed and people lost their previous submissive attitudes to authority by using direct action to change their lives for the better (see section A.5.4). Similarly, the Spanish Revolution occurred after the 19th of July, 1936, when workers again took over their workplaces, peasants

formed collectives and militias were organised to fight fascism (see section A.5.6)

Secondly, *"there **must** be a rapid modification of outgrown economical and political institutions, an overthrow of the injustices accumulated by centuries past, a displacement of wealth and political power."* [Kropotkin, **Op. Cit.**, p. 25] This aspect is the key one. Without the abolition of the state and capitalism, no real revolution has taken place. As Bakunin argued, *"the program of social revolution"* is *"the abolition of all exploitation and all political or juridical as well as governmental and bureaucratic oppression, in other words, to the abolition of all classes through the equalisation of economic conditions, and the abolition of their last buttress, the state."* That is, *"the total and definitive liberation of the proletariat from economic exploitation and state oppression."* [**Statism and Anarchy**, pp. 48-9]

We should stress here that, regardless of what Marxists may say, anarchists see the destruction of capitalism occurring **at the same time as** the destruction of the state. We do not aim to abolish the state first, then capitalism as Engels asserted we did (see section H.2.4). This perspective of a simultaneous political and economic revolution is clearly seen when Bakunin wrote that a city in revolt would *"naturally make haste to organise itself as best it can, in revolutionary style, after the workers have joined into associations and made a clean sweep of all the instruments of labour and every kind of capital and building; armed and organised by streets and **quartiers,** they will form the revolutionary federation of all the **quartiers,** the federative commune"* All *"the revolutionary communes will then send representatives to organise the necessary services and arrangements for production and exchange ... and to organise common defence against the enemies of the Revolution."* [**Michael Bakunin: Selected Writings**, p. 179]

As can be seen, an essential part of a social revolution is the *"expropriation of landowners and capitalists for the benefit of all."* [Malatesta, **Op. Cit.**, p. 198] This would be done by workers occupying their workplaces and placing them under workers' self-management. As Voltairine de Cleyre argued in 1910 *"the weapon of the future will be the general strike"* and is it not clear that *"it must be the strike which will **stay in** the factory, not **go out**? which will guard the machines and allow no scab to touch them? which will organise, not to inflict deprivation on itself, but on the enemy? which will take over industry and operate it for the workers, not for franchise holder, stockholders, and officeholders?"* [*"A Study of the General Strike in Philadelphia"*, pp. 307-14, **Anarchy! An Anthology of Emma Goldman's Mother Earth**, Peter Glassgold (ed.), p. 311] Individual self-managed workplaces would then federate on a local and industrial basis into workers' councils to co-ordinate joint activity, discuss common interests and issues as well as ensuring common ownership and universalising self-management: *"We must push the workers to take possession of the factories, to federate among themselves and work for the community, and similarly the peasants should take over the land and the produce usurped by the landlords, and come to an agreement with the industrial workers on the necessary exchange of goods."* [Malatesta, **Op. Cit.**, p. 165]

In this way capitalism is replaced by new economic system based the end of hierarchy, on self-managed work. These workplace assemblies and local, regional, etc., federations would start to organise production to meet human needs rather than capitalist profit. While most anarchists would like to see the introduction of communistic relations begin as quickly as possible in such an economy, most are realistic enough to recognise that tendencies towards libertarian communism will be depend on local conditions. As Malatesta argued:

> "It is then that graduation really comes into operation. We shall have to study all the practical problems of life: production, exchange, the means of communication, relations between anarchist groupings and those living under some kind of authority, between communist collectives and those living in an individualistic way; relations between town and country, the utilisation for the benefit of everyone of all natural resources of the different regions [and so on] … And in every problem [anarchists] should prefer the solutions which not only are economically superior but which satisfy the need for justice and freedom and leave the way open for future improvements, which other solutions might not." [**Op. Cit.**, p. 173]

No central government could organise such a transformation. No centralised body could comprehend the changes required and decide between the possibilities available to those involved. Hence the very complexity of life, and the needs of social living, will push a social revolution towards anarchism. *"Unavoidably,"* argued Kropotkin, *"the Anarchist system of organisation — free local action and free grouping — will come into play."* [**Op. Cit.**, p. 72] Unless the economy is transformed from the bottom up by those who work within it, socialism is impossible. If it is re-organised from the top-down by a centralised body all that will be achieved is state capitalism and rule by bureaucrats instead of capitalists. Without local action and free agreement between local groups to co-ordinate activity, a revolution would be dead in the water and fit only to produce a new bureaucratic class structure, as the experience of the Russian Revolution proves (see section H.6).

Therefore, the key economic aspect of a social revolution is the end of capitalist oppression by the direct action of the workers themselves and their re-organisation of their work and the economy by their own actions, organisations and initiative from the bottom-up:

> "To destroy radically this oppression without any danger of it re-emerging, all people must be convinced of their right to the means of production, and be prepared to exercise this basic right by expropriating the landowners, the industrialists and financiers, and putting all social wealth at the disposal of the people." [Malatesta, **Op. Cit.**, p. 167]

However, the economic transformation is but part of the picture. As Kropotkin argued, *"throughout history we see that each change in the economic relations of a community is accompanied by a corresponding change in what may be called political organisation … Thus, too, it will be with Socialism. If it contemplates a new departure in economics it **must** be prepared for a new departure in what is called political organisation."* [**Op. Cit.**, p. 39] Thus

the anarchist social revolution also aims to abolish the state and create a confederation of self-governing communes to ensure its final elimination. This destruction of the state is essential as *"those workers who want to free themselves, or even only to effectively improve their conditions, will be forced to defend themselves from the government … which by legalising the right to property and protecting it with brute force, constitutes a barrier to human progress, which must be beaten down … if one does not wish to remain indefinitely under present conditions or even worse."* Therefore, *"[f]rom the economic struggle one must pass to the political struggle, that is to the struggle against government."* [Malatesta, **Op. Cit.**, p. 195]

Thus a social revolution will have to destroy the state bureaucracy and its forces of violence and coercion (the police, armed forces, intelligence agencies, and so on). If this is not done then the state will come back and crush the revolution. As the CNT newspaper put it in the 1930s, the *"first step in the social revolution is to take control of Town Hall and proclaim the free commune. Once this occurs, self-management spreads to all areas of life and the people exercise their sovereign executive power through the popular assembly."* This free commune *"is the basic unit of libertarian communism … and, federated, it provides the basic structure of the new society in all its aspects: administrative, economic and political."* [quoted by Abel Paz, **Durruti in the Spanish Revolution**, p. 312]

Such a destruction of the state does not involve violence against individuals, but rather the end of hierarchical organisations, positions and institutions. It would involve, for example, the disbanding of the police, army, navy, state officialdom, etc. It would mean the transformation of police stations, military bases, the offices used by the bureaucracy into something more useful (or, as in the case of prisons, their destruction). Town halls would be occupied and used by community and industrial groups, for example. Offices of the mayor could be turned into crèches. Police stations, if they have not been destroyed, could be turned into storage centres for goods (William Morris, in his utopian novel **News from Nowhere**, imagined the Houses of Parliament being turned into a manure storage facility). And so on. Those who used to work in such occupations would be asked to pursue a more fruitful way of life or leave the community. In this manner, all harmful and useless institutions would be destroyed or transformed into something of benefit to society.

In addition, as well as the transformation/destruction of the buildings associated with the old state, the decision making process for the community previously usurped by the state would come back into the hands of the people. Alternative, self-managed organisations would be created in every community to manage community affairs. From these community assemblies, confederations would spring up to co-ordinate joint activities and interests. These neighbourhood assemblies and confederations would be means by which power would be dissolved in society and government finally eliminated in favour of freedom (both individual and collective).

Ultimately, anarchism means creating positive alternatives to those existing institutions which provide some useful function. For example, we propose self-management as an alternative to capitalist production. We propose self-governing communes to organise social life instead of the state. *"One only destroys, and effectively* and permanently," argued Malatesta, "that which one replaces by something else; and to put off to a later date the solution of problems which present themselves with the urgency of necessity, would be to give time to the institutions one is intending to abolish to recover from the shock and reassert themselves, perhaps under other names, but certainly with the same structure." [**Op. Cit.**, p. 159] This was the failure of the Spanish Revolution, which ignored the state rather than abolish it via new, self-managed organisations (see section I.8.13). It must be stressed that this was not due to anarchist theory (see section I.8.11).

Hence a social revolution would see the "[o]rganisation of social life by means of free association and federations of producers and consumers, created and modified according to the wishes of their members, guided by science and experience, and free from any kind of imposition which does not spring from natural needs, to which everyone, convinced by a feeling of overriding necessity, voluntarily submits." [Malatesta, **Op. Cit.**, p. 184] A revolution organises itself from the bottom up, in a self-managed way. As Bakunin summarised:

> "the federative Alliance of all working men's associations … will constitute the Commune … The Commune will be organised by the standing federation of the Barricades and by the creation of a Revolutionary Communal Council composed of one or two delegates from each barricade … vested with plenary but accountable and removable mandates … all provinces, communes and associations … **reorganising** on revolutionary lines … [would send] their representatives to an agreed meeting place … vested with similar mandates to constitute the federation of insurgent associations, communes and provinces in the name of the same principles and to organise a revolutionary force capable of defeating reaction … it is the very fact of the expansion and organisation of the revolution for the purpose of self-defence among the insurgent areas that will bring about the triumph of the revolution … There can no longer be any successful revolution unless the political revolution is transformed into social revolution … Since revolution everywhere must be created by the people, and supreme control must always belong to the people organised in a free federation of agricultural and industrial associations … organised from the bottom upwards by means of revolutionary delegation." [**Michael Bakunin: Selected Writings**, pp. 170-2]

Thus we have a dual framework of revolution, the federation of self-managed workplace and community assemblies based on mandated and recallable delegates. "Through its class organisations," Makhno argued, "the people yearned to lay the foundations of a new, free society intended, as it develops without interference, to eliminate from the body of society all the parasites and all the power exercised by some over others, these being deemed by the toilers to be stupid and harmful." [**Op. Cit.**, p. 79] These organisations, as we stressed in section I.2.3, are the products of the social struggle and revolution themselves:

> "Assembly and community must arise from within the revolutionary process itself; indeed, the revolutionary process must **be** the formation of assembly and community, and with it, the destruction of power. Assembly and community must become 'fighting words,' not distinct panaceas. They must be created as **modes of struggle** against existing society … The future assemblies of people in the block, the neighbourhood or the district — the revolutionary sections to come — will stand on a higher social level than all the present-day committees, syndicates, parties and clubs adorned by the most resounding 'revolutionary' titles. They will be the living nuclei of utopia in the decomposing body of bourgeois society … The specific gravity of society … must be shifted to its base — the armed people in permanent assembly." [Murray Bookchin, **Post-Scarcity Anarchism**, pp. 104-5]

Such organisations are required because "[f]reedom has its forms … a liberatory revolution always poses the question of what social forms will replace existing ones. At one point or another, a revolutionary people must deal with how it will manage the land and the factories from which it requires the means of life. It must deal with the manner in which it will arrive at decisions that affect the community as a whole. Thus if revolutionary thought is to be taken at all seriously, it must speak directly to the problems and forms of social management." [Bookchin, **Op. Cit.**, p. 86] If this is not done, capitalism and the state will not be destroyed and the social revolution will fail. Only by destroying hierarchical power, by abolishing state and capitalism by self-managed organisations, can individuals free themselves and society.

As well as these economic and political changes, there would be other changes as well — far too many to chronicle here. For example: "We will see to it that all empty and under-occupied houses are used so that no one will be without a roof over his [or her] head. We will hasten to abolish banks and title deeds and all that represents and guarantees the power of the State and capitalist privilege. And we will try to reorganise things in such a way that it will be impossible for bourgeois society to be reconstituted." [Malatesta, **Op. Cit.**, p. 165] Similarly, free associations will spring up on a whole range of issues, interests and needs. Social life will become transformed, as will many aspects of personal life and personal relationships. We cannot say in which way, bar there will be a general libertarian movement in all aspects of life as women resist and overcome sexism, gays resist and end homophobia, the young will expect to be treated as individuals, not property, and so on.

Society will become more diverse, open, free and libertarian in nature. And, hopefully, it and the struggle that creates it will be **fun** — anarchism is about making life worth living and so any struggle must reflect that. The use of fun in the struggle is important. There is no incongruity in conducting serious business and having fun. We are sure this will piss off the "serious" Left no end. The aim of revolution is to emancipate **individuals** not abstractions like "the proletariat," "society," "history" and so on. Having fun is part and parcel of that liberation. As Emma Goldman argued (and was paraphrased in the 1970s to "If I cannot dance, it is not my *revolution!"*), anarchism stands for *"release and freedom from conventions and prejudice"* and so she could *"not believe"* that it *"should demand the denial of life and joy"* (*"If it meant that, I did not want it"*): *"I want freedom, the right to self-expression, everybody's right to beautiful, radiant things."* [**Living My Life**, vol. 1, p. 56] As Bookchin suggested: *"Can we resolve the anarchic, intoxicating phase that opens all the great revolutions of history merely into an expression of class interest and the opportunity to redistribute social wealth?"* [Bookchin, **Op. Cit.**, p. 189f]

Therefore a social revolution involves a transformation of society from the bottom up by the creative action of working class people. This transformation would be conducted through self-managed organisations which will be the basis for abolishing hierarchy, state and capitalism: *"There can be no separation of the revolutionary process from the revolutionary goal. **A society based on self-administration must be achieved by means of self-administration** ... If we define 'power' as the power of man over man, power can only be destroyed by the very process in which man acquires power over his own life and in which he not only 'discovers' himself, but, more meaningfully, formulates his selfhood in all its social dimensions."* [Bookchin, **Op. Cit.**, p. 104]

J.7.5 What is the role of anarchists in a social revolution?

All the great social revolutions have been spontaneous. Indeed, it is cliché that the revolutionaries are usually the most surprised when a revolution breaks out. Nor do anarchists assume that a revolution will initially be totally libertarian in nature. All we assume is that there will be libertarian tendencies which anarchists work within to try and strengthen. Therefore the role of anarchists and anarchist organisations is to push a revolution towards a social revolution by encouraging the tendencies we discussed in the last section and by arguing for anarchist ideas and solutions. In the words of Vernon Richards:

> *"We do not for one moment assume that all social revolutions are necessarily anarchist. But whatever form the revolution against authority takes, the role of anarchists is clear: that of inciting the people to abolish capitalistic property and the institutions through which it exercises its power for the exploitation of the majority by a minority."* [**Lessons of the Spanish Revolution**, p. 44]

For anarchists, our role in a social revolution is clear — we try to spread anarchist ideas and encourage autonomous organisation and activity by the oppressed. For example, during the Russian Revolution anarchists and anarcho-syndicalists played a key role in the factory committee movement for workers' self-management. They combated Bolshevik attempts to substitute state control for workers' self-management and encouraged workplace occupations and federations of factory committees (see Maurice Brinton's **The Bolsheviks and Workers' Control** for a good introduction to this movement and Bolshevik hostility to it). Similarly, they supported the soviets (councils elected by workers in their workplaces) but opposed their transformation from revolutionary bodies into state organs (and so little more than organs of the Communist Party, rubber-stamping the decisions of the party leadership). The anarchists tried to *"work for their conversion from centres of authority and decrees into non-authoritarian centres, regulating and keeping things in order but not suppressing the freedom and independence of local workers' organisations. They must become centres which link together these autonomous organisations."* [G. P. Maksimov, **The Anarchists in the Russian Revolution**, p. 105]

Therefore, the role of anarchists, as Murray Bookchin put it, is to **"preserve and extend the anarchic phase that opens all the great social revolutions"** by working **"within the framework of the forms created by the revolution,** not within the forms created by the party. What this means is that their commitment is to the revolutionary organs of self-management ... to the **social** forms, not the **political** forms."* Revolutionary anarchists *"seek to persuade the factory committees, assemblies or soviets to make themselves into **genuine organs of popular self-management,** not to dominate them, manipulate them, or hitch them to an all-knowing political party,"* to organise to *"propagate ideas systematically ... **ideas which promote the concept of self-management**."* The revolutionary organisation *"presents the most advanced demands"* and *"formulate[s] — in the most concrete fashion — the immediate task that should be performed to advance the revolutionary process. It provides the boldest elements in action and in the decision-making organs of the revolution."* [**Post-Scarcity Anarchism**, pp. 139-140]

Equally as important, *"is that the people, all people, should lose their sheep-like instincts and habits with which their minds have been inculcated by an age-long slavery, and that they should learn to think and act freely. It is to this great task of spiritual liberation that anarchists must especially devote their attention."* Unless people think and act for themselves, no social revolution is possible and anarchy will remain just an opposition tendency within authoritarian societies. Practically, this means the encouragement of self-management and direct action. Anarchists thus *"push the people to expropriate the bosses and put all goods in common and organise their daily lives themselves, through freely constituted associations, without waiting for orders from outside and refusing to nominate or recognise any government or constituted body in whatever guise ... even in a provisional capacity, which ascribes to itself the right to lay down the law and impose with force its will on others."* [Malatesta, **Errico Malatesta: His Life and Ideas**, pp. 160-1 and p. 197] This is because, to quote Bakunin, anarchists do *"not accept, even in the process of revolutionary transition, either constituent assemblies, provisional governments or so-called revolutionary dictatorships; because we are convinced that revolution is only sincere, honest and real in the hands of the masses, and that when it is concentrated in those of a few ruling individuals it inevitably and immediately becomes reaction."* [**Michael Bakunin: Selected Writings**, p. 237]

The history of every revolution confirms Kropotkin (who echoed Proudhon) that *"revolutionary government"* is a contradiction in terms. Government bodies mean *"the transferring of initiative from the armed workers to a central body with executive powers. By* removing the initiative from the workers, the responsibility for the conduct of the struggle and its objectives [are] also transferred to a governing hierarchy, and this could have no other than an adverse effect on the morale of the revolutionary fighters." [Richards, **Op. Cit.**, pp. 42-3] Such a centralisation of power means the suppression of local initiatives, the replacing of self-management with bureaucracy and the creation of a new, exploitative and oppressive class of officials and party hacks. Only when power rests in the hands of everyone can a social revolution exist and a free society be created. If this is not done, if the state replaces the self-managed associations of a free people, all that happens is the replacement of one class system by another. This is because the state is an instrument of minority rule — it can never become an instrument of majority empowerment as its centralised, hierarchical and authoritarian nature excludes such a possibility (see section H.3.7 for more discussion on this issue).

Therefore an important role of anarchists is to undermine hierarchical organisation by creating self-managed ones, by keeping the management and direction of a struggle or revolution in the hands of those actually conducting it. It is **their** revolution, **not** a party's and so they should control and manage it. They are the ones who have to live with the consequences of it. As Bakunin argued, social revolution "should not only be made for the people's sake; it should also be made by the people." [**No Gods, No Masters**, vol. 1, p. 141] "The revolution is safe, it grows and becomes strong," correctly argued Alexander Berkman, "as long as the masses feel that they are direct participants in it, that they are fashioning their own lives, that **they** are making the revolution, that they **are** the revolution. But the moment that their activities are usurped by a political party or are centred in some special organisation, revolutionary effort becomes limited to a comparatively small circle from which the large masses are practically excluded. The natural result is that popular enthusiasm is dampened, interest gradually weakens, initiative languishes, creativeness wanes, and the revolution becomes the monopoly of a clique which presently turns dictator." [**What is Anarchism?**, p. 213] The history of every revolution proves this point, we feel, and so the role of anarchists is clear — to keep a revolution revolutionary by encouraging libertarian ideas, organisation, tactics and activity.

Anarchists, therefore, organise to influence social struggle in a libertarian manner and our role in any social revolution is to combat authoritarian tendencies and parties while encouraging working class self-organisation, self-activity and self-management (how we organise to achieve this is described in section J.3). Only by the spreading of libertarian ideas and values within society, encouraging libertarian forms of social organisation (i.e., self-management, decentralisation, federalism, etc.) and continually warning against centralising power into a few hands can a revolution become more than a change of masters.

J.7.6 How could an anarchist revolution defend itself?

To some, particularly Marxists, this section may seem in contradiction with anarchist ideas. As we discussed in section H.2.1, Marxists tend to assume, incorrectly, that anarchists are either against defending a revolution or see no need to. However, as will become very clear, nothing could be further from the truth. Anarchists have always argued for defending a revolution — by force, if necessary. Anarchists argue that Marx (and Marxists) confuse self-defence by "the people armed" with the state, a confusion which has horrific implications (as the history of the Russian Revolution shows).

So how would an anarchist revolution (and by implication, society) defend itself? Firstly, we should note that it will **not** defend itself by creating a centralised body, a new state. If it did this then the revolution will have failed and a new class society would have been created (a society based on state bureaucrats and oppressed workers as in the Soviet Union). Thus we reject the Marxist notion of a so-called "workers" or "revolutionary" state as confused in the extreme (as should be obvious from our analysis in section H). Rather, we seek libertarian means to defend a libertarian revolution. What would these libertarian means be?

In short, this would involve the "creation of a voluntary militia, without powers to interfere as militia in the life of the community, but only to deal with any armed attacks by the forces of reaction to re-establish themselves, or to resist outside intervention by countries as yet not in a state of revolution." The creation of a free militia would be part of the general social transformation as the "most powerful means for defending the revolution remains always that of taking away from the bourgeois the economic means on which their power rests, and of arming everybody (until such time as one will have managed to persuade everybody to throw away their arms as useless and dangerous toys), and of interesting the mass of the population in the victory of the revolution." [Malatesta, **Errico Malatesta: His Life and Ideas**, p. 166 and p. 173] As Bakunin stressed:

> "let us suppose … it is Paris that starts [the revolution] … Paris will naturally make haste to organise itself as best it can, in revolutionary style, after the workers have joined into associations and made a clean sweep of all the instruments of labour, every kind of capital and building; armed and organised by streets and **quartiers**, they will form the revolutionary federation of all the **quartiers**, the federative commune … All the French and foreign revolutionary communes will then send representatives to organise the necessary common services … and to organise common defence against the enemies of the Revolution, together with propaganda, the weapon of revolution, and practical revolutionary solidarity with friends in all countries against enemies in all countries."
> [**Michael Bakunin: Selected Writings**, pp. 178-9]

So anarchists have always seen the necessity to defend a revolution. There is no theoretical contradiction implied by this for while anarchism *"is opposed to any interference with your liberty"* and *"against all invasion and violence"*, it recognises that when *"any one attacks **you**, then it is **he** who is invading you, he who is employing violence against you. You have a right to defend yourself. More than that, it is your duty, as an anarchist to protect your liberty, to resist coercion and compulsion ... In other words, the social revolution will attack no one, but it will defend itself against invasion from any quarter."* [Alexander Berkman, **What is Anarchism?**, p. 231] These militias, in other words, do not seek to impose a revolution, for you cannot impose freedom or force people to be free against their will: *"The power of the people in arms can only be used in the defence of the revolution and the freedoms won by their militancy and their sacrifices."* [Vernon Richards, **Lessons of the Spanish Revolution**, p. 44]

Such activity, Berkman stressed, *"must be in consonance with th[e] spirit [of anarchism]. Self-defence excludes all acts of coercion, of persecution or revenge. It is concerned only with repelling attack and depriving the enemy of opportunity to invade you."* Any defence would be based on *"the strength of the revolution ... First and foremost, in the support of the people ... If they feel that they themselves are making the revolution, that they have become masters of their lives, that they have gained freedom and are building up their welfare, then in that very sentiment you have the greatest strength of the revolution ... Let them believe in the revolution, and they will defend it to the death."* Thus the *"armed workers and peasants are the only effective defence of the revolution."* [**Op. Cit.**, pp. 231-2] Malatesta stressed that a government is not required to defend freedom:

> *"But, by all means, let us admit that the governments of the still unemancipated countries were to want to, and could, attempt to reduce free people to a state of slavery once again. Would this people require a government to defend itself? To wage war men are needed who have all the necessary geographical and mechanical knowledge, and above all large masses of the population willing to go and fight. A government can neither increase the abilities of the former nor the will and courage of the latter. And the experience of history teaches us that a people who really want to defend their own country are invincible: and in Italy everyone knows that before the corps of volunteers (anarchist formations) thrones topple, and regular armies composed of conscripts or mercenaries disappear."* [**Anarchy**, p. 42]

As can be seen, anarchist theory has always addressed the necessity of defending a social revolution and proposed a solution — the voluntary, self-managed militia organised by the free communes and federations of workers' associations. The militias would be unified and co-ordinated by federations of communes while delegates from each militia unit would co-ordinate the actual fighting. In times of peace the militia members would be living and working among the rest of the populace, and, thus, they would tend to have the same outlook and interests as their fellows. Moreover, in the case of foreign intervention, the importance of international solidarity is important (*"a social revolution cannot be a revolution in one nation alone. It is by nature an international revolution."* [Bakunin, **Op.**

Cit., p. 49]). Thus any foreign intervention would face the problems of solidarity actions and revolts on its own doorstep and not dare send its troops abroad for long, if at all. Ultimately, the only way to support a revolution is to make your own.

Within the revolutionary area, it is the actions of liberated people that will defend it. Firstly, the population would be armed and so counter-revolutionaries would face stiff opposition to their attempts to recreate authority. Secondly, they would face liberated individuals who would reject and resist their attempts Thus, as we discuss in section I.5.11, any authoritarian would face the direct action of a free people, of free individuals, who would refuse to co-operate with the would-be authorities and join in solidarity with their friends and fellow workers to resist them. The only way a counter-revolution could spread internally is if the mass of the population had become alienated from the revolution and this is impossible in an anarchist revolution as power remains in their hands. A free society need not fear internal counter-revolutionaries gaining support.

History, as well as theory, points to such libertarian forms of self-defence. In all the major revolutions which anarchists took part in they formed militias to defend freedom. For example, anarchists in many Russian cities formed *"Black Guards"* to defend their expropriated houses and revolutionary freedoms. In the Ukraine, Nestor Makhno helped organise a peasant-worker army to defend the social revolution against authoritarians of right and left. In the Spanish Revolution, the CNT organised militias to free those parts of Spain under fascist rule after the military coup in 1936.

These anarchist militias were as self-managed as possible, with any "officers" elected and accountable to the troops and having the same pay and living conditions as them. Nor did they impose their ideas on others. When a militia liberated a village, town or city they called upon the population to organise their own affairs, as they saw fit. All the militia did was present suggestions and ideas to the population. For example, when the Makhnovists passed through a district they would put on posters announcing:

> *"The freedom of the workers and the peasants is their own, and not subject to any restriction. It is up to the workers and peasants to act, to organise themselves, to agree among themselves in all aspects of their lives, as they themselves see fit and desire ... The Makhnovists can do no more than give aid and counsel ... In no circumstances can they, nor do they wish to, govern."* [quoted by Peter Marshall, **Demanding the Impossible**, p. 473]

Needless to say, the Makhnovists counselled the workers and peasants *"to set up free peasants' and workers' councils"* as well as to expropriate the land and means of production. They argued that *"[f]reedom of speech, of the press and of assembly is the right of every toiler and any gesture contrary to that freedom constitutes an act of counter-revolution."* [**No Gods, No Masters**, vol. 2, pp. 157-8] The Makhnovists also organised regional congresses of peasants and workers to discuss revolutionary and social issues. The army's declared principles were voluntary enlistment, the election of officers and self-discipline according to the rules adopted by each unit themselves. Remarkably effective, the Makhnovists were the force that defeated Denikin's army and helped defeat Wrangel. After the Whites were defeated, the Bolsheviks turned against the Makhnovists and betrayed them. However, while they existed the Makhnovists defended the freedom of the working class to organise themselves against both right and left statists (see Voline's **The Unknown Revolution**, Peter Arshinov's **History of the Makhnovist Movement** or Alexandre Skirda's **Nestor Makhno Anarchy's Cossack** for more information).

A similar situation developed in Spain. After defeating the fascist military coup on 19th of July, 1936, the anarchists organised self-managed militias to liberate those parts of Spain under Franco. These groups were organised in a libertarian fashion from the bottom up:

> "The establishment of war committees is acceptable to all confederal militias. We start from the individual and form groups of ten, which come to accommodations among themselves for small-scale operations. Ten such groups together make up one **centuria,** which appoints a delegate to represent it. Thirty **centurias** make up one column, which is directed by a war committee, on which the delegates from the **centurias** have their say ... although every column retains its freedom of action, we arrive at co-ordination of forces, which is not the same thing as unity of command." [**Op. Cit.**, pp. 256-7]

Like the Makhnovists, the anarchist militias in Spain were not only fighting against reaction, they were fighting for a better world. As Durruti argued: "Our comrades on the front know for whom and for what they fight. They feel themselves revolutionaries and they fight, not in defence of more or less promised new laws, but for the conquest of the world, of the factories, the workshops, the means of transportation, their bread and the new culture." [**Op. Cit.**, p. 248] When they liberated towns and villages, the militia columns urged workers and peasants to collectivise the land and means of production, to re-organise life in a libertarian fashion. All across anti-Fascist Spain workers and peasants did exactly that. The militias only defended the workers' and peasants' freedom to organise their own lives as they saw fit and did not force them to create collectives or dictate their form.

In this, the CNT was not only following the suggestions of the likes of Bakunin and Malatesta, it was implementing its own stated policies. Thus before the revolution we find leading FAI member D. A. Santillan arguing that the "local Council of Economy will assume the mission of defence and raise voluntary corps for guard duty and if need be, for combat" in the "cases of emergency or danger of a counter-revolution." These Local Councils would be a federation of workplace councils and would be members of the Regional Council of the Economy which, like the Local Council, would be "constitute[d] by delegations or through assemblies." [**After the Revolution**, p. 80 and pp. 82-83] Thus defence of a free society is based on the federation of workers' councils and so directly controlled by the revolutionary population. This can also be seen in the Spanish CNT's 1936 resolution on Libertarian Communism in the section entitled **"Defence of the Revolution"**:

> "We acknowledge the necessity to defend the advances made through the revolution ... So ... the necessary steps will be taken to defend the new regime, whether against

the perils of a foreign capitalist invasion ... or against counter-revolution at home. It must be remembered that a standing army constitutes the greatest danger for the revolution, since its influence could lead to dictatorship, which would necessarily kill off the revolution ... The people armed will be the best assurance against any attempt to restore the system destroyed from either within or without ... Let each Commune have its weapons and means of defence ... the people will mobilise rapidly to stand up to the enemy, returning to their workplaces as soon as they may have accomplished their mission of defence... .

> "1. The disarming of capitalism implies the surrender of weaponry to the communes which be responsible for ensuring defensive means are effectively organised nationwide.

> "2. In the international context, we shall have to mount an intensive propaganda drive among the proletariat of every country so that it may take an energetic protest, calling for sympathetic action against any attempted invasion by its respective government. At the same time, our Iberian Confederation of Autonomous Libertarian Communes will render material and moral assistance to all the world's exploited so that these may free themselves forever from the monstrous control of capitalism and the State." [quoted by Jose Peirats, **The CNT in the Spanish Revolution**, vol. 1, p. 110]

Which was precisely what the CNT did do in July 1936 when faced with the fascist coup. Unfortunately, like the Makhnovists, the CNT militias were betrayed by their so-called allies on the left. The anarchist troops were not given enough arms and were left on the front to rot in inaction. The "unified" command of the Republican State preferred not to arm libertarian troops as they would use these arms to defend themselves and their fellow workers against the Communist led counter-revolution. Ultimately, the "people in arms" won the revolution and the "People's Army" which replaced it lost the war (see Jose Peirats' **The CNT in the Spanish Revolution**, Abel Paz's **Durruti in the Spanish Revolution**, Vernon Richard's **Lessons of the Spanish Revolution** or Noam Chomsky's **Objectivity and Liberal Scholarship**).

While the cynic may point out that, in the end, these revolutions and militias were defeated, it does not mean that their struggle was in vain or a future revolution will not succeed. That would be like arguing in 1940 that democracy is inferior to fascism because most democratic states had been (temporarily) defeated by the Axis powers. It does not mean that these methods will fail in the future or that we should embrace apparently more "successful" approaches which end in the creation of a society the total opposite of what we desire (means determine ends, after all, and statist means will create statist ends and apparent "successes" — like Bolshevism — are the greatest of failures in terms of our ideas and ideals). All we are doing here is pointing how anarchists have defended revolutions in the past and that these methods were successful for a long time in face of tremendous opposition forces.

Thus, in practice, anarchists have followed libertarian theory and created self-managed forms of self-defence against attempts to re-enslave a free people. In the end, an anarchist revolution can be defended only by applying its ideas as widely as possible. Its defence rests in those who make it. If the revolution is an expression of their needs, desires and hopes then it will be defended with the full passion of a free people. Such a revolution **may** be defeated by superior force, who can tell? But the possibility is that it will not and that is what makes it worth trying. To not act because of the possibility of failure is to live half a life.

Anarchism calls upon everyone to live the kind of life they deserve as unique individuals and desire as human beings. Individually we can make a difference, together we can change the world.

Bibliography

Bibliography for FAQ

Bibliography for FAQ 1126
Anarchist Anthologies 1126
Anarchist and Libertarian Works 1126
Works about Anarchism.. 1130
Non-Anarchist Works 1131

Bibliography for FAQ

This bibliography lists all the books quoted in the FAQ. However, details for some of these books is missing. Some books are listed in more than one edition. This is due to the process of revising the FAQ for publication and using the most recent versions of books quoted.

The bibliography is split into four sections: Anthologies of Anarchist authors; books by anarchists and other libertarians; books about anarchism, anarchists and anarchist history by non-libertarians; and books by non-anarchists/libertarians.

Anarchist Anthologies

Avrich, Paul (ed.), **The Anarchists in the Russian Revolution**, Thames and Hudson Ltd, London, 1973.

Brook, Frank H. (ed.), **The Individualist Anarchists: An Anthology of Liberty (1881-1908)**, Transaction Publishers, New Brunswick, 1994.

Dawn Collective (eds.), **Under the Yoke of the State: Selected Anarchist Responses to Prisons and Crime vol. 1, 1886-1929**, Dawn Collective/Kate Sharpley Library/PMB, Oakland/London/Berkeley, 2003.

Dark Star (ed.), **Quiet Rumours: An Anarcha-Feminist Reader**, AK Press/Dark Star, Edinburgh/San Francisco, 2002.
Beneath the Paving Stones: Situationists and the beach, May 1968, AK Press/Dark Star, Edinburgh/San Francisco, 2001.

Dolgoff, Sam (ed.), **The Anarchist Collectives: self-management in the Spanish revolution, 1936-1939**, Black Rose Books, Montreal, 1974.

Ehrlich, Howard J, Carol Ehrlich, David De Leon, Glenda Morris (eds.), **Reinventing Anarchy: What are Anarchists thinking these days?**, Routledge & Kegan Paul, London, 1979.

Ehrlich, Howard J. (ed.), **Reinventing Anarchy, Again**, AK Press, Edinburgh/San Francisco, 1996.

Glassgold, Peter (ed.), **Anarchy! An Anthology of Emma Goldman's Mother Earth**, Counterpoint, Washington D.C., 2001.

Graham, M. (ed.), **Man! An Anthology of Anarchist Ideas, Essays, Poetry and Commentaries**, Cienfuegos Press, London, 1974.

Graham, Robert (ed.), **Anarchism: A Documentary History of Libertarian Ideas -- Volume 1: From Anarchy to Anarchism (300CE to 1939)**, Black Rose Books, Montreal/New York/London, 2005.

Guerin, Daniel (ed.), **No Gods, No Masters: An Anthology of Anarchism** (in two volumes), AK Press, Edinburgh/San Francisco, 1998.

Krimerman, Leonard I. and Perry, Lewis, **Patterns of Anarchy: A Collection of Writings on the Anarchist Tradition**, Anchor Books, New York, 1966.

Woodcock, George (ed.), **The Anarchist Reader**, Fontana, Glasgow, 1987.

Anarchist and Libertarian Works

Ackelsberg, Martha A., **Free Women of Spain: anarchism and the struggle for the emancipation of women**, AK Press, Oakland/Edinburgh, 2005.

Anarchist Federation, **The Role of the Revolutionary Organisation**, Anarchist Communist Editions, London, 2008.

Anderson, Andy, **Hungary '56**, Phoenix Press, London, date unknown.

Anonymous, **Red Years, Black Years: Anarchist Resistance to Fascism in Italy**, ASP, London, 1989.

Arshinov, Peter, **The History of the Makhnovist Movement**, Freedom Press, London, 1987.
The Two Octobers available at: http://flag.blackened.net/revolt/russia/arshinov_2_oct.html

Avrich, Paul, **An American Anarchist: The Life of Voltairine de Cleyre**, Princeton University Press, Princeton, 1978.
Anarchist Voices: An Oral History of Anarchism in America, AK Press, Edinburgh/Oakland, 2005
Kronstadt 1921, W.W. Norton and Company Inc., New York, 1970.
The Russian Anarchists, W.W. Norton & Company, New York, 1978.
Anarchist Portraits, Princeton University Press, Princeton, 1988.
The Haymarket Tragedy, Princeton University Press, Princeton, 1984.
"Bolshevik Opposition To Lenin: G. Miasnikov and the Workers Group", pp. 1-29, **Russian Review**, vol. 43, no. 1

Bakunin, Micheal, **The Basic Bakunin**, Robert M. Cutler (ed.), Promethus Books, Buffalo, N.Y., 1994.
Bakunin on Anarchism, 2nd Edition, Sam Dolgoff (ed.), Black Rose Books, Montreal, 1980.
The Political Philosophy of Bakunin, G.P. Maximov (ed.), The Free Press, New York, 1953.
Michael Bakunin: Selected Writings, Arthur Lehning (ed.), Jonathan Cape, London, 1973.
Statism and Anarchy, Cambridge University Press, Cambridge, 1990.
God and the State, Dover, New York, 1970.
Marxism, Freedom and the State, K.J. Kenafick (ed.), Freedom Press, London, 1984.

Barclay, Harold, **The State**, Freedom Press, London, 2003.

Barrett, George, *"The Anarchist Revolution"* contained in **The Last War**, Pirate Press, Sheffield, 1990.
"Objections to Anarchism", **The Raven: Anarchist Quarterly**, no. 12 (Vol. 3, No. 4), Oct-Dec 1990, Freedom Press, pp. 339-364.

Bennello, George C., **From the Ground Up**, Black Rose Books, Montreal, 1992.

Berkman, Alexander, **What is Anarchism?**, AK Press, Edinburgh/London/Oakland, 2003.
The Russian Tragedy, Phoenix Press, London, 1986.
The Bolshevik Myth, Pluto Press, London, 1989.
Life of an Anarchist: The Alexander Berkman reader, Gene Fellner (ed.), Four Walls Eight Windows, New York, 1992.

Berkman, Alexander (ed.), **The Blast**, AK Press, Edinburgh/Oakland, 2005.

Berneri, Camillo, *"Peter Kropotkin: His Federalist Ideas"*, **The Raven: Anarchist Quarterly**, no. 31 (Vol. 8, No. 3), Autumn 1993, Freedom Press, pp. 268-82

Berneri, Marie-Louise, **Neither East Nor West: Selected Writings 1939-48**, Freedom Press, London, 1988.
Journey Through Utopia, Freedom Press, London, 1982.

Berry, David, **A History of the French Anarchist Movement, 1917-1945**, Greenwood Press, Westport, 2002.

Black, Bob, **The Abolition of Work and other essays**, Loompanics Unlimited, Port Townsend, 1986.
Friendly Fire, Autonomedia, New York, 1992.
Anarchy After Leftism, CAL Press, Columbia, 1997.

Bonanno, Alfredo M., **Anarchism and the National Liberation Struggle**, Bratach Dubh Editions, Catania, 1981.

Bookchin, Murray, **Post Scarcity Anarchism**, 3rd Edition, AK Press, Edinburgh/Oakland, 2004.
The Spanish Anarchists: The Heroic Years 1868-1936, AK Press, Edinburgh/San Francisco, 1998.
The Third Revolution: Popular Movements in the Revolutionary Era, Volume 1, Cassel, London, 1996.
The Third Revolution: Popular Movements in the Revolutionary Era, Volume 2, Cassel, London, 1998.
Toward an Ecological Society, Black Rose, Montreal, 1980.
Remaking Society: Pathways to a Green Future, South End Press, Boston, MA., 1990.
Social Anarchism and Lifestyle Anarchism, AK Press, Edinburgh/San Francisco, 1995.
The Modern Crisis, New Society Publishers, Philadelphia, 1986.
The Ecology of Freedom: The Emergence and Dissolution of Hierarchy, AK Press, Edinburgh/Oakland, 2005
Which Way for the Ecology Movement?, AK Press, Edinburgh/San Francisco, 1994.
The Philosophy of Social Ecology, Black Rose Books, Montreal/New York, 1990.
From Urbanisation to Cities: Toward a New Politics of Citizenship, Cassell, London, 1995.
The Murray Bookchin Reader, Janet Biehl (ed.), Cassell, London, 1997.

Anarchism, Marxism, and the Future of the Left: Interviews and Essays, 1993-1998, AK Press, Edinburgh/San Francisco, 1999.
To Remember Spain: The Anarchist and Syndicalist Revolution of 1936, AK Press, Edinburgh/San Francisco, 1994.

Bookchin, Murray and Dave Foreman, **Defending the Earth: A Dialogue between Murray Bookchin and Dave Foreman**, Black Rose Books, Montreal/New York.

Bradford, George, **How Deep is Deep Ecology?**, Times Change Press, California, 1989.
"Woman's Freedom: Key to the Population Question", pp. 65-84, **How Deep is Deep Ecology?**, Times Change Press, California, 1989.

Bricianer, Serge **Pannekoek and the Workers' Councils**, Telos Press, Saint Louis, 1978.

Brinton, Maurice, **For Workers' Power: The Selected Writings of Maurice Brinton**, David Goodway (ed.), AK Press, Edinburgh/Oakland, 2004.
The Bolsheviks and Workers' Control 1917 to 1921: the State and Counter-Revolution, Solidarity and Black and Red, London and Detroit, 1975.
The Irrational in Politics, Soldarity (London), London, 1975.

Brown, L. Susan, **The Politics of Individualism: Liberalism, Liberal Feminism and Anarchism**, Black Rose, Montreal/New York, 1993.

Brown, Tom, **Syndicalism**, Phoenix Press, London, 1990.

Buber, Martin, **Paths in Utopia**, Beacon Press, Boston, 1958.

Cardan, Paul, **Modern Capitalism and Revolution**, 2nd edition, Solidarity, London, 1974.

Carson, Kevin A., **The Iron Fist Behind the Invisible Hand**, available at: http://www.mutualist.org/id4.html
Studies in Mutualist Political Economy, available at: http://www.mutualist.org/id47.html

Carter, Alan, **Marx: A Radical Critique**, Wheatsheaf Books, Brighton, 1988.

Casa, Juan Gomez, **Anarchist Organisation: The History of the FAI**, Black Rose Books, Montreal, 1986.

Castoriadis, Cornelius, **Workers' Councils and the Economics of a Self-Managed Society**, Wooden Shoe Pamphlet, Philadelphia, 1984.
Political and Social Writings, vol. 1, translated and edited by David Ames Curtis, University of Minnesota Press, Minneapolis, 1988.
Political and Social Writings, vol. 2, translated and edited by David Ames Curtis, University of Minnesota Press, Minneapolis, 1988.
Political and Social Writings, vol. 3, translated and edited by David Ames Curtis, University of Minnesota Press, Minneapolis, 1993.
The Meaning of Socialism, Philadelphia Solidarity, Philadelphia, 1994.

Chomsky, Noam, **Chronicles of Dissent: Interviews with David Barsamian**, Common Courage and AK Press, Monroe, 1992.
Deterring Democracy, Vintage, London, 1992.
Keeping the Rabble in Line: Interviews with David Barsamian, AK Press, Edinburgh, 1994.
Noam Chomsky on Anarchism, available at: http://www.zmag.org/chomsky/interviews/9612-anarchism.html
Language and Politics, Expanded Second Edition, C.P. Otero (ed.), AK Press, Edinburgh/London/Oakland, 2004.
"Marxism, Anarchism, and Alternative Futures", pp. 775-785, **Language and Politics**, Expanded Second Edition.
World Orders, Old and New, Pluto Press, London, 1994.
Radical Priorities, Black Rose Books, Montreal, 1981.
Year 501: The Conquest Continues, Verso, London, 1993.
Necessary Illusions: Thought Control in Democratic Societies, Pluto Press, London, 1991.
Expanding the Floor of the Cage, available at: http://www.chomsky.info/interviews/199704--.htm
Rollback Parts I to IV, Z Magazine, January to May 1995 available at: http://www.chomsky.info/articles/199505--.htm
Interview on Pozner/Donahue in 1992, available at http://flag.blackened.net/liberty/chomskydon.html
For Reasons of State, Fontana/Collins, Suffolk, 1973.
The Chomsky Reader, James Peck (ed.), Pantheon Books, New York, 1987.
Turning the Tide: US Intervention in Central America and the Struggle for Peace, Pluto Press, 1985.
Rogue States: The Rule of Force in World Affairs, Pluto Press, London, 2000.
Understanding Power: The Indispensable Chomsky, Peter R. Mitchell and John Schoeffel (eds.), The New Press, New York, 2002.
Problems of Knowledge and Freedom: The Russell Lectures, The New Press, New York/London, 2003.
Hegemony or Survival: America's Quest for Global Dominance, Hamish Hamilton, London, 2003.
Powers and Prospects: Reflections on Human Nature and the Social Order, Pluto Press, London, 1996.
Class Warfare: Interviews with David Barsamian, Pluto Press, London, 1996.
American Power and the New Mandarins, Penguin Books, London, 1969.
Anarchism Interview: Noam Chomsky interviewed by Ziga Vodovnik, available at: http://www.chomsky.info/interviews/20040714.htm
Letters from Lexington: Reflections on Propaganda, Common Courage Press/AK Press, Monroe/Edinburgh, 1993.
Chomsky on Anarchism, AK Press, Edinburgh/Oakland, 2005.
Government in the Future, Seven Stories Press, New York, 2005.
Propaganda and the Public Mind: Conversations with Noam Chomsky, Pluto Press, London, 2001.
Failed States: The Abuse of Power and the Assault on Democracy, Hamish Hamilton, London, 2006.
The Culture of Terrorism, Pluto Press, London, 1989.
Imperial Ambitions: Conversations with Noam Chomsky on the post-9/11 World, Penguin Books, London, 2005.
Manufacturing Consent: Noam Chomsky and the Media, Mark Achbar (ed.), Black Rose Books, Quebec/New York, 1994.
Reluctant Icon: Noam Chomsky interviewed by Tim Halle available at http://www.chomsky.info/interviews/1999----.htm

Christie, Stuart, **We, the Anarchists! A Study of the Iberian Anarchist Federation (FAI) 1927-1927**, The Meltzer Press and Jura Media, Hastings/Petersham, 2000.
My Granny made me an Anarchist (The Christie File part 1, 1946-1964), Christie Books, Hastings, 2002.

Christie, Stuart and Meltzer, Albert, **The Floodgates of Anarchy**, Kahn & Averill, Southampton, 1984.

Ciliga, Ante, **The Russian Enigma**, Ink Links Ltd, London, 1979.

Clark, John, **The Anarchist Moment: Reflections on Culture, Nature and Power**, Black Rose Books, Montreal, 1984.

Clark, John P., **Max Stirner's Egoism**, Freedom Press, London, 1976.

Clark, John P and Martin, Camille (eds.), **Anarchy, Geography, Modernity: The Radical Social Thought of Elisée Reclus**, Lexington Books, Lanham, 2004.

Cleaver, Harry, **Reading Capital Politically**, AK Press/Anti-theses, London, 2000.

Cohn-Bendit, Daniel & Gabriel, **Obsolete Communism: The Left-Wing Alternative**, AK Press, Edinburgh, London & San Franciso, 2000.

Cole, G.D.H., **Guild Socialism Restated**, Transaction Books, New Brunswick, 1980.
Self-Government in Industry, Hutchinson Educational, London, 1972.

Comfort, Alex, **Authority and Delinquency in the Modern State: A Criminological Approach to the Problem of Power**, Routledge and Kegan Paul, 1950.
Writings against Power and Death: The Anarchist articles and Pamphlets of Alex Comfort, David Goodway (ed.), Freedom Press, London, 1994.

Crump, John, **Hatta Shuzo and Pure Anarchism in Interwar Japan**, St. Martin's Press, Inc., New York, 1993.

Dana, Charles A., **Proudhon and his "Bank of the People"**, Charles H. Kerr Publishing Co., Chicago, 1984.

de Cleyre, Voltairine, **The Voltairine de Cleyre Reader**, A.J. Brigati (ed.), AK Press, Oakland/Edinburgh, 2004.
Exquisite Rebel: The Essays of Voltairine de Cleyre -- Anarchist, Feminist, Genius, Sharon Presley and Crispin Sartwell (eds.), State University of New York Press, New York, 2005.
The First Mayday: The Haymarket Speeches 1895-1910, Cienfuegos Press, Libertarian Book Club and Soil of liberty, Orkney/Minneapolis, 1980

de Ligt, Bart, **The Conquest of Violence**, Pluto Press, London, 1989.

de Llorens, Ignaio, **The CNT and the Russian Revolution**, The Kate Sharpley Library, unknown, undated.

de Santillan, D. A., **After the Revolution: Economic Reconstruction in Spain Today**, Jura Media, Petersham, 1996

Debord, Guy, **Society of the Spectacle**, Rebel Press/Aim Publications, Exeter, 1987.

Direct Action Movement, **Winning the Class War: An Anarcho-Syndicalist Strategy**, Direct Action Movement-IWA, Manchester/Glasgow, 1991.
Direct Action in Industry, available at: http://www.spunk.org/texts/intro/practice/sp001703.html

Dobson, V.G., **Bringing the Economy Home from the Market**, Black Rose Books, Montreal, 1993.

Dolgoff, Sam, **The Cuban Revolution: A Critical Perspective**, Black Rose Books, Montreal, 1976.
The American Labour Movement: A New Beginning, Resurgence, Champaign, Il., 1980.
A Critique of Marxism, Soil of Liberty, Minneapolis, unknown.

Draughn, Jeff, **Between Anarchism and Libertarianism: Defining a New Movement**, available at http://flag.blackened.net/liberty/between.html

Ervin, Lorenzo Kom'boa, **Anarchism and the Black Revolution**, Monkeywrench Press and the Workers Self-Education Foundation, Philadelphia, 1994.

Fabbri, Luigi, **Bourgeois Influences on Anarchism**, Acrata Press, San Francisco, 1987.

Fernandez, Frank, **Cuban Anarchism: The History of a Movement**, See Sharp Press, Tucson, 2001.

Fleming, Marie, **The Geography of Freedom: The Odyssey of Elisée Reclus**, Black Rose Books, Montreal/New York, 1988.

Foner, Philip S. (ed.), **The Autobiographies of the Haymarket Martyrs**, Monad Press, New York, 1977.

Fontenis, Georges, **Manifesto of Libertarian Communism**, Anarchist Communist Editions, London, 1989.

For Ourselves, **The Right to Be Greedy: Thesis on the Practical Necessity of Demanding Everything**, Loompanics Unlimited, Port Townsend, Washington, 1983.

Fotopoulos, Takis, **Towards an Inclusive Democracy: The crisis of the growth economy and the need for a new liberatory Project**, Cassell, London/New York, 1997.

Ford, Earl C. and Foster, William Z., **Syndicalism**, Charles H. Keer Publishing Co., Chicago, 1990.

Franks, Benjamin, **Rebel Alliances: The means and ends of contemporary British anarchisms**, AK Press and Dark Star, Edinburgh/Oakland, 2006.

Fernandez, Neil C., **Capitalism and Class Struggle in the USSR: A Marxist Theory**, Ashgate, Aldershot, 1997.

Fromm, Erich, **To Have Or To Be?**, Abacus, London, 1993.
  Man for Himself: An Enquiry into the Psychology of Ethics, Ark Paperbacks, London, 1986.
  The Sane Society, Kegan Paul, 1959.
  The Fear of Freedom, Ark Paperbacks, London, 1989.

Galleani, Luigi, **The End of Anarchism?**, Cienfuegos Press, Orkney, 1982.

Godwin, William, **The Anarchist Writings of William Godwin**, Peter Marshall (ed.), Freedom Press, London, 1986.
  An Enquiry concerning Political Justice, Penguin, Harmondsworth, 1976

Goldman, Emma, **Red Emma Speaks: An Emma Goldman Reader**, 3rd Edition, Alix Kates Shulman (ed.), Humanity Books, New York, 1998.
  Anarchism and Other Essays, Dover Publications Ltd., New York, 1969.
  Vision on Fire: Emma Goldman on the Spanish Revolution, Commonground Press, New Paltz New York, 1985.
  My Disillusionment in Russia, Thomas Y. Crowell Company, New York, 1970.
  Living My Life (in 2 volumes), Dover Publications, New York, 1970.
  Emma Goldman: A Documentary History of the American Years volume 1: Made for America, 1890-1901, Candace Falk (ed.), University of California Press, Berkeley/Los Angeles/London, 2003.
  Emma Goldman: A Documentary History of the American Years volume 2: Making Speech Free, 1902-1909, Candace Falk (ed.), University of California Press, Berkeley/Los Angeles/London, 2005.

Goodway, David, **Anarchist Seeds Beneath the Snow: Left-Libertarian Thought and British Writers from William Morris to Colin Ward**, Liverpool University Press, Liverpool, 2006.

Goodway, David (ed.), **For Anarchism: History, Theory and Practice**, Routledge, London, 1989.

Gorter, Herman, **Open Letter to Comrade Lenin**, Wildcat, 1989.

Graeber, David, **Fragments of an Anarchist Anthropology**, Prickly Paradigm Press, Chicago, 2004.
  Possibilities: Essays on Hierarchy, Rebellion, and Desire, AK Press, Edinburgh/Oakland, 2007.

Green Anarchy, **Against Mass Society**, available at: http://www.primitivism.com/mass-society.htm

Greene, William B., **Mutual Banking**, West Brookfield, 1850.

Guerin, Daniel, **Anarchism: From Theory to Practice**, Monthly Review Press, New York/London, 1970.

Harper, Clifford, **Anarchy: A Graphic Guide**, Camden Press, London, 1987.

International Workers Association, **Principles, Aims and Statutes of the International Workers Association**, Monty Millar Press, Broadway, 1983.

Industrial Workers of the World, **How to fire your boss**, available at: http://fletcher.iww.org/direct_action/title.html

Kelman, James, **Some Recent Attacks: Essays Cultural and Political**, AK Press, Stirling, 1992.

Kelsey, Graham A., **Anarchosyndicalism, libertarian communism and the state: the CNT in Zaragoza and Aragon 1930-1937**, International Institute of Social History, Dordrecht, London, 1991.

Kenafick, K.J., **Michael Bakunin and Karl Marx**, Melbourne, 1948.

Klafta, Lance, *"Ayn Rand and the Perversion of Libertarianism"*, **Anarchy: A Journal of Desire Armed**, no. 34, pp. 59-62.

Knabb, Ken, **Public Secrets**, Bureau of Public Secrets, Berkeley, 1997.
  The Poverty of Primitivism, available at http://www.slip.net/~knabb/CF/primitivism.htm

Knabb, Ken (ed.), **Situationist International Anthology**, Bureau of Public Secrets, Berkeley, 1981.

Kropotkin, Peter, **Anarchism: A Collection of Revolutionary Writings**, Roger N. Baldwin (ed.), Dover Press, New York, 2002.
  Act for Yourselves: articles from Freedom 1886-1907, N. Walter and H. Becker (eds), Freedom Press, London, 1988.
  Ethics: Origin and Development, Blom, 1968.
  Mutual Aid, Freedom Press, London, 1987.
  The Conquest of Bread, Elephant Editions, Catania, 1985.
  The State: Its Historic Role, Freedom Press, London, 1987.
  Anarchism and Anarchist Communism: Its Basis and Principles, Freedom Press, London, 1987.
  The Great French Revolution (in two volumes), Elephant Editions, Catania, 1986.
  Words of a Rebel, Black Rose Books, Montreal, 1992.
  Evolution and Environment, Black Rose Books, Montreal, 1995.
  Fields, Factories and Workshops Tomorrow, Colin Ward (ed.), Freedom Press, London, 1985.
  Small Communal Experiments and Why They Fail, Jura Media, Sydney, 1997.
  The Place of Anarchism in Socialistic Evolution, Practical Parasite Publications, Cymru, 1990.
  Selected Writings on Anarchism and Revolution, Martin A. Miller (ed.), MIT Press, Cambridge, 1970.
  Memiors of a Revolutionist, Black Rose Books, Montreal/New York, 1989.
  The Conquest of Bread and Other Writings, Unversity Press, Cambridge, 1995.

Labadie, Joseph A., **Anarchism: What It Is and What It Is Not**, available at: http://alumni.umbc.edu/~akoont1/tmh/anar_jal.html
  Different Phases of the Labour Question, available at: http://members.aol.com/labadiejo/page11.html
  What is Socialism?, available at: http://members.aol.com/labadiejo/page7.html

Landauer, Gustav, **For Socialism**, Telos Press, St. Louis, 1978.

Law, Larry, **Spectacular Times: Bigger Cages, Longer Chains**, A-Distribution/Dark Star Press, London, 1991.

Le Guin, Ursula K., **The Dispossessed**, Grafton Books, London, 1986.

Leier, Mark, **Bakunin: The Creative Passion**, Thomas Dunne Books, New York, 2006.

Leval Gaston, **Collectives in the Spanish Revolution**, Freedom Press, London, 1975.

Levy, Carl, **Gramsci and the Anarchists**, Berg, Oxford, 1999.

Magón, Ricardo Flores, **Dreams of Freedom: A Ricardo Flores Magón Reader**, AK Press, Edinburgh/Oakland, 2005.
  Land and Liberty: Anarchist influences in the Mexican Revolution, David Poole (ed.), Cienfuegos Press, Sanday, 1977.

Mailer, Phil, **Portugal: The Impossible Revolution**, Solidarity, London, 1977.

Makhno, Nestor, **The Struggle Against the State and other Essays**, AK Press, Edinburgh/San Francisco, 1996.
  My Visit to the Kremlin, Kate Sharpley Library, London, 1993.

Makhno, Nestor, Ida Mett, Piotr Archinov, Valevsky, Linsky, **The Organisational Platform of the Libertarian Communists**, Workers Solidarity Movement, Dublin, 1989.

Malatesta, Errico, **Anarchy**, Freedom Press, London, 2001.
  Errico Malatesta: His Life and Ideas, 3rd Edition, Vernon Richards (ed.), Freedom Press, London, 1993.
  The Anarchist Revolution, Vernon Richards (ed.), Freedom Press, London, 1995.
  Fra Contadini: A Dialogue on Anarchy, Bratach Dudh Editions, Catena, 1981.

At the Cafe: Conversations on Anarchism, Freedom Press, London, 2005.
A Talk about Anarchist Communism, Freedom Press, London, 1894.
"Towards Anarchism", pp. 73-78, **Man!**, M. Graham (ed.), Cienfuegos Press, London, 1974.
"Anarchism and Syndicalism", pp. 146-52, Geoffrey Ostergaard, **The Tradition of Workers' Control**, Freedom Press, London, 1997.

Malet, Michael, **Nestor Makhno in the Russian Civil War**, MacMillan Press, London, 1982.

Martin, James J., **Men Against the State: The Expositors of Individualist Anarchism in America, 1827-1908**, Ralph Myles Publisher Inc., Colorado Springs, 1970.

Marshall, Peter, **Demanding the Impossible: A History of Anarchism**, Fontana, London, 1993.
Nature's Web: An Exploration of Ecological Thinking, Simon & Schuster, London, 1992.

Mattick, Paul, **Economic Crisis and Crisis Theory**, M.E. Sharpe, White Plains, New York, 1981.
Economics, Politics, and the Age of Inflation, Merlin Press, London, 1978.
Anti-Bolshevik Communism, Merlin Press, London, 1978.
Marx and Keynes: The Limits of the Mixed Economy, Merlin Press, London, 1971.
Marxism: The Last Refuge of the Bourgeoisie?, M. E. Sharpe, Inc./Merlin Press, Armonk/London, 1983.

Maximoff, G. P., **Program of Anarcho-Syndicalism**, Monty Miller Press, Sydney, 1985.
The Guillotine at Work: twenty years of terror in Russia (data and documents), Chicago Section of the Alexander Berkman Fund, Chicago, 1940.

Maximoff, G. P (ed.), **Constructive Anarchism**, Monty Miller Press, Sidney, 1988.

McKercher, William R., **Freedom and Authority**, Black Rose Books, Montreal/New York, 1989

Meltzer, Albert, **I Couldn't Paint Golden Angels**, AK Press, Edinburgh, 1996.
Anarchism: Arguments for and against, 7th Revised Edition, AK Press, Edinbrugh/San Francisco, 2000.
The Anarcho-Quiz Book, Simian Publications, Orkney, 1976.

Meltzer, Albert (ed.), **The Poverty of Statism**, Cienfuegos Press, Orkney, 1981.

Mett, Ida, **The Kronstadt Uprising**, Solidarity, London, date unknown.

Michel, Louise, **The Red Virgin: Memoirs of Louise Michel**, The University of Alabama Press, Alabama, 1981

Moore, John, **Primitivist Primer**, available at: http://lemming.mahost.org/johnmoore/primer.htm

Morris, Brian, **Bakunin: The Philosophy of Freedom**, Black Rose Books, Montreal, 1993.
Ecology and Anarchism: Essays and Reviews on Contemporary Thought, Images Publishing (Malvern) Ltd, Malvern Wells, 1996.
Kropotkin: The Politics of Community, Humanity Books, New York, 2004.

Morris, William, **Political Writings: Contributions to Justice and Commonweal 1883-1890**, Thoemmes Press, Bristol, 1994.
A Factory As it Might Be, Mushroom Bookshop, Nottingham, 1994.

Nettlau, Max, **A Short History of Anarchism**, Freedom Press, London, 1996.
Errico Malatesta: The Biography of an Anarchist, available at: http://dwardmac.pitzer.edu/anarchist_archives/malatesta/nettlau/nettlauonmalatesta.html

Nursey-Bray, Paul, **Anarchist Thinkers and Thought: an annotated bibliography**, Greenwood Press, New York, 1992.

Ostergaard, Geoffrey, **The Tradition of Workers' Control**, Freedom Press, London, 1997.

Pannekeok, Anton, **Workers' Councils**, AK Press, Oakland/Edinburgh, 2003.
Lenin as Philosopher: A Critical Examination of the Philosophical Basis of Leninism, Merlin Press, London, 1975.

Parsons, Albert R., **Anarchism: Its Philosophy and Scientific Basis**, University Press of the Pacific, Honolulu, 2003.

Parsons, Lucy, **Freedom, Equality & Solidarity: Writings & Speeches, 1878-1937**, Gale Ahrens (ed.), Charles H. Kerr, Chicago, 2004.

Pataud, Emile and Pouget, Emile, **How we shall bring about the Revolution: Syndicalism and the Co-operative Commonwealth**, Pluto Press, London, 1990.

Pateman, Carole, **The Problem of Political Obligation: A Critique of Liberal Theory**, Polity Press, Cambridge, 1985.
The Sexual Contract, Polity, Cambridge, 1988.
Participation and Democratic Theory, Cambridge University Press, Cambridge, 1970.
The Disorder of Women: Democracy, Feminism and Political theory, Polity, Cambridge, 1989.

Paz, Abel, **Durruti: The People Armed**, Black Rose Books, Montreal, 1976.
The Spanish Civil War, Pocket Archives, Hazan, Paris, 1997.
Durruti in the Spanish Revolution, AK Press, Edinburgh/Oakland, 2007.

Peacott, Joe, **Individualism and Inequality**, available at: http://world.std.com/~bbrigade/TL anarchy and inequality.htm
Individualism Reconsidered, available at: http://world.std.com/~bbrigade/badpp3.htm

Peirats, Jose, **Anarchists in the Spanish Revolution**, Freedom Press, London, 1990.
The CNT in the Spanish Revolution, vol. 1, The Meltzer Press, Hastings, 2001.
The CNT in the Spanish Revolution, vol. 2, ChristieBooks.com, Hastings, 2005.

Piercy, Marge, **Woman on the Edge of Time**, The Woman's Press, London, 1995.

Pouget, Emile , **Direct Action**, Kate Sharpley Library, London, 2003.
The Party Of Labour, available at: http://www.anarchosyndicalism.net/archive/display/190/index.php

Proudhon, P-J, **What is Property: an inquiry into the principle of right and of government**, William Reeves Bookseller Ltd., London, 1969.
System of Economical Contradictions or, the Philosophy of Misery, Benjamin Tucker, Boston, 1888.
The General Idea of the Revolution, Pluto Press, London, 1989.
Interest and Principal: A Loan is a Service available at: http://www.pitzer.edu/~dward/Anarchist_Archives/proudhon/interestletter1.html
Interest and Principal: The Circulation of Capital, Not Capital Itself, Gives Birth to Progress available at: http://www.pitzer.edu/~dward/Anarchist_Archives/proudhon/interestletter2.html
Selected Writings of Pierre-Joseph Proudhon, Stewart Edwards (ed.), MacMillan, London, 1969.
The Principle of Federation, University of Toronto Press, Canada, 1979.
Property is Theft! A Pierre-Joseph Proudhon Anthology, Iain McKay (ed.), AK Press, Edinburgh/Oakland, 2011.

Puente, Isaac, **Libertarian Communism**, Monty Miller Press, Sydney, 1985.

Purchase, Graham, **Evolution and Revolution: An Introduction to the Life and Thought of Peter Kropotkin**, Jura Books, Petersham, Australia, 1996.

Quail, John, **The Slow Burning Fuse: The Lost History of the British Anarchists**, Granada Publishing Ltd., London, 1978.

Read, Herbert, **Anarchy and Order: essays in politics**, Faber and Faber Ltd, London, 1954.
A One-Man Manifesto and other writings from Freedom Press, Freedom Press, London, 1994.

Richards, Vernon, **Lessons of the Spanish Revolution**, 3rd Edition, Freedom Press, London, 1983.
The Impossibilities of Social Democracy, Freedom Press, London, 1978.

Richards, Vernon (ed.), **Neither Nationalisation nor Privatisation: Selections from the Anarchist Journal Freedom 1945-1950**, Freedom Press, London, 1989.
Spain 1936-39 Social revolution and Counter Revolution: Selections from the Anarchist fortnightly Spain and the World, Freedom Press, London, 1990.
Why Work? Arguments for the Leisure Society, Freedom Press, London, 1997.
The May Days in Barcelona, Freedom Press, London, 1987.
World War - Cold War: Selections from the Anarchist Journals War Commentary and Freedom, 1939-1950, Freedom Press, London, 1989.
The Left and World War II: Selections from the Anarchist Journal War Commentary 1939-1943, Freedom Press, London, 1989.

Rocker, Rudolf, **Anarcho-Syndicalism: Theory and Practice**, AK Press, Edinburgh/Oakland, 2004.
Nationalism and Culture, Michael E. Coughlin, Minnesota, 1978.
The London Years, Five Leaves Publications/AK Press, Nottingham/Oakland, 2005.
The Tragedy of Spain, ASP, London & Doncaster, 1986.
Pioneers of American Freedom: Origin of Liberal and Radical Thought in America, Rocker Publications Committee, Los Angeles, 1949.

Root & Branch (ed.), **Root & Branch: The Rise of the Workers Movements**, Fawcett Publications, Greenwich, Conn., 1975.

Rooum, Donald, **What is Anarchism? An Introduction**, Freedom Press, London, 1992.

Roussopoulos, Dimitrios I. (ed.), **The Radical Papers**, Black Rose Books, Montreal/New York, 1987.
The Anarchist Papers, Black Rose Books, Montreal/New York, 2002.

Russell, Bertrand, **The Practice and Theory of Bolshevism**, George Allen and Unwin Ltd., London, 1949.
Roads to Freedom: Socialism, Anarchism and Syndicalism, George Allen and Unwin Ltd., London, 1973.

Sabatini, Peter, *"Libertarianism: Bogus Anarchy"*, **Anarchy: A Journal of Desire Armed**, no. 41, Fall/Winter 1994-5

Sacco, Nicola and Vanzetti, Bartolomeo, **The Letters of Sacco and Vanzetti**, Penguin Books, New York, 1997.

Schmidt, Michael and Walt, Lucien van der, **Black Flame: The Revolutionary Class Politics of Anarchism and Syndicalism**, AK Press, Edinburgh/Oakland, 2009.

Scott, James C., **Seeing like a State: How Certain Schemes to Improve the Human Condition Have Failed**, Yale University Press, New Haven and London, 1998.

Sheppard, Brian Oliver, **Anarchism vs. Primitivism**, See Sharp Press, Tuscon, 2003.

Shipway, Mark A. S., **Antiparliamentary Communism: The Movement for Workers' Councils in Britain, 1917-45**, Palgrave Macmillan, Basingstoke, 1988.

Sitrin, Marina (ed.), **Horizontalism: Voices of Popular Power in Argentina**, AK Press, Oakland/Edinburgh, 2006.

Skirda, Alexandre, **Nestor Makhno Anarchy's Cossack: The struggle for free soviets in the Ukraine 1917-1921**, AK Press, Edinburgh/Oakland, 2004
Facing the Enemy: A History of Anarchist Organisation from Proudhon to May 1968, AK Press, Edinburgh/Oakland, 2002.

Smart, D.A. (ed.), **Pannekoek and Gorter's Marxism**, Pluto Press, London, 1978.

Spooner, Lysander, **Natural Law**, available at http://flag.blackened.net/liberty/spoonnat.html
No Treason: The Constitution of No Authority, Ralph Myles Publisher, Inc., Colorado Springs, 1973.
An essay on the Trial by Jury, John P. Jewett and Co., Boston, 1852.
A Letter to Grover Cleveland, Benjamin R. Tucker, Boston, 1886.
Revolution: The Only Remedy For The Oppressed Classes Of Ireland, England, And Other Parts Of The British Empire, available at: http://www.lysanderspooner.org/Revolution.htm
Poverty: Its Illegal Causes and Legal Cure, Bela Marsh, Boston, 1846.
The Law of Intellectual Property, or, An Essay on the Right of Authors and Inventors to a Perpetual Property in Their Ideas, Boston, 1885.

Starhawk, *"Staying on the Streets,"* contained in **On Fire: The Battle of Genoa and the anti-capitalist movement**, One Off Press, unknown, 2001.

Stirner, Max, **The Ego and Its Own**, Rebel Press, London, 1993.

Tolstoy, Leo, **The Kingdom of God is Within You: Christianity Not as a Mystic Religion but as a New Theory of Life**, University of Nebraska Press, London, 1984.
The Slavery of Our Times, John Lawrence, London, 1972.

Trotwatch, **Carry on Recruiting! Why the Socialist Workers Party dumped the 'downturn' in a 'dash for growth' and other party pieces**, AK Press/Trotwatch, Glasgow, 1993.

Tucker, Benjamin R., **Instead of a Book, by a man too busy to write one: a fragmentary exposition of philosophical anarchism culled from the writings of Benj. R. Tucker**, Haskell House Publishers, New York, 1969.
Occupancy and Use verses the Single Tax available at: http://208.206.78.232/daver/anarchism/tucker/tucker32.html
"Why I am an Anarchist", pp. 132-136, **Man!**, M. Graham (ed.), Cienfuegos Press, London, 1974.

Unofficial Reform Committee, **The Miner's Next Step: Being a suggested scheme for the reorganisation of the Federation**, Germinal and Phoenix Press, London, 1991.

Vaneigem, Raoul, **The Revolution of Everyday Life**, Rebel Press/Left Bank Books, London, 1994.

Voline, **The Unknown Revolution**, Black & Red/Solidarity, Detroit/Chicago, 1974.

Walter, Nicolas, **About Anarchism**, Freedom Press, London, 2002.
The Anarchist Past and other essays, Five Leaves Publications, Nottingham, 2007.

Ward, Colin, **Anarchy in Action** (2nd Edition), Freedom Press, London, 1982.
Social Policy: an anarchist response, Freedom Press, London, 2000.
Talking Houses, Freedom Press, London, 1990.
Housing: An Anarchist Approach, Freedom Press, London, 1983
Reflected in Water: A Crisis of Social Responsibility, Cassel, London, 1997.
Freedom to go: after the motor age, Freedom Press, London, 1991.
Anarchism: A Very Short Introduction, Oxford University Press, Oxford, 2004.
Cotters and Squatters: Housing's Hidden History, Five Leaves, Nottingham, 2005.

Ward, Colin (ed.), **A Decade of Anarchy: Selections from the Monthly Journal Anarchy**, Freedom , London, 1987.

Ward, Colin and Goodway, David, **Talking Anarchy**, Five Leaves, Nottingham, 2003.

Watson, David, **Beyond Bookchin: Preface for a Future Social Ecology**, Autonomedia/Black and Red/Fifth Estate, USA, 1996.
Against the Megamachine: Essays on Empire and Its Enemies, Autonomedia/Fifth Estate, USA, 1997.

Weick, David, *"Anarchist Justice"*, pp. 215-36, **Anarchism: Nomos XIX**, J. Roland Pennock and John W. Chapman (eds.), New York University Press, New York, 1978.

Weil, Simone, **Oppression and Liberty**, Routledge, London, 2001.

Wildcat Group (ed.), **Class War on the Home Front: Revolutionary Opposition to the Second World War**, Wildcat Group, Manchester, 1986.

Wilde, Oscar, *"The Soul of Man Under Socialism"*, pp. 1174-1197, **Complete works of Oscar Wilde**, HarperCollins Publishers, Glasgow, 1994.

Wilson, Charlotte, **Anarchist Essays** , Freedom Press, London, 2000.

Wilson, Robert Anton, **Natural Law: or don't put a rubber on your willy**, Loompanics Ltd, Port Townsend, 1987.

Woodcock, George, **Anarchism: A History of libertarian ideas and movements** (2nd Edition), Penguin Books, England, 1986.
Pierre-Joseph Proudhon: A Biography, Black Rose Books, Montreal/New York, 1987.

Woodcock, George and Avakumovic, Ivan, **The Anarchist Prince: A Biographical Study of Peter Kropotkin**, T. V. Boardman & Co. Ltd., London, 1950.

Zerzan, John, **Elements of Refusal**, Left Bank Books, Seattle, 1988.
On the Transition: Postscript to Future Primitive, available at: http://www.insurgentdesire.org.uk/fp.htm

Zinn, Howard, **A People's History of the United States**, 2nd Edition, Longman, Essex, 1996.
Failure to Quit: Reflections of an Optimistic Historian, Common Courage Press, Monroe Main, 1993.
The Colorado Coal Strike, 1913-14, contained in **Three Strikes: Miners, Musicians, Salesgirls, and the Fighting Spirit of Labor's Last Century**, Howard Zinn, Dana Frank, Robin D. G. Kelly, Beacon Press, Boston, 2001.
The Zinn Reader: Writings on Disobedience and Democracy, Seven Stories Press, New York, 1997.
An Interview with Howard Zinn on Anarchism: Rebels Against Tyranny, available at: http://www.revolutionbythebook.akpress.org/an-interview-with-howard-zinn-on-anarchism-rebels-against-tyranny/

Zinn, Howard and Arnove, Anthony (eds.), **Voices of a People's History of the United States**, Seven Stories Press, New York, 2004.

Works about Anarchism

Alexander, Robert, **The Anarchists in the Spanish Civil War** (2 vols.), Janus Publishing Company, London, 1999.

Anderson, Carlotta R., **All-American Anarchist: Joseph A. Labadie and the Labor Movement**, Wayne State University Press, Detroit, 1998.

Apter, D. and Joll, J (Eds.), **Anarchism Today**, Macmillan, London, 1971.

Archer, Julian P. W., **The First International in France, 1864-1872: Its Origins, Theories, and Impact**, University Press of America, Inc., Lanham/Oxford, 1997.

Cahm, C., **Kropotkin and the Rise of Revolutionary Anarchism 1872-1886**, Cambridge University Press, Cambridge, 1989.

Carr, Edward Hallett, **Michael Bakunin**, Macmillan, London, 1937.

Coleman, Stephen and O'Sullivan, Paddy (eds.), **William Morris and News from Nowhere: A Vision for Our Time**, Green Books, Bideford, 1990.

Coughlin, Michael E., Hamilton, Charles H. and Sullivan, Mark A. (eds.), **Benjamin R. Tucker and the Champions of Liberty: A Centenary Anthology**, Michael E. Coughlin Publisher, St. Paul, Minnesota, 1986.

Delamotte, Eugenia C., **Gates of Freedom: Voltairine de Cleyre and the Revolution of the Mind -- With Selections from Her Writing**, The University of Michigan Press, Ann Arbor, 2004.

Dirlik, Arif, **Anarchism in the Chinese Revolution**, University of California Press, Berkeley and Los Angeles, 1991.

Ehrenberg, John, **Proudhon and his Age**, Humanity Books, New York, 1996.

Esenwein, George Richard, **Anarchist Ideology and the Working Class Movement in Spain, 1868-1898**, University of California Press, Berkeley, 1989.

Guthke, Karl S., **B. Traven: The life behind the legends**, Lawrence Hill Books, New York, 1991.

Hart, John M., **Anarchism and the Mexican Working Class, 1860-1931**, University of Texas Press, Austin, 1987.

Holton, Bob, **British Syndicalism: 1900-1914: Myths and Realities**, Pluto Press, London, 1976.

Hyams, Edward, **Pierre-Joseph Proudhon: His Revolutionary Life, Mind and Works**, John Murray, London, 1979.

Jennings, Jeremy, **Syndicalism in France: a study of ideas**, Macmillan, London, 1990

Kline, Wm. Gary, **The Individualist Anarchists: A Critique of Liberalism**, University Press of America, Lanham, Maryland, 1987.

Linden, Marcel van der and Thorpe, Wayne (eds.), **Revolutionary Syndicalism: An International Perspective**, Scolar Press, Aldershort, 1990.

Merithew, Caroline Waldron, *"Anarchist Motherhood: Toward the making of a revolutionary Proletariat in Illinois Coal towns"*, pp. 217-246, Donna R. Gabaccoia and Franca Iacovetta (eds.), **Women, Gender, and Transnational Lives: Italian Workers of the World**, University of Toronto Press, Toronto, 2002.

Miller, Martin A., **Kropotkin**, The University of Chicago Press, London, 1976.

Milner, Susan, **The Dilemmas of Internationalism: French Syndicalism and the International Labour Movement 1900-1914**, Berg, New York, 1990.

Mintz, Jerome R., **The Anarchists of Casas Viejas**, Indiana University Press, Bloomington, 1994.

Moya, Jose, *"Italians in Buenos Aires's Anarchist Movement: Gender Ideology and Women's Participation, 1890-1910,"* pp. 189-216, Donna R. Gabaccoia and Franca Iacovetta (eds.), **Women, Gender, and Transnational Lives: Italian Workers of the World**, University of Toronto Press, Toronto, 2002.

Oved, Yaacov, *"'Communsmo Libertario' and Communalism in Spanish Collectivisations (1936-1939)"*, **The Raven: Anarchist Quarterly**, no. 17 (Vol. 5, No. 1), Jan-Mar 1992, Freedom Press, pp. 39-61.

Palij, Michael, **The Anarchism of Nestor Makhno, 1918-1921: An Aspect of the Ukrainian Revolution**, University of Washington Press, Seattle, 1976.

Pernicone, Nunzio, **Italian Anarchism: 1864-1892**, Princeton University Press, Princeton, 1993.
 Carlo Tresca: Portrait of a Rebel, Palgrave MacMillian, New York, 2005.

Ravindranathan, T. R., **Bakunin and the Italians**, McGill-Queen's Univsersity Press, Kingston and Montreal, 1988.

Ritter, Alan, **The Political Thought of Pierre-Joseph Proudhon**, Princeton University Press, Princeton, 1969.

Salerno, Salvatore, **Red November, Black November: Culture and Community in the Industrial Workers of the World**, State University Press of New York, Albany, 1989.

Saltman, Richard B., **The Social and Political Thought of Michael Bakunin**, Greenwood Press, Westport Connecticut, 1983.

Schuster, Eunice, **Native American Anarchism : A Study of Left-Wing American Individualism**, De Capo Press, New Yprk, 1970.

Taylor, Michael, **Community, Anarchy and Liberty**, Cambrdige University Press, Cambridge, 1982.

Thomas, Edith, **Louise Michel**, Black Rose Books, Montreal, 1980.

Thomas, Matthew, **Anarchist ideas and counter-cultures in Britain, 1880-1914: revolutions in everyday life**, Aldershot, Ashgate, 2005.

Thorpe, Wayne, **"The Workers Themselves": Revolutionary Syndicalism and International Labour, 1913-1923**, Kluwer Academic Publishers, Dordrecht, 1989.

Vincent, K. Steven, **Pierre-Joseph Proudhon and the Rise of French Republican Socialism**, Oxford University Press, Oxford, 1984.

Zarrow, Peter, **Anarchism and Chinese Political Culture**, Columbia University Press, New York, 1990.

Non-Anarchist Works

Anderson, Terry L. and Leal, Donald R., **Free Market Environmentalism**, Pacific Research Institute for Public Policy, San Francisco, 1991.

Anweiler, Oskar, **The Soviets: The Russian Workers, Peasants, and Soldiers Councils 1905-1921**, Random House, New York, 1974.

Archer, Abraham (ed.), **The Mensheviks in the Russian Revolution**, Thames and Hudson Ltd, London, 1976.

Armstrong, Philip, Glyn, Andrew and Harrison, John, **Capitalism Since 1945**, Basil Blackwell, Oxford, 1991.

Aves, Jonathan, **Workers Against Lenin: Labour Protest and the Bolshevik Dictatorship**, Tauris Academic Studies, London, 1996.

Bakan, Joel, **The Corporation: The Pathological Pursuit of Profit and Power**, Constable, London, 2004.

Bukharin, Nikolai, **Economy Theory of the Leisure Class**, Monthly Press Review, New York/London, 1972.

Bagdikian, Ben H., **The New Media Monopoly**, Beacon Press, Boston, 2004.

Balogh, Thomas, **The Irrelevance of Conventional Economics**, Weidenfield and Nicolson, London, 1982.

Beder, Sharon, **Global Spin: The Corporate Assault on Environmentalism**, Green Books, Dartington, 1997.

Beevor, Antony, **The Spanish Civil War**, Cassell, London, 1999.
 The Battle for Spain: The Spanish Civil War 1936-1939, Phoenix, London, 2006.

Berghahn, V. R., **Modern Germany: society, economy and politics in the twentieth century**, 2nd ed., Cambridge University Press, Cambridge, 1987.

Beynon, Huw, **Working for Ford**, Penguin Education, London, 1973.

Blanchflower, David and Oswald, Andrew, **The Wage Curve**, MIT Press, Cambridge, Mass., 1994.

Blinder, Alan S. (ed.), **Paying for productivity: a look at the evidence**, Brookings Institution, Washington, D.C, 1990.

Böhm-Bawerk, Eugen, **Capital and Interest**, Libertarian Press, South Holland, Ill., 1959.

Bolloten, Burnett, **The Spanish Civil War: Revolution and Counter Revolution**, Harvester-Wheatsheaf, New York, 1991.

Boucher, Douglas H. (ed.), **The Biology of Mutualism: Biology and Evolution**, Croom Helm , London, 1985.

Bowles, Samuel and Edwards, Richard (Eds.), **Radical Political Economy**, (two volumes), Edward Elgar Publishing Ltd., Aldershot, 1990.

Bowles, Samuel and Gintis, Hebert, **Schooling in Capitalist America: Education Reform and the Contradictions of Economic Life**, Routledge & Kegan Paul, London, 1976.

Braverman, Harry, **Labour and Monopoly Capital: The Degradation of Work in the Twentieth Century**, Monthly Review Press, New York, 1974.

Brecher, Jeremy, **Strike!**, South End Press, Boston, 1972.

Brecher, Jeremy and Costello, Tim, **Common Sense for Hard Times**, Black Rose Books, Montreal, 1979.

Brenan, Gerald, **The Spanish Labyrinth: An Account of the Social and Political Background of the Spanish Civil War**, 2nd Edition, Cambridge University Press, Cambridge, 1976.

Broido, Vera, **Lenin and the Mensheviks: The Persecution of Socialists under Bolshevism**, Gower Publishing Company Limited, Aldershot, 1987.

Brovkin, Vladimir N., **The Mensheviks After October: Socialist Opposition and the Rise of the Bolshevik Dictatorship**, Cornell University Press, Ithaca, 1987.

Cahm, Eric and Fisera, Vladimir Claude (eds), **Socialism and Nationalism**, Spokesman, Nottingham, 1978-80.

Carr, Edward Hallett, **The Bolshevik Revolution: 1917-1923**, in three volumes, Pelican Books, 1966.

Carrier, James G. (ed.), **Meanings of the market: the free market in western culture**, Berg, Oxford, 1997.

Chang, Ha-Joon, **Kicking Away the Ladder: Development Strategy in Historic Perspective**, Anthem Press, London, 2002.
    Bad Samaritans: rich nations, poor policies and the threat to the developing world, Random House Business, London, 2007

Clark, J.B., **The Distribution of Wealth: A theory of wages, interest and profits**, Macmillan, New York, 1927

Cliff, Tony, **Lenin: The Revolution Besieged**, vol. 3, Pluto Press, London, 1978.
    Lenin: All Power to the Soviets, vol. 2, Pluto Press, London, 1976.
    State Capitalism in Russia, Bookmarks, London, 1988.

Collins, Joseph and Lear, John, **Chile's Free-Market Miracle: A Second Look**, Institute for Food and Development Policy, Oakland, 1995.

Communist International, **Proceedings and Documents of the Second Congress 1920**, (in two volumes), Pathfinder, New York, 1991.

Confino, Michael (ed.), **Daughter of a Revolutionary: Natalie Herzen and the Bakunin-Nechayev Circle**, Library Press, LaSalle Illinois, 1973.

Cowling, Keith, **Monopoly Capitalism**, MacMillian, London, 1982.

Cowling, Keith and Sugden, Roger, **Transnational Monopoly Capitalism**, Wheatshelf Books, Sussez, 1987.
    Beyond Capitalism: Towards a New World Economic Order, Pinter, London, 1994.

Daniels, Robert V., **The Conscience of the Revolution: Communist Opposition in Soviet Russia**, Harvard University Press, Cambridge, 1960.

Daniels, Robert V. (ed.), **A Documentary History of Communism**, vol. 1, Vintage Books, New York, 1960.

Davidson, Paul, **Controversies in Post-Keynesian Economics**, E. Elgar, Brookfield, Vt., USA, 1991.
    John Maynard Keynes, Palgrave Macmillan, Basingstoke, 2007

DeShazo, Peter, **Urban Workers and Labor Unions in Chile 1902-1927**, University of Wisconsin Press, Madison, 1983.

Devine, Pat, **Democracy and Economic Planning**, Polity, Cambridge, 1988.

Dobbs, Maurice, **Studies in Capitalist Development**, Routledge & Kegan Paul Ltd., London, 1963.

Domhoff, G. William, **Who Rules America Now? A view from the '80s**, Prentice-Hall, Englewood Cliffs, 1983.

Donaldson, Peter, **A Question of Economics**, Penguin Books, London, 1985.
    Economics of the Real World, 3rd edition, Penguin books, London, 1984.

Dorril, Stephen and Ramsay, Robin, **Smear! Wilson and the Secret State**, Fourth Estate Ltd., London, 1991.

Douglass, Frederick, **The Life and Writings of Frederick Douglass**, vol. 2, Philip S. Foner (ed.) International Publishers, New York, 1975.

Draper, Hal, **The 'dictatorship of the proletariat' from Marx to Lenin**, Monthly Review Press, New York, 1987.
    The Myth of Lenin's "Concept of The Party", available at: http://www.marxists.org/archive/draper/works/1990/myth/myth.htm

Du Boff, Richard B., **Accumulation and Power: an economic history of the United States**, M.E. Sharpe, London, 1989.

Dubois, Pierre, **Sabotage in Industry**, Penguin Books, London, 1979.

Eatwell, Roger and Wright, Anthony (eds.), **Contemporary political ideologies**, Pinter, London, 1993.

Edwards, Stewart, **The Paris Commune 1871**, Victorian (& Modern History) Book Club, Newton Abbot, 1972.

Edwards, Stewart (ed.), **The Communards of Paris, 1871**, Thames and Hudson, London, 1973.

Ellerman, David P., **Property and Contract in Economics: The Case for Economic Democracy**, Blackwell, Oxford, 1992.
    The Democratic Worker-Owned Firm: A New Model for East and West, Unwin Hyman, Boston, 1990.
    as "J. Philmore", **The Libertarian Case for Slavery**, available at: http://cog.kent.edu/lib/Philmore1/Philmore1.htm

Elliot, Larry and Atkinson, Dan, **The Age of Insecurity**, Verso, London, 1998.
    Fantasy Island: Waking Up to the Incredible Economic, Political and Social Illusions of the Blair Legacy, Constable, London, 2007.
    The Gods That Failed: Now the Financial Elite have Gambled Away our Futures, Vintage Books, London, 2009.

Engler, Allan, **Apostles of Greed: Capitalism and the myth of the individual in the market**, Pluto Press, London, 1995.

Farber, Samuel, **Before Stalinism: The Rise and Fall of Soviet Democracy**, Polity Press, Oxford, 1990.

Ferguson, C. E., **The Neo-classical Theory of Production and Distribution**, Cambridge University Press, London, 1969.

Figes, Orlando, **A People's Tragedy: The Russian Revolution 1891-1924**, Jonathan Cape, London, 1996.
    Peasant Russia, Civil War: the Volga countryside in revolution 1917-1921, Phoenix Press, London, 2001.

Forgacs, David (ed.), **Rethinking Italian fascism: capitalism, populism and culture**, Lawrence and Wishart, London, 1986.

Fraser, Ronald, **Blood of Spain: the experience of civil war, 1936-1939**, Allen Lane, London, 1979.

French, Marilyn, **Beyond Power: On Women, Men, and Morals**, Summit Books, 1985.

Friedman, David, **The Machinery of Freedom**, Harper and Row, New York, 1973.

Friedman, Milton, **Capitalism and Freedom**, University of Chicago Press, Chicago, 2002.
    Economic Freedom, Human Freedom, Political Freedom, available at: http://www.cbe.csueastbay.edu/~sbesc/frlect.html
    The Hong Kong Experiment, available at: http://www.hoover.org/publications/digest/3532186.html

Galbraith, James K., **Created Unequal: The Crisis in American Pay**, The Free Press, New York, 1999.

Galbraith, John Kenneth, **The Essential Galbraith**, Houghton Mifflin Company, New York, 2001.
    The New Industrial State, 4th edition, Princeton University Press, Princeton and Oxford, 2007.

Gemie, Sharif, **French Revolutions, 1815-1914**, Edinburgh University Press, Edinburgh, 1999.

Getzler, Israel, **Martov: A Political Biography of a Russian Social Democrat**, Melbourne University Press, Carlton, 1967.
    "Marxist Revolutionaries and the Dilemma of Power", pp. 88-112, **Revolution and Politics in Russia**, Alexander and Janet Rabinowitch with Ladis K.D. Kristof (eds.)

Gilmour, Ian, **Dancing with Dogma, Britain Under Thatcherism**, Simon and Schuster, London, 1992.

Glennerster, Howard and Midgley, James (eds.), **The Radical Right and the Welfare State: an international assessment**, Harvester Wheatsheaf, 1991.

Gluckstein, Donny, **The Paris Commune: A Revolutionary Democracy**, Bookmarks, London, 2006

Glyn, Andrew, **Capitalism Unleashed: Finance Globalisation and Welfare**, Oxford University Press, Oxford, 2006.

Glyn, Andrew and Miliband, David (eds.), **Paying for Inequality: The Economic Costs of Social Injustice**, IPPR/Rivers Oram Press, London, 1994.

Goodstein, Phil H., **The Theory of the General Strike from the French Revolution to Poland**, East European Monographs, Boulder, 1984.

Gould, Stephan Jay, **Ever Since Darwin: Reflections in Natural History**, Penguin Books, London, 1991.
    Bully for Brontosaurus: Reflections in Natural History, Hutchinson Radius, London, 1991.

Gramsci, Antonio, **Selections from Political Writings (1921-1926)**, Lawrence and Wishart, London, 1978.

Gray, John, **False Dawn: The Delusions of Global Capitalism**, Granta Books, London, 1998.

Green, Duncan, **Silent Revolution: The Rise of Market Economics in Latin America**, Cassell, London, 1995.

Greider, William, **One World, Ready or Not: The Manic Logic of Global Capitalism**, Penguin Books, London, 1997.

Gross, Bertram, **Friendly Fascism**, South End Press, Boston, 1989.

Gunn, Christopher Eaton, **Workers' Self-Management in the United States**, Cornell University Press, Ithaca and London, 1984.

Gunson, P., Thompson, A. and Chamberlain, G., **The Dictionary of Contemporary Politics of South America**, Routledge, 1989.

Hahnel, Robin and Albert, Michael, **The Quiet Revolution in Welfare Economics**, Princeton University Press, Princeton, 1990.
   The Political Economy of Participatory Economics, Princeton University Press, Princeton, 1991.
   Looking Forward: Participatory Economics for the Twenty First Century, South End Press, Boston, 1991.

Hallas, Duncan, *"Towards a revolutionary socialist party"*, contained in Tony Cliff, Duncan Hallas, Chris Harman and Leon Trotsky, **Party and Class**, Bookmarks, London, 1996.

Harding, Neil, **Leninism**, MacMillan Press, London, 1996.
   Lenin's political thought, vol. 1, Macmillan, London, 1977.

Harman, Chris, **Bureaucracy and Revolution in Eastern Europe**, Pluto Press, London, 1974.
   "Party and Class", contained in Tony Cliff, Duncan Hallas, Chris Harman and Leon Trotsky, **Party and Class**, Bookmarks, London, 1996.

Haworth, Alan, **Anti-Libertarianism: Markets, Philosophy and Myth**, Routledge, London, 1994.

Hayek, F. A. von, **The Essence of Hayek**, Chiaki Nishiyama and Kurt Leube (Eds.), Hoover Institution Press, Stanford, 1984
   Individualism and Economic Order, Henry Regnery Company, Chicago, 1948
   "1980s Unemployment and the Unions" contained in Coates, David and Hillard, John (Eds.), **The Economic Decline of Modern Britain: The Debate between Left and Right**, Wheatsheaf Books Ltd., 1986.
   New Studies in Philosophy, Politics, Economics and the History of Ideas, Routledge & Kegan Paul. London/Henley, 1978.
   Law, Legislation and Liberty, Routledge and Kegan Paul, London, 1982.

Hayek, F. A. von (ed.), **Collectivist Economic Planning**, Routledge and Kegan Paul, London, 1935.

Hayward, Jack, **After the French Revolution: Six critics of Democracy and Nationalism**, Harvester Wheatsheaf, Hemel Hempstead, 1991.

Heider, Ulrike, **Anarchism: left, right, and green**, City Lights Books, San Francisco, 1994.

Hein, Eckhard and Schulten, Thorsten, **Unemployment, Wages and Collective Bargaining in the European Union**, WSI_Discussion Paper No. 128, Witschafts- und Sozialwissenschaftliches Institut, Dusseldorf, 2004.

Henwood, Doug, **Wall Street: How it works and for whom**, Verso, London, 1998.
   "Booming, Borrowing, and Consuming: The US Economy in 1999", **Monthly Review**, vol. 51, no. 3, July-August 1999, pp.120-33.
   After the New Economy, The New Press, New York, 2003.
   Wall Street: Class Racket, available at: http://www.panix.com/~dhenwood/WS_Brecht.html

Herbert, Auberon, *"Essay X: The Principles Of Voluntaryism And Free Life"*, **The Right And Wrong Of Compulsion By The State, And Other Essays**, available at: http://oll.libertyfund.org/Texts/LFBooks/Herbert0120/CompulsionByState/HTMLs/0146_Pt11_Principles.html
   "Essay III: A Politician In Sight Of Haven", **The Right And Wrong Of Compulsion By The State, And Other Essays**, available at: http://oll.libertyfund.org/Texts/LFBooks/Herbert0120/CompulsionByState/HTMLs/0146_Pt04_Politician.html

Herman, Edward S., **Beyond Hypocrisy**, South End Press, Boston, 1992.
   Corporate Control, Corporate Power, Cambridge University Press, Cambridge, 1981.
   "Immiserating Growth: The First World", **Z Magazine**, January 1994.
   "The Economics of the Rich", **Z Magazine**, July, 1997

Herman, Edward S. and Chomsky, Noam, **Manufacturing Consent: the political economy of the mass media**, Pantheon Books, New York, 1988.

Hicks, J. R., **Value and Capital : an inquiry into some fundamental principles of economic theory**, 2nd edition, Clarendon Press, Oxford, 1975.

Hills, John, **Inequality and the State**, Oxford University Press, Oxford, 2004.

Hobsbawm, Eric, **Revolutionaries**, rev. ed., Abacus, London, 2007.

Hodgskin, Thomas, **Labour Defended against the Claims of Capital**, available at: http://socserv2.socsci.mcmaster.ca/~econ/ugcm/3ll3/hodgskin/labdef.txt

Hodgson, Geoffrey Martin, **Economics and Utopia: why the learning economy is not the end of history**, Routledge, London/New York, 1999.

Hoppe, Hans-Hermann, **Democracy: The God That Failed: The Economics and Politics of Monarchy, Democracy, and Natural Order**, Transaction, 2001.
   Anarcho-Capitalism: An Annotated Bibliography, available at: http://www.lewrockwell.com/hoppe/hoppe5.html

Holt, Richard P. F. and Pressman, Steven (eds.), **A New Guide to Post Keynesian Economics**, Routledge, London, 2001.

Howell, David R. (ed.), **Fighting Unemployment: The Limits of Free Market Orthodoxy**, Oxford University Press, New York, 2005.

Hutton, Will, **The State We're In**, Vintage, London, 1996.
   The World We're In, Little, Brown, London, 2002.

Hutton, Will and Giddens, Anthony (eds.), **On The Edge: living with global capitalism**, Jonathan Cape, London, 2000.

ISG, **Discussion Document of Ex-SWP Comrades**, available at: http://www.angelfire.com/journal/iso/isg.html
   Lenin vs. the SWP: Bureaucratic Centralism Or Democratic Centralism?, available at: http://www.angelfire.com/journal/iso/swp.html

Jackson, Gabriel, **The Spanish Republic and the Civil War, 1931-1939**, Princeton University Press, Princeton, 1965.

Johnson, Martin Phillip, **The Paradise of Association: Political Culture and Popular Organisation in the Paris Commune of 1871**, University of Michigan Press, Ann Arbor, 1996

Kaldor, Nicholas, **Further Essays on Applied Economics**, Duckworth, London, 1978.
   The Essential Kaldor, F. Targetti and A.P. Thirlwall (eds.), Holmes & Meier, New York, 1989.
   The Economic Consequences of Mrs Thatcher, Gerald Duckworth and Co. Ltd, London, 1983.

Kaplan, Frederick I., **Bolshevik Ideology and the Ethics of Soviet Labour, 1917-1920: The Formative Years**, Peter Owen, London, 1969.

Kaplan, Temma, **Anarchists of Andalusia: 1868-1903**, Princeton University Press, Princeton, N.J., 1965.

Katouzian, Homa, **Ideology and Method in Economics**, MacMillan Press Ltd., London, 1980.

Kautsky, Karl, **The road to power: political reflections on growing into the revolution**, Humanities Press, Atlantic Highlands, 1996.

Keen, Steve, **Debunking Economics: The Naked Emperor of the social sciences**, Pluto Press Australia, Annandale, 2001.

Keynes, John Maynard, **The General Theory of Employment, Interest and Money**, MacMillan Press, London, 1974.

Kindleberger, Charles P., **Manias, Panics, and Crashes: a history of financial crises**, 2nd Edition, Macmillan, London, 1989.

King, J.E., **A history of post Keynesian economics since 1936**, Edward Elgar, Cheltenham, 2002

Kirzner, Israel M., **Perception, Opportunity, and Profit**, University of Chicago Press, Chicago, 1979.

Klein, Naomi, **No Logo**, Flamingo, London, 2001.
   Fences and Windows: Dispatches from the front lines of the Globalisation Debate, Flamingo, London, 2002.

Koenker, Diane P., Rosenberg, William G. and Suny, Ronald Grigor (eds.), **Party, State, and Society in the Russian Civil War**, Indiana University Press, Indiana, 1989.

Kohn, Alfie, **No Contest: The Case Against Competition**, Houghton Mufflin Co., New York, 1992.
   Punished by Rewards: The Trouble with Gold Stars, Incentive Plans, A's, Praise and Other Bribes, Houghton Mifflin Company, Boston, 1993.

Krause, Peter, **The Battle for Homestead, 1880-1892: politics, culture, and steel**, University of Pittsburgh Press, Pittsburgh/London, 1992

Krugman, Paul, **Peddling Prosperity: Economic Sense and Nonsense in the Age of Diminished Expectations**, NW Norton & Co., New York/London, 1994.
> **The Conscience of a Liberal**, W.W. Norton & Co., New York/London, 2007.

Krugman, Paul and Wells, Robin, **Economics**, W. H. Freeman, New York, 2006.

Kuznets, Simon, **Economic Growth and Structure: Selected Essays**, Heineman Educational Books, London, 1966.
> **Capital in the American Economy**, Princeton University Press, New York, 1961.

Lazonick, William, **Business Organisation and the Myth of the Market Economy**, Cambridge University Press, Cambridge, 1991.
> **Competitive Advantage on the Shop Floor**, Havard University Press, Cambridge, Mass., 1990.
> **Organisation and Technology in Capitalist Development**, Edward Elgar, Brookfield, Vt, 1992.

Lear, John, **Workers, Neighbors, and Citizens: The Revolution in Mexico City**, University of Nebraska Press, Lincoln, 2001.

Lee, Frederic S., **Post Keynesian Price Theory**, Cambridge University Press, Cambridge, 1998

Leggett, George, **The Cheka: Lenin's Political Police**, Clarendon Press, Oxford, 1981.

Lenin, V. I., **Essential Works of Lenin**, Henry M. Christman (ed.), Bantam Books, New York, 1966.
> **The Lenin Anthology**, Robert C. Tucker (ed.), W.W. Norton & Company, New York, 1975.

Lenin, V. I., and Trotsky, Leon, **Kronstadt**, Monad Press, New York, 1986.

Lichtenstein, Nelson and Howell, John Harris (eds.), **Industrial Democracy in America: The Ambiguous Promise**, Cambridge University Press, Cambridge, 1992

List, Friedrich, **The Natural System of Political Economy**, Frank Cass, London, 1983.

Lovell, David W., **From Marx to Lenin: An evaluation of Marx's responsibility for Soviet authoritarianism**, Cambridge University Press, Cambridge, 1984.

Luxemburg, Rosa, **Rosa Luxemburg Speaks**, Mary-Alice Waters (ed.), Pathfinder Press, New York, 1970.

MacPherson, C.B., **The Political Theory of Possessive Individualism: Hobbes to Locke**, Oxford University Press, Oxford, 1964.

Malle, Silvana, **The Economic Organisation of War Communism, 1918-1921**, Cambridge University Press, Cambridge, 1985.

Mandel, David, **The Petrograd Workers and the Soviet Seizure of Power: from the July days 1917 to July 1918**, MacMillan, London, 1984.

Marshall, Alfred, **Principles of Economics: An Introductory Volume**, 9th Edition (in 2 volumes), MacMillian, London, 1961.

Martin, Benjamin, **The Agony of Modernisation: Labour and Industrialisation in Spain**, ICR Press, Cornell University, 1990.

Martov, J., **The State and Socialist Revolution**, Carl Slienger, London, 1977.

Marx, Karl, **Capital: A Critique of Political Economy**, vol. 1, Penguin Books, London, 1976.
> **Capital: A Critique of Political Economy**, vol. 3, Penguin Books, London, 1981.
> **Theories of Surplus Value**, vol. 3, Progress Publishers, Moscow, 1971.
> **A Contribution to the Critique of Political Economy**, Progress Publishers, Moscow, 1970.

Marx, Karl and Engels, Frederick, **Selected Works**, Progress Publishers, Moscow, 1975.
> **The Marx-Engels Reader**, Second Edition, Robert C. Tucker (ed.), W.W. Norton & Co, London & New York, 1978.
> **The socialist revolution**, F. Teplov and V. Davydov (eds.) Progess, Moscow, 1978.

Marx, Karl, Engels, Federick and Lenin, V.I., **Anarchism and Anarcho-Syndicalism**, Progress Publishers, Moscow, 1974.

Matthews, R.C.O. (ed.), **Economy and Democracy**, MacMillan Press Ltd., London, 1985.

McAuley, Mary, **Bread and Justice: State and Society in Petrograd 1917-1922**, Clarendon Press, Oxford, 1991.

McElroy, Wendy, **Anarchism: Two Kinds**, available at: http://www.wendymcelroy.com/mises/twoanarchism.html

McLay, Farguhar (ed.), **Workers City: The Real Glasgow Stands Up**, Clydeside Press, Glasgow, 1988.

McNally, David, **Against the Market: Political Economy, Market Socialism and the Marxist Critique**, Verso, London, 1993.

Miliband, Ralph, **Divided societies: class struggle in contemporary capitalism**, Clarendon Press, Oxford, 1989.

Mill, John Stuart, **Principles of Political Economy**, Oxford University Press, Oxford, 1994.

Minsky, Hyman, **Inflation, Recession and Economic Policy**, Wheatsheaf Books, Sussex, 1982.
> "The Financial Instability Hypothesis" in **Post-Keynesian Economic Theory**, pp. 24-55, Arestis, Philip and Skouras, Thanos (eds.), Wheatsheaf Books, Sussex, 1985.

Mises, Ludwig von, **Liberalism: A Socio-Economic Exposition**, Sheed Andres and McMeek Inc., Kansas City, 1978.
> **Human Action: A Treatise on Economics**, William Hodge and Company Ltd., London, 1949.
> **Socialism: an economic and sociological analysis**, Cape, London, 1951.

Montgomery, David, **The Fall of the House of Labour: The Workplace, the state, and American labour activism, 1865-1925**, Cambridge University Press, Cambridge, 1987.

Morrow, Felix, **Revolution and Counter-Revolution in Spain**, Pathfinder Press, New York, 1974.

Mumford, Lewis, **The Future of Technics and Civilisation**, Freedom Press, London, 1986.

Negri, Antonio, **Marx Beyond Marx**, Autonomedia, Brooklyn, 1991.

Neill, A.S, **Summerhill: a Radical Approach to Child Rearing**, Penguin, 1985.

Newman, Stephen L., **Liberalism at wit's end: the libertarian revolt against the modern state**, Cornell University Press, 1984.

Noble, David, **America by Design: Science, technology, and the rise of corporate capitalism**, Oxford University Press, Oxford, 1979.
> **Progress without People: In defense of Luddism**, Charles H. Kerr Publishing Ltd., Chicago, 1993.
> **Forces of Production: A Social History of Industrial Automation**, Oxford University Press, New York, 1984.

Nove, Alec, **An economic history of the USSR: 1917-1991**, 3rd ed., Penguin, Harmondsworth, 1992.

Nozick, Robert, **Anarchy, State and Utopia**, B. Blackwell, Oxford, 1974.

Oestreicher, Richard Jules, **Solidarity and fragmentation: working people and class consciousness in Detroit, 1875-1900**, University of Illinois Press, Urbana, 1986.

Ollman, Bertell (ed.), **Market Socialism: The Debate Among Socialists**, Routledge, London, 1998.

O'Neill, John, **Markets, Deliberation and Environment**, Routledge, Oxon, 2007.
> **The market: ethics, knowledge, and politics**, Routledge, London, 1998.
> **Ecology, policy, and politics: human well-being and the natural world**, Routledge, London/New York, 1993.

Oppenheimer, Franz, **The State**, Free Life Editions, New York, 1975.

Ormerod, Paul, **The Death of Economics**, Faber and Faber Ltd., London, 1994.

Orwell, George, **Homage to Catalonia**, Penguin, London, 1989.
> **The Road to Wigan Pier**, Penguin, London, 1954.
> **Nineteen Eighty-Four**, Penguin, Middlesex, 1982.
> **Orwell in Spain**, Penguin Books, London, 2001.
> **Inside the Whale and Other Essays**, Penguin Books, Harmondsworth, 1986.

Pagano, U. and Rowthorn, R. E. (eds.), **Democracy and Efficiency in Economic Enterprises**, Routledge, London, 1996.

Palley, Thomas I., **Plenty of Nothing: The Downsizing of the American Dream and the case for Structural Keynesian**, Princeton University Press, Princeton, 1998.

Paul, Ellen Frankel. Miller, Jr., Fred D. Paul, Jeffrey and Greenberg, Dan (eds.), **Socialism,** Basil Blackwell, Oxford, 1989.

Petras, James and Leiva, Fernando Ignacio, **Democracy and Poverty in Chile: The Limits to Electoral Politics**, Westview Press, Boulder, 1994.

Pipes, R., **Russia Under the Bolshevik Regime, 1919-1924**, Fontana Press, London, 1995.

Pirani, Simon, **The Russian revolution in retreat, 1920-24: Soviet workers and the new Communist elite**, Routledge, New York, 2008

Polanyi, Karl, **The Great Transformation: the political and economic origins of our time**, Beacon Press, Boston, 1957.

Preston, Paul, **The coming of the Spanish Civil War: reform, reaction, and revolution in the Second Republic**, 2nd ed., Routledge, London/ New York, 1994.

Prychitko, David L., **Markets, Planning and Democracy: essays after the collapse of communism**, Edward Elgar, Northampton, 2002.

Rabinowitch, Alexander, **Prelude to Revolution: The Petrograd Bolsheviks and the July 1917 Uprising**, Indiana University Press, Bloomington, 1991.
The Bolsheviks Come to Power: The Revolution of 1917 in Petrograd, W.W. Norton & Co., New York, 1976.
The Bolsheviks in Power: The first year of Soviet rule in Petrograd, Indiana University Press, Bloomington, 2007.
"Early Disenchantment with Bolshevik Rule: New Data form the Archives of the Extraordinary Assembly of Delegates from Petrograd Factories", **Politics and Society under the Bolsheviks**, Dermott, Kevin and Morison, John (eds.), Macmillan, Basingstoke, 1999.

Radcliff, Pamela Beth, **From mobilization to civil war: the politics of polarization in the Spanish city of Gijon, 1900-1937**, Cambridge University Press, New York, 1996.

Radin, Paul, **The World of Primitive Man**, Grove Press, New York, 1960.

Raleigh, Donald J., **Experiencing Russia's Civil War: Politics, Society, and Revolutionary Culture in Saratov, 1917-1921**, Princeton University Press, Woodstock, 2002.

Rand, Ayn, **Capitalism: The Unknown Ideal**, New American Library, New York, 1966.
The Ayn Rand Lexicon: Objectivism from A to Z, Harry Binswanger (ed.), Meridian, New York, 1986.
The Virtue of Selfishness, New American Library, New York, 1964.

Rayack, Elton, **Not So Free To Choose: The Political Economy of Milton Friedman and Ronald Reagan**, Praeger, New York, 1987.

Read, Christopher, **From Tsar to Soviets: The Russian people and their revolution, 1917-21**, UCL Press, London, 1996.

Reed, John, **Ten Days that shook the World**, Penguin Books, 1982.
Shaking the World: John Reed's revolutionary journalism, Bookmarks, London, 1998.

Reekie, W. Duncan, **Markets, Entrepreneurs and Liberty: An Austrian View of Capitalism**, Wheatsheaf Books Ltd., Sussex, 1984.

Reich, Wilhelm, **The Mass Psychology of Fascism**, Condor Book, Souvenir Press (E&A) Ltd., USA, 1991.

Reitzer, George, **The McDonaldization of Society: An Investigation into the changing character of contemporary social life**, Pine Forge Press, Thousand Oaks, 1993.

Remington, Thomas F., **Building Socialism in Bolshevik Russia: Ideology and Industrial Organisation 1917-1921**, University of Pittsburgh Press, London, 1984.

Ricardo, David, **The Principles of Political Economy and Taxation**, J.M. Dent & Sons/Charles E. Tuttle Co., London/Vermont, 1992.

Roberts, David D., **The Syndicalist Tradition and Italian Fascism**, University of North Carolina Press, Chapel Hill, 1979.

Robertson, Dennis, *"Wage-grumbles"*, **Economic Fragments**, pp. 42-57, in W. Fellner and B. Haley (eds.), **Readings in the theory of income distribution**, The Blakiston, Philadephia, 1951.

Robinson, Joan, **The Accumulation of Capital** (2nd Edition), MacMillan, St. Martin's Press, 1965.
Contributions to Modern Economics, Basil Blackwell, Oxford, 1978.
Collected Economic Papers, vol. 4, Basil Blackwell, Oxford, 1973.
Collected Economic Papers, vol. 5, Basil Blackwell, Oxford, 1979.

Rodrik, Dani, **Comments on 'Trade, Growth, and Poverty by D. Dollar and A. Kraay**, available at: http://ksghome.harvard.edu/~drodrik/ Rodrik%20on%20Dollar-Kraay.PDF

Rollins, L.A., **The Myth of Natural Rights**, Loompanics Unlimited, Port Townsend, 1983.

Rosenberg, William G., *"Russian Labour and Bolshevik Power"*, pp. 98-131, **The Workers Revolution in Russia: the view from below**, D. Kaiser (ed.), Cambridge University Press, Cambridge, 1987.
"Workers' Control on the Railroads and Some Suggestions Concerning Social Aspects of Labour Politics in the Russian Revolution", pp. D1181-D1219, **The Journal of Modern History**, vol. 49, no. 2.

Rosnick, David and Weisbrot, Mark, **Are Shorter Work Hours Good for the Environment? A Comparison of U.S. and European Energy Consumption**, available at: http://www.cepr.net/documents/publications/ energy_2006_12.pdf

Rothbard, Murray N., **The Ethics of Liberty**, Humanities Press, Atlantic Highlands, N.J., 1982.
For a New Liberty, MacMillan, New York, 1973.
Egalitarianism as a Revolt against Nature and Other Essays, Libertarian Press Review, 1974.
"Nations by Consent: Decomposing the Nation-State," in **Secession, State and Liberty**, David Gordon (ed.), Transaction Publishers, New Brunswick, 1998.
Power and Market, Institute for Humane Studies, Menlo Park, 1970.
Man, Economy, and State, with Power and Market, Ludwig von Mises Institute, Auburn, 2004.
"Society Without A State", pp. 191-207, **Anarchism: Nomos XIX**, J. Roland Pennock and John W. Chapman (eds.), New York University Press, New York, 1978.
America's great depression, Van Nostrand, Princeton/London, 1963.
Conceived in Liberty (in four volumes), Arlington House Publishers, New Rochell, 1975.
The Logic of Action II: Applications and Criticism from the Austrian School, Edward Elgar, Cheltenham/Lyme, 1997.
Classical Economics: An Austrian Perspective on the History of Economic Thought, Edward Elgar, Brookfield, 1995.
The Betrayal of the American Right, Ludwig von Mises Institute, Auburn, 2007.
Konkin on Libertarian Strategy, available at: http://www. anthonyflood.com/rothbardkonkin.htm
Are Libertarian 'Anarchists'?, available at: http://www. lewrockwell.com/rothbard/rothbard167.html

Rousseau, J-J, **The Social Contract and Discourses**, Everyman, London, 1996.

Rowbotham, Sheila, **Hidden from History: 300 Years of Women's Oppression and the fight against it**, Pluto Press, London, 1977.
"Edward Carpenter: Prophet of the New Life", Rowbotham, Sheila and Weeks, Jeffrey, **Socialism and the New Life: The Personal and Sexual Politics of Edward Carpenter and Havelock Ellis**, Pluto Press, London 1977.

Sakwa, Richard, **Soviet Communists in Power: a study of Moscow during the Civil War, 1918-21**, Macmillan, Basingstoke, 1987.

Sawyer, Malcolm C., **The Economics of Michal Kalecki**, MacMillan, Basingstoke, 1985.
The Economics of Industries and Firms: theories, evidence and policy (2nd ed.), Croom Helm, London, 1985.

Schapiro, Leonard, **The Origin of the Communist Autocracy: Political Opposition in the Soviet State: The First Phase, 1917-1922**, Frederick A. Praeger, New York, 1965.

Schlosser, Eric, **Fast Food Nation: What the all-american meal is doing to the world**, Allen Lane, London, 2001.

Schneider, Cathy Lisa, **Shantytown protest in Pinochet's Chile**, Temple University Press, Philadelphia, 1995.

Schor, Juliet B., **The Overworked American: The Unexpected Decline of Leisure**, BasicBooks, New York, 1992.

Schorske, C., **German Social Democracy, 1905-1917**, Cambridge, Mass., 1955.

Schulkind, Eugene (ed.), **The Paris Commune of 1871: The View from the Left**, Jonathan Cape, London, 1972.

Schumacher, E.F., **Small is Beautiful: A Study of Economics as if people mattered**, Vintage, London, 1993.

Schweickart, David **Against Capitalism**, Cambridge, Cambridge University Press, 1993.
After Capitalism, Rowman & Littlefield Publishers, inc., Lanham, 2002.

Sen, Amartya, **Resources, Values and Development**, Basil Blackwell, Oxford, 1984.
Development as Freedom, Oxford University Press, Oxford, 1999.

Senior, Nassau, **An Outline of the Science of Political Economy**, Alan & Unwin, London, 1951

Serge, Victor, **Memoirs of a Revolutionary 1901-41**, Oxford University Press, Oxford, 1963.
Revolution in Danger: Writings from Russia, 1919-1921, Redwords, London, 1997.
Year One of the Russian Revolution, Bookmarks, Pluto Press and Writers and Readers, London/New York, 1992.
The Serge-Trotsky Papers, D. J. Cotterill (ed.), Pluto Press, London, 1994.

Service, Robert, **The Bolshevik Party in Revolution: A Study of Organisational change**, Macmillan, London, 1979.

Silk L., and Vogel, D., **Ethics and Profits: The Crisis of Confidence in American Business**, Simon and Schuster, New York, 1976.

Sirianni, Carmen, **Workers' Control and Socialist Democracy**, Verso/NLB, London, 1982.

Shanin, Teodor, **The Awkward Class: Political Sociology of Peasantry in a Developing Society: Russia 1910-1925**, Oxford University Press, London, 1972.

Skidelsky, Robert (ed.), **Thatcherism**, Chatto & Windus, London, 1988.

Skidmore, Thomas E. and Smith, Peter H., **Modern Latin America**, Second Edition, Oxford University Press, 1989.

Smith, Adam, **The Wealth of Nations**, Everyman's Library, London, 1991.
    The Wealth of Nations, book 5, contained in **An Inquiry into the Nature and Causes of the Wealth of Nations: A Selected Edition**, Oxford University Press, Oxford/New York, 1998.

Smith, S.A., **Red Petrograd: Revolution in the Factories 1917-1918**, Cambridge University Press, Cambridge, 1983.

Sorenson, Jay B., **The Life and Death of Soviet Trade Unionism: 1917-1928**, Atherton Press, New York, 1969.

Spriano, Paolo, **The Occupation of the Factories: Italy 1920**, Pluto Press, London, 1975.

Stauber, John, and Sheldon Rampton, **Toxic Sludge is good for you! Lies, Damn Lies and the Public Relations Industry**, Common Courage Press, Monroe, Maine, 1995.

Steinbeck, John, **The Grapes of Wrath**, Mandarin, London, 1990.

Stewart, Michael, **Keynes in the 1990s: A Return to Economic Sanity**, Penguin Books, London, 1993.
    Keynes and After, 3rd edition, Penguin Books, London, 1987.

Stiglitz, Joseph, **Globalisation and its Discontents**, Penguin Books, London, 2002.

Stretton, Hugh, **Economics: A New Introduction**, Pluto Press, London, 2000.

Swain, Geoffrey, **The Origins of the Russian Civil War**, Longman, London/New York, 1996.

Sweezy, Paul, **Theory of Capitalist Development**, Monthly Review Press, New York, 1942.

Targetti, Ferdinando, **Nicholas Kaldor: The Economics and Politics of Capitalism as a Dynamic System**, Clarendon Press, Oxford, 1992.

Taylor, M. W., **Men versus the state: Herbert Spencer and late Victorian individualism**, Clarendon Press, Oxford, 1992.

Taylor, Michael W. (ed.), **Herbert Spencer and the Limits of the State: The Late Nineteenth-Century Debate Between Individualism and Collectivism**, St. Augustine's Press, 1997.

Thomas, Paul, **Karl Marx and the Anarchists**, Routledge & Kegan Paul plc, London, 1985.

Tomlins, Christopher L., **Law, Labor, and Ideology in the Early American Republic**, Cambridge University Press, New York, 1993.

Thompson, E.P., **The Making of the English Working Class**, Penguin Books, London, 1991.
    Customs in Common, Penguin Books, London, 1993.

Ticktin, Hillel and Cox, Michael (eds.), **The Ideas of Leon Trotsky**, Porcupine Press, London, 1995.

Trotsky, Leon, **History of the Russian Revolution**, in three volumes, Gollancz and Sphere Books, London, 1967.
    Writings of Leon Trotsky: Supplement (1934-40), Pathfinder Press, New York, 1979.
    Writings 1936-37, Pathfinder Press, New York, 1978.
    Terrorism and Communism, Ann Arbor, 1961.
    The Revolution Betrayed: What is the Soviet Union and where is it going?, Faber and Faber Ltd, London, 1937.
    Leon Trotsky Speaks, Pathfinder, New York, 1972.
    How the Revolution Armed: the military writings and speeches of Leon Trotsky, vol. 1, New Park Publications, London, 1979.
    How the Revolution Armed: the military writings and speeches of Leon Trotsky, vol. II, New Park Publications, London, 1979.
    How the Revolution Armed: the military writings and speeches of Leon Trotsky, vol. IV, New Park Publications, London, 1979.
    Stalin: An Appraisal of the man and his influence, in two volumes, Panther History, London, 1969.
    The Death Agony of Capitalism and the Tasks of the Fourth International, contained in **How Solidarity can change the world**, Alliance for Workers' Liberty, London, 1998.
    First Year Years of the Communist International, (in 2 volumes), New Park Publications, London, 1974.
    The Third International After Lenin, Pioneer Publishers, New York, 1957.
    The Challenge of the Left Opposition (1923-25), Pathfinder Press, New York, 1975.
    The Challenge of the Left Opposition (1926-27), Pathfinder, New York, 1980.
    On Lenin: Notes towards a Biography, George G. Harrap & Co. Ltd., London, 1971.
    "Lessons of October", pp. 113-177, **The Essential Trotsky**, Unwin Books, London, 1963.
    Leon Trotsky on China, Monad Press, New York, 2002
    In Defense of Marxism, Pathfinder, New York, 1995.
    Writings 1936-37, Pathfinder Press, New York, 2002.
    The Moralists and Sycophants against Marxism, contained in **Their Morals and Ours**, pp. 53-66, Pathfinder, New York, 1973.

Turner, Adai, **Just Capital: The Liberal Economy**, Pan Books, London, 2002.

Utton, M. A., **The Political Economy of Big Business**, Martin Robinson, Oxford, 1982.

Wade, Robert, **Governing the Market: Economic Theory and the role of government in East Asian Industrialisation**, Princeton University Press, Princeton, 1990.

Walford, George, **George Walford on Anarcho-Capitalism**, available at http://flag.blackened.net/liberty/walford-on-anarcap.html

Walras, L, **Elements of Pure Political Economy**, Allen and Unwin, London, 1954.

Ward, Benjamin, **What's Wrong with Economics?**, Basic Books, New York, 1972

Ware, Norman, **The Industrial Worker 1840-1860: The Reaction of American Industrial Society to the Advance of the Industrial Revolution**, Elephant Paperbacks, Chicago, 1924.

Watson, Andrew, **From Green to Red: Green Politics and environmentalism cannot save the environment. A socialist politics can**, Privately Published, 1990.

Weisbrot, Mark, **Globalisation for Whom?**, available at: http://www.cepr.net/Globalization.html

Weisbrot, Mark, Baker, Dean, Kraev, Egor and Chen, Judy, **The Scorecard on Globalization 1980-2000: Twenty Years of Diminished Progress**, available at: http://www.cepr.net/publications/globalization_2001_07_11.htm

Weisbrot, Mark, Baker, Dean, Naiman, Robert and Neta, Gila, **Growth May Be Good for the Poor -- But are IMF and World Bank Policies Good for Growth?** available at: http://www.cepr.net/publications/econ_growth_2001_05.htm

Weisbrot, Mark and Rosnick, David, **Another Lost Decade?: Latin America's Growth Failure Continues into the 21st Century**, available at: http://www.cepr.net/publications/latin_america_2003_11.htm

Wilkinson, Richard and Pickett, Kate, **The Spirit Level: Why More Equal Societies Almost Always Do Better**, Allen Lane, London, 2009.

Williams, Gwyn A., **Proletarian Order: Antonio Gramsci, factory councils and the origins of Italian Communism, 1911-1921**, Pluto Press, London, 1975.
    Artisans and Sans-Culottes: Popular Movements in France and Britain during the French Revolution, Edward Arnold, London, 1981.

Wilson, H., **The Labour Government 1964-1970**, London, 1971.

Winn, Peter (ed.), **Victims of the Chilean Miracle: Workers and Neoliberalism in the Pinochet Era, 1973-2002**, Duke University Press, Durham and London, 2004.

Wolff, Edward N., **Top Heavy: A Study of Increasing Inequality in America**, Twentieth Century Fund, 1995

Zinoviev, Grigorii, **History of the Bolshevik Party: A Popular Outline**, New Park Publications, London, 1973.